EXPERIENCING LAW SERIES™

EXPERIENCING BUSINESS ORGANIZATIONS

SECOND EDITION

Michael A. Chasalow
Director, Small Business Clinic
Clinical Professor of Law
USC Gould School of Law

WEST ACADEMIC PUBLISHING

444 Cedar Street, Suite 700
St. Paul, MN 55101
1-877-888-1330

Printed in the United States of America

ISBN: 978-1-68328-352-2

To my wonderful wife Emily, who is a true partner in my life.

Acknowledgments

I WOULD LIKE TO THANK all of my Business Organizations students who, over the years, have participated in a number of the *Experiencing Assignments* included in this book and have, through their questions and feedback, improved these materials. I would also like to specifically thank certain students who have contributed their time and effort to research, draft, correct, and proofread many of the materials included in this book: Rachel Grant, Emma Tehrani, Colleen Bazak, Kathryn Neubauer, Veronica Cook, Jack Altura, Cindy Organ, Sam Petty, Jessica Tober, Michael Davis, Sam Katz, Olivia Su, Danielle Richards, Jessica Sabbah-Mani, Tony Thai, Ramin Savar, Melissa Zonne, Jacob Agi, Ben Jakovljevic, Jaysen Borja, Christopher Partin, David Vences and Yvette Walker. This second edition of this book would not have been possible without the tremendous contributions made by Ali DeGolia, who deserves special thanks.

As with any casebook, this book adopts a number of stylistic conventions in reproducing cases. When text has been omitted from a case, the omission is indicated by an ellipses of ". . ." or by four asterisks "* * * *", depending upon the placement and the length of the omission. However, such indications have not been used when footnotes have been omitted or when we have omitted citations and inserted a "[*Citations omitted.*]" notation. In some instances, we have determined that certain case footnotes should be included in the materials, either because they enhance the reader's understanding of an important principle in the case or because they raise an interesting issue that some instructors might wish to discuss. In such instances, those footnotes have been retained and are reproduced using the same number or notation used in the original case.

Comments by the author are typically noted by an asterisk "*" or placed in brackets within the cited material.

There are also a number of resources which were helpful in the compilation of the materials in this book. They include:

William T. Allen, Reinier Kraakman & Guhan *Subramanian, Commentaries and Cases on the Law of Business Organization*, Aspen, 3rd Edition, 2009; Eric A. Chiappinelli, *Cases and Materials on Business Entities*, Aspen, 2nd Edition, 2010; Jesse H. Choper, John C. Coffee, Jr. & Ronald J. Gilson, *Cases and Material on Corporations*, Aspen, 7th Edition, 2008; Melvin Aron Eisenberg, *Corporations and Other Business Organizations*, Foundation Press, Concise 9th Edition, 2005; J. Dennis Hynes & Mark J. Loewenstein, *Agency, Partnership, and the LLC: The Law of Unincorporated Business Enterprises: Cases, Materials, Problems*, LexisNexis, 6th

Edition, 2003; Thomas Lee Hazen & Jerry W. Markham, *Corporations and Other Business Enterprises: Cases and Materials*, West, Standard Edition, 3rd Edition, 2009; Robert W. Hamilton, Jonathan R. Macey & Douglas K. Moll, *Cases and Materials on Corporations Including Partnerships and Limited Liability Companies*, West, 11th Edition, 2010; William A. Klein, J. Mark Ramseyer & Stephen M. Bainbridge, *Business Associations: Agency, Partnerships, and Corporations*, Foundation Press, 7th Edition, 2009; Jonathan R. Macey, *The Iconic Cases in Corporate Law*, West, 2008; Charles R.T. O'Kelley & Robert B. Thompson, *Corporations and Other Business Associations: Cases and Materials*, Aspen, 5th Edition, 2006; Stephen B. Presser, *An Introduction to the Law of Business Organizations: Cases, Notes and Questions*, West, 2nd Edition, 2008; Alan Palmiter & Frank Partnoy, *Corporations: A Contemporary Approach*, West, 2010; Larry E. Ribstein & Jeffrey M. Lipshaw, *Unincorporated Business Entities*, LexisNexis, 4th Edition, 2009; Linda O. Smiddy & Lawrence A. Cunningham, *Corporations and Other Business Organizations: Cases, Materials, Problems*, LexisNexis, 7th Edition, 2010; D. Gordon Smith & Cynthia A. Williams, *Business Organizations: Cases, Problems, and Case Studies*, Aspen, 2nd Edition, 2008; John C. Coffee, Jr. & Hillary A. Sale, *Securities Regulation*, Foundation Press, 11th Edition, 2009; and Stephen J. Choi & A.C. Pritchard, *Securities Regulation: Cases and Analysis*, Foundation Press 3rd Edition, 2012; and Michael A. Chasalow, *Acing Business Associations*, West, 2010.

I also want to thank my incredible colleagues that comprise the USC Gould School of Law faculty whose feedback, insight and support over the years has made me a better teacher and, has been invaluable throughout the process of writing this book.

And finally, B, J and R, who are a part of, and an inspiration in, all that I do.

Introduction

THE STUDY OF BUSINESS ORGANIZATIONS is filled with a large number of rules. At its worst, the study of these rules can obscure the interesting elements of the field. At its best, students are brought to understand that these "rules" are the foundations that govern the actions, structures and processes of the business world. The goal of this book is to create a law school textbook which both covers the fundamental material addressed in most traditional Business Organizations courses AND includes materials designed to teach students about how they will use that traditional material in the practice of business law. The inspiration behind this book came from my many years of teaching a traditional business organizations course combined with many years of work with actual businesses.

There are different approaches to teaching the subjects addressed under the heading "Business Law." Some professors focus heavily on the fundamentals present in a more traditional course. There are also many voices in legal education these days that advocate a singular focus on developing and building the practical skills used by an attorney in the practice of law. Some professors create "real world" courses that teach a business law curriculum, almost exclusively, through simulations.

I believe that the best lawyers have a strong understanding of the legal theory in their field of expertise AND a strong understanding of the practical skills necessary in that field. Good lawyers must use both abilities. Because of individual professors' doctrinal or pedagogical beliefs, often the materials intended to be used in business law courses "lean" strongly, or even exclusively, either toward more theoretical instruction or toward a more skills based approach. As a result, professors are often required to choose which of these important skill sets to emphasize in any given course. It is my hope that this book allows for a wide range of approaches to the material and may be used to teach a large number of business law simulations or merely to increase the experiential component of a more traditional class. The goal of this book is to integrate, into a single manageable course, the traditional Business Organizations course subject matter with practical materials that business lawyers (regardless of whether they are a transactional attorney or a litigator) will need to learn early in practice.

The recent addition of experiential components to the ABA's requirements for law school curriculum and the additional requirements imposed or under consideration by other states underscore the importance of connecting substantive learning to the practice of law. One of the challenges with bringing "live" clinical experiences to students is the ability to have a sufficient number of teachers to provide the instruction that is critical in such work. My experience as the Director of the USC Law School Small Business Clinic has placed me in a unique situation. In addition to having taught a substantial number of traditional business courses, for many years I also have taught the specific skills critical for success in the practice of business law. While this book is not intended to substitute for a clinical experience with live clients, it does provide a large number of simulations, that might be used to meet certain simulation requirements. While much of the material in the book covers the substantive doctrinal matters addressed in a traditional Business Organizations course, this book also represents my efforts to transform some of the experiences a young attorney might encounter in the practice of law into a format that is accessible to a large class. My many years as a business attorney have provided a substantial number of real life examples to include in the materials used for this book, which (with a little luck) make the problems and simulations both interesting and relevant.

This book can be used in a variety of approaches. It is intended to fill a need for new and long-time instructors who want to address the shift in legal education toward practical education, without abandoning the traditional material. This book is not intended to change the subject matter covered in Business Organizations courses. Rather it is intended to facilitate the expansion of the traditional course to include practical material. The goal of *Experiencing Business Associations* is to provide business law professors and law schools a means to teach students the practical elements of businesses law, in addition to the traditional theory behind those laws.

Students using this book are provided with examples of assignments that they might receive if they were junior associates, working in a law firm. Every chapter in this book commences with an *Experiencing Assignment.* (Some of the more significant sections within chapters will also have their own *Experiencing Assignments.*) The material that follows each Experiencing Assignment is the substantive law and cases that will help the student complete the Assignment. Even if the bulk of the *Experiencing Assignments* are not formally assigned, they are intended to frame the substantive law that follows, and, therefore, each Experiencing Assignment should be read as an introduction to that chapter's material. The *Experiencing Assignments* are designed to provide a real world context for the traditional cases that follow and provide a concrete example of how the rules and laws being studied apply to the work performed by attorneys in the field of business law. The substantive material that follows the *Experiencing Assignments* is, for the most part, the cases and explanations that one might find in a more traditional casebook. However, the fact that the material is preceded by an actual assignment is designed to focus the student on the critical aspects of the traditional material, and I have found, makes the material more easily understood by students.

A Business Organizations course is the first step in building a strategic understanding of the rules, laws and regulations that are central to the business world. The best transactional attorneys are able to use these rules, laws and regulations strategically, as tools to advance or strengthen a client's position, or as a means to avoid problems that would otherwise have arisen in the future. In litigation, mastery of these rules, laws and regulations enables an attorney to better advocate for a client's position or to build a more sophisticated understanding of the strengths or weaknesses in a case. At every level of business, attorneys are called upon to provide advice to their clients. This advice is not whether the client should pay more or pay less in a transaction. Rather, it relates to the structure of a transaction and to the steps required to accomplish a transaction so that the client has legal protections (at least to the extent possible) from the many pitfalls that arise in business dealings. A good business attorney can help her client to avoid unnecessary risk, and can often suggest alternative approaches or structures to a transaction that will accomplish the client's goals and provide increased protection if there are issues in the future.

In order to provide this strategic advice to their business clients, attorneys must have a thorough understanding of the principles of agency, limited liability, fiduciary duty, corporate governance and the many other concepts, structures and laws discussed in the pages that follow. These principles are critical to understanding the fundamental concepts of business law. However, the rules alone can be dry and, without context, difficult to grasp. The *Experiencing Assignments* in this book are intended to provide context for these principles. In creating these *Assignments*, we have endeavored to create short assignments that an associate in a law firm might encounter in the real world, and have attempted to avoid the more theoretical questions that law students are so often asked to ponder in the classroom. While the *Experiencing Assignments* are fictionalized, these *Assignments* are intended to mirror what an associate might be asked to do for a client. While no single course in Business Organizations is sufficient to instantly transform, even a top law student, into a great business attorney, it is our hope that this book will provide the initial training to establish a strong theoretical foundation as well as an introduction to the practical skills that are both necessary for any attorney who engages in any practice of law that involves the business concepts encountered in this course.

This second edition maintains the structure and substance of the original edition, but has been updated to include recent developments such as the increased use of special committees to approve freeze out mergers by dominant shareholders, material on *Salman v. United States* (a recent Supreme Court case on insider trading), a note on initial coin offerings and digital currencies, and a number of updates and corrections.

Summary of Contents

Table of Contents

Table of Cases

The principal cases are in bold type.

EXPERIENCING BUSINESS ORGANIZATIONS

SECOND EDITION

CHAPTER ONE

Agency

CONGRATULATIONS! You have just started work at a law firm. The following is your first assignment. The following fact pattern and questions are designed to help you learn the material in this chapter and to begin developing skills that you will use as an attorney. A good business attorney needs to be able to use his or her understanding of the law and the cases to assess situations and to provide advice to clients. The following fact pattern and questions do not need to be answered, and should not be answered, until the end of the section. However, as you study the cases and other materials in this chapter, it might be helpful to do so with a view toward providing assistance to Burger Barn, your client in the matter outlined below. Some of the materials in this chapter will relate more than others to the issues facing Burger Barn. However, the materials are designed to build your understanding of the issues that arise in agency and assist you in addressing your client's concerns and putting them in context. Please carefully read the following "assignment" and keep your client's issues and the questions presented in mind while reading the chapter materials that follow.

Experiencing Assignment 1: Burger Barn

FACTS:

Your client, **Burger Barn, Inc.** ("BB") owns and operates fast food restaurants throughout the country. Burger Barn has a "wild west" theme. Its restaurants are adorned with a significant amount of wood and rope and other decorations that remind customers of the Old West.

Lately, Burger Barn's sales have been declining. Fred Barns, the president of Burger Barn, is concerned that the declining sales might be the result of people no longer responding to the wild west theme. Fred hired a marketing consultant, Astrid Jet, to study this issue and to do research. Fred asked Astrid to concentrate her research in one region where there are three Burger Barn locations. Astrid was introduced to the regional manager, Rita Pushover, who was asked to cooperate and assist Astrid with any needs she had for her research. Fred asked Rita to report back to him in three months. After one month, Fred received a call from Rita who explained that she needed more money in her budget to cover the construction and decorating bills. It turns out that Astrid's "research" included changing the themes of the three regional Burger Barn restaurants to an "outer space" theme. Astrid had ordered new decorations and signage and had hired contractors to rebuild the interiors of the locations.

As soon as Fred heard this, he was furious. He called Astrid and told her that she was supposed to gather data. Astrid explained that she believes data provides limited information and that her research always involves "live" trials. Fred fired Astrid immediately. However, he is now facing bills totaling over $300,000 (approximately $100,000 for each location) from outer space decorations (ordered through Deco Designs), signage (from Sign Company Inc.) and the contractor (Connie Tractor). No construction has commenced, but the outer space decorations have arrived at the locations and Sign Company, Inc. has already started working on the new signs. All of the third parties (Deco Designs, Sign Company and Connie) want to be paid in full for products ordered and/or work that has been done or agreed to.

Assume that Deco Designs, Sign Company and Connie each have a written contract signed by Astrid as "Astrid Jet, agent for Burger Barn."

ASSIGNMENT:

Fred (who has never spoken directly to Deco Designs, Sign Company or Connie) explains the situation to you and wants to know if he needs to pay these bills. He also wants to know if he decides to fight them and not pay, whether it is likely that he will prevail. He also tells you that Astrid does not have any money, so it is unlikely that Burger Barn will be able to collect any money from her.

You explain to Fred that, while you are very bright, you are new to the practice of law, and you need some time to familiarize yourself with the issues of law involved. Fred says, "That's fine. Please write me a brief memo answering my questions, and making a recommendation and telling me why you are making that recommendation." If you are missing information, you should feel free to make reasonable assumptions. Just make it clear that you are making assumptions and the impact the accuracy of those assumptions will have on any conclusions you reach. Fred does not want to pay for a 10-page memo. He wants you to keep your memo under 1000 words. He also tells you that those 1000 words should not include too many "fancy lawyer words." Fred also makes it clear that he is not interested in case citations. He just wants to have enough information to decide whether to pay the bills or fight.

SECTION I: Agency in General

Agency law is about determining when or whether one party may be held responsible for, or bound by, the actions of another and what rights and obligations those parties have to one another.

Agency is a fundamental concept in the law. It is central to a number of legal practices and precepts. Because agency involves the most basic example of one person acting on behalf of another, agency concepts are present in most business transactions in which one party provides services on behalf of, or in conjunction with another. Agency concepts also arise throughout the study of Business Associations because an officer of a corporation or employee of a business is typically an agent for that corporation or business. The agency principles that determine whether an agent has the authority to act on behalf of a business, when the business is bound by, or liable for, the actions of its agents, and what duties and responsibilities an agent might have to a business, are core concepts that also arise in the study of partnerships, limited liability companies and corporations.

A. The Existence of a Principal-Agent Relationship

> "Agency is the fiduciary relationship that arises when one person (a 'principal') manifests assent to another person (an 'agent') that the agent shall act on the principal's behalf and subject to the principal's control, and the agent manifests assent or otherwise consents so to act." **Restatement of the Law—Agency; Restatement (Third) of Agency** Copyright © 2006 by the American Law Institute (referred to throughout these materials as the "*Third Restatement*") § 1.01

In order to create an agency relationship there must be some form of agreement or understanding between the parties, but not necessarily a contract between the parties. The existence of an agency relationship may be proved by an evaluation of the facts in each particular situation. Courts might look at what the parties said, what they did, how they acted, their course of dealing over time, even silence may be used to show a party's consent. It is not essential that the agent even receive compensation.

There are potentially three parties in agency situations:

1. The Principal
2. The Agent
3. The Third Party

Agency law involves a determination of the rights and responsibilities between and among these parties. There are several basic tenets that arise out of an agency relationship: the agent has certain duties and obligations to the principal; the principal has certain duties and obligations to the agent; the principal is responsible for tortious acts committed by the agent against a third party that fall within the scope of the agency; the agent has the ability to enter into binding agreements with third parties on the principal's behalf, as long as the agreement may be traced to the principal's authority; and the agent's knowledge (in the subject matter of the agency) is imputed to the principal.

When evaluating a situation involving an agency relationship, it is helpful to distinguish between fact patterns that involve tort issues and fact patterns that involve contract issues. In a tort context, the underlying issue typically involves a determination of which party or parties are responsible for a wrongful act or for some harm done. In the contract context, the underlying issue typically involves a determination of which party or parties are bound by a contractual commitment.

Excerpts from the Third Restatement

§ 1.01 Agency Defined

Agency is the fiduciary relationship that arises when one person (a "principal") manifests assent to another person (an "agent") that the agent shall act on the principal's behalf and subject to the principal's control, and the agent manifests assent or otherwise consents so to act.

§ 1.02 Parties' Labeling and Popular Usage Not Controlling

An agency relationship arises only when the elements stated in § 1.01 are present. Whether a relationship is characterized as agency in an agreement between parties or in the context of industry or popular usage is not controlling.

§ 2.04 Respondeat Superior

An employer is subject to liability for torts committed by employees while acting within the scope of their employment.

§ 7.03 Principal's Liability—In General

(1) A principal is subject to direct liability to a third party harmed by an agent's conduct when

(a) as stated in § 7.04, the agent acts with actual authority or the principal ratifies the agent's conduct and

(i) the agent's conduct is tortious, or

(ii) the agent's conduct, if that of the principal, would subject the principal to tort liability; or

(b) as stated in § 7.05, the principal is negligent in selecting, supervising, or otherwise controlling the agent; or

(c) as stated in § 7.06, the principal delegates performance of a duty to use care to protect other persons or their property to an agent who fails to perform the duty.

(2) A principal is subject to vicarious liability to a third party harmed by an agent's conduct when

(a) as stated in § 7.07, the agent is an employee who commits a tort while acting within the scope of employment; or

(b) as stated in § 7.08, the agent commits a tort when acting with apparent authority in dealing with a third party on or purportedly on behalf of the principal.

§ 7.07 Employee Acting Within Scope of Employment

(1) An employer is subject to vicarious liability for a tort committed by its employee acting within the scope of employment.

(2) An employee acts within the scope of employment when performing work assigned by the employer or engaging in a course of conduct subject to the employer's control. An employee's act is not within the scope of employment when it occurs within an independent course of conduct not intended by the employee to serve any purpose of the employer.

(3) For purposes of this section,

(a) an employee is an agent whose principal controls or has the right to control the manner and means of the agent's performance of work, and

(b) the fact that work is performed gratuitously does not relieve a principal of liability.

§ 7.08 Agent Acts with Apparent Authority

A principal is subject to vicarious liability for a tort committed by an agent in dealing or communicating with a third party on or purportedly on behalf of the principal when actions taken by the agent with apparent authority constitute the tort or enable the agent to conceal its commission.

The following cases turn upon a determination of whether an agency relationship existed between certain parties and, if such a relationship did exist, whether the wrongful actions of the agent were within the scope of that agency. In reading these cases note the importance that the specific facts in each case play in the courts' determinations regarding the existence and scope of the agency relationship as well as the consequences to the respective principals that may result from such determinations.

Clover v. Snowbird Ski Resort

808 P.2d 1037 (Utah 1991)

HALL, C.J.

Plaintiff Margaret Clover sought to recover damages for injuries sustained as the result of a ski accident in which Chris Zulliger, an employee of defendant Snowbird Corporation ("Snowbird"), collided with her. From the entry of summary judgment in favor of defendants, Clover appeals.

. . . . At the time of the accident, Chris Zulliger was employed by Snowbird as a chef at the Plaza Restaurant. Zulliger was supervised by his father, Hans Zulliger, who was the head chef at both the Plaza, which was located at the base of the resort, and the Mid-Gad Restaurant, which was located halfway to the top of the mountain. Zulliger was instructed by his father to make periodic trips to the Mid-Gad to monitor its operations. Prior to the accident, the Zulligers had made several inspection trips to the restaurant. On at least one occasion, Zulliger was paid for such a trip. He also had several conversations with Peter Mandler, the manager of the Plaza and Mid-Gad Restaurants, during which Mandler directed him to make periodic stops at the Mid-Gad to monitor operations.

On December 5, 1985, the date of the accident, Zulliger was scheduled to begin work at the Plaza Restaurant at 3 p.m. Prior to beginning work, he had planned to go skiing with Barney Norman, who was also employed as a chef at the Plaza. Snowbird preferred that their employees know how to ski because it made it easier for them to get to and from work. As part of the compensation for their employment, both Zulliger and Norman received season ski passes. On the morning of the accident, Mandler asked Zulliger to inspect the operation of the Mid-Gad prior to beginning work at the Plaza.

Zulliger and Norman stopped at the Mid-Gad in the middle of their first run. At the restaurant, they had a snack, inspected the kitchen, and talked to the personnel for approximately fifteen to twenty minutes. Zulliger and Norman then skied four runs before heading down the mountain to begin work. On their final run, Zulliger and Norman took a route that was often taken by Snowbird employees to travel from the top of the mountain to the Plaza. About mid-way down the mountain, at a point above the Mid-Gad, Zulliger decided to take a jump off a crest on the side of an intermediate run. He had taken this jump many times before. . . . Zulliger, . . . ignored the sign [to slow down] and skied over the crest at a significant speed. Clover, who had just entered the same ski run from a point below the crest, either had stopped or was traveling slowly below the crest. When Zulliger went over the jump, he collided with Clover, who was hit in the head and severely injured.

Clover brought claims against Zulliger and Snowbird, alleging that . . . Snowbird is liable for Zulliger's negligence because at the time of the collision, he was acting within the scope of his employment. . . .

* * * *

SCOPE OF EMPLOYMENT

Under the doctrine of respondeat superior, employers are held vicariously liable for the torts their employees commit when the employees are acting within the scope of their employment. Clover's respondeat superior claim was dismissed on the ground that as a matter of law, Zulliger's actions at the time of the accident were not within the scope of his employment. In a recent case, *Birkner v. Salt Lake County* [771 P.2d 1053 (Utah 1989)], this court addressed the issue of what types of acts fall within the scope of employment. In Birkner, we stated that acts within the scope of employment are " 'those acts which are so closely connected with what the servant is employed to do, and so fairly and reasonably incidental to it, that they may be regarded as methods, even though quite improper ones, of carrying out the objectives of the employment.' " The question of whether an employee is acting within the scope of employment is a question of fact. The scope of employment issue must be submitted to a jury "whenever reasonable minds may differ as to whether the [employee] was at a certain time involved wholly or partly in the performance of his [employer's] business or within the scope of employment." [*Birkner v. Salt Lake County,* 771 P.2d at 1056 (quoting W. Keeton, *Prosser and Keeton on the Law of Torts* § 70, at 502 (5th ed. 1984))] In situations where the activity is so clearly within or without the scope of employment that reasonable minds cannot differ, it lies within the prerogative of the trial judge to decide the issue as a matter of law.

In *Birkner,* we observed that the Utah cases that have addressed the issues of whether an employee's actions, as a matter of law, are within or without the scope of employment have focused on three criteria. "First, an employee's conduct must be of the general kind the employee is employed to perform. . . . In other words, the employee must be about the employer's business and the duties assigned by the employer, as opposed to being wholly involved in a personal endeavor." Second, the employee's conduct must occur substantially within the hours and ordinary spatial boundaries of the employment. "Third, the employee's conduct must be motivated at least in part, by the purpose of serving the employer's interest." Under specific factual situations, such as when the employee's conduct serves a dual purpose or when the employee takes a personal detour in the course of carrying out his employer's directions, this court has occasionally used variations of this approach. These variations, however, are not departures from the criteria advanced in *Birkner.* Rather, they are methods of applying the criteria in specific factual situations.

In applying the *Birkner* criteria to the facts in the instant case, it is important to note that if Zulliger had returned to the Plaza Restaurant immediately after he inspected the operations at the Mid-Gad Restaurant, there would be ample evidence to support the conclusion that on his return trip Zulliger's actions were within the scope of his employment. There is evidence that it was part of Zulliger's job to monitor the operations at the Mid-Gad and that he was directed to monitor the operations on the day of the accident. There is also evidence that Snowbird intended Zulliger to use the ski lifts and the ski runs on his trips to the Mid-Gad. It is clear, therefore, that Zulliger's actions could be considered to "be of the general kind that the employee is employed to perform." It is also clear that there would be evidence that Zulliger's actions occurred within the hours and normal spatial boundaries of his employment. Zulliger was expected to monitor the operations at the Mid-Gad during the time the lifts were operating and when he was not working as a chef at the Plaza. Furthermore, throughout the trip he would have been on his employer's premises. Finally, it is clear that Zulliger's actions in monitoring the operations at the Mid-Gad, per his employer's instructions, could be considered "motivated, at least in part, by the purpose of serving the employer's interest."

The difficulty, of course, arises from the fact that Zulliger did not return to the Plaza after he finished inspecting the facilities at the Mid-Gad. Rather, he skied four more runs and rode the lift to the top of the mountain before he began his return to the base. Snowbird claims that this fact shows that Zulliger's primary purpose for skiing on the day of the accident was for his own pleasure and that therefore, as a matter of law, he was not acting within the scope of his employment. In support of this proposition, Snowbird cites *Whitehead v. Variable Annuity Life Insurance*. [801 P.2d 934 (Utah 1989)] *Whitehead* concerned the dual purpose doctrine. Under this doctrine, if an employee's actions are motivated by the dual purpose of benefiting the employer and serving some personal interest, the actions will usually be considered within the scope of employment. *Id.* at 937. However, if the primary motivation for the activity is personal, "even though there may be some transaction of business or performance of duty merely incidental or adjunctive thereto, the [person] should not be deemed to be in the scope of his employment." *Id.* (citing *Martinson v. W-M Ins. Agency*, 606 P.2d 256, 285 (Utah 1980)). In situations where the scope of employment issue concerns an employee's trip, a useful test in determining if the transaction of business is purely incidental to a personal motive is "whether the trip is one which would have required the employer to send another employee over the same route or to perform the same function if the trip had not been made." *Id.*

In *Whitehead,* we held that an employee's commute home was not within the scope of employment, notwithstanding the plaintiff's contention that because the employee planned to make business calls from his house, there was a dual purpose for the commute. *Id.* In so holding, we noted that the business calls could have been made as easily from any other place as from the employee's home. *Id.* The instant case is distinguishable from *Whitehead* in that the activity of inspecting the Mid-Gad necessitates travel to the restaurant. Furthermore, there is evidence that the manager of both the Mid-Gad and the Plaza wanted an employee to inspect the restaurant and report back by 3 p.m. If Zulliger had not inspected the restaurant, it would have been necessary to send a second employee to accomplish the same purpose. Furthermore, the second employee would have most likely used the ski lifts and ski runs in traveling to and from the restaurant.

There is ample evidence that there was a predominant business purpose for Zulliger's trip to the Mid-Gad. Therefore, this case is better analyzed under our decisions dealing with situations where an employee has taken a personal detour in the process of carrying out his duties. This court has decided several cases in which employees deviated from their duties for wholly personal reasons and then, after resuming their duties, were involved in accidents. In situations where the detour was such a substantial diversion from the employee's duties that it constituted an abandonment of employment, we held that the employee, as a matter of law, was acting outside the scope of employment. However, in situations where reasonable minds could differ on whether the detour constituted a slight deviation from the employee's duties or an abandonment of employment, we have left the question for the jury.

Under the circumstances of the instant case, it is entirely possible for a jury to reasonably believe that at the time of the accident, Zulliger had resumed his employment and that Zulliger's deviation was not substantial enough to constitute a total abandonment of employment. First, a jury could reasonably believe that by beginning his return to the base of the mountain to begin his duties as a chef and to report to Mandler concerning his observations at the Mid-Gad, Zulliger had resumed his employment. In past cases, in holding that the actions of an employee were within the scope of employment, we have relied on the fact that the employee had resumed the duties of employment prior to the time of the accident. This is an important factor because if the employee has resumed the duties of employment, the employee is then "about the employer's business" and the employee's actions will be "motivated, at least in part, by the purpose of serving the employer's interest." The fact that due to Zulliger's deviation, the accident occurred at a spot above the Mid-Gad does not disturb this analysis. In situations where accidents have occurred substantially within the normal spatial boundaries of employment, we have held that employees may be within the scope of employment if, after a personal detour, they return to their duties and an accident occurs.

Second, a jury could reasonably believe that Zulliger's actions in taking four ski runs and returning to the top of the mountain do not constitute a complete abandonment of employment. It is important to note that by taking these ski runs, Zulliger was not disregarding his employer's directions. . . . In the instant case, far from directing its employees not to ski at the resort, Snowbird issued its employees season ski passes as part of their compensation.

These two factors, along with other circumstances—such as, throughout the day Zulliger was on Snowbird's property, there was no specific time set for inspecting the restaurant, and the act of skiing was the method used by Snowbird employees to travel among the different locations of the resort—constitute sufficient evidence for a jury to conclude that Zulliger, at the time of the accident, was acting within the scope of his employment.

Although we have held that Zulliger's actions were not, as a matter of law, outside the scope of his employment under the Birkner analysis, it is important to note that Clover also argues that Zulliger's conduct is within the scope of employment under two alternative theories. First, she urges this court to adopt a position taken by some jurisdictions that focuses, not on whether the employee's conduct is motivated by serving the employer's interest, but on whether the employee's conduct is foreseeable. Such an approach constitutes a significant departure from the *Birkner* analysis. *See Bushey & Sons, Inc. v. United States,* 398 F.2d 167, 171 (2d Cir. 1968); *Hinman v. Westinghouse Elec. Co.,* 2 Cal. 3d 956, 471 P.2d 988, 990, 88 Cal. Rptr. 188 (1970).

* * * *

Reversed and remanded for further proceedings.

A. Gay Jenson Farms Co. v. Cargill, Inc.

309 N.W.2d 285 (Minn. 1981)

Plaintiffs, 86 individual, partnership or corporate farmers, brought this action against defendant Cargill, Inc. (Cargill) and defendant Warren Grain & Seed Co. (Warren) to recover losses sustained when Warren defaulted on the contracts made with plaintiffs for the sale of grain. After a trial by jury, judgment was entered in favor of plaintiffs, and Cargill brought this appeal. We affirm.

This case arose out of the financial collapse of defendant Warren Seed & Grain Co., and its failure to satisfy its indebtedness to plaintiffs. Warren, which was located in Warren, Minnesota, was operated by Lloyd Hill and his son, Gary Hill. Warren operated a grain elevator and as a result was involved in the purchase of cash or market grain from local farmers. The cash grain would be resold through the Minneapolis Grain Exchange or to the terminal grain companies directly. Warren also stored grain for farmers and sold chemicals, fertilizer and steel storage bins. In addition, it operated a seed business which involved buying seed grain from farmers, processing it and reselling it for seed to farmers and local elevators.

Lloyd Hill decided in 1964 to apply for financing from Cargill. Cargill's officials from the Moorhead regional office investigated Warren's operations and recommended that Cargill finance Warren.

Warren and Cargill thereafter entered into a security agreement which provided that Cargill would loan money for working capital to Warren on "open account" financing up to a stated limit, which was originally set as $175,000.[2]

Under this contract, Warren would receive funds and pay its expenses by issuing drafts drawn on Cargill through Minneapolis banks. The drafts were imprinted with both Warren's and Cargill's names. Proceeds from Warren's sales would be deposited with Cargill and credited to its account. In return for this financing, Warren appointed Cargill as its grain agent for transaction with the Commodity Credit Corporation. Cargill was also given a right of first refusal to purchase market grain sold by Warren to the terminal market.

A new contract was negotiated in 1967, extending Warren's credit line to $300,000 and incorporating the provisions of the original contract. It was also stated in the contract that Warren would provide Cargill with annual financial statements and that either Cargill would keep the books for Warren or an audit would be conducted by an independent firm. Cargill was given the right of access to Warren's books for inspection.

In addition, the agreement provided that Warren was not to make capital improvements or repairs in excess of $5,000 without Cargill's prior consent. Further, it was not to become liable as guarantor on another's indebtedness, or encumber its assets except with Cargill's permission. Consent by Cargill was required before Warren would be allowed to declare a dividend or sell and purchase stock.

Officials from Cargill's regional office made a brief visit to Warren shortly after the agreement was executed. They examined the annual statement and the accounts receivable, expenses, inventory, seed, machinery and other financial matters. Warren was informed that it would be reminded periodically to make the improvements recommended by Cargill[3] At approximately this time, a memo was given to the Cargill official in charge of the Warren account, Erhart Becker, which stated in part: "This organization [Warren] needs very strong paternal guidance."

In 1970, Cargill contracted with Warren and other elevators to act as its agent to seek growers for a new type of wheat called Bounty 208. Warren, as

---

2 Loans were secured by a second mortgage on Warren's real estate and a first chattel mortgage on its inventories of grain and merchandise. . . .

3 Cargill headquarters suggested that the regional office check Warren monthly. Also, it was requested that Warren be given an explanation for the relatively large withdrawals from undistributed earnings made by the Hills, since Cargill hoped that Warren's profits would be used to decrease its debt balance. Cargill asked for written requests for withdrawals from undistributed earnings in the future.

Cargill's agent for this project, entered into contracts for the growing of the wheat seed, with Cargill named as the contracting party. Farmers were paid directly by Cargill for the seed and all contracts were performed in full. In 1971, pursuant to an agency contract, Warren contracted on Cargill's behalf with various farmers for the growing of sunflower seeds for Cargill. The arrangements were similar to those made in the Bounty 208 contracts, and all those contracts were also completed. Both these agreements were unrelated to the open account financing contract. In addition, Warren, as Cargill's agent in the sunflower seed business, cleaned and packaged the seed in Cargill bags.

During this period, Cargill continued to review Warren's operations and expenses and recommend that certain actions should be taken.[4] Warren purchased from Cargill various business forms printed by Cargill and received sample forms from Cargill which Warren used to develop its own business forms.

Cargill wrote to its regional office in 1970 expressing its concern that the pattern of increased use of funds allowed to develop at Warren was similar to that involved in two other cases in which Cargill experienced severe losses. Cargill did not refuse to honor drafts or call the loan, however. A new security agreement which increased the credit line to $750,000 was executed in 1972, and a subsequent agreement which raised the limit to $1,250,000 was entered into in 1976.

Warren was at that time shipping Cargill 90% of its cash grain. When Cargill's facilities were full, Warren shipped its grain to other companies. Approximately 25% of Warren's total sales was seed grain which was sold directly by Warren to its customers.

As Warren's indebtedness continued to be in excess of its credit line, Cargill began to contact Warren daily regarding its financial affairs. Cargill headquarters informed its regional office in 1973 that, since Cargill money was being used, Warren should realize that Cargill had the right to make some critical decisions regarding the use of the funds. Cargill headquarters also told Warren that a regional manager would be working with Warren on a day-to-day basis as well as in monthly planning meetings. In 1975, Cargill's regional office began to keep a daily debit position on Warren. A bank account was opened in Warren's name

[4] Between 1967 and 1973, Cargill suggested that Warren take a number of steps, including: (1) a reduction of seed grain and cash grain inventories; (2) improved collection of accounts receivable; (3) reduction or elimination of its wholesale seed business and its speciality [sic] grain operation; (4) marketing fertilizer and steel bins on consignment; (5) a reduction in withdrawals made by officers; (6) a suggestion that Warren's bookkeeper not issue her own salary checks; and (7) cooperation with Cargill in implementing the recommendations. These ideas were apparently never implemented, however.

on which Warren could draw checks in 1976. The account was to be funded by drafts drawn on Cargill by the local bank.

In early 1977, it became evident that Warren had serious financial problems. Several farmers, who had heard that Warren's checks were not being paid, inquired or had their agents inquire at Cargill regarding Warren's status and were initially told that there would be no problem with payment. In April 1977, an audit of Warren revealed that Warren was $4 million in debt. After Cargill was informed that Warren's financial statements had been deliberately falsified, Warren's request for additional financing was refused. In the final days of Warren's operation, Cargill sent an official to supervise the elevator, including disbursement of funds and income generated by the elevator.

After Warren ceased operations, it was found to be indebted to Cargill in the amount of $3.6 million. Warren was also determined to be indebted to plaintiffs in the amount of $2 million, and plaintiffs brought this action in 1977 to seek recovery of that sum. Plaintiffs alleged that Cargill was jointly liable for Warren's indebtedness as it had acted as principal for the grain elevator.

* * * *

The major issue in this case is whether Cargill, by its course of dealing with Warren, became liable as a principal on contracts made by Warren with plaintiffs. Cargill contends that no agency relationship was established with Warren, notwithstanding its financing of Warren's operation and its purchase of the majority of Warren's grain. However, we conclude that Cargill, by its control and influence over Warren, became a principal with liability for the transactions entered into by its agent Warren.

Agency is the fiduciary relationship that results from the manifestation of consent by one person to another that the other shall act on his behalf and subject to his control, and consent by the other so to act. *[Citations omitted.]* In order to create an agency there must be an agreement, but not necessarily a contract between the parties. *Restatement (Second) of Agency § 1, comment b* (1958). An agreement may result in the creation of an agency relationship although the parties did not call it an agency and did not intend the legal consequences of the relation to follow. *Id.* The existence of the agency may be proved by circumstantial evidence which shows a course of dealing between the two parties. *Rausch v. Aronson,* 211 Minn. 272, 1 N.W.2d 371 (1941). When an agency relationship is to be proven by circumstantial evidence, the principal must be shown to have consented to the agency since one cannot be the agent of another except by consent of the latter. *Larkin v. McCabe,* 211 Minn. 11, 299 N.W. 649 (1941).

Cargill contends that the prerequisites of an agency relationship did not exist because Cargill never consented to the agency, Warren did not act on behalf of Cargill, and Cargill did not exercise control over Warren. We hold that all three elements of agency could be found in the particular circumstances of this case. By directing Warren to implement its recommendations, Cargill manifested its consent that Warren would be its agent. Warren acted on Cargill's behalf in procuring grain for Cargill as the part of its normal operations which were totally financed by Cargill.[7] Further, an agency relationship was established by Cargill's interference with the internal affairs of Warren, which constituted de facto control of the elevator.

A creditor who assumes control of his debtor's business may become liable as principal for the acts of the debtor in connection with the business. Restatement (Second) of Agency § 14 O (1958). It is noted in comment a to section 14 O that:

> A security holder who merely exercises a veto power over the business acts of his debtor by preventing purchases or sales above specified amounts does not thereby become a principal. However, if he takes over the management of the debtor's business either in person or through an agent, and directs what contracts may or may not be made, he becomes a principal, liable as a principal for the obligations incurred thereafter in the normal course of business by the debtor who has now become his general agent. The point at which the creditor becomes a principal is that at which he assumes de facto control over the conduct of his debtor, whatever the terms of the formal contract with his debtor may be.

A number of factors indicate Cargill's control over Warren, including the following:

(1) Cargill's constant recommendations to Warren by telephone;

(2) Cargill's right of first refusal on grain;

(3) Warren's inability to enter into mortgages, to purchase stock or to pay dividends without Cargill's approval;

---

[7] Although the contracts with the farmers were executed by Warren, Warren paid for the grain with drafts drawn on Cargill. While this is not in itself significant—*see Lee v. Peoples Cooperative Sales Agency,* 201 Minn. 266, 276 N.W. 214 (1937)—it is one factor to be taken into account in analyzing the relationship between Warren and Cargill.

(4) Cargill's right of entry onto Warren's premises to carry on periodic checks and audits;

(5) Cargill's correspondence and criticism regarding Warren's finances, officers salaries and inventory;

(6) Cargill's determination that Warren needed "strong paternal guidance";

(7) Provision of drafts and forms to Warren upon which Cargill's name was imprinted;

(8) Financing of all Warren's purchases of grain and operating expenses; and

(9) Cargill's power to discontinue the financing of Warren's operations.

We recognize that some of these elements, as Cargill contends, are found in an ordinary debtor-creditor relationship. However, these factors cannot be considered in isolation, but, rather, they must be viewed in light of all the circumstances surrounding Cargill's aggressive financing of Warren.

It is also Cargill's position that the relationship between Cargill and Warren was that of buyer-supplier rather than principal-agent.

* * * *

Factors indicating that one is a supplier, rather than an agent, are:

> (1) That he is to receive a fixed price for the property irrespective of price paid by him. This is the most important. (2) That he acts in his own name and receives the title to the property which he thereafter is to transfer. (3) That he has an independent business in buying and selling similar property.

Restatement (Second) of Agency § 14K, Comment a (1958).

Under the Restatement approach, it must be shown that the supplier has an independent business before it can be concluded that he is not an agent. The record establishes that all portions of Warren's operation were financed by Cargill and that Warren sold almost all of its market grain to Cargill. Thus, the relationship which existed between the parties was not merely that of buyer and supplier.

* * * *

In this case, . . . Cargill furnished substantially all funds received by the elevator. Cargill did have a right of entry on Warren's premises, and . . . required maintenance of insurance against hazards of operation. Warren's activities . . . formed a substantial part of Cargill's business that was developed in that area. In addition, Cargill did not think of Warren as an operator who was free to become Cargill's competitor, but rather conceded that it believed that Warren owed a duty of loyalty to Cargill. The decisions made by Warren were not independent of Cargill's interest or its control.

Further, we are not persuaded by the fact that Warren was in one of the "line" elevators that Cargill operated in its own name. The Warren operation, like the line elevator, was financially dependent on Cargill's continual infusion of capital. The arrangement with Warren presented a convenient alternative to the establishment of a line elevator. Cargill became, in essence, the owner of the operation without the accompanying legal indicia.

The amici curiae assert that, if the jury verdict is upheld, firms and banks which have provided business loans to county elevators will decline to make further loans. The decision in this case should give no cause for such concern. We deal here with a business enterprise markedly different from an ordinary bank financing, since Cargill was an active participant in Warren's operations rather than simply a financier. Cargill's course of dealing with Warren was, by its own admission, a paternalistic relationship in which Cargill made the key economic decisions and kept Warren in existence.

Although considerable interest was paid by Warren on the loan, the reason for Cargill's financing of Warren was not to make money as a lender but, rather, to establish a source of market grain for its business. As one Cargill manager noted, "We were staying in there because we wanted the grain." For this reason, Cargill was willing to extend the credit line far beyond the amount originally allocated to Warren. It is noteworthy that Cargill was receiving significant amounts of grain and that, notwithstanding the risk that was recognized by Cargill, the operation was considered profitable.

On the whole, there was a unique fabric in the relationship between Cargill and Warren which varies from that found in normal debtor-creditor situations. We conclude that, on the facts of this case, there was sufficient evidence from which the jury could find that Cargill was the principal of Warren within the definitions of agency set forth in *Restatement (Second) of Agency §§ 1* and *140*.

* * * *

Affirmed.

Gorton v. Doty

57 Idaho 792, 69 P.2d 136 (Idaho 1937)

HOLDEN, J.:

In September, 1935, an action was commenced by R. S. Gorton, father of Richard Gorton, to recover expenses incurred by the father for hospitalization, physicians', surgeons', and nurses' fees, and another by the son, by his father as guardian *ad litem,* to recover damages for injuries sustained as a result of an accident. By stipulation the actions were consolidated for trial. Upon the trial of the cases so consolidated, the jury returned a verdict in favor of the father for $870 and another in favor of the son for $5,000. Separate judgments were then entered upon such verdicts. Thereafter a motion for a new trial was made and denied in each case. The cases come here upon an appeal from each judgment and order denying a new trial.

. . .

It appears that in September, 1934, Richard Gorton, a minor, was a junior in the Soda Springs High School and a member of the football team; that his high school team and the Paris High School team were scheduled to play a game of football at Paris on the 21st. Appellant was teaching at the Soda Springs High School and Russell Garst was coaching the Soda Springs team. On the day the game was played, the Soda Springs High School team was transported to and from Paris in privately owned automobiles. One of the automobiles used for that purpose was owned by appellant. Her car was driven by Mr. Garst, the coach of the Soda Springs High School team.

One of the most difficult questions, if not the most difficult, presented by the record, is, Was the coach, Russell Garst, the agent of appellant while and in driving her car from Soda Springs to Paris, and in returning to the point where the accident occurred?

Briefly stated, the facts bearing upon that question are as follows: That appellant knew the Soda Springs High School football team and the Paris High School football team were to play a game of football at Paris September 21, 1934; that she volunteered her car for use in transporting some of the members of the Soda Springs team to and from the game; that she asked the coach, Russell Garst, the day before the game, if he had all the cars necessary for the trip to Paris the next day; that he said he needed one more; that she told him he might use her car if he drove it; that she was not promised compensation for the use of her car and did not receive any; that the school district paid for the gasoline used on the trip to and from the game; that she testified she loaned the car to Mr. Garst; that she had not employed Mr. Garst at any time and that she had not at any time "directed his work or his services, or what he was doing."

. . .[T]he record before us does not present the question as to whether the customary relationship of master and servant did or did not exist between the appellant and Mr. Garst. Respondents do not bottom their right to recover upon the negligence of the coach, acting as the *servant* of appellant. They ground their right to recover upon the alleged negligence of the coach, acting as the *special agent* of appellant.

Broadly speaking, "agency" indicates the relation which exists where one person acts for another. It has these three principal forms: 1. The relation of principal and agent; 2. The relation of master and servant; and, 3. The relation of employer or proprietor and independent contractor. While all have points of similarity, there are, nevertheless, numerous differences. We are concerned here with the first form only.

Specifically, "agency" is the relationship which results from the manifestation of consent by one person to another that the other shall act on his behalf and subject to his control, and consent by the other so to act. (Restatement Agency, sec. 1, p. 7; *Sullivan v. Finch,* 140 Kan. 399, 36 P.2d 1023; *Georgeson v. Nielsen,* 214 Wis. 191, 252 N.W. 576).

* * * *

[In a previous case,] This court held, and correctly so, that one who undertakes to transact some business or manage some affair for another by authority and on account of the latter. . . . But this court did not thereby hold that the relationship of principal and agent must necessarily involve some matter of business, but only that where one undertakes to transact some business or manage some affair for another by authority and on account of the latter, the relationship of principal and agent arises.

To enable the Soda Springs football team to play football at Paris, it had to be transported to Paris. Automobiles were to be used and another car was needed. At that juncture, appellant volunteered the use of her car. For what purpose? Necessarily for the purpose of furnishing additional transportation. Appellant, of course, could have driven the car herself, but instead of doing that, she designated the driver (Russell Garst) and, in doing so, made it a condition precedent that the person she designated should drive her car. That appellant thereby at least consented that Russell Garst should act for her and in her behalf, in driving her car to and from the football game, is clear from her act in volunteering the use of her car upon the express condition that he should drive it, and, further, that Mr. Garst consented to so act for appellant is equally clear by his act in driving the car. It is not essential to the existence of authority that there be a contract between principal and agent or that the agent promise to act as such (Restatement Agency, secs. 15, 16, pp. 50–54), nor is it essential to the relationship of principal and agent that they, or either, receive compensation (Restatement Agency, sec. 16, p. 53).

Furthermore, this court held in *Willi v. Schaefer Hitchcock Co.,* 53 Idaho 367, 25 P.2d 167, in harmony with the clear weight of authority, that the fact of ownership alone (conceded here), regardless of the presence or absence of the owner in the car at the time of the accident, establishes a *prima facie* case against the owner for the reason that the presumption arises that the driver is the agent of the owner. . . .

It is vigorously contended, however, that the facts and circumstances bearing upon the question under discussion show appellant loaned her car to Mr. Garst. A determination of that question makes it necessary to quote appellant's testimony. She testified as follows:

"Q. On or about the 21st day of September, 1934, state whether or not you permitted Russell Garst to use that car?

"A. I did.

"Q. Under what circumstances?

"A. I loaned it to him.

"Q. When did you loan it to him? Was it that day, or the day before?

"A. On the day before I told him he might have it the next day.

"Q. Did you receive any compensation, or were you promised any compensation, for its use?

"A. No, sir.

"Q. What were the circumstances under which you permitted him to take it?

"A. Well,—"

After having so testified, appellant was then asked:

"Q. You may relate the conversation with him, if there was such conversation.

"A. I asked him if he had all the cars necessary for his trip to Paris the next day. He said he needed one more. I said that he might use mine if he drove it. That was the extent of it."

While it appears that appellant first testified that she permitted Russell Garst to use her car and also that she loaned it to him, it further appears that when she was immediately afterward asked to state the conversation she had with the coach about the matter, she stated that she asked him if he had all the cars necessary for the trip to Paris the next day, that he said he needed one more, that she said he might use her car if he drove it, and, finally, she said that that was the extent of it. It is clear, then, that appellant intended, in relating the conversation she had with the coach, to state the circumstances fully, because, after having testified to the conversation, she concluded by saying, "That was the extent of it." Thus she gave the jury to understand that those were the circumstances, and all of the circumstances, under which Russell Garst drove her car to the football game. If the appellant fully and correctly related the conversation she had with the coach and the circumstances under which he drove her car, as she unquestionably undertook to, and did, do, it follows that, as a matter of fact, she did not say anything whatever to him about loaning her car and he said nothing whatever to her about borrowing it.

We therefore conclude the evidence sufficiently supports the finding of the jury that the relationship of principal and agent existed between appellant and Russell Garst.

* * * *

The judgments and orders are affirmed with costs to respondents.

DISSENT

BUDGE, J., Dissenting.—I am unable to concur in the majority opinion.

As I read the entire record there is a total lack of evidence to support the allegation in the complaint that Garst was the agent of appellant Doty at or prior to the time of the accident in which respondent Richard Gorton was injured and as such agent was acting within the scope of his authority. An agent is one who acts for another by authority from him, one who undertakes to transact business or manage some affair for another by authority and on account of the latter. (*Moreland v. Mason,* 45 Idaho 143, 260 P. 1035.) Agency means more than mere passive permission. It involves request, instruction or command. (*Klee v. United States,* 53 F.2d 58.) The facts are not in dispute. Briefly they may be stated as follows: Appellant Doty and Garst were teachers at the Soda Springs High

School, not in the same but in different departments, the former being a teacher of Latin and Home Economics and the latter acting as Coach of Athletics and a teacher of Mathematics. Neither had any official connection with the other. Their employment was entirely separate and distinct. Miss Doty had no connection with, nor duty with respect to, the athletic activities of the school. Upon the day preceding the game, to which reference is made in the majority opinion, in a general conversation between Garst and Miss Doty she asked Garst if he had sufficient cars to transport the boys to Paris. Garst replied that he needed one more car and in answer to this statement Miss Doty stated he *might* use her car if he drove it himself. The next day Garst took Miss Doty's car to a garage in Soda Springs and purchased gasoline, charging it to the school district, the district subsequently paying for the same. Miss Doty received no compensation and none was to be paid her for the use of her car. As I read the record she simply loaned her car to Garst to enable him to furnish means of transportation for the team from Soda Springs to Paris. It was nothing more or less than a kindly gesture on her part to be helpful to Garst, the athletic coach, in arranging transportation for the team. The mere fact that she stated to Garst that he should drive the car was a mere precaution upon her part that the car should not be driven by any one of the young boys,—a perfectly natural thing for her to do. It is principally and particularly upon this statement of fact that the majority opinion holds that the relationship of principal and agent was created and that Garst became the agent of Miss Doty, authorized by her to undertake the transportation of the boys from Soda Springs to Paris for her and on her behalf. In other words, Miss Doty is held legally liable for each and every act done or performed by Garst as though she had been personally present and personally performed each and every act that was done or performed by Garst, this in the absence of any contractual relationship between her and Garst or between her and the school district. The rule would seem to be that one who borrows a car for his own use is a gratuitous bailee and not an agent of the owner. *(Gochee v. Wagner,* 257 N.Y. 344, 178 N.E. 553.)

* * * *

Appellant loaned her car to Garst, not for her benefit, but for his benefit or for the benefit of the school district. Garst was over the age of sixteen years, a careful driver, competent in every way to be entrusted with the loan of the car, and the accident happened before the purposes of the loan had been completed. Clearly the relationship of master and servant or that of principal and agent did not exist nor did any other legal relationship exist such as would create a liability against appellant. The rule announced in the foregoing case is applicable to the facts of the instant case. It is held in *S. B. McMaster, Inc., v. Chevrolet Motor Co.,* 3 F.2d 469, that:

"There are two distinctly essential elements in an 'agency.' The first is that the agent acts, not for himself, but, for another; and the second is that his acts, within the scope of his authority must be binding upon his principal."

* * * *

The judgment should be reversed and the cause remanded for further proceedings as herein indicated.

QUESTIONS

1. Apparently the jury received the following instruction at trial: "If you find from the evidence that Russell Garst, now deceased, was at the time of the accident, the agent of the defendant, then the defendant is chargeable with the acts of said agent as fully and to the same extent as though she had been driving the automobile herself." Does this sound like an accurate statement of the law?

2. As you are leaving class today, you run into the Dean of the college. She explains that the college's football team has a game across town, and she needs to borrow your car to drive the star linebacker to the game because he missed the bus. You really want to help the school team. Are there certain conditions under which you might let the Dean use your car? Would it matter if you noticed that, as she rushed away, her glasses fell and broke?

SECTION II: Agency Problems Involving Contracts

Many agency problems involve actions taken by an agent to bind the principal to an agreement with a third party. When a contract is involved, the central question is whether the principal is bound by the agent's actions, which generally depends upon whether the agent had authority and whether the agreement that was created was within the scope of that authority.

There are various forms of authority through which an agent may bind a principal to an agreement. These include: actual authority, apparent authority, liability of an undisclosed principal, ratification and estoppel.

A. Actual Authority

Actual authority (both express and implied) grants the agent the authority to bind the principal to agreements within the scope of the agency.

Excerpts from the Third Restatement

§ 1.03 Manifestation

A person manifests assent or intention through written or spoken words or other conduct.

§ 2.01 Actual Authority

An agent acts with actual authority when, at the time of taking action that has legal consequences for the principal, the agent reasonably believes, in accordance with the principal's manifestations to the agent, that the principal wishes the agent so to act.

§ 2.02 Scope of Actual Authority

(1) An agent has actual authority to take action designated or implied in the principal's manifestations to the agent and acts necessary or incidental to achieving the principal's objectives, as the agent reasonably understands the principal's manifestations and objectives when the agent determines how to act.

(2) An agent's interpretation of the principal's manifestations is reasonable if it reflects any meaning known by the agent to be ascribed by the principal and, in the absence of any meaning known to the agent, as a reasonable person in the agent's position would interpret the manifestations in light of the context, including circumstances of which the agent has notice and the agent's fiduciary duty to the principal.

(3) An agent's understanding of the principal's objectives is reasonable if it accords with the principal's manifestations and the inferences that a reasonable person in the agent's position would draw from the circumstances creating the agency.

§ 3.01 Creation of Actual Authority

Actual authority, as defined in § 2.01, is created by a principal's manifestation to an agent that, as reasonably understood by the agent, expresses the principal's assent that the agent take action on the principal's behalf.

An agent has actual authority when the principal "communicates" to the agent about the activities in which the agent may engage and the obligations the agent may undertake. This communication may be spoken or written, may occur through silence or even be implied by an occupation or a position. There are two forms of actual authority: express and implied. Determining whether express authority exists involves examining the principal's explicit instructions. Determining whether implied authority exists involves examining the principal's explicit instructions and asking what else might be reasonably included in those instructions (i.e., implied) in order to accomplish the job. Implied authority includes actions that are necessary to accomplish the principal's original instructions to the agent; it also includes those actions that the agent reasonably believes the principal wishes him to do, based on the agent's reasonable understanding of the authority granted by the principal.

Mill St. Church of Christ v. Hogan

785 S.W.2d 263 (Ky. App. 1990)

Mill Street Church of Christ and State Automobile Mutual Insurance Company petition for review of a decision of the New Workers' Compensation Board [hereinafter "New Board"] which had reversed an earlier decision by the Old Workers' Compensation Board [hereinafter "Old Board"]. The Old Board had ruled that Samuel J. Hogan was not an employee of the Mill Street Church of Christ and was not entitled to any workers' compensation benefits. The New Board reversed and ruled that Samuel Hogan was an employee of the church.

Samuel Hogan filed a claim for workers' compensation benefits for an injury he received while painting the interior of the Mill Street Church of Christ on December 15, 1986. In 1986, the Elders of the Mill Street Church of Christ decided to hire church member, Bill Hogan, to paint the church building. The Elders decided that another church member, Gary Petty, would be hired to assist if any assistance was needed. In the past, the church had hired Bill Hogan for similar jobs, and he had been allowed to hire his brother, Sam Hogan, the respondent, as a helper. Sam Hogan had earlier been a member of the church but was no longer a member. . . .

Dr. David Waggoner, an Elder of the church, soon contacted Bill Hogan, and he accepted the job and began work. Apparently Waggoner made no mention to Bill Hogan of hiring a helper at that time. Bill Hogan painted the church by himself until he reached the baptistry portion of the church. This was a very high, difficult portion of the church to paint, and he decided that he needed help. After Bill Hogan had reached this point in his work, he discussed the matter of a helper with Dr. Waggoner at his office. According to both Dr. Waggoner and Hogan, they discussed the possibility of hiring Gary Petty to help Hogan. None of the evidence indicates that Hogan was told that he had to hire Petty. In fact, Dr. Waggoner apparently told Hogan that Petty was difficult to reach. That was basically all the discussion that these two individuals had concerning hiring a helper. None of the other Elders discussed the matter with Bill Hogan.

On December 14, 1986, Bill Hogan approached his brother, Sam, about helping him complete the job. Bill Hogan told Sam the details of the job, including the pay, and Sam accepted the job. On December 15, 1986, Sam began working. A half hour after he began, he climbed the ladder to paint a ceiling corner, and a leg of the ladder broke. Sam fell to the floor and broke his left arm. . . .The church Elders did not know that Bill Hogan had approached Sam Hogan to work as a helper until after the accident occurred.

After the accident, Bill Hogan reported the accident and resulting injury to Charles Payne, a church Elder and treasurer. Payne stated in a deposition that he told Bill Hogan that the church had insurance. At this time, Bill Hogan told Payne the total number of hours worked which included a half hour that Sam Hogan had worked prior to the accident. Payne issued Bill Hogan a check for all of these hours. Further, Bill Hogan did not have to use his own tools and materials in the project. The church supplied the tools, materials, and supplies necessary to complete the project. Bill purchased needed items from Dunn's Hardware Store and charged them to the church's account.

. . . Mill Street Church of Christ is an insured employer under the Workers' Compensation Act. Sam Hogan filed a claim under the Workers' Compensation Act.

* * * *

As part of their argument, petitioners argue the New Board also erred in finding that Bill Hogan possessed implied authority as an agent to hire Sam Hogan. Petitioners contend there was neither implied nor apparent authority in the case at bar.

It is important to distinguish implied and apparent authority before proceeding further. Implied authority is actual authority circumstantially proven which the principal actually intended the agent to possess and includes such powers as are practically necessary to carry out the duties actually delegated.

Estell v. Barrickman, Ky. App., 571 S.W.2d 650 (1978). Apparent authority on the other hand is not actual authority but is the authority the agent is held out by the principal as possessing. It is a matter of appearances on which third parties come to rely. *Estell v. Barrickman, supra.*

Petitioners attack the New Board's findings concerning implied authority. In examining whether implied authority exists, it is important to focus upon the agent's understanding of his authority. It must be determined whether the agent reasonably believes because of present or past conduct of the principal that the principal wishes him to act in a certain way or to have certain authority. *3 Am.Jur.2d, Agency § 75.* The nature of the task or job may be another factor to consider. Implied authority may be necessary in order to implement the express authority. *3 Am.Jur.2d, Agency § 75, supra.* The existence of prior similar practices is one of the most important factors. Specific conduct by the principal in the past permitting the agent to exercise similar powers is crucial.

The person alleging agency and resulting authority has the burden of proving that it exists. [*Citations omitted.*] Agency cannot be proven by a mere statement, but it can be established by circumstantial evidence including the acts and conduct of the parties such as the continuous course of conduct of the parties covering a number of successive transactions. [*Citations omitted.*] Specifically one must look at what had gone on before to determine if the agent had certain authority. [*Citations omitted.*] If considering past similar acts done in a similar manner, it is found that the present action was taken with the apparent scope of the agent's authority, the act is binding upon the principal. [*Citations omitted.*]

It has been held that technical distinctions between implied or apparent authority are immaterial if a third party would suffer loss. . . . The principal will be bound to a third person by the act of the agent within his implied authority even if the third person was unaware that the agent's authority was only implied. *3 Am.Jur.2d Agency § 75, supra.*

In considering the above factors in the case at bar, Bill Hogan had implied authority to hire Sam Hogan as his helper. First, in the past the church had allowed Bill Hogan to hire his brother or other persons whenever he needed assistance on a project. Even though the Board of Elders discussed a different arrangement this time, no mention of this discussion was ever made to Bill or Sam Hogan. In fact, the discussion between Bill Hogan and Church Elder Dr. Waggoner, indicated that Gary Petty would be difficult to reach and Bill Hogan could hire whomever he pleased. Further, Bill Hogan needed to hire an assistant to complete the job for which he had been hired. The interior of the church simply could not be painted by one person. Maintaining a safe and attractive place of worship clearly is part of the church's function, and one for which it would designate an agent to ensure that the building is properly painted and maintained.

Finally, in this case, Sam Hogan believed that Bill Hogan had the authority to hire him as had been the practice in the past. To now claim that Bill Hogan could not hire Sam Hogan as an assistant, especially when Bill Hogan had never been told this fact, would be very unfair to Sam Hogan. Sam Hogan relied on Bill Hogan's representation. The church treasurer in this case even paid Bill Hogan for the half hour of work that Sam Hogan had completed prior to the accident. Considering the above facts, we find that Sam Hogan was within the employment of the Mill Street Church of Christ at the time he was injured. . . .

B. Apparent Authority

An agent acting under "apparent authority" appears to a third party to have the authority to bind the principal. Even if an agent lacks actual authority, a principal can be bound by an agent acting under apparent authority.

Excerpts from the Third Restatement

§ 2.03 Apparent Authority

Apparent authority is the power held by an agent or other actor to affect a principal's legal relations with third parties when a third party reasonably believes the actor has authority to act on behalf of the principal and that belief is traceable to the principal's manifestations.

§ 3.03 Creation of Apparent Authority

Apparent authority, as defined in § 2.03, is created by a person's manifestation that another has authority to act with legal consequences for the person who makes the manifestation, when a third party reasonably believes the actor to be authorized and the belief is traceable to the manifestation.

§ 3.11 Termination of Apparent Authority

(1) The termination of actual authority does not by itself end any apparent authority held by an agent.

(2) Apparent authority ends when it is no longer reasonable for the third party with whom an agent deals to believe that the agent continues to act with actual authority.

Real World Application: *The Mayor's Contracts*

Martin Resendiz was a congressional candidate and the mayor of a town called Sunland Park in New Mexico. In June of 2008 Resendiz was having drinks with executives of a company called Synthesis+ when he signed nine contracts related to a series of projects the city was planning. Synthesis+ is a California company that (following this incident in an effort to enforce these contracts) brought a suit against the town of Sunland Park for $1 million.

"The day I signed, I had way too much to drink. It was after 5 p.m. and I signed it [the contracts], and I didn't know what I was signing," Mayor (now former mayor) Resendiz acknowledged. "My sister had to pick me up." Resendiz is both a former El Paso, Texas, police officer and Sunland Park municipal judge.

In a deposition in the case brought by Synthesis+, Resendiz acknowledged signing the documents in May or June 2008 after several hours of drinking with Sythesis+ executives at Ardovino's Crossing, an Italian restaurant in Sunland Park. Resendiz explained: "Again, this was after two or three hours of us drinking, not exactly the best time to do business, not exactly the best time to read over legal documents, which he [David Soltero, an architect affiliated with Synthesis+] did not portray at any time to be legal documents. . ." [Transcript of Resendiz deposition.] Sunland Park City Councilor, Daniel Salinas, who was also deposed, said under oath that he was at the restaurant meeting and was also drunk.

Synthesis+ officials asserted that the mayor signed the documents in July 2008 at the Sunland Park city hall and that the mayor was sober. Sunland Park city officials asserted that, regardless of the place and circumstances of the signing, the contracts were not valid because they were not approved by the City. *Who is right?*

Apparent authority is not about what the principal wants the agent to do. It is about what a third party reasonably believes the principal has authorized the agent to do. Because of this dynamic, in evaluating whether apparent authority is present, it is critical to determine whether a principal made a manifestation to a third party that led that third party to reasonably believe that the agent had the authority to act on behalf of the principal. Apparent authority does not focus on communications between the principal and the agent or on whether a principal conferred authority on an agent to act. For purposes of apparent authority, it is irrelevant whether the agent has actual authority. Apparent authority is created when a person (principal or apparent principal) does something, says something or creates a reasonable impression (a "manifestation") that another person (the agent or even the apparent agent) has the authority to act on behalf of that apparent principal. A manifestation (*See* Section 1.03 of the Third Restatement, *supra.*) can either be an affirmative action, or a failure to do something. Another important feature of apparent authority is that, unlike estoppel, a third party need not show detrimental reliance to support a claim of apparent authority.

Three-Seventy Leasing Corp. v. Ampex Corp.

528 F.2d 993 (5th Cir. 1976)

DYER, CIRCUIT JUDGE:

Three-Seventy Leasing Corporation (370) seeks damages from Ampex Corporation (Ampex) for breach of a contract to sell six computer core memories. The district court, sitting without a jury, found that there was an enforceable contract between 370 and Ampex. . . . We find sufficient evidence to support the district court's finding of an enforceable contract, and agree that the terms of that contract precluded recovery of the type of compensatory damages which 370 sought below.

THE CONTRACT

Three-Seventy Leasing Corporation was formed by Joyce, at all times its only active employee, for the purpose of purchasing computer hardware from various manufacturers for lease to endusers. In August of 1972, Kays, a salesman of Ampex and friend of Joyce, initiated discussions with Joyce regarding the possibility of 370 purchasing computer equipment from Ampex. A meeting was arranged between Kays, Joyce, and Mueller, Kays' superior at Ampex. Joyce was informed at this meeting that Ampex could sell to 370 only if 370 could pass Ampex's credit requirements. Joyce informed the two that he did not think this would be a problem.

At approximately the same time, Joyce began negotiations with Electronic Data Systems (EDS), which resulted in EDS's verbal commitment to lease six units of Ampex computer core memory from 370. Desiring to close the two transactions simultaneously, Joyce continued negotiations with Kays. These negotiations resulted in a written document submitted by Kays to Joyce at the direction of Mueller. The document provided for the purchase by Joyce of six core memory units at a price of $100,000 each, with a down payment of $150,000 and the remainder to be paid over a five year period. The document specified that delivery was to be made to EDS. The document also contained a signature block for a representative of 370 and a signature block for a representative of Ampex.

Joyce received this document about November 3, 1972, and executed it on November 6, 1972. The document was never executed by a representative of Ampex. This document forms the core of the present controversy. 370 argues that the document was an offer to sell by Ampex, which was accepted upon Joyce's signature. Ampex contends that the document was nothing more than a solicitation which became an offer to purchase upon execution by Joyce, and that this offer was never accepted by Ampex. 370 counters by arguing in the alternative that even if the document when signed by Joyce was only an offer to purchase, the offer was later accepted by representatives of Ampex.

The district court, in concluding that there existed an enforceable contract, made no determination as to whether the document described above was an offer to sell accepted by Joyce's signature, or an offer to purchase when signed by Joyce which was later accepted by Ampex.

We reject the first alternative as being without evidentiary support. Elemental principles demand that there be a meeting of the minds and a communication that each party has consented to the terms of the agreement in order for a contract to exist. *Garcia v. Villarreal,* Tex. Civ. App. 1972, 478 S.W.2d 830. There is no evidence, either written or oral, other than the document itself, which shows that Ampex had the requisite intent necessary to the formation of a contract prior to November 6, 1972, the date the document was executed by Joyce. And the document on its face does not supply that intent. Rather, the fact that the document had a signature block for a representative of Ampex which was unsigned at the time it was submitted to Joyce, in the absence of other evidence, negates any interpretation that Ampex intended this to be an offer to Joyce, without any further acts necessary on the part of Ampex.

Thus, the document, when signed by Joyce, at most constituted an offer by him to purchase. In order for there to be a valid contract, we must therefore find some act of acceptance on the part of Ampex.

On November 9, 1972, Mueller issued an intra-office memorandum which stated in part that "on November 3, 1972, Ampex was awarded an Agreement by Three-Seventy Leasing, Dallas, Texas, for the purchase of six (6) ARM-3360 Memory Units", to be installed at EDS. This memorandum further informed those concerned at Ampex of Joyce's request that all contact with 370 be handled through Kays. On November 17, 1972, Kays sent a letter to Joyce which confirmed the delivery dates for the memory units.[2] We conclude, in light of the circumstances surrounding these negotiations, that the district court was not clearly erroneous when it found that Kays had apparent authority to accept Joyce's offer on behalf of Ampex, and we further conclude that the November 17 letter, in these circumstances, can reasonably be interpreted to be an acceptance.

An agent has apparent authority sufficient to bind the principal when the principal acts in such a manner as would lead a reasonably prudent person to suppose that the agent had the authority he purports to exercise. *Douglass v. Panama, Inc.,* Tex. 1974, 504 S.W.2d 776; *Tryad Service Corp. v. Machine Tool Center, Inc.,* Tex. App.1974, 512 S.W.2d 785. Further, absent knowledge on the part of third parties to the contrary, an agent has the apparent authority to do those things which are usual and proper to the conduct of the business which he is employed to conduct. *Mechanical Wholesale, Inc. v. Universal-Rundle Corp.,* 5 Cir. 1970, 432 F.2d 228 (interpreting Texas law).

In this case, Kays was employed by Ampex in the capacity of a salesman. It is certainly reasonable for third parties to presume that one employed as salesman has the authority to bind his employer to sell. And Ampex did nothing to dispel this reasonable inference. Rather, its actions and inactions provided a further basis for this belief. First, Kays, at the direction of Mueller, submitted the controversial document to Joyce for signature. The document contained a space for signature by an Ampex representative. Nothing in the document suggests that Kays did not have authority to sign it on behalf of Ampex.[3] Second, Joyce indicated to Kays and Mueller that he wished all communications to be channeled through Kays. Mueller agreed, and acknowledged this in the November 9 intra-company memorandum. Neither Mueller, nor anyone else at Ampex ever informed Joyce that communication regarding acceptance would

---

2 That letter stated:

Dear John:

With regard to delivery of equipment purchased by Three-Seventy Leasing: Ampex will ship three (3) million bytes of ARM-3360 magnetic core in sufficient time to install 1 1/2 million bytes the weekend of December 16, 1972. The remaining balance of 1 1/2 million bytes will be installed by the weekend of December 30, 1972.

The equipment will be installed in Camphill, Pennsylvania at a predetermined site by Electronic Data Systems.

Regards,

Thomas C. Kays, Sales Representative

3 It would have been an easy matter to provide in the document that only certain officers of Ampex had authority to sign on its behalf. Any inference to the contrary resulting from Ampex's failure to specify such a limitation must weigh against Ampex.

come through anyone other than Kays. In light of this request and Ampex's agreement, Joyce could reasonably expect that Kays would speak for the company.

Various individuals in the Ampex hierarchy testified at trial that only the contract manager or other supervisor in the company's contract department had authority to sign a contract on behalf of Ampex. However, there is no evidence that this limitation was ever communicated to Joyce in any manner. Absent knowledge of such a limitation by third parties, that limitation will not bar a claim of apparent authority. *Douglass v. Panama, Inc., supra.*

Thus, when Joyce received Kays' November 17 letter, he had every reason to believe, based upon Ampex's prior actions, that Kays spoke on behalf of the company. We thus agree with the district court's finding that Kays had apparent authority to act for Ampex.

Having determined that Kays had apparent authority to bind Ampex, we further conclude that his letter of November 17, in light of the pattern of negotiations, could reasonably be interpreted as a promise to ship the six memory units on the dates specified in the letter and on the terms previously set out in the document executed by Joyce and submitted to Ampex. The district court's finding that a contract was formed is therefore not clearly erroneous.[4]

* * * *

C. Liability of Undisclosed Principal

Liability of an undisclosed principal (a concept closely related to "inherent authority," a term that has been eliminated in the Third Restatement) may bind a principal to an agent's action even if the agent lacked actual authority AND even if the third party did not know the agent was acting on behalf of a principal. While this doctrine has been somewhat controversial over the years, it is an effort to address situations in which an agent, seemingly acting for himself, acts outside the scope of his authority and makes a commitment to a third party which is not fulfilled.

---

[4] Ampex contends that even if a contract is found to exist, it is unenforceable since there is no writing which complies with the statute of fraud. This argument falls along with their argument that there is no contract. The November 17 letter from Kays which constitutes the acceptance also satisfies the requirements of the statute of frauds.

no holding out, proof must be given of an agency in fact in order to make the principal liable.

Boydell Houghton, for the plaintiff. The defendants are liable in the present action. They are in fact undisclosed principals, who instead of carrying on the business in their own names employed a manager to carry it on for them, and clothed him with authority to do what was necessary to carry on the business. The case depends upon the same principles as *Edmunds v. Bushell,* where the manager of a business which was carried on in his own name with the addition "and Co." accepted a bill of exchange, notwithstanding a stipulation in the agreement with his principal that he should not accept bills; and the Court held that the principal was liable to an endorsee who took the bill without any knowledge of the relations between the principal and agent. In that case there was no holding out of the manager as an agent; it was the simple case of an agent being allowed to act as the ostensible principal without any disclosure to the world of there being any one behind him. Here the defendants have so conducted themselves as to enable their agent to hold himself out to the world as the proprietor of their business, and they are clearly undisclosed principals: *Ramazotti v. Bowring.* All that the plaintiff has to do, therefore, in order to charge the principals, is to show that the goods supplied were such as were ordinarily used in the business—that is to say, that they were within the reasonable scope of the agent's authority.

[Ed's. note: The opinion follows]

. . .LORD COLERIDGE, C.J.: The judgment which I am about to read has been written by my brother Wills, and I entirely concur in it. . .

WILLS, J: The plaintiff sues the defendants for the price of cigars supplied to the Victoria Hotel, Stockton-upon-Tees. The house was kept, not by the defendants, but by a person named Humble, whose name was over the door. The plaintiff gave credit to Humble, and to him alone, and had never heard of the defendants. The business, however, was really the defendants', and they had put Humble into it to manage it for them, and had forbidden him to buy cigars on credit. The cigars, however, were such as would usually be supplied to and dealt in at such an establishment. The learned county court judge held that the defendants were liable. I am of opinion that he was right.

There seems to be less of direct authority on the subject than one would expect. But I think that the Lord Chief Justice during the argument laid down the correct principle, viz., once it is established that the defendant was the real principal, the ordinary doctrine as to principal and agent applies—that the principal is liable for all the acts of the agent which are within the authority usually confided to an agent of that character, notwithstanding limitations, as between the principal and the agent, put upon that authority. It is said that it is only so where there has been a holding out of authority—which cannot be said of a case where the person supplying the goods knew nothing of the existence of a principal. But I do not think so. Otherwise, in every case of undisclosed principal, or at least in every case where the fact of there being a principal was undisclosed, the secret limitation of authority would prevail and defeat the action of the person dealing with the agent and then discovering that he was an agent and had a principal.

But in the case of a dormant partner it is clear law that no limitation of authority as between the dormant and active partner will avail the dormant partner as to things within the ordinary authority of a partner. The law of partnership is, on such a question, nothing but a branch of the general law of principal and agent, and it appears to me to be undisputed and conclusive on the point now under discussion.

The principle laid down by the Lord Chief Justice, and acted upon by the learned county court judge, appears to be identical with that enunciated in the judgments of Cockburn, C.J., and Mellor, J., in *Edmunds v. Bushell,* the circumstances of which case, though not identical with those of the present, come very near to them. There was no holding out, as the plaintiff knew nothing of the defendant. I appreciate the distinction drawn by Mr. Finlay in his argument, but the principle laid down in the judgments referred to, if correct, abundantly covers the present case. I cannot find that any doubt has ever been expressed that it is correct, and I think it is right, and that very mischievous consequences would often result if that principle were not upheld.

In my opinion this appeal ought to be dismissed with costs.

D. Ratification

The doctrine of ratification allows a principal to retroactively bind himself to an agent's agreement, even though, at the time the agent made the agreement, the agent had no authority to do so.

Excerpts from the Third Restatement

§ 4.01 Ratification Defined

(1) Ratification is the affirmance of a prior act done by another, whereby the act is given effect as if done by an agent acting with actual authority.

(2) A person ratifies an act by

(a) manifesting assent that the act shall affect the person's legal relations, or

(b) conduct that justifies a reasonable assumption that the person so consents.

(3) Ratification does not occur unless

(a) the act is ratifiable as stated in § 4.03,

(b) the person ratifying has capacity as stated in § 4.04,

(c) the ratification is timely as stated in § 4.05, and

(d) the ratification encompasses the act in its entirety as stated in § 4.07.

§ 4.02 Effect of Ratification

(1) Subject to the exceptions stated in subsection (2), ratification retroactively creates the effects of actual authority.

(2) Ratification is not effective:

(a) in favor of a person who causes it by misrepresentation or other conduct that would make a contract voidable;

(b) in favor of an agent against a principal when the principal ratifies to avoid a loss; or

(c) to diminish the rights or other interests of persons, not parties to the transaction, that were acquired in the subject matter prior to the ratification.

§ 4.04 Capacity to Ratify

(1) A person may ratify an act if

(a) the person existed at the time of the act, and

(b) the person had capacity as defined in § 3.04 at the time of ratifying the act.

(2) At a later time, a principal may avoid a ratification made earlier when the principal lacked capacity as defined in § 3.04.

§ 4.05 Timing of Ratification

A ratification of a transaction is not effective unless it precedes the occurrence of circumstances that would cause the ratification to have adverse and inequitable effects on the rights of third parties. These circumstances include:

(1) any manifestation of intention to withdraw from the transaction made by the third party;

(2) any material change in circumstances that would make it inequitable to bind the third party, unless the third party chooses to be bound; and

(3) a specific time that determines whether a third party is deprived of a right or subjected to a liability.

§ 4.06 Knowledge Requisite to Ratification

A person is not bound by a ratification made without knowledge of material facts involved in the original act when the person was unaware of such lack of knowledge.

§ 4.07 No Partial Ratification

A ratification is not effective unless it encompasses the entirety of an act, contract, or other single transaction.

Ratification is authority that is granted after a contract has been made. It involves situations in which an agent enters into an agreement on behalf of the principal without any authority (actual or apparent). There are two elements of ratification: (1) the principal, through word or deed, must manifest assent to ("affirm") the agreement; and (2) the law must give effect to that assent.

Affirmation may be express or implied; it is often implied by the principal accepting the benefits of the transaction. Once an agreement or transaction has been ratified, the law treats it as if it were originally entered into by the agent with actual authority. Both parties to the agreement are bound following a valid ratification.

Limitations on Ratification

Note that there are only certain circumstances in which an agreement may be ratified. For a ratification to be valid, the principal must know or have reason to know, at the time of the alleged ratification, the material facts relating to the transaction. A principal may not partially ratify a transaction. It is an "all or nothing" proposition. If the third party manifests an intention to withdraw from the transaction prior to the ratification, the principal may not subsequently ratify the agreement. Ratification may also be denied in order to protect the rights of innocent third parties. (This usually happens when there has been some material change in the circumstances between the time of the transaction and the time of the purported ratification.)

Once a contract has been ratified, it generally creates retroactive authority. In other words, the law treats the agreement as though the agent who entered into the agreement had actual authority at the time the agreement was made, even if the agent lacked authority at that time. One significant exception to this treatment occurs when the principal had no capacity to enter into the agreement at the time it was made. For example, if an agent enters into an agreement on behalf of a minor, and the minor does not ratify the agreement until she becomes an adult, then the agreement is effective with respect to that former minor upon ratification, not from the date of the original agreement.

Botticello v. Stefanovicz

177 Conn. 22, 411 A.2d 16 (Conn. 1979)

This case concerns the enforceability of an agreement for the sale of real property when that agreement has been executed by a person owning only an undivided half interest in the property. The plaintiff brought an action for specific performance against the defendants to compel conveyance of their land in accordance with the terms of a lease and option-to-purchase agreement signed by one of the defendants. . . . The defendants are now appealing from the consequent entry of a judgment ordering them to convey the real property in question to the plaintiff by warranty deed in consideration for the payment of $74,700.

The finding of the trial court discloses the following undisputed facts: The defendants, Mary and Walter Stefanovicz (hereinafter "Mary" and "Walter") in 1943 acquired as tenants in common a farm situated in the towns of Colchester and Lebanon. In the fall of 1965, the plaintiff, Anthony Botticello, became interested in the property. When he first visited the farm, Walter advised him that the asking price was $100,000. The following January, the plaintiff again visited the farm and made a counteroffer of $75,000. At that time, Mary stated that there was "no way" she could sell it for that amount. Ultimately the plaintiff and Walter agreed upon a price of $85,000 for a lease with an option to purchase; during these negotiations, Mary stated that she would not sell the property for less than that amount.

The informal agreement was finalized with the assistance of counsel for both Walter and the plaintiff. The agreement was drawn up by Walter's attorney after consultation with Walter and the plaintiff; it was then sent to, and modified by, the plaintiff's attorney. The agreement was signed by Walter and by the plaintiff. Neither the plaintiff nor his attorney, nor Walter's attorney, was then aware of the fact that Walter did not own the property outright. The plaintiff, although a successful businessman with considerable experience in real estate never requested his attorney to do a title search of any kind, and consequently no title search was done. Walter never represented to the plaintiff or the plaintiff's attorney, or to his own attorney, that he was acting for his wife, as her agent. Mary's part ownership came to light in 1968, when a third party sought an easement over the land in question.

Shortly after the execution of the lease and option-to-purchase agreement, the plaintiff took possession of the property. He made substantial improvements on the property and, in 1971, properly exercised his option to purchase. When the defendants refused to honor the option agreement, the plaintiff commenced the present action against both Mary and Walter, seeking specific performance, possession of the premises, and damages.

* * * *

The plaintiff alleged, and the trial court agreed, that although Mary was not a party to the lease and option-to-purchase agreement, its terms were nonetheless binding upon her because Walter acted as her authorized agent in the negotiations, discussions, and execution of the written agreement. The defendants have attacked several findings of fact and conclusions of law, claiming that the underlying facts and applicable law do not support the court's conclusion of agency. We agree.

Agency is defined as " 'the fiduciary relationship which results from manifestation of consent by one person to another that the other shall act on his behalf and subject to his control, and consent by the other so to act . . . .' Restatement (Second), 1 Agency § 1." *McLaughlin v. Chicken Delight, Inc.,* 164 Conn. 317, 322, 321 A.2d 456 (1973). Thus, the three elements required to show the existence of an agency relationship include: (1) a manifestation by the principal that the agent will act for him; (2) acceptance by the agent of the undertaking; and (3) an understanding between the parties that the principal will be in control of the undertaking. Restatement (Second), 1 Agency § 1, comment b (1958).[2]

The existence of an agency relationship is a question of fact. . . . The burden of proving agency is on the plaintiff. . .; and it must be proven by a fair preponderance of the evidence. . . . Marital status cannot in and of itself prove the agency relationship. . . . Nor does the fact that the defendants owned the land jointly make one the agent for the other. [*Citations omitted throughout.*]

The facts set forth in the court's finding are wholly insufficient to support the court's conclusion that Walter acted as Mary's authorized agent in the discussions concerning the sale of their farm and in the execution of the written agreement. The court's conclusion must be tested by the finding and not by the evidence. *Spicer v. Spicer,* 173 Conn. 161, 163, 377 A.2d 259 (1977). The finding indicates that when the farm was purchased, and when the couple transferred property to their sons, Walter handled many of the business aspects, including making payments for taxes, insurance, and mortgage. The finding also discloses that Mary and Walter discussed the sale of the farm, and that Mary remarked that she would not sell it for $75,000, and would not sell it for less than $85,000. A statement that one will not sell for *less than* a certain amount is by no means the equivalent of an agreement to sell for that amount. [*Citation omitted.*] Moreover, the fact that one spouse tends more to business matters than the other does not, absent other evidence of agreement or authorization, constitute the delegation of power as to an agent. What is most damaging to the plaintiff's case is the court's uncontradicted finding that, although Mary may have acquiesced in Walter's handling of many business matters, Walter *never* signed any documents as agent for Mary prior to 1966. Mary had consistently signed any deed, mortgage, or mortgage note in connection with their jointly held property.

---

[2] Agency may be either actual or apparent. "Apparent authority is that semblance of authority which a principal, through his own acts or inadvertences, causes or allows third persons to believe his agent possesses." *Lewis v. Michigan Millers Mutual Ins. Co.,* 154 Conn. 660, 665, 228 A.2d 803 (1967); *see* Restatement (Second), 1 Agency § 8 (1958). Apparent authority thus must be determined by the acts of the principal rather than by the acts of the agent. *Nowak v. Capitol Motors, Inc.,* 158 Conn. 65, 69, 255 A.2d 845 (1969). Since the plaintiff has admitted that he did not know of Mary's interest in the land at the time the agreement was signed, her actions cannot form the basis for a finding of apparent authority, and the plaintiff has not pursued that theory.

In light of the foregoing, it is clear that the facts found by the court fail to support its conclusion that Walter acted as Mary's authorized agent, and the conclusion therefore cannot stand. [*Citations omitted.*]

The plaintiff argues, alternatively, that even if no agency relationship existed at the time the agreement was signed, Mary was bound by the contract executed by her husband because she ratified its terms by her subsequent conduct. The trial court accepted this alternative argument as well, concluding that Mary had ratified the agreement by receiving and accepting payments from the plaintiff, and by acquiescing in his substantial improvements to the farm. The underlying facts, however, do not support the conclusion of ratification.

Ratification is defined as "the affirmance by a person of a prior act which did not bind him but which was done or professedly done on his account." Restatement (Second), 1 Agency § 82 (1958). Ratification requires "acceptance of the results of the act with an *intent* to ratify, and with *full knowledge of all the material circumstances." (Emphasis added.) Ansonia v. Cooper,* 64 Conn. 536, 544, 30 A. 760 (1894). [*Citations omitted.*]

The finding neither indicates an intent by Mary to ratify the agreement, nor establishes her knowledge of all the material circumstances surrounding the deal. At most, Mary observed the plaintiff occupying and improving the land, received rental payments from the plaintiff from time to time, knew that she had an interest in the property, and knew that the use, occupancy, and rentals were pursuant to a written agreement she had not signed. None of these facts is sufficient to support the conclusion that Mary ratified the agreement and thus bound herself to its terms. It is undisputed that Walter had the power to lease his own undivided one-half interest in the property; [*Citations omitted.*] and the facts found by the trial court could be referable to that fact alone. Moreover, the fact that the rental payments were used for "family" purposes indicates nothing more than one spouse providing for the other.

The plaintiff makes the further argument that Mary ratified the agreement simply by receiving its benefits and by failing to repudiate it. *See* Restatement (Second), 1 Agency § 98 (1958). The plaintiff fails to recognize that before the receipt of benefits may constitute ratification, the other requisites for ratification must first be present. "Thus if the original transaction was not purported to be done on account of the principal, the fact that the principal receives its proceeds does not make him a party to it." Restatement (Second), 1 Agency § 98, comment f (1958). Since Walter at no time purported to be acting on his wife's behalf, as is essential to effective subsequent ratification; . . . Mary is not bound by the terms of the agreement, and specific performance cannot be ordered as to her.

II

Our conclusion that there can be no recovery against Mary is not dispositive of the rights that the plaintiff may have against Walter. A person who contracts to convey full title to real property is not himself excused from performance, or immune from liability for breach, because of his inability to convey more than an undivided half interest in the property.

* * * *

In view of our holding that Mary never authorized her husband to act as her agent for any purpose connected with the lease and option-to-purchase agreement, recovery against her is precluded. As to Walter, the fact that his ownership was restricted to an undivided one-half interest in no way limited his capacity to contract. He contracted to convey full title and for breach of that contract he may be held liable. *Schneidau v. Manley, supra,* 288; *see Foster v. Civale, supra,* 474. The facts of the case are sufficient to furnish a basis for relief to the plaintiff by specific performance or by damages.

. . . .Since no third parties are here involved, the form of relief to be accorded must take into account the plaintiff's preference as well as the court's own discretion, "depending upon the equities of the case and based on reason and sound judgment." . . . .

Bullock v. State, Dept. of Transp.

966 P.2d 1215 (Utah App. 1998)

BILLINGS, JUDGE:

FACTS

Appellant and the individual defendants in this case were partners who owned land in Provo canyon. The Provo canyon property was the sole asset of the partnership. In October 1991, appellant's partners negotiated a contract between the partnership and UDOT [Utah Department of Transportation] to sell the Provo canyon property to the State of Utah. Appellant learned of this contract after it was negotiated but before the sale was finalized. Appellant opposed the sale because he felt it was below market value.

In January 1992, appellant discussed the contemplated sale with a UDOT employee. Appellant told the employee that he believed the sale would be invalid under the partnership agreement unless all of the partners consented to it. Appellant followed up this conversation with a letter to UDOT which indicated his familiarity with the terms of the sale. The letter concluded: "I have not yet received any information from you and would appreciate receiving whatever you are able to provide so hopefully a sale to the State of Utah can be effectuated."

In March 1992, the other partners deeded the Provo canyon property to UDOT in accordance with the 1991 contract of sale. Appellant did not sign the deed. In September 1992, the individual defendants, acting for the partnership, sent appellant a check for $67,198.43. This check was identified as appellant's share of the proceeds from the sale of the Provo canyon property, and it was accompanied by a note totaling the proceeds of the sale and explaining how they had been disbursed among the partners. Appellant endorsed and negotiated the check on September 18, 1992. Appellant did not respond in any other way to his receiving the check and the sales information.

In March 1993, one year after the title transfer and six months after appellant had accepted payment for the sale, he served notice of suit against the State of Utah. . . . In March 1996, appellant filed suit against UDOT and the individual defendants in state court and again tendered a check for his share of the sale proceeds. The state trial court dismissed appellant's claims against the State as untimely. The trial court also dismissed appellant's suit against the individual defendants, concluding appellant had ratified the sale. Appellant now appeals.

ANALYSIS

* * * *

II. Did the trial court err in dismissing appellant's claims against the individual defendants because appellant had ratified the sale to UDOT?

A. Did appellant ratify the sale to UDOT?

Appellant argues the trial court erroneously concluded that he ratified the sale of the Provo canyon property and thus erred in dismissing his claims against his partners. . . .

It is well-established under Utah law that " '[s]ubsequent affirmance by a principal of a contract made on his behalf by one who had at the time neither actual nor apparent authority constitutes a ratification, which in general is as effectual as an original authorization.' " *Moses v. Archie McFarland & Son,* 119 Utah 602, 607, 230 P.2d 571, 573 (1951).

A principal may impliedly or expressly ratify an agreement made by an unauthorized agent. Ratification of an agent's acts relates back to the time the unauthorized act occurred and is sufficient to create the relationship of principal and agent. Ratification is premised upon the knowledge of all material facts and upon an express or implied intention on the part of the principal to ratify.[*Citations omitted.*]

In *Moses,* the Utah Supreme Court explained the reasoning behind the doctrine of implied ratification:

> Ratification, like original authority, need not be express. Any conduct which indicates assent by the purported principal to become a party to the transaction or which is justifiable only if there is ratification is sufficient. Even silence with full knowledge of the facts may manifest affirmance and thus operate as a ratification. The person with whom the agent dealt will so obviously be deceived by assuming the professed agent was authorized to act as such, that the principal is under a duty to undeceive him. *So a purported principal may not be wilfully ignorant, nor may he purposely shut his eyes to means of information within his possession and control and thereby escape ratification "if the circumstances are such that he could reasonably have been expected to dissent unless he were willing to be a party to the transaction."*

Moses, 230 P.2d at 573–74 (*citation omitted*) (emphasis added).

In essence, the doctrine of implied ratification protects both a principal's agent and the co-parties to a contract by ensuring that the principal cannot repudiate the contract after the fact if any reasonable person would have concluded from the principal's actions at the time of the transaction that the principal endorsed the contract.

However, we will not infer ratification of a contract unless we conclude that the principal knowingly assented to the material terms of the contract. . . . Thus, " 'ratification requires the principal to have knowledge of all material facts and an intent to ratify.' " *Zions First Nat'l Bank,* 762 P.2d at 1098 (citations omitted).

Here, the trial court concluded, and we agree, that appellant had sufficient knowledge of the material facts of the sale to enable him to ratify the sale. Appellant knew in October 1991 that his partners were negotiating a sale to UDOT and was aware of the general terms of the sale. In September 1992, appellant was informed of the sale price and the manner in which the sale proceeds were distributed among the partners. Thus, appellant had unequivocal information that the sale had occurred and sufficient material facts about the sale that his ratification of the sale can reasonably be inferred from his actions. [*Citations Omitted.*]

The trial court also concluded that appellant ratified the sale by his conduct. "Under some circumstances failure to disaffirm may constitute ratification of the agent's acts." *Zions First Nat'l Bank,* 762 P.2d at 1098 (*citations omitted*). "Implied [ratification may arise] under circumstances of acquiescence or where a duty to disaffirm is not promptly exercised." *Lowe v. April Indus., Inc.,* 531 P.2d 1297, 1299 (Utah 1974) (footnote omitted).

Any conduct which indicates assent . . . which is justifiable only if there is ratification is sufficient [to ratify a contract]. Even silence with full knowledge of the facts may manifest affirmance and thus operate as a ratification [when t]he person with whom the agent dealt will so obviously be deceived [by the principal's silence] that the principal is under a duty to undeceive him. *Moses,* 230 P.2d at 574 (*citation omitted*). A duty to educate other parties to a contract arises whenever "the circumstances are such that [the principal] could reasonably have been expected to dissent unless he were a willing party to the transaction." *Id.*

A principal's retention of the fruits of a contract can also serve as an implied ratification of the contract. As the *Zions First Nat'l Bank* court noted:

> The retention by a purported principal, with knowledge of the facts *and before he has changed his position,* of something which he is not entitled to retain unless an act purported to be done on his account is affirmed, and to which he makes no claim except through such act, constitutes an affirmance unless at the time of such retention he repudiates the act. Even if he repudiates the act, his retention constitutes an affirmance at the election of the other party to the transaction.
>
> *Zions First Nat'l Bank,* 762 P.2d at 1099 (*citation omitted*).

In this case, appellant had knowledge both of the existence of the contract and of its material terms. Although appellant had voiced objections to the sale before it took place, he had framed his objections to imply that he would consent to a sale if the terms were satisfactory. When the other partners sent him a check for his portion of the proceeds and a note explaining the sale transaction and the disposition of the sale proceeds, appellant endorsed and negotiated the check and took no other action. Appellant made no objection until one year after the sale, by which time he had held his share of the sale proceeds for over six months. Under these circumstances, appellant "could reasonably be expected to dissent unless he were willing to be a party to the transaction." *Moses,* 230 P.2d at 574. Thus, the only reasonable conclusion the other parties to the transaction could draw from appellant's actions was that appellant had withdrawn his earlier objections to the sale and had ratified the contract.

* * * *

B. Did appellant's ratification release his partners from liability for violating the partnership agreement?

Finally, appellant argues even if he ratified the sale with respect to UDOT, his ratification was insufficient to release his partners from liability for their own breach of the partnership agreement. Appellant argues that his partners remain liable to him for damages because he was obligated to ratify his partners' act in order to protect his own interest and because his partners secured his ratification by means of duress and misrepresentation. Appellant cites *Kidd v. Maldonado,* 688 P.2d 461 (Utah 1984), to support his position. However, in *Maldonado,* the supreme court concluded that an agent who had violated his fiduciary duty to the principal was not liable to his principal because the principal failed to contest the agent's actions after they were brought to his attention, thereby implicitly ratifying them. *See Maldonado, 688 P.2d at 462.* The *Maldonado* court stated that "[w]hen a principal sees an act done by his agent and the act is not subject to misunderstanding by a reasonable person, the law does not permit the principal to ignore what is obvious, even if it be contrary to his instructions." *Id.* Thus the *Maldonado* court concluded, as we do in this case, that the principal's acquiescence in unauthorized acts *once he had reason to know about them,* constituted a ratification sufficient to release the agent from liability. *See id.*

CONCLUSION

. . .We. . .conclude that by accepting his portion of the sale proceeds and by failing to disaffirm the sale for over six months, appellant implicitly ratified the sale contract. This ratification validated the sale of the Provo canyon property to UDOT and released appellant's partners from liability for their violation of the partnership agreement. We therefore hold that the trial court correctly dismissed appellant's claims against the State and the individual defendants.

E. Estoppel

Estoppel is a doctrine that does not create a binding contract between the parties; rather, it prevents a principal from avoiding an obligation by arguing that no authority existed at the time the agent entered into a contract.

Excerpt from the Third Restatement

§ 2.05 Estoppel to Deny Existence of Agency Relationship

A person who has not made a manifestation that an actor has authority as an agent and who is not otherwise liable as a party to a transaction purportedly done by the actor on that person's account is subject to liability to a third party who justifiably is induced to make a detrimental change in position because the transaction is believed to be on the person's account, if

(1) the person intentionally or carelessly caused such belief, or

(2) having notice of such belief and that it might induce others to change their positions, the person did not take reasonable steps to notify them of the facts.

Rather than a specific form of authority, estoppel is an equitable doctrine which may prevent a principal from denying that an agency relationship exists. As a result, estoppel might be used to allow for the enforcement of an agreement made on behalf of a principal as though authority for such agreement had been given by the principal. Estoppel generally arises in agency situations in which the principal has done something improper. As used in agency, estoppel involves: (1) acts or omissions (generally wrongful) by the principal, either intentional or negligent, which create an appearance of authority in the purported agent; (2) a third party who reasonably and in good faith acts in reliance based upon that appearance of authority; and (3) the third party changing his or her position in reliance upon that appearance of authority.

The concepts of apparent authority and estoppel should not be confused. While it is certainly possible that both conditions could exist in the same circumstances, estoppel requires that the third party alter his or her position in reliance on the purported authority; apparent authority has no such requirement. In addition, apparent authority requires a manifestation by the principal (directly or indirectly) to the third party, whereas no such manifestation is required for estoppel, which merely requires some culpable act or omission by the principal.

While estoppel often arises when the principal takes some improper action, an improper action alone is not sufficient to amount to a "manifestation" to the third party. Therefore, in some circumstances it might be difficult to establish apparent authority even though a claim of estoppel might be available. One important facet to note is that, in the agency context, estoppel is not used to create a binding contract which may be enforced by both parties. Estoppel is used to prevent one party (typically the principal) from denying a purported agent's authority when the third party wants to enforce that contract. If the third party did not assert the doctrine of estoppel to enforce a contract, the principal would not have the right to enforce the same contract against the third party.

Hoddeson v. Koos Bros.

47 N.J. Super. 224, 135 A.2d 702 (N.J. Super.1957)

JAYNE, J.:

The occurrence which engages our present attention is a little more than conventionally unconventional in the common course of trade. Old questions appear in new styles. A digest of the story told by Mrs. Hoddeson will be informative and perhaps admonitory to the unwary shopper.

The plaintiff Mrs. Hoddeson was acquainted with the spacious furniture store conducted by the defendant, Koos Bros., a corporation, at No. 1859 St. George Avenue in the City of Rahway. On a previous observational visit, her eyes had fallen upon certain articles of bedroom furniture which she ardently desired to acquire for her home. It has been said that "the sea hath bounds but deep desire hath none." Her sympathetic mother liberated her from the grasp of despair and bestowed upon her a gift of $165 with which to consummate the purchase.

It was in the forenoon of August 22, 1956 that Mrs. Hoddeson, accompanied by her aunt and four children, happily journeyed from her home in South River to the defendant's store to attain her objective. Upon entering, she was greeted by a tall man with dark hair frosted at the temples and clad in a light gray suit. He inquired if he could be of assistance, and she informed him specifically of her mission. Whereupon he immediately guided her, her aunt, and the flock to the mirror then on display and priced at $29 which Mrs. Hoddeson identified, and next to the location of the designated bedroom furniture which she had described.

Upon confirming her selections the man withdrew from his pocket a small pad or paper upon which he presumably recorded her order and calculated the total purchase price to be $168.50. Mrs. Hoddeson handed to him the $168.50 in cash. He informed her the articles other than those on display were not in stock, and that reproductions would upon notice be delivered to her in September. Alas, she omitted to request from him a receipt for her cash disbursement. The transaction consumed in time a period from 30 to 40 minutes.

Mrs. Hoddeson impatiently awaited the delivery of the articles of furniture, but a span of time beyond the assured date of delivery elapsed, which motivated her to inquire of the defendant the cause of the unexpected delay. Sorrowful, indeed, was she to learn from the defendant that its records failed to disclose any such sale to her and any such monetary credit in payment.

Such were the essentialities of the narrative imparted to the judge and jury in the Union County District Court, where Mrs. Hoddeson and her husband obtained a final judgment against the defendant in reimbursement of her cash expenditure. The testimony of her aunt was corroborative of that of Mrs. Hoddeson.

Although the amount of money involved is relatively inconsiderable, the defendant has resolved to incur the expense of this appeal. This Division has heretofore had occasion to state that justice is not qualified by the monetary importance of the controversy. *Series Publishers, Inc. v. Greene,* 9 N.J. Super. 166 (App. Div. 1950). Obviously, the endeavor of the defendant is to elicit from us a precedential opinion concerning a merchant's liability in the exceptional circumstances. . . .

It eventuated that Mrs. Hoddeson and her aunt were subsequently unable *positively* to recognize among the defendant's regularly employed salesmen the individual with whom Mrs. Hoddeson had arranged for the purchase, although when she and her aunt were afforded the opportunities to gaze intently at one of the five salesmen assigned to that department of the store, both indicated a resemblance of one of them to the purported salesman, but frankly acknowledged the incertitude of their identification. The defendant's records revealed that the salesman bearing the alleged resemblance was on vacation and hence presumably absent from the store during the week of August 22, 1956.

As you will at this point surmise, the insistence of the defendant at the trial was that the person who served Mrs. Hoddeson was an impostor deceitfully impersonating a salesman of the defendant without the latter's knowledge.

It was additionally disclosed by the testimony that a relatively large number of salesmen were employed at the defendant's store, and that since they were remunerated in part on a sales commission basis, there existed considerable rivalry among them to serve incoming customers; hence the improbability of the unnoticed intrusion of an impersonator.

Fortifying the defense, each of the five salesmen, but not every salesman, denied that he had attended Mrs. Hoddeson on the stated occasion, and the defendant's comptroller and credit manager verified the absence in the store records of any notation of the alleged sale and of the receipt of the stated cash payment.

The credibility of the testimony of both Mrs. Hoddeson and her aunt was thus shadowed. The trial judge transmitted to the jury for determination the simple factual issue whether Mrs. Hoddeson and her co-plaintiff had established by a preponderance of the credible evidence that the $168.50 was paid in fact to an employee of the defendant; otherwise, the defendant should be acquitted of liability.

* * * *

There can be no doubt that the existence of the alleged relationship, or in the alternative an estoppel by the defendant to deny its existence, was an essential element of the legal right of the plaintiff, Mrs. Hoddeson, to recover her monetary disbursement from the company. Neither is it to be doubted that such a relationship of agency, actual or apparent, can be proved by means of circumstantial evidence.

We do not hastily yield to the temptation immediately to adopt the postulate that the person who waited upon Mrs. Hoddeson was without question a humbugger unassociated with the defendant. We recognize that the jurors, pursuant to the directions of the court, weighed on the scales of reasonable probabilities the inferences anent that issue which were to them derivable from the circumstantial evidence relating on the one hand to the described behavior and deportment of the individual and on the other to the revelatory state of the defendant's records.

* * * *

Where a party seeks to impose liability upon an alleged principal on a contract made by an alleged agent, as here, the party must assume the obligation of proving the agency relationship. It is not the burden of the alleged principal to disprove it.

Concisely stated, the liability of a principal to third parties for the acts of an agent may be shown by proof disclosing (1) express or real authority which has been definitely granted; (2) implied authority, that is, to do all that is proper, customarily incidental and reasonably appropriate to the exercise of the authority granted; and (3) apparent authority, such as where the principal by words, conduct, or other indicative manifestations has "held out" the person to be his agent.

Obviously the plaintiffs' evidence in the present action does not substantiate the existence of any basic express authority or project any question implicating implied authority. The point here debated is whether or not the evidence circumstantiates the presence of apparent authority, and it is at this very point we come face to face with the general rule of law that the apparency and appearance of authority must be shown to have been created by the manifestations of the alleged principal, and not alone and solely by proof of those of the supposed agent. Assuredly the law cannot permit apparent authority to be established by the mere proof that a mountebank in fact exercised it.

* * * *

Let us hypothesize for the purposes of our present comments that the acting salesman was not in fact an employee of the defendant, yet he behaved and deported himself during the stated period in the business establishment of the defendant in the manner described by the evidence adduced on behalf of the plaintiffs, would the defendant be immune as a matter of law from liability for the plaintiffs' loss? The tincture of estoppel that gives color to instances of apparent authority might in the law operate likewise to preclude a defendant's denial of liability. It matters little whether for immediate purposes we entitle or characterize the principle of law in such cases as "agency by estoppel" or "a tortious dereliction of duty owed to an invited customer." That which we have in mind are the unique occurrences where solely through the lack of the proprietor's reasonable surveillance and supervision an impostor falsely impersonates in the place of business an agent or servant of his. Certainly the proprietor's duty of care and precaution for the safety and security of the customer encompasses more than the diligent observance and removal of banana peels from the aisles. Broadly stated, the duty of the proprietor also encircles the exercise of reasonable care and vigilance to protect the customer from loss occasioned by the deceptions of an apparent salesman. The rule that those who bargain without inquiry with an apparent agent do so at the risk and peril of an absence of the agent's authority has a patently impracticable application to the customers who patronize our modern department stores. *Vide, 2 C.J.S. Agency* § 93, *p. 1193.*

Our concept of the modern law is that where a proprietor of a place of business by his dereliction of duty enables one who is not his agent conspicuously to act as such and ostensibly to transact the proprietor's business with a patron in the establishment, the appearances being of such a character as to lead a person of ordinary prudence and circumspection to believe that the impostor was in truth the proprietor's agent, in such circumstances the law will not permit the proprietor defensively to avail himself of the impostor's lack of authority and thus escape liability for the consequential loss thereby sustained by the customer.

* * * *

In reversing the judgment under review, the interests of justice seem to us to recommend the allowance of a new trial with the privilege accorded the plaintiffs to reconstruct the architecture of their complaint appropriately to project for determination the justiciable issue to which, in view of the inquisitive object of the present appeal, we have alluded. We do not in the exercise of our modern processes of appellate review permit the formalities of a pleading of themselves to defeat the substantial opportunities of the parties. *Cf. Marschalk v. Weber,* 11 N.J. Super. 16, 26 (App. Div. 1950), certification denied 6 N.J. 569 (1951).

Reversed and new trial allowed.

Atlantic Salmon A/S v. Curran

32 Mass. App. Ct. 488, 591 N.E.2d 206 (Mass. App. Ct. 1992)

These are the plaintiffs' appeals from a Superior Court judgment for the defendant. The issue presented is as to the personal liability of an agent who at the relevant times was acting on behalf of a partially disclosed or unidentified principal. *See Restatement (Second) of Agency § 4(2)* & *comment g* (1958).

. . . . The defendant began doing business with the plaintiffs, Salmonor A/S (Salmonor) and Atlantic Salmon A/S (Atlantic), Norwegian corporations and exporters of salmon, in 1985 and 1987, respectively. At all times, the defendant dealt with the plaintiffs as a representative of "Boston International Seafood Exchange, Inc.," or "Boston Seafood Exchange, Inc." The salmon purchased by the defendant was sold to other wholesalers. Payment checks from the defendant to the plaintiffs were imprinted with the name "Boston International Seafood Exchange, Inc.," and signed by the defendant, using the designation "Treas.," intending thereby to convey the impression that he was treasurer. Wire transfers of payments were also made in the name of Boston International

Seafood Exchange, Inc. The defendant gave the plaintiffs' representatives business cards which listed him as "marketing director" of "Boston International Seafood Exchange, Inc." Advertising placed by the defendant appeared in trade journals under both the names "Boston Seafood Exchange, Inc.," and "Boston International Seafood Exchange, Inc." (indicating in one instance as to the latter that it was "Est: 1982"). At the relevant times, no such Massachusetts or foreign corporation had been formed by the defendant or had existed.

On May 31, 1977, a Massachusetts corporation named "Marketing Designs, Inc.," was organized. It was created for the purpose of selling motor vehicles. As of 1983, the defendant was the president, treasurer, clerk, a director, and the sole stockholder of that corporation. The extent of activity or solvency of the corporation is not shown on the record. On October 19, 1983, however, Marketing Designs, Inc., was dissolved, apparently for failure to make requisite corporate filings. *See G. L. c. 156B, § 101.* On December 4, 1987, a certificate was filed with the city clerk of Boston declaring that Marketing Designs, Inc. (then dissolved), was conducting business under the name of Boston Seafood Exchange (not with the designation "Inc." and not also under the name Boston International Seafood Exchange, Inc.). *See G. L. c. 110, § 5.*

Salmonor is owed $101,759.65 and Atlantic $153,788.50 for salmon sold to a business known as Boston International Seafood Exchange or Boston Seafood Exchange during 1988. Marketing Designs, Inc., was dissolved at the time the debt was incurred. In that year, advertising in a trade journal appeared in the name of "Boston Seafood Exchange, Inc.," and listed the plaintiffs as suppliers, and the defendant delivered to representatives of the plaintiffs his business card on which he was described as "marketing director" of "Boston International Seafood Exchange, Inc." On July 8, August 19 and 30, and September 9, 1988, the defendant made checks, imprinted with the name "Boston International Seafood Exchange, Inc.," to one or the other of the plaintiffs as payments for shipments of salmon.

The defendant never informed the plaintiffs of the existence of Marketing Designs, Inc., and the plaintiffs did not know of it until after the commencement of the present litigation on November 25, 1988. Marketing Designs, Inc. was revived for all purposes on December 12, 1988. *See G. L. c. 156B, § 108.* In the fall of 1988, the defendant had communications with representatives of both plaintiffs, suggesting a "reorganization" or "restructuring" of Boston International Seafood Exchange, Inc., and a preferred stock position for the plaintiffs in exchange for debt.

In the course of his direct testimony, the defendant said: "We do business in seafood, and we're only in seafood. Boston Seafood Exchange is the name we use because it identifies us very closely with the industry and the products that we deal in. 'Marketing Designs, Inc.,' in the seafood business, would have absolutely no bearing or no recall or any factor at all. I picked the name Boston Seafood Exchange, Inc., because it defines where we are, who we deal with, the type of product we're into, and where our specialties are. The reason we have 'Inc.' on there is because also it seemed to me at the time—obviously it seemed to me at the time that it's incumbent upon me to tell people that I'm dealing with and to let them know that they're dealing with a corporation. So, we used 'Inc.' just to notify them; and I signed all my checks 'Treasurer' and so forth."

At trial and on appeal the defendant argues that he was acting as an agent of Marketing Designs, Inc., in 1988 when he incurred the debt which the plaintiffs seek to recover from him individually. It makes no difference that the plaintiffs thought they were dealing with corporate entities which did not exist, the defendant contends, because they were "aware" that they were transacting business with a corporate entity and not with the defendant individually. The judge essentially adopted the defendant's position. Further, relying on *Barker-Chadsey Co. v. W.C. Fuller Co.,* 16 Mass. App. Ct. 1 (1983), the judge placed no significance on the fact of the dissolution of Marketing Designs, Inc., at the time the debt was incurred. The plaintiffs argue that the defendant had no principal, as he was conducting business in the name of non-existent corporations, and he was, therefore, himself the principal, or, in the alternative, that he was acting for a partially disclosed principal (Marketing Designs, Inc.), not known to the plaintiffs, and, consequently, a party to the contracts with the plaintiffs. The judge seems to have treated the case as if it were one involving the defendant as an agent for a partially disclosed principal.[2] Then the analysis went astray.

"If the other party [to a transaction] has notice that the agent is or may be acting for a principal but has no notice of the principal's identity, the principal

---

[2] On the evidence in this case, one might view with considerable skepticism the good faith of the defendant's claim that he was in fact acting as the agent of Marketing Designs, Inc. His use of "Inc." in the description of the two fictitious corporations (a criminal violation, *see G. L. c. 110, §§ 4A* & *26*), the methods by which the business was conducted and advertised, the late filing of the business certificate, the purpose of Marketing Designs, Inc., and that in the defendant's own words that name "in the seafood business, would have absolutely no bearing or no recall or any factor at all," the use of only one fictitious name on the doing business certificate, the continuation thereafter of the use of business cards and checks in the other fictitious name of Boston International Seafood Exchange, Inc., and the suggestion to the plaintiffs of the reorganization of that nonentity strongly suggest manipulation and the attempted convenient illusion of personal liability by means of a corporation (then dissolved) never intended to conduct or be responsible for the business of salmon importing. Nevertheless, the judge found that the defendant was not culpable of any relevant "fraud or other reprehensible conduct."

for whom the agent is acting is a partially disclosed principal." *Restatement (Second) of Agency § 4(2)* (1958). Here, the plaintiffs had notice that the defendant was purporting to act for a corporate principal or principals but had no notice of the identity of the principal as claimed by the defendant in this litigation. "Unless otherwise agreed, a person purporting to make a contract with another for a partially disclosed principal is a party to the contract." *Id.* at § 321.

It is the duty of the agent, if he would avoid personal liability on a contract entered into by him on behalf of his principal, to disclose not only that he is acting in a representative capacity, but also the identity of his principal. [*Citations omitted.*]

The judge reasoned that since the defendant had filed a certificate with the city of Boston in December, 1987, that Marketing Designs, Inc., was doing business as Boston Seafood Exchange, the plaintiffs could have discerned "precisely with whom they were dealing by reference to public records before the 1988 credits were extended."[3] But the defendant had dealt with Salmonor, and probably Atlantic, before that date, continued to deal with both under the name Boston International Seafood Exchange, Inc., thereafter, and even proposed to the plaintiffs a corporate restructuring of that nonentity. In any event, it was not the plaintiffs' duty to seek out the identity of the defendant's principal; it was the defendant's obligation fully to reveal it. [*Citations omitted.*]

It is not sufficient that the plaintiffs may have had the means, through a search of the records of the Boston city clerk, to determine the identity of the defendant's principal. Actual knowledge is the test. [*Citations omitted.*] "The duty rests upon the agent, if he would avoid personal liability, to disclose his agency, and not upon others to discover it. It is not, therefore, enough that the other party has the means of ascertaining the name of the principal; the agent must either bring to him actual knowledge or, what is the same thing, that which to a reasonable man is equivalent to knowledge or the agent will be bound. There is no hardship to the agent in this rule, as he always has it in his power to relieve himself from personal liability by fully disclosing his principal and contracting only in the latter's name. If he does not do this, it may well be presumed that he intended to make himself personally responsible." 1 Mechem on Agency § 1413 (2d ed. 1914).

Finally, the defendant's use of trade names or fictitious names by which he claimed Marketing Designs, Inc., conducted its business is not in the

[3] Of course, had the plaintiffs checked the public corporate records, they would have found that Marketing Designs, Inc., had been dissolved.

circumstances a sufficient identification of the alleged principal so as to protect the defendant from personal liability. [*Citations omitted.*]. . . .

The judgment is reversed, and new judgments are to be entered against the defendant for Atlantic in the amount of $153,788.50 and for Salmonor in the amount of $101,759.65, both with appropriate interest and costs.

So ordered.

Additional Excerpts from the Third Restatement

§ 1.04 Terminology

(1) *Coagents.* Coagents have agency relationships with the same principal. A coagent may be appointed by the principal or by another agent actually or apparently authorized by the principal to do so.

(2) *Disclosed, undisclosed, and unidentified principals.*

(a) *Disclosed principal.* A principal is disclosed if, when an agent and a third party interact, the third party has notice that the agent is acting for a principal and has notice of the principal's identity.

(b) *Undisclosed principal.* A principal is undisclosed if, when an agent and a third party interact, the third party has no notice that the agent is acting for a principal.

(c) *Unidentified principal.* A principal is unidentified if, when an agent and a third party interact, the third party has notice that the agent is acting for a principal but does not have notice of the principal's identity.

(3) *Gratuitous agent.* A gratuitous agent acts without a right to compensation.

(4) *Notice.* A person has notice of a fact if the person knows the fact, has reason to know the fact, has received an effective notification of the fact, or should know the fact to fulfill a duty owed to another person. Notice of a fact that an agent knows or has reason to know is imputed to the principal as stated in §§ 5.03 and 5.04. A notification given to or by an agent is effective as notice to or by the principal as stated in § 5.02.

(5) *Person.* A person is (a) an individual; (b) an organization or association that has legal capacity to possess rights and incur obligations; (c) a

government, political subdivision, or instrumentality or entity created by government; or (d) any other entity that has legal capacity to possess rights and incur obligations.

* * * *

(8) *Subagent.* A subagent is a person appointed by an agent to perform functions that the agent has consented to perform on behalf of the agent's principal and for whose conduct the appointing agent is responsible to the principal. The relationship between an appointing agent and a subagent is one of agency, created as stated in § 1.01. . . .

§ 3.02 Formal Requirements

If the law requires a writing or record signed by the principal to evidence an agent's authority to bind a principal to a contract or other transaction, the principal is not bound in the absence of such a writing or record. A principal may be estopped to assert the lack of such a writing or record when a third party has been induced to make a detrimental change in position by the reasonable belief that an agent has authority to bind the principal that is traceable to a manifestation made by the principal.

§ 6.01 Agent for Disclosed Principal

When an agent acting with actual or apparent authority makes a contract on behalf of a disclosed principal,

(1) the principal and the third party are parties to the contract; and

(2) the agent is not a party to the contract unless the agent and third party agree otherwise.

§ 6.02 Agent for Unidentified Principal

When an agent acting with actual or apparent authority makes a contract on behalf of an unidentified principal,

(1) the principal and the third party are parties to the contract; and

(2) the agent is a party to the contract unless the agent and the third party agree otherwise.

§ 6.03 Agent for Undisclosed Principal

When an agent acting with actual authority makes a contract on behalf of an undisclosed principal,

(1) unless excluded by the contract, the principal is a party to the contract;

(2) the agent and the third party are parties to the contract; and

(3) the principal, if a party to the contract, and the third party have the same rights, liabilities, and defenses against each other as if the principal made the contract personally, subject to §§ 6.05–6.09.

§ 6.04 Principal Does Not Exist or Lacks Capacity

Unless the third party agrees otherwise, a person who makes a contract with a third party purportedly as an agent on behalf of a principal becomes a party to the contract if the purported agent knows or has reason to know that the purported principal does not exist or lacks capacity to be a party to a contract.

SECTION III: Agency Problems Involving Torts

When a tort occurs in an agency context, often the question is whether the principal is responsible for the agent's tort. The issue is not whether the principal acted negligently. If the principal were negligent, then he or she would be liable under tort law. Similarly, under basic tort law principles, a negligent agent is always liable for his own negligence. Agency problems involving torts focus on the question of whether an third party, whose injury resulted from an agent's negligence, can also recover from that agent's non-negligent principal. The fundamental "twist" of agency law is that it presents the possibility that the principal may be found liable for the torts of an agent, even though the principal was not negligent.

Under agency law, whether a principal is responsible for the wrongdoing of an agent depends upon the nature of the principal-agent relationship. It is critical to determine if the agent was an employee of the principal, because a principal is liable for torts committed by its employee that are within the scope of that employee's employment. This concept is known as "*respondeat superior*." If the agent was not an employee of the principal, then the principal might still incur liability, but the scope of actions that could potentially result in liability is reduced significantly.

Experiencing Assignment 2: Burger Barn II

Because of your excellent work on Burger Barn's previous matter, your firm has been retained for work on another assignment. However, please assume that this matter is completely independent from the prior matter and do not use facts from that assignment in addressing the issues raised in this assignment.

FACTS:

Burger Barn, Inc. owns and operates fast food restaurants throughout the country. Burger Barn has a "wild west" theme. Their restaurants are adorned with lots of wood and rope and other decorations that remind customers of the old west. Burger Barn also sells franchises. Burger Barn franchisees must use Burger Barn food products, paper products, and serving materials and must have their restaurants' décor conform to a design, look and feel that is approved by Burger Barn, so that customers will know that they are in a Burger Barn location. Furthermore, franchisees must only sell items from a menu approved by Burger Barn and must offer all items on the Burger Barn menu. While franchisees are free to hire their own employees, employees are trained through procedures, manuals and videos provided by Burger Barn. Burger Barn also sets the prices which its franchisees may charge for food. However, franchisees are free to pay employees any wage they see fit. Franchisees make all decisions about services provided to the restaurant such as utilities, trash, heating, air conditioning and maintenance (although franchisee's premises must be maintained to meet a certain minimum standard).

Hilda and Henry Slider own and operate a Burger Barn franchise in Anytown, USA (the "Slider BB Franchise"). One of their employees, named Miss Step, accidentally tripped a customer, named Vic, who was carrying a tray of food. As Vic fell, the tray flew out of his hand and struck another customer named Tim. The tray hit Tim in the head, causing him to lose consciousness, fall, and break his wrist. (Note that Burger Barn restaurants use wooden trays with the Burger Barn logo branded into the center of the tray.) Tim had been a very successful professional bowler. Unfortunately, the wrist injury ended his career. Tim plans to sue for $5.2 million. He is claiming both negligence and that the trays used by the Slider BB Franchise are too heavy, alleging that a plastic tray would not have knocked him out and, therefore, all of the other resulting injuries he suffered could have prevented (or substantially reduced).

ASSIGNMENT A:

Part I: The partner for whom you work has asked you to provide a brief assessment of this matter. She would like you, based on the cases included in this chapter and without doing outside research, to draft a letter to the Sliders addressing the following questions:

Does Tim have a claim against the Slider BB Franchise under Agency Law? What is the nature of that claim or claims? While it should not be the focus of the letter to the Sliders, you might also consider whether Tim has any claims against Burger Barn under Agency Law?

There is no need to do an analysis of the tort issues with respect to Miss Step's actions. For purposes of this assignment, you may assume that Miss Step acted negligently and that her negligence caused Tim's injuries. You may also assume that the question of whether the use of wooden trays increased the severity of Tim's injuries is a question of fact.

Part II: When investigating this case, you discover that another Slider BB Franchise employee, named Pete, who is also a part-time bowler, recognized Tim, to whom Pete had lost several tournaments. It is possible that when Tim was unconscious, Pete pretended to help Tim, but actually twisted Tim's wrist, increasing the severity of the break and making sure that Tim would never return to bowling. If it turns out that Pete did intentionally injure Tim, are the Slider's liable for damages caused by Pete's wrongful conduct?

The partner would like you to draft a letter to the Sliders outlining your analysis of the above questions. Your letter should include legal concepts, but the Sliders just want to understand their position on the above issues and do not want to have cases cited to them. Remember you are writing the letter to business people, not to attorneys. Your letter should not exceed 1000 words.

ASSIGNMENT B:

Your firm's client, Burger Barn, Inc., has another assignment for you. Burger Barn wishes to redesign the agreement through which each independent operator ("IO", formerly a franchisee) will be able to open a Burger Barn restaurant and use the Burger Barn name. Independent operators will not be owned by Burger Barn.

The following represents a "wish list" of the provisions that Burger Barn would like covered in the Agreement:

- IO will design a restaurant consistent with the décor and design of a Burger Barn restaurant.
- All designs must be approved by Burger Barn.
- Employees will be hired to meet Burger Barn minimum standards and training must be consistent with the Burger Barn manual.
- All IO employees will attend a two-week training at Burger Barn headquarters and must satisfactorily complete the course before they start working at the IO location.
- All IO employees will wear Burger Barn uniforms and any employee taking orders will greet each customer with the Burger Barn greeting, *"Howdeeee Do! Welcome to Burger Barn! What grub can we rustle up for you today?"*
- Burger Barn will approve all displays, all menus and all items sold in the IO's restaurant.
- IO must only sell items from the Burger Barn menu and must offer all items on the Burger Barn menu. No other food, services or merchandise may be sold on the IO's premises.
- All food, paper products and serving materials must be purchased from Burger Barn (including the signature wooden Burger Barn trays).
- IO will pay Burger Barn an annual fee of $50,0000 or 17% of all sales, whichever is greater.
- Burger Barn has the right to terminate the franchise at any time that the IO violates the agreement, does not meet Burger Barn standards or if Burger Barn believes that any action or practice of the IO jeopardizes the Burger Barn name, brand or trademark.

Burger Barn realizes this is a substantial list and is worried about liability. Burger Barn would like your advice about how to implement the maximum items on the above wish list without risking the liability that might arise out of the actions of an IO or an IO's employees. Burger Barn would also like you to provide an explanation of why certain items are excluded and why others are included. Feel free to suggest modifications to the wish list that might strengthen Burger Barn's position. Please limit your response to two pages and do not exceed 1250 words.

A. Employees Versus Non-Employee Agents (aka "Independent Contractors")

When evaluating whether an agent is an "employee" for the purposes of *respondeat superior,* a critical issue is whether the principal had the right to exert control over the manner and the means by which the agent performed his duties. Note, that it is not just the actual exercise of control that is critical, but also the right to exercise control that is evaluated. Various factors are involved in assessing whether a principal has the right to exert enough control over the agent for the agent to be considered an "employee."

These factors (set forth in *Comment f to Restatement (Third) of Agency* § 7.07) include:

- the extent of control that the agent and the principal have agreed the principal may exercise over the details of the work (Note that the extent of control that the principal actually exercises is relevant as well.);
- whether the agent is engaged in a distinct occupation or business;
- whether the type of work done by the agent is customarily done under a principal's direction or without supervision;
- the skill required in the agent's occupation;
- whether the agent or the principal supplies the tools or other instrumentalities required for the work and the place in which to perform it;
- the length of time during which the agent is engaged by a principal;
- whether the agent is paid by the job or by the time worked;
- whether the principal and agent believe they are creating an employment relationship; and
- whether the principal is or is not in business.

It is, of course, possible to have an agency relationship in which the agent is not an employee of the principal. Prior to the adoption of the *Third Restatement,* those who performed services for another, who were not employees, were called "independent contractors." The *Third Restatement* has adopted a new designation for this category of agent and now uses the term, "non-employee agent." Other sources still use the term "independent contractors." The distinction between an employee and a non-employee agent is important because the tortious actions of employees and non-employee agents create different potential liabilities for their respective principals. Under the doctrine of *respondeat superior,* principals/employers are vicariously liable (i.e., responsible) for the torts of their employee agents that arise within the scope of that agent's employment. However, principals are not responsible for the torts of their non-employee agents (or independent contractors) unless the tort arises out of an area over which the principal exercised control or the tort arises under one of the exceptions discussed below, such as an inherently dangerous activity, a non-delegable duty or a negligent hiring. It is important to recognize that even in the situation of a non-employee agent, the agency relationship exists on a continuum of control. In some agency situations, the principal exercises some control over the subject matter of the agency, but not enough control to create an employer/employee relationship. In others, virtually no control is exercised by the principal and the relationship involves a third party performing services on a truly independent basis.

Humble Oil & Ref. Co. v. Martin

148 Tex. 175, 222 S.W.2d 995 (Tex. 1949)

Petitioners Humble Oil & Refining Company and Mrs. A.C. Love and husband complain here of the judgments of the trial court and the Court of Civil Appeals in which they were held in damages for personal injuries following a special issue verdict at the suit of respondent George F. Martin acting for himself and his two minor daughters. The injuries were inflicted on the three Martins about the noon hour on May 12, 1947, in the City of Austin, by an unoccupied automobile belonging to the petitioners Love, which, just prior to the accident, had been left by Mrs. Love at a filling station owned by petitioner Humble for servicing and thereafter, before any station employee had touched it, rolled by gravity off the premises into and obliquely across the abutting street, striking Mr. Martin and his children from behind as they were walking into the yard of their home, a short distance downhill from the station.

The trial court rendered judgment against petitioners Humble and Mrs. Love jointly and severally and gave the latter judgment over against Humble for whatever she might pay the respondents. The Court of Civil Appeals affirmed the judgment after reforming it to eliminate the judgment over in favor of Mrs. Love, without prejudice to the right of contribution by either defendant .... The petitioners here respectively complain of the judgment in favor of the

Martins, and each seeks full indemnity (as distinguished from contribution) from the other.

The apparently principal contention of petitioner, Humble, is that it is liable neither to respondent Martin nor to petitioner Mrs. Love, since the station was in effect operated by an independent contractor, W. T. Schneider, and Humble is accordingly not responsible for his negligence nor that of W. V. Manis, who was the only station employee or representative present when the Love car was left and rolled away. In this conncetion, the jury convicted petitioner Humble of the following acts of negligence proximately causing the injuries in question: (a) Failure to inspect the Love car to see that the emergency brake was set or the gears engaged; (b) failure to set the emergency brake on the Love car; (c) leaving the Love car unattended on the driveway. The verdict also included findings that Mrs. Love "had delivered her car to the custody of the defendant Humble Oil & Refining Company, before her car started rolling from the position in which she had parked it"; that the accident was not unavoidable; and that no negligent act of either of petitioners was the sole proximate cause of the injuries in question. We think the Court of Civil Appeals properly held Humble responsible for the operation of the station, which admittedly it owned, as it did also the principal products there sold by Schneider under the so-called "Commission Agency Agreement" between him and Humble which was in evidence. The facts that neither Humble, Schneider nor the station employees considered Humble as an employer or master; that the employees were paid and directed by Schneider individually as their "boss", and that a provision of the agreement expressly repudiates any authority of Humble over the employees, are not conclusive against the master-servant relationship, since there is other evidence bearing on the right or power of Humble to control the details of the station work as regards Schneider himself and therefore as to employees which it was expressly contemplated that he would hire. The question is ordinarily one of fact, and where there are items of evidence indicating a master-servant relationship, contrary items such as those above mentioned cannot be given conclusive effect. [*Citations omitted*] Even if the contract between Humble and Schneider were the only evidence on the question, the instrument as a whole indicates a master-servant relationship quite as much as, if not more than, it suggests an arrangement between independent contractors. For example, paragraph 1 includes a provision requiring Schneider "to make reports *and perform other duties in connection with the operation of said station that may be required of him from time to time by Company*." (Emphasis supplied). And while paragraph 2 purports to require Schneider to pay all operational expenses, the schedule of commissions forming part of the agreement does just the opposite in its paragraph (F), which gives Schneider a 75% "commission" on "the net public utility bills paid" by him and thus requires Humble to pay three-fourths of one of the most important operational expense items. Obviously the main object of the enterprise was the retail marketing of Humble's products with title remaining in Humble until delivery to the consumer. This was done under a strict system of financial control and supervision by Humble, with little or no business discretion reposed in Schneider except as to hiring, discharge, payment and supervision of a few station employees of a more or less laborer status. Humble furnished the all important station location and equipment, the advertising media, the products and a substantial part of the current operating costs. The hours of operation were controlled by Humble. The "Commission Agency Agreement", which evidently was Schneider's only title to occupancy of the premise, was terminable at the will of Humble. The so-called "rentals" were, at least in part, based on the amount of Humble's products sold, being, therefore, involved with the matter of Schneider's remuneration and not rentals in the usual sense. And, as above shown, the agreement required Schneider in effect to do anything Humble might tell him to do. All in all, aside from the stipulation regarding Schneider's assistants, there is essentially little difference between his situation and that of a mere store clerk who happens to be paid a commission instead of a salary. The business was Humble's business, just as the store clerk's business would be that of the store owner. Schneider was Humble's servant, and so accordingly were Schneider's assistants who were contemplated by the contract.

* * * *

The evidence above discussed serves to distinguish the instant case from *The Texas Company v. Wheat,* 140 Texas 468, 168 S.W. (2d) 632, upon which petitioner Humble principally relies. In that case the evidence differed greatly from that now before us. It clearly showed a "dealer" type of relationship in which the lessee in charge of the filling station purchased from his landlord, The Texas Company, and sold as his own, and was free to sell at his own price and on his own credit terms, the company products purchased, as well as the products of other oil companies. The contracts contained no provision requiring the lessee to perform any duty The Texas Company might see fit to impose on him, nor did the company pay any part of the lessee's operating expenses, nor control the working hours of the station. . . .

Hoover v. Sun Oil Co.

58 Del. 553, 212 A.2d 214 (Del. 1965)

This case is concerned with injuries received as the result of a fire on August 16, 1962 at the service station operated by James F. Barone. The fire started at the rear of plaintiff's car where it was being filled with gasoline and was allegedly caused by the negligence of John Smilyk an employee of Barone. Plaintiffs brought suit against Smilyk, Barone and Sun Oil Company (Sun) which owned the service station.

Sun has moved for summary judgment as to it on the basis that Barone was an independent contractor and therefore the alleged negligence of his employee could not result in liability as to Sun. The plaintiffs contend instead that Barone was acting as Sun's agent and that Sun may therefore be responsible for plaintiff's injuries.

Barone began operating this business in October of 1960 pursuant to a lease dated October 17, 1960. The station and all of its equipment, with the exception of a tire-stand and rack, certain advertising displays and miscellaneous hand tools, were owned by Sun. The lease was subject to termination by either party upon thirty days' written notice after the first six months and at the anniversary date thereafter. The rental was partially determined by the volume of gasoline purchased but there was also a minimum and a maximum monthly rental.

At the same time, Sun and Barone also entered into a dealer's agreement under which Barone was to purchase petroleum products from Sun and Sun was to loan necessary equipment and advertising materials. Barone was required to maintain this equipment and to use it solely for Sun products. Barone was permitted under the agreement to sell competitive products but chose to do so only in a few minor areas As to Sun products, Barone was prohibited from selling them except under the Sunoco label and from blending them with products not supplied by Sun.

Barone's station had the usual large signs indicating that Sunoco products were sold there. His advertising in the classified section of the telephone book was under a Sunoco heading and his employees wore uniforms with the Sun emblem, the uniforms being owned by Barone or rented from an independent company.

Barone, upon the urging of Robert B. Peterson, Sun's area sales representative, attended a Sun school for service station operators in 1961. The school's curriculum was designed to familiarize the station operator with bookkeeping and merchandising, the appearance and proper maintenance of a Sun station, and the Sun Oil products. The course concluded with the operator working at Sun's model station in order to gain work experience in the use of the policy and techniques taught at the school.

Other facts typifying the company-service station relationship were the weekly visits of Sun's sales representative, Peterson, who would take orders for Sun products, inspect the restrooms, communicate customer complaints, make various suggestions to improve sales and discuss any problems that Barone might be having. Besides the weekly visits, Peterson was in contact with Barone on other occasions in order to implement Sun's "competitive allowance system" which enabled Barone to meet local price competition by giving him a rebate on the gasoline in his inventory roughly equivalent to the price decline and a similarly reduced price on his next order of gasoline.

While Peterson did offer advice to Barone on all phases of his operation, it was usually done on request and Barone was under no obligation to follow the advice. Barone's contacts and dealings with Sun were many and their relationship intricate, but he made no written reports to Sun and he alone assumed the overall risk of profit or loss in his business operation. Barone independently determined his own hours of operation and the identity, pay scale and working conditions of his employees, and it was his name that was posted as proprietor.

Plaintiffs contend in effect that the aforegoing facts indicate that Sun controlled the day-to-day operation of the station and consequently Sun is responsible for the negligent acts of Barone's employee. Specifically, plaintiffs contend that there is an issue of fact for the jury to determine as to whether or not there was an agency relationship.

The legal relationships arising from the distribution systems of major oil-producing companies are in certain respects unique. As stated in an annotation collecting many of the cases dealing with this relationship:

"This distribution system has grown up primarily as the result of economic factors and with little relationship to traditional legal concepts in the field of master and servant, so that it is perhaps not surprising that attempts by the court to discuss the relationship in the standard terms have led to some difficulties and confusion." *83 A.L.R.2d 1282, 1284 (1962).*

In some situations traditional definitions of principal and agent and of employer and independent contractor may be difficult to apply to service station operations, but the undisputed facts of the case at bar make it clear that Barone was an independent contractor.

Barone's service station, unlike retail outlets for many products, is basically a one-company outlet and represents to the public, through Sunoco's national and local advertising, that it sells not only Sun's quality products but Sun's quality service. Many people undoubtedly come to the service station because of that latter representation.

However, the lease contract and dealer's agreement fail to establish any relationship other than landlord-tenant, and independent contractor. Nor is there anything in the conduct of the individuals which is inconsistent with that relationship so as to indicate that the contracts were mere subterfuge or sham. The areas of close contact between Sun and Barone stem from the fact that both have a mutual interest in the sale of Sun products and in the success of Barone's business.

The cases cited by both plaintiffs and defendant indicate that the result varies according to the contracts involved and the conduct and evidence of control under those contracts. Both lines of cases indicate that the test to be applied is that of whether the oil company has retained the right to control the details of the day-to-day operation of the service station; control or influence over results alone being viewed as insufficient. . . . . It should be noted however that the same rule of law is applied in nearly all of the cases and that the differences in result are explained by different fact situations and greater evidence of oil company control. [*Citations omitted*] . . . .

The facts of this case differ markedly from those in which the oil company was held liable for the tortious conduct of its service station operator or his employees. Sun had no control over the retails [*sic*] of Barone's day-to-day operation. Therefore, no liability can be imputed to Sun from the allegedly negligent acts of Smilyk. Sun's motion for summary judgment is granted.

It is so ordered.

B. Franchise Arrangements

A franchise arrangement involves a company or an individual (the "franchisee") selling a product or a service or operating a business pursuant to a license to do so (typically referred to in this context as a "franchise agreement") from another company or individual (the "franchisor"). Whether a franchisor has exercised sufficient control over the franchisee to create an agency relationship through which the franchisor might be found to be liable for tortious conduct of the franchisee is often a question that must be determined by a court. That determination, as well as the extent of the agency relationship if one exists, is typically a question of fact. (*Kuchta v. Allied Builders Corp.* (1971), 21 Cal. App. 3d 541.) In order to make this determination, courts will typically look at the extent of the franchisor's involvement in day-to-day operations as well as the franchisor's rights to control a franchisee's operations (even if that control is not exercised), which might include provisions in the franchise agreement, such as pricing requirements, audit rights and approval of advertising. *Greil v. Travelodge International, Inc.* (186 Ill. App. 3d 1061; (Ill. App.1989)).

While franchisors frequently exert sufficient control to establish an employer/employee type relationship, the following excerpt from the dissent in *Greil v. Travelodge International, Inc.* cites several cases in which a franchise arrangement did not result in an employer/employee type relationship or give rise to the vicarious liability that might derive from such a relationship:

> The question of the responsibility of the owner of a franchise trademark for the torts of its franchisee was discussed in *Coty v. U.S. Slicing Machine Co.* (1978), 58 Ill. App. 3d 237, 272 N.E.2d 1371. In that case, an employee of a Yankee Doodle Dandy restaurant, the franchisee, sued the franchisor on a theory of negligence and willful and wanton misconduct, as well as the manufacturer of the machine she had been using when injured. Under the franchise agreement "numerous restrictions were imposed upon the franchisee relating to the general nature of the operation of the restaurant, [with the principal goal of] protecting the Yankee Doodle trademark and the good will associated with it." (58 Ill. App. 3d at 239.) The franchisee agreed that its managers would be trained by the franchisor, its employees would wear distinctive uniforms, and it would comply with the franchisor's rules on minimum hours and days of service and on contributions and participation in advertising programs. The franchisee was also required to comply with all Federal, State and local laws. The franchisor did not retain any day-to-day control, and it could not hire or fire anyone, stop work immediately or give orders to the franchisee's employees. The franchisor was required to give a 10-day written notice demanding cure of any breach of the franchise agreement by the franchisee, and could terminate the agreement if such cure was not forthcoming. (58 Ill. App. 3d at 240.) The appellate

court affirmed a directed verdict for the franchisor, holding that the "general right to rescind the contract or 'call off work' is insufficient * * * to subject the franchisor to liability under either agency or employer-independent contractor theories." 58 Ill. App. 3d at 242.

In so deciding the court relied on *Murphy v. Holiday Inns, Inc.* (1975), 216 Va. 490, 219 S.E.2d 874. In that case, plaintiff had slipped and fallen at a Holiday Inn owned by the Betsy-Len Corporation, a franchisee. She sued the franchisor on the theory that it owned and operated the motel and that its agents and employees were negligent. The appellate court affirmed the trial court's granting of summary judgment in favor of the franchisor, finding that there was no principal-agent or master-servant relationship under the franchise agreement. That agreement provided that the franchisee contribute to advertising campaigns and that its managers be trained by the franchisor, and that the franchisee operate its motel under the "system" which included the trademark, color schemes, furnishings, advertising services and methods of operation. (*Coty,* 58 Ill. App. 3d at 240.) The court stated:

" 'Having carefully considered all of the regulatory provisions in the agreement, we are of the opinion that they gave defendant no "control or right to control the methods or details of doing the work," * * * and, therefore, agree with the trial court that no principal-agent or master-servant relationship was created. * * * The regulatory provisions did not give defendant control over the day-to-day operation of Betsy-Len's motel. While defendant was empowered to regulate the architectural style of the buildings and the type and style of furnishings and equipment, defendant was given no power to control daily maintenance of the premises. Defendant was given no power to control Betsy-Len's current business expenditures, fix customer rates, or demand a share of the profits. Defendant was given no power to hire or fire Betsy-Len's employees, determine employee wages or working conditions, set standards for employee skills or productivity, supervise employee work routine, or discipline employees for nonfeasance or misfeasance. All such powers and other management controls and responsibilities customarily exercised by an owner and operator of an on-going business were retained by Betsy-Len.' " *Coty,* 58 Ill. App. 3d at 241, quoting *Murphy v. Holiday Inns, Inc.* (1975), 216 Va. at 495, 219 S.E.2d at 877–78.

Greil at 1075–1076.

Miller v. McDonald's Corp.

150 Ore. App. 274, 945 P.2d 1107 (Ore. App. 1997)

WARREN, P.J.:

Plaintiff seeks damages from defendant McDonald's Corporation for injuries that she suffered when she bit into a heart-shaped sapphire stone while eating a Big Mac sandwich that she had purchased at a McDonald's restaurant in Tigard. The trial court granted summary judgment to defendant on the ground that it did not own or operate the restaurant; rather, the owner and operator was a non-party, 3K Restaurants (3K), that held a franchise from defendant. Plaintiff appeals, and we reverse.

. . . . 3K owned and operated the restaurant under a License Agreement (the Agreement) with defendant that required it to operate in a manner consistent with the "McDonald's System." The Agreement described that system as including proprietary rights in trade names, service marks and trademarks, as well as

> "designs and color schemes for restaurant buildings, signs, equipment layouts, formulas and specifications for certain food products, methods of inventory and operation control, bookkeeping and accounting, and manuals covering business practices and policies."

The manuals contain "detailed information relating to operation of the Restaurant," including food formulas and specifications, methods of inventory control, bookkeeping procedures, business practices, and other management, advertising, and personnel policies. 3K, as the licensee, agreed to adopt and exclusively use the formulas, methods, and policies contained in the manuals, including any subsequent modifications, and to use only advertising and promotional materials that defendant either provided or approved in advance in writing.

The Agreement described the way in which 3K was to operate the restaurant in considerable detail. It expressly required 3K to operate in compliance with defendant's prescribed standards, policies, practices, and procedures, including serving only food and beverage products that defendant designated. 3K had to follow defendant's specifications and blueprints for the equipment and layout of the restaurant, including adopting subsequent reasonable changes that defendant made, and to maintain the restaurant building in compliance with defendant's standards. 3K could not make any changes in the basic design of the building without defendant's approval.

The Agreement required 3K to keep the restaurant open during the hours that defendant prescribed, including maintaining adequate supplies and employing adequate personnel to operate at maximum capacity and efficiency during those hours. 3K also had to keep the restaurant similar in appearance to all other McDonald's restaurants. 3K's employees had to wear McDonald's uniforms, to have a neat and clean appearance, and to provide competent and courteous service. 3K could use only containers and other packaging that bore McDonald's trademarks. The ingredients for the foods and beverages had to meet defendant's standards, and 3K had to use "only those methods of food handling and preparation that [defendant] may designate from time to time." In order to obtain the franchise, 3K had to represent that the franchisee had worked at a McDonald's restaurant; the Agreement did not distinguish in this respect between a company-run or a franchised restaurant. The manuals gave further details that expanded on many of these requirements.

In order to ensure conformity with the standards described in the Agreement, defendant periodically sent field consultants to the restaurant to inspect its operations. 3K trained its employees in accordance with defendant's materials and recommendations and sent some of them to training programs that defendant administered. Failure to comply with the agreed standards could result in loss of the franchise.

Despite these detailed instructions, the Agreement provided that 3K was not an agent of defendant for any purpose. Rather, it was an independent contractor and was responsible for all obligations and liabilities, including claims based on injury, illness, or death, directly or indirectly resulting from the operation of the restaurant.

Plaintiff went to the restaurant under the assumption that defendant owned, controlled, and managed it. So far as she could tell, the restaurant's appearance was similar to that of other McDonald's restaurants that she had patronized. Nothing disclosed to her that any entity other than defendant was involved in its operation. The only signs that were visible and obvious to the public had the name "McDonald's,"[2] the employees wore uniforms with McDonald's insignia, and the menu was the same that plaintiff had seen in other

[2] . . . . Representatives of 3K testified in their depositions that there was a sign near the front counter that identified Bob and Karen Bates and 3K Restaurants as the owners. There is no evidence of the size or prominence of the sign, nor is there evidence of any other non-McDonald's identification in the restaurant.

McDonald's restaurants. The general appearance of the restaurant and the food products that it sold were similar to the restaurants and products that plaintiff had seen in national print and television advertising that defendant had run. To the best of plaintiff's knowledge, only McDonald's sells Big Mac hamburgers.

In short, plaintiff testified, she went to the Tigard McDonald's because she relied on defendant's reputation and because she wanted to obtain the same quality of service, standard of care in food preparation, and general attention to detail that she had previously enjoyed at other McDonald's restaurants.

Under these facts, 3K would be directly liable for any injuries that plaintiff suffered as a result of the restaurant's negligence. The issue on summary judgment is whether there is evidence that would permit a jury to find defendant vicariously liable for those injuries because of its relationship with 3K. Plaintiff asserts two theories of vicarious liability, actual agency and apparent agency. We hold that there is sufficient evidence to raise a jury issue under both theories. We first discuss actual agency.

The kind of actual agency relationship that would make defendant vicariously liable for 3K's negligence requires that defendant have the right to control the *method* by which 3K performed its obligations under the Agreement. The common context for that test is a normal master-servant (or employer-employee) relationship. [*Citations omitted.*] The . . .Oregon Supreme Court, in common with most if not all other courts that have considered the issue, has applied the right to control test for vicarious liability. . . . We therefore apply that test to this case.[3]

In *Peeples,* the issue was whether a motorcycle distributor was liable for a dealer's allegedly negligent warranty service. The agreement between the distributor and the dealer gave the distributor the right to set standards governing the dealer's method of operation, service, and warranty repair, including to some extent the physical conduct of the dealer's employees in the performance of warranty work. The distributor could terminate the relation for a breach of those standards. The Supreme Court held that the record as a whole supported a finding that the distributor had the right to control the dealer's conduct in providing warranty service and, therefore, that the trial court properly submitted the issue of the distributor's vicarious liability to the jury. 288 Ore. at 149–50.

---

[3] Under the right to control test it does not matter whether the putative principal actually exercises control; what is important is that it has the right to do so. *See Peeples v. Kawasaki Heavy Indust., Ltd.,* 288 Ore. 143, 149, 603 P.2d 765 (1979).

A number of other courts have applied the right to control test to a franchise relationship. The Delaware Supreme Court, in *Billops v. Magness Const Co.,* 391 A.2d 196 (Del 1978), stated the test as it applies to that context:

> "If, in practical effect, the franchise agreement goes beyond the stage of setting standards, and allocates to the franchisor the right to exercise control over the daily operations of the franchise, an agency relationship exists." 391 A.2d at 197–98.

This statement expresses the general direction that courts have taken and is consistent with the Supreme Court's discussion in *Peeples.* We therefore adopt it for the purposes of this case.

As the various cases show, it may be difficult to determine when a franchisor has retained a right not only to set standards but also to control the daily operations of the franchisee. Two examples show the different conclusions that the courts have reached and provide some guidance for this case. In *Wood v. Shell Oil Co.,* 495 So. 2d 1034 (Ala 1986), the franchise agreement required a Shell gasoline dealer to maintain the station premises, including the appearance, design, color, style, and layout, in accordance with Shell's specifications or recommendations, to promote the sale of the products that the dealer purchased, to require all employees to wear Shell uniforms, and to let Shell inspect its books. The dealer had to maintain a competent staff of employees and to perform all mechanical work in a workmanlike manner, using only first class parts. Shell might offer supplemental training for the employees. The Alabama court held that the agreement did not establish actual agency because it did not control *how* the dealer complied with the requirements. [*Citations omitted.*]

In contrast, in *Billops* the franchise agreement for a Hilton Inn hotel incorporated a detailed and, in part, mandatory operating manual that covered identification, advertising, front office procedures, cleaning and inspection service for rooms and public areas, minimum room standards, food purchasing and preparation standards, staff procedures and standards for booking group meetings, function, and room reservations, accounting, insurance, engineering, maintenance and numerous other details. The franchisee had to keep detailed records so that the franchisor could ensure compliance with those guidelines, while the franchisor retained the right to enter the premises to ensure compliance. The franchisor could terminate on 20 days notice for an uncorrected violation. The court held that those facts created a jury issue of whether an actual agency relationship existed. 391 A.2d at 198. [*Citations omitted.*]

The essential distinction between *Wood* and *Billops* is the extent to which the franchisor retained control over the details of the franchisee's performance. In *Wood,* the franchisor required only that mechanical work be done in a workmanlike manner. In *Billops,* however, the franchisor issued a manual that described the methods by which the franchisee was to carry out its responsibilities in considerable detail. The agreement in *Wood,* thus, could only be read as providing standards that the franchisee had to meet, while the agreement in *Billops* could be read as retaining the right to exercise control over the franchisee's daily operations.

The facts of this case are close to those in *Billops*. For that reason, we believe that a jury could find that defendant retained sufficient control over 3K's daily operations that an actual agency relationship existed. The Agreement did not simply set standards that 3K had to meet. Rather, it required 3K to use the precise methods that defendant established, both in the Agreement and in the detailed manuals that the Agreement incorporated. Those methods included the ways in which 3K was to handle and prepare food. Defendant enforced the use of those methods by regularly sending inspectors and by its retained power to cancel the Agreement. That evidence would support a finding that defendant had the right to control the way in which 3K performed at least food handling and preparation. In her complaint, plaintiff alleges that 3K's deficiencies in those functions resulted in the sapphire being in the Big Mac and thereby caused her injuries. Thus, as in *Peeples,* there is evidence that defendant had the right to control 3K in the precise part of its business that allegedly resulted in plaintiff's injuries. That is sufficient to raise an issue of actual agency.

Plaintiff next asserts that defendant is vicariously liable for 3K's alleged negligence because 3K was defendant's apparent agent.[4] The relevant standard is in *Restatement (Second) of Agency, § 267, which we adopted in Themins v. Emanuel Lutheran* [*Citations omitted.*]:

> "One who represents that another is his servant or other agent and thereby causes a third person justifiably to rely upon the care or skill of such apparent agent is subject to liability to the third person for harm caused by the lack of care or skill of the one appearing to be a servant or other agent as if he were such." *See Themins,* 54 Ore. App. at 908.

[4] Apparent agency is a distinct concept from apparent authority. Apparent agency creates an agency relationship that does not otherwise exist, while apparent authority expands the authority of an actual agent. . . . In this case, the precise issue is whether 3K was defendant's apparent agent, not whether 3K had apparent authority. . . .

that *McDonald's Corporation* operated both it and the other McDonald's restaurants that she had previously patronized. It states:

> "All [that] the Plaintiff's affidavit proves is that she went to the Tigard McDonald's based in reliance on her past experiences at other McDonald's. But her affidavit does nothing to link her experiences with ownership of those restaurants by McDonald's Corporation."

Defendant's argument both demands a higher level of sophistication about the nature of franchising than the general public can be expected to have and ignores the effect of its own efforts to lead the public to believe that McDonald's restaurants are part of a uniform national system of restaurants with common products and common standards of quality. A jury could find from plaintiff's affidavit that she believed that all McDonald's restaurants were the same because she believed that one entity owned and operated all of them or, at the least, exercised sufficient control that the standards that she experienced at one would be the same as she experienced at others.

* * * *

Other courts have not required the specificity of reliance on which defendant insists. In *Crinkley,* the plaintiffs stayed at a Holiday Inn because they thought that it would be a good place to stay. They were unable to get a room at the first Holiday Inn that they tried and used a Holiday Inn directory to find the one where they did stay. One plaintiff testified that he did not know the difference between a franchised inn and a company-owned inn and would be greatly surprised to find that Holiday Inns (the franchisor) was not involved in the operation of the inn where he stayed. The court held that that evidence was sufficient to raise a jury issue of reliance. *844 F.2d at 167.*

* * * *

[P]laintiff testified that she relied on the general reputation of McDonald's in patronizing the Tigard restaurant and in her expectation of the quality of the food and service that she would receive. Especially in light of defendant's efforts to create a public perception of a common McDonald's system at all McDonald's restaurants, whoever operated them, a jury could find that plaintiff's reliance was objectively reasonable. The trial court erred in granting summary judgment on the apparent agency theory.

Reversed and remanded.

C. Apparent Agency

The preceding case raises the issue of apparent agency. Under the doctrine of apparent agency, a principal (or alleged principal) could incur liability for wrongdoing committed by an agent (or alleged agent), acting with apparent authority on behalf, or purportedly on behalf, of the principal. (*Third Restatement* § 7.08.) Typically, the analysis of a principal's responsibility for the actions of an agent turns upon issues of control and vicarious responsibility and not questions of appearances. The evaluation of the appearances of an agency relationship is usually seen when evaluating an agency fact pattern involving a contract and the issue is whether the agent acted with "apparent authority." (*See* Section II, *supra.*) However, while issues of apparent authority are a more integral part of a contract analysis than a tort analysis, there is one particular instance in which the question of the apparent role of the agent (or the apparent agent) is relevant to a tort analysis. That instance is known as "apparent agency."

Apparent agency arises in situations in which a person commits a tort, but that person is not an employee, or perhaps not even an agent, of the principal. Therefore, the principal would not be liable for the alleged agent's tort under the traditional agency analysis, discussed above. However, if there are circumstances which led the injured third party to reasonably believe that an employment or agency relationship existed between the principal and the alleged agent, and those circumstances existed because of some action or inaction (i.e., manifestation) on the part of the principal, then the principal might still be liable under a theory of apparent agency, even if no employment relationship existed. Many courts, but not all, will also require that the injury to the third party resulted because of the third party's reasonable, but incorrect, belief that the alleged agent was, in fact, an agent of the principal. In other words, some showing that if the alleged agent were under the control of the principal, then the principal would, or could, have exercised control to avoid the tort which took place.

Apparent agency involves: a reasonable belief by the third party that the alleged agent is an agent of the principal (i.e., reasonable reliance); some action or inaction by the principal to create (or to fail to dispel) that reasonable belief on the part of the third party; and some showing (in some jurisdictions) that the third party's injury could have been avoided had the alleged principal exercised control over the alleged agent. In other words, the third party's injury arose out of that third party's reasonable belief that an employee/agency relationship existed.

Butler v. McDonald's Corporation

110 F. Supp. 2d 62 (D.R.I. 2000)

LAGUEUX, DISTRICT JUDGE:

John D. and Corliss E. Butler have brought this action on behalf of their minor child, Bryan A. Butler ("plaintiff"), for injuries he sustained as the result of the alleged negligence of McDonald's Corporation ("defendant"), its agents, servants, and/or employees in maintaining the premises of a franchised restaurant and in training and supervision of its agents, servants and/or employees.

* * * *

For eleven years defendant has leased a restaurant building and premises at 6595 Post Road, North Kingstown, Rhode Island ("franchise restaurant") to James Cooper ("Cooper"). Defendant also has a license franchise agreement that allows Cooper to operate the business under the McDonald's name according to a variety of requirements and conditions typically found in franchise arrangements. It is undisputed that the employees working at the franchise restaurant are not employees of defendant but rather are employees of Cooper.

On or about July 25, 1997 plaintiff was a patron at the franchise restaurant. Plaintiff was in the company of other minors (young teens) who frequently visited this particular McDonald's restaurant and other "fast-food" establishments. Plaintiff and his companions were awaiting the arrival of Mr. Groves, father to one of the boys, for a ride back home. Plaintiff saw what he believed to be the Groves car in the parking lot and exited the south side door of the restaurant to inform Mr. Groves that the boys needed more time. After exiting plaintiff realized that he was mistaken—it was not the Groves car. Plaintiff turned to re-enter the restaurant. As plaintiff pushed against the door it shattered, resulting in injury to his right hand which has required two corrective surgeries and physical therapy.

Plaintiff, through his parents, filed this action on September 2, 1998 seeking damages. Plaintiff claims the injury was caused by the negligence of the franchise restaurant operator and/or his employees, but he seeks to hold defendant liable because of the nature of the relationship between defendant and the franchise restaurant.

Specifically, plaintiff alleges there was a "spider crack" in the glass portion of the door for a period of time exceeding two weeks, and that the franchise restaurant operator and/or his employees knew or should have known of this unsafe condition. As a result, plaintiff claims that the alleged unsafe condition should have been repaired, and that the failure to repair the alleged unsafe condition and the resultant structural weakness in the glass was the proximate cause of his injuries.

* * * *

Through the doctrine of respondeat superior, a party can be held vicariously liable for the torts of another. Vicarious liability often arises from a employer-employee relationship or a principal-agent relationship. [*Citations omitted*] Plaintiff does not allege the existence of an employer-employee relationship. The issue presented by this motion then, with regard to vicarious liability, is whether defendant can be made liable by application of an agency theory or the doctrine of apparent agency.

* * * *

Agency is " 'the fiduciary relation which results from the manifestation of consent by one person to another that the other shall act on behalf and subject to his control, and consent by the other so to act.' " *Toledo v. Van Waters & Rogers, Inc.,* 92 F. Supp. 2d 44, 52 (D.R.I. 2000)(citing *Lawrence v. Anheuser-Busch, Inc.,* 523 A.2d 864, 867 (R.I. 1987)(quoting *Restatement (Second) Agency § 1(1)*(1958))). The Rhode Island Supreme Court has outlined three elements that must be shown in order for an agency relationship to exist: (1) the principal must manifest that the agent will act for him, (2) the agent must accept the undertaking, and (3) the parties must agree that the principal will be in control of the undertaking. [*Citations omitted.*] "It is essential to the relationship that the principal have the right to control the work of the agent, and that the agent act primarily for the benefit of the principal." [*Citations omitted.*] In contrast, an independent contractor relationship exists where one is retained to perform a task independent of and not subject to the control of the employer. [*Citations omitted.*] Therefore, the key element of an agency relationship is the right of the principal to control the work of the agent. [*Citations omitted.*] The critical issue then in determining defendant's liability under an agency theory is whether defendant had the right to control the franchise restaurant operator's activities and operations.

* * * *

The strongest evidence put forward by defendant that an agency relationship does not exist is the franchise license agreement itself which explicitly states that no agency has been created thereby. However, a party cannot simply rely on statements in an agreement to establish or deny agency. *See Silvestri,* 1991 WL 789928 at *2. Rather, an agency relationship is essentially determined by examining whether there is a right of control of one party over another. *See id.* Further, defendant offers an affidavit from its Senior Corporate Attorney stating on behalf of defendant that defendant does not own, operate, or have a right to control the franchise restaurant.

Plaintiff claims that these representations are hollow since defendant maintains a right to control the operations and management of the franchise restaurant through operational and training manuals, a franchise license agreement, and an operator's lease and license agreement. Additionally, plaintiff claims defendant exercises a right to control through defendant's requirement that the restaurant conform to the McDonald's "comprehensive" system, the frequent and detailed inspections of the premises and its operations, the taking of profits, and the right of defendant to terminate the agreement for material breach.

Other courts have reached different conclusions as to whether these elements of a franchise agreement are sufficient to create an issue of fact regarding the existence of an agency relationship between a franchisor and a franchisee. For example, in *Hoffnagle v. McDonald's Corp.,* 522 N.W.2d 808, 809 (Iowa 1994), on which defendant relies, the Court examined the defendant's right to control the franchisee in the context of determining whether or not the defendant owed a duty of due care to an employee of the franchisee under the employer-independent contractor test contained in the Restatement (Second) of Torts Section 414. The Court, awarding summary judgment to the defendant franchisor, concluded that the defendant's "authority is no more than the authority to insure 'the uniformity and standardization of products and services offered by a [franchisor's] restaurant. [Such] obligations do not affect the control of daily operations.' " *Id.* at 814 (quoting *Little v. Howard Johnson Co.,* 183 Mich. App. 675, 455 N.W.2d 390, 394 (Mich. Ct. App. 1990)). *See also Folsom v. Burger King,* 135 Wn.2d 658, 958 P.2d 301, 303 (Wash. 1998).

However, in *Miller v. McDonald's Corp.,* 150 Ore. App. 274, 945 P.2d 1107, 1111 (Or. Ct. App. 1997), the Court, in examining the existence vel non of an agency relationship between the franchisor and the franchisee, reached the opposite conclusion. . . .

The Rhode Island Supreme Court has outlined the indicia for the right to control in an agency relationship. Relevant examples include a principal's beneficial interest in the agent's undertaking, written agreements between the parties, and instructions given to the agent by the principal relating to how to conduct business. *See Baker v. ICA Mortgage Corp.*, 588 A.2d 616, 617 (R.I. 1991); Lawrence, 523 A.2d at 867.

Because plaintiff has offered the aforesaid evidence to demonstrate defendant's requisite right to control the franchise restaurant, and because the Court finds the reasoning in *Miller* more persuasive than that in *Hoffnagle,* the Court concludes that a reasonable jury could find that an agency relationship exists and that defendant can be held vicariously liable. Therefore, on the issue of whether defendant can be held vicariously liable for the negligence of its franchised restaurant under an agency theory, summary judgment must be denied.

2. Apparent Agency

Since defendant's motion for summary judgment must be denied because there are disputed issues of fact as to whether the franchise restaurant operator is an agent of defendant, the Court does not need to address the applicability of the doctrine of apparent agency. However, since plaintiff will undoubtedly rely on that doctrine at trial, this Court should give the parties some guidance in that respect.

In Rhode Island the doctrine of apparent agency, sometimes called agency by estoppel or ostensible agency, was intended to provide recourse to third parties who justifiably contract under the belief that another is an agent of a principal and detrimentally suffer as a result of that reliance. [*Citations omitted.*] "The doctrine of apparent agency exists in order to allow third parties to depend on agents without investigating their agency before every single transaction. [*Citations omitted.*] The doctrine also serves the purpose of promoting responsible business practices and protecting third party reliance on reasonable perceptions of a party's agency.

* * * *

It is by no means clear that the Rhode Island Supreme Court will apply the doctrine of apparent agency to a franchisor/franchisee situation. But, if it did, clearly it would require the plaintiff to prove: (1) that the franchisor acted in a manner that would lead a reasonable person to conclude that the operator and/or employees of the franchise restaurant were employees or agents of the defendant; (2) that the plaintiff actually believed the operator and/or employees of the franchise restaurant were agents or servants of the franchisor; and (3) that the plaintiff thereby relied to his detriment upon the care and skill of the allegedly negligent operator and/or employees of the franchise restaurant. [*Citations omitted.*]

Other jurisdictions have used similar criteria in applying the apparent agency doctrine to torts in a franchise situation. *See Crinkley v. Holiday Inns, Inc.,* 844 F.2d 156, 157 (4th Cir. 1988)(apparent agency test applied to a hotel franchise relationship); *Gizzi v. Texaco, Inc.,* 437 F.2d 308, 309 (5th Cir.), cert. denied 404 U.S. 829, 30 L. Ed. 2d 57, 92 S. Ct. 65 (1971)(apparent agency test applied to a gas station franchise relationship); *Miller, 945 P.2d at 1112* (apparent agency test applied to the instant defendant in a similar franchise relationship); *Orlando Executive Park, Inc. v. P.D.R.,* 402 So. 2d 442, 449 (Fla. Dist. Ct. App. 1981)(apparent agency test applied to a hotel franchise relationship). These cases are instructive but by no means determinative as to what the Rhode Island Supreme Court would do in this case.

The first requirement, [is] whether defendant acted in manner that would lead a reasonable person to conclude that the operator and/or employees of the franchise restaurant were employees or agents of the defendant. . . .

Plaintiff argues that defendant encourages third persons to think that they are dealing with defendant when they visit one of defendant's franchised restaurants. This belief stems from a customer's difficulty in differentiating between a restaurant that is corporate-owned from one which is franchised. Plaintiff points to defendant's national advertising campaign, highly visible logos throughout the restaurant and on food packaging, a requirement that the employees wear uniforms of designated color, design and other specifications, and volumes of required standards with respect to nearly all aspects of the franchise restaurant's maintenance, appearance, and operation. Seemingly, the purpose of defendant's mandatory procedures and requirements for the appearance and operation of franchised restaurants is to promote uniformity in both product and environment.

Certainly it is arguable that plaintiff, as well as any other customer of defendant's restaurants, would reasonably conclude that the restaurant is owned by defendant and operated by defendant's employees. Because plaintiff has produced enough evidence to support the view that a reasonable person would conclude that the operator and/or employees of the franchise restaurant were employees or agents of defendant, the question must be resolved by the jury.

Second, plaintiff has indicated that he simply went to the franchise restaurant because he and his friends wanted "McDonald's" food, as they had done on numerous occasions. Nowhere does plaintiff indicate that he did or could differentiate a franchised restaurant from a corporate-owned restaurant. Therefore, whether plaintiff actually believed that the franchise restaurant operator and/or his employees were agents of defendant is a question of fact best left for trial and resolution by the jury.

Finally, whether plaintiff relied to his detriment upon the care and skill of the allegedly negligent operator and/or employees of the franchise restaurant again presents a factual issue.

It is obvious that the issue of apparent agency will have to be submitted to the jury and after the jury has answered interrogatories, the Court may decide to certify questions regarding the applicability of the doctrine of apparent agency to this case to the Rhode Island Supreme Court.

* * * *

IV. Conclusion

For the preceding reasons, defendant's motion for summary judgment is denied.

D. Intentional Torts

Typically, principals (even employers) are not held liable for the intentional torts of their agents. Such actions are usually found to be outside the scope of employment and are committed without any intent to serve the employer. However, many courts recognize an exception to this exclusion when the employee's job is such that some part of the intentional tort might be characterized as being done with the intent of "serving the employer." For example, a bouncer who ejects a patron from a club, seriously injuring the patron, might be said to have done so with, at least a partial, intent to serve his employer. Some other jurisdictions look beyond the test of whether the intentional tort was committed with the purpose of serving the employer and find that a principal may be liable for the harm done as a result of the intentional torts of an agent if it is foreseeable that some harm might arise out of the specific employment/agency relationship, even if the exact harm which occurred was not foreseeable. In an effort to assess whether a particular harm was foreseeable, courts in these jurisdictions will ask whether the tort was of "characteristic risk" associated with the agency relationship.

Ira S. Bushey & Sons, Inc. v. United States

398 F.2d 167 (2d Cir. 1968)

FRIENDLY, CIRCUIT JUDGE:

While the United States Coast Guard vessel Tamaroa was being overhauled in a floating drydock located in Brooklyn's Gowanus Canal, a seaman returning from shore leave late at night, in the condition for which seamen are famed, turned some wheels on the drydock wall. He thus opened valves that controlled the flooding of the tanks on one side of the drydock. Soon the ship listed, slid off the blocks and fell against the wall. Parts of the drydock sank, and the ship partially did—fortunately without loss of life or personal injury. The drydock owner sought and was granted compensation by the District Court for the Eastern District of New York in an amount to be determined, *276 F. Supp. 518;* the United States appeals.

* * * *

The Tamaroa had gone into drydock on February 28, 1963; her keel rested on blocks permitting her drive shaft to be removed and repairs to be made to her hull. The contract between the Government and Bushey provided in part:

> (*o*) The work shall, whenever practical, be performed in such manner as not to interfere with the berthing and messing of personnel attached to the vessel undergoing repair, and provision shall be made so that personnel assigned shall have access to the vessel at all times, it being understood that such personnel will not interfere with the work or the contractor's workmen.

Access from shore to ship was provided by a route past the security guard at the gate, through the yard, up a ladder to the top of one drydock wall and along the wall to a gangway leading to the fantail deck, where men returning from leave reported at a quartermaster's shack.

Seaman Lane, whose prior record was unblemished, returned from shore leave a little after midnight on March 14. He had been drinking heavily; the quartermaster made mental note that he was "loose." For reasons not apparent to us or very likely to Lane,[4] he took it into his head, while progressing along the gangway wall, to turn each of three large wheels some twenty times; unhappily, as previously stated, these wheels controlled the water intake valves. After boarding ship at 12:11 A.M., Lane mumbled to an off-duty seaman that he had

[4] Lane disappeared after completing the sentence imposed by a court-martial and being discharged from the Coast Guard.

"turned some valves" and also muttered something about "valves" to another who was standing the engineering watch. Neither did anything; apparently Lane's condition was not such as to encourage proximity. At 12:20 A.M. a crew member discovered water coming into the drydock. By 12:30 A.M. the ship began to list, the alarm was sounded and the crew were ordered ashore. Ten minutes later the vessel and dock were listing over 20 degrees; in another ten minutes the ship slid off the blocks and fell against the drydock wall.

The Government attacks imposition of liability on the ground that Lane's acts were not within the scope of his employment. It relies heavily on § 228(1) of the Restatement of Agency 2d which says that "conduct of a servant is within the scope of employment if, but only if: * * * (c) it is actuated, at least in part by a purpose to serve the master." Courts have gone to considerable lengths to find such a purpose, as witness a well-known opinion in which Judge Learned Hand concluded that a drunken boatswain who routed the plaintiff out of his bunk with a blow, saying "Get up, you big son of a bitch, and turn to," and then continued to fight, might have thought he was acting in the interest of the ship. *Nelson v. American-West African Line,* 86 F.2d 730 (2 Cir. 1936), cert. denied, 300 U.S. 665, 57 S. Ct. 509, 81 L. Ed. 873 (1937). It would be going too far to find such a purpose here; while Lane's return to the Tamaroa was to serve his employer, no one has suggested how he could have thought turning the wheels to be, even if—which is by no means clear—he was unaware of the consequences.

In light of the highly artificial way in which the motive test has been applied, the district judge believed himself obliged to test the doctrine's continuing vitality by referring to the larger purposes *respondeat superior* is supposed to serve. He concluded that the old formulation failed this test. We do not find his analysis so compelling, however, as to constitute a sufficient basis in itself for discarding the old doctrine. It is not at all clear, as the court below suggested, that expansion of liability in the manner here suggested will lead to a more efficient allocation of resources. As the most astute exponent of this theory has emphasized, a more efficient allocation can only be expected if there is some reason to believe that imposing a particular cost on the enterprise will lead it to consider whether steps should be taken to prevent a recurrence of the accident. Calabresi, The Decision for Accidents: An Approach to Non-fault Allocation of Costs, 78 Harv.L.Rev. 713, 725–34 (1965). And the suggestion that imposition of liability here will lead to more intensive screening of employees rests on highly questionable premises, *see* Comment, *Assessment of Punitive Damages Against an Entrepreneur for the Malicious Torts of His Employees,* 70 Yale L.J. 1296, 1301–04

(1961).[5] The unsatisfactory quality of the allocation of resource rationale is especially striking on the facts of this case. It could well be that application of the traditional rule might induce drydock owners, prodded by their insurance companies, to install locks on their valves to avoid similar incidents in the future,[6] while placing the burden on shipowners is much less likely to lead to accident prevention.[7] It is true, of course, that in many cases the plaintiff will not be in a position to insure, and so expansion of liability will, at the very least, serve *respondeat* superior's loss spreading function. *See* Smith, *Frolic and Detour,* 23 Colum.L.Rev. 444, 456 (1923). But the fact that the defendant is better able to afford damages is not alone sufficient to justify legal responsibility, *see* Blum & Kalven, *Public Law Perspectives on a Private Law Problem* (1965), and this overarching principle must be taken into account in deciding whether to expand the reach of *respondeat superior.*

A policy analysis thus is not sufficient to justify this proposed expansion of vicarious liability. This is not surprising since *respondeat superior,* even within its traditional limits, rests not so much on policy grounds consistent with the governing principles of tort law as in a deeply rooted sentiment that a business enterprise cannot justly disclaim responsibility for accidents which may fairly be said to be characteristic of its activities. It is in this light that the inadequacy of the motive test becomes apparent. Whatever may have been the case in the past, a doctrine that would create such drastically different consequences for the actions of the drunken boatswain in *Nelson* and those of the drunken seaman here reflects a wholly unrealistic attitude toward the risks characteristically attendant upon the operation of a ship. We concur in the statement of Mr. Justice Rutledge in a case involving violence injuring a fellow-worker, in this instance in the context of workmen's compensation:

> "Men do not discard their personal qualities when they go to work. Into the job they carry their intelligence, skill, habits of care and rectitude. Just as inevitably they take along also their tendencies to carelessness and camaraderie, as well as emotional make-up. In bringing men together, work brings these qualities together, causes frictions between them, creates occasions for lapses into carelessness,

---

5 We are not here speaking of cases in which the enterprise has negligently hired an employee whose undesirable propensities are known or should have been. [*Citations omitted.*]

6 The record reveals that most modern drydocks have automatic locks to guard against unauthorized use of valves.

7 Although it is theoretically possible that shipowners would demand that drydock owners take appropriate action, *see* Coase, The Problem of Social Cost, 3 J.L. & Economics 1 (1960), this would seem unlikely to occur in real life.

> and for fun-making and emotional flare-up. * * * These expressions of human nature are incidents inseparable from working together. They involve risks of injury and these risks are inherent in the working environment."

Hartford Accident & Indemnity Co. v. Cardillo, 72 App.D.C. 52, 112 F.2d 11, 15, cert. denied, 310 U.S. 649, 60 S. Ct. 1100, 84 L. Ed. 1415 (1940). . . .

Put another way, Lane's conduct was not so "unforeseeable" as to make it unfair to charge the Government with responsibility. We agree with a leading treatise that "what is reasonably foreseeable in this context [of *respondeat superior*] * * * is quite a different thing from the foreseeably unreasonable risk of harm that spells negligence * * *. The foresight that should impel the prudent man to take precautions is not the same measure as that by which he should perceive the harm likely to flow from his long-run activity in spite of all reasonable precautions on his own part. The proper test here bears far more resemblance to that which limits liability for workmen's compensation than to the test for negligence. The employer should be held to expect risks, to the public also, which arise 'out of and in the course of' his employment of labor." 2 Harper & James, *The Law of Torts* 1377–78 (1956). *See also* Calabresi, *Some Thoughts on Risk Distribution and the Law of Torts,* 70 Yale L.J. 499, 544 (1961). Here it was foreseeable that crew members crossing the drydock might do damage, negligently or even intentionally, such as pushing a Bushey employee or kicking property into the water. Moreover, the proclivity of seamen to find solace for solitude by copious resort to the bottle while ashore has been noted in opinions too numerous to warrant citation. Once all this is granted, it is immaterial that Lane's precise action was not to be foreseen. . . . Consequently, we can no longer accept our past decisions that have refused to move beyond the *Nelson rule, Brailas v. Shepard S.S. Co.,* 152 F.2d 849 (2d Cir. 1945), cert. denied, 327 U.S. 807, 66 S. Ct. 970, 90 L. Ed. 1032 (1946); *Kable v. United States,* 169 F.2d 90, 92 (2 Cir. 1948), since they do not accord with modern understanding as to when it is fair for an enterprise to disclaim the actions of its employees.

One can readily think of cases that fall on the other side of the line. If Lane had set fire to the bar where he had been imbibing or had caused an accident on the street while returning to the drydock, the Government would not be liable; the activities of the "enterprise" do not reach into areas where the servant does not create risks different from those attendant on the activities of the community in general. [*Citations omitted.*] We agree with the district judge that if the seaman "upon returning to the drydock, recognized the Bushey security guard as his wife's lover and shot him," *276 F. Supp. at 530,* vicarious liability would not follow; the incident would have related to the seaman's domestic life, not to his seafaring activity [*Citations omitted.*], and it would have been the most unlikely happenstance that the confrontation with the paramour occurred on a drydock rather than at the traditional spot. Here Lane had come within the closed-off area where his ship lay [*Citations omitted.*], to occupy a berth to which the Government insisted he have access [*Citation omitted.*], and while his act is not readily explicable, at least it was not shown to be due entirely to facets of his personal life. The risk that seamen going and coming from the Tamaroa might cause damage to the drydock is enough to make it fair that the enterprise bear the loss. It is not a fatal objection that the rule we lay down lacks sharp contours; in the end, as Judge Andrews said in a related context, "it is all a question [of expediency,] * * * of fair judgment, always keeping in mind the fact that we endeavor to make a rule in each case that will be practical and in keeping with the general understanding of mankind." *Palsgraf v. Long Island R.R. Co.,* 248 N.Y. 339, 354–355, 162 N.E. 99, 104, 59 A.L.R. 1253 (1928) (dissenting opinion). . . .

E. Frolic and Detour

Of course, there are times when an agent acts on her own behalf outside of the scope of her employment. For example, if an agent has gone home for the evening, and then drives to a party and gets into a car accident, that accident has not occurred within the scope of the agent's employment. Sometimes it can be difficult to determine whether or not an agent has "left" employment. When an employee leaves employment to do something for personal reasons, that is known as a "frolic." If an employee is still engaged in employment but strays only slightly from the direct assignment, that is known as a mere "detour." An agent who is driving to the bank to deposit money for the store which employs him and takes a longer route so he can drive by the new sculpture in the park is on a "detour." If he gets into an accident while driving by the sculpture, his employer will still be liable. However, if that same agent, instead of going to the bank, goes to see a movie, and spills his soda on the person sitting next to him, the person with the soda-stained garment cannot charge the agent's employer for the cleaning bill since the agent's leaving work to attend the movie would be considered a frolic.

In *Clover v. Snowbird Ski Resort,* 808 P.2d 1037 (Utah 1991), the court stated: "it is important to note that if Zulliger had returned to the Plaza Restaurant immediately after he inspected the operations at the Mid-Gad Restaurant, there would be ample evidence to support the conclusion that on his return trip

Zulliger's actions were within the scope of his employment. [. . .] The difficulty, of course, arises from the fact that Zulliger did not return to the Plaza after he finished inspecting the facilities at the Mid-Gad. Rather, he skied four more runs and rode the lift to the top of the mountain before he began his return to the base." (*Id* at 1041.) In other words, the question is whether skiing "four more runs" was a detour or a frolic. Detours are generally considered to fall within the course of employment, and an employer would, therefore, be liable under *respondeat superior* for torts arising during an employee's detours. By contrast, a frolic takes an employee's action outside the course of his employment, and an employer would probably not be held liable for torts arising during an employee's frolic. Whether a tort arises during a detour or a frolic is a factual inquiry.

As one Illinois court put it: ". . .long ago [we] recognized a distinction between 'frolic,' where the employee's personal business is seen as unrelated to employment and a 'detour,' where the employee's deviation for personal reasons is nonetheless seen as sufficiently related to the employment. . . . An employer will not necessarily be relieved of liability for an employee's negligence even if the employee was combining personal business with the employer's business: 'Where an employee's deviation from the course of employment is slight and not unusual, a court may find as a matter of law that the employee was still executing the employer's business. . . .' [*Citation omitted.*] Conversely, when a deviation is exceedingly marked and unusual, as a matter of law the employee may be found to be outside the scope of employment. . . ." *Laird v. Baxter Health Care Corp,* 650 N.E.2d 215 (Ill. App. Ct. 1994).

F. Inherently Dangerous Activities

As discussed above, there are certain specific circumstances in which a principal may be held liable for the actions of an agent, even if that agent is not an employee. These circumstances include: (1) inherently dangerous activities; (2) non-delegable duties; and (3) negligent hiring. Inherently dangerous activities include any activity which is likely to cause harm or damage unless some precautions are taken. A non-delegable duty is one that a person may not avoid by the mere delegation of a task to another person. For example, landlords have certain non-delegable duties to their tenants. Attorneys have certain non-delegable duties to their clients. If something is "non-delegable," it does not mean that an agent may not be hired to perform the task. It means that hiring an agent to perform the task will not discharge or transfer the principal's responsibility or liability. The last category, negligent hiring, is not really about vicarious liability. It refers to circumstances in which the principal may be found liable for the torts of a non-employee agent. However, that liability is based on the principal's negligence in hiring the agent, not on attributing the tortious act of an agent to an innocent principal.

Majestic Realty Assocs., Inc. v. Toti Contracting Co.

30 N.J. 425, 153 A.2d 321 (N.J. 1959)

Plaintiffs Majestic Realty Associates, Inc., and Bohen's, Inc., owner and tenant, sought compensation from defendants Toti Contracting Co., Inc. and Parking Authority of the City of Paterson, New Jersey, for damage to Majestic's building and to Bohen's goods. The claim arose out of the activity of Toti in demolishing certain structures owned by the Authority. In the trial court, the action against the Authority was dismissed at the close of the plaintiffs' proof on the ground that Toti was an independent contractor for whose negligence the Authority could not be held responsible. The issue of the contractor's liability was submitted to the jury, which returned substantial verdicts for both plaintiffs. Majestic and Bohen's appealed from the dismissal in favor of the Authority. Toti did not seek a review. . . .

Majestic is the owner of the two-story premises at 297 Main Street, Paterson, New Jersey. Bohen's is the tenant of the first floor and basement thereof in which it conducted a dry goods business. The Authority acquired properties along Main Street beginning immediately adjacent to Majestic's building on the south and continuing to Ward Street, the next intersecting street, and then east on the latter street for 150 feet. The motive for the acquisition was to establish a public parking area. Main Street is one of the principal business arteries of the city and the locality was completely built up.

Accomplishment of the Authority's object required demolition of the several buildings on both streets. Some time prior to October 26, 1956, a contract was entered into by the Authority with Toti to do the work. The razing began on the Ward Street side and moved north. . . until the structure next to Majestic's premises was reached. It was at least a story (about 20 feet) higher than Majestic's roof; the northerly wall of the one was "right up against" the southerly wall of the other and the two walls ran alongside each other for 40 feet.

In the process of leveling this adjacent building, the contractor first removed the roof, then the front and south sidewalls and all of the interior partitions and floors. Thus, the north wall of brick and masonry next to

Majestic's structure was left standing free. Expert testimony was adduced to show that the proper method of demolition under the existing circumstances would have been to remove the roof, leaving the interior partition work for support, and to begin to take the north wall down "never leaving any portion [of it] at a higher point than the interior construction of the building would form a brace."

In demolishing the walls, Toti used a large metal ball, said to weigh 3,500 pounds, suspended from a crane which was stationed in the street. There was testimony that during the week prior to the accident, every time the ball would strike a wall, debris and dirt would fly and the Majestic building "rocked."

Further expert testimony indicated that in dealing with the free-standing north wall, the ball should have been made to hit the very top on each occasion so as to level it a few bricks at a time. This course was followed at first; the ball was swung from north to south and the dislodged bricks were catapulted away from Majestic's building and onto the adjoining lot. After a time, work ceased for a few minutes. On resumption, the operator of the crane swung the ball in such a manner that it struck at a point some 15 feet below the top of the wall. The impact propelled the uppermost section of the wall back in the direction from which the blow had come with the result that a 15 by 40 foot section fell on Majestic's roof, causing a 25 by 40 foot break therein. One of Bohen's employees, who saw the incident, asked the crane operator in the presence of Toti's president: "What did you do to our building?" He replied, "I goofed."

In characterizing a demolition undertaking of this type in a built up and busy section of a city, and in particular where one building to be razed adjoined another which was to remain untouched, plaintiffs' expert witness said it was "hazardous work"; "one of the most hazardous operations in the building business." And with reference to the leveling of a building so close to another structure which was not to be harmed, he asserted that the recognized procedure is to take it down in small sections so as not to lose control of the operation. . . .

On the proof outlined, the trial court recognized that the work was hazardous in its very nature, but did not feel that it constituted a nuisance *per se*. Therefore, he ruled that the Authority, not having had or exercised control over the manner and method or means of performing the demolition operation, could not be held for the negligent act of its independent contractor. The majority of the Appellate Division took the position that where the activity contracted to be undertaken is such that potential danger exists regardless of reasonable care on the part of the contractor, the landowner cannot, by contractual delegation, immunize himself against liability for negligence of the contractor which causes injury to a member of the public or to an adjoining property owner. Thc dissent expressed the view that under the evidence the mishap resulted from a negligent failure to follow the standard procedure for the destruction of the wall and not from a danger which inhered in the work itself regardless of the exercise of care. Thus, it was declared that the contract protected the Authority against liability for Toti's negligence in the performance of the work. It remains for this court to search out the just rule to be applied in the circumstances.

The problem must be approached with an awareness of the long settled doctrine that ordinarily where a person engages a contractor, who conducts an independent business by means of his own employees, to do work not in itself a nuisance (as our cases put it), he is not liable for the negligent acts of the contractor in the performance of the contract. [*Citations omitted.*] Certain exceptions have come to be accepted, *i.e.,* (a) where the landowner retains control of the manner and means of the doing of the work which is the subject of the contract; (b) where he engages an incompetent contractor; or (c) where, as noted in the statement of the general rule, the activity contracted for constitutes a nuisance *per se.* [*Citations omitted.*]

In the present case, the suggestion is made that the language of the contract reveals a retention of control by the Authority of the method of Toti's performance sufficient to warrant the application of principles of *respondeat superior* in the interest of injured third persons. Our examination of the document convinces us otherwise. The plain import of the provisions is not to confer on the Authority the right to say how the job shall be done; the reservation is limited to supervision for the purpose of seeing that the work is done in accordance with the contract and specifications. The supervisory interest relates to the result to be accomplished, not to the means of accomplishing it. [*Citations omitted.*]

As to exception (b), noted above, it is not claimed that the proof makes out a jury question on the charge that an incompetent contractor was hired for the task of demolition. . . .

But this precise facet of the problem of Toti's competency was not raised at the trial or in the briefs. It arose as an emanation of the oral argument. Consequently, no decision is rendered with respect to it and the matter is expressly reserved.

Under exception (c), on which plaintiffs rely principally, liability will be imposed upon the landowner in spite of the engagement of an independent contractor if the work to be done constitutes a nuisance *per se.*

* * * *

Without undertaking an exhaustive review of the cases in our State where the expression appears, it seems proper to say that the legal content of "nuisance *per se*" and the application thereof in a factual framework such as that now before us, is anything but clear. And we agree with the Appellate Division that in these times it is of doubtful utility. In *Sarno v. Gulf Refining Co.,* 99 N.J.L. 340, 342 (Sup. Ct. 1924), affirmed 102 N.J.L. 223 (E. & A. 1925), the court equated it with "inherently dangerous" and this appears to have set in motion a trend toward the view now espoused by the *Restatement, Torts,* §§ 835(*e*), 416. [*Citations omitted.*]

Section 416 of the Restatement propounds a rule which would impose liability upon the landowner who engages an independent contractor to do work which he should recognize as necessarily requiring the creation during its progress of a condition involving a peculiar risk of harm to others unless special precautions are taken, if the contractor is negligent in failing to take those precautions. Such work may be said to be inherently dangerous, *i.e.,* an activity which can be carried on safely only by the exercise of special skill and care, and which involves grave risk of danger to persons or property if negligently done. *Restatement, supra, § 835, comment on clause (e), page* 285. The term signifies that danger inheres in the activity itself at all times, so as to require special precautions to be taken with regard to it to avoid injury. It means more than simply danger arising from the casual or collateral negligence of persons engaged in it under particular circumstances. . . .

It is important to distinguish an operation which may be classed as inherently dangerous from one that is ultra-hazardous. The latter is described as one which "(a) necessarily involves a serious risk of harm to the person, land or chattels of others which cannot be eliminated by the exercise of the utmost care, and (b) is not a matter of common usage." *Restatement, supra,* § 520. The distinction is important because liability is absolute where the work is ultra-hazardous, ... but it is contingent on proof of negligence in cases of inherently dangerous activity. . . . In our judgment in the future in a factual context, such as is present here, decision will be facilitated if liability is tested in terms of these distinctions.

There is no doubt that the line between work which is ordinary, usual and commonplace, and that which is inherently dangerous because its very nature involves a peculiar and high risk of harm to members of the public or adjoining proprietors of land unless special precautions are taken, is somewhat shadowy. At least one basis for classification must stem from a common realization by reasonable men that a higher incidence of accidents is ordinarily associated with the latter type of work. The perimeter of an all-inclusive category cannot be drawn except in the general terms of the rule, and its application must be left in large measure to the gradual accumulation of precedents. *See* 23 *A.L.R., at pages* 1026, 1027. For the present, we need deal only with the case before us.

There is some conflict in the decisions as to whether demolition activity is one which necessarily involves a peculiar risk of harm to members of the public or to adjoining property. The current New York rule is that the razing of buildings in a busy, built-up section of a city is inherently dangerous within the contemplation of section 416 of the Restatement. [*Citations omitted.*]

* * * *

It is urged that such a burden ought not to be imposed upon a landowner who is not competent to do the work himself and so must turn to a person following the necessary independent calling in the particular field to accomplish the result sought. But in the resolution of the conflicting interests of the innocent injured person and the landowner who chose the contractor, justice and equity demand recognition of the absolute duty.

* * * *

For the reasons stated herein, the judgment of the Appellate Division is affirmed and the matter is remanded for a new trial against the Parking Authority.

SECTION IV: Rights, Duties and Liabilities of Agents and Principals

A. Agent's Liability

Agent's Liability for Torts

An agent is liable for his or her tortious conduct, regardless of whether the principal is also liable through vicarious liability. The *Third Restatement* § 7.01 states: "An agent is subject to liability to a third party harmed by the agent's tortious conduct. Unless an applicable statute provides otherwise, an actor remains subject to liability although the actor acts as an agent or an employee, with actual or apparent authority, or within the scope of employment." Thus, unless some applicable statute provides otherwise, a person is liable for his or her wrongdoing. The fact that an agent might have been acting as an employee and/or under the authority of a principal does not eliminate the agent's liability.

Even if a principal is vicariously liable for an agent's tortious conduct, such liability is typically accompanied by a claim against the agent by the principal for any liability the principal incurred as a result of the agent's conduct. Of course, it is often fruitless to bring such a claim if the agent is judgment proof, but the right exists nonetheless.

Agent's Liability for Contracts

Typically an agent is not liable as a party to the contracts that the agent enters into on behalf of a disclosed principal, unless there are special circumstances and/or the parties agree that the agent will be liable under the contract. However, there are situations in which the agent will usually be treated as a party to a contract. These situations occur when the agent is acting on behalf of: (1) an undisclosed principal; or (2) an unidentified principal (also known as a partially disclosed principal).

A principal is "undisclosed" when an agent is acting on behalf of that principal, but the agent does not tell the third party (and the third party does not know) that the agent is acting on behalf of a principal. Since the third party thinks it is entering into an agreement with the agent, and no other person is disclosed, the agent is presumed to be a party to the agreement and is bound by the agreement.

A principal is "unidentified" (or "partially disclosed") when an agent tells the third party that the agent is acting on behalf of a principal, but the identity of the principal is not disclosed. Even though the third party is aware of the existence of a principal, since an unidentified party may not enter into a contract, the agent, is usually treated as a party to the agreement and is bound by the agreement.

In either of these instances, once the agreement is signed (or otherwise "agreed to"), the agent is bound by the agreement, even if the principal is subsequently disclosed or identified, unless the parties specifically agree that the agent will not be bound or the original agreement provides that, upon identification of the principal, the agent will no longer be bound. However, the principal might also be bound by the agreement. When both the agent and the principal are bound, if the third party wishes to sue for a breach of the contract, in many states, the third party must often elect whether to sue the agent or the principal. (In other states, the third party may sue both the agent and the principal, but may only recover for damages once.) It is important to note that in most situations in which an agent would be found liable under an agreement entered into for a principal, the agent would have a claim for indemnification against the principal, provided, of course, that the agent acted with the principal's authority and did not cause the breach of the agreement.

An agent might also incur liability if the agent were to enter into an agreement without the authority to do so from the principal. If the agent enters into an agreement with a third party purporting to bind a principal, yet the agent actually lacks the authority to do so, the agent could be liable to the third party for breach of the agent's warranty of authority. Alternatively, if the principal were to be bound by such an agreement (for example, under an apparent authority claim), the principal might have a claim against the agent for the agent's actions which were taken without authority.

B. Duties in Agency

One of the concepts that is introduced in agency (but will arise in the context of partnerships and corporations as well as other entities and frameworks) is the idea that when one person takes responsibility to act on behalf of another, that responsibility carries with it certain duties beyond the mere completion of the task involved. These duties often relate to the ways in which the task is performed and the responsibilities that accompany the trusted role of the agent. Of course, an agent will have obligations to act consistently with any contractual duties the agent might have to the principal, to act within the scope of the agent's actual authority and to comply with the principal's lawful instructions. However, there is a long list of additional duties for which an agent is responsible under the *Third Restatement.* If an agent violates these duties without the consent of the fully informed principal, the agent could be liable to the principal for any resulting damages. Alternatively, the agent could also be liable to disgorge to the principal any profit made by the agent in violation of a duty, even if the principal could not have made the same profit. It is also important to be aware that the principal has certain duties to the agent who is taking the responsibility to act on the principal's behalf. These duties include:

Excerpts from the Third Restatement

Chapter 8. Duties of Agent and Principal to Each Other

§ 8.01 General Fiduciary Principle

An agent has a fiduciary duty to act loyally for the principal's benefit in all matters connected with the agency relationship.

§ 8.02 Material Benefit Arising out of Position

An agent has a duty not to acquire a material benefit from a third party in connection with transactions conducted or other actions taken on behalf of the principal or otherwise through the agent's use of the agent's position.

§ 8.03 Acting as or on Behalf of an Adverse Party

An agent has a duty not to deal with the principal as or on behalf of an adverse party in a transaction connected with the agency relationship.

§ 8.04 Competition

Throughout the duration of an agency relationship, an agent has a duty to refrain from competing with the principal and from taking action on behalf of or otherwise assisting the principal's competitors. During that time, an agent may take action, not otherwise wrongful, to prepare for competition following termination of the agency relationship.

§ 8.05 Use of Principal's Property; Use of Confidential Information

An agent has a duty

(1) not to use property of the principal for the agent's own purposes or those of a third party; and

(2) not to use or communicate confidential information of the principal for the agent's own purposes or those of a third party.

§ 8.06 Principal's Consent

(1) Conduct by an agent that would otherwise constitute a breach of duty as stated in §§ 8.01, 8.02, 8.03, 8.04, and 8.05 does not constitute a breach of duty if the principal consents to the conduct, provided that

(a) in obtaining the principal's consent, the agent

(i) acts in good faith,

(ii) discloses all material facts that the agent knows, has reason to know, or should know would reasonably affect the principal's judgment unless the principal has manifested that such facts are already known by the principal or that the principal does not wish to know them, and

(iii) otherwise deals fairly with the principal; and

(b) the principal's consent concerns either a specific act or transaction, or acts or transactions of a specified type that could reasonably be expected to occur in the ordinary course of the agency relationship.

(2) An agent who acts for more than one principal in a transaction between or among them has a duty

(a) to deal in good faith with each principal,

(b) to disclose to each principal

(i) the fact that the agent acts for the other principal or principals, and

(ii) all other facts that the agent knows, has reason to know, or should know would reasonably affect the principal's judgment unless the principal has manifested that such facts are already known by the principal or that the principal does not wish to know them, and

(c) otherwise to deal fairly with each principal.

§ 8.07 Duty Created by Contract

An agent has a duty to act in accordance with the express and implied terms of any contract between the agent and the principal.

§ 8.08 Duties of Care, Competence, and Diligence

Subject to any agreement with the principal, an agent has a duty to the principal to act with the care, competence, and diligence normally exercised by agents in similar circumstances. Special skills or knowledge possessed by an agent are circumstances to be taken into account in determining whether the agent acted with due care and diligence. If an agent claims to possess special skills or knowledge, the agent has a duty to the principal to act with the care, competence, and diligence normally exercised by agents with such skills or knowledge.

§ 8.09 Duty to Act Only within Scope of Actual Authority and to Comply with Principal's Lawful Instructions

(1) An agent has a duty to take action only within the scope of the agent's actual authority.

(2) An agent has a duty to comply with all lawful instructions received from the principal and persons designated by the principal concerning the agent's actions on behalf of the principal.

§ 8.10 Duty of Good Conduct

An agent has a duty, within the scope of the agency relationship, to act reasonably and to refrain from conduct that is likely to damage the principal's enterprise.

§ 8.11 Duty to Provide Information

An agent has a duty to use reasonable effort to provide the principal with facts that the agent knows, has reason to know, or should know when

(1) subject to any manifestation by the principal, the agent knows or has reason to know that the principal would wish to have the facts or the facts are material to the agent's duties to the principal; and

(2) the facts can be provided to the principal without violating a superior duty owed by the agent to another person.

§ 8.12 Duties Regarding Principal's Property—Segregation, Record-Keeping, and Accounting

An agent has a duty, subject to any agreement with the principal,

(1) not to deal with the principal's property so that it appears to be the agent's property;

(2) not to mingle the principal's property with anyone else's; and

(3) to keep and render accounts to the principal of money or other property received or paid out on the principal's account.

* * * *

§ 8.14 Duty to Indemnify

A principal has a duty to indemnify an agent

(1) in accordance with the terms of any contract between them; and

(2) unless otherwise agreed,

  (a) when the agent makes a payment

    (i) within the scope of the agent's actual authority, or

    (ii) that is beneficial to the principal, unless the agent acts officiously in making the payment; or

  (b) when the agent suffers a loss that fairly should be borne by the principal in light of their relationship.

§ 8.15 Principal's Duty to Deal Fairly and in Good Faith

A principal has a duty to deal with the agent fairly and in good faith, including a duty to provide the agent with information about risks of physical harm or pecuniary loss that the principal knows, has reason to know, or should know are present in the agent's work but unknown to the agent.

The following cases involve breaches (or allegations of breaches) of one or more of the duties set forth above. In each instance try to determine which duty or duties were violated.

Reading v. Regem

[1948] 2 KB 268, [1948] 2 All ER 27, [1948] WN 205

The supplicant [*Eds. Note: "supplicant" would be the "plaintiff" in a U.S. court.*] joined the army in 1936, and at the beginning of 1944 he was a sergeant in the Royal Army Medical Corps stationed at the general hospital in Cairo, where he was in charge of the medical stores.

The suppliant had not had any opportunities, in his life as a soldier, of making money, but in March, 1944, there were found standing to his credit at banks in Egypt, several thousands of pounds, and he had more thousands of pounds in notes in his flat. He had also acquired a motor car worth £ 1,500. The Special Investigation Branch of the army looked into the matter, and he was asked how he came by these moneys. He made a statement, from which it appears that they were paid to him by a man by the name of Manole in these circumstances. A lorry used to arrive loaded with cases, the contents of which were unknown. Then the suppliant, in full uniform, boarded the lorry, and escorted it through Cairo, so that it was able to pass the civilian police without being inspected. When it arrived at its destination, it was unloaded, or the contents were transferred to another lorry. After the first occasion when this happened, the suppliant saw Manole in a restaurant in Cairo. Manole handed him an envelope which he put in his pocket. On examining it when he arrived home, he found that it contained £ 2,000. Two or three weeks later, another load arrived, and another £ 2,000 was *paid* £ 3,000 was paid after the third load, and so it went on until eventually some £ 20,000 had gone into the pocket of the suppliant. The services which he rendered for that money were that he accompanied this lorry from one part of Cairo to another, and it is plain that he got it because he was a sergeant in the British army, and, while in uniform, escorted these lorries through Cairo. It is also plain that he was clearly violating his duty in so doing. The military authorities took possession of the money. . . .

In this petition of right, the suppliant alleges that these moneys are his and should be returned to him by the Crown. In answer, the Crown say: "These were bribes received by you by reason of your military employment, and you hold the money for the Crown. Even if we were wrong in the way in which we seized them, we are entitled to recover the amount of them, and to set off that amount against any claim you may have." In these circumstances, it is not necessary to dwell on the form of the claim. The question is whether or not the Crown is entitled to the money. It is not entitled to it simply because it is the Crown-moneys which are unlawfully obtained are not ipso facto forfeited to the Crown. The claim of the Crown rests on the fact that at the material time it was the suppliant's employer.

There are many cases in the books where a master has been held entitled to the unauthorised gains of his servant or agent. At law, the action took the form of money had and received. In equity it was put on the basis of a constructive trust due to a fiduciary relationship. Nowadays it is unnecessary to draw a distinction between law and equity. The real cause of action is a claim for restitution of moneys which, in justice, ought to be paid over. In my judgment, it is a principle of law that, if a servant takes advantage of his service and violates his duty of honestly and good faith to make a profit for himself, in the sense that the assets of which he has control, the facilities which he enjoys, or the position which he occupies, are the real cause of his obtaining the money as distinct from merely affording the opportunity for getting it, that is to say, if they play the predominant part in his obtaining the money, then he is accountable for it to his master. It matters not that the master has not lost any profit nor suffered any damage, nor does it matter that the master could not have done the act himself. If the servant has unjustly enriched himself by virtue of his service without his master's sanction, the law says that he ought not to be allowed to keep the money, but it shall be taken from him and given to his master, because he got it solely by reason of the position which he occupied as a servant of his master. Instances readily occur to mind. Take the case of the master who tells his servant to exercise his horses, and while the master is away, the servant lets them out and makes a profit by so doing. There is no loss to the master, the horses have been exercised, but the servant must account for the profits he makes. The Attorney-General put in argument the case of a uniformed policeman who, at the request of thieves and in return for a bribe, directs traffic away from the site of the crime. Is he to be allowed to keep the money? So, also, here, the use of the facilities provided by the Crown in the shape of the uniform and the use of his position in the army were the only reason why the suppliant was able to get this money. It was solely on that account that he was able to sit in the front of these lorries and give them a safe conduct through Cairo. There was no loss of profit to the Crown. The Crown would have been violating its duty if it had undertaken the task, but the suppliant was certainly violating his duty, and it is money which must be paid over to his master-in this case, the Crown.

. . .[I]n this case, . . . [t]he suppliant was not acting in the course of his employment. In my opinion, however, those are not essential ingredients of the cause of action. The uniform of the Crown and the position of the suppliant as a servant of the Crown were the only reasons why he was able to get this money, and that is sufficient to make him liable to hand it over to the Crown. The case is to be distinguished from cases where the service merely gives the opportunity of making money. A servant may, during his master's time, in breach of his contract, do other things to make money for himself, such as gambling, but he is entitled to keep that money himself. The master has a claim for damages for breach of contract, but he has no claim to the money. So, also, the fact that a soldier is stationed in a certain place may give him the opportunity, contrary to the King's Regulations, of engaging in trade and making money in that way. In such a case, the mere fact that his service gave the opportunity for getting the money would not entitle the Crown to it, but if, as here, the wearing of the King's uniform and his position as a soldier is the sole cause of his getting the money and he gets it dishonestly, that is an advantage which he is not allowed to keep. Although the Crown, has suffered no loss, the court orders the money to be handed over to the Crown, because the Crown is the only person to whom it can properly be *paid* The suppliant must not be allowed to enrich himself in this way. He got the money by virtue of his employment, and must hand it over.

QUESTIONS

1. Why should the government get to keep the money made from smuggling, an activity in which it never could have engaged?

2. If the soldier in the Reading case had not accepted money for assisting the smugglers, and instead had just been helping out "friends," would that have violated any of his duties as an agent? If so, which duty or duties would be violated?

Tarnowski v. Resop

236 Minn. 33, 51 N.W.2d 801 (Minn. 1952)

Plaintiff desired to make a business investment. He engaged defendant as his agent to investigate and negotiate for the purchase of a route of coin-operated music machines. On June 2, 1947, relying upon the advice of defendant and the investigation he had made, plaintiff purchased such a business from Phillip Loechler and Lyle Mayer of Rochester, Minnesota, who will be referred to hereinafter as the sellers. . . . Plaintiff alleges that defendant represented to him that he had made a thorough investigation of the route; that it had 75 locations in operation; that one or more machines were at each location; that the equipment at each location was not more than six months old; and that the gross income from all locations amounted to more than $3,000 per month. As a matter of fact, defendant had made only a superficial investigation and had investigated only five of the locations. Other than that, he had adopted false representations of the sellers as to the other locations and had passed them on to plaintiff as his own. Plaintiff was to pay $30,620 for the business. He paid $11,000 down. About six weeks after the purchase, plaintiff discovered that the representations made to him by defendant were false, in that there were not more than 47 locations; that at some of the locations there were no machines and at others there were machines more than six months old, some of them being seven years old; and that the gross income was far less than $3,000 per month. Upon discovering the falsity of defendant's representations and those of the sellers, plaintiff rescinded the sale. He offered to return what he had received, and he demanded the return of his money. The sellers refused to comply, and he brought suit against them in the district court of Olmsted county. The action was tried, resulting in a verdict of $10,000 for plaintiff. Thereafter, the sellers paid plaintiff $9,500, after which the action was dismissed with prejudice pursuant to a stipulation of the parties.

In this action . . . plaintiff alleges that defendant, while acting as agent for him, collected a secret commission from the sellers for consummating the sale, which plaintiff seeks to recover under his first cause of action. . . . The case was tried to a jury, and plaintiff recovered a verdict of $5,200. . . .

* * * *

1. With respect to plaintiff's first cause of action, the principle that all profits made by an agent in the course of an agency belong to the principal, whether they are the fruits of performance or the violation of an agent's duty, is firmly established and universally recognized. [*Citations omitted.*]

It matters not that the principal has suffered no damage or even that the transaction has been profitable to him. [*Citation omitted.*]

The rule and the basis therefor are well stated in *Lum v. McEwen,* 56 Minn. 278, 282, 57 N.W. 662, where, speaking through Mr. Justice Mitchell, we said:

"Actual injury is not the principle the law proceeds on, in holding such transactions void. Fidelity in the agent is what is aimed at, and, as a means of securing it, the law will not permit him to place himself in a position in which he may be tempted by his own private interests to disregard those of his principal. * * * It is not material that no actual injury to the company [principal] resulted. . . ."

The right to recover profits made by the agent in the course of the agency is not affected by the fact that the principal, upon discovering a fraud, has rescinded the contract and recovered that with which he parted. Restatement, Agency, § 407(2). Comment e on Subsection (2) reads:

"If an agent has violated a duty of loyalty to the principal so that the principal is entitled to profits which the agent has thereby made, the fact that the principal has brought an action against a third person and has been made whole by such action does not prevent the principal from recovering from the agent the profits which the agent has made. Thus, if the other contracting party has given a bribe to the agent to make a contract with him on behalf of the principal, the principal can rescind the transaction, recovering from the other party anything received by him, or he can maintain an action for damages against him; in either event the principal may recover from the agent the amount of the bribe."

It follows that, insofar as the secret commission of $2,000 received by the agent is concerned, plaintiff had an absolute right thereto, irrespective of any recovery resulting from the action against the sellers for rescission.

. . . .Our inquiry is limited to a consideration of the question whether a principal may recover of an agent who has breached his trust the items of damage mentioned after a successful prosecution of an action for rescission against the third parties with whom the agent dealt for his principal.

The general rule is stated in Restatement, Agency, § 407(1), as follows:

"If an agent has received a benefit as a result of violating his duty of loyalty, the principal is entitled to recover from him what he has so received, its value, or its proceeds, and also the amount of damage thereby caused, except that if the violation consists of the wrongful disposal of the principal's property, the principal cannot recover its value and also what the agent received in exchange therefor."

In Comment a on Subsection (1) we find the following:

"* * * In either event, whether or not the principal elects to get back the thing improperly dealt with or to recover from the agent its value or the amount of benefit which the agent has improperly received, he is, in addition, entitled to be indemnified by the agent for any loss which has been caused to his interests by the improper transaction.

* * * *

Defendant [also] contends that plaintiff had an election of remedies and, having elected to proceed against the sellers to recover what he had paid, is now barred from proceeding against defendant. It is true that upon discovery of the fraud plaintiff had an election of remedies against the sellers. It is not true, however, that, having elected to sue for recovery of that with which he had parted, he is barred from proceeding against his agent to recover damages for his tortious conduct. . . . Plaintiff may recover profits made by the agent, irrespective of his recovery against the sellers. . . .

Nor is the settlement and dismissal of the action against the sellers a bar to an action against the agent, for the same reasons as stated above. The sellers and agent are not joint tortfeasors in the sense that their wrongful conduct necessarily grows out of the same wrong. Their individual torts may have been based on the same fraud, but their liabilities to plaintiff do not have the same limitations. In simple terms, the causes of action are not the same. . . .

Gen. Auto. Mfg. Co. v. Singer

19 Wis. 2d 528, 120 N.W.2d 659 (Wis. 1963)

Action commenced by General Automotive Manufacturing Company, hereinafter referred to as 'Automotive', against John Singer, a former employee, to account for secret profits received while in its employ. . . .

John Singer, defendant-appellant, is a machinist-consultant and manufacturer's representative. Singer has worked in the machine shop field for over thirty years. He is adept at machine work and had ability not only as a machinist but also as to metal treatment, grinding techniques and special techniques. He enjoys this reputation in machine shop circles. None of Automotive's employees has defendant's ability to handle these machines. He is also known to be qualified in estimating the costs of machine-shop products and the competitive prices for which such products can be sold.

* * * *

We have . . . ourselves reached conclusions as stated by the trial court and set forth in its Findings of Fact, as follows:

'3. That heretofore and on or about the 28th day of March 1953, the plaintiff hired and employed the defendant as general manager of its business and affairs and the defendant accepted such employment under and pursuant to a written contract.

'4. That said contract of employment was for a term of one (1) year from March 30, 1953, to March 29, 1954, and was renewed for a period of two (2) years to March 28, 1956 and thereafter was extended for an indefinite period of time and continued in existence with no change either in the duties the defendant performed or the compensation the defendant received (one reduction in rate mutually agreed to) including the commission of 3% of the plaintiff's gross sales. That the said contract was finally terminated and the defendant left the employ of the plaintiff on or about May 7, 1959.

* * * *

'8. That in and by said contract, in consideration of compensation to be paid by the plaintiff to the defendant, the defendant promised and agreed:

'A. To devote his entire time, skill, labor and attention to said employment, during the term of this employment, and not to engage in any other business or vocation of a permanent nature during the term of this employment, and to observe working hours for 5 1/2 days.

'B. Not to, either during the term of his employment, or at any time thereafter, disclose to any person, firm or corporation any information concerning the business or affairs of the Employer which he may have acquired in the course of or as incident to his employment hereunder, for his own benefit, or to the detriment or intended or probable detriment of the Employer.

'9. That the defendant under the agreement as manager was a fiduciary agent with respect to solicitation of business for the plaintiff and as such was bound to the exercise of the utmost faith and loyalty to his principal and employer.'

Although stated as a Finding of Fact, Finding No. 10 is mainly a conclusion of law. It produces the principal issue in the case and deserves further discussion. It reads:

'10. That the defendant breached his contract of employment with the plaintiff and violated the duty of loyalty which he owed to the plaintiff and his fiduciary duty of general manager thereof during the existence of such employment by engaging in business activities directly competitive with the plaintiff, to-wit by obtaining orders from a customer for his own account.'

The record leaves no room for doubt of the correctness of Finding 11, as follows:

'11. That thereafter, instead of turning such orders over to the plaintiff the defendant turned such orders over to other concerns to be filled, collected the proceeds thereof from the customers for his own account and kept the profits accruing therefrom.'

* * * *

Further Findings of Fact that Singer breached his contract of employment, violated his fiduciary duty of general manager of Automotive, secretly engaged in competition with Automotive and kept the profits accruing from such competition are hotly disputed. . . .

Study of the record discloses that Singer was engaged as general manager of Automotive's operations. Among his duties was solicitation and procurement of machine shop work for Automotive. Because of Singer's high reputation in the trade he was highly successful in attracting orders.

Automotive is a small concern and has a low credit rating. Singer was invaluable in bolstering Automotive's credit. For instance, when collections were slow for work done by Automotive Singer paid the customer's bill to Automotive and waited for his own reimbursement until the customer remitted. Also, when work was slack, Singer set Automotive's shop to make parts for which there were no present orders and himself financed the cost of materials for such parts, waiting for recoupment until such stock-piled parts could be sold. Some parts were never sold and Singer personally absorbed the loss upon them.

As time went on a large volume of business attracted by Singer was offered to Automotive but which Singer decided could not be done by Automotive at all, for lack of suitable equipment, or which Automotive could not do at a competitive price. When Singer determined that such orders were unsuitable for Automotive he neither informed Automotive of these facts nor sent the orders back to the customer. Instead, he made the customer a price, then dealt with another machine shop to do the work at a less price, and retained the difference between the price quoted to the customer and the price for which the work was done. Singer was actually behaving as a broker for his own profit in a field where by contract he had engaged to work only for Automotive. We concur in the decision of the trial court that this was inconsistent with the obligations of a faithful agent or employee.

Singer finally set up a business of his own, calling himself a manufacturer's agent and consultant, in which he brokered orders for products of the sort manufactured by automotive,—this while he was still Automotive's employee and without informing Automotive of it. Singer had broad powers of management and conducted the business activities of Automotive. In this capacity he was Automotive's agent and owed a fiduciary duty to it. 13 Am.Jur., Corporations, sec. 997, page 948. Under his fiduciary duty to Automotive Singer was bound to the exercise of the utmost good faith and loyalty so that he did not act adversely to the interests of Automotive by serving or acquiring any private interest of his own. [*Citation omitted.*] He was also bound to act for the furtherance and advancement of the interest of *Automotive.* [*Citation omitted.*]

* * * *

The present controversy centers around the question whether the operation of Singer's side line business was a violation of his fiduciary duty to Automotive. The trial court found this business was conducted in secret and without the knowledge of Automotive. There is conflicting evidence regarding this finding but it is not against the great weight and clear preponderance of the evidence and, therefore, cannot be disturbed. *Central Refrigeration, Inc. v. Monroe* (1951), 259 Wis. 23, 47 N.W.2d 438.

The trial court found that Singer's side line business, the profits of which were $64,088.08, was in direct competition with Automotive. However, Singer argues that in this business he was a manufacturer's agent or consultant, whereas Automotive was a small manufacturer of automotive parts. The title of an activity does not determine the question whether it was competitive but an examination of the nature of the business must be made. In the present case the conflict of interest between Singer's business and his position with Automotive arises from the fact that Singer received orders, principally from a third-party called Husco, for the manufacture of parts. As a manufacturer's consultant he had to see that these orders were filled as inexpensively as possible, but as Automotive's general manager he could not act adversely to the corporation and serve his own interests. On this issue Singer argues that when Automotive had the shop capacity to fill an order he would award Automotive the job, but he contends that it was in the exercise of his duty as general manager of Automotive to refuse orders which in his opinion Automotive could not or should not fill and in that case he was free to treat the order as his own property. However, this argument ignores, as the trial court said, 'defendant's agency with plaintiff and the fiduciary duties of good faith and loyalty arising therefrom.'

Rather than to resolve the conflict of interest between his side line business and Automotive's business in favor of serving and advancing his own personal interests, Singer had the duty to exercise good faith by disclosing to Automotive all the facts regarding this matter. 2 Am.Jur., Agency, sec. 269, page 217. Upon disclosure to Automotive it was in the latter's discretion to refuse to accept the orders from Husco or to fill them if possible or to sub-job them to other concerns with the consent of Husco if necessary, and the profit, if any, would belong to Automotive. Automotive would then be able also to decide whether to expand its operations, install suitable equipment, or to make further arrangements with Singer or Husco. By failing to disclose all the facts relating to the orders from Husco and by receiving secret profits from these orders, Singer violated his fiduciary duty to act solely for the benefit of Automotive. Therefore he is liable for the amount of the profits he earned in his side line business.

Singer contends that the doctrine of 'Corporate Opportunity' applies in the case at bar and that the elements of the doctrine are not satisfied under the facts of this case.

The doctrine of corporate opportunity is a species of the duty of fiduciary to act with undivided loyalty. This doctrine applies to the acquisition of property, tangible or intangible, present or future, of a person who occupies a fiduciary relationship to a corporation which is in opposition to the corporation. *Gauger v. Hintz* (1952), 262 Wis. 333, 351, 55 N.W.2d 426. Although the elements of the breach of the fiduciary duty in this doctrine are similar to those in the present case presently we are concerned with the operation of a business by an agent in competition with a corporation and the retention of secret profits arising therefrom and not with the narrow question of the acquisition of property in opposition to a corporation.

We conclude that Singer's independent activities were in competition with Automotive and were in violation of his obligation of fidelity to that corporation, as stated in Finding of Fact No. 10 and Singer must account for his profits so obtained.

* * * *

Concurring with the learned trial court, we conclude that Singer's operations were in competition with his employer, Automotive, and from which he received undisclosed personal profits for which he must account. . . .

Agents Competing with Former Employers

Section 8.04 of the Third Restatement restricts an agent from competing with the principal during the agency relationship. While the *Third Restatement* does not prevent an agent from competing with the principal after the termination of the agency relationship, there are often other duties that are violated by an agent engaging in such competition. Attorneys are often asked to evaluate what steps should be taken by an employee about to leave a job and compete with the soon-to-be former employer. Conversely, employers will often seek an attorney's guidance as to how best to prevent competition by former employees. Of course, there are often contractual as well as statutory rights which factor into such assessments. However, it is important to understand the extent as well as the limitations of the protections provided through agency law. The following cases examine some of these parameters that often arise when employees compete with former employers. Consider what counsel you might provide to both employer and employee in similar circumstances to the cases that follow.

Hamburger v. Hamburger

4 Mass. L. Rptr. 409 (1995)

THAYER FREMONT-SMITH, J.:

* * * *

David Hamburger (David), son of Joseph Hamburger (Joseph) and nephew of Jacob (Ted), began working at Ace Wire and Burlap, Inc. (Ace) and A. Hamburger & Sons (A. Hamburger) summers as a high school student beginning in 1978. His work was primarily that of a warehouseman, loading and unloading trucks, assisting in delivering wire and picking up wool and other manual labor.

In November 1984, after graduating from the University of Bridgeport, David began working at Ace full time. His responsibilities were similar to the work he had done during preceding summers, i.e., general warehouse work for both the wire and wool business. At the time he began full-time employment at Ace, David was aware of a strained relationship between his father, Joe, and uncle, Ted. Nevertheless, both brothers agreed to his employment and welcomed him into the business.

David continued to work, primarily as a warehouseman. Beginning around 1986, however, he began to become involved in the sales activities of Ace. He increasingly began to call on customers and to learn from his father about the pricing and uses for different types of wire. His father also introduced him to customers and suppliers. In subsequent years, David built the business of Ace from about 300 suppliers and $500,000 in sales to over 700 accounts and over $1,000,000 in sales.

Although Ted had originally welcomed David as a general helper and warehouseman, he became increasingly resentful of David's gradual ascent to the role of sales manager and general manager of the wire business which resulted in a further deterioration of the relationship between Ted and Joseph. Heated and sometimes physical altercations between the brothers ensued, into which David was sometimes drawn on the side of his father. Periodically, Ted attempted to fire David from the business but Joe successfully resisted these efforts. In 1987, Ted went so far as to retain an attorney and brought suit to remove his nephew from the business, but this effort also failed. Things deteriorated to the point where Ted would berate and insult David in front of other employees, and David, on at least one occasion, responded in kind.

In early 1992 David, concerned about his long-term future at Ace, consulted with Ted to inquire about his prospects in the business. Ted rejected David's request for increased compensation or a commission on sales and told him words to the effect that "in 10 years your father or I will probably die; when that happens you'll know what your future is." David, not unreasonably, understood this to signify that he could expect to be fired if his father died before Ted.

In February or March of 1983, David had a dinner meeting with Robert Yates, Jr. of Eastern Wire Products, Inc. (Eastern Wire), one of Ace's four suppliers of wire. At this meeting David expressed his unhappiness at Ace and told Yates that he was contemplating going into business for himself. He inquired whether Yates would be willing to help finance a wire company that David would start. Yates subsequently agreed to loan David $50,000 in order to start his new company, $30,000 of which David received and deposited in an account under the name of his new company, New England Baling Wire, Inc. (NEBW), in early May 1993. He also leased space for his new company in Avon, Massachusetts.

On May 13, 1993, David resigned without prior notice, formally incorporated NEBW and commenced work the following day at his new quarters in Avon, Massachusetts. He also immediately hired Ace's book-keeper, Ray Brennan, who had resigned a week earlier, and Ace's truck driver was employed on May 20, 1993. Beginning on May 13, David and Brennan began to actively solicit, by telephone, many of Ace's customers, with the result that several hundred of them are now customers of David's NEBW.

Ted contends that David's arrangement for financing and leasehold arrangements for NEBW and his solicitation of Ace's customers were wrongful because they not only had commenced while he was still an Ace employee, but because the customer solicitation was facilitated by David's wrongful appropriation of confidential customer lists and pricing information of Ace, which David is alleged to have obtained with Joseph's connivance, in violation of David's and Joseph's fiduciary obligations to Ace and to Ted. [*Citations omitted.*]

The Court rules, however, that David's having arranged financing and leased space for NEBW while he was still an Ace employee was not illegal, as an employee is free to make such logistical arrangements while still an employee. *See . . . Meehan v. Shaughnessey; Cohen,* 404 Mass. 419, 435, 535 N.E.2d 1255 (1989).

With respect to David's solicitation of Ace customers, there was no evidence that this had commenced, in any significant way, prior to his May 13, 1993 resignation. As Ace's sales manager, he had been intimately familiar with its customers and pricing, so that he was familiar with such information when he left Ace's employ. He was entitled to use his general knowledge, experience, memory and skill in establishing NEBW, including "remembered information." *J.T. Healy & Son, Inc. v. James A. Murphy & Son, Inc.,* 357 Mass. 728, 740, 260 N.E.2d 723 (1970). Although he was certainly a key employee, an employer who wishes to restrict the post-employment competitive activities of a key employee, where the activities do not entail misuse of proprietary information, must protect that goal through a noncompetition agreement. . . . This the plaintiff neglected to do. Moreover, while David may have made some use of personal notes relating to Ace customers, customer lists are not considered trade secrets if the information is readily available from published sources, such as business directories. Such directories were in fact available to him and were used by him and Brennan to contact customers on and after May 13. While Ted suspected that Joseph was providing David with such information from Ace, there was no hard evidence of this such as would convince the Court that this occurred to any significant extent. And, while Ted and Joseph were certainly at logger-heads with respect to customer pricing after David left, the Court concludes that Joseph's contradiction of Ted's quoted prices to customers resulted from their convergent views as to what was best for the company, rather than from any attempt by Joseph to sabotage the wire business for the benefit of his son.[1]

By the same token, the Court is not convinced that Ted, on his part, acted in bad faith in his conduct of the business or in filing this lawsuit. Ted's views were so colored by his animosity for his brother and nephew that Ted suspected the worst of them and reacted accordingly in bringing the lawsuit.

The sad and ironic thing about this case is that this festering hatred between two brothers caused the ruination of a good family business, by driving away the very person who had built the business up since 1984 and who was the only person around who had the energy, personality, knowledge and love for the business that could have preserved it for the long run. Under the circumstances in which he found himself, David took the only reasonable course open to him and did so in a way which the court finds did not violate any legal obligation to Ted or Ace.

QUESTIONS

1. Are there steps that could have been taken before David started working at Ace that might have avoided the "sad and ironic" result to which the court refers?

2. Is it appropriate for an attorney to provide advice about family dynamics when dealing with a family business?

Town & Country House & Home Serv., Inc. v. Newbery

3 N.Y. 2d 554, 170 N.Y.S.2d 328, 147 N.E.2d 724 (N.Y. 1958)

This action was brought for an injunction and damages against appellants on the theory of unfair competition. The complaint asks to restrain them from engaging in the same business as plaintiff, from soliciting its customers, and for an accounting and damages. The individual appellants were in plaintiff's employ for about three years before they severed their relationships and organized the corporate appellant through which they have been operating. The theory of the

---

1 Ted testified that he believed Ace should meet the lower price competition of NEBW even if this meant selling wire at below fully-accounted cost, whereas Joseph testified that he believed that sales should only be made at prices which could return a net profit to the company.

complaint is that plaintiff's enterprise "was unique, personal and confidential", and that appellants cannot engage in business at all without breach of the confidential relationship in which they learned its trade secrets, including the names and individual needs and tastes of its customers.

The nature of the enterprise is house and home cleaning by contract with individual householders. Its "unique" quality consists in superseding the drudgery of ordinary house cleaning by mass production methods. The house cleaning is performed by a crew of men who descend upon a home at stated intervals of time, and do the work in a hurry after the manner of an assembly line in a factory. They have been instructed by the housewife but work without her supervision. The householder is supplied with liability insurance, the secrets of the home are kept inviolate, the tastes of the customer are served and each team of workmen is selected as suited to the home to which it is sent. The complaint says that the customer relationship is "impregnated" with a "personal and confidential aspect".

The complaint was dismissed at Special Term on the ground that the individual appellants were not subjected to negative covenants under any contract with plaintiff, and that the methods and techniques used by plaintiff in conducting its business are not confidential or secret as in the case of a scientific formula; that house cleaning and housekeeping "are old and necessary chores which accompany orderly living" and that no violation of duty was involved in soliciting plaintiff's customers by appellants after resigning from plaintiff's employ. The contacts and acquaintances with customers were held not to have been the result of a confidential relationship between plaintiff and defendants or the result of the disclosure of secret or confidential material.

By a divided vote the Appellate Division reversed, but on a somewhat different ground, namely, that while in plaintiff's employ, appellants conspired to terminate their employment, form a business of their own in competition with plaintiff and solicit plaintiff's customers for their business. The overt acts under this conspiracy were found by the Appellate Division to have been that, in pursuance of this plan, they formed the corporate appellant and bought equipment and supplies for their operations—not on plaintiff's time—but during off hours, before they had severed their relations as employees of plaintiff. The Appellate Division concluded that "it is our opinion that their agreement and encouragement to each other to carry out the course of conduct thus planned by them, and their consummation of the plan, particularly their termination of employment virtually en masse, were inimical to, and violative of, the obligations owed by them to appellant as its employees; and that therefore appellant was entitled to relief. (Cf. *Duane Jones Co. v. Burke,* 306 N. Y. 172.)"

The *Duane Jones* case involved unusual facts. There the defendants appropriated overnight upwards of 50% of the business of their previous employer, and 90% of its skilled employees as well as a majority of the entire working force. . . . . [I]n *Duane Jones* there had been solicitation of the customers of plaintiff while the defendants were still employed; there was an attempt to panic and break the morale of the employees, again with the over-all purpose of paralyzing the plaintiff in order to seize it. Here, although these three employees and their wives left at the same time, there was no abrupt departure of most of the key men and nothing in reference to the interruption or paralysis of plaintiff's business. In fact, at the time of the trial, Mrs. Rossmoore testified that they had 280 customers and 8 crews, which were 40 more customers and 1 more crew than at the time when appellants departed.

Although the Appellate Division implied more relief than we consider to have been warranted, we think that the trial court erred in dismissing the complaint altogether. The only trade secret which could be involved in this business is plaintiff's list of customers. Concerning that, even where a solicitor of business does not operate fraudulently under the banner of his former employer, he still may not solicit the latter's customers who are not openly engaged in business in advertised locations or whose availability as patrons cannot readily be ascertained but "whose trade and patronage have been secured by years of business effort and advertising, and the expenditure of time and money, constituting a part of the good-will of a business which enterprise and foresight have built up" (*Witkop & Holmes Co. v. Boyce,* 61 Misc. 126, 131, affd. 131 App. Div. 922, followed in *People's Coat, Apron & Towel Supply Co. v. Light,* 171 App. Div. 671, 673, affd. 224 N. Y. 727). In the latter case it was pointed out by the Appellate Division that although there was no evidence that the former employee had a written customers list, "There was in his head what was equivalent. They were on routes, in streets and at numbers revealed to him through his service with plaintiff. Their faces were familiar to him, and their identity known because of such employment." That case was not overruled by *Scott & Co. v. Scott* (186 App. Div. 518, 525), as is clear from the opinion by Justice Callahan in *Kleinfeld v. Roburn Agencies* (270 App. Div. 509, 511), where it is said: "A distinction is made in the cases between a former employee soliciting customers of his former employer who are openly engaged in business in advertised locations and his soliciting unadvertised customers who became known to the employee only because of information obtained during his employment.[*Citations omitted*]"

* * * *

The testimony in the instant record shows that the customers of plaintiff were not and could not be obtained merely by looking up their names in the telephone or city directory or by going to any advertised locations, but had to be screened from among many other housewives who did not wish services such as respondent and appellants were equipped to render, but preferred to do their own housework. In most instances housewives do their own house cleaning. The only appeal which plaintiff could have was to those whose cleaning had been done by servants regularly or occasionally employed, except in the still rarer instances where the housewife was on the verge of abandoning doing her own work by hiring some outside agency. In the beginning, prospective customers of plaintiff were discovered by Dorothy Rossmoore, wife of plaintiff's president, by telephoning at random in "sections of Nassau that we thought would be interested in this type of cleaning, and from that we got directories, town directories, and we marked the streets that we had passed down, and I personally called, right down the list". In other words, after selecting a neighborhood which they felt was fertile for their kind of business, they would telephone to all of the residents of a street in the hope of discovering likely prospects. On the first day Mrs. Rossmoore called 52 homes. If she enlisted their interest, an appointment would be made for a personal call in order to sell them the service. At the end of the first year, only 40 to 50 customers had thus been secured. Two hundred to three hundred telephone calls netted 8 to 12 customers. Moreover, during the first year it was not possible to know how much to charge these customers with accuracy, inasmuch as the cleaning requirements of each differed from the others, so that special prices had to be set. In the beginning the customer usually suggested the price which was paid until some kind of cost accounting could demonstrate whether it should be raised or lowered. These costs were entered on cards for every customer, and this represented an accumulated body of experience of considerable value. After three years of operation, and by August, 1952, when the individual appellants resigned their employment by plaintiff, the number of customers amounted to about 240. By that time plaintiff had 7 or 8 crews doing this cleaning work, consisting of 3 men each.

Although appellants did not solicit plaintiff's customers until they were out of plaintiff's employ, nevertheless plaintiff's customers were the only ones they did solicit. Appellants solicited 20 or 25 of plaintiff's customers who refused to do business with appellants and about 13 more of plaintiff's customers who transferred their patronage to appellants. These were all the people that appellants' firm solicited. It would be different if these customers had been equally available to appellants and respondent, but, as has been related, these customers had been screened by respondent at considerable effort and expense, without which their receptivity and willingness to do business with this kind of a service organization could not be known. So there appears to be no question that plaintiff is entitled to enjoin defendants from further solicitation of its customers, or that some profits or damage should be paid to plaintiff by reason of these customers whom they enticed away.

For more than this appellants are not liable. . . . Inasmuch as the complaint asks that appellants be enjoined, severally and jointly, from engaging directly or indirectly in the business of house and home cleaning in any manner, shape or form adopted by the plaintiff, it is necessary for us to point out that plaintiff is not entitled to that much relief. The business of plaintiff has not been found to be unique . . . and the evidence demonstrates that it is not so. No trade secrets are involved, as has been stated, except the customers list. . . .

. . . .Plaintiff is entitled to enjoin appellants from soliciting its former customers, and to recover such damages or loss of profits as may be established to have resulted from those that have been solicited to date. Further than that the complaint is dismissed. . . .

Since agency duties typically prevent competition during, but not after the agency, businesses have long sought ways to restrict such competition. One way to expand the limitations on an employee's ability to compete with a former employer is through a covenant not to compete. However, many states will not enforce such covenants, and, those that do, require that any limitations on competition are reasonable. Consider the circumstances in the case that follows, *Robbins v. Finlay*.

Robbins v. Finlay

645 P.2d 623 (1982 Utah)

STEWART, J.:

Douglas Finlay, defendant, was employed by plaintiff Robbins, dba Beltone Utah (hereafter "Beltone"), until December, 1975, to sell hearing aids. Beltone is a distributor of Beltone brand hearing aids. At that time, Finlay terminated his employment with Robbins and went into business for himself selling hearing aids. Beltone thereafter sued Finlay for breach of a covenant prohibiting unauthorized use of customer leads provided by Beltone and for breach of a covenant not to compete.

This is an appeal by defendant Finlay from a judgment entered on a jury verdict finding that Finlay had breached the covenants of his employment contract with Beltone. The judgment awarded Beltone damage amounts stipulated in the employment contract: $5000 for breach of a covenant not to misuse customer leads supplied by Beltone[1], and $3000 for breach of a covenant not to compete with Beltone in its service area for a period of one year following termination of employment.[2] Plaintiff was also awarded $2500 as attorney's fees.

Finlay began working for Beltone in 1971 under an employment contract substantially the same as the one involved here. The covenants at issue here are part of an employment contract entered into April 3, 1974. Finlay was an experienced hearing aid salesman, having worked previously for six Beltone distributors, and therefore did not receive the training provided for in the Beltone employment contract.

In August of 1975, Finlay in a letter to Mr. Robbins expressed dissatisfaction with the terms of his employment agreement with Beltone. The letter requested that he be put in charge of hiring and firing the sales staff, and that he be given a 5% override on their sales. He also requested an increase in his advertising allowance and an increase in his commission percentage. The testimony indicated that both parties intended to enter into a new employment agreement based at least partially on Finlay's demands, but no revised agreement

---

1 The pertinent provision of the employment contract provides:

The Company agrees to furnish the Consultant with a list of prospects for, and users of hearing aids, which list is herewith recognized by both parties as a trade secret of the business, and the Consultant agrees to make no copies of said list; to use it only in the course of the Company's business; and to return it to the Company immediately upon the termination of this Agreement. Consultant further agrees that in the event the said list is used for any other purpose to the detriment or damage of the Company by the Consultant or any other person as a result of his negligence or connivance that the stipulated damages and detriments to be paid by the Consultant shall amount to the sum of Five Thousand Dollars ($ 5,000.00) to the Company on demand. Consultant further agrees that all new names added to such list, on account of new prospects and users of hearing aids, whether discovered by the Company or by the Consultant, shall be a part of the trade secret of the business as aforesaid.

2 The noncompetition clause provides:

After the termination of his employment for the Company for whatsoever cause, Consultant agrees that he will not engage in the business of selling or servicing hearing aids in the areas serviced by the Company in the State of Utah for a period of one year following the termination of his employment; and it is specifically agreed that if the Consultant violates this provision of the Agreement he shall be liable to the Company for stipulated damages in the sum of Three Thousand Dollars ($ 3,000.00), together with reasonable attorneys fees.

was consummated. In December 1975 Finlay left Beltone and opened his own office in Salt Lake City for selling hearing aids.

Beltone presented testimony at trial establishing the following:

1. In November 1975 Finlay sold hearing aids other than Beltone products to three persons from Kamas, Utah, who had been identified as potential customers through a hearing clinic conducted under the auspices of Beltone. Beltone received no compensation from those sales.

2. Finlay had in his possession at least as late as November 1976 the names and addresses of 154 potential Beltone customers whose names had been given Finlay by Beltone.

3. In late 1975 Finlay induced another employee of Beltone to sell two hearing aids for a company which Finlay had formed. The sales were made through customer leads produced from a Beltone hearing clinic.

4. Beltone's service area is a strip running east and west across the State of Utah with the northern boundary defined by a line running through Farmington, Utah, and the southern boundary by a line running through the Point of the Mountain in southern Salt Lake County. Finlay does not dispute that he has competed with Beltone within Beltone's service area.

* * * *

The testimony at trial indicated that it was Beltone policy to restrict the number of leads a salesman had out at one time to twenty or thirty. As of November 1976, Finlay had 154 leads in his possession, and they did not include those individuals to whom he eventually sold a competing brand of hearing aid in Kamas, Utah.

* * * *

The second issue raised by Finlay is whether the anti-competition clause in the employment contract is unenforceable because it is unreasonable and because the position of hearing aid salesman is a common calling.

Covenants not to compete are enforceable if carefully drawn to protect only the legitimate interests of the employer. The reasonableness of a covenant depends upon several factors, including its geographical extent; the duration of the limitation; the nature of the employee's duties; and the nature of the interest which the employer seeks to protect such as trade secrets, the goodwill of his business, or an extraordinary investment in the training or education of the employee. [*Citations omitted.*]

In a general sense, the law balances the nature of the interest of one seeking to enforce such a covenant, whether by injunction or by stipulated damages, against the hardship imposed on the employee as the result of the restraint. *Allen v. Rose Park Pharmacy, supra. See also*, R. Callmann, *The Law of Unfair Competition, Trademarks and Monopolies* vol. 2 § 64.4 (3d ed. 1968); *Beltone Electronics Corp. v. Smith,* 44 Ill. App.2d 112, 194 N.E.2d 21 (1963). Covenants not to compete which are primarily designed to limit competition or restrain the right to engage in a common calling are not enforceable.

The case is clearly distinguishable from *Allen v. Rose Park Pharmacy, supra,* where a covenant not to compete was enforced because all the goodwill of the employer was associated with, and created by, the employee. In this case, the covenant served no purpose other than restricting an employee from competing with a former employer. There is nothing to indicate that Finlay was largely responsible for plaintiff's goodwill, and there is no contention or proof that Finlay was privy to any trade secrets plaintiff may have possessed. Nor is there any indication that his competition (except for the use of the customer leads) had any greater effect on plaintiff's goodwill, or other legally protectable interests, than the competition of any other salesman employed by a competitor of plaintiff. Indeed, although Robbins was an authorized dealer of Beltone hearing aids, he was not restricted from handling hearing aids of other manufacturers.

The record shows that Finlay's job required little training and is not unlike the job of many other types of salesmen. The company's investment in training him was small. In fact, he had previously worked as a Beltone salesman for other dealers in Canada. Furthermore, there is no showing that his services were special, unique, or extraordinary, even if their value to his employer was high. Thus, this case is similar to *Columbia Ribbon & Carbon Mfg. Co. v. A-1-A Corp.,* 42 N.Y.2d 496, 369 N.E.2d 4, 398 N.Y.S.2d 1004 (1977), where the court stated:[9]

---

[9] The Covenant in that case stated:

The Employee further expressly covenants that he will not, for a period of twenty-four months after the termination of his employment with the Company, directly or indirectly, for himself, or his agent or employee of, or on behalf of or in conjunction with any person, firm or corporation, sell or deliver any goods, wares and merchandise of the kind or character sold by the Company at any time during the term of his employment with the Company, or in any other manner, engage in the sale and delivery thereof within any territory to which the Employee was assigned during the last twenty-four months prior to termination. [*369 N.E.2d at 6*]

> It is clear that [the covenant's] broad-sweeping language is unrestrained by any limitations keyed to uniqueness [of the employee's services], trade secrets, confidentiality or even competitive unfairness. It does no more than baldly restrain competition. This it may not do. [*Id.,* 369 N.E. 2d at 6.]

It is of no moment that defendant may have been especially proficient in his work. General knowledge or expertise acquired through employment in a common calling cannot be appropriated as a trade secret. "The efficiency and skills which an employee develops through his work belong to him and not to his former employer." *Hallmark Personnel of Texas, Inc. v. Franks, Texas,* 562 S.W.2d 933, 936 (1978). The same principles apply to the covenant here. We hold that the covenant not to compete had the effect of preventing the defendant from exploiting skills and experience which he had a right to exploit. It makes no difference that the plaintiff sought to enforce the covenant by a damage remedy rather than by injunction. Plaintiff had no right to extract a toll from defendant for entering into competition.

We recognize that to some extent the customer leads which Finlay had were in the nature of trade secrets due to the time, expense, and effort which went into discovering the leads.[10] However, the customer leads were specifically protected by the provision analyzed in the first part of this opinion and the covenant not to compete was not justified as an additional protection.

We therefore conclude that the covenant not to compete is unreasonable and unenforceable. Due to this conclusion, it is unnecessary to address Finlay's other contention that the covenant not to compete was unreasonable because of the geographical area covered and the duration of the covenant.

QUESTION

1. What could Beltone have done to protect itself in a way that might have been more reasonable" to a Utah court?

---

[10] *Cf. Microbiological Research Corp. v. Muna, Utah,* 625 P.2d 690 (1981) where the company's customer list was found to be readily reproducible through the simple expedient of looking up the names and addresses of hospitals and clinics in the telephone directory and hence was not protectable as a trade secret. Such is not the case here.

CHAPTER TWO

Partnerships

THE LAW FIRM THAT YOU WORK FOR has a new client, named Pete, who is starting a business. The business is relatively small, so the partner on the project is going to let you "run with it."

Experiencing Assignment 3: Pete's Products

FACTS:

Pete has a new business, called "Pete's Products," which plans to sell and distribute handmade textile and craft products from a small country in South America. Because of various licenses and regulations, Pete is one of the few individuals who is allowed to import to, and sell these products in, the United States. Pete is very proud of the innovative business model he has developed to help distribute the products. Pete will import the products and list them on a website. While anyone can purchase Pete's products from his website, Pete has made special arrangements with a group of individuals who will be able to purchase products from Pete at a discount. These individuals, whom Pete refers to as "Pete's Partners" must deposit at least $25,000 with Pete. When these individuals purchase products the price of the items purchased is deducted from their respective accounts. Each "Partner's" account may be replenished at any time, but a requirement for future purchases is that the balance in the account must exceed $10,000 as well as the price of the products purchased. The balance in the account is non-refundable, but may be applied to any of the products that are available on the Pete's Products website. Pete also has an arrangement (that he has called a "profit sharing arrangement") with the Partners through which the Partners receive a discount on any product purchased from Pete. The discount is equal to 30% of Pete's retail profit. (Pete's retail profit is equal to the difference between the product price, listed on Pete's website, and Pete's cost for that product.) Any Partner who purchases products from Pete, even at a discount, is entitled to resell those products for any price he or she chooses.

Recently Pete has learned that there are many liabilities associated with partnership. Pete is also very concerned about liability that might result from the Pete's Partners program and does not want any of his so-called Partners to create liability for him. Pete also provides each Partner with business cards that say "Pete's Products," but Partners have no right to participate in management.

ASSIGNMENT:

Pete would like you to revise a portion of his form Letter Agreement with the Partners with a view toward *minimizing Pete's liability under partnership law*. You should not re-write the entire Agreement. Pete wants your input about some ways to strengthen his protection from liability that might be created by Pete's Partners. You should assume that Pete's Partners will probably not have sufficient resources to indemnify Pete's for any liabilities that might result. In addition, please assume that there are other provisions which address any other concerns you think that Pete might have about the Agreement. Furthermore, please do not revise the "Miscellaneous" provisions. Those provisions were included merely to provide context. At this point Pete is most interested in minimizing his exposure to liability under partnership law. Therefore, please limit your efforts to revising the section of the Agreement below. If you feel that it might be beneficial to include a few sentences, explaining your revisions to Pete, please feel free to do so, but Pete does not want a memo on every reason for every change you suggest.

TEXT FROM PETE'S LETTER AGREEMENT

Dear Pete's Partner:

Welcome! I am so glad that you are going to join the Pete's Partner program. By signing this Letter Agreement with Pete's Products ("Pete's"), you are entitled to participate in the Pete's Partner benefits. The terms of participation follow.

In exchange for providing Pete's with at least $25,000 (the "Payment Amount"), you will be entitled to purchase products from Pete's at the Authorized Partner Rate. These products may be kept or resold by you anywhere in the U.S., unless prohibited by law.

The Authorized Partner Rate is equal to the retail price shown for a product on the Pete's website, reduced by the Partner Profit Share. The Partner Profit Share equals 30% of Pete's retail profit. (Pete's retail profit is equal to the difference between the price of the product, as listed on Pete's website, and Pete's cost for that product.) For example, if a product is listed on Pete's

Product's website for a retail price of $30, and Pete's costs is $10, then Pete's retail profit is $20. The Partner Profit Share on $20 is $6 (which is 30% of $20). Therefore, Pete's Partners would pay $24 for the product, rather than $30 for the product. All calculations of Pete's retail profit and Partner Profit Share shall be done by Pete's in Pete's sole and absolute discretion.

The cost of any product purchased from Pete's website will be deducted from the Payment Amount. The Payment Amount may be increased by you at any time but it must always exceed the amount of any products you purchase from Pete's website. If the Payment Amount is ever less than $10,000, the amount must be increased to $25,000, or you will not receive the Partner Profit Share. Furthermore, the Payment is NON-REFUNDABLE. It may be applied to purchases from Pete's website, but it may never be repaid.

Pete's will also provide you with Business cards identifying you as one of Pete's Partners.

[Other provisions in the Letter Agreement omitted from the excerpt include rights, requirements, reporting, and termination provisions.]

Miscellaneous Provisions:

If any provision in this Agreement is held by a court of competent jurisdiction to be invalid, void or unenforceable, the remaining provisions shall still continue in full force without being impaired or invalidated in any way. This Agreement constitutes the entire agreement between you and Pete's and may not be released, discharged, changed or modified except by an instrument in writing, signed by both you and Pete's. A waiver of, or failure to enforce any provision contained in this Agreement on any occasion shall not be deemed to be a continuing waiver or a waiver on any other occasion. Pete's may terminate this Agreement or your Pete's Partner status for any reason upon 30 days' notice to you, or at any time, with or without notice, for any conduct that Pete's in its sole discretion believes violates this Agreement, or is harmful to another buyer, third-party, or Pete's interests. You agree to comply with any and all applicable laws and regulations and shall indemnify and hold Pete's harmless for any failure, on your part, to do so.

We are excited to welcome you as one of Pete's Partners.

Pete,

Pete's Products, Owner

I HAVE REVIEWED THE ABOVE LETTER AGREEMENT AND UNDERSTAND AND AGREE TO ALL OF ITS TERMS AND CONDITIONS.

By: ______________________ Date: __________

[PRINT NAME], Pete's Partner

____

This Assignment does not need to be completed, and should not be completed, until the end of the section. However, as you study the cases and other materials that follow, it might be helpful to do so with a view toward providing assistance to Pete, your client in matter outlined above. Some of the materials in the chapter will relate more than others to the issues facing Pete. However, the materials are designed to build your understanding of some of the issues that arise in partnership law and assist you in addressing Pete's concerns and putting them in context. Please keep Pete's issues and the questions presented by the assignment in mind while reading the chapter materials that follow.

SECTION I: The Partnership Form

A partnership is the simplest form of entity, formed by two or more people working together. Partnerships have existed longer than any other business entity. The rules governing partnerships are generally straightforward, but they form the building blocks for an understanding of other entities. Because partnerships, by definition, involve more than one partner, any partnership requires rules and principles that govern the relationships between or among the partners, the relationship between each partner and the partnership, and the relationships between the partnership and outside parties.

While courts look to various elements to determine whether a business relationship constitutes a partnership, at its core, a partnership is "an association of two or more persons to carry on as co-owners of a business for profit." Section 6(1) of the *Uniform Partnership Act* (the "*UPA*"). The association between partners must be voluntary, although it does not need to be with the knowledge or intent to form a partnership, and no formal contract is required. The association can be an understanding between or among two or more persons who are working together. Further, there is no requirement that the "persons" be two individuals. The association may involve any two entities that are considered "persons" under law.

A. Characteristics of a Typical Partnership

There are a number of characteristics that are typically found in general partnerships. While not all these characteristics are required for a partnership to exist, courts will look to them to help evaluate if an endeavor is a partnership. The best test to evaluate whether a partnership exists is to ask the question: "Is it the intent of the parties to carry on as co-owners a definite business?" The question of whether an endeavor is a partnership is a question of fact. Relevant factors include:

(1) *Profit Sharing.* Sharing profits in a business is prima facie evidence that a partnership exists, except where those profits are received as debt service, wages, rent, or an annuity.

(2) *Contribution.* Owners in a partnership generally make some contribution (which need not be monetary) in exchange for their interest in the partnership. Joint ownership alone does not automatically mean that a partnership exists.

(3) *Participation in Management.* Partners jointly participate in the management of the endeavor, but joint participation does not require that partners have equal votes or that control is divided equally.

(4) *Risk of Loss.* Partners generally share in the financial losses of the partnership. Employees and lenders do not typically "share" in the losses, short of a failure of the business endeavor itself

(5) *Absence of Alternative Classification.* While the above characteristics might very well be present in another form of entity, if the endeavor is registered as another entity (such as an LLC), then it is not a partnership.

Partnerships may hire individuals as associates or employees who are not partners. The question sometimes arises whether a person working in a partnership is a partner or an employee. To resolve this question, courts look to the relationship among the parties. What was the intent of the parties? Is there an agreement among the parties, and if so, does the language specify the person is a partner? Do the other partners permit the purported partner to act like a partner toward third parties? Does the purported partner share in the profits of the partnership? Merely receiving a portion of profits in the form of wages or a commission does not make someone a partner. Finally, who bears the risk of financial loss? It is very rare for an employee to be liable for partnership debts.

B. Partnership Features

The determination of whether an endeavor is a "partnership" can be critical because once an entity is classified as a partnership, there are certain attributes which are associated with the partnership. Many of these attributes arise in the following categories:

- **Liabilities**—Each partner is jointly and severally liable for the debts of the partnership. In addition, each partner has the power to create obligations and liabilities for the partnership. This feature of general partnerships means that if the partnership's assets are not sufficient to cover a debt, the partners are *personally* liable for that debt.
- **Control**—Each partner has the ability to participate in the control and management of the partnership. Under the *Uniform Partnership Act (1997)* ("RUPA")*, each partner is entitled to one vote, regardless of how much capital he or she contributed. Alternative voting standards may be established by agreement among the partners.
- **Returns**—In a partnership, profits are shared equally among partners. Therefore, when a partnership is dissolved, the money is divided up among the partners. Most states provide that profits are allocated among partners equally (per captita), regardless of how much money was contributed by each partner. The partners can also change this feature by an agreement to allocate profits based on the amount contributed to the partnership or using some other measure they might determine appropriate.
- **Tax treatment**—Partnerships are not taxed on their income. Instead, the tax responsibility (or credit, as the case may be) for the profits or losses of the partnership is "passed through" to the partners to include on their respective "personal" tax returns.
- **Fiduciary duties**—Partners owe fiduciary duties to each other and to the partnership. These duties are detailed below.

---

* Ed's note: Because the Uniform Partnership Act has been revised on many occasions, the National Conference of Commissioners on Uniform State Laws uses the year the revision was approved to describe different revisions of the Act. However, many people (including the author of this book) still use "RUPA" as a distinguishing abbreviation for the revised version of the ACT.

- **Distinct entity**—A partnership is treated as a distinct entity, separate from its partners. It may enter into contracts, own property and hold rights under the law.

C. The Default Rules

Partnerships are generally governed by state law. A majority of states have adopted some version of RUPA (which stands for the "Revised Uniform Partnership Act" as it was formerly called). Note that often versions or revisions of the Uniform Partnership Act are also referred to as the "UPA" with the year of the version following in parenthesis, for example: UPA (1997). However, there are several states that continue to operate under some version of the original UPA (1914). (These states include Georgia, Indiana, Massachusetts, Michigan, Missouri, New Hampshire New York, North Carolina, Pennsylvania, Rhode Island, South Carolina, and Wisconsin.) The rules in each state's adopted version of the RUPA or the UPA outline the rules which will govern partnerships in that state. These respective codified versions of UPA or RUPA are also referred to as the partnership "default rules" because these rules typically apply if the partnership is not governed by a partnership agreement or if a partnership agreement does not cover a particular area. The default rules are intended to fill any gaps in the partnership agreement or to provide guidelines for governance when there is no such agreement. While most provisions of the default rules may be modified by agreement among the partners, there are certain areas which may not be modified. Some significant examples of these limitations are set forth in section 103 of RUPA and may not be limited by a partnership agreement, including that a partnership agreement may NOT:

- Unreasonably restrict a partner's access to books and records of the partnership;
- Eliminate the general duty of loyalty (although specific exceptions may be approved);
- Unreasonably reduce the duty of care;
- Eliminate the obligation of good faith and fair dealing (although certain reasonable standards by which this performance of this duty is measured may be established);
- Vary the power of a partner to dissociate;
- Vary the right of a court to expel a partner under specific circumstances;

- Vary the requirement to wind up the partnership business in certain circumstances; or
- Restrict the rights of third parties under the RUPA.

Because so much of the case law in this area arises under the UPA (and because there is a variance among states of the default rules), it is important to be familiar with the provisions of both the UPA and the RUPA. While there are some significant variations between the UPA and the RUPA (as well as among the various versions of each), most of the fundamental principles of partnership are the same. It is important to recognize that the default rules are not necessarily the best rules, or even the rules that a particular state's legislature thinks provide the best outcome, regardless of whether a state's default rules arise out of the UPA or the RUPA. The default rules are simply the rules that apply in the absence of a partnership agreement. Other than some of the limited areas above, partners often alter the default rules through the partnership agreement to suit the needs of a business or the particular provisions desired or negotiated by the partners.

D. Joint Ventures

A joint venture is a business endeavor undertaken by two or more parties. Joint ventures typically have a limited scope and are usually for a limited time. For these reasons, some people will distinguish joint ventures from traditional partnerships. However, to the extent that any joint endeavor, whether it is called a "joint venture," "partnership" or something else, represents an association of two or more persons to carry on as co-owners a business for profit, then it will be treated as a partnership. Even if the scope of a joint venture represents a very limited business venture, it will still be treated as a partnership. On the other hand, merely because an endeavor is called a joint venture does not make it a partnership. The factual circumstances of the undertaking must meet the requirement of the applicable statutory default rules. Assuming it does, then the partnership rules will apply.

E. Partnership by Estoppel

There are instances when, even if someone is not a partner in a partnership, he or she might still be responsible for the debts of the partnership. The most common situation is known as "partnership by estoppel." In partnership by estoppel, if A, B, and C are partners, and X is not a partner X still might be incur liability as a partner if X allows the partners to act in a way that third parties reasonably believe X to be a partner, and the following conditions are met. In order to be responsible under partnership by estoppel, X must make some manifestation which creates an impression, allowing others outside the partnership to reasonably believe that X is a partner, and the third party claiming partnership by estoppel must rely on that impression to his/her detriment. Partnership by estoppel requires that the alleged partner make some manifestation to another individual or entity that creates a reasonable belief in the third party claiming partnership by estoppel that the alleged partner is, in fact, a partner. Even if the manifestation is not made directly to the third party, it must be traceable back to some action or inaction of the alleged partner. In addition, the party claiming partnership by estoppel must actually rely on the manifestation and the reliance must be reasonable.

A similar concept arises in situations in which a partnership may be held liable for the actions of a non-partner. In these situations a "non-partner" is treated as though he or she had the authority of an actual partner, to bind the partnership. These situations actually involve the agency concept of apparent authority (discussed in Chapter 1, Section II, above). In these instances, a partnership which creates the (albeit incorrect) appearance that a person who is not actually a partner is in fact a partner, may be held liable for the actions of that non-partner, taken on behalf of the partnership if the third party dealing with the non-partner reasonably believes that the non-partner is a partner. This concept is known as the apparent authority of a purported partner.

In order for an apparent partner to be able to bind the partnership, the partnership must have done (or failed to do) something to make it appear that there was a partnership with the non-partner, and a third party must reasonably believe that the "non-partner" had the authority to act on behalf of the partnership in the transaction in question.

Partnership by estoppel and the apparent authority of a purported partner are two separate concepts: one involves the possibility that a non-partner will be held liable as a partner by estoppel, and the other involves the ability of a non-partner to bind the partnership. These concepts are not necessarily reciprocal. They exist independently of one another.

The issue in the partnership by estoppel is the reasonable understanding of the third party, and the understanding of the third party must be traceable back to something the non-partner did (or failed to do) to create that understanding. The issue in the apparent authority of a purported partner involves the same language but, although we are still interested in the reasonable understanding of the third party, it must be traceable back to something the partnership did to create that understanding. Furthermore, there is no requirement that the party claiming apparent authority show detrimental reliance.

Nevertheless, both of these concepts underscore the importance of avoiding circumstances which could create an impression with some third party that a partnership relationship exists when it does not. Both partnership by estoppel and the apparent authority of a purported partner could result in unwanted obligations or even liability merely because of a mistaken impression. Careful attorneys, therefore, will caution their clients about the improper use of the term "partner" or taking other actions which might create an incorrect impression that a partnership exists.

Martin v. Peyton

246 N.Y. 213, 158 N.E. 77 (1927)

ANDREWS, J.:

Much ancient learning as to partnership is obsolete. Today only those who are partners between themselves may be charged for partnership debts by others. (Partnership Law [Cons. Laws, ch. 39], sec. 11.) There is one exception. Now and then a recovery is allowed where in truth such relationship is absent. This is because the debtor may not deny the claim.

Partnership results from contract, express or implied. If denied it may be proved by the production of some written instrument; by testimony as to some conversation; by circumstantial evidence. If nothing else appears, the receipt by the defendant of a share of the profits of the business is enough.

Assuming some written contract between the parties the question may arise whether it creates a partnership. If it be complete; if it expresses in good faith the full understanding and obligation of the parties, then it is for the court to say whether a partnership exists. It may, however, be a mere sham intended to hide the real relationship. Then other results follow. In passing upon it effect is to be given to each provision. Mere words will not blind us to realities. Statements that no partnership is intended are not conclusive. If as a whole a contract contemplates an association of two or more persons to carry on as co-owners a business for profit a partnership there is. On the other hand, if it be less than this no partnership exists. Passing on the contract as a whole, an arrangement for sharing profits is to be considered. It is to be given its due weight. But it is to be weighed in connection with all the rest. It is not decisive. It may be merely the method adopted to pay a debt or wages, as interest on a loan or for other reasons. . . .

In the case before us the claim that the defendants became partners in the firm of Knauth, Nachod & Kuhne, doing business as bankers and brokers, depends upon the interpretation of certain instruments. There is nothing in their subsequent acts determinative of or indeed material upon this question. And we are relieved of questions that sometimes arise. "The plaintiff's position is not," we are told, "that the agreements of June 4, 1921, were a false expression or incomplete expression of the intention of the parties. We say that they express defendants' intention and that that intention was to create a relationship which as a matter of law constitutes a partnership." Nor may the claim of the plaintiff be rested on any question of estoppel. "The plaintiff's claim," he stipulates, "is a claim of actual partnership, not of partnership by estoppel. . . ."

Remitted then, as we are, to the documents themselves, we refer to circumstances surrounding their execution only so far as is necessary to make them intelligible. And we are to remember that although the intention of the parties to avoid liability as partners is clear, although in language precise and definite they deny any design to then join the firm of K. N. & K.; although they say their interests in profits should be construed merely as a measure of compensation for loans, not an interest in profits as such; although they provide that they shall not be liable for any losses or treated as partners, the question still remains whether in fact they agree to so associate themselves with the firm as to "carry on as co-owners a business for profit."

In the spring of 1921 the firm of K. N. & K. found itself in financial difficulties. John R. Hall was one of the partners. He was a friend of Mr. Peyton. From him he obtained the loan of almost $500,000 of Liberty bonds, which K. N. & K. might use as collateral to secure bank advances. This, however, was not sufficient. The firm and its members had engaged in unwise speculations, and it was deeply involved. Mr. Hall was also intimately acquainted with George W. Perkins, Jr., and with Edward W. Freeman. He also knew Mrs. Peyton and Mrs. Perkins and Mrs. Freeman. All were anxious to help him. He, therefore, representing K. N. & K., entered into negotiations with them. While they were pending a proposition was made that Mr. Peyton, Mr. Perkins and Mr. Freeman or some of them should become partners. It met a decided refusal. Finally an agreement was reached. It is expressed in three documents, executed on the same day, all a part of the one transaction. They were drawn with care and are unambiguous. We shall refer to them as "the agreement," "the indenture" and "the option."

We have no doubt as to their general purpose. The respondents were to loan K. N. & K. $2,500,000 worth of liquid securities, which were to be returned to them on or before April 15, 1923. The firm might hypothecate them to secure loans totaling $2,000,000, using the proceeds as its business necessities required. To insure respondents against loss K. N. & K. were to turn over to them a large number of their own securities which may have been valuable, but which were of so speculative a nature that they could not be used as collateral for bank loans. In compensation for the loan the respondents were to receive 40 per cent of the profits of the firm until the return was made, not exceeding, however, $500,000 and not less than $100,000. Merely because the transaction involved the transfer of securities and not of cash does not prevent its being a loan within the meaning of section 11. The respondents also were given an option to join the firm if they or any of them expressed a desire to do so before June 4, 1923.

Many other detailed agreements are contained in the papers. Are they such as may be properly inserted to protect the lenders? Or do they go further? Whatever their purpose, did they in truth associate the respondents with the firm so that they and it together thereafter carried on as co-owners a business for profit? The answer depends upon an analysis of these various provisions.

As representing the lenders, Mr. Peyton and Mr. Freeman are called "trustees." The loaned securities when used as collateral are not to be mingled with other securities of K. N. & K., and the trustees at all times are to be kept informed of all transactions affecting them. To them shall be paid all dividends and income accruing therefrom. They may also substitute for any of the securities loaned securities of equal value. With their consent the firm may sell any of its securities held by the respondents, the proceeds to go, however, to the trustees. In other similar ways the trustees may deal with these same securities, but the securities loaned shall always be sufficient in value to permit of their hypothecation for $2,000,000. If they rise in price the excess may be withdrawn by the defendants. If they fall they shall make good the deficiency.

So far there is no hint that the transaction is not a loan of securities with a provision for compensation. Later a somewhat closer connection with the firm appears. Until the securities are returned the directing management of the firm is to be in the hands of John R. Hall, and his life is to be insured for $1,000,000, and the policies are to be assigned as further collateral security to the trustees. These requirements are not unnatural. Hall was the one known and trusted by the defendants. Their acquaintance with the other members of the firm was of the slightest. These others had brought an old and established business to the verge of bankruptcy. As the respondents knew, they also had engaged in unsafe speculation. The respondents were about to loan $2,500,000 of good securities. As collateral they were to receive others of problematical value. What they required seems but ordinary caution. Nor does it imply an association in the business.

The trustees are to be kept advised as to the conduct of the business and consulted as to important matters. They may inspect the firm books and are entitled to any information they think important. Finally they may veto any business they think highly speculative or injurious. Again we hold this but a proper precaution to safeguard the loan. The trustees may not initiate any transaction as a partner may do. They may not bind the firm by any action of their own. Under the circumstances the safety of the loan depended upon the business success of K. N. & K. This success was likely to be compromised by the inclination of its members to engage in speculation. No longer, if the respondents were to be protected, should it be allowed. The trustees, therefore, might prohibit it, and that their prohibition might be effective, information was to be furnished them. Not dissimilar agreements have been held proper to guard the interests of the lender.

As further security each member of K. N. & K. is to assign to the trustees their interest in the firm. No loan by the firm to any member is permitted and the amount each may draw is fixed. No other distribution of profits is to be made. So that realized profits may be calculated the existing capital is stated to be $700,000, and profits are to be realized as promptly as good business practice will permit. In case the trustees think this is not done, the question is left to them and to Mr. Hall, and if they differ then to an arbitrator. There is no obligation that the firm shall continue the business. It may dissolve at any time. Again we conclude there is nothing here not properly adapted to secure the interest of the respondents as lenders. If their compensation is dependent on a percentage of the profits still provision must be made to define what these profits shall be.

The "indenture" is substantially a mortgage of the collateral delivered by K. N. & K. to the trustees to secure the performance of the "agreement." It certainly does not strengthen the claim that the respondents were partners.

Finally we have the "option." It permits the respondents or any of them or their assignees or nominees to enter the firm at a later date if they desire to do so by buying 50 per cent or less of the interests therein of all or any of the members at a stated price. Or a corporation may, if the respondents and the members agree, be formed in place of the firm. Meanwhile, apparently with the design of protecting the firm business against improper or ill-judged action which might render the option valueless, each member of the firm is to place his resignation in the hands of Mr. Hall. If at any time he and the trustees agree that such resignation should be accepted, that member shall then retire, receiving the value of his interest calculated as of the date of such retirement.

This last provision is somewhat unusual, yet it is not enough in itself to show that on June 4, 1921, a present partnership was created nor taking these various papers as a whole do we reach such a result. It is quite true that even if one or two or three like provisions contained in such a contract do not require this conclusion, yet it is also true that when taken together a point may come where stipulations immaterial separately cover so wide a field that we should hold a partnership exists. As in other branches of the law a question of degree is often the determining factor. Here that point has not been reached. . . . The judgment appealed from should be affirmed, with costs.

F. Partner or Employee?

As in the preceding case, a substantial number of cases involving partnership law involve a determination as to whether a particular relationship constitutes a partnership, even though the term "partnership" is not used. There are also circumstances (although they occur less frequently) when an individual might be described as a partner and, based on the circumstances, is not. In addition, there are circumstances in which a person plays more than one role in an enterprise and that person might be treated both as a partner for some purposes and as something else for other purposes.

There are also situations in which a court is asked to determine whether an individual providing services to a partnership is a partner or an employee. Whether someone is an employee or a partner can be significant for many reasons. While employees do owe agency-based fiduciary duties to an employee, these duties are typically narrower in scope than the duties that partners owe a partnership. (*See Meinhard v. Salmon* (249 N.Y. 458, 164 N.E. 545 (N.Y. 1928)) below and its well-known characterization of a partner's duties as requiring "the punctilio of an honor most sensitive. . . .") In addition, the default rules of the RUPA do not apply to employees. Employees, without a specific contractual provision, may not claim a partnership owes them a share of profits. Additionally, certain laws designed to protect employees, such as the federal employment anti-discrimination laws or minimum wage laws, apply to employees, not to partners. Non-employee partners may not sue for discrimination in the workplace under Title VII and its related laws or for violations of the minimum wage law. (*See Fitzsimons v. Cal. Emergency Physicians Med. Group*, 205 Cal. App. 4th 1423 (2012), holding that a partnership could incur liability under the California Fair Employment and Housing Act, based upon the partnership's retaliation against a partner who complained about discrimination or harassment of partnership employees, notwithstanding the fact that the complaining partner was not a partnership "employee" and would not herself have been protected against such discrimination of harassment.)

The court in *Serapion v. Martinez*, 119 F.3d 982 (1st Cir. 1997), considered the question of what circumstances determines one's status in a partnership. In *Serapion*, the plaintiff, Margarita Serapin, sued under Title VII for sex-based discrimination. Although the plaintiff's title was "senior partner," Serapin claimed she was not actually a partner because she did not have the responsibility nor was she given the pay that the male partners in the firm enjoyed. (These allegations also formed the basis of her Title VII claim.) In affirming the district court's determination that Serapion was not an "employee" of the firm, the Court of Appeals for the First Circuit distinguished three categories which it considered in its determination that the plaintiff could not be considered an employee who was eligible to sue under Title VII. Note that the factors considered below would also be useful in evaluating whether any relationship constituted a partnership.

> We think that these cases provide valuable guidance concerning the factors which courts must consider in making status determinations under Title VII. In large, the critical attributes of proprietary status involve three broad, overlapping categories: ownership, remuneration, and management. Within these categories, emphasis will vary depending on the circumstances of particular cases. Nonetheless, although myriad factors may influence a court's ultimate decision in a given case, we recount a non-exclusive list of factors that frequently will bear upon such determinations.
>
> Under the first category, relevant factors include investment in the firm, ownership of firm assets, and liability for firm debts and obligations. To the extent that these factors exist, they indicate a proprietary role; to the extent that they do not exist, they indicate a status more akin to that of an employee.
>
> Under the second category, the most relevant factor is whether (and if so, to what extent) the individual's compensation is based on the firm's profits. To the extent that a partner's remuneration is subject to the vagaries of the firm's economic fortunes, her status more closely resembles that of a proprietor; conversely, to the extent that a partner is paid on a straight salary basis, the argument for

treating her as an ordinary employee will gain strength. A second potentially relevant factor in this regard relates to fringe benefits. An individual who receives benefits of a kind or in an amount markedly more generous than similarly situated employees who possess no ownership interest is more likely to be a proprietor.

Under the third category, relevant factors include the right to engage in policymaking; participation in, and voting power with regard to, firm governance; the ability to assign work and to direct the activities of employees within the firm; and the ability to act for the firm and its principals. Once again, to the extent that these factors exist, they indicate a proprietary role.

We add a note of caution. Status determinations are necessarily made along a continuum. The cases that lie at the polar extremes will prove easy to resolve. The close cases, however, will require a concerned court to make a case-specific assessment of whether a particular situation is nearer to one end of the continuum or the other. In performing this assessment, no single factor should be accorded talismanic significance. Rather, a status determination under Title VII must be founded on the totality of the circumstances which pertain in a particular case. Given these verities, any effort to formulate a hard-and-fast rule would likely result in a statement that was overly simplistic, or too general to be of any real help, or both.

Serapion v. Martinez, supra, at 990.

DISCUSSION PROBLEM—SEEKING ASSISTANCE

Consider a situation in which David and Mindy are starting a business to develop applications which will eventually be sold on "smartphone" devices. David and Mindy are about to graduate from the business school of Ivy League University ("ILU"). They post a notice in the engineering department of ILU, requesting assistance with creating and programming the applications for their business. An eager and capable engineering student, named Rocky, responds to the request and offers to help "build" and program the initial applications for David and Mindy's business.

Rocky does not want any money, even though he will spend hundreds of hours on the work. Rocky just wants experience. Rocky says, "I'll tell you what. Don't pay me anything now, and if the business is ever a big hit, you can pay me whatever you think is fair." David and Mindy do not know Rocky well and don't want to get into trouble. One day you meet David and Mindy on the ILU campus, and they ask for your assistance in structuring the arrangement with Rocky. Assume they are not yet prepared to form an entity. They hope to have investors in the future, and recognize that these investors will, no doubt, scrutinize whether there are any potential claims against the business. They can't afford to pay Rocky the minimum wage that the state law requires be received by all employees. What should they do?

SECTION II: Partnership Management

An important aspect of partnership law is that each partner is an agent of the partnership for the purpose of conducting the partnership's business. Any partner has the authority to bind the partnership in the ordinary course of business (unless the partnership agreement says otherwise). However, when a partnership wishes to make a decision about, or a change in, some aspect of its day-to-day operations, a vote is typically appropriate. A majority of the partners will usually have the right to make decisions relating to the day-to-day operations of the partnership business. The standard default rule is that each partner will have one vote, regardless of the amount of money he or she contributed to the partnership. Matters outside the ordinary course of business, such as selling all of the partnership assets, typically require unanimous approval. Of course, these standards may be altered by the partnership agreement. Sometimes these requirements can create difficulties, especially with an even number of partners. (*See National Biscuit Co. v. Stroud* (249 N.C. 467, 106 S.E.2d 692 (N.C. 1959)) below.)

A related management rights issue involves a partner's ability to bind the partnership even though that partner might lack actual authority to do so. Since any partner has the power to bind a partnership for the purpose of carrying on the partnership business, one partner might be able to act with apparent authority to bind the partnership. If such an act was in violation of the partnership agreement, the partnership would have a claim against the partner who acted without actual authority. However, the partnership might still be bound if the third party reasonably believed that the partner was acting with actual authority. Note that because unanimity is required for matters outside the ordinary course of business, it is less reasonable for a third party to rely on the apparent authority of a partner, purporting to act on behalf of the partnership, with regard to a transaction outside of the ordinary course of business.

National Biscuit Co. v. Stroud

249 N.C. 467, 106 S.E.2d 692 (N.C. 1959)

PARKER, J.:

C. N. Stroud and Earl Freeman entered into a general partnership to sell groceries under the firm name of Stroud's Food Center. There is nothing in the agreed statement of facts to indicate or suggest that Freeman's power and authority as a general partner were in any way restricted or limited by the articles of partnership in respect to the ordinary and legitimate business of the partnership. Certainly, the purchase and sale of bread were ordinary and legitimate business of Stroud's Food Center during its continuance as a going concern.

Several months prior to February 1956 Stroud advised plaintiff that he personally would not be responsible for any additional bread sold by plaintiff to Stroud's Food Center. After such notice to plaintiff, it from 6 February 1956 to 25 February 1956, at the request of Freeman, sold and delivered bread in the amount of $171.04 to Stroud's Food Center.

In *Johnson v. Bernheim*, 76 N.C. 139, this Court said: 'A and B are general partners to do some given business; the partnership is, by operation of law, a power to each to bind the partnership in any manner legitimate to the business. If one partner go to a third person to buy an article on time for the partnership, the other partner cannot prevent it by writing to the third person not to sell to him on time; or, if one party attempt to buy for cash, the other has no right to require that it shall be on time. And what is true in regard to buying is true in regard to selling. What either partner does with a third person is binding on the partnership. It is otherwise where the partnership is not general, but is upon special terms, as that purchases and sales must be with and for cash. There the power to each is special, in regard to all dealings with third persons at least who have notice of the terms.' There is contrary authority. 68 C.J.S. Partnership § 143, pp. 578–579. However, this text of C.J.S. does not mention the effect of the provisions of the Uniform Partnership Act.

The General Assembly of North Carolina in 1941 enacted a Uniform Partnership Act, which became effective 15 March 1941. G.S. Ch. 59, Partnership, Art. 2.

G.S. § 59–39 is entitled 'Partner Agent of Partnership as to Partnership Business', and subsection (1) reads: 'Every partner is an agent of the partnership for the purpose of its business, and the act of every partner, including the execution in the partnership name of any instrument, for apparently carrying on in the usual way the business of the partnership of which he is a member binds the partnership, unless the partner so acting has in fact no authority to act for the partnership in the particular matter, and the person with whom he is dealing has knowledge of the fact that he has no such authority.' . . . .

G.S. § 59–45 provides that 'all partners are jointly and severally liable for the acts and obligations of the partnership.'

G.S. § 59–48 is captioned 'Rules Determining Rights and Duties of Partners'. Subsection (e) thereof reads: 'All partners have equal rights in the management and conduct of the partnership business. 'Subsection (h) hereof is as follows: 'Any difference arising as to ordinary matters connected with the partnership business may be decided by a majority of the partners; but no act in contravention of any agreement between the partners may be done rightfully without the consent of all the partners.'

Freeman as a general partner with Stroud, with no restrictions on his authority to act within the scope of the partnership business so far as the agreed statement of facts shows, had under the Uniform Partnership Act 'equal rights in the management and conduct of the partnership business.' Under G.S. § 59–48(h) Stroud, his co-partner, could not restrict the power and authority of Freeman to buy bread for the partnership as a going concern, for such a purchase was an 'ordinary matter connected with the partnership business,' for the purpose of its business and within its scope, because in the very nature of things Stroud was not, and could not be, a majority of the partners. Therefore, Freeman's purchases of bread from plaintiff for Stroud's Food Center as a going concern bound the partnership and his co-partner Stroud. . .

In *Crane on Partnership*, 2d Ed., p. 277, it is said: 'In cases of an even division of the partners as to whether or not an act within the scope of the business should be done, of which disagreement a third person has knowledge, it seems that logically no restriction can be placed upon the power to act. The partnership being a going concern, activities within the scope of the business should not be limited, save by the expressed will of the majority deciding a disputed question; half of the members are not a majority.'

* * * *

At the close of business on 25 February 1956 Stroud and Freeman by agreement dissolved the partnership. By their dissolution agreement all of the partnership assets, including cash on hand, bank deposits and all accounts receivable, with a few exceptions, were assigned to Stroud, who bound himself by such written dissolution agreement to liquidate the firm's assets and discharge its liabilities. It would seem a fair inference from the agreed statement of facts that the partnership got the benefit of the bread sold and delivered by plaintiff to Stroud's Food Center, at Freeman's request, from 6 February 1956 to 25 February 1956. [*Citation omitted.*] But whether it did or not, Freeman's acts, as stated above, bound the partnership and Stroud.

The judgment of the court below is

Affirmed.

Summers v. Dooley

94 Idaho 87, 481 P.2d 318 (Idaho 1971)

DONALDSON, J.:

This lawsuit, tried in the district court, involves a claim by one partner against the other for $6,000. . . . The expenditure in question was incurred by the complaining partner (John Summers, plaintiff-appellant) for the purpose of hiring an additional employee. . . .

. . . . Summers entered a partnership agreement with Dooley (defendant-respondent) in 1958 for the purpose of operating a trash collection business. The business was operated by the two men and when either was unable to work, the non-working partner provided a replacement at his own expense. In 1962, Dooley became unable to work and, at his own expense, hired an employee to take his place. In July, 1966, Summers approached his partner Dooley regarding the hiring of an additional employee but Dooley refused. Nevertheless, on his own initiative, Summers hired the man and paid him out of his own pocket. Dooley, upon discovering that Summers had hired an additional man, objected, stating that he did not feel additional labor was necessary and refused to pay for the new employee out of the partnership funds. Summers continued to operate the business using the third man and in October of 1967 instituted suit in the district court for $6,000 against his partner, the gravamen of the complaint being that Summers has been required to pay out more than $11,000 in expenses, incurred in the hiring of the additional man, without any reimbursement from either the partnership funds or his partner. . . .

The principal thrust of appellant's contention is that in spite of the fact that one of the two partners refused to consent to the hiring of additional help, nonetheless, the non-consenting partner retained profits earned by the labors of the third man and therefore the non-consenting partner should be stopped from denying the need and value of the employee, and has by his behavior ratified the act of the other partner who hired the additional man.

The issue presented for decision by this appeal is whether an equal partner in a two man partnership has the authority to hire a new employee in disregard of the objection of the other partner and then attempt to charge the dissenting partner with the costs incurred as a result of his unilateral decision.

The State of Idaho has enacted specific statutes with respect to the legal concept known as 'partnership. Therefore any solution of partnership problems should logically begin with an application of the relevant code provision.

In the instant case the record indicates that although Summers requested his partner Dooley to agree to the hiring of a third man, such requests were not honored. In fact Dooley made it clear that he was 'voting no' with regard to the hiring of an additional employee.

An application of the relevant statutory provisions and pertinent case law to the factual situation presented by the instant case indicates that the trial court was correct in its disposal of the issue since a majority of the partners did not consent to the hiring of the third man. I.C. § 53–318(8) [UPA (1914) § 18 (h)] provides:

> 'Any difference arising as to ordinary matters connected with the partnership business may be decided by a *majority of the partners* * * *.' (emphasis supplied)

* * * *

A careful reading of the statutory provision [UPA (1914) § 18] indicates that subsection 5 bestows equal rights in the management and conduct of the partnership business upon all of the partners. [In the absence of an agreement to the contrary. . . .] The concept of equality between partners with respect to management of business affairs is a central theme and recurs throughout the Uniform Partnership law . . . which has been enacted in this jurisdiction. Thus the only reasonable interpretation of I.C. § 53–318(8) [UPA (1914) § 18 (h)] is that business differences must be decided by a majority of the partners provided no other agreement between the partners speaks to the issues.

A noted scholar has dealt precisely with the issue to be decided.

'* * * if the partners are equally divided, those who forbid a change must have their way.' Walter B. Lindley, *A Treatise on the Law of Partnership*, Ch. II, s III, 24–8, p. 403 (1924).

* * * *

In the case at bar one of the partners continually voiced objection to the hiring of the third man. He did not sit idly by and acquiesce in the actions of his partner. Under these circumstances it is manifestly unjust to permit recovery of an expense which was incurred individually and not for the benefit of the partnership but rather for the benefit of one partner.

Judgment affirmed.

SECTION III: Partnership Financial Structure

As discussed above, each partner is jointly and severally liable for the debts of the partnership. This feature of personal liability means that (subject to various procedural requirements that can vary from state to state and to any contractual provisions to the contrary) an outside creditor of a partnership may make a claim against any partner in that partnership for the total amount of an obligation owed by the partnership to that creditor. Nevertheless, the rights of a creditor to make claims against the partners in a partnership do not define the rights of the partners with respect to each other or to the partnership. The RUPA provides guidelines for allocation of the obligations of any partner arising out of the partnership. These guidelines arise in the context of a partner's rights to the profits of a partnership and a partner's obligations with respect to losses of a partnership.

Under the default provisions of RUPA, each partner in a partnership is entitled to share equally in the partnerships profits (RUPA § 401(b)). Similarly, absent an agreement to the contrary, each partner is chargeable for the losses of a partnership in the same proportion that the partners share profits. (*Id.*) Upon the formation of a partnership, each partner has a capital account established. A partner's capital account keeps track of the balance of that partner's "capital" that is invested with the partnership. A capital account balance may increase or decrease during the term of the partnership. The balance in a partner's capital account is increased by contributions made by (or on behalf of) a partner (less any liabilities) and decreases by any distributions made by the partnership to (or on behalf of) that partner. A partner's capital account balance may also increase or decrease based on allocations of profit or loss. The capital account balance is increased for any profits allocated to a partner and decreased for any losses allocated to the partner. A partner's capital account balance is not necessarily a measure of the value of a partner's stake in the partnership. It is merely an accounting device to keep track of the capital that a partner has contributed or received and the profits and losses allocated to that partner. If a partner has a negative balance in his or her capital account, then, following the dissolution of the partnership, that partner has an obligation to the partnership for the amount of that negative balance, unless the partnership agreement provides otherwise. (RUPA § 807(b)).

To the extent that any one partner makes payments or incurs liabilities in excess of that partner's share of the liabilities of a partnership then that partner has the right to indemnification from the partnership. (RUPA § 401(c)). Furthermore, to the extent the partnership does not have assets that are sufficient to indemnify the partner, the partnership (or the partner) may seek contribution from the other partners (RUPA § 405).

Often individuals or entities, desiring a more complex business arrangement, will modify the provisions of a partnership agreement to provide for different allocations and financial structures than those provided above. For example, consider the situation that arises in the *Kessler v. Antinora* case below, in which one partner contributed labor but not capital and the other contributed all of the capital.

Kessler v. Antinora

279 N.J. Super. 471, 653 A.2d 579 (1995)

KING, P.J.A.D.:

I

Plaintiff Robert H. Kessler and defendant Richard Antinora entered into a written agreement for the purpose of building and selling a single-family residence on a lot in Wayne in Passaic County. The concept of the agreement seemed simple: Kessler was to provide the money and Antinora was to act as general contractor. Profits would be divided—60% to Kessler, 40% to Antinora—after Kessler was repaid. No thought was given to losses. The venture lost money. Kessler sued Antinora to recover 40% of his financial losses or $65,742. The Law Division judge ruled in Kessler's favor on summary judgment. The judge denied Antinora's cross-motion for summary judgment of dismissal. We disagree, reverse the judgment in Kessler's favor, and order judgment in Antinora's favor.

II

On April 15, 1987 Kessler and Antinora executed a seven-page written agreement titled "JOINT VENTURE PARTNERSHIP AGREEMENT." The agreement contemplated a single venture: buying a lot in Wayne and building and selling a residence on it. Under the agreement Kessler agreed to "provide all necessary funds to purchase land and construct a one-family dwelling and disburse all funds to pay bills." Antinora agreed to "actually construct the dwelling and be the general contractor of the job."

The agreement provided for distribution of the proceeds of the venture:

> 9. *Distribution.* Upon or about completion of the dwelling it shall be placed for sale. Upon sale of same, and after deducting all monies expended by Robert Kessler plus interest [sic] at prime plus one point and/or including interest or any funds borrowed for the project, not to exceed prime plus one point, engineering fees, architectural fees, legal fees, broker fees, if any, and any other costs connected with the project, the parties, Robert Kessler and Richard Antinora, shall divide the net profits as follows: . . .
>
> Robert Kessler—sixty (60%) percent
>
> Richard Antinora—forty (40%) percent

The agreement was silent about losses. There was no provision to compensate Antinora for any services other than the 40% profit clause.

Both parties complied with the agreement. Kessler provided the funds; Antinora supervised and delivered the finished house. This took over three years. Meanwhile, the real estate market soured. The house sold on September 1, 1991 for $420,000. The cost incurred in building and selling the house was $498,917.

Kessler was repaid all but $78,917 of the money he advanced pursuant to the contract. He also claimed unreimbursed interest of $85,440 for his self-characterized "loan" to the partnership. This claim for interest is disputed as to amount. Kessler thus claimed a total loss of $164,357. He sought and obtained his summary judgment in the Law Division for 40% of this amount, or $65,742.80. No amount was presented on the value of Antinora's services over the three-year period as general contractor.

Antinora contended that the agreement was basically for a joint venture, silent as to losses, and that both parties risked and lost their unrecovered contributions—Kessler's money and Antinora's labor. The Law Division judge disagreed and found that statutory partnership law governed. The judge ruled that N.J.S.A. 42:1–18a required each partner to "contribute towards the losses, whether of capital or otherwise, sustained by the partnership according to his share in the profits." N.J.S.A. 42:1–18a. The judge ruled that Antinora was liable for 40% of Kessler's monetary losses and inferentially rejected any recognition of Antinora's "in kind" loss.

III

We conclude that New Jersey's allegedly applicable section of the Uniform Partnership Law, N.J.S.A. 42:1–18a, does not control here because of the specific terms of the agreement between the parties. The pertinent statutory section states:

> 42:1–18. Rights and Duties of Partners
>
> The rights and duties of the partners in relation to the partnership shall be determined, *subject to any agreement between them,* by the following rules:
>
> a. Each partner shall be repaid his contributions, whether by way of capital or advances to the partnership property and share equally in the profits and surplus remaining after all liabilities, including those to partners, are satisfied; and must contribute towards the losses, whether of capital or otherwise, sustained by the partnership according to his share in the profits.
>
> * * * *
>
> [N.J.S.A. 42:1–18a.] (emphasis added)

We find the agreement controlling over the statute. The agreement said that upon sale of the house "and after deducting all monies expended by Robert Kessler plus interest," fees, and other costs the "parties [Kessler and Antinora] shall divide net profits" 60% and 40%. We conclude that the agreement evinced a clear intent that Kessler would be repaid his investment from the sale of the house only, not by Antinora. There is no suggestion in the agreement that any of Kessler's risked and lost money would be repaid in part by Antinora. Nor is there any suggestion that Antinora's risked labor would be repaid in part by Kessler.

We find particularly persuasive the reasoning of the California Supreme Court in *Kovacik v. Reed,* 49 Cal. 2d 166, 315 P.2d 314 (1957). There the parties orally agreed to participate in a kitchen remodeling venture for Sears Roebuck & Company. Kovacik agreed to invest $10,000 in the venture and Reed agreed to become the job estimator and supervisor. They agreed to share the profits on a 50-50 basis. Possible losses were not discussed. Despite their efforts, the venture was unsuccessful and Kovacik sued Reed to recover one-half the money losses he endured. Kovacik prevailed in the trial court and recovered $4,340, or one-half the net monetary loss of $8,680.

The California Supreme Court acknowledged the general rule of partnership law that in the absence of an agreement, "the law presumes that partners and joint adventurers intended to participate equally in the profits and losses of the common enterprise, irrespective of any inequality in the amounts each contributed to the capital employed in the venture, with the losses being shared by them in the same proportions as they share the profits." [*Citations omitted.*]

The California court then observed that this "general rule" did not obtain where one party contributed the money and the other the labor, stating:

> However, it appears that in the cases in which the above stated general rule has been applied, each of the parties had contributed capital consisting of either money or land or other tangible property, or was to receive compensation for services rendered to the common undertaking which was to be paid before computation of the profits or losses. Where, however, as in the present case, one partner or joint adventurer contributes the money capital as against the other's skill and labor, all the cases cited, and which our research has discovered, hold that neither party is liable to the other for contribution for any loss sustained. Thus, upon loss of the money the party who contributed it is not entitled to recover any part of it from the party who contributed only services.

[*Citations omitted.*]

The rationale which the California decision and the earlier cited cases adopted was where one party contributes money and the other services, in the event of a loss, each loses his own capital—one in the form of money, the other in labor. *Ibid.* A corollary view was that the parties have implicitly agreed, by their conduct and contract, to share profits and that their contributions of money and sweat equity have been valued in an equal ratio. Thus, upon the loss of both some money and labor, the loss falls upon each proportionately without any legal recourse. Thus, Kovacik lost $8,680 of his $10,000 while Reed lost all of his labor.

Likewise, in the case before us, Kessler lost some of his money—$65,472, plus disputed interest, but Antinora lost all of the value of his labor on the three-year project. The Arizona Court of Appeals in *Ellingson v. Sloan,* 22 Ariz. App. 383, 527 P.2d 1100 (1974), has also recognized that in a joint venture "[t]he term 'losses' is not limited to monetary losses, but includes time expenditures and out-of-pocket expenses, especially where one party in a joint venture furnishes property and the other only services." *Id.* 527 P.2d at 1103, citing *Kovacik v. Reed, supra.* The point of the Arizona case is that rendering services to an ultimately losing venture represents a valuable contribution, even though the laboring venturer risked no money capital. * * *

We conclude that the "JOINT VENTURE PARTNERSHIP AGREEMENT" here did contemplate repayment to Kessler of his investment but only from the proceeds of the sale of the house, not from his coventurer Antinora. This is what the parties said, the only truly reliable evidence of what they intended. Our interpretation of the agreement between the parties accords with the result reached under the common-law cases discussed, and with our overall sense of fairness. Each party shoulders a loss, one in determinative dollars; the other in labor, difficult, if not impossible, to quantify. The parties did not think about losses in casting their agreement and any attempt by the law now to reconstruct their then non-existent intent on the subject would be speculative.

Reversed for entry of summary judgment for the defendant Antinora.

QUESTIONS

1. If the parties in the preceding case had known that the venture would result in a loss, what agreement do you think they would have reached?

2. In situations in which the parties have not anticipated the outcome, and, therefore, not provided for it in their agreement, should courts attempt to determine what the parties would have agreed had they known the facts or should the question be what are the parties' obligations under the default rules? Under RUPA the default rules provide that, absent an agreement to the contrary, the partnership losses should be divided equally among the partners. However, there are other cases which have concluded that a contrary result was more appropriate. *See Kovacik v. Reed,* 49 Cal.2d 166, 315 P.2d 314 (1957); *Becker v. Killarney,* 177 Ill.App.3d 793, 532 N.E.2d 931 (1988).

3. Consider what provisions you would have included in an agreement to be drafted before the parties in the preceding case embarked upon their venture if you were the attorney representing Kessler or if you were the attorney representing Antinora.

A. The Nature of Partnership Interests

The "interest" that partners typically hold in a partnership is comprised of two sets of rights: "economic rights" and "management rights." Economic rights include the right to receive money which is distributed from the partnership to the holder of the economic right. Management rights (discussed above) include the right to vote and participate in management of the partnership.

In general, economic rights are transferable but management rights are not, without the consent of all of the partners. When a partner transfers economic rights, the recipient transferee has the right to obtain money (or other distributions) which otherwise would have been paid by the partnership to the transferor partner. Unless additional rights are specifically granted by a court, by the other partners or by the partnership agreement, the transferee (or "assignee") is not considered to be a "partner" and does not have the right to vote or to become a partner merely by holding economic rights in the partnership.

Transferees may obtain an economic interest in several ways: by a voluntary transfer by the transferor partner; by an involuntary transfer by the transferor partner which may occur due to the enforcement of a judgment against him or her; or following the death of the transferor partner. When economic rights are transferred, the transferor partner will sometimes still hold management rights in the partnership. This dynamic can create difficult situations for the transferee since the transferee does not have the right to vote or even to enforce fiduciary obligations which might be owed to the transferor partner. The transferee is, therefore, dependent on the transferor to enforce certain fiduciary protections and to vote in the transferee's interest. In the case of an involuntary transfer or the death of the transferor, the "support" of the transferor is not available to a transferee, and the transferee is often at the mercy of the remaining partners and can only receive a share of the funds, if any, that the partnership decides to distribute. A transferee of a partnership interest may not become a new partner without the vote of all of the other partners in the partnership. Note that these restrictions may be altered by the partnership agreement which could provide for free transferability or for a different vote on the admission of a new partner.

B. Partnership Property

Economic rights entitle a partner (or other holder of such rights) to funds that are distributed by the partnership. However, economic rights do not entitle the holder to any right in any of the specific property of the partnership. In fact, a fundamental axiom of partnership law is that all property acquired by the partnership is the property of the partnership and not of the partners individually. (RUPA § 203). This construct means that no single partner has an interest in, or right to, any specific property owned by the partnership. While the theory behind this principal may seem innocuous, it can produce results in certain circumstances that may seem unfair. Consider the following case.

Putnam v. Shoaf

620 S.W.2d 510 (Tenn. Ct. App. 1981)

NEARN, J.

This dispute is over the sale of a partnership interest in the Frog Jump Gin Company.

The Frog Jump Gin had operated for a number of years showing losses in some years and profits in others. In the time immediately preceding February, 1976, it appears that the gin operated at a loss. Originally, the gin was operated as an equal partnership between E. C. Charlton, Louise H. Charlton, Lyle Putnam and Carolyn Putnam. In 1974 Mr. Putnam died and Mrs. Putnam, by agreement, succeeded to her husband's interest. The gin operated under that control and management until February 19, 1976, when Mrs. Putnam desired to sever her relationship with the other partners in Frog Jump Gin. At that time the gin was heavily indebted to the Bank of Trenton and Trust Company, and Mrs. Putnam desired to be relieved of this liability. John A. and Maurine H. Shoaf displayed an interest in obtaining Mrs. Putnam's one-half interest in the partnership. An examination by the Shoafs of the financial records of the gin, evidenced by a statement from the gin bookkeeper, indicated a negative financial position of approximately $90,000.00. The Shoafs agreed to take over Mrs. Putnam's position in the partnership if Mrs. Putnam and the Charltons would each pay $21,000.00 into the partnership account. The Shoafs agreed to assume personal liability for all partnership debts, including Putnam's share of any partnership debts made prior to their coming into the partnership, although the Uniform Partnership Act would only make him personally liable for debts made after his entry into the partnership unless he agreed to more. [*Citation omitted.*] Both the Charltons and Mrs. Putnam paid their respective amounts into the partnership account, and Shoaf assumed all partnership obligations as aforesaid.

At the time of his agreement the known assets of the Frog Jump Gin consisted primarily of the gin, its equipment, and the land upon which they were located. All gin assets, including the land, were held in the name of the partnership. Mrs. Putnam conveyed her interest in the partnership to the Shoafs by means of a quit claim deed. Upon Shoaf's assumption of the position of a partner, the services of the old bookkeeper were terminated and a new bookkeeper was hired.

In April, 1977, with the assistance of the new bookkeeper, it was learned that the old bookkeeper had engaged in a scheme of systematic embezzlement from the Frog Jump Gin Company from the time of Mr. Putnam's death until the bookkeeper's services were terminated. This disclosure led to suits being filed by the gin against the bookkeeper and the banks that had honored checks forged by the bookkeeper. There is no need to go into the details of all that litigation. Suffice it to say that Mrs. Putnam was allowed to intervene claiming an interest in any fund paid by the banks and the upshot of it all was a judgment paid into Court by the banks in excess of $68,000.00. One-half of that sum, by agreement, has been paid to the Charltons as owners of a one-half interest in the gin, and the other half is the subject of this dispute between the Shoafs and Mrs. Putnam's estate. She has died pending this litigation and the case revived.

* * * *

The basis of the Trial Judge's decision was that Mrs. Putnam intended to convey all of her interest in the partnership to Shoaf and, therefore, the Court could not reform the sale and hold that the unknown right of action against the banks for payment of forged checks was not conveyed by Mrs. Putnam in the conveyance to the Shoafs.

The conveyance between Mrs. Putnam and the Shoafs is evidenced by what is styled a "Quitclaim Deed" executed by Mrs. Putnam on February 19, 1976, which is as follows:

> "FOR AND IN CONSIDERATION of the sum of One Dollar ($1.00), cash in hand paid, the receipt of which is hereby acknowledged, and the assumption by Grantees of all Grantor's obligations arising or by virtue of her partnership interest in the Frog Jump Gin Company, . . . a widow, have this day bargained and sold and by these presents so hereby sell, transfer, convey and forever quitclaim unto JOHN A. SHOAF and wife, MAURINE H. SHOAF, their heirs and assigns, all the right, title and interest (it being a one-half (1/2) undivided interest) I have in and to the following described real and personal property located in the 25th Civil District of Gibson County, Tennessee, and described as follows; to-wit:"

(The legal description of the real property follows.)

"PERSONAL PROPERTY:

"All of the personal property and machinery in said Frog Jump Gin Company's buildings and on said properties described and used in the operation of its cotton gin plant on the above described parcel of land, including two Moss Gordin 75 saw gin stands; one Overhead incline cleaner; stick and green leaf machine; two Moss Gordin lint cleaners; two Mitchell Feeders; two Mitchell burners; one Hardwick Etter all steel press; condensers; fans; motors; pulleys; shafting; all piping; belting and machinery and appliances and other personal property, including all cotton trailers, on said parcel of land and used in connection with the operation of said cotton gin, accounts receivable, inventory and all other assets of Frog Jump Gin Company.

"TO HAVE AND TO HOLD the said real and personal property with the appurtenances, estate, title and interest thereto belonging unto the said John A. Shoaf and wife, Maurine H. Shoaf, their heirs and assigns, forever. . . ."

On the same day Mrs. Putnam and the Charltons executed the following agreement:

"This Agreement made and entered into on this the 19th day of February, 1976, by and between E. C. Charlton and wife, Louise H. Charlton, party of one part, and Carolyn B. Putnam, party of the other part, all of Trenton, Gibson County, Tennessee;

"WITNESSETH: THAT WHEREAS, the parties have heretofore been conducting a business, as partners, under the firm name and style of Frog Jump Gin Company; and

"WHEREAS, Carolyn B. Putnam has agreed to pay into the partnership the sum of Twenty-one Thousand Dollars ($21,000.00), the receipt of which is hereby acknowledged, and has sold and conveyed her interest in the partnership to John A. Shoaf and wife, Maurine H. Shoaf.

"NOW, THEREFORE, it is mutually agreed that the partnership be and hereby is dissolved. It is further mutually agreed that the parties do hereby release and forever discharge each other from any and all claims and demands on account of, connected with, or growing out of the said partnership, or the division of the assets thereof; and it is expressly understood and agreed that Carolyn B. Putnam is completely released and discharged from any and all

> liability, debts, or causes of action of the Frog Jump Gin Company, presently existing, contingent, or otherwise, including notes owed to Bank of Trenton and Trust Company, and that E. C. Charlton and wife, Louise H. Charlton assume all liability and indebtedness of the said partnership and covenant to indemnify and save harmless the said Carolyn B. Putnam in the premises. . . ."

At approximately the same time, Mrs. Putnam obtained from the Bank of Trenton a complete release from all personal liability for note indebtednesses to the Bank in the face amount of $105,000.00 in consideration of the Shoafs' assumption of all obligations of the Frog Jump Gin.

* * * *

First, we must discover the nature of the ownership interest of Mrs. Putnam in that which she conveyed. Under the Uniform Partnership Act, . . . her partnership property rights consisted of her (1) rights in specific partnership property, (2) interest in the partnership and (3) right to participate in management. [*Citation omitted.*] The right in "specific partnership property" is the partnership tenancy possessory right of equal use or possession by partners for partnership purposes. This possessory right is incident to the partnership and the possessory right does not exist absent the partnership. The possessory right is not the partner's "interest" in the assets of the partnership. [*Citation omitted.*] The real interest of a partner, as opposed to that incidental possessory right before discussed, is the partner's interest in the partnership which is defined as "his share of the profits and surplus and the same is personal property." [*Citation omitted.*] Therefore, a co-partner owns no personal specific interest in any specific property or asset of the partnership. The partnership owns the property or the asset. [*Citation omitted.*] The partner's interest is an undivided interest, as a co-tenant in all partnership property. [*Citation omitted.*] That interest is the partner's pro rata share of the net value or deficit of the partnership. [*Citation omitted.*] For this reason a conveyance of partnership property held in the name of the partnership is made in the name of the partnership and not as a conveyance of the individual interests of the partners. [*Citation omitted.*]

This being true, all Mrs. Putnam had to convey was her interest in the partnership. Accordingly, she had no specific interest in the admittedly unknown choices in action to separately convey or retain. Therefore, the determinative question is: Did Mrs. Putnam intend to convey her interest in the partnership to the Shoafs? There can be no doubt that such was the intent of Mrs. Putnam, as she had no other interest to convey. To give any other intent to the actions of Mrs. Putnam would require a fraudulent intent on her part, which intent certainly did not exist. Therefore, the intent of Mrs. Putnam was to convey the interest she owned which was "her share of the profits and surplus." T.C.A. § 61–1–125. If we would say otherwise, that is that she intended to convey less, and thereby retain a partnership interest, Mrs. Putnam would have remained a partner unknown to the other parties and, in reality, unknown to herself. It is abundantly evident that the last thing Mrs. Putnam wanted was to remain a partner. She wanted out, and out she got.

Since neither the Shoafs nor Mrs. Putnam knew of the embezzlement by accountant Bennie Johnston, there can be no doubt that neither the Shoafs no Mrs. Putnam knew of the valuable asset that the partnership possessed in its claim against the banks. However, it was the partnership's asset and not her personal asset. Just as she could not have retained it, had she known of it, and at the same time conveyed her partnership interest, we cannot now say she conveyed her partnership interest in 1976, but is still entitled to a share in it. This situation is no different from a hypothetical oil discovery on the partnership real property after transfer of a partnership interest with neither party believing oil to be present at the time of the conveyance. The interest in the real property always was and remained in the partnership. Of course, the transferor would not have transferred his partnership interest had he known of the existence of oil on partnership property; but, mutual ignorance of the existence of the oil would not, in our opinion, warrant a "reformation" of the contract for sale of the partnership interest, or warrant a decree in favor of the transferor for a share of the value of the oil.

* * * *

This is not a case of mutual mistake but one of mutual ignorance. They are not necessarily the same thing. . . . . Mrs. Putnam had to intend to convey her interest in the partnership. Hindsight now shows that it had more value than either party thought. But, hindsight is not a basis for a money judgment, a revision or a reformation. We wonder what would be the position of Mrs. Putnam, or the estate, had the Frog Jump Gin failed, leaving a sizeable deficit, even after the influx of the bank's refund. Would she except a partner's share of the Frog Jump Gin's liabilities for a share of the bank's refund? The question answers itself and we pose it only to show that she did not have a specific interest in any specific assets of the Frog Jump Gin, either to retain or convey. All she had was a partner's interest in a "share of the profits" (and losses) which she certainly intended to convey. . . .

QUESTIONS

1. If Sam buys Paul's house, and, several years later, finds a diamond ring stuck in a drain in the house, is Sam entitled to keep the ring? Is the preceding case analogous to the sale of Paul's house? Why or why not?

2. How could or should Mrs. Putnam's attorney have protected her from the outcome in the preceding case?

3. If Mrs. Putnam had requested certain protections against "windfall gains," do you think the Shoafs would or should have agreed to those protections?

SECTION IV: Fiduciary and Other Duties in Partnership

Experiencing Assignment 4: Proplimb's Problems

One day you arrive at work at the firm and are called into a meeting with a senior partner and a client named Emma Proplimb. Emma was a partner in a general partnership, called the NWFP Real Estate Partnership ("NWFP"). Emma is very angry and feels that the other partners at NWFP have cheated her out of a substantial sum of money. She relates to you the following facts:

FACTS:

Until about nine months ago, NWFP consisted of four partners, Nancy Nyce, Will Wrotten, Phil Fayer, and Emma Proplimb. NWFP owned various real estate holdings throughout the state. Each partner had management responsibilities in the business. These duties included property management responsibilities such as securing tenants, collecting rents and handling maintenance and repair issues as they arose. In addition, each partner would spend time seeking new properties which NWFP could purchase and/or develop. The partnership was formed in 2005. At that time, each partner contributed $200,000 for their respective interests in NWFP. All profits, losses and distributions were divided equally among the partners, and each partner had one vote.

The partnership had been extremely successful and owned several properties, worth approximately $30 million and owed approximately $20 million to banks and other lenders that had financed the purchase of the partnership properties. The partnership was scheduled to dissolve in 2025 or upon a vote of 75% of the partners (the "Term"). The partnership agreement provided that any partner who left the partnership before the completion of the Term, whether voluntarily, by death, or by expulsion was entitled to receive the lesser of (a) a return of his or her capital contribution, plus 10% interest for each year in which the partner was in the partnership; or (b) 25% of the value of the partnership assets minus partnership liabilities. The Partnership agreement also provided that any partner could be expelled from the partnership by a vote of three of the four partners. While most partnership decisions were made based on a majority vote, the partnership agreement could only be amended by a unanimous vote of the partners.

Each partner handled his or her property management responsibilities adequately. However, only Nancy and Will had been successful in finding properties in which NWFP could invest. In fact, NWFP's entire holdings were the result of deals made by Nancy and Will. In 2012, Emma accused Will of poor management of certain NWFP real estate holdings. Will had taken depreciation losses for tax reasons which resulted in large and beneficial deductions for the partners. However, because Emma did not understand the accounting procedures or the tax benefits, she just thought that Will was losing money on his properties. Emma accused Will in front of the other partners and tried to have Will expelled. However, after an investigation by Phil, Will was cleared of any wrongdoing.

Approximately six months after the matter involving Emma's allegations about Will, Will called a meeting of the partners and made a motion to amend the partnership agreement to reflect that he and Nancy had made more significant contributions than the other partners. Will wanted the profits, losses and distributions to be divided as follows: 30% to Will, 30% to Nancy, 20% to Phil and 20% to Emma. Everyone voted for the motion except Emma, who voted "no." Because the partnership agreement required unanimous approval for such an amendment, the motion did not pass. However, after the motion, the office environment changed. Emma was somewhat aloof and "frosty" toward the other partners and the other partners were somewhat "cold and distant" to Emma. After a few months had passed, Will called another meeting. At this meeting he made a motion to expel Emma from the partnership on the basis that her attitude was not conducive to the positive environment that the partnership strove to create. This motion passed.

Emma was expelled in 2013 after 8 years with the partnership and received approximately $430,000 in accordance with the provisions of the partnership agreement. Four months after Emma was expelled from the partnership, the partnership decided to accept an offer to sell all of its properties. Will, Phil and

Nancy split the profits three ways, and each made $4 million dollars. Emma is furious and wants "her" share of the money.

ASSIGNMENT:

The partner at your firm who is handling this matter instructs you to write a letter to the NWFP partnership in which Emma demands that NWFP provide her with her share of the $12 million profit. Your letter is not a legal brief. Therefore you do not need to cite cases to support your assertions of the law. However, if there is a lawsuit, the letter will probably become a part of the court record. So, it should provide support for Emma's position. Your letter should not exceed 850 words. (If you wish to address the letter or put a heading on it, these "words" will not be included in the 850 count.)

This Assignment does not need to be completed, and should not be completed, until the end of the section. However, as you study the cases and other materials that follow, it might be helpful to do so with a view toward providing assistance to Emma. Some of the materials in the chapter will relate more than others to the issues facing Emma. However, the materials are designed to build your understanding of the fiduciary duty issues that arise in a partnership and assist you in addressing Emma's concerns and putting them in context. Please keep Emma's issues and the questions presented by the assignment in mind while reading the materials that follow.

A. Fiduciary Obligations of Partners

Each partner has fiduciary obligations to the partnership itself and to the other partners in the partnership. These fiduciary obligations fall within the two general duties: the duty of loyalty and the duty of care. (*See* RUPA § 404.)

Partnership Duty of Care

The duty of care encompasses the standard by which a partner must evaluate and make partnership decisions. A partner typically does not violate his duty of care for mere negligence. Under the duty of care standards articulated in section 404(c) of the RUPA a partner must not engage in gross negligence, reckless conduct, intentional misconduct, or a knowing violation of the law.

Partnership Duty of Loyalty

There are several specific obligations that arise under a partner's duty of loyalty. Partners have obligations to account to the partnership for profits, property or benefits from the conduct (or winding up) of partnership business or the use of partnership property; to refrain from acting as or on behalf of a party with an adverse interest to the partnership (e.g. avoiding conflicts of interest); and to refrain from competing with the partnership in the subject matter of the partnership business.

B. The Implied Covenant of Good Faith and Fair Dealing

In addition to the preceding "fiduciary" duties, every partner has the obligation to discharge his, her or its duties to the partnership and to the other partners (and to exercise any rights that he or she might have under partnership law or the partnership agreement) consistent with the implied covenant of good faith and fair dealing. This implied covenant of good faith and fair dealing is not considered to be a "fiduciary" duty. However, it is a principle that is central to the conduct and operation of every partnership and a standard by which partners may not violate even by actions which might otherwise be valid under a partnership agreement.

Page v. Page

359 P.2d 41 (Cal. 1961)

TRAYNOR, JUSTICE:

Plaintiff and defendant are partners in a linen supply business in Santa Maria, California. Plaintiff appeals from a judgment declaring the partnership to be for a term rather than at will.

The partners entered into an oral partnership agreement in 1949. Within the first two years each partner contributed approximately $43,000 for the purchase of land, machinery, and linen needed to begin the business. From 1949 to 1957 the enterprise was unprofitable, losing approximately $62,000. The partnership's major creditor is a corporation, wholly owned by plaintiff, that supplies the linen and machinery necessary for the day-to-day operation of the business. This corporation holds a $47,000 demand note of the partnership. The partnership operations began to improve in 1958. The partnership earned $3,824.41 in that year and $2,282.30 in the first three months of 1959. Despite this improvement plaintiff wishes to terminate the partnership.

The Uniform Partnership Act provides that a partnership may be dissolved 'By the express will of any partner when no definite term or particular undertaking is specified.' Corp.Code, § 15031, subd. (1)(b). The trial court found that the partnership is for a term, namely, 'such reasonable time as is necessary to enable said partnership to repay from partnership profits, indebtedness incurred for the purchase of land, buildings, laundry and delivery equipment and linen for the operation of such business. * * *' Plaintiff correctly contends that this finding is without support in the evidence.

Defendant testified that the terms of the partnership were to be similar to former partnerships of plaintiff and defendant, and that the understanding of these partnerships was that 'we went into partnership to start the business and let the business operation pay for itself, put in so much money, and let the business pay itself out.' There was also testimony that one of the former partnership agreements provided in writing that the profits were to be retained until all obligations were paid.

Upon cross-examination defendant admitted that the former partnership in which the earnings were to be retained until the obligations were repaid was substantially different from the present partnership. The former partnership was a limited partnership and provided for a definite term of five years and a partnership at will thereafter. Defendant insists, however, that the method of operation of the former partnership showed an understanding that all obligations were to be repaid from profits. He nevertheless concedes that there was no understanding as to the term of the present partnership in the event of losses. He was asked: '(W)as there any discussion with reference to the continuation of the business in the event of losses?' He replied, 'Not that I can remember.' He was then asked, 'Did you have any understanding with Mr. Page, your brother, the plaintiff in this action, as to how the obligations were to be paid if there were losses?' He replied, 'Not that I can remember. I can't remember discussing that at all. We never figured on losing, I guess.'

Viewing this evidence most favorably for defendant, it proves only that the partners expected to meet current expenses from current income and to recoup their investment if the business were successful.

Defendant contends that such an expectation is sufficient to create a partnership for a term under the rule of *Owen v. Cohen*, 19 Cal.2d 147, 150, 119 P.2d 713. In that case we held that when a partner advances a sum of money to a partnership with the understanding that the amount contributed was to be a loan to the partnership and was to be repaid as soon as feasible from the prospective profits of the business, the partnership is for the term reasonably required to repay the loan. It is true that *Owen v. Cohen*, supra, and other cases hold that partners may impliedly agree to continue in business until a certain sum of money is earned (*Mervyn Investment Co. v. Biber*, 184 Cal. 637, 641–642, 194 P. 1037), or one or more partners recoup their investments (*Vangel v. Vangel*, 116 Cal.App.2d 615, 625, 254 P.2d 919), or until certain debts are paid (*Owen v.

Cohen, supra, 19 Cal.2d at page 150, 119 P.2d at page 714), or until certain property could be disposed of on favorable terms (*Shannon v. Hudson*, 161 Cal.App.2d 44, 48, 325 P.2d 1022). In each of these cases, however, the implied agreement found support in the evidence.

In *Owen v. Cohen, supra,* the partners borrowed substantial amounts of money to launch the enterprise and there was an understanding that the loans would be repaid from partnership profits. In *Vangel v. Vangel*, supra, one partner loaned his co-partner money to invest in the partnership with the understanding that the money would be repaid from partnership profits. In *Mervyn Investment Co. v. Biber*, supra, one partner contributed all the capital, the other contributed his services, and it was understood that upon the repayment of the contributed capital from partnership profits the partner who contributed his services would receive a one-third interest in the partnership assets. In each of these cases the court properly held that the partners impliedly promised to continue the partnership for a term reasonably required to allow the partnership to earn sufficient money to accomplish the understood objective. In *Shannon v. Hudson*, supra, the parties entered into a joint venture to build and operate a motel until it could be sold upon favorable and mutually satisfactory terms, and the court held that the joint venture was for a reasonable term sufficient to accomplish the purpose of the joint venture.

In the instant case, however, defendant failed to prove any facts from which an agreement to continue the partnership for a term may be implied. The understanding to which defendant testified was no more than a common hope that the partnership earnings would pay for all the necessary expenses. Such a hope does not establish even by implication a 'definite term or particular undertaking' as required by section 15031, subdivision (1)(b) of the Corporations Code. All partnerships are ordinarily entered into with the hope that they will be profitable, but that alone does not make them all partnerships for a term and obligate the partners to continue in the partnerships until all of the losses over a period of many years have been recovered.

Defendant contends that plaintiff is acting in bad faith and is attempting to use his superior financial position to appropriate the now profitable business of the partnership. Defendant has invested $43,000 in the firm, and owing to the long period of losses his interest in the partnership assets is very small. The fact that plaintiff's wholly-owned corporation holds a $47,000 demand note of the partnership may make it difficult to sell the business as a going concern. Defendant fears that upon dissolution he will receive very little and that plaintiff, who is the managing partner and knows how to conduct the operations of the partnership, will receive a business that has become very profitable because of the establishment of Vandenberg Air Force Base in its vicinity. Defendant charges that plaintiff has been content to share the losses but now that the business has become profitable he wishes to keep all the gains.

There is no showing in the record of bad faith or that the improved profit situation is more than temporary. In any event these contentions are irrelevant to the issue whether the partnership is for a term or at will. Since, however, this action is for a declaratory judgment and will be the basis for future action by the parties, it is appropriate to point out that defendant is amply protected by the fiduciary duties of co-partners.

Even though the Uniform Partnership Act provides that a partnership at will may be dissolved by the express will of any partner (Corp.Code, § 15031, subd. (1) (b)), this power, like any other power held by a fiduciary, must be exercised in good faith.

We have often stated that 'partners are trustees for each other, and in all proceedings connected with the conduct of the partnership every partner is bound to act in the highest good faith to his copartner, and may not obtain any advantage over him in the partnership affairs by the slightest misrepresentation, concealment, threat, or adverse pressure of any kind." [*Citations omitted.*] . . . .

A partner at will is not bound to remain in a partnership, regardless of whether the business is profitable or unprofitable. A partner may not, however, by use of adverse pressure 'freeze out' a co-partner and appropriate the business to his own use. A partner may not dissolve a partnership to gain the benefits of the business for himself, unless he fully compensates his co-partner for his share of the prospective business opportunity. In this regard his fiduciary duties are at least as great as those of a shareholder of a corporation.

In the case of In re Security Finance Co., 49 Cal.2d 370, 376–377, 317 P.2d 1, 5 we stated that although shareholders representing 50 per cent of the voting power have a right under Corporations Code,§ 4600 to dissolve a corporation, they may not exercise such right in order 'to defraud the other shareholders [*Citation omitted.*], to 'freeze out' minority shareholders [*Citation omitted.*] or to sell the assets of the dissolved corporation at an inadequate price [*Citation omitted.*].

Likewise in the instant case, plaintiff has the power to dissolve the partnership by express notice to defendant. If, however, it is proved that plaintiff acted in bad faith and violated his fiduciary duties by attempting to appropriate to his own use the new prosperity of the partnership without adequate compensation to his co-partner, the dissolution would be wrongful and the plaintiff would be liable as provided by subdivision (2)(a) of Corporations Code,§ 15038 (rights of partners upon wrongful dissolution) for violation of the implied agreement not to exclude defendant wrongfully from the partnership business opportunity.

The judgment is reversed.

Bohatch v. Butler & Binion

977 S.W.2d 543 (Tex. 1998)

ENOCH, JUSTICE, delivered the opinion of the Court, in which GONZALEZ, OWEN, BAKER, and HANKINSON, JUSTICES, join.

Partnerships exist by the agreement of the partners; partners have no duty to remain partners. The issue in this case is whether we should create an exception to this rule by holding that a partnership has a duty not to expel a partner for reporting suspected overbilling by another partner. The trial court rendered judgment for Colette Bohatch on her breach of fiduciary duty claim against Butler & Binion and several of its partners (collectively, "the firm"). The court of appeals held that there was no evidence that the firm breached a fiduciary duty and reversed the trial court's tort judgment; however, the court of appeals found evidence of a breach of the partnership agreement and rendered judgment for Bohatch on this ground. 905 S.W.2d 597. We affirm the court of appeals' judgment.

I. FACTS

Bohatch became an associate in the Washington, D.C., office of Butler & Binion in 1986 after working for several years as Deputy Assistant General Counsel at the Federal Energy Regulatory Commission. John McDonald, the managing partner of the office, and Richard Powers, a partner, were the only other attorneys in the Washington office. The office did work for Pennzoil almost exclusively.

Bohatch was made partner in February 1990. She then began receiving internal firm reports showing the number of hours each attorney worked, billed, and collected. From her review of these reports, Bohatch became concerned that McDonald was overbilling Pennzoil and discussed the matter with Powers. Together they reviewed and copied portions of McDonald's time diary. Bohatch's review of McDonald's time entries increased her concern.

On July 15, 1990, Bohatch met with Louis Paine, the firm's managing partner, to report her concern that McDonald was overbilling Pennzoil. Paine said he would investigate. Later that day, Bohatch told Powers about her conversation with Paine.

The following day, McDonald met with Bohatch and informed her that Pennzoil was not satisfied with her work and wanted her work to be supervised. Bohatch testified that this was the first time she had ever heard criticism of her work for Pennzoil.

The next day, Bohatch repeated her concerns to Paine and to R. Hayden Burns and Marion E. McDaniel, two other members of the firm's management committee, in a telephone conversation. Over the next month, Paine and Burns investigated Bohatch's complaint. They reviewed the Pennzoil bills and supporting computer print-outs for those bills. They then discussed the allegations with Pennzoil in-house counsel John Chapman, the firm's primary contact with Pennzoil. Chapman, who had a long-standing relationship with McDonald, responded that Pennzoil was satisfied that the bills were reasonable.

In August, Paine met with Bohatch and told her that the firm's investigation revealed no basis for her contentions. He added that she should begin looking for other employment, but that the firm would continue to provide her a monthly draw, insurance coverage, office space, and a secretary. After this meeting, Bohatch received no further work assignments from the firm.

In January 1991, the firm denied Bohatch a year-end partnership distribution for 1990 and reduced her tentative distribution share for 1991 to zero. In June, the firm paid Bohatch her monthly draw and told her that this draw would be her last. Finally, in August, the firm gave Bohatch until November to vacate her office.

By September, Bohatch had found new employment. She filed this suit on October 18, 1991, and the firm voted formally to expel her from the partnership three days later, October 21, 1991.

. . . . The jury found that the firm breached the partnership agreement and its fiduciary duty. It awarded Bohatch $57,000 for past lost wages, $250,000 for past mental anguish, $4,000,000 total in punitive damages (this amount was apportioned against several defendants), and attorney's fees. The trial court rendered judgment for Bohatch in the amounts found by the jury, except it disallowed attorney's fees because the judgment was based in tort. After suggesting remittitur, which Bohatch accepted, the trial court reduced the punitive damages to around $237,000.

All parties appealed. The court of appeals held that the firm's only duty to Bohatch was not to expel her in bad faith. 905 S.W.2d at 602. The court of appeals stated that " '[b]ad faith' in this context means only that partners cannot expel another partner for self-gain." *Id.* Finding no evidence that the firm expelled Bohatch for self-gain, the court concluded that Bohatch could not recover for breach of fiduciary duty. *Id.* at 604. However, the court concluded that the firm breached the partnership agreement when it reduced Bohatch's tentative partnership distribution for 1991 to zero without notice, and when it terminated her draw three months before she left. *Id.* at 606. The court concluded that Bohatch was entitled to recover $35,000 in lost earnings for 1991 but none for 1990, and no mental anguish damages. *Id.* at 606–07. Accordingly, the court rendered judgment for Bohatch for $35,000 plus $225,000 in attorney's fees. *Id.* at 608.

II. BREACH OF FIDUCIARY DUTY

We have long recognized as a matter of common law that "[t]he relationship between . . . partners . . . is fiduciary in character, and imposes upon all the participants the obligation of loyalty to the joint concern and of the utmost good faith, fairness, and honesty in their dealings with each other with respect to matters pertaining to the enterprise." *Fitz-Gerald v. Hull,* 150 Tex. 39, 237 S.W.2d 256, 264 (1951) (quotation omitted). Yet, partners have no obligation to remain partners; "at the heart of the partnership concept is the principle that partners may choose with whom they wish to be associated." *Gelder Med. Group v. Webber,* 41 N.Y.2d 680, 394 N.Y.S.2d 867, 870–71, 363 N.E.2d 573, 577 (1977). The issue presented, one of first impression, is whether the fiduciary relationship between and among partners creates an exception to the at-will nature of partnerships; that is, in this case, whether it gives rise to a duty not to expel a partner who reports suspected overbilling by another partner.

. . . . [T]he partnership agreement contemplates expulsion of a partner and prescribes procedures to be followed, but it does not specify or limit the grounds for expulsion. Thus, while Bohatch's claim that she was expelled in an *improper way* is governed by the partnership agreement, her claim that she was expelled for an *improper reason* is not. Therefore, we look to the common law to find the principles governing Bohatch's claim that the firm breached a duty when it expelled her.

Courts in other states have held that a partnership may expel a partner for purely business reasons. *See St. Joseph's Reg'l Health Ctr. v. Munos,* 326 Ark. 605, 934 S.W.2d 192, 197 (1996) (holding that partner's termination of another partner's contract to manage services performed by medical partnership was not breach of fiduciary duty because termination was for business purpose); *Waite v. Sylvester,* 131 N.H. 663, 560 A.2d 619, 622–23 (1989) (holding that removal of partner as managing partner of limited partnership was not breach of fiduciary duty because it was based on legitimate business purpose); *Leigh v. Crescent Square, Ltd.,* 80 Ohio App.3d 231, 608 N.E.2d 1166, 1170 (1992) ("Taking into account the general partners' past problems and the previous litigation wherein Leigh was found to have acted in contravention of the partnership's best interests, the ouster was instituted in good faith and for legitimate business purposes."). Further, courts recognize that a law firm can expel a partner to protect relationships both within the firm and with clients. *See Lawlis v. Kightlinger & Gray,* 562 N.E.2d 435, 442 (Ind.App.1990) (holding that law firm did not breach fiduciary duty by expelling partner after partner's successful struggle against alcoholism because "if a partner's propensity toward alcohol has the potential to damage his firm's good will or reputation for astuteness in the practice of law, simple prudence dictates the exercise of corrective action . . . since the survival of the partnership itself potentially is at stake"); *Holman v. Coie,* 11 Wash.App. 195, 522 P.2d 515, 523 (1974) (finding no breach of fiduciary duty where law firm expelled two partners because of their contentious behavior during executive committee meetings and because one, as state senator, made speech offensive to major client). Finally, many courts have held that a partnership can expel a partner without breaching any duty in order to resolve a "fundamental schism." *See Waite,* 560 A.2d at 623 (concluding that in removing partner as managing partner "the partners acted in good faith to resolve the 'fundamental schism' between them"); *Heller v. Pillsbury Madison & Sutro,* 50 Cal.App.4th 1367, 58 Cal.Rptr.2d 336, 348 (1996) (holding that law firm did not breach fiduciary duty when it expelled partner who was not as productive as firm expected and who was offensive to some of firm's major clients); *Levy v. Nassau Queens Med. Group,* 102 A.D.2d 845, 476 N.Y.S.2d 613, 614 (1984) (concluding that expelling partner because of "[p]olicy disagreements" is not "bad faith").

The fiduciary duty that partners owe one another does not encompass a duty to remain partners or else answer in tort damages. Nonetheless, Bohatch and several distinguished legal scholars urge this Court to recognize that public policy requires a limited duty to remain partners—*i.e.,* a partnership must retain a whistleblower partner. They argue that such an extension of a partner's fiduciary duty is necessary because permitting a law firm to retaliate against a partner who in good faith reports suspected overbilling would discourage compliance with rules of professional conduct and thereby hurt clients.

While this argument is not without some force, we must reject it. A partnership exists solely because the partners choose to place personal confidence and trust in one another. *See Holman,* 522 P.2d at 524 ("The foundation of a professional relationship is personal confidence and trust."). Just as a partner can be expelled, without a breach of any common law duty, over disagreements about firm policy or to resolve some other "fundamental schism," a partner can be expelled for accusing another partner of overbilling without subjecting the partnership to tort damages. Such charges, whether true or not, may have a profound effect on the personal confidence and trust essential to the partner relationship. Once such charges are made, partners may find it impossible to continue to work together to their mutual benefit and the benefit of their clients.

We are sensitive to the concern expressed by the dissenting Justices that "retaliation against a partner who tries in good faith to correct or report perceived misconduct virtually assures that others will not take these appropriate steps in the future." 977 S.W.2d at 561 (Spector, J., dissenting). However, the dissenting Justices do not explain how the trust relationship necessary both for the firm's existence and for representing clients can survive such serious accusations by one partner against another. The threat of tort liability for expulsion would tend to force partners to remain in untenable circumstance—suspicious of and angry with each other—to their own detriment and that of their clients whose matters are neglected by lawyers distracted with intra-firm frictions.

Although concurring in the Court's judgment, Justice Hecht criticizes the Court for failing to "address amici's concerns that failing to impose liability will discourage attorneys from reporting unethical conduct." 977 S.W.2d at 556 (Hecht, J., concurring). To address the scholars' concerns, he proposes that a whistleblower be protected from expulsion, but only if the report, irrespective of being made in good faith, is proved to be correct. We fail to see how such an approach encourages compliance with ethical rules more than the approach we adopt today. Furthermore, the amici's position is that a reporting attorney must be in good faith, not that the attorney must be right. In short, Justice Hecht's approach ignores the question Bohatch presents, the amici write about, and the firm challenges—whether a partnership violates a fiduciary duty when it expels a partner who in good faith reports suspected ethical violations. The concerns of the amici are best addressed by a rule that clearly demarcates an attorney's ethical duties and the parameters of tort liability, rather than redefining "whistleblower."

We emphasize that our refusal to create an exception to the at-will nature of partnerships in no way obviates the ethical duties of lawyers. Such duties sometimes necessitate difficult decisions, as when a lawyer suspects overbilling by a colleague. The fact that the ethical duty to report may create an irreparable schism between partners neither excuses failure to report nor transforms expulsion as a means of resolving that schism into a tort.

We hold that the firm did not owe Bohatch a duty not to expel her for reporting suspected overbilling by another partner.

III. BREACH OF THE PARTNERSHIP AGREEMENT

The court of appeals concluded that the firm breached the partnership agreement by reducing Bohatch's tentative distribution for 1991 to zero without the requisite notice. 905 S.W.2d at 606. The firm contests this finding on the ground that the management committee had the right to set tentative and year-end bonuses. However, the partnership agreement guarantees a monthly draw of $7,500 per month regardless of the tentative distribution. Moreover, the firm's right to reduce the bonus was contingent upon providing proper notice to Bohatch. The firm does not dispute that it did not give Bohatch notice that the firm was reducing her tentative distribution. Accordingly, the court of appeals did not err in finding the firm liable for breach of the partnership agreement. Moreover, because Bohatch's damages sound in contract, and because she sought attorney's fees at trial under section 38.001(8) of the Texas Civil Practice and Remedies Code, we affirm the court of appeals' award of Bohatch's attorney's fees.

* * * *

We affirm the court of appeals' judgment.

* * * *

HECHT, JUSTICE, concurring in the judgment.

The Court holds that partners in a law firm have no common-law liability for expelling one of their number for accusing another of unethical conduct. The dissent argues that partners in a law firm are liable for such conduct. Both views are unqualified; neither concedes or even considers whether "always" and "never" are separated by any distance. I think they must be. The Court's position is directly contrary to that of some of the leading scholars on the subject who have appeared here as amici curiae. . . .

The issue is not well developed; in fact, to our knowledge we are the first court to address it. It seems to me there must be some circumstances when expulsion for reporting an ethical violation is culpable and other circumstances when it is not. I have trouble justifying a 500-partner firm's expulsion of a partner for reporting overbilling of a client that saves the firm not only from ethical complaints but from liability to the client. But I cannot see how a five-partner firm can legitimately survive one partner's accusations that another is unethical. Between two such extreme examples I see a lot of ground.

This case does not force a choice between diametrically opposite views. Here, the report of unethical conduct, though made in good faith, was incorrect. That fact is significant to me because I think a law firm can always expel a partner for bad judgment, whether it relates to the representation of clients or the relationships with other partners, and whether it is in good faith. I would hold that Butler & Binion did not breach its fiduciary duty by expelling Colette Bohatch because she made a good-faith but nevertheless extremely serious charge against a senior partner that threatened the firm's relationship with an important client, her charge proved groundless, and her relationship with her partners was destroyed in the process. I cannot, however, extrapolate from this case, as the Court does, that no law firm can ever be liable for expelling a partner for reporting unethical conduct. Accordingly, I concur only in the Court's judgment.

* * * *

In only one case has an appellate court confronted circumstances which it believed might give rise to liability for a breach of fiduciary duty in expelling a partner. In *Nosal,* an attorney claimed that he had been expelled from his firm because of his insistence on his right under the partnership agreement to inspect firm records which he believed would show misconduct by the firm's management. The court reversed summary judgment for the firm, holding that Nosal's evidence raised a fact issue that his expulsion was in breach of the fiduciary duty owed him. *Nosal,* 215 Ill.Dec. at 849, 664 N.E.2d at 246.

Scholars are divided over not only how but whether partners' common-law fiduciary duty to each other limit expulsion of a partner. There is also disagreement over the impact of the Revised Uniform Partnership Act (which, as I have noted, has been adopted in Texas) on this issue. [*Citations Omitted.*] Nine distinguished law professors [*Professors Omitted.*] have argued in amicus curiae briefs that expulsion of a partner in bad faith is a breach of fiduciary duty, and that expulsion for self-gain is in bad faith, but so is expulsion for reporting unethical conduct. From a canvass of the various commentators' arguments it is fair to say that the law governing liability for expulsion of a partner is relatively uncertain.

B

No court has considered whether expulsion of a partner from a law firm for reporting unethical conduct is a breach of fiduciary duty. Several courts have concluded that expulsion to remedy a fundamental schism in a professional firm is not a breach of fiduciary duty. There is hardly a schism more fundamental than that caused by one partner's accusing another of unethical conduct. If a partner can be expelled because of disagreements over nothing more significant than firm policy and abrasive personal conduct, as cases have held, surely a partner can be expelled for accusing another partner of something as serious as unethical conduct. Once such charges are raised, I find it hard to imagine how partners could continue to work together to their mutual benefit and the benefit of their clients. The trust essential to the relationship would have been destroyed. Indeed, I should think that a lawyer who was unable to convince his or her partners to rectify the unethical conduct of another would choose to withdraw from the firm rather than continue in association with lawyers who did not adhere to high ethical standards.

But I am troubled by the arguments of the distinguished amici curiae that permitting a law firm to retaliate against a partner for reporting unethical behavior would discourage compliance with rules of conduct, hurt clients, and contravene public policy. Their arguments have force, but they do not explain how a relationship of trust necessary for both the existence of the firm and the representation of its clients can survive such serious accusations by one partner against another. The threat of liability for expulsion would tend to force partners to remain in untenable circumstances—suspicious of and angry with each other—to their own detriment and that of their clients whose matters are neglected by lawyers distracted with intra-firm frictions. If "at the heart of the partnership concept is the principle that partners may choose with whom they wish to be associated", *Gelder,* 394 N.Y.S.2d at 870–871, 363 N.E.2d at 577, surely partners are not obliged to continue to associate with someone who has accused one of them of unethical conduct.

This very difficult issue need not be finally resolved in this case. Bohatch did not report unethical conduct; she reported what she *believed,* presumably in good faith but nevertheless mistakenly, to be unethical conduct. At the time, the District of Columbia Code of Professional Responsibility provided that "[a] lawyer shall not . . . collect a[ ] . . . clearly excessive fee." D.C.CODE OF PROF'L. RESP. DR 2–106(A) (1990). Pennzoil's conclusion that Butler & Binion's fees were reasonable, reached after being made aware of Bohatch's concerns that McDonald's time was overstated, establishes that Butler & Binion did not collect excessive fees from Pennzoil. A fee that a client as sophisticated as Pennzoil considers reasonable is not clearly excessive simply because a lawyer believes it could have been less. Bohatch's argument that Pennzoil had other reasons not to complain of Butler & Binion's bills is simply beside the point. Whatever its motivations, Pennzoil found the bills reasonable, thereby establishing that McDonald had not overbilled in violation of ethical rules. Bohatch's argument that Pennzoil's assessment of the bills was prejudiced by Butler & Binion's misrepresentations about her is implausible. There is nothing to suggest that Pennzoil would have thought clearly excessive legal fees were reasonable simply because it did not like Bohatch.

Bohatch's real concern was not that fees to Pennzoil were excessive—she had never even seen the bills and had no idea what the fees, or fee arrangements, were—but that McDonald was misrepresenting the number of hours he worked. The District of Columbia Code of Professional Responsibility at the time also prohibited lawyers from engaging in "conduct involving dishonesty, fraud, deceit or misrepresentation." *Id.* DR 1–102(A)(4). But there is no evidence that McDonald actually engaged in such conduct. At most, Bohatch showed only that McDonald kept sloppy time records, not that he deceived his partners or clients. Neither his partners nor his major client accused McDonald of dishonesty, even after reviewing his bills and time records. Bohatch complains that Butler & Binion did not fully investigate McDonald's billing practices. Assuming Butler & Binion had some duty to investigate Bohatch's charges, it discharged that duty by determining that Pennzoil considered its bills reasonable. (The district court, as the court of appeals noted, excluded evidence that Paine and McDonald himself went so far as to report the charges against McDonald to the lawyer disciplinary authority, which exonerated him. 905 S.W.2d at 607.)

Even if expulsion of a partner for reporting unethical conduct might be a breach of fiduciary duty, expulsion for *mistakenly* reporting unethical conduct cannot be a breach of fiduciary duty. At the very least, a mistake so serious indicates a lack of judgment warranting expulsion. No one would argue that an attorney could not be expelled from a firm for a serious error in judgment about a client's affairs or even the firm's affairs. If Bohatch and McDonald had disagreed over what position to take in a particular case for Pennzoil, or over whether Butler & Binion should continue to operate its Washington office, the firm could have determined that she should be expelled for the health of the firm, even if Bohatch had acted in complete good faith. Reporting unethical conduct where none existed is no different. If, as in *Gelder,* a partner can be expelled for being blunt, surely a partner can be expelled for a serious error in judgment.

Butler & Binion's expulsion of Bohatch did not discourage ethical conduct; it discouraged errors of judgment, which ought to be discouraged. Butler & Binion did not violate its fiduciary duty to Bohatch.

III

* * * *

. . . . The issue is not whether partners have a fiduciary duty to remain partners, but whether in choosing not to they can breach their fiduciary duty to one another. The cases I have cited indicate that partners cannot withdraw from a partnership or expel another partner solely to prevent a partner from obtaining the benefit of a financial opportunity that should have been the partnership's. *E.g. Leigh*, 608 N.E.2d at 1170; *Holman,* 522 P.2d at 523. That is not Bohatch's claim, but her claim is similar. She argues that Butler & Binion breached its fiduciary duty to her, not merely by expelling her, but by expelling her for reporting McDonald's unethical conduct.

The Court's claim that it is "sensitive" to the concerns of the amici curiae is belied by its failure even to understand those concerns. The amici plainly argue that "breach of fiduciary duty should be established if it can be shown that the expelling partner violated his ethical duties or that the expelled partner was terminated for complying with her ethical responsibilities." The Court never addresses this issue directly, holding only that people cannot be forced to remain partners. The Court makes no mention of the amici's breach of fiduciary duty argument. Nor does the Court address amici's concerns that failing to impose liability will discourage attorneys from reporting unethical conduct. The Court states only that its decision "in no way obviates the ethical duties of lawyers." Again, the statement is correct but irrelevant. The argument is that failing to punish retaliation for reporting ethics violations discourages such reporting because it leaves the reporting attorney without any defense to such retaliation. The concern is a legitimate one, but the Court simply ignores it.

It is no answer to say, as the Court does, that those who share this concern cannot convincingly explain how partners can share the trust requisite for a law firm (or at least some law firms) if they resent another partner for having "snitched" or "ratted on" another, as they might refer to the reporting of an ethical violation. Bohatch and the amici do not even attempt to explain away this practical reality. Still, the fact that their concerns raise others does not mean that their concerns are not real.

Finally, the Court mischaracterizes my position, just as it does the amici's arguments. It simply is not true that I "propose[ ] that a whistle blower be protected from expulsion, but only if the report, irrespective of being made in good faith, is proved to be correct." *Ante* at 547. As I have explained, I would not attempt to define when a law firm partner expelled for reporting unethical conduct can recover damages because I do not regard it as essential to the disposition of this case to do so. I would not hold that being correct is enough, only that being incorrect precludes recovery, at least in these circumstances. My criticism of the Court is not that another bright-line rule—one based on whether a report was correct—would be better, but that no bright-line rule should be adopted when the full ramifications of so broad a rule have not been adequately considered. It should come as no surprise to anyone that a lawyer can be fired for being incorrect, albeit in good faith. A lawyer can always be terminated for being incorrect about legal matters. It is, after all, a lawyer's judgment that is important, not her sincerity. Bohatch's charges were not merely an innocent mistake. They caused the expenditure of a significant amount of time in investigation, the report of possible overbilling to one of the firm's major clients, potentially jeopardizing that relationship, and an impossible strain on three lawyers working together on the same business for the same client in a small but important office of the firm.

Without offering a solution to the problems the amici raise, the Court adopts an absolute rule: a law firm that expels a partner for reporting ethics violations has no liability to the partner under any circumstances. The rule is ill-advised, particularly when it is far broader than necessary to address Bohatch's claims.

* * * *

I do not disagree with the Court's treatment of Bohatch's claim for breach of contract. Accordingly, I concur in the Court's judgment but not in its opinion.

JUSTICE SPECTOR, joined by CHIEF JUSTICE PHILLIPS, dissenting.

> [W]hat's the use you learning to do right when it's troublesome to do right and ain't no trouble to do wrong, and the wages is just the same?
>
> —*The Adventures of Huckleberry Finn*

The issue in this appeal is whether law partners violate a fiduciary duty by retaliating against one partner for questioning the billing practices of another partner. I would hold that partners violate their fiduciary duty to one another by punishing compliance with the Disciplinary Rules of Professional Conduct. Accordingly, I dissent.

I.

This dispute arose after Colette Bohatch, a partner in Butler & Binion's Washington, D.C. office, expressed concerns to the firm's managing partner, Louis Paine, about possible overbilling by another partner, John McDonald. The firm had hired Bohatch to join McDonald as one of three attorneys in the firm's Washington office, which was devoted almost exclusively to Pennzoil matters. Bohatch had several years' experience working at the Federal Energy Regulatory Commission, ending her tenure there as Deputy Assistant General Counsel for Gas and Oil Litigation.

Once Bohatch became a partner in Butler & Binion, just over two years after being hired, she began receiving billing reports that indicated McDonald was charging Pennzoil for eight to twelve hours of work each day. Bohatch developed doubts about McDonald's billing practices after observing that he only worked an average of three to four hours per day.

She first expressed her suspicions about McDonald's billing practices to Richard Powers, the other partner in the Washington office, when he approached her with similar concerns. Together, Powers and Bohatch examined McDonald's time diary. They saw many vague entries that did not comply with firm requirements for keeping time records; Bohatch thought the records might have been falsified in an attempt to conceal overbilling. Powers told Bohatch that she should do something about her concerns.

Before reporting her suspicions, Bohatch reviewed the District of Columbia's ethical rules and consulted counsel. She ultimately met with Louis Paine, the firm's managing partner, to report that she suspected McDonald was overbilling Pennzoil on the level of $20,000 to $25,000 each month. Paine told Bohatch that she was right to report her concerns to him. Within a few hours, Bohatch informed Powers, upon his inquiry, that she had made a report to Paine.

The *day after* Bohatch made her report and immediately after an hour-long conversation with Powers, McDonald, the partner whose billing was in question, told Bohatch that Pennzoil had been dissatisfied with her work and that he would be supervising her future work. Bohatch testified that McDonald delivered this criticism with "red-faced anger." She also maintained that she had never before heard any criticism of her work for Pennzoil. Bohatch phoned Paine that night and expressed fear that McDonald's criticism was a response to her report. Within a few weeks, McDonald removed her from a pending Pennzoil case, reassigning it to an associate of one month's tenure, and barred her from taking on any new work for Pennzoil.

Within six weeks of Bohatch's initial report, Paine met with her and told her she should look for a new position. . . .

Bohatch contends that instead of properly investigating and responding to the allegations, McDonald, Paine, and the firm's management committee immediately began a retaliatory course of action that culminated in her expulsion from the partnership. The partners deny these claims.

Paine and another partner on the management committee, Hayden Burns, conducted an investigation of the overbilling allegations and testified at trial that they concluded the allegations were groundless. They maintain that Bohatch made her report for selfish or spiteful reasons, not out of a desire to fulfill her ethical responsibilities as a lawyer.

The jury heard Bohatch's and the firm's versions of the events and weighed the credibility of Bohatch, McDonald, Paine, and other witnesses. It returned a verdict in favor of Bohatch, finding that the defendants had failed to comply with the partnership agreement and had breached their fiduciary duty to Bohatch. . . .

* * * *

It is true that no high court has considered the issue of whether expulsion of a partner for complying with ethical rules violates law partners' fiduciary duty. The dearth of authority in this area does not, however, diminish the significance of this case. Instead, the scarcity of guiding case law only heightens the importance of this Court's decision.

* * * *

In light of this Court's role in setting standards to govern attorneys' conduct, it is particularly inappropriate for the Court to deny recourse to attorneys wronged for adhering to the Disciplinary Rules. [*Citation Omitted.*] I would hold that in this case the law partners violated their fiduciary duty by retaliating against a fellow partner who made a good-faith effort to alert her partners to the possible overbilling of a client.

C.

The duty to prevent overbilling and other misconduct exists for the protection of the client. Even if a report turns out to be mistaken or a client ultimately consents to the behavior in question, as in this case, retaliation against a partner who tries in good faith to correct or report perceived misconduct virtually assures that others will not take these appropriate steps in the future. Although I agree with the majority that partners have a right not to continue a partnership with someone against their will, they may still be liable for damages directly resulting from terminating that relationship. [*Citation Omitted.*]

III.

The Court's writing in this case sends an inappropriate signal to lawyers and to the public that the rules of professional responsibility are subordinate to a law firm's other interests. Under the majority opinion's vision for the legal profession, the wages would not even be the same for "doing right"; they diminish considerably and leave an attorney who acts ethically and in good faith without recourse. Accordingly, I respectfully dissent.

QUESTIONS

1. Given the outcome in the *Bohatch* case above, if a partner at a firm were to seek your advice about how to handle a situation in which he or she suspected a colleague of overbilling clients, how would you advise them to proceed? Note that Rule 8.3(a) of the ABA Model Rules of Professional Conduct (the "RPC") provides that: "A lawyer who knows that another lawyer has committed a violation of the Rules of Professional Conduct that raises a substantial question as to that lawyer's honesty, trustworthiness or fitness as a lawyer in other respects, shall inform the appropriate professional authority." In addition Rule 5.1(c) of the RPC provides that: "A lawyer shall be responsible for another lawyer's violation of the Rules of Professional Conduct if: . . . (2) the lawyer is a partner or has comparable managerial authority in the law firm in which the other lawyer practices, or has direct supervisory authority over the other lawyer, and knows of the conduct at a time when its consequences can be avoided or mitigated but fails to take reasonable remedial action." *See also In re Cohen,* 847 A.2d 1162, 1163 (D.C. 2004) (holding a senior attorney responsible for a subordinate lawyer's violation of the D.C. Rules of Professional Conduct); and *People v. Reuler,* 2002 WL 31151184 (Colo. O.P.D.J. 2002)(suspending an attorney for nine months for, *inter alia,* ratifying and failing to take remedial action with respect to another attorney's false or inaccurate billing statement in violation of the Colorado Rules of Professional Conduct 5.1 and 8.4(c)).

2. As discussed above in the note regarding *Serapion v. Martinez, supra,* there are many protections afforded to employees that are not necessarily available to partners in a partnership. Might Colette Bohatch been treated differently if she were an associate at Butler & Binion rather than a partner? Is it appropriate to provide different protections for employees than for partners?

3. Note that the Sarbanes-Oxley Act of 2002 ("SOX") requires attorneys to take certain actions when they encounter evidence of a "material violation" of securities law a breach of fiduciary duty or a similar violation. SOX, as well as the Dodd-Frank Wall Street Reform and Consumer Protection Act (the "Dodd-Frank Act"), also provides protections for "whistleblower" attorneys who provide information about material violations of securities laws to the Securities and Exchange Commission (the "SEC"). Is there any reason to extend such protections to attorneys who act as "whistleblowers" with respect to partners in their own firms?

C. Partnership Opportunities and the Specific Rules Applied to Such Opportunities

The following case, *Meinhard v. Salmon* (164 N.E. 545 (N.Y. 1928)), is one of the best known partnership cases relating to the fiduciary duty of loyalty. This seminal case is about the rights of other partners to share in a partnership opportunity and the right and/or ability of one partner to take advantage of an opportunity which might rightfully belong to the partnership or its partners. In the *Meinhard v. Salmon* opinion, Judge Cardozo coined the famous punctilio of honor phrase. ("Many forms of conduct permissible in a workaday world for those acting at arm's length, are forbidden to those bound by fiduciary ties. . . . Not honesty alone, but the punctilio of an honor the most sensitive, is then the standard of behavior." (*Id.* at 546.)) Even though the holding itself and the subsequent law create a balanced assessment of the extent of a partner's right to take advantage of an opportunity, this phrase is often quoted to support any proposition involving fiduciary duty among partners to emphasize the high duty one partner owes to another.

Meinhard v. Salmon

249 N.Y. 458, 164 N.E. 545 (N.Y. 1928)

CARDOZO, C. J.:

On April 10, 1902, Louisa M. Gerry leased to the defendant Walter J. Salmon the premises known as the Hotel Bristol at the northwest corner of Forty-Second street and Fifth avenue in the city of New York. The lease was for a term of 20 years, commencing May 1, 1902, and ending April 30, 1922. The lessee undertook to change the hotel building for use as shops and offices at a cost of $200,000. Alterations and additions were to be accretions to the land.

Salmon, while in course of treaty with the lessor as to the execution of the lease, was in course of treaty with Meinhard, the plaintiff, for the necessary funds. The result was a joint venture with terms embodied in a writing. Meinhard was to pay to Salmon half of the moneys requisite to reconstruct, alter, manage, and operate the property. Salmon was to pay to Meinhard 40 per cent. of the net profits for the first five years of the lease and 50 per cent. for the years thereafter. If there were losses, each party was to bear them equally. Salmon, however, was to have sole power to 'manage, lease, underlet and operate' the building. There were to be certain pre-emptive rights for each in the contingency of death.

The two were coadventures, subject to fiduciary duties akin to those of partners. *King v. Barnes,* 109 N. Y. 267, 16 N. E. 332. As to this we are all agreed. The heavier weight of duty rested, however, upon Salmon. He was a coadventurer with Meinhard, but he was manager as well. During the early years of the enterprise, the building, reconstructed, was operated at a loss. If the relation had then ended, Meinhard as well as Salmon would have carried a heavy burden. Later the profits became large with the result that for each of the investors there came a rich return. For each the venture had its phases of fair weather and of foul. The two were in it jointly, for better or for worse.

When the lease was near its end, Elbridge T. Gerry had become the owner of the reversion. He owned much other property in the neighborhood, one lot adjoining the Bristol building on Fifth avenue and four lots on Forty-Second street. He had a plan to lease the entire tract for a long term to some one who would destroy the buildings then existing and put up another in their place. In the latter part of 1921, he submitted such a project to several capitalists and dealers. He was unable to carry it through with any of them. Then, in January, 1922, with less than four months of the lease to run, he approached the defendant Salmon. The result was a new lease to the Midpoint Realty Company, which is owned and controlled by Salmon, a lease covering the whole tract, and involving a huge outlay. The term is to be 20 years, but successive covenants for renewal will extend it to a maximum of 80 years at the will of either party. The existing buildings may remain unchanged for seven years. They are then to be torn down, and a new building to cost $3,000,000 is to be placed upon the site. The rental, which under the Bristol lease was only $55,000, is to be from $350,000 to $475,000 for the properties so combined. Salmon personally guaranteed the performance by the lessee of the covenants of the new lease until such time as the new building had been completed and fully paid for.

The lease between Gerry and the Midpoint Realty Company was signed and delivered on January 25, 1922. Salmon had not told Meinhard anything about it. Whatever his motive may have been, he had kept the negotiations to himself. Meinhard was not informed even of the bare existence of a project. The first that he knew of it was in February, when the lease was an accomplished fact. He then made demand on the defendants that the lease be held in trust as an asset of the venture, making offer upon the trial to share the personal obligations incidental to the guaranty. The demand was followed by refusal, and later by this suit. A referee gave judgment for the plaintiff, limiting the plaintiff's interest in the lease, however, to 25 percent. The limitation was on the theory that the plaintiff's equity was to be restricted to one-half of so much of the value of the lease as was contributed or represented by the occupation of the Bristol site. Upon cross-appeals to the Appellate Division, the judgment was modified so as to enlarge the equitable interest to one-half of the whole lease. With this enlargement of plaintiff's interest, there went, of course, a corresponding enlargement of his attendant obligations. The case is now here on an appeal by the defendants.

Joint adventurers, like copartners, owe to one another, while the enterprise continues, the duty of the finest loyalty. Many forms of conduct permissible in a workaday world for those acting at arm's length, are forbidden to those bound by fiduciary ties. A trustee is held to something stricter than the morals of the market place. Not honesty alone, but the punctilio of an honor the most sensitive, is then the standard of behavior. As to this there has developed a tradition that is unbending and inveterate. Uncompromising rigidity has been the attitude of courts of equity when petitioned to undermine the rule of undivided loyalty by the 'disintegrating erosion' of particular exceptions. *Wendt v. Fischer,* 243 N. Y. 439, 444, 154 N. E. 303. Only thus has the level of conduct for fiduciaries been kept at a level higher than that trodden by the crowd. It will not consciously be lowered by any judgment of this court.

The owner of the reversion, Mr. Gerry, had vainly striven to find a tenant who would favor his ambitious scheme of demolition and construction. Baffled in the search, he turned to the defendant Salmon in possession of the Bristol, the keystone of the project. He figured to himself beyond a doubt that the man in possession would prove a likely customer. To the eye of an observer, Salmon held the lease as owner in his own right, for himself and no one else. In fact he held it as a fiduciary, for himself and another, sharers in a common venture. If this fact had been proclaimed, if the lease by its terms had run in favor of a partnership, Mr. Gerry, we may fairly assume, would have laid before the partners, and not merely before one of them, his plan of reconstruction. The pre-emptive privilege, or, better, the pre-emptive opportunity, that was thus an incident of the enterprise, Salmon appropriate to himself in secrecy and silence. He might have warned Meinhard that the plan had been submitted, and that either would be free to compete for the award. If he had done this, we do not need to say whether he would have been under a duty, if successful in the competition, to hold the lease so acquired for the benefit of a venture than about to end, and thus prolong by indirection its responsibilities and duties. The trouble about his conduct is that he excluded his coadventurer from any chance to compete, from any chance to enjoy the opportunity for benefit that had come to him alone by virtue of his agency. This chance, if nothing more, he was under a duty to concede. The price of its denial is an extension of the trust at the option and for the benefit of the one whom he excluded.

No answer is it to say that the chance would have been of little value even if seasonably offered. Such a calculus of probabilities is beyond the science of the chancery. Salmon, the real estate operator, might have been preferred to Meinhard, the woolen merchant. On the other hand, Meinhard might have offered better terms, or reinforced his offer by alliance with the wealth of others. Perhaps he might even have persuaded the lessor to renew the Bristol lease alone, postponing for a time, in return for higher rentals, the improvement of adjoining lots. We know that even under the lease as made the time for the enlargement of the building was delayed for seven years. All these opportunities were cut away from him through another's intervention. He knew that Salmon was the manager. As the time drew near for the expiration of the lease, he would naturally assume from silence, if from nothing else, that the lessor was willing to extend it for a term of years, or at least to let it stand as a lease from year to year. Not impossibly the lessor would have done so, whatever his protestations of unwillingness, if Salmon had not given assent to a project more attractive. At all events, notice of termination, even if not necessary, might seem, not unreasonably, to be something to be looked for, if the business was over the another tenant was to enter. In the absence of such notice, the matter of an extension was one that would naturally be attended to by the manager of the enterprise, and not neglected altogether. At least, there was nothing in the situation to give warning to any one that while the lease was still in being, there had come to the manager an offer of extension which he had locked within his breast to be utilized by himself alone. The very fact that Salmon was in control with exclusive powers of direction charged him the more obviously with the duty of disclosure, since only through disclosure could opportunity be equalized. . . .

Little profit will come from a dissection of the precedents. None precisely similar is cited in the briefs of counsel. What is similar in many, or so it seems to us, is the animating principle. Authority is, of course, abundant that one partner may not appropriate to his own use a renewal of a lease, though its term is to begin at the expiration of the partnership. *Mitchell v. Read,* 61 N. Y. 123, 19 Am. Rep. 252; *Id.*, 84 N. Y. 556. The lease at hand with its many changes is not strictly a renewal. Even so, the standard of loyalty for those in trust relations is without the fixed divisions of a graduated scale. . . .

We have no thought to hold that Salmon was guilty of a conscious purpose to defraud. Very likely he assumed in all good faith that with the approaching end of the venture he might ignore his coadventurer and take the extension for himself. He had given to the enterprise time and labor as well as money. He had made it a success. Meinhard, who had given money, but neither time nor labor, had already been richly paid. There might seem to be something grasping in his insistence upon more. Such recriminations are not unusual when coadventurers fall out. They are not without their force if conduct is to be judged by the common standards of competitors. That is not to say that they have pertinency here. Salmon had put himself in a position in which thought of self was to be renounced, however hard the abnegation. He was much more than a coadventurer. He was a managing coadventurer. *Clegg v. Edmondson,* 8 D. M. & G. 787, 807. For him and for those like him the rule of undivided loyalty is relentless and supreme. [*Citations omitted.*] A different question would be here if there were lacking any nexus of relation between the business conducted by the manager and the opportunity brought to him as an incident of management. [*Citations omitted.*] For this problem, as for most, there are distinctions of degree. If Salmon had received from Gerry a proposition to lease a building at a location far removed, he might have held for himself the privilege thus acquired, or so we shall assume. Here the subject-matter of the new lease was an extension and enlargement of the subject-matter of the old one. A managing coadventurer appropriating the benefit of such a lease without warning to his partner might fairly expect to be reproached with conduct that was underhand, or lacking, to say the least, in reasonable candor, if the partner were to surprise him in the act of signing the new instrument. Conduct subject to that reproach does not receive from equity a healing benediction.

A question remains as to the form and extent of the equitable interest to be allotted to the plaintiff. The trust as declared has been held to attach to the lease which was in the name of the defendant corporation. We think it ought to attach at the option of the defendant Salmon to the shares of stock which were owned by him or were under his control. The difference may be important if the lessee shall wish to execute an assignment of the lease, as it ought to be free to do with the consent of the lessor. On the other hand, an equal division of the shares might lead to other hardships. It might take away from Salmon the power of control and management which under the plan of the joint venture he was to have from first to last. The number of shares to be allotted to the plaintiff should, therefore, be reduced to such an extent as may be necessary to preserve to the defendant Salmon the expected measure of dominion. To that end an extra share should be added to his half.

* * * *

The judgment should be modified by providing that at the option of the defendant Salmon there may be substituted for a trust attaching to the lease a trust attaching to the shares of stock, with the result that one-half of such shares together with one additional share will in that event be allotted to the defendant Salmon and the other shares to the plaintiff, and as so modified the judgment should be affirmed with costs.

ANDREWS, J. (dissenting).

A tenant's expectancy of the renewal of a lease is a thing, tenuous, yet often having a real value. It represents the probability that a landlord will prefer to relet his premises to one already in possession rather than to strangers. Less tangible than 'good will,' it is never included in the tenant's assets, yet equity will not permit one standing in a relation of trust and confidence toward the tenant unfairly to take the benefit to himself. . . .

At other times some inquiry is allowed as to the facts involved. Fair dealing and a scrupulous regard for honesty is required. But nothing more. It may be stated generally that a partner may not for his own benefit secretly take a renewal of a firm lease to himself. *Mitchell v. Reed,* 61 N. Y. 123, 19 Am. Rep. 252. Yet under very exceptional circumstances this may not be wholly true. . . .

Where the trustee, or the partner or the tenant in common, takes no new lease but buys the reversion in good faith a somewhat different question arises. Here is no direct appropriation of the expectancy of renewal. Here is no offshoot of the original lease. We so held in *Anderson v. Lemon,* 8 N. Y. 236, and although Judge Dwight casts some doubt on the rule in *Mitchell v. Reed*, it seems to have the support of authority. [*Citations omitted.*] The issue, then, is whether actual fraud, dishonesty, or unfairness is present in the transaction. If so, the purchaser may well be held as a trustee. . . .

With this view of the law I am of the opinion that the issue here is simple. Was the transaction, in view of all the circumstances surrounding it, unfair and inequitable? I reach this conclusion for two reasons. There was no general partnership, merely a joint venture for a limited object, to end at a fixed time. The new lease, covering additional property, containing many new and unusual terms and conditions, with a possible duration of 80 years, was more nearly the purchase of the reversion than the ordinary renewal with which the authorities are concerned.

* * * *

Were this a general partnership between Mr. Salmon and Mr. Meinhard, I should have little doubt as to the correctness of this result, assuming the new lease to be an offshoot of the old. Such a situation involves questions of trust and confidence to a high degree; it involves questions of good, will; many other considerations. As has been said, rarely if ever may one partner without the knowledge of the other acquire for himself the renewal of a lease held by the firm, even if the new lease is to begin after the firm is dissolved. Warning of such an intent, if he is managing partner, may not be sufficient to prevent the application of this rule.

We have here a different situation governed by less drastic principles. I assume that where parties engage in a joint enterprise each owes to the other the duty of the utmost good faith in all that relates to their common venture. Within its scope they stand in a fiduciary relationship. I assume . . . . that Mr. Meinhard had an equitable interest in the Bristol Hotel lease. Further, that an expectancy of renewal inhered in that lease. Two questions then arise. Under his contract did he share in that expectancy? And if so, did that expectancy mature into a graft of the original lease? To both questions my answer is 'No.'

The one complaint made is that Mr. Salmon obtained the new lease without informing Mr. Meinhard of his intention. Nothing else. There is no claim of actual fraud. No claim of misrepresentation to any one. . . . Here was a refusal of the landlord to renew the Bristol lease on any terms; a proposal made by him, not sought by Mr. Salmon, and a choice by him and by the original lessor of the person with whom they wished to deal . . ., and by their ignorance of the arrangement with Mr. Meinhard.

What then was the scope of the adventure into which the two men entered? It is to be remembered that before their contract was signed Mr. Salmon had obtained the lease of the Bristol property. . . .

It seems to me that the venture so inaugurated had in view a limited object and was to end at a limited time. There was no intent to expand it into a far greater undertaking lasting for many years. The design was to exploit a particular lease. Doubtless in it Mr. Meinhard had an equitable interest, but in it alone. This interest terminated when the joint adventure terminated. . . . Mr. Salmon has done all he promised to do in return for Mr. Meinhard's undertaking when he distributed profits up to May 1, 1922. . . . The adventure by its express terms ended on May 1, 1922. The contract by its language and by its whole import excluded the idea that the tenant's expectancy was to subsist for the benefit of the plaintiff. On that date whatever there was left of value in the lease reverted to Mr. Salmon, as it would had the lease been for thirty years instead of twenty. Any equity which Mr. Meinhard possessed was in the particular lease itself, not in any possibility of renewal. There was nothing unfair in Mr. Salmon's conduct.

* * * *

So far I have treated the new lease as if it were a renewal of the old. As already indicated, I do not take that view. Such a renewal could not be obtained. Any expectancy that it might be had vanished. What Mr. Salmon obtained was not a graft springing from the Bristol lease, but something distinct and different-as distinct as if for a building across Fifth avenue. . . .

The judgment of the courts below should be reversed and a new trial ordered, with costs in all courts to abide the event.

QUESTIONS AND COMMENTS

1. Had Mr. Salmon approached you and told you about the potential new venture with Mr. Gerry, what advice would you give him as to how to best deal with Mr. Meinhard?

2. As we learn from the preceding case, partners are restricted (as part of their duty of loyalty) in their ability to take opportunities which belong to the

partnership, for their personal benefit. With regard to an opportunity presented to the partnership, often the question is: What is the nature of the opportunity? Is the "opportunity" just information about the potential to profit in an enterprise outside the scope of the partnership business? If so, disclosure alone might be sufficient. However, if the business opportunity *falls within the scope of the partnership business,* then disclosure alone is probably not enough. If the opportunity belongs to the partnership, then no partner may make a unilateral determination to take the partnership opportunity for him or herself. When faced with a new opportunity that arises out of, or relates to, the partnership business, a partner must disclose the business opportunity to the other partners. Then a decision must be made by the managing partner or the partnership as to whether or not to act on behalf of the partnership and take the opportunity. Of course, any decision by any partner or the partnership of whether or not to take advantage of an opportunity must be made in good faith.

D. The Ability to Waive Fiduciary Duties in a Partnership

Often partners wish to waive or limit certain fiduciary duties in a partnership. While waiver is permissible, there are also limitations regarding the extent to which fiduciary duties may be waived, and, of course there is variation among the states. Notwithstanding these variations, partners are typically permitted to waive specific duties, but not general duties, such as the duty of loyalty. Even when permitted by statute, many courts tend to frown upon blanket waivers of rights, such as the duty of care and the duty of loyalty. On the other hand, consider Delaware Revised Uniform Partnership Act § 15–103(f) which provides:

> A partnership agreement may provide for the limitation or elimination of any and all liabilities for breach of contract and breach of duties (*including fiduciary duties*) of a partner or other person to a partnership or to another partner or to another person that is a party to or is otherwise bound by a partnership agreement; *provided, that a partnership agreement may not limit or eliminate liability for any act or omission that constitutes a bad faith violation of the implied contractual covenant of good faith and fair dealing.* (Emphasis added).

The RUPA itself does not allow for a partnership agreement to unreasonably reduce the duty of care (RUPA § 103(b)(4)) or eliminate the duty of loyalty, but does provide that "the partnership agreement may identify specific types or categories of activities that do not violate the duty of loyalty, if not manifestly unreasonable." (RUPA § 103(b)(3)).

Directly related to a partnership's right to waive duties is the ability to ratify an action which would otherwise violate a duty. In general, waiver occurs before the fact, and ratification occurs after the fact. Since it occurs after an action has been taken, ratification almost always involves a specific action and so may encompass more questionable actions than might be allowed under a broad but more general waiver. By definition, ratification, at least in theory, is a more informed action. However, in order to be effective, the partners ratifying an action must be fully informed. (RUPA § 103(b)(3)(ii)).

SECTION V: Partnership Dissolution and Dissociation

When a partnership ends, it goes through three "phases": (1) dissolution, (2) winding up, and (3) termination. The terminology associated with this process can be somewhat confusing because we are used to thinking of "dissolution" as the end of something. However, in the partnership world, dissolution signals the end of the prior constitution of the partnership. Most partnership dissolutions are followed by winding up and termination. The winding up phase is a neutral period prior to termination when the partnership must conclude its business, sell its assets, pay creditors and make distributions to its partners. Once the winding up phase has been concluded, the partnership is terminated. Note that during the winding up phase, the partnership may not embark upon new business. However, even following a dissolution, the partners may vote to continue the partnership, rather than proceeding to termination. In order to continue a partnership, following dissolution, a vote of all of the partners is required.

Prior to the adoption of RUPA, when a partner left a firm, that was deemed to be a "dissolution," and the remaining partners, under most circumstances, could vote to continue the partnership if they did not wish to wind up and terminate the partnership. (UPA § 38.) However, RUPA created a new term to describe circumstances of a partner leaving a partnership: "dissociation." When a partner leaves a firm, either voluntarily or involuntarily (by expulsion or even death), that is known as dissociation. If the partner does not have the right to leave the partnership, then the dissociation is "wrongful," and the dissociated partner might be liable to the partnership for damages. (RUPA § 602.)

When evaluating whether a dissociation is wrongful, the term of a partnership has significant implications. A partnership may be "at will" which means that the partnership is not for any term or undertaking, or a partnership may be established for a term or particular undertaking. The default rules provide for different treatment of the rights and obligations of partners in an "at will" partnership than those of partners in a partnership for a term or particular undertaking, especially those rights and obligations that arise in connection with the termination of a partner's relationship to the partnership. For example, if a partnership is for a term or an undertaking, then dissociation prior to the completion of the term or the undertaking (unless provided for in the partnership agreement) would be "wrongful." Also, any dissociation in violation of the partnership agreement would be "wrongful." However, a partner may dissociate from an at-will partnership at any time, provided the partnership agreement does not provide otherwise.

Whether or not the dissociation was wrongful, the dissociated partner is entitled to receive funds, representing his or her share of the partnership (minus any damages). The biggest questions surrounding dissociation are: 1) to what amount is the dissociated partner entitled, and 2) when is this amount due. Although partnership agreements may, and often do, provide differently, under RUPA, assuming that the partner's dissociation does not result in a dissolution and winding up of the partnership business, dissociated partners are usually entitled to the greater of their share of the "going concern" value of the partnership or the liquidation value of the partnership, minus damages, if any, for the partner's wrongful dissociation and minus other amounts that might be owed to the partnership. (RUPA § 701). The going concern value is the value of the partnership as an operating entity (without the dissociated partner). The liquidation value of the partnership is the value one could get for selling all of the assets of the business. If the partnership is "at-will," then the dissociated partner is typically entitled to his or her share of the business within 120 days after dissociating. If the partnership is for a term or an undertaking, then the dissociated partner is not entitled to be paid for his or her share of the partnership until the end of the term or the completion of the undertaking. (RUPA § 701(h)). Often there is an exception to this delay in payment, if the dissociated partner can show that payment for his or her share would not create a hardship for the partnership.

NOTE ON GOING CONCERN AND LIQUIDATION VALUE

Students often struggle with the difference between going concern value and liquidation value. There is no way to have a blanket rule about which value is greater, without facts about the specific business. For example, an internet social networking business, which sells advertising and memberships, might have a very small liquidation value, but a larger going concern value. If the business were liquidated, its members would disappear, and it would not be able to sell advertising. It probably has very few assets. However, as a "going concern," it might bring in a great deal of money each year. That business would have a much larger going concern value than liquidation value. On the other hand, consider a business which manufactures diamond drill bits. Diamond drill bits are used to penetrate very hard surfaces without breaking. Imagine that this business has collected a large amount of raw material inventory (i.e., diamonds) when the price of diamonds skyrockets. There is a limit on how much people will pay for diamond drill bits. So, the business is not making very many sales. It probably has a relatively low going concern value. However, if it were to sell its inventory of diamonds, it could make a substantial amount of money. This business has a much higher liquidation value than going concern value.

When a partnership is dissolved, there may also be questions about the amount of money to which a partner is entitled, particularly in situations in which one or more of the partners wishes to purchase or continue the partnership business. Consider the following case involving a family dispute over a ranching partnership, and ask yourself what steps each partner might have taken to secure the desired result and avoid years of litigation.

McCormick v. Brevig

2004 MT 179, 322 Mont. 112, 96 P.3d 697 (2004)

JUSTICE JIM RICE delivered the Opinion of the Court.

This case involves a protracted dispute between a brother and sister concerning their respective interests in a ranching partnership that is before the Court a second time. The litigation began in 1995 when Joan McCormick ("Joan") brought this action against her brother, Clark Brevig ("Clark"), and their Partnership, Brevig Land Live and Lumber (hereinafter, "the Partnership"), seeking a Partnership accounting and dissolution. Clark counterclaimed for fraud, deceit, negligent misrepresentation, and to quiet title. He also filed a third-party complaint against several accounting defendants for professional negligence and against his sister for breach of fiduciary duty. Thereafter, Joan moved for partial summary judgment in relation to Clark's counterclaim and third-party complaint, and Clark moved for partial summary judgment on the issue of liability raised in his counterclaim and third-party complaint against Joan. Clark also moved for partial summary judgment on the issue of liability against the third-party accounting defendants. The District Court of the Tenth Judicial District, Fergus County, granted Joan's motion for partial summary judgment on her claims and denied Clark's motion for partial summary judgment against Joan. . . .

. . . . We affirmed the District Court's entry of summary judgment in favor of Joan, but concluded that the court had erred in granting summary judgment to the accounting defendants, and therefore reversed and remanded for further proceedings. *McCormick v. Brevig*, 1999 MT 86, 294 Mont. 144, 980 P.2d 603 (hereinafter referred to as, "*McCormick I*").

* * * *

. . . . On December 27, 2001, the District Court concluded that the parties' Partnership agreement did not apply, and that a judicial dissolution of the Partnership was warranted pursuant to § 35–10–624(5), MCA. The court further recognized that § 35–10–629, MCA, explicitly required any surplus assets after paying creditors to be paid to the partners in cash in accordance with their right to distribution. Nonetheless, the court found that it would be inequitable to order the liquidation of the Partnership assets in order to satisfy Joan's interest in the Partnership. Therefore, in keeping with its desire to preserve the family farm, the court ordered Joan to sell her interest in the Partnership to her brother following an appraisal and determination of the value of her share. With the assistance of a special master, and following an accounting of Partnership assets, the District Court eventually fixed a price of $1,107,672 on Joan's 50 percent interest in the Partnership. Joan appeals from the District Court's accounting and order requiring her to sell her interest in the Partnership to her brother, and Clark cross-appeals from the court's determination regarding certain Partnership assets . . . . We affirm in part, reverse in part, and remand for further proceedings.

The following issues are presented on appeal:

1. After ordering dissolution of the Partnership, did the District Court err by failing to order liquidation of the Partnership assets, and instead granting Clark the right to purchase Joan's Partnership interest at a price determined by the court?

2. Did the District Court err by failing to grant Joan's petition for an accounting of the Partnership's business affairs?

* * * *

FACTUAL AND PROCEDURAL BACKGROUND

Joan and Clark are the children of Charles and Helen Brevig (hereinafter, "Charles" and "Helen"). In 1960 Charles purchased the Brevig Ranch outside of Lewistown from his parents. . . . [Ultimately, Joan and Clark each held a 50% interest in the partnership which owned the Ranch. The partnership was governed by a written partnership agreement.]

* * * *

Disagreements concerning management of the ranch, and particularly, management of the debt load on the ranch, caused Clark and Joan's relationship to deteriorate. By the early 1990s, cooperation between Clark and Joan regarding the operation of the ranch and securing of loans necessary to fund the ranch had essentially ceased, and they began looking for ways to dissolve the Partnership.

In 1995, Joan brought suit against Clark and the Partnership, alleging that Clark had converted Partnership assets to his own personal use, and sought an accounting of the Partnership's affairs. She also requested a determination that Clark had engaged in conduct warranting a decree of expulsion. Alternatively, Joan sought an order dissolving and winding up the Partnership.

* * * *

. . .On April 3, 2000, the District Court issued findings of fact and conclusions of law, finding that . . . Joan was a 50 percent partner and should be credited for any excess capital contributions she made to the Partnership, and that Clark was not entitled to receive compensation as a partner. The court further concluded that the Partnership should be dissolved and its business wound up, and reasoned that appointment of a special master was appropriate in order to determine the amount of the parties' respective capital contributions and Partnership assets.

* * * *

. . .On December 27, 2001, the District Court ordered the value of Joan's interest in the Partnership to be determined following an appraisal conducted and paid for by the Partnership. Following such determination, Clark would have sixty days in which to purchase Joan's interest, or the Partnership assets would be liquidated and the net assets distributed to the partners.

* * * *

DISCUSSION

After ordering dissolution of the Partnership, did the District Court err by failing to order liquidation of the Partnership assets, and instead granting Clark the right to purchase Joan's Partnership interest at a price determined by the court?

Joan contends that when a partnership is dissolved by judicial decree, Montana's Revised Uniform Partnership Act, § 35–10–101 et seq., MCA (2001), requires liquidation by sale of partnership assets and distribution in cash of any surplus to the partners. In response, Clark asserts that there are other judicially acceptable methods of distributing partnership assets upon dissolution besides liquidating assets through a forced sale. For the reasons set forth below, we conclude that the Revised Uniform Partnership Act requires liquidation of partnership assets and distribution of the net surplus in cash to the partners upon dissolution entered by judicial decree when it is no longer reasonably practicable to carry on the business of the partnership.

We begin our analysis by reviewing the law of partnerships as it pertains to the issues in this case. A partnership is an association of two or more persons to carry on as co-owners a business for profit. [*Citations omitted.*] An informal or oral agreement will usually suffice to create a partnership, and where a partnership agreement exists, it will generally govern relations among partners. Thus, statutory rules are merely default rules, which apply only in the absence of a partnership agreement to the contrary. . . . In the present case, the parties do not dispute that the partnership agreement did not apply to situations involving a court ordered dissolution of a partnership.

Partnership law in Montana and throughout the United States has been primarily derived from the Uniform Partnership Act ("UPA"), which was originally promulgated by the Uniform Law Commissioners in 1914. Under the UPA, the law of partnership breakups was couched in terms of dissolution. A partnership was dissolved and its assets liquidated upon the happening of specific events, the most significant of which was the death of a partner or any partner expressing a will to leave the partnership. Montana adopted the UPA in 1947.

In 1993, our legislature significantly amended the UPA by adopting the Revised Uniform Partnership Act, or RUPA. Unlike the UPA, RUPA now provides two separate tracks for the exiting partner. The first track applies to the dissociating partner, and does not result in a dissolution, but in a buy-out of the dissociating partner's interest in the partnership. *See* § 35–10–616, MCA. The term "dissociation" is new to the act, and occurs upon the happening of any one of ten events specified in § 35–10–616, MCA. Examples of events leading to dissociation include bankruptcy of a partner and death, . . . but does not include a judicially ordered dissolution of the partnership.

The second track for the exiting partner does involve dissolution and winding up of the partnership's affairs. Section 35–10–624, MCA, sets forth the events causing dissolution and winding up of a partnership, and includes the following:

Events causing dissolution and winding up of partnership business.

* * * *

(5) a judicial decree, issued upon application by a partner, that:

(a) the economic purpose of the partnership is likely to be unreasonably frustrated;

(b) another partner has engaged in conduct relating to the partnership business that makes it not reasonably practicable to carry on the business in partnership with that partner; or

(c) it is not otherwise reasonably practicable to carry on the partnership business in conformity with the partnership agreement[.]

In this case, the District Court dissolved the Partnership pursuant to § 35–10–624(5), MCA. In so doing, it recognized that, in the absence of a partnership agreement to the contrary, the only possible result under RUPA was for the partnership assets to be liquidated and the proceeds distributed between the partners proportionately. The court reasoned, however, that the term "liquidate" had a variety of possible meanings, one of which was "to assemble and mobilize the assets, settle with the creditors and debtors and apportion the remaining assets, if any, among the stockholders or owners." Applying this definition, which the court had obtained from *Black's Law Dictionary,* the court concluded that a judicially ordered buy-out of Joan's interest in the Partnership by Clark was an acceptable alternative to liquidation of the partnership assets through a compelled sale.

* * * *

It is true that this Court has previously utilized dictionaries when seeking to define the common use and meaning of terms. [*Citation omitted.*] However, in this case, we conclude that it was not necessary for the District Court to resort to such devices. Section 35–10–629(1), MCA, clearly provides that "[i]n winding up a partnership's business, the assets of the partnership must be applied to discharge its obligations to creditors, including partners who are creditors. Any surplus must be applied to pay *in cash* the net amount distributable to partners in accordance with their right to distributions pursuant to subsection (2)." (Emphasis added.) Furthermore, subsection (2) of the statute provides:

> Each partner is entitled to a settlement of all partnership accounts upon winding up the partnership business. In settling accounts among the partners, the profits and losses that result from the *liquidation of the partnership assets* must be credited and charged to the partners' accounts. The partnership shall make a distribution to a partner in an amount equal to that partner's positive account balance. (Emphasis added.)

Thus, the common purpose and plain meaning of the term "liquidation," as it is used in § 35–10–629(2), MCA, is to reduce the partnership assets to cash, pay creditors, and distribute to partners the value of their respective interest. *See also* 59A Am.Jur.2d *Partnership* § 1100 (2003). This is all part of the process of "winding up" the business of a partnership and terminating its affairs.

Clark invites this Court to take a liberal reading of § 35–10–629, MCA, and cites *Creel v. Lilly* (1999), 354 Md. 77, 729 A.2d 385, in support of the proposition that judicially acceptable alternatives exist to compelled liquidation in a dissolution situation. . . .

However, of critical distinction between the facts in *Creel* and the case *subjudice* is the manner in which the partners exited the entity. In *Creel* one of the partners had died. Here, Joan sought a court ordered dissolution of the Partnership. Under RUPA, the death of a partner triggers the provisions of § 35–10–619, MCA, which allows for the purchase of the dissociated partner's interest in the partnership. . . . Conversely, a court ordered dissolution pursuant to § 35–10–624(5), MCA, as in this case, results in the dissolution and winding up of the partnership. . . .

* * * *

Accordingly, we conclude that when a partnership's dissolution is court ordered pursuant to § 35–10–624(5), MCA, the partnership assets necessarily must be reduced to cash in order to satisfy the obligations of the partnership and distribute any net surplus in cash to the remaining partners in accordance with their respective interests. By adopting a judicially created alternative to this statutorily mandated requirement, the District Court erred.

Did the District Court err by failing to grant Joan's petition for an accounting of the Partnership's business affairs?

Joan maintains that the accounting performed by special master Blakely was inadequate as it was limited to a review of tax returns, some of which were unfiled drafts, for the years 1985 to 2001. She argues that the partnership tax returns failed to account for the nearly $400,000 Clark allegedly removed from the Partnership for his own personal use. Clark responds that the District Court found no competent evidence supporting Joan's claim that he wrongfully took funds from the Partnership, and argues that Joan agreed to the special master's limited accounting. However, the record reveals no such stipulation by Joan.

Every partner is generally entitled to have an accounting of the partnership's affairs, even in the absence of an express contract so providing. 59A Am.Jur.2d Partnership § 617. Moreover, RUPA provides that a partner may maintain an action against the partnership or another partner for legal or equitable relief, including an accounting as to partnership business, or to enforce a right to compel a dissolution and winding up of the partnership business under § 35–10–624, MCA. *See* § 35–10–409(2) (b)(iii), MCA.

The purpose of an accounting is to determine the rights and liabilities of the partners, and to ascertain the value of the partners' interests in the partnership as of a particular date, such as the date of dissolution. 59A Am.Jur.2d *Partnership* at § 667. "When an action for an accounting is being used to wind up the partnership's affairs, the court is obligated to provide 'for a full accounting of the partnership assets and obligations and distribution of any remaining assets or liabilities to the partners in accordance with their interests in the partnership.' " *Guntle v. Barnett* (1994), 73 Wash.App. 825, 871 P.2d 627, 630. This is often accomplished through the appointment of a special master subject to court review, who conducts a comprehensive investigation of the transactions of the partnership and the partners... In rendering the accounting, mere summaries or lump listings of types of items, or schedules of cash to be distributed without detailing the firm's transactions, are generally insufficient, as are mere tax returns. 59A Am.Jur.2d *Partnership* at § 621; *Juliano v. Rea* (1982), 89 A.D.2d 618, 452 N.Y.S.2d 668, 669.

* * * *

Because we conclude . . . the Partnership's assets must be liquidated in order to satisfy the Partnership's obligations to its creditors and distribute the net surplus of any assets in cash to the partners, on remand it will become necessary for the District Court to perform a full accounting of the Partnership's affairs. Once again, this requires a detailed accounting of all the Partnership's assets and liabilities, as well as distributions of assets and liabilities to the partners in accordance with their respective interests in the Partnership. . . .

* * * *

Affirmed in part, reversed in part, and remanded for further proceedings consistent with this opinion.

Not all courts agree that the dissolution of a partnership requires a sale of the partnership assets. In *Horne v. Aune,* 121 P.3d 1227 (Wash. Ct. App. 2005), a Washington appellate court explored this question. Horne and Aune, intending to pursue a family life together, purchased a house as tenants in common. After some initial disagreements, Horne and Aune entered into an agreement which provided that they were "equal partners in said property sharing equally in ownership, care, upkeep and title and mortgage obligations. . ." (*Id.* at 1228.) Things went from bad to worse when Aune assaulted Horne's teenage son during an argument. Aune then left for a "cooling off period" and Horne sought and obtained a protective order prohibiting Aune from contact with Horne or her son with the limited exception that the couple could discuss a property settlement. Aune wanted the property sold at a public sale, but Horne wanted to purchase Aune's half of the property. The issue went to court, and the judge ordered a distribution in kind requiring Aune to quitclaim his interest in the property to Horne in exchange for a cash payment. Aune appealed the ruling.

The court noted that under the § 38 of the old UPA, absent agreement to the contrary, the departure of any partner resulted in dissolution and winding up of the partnership. Many states, including Washington, adopted the RUPA which substantially modified this rule. Under RUPA, when a partner dissociates from a partnership, dissolution is not automatically triggered. Rather, the remaining partners must purchase the dissociated partner's interest under Article 7 of RUPA unless there is a dissolution and winding up of the partnership business under Article 8 of RUPA. *See* RUPA § 603, cmts. 1–2 (2011–2012). The

Washington Court in *Horne v. Aune* specifically declined to follow the Montana Supreme Court's ruling in *McCormick v. Brevig, supra,* which had forced partnership dissolution in the absence of a specific partnership agreement to the contrary. Rather, the court sustained the lower court's order, agreeing with cases it cited from Oregon, Maryland, and Alaska in allowing a remaining partner, Horne, to purchase the interest of a departing partner, Aune.

A. Books, Records and the Right to a Partnership Accounting

In the preceding case the Plaintiff also brought an action for an accounting. The RUPA provides partners with broad rights to bring an action against the partnership or another partner in order to protect the rights or interests of the partner bringing such an action. (RUPA § 405(b)). Any such action may also be accompanied by an action for an accounting. *Id.* The ability to demand an accounting can be a powerful tool because an accounting can produce information that goes well beyond an individual partner's concerns. An account can expose illegal or improper behavior on the part of careless or unscrupulous partners and may expose finances that other partners wish to keep private. These concerns can often provide negotiating leverage to the partner requesting the accounting. Of course a partner's rights to an accounting (as well as her right to inspect books and records provided in RUPA § 403) underscore the importance of diligence in recording keeping, in maintaining accurate records and in carefully adhering to proper procedures, rules, laws and regulations.

B. Liabilities for Departing Partners

When partners dissociate, they are no longer partners in the partnership. Because they have changed status, they are not personally liable for debts of the partnership which arise following dissociation. There is an exception to this limitation for any third party who does not have actual or constructive notice of the partner's dissociation and enters into a transaction with the partnership within two years after the dissociation in reliance upon that third party's reasonable belief that the dissociated partner is a partner. This exception only applies if the third party did not have notice (regardless of his or her reasonable belief) of the partner's dissociation or is not deemed to have notice based on the filing of a Statement of Dissociation. (RUPA § 703). This structure provides an incentive for dissociated partners to provide notice of their dissociation to third parties. Note that a dissociated partner might also have apparent authority to bind a partnership. The potential for apparent authority provides incentive for the partnership to provide notice of the dissociation to third parties.

The dissociated partner is still liable to creditors of the partnership for partnership debts which arose prior to the dissociation. (RUPA § 703(a)). This might seem unfair if the dissociated partner's share of these liabilities has already been deducted from any payments to the dissociated partner. However, the law does not allow an agreement between the partnership and a departing partner to alter a third party's claim or potential claim. Therefore, the dissociated partner remains personally liable for pre-dissociation debts, even after receiving payment for his or her interest from the partnership, but the dissociated partner has the right to seek indemnification from the partnership and, ultimately from the partners for any claims made against that dissociated partner, following the purchase of that dissociated partner's interest in the partnership. (RUPA § 701(d)).

C. Liabilities for New Partners

Conversely, if a new partner joins the partnership, that partner is only personally liable for new debts that are incurred once that person joins the firm. (RUPA § 306(b)). Of course any capital contribution made by the new partner will be subject to a judgment against the partnership irrespective of whether it arises out of an event that occurred before the new partner joined the firm. However, the new partner would not have personal liability for such a debt.

D. Obligations to Dissociated Partners

Dissociated partners may have obligations to third parties and certain rights that arise out of those obligations. Upon dissociation by a partner and a buyout of that partner's interest in the firm, the partner no longer has an interest in the partnership, and, therefore, would no longer be owed any fiduciary duties by the partners or the partnership. However, in certain situations, for example, when there is a delay in the buyout of a partner's interest in the partnership, the dissociated partner might still claim that he or she is owed certain fiduciary duties. (Note that partners are owed certain fiduciary duties during the winding up of the partnership business. RUPA § 404.) On the other hand, even a dissociated partner with some continuing interest in the partnership might only be entitled to the rights of a transferee of an economic interest and would not be entitled to fiduciary claims relating to alleged mismanagement of a firm. Consider the case below and what you might have done to protect the retired partner, Charles Bane, if you were his attorney.

Bane v. Ferguson

890 F.2d 11 (7th Cir. 1989)

POSNER, CIRCUIT JUDGE:

The question presented by this appeal from the dismissal of the complaint (*see* 707 F.Supp. 988 (N.D.Ill.1989)) is whether a retired partner in a law firm has either a common law or a statutory claim against the firm's managing council for acts of negligence that, by causing the firm to dissolve, terminate his retirement benefits. It is a diversity case governed by the law of Illinois, rather than a federal-question case governed by the Employee Retirement Income Security Act, 29 U.S.C. §§ 1001 *et seq.,* because ERISA excludes partners from its protections. [*Citation omitted.*]

Charles Bane practiced corporate and public utility law as a partner in the venerable Chicago law firm of Isham, Lincoln & Beale, founded more than a century ago by Abraham Lincoln's son Robert Todd Lincoln. In August 1985 the firm adopted a noncontributory retirement plan that entitled every retiring partner to a pension, the amount depending on his earnings from the firm on the eve of retirement. The plan instrument provided that the plan, and the payments under it, would end when and if the firm dissolved without a successor entity, and also that the amount paid out in pension benefits each year could not exceed five percent of the firm's net income in the preceding year. Four months after the plan was adopted, the plaintiff retired, moved to Florida with his wife, and began drawing his pension (to continue until his wife's death if he died first) of $27,483 a year. Bane was 72 years old when he retired. So far as appears, he had, apart from social security, no significant source of income other than the pension.

Several months after Bane's retirement, Isham, Lincoln & Beale merged with Reuben & Proctor, another large and successful Chicago firm. The merger proved to be a disaster, and the merged firm was dissolved in April 1988 without a successor-whereupon the payment of pension benefits to Bane ceased and he brought this suit. The suit alleges that the defendants were the members of the firm's managing council in the period leading up to the dissolution and that they acted unreasonably in deciding to merge the firm with Reuben & Procter, in purchasing computers and other office equipment, and in leaving the firm for greener pastures shortly before its dissolution. The suit does not allege that the defendants committed fraud, engaged in self-dealing, or deliberately sought to destroy or damage the law firm or harm the plaintiff; the charge is negligent mismanagement, not deliberate wrongdoing. The suit seeks damages, presumably the present value of the pension benefits to which the Banes would be entitled had the firm not dissolved.

* * * *

Bane has four theories of liability. The first is that the defendants, by committing acts of mismanagement that resulted in the dissolution of the firm, violated the Uniform Partnership Act, . . . which provides that "unless authorized by the other partners . . . one or more but less than all the partners have no authority to: Do any . . . act which would make it impossible to carry on the ordinary business of the partnership." This provision is inapplicable. Its purpose is not to make negligent partners liable to persons with whom the partnership transacts (such as Bane), but to limit the liability of the other partners for the unauthorized act of one partner. See *Hackney v. Johnson,* 601 S.W.2d 523, 525 (Tex.Civ.App.1980). The purpose in other words is to protect partners. Bane ceased to be a partner when he retired in 1985.

Nor can Bane obtain legal relief on the theory that the defendants violated a fiduciary duty to him; they had none. A partner is a fiduciary of his partners, but not of his former partners, for the withdrawal of a partner terminates the partnership as to him. *Adams v. Jarvis,* 23 Wis.2d 453, 458, 127 N.W.2d 400, 403 (1964). Bane must look elsewhere for the grounds of a fiduciary obligation running from his former partners to himself. The pension plan did not establish a trust, and even if, notwithstanding the absence of one, the plan's managers were fiduciaries of its beneficiaries (there are myriad sources of fiduciary duty besides a trust), the mismanagement was not of the plan but of the firm. There is no suggestion that the defendants failed to inform the plaintiff of his rights under the plan or miscalculated his benefits or mismanaged or misapplied funds set aside for the plan's beneficiaries; no funds *were* set aside for them. Even if the defendants were fiduciaries of the plaintiff, moreover, the business-judgment rule would shield them from liability for mere negligence in the operation of the firm, just as it would shield a corporation's directors and officers, who are fiduciaries of the shareholders. *See Cottle v. Hilton Hotels Corp.,* 635 F.Supp. 1094, 1099 (N.D.Ill.1986).

* * * *

The last question, which is the most interesting because the most fundamental, is whether the defendants violated a duty of care to the plaintiff founded on general principles of tort law. What is the liability of the managers of a failed enterprise to persons harmed by the failure? When a large firm-whether a law firm, or a manufacturing enterprise, or a bank, or a railroad-fails, and shuts its doors, many persons besides the owners of the firm may be hurt in their pocketbooks-workers, suppliers, suppliers' workers, creditors (like Mr. Bane), and members of these persons' families. . . . We can find no precedent in Illinois law or elsewhere for imposing tort liability on careless managers for the financial consequences of the collapse of the firm to all who are hurt by that collapse. . . .

There are a number of reasons for the principle. . . . In addition, potential victims of a firm's dissolution can protect themselves through contract, and therefore do not need the protection of tort law; people should be encouraged to protect themselves through voluntary transactions rather than to look to tort law to repair the consequences of their improvidence. Finally, so massive and uncertain a contingent liability would be difficult to quantify, and hence difficult and costly to insure against, and as a result it might curtail risk-taking and entrepreneurship. Concretely, the threat of such liability in the present case might have deterred any partner from accepting election to the managing council of Isham, Lincoln & Beale and might have deterred the firm from establishing the retirement plan at all-the benefits of which were then so cruelly, but not maliciously, cut off.

We are sorry about the financial blow to the Banes but we agree with the district judge that there is no remedy under the law of Illinois.

AFFIRMED.

E. Attorneys and Their Duties to Their Firms

Several partnership cases involve attorneys leaving law firms. These cases center around two concepts. One is what lawyers may do with regard to the cases and clients of the firm they are leaving while preparing to leave a firm and after leaving a firm. The second involves the question of what, if anything, are the lawyers who leave the firm entitled to receive with regard to work that remains at the firm and what, if anything, are the departing partner's former partners entitled to receive with regard to clients/cases that accompany the departing partner(s). These cases provide examples of the operation of fiduciary duties within a partnership, but they have the added element of the ethical obligations associated with the practice of law. An attorney's ethical obligations will often provide more specific and broader constraints on an attorney's behavior when leaving a firm.

Meehan v. Shaughnessy

404 Mass. 419, 535 N.E.2d 1255 (Mass. 1989)

HENNESSEY, CHIEF JUSTICE:

The plaintiffs, James F. Meehan (Meehan) and Leo V. Boyle (Boyle), were partners of the law firm, Parker, Coulter, Daley & White (Parker Coulter). After Meehan and Boyle terminated their relationship with Parker Coulter to start their own firm, they commenced this action both to recover amounts they claim the defendants, their former partners, owed them under the partnership agreement, and to obtain a declaration as to amounts they owed the defendants for work done at Parker Coulter on cases they removed to their new firm. The defendants (hereinafter collectively Parker Coulter) counterclaimed that Meehan and Boyle violated their fiduciary duties, breached the partnership agreement, and tortiously interfered with their advantageous business and contractual relationships. As grounds for these claims, Parker Coulter asserted that Meehan and Boyle engaged in improper conduct in withdrawing cases and clients from the firm, and in inducing employees to join the new firm of Meehan, Boyle & Cohen, P.C. (MBC). . .

After a jury-waived trial, a Superior Court judge rejected all of Parker Coulter's claims for relief, and found that Meehan and Boyle were entitled to recover amounts owed to them under the partnership agreement. The judge also found, based on the partnership agreement and a quantum meruit theory, that Parker Coulter was entitled to recover from Meehan and Boyle for time billed and expenses incurred on the cases Meehan and Boyle removed to their own firm. Parker Coulter appealed from the judgment, and we granted direct appellate review.

* * * *

. . . .Parker, Coulter, Daley & White is a large partnership which specializes in litigation on behalf of both defendants and plaintiffs. Meehan joined the firm in 1959, and became a partner in 1963; his practice focuses primarily on complex tort litigation, such as product liability and aviation defense work. Boyle joined Parker Coulter in 1971, and became a partner in 1980; he has concentrated on plaintiffs' work. Both have developed outstanding reputations as trial lawyers in the Commonwealth. Meehan and Boyle each were active in the management of Parker Coulter. . . . . At the time of their leaving, Meehan's interest in the partnership was 6% and Boyle's interest was 4.8%.

Meehan and Boyle had become dissatisfied at Parker Coulter. On June 27, 1984, after unsuccessfully opposing the adoption of a firm-wide pension plan, the two first discussed the possibility of leaving Parker Coulter. Another partner met with them to discuss leaving but told them their proposed firm would not be suitable for his type of practice. On July 1, Meehan and Boyle decided to leave Parker Coulter and form their own partnership.

Having decided to establish a new firm, Meehan and Boyle then focused on whom they would invite to join them. The two spoke with Cohen, a junior partner and the de facto head of Parker Coulter's appellate department, about joining the new firm as a partner. They arranged to meet with her on July 5, and told her to keep their conversations confidential. The day before the July 5 meeting, Boyle prepared two lists of what he considered to be his cases. The lists contained approximately eighty to 100 cases, and for each case indicated the status, fee arrangement, estimated settlement value, and potential fee to MBC. Boyle gave these lists to Cohen for her to examine in preparation for the July 5 meeting.

At the July 5 meeting, Meehan and Boyle outlined to Cohen their plans for the new firm, including their intent to offer positions to Schafer, Peter Black (Black), and Warren Fitzgerald (Fitzgerald), who were associates at Parker Coulter. Boyle stated that he hoped the clients he had been representing would go with him to the new firm; Meehan said he would take the aviation work he had at Parker Coulter with him. Both stated that they felt others at Parker Coulter were getting paid as much as or more than they were, but were not working as hard. Cohen decided to consider the offer from Meehan and Boyle, and agreed to keep the plans confidential until formal notice of the separation was given to the partnership. Although the partnership agreement required a notice period of three months, the three decided to give only thirty days' notice. They chose to give shorter notice to avoid what they believed would be an uncomfortable situation at the firm, and possible retaliatory measures by the partnership. Meehan and Boyle had agreed that they would leave Parker Coulter on December 31, 1984, the end of Parker Coulter's fiscal year.

During the first week of August, Cohen accepted the offer to join the new firm as a partner. Her primary reason for leaving Parker Coulter to join MBC was that she enjoyed working with Meehan and Boyle.

In July, 1984, Boyle offered a position at MBC to Schafer, who worked closely with Boyle in the plaintiffs department. Boyle told Schafer to organize his cases, and "to keep an eye towards cases to be resolved in 1985 and to handle these cases for resolution in 1985 rather than 1984." He also told Schafer to make a list of cases he could take with him to MBC, and to keep all their conversations confidential.

Late in the summer of 1984, Meehan asked Black and Fitzgerald to become associates at MBC. Fitzgerald had worked with Meehan in the past on general defense work, and Black worked with Meehan, particularly in the aviation area. Meehan was instrumental in attracting Black, who had previously been employed by U.S. Aviation Underwriters (USAU), to Parker Coulter. Although Black had already considered leaving Parker Coulter, he was concerned about whether USAU would follow him to a small firm like MBC, and wanted to discuss his leaving Parker Coulter with the vice president of USAU. In October, 1984, Black and Meehan met with the USAU vice president in New York. They later received assurances from him that he would be interested in sending USAU business to the proposed new firm. Black then accepted the offer to join MBC. Fitzgerald also accepted. Schafer, Black, and Fitzgerald were the only associates Meehan, Boyle, and Cohen approached concerning the new firm.

During July and the following months, Meehan, Boyle, and Cohen made arrangements for their new practice apart from seeking associates. They began to look for office space and retained an architect. In early fall, a lease was executed on behalf of MBC in the name of MBC Realty Trust. They also retained an attorney to advise them on the formation of the new firm.

* * * *

Toward the end of November, Boyle prepared form letters to send to clients and referring attorneys as soon as Parker Coulter was notified of the separation. He also drafted a form for the clients to return to him at his home address authorizing him to remove cases to MBC. An outside agency typed these materials on Parker Coulter's letterhead. Schafer prepared similar letters and authorization forms.

While they were planning their departure, from July to approximately December, Meehan, Boyle, Cohen, Schafer, Black, and Fitzgerald all continued to work full schedules. They settled cases appropriately, made reasonable efforts to avoid continuances, tried cases, and worked on discovery. Each generally maintained his or her usual standard of performance.

Meehan and Boyle had originally intended to give notice to Parker Coulter on December 1, 1984. Rumors of their leaving, however, began to circulate before then. During the period from July to early fall, different Parker Coulter partners approached Meehan individually on three separate occasions and asked him if the rumors about his leaving were true. On each occasion, Meehan denied that he was leaving. On November 30, 1984, a partner, Maurice F. Shaughnessy (Shaughnessy), approached Boyle and asked him whether Meehan and Boyle intended to leave the firm. Shaughnessy interpreted Boyle's evasive response as an affirmation of the rumors. Meehan and Boyle then decided to distribute their notice that afternoon, which stated, as their proposed date for leaving, December 31, 1984. A notice was left on the desk of each partner. . .

On December 3, the Parker Coulter partners appointed a separation committee and decided to communicate with "important sources of business" to tell them of the separation and of Parker Coulter's desire to continue representing them. Meehan and Boyle asked their partners for financial information about the firm, discussed cases and clients with them, and stated that they intended to communicate with clients and referring attorneys on the cases in which they were involved. Sometime during the week of December 3, the partners sent Boyle a list of cases and requested that he identify the cases he intended to take with him.

Boyle had begun to make telephone calls to referring attorneys on Saturday morning, December 1. He had spoken with three referring attorneys by that date and told them of his departure from Parker Coulter and his wish to continue handling their cases. On December 3, he mailed his previously typed letters and authorization forms, and by the end of the first two weeks of December he had spoken with a majority of referring attorneys, and had obtained authorizations from a majority of clients whose cases he planned to remove to MBC.

Although the partners previously were aware of Boyle's intention to communicate with clients, they did not become aware of the extent of his communications until December 12 or 13. Boyle did not provide his partners with the list they requested of cases he intended to remove until December 17. Throughout December, Meehan, Boyle, and Schafer continued to communicate with referring attorneys on cases they were currently handling to discuss authorizing their transfer to MBC. On December 19, 1984, one of the partners accepted on behalf of Parker Coulter the December 31 departure date and waived the three-month notice period provided for by the partnership agreement. Meehan, Boyle, and Cohen formalized their arrangement as a professional corporation on January 1, 1985.

MBC removed a number of cases from Parker Coulter. Of the roughly 350 contingent fee cases pending at Parker Coulter in 1984, Boyle, Schafer, and Meehan removed approximately 142 to MBC. Meehan advised Parker Coulter that the 4,000 asbestos cases he had attracted to the firm would remain, and he did not seek to take certain other major clients. Black removed thirty-five cases;

Fitzgerald removed ten; and Cohen removed three. A provision in the partnership agreement in effect at the separation provided that a voluntarily retiring partner, upon the payment of a "fair charge," could remove "any matter in which the partnership had been representing a client who came to the firm through the personal effort or connection of the retiring partner," subject to the right of the client to stay with the firm. Approximately thirty-nine of the 142 contingent fee cases removed to MBC came to Parker Coulter at least in part through the personal efforts or connections of Parker Coulter attorneys other than Meehan, Boyle, Cohen, Schafer, Black, or Fitzgerald. In all the cases removed to MBC, however, MBC attorneys had direct, existing relationships with the clients. In all the removed cases, MBC attorneys communicated with the referring attorney or with the client directly by telephone or letter. In each case, the client signed an authorization.

* * * *

The Parker Coulter partnership agreement . . . . provides for an allocation to the departing partner of a share of the firm's current net income, and a return of his or her capital contributions. In addition, the agreement also recognizes that a major asset of a law firm is the expected fees it will receive from unfinished business currently being transacted. Instead of assigning a value to the departing partner's interest in this unfinished business, or waiting for the unfinished business to be "wound up" and liquidated, which is the method [set forth for in the statutory provisions], the agreement gives the partner the right to remove any case which came to the firm "through the personal effort or connection" of the partner, if the partner compensates the dissolved partnership "for the services to and expenditures for the client." Once the partner has removed a case, the agreement provides that the partner is entitled to retain all future fees in the case, with the exception of the "fair charge" owed to the dissolved firm.

Although the provision in the partnership agreement which divides the dissolved firm's unfinished business does not expressly apply to the removal of cases which did not come to Parker Coulter through the efforts of the departing partner, we believe that the parties intended this provision to apply to these cases also. . . .The strong public interest in allowing clients to retain counsel of their choice outweighs any professional benefits derived from a restrictive covenant. Thus, the Parker Coulter partners could not restrict a departing partner's right to remove any clients who freely choose to retain him or her as their legal counsel. Second, we believe the agreement's carefully drawn provisions governing dissolution and the division of assets indicate the partners' strong intent [to waive statutory provisions which might otherwise govern]. Therefore, based on the partners' intent, and on the prohibition against restrictive covenants between attorneys, we interpret the agreement to provide that, upon the payment of a fair charge, any case may be removed regardless of whether the case came to the firm through the personal efforts of the departing partner. This privilege to remove, as is shown in our later discussion, is of course dependent upon the partner's compliance with fiduciary obligations.

* * * *

In sum, the statute gives a partner the power to dissolve a partnership at any time. Under the statute, the assets of the dissolved partnership are divided among the former partners through the process of liquidation and windup. The statute, however, allows partners to design their own methods of dividing assets and, provided the dissolution is not premature, expressly states that the partners' method controls. Here, the partners have fashioned a division method which immediately winds up unfinished business, allows for a quick separation of the surviving practices, and minimizes the disruptive impact of a dissolution.

* * * *

Parker Coulter claims that the judge erred in finding that Meehan, Boyle, Cohen, and Schafer fulfilled their fiduciary duties to the former partnership. In particular, Parker Coulter argues that these attorneys breached their duties (1) by improperly handling cases for their own, and not the partnership's benefit, (2) by secretly competing with the partnership, and (3) by unfairly acquiring from clients and referring attorneys consent to withdraw cases to MBC. We do not agree with Parker Coulter's first two arguments but agree with the third. . . .

It is well settled that partners owe each other a fiduciary duty of "the utmost good faith and loyalty." [*Citations omitted.*] As a fiduciary, a partner must consider his or her partners' welfare, and refrain from acting for purely private gain. [*Citations omitted.*] Partners thus "may not act out of avarice, expediency or self-interest in derogation of their duty of loyalty." [*Citations omitted.*] Meehan and Boyle owed their copartners at Parker Coulter a duty of the utmost good faith and loyalty, and were obliged to consider their copartners' welfare, and not merely their own.

Parker Coulter first argues that Meehan and Boyle violated their fiduciary duty by handling cases for their own benefit, and challenges the judge's finding that no manipulation occurred.[13]

---

[13] The judge found, specifically, that: "MBC, Schafer, Black and Fitzgerald worked full schedules from July to November 30, 1984, and some beyond. There was no manipulation of the cases nor were the cases handled differently as a result of the decision by MBC to leave Parker Coulter. They tried

Parker Coulter also claims that we should disregard the judge's finding of no manipulation because the finding is clearly contradicted by other subsidiary findings, namely that Boyle planned to, and told Schafer to, handle cases for resolution at MBC rather than at Parker Coulter; that Boyle reassigned a number of a departing attorney's cases to himself and Schafer; and that a number of cases which were ready to resolve at Parker Coulter were, in fact, not resolved there. We do not agree that there is a conflict. The judge's finding that Boyle spoke of engaging in improper conduct does not require the conclusion that this conduct actually took place. Similarly, his finding that the reassignment of cases did not establish manipulation is consistent with a determination that the reassignment was based on merit and workload. . . . Parker Coulter points to no specific case which the MBC attorneys manipulated for their own benefit. . . . We have reviewed the record, and conclude that the judge was warranted in determining that Meehan and Boyle handled cases no differently as a result of their decision to leave Parker Coulter, and that they thus fulfilled their fiduciary duty in this respect.

Parker Coulter next argues that the judge's findings compel the conclusion that Meehan and Boyle breached their fiduciary duty not to compete with their partners by secretly setting up a new firm during their tenure at Parker Coulter. We disagree. We have stated that fiduciaries may plan to compete with the entity to which they owe allegiance, "provided that in the course of such arrangements they [do] not otherwise act in violation of their fiduciary duties." *Chelsea Indus. v. Gaffney,* 389 Mass. 1, 10, 11–12, 449 N.E.2d 320 (1983). Here, the judge found that Meehan and Boyle made certain logistical arrangements for the establishment of MBC. These arrangements included executing a lease for MBC's office, preparing lists of clients expected to leave Parker Coulter for MBC, and obtaining financing on the basis of these lists. We believe these logistical arrangements to establish a physical plant for the new firm were permissible under *Chelsea Indus.,* especially in light of the attorneys' obligation to represent adequately any clients who might continue to retain them on their departure from Parker Coulter. . . .

Lastly, Parker Coulter argues that the judge's findings compel the conclusion that Meehan and Boyle breached their fiduciary duties by unfairly acquiring consent from clients to remove cases from Parker Coulter. We agree that Meehan and Boyle, through their preparation for obtaining clients' consent,

cases, worked on discovery, settled cases and made reasonable efforts to avoid continuances, to try their cases when reached, and settle where appropriate and in general maintain the same level of industry and professionalism that they had always demonstrated."

their secrecy concerning which clients they intended to take, and the substance and method of their communications with clients, obtained an unfair advantage over their former partners in breach of their fiduciary duties.

A partner has an obligation to "render on demand true and full information of all things affecting the partnership to any partner." [UPA] § 20. . . . . On three separate occasions Meehan affirmatively denied to his partners, on their demand, that he had any plans for leaving the partnership. During this period of secrecy, Meehan and Boyle made preparations for obtaining removal authorizations from clients. Meehan traveled to New York to meet with a representative of USAU and interest him in the new firm. Boyle prepared form letters on Parker Coulter's letterhead for authorizations from prospective MBC clients. Thus, they were "ready to move" the instant they gave notice to their partners. [*Citations omitted.*]

On giving their notice, Meehan and Boyle continued to use their position of trust and confidence to the disadvantage of Parker Coulter. The two immediately began communicating with clients and referring attorneys. Boyle delayed providing his partners with a list of clients he intended to solicit until mid-December, by which time he had obtained authorization from a majority of the clients.

Finally, the content of the letter sent to the clients was unfairly prejudicial to Parker Coulter. The ABA Committee on Ethics and Professional Responsibility, in Informal Opinion 1457 (April 29, 1980), set forth ethical standards for attorneys announcing a change in professional association. Because this standard is intended primarily to protect clients, proof by Parker Coulter of a technical violation of this standard does not aid them in their claims [*Citation omitted.*] We will, however, look to this standard for general guidelines as to what partners are entitled to expect from each other concerning their joint clients on the division of their practice. The ethical standard provides that any notice explain to a client that he or she has the right to decide who will continue the representation. Here, the judge found that the notice did not "clearly present to the clients the choice they had between remaining at Parker Coulter or moving to the new firm." By sending a one-side announcement, on Parker Coulter letterhead, so soon after notice of their departure, Meehan and Boyle excluded their partners from effectively presenting their services as an alternative to those of Meehan and Boyle.

Meehan and Boyle could have foreseen that the news of their departure would cause a certain amount of confusion and disruption among their partners. The speed and preemptive character of their campaign to acquire clients' consent took advantage of their partners' confusion. By engaging in these preemptive tactics, Meehan and Boyle violated the duty of utmost good faith and loyalty which they owed their partners. Therefore, we conclude that the judge erred in deciding that Meehan and Boyle acted properly in acquiring consent to remove cases to MBC.

* * * *

We conclude that Meehan and Boyle had the burden of proving no causal connection between their breach of duty and Parker Coulter's loss of clients. [*Citations omitted.*] Proof of the circumstances of the preparations for obtaining authorizations and of the actual communications with clients was more accessible to Meehan and Boyle than to Parker Coulter. Furthermore, requiring these partners to disprove causation will encourage partners in the future to disclose seasonably and fully any plans to remove cases. This disclosure will allow the partnership and the departing partner an equal opportunity to present to clients the option of continuing with the partnership or retaining the departing partner individually.

* * * *

In sum, we conclude that the MBC attorneys' breach of duty consisted of their method of acquiring consent from clients to remove cases. We therefore limit Parker Coulter's recovery to only those losses which were caused by this breach of duty, but place on the MBC attorneys the burden of disproving causation. On remand, the judge is to determine, based on the record and his findings as they now stand, whether the MBC attorneys have met their burden as to each case removed from Parker Coulter. A constructive trust for the benefit of the former partnership is to be imposed on any profits which Meehan, Boyle, Cohen, or Schafer receive on cases which the judge determines they unfairly removed. Because the fair charge which Meehan and Boyle owe on all removed cases is an asset of the former partnership, and because the constructive trust we impose is for the benefit of the former partnership, each former partner is entitled to his or her partnership share of these amounts. . . . . Meehan and Boyle are entitled to 6% and 4.8%, respectively, of these amounts. Additionally, under the agreement's terms, Meehan and Boyle are to receive the return of their capital contributions and their profit shares. . . .

NOTES

1. The American Bar Association (the "ABA") has outlined "best practices" which should be followed when an attorney leaves a firm. (ABA Formal Ethics Op. 99–414, 16 Law. Man. Prof. Conduct 122 (1999).) The ABA guidelines explain that the departing attorney should mail notice to each client with whom the lawyer had an active attorney-client relationship. The notice should not encourage the client to sever relations with the firm and should be brief, dignified, and not disparage the former firm.

2. While attorneys have an obligation to keep their clients informed of a departure if the attorney has significant personal contact with the client, attorneys must not engage in behavior that rises to the level of luring clients away from a firm. Several attorneys have been sued for alleged violations of this limitation by their former firms levying allegations that the departing attorneys actions constituted interference with the contractual relationships that the firm had with its clients. *See e.g., Graubard Mollen Dannett & Horowitz v. Moskovitz,* 86 N.Y.2d 112, 653 N.E.2d 1179, 629 N.Y.S.2d 1009 (1995); *Adler, Barish, Daniels, Levin and Creskoff v. Epstein,* 482 Pa. 416, 393 A.2d 1175 (1978); *Reeves v. Hanlon,* 106 Cal. App. 4th 433, 130 Cal. Rptr. 2d 793 (Cal. App. 2d Dist., 2003). The ethical obligation to notify clients and to allow clients a "choice" in their representation might augment aspects of more traditional partnership fiduciary duties which would prevent competition and would not allow a partner to take a partnership opportunity. However, these obligations are still present and are not invalidated merely by an attorney's obligation to provide notice to his or her clients.

F. Expulsion

RUPA provides for the expulsion of partners from a partnership under certain circumstances. A partner may be expelled under RUPA if expulsion is provided for in the partnership agreement. (RUPA § 601(3)). However, there are additional circumstances under which a partner may be expelled under RUPA, including by the unanimous vote of the other partners if it is unlawful to carry on the partnership business with that partner; if there has been a transfer of all (or substantially all) of that partner's transferable interest; or if the partner to be expelled is another entity which is ending its existence. (RUPA § 601(4)). Under RUPA § 601(5) a partner may also be expelled by judicial determination if that partner engaged in wrongful conduct that adversely and materially affected the partnership business; if that partner willfully or persistently breached the partnership agreement or that partner's duties to the other partners or to the partnership; or if that partner engaged in conduct relating to the partnership business, making it not reasonably practicable to carry on the partnership business with that partner. These provisions contained in RUPA § 601(5) may not be waived in the partnership agreement. (RUPA § 103(b)(7)).

As discussed above, most of the provisions of RUPA may be altered. Except with respect to expulsion by judicial determination, if the partners agree, the partnership agreement may include provisions making it much easier (or more difficult) to expel a partner. However, even permissible expulsion provisions (and in fact all partnership rights and remedies) must be exercised consistent with the obligation of good faith and fair dealing. Whether a partner is expelled under RUPA or pursuant to the partnership agreement, if the power to expel is exercised in bad faith or for predatory reasons, such an expulsion frequently gives rise to an action for damages the affected partner has suffered as a result of the other partners' violation of the duty of good faith and fair dealing.

Cadwalader, Wickersham & Taft v. Beasley

728 So. 2d 253 (1998)

POLEN, J.:

* * * *

Beasley laterally transferred to become a partner at CW & T [Cadwalader, Wickersham & Taft] in its Palm Beach office in 1989. After his arrival, the Palm Beach office suffered from internal discord and, by 1994, the office was operating at a loss. In response to this situation, the firm's management committee began discussions regarding the termination of up to 30 partners nationwide, including the Palm Beach partners. During this time, and allegedly unbeknownst to CW & T, Beasley was planning to leave the firm. He met secretly with associates in CW & T's Palm Beach office about leaving with him.

The management committee eventually held a day-long meeting on August 7, 1994. Prior to the meeting, the committee members were asked to submit lists of less productive partners to be considered for possible termination. All of the Palm Beach partners were identified on the lists actually submitted. A tentative vote was reached at that meeting and, later that month, the committee formally decided to close its Palm Beach office by year-end 1994. It informed its partners, including Beasley, of its decision on August 30, 1994.

After the announcement, Beasley retained Professor Robert Hillman, who opined that CW & T, pursuant to the partnership agreement, lacked the legal authority to expel him from the partnership. In response to this opinion, CW & T sent a memorandum to Beasley informing him that he was still a partner in the firm. It then offered Beasley either relocation within the firm but in the New York or Washington, D.C. offices, or, a compensation/severance package which included his return of capital, departure bonus, and full shares through December 31, 1994. He was presented with a written withdrawal agreement confirming the same. Beasley, a member of both the Florida and New York bars, rejected the same as impractical.

Settlement negotiations between CW & T and Beasley then continued. On November 9, he sued the firm for fraud and breach of fiduciary duty, among other counts. On November 10, 1994, CW & T sent a letter to Beasley informing him to vacate the premises by 5:00 p.m. the next day. The letter specifically prohibited him from continuing to represent himself as associated with the firm.

After a nine-day bench trial, Judge Cook authored a meticulous and, we believe, exceptionally well-reasoned final judgment. He found that CW & T was authorized to close the Palm Beach office pursuant to the partnership agreement, and that Beasley would have voluntarily left CW & T by year-end 1994 in any event. Nevertheless, since the partnership agreement lacked provisions for the expulsion of a partner except in one limited situation, he found that CW & T had anticipatorily breached the partnership agreement when it announced its plans to close the Palm Beach office in August, and then actually breached the agreement when it sent him the November 10, 1994 letter. The final judgment awarded Beasley his paid-in capital plus interest (which CW & T does not dispute), his percentage interest in the firm's accounts receivables and assets and interest thereon, and punitive damages, all totaling $2.5+ million. The later judgment awarded Beasley's attorneys fees and costs. These amounts . . . [include Beasley's] percentage interest in the firm's accounts receivable, work-in-progress, office building and other assets. . . . $867,110.00—his profits attributable to the use of his right in the property of the dissolved partnership. . . . $935,261.52—punitive damages. . . . $500,000.00—attorney's fees and costs. . . . $1,108,247.92. . . .

* * * *

I. WHETHER BEASLEY WAS EXPELLED OR VOLUNTARILY WITHDREW

Under New York Partnership Law's adoption of the Uniform Partnership Act (UPA), partners have no common law or statutory right to expel or dismiss another partner from the partnership; they may, however, provide in their partnership agreement for expulsion under prescribed conditions which must be strictly applied. [*Citations omitted.*] Absent such a provision, as here, the removal of a partner may be accomplished only through dissolution of the firm. [*Citations omitted.*]

The evidence supports Judge Cook's finding that CW & T intended to remove Beasley as a partner in the firm when it announced it was closing its Palm Beach office by year-end 1994. This finding, in turn, supports the conclusion that CW & T anticipatorily expelled Beasley from the firm. [*Citations omitted.*]

In reaching this conclusion, we necessarily reject CW & T's argument that Beasley voluntary withdrew from the firm rather than having been expelled. Beasley had been practicing exclusively in South Florida for 22 years, where he built a substantial client base. As the trial court observed, to suddenly uproot to New York or Washington and leave his clients and contacts behind, as the court suggested, would have severely diminished his rainmaking abilities. Under these circumstances, we conclude that his rejecting the offer as impractical was not tantamount to a voluntary withdrawal.

Even assuming that CW & T did not anticipatorily breach the agreement on August 29, 1994, we conclude that the November 10, 1994 letter actually expelled him. Even though CW & T notes that Beasley planned on eventually leaving the firm even before it announced the decision to close the Palm Beach office, and that he most likely would not have stayed past 1994, the record does not reflect that he actually had definite plans to leave.

We further reject CW & T's argument that Beasley's suing the firm on November 9, 1994 was tantamount to a voluntary withdrawal. Since CW & T does not dispute the lack of frivolousness of Beasley's lawsuit, but merely takes issue with its allegations, we find its argument unpersuasive. [*Citations omitted.*]

II. THE AWARD OF INTEREST

CW & T then argues the trial court erred in finding that a dissolution occurred and contends that, as a "withdrawn partner" pursuant to the agreement, Beasley was entitled to only his paid-in capital. Even if dissolution had occurred, it argues he still only would be entitled to an amount significantly less than that awarded to him. Beasley disputes that he was a "withdrawn" partner pursuant to the agreement, and contends that dissolution was mandated.

Under the partnership agreement, a "withdrawn Partner" is anyone "who was a Partner under this or a prior Firm Agreement." More specifically, the agreement provides that a partner, upon 60 days written notice, may withdraw from the firm at the end of any fiscal year. CW & T argues that, under these provisions, Beasley was technically a withdrawn partner and, thus, was only entitled to his capital contribution plus interest under Paragraph F(2)(a)(i) of the agreement. We, instead, agree with Judge Cook that the term "withdrawn" neither contemplated nor encompassed a partner expelled in the same manner as Beasley, especially since Beasley never provided any written notice of a voluntary withdrawal, and since CW & T conceded at trial that it did not treat Beasley as a "withdrawn partner" after his departure.

Antidissolution Provision

CW & T then argues that concluding a dissolution occurred would conflict with that portion of the agreement which states, "Neither withdrawal of a Partner nor the death of a Partner, nor *any other event* shall cause dissolution of the Firm [unless 75% of the remaining partners agreed in writing]." (Emphasis added.) It reasons that expulsion of a partner, however wrongful, is an "event" for purposes of this antidissolution clause. We disagree, for to construe this anti-dissolution provision strictly would recognize an implicit expulsion provision where no provision exists. Such an interpretation would be inconsistent with existing law. [*Citations omitted.*]

Even if the provision were broad enough to cover expulsions, we believe Beasley would still be allowed to seek dissolution of the partnership. Under New York law, any partner has the right to a formal accounting as to partnership affairs if he is wrongfully excluded from the partnership business or possession of its property by his co-partners, or "whenever other circumstances render it just and reasonable." *N.Y. Partnership Law § 44* (McKinney 1993). Thus, a wrongful exclusion of one partner by a co-partner from participation in the conduct of the business may be grounds for judicial dissolution. [*Citations omitted.*]

Since Beasley was expelled, his damages are to be assessed under *§ 71 of New York Partnership Law,* and not under the partnership agreement. Since there is competent, substantial evidence in the record to support both the method and result used to calculate his interest in the firm's assets, we affirm the award of interest in the amount of $867,110.00.

III. THE AWARD OF PROFITS

Under New York law, when a partnership continues following the expulsion of a partner, that partner has the right to receive the value of his partnership interest as of the date of dissolution, either with interest from the date of dissolution, or, at his election, the profits attributable to the use of his right in the property of the dissolved partnership. *N.Y. Partnership Law § 73* (McKinney 1993).

Strictly construing this statute, Beasley was entitled to either interest *on the value* of his interest in the dissolved partnership ($867,110) *or* profits attributable to the use of his right in the property of the firm *on top of* the $867,110. Beasley elected to receive the profits attributable to his use through the date of judgment instead of interest at 3% over prime (as defined in the agreement). Based on his expert, Mr. Burgher, having calculated the profits attributable to the use of his right in the property based on the firm's total earnings to reflect what Beasley's total income would have been had he stayed at the firm from November, 1994 through May, 1996, the court awarded Beasley profits in the amount of $935,261.52.

CW & T argues that, as a matter of law, awarding Beasley $935,261.52 in "profits" based on this calculation was incorrect. Relying on *Kirsch v. Leventhal,* 181 A.D.2d 222, 586 N.Y.S.2d 330 (App. Div. 1992), it reasons that Beasley should not be entitled to profits resulting from the postdissolution services of the remaining partners. We agree. To the extent that some of the firm's postdissolution profits may be attributable to the postdissolution efforts, skill, and diligence of the remaining partners, the firm's fee as a result of those services should not be proportionately attributable to the use of the departing partner's right in the property of the dissolved partnership. [*Citations omitted.*] As the record does not clarify what portion, if any, of the postdissolution profits earned on services (as opposed to firm assets) was attributable to Beasley, we find that Beasley failed to carry his burden of showing what the quantum meruit value of his services was after he left the firm.

Beasley tries to distinguish *Kirsch* and the other cases upon which CW & T relies based on the fact that the partners in those cases were not wrongfully expelled. If recognized, this distinction may help justify the court's award, but it would seem to be an impermissible extension of *§ 73*. As an equitable consideration, although the facts underlying Beasley's departure appear much more egregious than in the cases CW & T cites, Beasley still had "dirt under his fingernails." While CW & T should not be unjustly enriched through its wrongful expulsion of Beasley, neither should Beasley be unjustly enriched by reaping the rewards of other partners' individual efforts. Accordingly, we reverse this portion of the award and remand the case to the trial court to calculate Beasley's interest on $867,110 at 3% over prime, the defined rate pursuant to the agreement, under *§ 73*.

IV. THE IMPOSITION OF PUNITIVE DAMAGES

CW & T then argues that the court's award of punitive damages was both unwarranted and erroneous as a matter of law. It asserts that the court's failure to award Beasley compensatory damages on his breach of fiduciary duty claim barred an award of punitive damages under New York law. Under New York law, the nature of the conduct which justifies an award of punitive damages is conduct having a high degree of moral culpability, or, in other words, conduct which shows a "conscious disregard of the rights of others or conduct so reckless as to amount to such disregard." [*Citations omitted.*] CW & T is correct in arguing that punitive damages are generally recovered only after compensatory damages have been awarded; [*Citations omitted.*] [H]owever, since the purpose of punitive damages is to both punish the wrongdoer and deter others from such wrongful behavior, as a matter of policy, courts have the discretion to award punitive damages even where compensatory damages are found lacking. [*Citations omitted.*]

We believe CW &T should not be insulated from the consequences of its wrongdoing simply because Beasley suffered no compensatory damages. As the court found, CW & T "was participating in a clandestine plan to wrongfully expel some partners for the financial gain of other partners. Such activity cannot be said to be honorable, much less to comport with the 'punctilio of an honor.' " Because these findings establish that CW & T consciously disregarded the rights of Beasley, we affirm the award of punitive damages.

V. THE AWARD OF ATTORNEY'S FEES, EXPERT WITNESS COSTS AND TRIAL COSTS

* * * *

[We] reverse the award of costs [and attorney's fees].

QUESTIONS

1. If you were asked to draft the partnership agreement for your law firm, would you make the expulsion provisions moderate, extremely limited or extremely broad?

2. Would it make a difference if you were one of the founders or one of hundreds of partners?

3. Would you be less inclined to join a firm if the partnership agreement made it easy for the firm to expel you?

4. What concerns or questions would dictate the type of expulsion provisions one should include in a partnership agreement?

SECTION VI: Limited Partnerships

A limited partnership is a partnership entity that is required to have at least one limited partner and one general partner. The general partner or partners have personal liability for the debts and obligations of the limited partnership. However, the limited partner or partners, subject to certain limitations discussed below, are not personally liable for debts and obligations of the limited partnership. The liability of a limited partner is typically limited to the amount invested (or committed) to the limited partnership.

In a limited partnership the general partner manages the operation of the business while the limited partner (or partners) are not involved in the day to day management of the business. The rules governing the general partner of a general partnership are similar to the rules that govern general partners of limitedpartnerships. Like a general partnership, limited partnerships are governed by a Partnership Agreement. If there is not a partnership agreement or if there are issues not addressed in the partnership agreement, limited partnerships are subject to default rules. Default rules are similar, but not identical to the default rules for general partnerships. Limited partnerships are governed by state law and may only be created by a filing with a state regulatory agency, which is usually the Secretary of State.

Limited partners do not take part in the management of the business and are not subject to personal liability for the debts and obligations of the business. Their involvement, like their liability, is limited. Furthermore, a limited partnership (at least under existing law) is not subject to veil piercing (discussed *infra*). Therefore, limited partners are protected from unlimited liability to creditors of the firm. However, limited partners may still incur liability for money they receive in the form of improper distributions or fraudulent transfers. (*See Henkels & McCoy, Inc. v. Adochio, et al, infra.*)

If limited partners do participate in the control of the partnership, they risk losing their "limited" status and being treated as general partners and, as such, may incur personal liability. This restriction on participation in the business is known as the "control rule." While historically there was a greater risk of a limited partner losing his or her "limited" status by virtue of the control rule, in states that have adopted the Uniform Limited Partnership Act (2001), limited partners will not risk personal liability for participating in management unless they take other action to incur liability. In other states, a limited partner incurs liability only if that limited partner participated in the control of the limited partnership, a third party is aware of the limited partner's participation in control, and that third party transacts business with the limited partner with the reasonable belief that the limited partner is a general partner. Even under these circumstances, the limited partner's liability would be limited to the specific third party who believed the limited partner to be a general partner, not to all creditors.

Even in states that have not adopted the protections for limited partners contained in the Uniform Limited Partnership Act of 2001, there are a number of "safe harbors" that allow limited partners to participate in management on some level without risking liability. However, as the "control rule" erodes, the existence of the "safe harbor" becomes less necessary. The safe harbor areas include: being a contractor for or an agent or employee of the limited partnership or of a general partner of the limited partnership; being an officer, director, or shareholder of a corporate general partner of the limited partnership; consulting with and advising a general partner with respect to the limited partnership's business; acting as a surety or guarantor of the limited partnership; requesting or attending a meeting of the partners; voting; and winding up the partnership.

There is no requirement that a general partner be an individual, and often more sophisticated ventures will form a corporation to serve as the general partner of a limited partnership. This structure allows a limited partnership to take advantage of the limited liability protections of a corporation and protect the shareholders in the corporate general partner from the liability they could incur if they were to act as individual general partners. Corporations and limited liability are discussed in subsequent chapters of this book.

Limited partners do not have the right to bind the limited partnership and, therefore, may not exercise actual or "apparent authority" over the limited partnership while acting in the capacity of a limited partner.

A limited partnership is a pass through entity for tax purposes, and its partners are taxed on the profits from, and may deduct the losses of, the business. Profits, losses, and distributions may be allocated among the limited and general partners as provided by the Partnership Agreement. If no provision is made for allocations, they typically will be allocated on a percentage basis, based upon capital contributions (i.e., investments) in the limited partnership.

General partners have fiduciary duties that are akin to the fiduciary duties of partners in a general partnership, while limited partners typically do not. However, limited partners are still bound to discharge all duties to the partnership and to the other partners and to exercise any rights they might have, consistent with the obligation of good faith and fair dealing.

Transferability of a limited partner's interest follows similar rules as transferring a general partnership interest. A limited partner may transfer its economic interest without the consent of the other partners, but requires the consent of the other partners to transfer "limited partner" status. The transferee would have the right only to receive funds which would have been distributed to the transferring limited partner on the interest transferred. (Since limited partners are not entitled to participate in the control of the limited partnership, even though a transferee of an economic interest would not have the right to vote, there would be a smaller variation between economic interest and management rights in a limited partnership than there would be in other entities.) General partners will be more restricted in their rights to transfer their general partner interest in the limited partnership. These restrictions are similar to those found in a general partnership.

Limited partners have the right to dissociate from the partnership if it is an "at will" partnership.* However, if the partnership is for a term or a particular undertaking, limited partners may not dissociate without incurring liability for wrongful dissociation. If there is no definite time for the limited partnership to end, then a limited partner may typically withdraw upon six months' notice. A general partner may also withdraw by providing notice, but, if the withdrawal violates the partnership agreement, then the withdrawing general partner is liable for damages. Within a reasonable time following withdrawal, and subject to the

* Note that some statutes use the term "withdraw" and some us the term "dissociate". For these purposes, the terms are interchangeable.

partnership agreement in all respects, (a) the withdrawing limited partner is entitled to the "fair" valuc of his or her interest; (b) the withdrawing general partner is entitled to the "fair" value of his or her interest, less any damages arising out of a breach of the partnership agreement.

Limited partnerships have been used as investment vehicles for years. The structure of a pass through entity for passive investors makes the structure very appealing. (Importantly, limited partnership interests are generally considered securities and subject to the securities laws (discussed *infra*).) While in recent years, limited liability companies have been used more frequently than limited partnerships, limited partnerships still serve an important role as an alternative entity in many situations. Often limited partnerships involve a more complex structure, and, while such structures play an important role in many sophisticated business endeavors and operations they are beyond the scope of this book.

One advantage of a limited partnership is the clear separation between the management role of a general partner and the limited role of the limited partner. As discussed above, when these roles are not respected, the limited partner might be exposed to liability. The *Gateway Potato Sales v. GB Inv. Co.* case below is one example of the potential risk for limited partners who fail to respect these roles.

Gateway Potato Sales v. G.B. Inv. Co.

170 Ariz. 137, 822 P.2d 490 (Ariz.App. Div. 1 1991)

TAYLOR, J.:

Gateway Potato Sales (Gateway), a creditor of Sunworth Packing Limited Partnership (Sunworth Packing), brought suit to recover payment for goods it had supplied to the limited partnership. Gateway sought recovery from Sunworth Packing, from Sunworth Corporation as general partner, and from G.B. Investment Company (G.B. Investment) as a limited partner, pursuant to Arizona Revised Statutes Annotated (A.R.S.) § 29–319. Under § 29–319, a limited partner may become liable for the obligations of the limited partnership under certain circumstances in which the limited partner has taken part in the control of the business.

* * * *

. . . Sunworth Corporation and G.B. Investment formed Sunworth Packing in November 1985 for the purpose of engaging in potato farming in Arizona. The limited partnership certificate and agreement of Sunworth Packing, filed with the office of the Arizona Secretary of State, specified Sunworth Corporation as the general partner and G.B. Investment Company as the limited partner. The agreement recited that the limited partner would not participate in the control of the business. The agreement further stated that the limited partner would not become liable to the creditors of the partnership, except to the extent of its initial contribution and any liability it may incur with an Arizona bank as a signatory party or guarantor of a loan and/or line of credit.

In late 1985, Robert C. Ellsworth, the president of Sunworth Corporation, called Robert Pribula, the owner of Gateway, located in Minnesota, to see if Gateway would supply Sunworth Packing with seed potatoes. Pribula hesitated to supply the seed potatoes without receiving assurance of payment because Pribula was aware that Ellsworth had previously undergone bankruptcy. Pribula, however, decided to sell the seed potatoes to Sunworth Packing after being assured by Ellsworth that he was in partnership with a large financial institution, G.B. Investment Company, and that G.B. Investment was providing the financing, was actively involved in the operation of the business, and had approved the purchase of the seed potatoes. Thereafter, from February 1986 through April 1986, Gateway sold substantial quantities of seed potatoes to Sunworth Packing.

While supplying the seed potatoes, Pribula believed that he was doing business with a general partnership (i.e., Sunworth Packing Company, formed by Sunworth Corporation and G.B. Investment Company). The sales documents used by the parties specified "Sunworth Packing Company" as the name of the partnership. Pribula was neither aware of the true name of the partnership nor that it was a limited partnership.

All of Gateway's dealings were with Ellsworth. Pribula neither contacted G.B. Investment prior to selling the seed potatoes to the limited partnership nor did he otherwise attempt to verify any of the statements Ellsworth had made about G.B. Investment's involvement. The only direct contact between G.B. Investment and Gateway occurred some time after the sale of the seed potatoes. It is, however, disputed whether G.B. Investment ever provided any assurance of payment to Gateway.

G.B. Investment's vice-president, Darl Anderson, testified in his affidavit that G.B. Investment had exerted no control over the daily management and operation of the limited partnership, Sunworth Packing. This testimony was contradicted, however, by the affidavit testimony of Ellsworth which was presented by Gateway in opposing G.B. Investment's motion for summary judgment. According to Ellsworth, G.B. Investment's employees, Darl Anderson and Thomas McHolm, controlled the day-to-day affairs of the limited partnership and made Ellsworth account to them for nearly everything he did. This day-to-day contact included but was not limited to approval of most of the significant operational decisions and expenditures and the use and management of partnership funds without Ellsworth's involvement.[1]

Ellsworth testified further that he had described G.B. Investment's control of the business operation to Pribula. Pribula confirmed that Ellsworth had informed him that G.B. Investment's employees, McHolm and Anderson, were at the partnership's office on a frequent basis, that Ellsworth reported directly to them, that daily operations of the partnership were reviewed by representatives of G.B. Investment, and that Ellsworth had to get their approval before making certain business decisions.

* * * *

Subsection (a) of A.R.S. § 29–319 sets forth the general rule that a limited partner who is not also a general partner is not liable for the obligations of the limited partnership.

> [A] limited partner is not liable for the obligations of a limited partnership unless he is also a general partner or, in addition to the exercise of his rights and powers as a limited partner, he takes part in the control of the business. However, if the limited partner's

---

[1] Ellsworth described with some specificity the ways in which G.B. Investment's control was exerted:

> . . . .b. G.B. Investment Company was solely responsible for obtaining a $150,000.00 line-of-credit loan for the Partnership with Valley National Bank of Arizona, and it also signed documents guaranteeing the repayment of the loan; c. As the President of the general partner, I was not permitted to make any significant independent business decisions concerning the operations of the Partnership, but was directed to have all business decisions approved with Darl Anderson and/or Thomas McHolm. . . . d. Prior to constructing improvements to the packaging facilities of the Partnership, Thomas McHolm and/or Darl Anderson had to approve all construction bids, ... e. Thomas McHolm and/or Darl Anderson dictated the accounting procedures to be followed by the Partnership, reviewed the Partnership's books and accounts almost continually. . . . f. During a great portion of the duration of the Partnership, Thomas McHolm and/or Darl Anderson . . . I had to have all expenditures approved by Thomas McHolm and/or Darl Anderson and Darl Anderson had to approve and sign checks issued by the Partnership . . . . i. At least on two separate occasions, . . . Darl Anderson caused sums of monies (approximately $8,000 and $7,000 respectively) to be withdrawn from the Partnership account . . . with Valley National Bank without the prior knowledge or consent of myself, as the President of the general partner of the Partnership. These monies were paid directly to G.B. Investment, and the withdrawals caused other checks of the Partnership to be dishonored due to insufficient funds. . . .

> participation in the control of the business is not substantially the same as the exercise of the powers of a general partner, he is liable only to persons who transact business with the limited partnership with actual knowledge of his participation in control.

Subsection (a) does not discuss the types of activities that might be undertaken by a limited partner which would amount to "control of the business." Subsection (b), however, does contain a listing of activities that are permissible for a limited partner to undertake without being deemed to be taking part in "control of the business."[2]

A limited partner does not participate in the control of the business within the meaning of subsection (a) solely by doing one or more of the following:

(1) Being a contractor for or an agent or employee of the limited partnership or of a general partner;

(2) Consulting with and advising a general partner with respect to the business of the limited partnership;

(3) Acting as surety for the limited partnership;

(4) Approving or disproving an amendment to the partnership agreement; or

(5) Voting on one or more of the following matters:

  (i) The dissolution and winding up of the limited partnership;

  (ii) The sale, exchange, lease, mortgage, pledge or other transfer of all or substantially all of the assets of the limited partnership other than in the ordinary course of its business;

  (iii) The incurrence of indebtedness by the limited partnership other than in the ordinary course of its business;

  (iv) A change in the nature of the business; or

  (v) The removal of a general partner.

In addition, subsection (c) of A.R.S. § 29–319 provides that "[t]he enumeration in subsection (b) does not mean that the possession or exercise of any other powers by a limited partner constitutes participation by him in the business of the limited partnership."

---

2 The drafters of the Revised Uniform Limited Partnership Act (RULPA) . . ., refer to this listing as a "safe harbor." Revised Uniform Limited Partnership Act § 303. . . .

* * * *

In granting G.B. Investment's motion for summary judgment, the trial court gave two reasons for concluding that G.B. Investment could not be found liable under A.R.S. § 29–319(a) as a matter of law. First, as we interpret the trial court's comments, it read the statute as having a threshold requirement-that is, under all circumstances, a creditor of the limited partnership must have contact with the limited partner in order to impose liability on the limited partner. The evidence before the trial court showed that Gateway merely relied upon the statements made by Ellsworth, president of the general partner, and that Gateway did not contact G.B. Investment prior to transacting business with the limited partnership. Based upon these facts, the trial court concluded that liability could not be imposed upon G.B. Investment. . . .

> . . .Consequently, plaintiff fails to leap the first "hurdle"; and neither the court nor the trier-of-fact need review plaintiff's factual assertions regarding "safe harbor" excesses or violations, if any, under A.R.S. § 29–319(B). The only purported contact between plaintiff and defendant G.B. Investment Company occurred in the fall of 1986, well after the last of the seed potatoes were delivered by plaintiff to the limited partnership. . . .

* * * *

To the extent that the trial court's ruling may have been based on a belief that a limited partner could never be liable under the statute unless the creditor had contact with the limited partner and learned directly from him of his participation and control of the business, we believe that ruling to be in error.

In A.R.S. § 29–319(a), the legislature stopped short of expressly stating that if the limited partner's participation in the control of the business is substantially the same as the exercise of the powers of a general partner, he is liable to persons who transact business with a limited partnership even though they have no knowledge of his participation and control. It has made this statement by implication, though, by stating to the opposite effect that "if the limited partner's participation in the control of the business is not substantially the same as the exercise of the powers of a general partner, he is liable only to persons who transact business with the limited partnership with actual knowledge of his participation in control." A.R.S. § 29–319(a).

* * * *

In 1985, the drafters of the RULPA backtracked from the position taken in section 303(a) of the 1976 Act. The new amendments reflect a reluctance to hold a limited partner liable if the limited partner had no direct contact with the creditor. The 1985 revised RULPA section 303(a) was amended to provide as follows:

> Except as provided in Subsection (d), a limited partner is not liable for the obligations of a limited partnership unless he is also a general partner or, in addition to the exercise of his rights and powers as a limited partner, he participates in the control of the business. *However, if the limited partner participates in the control of the business, he is liable only to persons who transact business with the limited partnership reasonably believing, based upon the limited partner's conduct, that the limited partner is a general partner.*

Id. at 325 (emphasis added).

* * * *

The Arizona legislature, however, has not revised A.R.S. § 29–319(a) to correspond to the section 303 amendments. The Arizona statute continues to impose liability on a limited partner whenever the "substantially the same as" test is met, even though the creditor has no knowledge of the limited partner's control. It follows then that no contact between the creditor and the limited partner is required to impose liability.

Moreover, whereas section 303 of the RULPA states that the creditor's reasonable belief must be "based upon the limited partner's conduct," under A.R.S. § 29–319 the only requirement is that the creditor has had "actual knowledge of [the limited partner's] participation in control." The statute does not state that this knowledge must be based upon the limited partner's conduct. The comments to the original version of section 303 of the RULPA, from which Arizona's statute is taken, make it clear that only when the "substantially the same as" test is met is direct contact not a requirement. Conversely, if the "substantially the same as" test is not met, direct contact is required. Under the facts presented in this case, Gateway had no direct contact with G.B. Investment until after the sales were concluded. We conclude, therefore, that G.B. Investment would be liable only if the "substantially the same as" test was met.

Whether a limited partner has exercised the degree of control that will make him liable to a creditor has always been a factual question. This is so regardless of whether the particular statute involved is patterned after section 7 of the ULPA or after section 303 of the RULPA. [*Citations omitted.*] Our current Arizona statute lists activities that a limited partner may undertake without participating in controlling the business. It also states that other activities may be excluded from the definition of such control. Where activities do not fall within the "safe harbor" of A.R.S. § 29–319(b), it is necessary for a trier-of-fact to determine whether such activities amount to "control." In the absence of actual knowledge of the limited partner's participation in the control of the partnership business, there must be evidence from which a trier-of-fact might find not only control, but control that is "substantially the same as the exercise of powers of a general partner."

We conclude that the evidence Gateway presented in this case should have allowed it to withstand summary judgment. The affidavit testimony of Ellsworth raises the issue whether he was merely a puppet for the limited partner, G.B. Investment. While a few of the activities Ellsworth listed may have fallen within the protected areas listed in A.R.S. § 29–319(b), others did not. Ellsworth's detailed statement raises substantial issues of material facts.

Viewing the facts in the light most favorable to Gateway, we cannot say as a matter of law that G.B. Investment was entitled to summary judgment. We conclude that Gateway is entitled to a determination by trial of the extent of control exercised by G.B. Investment over Sunworth Packing.

For the foregoing reasons, we reverse the judgment of the trial court and remand for further proceedings.

Improper Distributions

While limited partners are typically protected from liability for the debts and obligations of the limited partnership, they might still incur personal liability for an improper distribution. Most states have restrictions on limited partnerships (as well as on corporations and LLCs) restricting the entities ability to take money out of the entity and distribute that money to the owners if such a distribution would leave the entity unable to satisfy its obligations to its creditors. Section 508 of the Uniform Limited Partnership Act (2001) ("U.L.P.A.") provides:

SECTION 508. LIMITATIONS ON DISTRIBUTION.

(a) A limited partnership may not make a distribution in violation of the partnership agreement.

(b) A limited partnership may not make a distribution if after the distribution:

(1) the limited partnership would not be able to pay its debts as they become due in the ordinary course of the limited partnership's activities; or

(2) the limited partnership's total assets would be less than the sum of its total liabilities plus the amount that would be needed, if the limited partnership were to be dissolved, wound up, and terminated at the time of the distribution, to satisfy the preferential rights upon dissolution, winding up, and termination of partners whose preferential rights are superior to those of persons receiving the distribution.

A limited partner who receives an improper distribution is typically not subject to unlimited liability (as might happen if the limited partner were deemed to be a general partner). A limited partner who receives an improper distribution is typically liable (for some period of time) to the extent of that distribution. Some states will further limit the limited partner's potential liability to the extent that the partner received the distribution with knowing that the distribution was improper and "only to the extent that the distribution received by the partner or transferee exceeded the amount that could have been properly paid. . ." (*See U.L.P.A. § 509.*) In other words, most statutes will not allow a limited partner to avoid returning an improper distribution by claiming the protections of limited liability. While such safeguards seem reasonable, consider the result in the following case as an example of the potential consequences of receiving a distribution that might subsequently be characterized as "improper."

Henkels & McCoy, Inc. v. Adochio, et al

138 F.3d 491 (1998)

ROSENN, CIRCUIT JUDGE.:

This appeal presents an important question pertaining to the obligation of limited partners to return capital contributions distributed to them in violation of their partnership agreement which required that they establish reasonably necessary reserves. The issue is rendered complex by an interrelated maze of corporations and partnerships devised by the limited partners and the general partner in their efforts to develop two separate real estate projects. One of these, Timber Knolls, was aborted shortly after conception, and the other, Chestnut Woods, became the genesis of protracted litigation and of this appeal.

The defendants-appellants are limited partners of Red Hawk North Associates, L.P. (Red Hawk) L.P., a New Jersey limited partnership. G&A

Development Corporation (G&A) is the general partner of Red Hawk. Cedar Ridge Development Corporation (Cedar Ridge), a New Jersey corporation, and Red Hawk entered into a joint venture agreement, the Chestnut Woods Partnership (Chestnut), to develop, construct, and market residential homes in Bucks County, Pennsylvania. Red Hawk and Cedar Ridge are both general partners of Chestnut Woods. Under the joint venture agreement, Red Hawk would provide the funding and Cedar Ridge would provide the land which it previously had agreed to purchase. Cedar Ridge would act as the managing partner and general contractor.

On December 29, 1988, Cedar Ridge, as general contractor for Chestnut Woods, entered into a written subcontract with Henkels & McCoy, Inc. (Henkels), the plaintiff herein, to have it furnish the labor, materials, and equipment for the installation of the storm and sanitary sewer systems for the project. Cedar Ridge agreed to pay Henkels a fixed-price of $300,270 under the contract. Henkels completed the installation of the storm and sewer systems but Chestnut Woods defaulted in making the payments due under the contract. Henkels, a Pennsylvania corporation, then filed three actions in the United States District Court for the Eastern District of Pennsylvania; Henkels filed the first in December 1990 against Cedar Ridge and Red Hawk, trading as Chestnut Woods, for the balance due on the contract plus interest. The court entered a default judgment which was not satisfied in whole or part.

Henkels then filed suit against G&A in its capacity as a general partner of Red Hawk and obtained a default judgment in the same amount as it had obtained against Cedar Ridge and Red Hawk. Efforts to obtain payment on this judgment also proved fruitless and counsel for the defendants advised plaintiff's counsel by letter dated October 26, 1993 that Red Hawk was worthless. Henkels' counsel also had been advised that G&A was unable to pay the judgment out of its assets.

Henkels finally brought this suit against the nineteen limited partners of Red Hawk (the Partners), standing in the shoes of the Red Hawk limited partnership; sixteen of the partners are parties to this appeal. Henkels sought, *inter alia,* to compel replacement of certain capital distributions made by Red Hawk to the limited partners aggregating $492,000 during the period that Cedar Ridge was obligated under its contract with Henkels to pay Henkels $300,270. Henkels alleged that the capital distributions were made in violation of the Red Hawk limited partnership agreement and *§ 42:2A–46(b)* of the New Jersey Uniform Limited Partnership Law of 1976 (New Jersey ULPL). . . .

After the district court denied both Henkels's and the Partners' motions for summary judgment, it conducted a bench trial and on January 6, 1997, entered judgment in favor of Henkels. The court held each limited partner of Red Hawk liable to Henkels for his proportionate share of liability in the total amount of $371,101.84 plus interest to the date of payment of any judgment. The Partners appealed. We affirm.

I.

* * * *

In 1987, Red Hawk and Cedar Ridge entered into a joint venture agreement forming the Chestnut Woods Partnership, with both Red Hawk and Cedar Ridge as general partners. Under the joint venture agreement, Red Hawk would provide the capital funds for the project and Cedar Ridge would provide the general management and assign its contract for the purchase of the land. Red Hawk funded the Partnership with an initial capital contribution of $650,000 (and an additional contribution of $200,000 in 1988). Cedar Ridge agreed to act as both the managing partner and the general contractor of the Chestnut Woods project. In addition, Cedar Ridge had the right to incur liabilities on behalf of the partnership in connection with the partnership's reasonable and legitimate business, borrow money in the name of the partnership, and incur reasonable and legitimate expenses related to the Chestnut Woods property. Work on the Chestnut Woods project subsequently commenced.

In 1988, Red Hawk and Cedar Ridge entered into a second and distinct joint venture agreement to form the Timber Knolls partnership, under which both Red Hawk and Cedar Ridge were also general Partners. Red Hawk contributed $2.3 million to the Timber Knolls partnership and Cedar Ridge again agreed to act as both the managing partner and the general contractor of the project. Unlike the Chestnut Woods project, the Timber Knolls project never commenced operations. Therefore, in 1988, the Red Hawk Partners entered into an agreement with Cedar Ridge requiring the latter to return Red Hawk's $2.3 million capital contribution. As evidence of this obligation, Cedar Ridge executed promissory notes aggregating $2.3 million with interest and principal payable quarterly. 4 Cedar Ridge made quarterly payments to Red Hawk on the notes, and G&A distributed these payments to the individual Red Hawk Partners, [in January, April and Jul of 1989].

Meanwhile, on December 29, 1988, Cedar Ridge, in its role as general contractor of Chestnut Woods, bound itself to a $300,270 fixed-price contract with Henkels, under which Henkels agreed to furnish and install storm and sanitary sewer systems for the Chestnut Woods development. The contract identified Cedar Ridge as the "General Contractor," Henkels as the "Subcontractor," and Chestnut Woods as the "Property Owner." The contract did not mention the relationship between Cedar Ridge and the Chestnut Woods Partnership, and made no reference to Red Hawk. It provided that the General Contractor, Cedar Ridge, was obligated to pay Henkels, payments to be made against billed invoices 30 days after approved inspection. At that time, Henkels was unaware that Cedar Ridge and Red Hawk were partners in Chestnut Woods.

On January 16, 1989, Henkels commenced the installation of the Chestnut Woods storm and sewer systems and completed the work according to the contract in late 1989. . . .

. . .Henkels received a partial payment in October on its August invoice and no payments on its September and November invoices, leaving a total unpaid balance of $237,943. G&A, the general partner for Red Hawk, failed to establish any reserves from the cash receipts of the limited partnership. . . .

* * * *

II.

On appeal, the Partners contend that the district court erred in holding that at the times of the distributions by Red Hawk to its limited partners, Henkels was a creditor of Red Hawk and that the distributions were made in violation of the partnership agreement.

* * * *

. . . .Henkels . . . allege[s] that the distributions made by G&A to the Partners were illegal under Section 42:2A–46(b) of the New Jersey ULPL. Henkels specifically alleges that the distributions violated the New Jersey ULPL because they were made in violation of the Red Hawk partnership agreement. Accordingly, we confine our analysis to the relevant sections of the partnership agreement in conjunction with Section 42:2A–46(b) which, in its entirety, reads as follows:

> b. If a limited partner has received the return of any part of his contribution *in violation of the partnership agreement* or this chapter, he is liable to the limited partnership for a period of six years thereafter for the amount of the contribution wrongfully returned. (Emphasis added).

Section 12(a) of the Red Hawk partnership agreement specifically provided that cash receipts be used for the establishment of reasonable reserves (for creditors) before such receipts be distributed to the Partners.[5] The Partners contend that the distributions were not made in violation of the partnership agreement because Henkels, under the sewer subcontract, at most was a creditor of only Cedar Ridge, not of either Chestnut Woods or Red Hawk. Thus Red Hawk, they argue, was not required to establish reserves. Pursuant to this reasoning, the Partners assert that because Henkels was not a creditor, they did not receive the 1989 distributions in violation of the partnership agreement and thus did not violate the New Jersey ULPL.

[The court held that the district court did not err in its finding that Henkels was a creditor of Red Hawk, despite dealing only with Cedar Ridge because Cedar Ridge acted as the managing partner of Chestnut Woods, which was an undisclosed principal.]

* * * *

The Partners also argue that the district court erred in finding that Henkels was a creditor of Red Hawk, because, even assuming *arguendo* that a contractual relationship existed between Red Hawk and Henkels, Henkels had not extended any credit to Cedar Ridge, Chestnut Woods, or Red Hawk. The unpaid invoices at issue here are from August, September, and November 1989, whereas the distributions to the Red Hawk Partners were made prior, in January, April, and July 1989. Therefore, the Partners claim that this is in itself prima facie proof that Henkels was not a creditor—i.e., Henkels was not owed any money at the time of the distributions. These arguments, however, take a very narrow and ultimately erroneous legal view of the contractual relationship with Henkels and even a more constricted view of the definition of creditor.

Although the term creditor is undefined in the New Jersey ULPL and there is no New Jersey case law interpreting the term in this context, the term creditor is not foreign to New Jersey law. For instance, many New Jersey statutes define creditor very broadly to include "the holder of any claim, of whatever character, ... whether secured or unsecured, matured or unmatured, liquidated or unliquidated, absolute or contingent." .... In addition, the generic common law definition of creditor is very broad and

5 Section 12, in pertinent part, provides that:

(a) *Application of Cash Receipts.* Cash receipts shall be applied in the following order of priority:

...

(iv) to the establishment of such reserves as the General Partner shall reasonably deem necessary; and

(v) to distributions to the Partners ...

> includes every one having [the] right to require the performance of *any* legal obligation [or] contract, . . . or a legal right to damages growing out of [a] contract or tort, and includes not merely the holder of a fixed and certain present debt, but *every one* having a right to require the performance of *any* legal obligation [or] contract, . . . or a legal right to damages growing out of [a] contract or tort.
>
> *Black's Law Dictionary 368* (6th ed. 1990) (emphasis added).

Finally, the failure of the statute to define creditor is indicative of the New Jersey legislature's intent that the term "creditor" be construed consistent with the New Jersey ULPL's broad remedial purpose and its common usage. *See N.J. Stat. Ann. § 1:1–1* (General rules of construction). . . .

Pursuant to the subcontract agreement, Henkels had a claim to payment for a fixed contract price to be paid in installments upon progressive completion of the sewer work. Although the Partners argue that Henkels did not have a claim at the time of the 1989 distributions, the contract between Henkels and Cedar Ridge was entered into on December 29, 1988. Thus Henkels and Cedar Ridge had definite obligations to each other under the contract over a week *prior* to the first distribution by the general partner to the Red Hawk limited partners. Those obligations required Henkels to make the site improvements and Cedar Ridge to make scheduled payments as performance was rendered. In addition, G&A made the bulk of the distributions *after* Henkels had commenced work and was incurring costs and expenses in fulfilling its commitments under the contract. Thus Chestnut Woods and Red Hawk had incurred liability as early as December 29, 1988, although the bulk of the payment matured the month after the last distribution by Red Hawk to the Partners.

The Partners' overly narrow definition of creditor is inconsistent with the obvious financial realities that existed at the time, the generally accepted common law meaning of the term, the broad definition used in other New Jersey statutory contexts, and the broad remedial purpose of the statute. Accordingly, we hold that under this broad definition and consistent with the principles of agency and partnership law previously discussed, Henkels was not only a creditor of Cedar Ridge, but of Chestnut Woods, and thus Red Hawk and its partners. The Partners further argue that even if we conclude that Henkels was a creditor of Chestnut Woods, Red Hawk was not "jointly and severally" liable for the partnership's debts, but only "jointly" liable, as it was only a partner in Chestnut Woods. The Partners find this significant and contend that as a partner Red Hawk was only contingently liable as a guarantor of collection, not as a guarantor of payment. Furthermore, the Partners contend that even then Red

Hawk was not liable until Henkels had obtained a judgment against the Chestnut Woods partnership, was unable to collect, and then sought payment from Chestnut Woods's partner, Red Hawk. Therefore, the Partners conclude, Henkels was not a creditor of Red Hawk until this eventuality ultimately did occur in October 1991—more than two years *after* the distributions. Thus, they assert there was no violation of Section 42:2A–46(b) or the partnership agreement. Although the Partners make much of the distinction between "joint" and "joint and several liability," and between "guarantor of *collection*" and "guarantor of *payment*," the distinctions between these terms are illusory here and are not dispositive. . . .

* * * *

. . .Although the Partners' individual assets were only contingently at risk, the Partners nonetheless were liable to Henkels from the time the contract was signed and, as ultimately did happen, their assets did become available when the Red Hawk partnership's assets proved insufficient to meet its debt with Henkels.

Accordingly, we hold that the district court's finding that Henkels was a creditor of Red Hawk was correct. *See Henkels & McCoy,* 906 F. Supp. at 252–53. At the time of the 1989 distributions, Henkels was a creditor of Red Hawk and the individual Red Hawk partners were liable for that debt.[8]

III.

Although Henkels was a creditor of Red Hawk, the 1989 distributions were in violation of the partnership agreement only if, as Henkels argues, Red Hawk's distributions constituted a failure to abide by the partnership agreement's requirement to establish reasonably necessary reserves. The Partners, however, contend that the district court made several errors in interpreting the Red Hawk partnership agreement which resulted in its finding that the distributions were in violation of the agreement by failing to establish such reasonable reserves.

Section 9(b) of the partnership agreement grants the general partner, G&A, certain rights and powers, including, under subsection (ix), the power "to

---

[8] The dissent would extend our holding far beyond its limit. It concludes that the majority holds "by necessary implication. . . that a distribution could not be made to Red Hawk partners unless cash reserves had been established to fund the payment of all anticipated future liabilities of the joint venture partnerships (owned in part by others) that might accrue over some unspecified period of time . . . ." Dissent at p. 30. We are not called upon in this case to decide whether reserves are required for "all anticipated future liabilities" and therefore the majority does not decide that question, either directly or by implication. The focus of our holding is merely that when there is clear liability under an existing contract, the equity partners cannot ignore that liability, recapture their capital investments, and leave the creditor spinning in the wind.

establish reasonable reserve funds from income derived from the Partnership's operations to provide for future . . . debt service or similar requirements." The Partners argue that this subsection is the *only* subsection of the agreement that permits or authorizes the general partner to reserve funds. Thus, according to the Partners, all reserves had to be (1) authorized by this subsection, (2) taken from income derived from operations, and (3) used for debt service. Therefore, had G&A reserved funds against the Henkels contract, the Partners contend that such reserves would have been taken in violation of this subsection of the partnership agreement because the funds would not have been derived from operations but from distributions of capital.

The Partners' argument fails, however, because it selectively presents the language of Sections 9 and 12 and omits other relevant language which demonstrates that the Partners greatly overemphasize the significance of subsection (ix). First, the express language of Section 9(b) provides that the general partner possess all "rights and powers required for or appropriate to its management of the partnership's business which, *by way of illustration but not by way of limitation,* shall include the following: . . . (ix) to establish reasonable reserve funds from income derived from the partnership's operations to provide for future . . . debt service or similar requirements." This unambiguous language demonstrates that G&A had the right and power to establish reserves, even if not expressly authorized under subsection (ix), if it deemed them required or appropriate for the management of Red Hawk's business. The list of rights and powers in subsection (ix) is merely illustrative and is not an exclusive limitation on the general partner's rights and powers.

Equally important, as the district court properly found, the distributions at issue here were not taken from income derived from operations, but were merely returns of capital of the aborted Timber Knolls partnership, which, as Red Hawk admits, "never got off the ground." Income from "operations," as used in this subsection, refers to income derived from the active, normal, on-going activities of the partnership. Timber Knolls never functioned, and thus there never was any income from operations. Therefore, subsection (ix) is not applicable to the distributions at issue here. It is completely irrelevant because the distributions constituted capital funds retrieved by Red Hawk from its abandoned project, Timber Knolls. Although the Partners emphasize that the funds were derived from the Timber Knolls project, Subsection (ix) only addresses the reserving of funds derived from *operations;* the germinating *project* is immaterial.

Finally, as previously discussed, Henkels qualified as a creditor of Red Hawk at the time the distributions were made. Therefore, pursuant to Section

12(a) of the Red Hawk limited partnership agreement governing the distribution of *all* cash receipts, the Red Hawk general partner was required to establish reasonable reserves from the cash received on the Timber Knolls promissory notes to meet its ongoing liability *before* distributing such cash to the individual limited partners. We, therefore, turn to the issue as to what would constitute a "reasonable" reserve to meet the outstanding liability under the Henkels subcontract. Although neither party provided the district court with any case law or treatise defining reasonable reserves, the court used the Black's Law Dictionary definition of "reasonable" and of "reserves" in the insurance context to define reasonable reserves in the business context before us. We agree with them that the insurance context is inappropriate for analysis because the nature of the insurance business differs significantly from that of an ordinary business partnership. Unlike an ordinary business partnership, an insurance company essentially is required to meet future, contingent obligations, and these reserves are required. The Partners instead propose that the highly deferential corporate "business judgment" standard is the appropriate standard. However, as Henkels correctly argues, the business judgment rule also is inapposite in the partnership context because it is a function of a unique corporate setting. . . .

. . . Regardless of what standard the New Jersey courts will ultimately adopt, under any standard and using any definition of reasonable reserves, the Red Hawk general partner's failure to establish any reserves in the face of the fixed obligation and imminent payments due under the contract with Henkels and the operations of the Chestnut Woods development was callous and not reasonable.

It is undisputed that of the approximately $500,000 monies received by Red Hawk in 1989, the Red Hawk general partner (G&A) did not set aside any of these funds to establish reserves, even in the face of a contracted liability. Red Hawk argues, however, that this was not unreasonable because (1) the Red Hawk partnership had no liabilities and $3 million in assets at the time of the distributions; (2) Henkels had not yet invoiced Chestnut Woods; (3) the financial outlook of Red Hawk (& Chestnut Woods) was healthy; and (4) the express terms of the partnership agreement prohibited the taking of such reserves. Each of these contentions is without merit.

First, the $3 million of assets included on Red Hawk's January 1, 1989 balance sheet is somewhat illusory. Of the $3 million in assets, a scant $22,000 was in the form of cash or other liquid assets. The remaining were almost exclusively illiquid: the $800,000 investment in the Chestnut Woods project itself which consisted of land and infrastructure and the $2.1 million Timber Knolls notes receivable from Cedar Ridge—which were substantially distributed to the limited partners. Neither of these assets were readily available to satisfy Red Hawk obligations, especially not after the payments on the notes were distributed to the partners. Moreover, Red Hawk repeatedly left almost no money in its checking account after each distribution to the Partners, other than several thousand dollars to cover incidental operating expenses. Additionally, the absence of any formal liabilities from its balance sheet and the failure of Henkels to physically invoice Cedar Ridge did not mean that Red Hawk had no liabilities; it simply was an "off-balance sheet" liability. In the accounting profession, an "off-balance sheet" liability is a financial obligation that is not formally recognized in an entity's accounting statements because no "accounting" obligation arises until the exchange transactions is completed; nonetheless, they do have real current and future cash flow consequences. *See Accountant's Handbook,* 10.29 (7th ed. 1991). Under the broad definition of creditor established above, Red Hawk had an unmatured, fixed, off-balance sheet liability to Henkels.

Although by itself this may be not determinative, more telling is the Partners' failure to identify any other source of funds from which the Red Hawk Partnership would be able to meet its obligations, including its contract obligation to Henkels. . . . Without any other source of cash or liquid assets, short of liquidating the Chestnut Woods property itself, it clearly was unreasonable for G&A to distribute to the Partners Red Hawk's only available source of payment without setting aside any reserves to meet the Henkels debt.

Second, and equally telling, G&A knew, or at least had ample notice, that the financial outlook of Red Hawk and Chestnut Woods was not as rosy at the time of the distributions as the Partners attempt to assert now. For example, the Partners fail to mention or accurately state many of the following facts: (1) Red Hawk and G&A, in December 1988, received notification from Cedar Ridge that four separate and distinct types of delays in the Chestnut Woods project were resulting in additional financial burdens to it; (2) Cedar Ridge also informed Red Hawk that these financial burdens were worrisome given the decline already experienced in the housing market; (3) Red Hawk had a scant $22,000 in cash or other liquid assets on hand as of January 1, 1989; (4) Chestnut Woods had an equally scant $12,000 in cash or other liquid assets on hand as of January 1, 1989; (5) Chestnut Woods' January 1, 1989 balance sheet showed over $1.7 million in current liabilities, with the land and construction in progress of Chestnut Woods comprising over 90% of its $2.4 million in assets, leaving meager resources available to pay for the planned 1989 site improvements, such as the $300,000 of sewer systems from Henkels; 12 (6) as of March 7, 1989, Red Hawk had, at a minimum, imputed knowledge from its bank's written notice that interest on the Chestnut Woods mortgage would no longer be paid out of the interest reserve fund and that Cedar Ridge was responsible to pay interest out of its own funds due to "the past unfortunate circumstances [which] caused slower than expected [progress on the Chestnut Woods project,]" and which caused the remaining interest reserve to become substantially depleted and potentially "insufficient to carry this loan;" and (7) the August 1989 $2.7 million appraisal of the Chestnut Woods project was merely a *potential future retail* estimate and contained the express caveat that this "value estimate[ ] assumes that all site improvements will be completed in a workmanlike manner and within a reasonable period of time."

Finally, as previously discussed, the Red Hawk partnership agreement did not prohibit G&A from reserving funds for the payment of Henkels. Section 9(b)(ix) is merely an illustration of G&A's rights and powers and, because the funds at issue were not derived from operations, ultimately was irrelevant to the funds at issue. More importantly, Section 12(a) expressly required that the available cash funds be used to establish reserves before they were distributed to the Partners.

Although neither Henkels nor the district court attempted to determine what level of reserves was reasonable, no determination was needed because Red Hawk and G&A failed to establish *any* reserves. It is patently obvious that at least *some* level of reserves was reasonably necessary, and that the general partners' distributions and failure to reserve *any* money for the Henkels contract obligation, in light of Chestnut Woods' and Red Hawk's precarious financial condition, was unreasonable. Thus, the district court did not need to determine what level of reserves was reasonable; it clearly had an ample factual basis upon which to determine that the complete failure to establish any reserves was a violation of the Red Hawk partnership agreement's requirement that G&A establish some level of reserves before making distributions to the Partners. Accordingly, we hold that Red Hawk's failure to establish any reserves in light of both partnerships' then existing financial condition was not reasonable.

IV.

. . . . The Partners are therefore obligated to return the improper capital distributions to Red Hawk. Because the plaintiff stands in the shoes of Red Hawk for the purpose of recovering these funds on behalf of the partnership, *In re: Sharps Run Associates, 157 B.R. 766, 772–73 (D.N.J. 1993)*, and because of the multiple suits it already has been compelled to undergo to enforce collection of its debt, judicial resources will be conserved and economies of time and expenses effectuated, to hold the Partners directly liable to Henkels.

Accordingly, the judgment of the district court will be affirmed. . . .

QUESTIONS

1. In the preceding case, the money that was distributed from the Timber Knolls project was found to be recoverable based upon a claim arising out of the Cedar Ridge project. How might a forward-thinking attorney have avoided this result when Red Hawk was structured?

2. If you were the attorney for a limited partnership contemplating a large distribution, but concerned that there could be unknown, contingent liabilities, how would you advise your client to proceed?

3. If your client was a limited partner in such a partnership should they accept a distribution without some certification that the distribution was "proper"?

SECTION VII: Limited Liability Companies

Limited liability companies have become increasingly popular in recent years. These entities are frequently used in privately held businesses for variety of endeavors. LLCs are so appealing because they offer the tax structure and flexibility of partnership and the limited liability of a corporation. LLCs may accommodate a variety of ownership and management structures. While and entire course could be filled with a detailed study of the rules and structures of partnerships and limited liability companies, this book outlines some of the basic structural features of the LLC. However, students should be aware that the many of the concepts addressed in the partnership section will apply to certain aspects of the LLC, while elements of the law of corporations will apply to other aspects LLCs. In some of these instances, cases involving LLCs have been included with the cases relating to the relevant area of corporate law to highlight the connection between the specific rules that span these organizations. (*See e.g.* Chapter 3, Section III, regarding piercing the veil and; Chapter 8, Section I, regarding information about securities in partnerships and LLCs.) Nevertheless, this book only provides a basic introduction to LLCs. Students with an interest in business should take subsequent courses which explore in more detail the rules of LLCs and the wide range of structures that may be implemented in an LLC. The many business associations covered in this book, even those addressed in the context of partnerships or corporations, should provide a strong foundation for such subsequent study. The following is a summary of some of the major structural features of limited liability companies.

A. Structure

As mentioned above, the structure of an LLC combines the limited liability of a corporation with the flexibility of a partnership. The owners of an LLC are referred to as "Members." The person, or people, who operate the LLC, are called the "Manager(s)." An LLC may be "member managed" or "manager managed." An LLC is formed by filing Articles of Organization with the Secretary of State's office in the state in which the LLC organizer(s) wish to form the entity. An LLC is governed by both the statutory rules of the state and an "Operating Agreement." In most instances, the Operating Agreement will dictate how the LLC is governed, and the state's LLC statute will fill in any gaps not addressed in the Operating Agreement. As is the situation with partnerships, the statutory rules are known as the "default" rules. The default rules will also put limitations on just how far an Operating Agreement can alter the statutory framework. For example, most states will not allow the Operating Agreement to provide for a blanket waiver of all fiduciary duties of a manager. LLCs are typically not required to follow as many formalities as corporations. For example, unless required in the Operating Agreement, there is no requirement that the members of an LLC hold regular meetings.

The most significant features of an LLC are: (1) limited liability; (2) flow-through (also known as "pass through") taxation; (3) the ability of owners to participate in management without risking personal liability; (4) flexibility in the ability to allocate profits and losses to members; (5) flexibility and choices in the entity's management structure (centralized or decentralized); and (6~~5~~) partnership-like fiduciary duties.

B. Member Managed

In a member managed LLC, the entity has more of the "feel" of a partnership. The owners are engaged in the daily operation of the business as agents of the LLC. They will vote on matters related to governance and will have responsibilities consistent with the organization's Operating Agreement. States are split on whether the default rules for member voting should be pro rata (by percentage) as in a corporation or "per capita" (one vote per person) as in a partnership. In any event the voting rights of the members are typically set forth in the Operating Agreement. In a member managed LLC, the members have fiduciary duties to the LLC and to each other, similar to the duties owed among partners in a partnership. Each member has the apparent authority to bind the LLC in transactions in the ordinary course of business, unless the member lacks the actual authority to act and the person with whom the member was dealing had actual knowledge that the member lacked authority.

C. Manager Managed

In a manager managed LLC, the operation of the entity is handled by a "manager." The manager may be one person or several people, and those people may be members, but there is no requirement that a manager also be a member. The scope of the manager's responsibility may be set forth in the Operating Agreement. So, the manager may have a great deal of power over the entity or very limited power. Managers owe fiduciary duties to the LLC and to its members. Managers also have the apparent authority to bind the LLC in transactions in the ordinary course of business, unless the manager had no actual authority and the person with whom the manager was dealing had actual knowledge that the manager lacked authority. Members (who are not also managers) of a manager managed LLC do not have the apparent authority to bind the LLC.

D. Taxation

LLCs are typically taxed like partnerships and follow partnership accounting. The profits and losses of an LLC are "passed through" to the members who are responsible for paying tax on the profits and will be able to report the losses on their respective personal income tax returns. The LLC does not pay its own taxes. (Note however, that many states impose small fees and taxes on the LLC itself.) The IRS does allow an LLC to elect to be taxed as a corporation. However, this option is rarely selected since partnership taxation is one of the significant benefits of an LLC.

E. Liability for the Members

In general, the owners of an LLC have limited liability and are not personally liable for the debts and obligations of the business. However, it is possible to "pierce" the LLC veil and the standard is typically the same as the standard for piercing the corporate veil: a unity of interest (or disregard for the entity's separate existence) and some type of "fraud-like conduct" or injustice. The difference in LLC cases is that LLCs are required to follow fewer formalities. Therefore, an LLC does not violate the unity of interest test by not having formal meetings or keeping minutes (as can happen with a corporation), unless the Operating Agreement requires meetings. (Most Operating Agreements don't require meetings because they do not want to establish a basis for veil piercing down the road.) A member and an LLC may still violate the unity of interest test by co-mingling funds, by not keeping separate financial records or bank accounts, by failing to respect the separate existence of the LLC or by undercapitalization. However, because a common issue in the context of piercing a corporation's veil is failure to have meetings, keep minutes or issue stock, there are fewer instances of LLC piercing than piercing the corporate veil. Assuming the LLC veil is not pierced, members do not have personal liability for the debts of the LLC, regardless of how much they participate in management. Members might have some personal liability for distributions they receive, or vote for, in excess of the amount the LLC needs to retain in order to satisfy its obligations to creditors. *See Kaycee Land and Livestock v. Flahive*, 46 P.3d 323 (Wyo. 2002) in the following chapter.

As in a limited partnership, LLC members in an LLC also have liability for improper distributions which they receive from the LLC. However, in such instances the personal liability of the member cannot exceed the amount of the improper distribution.

F. Transferability

The transfer limitations in an LLC are similar to those in a partnership. Typically, membership interests in an LLC are not transferable without the consent of the other members. An attempted transfer would usually wind up in a transfer of the member's "economic" interest but not her management interest, and the transferee would have no management rights, and could not become a member without the consent of the other members. The transferee would only have the right to receive funds which would have been distributed to the transferring member on the economic interest transferred.

G. Dissociation

When a member leaves an LLC, that departure is known as "dissociation." (Note that this same term is used in partnerships.) Dissociation may be voluntary ("I'm leaving") or involuntary ("You've been expelled"). In either instance the dissociating member is usually entitled to receive the value of her interest, less any damages caused by the dissociation if the dissociation is "wrongful." If the LLC is for a term or for a particular undertaking, the dissociating member may need to wait to receive payment for her interest until the end of the term or undertaking. Rules governing transfers and dissociation are typically dealt with in the Operating Agreement, and may be different than those outlined above.

H. Dissolution

Most LLC statutes provide that an LLC's existence will continue until it is dissolved. An LLC will typically be dissolved and its affairs wound up, as provided in its Operating Agreement or upon a vote of its members. LLCs are subject to judicial dissolution as well and the state statutes, under certain circumstances that vary from state to state, will give courts the power to dissolve an LLC as well.

CHAPTER THREE

Introduction to Corporations

YOU HAVE BEEN WORKING AT the firm for several months, and, because work has been very demanding and you have a free evening, you decide to join some of your friends at a party. At this party you find yourself talking with Carl Cooker. Carl is a chef and is going to be opening a barbeque restaurant called "Carl's Corral". When he finds out that you are an attorney, Carl is very excited because he needs legal advice.

Experiencing Assignment 5: Carl's Corral, Inc.

FACTS:

Carl is excited because a local bank has agreed to give Carl a $100,000 line of credit to fund the opening and initial operations of the restaurant. Carl also tells you that he is going to sign a lease in the next few days and that it will take some time to build out the space for the restaurant. So, Carl's Corral will not open for a few months. In addition, he mentions that several people have been suggesting that he form a corporation, and Carl would like to form the corporation before the restaurant opens. As you speak more about the restaurant, Carl explains that one of the "benefits" of the restaurant business is that many people pay in cash. He relates his understanding that you do not need to report the cash and can just deposit it into your personal account, which will save money on taxes. When you ask Carl about the bank loan, Carl explains that he also plans to sign the loan documents in the next few weeks. However, the bank will only allow him to draw down on the credit line once the restaurant is open. Carl says this is probably fine, since Carl is planning to put all of the restaurant expenses on his personal credit cards, until the restaurant is open. Carl has already ordered some furniture and equipment for the restaurant and plans to pay for that furniture and for the construction work on the restaurant space by using his credit cards as well. Carl plans to use a portion of the line of credit to pay off his credit card bill once the restaurant opens and he has access to the money. Carl asks if he can meet with you at your office the next day. He would like your help forming a corporation sometime in the next few months and with some of the logistics associated with setting up a new business as a corporation and maximizing the benefits of operating his business as a corporation. He does mention that he does not have any cash to invest in a corporation right now, but that he is planning to assign the line of credit to the corporation. You are excited to be generating business for the firm and that you have a client of your own. You tell Carl that you can meet with him tomorrow at 3:00.

ASSIGNMENT:

You realize that you should spend the morning preparing for the meeting. Please outline the points that you plan to address with Carl in the meeting. Your outline should include any issues you identify that relate to the formation, operation and organization of Carl's Corral as a corporation. While you may assist Carl with other matters in the future, at present you do not have enough information to discuss the specific terms of the credit line or the lease. Your outline does not need to include the terms of your engagement. Your outline should be clear about the matters you intend to cover with Carl, the important points you would like to make, questions you would like to ask him and the information you might need from him. Carl is a "no-nonsense" guy, and he does not want elaborate or fancy talk. Please keep your points as simple as possible and limit your outline to two pages.

This Assignment does not need to be completed, and should not be completed, until the end of the section. However, as you study the cases and other materials that follow, it might be helpful to do so with a view toward providing assistance to Carl. Some of the materials in the chapter will relate more than others to the issues facing Carl. However, the materials are designed to build your understanding of the rules that arise in the formation and operation of a corporation and assist you in addressing Carl's concerns and the issues he might face. Please keep Carl's issues and the questions presented by the assignment in mind while reading the materials that follow.

SECTION I: Promoters

Before a corporation is even formed, someone needs to take some action. The action may be merely filing the Articles of Incorporation to create the corporation, or it may involve months of planning and preparation. The individuals who organize and/or make financing or other arrangements for a corporation before it is formed are called "Promoters." They will often perform work for the soon-to-be formed corporation and enter into contracts. While often the promoter is also the incorporator, this does not need to be the case. Incorporators are the people who actually form the corporation and execute the Articles of Incorporation. Promoters often do work related to laying the "ground work" for the corporation's business or operations, such as entering into initial contracts, prospectively, on behalf of the yet-to-be-formed corporation. These contracts might be intended to secure or provide important elements of the soon-to-be-formed corporation's business, such as potential customers, supplies or inventory, distribution channels, or rental space. Sometimes promoters will also coordinate the investment that is to be made in the new corporation before it is formed.

Promoters have fiduciary duties (both a duty of care and a duty of loyalty) to the corporation they promote and to those who will eventually buy stock in the corporation. These duties are the same fiduciary duties that one sees in agency because a promoter is an agent for the proposed corporation.

A question that frequently arises in this area involves the contracts into which the promoter has entered on behalf of the corporation. The basic rules are that the promoter is bound by any contract entered into on behalf of a corporation that has not yet been formed (whether the contract was entered into in the promoter's name or in the name of the proposed corporation), unless there is a clear intent that the promoter not be bound or the circumstances are such that the promoter could not perform the agreement. (Notice that these rules mirror the rules governing a contract entered into by an agent for an undisclosed or unidentified principal discussed in Chapter 1, *supra.*) Once the corporation is formed, it may be bound by the contract, but only if the corporation agrees to be bound. A corporation may agree to be bound by adopting the contract, either by expressly ratifying the contract (often through a novation) or by impliedly ratifying the contract through the corporation's actions (for example, by paying the rent on a lease) or accepting or acknowledging the benefits of the contract.

Ratification by the corporation does not, however, release the promoter from liability. The promoter remains bound under the agreement, unless there is an agreement (a novation) from the other parties to the contract to release the promoter from liability. Typically, such an agreement would provide that only the corporation is bound and not the promoter. If both the promoter and the corporation are bound, and the other party to the contract wishes to sue for breach of contract, that party usually must choose whether it is going to sue the promoter or the corporation. If the corporation has adopted the contract and the promoter is sued, the promoter will usually have a claim for indemnification against the corporation. However, the value of any such claim would be dependent upon whether there were resources remaining in the corporation. If the corporation is never formed, then the promoter is still liable under the contract and has the right to enforce the contract, unless formation of the corporation was an express condition to the contract.

Moneywatch Cos. v. Wilbers

106 Ohio App. 3d 122, 665 N.E.2d 689 (Ohio Ct. App. 1995)

POWELL, J.:

Defendant-appellant, Jeffrey Wilbers, appeals a decision of the Butler County Court of Common Pleas in favor of plaintiff-appellee, Moneywatch Companies, in a breach of contract action.

In December 1992, appellant entered into negotiations with appellee, through its property manager, Rebecca Reed, for the lease of commercial property space in the Kitty Hawk Center located in Middletown, Ohio. During the negotiations, appellant indicated that he intended to create a corporation and needed the space for a golfing business he wanted to open. Reed testified that while appellant told her that he would be forming a corporation, she advised appellant that he would have to remain personally liable on the lease even if a corporation was subsequently created. Appellant testified that he never intended to assume personal liability on the lease and that appellee never advised him that he would have to be personally liable under the lease. At appellee's request, appellant submitted a personal financial statement and business plan.

On December 23, 1992, a lease agreement was signed naming appellee as landlord and "Jeff Wilbers, dba Golfing Adventures" as tenant. The lease agreement provided that rent would not be due until March 1, 1993. On January 11, 1993, articles of incorporation for "J & J Adventures, Inc." were signed by "Jeff Wilbers, Incorporator." On February 3, 1993, a Trade Name Registration was signed for "Golfing Adventures" to be used by J & J Adventures, Incorporated. On February 8, 1993, the Ohio Secretary of State certified the corporation and approved the Trade Name Registration.

Appellant notified appellee of the incorporation of J & J Adventures, Inc. and asked that the name of the tenant on the lease be changed from "Jeff Wilbers, dba Golfing Adventures" to "J & J Adventures, Inc., dba Golfing Adventures." In a letter dated March 1, 1993, from appellee to appellant, appellee informed appellant that the name of the tenant on the lease would be so changed and that "this name change shall be deemed a part of the entire Lease Agreement." Reed testified that appellant did not request a release of personal liability under the lease at this time. Appellant testified that he did not seek release of personal liability because he never thought he was personally liable under the lease.

Throughout the lease period, rent was paid with checks bearing the corporation's name and address. The address listed on the checks was the address of the leased property. The rent checks for March and April, 1993, were signed by "Judy G. Wilbers—Secretary/Treasurer" and rent checks signed in July and August, 1993, were signed by "J & J Adventures, Inc. by Jeffrey Wilbers—president." However, all correspondence from appellee to appellant was addressed to "Jeff Wilbers" and mailed to his home address.

At some time during 1993, the corporation defaulted and vacated the premises. Appellee brought a breach of contract action against appellant in his personal capacity. After a bench trial, the trial court entered judgment in favor of appellee and ordered appellant to pay appellee the sum of $13,922.67 plus interest and costs. It is from this decision that appellant now appeals, setting forth the following assignment of error:

THE TRIAL COURT ERRED IN GRANTING JUDGMENT IN FAVOR OF THE PLAINTIFF.

In his sole assignment of error, appellant contends that he is not personally liable under the lease agreement because a novation was accomplished by the substitution of "J & J Adventures, Inc., dba Golfing Adventures," a corporate party, for "Jeff Wilbers, dba Golfing Adventures," an individual party. A novation occurs "where a previous valid obligation is extinguished by a new valid contract, accomplished by substitution of parties or of the undertaking, with the consent of all the parties, and based on valid consideration." *McGlothin v. Huffman* (1994), 94 Ohio App. 3d 240, 244, 640 N.E.2d 598. In order to effect a valid novation, all parties to the original contract must clearly and definitely intend the second agreement to be a novation and intend to completely disregard the original contract obligation. *Citizens State Bank v. Richart* (1984), 16 Ohio App. 3d 445, 446, 476 N.E.2d 383; *Sherwin Williams Co. v. Glenn Paint & Wall Paper Co.* (C.A. 1927), 6 Ohio L. Abs. 101 (novation is an agreement to release a previous debtor and look only to a subsequent debtor). In addition, a novation requires sufficient and valuable consideration to be valid and enforceable. *Wilson v. Lynch & Lynch Co.,* L.P.A. (Dec. 23, 1994), Geauga App. Nos. 93–G–1804 and 94–G–1814, unreported. A novation can never be presumed. *Citizens State Bank,* 16 Ohio App. 3d at 446.

In this case, it is undisputed that both parties agreed to the substitution of the corporation in place of appellant as tenant on the lease. However, there is no clear and definite intent on appellee's part to create a new contract through novation. The record indicates that appellee made statements during the negotiation and execution of the lease to the effect that appellant would have to be personally liable on the lease even if a corporation were formed, that all correspondence from appellee to appellant was mailed to appellant, individually, at his home address, that there was no release of appellant from personal liability under the lease at the time of the name change, and that the lease was not re-executed at the time of the name change and appellant's personal signature, rather than a signature on behalf of the corporation, remained on the lease. Thus, we find insufficient evidence in the record which would indicate an intent on appellee's part to release appellant from individual liability and look solely to the corporation in the event of a breach.

Further, a review of the record indicates a lack of consideration for the novation alleged to have occurred by the substitution of the corporation for appellant as tenant on the lease agreement. A novation must have consideration to be enforceable. *Wilson, supra.* Where the parties to a contract and a third party are all in agreement that one party will be released from the contract obligations and the third party substituted in its place, a novation has occurred and additional consideration, over and above the release and substitution, is not required. *Bacon v. Daniels (1881),* 37 Ohio St. 279, 281–282. As this court stated in *McGlothin, supra,* at 244, "the discharge of the existing obligation of a party to a contract is sufficient consideration for a contract of novation."

In this case, the substitution of tenant names on the lease does not constitute a novation because there was no discharge of appellant from his original obligations under the lease. *Grant-Holub Co. v. Goodman* (1926), 23 Ohio App. 540, 547, 156 N.E. 151. Likewise, the record does not indicate a benefit flowing to appellee by accepting the substitution of tenants. In the absence of a release and benefit to the respective parties, there is insufficient consideration to support a novation. Under the circumstances, we find that the substitution of tenant names on the lease agreement does not constitute a novation.

Appellant also contends that he is not personally liable under the lease agreement because he executed the lease as a corporate promoter on behalf of a future corporation.

Corporate promoters are "those who participate in bringing about the organization of an incorporated company, and in getting it in condition for transacting the business for which it is organized * * *." *Yeiser v. United States Bd.*

& Paper Co. (C.A.6, 1901), 107 F. 340, 344; *Cooper v. Stetler* (June 18, 1981), Cuyahoga App. No. 42885, unreported. A promoter is not personally liable on a contract made prior to incorporation which is made "in the name and solely on the credit of a future corporation * * *." *Stewart Realty Co., Inc. v. Keller* (1962), 118 Ohio App. 49, 51, 193 N.E.2d 179. Further, a corporation does not assume a contract made on its behalf by the mere act of incorporation. *Hamilton Hotel Corp. v. Bee Hotel Mgt., Inc.* (C.P.1965), 12 Ohio Misc. 114, 117–118, 230 N.E.2d 742.

In addressing the issue of promoter liability on contracts executed on behalf of a corporation to be formed in the future, the Ohio Supreme Court recently stated:

> It is axiomatic that the promoters of a corporation are at least initially liable on any contracts they execute in furtherance of the corporate entity prior to its formation. The promoters are released from liability only where the contract provides that performance is to be the obligation of the corporation, the corporation is ultimately formed, and the corporation then formally adopts the contract.
>
> * * * *
>
> Moreover, mere adoption of the contract by the corporation will not relieve promoters from liability in the absence of a subsequent novation. * * * Consequently, the promoters of a corporation who execute a contract on its behalf are personally liable for the breach thereof irrespective of the later adoption of the contract by the corporation unless the contract provides that performance thereunder is solely the responsibility of the corporation. [Citations omitted.]

Illinois Controls, Inc. v. Langham (1994), 70 Ohio St. 3d 512, 523–524, 639 N.E.2d 771.

In this case, appellant can be deemed a promoter because he participated in bringing about the organization of the corporation and in getting it ready for business. However, the original lease was not made "in the name and solely on the credit of the future corporation." *Stewart Realty Co., supra.* To the contrary, the lease was executed by appellant, individually, on his own credit, as evidenced by the submission of appellant's personal financial statement during the negotiation and execution of the lease.

Promoters are released from personal liability under the terms of a contract only where the contract provides that performance is to be the obligation of the corporation, the corporation is ultimately formed and the corporation formally adopts the contract. *Illinois Controls, supra, at 523.* In this case, the lease agreement does not provide that the corporation will be exclusively liable under its terms even though the corporation is now listed as tenant. In fact, appellant's individual signature remains on the lease agreement. *See Spicer v. James* (1985), 21 Ohio App. 3d 222, 223, 487 N.E.2d 353 (where lease agreement involving a corporate tenant is signed by corporate officers twice, once individually and once in their corporate capacities, corporate officers remain individually liable under the lease). In addition, there is no evidence that the corporation, once formed, formally adopted the lease agreement as executed by appellant. In the absence of the necessary steps which must be taken to ensure that appellant is not personally liable and the corporation is solely liable under the lease, appellant is liable under the lease.

* * * *

After thoroughly reviewing the record, we find competent, credible evidence to support the trial court's decision to hold appellant personally liable under the lease. We will not substitute our judgment for that of the trial court. . . . Accordingly, appellant's sole assignment of error is overruled.

Judgment affirmed.

YOUNG, P.J., and KOEHLER, J., concur.

The question of when a promoter is liable on a contract entered into on behalf of a corporation (or for the benefit of a corporation) often turns on the intent and the understanding of the parties. However, in other instances when the corporate entity referred to in a contract is never formed or is organized in a different form than anticipated in the contract, courts will often consider the doctrines of corporation by estoppel and/or de facto corporation in evaluating promoter liability. This concept is reflected in the following case.

Southern-Gulf Marine Co. No. 9, Inc. v. Camcraft, Inc.

410 So. 2d 1181 (La. Ct. App. 1982)

DOUCET, J.:

Plaintiff, a corporation chartered under the laws of Cayman, British West Indies, filed suit alleging breach of a contract to furnish a ship. Defendant responded with a peremptory exception of no cause of action based upon the plaintiff's lack of corporate existence at the time of entering into the contract, and the plaintiff's subsequent incorporation under the laws of a sovereign different than that represented in the contract. The motion was sustained and plaintiff appeals. We reverse.

On December 6, 1978 a "Letter of Agreement" was entered into, which by its terms obligated "Southern-Gulf Marine Co. No. 9, Inc., a company to be formed, to purchase one 156 foot supply vessel from Camcraft, Inc. for a price of $1,350,000.00." The agreement further provided for an anticipated delivery date, authority for Camcraft to begin purchasing components, and stated that a definite set of specifications and a Vessel Construction Contract would be written in the near future. The agreement was signed by Mr. Dudley Bowman, as President of Camcraft, Inc., and by Mr. D. W. Barrett, both individually and as President of Southern-Gulf Marine Co. No. 9, Inc.

Thereafter, on May 30, 1979, the Vessel Construction Contract was executed between Camcraft and Southern-Gulf Marine Co. No. 9, Inc., the latter of which was listed in the preamble as a corporation organized by virtue of the laws of Texas, appearing through D. W. Barrett, its President. The contract, prepared on a form supplied by Camcraft, recited that both parties acknowledge receipt of valuable consideration, then went on to list the mutual promises of Builder (Camcraft) and Owner (Southern-Gulf). Among the conditions which followed on the form contract was one entitled "Shipping Act of 1916", whereby the owner warranted that it was a citizen of the United States within the meaning of the Shipping Act of 1916, as amended . . . and that provisions of said act restricting transfer of ownership are inapplicable. The agreement further listed causes for default and the effect thereof. Another provision afforded Builder the right to assign its interest provided such would not violate any law of the United States.

Subsequently Mr. D. W. Barrett, President of Southern-Gulf Marine Co. No. 9, Inc., wrote to Mr. Bowman in a letter dated February 21, 1980, informing him that his organization was incorporated in the Cayman Islands of British West Indies on February 15, 1980. Mr. Barrett explained that such incorporation was done to make the vessel's use in foreign commerce more economical. As President and Managing Director, he further informed Camcraft of the Board of Directors' resolution to ratify, confirm, and adopt the aforesaid agreements. The letter was signed by Mr. Barrett individually and as President. Mr. Bowman signed a written acceptance and agreement to the letter on February 22, 1980.

Defendant subsequently defaulted on its obligation and this suit followed, wherein plaintiff sought to sequester the vessel involved and demanded specific performance and damages occasioned by defendant's failure to timely deliver the vessel. The defendant then sought to escape liability via a peremptory exception of no cause of action based upon the legal status of plaintiff.

The trial judge, in his Reasons for Judgment, reasoned that a contract requires two parties, and as plaintiff was not incorporated as of the date of the Vessel Construction Contract, there was no contract. He further reasoned that the purported ratification by Southern-Gulf Marine Co. No. 9, Inc., as evidenced by the letter of February 21, 1980, was ineffective because Southern-Gulf Marine Co. No. 9, Inc. never appeared as a Texas corporation and approved of any substitution of parties or assignment. The trial judge also rejected plaintiff's claim that D. W. Barrett could enforce the contract individually.

. . . . Although we find merit in the argument that D. W. Barrett could enforce the contract individually, this was not urged on appeal, and thus is considered abandoned.

We address ourselves first to whether the defendant should be estopped from asserting the plaintiff's lack of corporate capacity at the time the Vessel Construction Contract was executed after dealing with the plaintiff as a corporation. We believe the defendant, having given its promise to construct the vessel, should not be permitted to escape performance by raising an issue as to the character of the organization to which it is obligated, unless its substantial rights might thereby be affected. As was stated in *Latiolais v. Citizens Bank,* 33 La.Ann. 1444 (1881), overruled on other grounds in *General Motors Acceptance Corp. v. Anzelmo,* 222 La. 1019, 64 So.2d 417, 418–419 (1953).

"It is settled, by an overwhelming array of indisputable precedents, that, as a rule, one who contracts with what he acknowledges to be and treats as a corporation, incurring obligations in its favor, is estopped from denying its corporate existence, particularly when the obligations are sought to be enforced. It is right that it should be so. If a party have no other objection to oppose to the enforcement of the contract than that the obligee is incompetent to sue, for reasons anterior to his contract, or last acknowledgement, he should not be permitted to escape liability. The case would be different where the incompetency is the result of something happening subsequent to the contract, or last acknowledgement of existence and capacity. It is a familiar principle that one cannot be permitted to play fast and loose, so as to take advantage of his own unfair vacillations."

* * * *

The rule was stated in *Casey v. Galli,* 94 U.S. 673, 680, . . . (1877) as follows:

"Where a party has contracted with a corporation, and is sued upon the contract, neither is permitted to deny the existence, or the legal validity of such corporation. To hold otherwise would be contrary to the plainest principles of reason and of good faith, and involve a mockery of justice."

The record discloses nothing indicating that the substantial rights of defendant were affected by the plaintiff's de facto status. The plaintiff relied upon the contract and secured financing. The defendant likewise relied on the contract and began construction of the vessel. We have no doubts that defendant would assert that plaintiff and D. W. Barrett were liable on the contract had they defaulted and enforcement was advantageous, but defendants refuse to recognize any rights they may have therein. In all likelihood, the true state of affairs is as represented by plaintiff's counsel: the vessel appreciated in value above the contract price between the time of the contract and the agreed delivery date. We hold the defendant estopped to deny the corporate existence of plaintiff in this regard. . . . .

The question remains whether defendant should be able to inject into the case the fact that plaintiff subsequently did incorporate in the Cayman Islands rather than in Texas, as originally represented. Paragraph 25 of the contract provides that an assignment or transfer shall not violate the Shipping Act of 1916 which prohibits transfer in the event of war or national emergency. Defendant apparently had no objections to the plaintiff's altered status, as a Cayman rather de facto corporation, at the time the letter of February 21, 1980 was accepted and agreed to. And we all know that no war or national emergency existed. Thus the evidence indicates that the plaintiff's legal status is not germane to any cause for the contract and as such should not be grounds for avoidance of the contract. However, as the trial judge did not reach this consideration, we reserve unto defendant, upon remand, the right to raise the issue of the relevance of Cayman incorporation rather than Texan. . . .

The judgment appealed from is reversed and remanded to the trial court for further consideration consistent with the views herein. . . . .

REVERSED AND REMANDED.

SECTION II: The Structure of the Corporation

A. Characteristics of a Typical Corporation

Under the law a corporation is considered to be a "person," and that corporate person is separate from its owners. This means it can own property, it has certain "rights," and it can sue and be sued. Corporations have certain features that are associated with corporate existence. In order to better understand this "person," it is important to examine these features and the functions associated with these features. The corporation is owned by shareholders, and, as owners, the shareholders are entitled to the residual value of the corporation after it has satisfied its obligations to its creditors. Shareholders do not participate in the management of the corporation. They merely elect the board of directors. The board of directors then appoints officers, such as the president, treasurer, and secretary of the corporation. The diagram below represents a typical structure for a fictional corporation, named ABC Corporation:

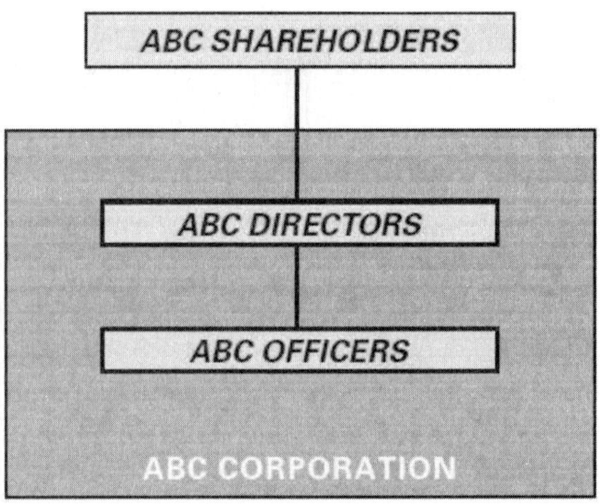

In general, the rights and responsibilities of the shareholders, directors and officers are divided as follows:

Shareholders

Shareholders do not participate directly in the management of the corporation. Corporations are run by a board of directors, who are elected by the shareholders. This type of structure, in which a core group manages the firm is known as "centralized management." Note the variation from a typical partnership, which is characterized by "decentralized management" since all partners participate in the management of the firm. While shareholders do not directly manage, they do have the right to vote on certain matters. Shareholders typically vote on (1) the election of directors (While at present, shareholders of publicly held companies do not have the right to nominate directors and typically may only vote on a 'slate' of directors proposed by the Board, the Dodd-Frank Wall Street Reform and Consumer Protection Act of 2010 (the "Dodd Frank Act") authorizes the Securities and Exchange Commission to create mechanisms through which shareholders may nominate, and solicit votes for, directors.); (2) amendments to the Articles of Incorporation and (usually) the Bylaws; (3) fundamental transactions such as mergers and acquisitions; and (4) miscellaneous matters such as the approval of independent auditors and non-binding resolutions.

Shareholders are entitled to the residual interest in the assets of the corporation. This means that upon liquidation of a corporation, the shareholders are entitled to receive the value of the assets remaining in the corporation after all of the corporation's obligations have been satisfied.

Board of Directors

The directors of the corporation are responsible to the shareholders for managing the corporate assets. They typically serve for a set term such as a year or two years (although they are often re-elected to their board seats). The directors of a corporation are charged with making major decisions relating to the operation of the corporation. Directors also appoint the corporation's officers (who handle the day-to-day affairs of the corporation).

Officers

The officers of a corporation are selected by the board of directors and manage the day-to-day operations of the corporation. The typical officers in a corporation are the President (also sometimes called the Chief Executive Officer or "CEO."), the Chief Financial Officer (also sometimes called the Treasurer or "CFO"), and the Secretary. Other officers may include a Chief Operating Officer (also sometimes called the "COO") and various Vice Presidents.

B. Forming a Corporation

Corporations are created under state law. In order to form a corporation, Articles of Incorporation must be filed with the Secretary of State in the state that has been selected for the corporation's formation. Once the Articles have been properly filed, a corporation is established. Assuming the Articles of

Incorporation are properly filed, the corporation is known as a "*de jure*" corporation.

De Facto Corporations

Occasionally, corporations are not properly formed. However, the would-be shareholders believe that, and act as though, the corporation was properly formed. In these instances, the shareholders of the organization are sometimes given corporate protection under an equitable doctrine known as "*de facto*" corporation status. In order to assert the protections of a de facto corporation, the owners of the business must establish that they made a good faith, substantial effort to comply with the state's incorporation statute; that the business had a legal right to incorporate; and that the parties involved had a good faith belief that they had actually formed a corporation, and acted as though they had, in fact, formed a corporation.

If these standards are met, the organization may be granted de facto corporation status, which means that the principals will have limited liability from the debts of the corporation as though the corporation had been properly formed. Because most states provide notice when Articles of Incorporation are properly filed and notice when the Articles of Incorporation are not properly filed, Incorporators will almost always have notice (or constructive notice) of whether the Articles of Incorporation were successfully filed. Therefore, it is much more difficult to have a good faith belief that the corporation has been formed when it has not. Given the simplicity and clarity of modern filing procedures, many states refuse to apply the *de facto* corporation doctrine. However, in other states, although still unlikely, it is not impossible that de facto corporation status will arise.

Corporation by Estoppel

Even when de facto corporation status is not available, it is still possible that the principals of a would-be corporation will be protected by the doctrine of corporation by estoppel. Under this doctrine, if a third party treats an organization as though it were a corporation, that third party may be estopped from denying the organization's corporate existence if the denial would result in unjust harm to the principals. Conversely, if an organization holds itself out as a corporation (even though it is not), that organization will be estopped from denying its own corporate existence to avoid an obligation or to obtain an unfair benefit. In order for the doctrine of corporation by estoppel to apply, the parties need to have consistently treated the organization as though it were a corporation; and an unfair advantage or benefit would be obtained by one of the parties if that party were allowed to deny the existence of the corporation.

Consider the case of ***Cranson v. IBM***, 234 Md. 477, 200 A.2D 33 (Md. 1964):

> . . .in April 1961, Cranson was asked to invest in a new business corporation which was about to be created. Towards this purpose he met with other interested individuals and an attorney and agreed to purchase stock and become an officer and director. Thereafter, upon being advised by the attorney that the corporation had been formed under the laws of Maryland, he paid for and received a stock certificate evidencing ownership of shares in the corporation, and was shown the corporate seal and minute book. The business of the new venture was conducted as if it were a corporation, through corporate bank accounts, with auditors maintaining corporate books and records, and under a lease entered into by the corporation for the office from which it operated its business. Cranson was elected president and all transactions conducted by him for the corporation, including the dealings with I.B.M., were made as an officer of the corporation. At no time did he assume any personal obligation or pledge his individual credit to I.B.M. Due to an oversight on the part of the attorney, of which Cranson was not aware, the certificate of incorporation, which had been signed and acknowledged prior to May 1, 1961, was not filed until November 24, 1961. Between May 17 and November 8, the Bureau [the business which Cranson believed to be a corporation] purchased eight typewriters from I.B.M., on account of which partial payments were made, leaving a balance due of $4,333.40 . . .

Id. at 479–480.

In finding that Cranson was not liable for the balance due for the typewriters, the court explained: "I.B.M. contends that the failure of the Bureau to file its certificate of incorporation debarred *all* corporate existence. But, in spite of the fact that the omission might have prevented the Bureau from being either a corporation *de jure* or *de facto*,. . . we think that I.B.M. having dealt with the Bureau as if it were a corporation and relied on its credit rather than that of Cranson, is estopped to assert that the Bureau was not incorporated at the time the typewriters were purchased." *Id.* at 488.

---

plaintiff asserts that he is also entitled to hold their stockholders personally liable for the damages sought because the multiple corporate structure constitutes an unlawful attempt "to defraud members of the general public" who might be injured by the cabs.

The defendant Carlton has moved . . . to dismiss the complaint on the ground that as to him it "fails to state a cause of action". The court at Special Term granted the motion but the Appellate Division, by a divided vote, reversed, holding that a valid cause of action was sufficiently stated. The defendant Carlton appeals to us, from the nonfinal order, by leave of the Appellate Division on a certified question.

The law permits the incorporation of a business for the very purpose of enabling its proprietors to escape personal liability [*Citations omitted.*] but, manifestly, the privilege is not without its limits. Broadly speaking, the courts will disregard the corporate form, or, to use accepted terminology, "pierce the corporate veil", whenever necessary "to prevent fraud or to achieve equity". (*International Aircraft Trading Co. v. Manufacturers Trust Co.,* 297 N. Y. 285, 292.) In determining whether liability should be extended to reach assets beyond those belonging to the corporation, we are guided, as Judge Cardozo noted, by "general rules of agency". (*Berkey v. Third Ave. Ry. Co.,* 244 N. Y. 84, 95.) In other words, whenever anyone uses control of the corporation to further his own rather than the corporation's business, he will be liable for the corporation's acts "upon the principle of respondeat superior applicable even where the agent is a natural person [*Citations omitted.*] Such liability, moreover, extends not only to the corporation's commercial dealings [*Citations omitted.*] but to its negligent acts as well. . . .

In the *Mangan* case (247 App. Div. 853 . . .), the plaintiff was injured as a result of the negligent operation of a cab owned and operated by one of four corporations affiliated with the defendant Terminal. Although the defendant was not a stockholder of any of the operating companies, both the defendant and the operating companies were owned, for the most part, by the same parties. The defendant's name (Terminal) was conspicuously displayed on the sides of all of the taxis used in the enterprise and, in point of fact, the defendant actually serviced, inspected, repaired and dispatched them. These facts were deemed to provide sufficient cause for piercing the corporate veil of the operating company—the nominal owner of the cab which injured the plaintiff—and holding the defendant liable. The operating companies were simply instrumentalities for carrying on the business of the defendant without imposing upon it financial and other liabilities incident to the actual ownership and operation of the cabs. [*Citations omitted.*]

In the case before us, the plaintiff has explicitly alleged that none of the corporations "had a separate existence of their own" and, as indicated above, all are named as defendants. However, it is one thing to assert that a corporation is a fragment of a larger corporate combine which actually conducts the business. [*Citations omitted.*] It is quite another to claim that the corporation is a "dummy" for its individual stockholders who are in reality carrying on the business in their personal capacities for purely personal rather than corporate ends. [*Citations omitted.*] Either circumstance would justify treating the corporation as an agent and piercing the corporate veil to reach the principal but a different result would follow in each case. In the first, only a larger *corporate* entity would be held financially responsible [*citations omitted*], while, in the other, the stockholder would be personally liable. [*Citations omitted.*] Either the stockholder is conducting the business in his individual capacity or he is not. If he is, he will be liable; if he is not, then, it does not matter—insofar as his personal liability is concerned—that the enterprise is actually being carried on by a larger "enterprise entity". [*Citations omitted.*]

At this stage in the present litigation, we are concerned only with the pleadings and, since CPLR 3014 permits causes of action to be stated "alternatively or hypothetically", it is possible for the plaintiff to allege both theories as the basis for his demand for judgment. . . .Reading the complaint in this case most favorably and liberally, we do not believe that there can be gathered from its averments the allegations required to spell out a valid cause of action against the defendant Carlton.

The individual defendant is charged with having "organized, managed, dominated and controlled" a fragmented corporate entity but there are no allegations that he was conducting business in his individual capacity. Had the taxicab fleet been owned by a single corporation, it would be readily apparent that the plaintiff would face formidable barriers in attempting to establish personal liability on the part of the corporation's stockholders. The fact that the fleet ownership has been deliberately split up among many corporations does not ease the plaintiff's burden in that respect. The corporate form may not be disregarded merely because the assets of the corporation, together with the mandatory insurance coverage of the vehicle which struck the plaintiff, are insufficient to assure him the recovery sought. If Carlton were to be held individually liable on those facts alone, the decision would apply equally to the thousands of cabs which are owned by their individual drivers who conduct their businesses through corporations organized pursuant to section 401 of the Business Corporation Law and carry the minimum insurance required by . . . the Vehicle and Traffic Law. These taxi owner-operators are entitled to form such [*Citations omitted.*], and we agree with the court at Special Term that, if the insurance coverage required by statute "is inadequate for the protection of the public, the remedy lies not with the courts but with the Legislature." It may very well be sound policy to require that certain corporations must take out liability insurance which will afford adequate compensation to their potential tort victims. However, the responsibility for imposing conditions on the privilege of incorporation has been committed by the Constitution to the Legislature . . . and it may not be fairly implied, from any statute, that the Legislature intended, without the slightest discussion or debate, to require of taxi corporations that they carry automobile liability insurance over and above that mandated by the Vehicle and Traffic Law.

This is not to say that it is impossible for the plaintiff to state a valid cause of action against the defendant Carlton. However, the simple fact is that the plaintiff has just not done so here. While the complaint alleges that the separate corporations were undercapitalized and that their assets have been intermingled, it is barren of any "sufficiently [particularized] statements" [*Citations omitted.*] that the defendant Carlton and his associates are actually doing business in their individual capacities, shuttling their personal funds in and out of the corporations" without regard to formality and to suit their immediate convenience." [*Citations omitted.*] Such a "perversion of the privilege to do business in a corporate form" (*Berkey v. Third Ave. Ry. Co.,* 244 N. Y. 84, 95, *supra*) would justify imposing personal liability on the individual stockholders. [*Citations omitted.*] Nothing of the sort has in fact been charged, and it cannot reasonably or logically be inferred from the happenstance that the business of Seon Cab Corporation may actually be carried on by a larger corporate entity composed of many corporations which, under general principles of agency, would be liable to each other's creditors in contract and in tort.[3]

In point of fact, the principle relied upon in the complaint to sustain the imposition of personal liability is not agency but fraud. Such a cause of action cannot withstand analysis. If it is not fraudulent for the owner-operator of a

---

[3] In his affidavit in opposition to the motion to dismiss, the plaintiff's counsel claimed that corporate assets had been "milked out" of, and "siphoned off" from the enterprise. Quite apart from the fact that these allegations are far too vague and conclusory, the charge is premature. If the plaintiff succeeds in his action and becomes a judgment creditor of the corporation, he may then sue and attempt to hold the individual defendants accountable for any dividends and property that were wrongfully distributed. . .

single cab corporation to take out only the minimum required liability insurance, the enterprise does not become either illicit or fraudulent merely because it consists of many such corporations. The plaintiff's injuries are the same regardless of whether the cab which strikes him is owned by a single corporation or part of a fleet with ownership fragmented among many corporations. Whatever rights he may be able to assert against parties other than the registered owner of the vehicle come into being not because he has been defrauded but because, under the principle of *respondeat superior*, he is entitled to hold the whole enterprise responsible for the acts of its agents.

In sum, then, the complaint falls short of adequately stating a cause of action against the defendant Carlton in his individual capacity. . . .

KEATING, J. (dissenting).

The defendant Carlton, the shareholder here sought to be held for the negligence of the driver of a taxicab, was a principal shareholder and organizer of the defendant corporation which owned the taxicab. The corporation was one of 10 organized by the defendant, each containing two cabs and each cab having the "minimum liability" insurance coverage mandated by section 370 of the Vehicle and Traffic Law. The sole assets of these operating corporations are the vehicles themselves and they are apparently subject to mortgages.*

From their inception these corporations were intentionally undercapitalized for the purpose of avoiding responsibility for acts which were bound to arise as a result of the operation of a large taxi fleet having cars out on the street 24 hours a day and engaged in public transportation. And during the course of the corporations' existence all income was continually drained out of the corporations for the same purpose.

In his affidavit in opposition to the motion to dismiss, the plaintiff's counsel claimed that corporate assets had been "milked out" of, and "siphoned off" from the enterprise. Quite apart from the fact that these allegations are far too vague and conclusory, the charge is premature. If the plaintiff succeeds in his action and becomes a judgment creditor of the corporation, he may then sue and attempt to hold the individual defendants accountable for any dividends and property that were wrongfully distributed. . . It appears that the medallions, which are of considerable value, are judgment proof. (Administrative Code of City of New York, § 436–2.0.)

* It appears that the medallions, which are of considerable value, are judgment proof. (Administrative Code of City of New York, § 436–2.0.)

The issue presented by this action is whether the policy of this State, which affords those desiring to engage in a business enterprise the privilege of limited liability through the use of the corporate device, is so strong that it will permit that privilege to continue no matter how much it is abused, no matter how irresponsibly the corporation is operated, no matter what the cost to the public. I do not believe that it is.

Under the circumstances of this case the shareholders should all be held individually liable to this plaintiff for the injuries he suffered.

* * * *

The policy of this State has always been to provide and facilitate recovery for those injured through the negligence of others. The automobile, by its very nature, is capable of causing severe and costly injuries when not operated in a proper manner. The great increase in the number of automobile accidents combined with the frequent financial irresponsibility of the individual driving the car led to the adoption of section 388 of the Vehicle and Traffic Law which had the effect of imposing upon the owner of the vehicle the responsibility for its negligent operation. It is upon this very statute that the cause of action against both the corporation and the individual defendant is predicated.

In addition the Legislature, still concerned with the financial irresponsibility of those who owned and operated motor vehicles, enacted a statute requiring minimum liability coverage for all owners of automobiles. The important public policy represented by both these statutes is outlined in section 310 of the Vehicle and Traffic Law. That section provides that: "The legislature is concerned over the rising toll of motor vehicle accidents and the suffering and loss thereby inflicted. The legislature determines that it is a matter of grave concern that motorists shall be financially able to respond in damages for their negligent acts, so that innocent victims of motor vehicle accidents may be recompensed for the injury and financial loss inflicted upon them."

The defendant Carlton claims that, because the minimum amount of insurance required by the statute was obtained, the corporate veil cannot and should not be pierced despite the fact that the assets of the corporation which owned the cab were "trifling compared with the business to be done and the risks of loss" which were certain to be encountered. I do not agree.

The Legislature in requiring minimum liability insurance of $10,000, no doubt, intended to provide at least some small fund for recovery against those individuals and corporations who just did not have and were not able to raise or accumulate assets sufficient to satisfy the claims of those who were injured as a result of their negligence. It certainly could not have intended to shield those individuals who organized corporations, with the specific intent of avoiding responsibility to the public, where the operation of the corporate enterprise yielded profits sufficient to purchase additional insurance. Moreover, it is reasonable to assume that the Legislature believed that those individuals and corporations having substantial assets would take out insurance far in excess of the minimum in order to protect those assets from depletion. Given the costs of hospital care and treatment and the nature of injuries sustained in auto collisions, it would be unreasonable to assume that the Legislature believed that the minimum provided in the statute would in and of itself be sufficient to recompense "innocent victims of motor vehicle accidents * * * for the injury and financial loss inflicted upon them".

* * * *

The defendant contends that a decision holding him personally liable would discourage people from engaging in corporate enterprise.

What I would merely hold is that a participating shareholder of a corporation vested with a public interest, organized with capital insufficient to meet liabilities which are certain to arise in the ordinary course of the corporation's business, may be held personally responsible for such liabilities. Where corporate income is not sufficient to cover the cost of insurance premiums above the statutory minimum or where initially adequate finances dwindle under the pressure of competition, bad times or extraordinary and unexpected liability, obviously the shareholder will not be held liable. [*Citations omitted.*]

The only types of corporate enterprises that will be discouraged as a result of a decision allowing the individual shareholder to be sued will be those such as the one in question, designed solely to abuse the corporate privilege at the expense of the public interest.

For these reasons I would vote to affirm the order of the Appellate Division. . . .

NOTE ON ENTERPRISE LIABILITY

Enterprise liability (which is discussed in the preceding case) is often addressed at the same time a typical Business Associations course addresses piercing the corporate veil. However, enterprise liability (even though it is sometimes referred to as "horizontal piercing") is NOT piercing. In enterprise liability, a creditor claims there are several related corporations and all or some are really part of the same corporation or enterprise. It is an effort to impose a claim against one corporation on other, related corporations. Enterprise liability is typically claimed when there is common ownership among two or more corporations. These commonly owned corporations are typically known as "sister corporations." Enterprise liability may be thought of as an agency theory of liability applied to related corporations. However, even when a court determines that there is enterprise liability, and a creditor can reach the assets of other corporations, it does NOT mean that the creditor can reach the assets of the shareholders.

Kinney Shoe Corp. v. Polan

939 F.2d 209 (4th Cir. 1991)

CHAPMAN S.C.J.:

Plaintiff-appellant Kinney Shoe Corporation ("Kinney") brought this action in the United States District Court for the Southern District of West Virginia against Lincoln M. Polan ("Polan") seeking to recover money owed on a sublease between Kinney and Industrial Realty Company ("Industrial"). Polan is the sole shareholder of Industrial. The district court found that Polan was not personally liable on the lease between Kinney and Industrial. Kinney appeals asserting that the corporate veil should be pierced, and we agree.

I.

The district court based its order on facts which were stipulated by the parties. In 1984 Polan formed two corporations, Industrial and Polan Industries, Inc., for the purpose of re-establishing an industrial manufacturing business. The certificate of incorporation for Polan Industries, Inc. was issued by the West Virginia Secretary of State in November 1984. The following month the certificate of incorporation for Industrial was issued. Polan was the owner of both corporations. Although certificates of incorporation were issued, no organizational meetings were held, and no officers were elected.

In November 1984 Polan and Kinney began negotiating the sublease of a building in which Kinney held a leasehold interest. The building was owned by the Cabell County Commission and financed by industrial revenue bonds issued in 1968 to induce Kinney to locate a manufacturing plant in Huntington, West Virginia. Under the terms of the lease, Kinney was legally obligated to make payments on the bonds on a semi-annual basis through January 1, 1993, at which time it had the right to purchase the property. Kinney had ceased using the building as a manufacturing plant in June 1983.

The term of the sublease from Kinney to Industrial commenced in December 1984, even though the written lease was not signed by the parties until April 5, 1985. On April 15, 1985, Industrial subleased part of the building to Polan Industries for fifty percent of the rental amount due Kinney. Polan signed both subleases on behalf of the respective companies.

Other than the sublease with Kinney, Industrial had no assets, no income and no bank account. Industrial issued no stock certificates because nothing was ever paid in to this corporation. Industrial's only income was from its sublease to Polan Industries, Inc. The first rental payment to Kinney was made out of Polan's personal funds, and no further payments were made by Polan or by Polan Industries, Inc. to either Industrial or to Kinney.

Kinney filed suit against Industrial for unpaid rent and obtained a judgment in the amount of $166,400.00 on June 19, 1987. A writ of possession was issued, but because Polan Industries, Inc. had filed for bankruptcy, Kinney did not gain possession for six months. Kinney leased the building until it was sold on September 1, 1988. Kinney then filed this action against Polan individually to collect the amount owed by Industrial to Kinney. Since the amount to which Kinney is entitled is undisputed, the only issue is whether Kinney can pierce the corporate veil and hold Polan personally liable.

The district court held that Kinney had assumed the risk of Industrial's undercapitalization and was not entitled to pierce the corporate veil. Kinney appeals, and we reverse.

II.

We have long recognized that a corporation is an entity, separate and distinct from its officers and stockholders, and the individual stockholders are not responsible for the debts of the corporation. *[Citation omitted.]* This concept, however, is a fiction of the law " 'and it is now well settled, as a general principle, that the fiction should be disregarded when it is urged with an intent not within its reason and purpose, and in such a way that its retention would produce injustices or inequitable consequences.' " *Laya v. Erin Homes, Inc.,* 352 S.E.2d 93, 97–98 (W. Va. 1986) (*quoting Sanders v. Roselawn Memorial Gardens, Inc.,* 152 W. Va. 91, 159 S.E.2d 784, 786 (1968).

Piercing the corporate veil is an equitable remedy, and the burden rests with the party asserting such claim. . . .A totality of the circumstances test is used in determining whether to pierce the corporate veil, and each case must be decided on its own facts. . . .

Kinney seeks to pierce the corporate veil of Industrial so as to hold Polan personally liable on the sublease debt. The Supreme Court of Appeals of West Virginia has set forth a two prong test to be used in determining whether to pierce a corporate veil in a breach of contract case. This test raises two issues: first, is the unity of interest and ownership such that the separate personalities of the corporation and the individual shareholder no longer exist; and second, would an equitable result occur if the acts are treated as those of the corporation alone. *Laya,* 352 S.E.2d at 99. Numerous factors have been identified as relevant in making this determination.*

---

* The following factors were identified in *Laya*:

(1) commingling of funds and other assets of the corporation with those of the individual shareholders;

(2) diversion of the corporation's funds or assets to noncorporate uses (to the personal uses of the corporation's shareholders);

(3) failure to maintain the corporate formalities necessary for the issuance of or subscription to the corporation's stock, such as formal approval of the stock issue by the board of directors;

(4) an individual shareholder representing to persons outside the corporation that he or she is personally liable for the debts or other obligations of the corporation;

(5) failure to maintain corporate minutes or adequate corporate records;

(6) identical equitable ownership in two entities;

(7) identity of the directors and officers of two entities who are responsible for supervision and management (a partnership or sole proprietorship and a corporation owned and managed by the same parties);

(8) failure to adequately capitalize a corporation for the reasonable risks of the corporate undertaking;

(9) absence of separately held corporate assets;

(10) use of a corporation as a mere shell or conduit to operate a single venture or some particular aspect of the business of an individual or another corporation;

(11) sole ownership of all the stock by one individual or members of a single family;

(12) use of the same office or business location by the corporation and its individual shareholder(s);

(13) employment of the same employees or attorney by the corporation and its shareholder(s);

(14) concealment or misrepresentation of the identity of the ownership, management or financial interests in the corporation, and concealment of personal business activities of the shareholders (sole shareholders do not reveal the association with a corporation, which makes loans to them without adequate security);

(15) disregard of legal formalities and failure to maintain proper arm's length relationships among related entities;

The district court found that the two prong test of *Laya* had been satisfied. The court concluded that Polan's failure to carry out the corporate formalities with respect to Industrial, coupled with Industrial's gross undercapitalization, resulted in damage to Kinney. We agree.

It is undisputed that Industrial was not adequately capitalized. Actually, it had no paid in capital. Polan had put nothing into this corporation, and it did not observe any corporate formalities. As the West Virginia court stated in *Laya,* " 'individuals who wish to enjoy limited personal liability for business activities under a corporate umbrella should be expected to adhere to the relatively simple formalities of creating and maintaining a corporate entity.' " *Laya,* 352 S.E.2d at 100 n. 6 *(quoting Labadie Coal Co. v. Black,* 217 U.S. App. D.C. 239, 672 F.2d 92, 96–97 (D.C. Cir. 1982)). This, the court stated, is " 'a relatively small price to pay for limited liability.' " Id. Another important factor is adequate capitalization. "Grossly inadequate capitalization combined with disregard of corporate formalities, causing basic unfairness, are sufficient to pierce the corporate veil in order to hold the shareholder(s) actively participating in the operation of the business personally liable for a breach of contract to the party who entered into the contract with the corporation." *Laya, 352 S.E.2d at 101–02.*

In this case, Polan bought no stock, made no capital contribution, kept no minutes, and elected no officers for Industrial. In addition, Polan attempted to protect his assets by placing them in Polan Industries, Inc. and interposing Industrial between Polan Industries, Inc. and Kinney so as to prevent Kinney from going against the corporation with assets. Polan gave no explanation or justification for the existence of Industrial as the intermediary between Polan Industries, Inc. and Kinney. Polan was obviously trying to limit his liability and the liability of Polan Industries, Inc. by setting up a paper curtain constructed of nothing more than Industrial's certificate of incorporation. These facts present the classic scenario for an action to pierce the corporate veil so as to reach the

---

(16) use of a corporate entity as a conduit to procure labor, services or merchandise for another person or entity;

(17) diversion of corporate assets from the corporation by or to a stockholder or other person or entity to the detriment of creditors, or the manipulation of assets and liabilities between entities to concentrate the assets in one and the liabilities in another;

(18) contracting by the corporation with another person with the intent to avoid risk of nonperformance by use of the corporate entity; or the use of a corporation as a subterfuge for illegal transactions;

(19) the formation and use of the corporation to assume the existing liabilities of another person or entity.

Laya, 352 S.E.2d at 98–99. . . .

responsible party and produce an equitable result. Accordingly, we hold that the district court correctly found that the two prong test in *Laya* had been satisfied.

* * * *

. . .This corporation was no more than a shell—a transparent shell. When nothing is invested in the corporation, the corporation provides no protection to its owner; nothing in, nothing out, no protection. If Polan wishes the protection of a corporation to limit his liability, he must follow the simple formalities of maintaining the corporation. This he failed to do, and he may not relieve his circumstances by saying Kinney should have known better.

III.

For the foregoing reasons, we hold that Polan is personally liable for the debt of Industrial, and the decision of the district court is reversed and this case is remanded with instructions to enter judgment for the plaintiff.

REVERSED AND REMANDED WITH INSTRUCTIONS.

NOTE REGARDING PIERCING THE VEIL OF LIMITED LIABILITY COMPANIES

Following the same principles set forth in the corporate veil-piercing cases, virtually all jurisdictions allow for the piercing of the limited liability veil of an LLC. The test is the same, which is typically the showing of a unity of interest between the owner and the entity and that some inequity or injustice would result or go unaddressed (other than the plaintiffs failure to get paid) if piercing were not allowed. However, as discussed at the end of the previous chapter, LLCs typically have fewer formalities to follow than corporations, so it might be more difficult to show a unity of interest based upon a failure to follow formalities. This distinction did not seem to be an obstacle in *Kaycee Land and Livestock v. Flahive* 2002 WY 73; 46 P. 3d 323 (2002) set forth below, in which the court allowed for an LLC's veil to be pierced. In explaining its decision, the court noted: "We can discern no reason, in either law or policy, to treat LLCs differently than we treat corporations. If the members and officers of an LLC fail to treat it as a separate entity as contemplated by statute, they should not enjoy immunity from individual liability for the LLC's acts that cause damage to third parties. Most, if not all, of the expert LLC commentators have concluded the doctrine of piercing the veil should apply to LLCs." *Id.* at 327–328.

C. Piercing the Veil in an LLC

Kaycee Land and Livestock v. Flahive

2002 WY 73, 46 P.3d 323 (2002)

KITE, J.:

This matter comes before this court as a question certified to us by the district court for resolution under W.R.A.P. 11. The certified question seeks resolution of whether, in the absence of fraud, the entity veil of a limited liability company (LLC) can be pierced in the same manner as that of a corporation. We answer the certified question in the affirmative.

CERTIFIED QUESTION

The question we have agreed to answer is phrased as follows:

> In the absence of fraud, is a claim to pierce the Limited Liability entity veil or disregard the Limited Liability Company entity in the same manner as a court would pierce a corporate veil or disregard a corporate shield, an available remedy against a Wyoming Limited Liability Company under Wyoming's Limited Liability Company Act, Wyo. Stat. § [§] 17–15–101 through 17–15–144 (2000)

FACTS

* * * *

.... The district court submitted the following statement of facts in its order certifying the question of law:

> 1. Flahive Oil & Gas is a Wyoming Limited Liability Company with no assets at this time.
> 2. [Kaycee Land and Livestock] entered into a contract with Flahive Oil & Gas LLC allowing Flahive Oil & Gas to use the surface of its real property.
> 3. Roger Flahive is and was the managing member of Flahive Oil & Gas at all relevant times.
> 4. [Kaycee Land and Livestock] alleges that Flahive Oil & Gas caused environmental contamination to its real property located in Johnson County, Wyoming.

5. [Kaycee Land and Livestock] seeks to pierce the LLC veil and disregard the LLC entity of Flahive Oil & Gas Limited Liability Company and hold Roger Flahive individually liable for the contamination.

6. There is no allegation of fraud.

DISCUSSION

The question presented is limited to whether, in the absence of fraud, the remedy of piercing the veil is available against a company formed under the Wyoming Limited Liability Company Act (*Wyo. Stat. Ann.* §§ 17–15–101 to –144 (LexisNexis 2001)). To answer this question, we must first examine the development of the doctrine within Wyoming's corporate context. . . .

Wyoming courts, as well as courts across the country, have typically utilized a fact driven inquiry to determine whether circumstances justify a decision to pierce a corporate veil. *Opal Mercantile,* 616 P.2d at 778. This case comes to us as a certified question in the abstract with little factual context, and we are asked to broadly pronounce that there are no circumstances under which this court will look through a failed attempt to create a separate LLC entity and prevent injustice. We simply cannot reach that conclusion and believe it is improvident for this court to prohibit this remedy from applying to any unforeseen circumstance that may exist in the future.

* * * *

We have long recognized that piercing the corporate veil is an equitable doctrine. *State ex rel. Christensen v. Nugget Coal Co.,* 60 Wyo. 51, 144 P.2d 944, 952 (1944). The concept of piercing the corporate veil is a judicially created remedy for situations where corporations have not been operated as separate entities as contemplated by statute and, therefore, are not entitled to be treated as such. The determination of whether the doctrine applies centers on whether there is an element of injustice, fundamental unfairness, or inequity. The concept developed through common law and is absent from the statutes governing corporate organization. *See* Wyo. Stat. Ann. §§ 17–16–101 to –1803 (LexisNexis 2001). Appellee Roger Flahive suggests that, by the adoption of § 17–16–622(b)—a provision from the revised Model Business Corporation Act-the Wyoming legislature intended to explicitly authorize piercing in the corporate context and, by inference, prevent its application in the LLC context. A careful review of the statutory language and legislative history leads to a different conclusion. Section 17–16–622(b) reads: "Unless otherwise provided in the articles of incorporation, a shareholder of a corporation is not personally liable for the acts or debts of the corporation except that he may become personally liable by reason of his own acts or conduct." Mr. Flahive contrasts that language with the LLC statute which simply states the underlying principle of limited liability for individual members and managers. Wyo. Stat. Ann. § 17–15–113 *(LexisNexis 2001)*. Section 17–15–113 provides:

> Neither the members of a limited liability company nor the managers of a limited liability company managed by a manager or managers are liable under a judgment, decree or order of a court, or in any other manner, for a debt, obligation or liability of the limited liability company.

However, we agree with Commentator Gelb that: "It is difficult to read statutory § 17–15–113 as intended to preclude courts from deciding to disregard the veil of an improperly used LLC." Harvey Gelb, *Liabilities of Members and Managers of Wyoming Limited Liability Companies,* 31 Land & Water L. Rev. 133 at 142 (1996).

* * * *

.... It is true that some other states have adopted specific legislation extending the doctrine to LLCs while Wyoming has not. However, that situation seems more attributable to the fact that Wyoming was a pioneer in the LLC arena and states which adopted LLC statutes much later had the benefit of years of practical experience during which this issue was likely raised.

* * * *

With the dearth of legislative consideration on this issue in Wyoming, we are left to determine whether applying the well established common law to LLCs somehow runs counter to what the legislature would have intended had it considered the issue. In that regard, it is instructive that: "Every state that has enacted LLC piercing legislation has chosen to follow corporate law standards and not develop a separate LLC standard." Philip P. Whynott, *The Limited Liability Company* § 11:140 at 11–5 (3d ed. 1999). Statutes which create corporations and LLCs have the same basic purpose-to limit the liability of individual investors with a corresponding benefit to economic development. Eric Fox, *Piercing the Veil of Limited Liability Companies,* 62 Geo. Wash. L. Rev. 1143, 1145–46 (1994). Statutes created the legal fiction of the corporation being a completely separate entity which could act independently from individual persons. If the corporation were created and operated in conformance with the statutory requirements, the law would treat it as a separate entity and shelter the individual shareholders from any liability caused by corporate action, thereby encouraging investment. However, courts throughout the country have consistently recognized certain unjust circumstances can arise if immunity from liability shelters those who have failed to operate a corporation as a separate entity. Consequently, when corporations fail to follow the statutorily mandated formalities, co-mingle funds, or ignore the restrictions in their articles of incorporation regarding separate treatment of corporate property, the courts deem it appropriate to disregard the separate identity and do not permit shareholders to be sheltered from liability to third parties for damages caused by the corporations' acts.

We can discern no reason, in either law or policy, to treat LLCs differently than we treat corporations. If the members and officers of an LLC fail to treat it as a separate entity as contemplated by statute, they should not enjoy immunity from individual liability for the LLC's acts that cause damage to third parties. Most, if not all, of the expert LLC commentators have concluded the doctrine of piercing the veil should apply to LLCs. *See generally* Fox, *supra;* Gelb, *supra;* Robert G. Lang, Note, *Utah's Limited Liability Company Act: Viable Alternative or Trap for the Unwary?,* 1993 Utah L. Rev. 941, 966 (1993) (Part 2); Stephen B. Presser, *Piercing the Corporate Veil* § 4.01[2] (2002); Ann M. Seward & Laura Stubberud, *The Limits of Limited Liability-Part Two,* Limited Liability Company Reporter 94–109 (January/February 1994);. . . It also appears that most courts faced with a similar situation—LLC statutes which are silent and facts which suggest the LLC veil should be pierced—have had little trouble concluding the common law should be applied and the factors weighed accordingly. . . .

Certainly, the various factors which would justify piercing an LLC veil would not be identical to the corporate situation for the obvious reason that many of the organizational formalities applicable to corporations do not apply to LLCs. The LLC's operation is intended to be much more flexible than a corporation's. Factors relevant to determining when to pierce the corporate veil have developed over time in a multitude of cases. It would be inadvisable in this case, which lacks a complete factual context, to attempt to articulate all the possible factors to be applied to LLCs in Wyoming in the future. . . .

* * * *

[E]ven absent fraud, courts have the power to impose liability on corporate shareholders. . . . The district court must complete a fact intensive inquiry and exercise its equitable powers to determine whether piercing the veil is appropriate under the circumstances presented in this case.

CONCLUSION

No reason exists in law or equity for treating an LLC differently than a corporation is treated when considering whether to disregard the legal entity. We conclude the equitable remedy of piercing the veil is an available remedy under the Wyoming Limited Liability Company Act.

QUESTION

1. The court in the preceding case remarked on the differences between LLCs and corporations. "Certainly, the various factors which would justify piercing an LLC veil would not be identical to the corporate situation for the obvious reason that many of the organizational formalities applicable to corporations do not apply to LLCs. The LLC's operation is intended to be much more flexible than a corporation's. . . ." *Id.* at 328. If you were asked by a client about what different formalities might be required in an LLC than would be required in a corporation, what might you tell them?

D. Reverse Piercing

Reverse piercing (as occurred with respect to Tie-Net in the *Sea-Land Services* case above) occurs when a claim against an individual shareholder is found to be enforceable directly against the corporation in which the individual is a shareholder. While the direction of the piercing is different (a claim against a shareholder is treated also as a claim against the corporation), the test is the same.

Sea-Land Services, Inc. v. Pepper Source

941 F.2d 519 (7th Cir. 1991)

BAUER, C.J.:

This spicy case finds its origin in several shipments of Jamaican sweet peppers. Appellee Sea-Land Services, Inc. ("Sea-Land"), an ocean carrier, shipped the peppers on behalf of The Pepper Source ("PS"), one of the appellants here. PS then stiffed Sea-Land on the freight bill, which was rather substantial. Sea-Land filed a federal diversity action for the money it was owed. On December 2, 1987, the district court entered a default judgment in favor of Sea-Land and against PS in the amount of $86,767.70. But PS was no-where to be found; it had been "dissolved" in mid-1987 for failure to pay the annual state franchise tax. Worse yet for Sea-Land, even had it not been dissolved, PS apparently had no assets. With the well empty, Sea-Land could not recover its judgment against PS. Hence the instant lawsuit.

In June 1988, Sea-Land brought this action against Gerald J. Marchese and five business entities he owns: PS, Caribe Crown, Inc., Jamar Corp., Salescaster Distributors, Inc., and Marchese Fegan Associates. Marchese also was named individually. Sea-Land sought by this suit to pierce PS's corporate veil and render Marchese personally liable for the judgment owed to Sea-Land, and then "reverse pierce" Marchese's other corporations so that they, too, would be on the hook for the $87,000. Thus, Sea-Land alleged in its complaint that all of these corporations "are alter egos of each other and hide behind the veils of alleged separate corporate existence for the purpose of defrauding plaintiff and other creditors." . . . . Not only are the corporations alter egos of each other, alleged Sea-Land, but also they are alter egos of Marchese, who should be held individually liable for the judgment because he created and manipulated these corporations and their assets for his own personal uses. . . . . (Hot on the heels of the filing of Sea-Land's complaint, PS took the necessary steps to be reinstated as a corporation in Illinois.)

In early 1989, Sea-Land filed an amended complaint adding Tie-Net International, Inc., as a defendant. Unlike the other corporate defendants, Tie-Net is not owned solely by Marchese: he holds half of the stock, and an individual named George Andre owns the other half. Sea-Land alleged that, despite this shared ownership, Tie-Net is but another alter ego of Marchese and the other corporate defendants, and thus it also should be held liable for the judgment against PS.

* * * *

In an order dated June 22, 1990, the court granted Sea-Land's motion. The court discussed and applied the test for corporate veil-piercing explicated in *Van Dorn Co. v. Future Chemical and Oil Corp.*, 753 F.2d 565 (7th Cir. 1985). Analyzing Illinois law, we held in *Van Dorn* that

> a corporate entity will be disregarded and the veil of limited liability pierced when two requirements are met:
>
> First, there must be such unity of interest and ownership that the separate personalities of the corporation and the individual [or other corporation] no longer exist; and second, circumstances must be such

that adherence to the fiction of separate corporate existence would sanction a fraud or promote injustice.

. . . . As for determining whether a corporation is so controlled by another to justify disregarding their separate identities, the Illinois cases, as we summarized them in *Van Dorn*, focus on four factors: "(1) the failure to maintain adequate corporate records or to comply with corporate formalities, (2) the commingling of funds or assets, (3) undercapitalization, and (4) one corporation treating the assets of another corporation as its own." *753 F.2d at 570* (citations omitted). [*Citations omitted.*]

Following the lead of the parties, the district court in the instant case laid the template of *Van Dorn* over the facts of this case. Dist. Ct. Op. at 3–12. The court concluded that both halves and all features of the test had been satisfied, and, therefore, entered judgment in favor of Sea-Land and against PS, Caribe Crown, Jamar, Salescaster, Tie-Net, and Marchese individually. These defendants were held jointly liable for Sea-Land's $87,000 judgment, as well as for post-judgment interest under Illinois law. From that judgment Marchese and the other defendants brought a timely appeal.

Because this is an appeal from a grant of summary judgment, our review is *de novo*. . . . The first and most striking feature that emerges from our examination of the record is that these corporate defendants are, indeed, little but Marchese's playthings. Marchese is the sole shareholder of PS, Caribe Crown, Jamar, and Salescaster. He is one of the two shareholders of Tie-Net. Except for Tie-Net, none of the corporations ever held a single corporate meeting. (At the handful of Tie-Net meetings held by Marchese and Andre, no minutes were taken.) During his deposition, Marchese did not remember any of these corporations ever passing articles of incorporation, bylaws, or other agreements. As for physical facilities, Marchese runs all of these corporations (including Tie-Net) out of the same, single office, with the same phone line, the same expense accounts, and the like. And how he does "run" the expense accounts! When he fancies to, Marchese "borrows" substantial sums of money from these corporations—interest free, of course. The corporations also "borrow" money from each other when need be, which left at least PS completely out of capital when the Sea-Land bills came due. What's more, Marchese has used the bank accounts of these corporations to pay all kinds of personal expenses, including alimony and child support payments to his ex-wife, education expenses for his children, maintenance of his personal automobiles, health care for his pet—the list goes on and on. Marchese did not even have a personal bank account! (With "corporate" accounts like these, who needs one?)

And Tie-Net is just as much a part of this as the other corporations. On appeal, Marchese makes much of the fact that he shares ownership of Tie-Net, and that Sea-Land has not been able to find an example of funds flowing from PS to Tie-Net to the detriment of Sea-Land and PS's other creditors. So what? The record reveals that, in all material senses, Marchese treated Tie-Net like his other corporations: he "borrowed" over $30,000 from Tie-Net; money and "loans" flowed freely between Tie-Net and the other corporations; and Marchese charged up various personal expenses (including $460 for a picture of himself with President Bush) on Tie-Net's credit card. Marchese was not deterred by the fact that he did not hold all of the stock of Tie-Net; why should his creditors be?[2]

In sum, we agree with the district court that their [*sic*] can be no doubt that the "shared control/unity of interest and ownership" part of the *Van Dorn* test is met in this case: corporate records and formalities have not been maintained; funds and assets have been commingled with abandon; PS, the offending corporation, and perhaps others have been undercapitalized; and corporate assets have been moved and tapped and "borrowed" without regard to their source. Indeed, Marchese basically punted this part of the inquiry before the district court by coming forward with little or no evidence in response to Sea-Land's extensively supported argument on these points. . . .

The second part of the *Van Dorn* test is more problematic, however. "Unity of interest and ownership" is not enough; Sea-Land also must show that honoring the separate corporate existences of the defendants "would sanction a fraud or promote injustice." *Van Dorn,* 753 F.2d at 570. This last phrase truly is disjunctive:

> Although an intent to defraud creditors would surely play a part if established, the Illinois test does not require proof of such intent. Once the first element of the test is established, *either* the sanctioning of a fraud (intentional wrongdoing) or the promotion of injustice, will satisfy the second element.

---

[2] We note that the record evidence in this case, if true, establishes that for years Marchese flagrantly has disregarded the tax code concerning the treatment of corporate funds. Yet, when we inquired at oral argument whether Marchese currently is under investigation by the IRS, his counsel informed us that to his knowledge he is not. Marchese also stated in his deposition that he never has been audited by the IRS. If these statements are true, and the IRS has so far shown absolutely no interest in Marchese's financial shenanigans with his "corporations," how and why that has occurred may be the biggest puzzles in this litigation. [On remand, the finding that Marchese had committed tax fraud was one of the findings used to satisfy the second prong of the *Van Dorn* test.—*Eds.*]

Id. (emphasis in original). Seizing on this, Sea-Land has abandoned the language in its two complaints that make repeated references to "fraud" by Marchese, and has chosen not to attempt to *prove* that PS and Marchese intended to defraud it—which would be quite difficult on summary judgment. Instead, Sea-Land has argued that honoring the defendants' separate identities would "promote injustice."

But what, exactly, does "promote injustice" mean, and how does one establish it on summary judgment? These are the critical, troublesome questions in this case. To start with, as the above passage from *Van Dorn* makes clear, "promote injustice" means something less than an affirmative showing of fraud—but how much less? In its one-sentence treatment of this point, the district court held that it was enough that "Sea-Land would be denied a judicially-imposed recovery." Dist. Ct. Op. at 11–12. Sea-Land defends this reasoning on appeal, arguing that "permitting the appellants to hide behind the shield of limited liability would clearly serve as an injustice against appellee" because it would "impermissibly deny appellee satisfaction." . . . . But that cannot be what is meant by "promote injustice." The prospect of an unsatisfied judgment looms in every veil-piercing action; why else would a plaintiff bring such an action? Thus, if an unsatisfied judgment is enough for the "promote injustice" feature of the test, then *every* plaintiff will pass on that score, and *Van Dorn* collapses into a one-step "unity of interest and ownership" test.

Because we cannot abide such a result, we will undertake our own review of Illinois cases to determine how the "promote injustice" feature of the veil-piercing inquiry has been interpreted. In *Pederson,* a recent case from the Illinois court of appeals, the court offered the following summary: "Some element of unfairness, something akin to fraud or deception or the existence of a compelling public interest must be present in order to disregard the corporate fiction." 214 Ill. App. 3d at 822. . . . (The court ultimately refused to pierce the corporate veil in *Pederson,* at least in part because "nothing in these facts provides evidence of scheming on the part of defendant to commit a fraud on potential creditors [of the two defendant corporations]." *Id.* at 823).

* * * *

[*The court's examination of a number of Illinois veil piercing cases is omitted.*]

Generalizing from these cases, we see that the courts that properly have pierced corporate veils to avoid "promoting injustice" have found that, unless it did so, some "wrong" beyond a creditor's inability to collect would result: the common sense rules of adverse possession would be undermined; former partners would be permitted to skirt the legal rules concerning monetary obligations; a party would be unjustly enriched; a parent corporation that caused a sub's liabilities and its inability to pay for them would escape those liabilities; or an intentional scheme to squirrel assets into a liability-free corporation while heaping liabilities upon an asset-free corporation would be successful. Sea-Land, although it alleged in its complaint the kind of intentional asset-and liability-shifting found in *Van Dorn,* has yet to come forward with evidence akin to the "wrongs" found in these cases. Apparently, it believed, as did the district court, that its unsatisfied judgment was enough. That belief was in error, and the entry of summary judgment premature. We, therefore, reverse the judgment and remand the case to the district court.

On remand, the court should require that Sea-Land produce, if it desires summary judgment, evidence and argument that would establish the kind of additional "wrong" present in the above cases. For example, perhaps Sea-Land could establish that Marchese, like Roth in *Van Dorn,* used these corporate facades to avoid its responsibilities to creditors; or that PS, Marchese, or one of the other corporations will be "unjustly enriched" unless liability is shared by all. Of course, Sea-Land is not required fully to prove intent to defraud, which it probably could not do on summary judgment anyway. But it is required to show the kind of injustice to merit the evocation of the court's essentially equitable power to prevent "injustice." It may well be that, after more of such evidence is adduced, no genuine issue of fact exists to prevent Sea-Land from reaching Marchese's other pet corporations for PS's debt. Or it may be that only a finder of fact will be able to determine whether fraud or "injustice" is involved here. In any event, the record as it currently stands is insufficient to uphold the entry of summary judgment.

REVERSED and REMANDED with instructions.

NOTES ABOUT SEA-LAND SERVICES

1. On remand, the District Court entered a judgment for Sea-Land. The court found that the fraud or injustice requirement was satisfied, based upon the tax fraud mentioned in the case (Marchese's practice of manipulating the corporations' assets to avoid liability to other creditors, and the fact that Marchese had assured Sea-Land that it would receive payment even though Marchese intended to manipulate the funds of PS to insure that Sea-Land would not be paid).

2. One difference of reverse piercing is that it does not enable a creditor to collect on a claim which otherwise would *necessarily* be unpaid by the party reached by the piercing. It changes the status of the claim holder. In conventional piercing, a creditor of the corporation may not proceed against the shareholder(s) of that corporation unless piercing is allowed (or some other exception to limited liability exists). However, in a situation in which a creditor has a claim against an individual shareholder, it is possible, even likely, that the creditor could foreclose on the individual shareholder's stock and become a shareholder of the corporation. As a shareholder of the corporation (especially a controlling shareholder), the creditor might be able to cause the corporation to make distributions to the shareholder(s). Those dividends could reduce the losses of the creditor. However, in that scenario, the creditor of the individual shareholder is not a creditor of the corporation, and, therefore, does not have the right to distribute funds before the creditors of the corporation are paid. Reverse piercing enables the individual shareholder's creditor to be treated as a creditor of the corporation and avoid a situation in which the corporation's creditors have priority over the individual shareholder's creditor's claim.

Piercing in a Corporation with Multiple Shareholders

The cases that involve piercing the corporate veil frequently arise in situations where there are only one or two shareholders because in situations in which there are only a few shareholders it is easier to show a unity of interest. Students often ask whether it is possible to pierce the corporate veil in a situation in which there are shareholders who have violated the rules, but also "innocent" shareholders who have not. Most courts will not allow piercing against the shareholders with no involvement in the misconduct, allowing piercing to remove the protection from liability only with respect to the shareholders who have violated the rules, while the innocent shareholders remain protected. However, there can be no guarantee that courts will apply the rules to protect the innocent shareholders. Note that piercing the corporate veil does not occur in public companies. All piercing cases involve closely held corporations.

E. Piercing Between Parent and Subsidiary Corporations

Sometimes there is an effort to pierce the veil of a subsidiary corporation in order to get to the assets of the parent corporation. While the standard for piercing is basically the same in these situations, courts are frequently less rigorous in the requirement that fraud-like conduct or injustice be shown. In addition to the other more traditional factors, courts will often look for interlocking boards of directors between the parent and the subsidiary as an indication that the subsidiary is not "separate" or independent. Just as a corporation that is not a subsidiary must be separate from its shareholders, a subsidiary corporation must be separate and independent from its parent or it will risk piercing as well.

Gardemal v. Westin Hotel Co.

186 F.3d 588 (5th Cir. 1999)

DEMOSS, C.J.:

Plaintiff-appellant, Lisa Cerza Gardemal ("Gardemal"), sued defendants-appellees, Westin Hotel Company ("Westin") and Westin Mexico, S.A. de C.V. ("Westin Mexico"), under Texas law, alleging that the defendants were liable for the drowning death of her husband in Cabo San Lucas, Mexico. The district court dismissed the suit in accordance with the magistrate judge's recommendation that the court grant Westin's motion for summary judgment, and Westin Mexico's motion to dismiss for lack of personal jurisdiction. We affirm the district court's rulings.

I.

In June 1995, Gardemal and her husband John W. Gardemal, a physician, traveled to Cabo San Lucas, Baja California Sur, Mexico, to attend a medical seminar held at the Westin Regina Resort Los Cabos ("Westin Regina"). The Westin Regina is owned by Desarollos Turisticos Integrales Cabo San Lucas, S.A. de C.V. ("DTI"), and managed by Westin Mexico. Westin Mexico is a subsidiary of Westin, and is incorporated in Mexico. During their stay at the hotel, the Gardemals decided to go snorkeling with a group of guests. According to Gardemal, the concierge at the Westin Regina directed the group to "Lovers Beach" which, unbeknownst to the group, was notorious for its rough surf and strong undercurrents. While climbing the beach's rocky shore, five men in the group were swept into the Pacific Ocean by a rogue wave and thrown against the rocks. Two of the men, including John Gardemal, drowned.

Gardemal, as administrator of her husband's estate, brought wrongful death and survival actions under Texas law against Westin and Westin Mexico, alleging that her husband drowned because Westin Regina's concierge negligently directed the group to Lovers Beach and failed to warn her husband of its dangerous condition. Westin then moved for summary judgment, alleging that although it is the parent company of Westin Mexico, it is a separate corporate entity and thus could not be held liable for acts committed by its subsidiary. The magistrate judge agreed with Westin, and recommended that Westin be dismissed from the action. In reaching its decision the magistrate judge rejected Gardemal's assertion that the state-law doctrines of alter-ego and single business enterprise allowed the court to disregard Westin's separate corporate identity.

* * * *

III.

Two separate issues confront us in this appeal. The first is whether the district court properly granted Westin's motion for summary judgment. . . .

In this action Gardemal seeks to hold Westin liable for the acts of Westin Mexico by invoking two separate, but related, state-law doctrines. Gardemal first argues that liability may be imputed to Westin because Westin Mexico functioned as the alter ego of Westin. [*Citation omitted.*] Gardemal next contends that Westin may be held liable on the theory that Westin Mexico operated a single business enterprise. *See Old Republic Ins. Co. v. Ex-Im Servs. Corp.,* 920 S.W.2d 393, 395–96 (Tex. App—Houston [1st Dist.] 1996, no writ) (explaining that under Texas law corporate form may be disregarded when corporations are not operated as separate entities but rather integrate their resources to achieve a common business purpose). We consider first the issue of whether Westin may be held liable on an alter-ego theory.

1.

Under Texas law the alter ego doctrine allows the imposition of liability on a corporation for the acts of another corporation when the subject corporation is organized or operated as a mere tool or business conduit. [*Citation omitted.*] It applies "when there is such unity between the parent corporation and its subsidiary that the separateness of the two corporations has ceased and holding only the subsidiary corporation liable would result in injustice." *Harwood Tire-Arlington, Inc. v. Young,* 963 S.W.2d 881, 885. . . . Alter ego is demonstrated "by evidence showing a blending of identities, or a blurring of lines of distinction, both formal and substantive, between two corporations. *Hideca Petroleum Corp. v. Tampimex Oil Int'l Ltd.,* 740 S.W.2d 838, 843. . . . An important consideration is whether a corporation is underfunded or undercapitalized, which is an indication that the company is a mere conduit or business tool. *Lucas v. Texas Indus., Inc.,* 696 S.W.2d 372, 374 (Tex. 1984).[2]

On appeal Gardemal points to several factors which, in her opinion, show that Westin is operating as the alter ego of Westin Mexico. She claims, for example, that Westin owns most of Westin Mexico's stock; that the two companies share common corporate officers; that Westin maintains quality control at Westin Mexico by requiring Westin Mexico to use certain operations manuals; that Westin oversees advertising and marketing operations at Westin Mexico through two separate contracts; and that Westin Mexico is grossly undercapitalized. *See United States v. Jon-T Chemicals, Inc.,* 768 F.2d 686, 691–92 (5th Cir. 1985) (listing the numerous factors used in alter ego analysis); [*Citation omitted.*] Gardemal places particular emphasis on the last purported factor, that Westin Mexico is undercapitalized. She insists that this factor alone is sufficient evidence that Westin Mexico is the alter ego of Westin. [*Citation omitted.*] We are not convinced.

The record, even when viewed in a light most favorable to Gardemal, reveals nothing more than a typical corporate relationship between a parent and subsidiary. It is true, as Gardemal points out, that Westin and Westin Mexico are closely tied through stock ownership, shared officers, financing arrangements, and the like. But this alone does not establish an alter-ego relationship. As we explained in *Jon-T Chemicals, Inc.,* there must be evidence of complete domination by the parent.

> The control necessary . . . is not mere majority or complete stock control but such domination of finances, policies and practices that the controlled corporation has, so to speak, no separate mind, will or existence of its own and is but a business conduit for its principal.

Id. at 691 (citation and quotation omitted). Thus, "one-hundred percent ownership and identity of directors and officers are, even together, an insufficient basis for applying the alter ego theory to pierce the corporate veil." *Id.*

In this case, there is insufficient record evidence that Westin dominates Westin Mexico to the extent that Westin Mexico has, for practical purposes,

[2] The rationale behind the "alter ego" theory is that if the shareholders themselves, or the corporations themselves, disregard the legal separation, distinct properties, or proper formalities of the different corporate enterprises, then the law will likewise disregard them so far as is necessary to protect individual and corporate creditors. *Castleberry, 721 S.W.2d at 272.*

surrendered its corporate identity. In fact, the evidence suggests just the opposite, that Westin Mexico functions as an autonomous business entity.

There is evidence, for example, that Westin Mexico banks in Mexico and deposits all of the revenue from its six hotels into that account. The facts also show that while Westin is incorporated in Delaware, Westin Mexico is incorporated in Mexico and faithfully adheres to the required corporate formalities. Finally, Westin Mexico has its own staff, its own assets, and even maintains its own insurance policies.

Gardemal is correct in pointing out that undercapitalization is a critical factor in our alter-ego analysis, especially in a tort case like the present one. *See Jon-T Chemicals, Inc.,* 768 F.2d at 693. But as noted by the district court, there is scant evidence that Westin Mexico is in fact undercapitalized and unable to pay a judgment, if necessary. This fact weighs heavily against Gardemal because the alter ego doctrine is an equitable remedy which prevents a company from avoiding liability by abusing the corporate form. "We disregard the corporate fiction . . . when the corporate form has been used as part of a basically unfair device to achieve an inequitable result." *Castleberry,* 721 S.W.2d at 271–72 (citation and quotation omitted) . . . . In this case, there is insufficient evidence that Westin Mexico is undercapitalized or uninsured. Moreover, there is no indication that Gardemal could not recover by suing Westin Mexico directly. As a result, equity does not demand that we merge and disregard the corporate identities of Westin and Westin Mexico. We reject Gardemal's attempt to impute liability on Westin based on the alter-ego doctrine.

2.

Likewise, we reject Gardemal's attempt to impute liability to Westin based on the single business enterprise doctrine. Under that doctrine, when corporations are not operated as separate entities, but integrate their resources to achieve a common business purpose, each constituent corporation may be held liable for the debts incurred in pursuit of that business purpose. *Old Republic Ins. Co. v. Ex-Im Serv. Corp.* . . . the alter-ego doctrine, the single business enterprise doctrine is an equitable remedy which applies when the corporate form is "used as part of an unfair device to achieve an inequitable result." *Id.* at 395.

On appeal, Gardemal attempts to prove a single business enterprise by calling our attention to the fact that Westin Mexico uses the trademark "Westin Hotels and Resorts." She also emphasizes that Westin Regina uses Westin's operations manuals. Gardemal also observes that Westin allows Westin Mexico to use its reservation system. Again, these facts merely demonstrate what we would describe as a typical, working relationship between a parent and subsidiary. Gardemal has pointed to no evidence in the record demonstrating that the operations of the two corporations were so integrated as to result in a blending of the two corporate identities. Moreover, Gardemal has come forward with no evidence that she has suffered some harm, or injustice, because Westin and Westin Mexico maintain separate corporate identities.

Reviewing the record in the light most favorable to Gardemal, we conclude that there is insufficient evidence that Westin Mexico was Westin's alter ego. Similarly, there is insufficient evidence that the resources of Westin and Westin Mexico are so integrated as to constitute a single business enterprise. Accordingly, we affirm the district court's grant of Westin's motion for summary judgment on that issue. . . .

* * * * [*The court also upheld the lower court's dismissal of Gardemal's suit against Westin Mexico on the basis that there was neither general nor specific jurisdiction over Westin Mexico and that personal jurisdiction was lacking.—Eds.*]

AFFIRMED.

NOTES ON PARENT SUBSIDIARY PIERCING

In contrast to the foregoing case, in the case *In re Silicone Gel Breast Implants Products Liability Litigation,* 887 F. Supp. 1447 (N.D. Ala. 1995), Bristol-Myers Squibb Co. ("BMS") was the sole shareholder of Medical Engineering Corporation ("MEC"), a major supplier of breast implants, but had never itself manufactured or distributed breast implants. In a suit seeking to hold BMS liable for claims against MEC, the district court found that there was ample evidence from which a jury could find that BMS was MEC's alter ego.

This included evidence that parent and subsidiary shared directors; that the subsidiary manufacturer was part of Bristol-Myers Squibb's health care group and used its legal, auditing, and communications departments; that they filed consolidated federal tax returns; that defendant prepared consolidated financial reports; that BMS operated as MEC's finance company, providing loans for the purchase of other entities; that MEC funds were deposited with BMS and, although segregated, BMS effectively "used MEC's resources as its own by obtaining interest on MEC's money and requiring MEC to make requests for capital appropriations to obtain its own funds"; that some members of MEC's board were not aware that MEC had a board of directors, let alone that they were members; and that the senior BMS member of MEC's board could not be out-voted by the other two directors.

The district court in the *Silicone Gel Breast Implants* case also cited *Jon-T Chemicals, Inc.,* which provides the following guidelines:*

> The totality of circumstances must be evaluated in determining whether a subsidiary may be found to be the alter ego or mere instrumentality of the parent corporation. Although the standards are not identical in each state, all jurisdictions require a showing of substantial domination. Among the factors to be considered are whether:
>
> - the parent and the subsidiary have common directors or officers
> - the parent and the subsidiary have common business departments
> - the parent and the subsidiary file consolidated financial statements and tax returns
> - the parent finances the subsidiary
> - the parent caused the incorporation of the subsidiary
> - the subsidiary operates with grossly inadequate capital
> - the parent pays the salaries and other expenses of the subsidiary
> - the subsidiary receives no business except that given to it by the parent
> - the parent uses the subsidiary's property as its own
> - the daily operations of the two corporations are not kept separate
> - the subsidiary does not observe the basic corporate formalities, such as keeping separate books and records and holding shareholder and board meetings.
>
> *Id.* at 1452

---

* *United States v. Jon-T Chemicals, Inc.,* 768 F.2d 686, 691–92 (5th Cir. 1985), cert. denied 475 U.S. 1014, 89 L. Ed. 2d 309, 106 S. Ct. 1194 (1986).

F. Other Claims That Might Be Made Against the Personal Assets of Shareholders

As mentioned above, there are other instances in which a creditor of the corporation may also make a claim against the shareholders' personal assets. The most common situations creating such claims involve: actual fraud; fraudulent conveyances/transfers; improper dividends; negligence; and personal guaranty of a corporate obligation by a shareholder.

In the situation of a fraudulent conveyance or an improper dividend, creditors may be able to recover funds or assets that were supposed to stay in the corporation but were distributed to shareholders, officers, or even third parties. If a person receives money that was not supposed to be paid or distributed by the corporation, creditors of the corporation may be able to make that person give that money back.* Note that a corporation may not pay dividends if it is insolvent or if the dividend renders the corporation insolvent. Dividends paid under such circumstances are "improper" and may be recovered by, or on behalf of, the corporation. Both of these types of claims are different from "piercing the veil" because they do not allow creditors to collect ALL the money they are owed by the corporation from a shareholder. Creditors may only collect to the extent of the fraudulent transfer or improper dividend.

In situations that involve the negligence of a shareholder, the law is not disregarding the protections of a corporation. Instead, the law recognizes that shareholders may play additional roles in the corporation, for which they might incur liability. If a shareholder commits a negligent act on behalf of a corporation and, as a direct result, someone is injured, the injured party may sue the corporation, but may also sue the negligent individual. The fact that the individual also happens to be a shareholder of the corporation will not shield them from liability. (Recall the discussion of an agent's liability for that agent's tortious conduct, above.)

Sometimes a shareholder may voluntarily assume liability for the debts of the corporation by promising to pay a debt if it turns out that the corporation is unable to pay that debt, by guaranteeing, bonding, or acting as a surety for the corporation. In these instances, piercing the corporate veil is not necessary. The shareholder is already personally liable under the contractual promise to pay on behalf of the corporation. For example, a landlord who does not wish to be subject to the liability limitations of a corporate tenant, may negotiate for the shareholders of that corporation to personally guarantee the lease obligations of the corporation as a means to provide additional contractual protections.

* While beyond the scope of this book, a fraudulent conveyance typically involves the transfer of money or assets without the receipt of equivalent value.

CHAPTER FOUR

Duty of Care and Obligations of Good Faith

ONE DAY WHILE YOU ARE hard at work, a senior partner in the firm's corporate department calls you into her office and tells you about a client, a public company called Heavenly Chocolates, Inc. ("HCI").

Experiencing Assignment 6: Heavenly Chocolates, Inc.

FACTS:

The partner explains that HCI has been a client of the firm for quite some time and asks you to "sit in" on a conference call with the President of HCI, Olive Sweetz. The call is going to start in an hour, but you have some time before the call to do some quick research on HCI. You learn the following information: HCI is a Delaware corporation that manufactures and distributes high-quality chocolates. HCI has been very successful for many years. The company operates based upon a core philosophy that HCI customers have refined tastes and appreciate the care and quality that goes into HCI's chocolate products.

You also learn that chocolate is grown on a small tropical tree known as the *Theobroma cacao*, usually called simply "cacao." (Pronounced: ka-KOW. *Theobroma* is Greek for "food of the gods.") Cacao is native to Central and South America, but it is grown commercially throughout the tropics. About 70% of the world's cacao is grown in Africa. There are three main kinds of cacao trees grown throughout the world, Forastero, Criollo and Trinitario, each with their own flavor profiles and growth characteristics. As a general rule, Forastero beans are used as bulk beans and Trinitario and Criollo are used as "flavor beans." Many chocolate bars combine both kinds of beans, bulk beans for consistent chocolate flavor and flavor beans for unique tasting notes. Although the overwhelming majority of cacao beans produced today are of the bulk variety,

HCI uses almost exclusively "flavor beans" in its chocolate, which account for its superior taste and quality.

During the conference call, you learn that Ms. Sweetz, and HCI's senior management has decided that HCI should purchase a chocolate plantation, located on a small island in the Caribbean. The plantation produces only flavor beans. The purchase represents a substantial expenditure for HCI and could create financial problems down the road. However, if the risk pays off, it will assure a good supply source for HCI, especially in the event of price fluctuations in the market for flavor beans. Ms. Sweetz also explains that, even if the move does not produce any business advantages, it will ensure that HCI is producing a higher quality chocolate product of which all of HCI can be proud. Ms. Sweetz feels that this, in and of itself, makes the transaction "worthwhile." However, Ms. Sweetz is concerned that this transaction (because of its size and the risk involved) might result in a suit from some disgruntled HCI shareholders. HCI has a total of seven directors on its board of directors. Ms. Sweetz and two other senior managers hold three of the board seats. The other four directors are not employed by HCI in any other capacity. HCI would like your firm to guide the HCI board of directors through the approval of the purchase to strengthen its position in the event of any such lawsuit.

As the discussion continues, you also learn that HCI has recently discovered that the purchase of the plantation might require payments to local officials in order to "process" and approve the sale. It is possible that such payments could be construed as bribes, which would violate U.S. Federal law. The HCI board is confident that even if the company were found to have violated a law by making these payments, the penalty for any such payments would be a fine, and there would be no further consequences. HCI is willing to pay the fine, but HCI wants you to have this information just in case it would alter your analysis about the plantation purchase. (The board does not want you to investigate or evaluate the illegality of any such payments or to make any independent evaluation of any potential criminal penalty.)

ASSIGNMENT:

The partner from your firm asks you to prepare guidelines for the HCI directors to follow in evaluating (and approving) the purchase of the Caribbean plantation. In addition please include an explanation of the standard by which any shareholder's claim against HCI arising out of the plantation purchase would be evaluated. The HCI directors do not want case citations. They want to understand the proper procedures, the risks involved and the legal standards by which their actions might be judged.

This Assignment does not need to be completed, and should not be completed, until the end of the section. However, as you study the cases and other materials that follow, it might be helpful to do so with a view toward providing assistance to the HCI directors. Some of the materials in the chapter will relate more than others to the issues facing HCI. However, the materials are designed to build your understanding of the fiduciary duty issues that arise in evaluating actions taken by a corporation's board of directors and assist you in addressing HCI's concerns and putting them in context. Please keep HCI's issues and the questions presented by the assignment in mind while reading the materials that follow.

SECTION I: The Power and Scope of Corporate Authority

The directors who serve on a corporation's board of directors are not the owners of the corporation. They are stewards or trustees who are charged with guiding the corporation for the benefit of its shareholders. Because of that role, there are guidelines about the actions that may be taken on behalf of the corporation and guidelines about how the directors perform their roles and the duties associated with those roles. Typically, a board of directors is charged with the responsibility of maximizing the value of the corporation for its shareholders. Actions that are not consistent with this objective may not be deemed to be within the "scope" of the corporation's authority. In addition, there may be limits that are set in the corporation's Articles of Incorporation or bylaws, which might further limit the scope of corporate actions. In evaluating a decision of a corporation's board of directors, there is often significant latitude granted with respect to the question of how the board might maximize the corporation's value. However, because of the board's obligations to the corporation's shareholders, it is not permitted to ask whether to maximize the corporation's value, only *how* to maximize the corporation's value.

A. Purpose of the Corporation

The significant actions taken by a corporation must be authorized or sanctioned by its board of directors. Corporations formed in the current business environment are typically authorized to act for any lawful purpose. This broad statement of purpose often raises questions about what limitations (beyond the limits imposed by law) are placed on a corporation or its board that is already authorized to act for any lawful purpose. Historically, when corporations had more limited purposes, actions taken "outside of the corporate purpose" were considered to be void or voidable as *ultra vires*. Currently, this doctrine is seldom used, and issues that arise with respect to the actions of a corporation that historically might have been challenged as "ultra vires" would now typically be challenged under the category of "waste." However, it remains important to understand the concept that certain actions are beyond the corporate purpose.

Wiswall v. The Greenville and Raleigh Plank Road Company

56 N.C. 183, 3 Jones Eq. 183 (N.C. 1857)

PEARSON, J.:

It was conceded in the argument that a corporation has a right to restrain by injunction the corporators from doing any act which is not embraced within the scope and purpose for which the corporate body was created, and which would be a violation of the charter; not only on the ground that such act would operate injuriously upon the rights and interests of the corporators, but on the further ground that a forfeiture of the charter would be thereby incurred.

So, the only question made by the demurrer is this: Has the company power to purchase stages and horses to be run upon the said road?—and has it likewise power to enter into a contract to carry the United States mail on the road by means of such stages?

This question must be decided by a construction of the charter. We have examined it, and declare our opinion to be, that no such power is given to the company.

The first section sets out the object of the incorporation, to wit, "for the purpose of effecting a communication by means of a plank road from Greenville to Raleigh."

The third section grants the franchise of incorporation, and gives all the powers, rights and privileges necessary "for the purposes mentioned in this act."

The ninth section invests the president and directors of the company "with all the rights and powers necessary for the *construction, repairs and maintaining* of a plank road to be located as aforesaid."

The fourteenth section provides for the erection of toll-houses and gates.

The fifteenth section provides for the collection of toll to be "*demanded and received from all persons using the said plank road,*" with a proviso that the tolls shall be so regulated that the profits shall not exceed twenty-five per cent on the capital in any one year.

These sections contain the substantive provisions; the others merely embrace the details necessary for the formation of the company, &c.

The mere statement makes the question too plain for observation. If, under the power to construct, repair and maintain a plank road, a power can be implied to buy stages and horses and become a mail contractor, the company, by a parity of reasoning, has an implied power to set up establishments at convenient points along the road for the purchase of produce to be carried over its road. Besides, how are tolls to be demanded and received, and how are the profits of this enlarged operation to be regulated? How are losses from such speculations to be guarded against?

It may as well be contended that a turn-pike company, from its power to construct, repair and maintain the road, has, by implication, power to embark in the business of mail contractor, or in buying and selling horses, cattle, or produce, under the suggestion that the road would be subservient to these purposes.

Let the demurrer be overruled.

PER CURIAM,

Decree accordingly.

While corporations are limited by their corporate purpose, it is also true that a shareholder who participates in an ultra vires act cannot subsequently attack the act as ultra vires. *Goodman v. Ladd Estate Co.* (246 Ore. 621; 427 P.2d 102 (Or. 1967)).

B. Charitable Acts

A situation commonly addressed when evaluating whether an act was within the corporation's "purpose" is an excessive charitable act. This notion of "excessive charity" is perhaps a backhanded way of addressing the question of who is the real party in interest in the corporation. There are many scholars who argue for broadening of the constituencies which fall within the parties whose interests are relevant in evaluating a corporation's actions. These constituencies may include a corporation's customers, employees, creditors, and communities.

However, ultimately, the primary party in interest is the shareholders. While the interests of other constituencies may occasionally be considered, this may not be done at the expense of the shareholders.

The guiding principle that arises out of this concept is that the corporation's duty/purpose is to maximize wealth or value for its shareholders. While the law grants great latitude to the ways in which a corporation may go about maximizing wealth or value for its shareholders, it does not allow corporations to act contrary to that goal. If, for example, a corporation were to donate all of its assets to charity, while that might be an action of great generosity, it would not be permitted without the consent of all of the shareholders. Whether the term *ultra vires* or waste is used, the result is the same. Assets must be used toward the corporate purpose of maximizing shareholder value and to accomplish this goal, the company may not engage in "wasteful" acts. Even in the case of a "worthwhile" charitable donation, many shareholders would argue that they should receive the money and make their own decisions about which charity, if any, they wished to support with their portion of the money.

A.P. Smith Mfg. Co. v. Barlow

13 N.J. 145, 98 A.2d 581 (N.J. 1953)

JACOBS, J.:

The Chancery Division, in a well-reasoned opinion by Judge Stein, determined that a donation by the plaintiff The A.P. Smith Manufacturing Company to Princeton University was *intra vires*. Because of the public importance of the issues presented, the appeal duly taken to the Appellate Division has been certified directly to this court under *Rule 1:5–1*(a).

The company was incorporated in 1896 and is engaged in the manufacture and sale of valves, fire hydrants and special equipment, mainly for water and gas industries. Its plant is located in East Orange and Bloomfield and it has approximately 300 employees. Over the years the company has contributed regularly to the local community chest and on occasions to Upsala College in East Orange and Newark University, now part of Rutgers, the State University. On July 24, 1951 the board of directors adopted a resolution which set forth that it was in the corporation's best interests to join with others in the 1951 Annual Giving to Princeton University, and appropriated the sum of $1,500 to be transferred by the corporation's treasurer to the university as a contribution towards its maintenance. When this action was questioned by stockholders the corporation instituted a declaratory judgment action in the Chancery Division and trial was had in due course.

Mr. Hubert F. O'Brien, the president of the company, testified that he considered the contribution to be a sound investment, that the public expects corporations to aid philanthropic and benevolent institutions, that they obtain good will in the community by so doing, and that their charitable donations create favorable environment for their business operations. In addition, he expressed the thought that in contributing to liberal arts institutions, corporations were furthering their self-interest in assuring the free flow of properly trained personnel for administrative and other corporate employment. Mr. Frank W. Abrams, chairman of the board of the Standard Oil Company of New Jersey, testified that corporations are expected to acknowledge their public responsibilities in support of the essential elements of our free enterprise system. He indicated that it was not "good business" to disappoint "this reasonable and justified public expectation," nor was it good business for corporations "to take substantial benefits from their membership in the economic community while avoiding the normally accepted obligations of citizenship in the social community." Mr. Irving S. Olds, former chairman of the board of the United States Steel Corporation, pointed out that corporations have a self-interest in the maintenance of liberal education as the bulwark of good government. He stated that "Capitalism and free enterprise owe their survival in no small degree to the existence of our private, independent universities" and that if American business does not aid in their maintenance it is not "properly protecting the long-range interest of its stockholders, its employees and its customers." . . . .

The objecting stockholders have not disputed any of the foregoing testimony nor the showing of great need by Princeton and other private institutions of higher learning and the important public service being rendered by them for democratic government and industry alike. Similarly, they have acknowledged that for over two decades there has been state legislation on our books which expresses a strong public policy in favor of corporate contributions such as that being questioned by them. Nevertheless, they have taken the position that (1) the plaintiff's certificate of incorporation does not expressly authorize the contribution and under common-law principles the company does not possess any implied or incidental power to make it, and (2) the New Jersey statutes which expressly authorize the contribution may not constitutionally be applied to the plaintiff, a corporation created long before their enactment. . . .

In his discussion of the early history of business corporations Professor Williston refers to a 1702 publication where the author stated flatly that "The general intent and end of all civil incorporations is for better government." And he points out that the early corporate charters, particularly their recitals, furnish additional support for the notion that the corporate object was the public one of managing and ordering the trade as well as the private one of profit for the members. . . . . However, with later economic and social developments and the free availability of the corporate device for all trades, the end of private profit became generally accepted as the controlling one in all businesses other than those classed broadly as public utilities. *Cf. Dodd, For Whom Are Corporate Managers Trustees,* 45 Harv. L. Rev. 1145, 1148 (1932). As a concomitant the common-law rule developed that those who managed the corporation could not disburse any corporate funds for philanthropic or other worthy public cause unless the expenditure would benefit the corporation. [*Citations omitted.*]. . . .

Thus, in the leading case of *Evans v. Brunner, Mond & Company, Ltd.* [1921] 1 Ch. 359, the court held that it was within the incidental power of a chemical company to grant # 100,000 to universities or other scientific institutions selected by the directors "for the furtherance of scientific education and research." The testimony indicated that the company desired to encourage and assist men who would devote their time and abilities to scientific study and research generally, a class of men for whom the company was constantly on the lookout. . . . . Similarly, in *Armstrong Cork Co. v. H.A. Meldrum Co.,* 285 F. 58 (D.C.W.D.N.Y. 1922), the court sustained contributions made by the corporation to the University of Buffalo and Canisius College. In the course of its opinion the court quoted the familiar comment from *Steinway v. Steinway & Sons,* 17 Misc. 43, 40 N.Y.S. 718 (Sup. Ct. 1896) . . . on the issue as to whether the corporation had received any corporate benefit it said:

> "It was also considered, in making the subscriptions or donations, that the company would receive advertisement of substantial value, including the good will of many influential citizens and of its patrons, who were interested in the success of the development of these branches of education, and, on the other hand, suffer a loss of prestige if the contributions were not made, in view of the fact that business competitors had donated and shown a commendable public spirit in that relation. In the circumstances the rule of law that may fairly be applied is that the action of the officers of the company was not *ultra vires*, but was in fact within their corporate powers, since it tended to promote the welfare of the business in which the corporation was engaged."

* * * *

The foregoing authorities illustrate how courts, while adhering to the terms of the common-law rule, have applied it very broadly to enable worthy corporate donations with indirect benefits to the corporations. In *State ex rel. Sorensen v. Chicago B. & Q.R. Co.,* 112 Neb. 248, 199 N.W. 534, 537 (1924), the Supreme Court of Nebraska, through Justice Letton, went even further and without referring to any limitation based on economic benefits to the corporation said that it saw . . . . "no reason why a railroad corporation may not, to a reasonable extent, donate funds or services to aid in good works."

* * * *

When the wealth of the nation was primarily in the hands of individuals they discharged their responsibilities as citizens by donating freely for charitable purposes. With the transfer of most of the wealth to corporate hands and the imposition of heavy burdens of individual taxation, they have been unable to keep pace with increased philanthropic needs. They have therefore, with justification, turned to corporations to assume the modern obligations of good citizenship in the same manner as humans do. Congress and state legislatures have enacted laws which encourage corporate contributions, and much has recently been written to indicate the crying need and adequate legal basis therefor. [*Citations omitted.*] In actual practice corporate giving has correspondingly increased. Thus, it is estimated that annual corporate contributions throughout the nation aggregate over 300 million dollars with over 60 million dollars thereof going to universities and other educational institutions. Similarly, it is estimated that local community chests receive well over 40% of their contributions from corporations; these contributions and those made by corporations to the American Red Cross, to Boy Scouts and Girl Scouts, to 4-H Clubs and similar organizations have almost invariably been unquestioned.

During the first world war corporations loaned their personnel and contributed substantial corporate funds in order to insure survival; during the depression of the '30s they made contributions to alleviate the desperate hardships of the millions of unemployed; and during the second world war they again contributed to insure survival. They now recognize that we are faced with other, though nonetheless vicious, threats from abroad which must be withstood without impairing the vigor of our democratic institutions at home and that otherwise victory will be pyrrhic indeed. More and more they have come to recognize that their salvation rests upon sound economic and social environment which in turn rests in no insignificant part upon free and vigorous non-governmental institutions of learning. It seems to us that just as the conditions prevailing when corporations were originally created required that they serve public as well as private interests, modern conditions require that corporations acknowledge and discharge social as well as private responsibilities as members of the communities within which they operate. Within this broad concept there is no difficulty in sustaining, as incidental to their proper objects and in aid of the public welfare, the power of corporations to contribute corporate funds within reasonable limits in support of academic institutions. But even if we confine ourselves to the terms of the common-law rule in its application to current conditions, such expenditures may likewise readily be justified as being for the benefit of the corporation. . . .

In 1930 a statute was enacted in our State which expressly provided that any corporation could cooperate with other corporations and natural persons in the creation and maintenance of community funds and charitable, philanthropic or benevolent instrumentalities conducive to public welfare, and could for such purposes expend such corporate sums as the directors "deem expedient and as in their judgment will contribute to the protection of the corporate interests.". . . In 1950 a more comprehensive statute was enacted . . . . [which] declared that it shall be the public policy of our State and in furtherance of the public interest and welfare that encouragement be given to the creation and maintenance of institutions engaged in community fund, hospital, charitable, philanthropic, educational, scientific or benevolent activities or patriotic or civic activities conducive to the betterment of social and economic conditions; and it expressly empowered corporations acting singly or with others to contribute reasonable sums to such institutions, provided, however, that the contribution shall not be permissible if the donee institution owns more than 10% of the voting stock of the donor and provided, further, that the contribution shall not exceed 1% of capital and surplus unless the excess is authorized by the stockholders at a regular or special meeting. To insure that the grant of express power in the 1950 statute would not displace preexisting power at common law or otherwise, the Legislature provided that the "act shall not be construed as directly or indirectly minimizing or interpreting the rights and powers of corporations, as heretofore existing, with reference to appropriations, expenditures or contributions of the nature above specified." N.J.S.A. 14:3–13.3. It may be noted that statutes relating to charitable contributions by corporations have now been passed in 29 states. . . .

The appellants contend that the foregoing New Jersey statutes may not be applied to corporations created before their passage. Fifty years before the incorporation of The A.P. Smith Manufacturing Company our Legislature provided that every corporate charter thereafter granted "shall be subject to alteration, suspension and repeal, in the discretion of the legislature." *L.* 1846, *p.* 16;

R.S. 14:2–9. A similar reserved power was placed into our State Constitution in 1875 (*Art.* IV, Sec. VII, *par.* 11), and is found in our present Constitution. . . .

* * * *

We are entirely satisfied that within the orbit of above authorities the legislative enactments found in R.S. 14:3–13 and N.J.S.A. 14:3–13.1 *et seq.* and applied to pre-existing corporations do not violate any constitutional guarantees afforded to their stockholders.

. . . . It is significant that in its enactments the State had not in anywise sought to impose any compulsory obligations or alter the corporate objectives. And since in our view the corporate power to make reasonable charitable contributions exists under modern conditions, even apart from express statutory provision, its enactments simply constitute helpful and confirmatory declarations of such power, accompanied by limiting safeguards.

In the light of all of the foregoing we have no hesitancy in sustaining the validity of the donation by the plaintiff. There is no suggestion that it was made indiscriminately or to a pet charity of the corporate directors in furtherance of personal rather than corporate ends. On the contrary, it was made to a preeminent institution of higher learning, was modest in amount and well within the limitations imposed by the statutory enactments, and was voluntarily made in the reasonable belief that it would aid the public welfare and advance the interests of the plaintiff as a private corporation and as part of the community in which it operates. We find that it was a lawful exercise of the corporation's implied and incidental powers under common-law principles and that it came within the express authority of the pertinent state legislation. . . . . [T]he appellants, as individual stockholders whose private interests rest entirely upon the well-being of the plaintiff corporation, ought not be permitted to close their eyes to present-day realities and thwart the long-visioned corporate action in recognizing and voluntarily discharging its high obligations as a constituent of our modern social structure.

The judgment entered in the Chancery Division is in all respects

Affirmed.

NOTES

1. In evaluating a charitable bequest made by a corporation, a determination of the propriety of such a bequest can vary greatly from state to state, but the underlying assessment involves the question of whether there is some direct or indirect benefit to the shareholders and/or the corporation.

2. Some of the factors most frequently examined include: whether the gift was made to a "pet charity" (Mentioned in the preceding case, a "pet charity" is a charity which does not have widespread appeal but is merely an interest of an officer or director of the corporation and is more suspect in that it is less likely that a gift made to such a charity is truly for the benefit of the corporation.); whether the gift was anonymous (This would reduce the value to the firm if the gift was made for marketing purposes or to create good public relations.); and whether the amount donated was significant when compared to the corporation's earnings.

C. Scrutiny of Corporate Actions

The question of whether or not a corporation's actions fall within its corporate purpose or constitute waste can expand well beyond the realm of a charitable bequest. Examining these issues often leads to the question of when and whether a court should have the ability to scrutinize the actions taken by a corporation. Such questions often lead to debate as to which circumstances should be present in order to justify a court substituting its own judgment for the judgment of a corporation's board of directors or management. The case of *Ford v. Dodge* highlights these issues and provides an early example of a court's assessment of certain decisions made by the Ford corporation, but to which a few of Ford's shareholders objected.

Dodge v. Ford Motor Co.

204 Mich. 459, 170 N.W. 668 (Mich. 1919)

OSTRANDER, C.J.:

[Plaintiffs are the "Dodge Brothers," who owned 10% of the outstanding Ford Motor Company capital stock, Henry Ford, the president of the Ford Motor owned 58% and five other shareholders owned the balance. The Dodge Brothers had brought a suit, seeking to force Ford Motor to declare a dividend equal to 75% of the accumulated cash surplus. The lower court order Ford

Motor to pay a dividend of $19.3 million (approximately half of its cash surplus).—*Eds.*]

* * * *

This court, in *Hunter v. Roberts, Throp & Co.,* 83 Mich. 63, 71, recognized the rule [regarding discretion to declare dividends] in the following language:

"It is a well-recognized principle of law that the directors of a corporation, and they alone, have the power to declare a dividend of the earnings of the corporation, and to determine its amount. 5 Am. & Eng. Enc. Law [1st Ed.], p. 725. Courts of equity will not interfere in the management of the directors unless it is clearly made to appear that they are guilty of fraud or misappropriation of the corporate funds, or refuse to declare a dividend when the corporation has a surplus of net profits which it can, without detriment to its business, divide among its stockholders, and when a refusal to do so would amount to such an abuse of discretion as would constitute a fraud, or breach of that good faith which they are bound to exercise towards the stockholders."

In *2 Cook on Corporations* (7th Ed.), § 545, it is expressed as follows:

"The board of directors declare the dividends, and it is for the directors, and not the stockholders, to determine whether or not a dividend shall be declared.

"When, therefore, the directors have exercised this discretion and refused to declare a dividend, there will be no interference by the courts with their decision, unless they are guilty of a willful abuse of their discretionary powers, or of bad faith or of a neglect of duty. It requires a very strong case to induce a court of equity to order the directors to declare a dividend, inasmuch as equity has no jurisdiction, unless fraud or a breach of trust is involved. There have been many attempts to sustain such a suit, yet, although the court do not disclaim jurisdiction, they have quite uniformly refused to interfere. The discretion of the directors will not be interfered with by the courts, unless there has been bad faith, willful neglect, or abuse of discretion. . . ."

* * * *

When plaintiffs made their complaint and demand for further dividends the Ford Motor Company had concluded its most prosperous year of business. The demand for its cars at the price of the preceding year continued. It could make and could market in the year beginning August 1, 1916, more than 500,000 cars. Sales of parts and repairs would necessarily increase. The cost of materials was likely to advance, and perhaps the price of labor, but it reasonably might have expected a profit for the year of upwards of $60,000,000. It had assets of more than $132,000,000, a surplus of almost $112,000,000, and its cash on hand and municipal bonds were nearly $54,000,000. Its total liabilities, including capital stock, was a little over $20,000,000. It had declared no special dividend during the business year except the October, 1915, dividend. It had been the practice, under similar circumstances, to declare larger dividends. Considering only these facts, a refusal to declare and pay further dividends appears to be not an exercise of discretion on the part of the directors, but an arbitrary refusal to do what the circumstances required to be done. These facts and others call upon the directors to justify their action, or failure or refusal to act. In justification, the defendants have offered testimony tending to prove, and which does prove, the following facts. It had been the policy of the corporation for a considerable time to annually reduce the selling price of cars, while keeping up, or improving, their quality. As early as in June, 1915, a general plan for the expansion of the productive capacity of the concern by a practical duplication of its plant had been talked over by the executive officers and directors and agreed upon, not all of the details having been settled and no formal action of directors having been taken. The erection of a smelter was considered, and engineering and other data in connection therewith secured. In consequence, it was determined not to reduce the selling price of cars for the year beginning August 1, 1915, but to maintain the price and to accumulate a large surplus to pay for the proposed expansion of plant and equipment, and perhaps to build a plant for smelting ore. It is hoped, by Mr. Ford, that eventually 1,000,000 cars will be annually produced. The contemplated changes will permit the increased output.

The plan, as affecting the profits of the business for the year beginning August 1, 1916, and thereafter, calls for a reduction in the selling price of the cars. It is true that this price might be at any time increased, but the plan called for the reduction in price of $80 a car. The capacity of the plant, without the additions thereto voted to be made (without a part of them at least), would produce more than 600,000 cars annually. This number, and more, could have been sold for $440 instead of $360, a difference in the return for capital, labor and materials employed of at least $48,000,000. In short, the plan does not call for and is not intended to produce immediately a more profitable business but a less profitable one; not only less profitable than formerly but less profitable than it is admitted it might be made. The apparent immediate effect will be to diminish the value of shares and the returns to shareholders.

It is the contention of plaintiffs that the apparent effect of the plan is intended to be the continued and continuing effect of it and that it is deliberately proposed, not of record and not by official corporate declaration, but nevertheless proposed, to continue the corporation henceforth as a semi-eleemosynary institution and not as a business institution. In support of this contention they point to the attitude and to the expressions of Mr. Henry Ford.

Mr. Henry Ford is the dominant force in the business of the Ford Motor Company. No plan of operations could be adopted unless he consented, and no board of directors can be elected whom he does not favor. One of the directors of the company has no stock. One share was assigned to him to qualify him for the position, but it is not claimed that he owns it. A business, one of the largest in the world, and one of the most profitable, has been built up. It employs many men, at good pay.

"My ambition," said Mr. Ford, "is to employ still more men, to spread the benefits of this industrial system to the greatest possible number, to help them build up their lives and their homes. To do this we are putting the greatest share of our profits back in the business."

"With regard to dividends, the company paid sixty percent on its capitalization of two million dollars, or $1,200,000, leaving $58,000,000 to reinvest for the growth of the company. This is Mr. Ford's policy at present, and it is understood that the other stockholders cheerfully accede to this plan."

He had made up his mind in the summer of 1916 that no dividends other than the regular dividends should be paid, "for the present."

> "*Q.* For how long? Had you fixed in your mind any time in the future, when you were going to pay—
>
> "*A.* No.
>
> "*Q.* That was indefinite in the future?
>
> "*A.* That was indefinite, yes, sir."

The record, and especially the testimony of Mr. Ford, convinces that he has to some extent the attitude towards shareholders of one who has dispensed and distributed to them large gains and that they should be content to take what he chooses to give. His testimony creates the impression, also, that he thinks the Ford Motor Company has made too much money, has had too large profits, and that although large profits might be still earned, a sharing of them with the public, by reducing the price of the output of the company, ought to be undertaken. We have no doubt that certain sentiments, philanthropic and altruistic, creditable to Mr. Ford, had large influence in determining the policy to be pursued by the Ford Motor Company—the policy which has been herein referred to.

* * * *

The difference between an incidental humanitarian expenditure of corporate funds for the benefit of the employees, like the building of a hospital for their use and the employment of agencies for the betterment of their condition, and a general purpose and plan to benefit mankind at the expense of others, is obvious. There should be no confusion (of which there is evidence) of the duties which Mr. Ford conceives that he and the stockholders owe to the general public and the duties which in law he and his co-directors owe to protesting, minority stockholders. A business corporation is organized and carried on primarily for the profit of the stockholders. The powers of the directors are to be employed for that end. The discretion of directors is to be exercised in the choice of means to attain that end and does not extend to a change in the end itself, to the reduction of profits or to the nondistribution of profits among stockholders in order to devote them to other purposes.

There is committed to the discretion of directors, a discretion to be exercised in good faith, the infinite details of business, including the wages which shall be paid to employees, the number of hours they shall work, the conditions under which labor shall be carried on, and the prices for which products shall be offered to the public. It is said by appellants that the motives of the board members are not material and will not be inquired into by the court so long as their acts are within their lawful powers. As we have pointed out, and the proposition does not require argument to sustain it, it is not within the lawful powers of a board of directors to shape and conduct the affairs of a corporation for the merely incidental benefit of shareholders and for the primary purpose of benefiting others, and no one will contend that if the avowed purpose of the defendant directors was to sacrifice the interests of shareholders it would not be the duty of the courts to interfere.

We are not, however, persuaded that we should interfere with the proposed expansion of the business of the Ford Motor Company. In view of the fact that the selling price of products may be increased at any time, the ultimate results of the larger business cannot be certainly estimated. The judges are not business experts. It is recognized that plans must often be made for a long future, for expected competition, for a continuing as well as an immediately profitable venture. The experience of the Ford Motor Company is evidence of capable management of its affairs. It may be noticed, incidentally, that it took from the public the money required for the execution of its plan and that the very considerable salaries paid to Mr. Ford and to certain executive officers and employees were not diminished. We are not satisfied that the alleged motives of the directors, in so far as they are reflected in the conduct of the business, menace the interests of shareholders. It is enough to say, perhaps, that the court of equity is at all times open to complaining shareholders having a just grievance.

Assuming the general plan and policy of expansion and the details of it to have been sufficiently, formally, approved at the October and November, 1917, meetings of directors, and assuming further that the plan and policy and the details agreed upon were for the best ultimate interest of the company and therefore of its shareholders, what does it amount to in justification of a refusal to declare and pay a special dividend, or dividends? The Ford Motor Company was able to estimate with nicety its income and profit. It could sell more cars than it could make. Having ascertained what it would cost to produce a car and to sell it, the profit upon each car depended upon the selling price. That being fixed, the yearly income and profit was determinable, and, within slight variations, was certain.

There was appropriated—voted—for the smelter $11,325,000. As to the remainder voted there is no available way for determining how much had been paid before the action of directors was taken and how much was paid thereafter, but assuming that the plans required an expenditure sooner or later of $9,895,000 for duplication of the plant, and for land and other expenditures $3,000,000, the total is $24,220,000. The company was continuing business, at a profit—a cash business. If the total cost of proposed expenditures had been immediately withdrawn in cash from the cash surplus (money and bonds) on hand August 1, 1916, there would have remained nearly $30,000,000.

Defendants say, and it is true, that a considerable cash balance must be at all times carried by such a concern. But, as has been stated, there was a large daily, weekly, monthly, receipt of cash. The output was practically continuous and was continuously, and within a few days, turned into cash. Moreover, the contemplated expenditures were not to be immediately made. The large sum appropriated for the smelter plant was payable over a considerable period of time. So that, without going further, it would appear that, accepting and approving the plan of the directors, it was their duty to distribute on or near the first of August, 1916, a very large sum of money to stockholders.

In reaching this conclusion, we do not ignore, but recognize, the validity of the proposition that plaintiffs have from the beginning profited by, if they have not lately, officially, participated in, the general policy of expansion pursued by this corporation. We do not lose sight of the fact that it had been, upon an occasion, agreeable to the plaintiffs to increase the capital stock to $100,000,000 by a stock dividend of $98,000,000. These things go only to answer other contentions now made by plaintiffs and do not and cannot operate to estop them to demand proper dividends upon the stock they own. It is obvious that an annual dividend of sixty percent upon $2,000,000, or $1,-$200,000, is the equivalent of a very small dividend upon $100,000,000, or more.

The decree of the court below fixing and determining the specific amount to be distributed to stockholders is affirmed. In other respects, except as to the allowance of costs, the said decree is reversed. . . .

MOORE, J. *(concurring)*. I agree with what is said by Justice OSTRANDER upon the subject of capitalization. I agree with what he says as to the smelting enterprise on the River Rouge. I do not agree with all that is said by him in his discussion of the question of dividends. I do agree with him in his conclusion that the accumulation of so large a surplus establishes the fact that there has been an arbitrary refusal to distribute funds that ought to have been distributed to the stockholders as dividends. I therefore agree with the conclusion reached by him upon that phase of the case.

NOTES AND QUESTIONS

1. *Dodge v. Ford Motor Co.* is an important case in the development of the modern business judgment rule discussed below. It raises the issues of how much autonomy should be given to the corporation's management and under what circumstances management actions should be scrutinized, and perhaps overturned, by the courts.

2. Are there arguments that might have been presented to justify the higher wages and cheaper cars?

3. Are there business reasons for not paying the dividend?

4. Do you agree with the court's determination? Would your answer be different if you were told that the Dodge brothers wanted Ford to issue a dividend so that they would have sufficient capital to fund a competing car company?

5. How would you have handled a client like Henry Ford?

SECTION II: Fiduciary Duties—Duty of Care

The most significant guidelines as to how directors should act in their roles as stewards of the corporation are known as fiduciary duties. These duties create parameters within which the conduct of a corporation's officers and directors may be measured. There are two major categories of fiduciary duties: the duty of care and the duty of loyalty. When attorneys are advising corporations, whether it be with respect to a transaction, litigation or general business matters, the issues that arise from the requirement that a corporation's officers and directors act in accordance with their fiduciary duties, are always present if not paramount.

A. Duty of Care

The duty of care requires that each member of the board of directors, when performing the duties of a director, act in good faith and in a manner the director reasonably believes to be in the best interests of the corporation.

> § 4.01(a): A director or officer has a duty to the corporation to perform the director's or officer's functions in good faith, in a manner that he or she reasonably believes to be in the best interests of the corporation, and with the care that an ordinarily prudent person would reasonably be expected to exercise in a like position and under similar circumstances.
>
> —American Law Institute, *Principles of Corporate Governance Part IV: Duty of Care and the Business Judgment Rule. See also* Model Business Corporations Act § 830(a).

While the exact language of the duty of care may vary slightly from jurisdiction to jurisdiction, the fundamental standard is consistent from state to state. Although the duty of care establishes a standard of conduct, any allegation that a director has breached that duty is still subject to the fundamental principles of tort law. In *Barnes v. Andrews* (298 F. 614 (S.D.N.Y 1924)) the receiver of a failed company sued a director for general negligence in failing to carry out his duty as director. In failing to hold the director liable, the court made clear that even if a director fails to fulfill his duty of care, a plaintiff must still show that the director's failure led to, or was the cause of, the loss which the plaintiff was alleged to have suffered. "The plaintiff must, however, go further than to show that [the director] should have been more active in his duties. . . . The plaintiff must accept the burden of showing that the performance of the defendant's duties would have avoided loss, and what loss it would have avoided." (*Id.* at 616.)

Shlensky v. Wrigley

95 Ill. App. 2d 173, 237 N.E.2d 776 (Ill. App. Ct. 1968)

SULLIVAN, J.:

This is an appeal from a dismissal of plaintiff's amended complaint on motion of the defendants. The action was a stockholders' derivative suit against the directors for negligence and mismanagement. The corporation was also made a defendant. Plaintiff sought damages and an order that defendants cause the installation of lights in Wrigley Field and the scheduling of night baseball games.

Plaintiff is a minority stockholder of defendant corporation, Chicago National League Ball Club (Inc.), a Delaware corporation with its principal place of business in Chicago, Illinois. Defendant corporation owns and operates the major league professional baseball team known as the Chicago Cubs. The corporation also engages in the operation of Wrigley Field, the Cubs' home park, the concessionaire sales during Cubs' home games, television and radio broadcasts of Cubs' home games, the leasing of the field for football games and other events and receives its share, as visiting team, of admission moneys from games played in other National League stadia. The individual defendants are directors of the Cubs and have served for varying periods of years. Defendant Philip K. Wrigley is also president of the corporation and owner of approximately 80% of the stock therein.

Plaintiff alleges that since night baseball was first played in 1935 nineteen of the twenty major league teams have scheduled night games. In 1966, out of a total of 1,620 games in the major leagues, 932 were played at night. Plaintiff alleges that every member of the major leagues, other than the Cubs, scheduled substantially all of its home games in 1966 at night, exclusive of opening days, Saturdays, Sundays, holidays and days prohibited by league rules. Allegedly this has been done for the specific purpose of maximizing attendance and thereby maximizing revenue and income.

The Cubs, in the years 1961–65, sustained operating losses from its direct baseball operations. Plaintiff attributes those losses to inadequate attendance at Cubs' home games. He concludes that if the directors continue to refuse to install lights at Wrigley Field and schedule night baseball games, the Cubs will continue to sustain comparable losses and its financial condition will continue to deteriorate.

Plaintiff alleges that, except for the year 1963, attendance at Cubs' home games has been substantially below that at their road games, many of which were played at night.

Plaintiff compares attendance at Cubs' games with that of the Chicago White Sox, an American League club, whose weekday games were generally played at night. The weekend attendance figures for the two teams were similar; however, the White Sox week-night games drew many more patrons than did the Cubs' weekday games.

Plaintiff alleges that the funds for the installation of lights can be readily obtained through financing and the cost of installation would be far more than offset and recaptured by increased revenues and incomes resulting from the increased attendance.

Plaintiff further alleges that defendant Wrigley has refused to install lights, not because of interest in the welfare of the corporation but because of his personal opinions "that baseball is a 'daytime sport' and that the installation of lights and night baseball games will have a deteriorating effect upon the surrounding neighborhood." It is alleged that he has admitted that he is not interested in whether the Cubs would benefit financially from such action because of his concern for the neighborhood, and that he would be willing for the team to play night games if a new stadium were built in Chicago.

Plaintiff alleges that the other defendant directors, with full knowledge of the foregoing matters, have acquiesced in the policy laid down by Wrigley and have permitted him to dominate the board of directors in matters involving the installation of lights and scheduling of night games, even though they knew he was not motivated by a good faith concern as to the best interests of defendant corporation, but solely by his personal views set forth above. It is charged that the directors are acting for a reason or reasons contrary and wholly unrelated to the business interests of the corporation; that such arbitrary and capricious acts constitute mismanagement and waste of corporate assets, and that the directors have been negligent in failing to exercise reasonable care and prudence in the management of the corporate affairs.

The question on appeal is whether plaintiff's amended complaint states a cause of action. It is plaintiff's position that fraud, illegality and conflict of interest are not the only bases for a stockholder's derivative action against the directors. Contrariwise, defendants argue that the courts will not step in and interfere with honest business judgment of the directors unless there is a showing of fraud, illegality or conflict of interest.

The cases in this area are numerous and each differs from the others on a factual basis. However, the courts have pronounced certain ground rules which appear in all cases and which are then applied to the given factual situation. The court in *Wheeler v. The Pullman Iron & Steel Co.,* 143 Ill 197, 207, 32 NE 420 said:

> "It is, however, fundamental in the law of corporations, that the majority of its stockholders shall control the policy of the corporation, and regulate and govern the lawful exercise of its franchise and business. . . . ."

The standards set in Delaware are also clearly stated in the cases. In *Davis v. Louisville Gas & Electric Co.,* 6 NJ Misc 706, 142 A. 654, a minority shareholder sought to have the directors enjoined from amending the certificate of incorporation. The court said on page 659:

> "We have then a conflict in view between the responsible managers of a corporation and an overwhelming majority of its stockholders on the one hand and a dissenting minority on the other—a conflict touching matters of business policy, such as has occasioned innumerable applications to courts to intervene and determine which of the two conflicting views should prevail. The response which courts make to such applications is that it is not their function to resolve for corporations questions of policy and business management. The directors are chosen to pass upon such questions and their judgment *unless shown to be tainted with fraud* is accepted as final. The judgment of the directors of corporations enjoys the benefit of a presumption that it was formed in good faith and was designed to promote the best interests of the corporation they serve." (*Emphasis supplied.*)

Similarly, the court in *Toebelman v. Missouri-Kansas Pipe Line Co.,* 41 F Supp. 334, said at page 339:

> "The general legal principle involved is familiar. . . . Reference may be made to the statement of the rule in *Helfman v. American Light & Traction Company,* 121 NJ Eq. 1, 187 A 540, 550, in which the Court stated the law as follows: 'In a purely business corporation . . . the authority of the directors in the conduct of the business of the corporation must be regarded as absolute when they act within the

law, and the court is without authority to substitute its judgment for that of the directors.' "

Plaintiff argues that the allegations of his amended complaint are sufficient to set forth a cause of action under the principles set out in *Dodge v. Ford Motor Co.,* 204 Mich. 459, 170 NW 668. In that case plaintiff, owner of about 10% of the outstanding stock, brought suit against the directors seeking payment of additional dividends and the enjoining of further business expansion. In ruling on the request for dividends the court indicated that the motives of Ford in keeping so much money in the corporation for expansion and security were to benefit the public generally and spread the profits out by means of more jobs, etc. The court felt that these were not only far from related to the good of the stockholders, but amounted to a change in the ends of the corporation and that this was not a purpose contemplated or allowed by the corporate charter. The court relied on language found in *Hunter v. Roberts, Throp & Co.,* 83 Mich. 63, 47 NW 131, 134, wherein it was said:

> "Courts of equity will not interfere in the management of the directors unless it is clearly made to appear that they are guilty of fraud or misappropriation of the corporate funds, or refuse to declare a dividend when the corporation has a surplus of net profits which it can, without detriment to its business, divide among its stockholders, and when a refusal to do so would amount to such an abuse of discretion as would constitute a fraud or breach of that good faith which they are bound to exercise toward the stockholders."

From the authority relied upon in that case it is clear that the court felt that there must be fraud or a breach of that good faith which directors are bound to exercise toward the stockholders in order to justify the courts entering into the internal affairs of corporations. . . .

Plaintiff in the instant case argues that the directors are acting for reasons unrelated to the financial interest and welfare of the Cubs. However, we are not satisfied that the motives assigned to Philip K. Wrigley, and through him to the other directors, are contrary to the best interests of the corporation and the stockholders. For example, it appears to us that the effect on the surrounding neighborhood might well be considered by a director who was considering the patrons who would or would not attend the games if the park were in a poor neighborhood. Furthermore, the long run interest of the corporation in its property value at Wrigley Field might demand all efforts to keep the neighborhood from deteriorating. By these thoughts we do not mean to say that we have decided that the decision of the directors was a correct one. That is beyond our jurisdiction and ability. We are merely saying that the decision is one properly before directors and the motives alleged in the amended complaint showed no fraud, illegality or conflict of interest in their making of that decision.

While all the courts do not insist that one or more of the three elements must be present for a stockholder's derivative action to lie, nevertheless we feel that unless the conduct of the defendants at least borders on one of the elements, the courts should not interfere. The trial court in the instant case acted properly in dismissing plaintiff's amended complaint.

We feel that plaintiff's amended complaint was also defective in failing to allege damage to the corporation. . . .

There is no allegation that the night games played by the other nineteen teams enhanced their financial position or that the profits, if any, of those teams were directly related to the number of night games scheduled. There is an allegation that the installation of lights and scheduling of night games in Wrigley Field would have resulted in large amounts of additional revenues and incomes from increased attendance and related sources of income. Further, the cost of installation of lights, funds for which are allegedly readily available by financing, would be more than offset and recaptured by increased revenues. However, no allegation is made that there will be a net benefit to the corporation from such action, considering all increased costs.

Plaintiff claims that the losses of defendant corporation are due to poor attendance at home games. However, it appears from the amended complaint, taken as a whole, that factors other than attendance affect the net earnings or losses. For example, in 1962, attendance at home and road games decreased appreciably as compared with 1961, and yet the loss from direct baseball operation and of the whole corporation was considerably less.

The record shows that plaintiff did not feel he could allege that the increased revenues would be sufficient to cure the corporate deficit. The only cost plaintiff was at all concerned with was that of installation of lights. No mention was made of operation and maintenance of the lights or other possible increases in operating costs of night games and we cannot speculate as to what other factors might influence the increase or decrease of profits if the Cubs were to play night home games.

* * * *

[I]n the instant case, plaintiff's allegation that the minority stockholders and the corporation have been seriously and irreparably damaged by the wrongful conduct of the defendant directors is a mere conclusion and not based on well pleaded facts in the amended complaint.

Finally, we do not agree with plaintiff's contention that failure to follow the example of the other major league clubs in scheduling night games constituted negligence. Plaintiff made no allegation that these teams' night schedules were profitable or that the purpose for which night baseball had been undertaken was fulfilled. Furthermore, it cannot be said that directors, even those of corporations that are losing money, must follow the lead of the other corporations in the field. Directors are elected for their business capabilities and judgment and the courts cannot require them to forego their judgment because of the decisions of directors of other companies. Courts may not decide these questions in the absence of a clear showing of dereliction of duty on the part of the specific directors and mere failure to "follow the crowd" is not such a dereliction.

For the foregoing reasons the order of dismissal entered by the trial court is affirmed.

Affirmed.

QUESTIONS

1. What recourse should shareholders have if they don't like the decisions made by a corporation's management?

2. If a shareholder came to you and wanted to prevent future "bad" decisions of management, is there a course of action you would recommend?

B. The Business Judgment Rule

When a director is sued for breach of the duty of care, the director is usually protected from liability by the business judgment rule. The business judgment rule protects directors from lawsuits that challenge the business judgment of those directors. Transactions frequently litigated involve setting executive compensation, dividend payouts, and mergers and acquisitions. However, litigation may involve any action or failure to take action, by a corporation's board of directors. Of course, if shareholders were permitted to challenge any corporate decision, for any reason, the volume of litigation would be huge, and corporate boards of directors would have a difficult time taking any action without fear of challenge. The idea underlying the business judgment rule is to give directors wide latitude in taking steps to benefit a corporation. In addition, the business judgment rule prevents courts from second guessing the business judgment of directors, provided that the judgments are made in accordance with the parameters discussed below.

While some describe the business judgment rule as a shield that protects directors from lawsuits, others view the rule as limiting a director's potential liability to acts involving gross negligence. The basic rule is that the business judgment rule applies to informed business decisions made by directors unless a plaintiff can show any of the following conditions: fraud, illegality, conflict of interest, bad faith, egregious decision, or waste. The existence of some of these conditions will result in liability, while others typically lead to a different analysis involving significantly greater scrutiny of the transaction in question. Importantly, directors are not subject to liability merely because a court finds a challenged action not protected by the business judgment rule. Rather, the directors must also have breached the duty of care.

C. Procedural and Substantive Requirements for the Business Judgment Rule

Because the business judgment rule has the potential to shield significant corporate decisions from scrutiny, it is important that there be some safeguards on the conditions under which the rule will apply. While most corporate actions do satisfy these conditions, it is important to assure that a decision protected by the business judgment rule be free from the taint of impropriety. Therefore, in order to obtain the protection afforded by the business judgment rule, directors must satisfy both procedural and substantive requirements.

Procedural Requirements of the Business Judgment Rule

The procedural requirements of the business judgment rule act as a trigger to the protection. Only *informed decisions* are protected by the business judgment rule. Attorneys will frequently advise their clients, not just to inform themselves before making a decision, but also to keep sufficient records as evidence to document that their decisions are indeed informed.

The business judgment rule protects decisions, not the people who are charged with making them. In order for a director to be protected by the business judgment rule, the director must actually make a decision. If the director fails to make a decision, there is no business judgment rule protection because there has been no business judgment. The business judgment rule does not protect directors solely because of their status in a corporation. Directors cannot shut their eyes to corporate misconduct and pretend they did not see the conduct. However, this does not mean there is automatic liability; even if a decision or a failure to make a decision does not meet the standard to obtain the protection of the business judgment rule, a plaintiff bringing an action against a director would still have to prove that the director had violated his or her duty of care.

Because business judgment rule protection is not available if directors do not make a decision, or if they make an uninformed decision, many decisions are challenged on these grounds. In order to prevail in such a challenge, in most jurisdictions, a plaintiff must show that the board was grossly negligent in failing to inform itself of all material information reasonably available to it and that the decision itself was grossly negligent.

In order to avoid liability for violating the duty of care on procedural grounds, directors should keep informed about and properly "oversee" the corporation's activities and policies; be adequately informed about the corporation's business, its interests and the relevant issues, before making decisions; possess a minimum level of skill and expertise with regard to the role of director for the specific business; and be aware of the financial status of the corporation (e.g. regularly review the firm's financial statements).

Substantive Requirements of the Business Judgment Rule

The substantive requirements of the business judgment rule require the board to refrain from certain actions. With respect to any decision it makes, the board may not commit fraud, make an egregious decision, engage in a conflict of interest, act in bad faith, make a wasteful decision or make an illegal decision. If the board has met the procedural conditions outlined above, and the board's decision is not tainted by any of these conditions, the decision meets the substantive requirements and is protected by the business judgment rule. A plaintiff challenging an informed decision (one that meets procedural requirements outlined above) must show that one of the above substantive conditions has occurred. Importantly, even if a plaintiff can show a violation of a substantive requirement, a plaintiff bringing an action against a director would still have to prove a violation of the underlying duty of care. In most jurisdictions, the standard for breach of the duty of care is gross negligence.

For example, a board of directors of an overnight delivery service sets forth a policy that drivers are to double-park illegally, rather than park farther away, because it is in the interest of the company to deliver packages on time. In the judgment of the board, the value of delivering packages on time is greater than the cost of occasionally getting parking tickets. However, since the board is asking drivers to break the law by parking illegally, this decision is not protected by the business judgment rule. Even though the decision is not protected by the business judgment rule, the board is not subject to liability unless it also breached the duty of care. In this case, there is a strong argument that the decision is probably not a breach of the duty of care, because it involved a minor violation and resulted in a net financial gain for the company.

A key point to remember about the business judgment rule is that directors can make a bad or wrong decision and still have that decision protected by the business judgment rule if they act in good faith, have a business reason for their action, and make an informed decision. Making the best decision is not a prerequisite to business judgment rule protection.

Kamin v. American Express Co.

86 Misc. 2d 809, 383 N.Y.S.2d 807 (N.Y. Sup. Ct. 1976)

GREENFIELD, J.:

In this stockholders' derivative action, the individual defendants, who are the directors of the American Express Company, move for an order dismissing the complaint for failure to state a cause of action . . . and alternatively, for summary judgment. . . .

The complaint is brought derivatively by two minority stockholders of the American Express Company, asking for a declaration that a certain dividend in kind is a waste of corporate assets, directing the defendants not to proceed with the distribution, or, in the alternative, for monetary damages. The motion to dismiss the complaint requires the court to presuppose the truth of the allegations. It is the defendants' contention that, conceding everything in the complaint, no viable cause of action is made out.

After establishing the identity of the parties, the complaint alleges that in 1972 American Express acquired for investment 1,954,418 shares of common stock of Donaldson, Lufken and Jenrette, Inc. (hereafter DLJ), a publicly traded corporation, at a cost of $29,900,000. It is further alleged that the current market value of those shares is approximately $4,000,000. On July 28, 1975, it is alleged, the board of directors of American Express declared a special dividend to all stockholders of record pursuant to which the shares of DLJ would be distributed in kind. Plaintiffs contend further that if American Express were to sell the DLJ shares on the market, it would sustain a capital loss of $25,000,000 which could be offset against taxable capital gains on other investments. Such a sale, they allege, would result in tax savings to the company of approximately $8,000,000, which would not be available in the case of the distribution of DLJ shares to stockholders. It is alleged that on October 8, 1975 and October 16, 1975, plaintiffs demanded that the directors rescind the previously declared dividend in DLJ shares and take steps to preserve the capital loss which would result from selling the shares. This demand was rejected by the board of directors on October 17, 1975.

It is apparent that all the previously-mentioned allegations of the complaint go to the question of the exercise by the board of directors of business judgment in deciding how to deal with the DLJ shares. The crucial allegation which must be scrutinized to determine the legal sufficiency of the complaint is paragraph 19, which alleges:

> "19. All of the defendant Directors engaged in or acquiesced in or negligently permitted the declaration and payment of the Dividend in violation of the fiduciary duty owed by them to Amex to care for and preserve Amex's assets in the same manner as a man of average prudence would care for his own property."

Plaintiffs never moved for temporary injunctive relief, and did nothing to bar the actual distribution of the DLJ shares. The dividend was in fact paid on October 31, 1975. Accordingly, that portion of the complaint seeking a direction not to distribute the shares is deemed to be moot, and the court will deal only with the request for declaratory judgment or for damages.

Examination of the complaint reveals that there is no claim of fraud or self-dealing, and no contention that there was any bad faith or oppressive conduct. The law is quite clear as to what is necessary to ground a claim for actionable wrongdoing.

> "In actions by stockholders, which assail the acts of their directors or trustees, courts will not interfere unless the powers have been illegally or unconscientiously executed, or unless it be made to appear that the acts were fraudulent or collusive and destructive of the rights of the stockholders. Mere errors of judgment are not sufficient as grounds for equity interference; for the powers of those entrusted with corporate management are largely discretionary." *(Leslie v Lorillard, 110 NY 519, 532* [*Citations omitted.*])

More specifically, the question of whether or not a dividend is to be declared or a distribution of some kind should be made is exclusively a matter of business judgment for the board of directors.

> "Courts will not interfere with such discretion unless it be first made to appear that the directors have acted or are about to act in bad faith and for a dishonest purpose. It is for the directors to say, acting in good faith of course, when and to what extent dividends shall be declared. The statute confers upon the directors this power, and the minority stockholders are not in a position to question this right, so long as the directors are acting in good faith" [*Citations omitted.*]

Thus, a complaint must be dismissed if all that is presented is a decision to pay dividends rather than pursuing some other course of conduct. [*Citations omitted.*] A complaint which alleges merely that some course of action other than that pursued by the board of directors would have been more advantageous gives rise to no cognizable cause of action. Courts have more than enough to do in adjudicating legal rights and devising remedies for wrongs. The directors' room rather than the courtroom is the appropriate forum for thrashing out purely business questions which will have an impact on profits, market prices, competitive situations, or tax advantages. . . .

It is not enough to allege, as plaintiffs do here, that the directors made an imprudent decision, which did not capitalize on the possibility of using a potential capital loss to offset capital gains. More than imprudence or mistaken judgment must be shown. . . .

[T]he Business Corporation Law permits an action against directors for "[the] neglect of, or failure to perform, or other violation of his duties in the management and disposition of corporate assets committed to his charge." This does not mean that a director is chargeable with ordinary negligence for having made an improper decision, or having acted imprudently. The "neglect" referred to in the statute is neglect of duties (i.e., malfeasance or nonfeasance) and not misjudgment. To allege that a director "negligently permitted the declaration and payment" of a dividend without alleging fraud, dishonesty or nonfeasance, is to state merely that a decision was taken with which one disagrees.

Nor does this appear to be a case in which a potentially valid cause of action is inartfully stated. . . . The affidavits of the defendants and the exhibits annexed thereto demonstrate that the objections raised by the plaintiffs to the proposed dividend action were carefully considered and unanimously rejected by the board at a special meeting called precisely for that purpose at the plaintiffs' request. The minutes of the special meeting indicate that the defendants were fully aware that a sale rather than a distribution of the DLJ shares might result in the realization of a substantial income tax saving. Nevertheless, they concluded that there were countervailing considerations primarily with respect to the adverse effect such a sale, realizing a loss of $25,000,000, would have on the net income figures in the American Express financial statement. Such a reduction of net income would have a serious effect on the market value of the publicly traded American Express stock. This was not a situation in which the defendant directors totally overlooked facts called to their attention. They gave them consideration, and attempted to view the total picture in arriving at their decision. While plaintiffs contend that according to their accounting consultants the loss on the DLJ stock would still have to be charged against current earnings even if the stock were distributed, the defendants' accounting experts assert that the loss would be a charge against earnings only in the event of a sale, whereas in the event of distribution of the stock as a dividend, the proper accounting treatment would be to charge the loss only against surplus. While the chief accountant for the SEC raised some question as to the appropriate accounting treatment of this transaction, there was no basis for any action to be taken by the SEC with respect to the American Express financial statement.

The only hint of self-interest which is raised . . . is that 4 of the 20 directors were officers and employees of American Express and members of its executive incentive compensation plan. Hence, it is suggested, by virtue of the action taken earnings may have been overstated and their compensation affected thereby. Such a claim is highly speculative and standing alone can hardly be regarded as sufficient to support an inference of self-dealing. There is no claim or showing that the four company directors dominated and controlled the 16 outside members of the board. Certainly, every action taken by the board has some impact on earnings and may therefore affect the compensation of those whose earnings are keyed to profits. That does not disqualify the inside directors, nor does it put every policy adopted by the board in question. All directors have an obligation, using sound business judgment, to maximize income for the benefit of all persons having a stake in the welfare of the corporate entity. [*Citation omitted.*] What we have here . . . is that a disagreement exists between two minority stockholders and a unanimous board of directors as to the best way to handle a loss already incurred on an investment. The directors are entitled to exercise their honest business judgment on the information before them, and to act within their corporate powers. That they may be mistaken, that other courses of action might have differing consequences, or that their action might benefit some shareholders more than others present no basis for the superimposition of judicial judgment, so long as it appears that the directors have been acting in good faith. The question of to what extent a dividend shall be declared and the manner in which it shall be paid is ordinarily subject only to the qualification that the dividend be paid out of surplus (Business Corporation Law, § 510, subd

[b]). The court will not interfere unless a clear case is made out of fraud, oppression, arbitrary action, or breach of trust.

* * * *

In this case it clearly appears that the plaintiffs have failed as a matter of law to make out an actionable claim. Accordingly, the motion by the defendants for summary judgment and dismissal of the complaint is granted.

QUESTIONS

1. The court found the defendant's actions did not constitute waste. Consider the American Law Institute's *Principles of Corporate Governance* § 1.42:

> "A transaction constitutes a 'waste of corporate assets' if it involves an expenditure of corporate funds or a disposition of corporate assets for which no consideration is received in exchange and for which there is no rational business purpose, or, if consideration is received in exchange, the consideration the corporation receives is so inadequate in value that no person of ordinary sound business judgment would deem it worth that which the corporation has paid."

Do you think the American Express directors' actions constituted a "waste of corporate assets?"

2. What rationale could exist for protecting bad decisions by directors? Would you prefer a rule that allowed for greater scrutiny of such decisions?

3. What advice would you give to Mr. Henry Ford if he had come to you for guidance about how to protect the decision not to issue a dividend and to build the plant?

4. If the same factual circumstances occurred with respect to another failed purchase by American Express two years after the decision in the *Kamin* case, and the directors decided to handle the situation in the same manner (i.e., by distributing the stock of the failed company), do you think that such a decision would be afforded the same protection if shareholders again filed a claim for waste? Why or why not?

In *Lewis v. Vogelstein* (699 A.2d 327 (Del. 1997)) the court was evaluating whether the grant of stock options to officers and directors of Mattel, Inc. (the

"Plan"), violated directors' fiduciary duties because of the allegation that the Plan "did not offer reasonable assurance to the corporation that it would receive adequate value in exchange for such grants, and that such grants represent[ed] excessively large compensation for the directors in relation to the value of their service to Mattel." In evaluating whether the action for waste should be dismissed, Chancellor Allen explained:

> The judicial standard for determination of corporate waste is well developed. Roughly, a waste entails an exchange of corporate assets for consideration so disproportionately small as to lie beyond the range at which any reasonable person might be willing to trade. . . . Most often the claim is associated with a transfer of corporate assets that serves no corporate purpose; or for which no consideration at all is received. Such a transfer is in effect a gift. If, however, there is *any substantial* consideration received by the corporation, and if there is a *good faith judgment* that in the circumstances the transaction is worthwhile, there should be no finding of waste, even if the fact finder would conclude *ex post* that the transaction was unreasonably risky. Any other rule would deter corporate boards from the optimal rational acceptance of risk . . . . Courts are ill-fitted to attempt to weigh the "adequacy" of consideration under the waste standard or, *ex post,* to judge appropriate degrees of business risk.

Id. at 336.

Smith v. Van Gorkom

488 A.2d 858 (Del. 1985)

HORSEY, J.:

This appeal from the Court of Chancery involves a class action brought by shareholders of the defendant Trans Union Corporation ("Trans Union" or "the Company") . . .against the defendant members of the Board of Directors of Trans Union. . . .

Following trial, the former Chancellor granted judgment for the defendant directors . . . . based on two findings: (1) that the Board of Directors had acted in an informed manner so as to be entitled to protection of the business judgment rule in approving the cash-out merger; and (2) that the shareholder vote approving the merger should not be set aside because the stockholders had been "fairly informed" by the Board of Directors before voting thereon.

* * * *

Speaking for the majority of the Court, . . . we reverse and direct that judgment be entered in favor of the plaintiffs and against the defendant directors for the fair value of the plaintiffs' stockholdings in Trans Union, in accordance with *Weinberger v. UOP, Inc., Del.Supr.,* 457 A.2d 701 (1983).

We hold: (1) that the Board's decision, reached September 20, 1980, to approve the proposed cash-out merger was not the product of an informed business judgment; (2) that the Board's subsequent efforts to amend the Merger Agreement and take other curative action were ineffectual, both legally and factually; and (3) that the Board did not deal with complete candor with the stockholders by failing to disclose all material facts, which they knew or should have known, before securing the stockholders' approval of the merger.

I.

The nature of this case requires a detailed factual statement. . . .

Trans Union was a publicly-traded, diversified holding company, the principal earnings of which were generated by its railcar leasing business. During the period here involved, the Company had a cash flow of hundreds of millions of dollars annually. However, the Company had difficulty in generating sufficient taxable income to offset increasingly large investment tax credits (ITCs). . . .

* * * *

On August 27, 1980, Van Gorkom [Jerrome W. Van Gorkom was Trans Union's Chairman and CEO.] met with Senior Management of Trans Union. Van Gorkom reported on . . . his desire to find a solution to the tax credit problem more permanent than a continued program of acquisitions. Various alternatives were suggested and discussed preliminarily, including the sale of Trans Union to a company with a large amount of taxable income.

Donald Romans, Chief Financial Officer of Trans Union, stated that his department had done a "very brief bit of work on the possibility of a leveraged buy-out."* . . . . The work consisted of a "preliminary study" of the cash which could be generated by the Company if it participated in a leveraged buy-out. . .

On September 5, at another Senior Management meeting which Van Gorkom attended, Romans again brought up the idea of a leveraged buy-out

* A leveraged buyout (or "LBO") is a transaction in which the purchase price of a company is financed by borrowing against the assets of that company.—*Eds.*

. . . . Romans and Bruce S. Chelberg, President and Chief Operating Officer of Trans Union, had been working on the matter in preparation for the meeting. According to Romans: They did not "come up" with a price for the Company. They merely "ran the numbers" at $50 a share and at $60 a share with the "rough form" of their cash figures at the time. Their "figures indicated that $50 would be very easy to do but $60 would be very difficult to do under those figures." This work did not purport to establish a fair price for either the Company or 100% of the stock. It was intended to determine the cash flow needed to service the debt that would "probably" be incurred in a leveraged buy-out, based on "rough calculations" without "any benefit of experts to identify what the limits were to that, and so forth." . . . .

At this meeting, Van Gorkom stated that he would be willing to take $55 per share for his own 75,000 shares. He vetoed the suggestion of a leveraged buy-out by Management, however, as involving a potential conflict of interest for Management. Van Gorkom, a certified public accountant and lawyer, had been an officer of Trans Union for 24 years, its Chief Executive Officer for more than 17 years, and Chairman of its Board for 2 years. It is noteworthy in this connection that he was then approaching 65 years of age and mandatory retirement.

For several days following the September 5 meeting, Van Gorkom pondered the idea of a sale. He had participated in many acquisitions as a manager and director of Trans Union and as a director of other companies. He was familiar with acquisition procedures, valuation methods, and negotiations; and he privately considered the pros and cons of whether Trans Union should seek a privately or publicly-held purchaser.

Van Gorkom decided to meet with Jay A. Pritzker, a well-known corporate takeover specialist and a social acquaintance. However, rather than approaching Pritzker simply to determine his interest in acquiring Trans Union, Van Gorkom assembled a proposed per share price for sale of the Company and a financing structure by which to accomplish the sale. Van Gorkom did so without consulting either his Board or any members of Senior Management except one: Carl Peterson, Trans Union's Controller. Telling Peterson that he wanted no other person on his staff to know what he was doing, but without telling him why, Van Gorkom directed Peterson to calculate the feasibility of a leveraged buy-out at an assumed price per share of $55. Apart from the Company's historic stock market price, and Van Gorkom's long association with Trans Union, the record is devoid of any competent evidence that $55 represented the per share intrinsic value of the Company.

Having thus chosen the $55 figure, based solely on the availability of a leveraged buy-out, Van Gorkom multiplied the price per share by the number of shares outstanding to reach a total value of the Company of $690 million. Van Gorkom told Peterson to use this $690 million figure and to assume a $200 million equity contribution by the buyer. Based on these assumptions, Van Gorkom directed Peterson to determine whether the debt portion of the purchase price could be paid off in five years or less if financed by Trans Union's cash flow as projected in the Five Year Forecast, and by the sale of certain weaker divisions identified in a study done for Trans Union by the Boston Consulting Group ("BCG study"). Peterson reported that, of the purchase price, approximately $50–80 million would remain outstanding after five years. Van Gorkom was disappointed, but decided to meet with Pritzker nevertheless.

Van Gorkom arranged a meeting with Pritzker at the latter's home on Saturday, September 13, 1980. Van Gorkom prefaced his presentation by stating to Pritzker: "Now as far as you are concerned, I can, I think, show how you can pay a substantial premium over the present stock price and pay off most of the loan in the first five years. If you could pay $55 for this Company, here is a way in which I think it can be financed."

Van Gorkom then reviewed with Pritzker his calculations based upon his proposed price of $55 per share. Although Pritzker mentioned $50 as a more attractive figure, no other price was mentioned. However, Van Gorkom stated that to be sure that $55 was the best price obtainable, Trans Union should be free to accept any better offer. Pritzker demurred, stating that his organization would serve as a "stalking horse" for an "auction contest" only if Trans Union would permit Pritzker to buy 1,750,000 shares of Trans Union stock at market price which Pritzker could then sell to any higher bidder. . . .

On Monday, September 15, Pritzker advised Van Gorkom that he was interested in the $55 cash-out merger proposal and requested more information on Trans Union. Van Gorkom agreed to meet privately with Pritzker, accompanied by Peterson, Chelberg, and Michael Carpenter, a consultant from the Boston Consulting Group. The meetings took place on September 16 and 17. Van Gorkom was "astounded that events were moving with such amazing rapidity."

On Thursday, September 18, Van Gorkom met again with Pritzker. At that time, Van Gorkom knew that Pritzker intended to make a cash-out merger offer at Van Gorkom's proposed $55 per share. Pritzker instructed his attorney, a merger and acquisition specialist, to begin drafting merger documents. There was no further discussion of the $55 price. However, the number of shares of

Trans Union's treasury stock to be offered to Pritzker was negotiated down to one million shares; the price was set at $38—75 cents above the per share price at the close of the market on September 19. At this point, Pritzker insisted that the Trans Union Board act on his merger proposal within the next three days, stating to Van Gorkom: "We have to have a decision by no later than Sunday [evening, September 21] before the opening of the English stock exchange on Monday morning." . . . .

On Friday, September 19, Van Gorkom, Chelberg, and Pritzker consulted with Trans Union's lead bank regarding the financing of Pritzker's purchase of Trans Union. The bank indicated that it could form a syndicate of banks that would finance the transaction. On the same day, Van Gorkom retained James Brennan, Esquire, to advise Trans Union on the legal aspects of the merger. Van Gorkom did not consult with William Browder, a Vice-President and director of Trans Union and former head of its legal department, or with William Moore, then the head of Trans Union's legal staff.

On Friday, September 19, Van Gorkom called a special meeting of the Trans Union Board for noon the following day. He also called a meeting of the Company's Senior Management to convene at 11:00 a.m., prior to the meeting of the Board. . . .

Of those present at the Senior Management meeting on September 20, only Chelberg and Peterson had prior knowledge of Pritzker's offer. Van Gorkom disclosed the offer and described its terms, but he furnished no copies of the proposed Merger Agreement. Romans announced that his department had done a second study which showed that, for a leveraged buy-out, the price range for Trans Union stock was between $55 and $65 per share. Van Gorkom neither saw the study nor asked Romans to make it available for the Board meeting.

Senior Management's reaction to the Pritzker proposal was completely negative. No member of Management, except Chelberg and Peterson, supported the proposal. Romans objected to the price as being too low; he was critical of the timing and suggested that consideration should be given to the adverse tax consequences of an all-cash deal for low-basis shareholders; and he took the position that the agreement to sell Pritzker one million newly-issued shares at market price would inhibit other offers, as would the prohibitions against soliciting bids and furnishing inside information to other bidders. Romans argued that the Pritzker proposal was a "lock up" and amounted to "an agreed merger as opposed to an offer." Nevertheless, Van Gorkom proceeded to the Board meeting as scheduled without further delay.

Van Gorkom began the Special Meeting of the Board with a twenty-minute oral presentation. Copies of the proposed Merger Agreement were delivered too late for study before or during the meeting. He reviewed the Company's ITC and depreciation problems and the efforts theretofore made to solve them. He discussed his initial meeting with Pritzker and his motivation in arranging that meeting. Van Gorkom did not disclose to the Board, however, the methodology by which he alone had arrived at the $55 figure, or the fact that he first proposed the $55 price in his negotiations with Pritzker.

Van Gorkom outlined the terms of the Pritzker offer as follows: Pritzker would pay $55 in cash for all outstanding shares of Trans Union stock upon completion of which Trans Union would be merged into New T Company, a subsidiary wholly-owned by Pritzker and formed to implement the merger; for a period of 90 days, Trans Union could receive, but could not actively solicit, competing offers; the offer had to be acted on by the next evening, Sunday, September 21; Trans Union could only furnish to competing bidders published information, and not proprietary information; the offer was subject to Pritzker obtaining the necessary financing by October 10, 1980; if the financing contingency were met or waived by Pritzker, Trans Union was required to sell to Pritzker one million newly-issued shares of Trans Union at $38 per share.

Van Gorkom took the position that putting Trans Union "up for auction" through a 90-day market test would validate a decision by the Board that $55 was a fair price. He told the Board that the "free market will have an opportunity to judge whether $55 is a fair price." Van Gorkom framed the decision before the Board not as whether $55 per share was the highest price that could be obtained, but as whether the $55 price was a fair price that the stockholders should be given the opportunity to accept or reject.

Attorney Brennan advised the members of the Board that they might be sued if they failed to accept the offer and that a fairness opinion was not required as a matter of law.

Romans attended the meeting as chief financial officer of the Company. He told the Board that he had not been involved in the negotiations with Pritzker and knew nothing about the merger proposal until the morning of the meeting; that his studies did not indicate either a fair price for the stock or a valuation of the Company; that he did not see his role as directly addressing the fairness issue; and that he and his people "were trying to search for ways to justify a price in connection with such a [leveraged buy-out] transaction, rather than to say what the shares are worth.". . . .

Romans told the Board that, in his opinion, $55 was "in the range of a fair price," but "at the beginning of the range."

* * * *

The Board meeting of September 20 lasted about two hours. Based solely upon Van Gorkom's oral presentation, Chelberg's supporting representations, Romans' oral statement, Brennan's legal advice, and their knowledge of the market history of the Company's stock, the directors approved the proposed Merger Agreement. . . .While the Board now claims to have reserved the right to accept any better offer received after the announcement of the Pritzker agreement (even though the minutes of the meeting do not reflect this), it is undisputed that the Board did not reserve the right to actively solicit alternate offers.

The Merger Agreement was executed by Van Gorkom during the evening of September 20 at a formal social event that he hosted for the opening of the Chicago Lyric Opera. Neither he nor any other director read the agreement prior to its signing and delivery to Pritzker.

* * * *

Within 10 days of the public announcement, dissent among Senior Management over the merger had become widespread. Faced with threatened resignations of key officers, Van Gorkom met with Pritzker who agreed to several modifications of the Agreement. Pritzker was willing to do so provided that Van Gorkom could persuade the dissidents to remain on the Company payroll for at least six months after consummation of the merger.

Van Gorkom reconvened the Board on October 8 and secured the directors' approval of the proposed amendments—sight unseen. The Board also authorized the employment of Salomon Brothers, its investment banker, to solicit other offers for Trans Union during the proposed "market test" period.

* * * *

Salomon Brothers' efforts over a three-month period from October 21 to January 21 produced only one serious suitor for Trans Union—General Electric Credit Corporation ("GE Credit"), a subsidiary of the General Electric Company. However, GE Credit was unwilling to make an offer for Trans Union unless Trans Union first rescinded its Merger Agreement with Pritzker. When Pritzker refused, GE Credit terminated further discussions with Trans Union in early January.

In the meantime, in early December, the investment firm of Kohlberg, Kravis, Roberts & Co. ("KKR"), the only other concern to make a firm offer for Trans Union, withdrew its offer under circumstances hereinafter detailed.

* * * *

On February 10, the stockholders of Trans Union approved the Pritzker merger proposal. Of the outstanding shares, 69.9% were voted in favor of the merger; 7.25% were voted against the merger; and 22.85% were not voted.

II.

We turn to the issue of the application of the business judgment rule to the September 20 meeting of the Board.

* * * *

Under Delaware law, the business judgment rule is the offspring of the fundamental principle, codified in 8 Del. C. § 141 (a), that the business and affairs of a Delaware corporation are managed by or under its board of directors. [*Citations omitted.*] In carrying out their managerial roles, directors are charged with an unyielding fiduciary duty to the corporation and its shareholders. [*Citations omitted.*] The business judgment rule exists to protect and promote the full and free exercise of the managerial power granted to Delaware directors. *Zapata Corp. v. Maldonado, supra* at 782. The rule itself "is a presumption that in making a business decision, the directors of a corporation acted on an informed basis, in good faith and in the honest belief that the action taken was in the best interests of the company." . . . Thus, the party attacking a board decision as uninformed must rebut the presumption that its business judgment was an informed one. . . .

The determination of whether a business judgment is an informed one turns on whether the directors have informed themselves "prior to making a business decision, of all material information reasonably available to them.". . . .

Under the business judgment rule there is no protection for directors who have made "an unintelligent or unadvised judgment." . . . A director's duty to inform himself in preparation for a decision derives from the fiduciary capacity in which he serves the corporation and its stockholders. . . . . Since a director is vested with the responsibility for the management of the affairs of the corporation, he must execute that duty with the recognition that he acts on behalf of others. Such obligation does not tolerate faithlessness or self-dealing. But fulfillment of the fiduciary function requires more than the mere absence of bad faith or fraud. Representation of the financial interests of others imposes on a director an affirmative duty to protect those interests and to proceed with a critical eye in assessing information of the type and under the circumstances present here. [*Citations omitted.*]

Thus, a director's duty to exercise an informed business judgment is in the nature of a duty of care, as distinguished from a duty of loyalty. Here, there were no allegations of fraud, bad faith, or self-dealing, or proof thereof. Hence, it is presumed that the directors reached their business judgment in good faith . . . and considerations of motive are irrelevant to the issue before us.

The standard of care applicable to a director's duty of care has also been recently restated by this Court [as gross negligence]. . . . We think the concept of gross negligence is also the proper standard for determining whether a business judgment reached by a board of directors was an informed one.

In the specific context of a proposed merger of domestic corporations, a director has a duty under 8 Del. C. § 251(b), along with his fellow directors, to act in an informed and deliberate manner in determining whether to approve an agreement of merger before submitting the proposal to the stockholders. Certainly in the merger context, a director may not abdicate that duty by leaving to the shareholders alone the decision to approve or disapprove the agreement. . . . Only an agreement of merger satisfying the requirements of 8 Del. C. § 251 (b) may be submitted to the shareholders under § 251 (c). . . .

III.

* * * *

[T]he question of whether the directors reached an informed business judgment in agreeing to sell the Company, pursuant to the terms of the September 20 Agreement presents, in reality, two questions: (A) whether the directors reached an informed business judgment on September 20, 1980; and (B) if they did not, whether the directors' actions taken subsequent to September 20 were adequate to cure any infirmity in their action taken on September 20. . . .

A

On the record before us, we must conclude that the Board of Directors did not reach an informed business judgment on September 20, 1980 in voting to "sell" the Company for $55 per share pursuant to the Pritzker cash-out merger proposal. Our reasons, in summary, are as follows:

The directors (1) did not adequately inform themselves as to Van Gorkom's role in forcing the "sale" of the Company and in establishing the per share purchase price; (2) were uninformed as to the intrinsic value of the Company; and (3) given these circumstances, at a minimum, were grossly negligent in approving the "sale" of the Company upon two hours' consideration, without prior notice, and without the exigency of a crisis or emergency.

As has been noted, the Board based its September 20 decision to approve the cash-out merger primarily on Van Gorkom's representations. None of the directors, other than Van Gorkom and Chelberg, had any prior knowledge that the purpose of the meeting was to propose a cash-out merger of Trans Union. No members of Senior Management were present, other than Chelberg, Romans and Peterson; and the latter two had only learned of the proposed sale an hour earlier. . . .

Without any documents before them concerning the proposed transaction, the members of the Board were required to rely entirely upon Van Gorkom's 20-minute oral presentation of the proposal. No written summary of the terms of the merger was presented; the directors were given no documentation to support the adequacy of $55 price per share for sale of the Company; and the Board had before it nothing more than Van Gorkom's statement of his understanding of the substance of an agreement which he admittedly had never read, nor which any member of the Board had ever seen.

Under 8 Del.C. § 141 (e), "directors are fully protected in relying in good faith on reports made by officers." [*Citations omitted.*] The term "report" has been liberally construed to include reports of informal personal investigations by corporate officers, *Cheff v. Mathes,* [*Citations omitted.*] However, there is no evidence that any "report," as defined under § 141 (e), concerning the Pritzker proposal, was presented to the Board on September 20. Van Gorkom's oral presentation of his understanding of the terms of the proposed Merger Agreement, which he had not seen, and Romans' brief oral statement of his preliminary study regarding the feasibility of a leveraged buy-out of Trans Union do not qualify as § 141 (e) "reports" for these reasons: The former lacked substance because Van Gorkom was basically uninformed as to the essential provisions of the very document about which he was talking. Romans' statement was irrelevant to the issues before the Board since it did not purport to be a valuation study. At a minimum for a report to enjoy the status conferred by § 141 (e), it must be pertinent to the subject matter upon which a board is called to act, and otherwise be entitled to good faith, not blind, reliance. Considering all of the surrounding circumstances . . . the directors were duty bound to make reasonable inquiry of Van Gorkom and Romans, and if they had done so, the inadequacy of that upon which they now claim to have relied would have been apparent.

The defendants rely on the following factors to sustain the Trial Court's finding that the Board's decision was an informed one: (1) the magnitude of the premium or spread between the $55 Pritzker offering price and Trans Union's current market price of $38 per share; (2) the amendment of the Agreement as submitted on September 20 to permit the Board to accept any better offer during the "market test" period; (3) the collective experience and expertise of the Board's "inside" and "outside" directors; and (4) their reliance on Brennan's legal advice that the directors might be sued if they rejected the Pritzker proposal. . . .

(1)

A substantial premium may provide one reason to recommend a merger, but in the absence of other sound valuation information, the fact of a premium alone does not provide an adequate basis upon which to assess the fairness of an offering price. Here, the judgment reached as to the adequacy of the premium was based on a comparison between the historically depressed Trans Union market price and the amount of the Pritzker offer. Using market price as a basis for concluding that the premium adequately reflected the true value of the Company was a clearly faulty, indeed fallacious, premise. . . .

The record is clear that before September 20, Van Gorkom and other members of Trans Union's Board knew that the market had consistently undervalued the worth of Trans Union's stock, despite steady increases in the Company's operating income in the seven years preceding the merger. The Board related this occurrence in large part to Trans Union's inability to use its ITCs as previously noted. . . .

The parties do not dispute that a publicly-traded stock price is solely a measure of the value of a minority position and, thus, market price represents only the value of a single share. Nevertheless, on September 20, the Board assessed the adequacy of the premium over market, offered by Pritzker, solely by comparing it with Trans Union's current and historical stock price. . . .

Indeed, as of September 20, the Board had no other information on which to base a determination of the intrinsic value of Trans Union as a going concern. As of September 20, the Board had made no evaluation of the Company designed to value the entire enterprise, nor had the Board ever previously considered selling the Company or consenting to a buy-out merger. . . .

* * * *

The record also establishes that the Board accepted without scrutiny Van Gorkom's representation as to the fairness of the $55 price per share for sale of the Company—a subject that the Board had never previously considered. The Board thereby failed to discover that Van Gorkom had suggested the $55 price to Pritzker and, most crucially, that Van Gorkom had arrived at the $55 figure based on calculations designed solely to determine the feasibility of a leveraged buy-out. No questions were raised either as to the tax implications of a cash-out merger or how the price for the one million share option granted Pritzker was calculated.

* * * *

(2)

This brings us to the post-September 20 "market test" upon which the defendants ultimately rely to confirm the reasonableness of their September 20 decision to accept the Pritzker proposal. In this connection, the directors present a two-part argument: (a) that by making a "market test" of Pritzker's $55 per share offer a condition of their September 20 decision to accept his offer, they cannot be found to have acted impulsively or in an uninformed manner on September 20; and (b) that the adequacy of the $17 premium for sale of the Company was conclusively established over the following 90 to 120 days by the most reliable evidence available—the marketplace. . . .

Again, the facts of record do not support the defendants' argument. There is no evidence: (a) that the Merger Agreement was effectively amended to give the Board freedom to put Trans Union up for auction sale to the highest bidder; or (b) that a public auction was in fact permitted to occur. . . .

* * * *

Van Gorkom states that the Agreement as submitted incorporated the ingredients for a market test by authorizing Trans Union to receive competing offers over the next 90-day period. However, he concedes that the Agreement barred Trans Union from actively soliciting such offers and from furnishing to interested parties any information about the Company other than that already in the public domain. . . .

* * * *

(3)

The directors' unfounded reliance on both the premium and the market test as the basis for accepting the Pritzker proposal undermines the defendants' remaining contention that the Board's collective experience and sophistication was a sufficient basis for finding that it reached its September 20 decision with informed, reasonable deliberation. . . . .

* * * *

B

We now examine the Board's post-September 20 conduct for the purpose of determining . . . whether it was informed and not grossly negligent. . . .

(1)

* * * *

First, as to the Board meeting of October 8: Its purpose arose in the aftermath of the September 20 meeting: (1) the September 22 press release announcing that Trans Union "had entered into definitive agreements to merge with an affiliate of Marmon Group, Inc.;" and (2) Senior Management's ensuing revolt.

* * * *

The press release made no reference to provisions allegedly reserving to the Board the rights to perform a "market test" and to withdraw from the Pritzker Agreement if Trans Union received a better offer before the shareholder meeting. . . .

Instead of reconvening the Board, Van Gorkom again privately met with Pritzker, informed him of the developments, and sought his advice. Pritzker then made the following suggestions for overcoming Management's dissatisfaction: (1) that the Agreement be amended to permit Trans Union to solicit, as well as receive, higher offers; and (2) that the shareholder meeting be postponed from early January to February 10, 1981. In return, Pritzker asked Van Gorkom to obtain a commitment from Senior Management to remain at Trans Union for at least six months after the merger was consummated.

Van Gorkom then advised Senior Management that the Agreement would be amended to give Trans Union the right to solicit competing offers through January, 1981, if they would agree to remain with Trans Union. Senior Management was temporarily mollified; and Van Gorkom then called a special meeting of Trans Union's Board for October 8.

Thus, the primary purpose of the October 8 Board meeting was to amend the Merger Agreement, in a manner agreeable to Pritzker, to permit Trans Union to conduct a "market test." Van Gorkom understood that the proposed amendments were intended to give the Company an unfettered "right to openly solicit offers down through January 31." Van Gorkom presumably so represented the amendments to Trans Union's Board members on October 8. In a brief session, the directors approved Van Gorkom's oral presentation of the substance of the proposed amendments, the terms of which were not reduced to writing until October 10. But rather than waiting to review the amendments, the Board again approved them sight unseen and adjourned, giving Van Gorkom authority to execute the papers when he received them.

* * * *

The next day, October 9, and before the Agreement was amended, Pritzker moved swiftly to off-set the proposed market test amendment. First, Pritzker informed Trans Union that he had completed arrangements for financing its acquisition and that the parties were thereby mutually bound to a firm purchase and sale arrangement. Second, Pritzker announced the exercise of his option to purchase one million shares of Trans Union's treasury stock at $38 per share—75 cents above the current market price. . . .

The next day, October 10, Pritzker delivered to Trans Union the proposed amendments to the September 20 Merger Agreement. Van Gorkom promptly proceeded to countersign all the instruments on behalf of Trans Union without reviewing the instruments to determine if they were consistent with the authority previously granted him by the Board. . . .

The October 10 amendments to the Merger Agreement did authorize Trans Union to solicit competing offers, but the amendments had more far-reaching effects. The most significant change was in the definition of the third-party "offer" available to Trans Union as a possible basis for withdrawal from its Merger Agreement with Pritzker. Under the October 10 amendments, a better offer was no longer sufficient to permit Trans Union's withdrawal. Trans Union was now permitted to terminate the Pritzker Agreement and abandon the merger only if, prior to February 10, 1981, Trans Union had either consummated a merger (or sale of assets) with a third party or had entered into a "definitive" merger agreement more favorable than Pritzker's and for a greater consideration—subject only to stockholder approval. Further, the "extension" of the market test period to February 10, 1981 was circumscribed by other amendments which required Trans Union to file its preliminary proxy statement on the Pritzker merger proposal by December 5, 1980 and use its best efforts to mail the statement to its shareholders by January 5, 1981. Thus, the market test period was effectively reduced, not extended. . . .

In our view, the record compels the conclusion that the directors' conduct on October 8 exhibited the same deficiencies as did their conduct on September 20. The Board permitted its Merger Agreement with Pritzker to be amended in a manner it had neither authorized nor intended. . . .

We conclude that the Board acted in a grossly negligent manner on October 8; and that Van Gorkom's representations on which the Board based its actions do not constitute "reports" under § 141 (e) on which the directors could reasonably have relied. Further, the amended Merger Agreement imposed on Trans Union's acceptance of a third party offer conditions more onerous than those imposed on Trans Union's acceptance of Pritzker's offer on September 20. . . .

* * * *

Our review of the record compels a finding that confirmation of the appropriateness of the Pritzker offer by an unfettered or free market test was virtually meaningless in the face of the terms and time limitations of Trans Union's Merger Agreement with Pritzker as amended October 10, 1980.

* * * *

. . .[W]e hold that the defendants' post-September conduct did not cure the deficiencies of their September 20 conduct; and that, accordingly, the Trial Court erred in according to the defendants the benefits of the business judgment rule.

* * * *

VI.

To summarize: we hold that the directors of Trans Union breached their fiduciary duty to their stockholders (1) by their failure to inform themselves of all information reasonably available to them and relevant to their decision to recommend the Pritzker merger; and (2) by their failure to disclose all material information such as a reasonable stockholder would consider important in deciding whether to approve the Pritzker offer.

We hold, therefore, that the Trial Court committed reversible error in applying the business judgment rule in favor of the director defendants in this case.

On remand, the Court of Chancery shall conduct an evidentiary hearing to determine the fair value of the shares represented by the plaintiffs' class, based on the intrinsic value of Trans Union on September 20, 1980. . . . Thereafter, an award of damages may be entered to the extent that the fair value of Trans Union exceeds $55 per share.

* * * *

REVERSED and REMANDED for proceedings consistent herewith.

DISSENT

MCNEILLY, JUSTICE, dissenting:

The majority opinion reads like an advocate's closing address to a hostile jury. And I say that not lightly. Throughout the opinion great emphasis is directed only to the negative, with nothing more than lip service granted the positive aspects of this case. . . . . The first and most important error made is the majority's assessment of the directors' knowledge of the affairs of Trans Union and their combined ability to act in this situation under the protection of the business judgment rule.

Trans Union's Board of Directors consisted of ten men, five of whom were "inside" directors and five of whom were "outside" directors. The "inside" directors were Van Gorkom, Chelberg, Bonser, William B. Browder, Senior Vice-President-Law, and Thomas P. O'Boyle, Senior Vice-President-Administration. At the time the merger was proposed the inside five directors had collectively been employed by the Company for 116 years and had 68 years of combined experience as directors. The "outside" directors were A. W. Wallis, William B. Johnson, Joseph B. Lanterman, Graham J. Morgan and Robert W. Reneker. With the exception of Wallis, these were all chief executive officers of Chicago based corporations that were at least as large as Trans Union. The five "outside" directors had 78 years of combined experience as chief executive officers, and 53 years cumulative service as Trans Union directors. . . .

Directors of this caliber are not ordinarily taken in by a "fast shuffle". I submit they were not taken into this multi-million dollar corporate transaction without being fully informed and aware of the state of the art as it pertained to the entire corporate panoroma [sic] of Trans Union. True, even directors such as these, with their business acumen, interest and expertise, can go astray. I do not believe that to be the case here. These men knew Trans Union like the back of their hands and were more than well qualified to make on the spot informed business judgments concerning the affairs of Trans Union including a 100% sale of the corporation. Lest we forget, the corporate world of then and now operates on what is so aptly referred to as "the fast track". These men were at the time an integral part of that world, all professional business men, not intellectual figureheads. . . .

NOTE ON THE DELAWARE LEGISLATIVE RESPONSE TO DIRECTOR LIABILITY

The Delaware General Assembly adopted section 102(b)(7) in 1986, following a directors and officers insurance "liability crisis" and the 1985 Delaware Supreme Court decision in *Smith v. Van Gorkom*. "The purpose of this statute was to permit stockholders to adopt a provision in the certificate of incorporation to free directors of personal liability in damages for due care violations, but not duty of loyalty violations, bad faith claims and certain other conduct. Such a charter provision, when adopted, would not affect injunctive proceedings based on gross negligence. Once the statute was adopted, stockholders usually approved charter amendments containing these provisions because it freed up directors to take business risks without worrying about negligence lawsuits." *Malpiede v. Townson* (780 A.2d 1075 at 1095 (Del. 2001)).

Del. Gen. Corp. Law 102(b)(7)

§ 102 Contents of Certificate of Incorporation

* * * *

(b) In addition to the matters required to be set forth in the certificate of incorporation by subsection (a) of this section, the certificate of incorporation may also contain any or all of the following matters:

* * * *

7) A provision eliminating or limiting the personal liability of a director to the corporation or its stockholders for monetary damages for breach of fiduciary duty as a director, provided that such provision shall not eliminate or limit the liability of a director: (i) For any breach of the director's duty of loyalty to the corporation or its stockholders; (ii) for acts or omissions not in good faith or which involve intentional misconduct or a knowing violation of law; (iii) under § 174 of this title; or (iv) for any transaction from which the director derived an improper personal benefit. No such provision shall eliminate or limit the liability of a director for any act or

omission occurring prior to the date when such provision becomes effective. All references in this paragraph to a director shall also be deemed to refer to such other person or persons, if any, who, pursuant to a provision of the certificate of incorporation in accordance with § 141(a) of this title, exercise or perform any of the powers or duties otherwise conferred or imposed upon the board of directors by this title.

D. Intrinsic and Entire Fairness as a Defense in Duty of Care Actions

Directors are not subject to liability for transactions beneficial, "fair" or causing no injury to the corporation even if the transaction constituted a breach of the duty of care. This affirmative defense, called the "intrinsic fairness" defense, looks to whether the consideration received by the corporation in a particular transaction was "fair." Consider a situation in which a deal was approved by an uninformed board of directors. However, the deal was not just fair, but extremely beneficial for the corporation. Should the board be liable for a breach of its duty if no injury results from that breach? In such circumstances, the board would still have violated its duty, but it would have an affirmative defense that the outcome was intrinsically fair to the shareholders.

Most decisions that are "intrinsically fair" (fair price) will not result in director liability. However, in the case of a merger or acquisition, courts require the decision to meet the "entire fairness" standard. Entire fairness involves both procedural fairness and intrinsic fairness. Both the manner in which the board made the decision and the price itself must be fair. This standard is more difficult for a board to satisfy.

Cinerama Inc. v. Technicolor, 663 A.2d 1156 (Del. 1995) (*with facts adapted from Cede & Co. v. Technicolor, Inc.* 634 A.2d 345 (Del. 1993). [In 1970 Technicolor was a corporation with a long and prominent history in the film/audio-visual industries. Technicolor's core business for over thirty years had been the processing of film for Hollywood movies through facilities in the United States, England and Italy. In its field, Technicolor was the most prominent of a handful of companies. Notwithstanding Technicolor's dominance within its field, the company, by the late seventies, decreased in competitiveness. Its major film processing laboratory was, in the words of Morton Kamerman ("Kamerman"), its Chief Executive Officer and Board

Chairman, "totally out of control" and it was taking losses that were "unacceptable."

In response, Technicolor's Chief Executive Officer initiated efforts to reduce costs at Technicolor's film laboratories and to eliminate other inefficiencies. Through Kamerman's initiative, in the late seventies Technicolor's market share and earnings improved. However, by the early eighties, Technicolor's increase in market share had leveled off and the company's core business earnings had stagnated. Kamerman concluded that Technicolor's principal business, theatrical film processing, did not offer sufficient long-term growth for Technicolor, even though it still represented more than fifty percent of Technicolor's net income.

Kamerman proposed that Technicolor enter the field of rapid processing of consumer film by establishing a network of stores across the country offering one-hour development of film, with quality service at competitive prices. The business, named "One Hour Photo" ("OHP"), would require Technicolor to open approximately one thousand stores over a five year period and to invest about $150 million. In May 1981, Technicolor's Board of Directors approved Kamerman's plan. The following month Technicolor announced its ambitious venture with considerable fanfare. On the date of its OHP announcement, Technicolor's stock had risen to a high of $22.13.

The securities market reacted negatively to Technicolor's announcement. Technicolor's stock dropped by almost $4 a share; and over the next month no Technicolor store had opened. The market had reacted to concern over the size of Technicolor's investment in the new venture, $150 million, in proportion to the shareholders' equity, $78 million.

In late summer 1982, MacAndrews & Forbes Group, Inc. (MAF), identified Technicolor as an attractive takeover target. Negotiations between Ronald Perelman, MAF's controlling shareholder and Kamerman resulted in MAF and Technicolor's agreement to MAF's two-step acquisition of Technicolor. The first step was an all-cash tender offer of $23 per share for all of Technicolor's outstanding shares; if not all Technicolor shareholders tendered their shares to MAF, the second step was a merger of MAF and Technicolor, by which all remaining Technicolor shareholders would receive $23 per share and Technicolor would merge with MAF. Several Technicolor shareholders, including Cinerama, challenged the transaction. After years of litigation, the Delaware Supreme Court found that, although Technicolor directors had breached their duty of care in approving the merger, Cinerama had failed to prove that it had been damaged. The Delaware Supreme Court went on to evaluate the Court of Chancery's determination that Technicolor had met its burden of showing entire fairness.]

. . . .Where, as in this case, the presumption of the business judgment rule has been rebutted, the board of directors' action is examined under the entire fairness standard. *Unitrin, Inc. v. American Gen. Corp.,* 651 A.2d at 1371 n. 7 (collecting cases). This Court has described the dual aspects of entire fairness, as follows:

> The concept of fairness has two basic aspects: fair dealing and fair price. The former embraces questions of when the transaction was timed, how it was initiated, structured, negotiated, disclosed to the directors, and how the approvals of the directors and the stockholders were obtained. The latter aspect of fairness relates to the economic and financial considerations of the proposed merger, including all relevant factors: assets, market value, earnings, future prospects, and any other elements that affect the intrinsic or inherent value of a company's stock. . . . However, the test for fairness is not a bifurcated one as between fair dealing and price. All aspects of the issue must be examined as a whole since the question is one of entire fairness.

Weinberger v. UOP, Inc., 457 A.2d at 711. Thus, the entire fairness standard requires the board of directors to establish "to the *court's* satisfaction that the transaction was the product of both fair dealing *and* fair price." *Cede II*, 634 A.2d at 361. In this case, because the contested action is the sale of a company, the "fair price" aspect of an entire fairness analysis requires the board of directors to demonstrate "that the price offered was the highest value reasonably available under the circumstances." *Id.*

Because the decision that the *procedural* presumption of the business judgment rule has been rebutted does not establish *substantive* liability under the entire fairness standard, such a ruling does not necessarily present an insurmountable obstacle for a board of directors to overcome. Thus, an initial judicial determination that a given breach of a board's fiduciary duties has rebutted the presumption of the business judgment rule does not preclude a subsequent judicial determination that the board action was entirely fair, and is, therefore, not outcome—determinative *per se. Id.* at 371; *accord Nixon v. Blackwell,* 626 A.2d at 1381. To avoid substantive liability *notwithstanding* the quantum of adverse evidence that has defeated the business judgment rule's protective procedural presumption, the board will have to demonstrate entire fairness by presenting evidence of the cumulative manner by which it otherwise discharged all of its fiduciary duties.

Although the *procedural* decision to shift the evidentiary burden to the board of directors to show entire fairness does not create liability *per se,* the aspect of fair dealing to which *Weinberger* devoted the most attention—*disclosure*—has a unique position in a *substantive* entire fairness analysis. A combination of the fiduciary duties of care and loyalty gives rise to the requirement that "a director disclose to shareholders all material facts bearing upon a merger vote. . . ." Moreover, in Delaware, "existing law and policy have evolved into a virtual *per se* rule of [awarding] damages for breach of the fiduciary duty of disclosure." *In re Tri-Star Pictures, Inc.* Litig., 634 A.2d at 333.

[Ultimately the transaction was determined to have met the entire fairness standard. After approximately 10 years of litigation, Cinerama was entitled to receive $21.60 per share (*Cede & Co. v. Technicolor, Inc.,* Del. Ch., C.A. No. 7129 (Oct. 19, 1990)), $1.40 less than the $23 per share it would have received had it voted for the merger.]

E. Informed Decisions

The preceding material emphasizes the importance of a director or officer being "informed" prior to taking any action. In fact, the business judgment rule only protects informed decisions. This, of course, leads to the question of what does it mean to be informed, and how much information is sufficient to meet the standard of "an informed decision."

Francis v. United Jersey Bank

87 N.J. 15, 432 A. 2d 814 (N.J. 1981)

POLLOCK, J.:

The primary issue on this appeal is whether a corporate director is personally liable in negligence for the failure to prevent the misappropriation of trust funds by other directors who were also officers and shareholders of the corporation.

Plaintiffs are trustees in bankruptcy of Pritchard & Baird Intermediaries Corp. (Pritchard & Baird), a reinsurance broker or intermediary. Defendant Lillian P. Overcash is the daughter of Lillian G. Pritchard and the executrix of her estate. At the time of her death, Mrs. Pritchard was a director and the largest single shareholder of Pritchard & Baird. Because Mrs. Pritchard died after the institution of suit but before trial, her executrix was substituted as a defendant. . . .

This litigation focuses on payments made by Pritchard & Baird to Charles Pritchard, Jr. and William Pritchard, who were sons of Mr. and Mrs. Charles Pritchard, Sr., as well as officers, directors and shareholders of the corporation. Claims against Charles, Jr. and William are being pursued in bankruptcy proceedings against them.

* * * *

[T]he initial question is whether Mrs. Pritchard was negligent in not noticing and trying to prevent the misappropriation of funds held by the corporation in an implied trust. . . .

I

. . . . Reinsurance involves a contract under which one insurer agrees to indemnify another for loss sustained under the latter's policy of insurance. Insurance companies that insure against losses arising out of fire or other casualty seek at times to minimize their exposure by sharing risks with other insurance companies. Thus, when the face amount of a policy is comparatively large, the company may enlist one or more insurers to participate in that risk. Similarly, an insurance company's loss potential and overall exposure may be reduced by reinsuring a part of an entire class of policies. . . . The selling insurance company is known as a ceding company. The entity that assumes the obligation is designated as the reinsurer.

* * * *

The "loans" to Charles, Jr. and William far exceeded their salaries and financial resources. If the payments to Charles, Jr. and William had been treated as dividends or compensation, then the balance sheets would have shown an excess of liabilities over assets. If the "loans" had been eliminated, the balance sheets would have depicted a corporation not only with a working capital deficit, but also with assets having a fair market value less than its liabilities. The balance sheets for 1970–1975, however, showed an excess of assets over liabilities. This result was achieved by designating the misappropriated funds as "shareholders' loans" and listing them as assets offsetting the deficits. Although the withdrawal of the funds resulted in an obligation of repayment to Pritchard & Baird, the more significant consideration is that the "loans" represented a massive misappropriation of money belonging to the clients of the corporation.

* * * *

Mrs. Pritchard was not active in the business of Pritchard & Baird and knew virtually nothing of its corporate affairs. She briefly visited the corporate offices in Morristown on only one occasion, and she never read or obtained the annual financial statements. She was unfamiliar with the rudiments of reinsurance and made no effort to assure that the policies and practices of the corporation, particularly pertaining to the withdrawal of funds, complied with industry custom or relevant law. Although her husband had warned her that Charles, Jr. would "take the shirt off my back," Mrs. Pritchard did not pay any attention to her duties as a director or to the affairs of the corporation. . . .

After her husband died in December 1973, Mrs. Pritchard became incapacitated and was bedridden for a six-month period. She became listless at this time and started to drink rather heavily. Her physical condition deteriorated, and in 1978 she died. The trial court rejected testimony seeking to exonerate her because she "was old, was grief-stricken at the loss of her husband, sometimes consumed too much alcohol and was psychologically overborne by her sons." 162 N.J. Super. at 371. That court found that she was competent to act and that the reason Mrs. Pritchard never knew what her sons "were doing was because she never made the slightest effort to discharge any of her responsibilities as a director of Pritchard & Baird." 162 N.J. Super. at 372.

* * * *

Individual liability of a corporate director for acts of the corporation is a prickly problem. Generally directors are accorded broad immunity and are not insurers of corporate activities. The problem is particularly nettlesome when a third party asserts that a director, because of nonfeasance, is liable for losses caused by acts of insiders, who in this case were officers, directors and shareholders. Determination of the liability of Mrs. Pritchard requires findings that she had a duty to the clients of Pritchard & Baird, that she breached that duty and that her breach was a proximate cause of their losses.

The New Jersey Business Corporation Act, which took effect on January 1, 1969, was a comprehensive revision of the statutes relating to business corporations. One section, N.J.S.A. 14A:6–14, concerning a director's general obligation had no counterpart in the old Act. That section makes it incumbent upon directors to discharge their duties in good faith and with that degree of diligence, care and skill which ordinarily prudent men would exercise under similar circumstances in like positions. . . .

* * * *

Because N.J.S.A. 14A:6–14 is modeled in part upon section 717 of the New York statute, . . . we consider also the law of New York in interpreting the New Jersey statute. . .

Prior to the enactment of section 717, the New York courts, like those of New Jersey, had espoused the principle that directors owed that degree of care that a businessman of ordinary prudence would exercise in the management of his own affairs. [*Citations omitted.*] In addition to requiring that directors act honestly and in good faith, the New York courts recognized that the nature and extent of reasonable care depended upon the type of corporation, its size and financial resources. Thus, a bank director was held to stricter accountability than the director of an ordinary business.[2]

* * * *

As a general rule, a director should acquire at least a rudimentary understanding of the business of the corporation. Accordingly, a director should become familiar with the fundamentals of the business in which the corporation is engaged. . . . Because directors are bound to exercise ordinary care, they cannot set up as a defense lack of the knowledge needed to exercise the requisite degree of care. If one "feels that he has not had sufficient business experience to qualify him to perform the duties of a director, he should either acquire the knowledge by inquiry, or refuse to act." *Ibid.*

Directors are under a continuing obligation to keep informed about the activities of the corporation. Otherwise, they may not be able to participate in the overall management of corporate affairs. . . . Directors may not shut their eyes to corporate misconduct and then claim that because they did not see the misconduct, they did not have a duty to look. The sentinel asleep at his post contributes nothing to the enterprise he is charged to protect. . . .

Directorial management does not require a detailed inspection of day-to-day activities, but rather a general monitoring of corporate affairs and policies. . . .

While directors are not required to audit corporate books, they should maintain familiarity with the financial status of the corporation by a regular review of financial statements. . . .

Of some relevance in this case is the circumstance that the financial records disclose the "shareholders' loans". Generally directors are immune from liability if, in good faith, they rely upon the opinion of counsel for the corporation or upon written reports setting forth financial data concerning the corporation and

[2] The obligations of directors of banks involve some additional consideration because of their relationship to the public generally and depositors in particular. Statutes impose certain requirements on bank directors. For example, directors of national banks must take an oath that they will diligently and honestly administer the affairs of the bank and will not permit violation of the banking laws. . . .

prepared by an independent public accountant or certified public accountant or firm of such accountants or upon financial statements, books of account or reports of the corporation represented to them to be correct by the president, the officer of the corporation having charge of its books of account, or the person presiding at a meeting of the board. [N.J.S.A. 14A:6–14.]

The review of financial statements, however, may give rise to a duty to inquire further into matters revealed by those statements. . . . Upon discovery of an illegal course of action, a director has a duty to object and, if the corporation does not correct, the conduct, to resign.

* * * *

In certain circumstances, the fulfillment of the duty of a director may call for more than mere objection and resignation. Sometimes a director may be required to seek the advice of counsel. . . . A director may require legal advice concerning the propriety of his or her own conduct, the conduct of other officers and directors or the conduct of the corporation. . . . A director may have a duty to take reasonable means to prevent illegal conduct by co-directors; in an appropriate case, this may include threat of suit. . . .

* * * *

A director's duty of care does not exist in the abstract, but must be considered in relation to specific obligees. In general, the relationship of a corporate director to the corporation and its stockholders is that of a fiduciary. *Whitfield v. Kern,* 122 N.J. Eq. 332, 341 (E. & A. 1937). Shareholders have a right to expect that directors will exercise reasonable supervision and control over the policies and practices of a corporation. The institutional integrity of a corporation depends upon the proper discharge by directors of those duties.

. . . . With certain corporations, however, directors are seemed to owe a duty to creditors and other third parties even when the corporation is solvent. Although depositors of a bank are considered in some respects to be creditors, courts have recognized that directors may owe them a fiduciary duty. . . . Directors of nonbanking corporations may owe a similar duty when the corporation holds funds of others in trust. . . .

* * * *

The most striking circumstances affecting Mrs. Pritchard's duty as a director are the character of the reinsurance industry, the nature of the misappropriated funds and the financial condition of Pritchard & Baird. The hallmark of the reinsurance industry has been the unqualified trust and confidence reposed by ceding companies and reinsurers in reinsurance brokers. Those companies entrust money to reinsurance intermediaries with the justifiable expectation that the funds will be transmitted to the appropriate parties. Consequently, the companies could have assumed rightfully that Mrs. Pritchard, as a director of a reinsurance brokerage corporation, would not sanction the commingling and the conversion of loss and premium funds for the personal use of the principals of Pritchard & Baird.

* * * *

As a director of a substantial reinsurance brokerage corporation, she should have known that it received annually millions of dollars of loss and premium funds which it held in trust for ceding and reinsurance companies. Mrs. Pritchard should have obtained and read the annual statements of financial condition of Pritchard & Baird. Although she had a right to rely upon financial statements prepared in accordance with [New Jersey statutory requirements], such reliance would not excuse her conduct. The reason is that those statements disclosed on their face the misappropriation of trust funds.

From those statements, she should have realized that, as of January 31, 1970, her sons were withdrawing substantial trust funds under the guise of "Shareholders' Loans." The financial statements for each fiscal year commencing with that of January 31, 1970, disclosed that the working capital deficits and the "loans" were escalating in tandem. Detecting a misappropriation of funds would not have required special expertise or extraordinary diligence; a cursory reading of the financial statements would have revealed the pillage. Thus, if Mrs. Pritchard had read the financial statements, she would have known that her sons were converting trust funds. When financial statements demonstrate that insiders are bleeding a corporation to death, a director should notice and try to stanch the flow of blood.

In summary, Mrs. Pritchard was charged with the obligation of basic knowledge and supervision of the business of Pritchard & Baird. Under the circumstances, this obligation included reading and understanding financial statements, and making reasonable attempts at detection and prevention of the illegal conduct of other officers and directors. She had a duty to protect the clients of Pritchard & Baird against policies and practices that would result in the misappropriation of money they had entrusted to the corporation. She breached that duty.

IV

Nonetheless, the negligence of Mrs. Pritchard does not result in liability unless it is a proximate cause of the loss. . .

Cases involving nonfeasance present a much more difficult causation question than those in which the director has committed an affirmative act of negligence leading to the loss. Analysis in cases of negligent omissions calls for determination of the reasonable steps a director should have taken and whether that course of action would have averted the loss.

Usually a director can absolve himself from liability by informing the other directors of the impropriety and voting for a proper course of action. [*Citation omitted.*] Conversely, a director who votes for or concurs in certain actions may be "liable to the corporation for the benefit of its creditors or shareholders, to the extent of any injuries suffered by such persons, respectively, as a result of any such action." . . . . A director who is present at a board meeting is presumed to concur in corporate action taken at the meeting unless his dissent is entered in the minutes of the meeting or filed promptly after adjournment. N.J.S.A. 14A:6–13. In many, if not most, instances an objecting director whose dissent is noted in accordance with N.J.S.A. 14A:6–13 would be absolved after attempting to persuade fellow directors to follow a different course of action. . . .

Even accepting the hypothesis that Mrs. Pritchard might not be liable if she had objected and resigned, there are two significant reasons for holding her liable. First, she did not resign until just before the bankruptcy. Consequently, there is no factual basis for the speculation that the losses would have occurred even if she had objected and resigned. . . .

In this case, the scope of Mrs. Pritchard's duties was determined by the precarious financial condition of Pritchard & Baird, its fiduciary relationship to its clients and the implied trust in which it held their funds. Thus viewed, the scope of her duties encompassed all reasonable action to stop the continuing conversion. Her duties extended beyond mere objection and resignation to reasonable attempts to prevent the misappropriation of the trust funds. . . .

* * * *

Within Pritchard & Baird, several factors contributed to the loss of the funds: comingling of corporate and client monies, conversion of funds by Charles, Jr. and William and dereliction of her duties by Mrs. Pritchard. The wrongdoing of her sons, although the immediate cause of the loss, should not excuse Mrs. Pritchard from her negligence which also was a substantial factor contributing to the loss. . . . . Her sons knew that she, the only other director, was not reviewing their conduct; they spawned their fraud in the backwater of her neglect. Her neglect of duty contributed to the climate of corruption; her failure to act contributed to the continuation of that corruption. . . .

Analysis of proximate cause is especially difficult in a corporate context where the allegation is that nonfeasance of a director is a proximate cause of damage to a third party. . . Nonetheless, where it is reasonable to conclude that the failure to act would produce a particular result and that result has followed, causation may be inferred. . . . We conclude that even if Mrs. Pritchard's mere objection had not stopped the depredations of her sons, her consultation with an attorney and the threat of suit would have deterred them. That conclusion flows as a matter of common sense and logic from the record. Whether in other situations a director has a duty to do more than protest and resign is best left to case-by-case determinations. In this case, we are satisfied that there was a duty to do more than object and resign. Consequently, we find that Mrs. Pritchard's negligence was a proximate cause of the misappropriations.

To conclude, by virtue of her office, Mrs. Pritchard had the power to prevent the losses sustained by the clients of Pritchard & Baird. With power comes responsibility. She had a duty to deter the depredation of the other insiders, her sons. She breached that duty and caused plaintiffs to sustain damages. . .

The American Law Institute's View on Informed Decisions

While it is clear that, whatever the standard of an informed decision is, Mrs. Pritchard did not meet that standard, § 4.01(c) of the American Law Institute's *Principles of Corporate Governance* and comments to that section, provide additional insight.

> § 4.01(c)(2): A director or officer who makes a business judgment in good faith fulfills the duty under this Section if the director or officer: . . .
>
> (2) is *informed* with respect to the subject of the business judgment to the extent the director or officer reasonably believes to be appropriate under the circumstances (emphasis added).
>
> . . . . The informed decision prerequisite in § 4.01(c)(2) focuses on the preparedness of a director or officer in making a business decision as opposed to the quality of the decision itself. Fundamental

to an understanding of the standard set forth in § 4.01(c) is the recognition that the extent of the information required is that which the director or officer "reasonably believes to be appropriate under the circumstance." . . . .

Some business decisions must be made under severe time pressure while others afford time for the orderly marshaling of material information. Section 4.01(c)(2) permits a director or officer to take into account the time that is realistically available in deciding the extent to which he or she should be informed. The time realistically available may compel risk taking, which includes the risk of not having all relevant facts concerning a proposed transaction as well as the risks related to the economic consequences of the transaction itself. A decision to accept the risk of incomplete information, so long as the director reasonably believes such informational risk taking to be appropriate under the circumstances, will be fully consistent with the application of the business judgment rule to decisions made with respect to the principal transaction. . . .

There is no precise way to measure how much information will be required to meet the "reasonable belief" test in given circumstances. Among the factors that may have to be taken into account in judging a director's reasonable belief as to what was "appropriate under the circumstances" are: (i) the importance of the business judgment to be made; (ii) the time available for obtaining information; (iii) the costs related to obtaining information; (iv) the director's confidence in those who explored a matter and those making presentations; and (v) the state of the corporation's business at the time and the nature of competing demands for the board's attention. The different backgrounds of individual directors, the distinct role each plays in the corporation, and the general value of maintaining board cohesiveness may all be relevant when determining whether a director acted "reasonably" in believing that the information before him or her was "appropriate under the circumstances."

Of course, the business or professional experience of directors or officers may help to inform them about a decision. They may also be informed by the general views or specialized experience of colleagues. Reliance on reports, representations, statements, and opinions prepared by officers and employees of the corporation and

> by outside professionals and experts will often be necessary and will, in many situations, satisfy the informational requirement of § 4.01(c)(2). . . .

American Law Institute, *Principles of Corporate Governance,* Comments to § 4.01(c), Comment e.

Protection by Consulting an Expert

A corollary to the question of what level of information is required to make an informed decision, is the question: to what extent may an officer or director rely upon the knowledge or expertise of others in becoming informed about a particular situation. It is important that directors be able to retain and to rely on experts because directors do not possess expertise in every matter concerning the operations of a given corporation's business. If the corporation hires or consults an expert regarding certain matters, the board of directors' decisions and actions taken with regard to those matters are protected under the business judgment rule as informed decisions (provided, of course, that the decision does not violate some other requirement of the business judgment rule). Of course, the decision to hire or consult a particular expert is itself subject to the business judgment rule and duty of care requirements. A director may not rely on an expert who was hired in a manner that violated the duty of care. Furthermore, directors may only rely upon an expert to the extent that matters addressed by the expert fall within the scope of the expert's competence. An expert hired to evaluate whether a compensation package was fair and consistent with industry practices cannot be relied upon to provide advice on whether to acquire a company, unless the expert has expertise in that area as well. Further, decisions based on the advice of an expert are protected by the business judgment rule only if the board relied on the expert's opinion. Thus, if an expert produced a report, that report must be read prior to, not after, the board of directors acts. Finally, reliance on an expert must be reasonable. A board may not rely on an expert when the directors know, or should know, that the expert is wrong.

The Delaware Code § 141(e) provides that:

> A member of the board of directors, or a member of any committee designated by the board of directors, shall, in the performance of such member's duties, be fully protected in relying in good faith upon the records of the corporation and upon such information, opinions, reports or statements presented to the corporation by any of the corporation's officers or employees, or committees of the board of directors, or by any other person as to matters the member reasonably

> believes are within such other person's *professional or expert competence* and who has been selected with reasonable care by or on behalf of the corporation. (Emphasis added). 8 Del. C. § 141(e).

See also American Law Institute, *Principles of Corporate Governance* § 4.02.

Subsections 8.30(d–f) of the Model Business Corporations Act permit reliance by a director on "outside advisers." The outside advisers contemplated extend beyond lawyers and accountants to include "other persons retained by the corporation as to matters involving skills or expertise the director reasonably believes are matters (i) within the particular person's professional or expert competence or (ii) as to which the particular person merits confidence." (*Id.* at § 8.30(f)(2).) The comments to this section make clear that "The concept of 'expert competence' embraces a wide variety of qualifications and is not limited to the more precise and narrower recognition of experts under the Securities Act of 1933. In this respect, subsection (f)(2) goes beyond the reliance provision found in many existing state business corporation acts." Model Business Corporations Act § 8.30(f), Comment 6. § 8.30(f).

In re The Walt Disney Co. Derivative Litigation (906 A.2d 27 (Del. 2006)). The question of the extent to which a board of directors may rely on an expert was examined in the *In re The Walt Disney Co. Derivative Litigation (infra).* This case arose when the Walt Disney Company was looking for a new president, and Michael Ovitz, a longtime friend of Michael Eisner (who was at the time the CEO of Disney), was the top candidate. Knowing the question of executive compensation would be the determining factor in whether Walt Disney could persuade Ovitz to join the company, the Disney board of directors delegated the task to an executive compensation committee; the committee hired a compensation expert, Graef Crystal, to put together a competitive package.

> The compensation committee reasonably believed that the analysis of the terms of Ovitz' compensation package was within Crystal's professional or expert competence, and together with Russell and Watson's [two Disney directors] professional competence in those same areas, the committee relied on the information, opinions, reports and statements made by Crystal, even if Crystal did not relay the information, opinions, reports and statements in person to the committee as a whole. Crystal's analysis was not so deficient that the compensation committee would have reason to question it.

> Furthermore, Crystal appears to have been selected with reasonable care, especially in light of his previous engagements with the Company in connection with past executive compensation contracts that were structurally, at least, similar to the OEA. For all these reasons, the compensation committee also is entitled to the protections of 8 *Del. C.* § 141(e) in relying upon Crystal.

Id. at 59.

Reliance on a Committee

However, in the facts leading up to this case, Crystal, the compensation expert, did not present findings to the full Disney board of directors, but rather presented recommendations to the special compensation committee referred to above. The committee deliberated on the compensation package to be offered to Ovitz and forwarded the committee's recommendation to the board of directors, which approved the package. In evaluating the steps taken by the compensation committee, the Delaware Supreme Court found that the committee had informed itself of the material facts relating to the compensation package. When the plaintiffs challenged the full board of directors' decision to approve the package, the Court dismissed the claim, finding that the question of whether to approve the compensation package had already been determined by the committee.

Best Practices

Although the Court in this case found the compensation committee had properly relied on the compensation expert and had sufficiently informed themselves about the compensation package to meet the threshold required to garner the protection of the business judgment rule, the court felt that the process could have been handled better:

> In our view, a helpful approach is to compare what actually happened here to what would have occurred had the committee followed a "best practices" (or "best case") scenario, from a process standpoint. In a "best case" scenario, all committee members would have received, before or at the committee's first meeting a spreadsheet or similar document prepared by (or with the assistance of) a compensation expert. Making different, alternative assumptions, the spreadsheet would disclose the amounts that Ovitz could receive under the deal in each circumstance that might foreseeably arise. The contents of the spreadsheet would be explained to the committee

> members, either by the expert who prepared it or by a fellow committee member similarly knowledgeable about the subject. That spreadsheet, which ultimately would become an exhibit to the minutes of the compensation committee meeting, would form the basis of the committee's deliberations and decision.
>
> Had that scenario been followed, there would be no dispute (and no basis for litigation) over what information was furnished to the committee members or when it was furnished. Regrettably, the committee's informational and decision making process used here was not so tidy.

Id. at 56.

F. Do Officers and Directors Have Different Duties?

There is some question about the different standards applied to officers and directors. Because officers and directors play different roles, they may have different responsibilities in acting in accordance with their respective duties of care. Furthermore, at least some courts do not allow the officers of a corporation to avail themselves of the business judgment rule. (*See e.g. FDIC v. Perry,* below.)

In *Bates v. Dresser* (251 U.S. 524 (1920)) the bookkeeper of a small bank was stealing deposits and falsifying the bank's records over a period of seven years. By the time the bank was shut down, the bookkeeper had stolen more than $310,000; average deposits for the bank were approximately $300,000. The Court agreed that the bank's directors had not been negligent and had not violated their duties merely because they took the bank cashier's statements of liabilities to be correct and failed to inspect the depositors' ledger, especially given that the statement of assets was always correct. However, the actions of the bank's president, Edwin Dresser, were viewed more harshly.

> The position of the president is different. Practically he was the master of the situation. He was daily at the bank for hours, he had the deposit ledger in his hands at times and might have had it at any time. He had had hints and warnings . . . that should not be magnified unduly, but still that taken with the auditor's report of 1903, the unexplained shortages, the suggestion of the teller . . ., and the final seeming rapid decline in deposits, would have induced scrutiny but for an invincible repose upon the status quo. In 1908 one Fillmore learned that a package containing $150 left with the bank for safe keeping was not to be found, told Dresser of the loss, wrote to him that he could not conclude that the package had been destroyed or

> removed by someone connected with the bank, and in later conversation said that it was evident that there was a thief in the bank. He added that he would advise the president to look after Coleman, that he believed he was living at a pretty fast pace, and that he had pretty good authority for thinking that he was supporting a woman. In the same year or the year before, Coleman, whose pay was never more than twelve dollars a week, set up an automobile, as was known to Dresser and commented on unfavorably, to him. There was also some evidence of notice to Dresser that Coleman was dealing in copper stocks. In 1909 came the great and inadequately explained seeming shrinkage in the deposits. No doubt plausible explanations of his conduct came from Coleman and the notice as to speculations may have been slight, but taking the whole story of the relations of the parties, we are not ready to say that the two courts below erred in finding that Dresser had been put upon his guard. However little the warnings may have pointed to the specific facts, had they been accepted they would have led to an examination of the depositors' ledger, a discovery of past and a prevention of future thefts.

Id. at 530–531.

The Court explained its justification for affirming Dresser's liability as follows: "In accepting the presidency Dresser must be taken to have contemplated responsibility for losses to the bank, whatever they were, if chargeable to his fault. Those that happened were chargeable to his fault, after he had warnings that should have led to steps that would have made fraud impossible, even though the precise form that the fraud would take hardly could have been foreseen." *Id.* at 531. Notwithstanding the fact that the *Bates* case focused on the liability of a corporate officer and held that the bank's directors were not obliged by their duty to uncover or prevent the theft from the bank, there are other circumstances in which directors might still incur liability with respect to a fraud perpetrated on a corporation, either because the directors were aware of the malfeasance or, it can be shown that, had the directors performed their duties, they would have been aware of the malfeasance.

Many jurisdictions do not even permit the officers of a corporation to rely on the business judgment rule, but at least eighteen jurisdictions do. In *FDIC v. Perry*, No. CV 11-4461, 2011 WL 6178544 (C.D. Cal. Dec. 13, 2011), the FDIC sued Matthew Perry (the former chief executive officer of Indymac Bank, not the actor from *Friends*), alleging that he breached his fiduciary duties to Indymac by negligently permitting the generation and purchase of more than $10 billion in risky residential loans for sale into the secondary market. Perry was both an officer (in fact, the chief executive officer) and a director of Indymac. Perry argued that his actions were protected by the business judgment rule. The FDIC argued that it was suing Perry for his actions as an officer rather than a director and that, therefore, the business judgment rule did not protect his actions. In denying Perry's motion to dismiss, the court found that, at least under California law, the business judgment rule did not apply to corporate officers or protect their decisions and allowed the FDIC's case against Perry to proceed. While this matter involved a construction of California law and legislative history, it raises the question of whether corporate officers may rely on the business judgment rule for protection of their actions, at least in jurisdictions that have not specifically addressed the issue and determined that the business judgment rule applies to officers as well. Note that, as discussed above, the business judgment rule is typically viewed as providing enhanced protection; it is not, in and of itself, a standard of liability. Therefore, even in jurisdictions in which the protections of the business judgment rule are not available to a corporation's officers, a plaintiff still must show that those officers breached their duty of care in order to prevail in any such action.

SECTION III: Failure to Act or to Monitor the Firm

In some situations in which the entire board is accused of failing to act, the business judgment rule is not available. Recall that the business judgment rule only protects "judgments." It does not apply when the board has not taken an action (unless, possibly, if the board has made an affirmative informed decision not to take action). Situations in which the directors on the board are accused of failing to act often involve instances of corporate wrongdoing which the board of directors is accused of failing to detect, prevent, or stop. These types of claims are often called "*Caremark claims*" for the well-known case in which the rule was established. Even though the business judgment rule does not apply in these "failure to act" cases, the courts still needed to develop a standard to evaluate the actions (or more accurately, inactions) of a board of directors. In the case, *In re Caremark International Inc. Derivative Litigation* (698 A.2d 959 (Del. Ch. 1996)), the Delaware court established standards, regarding the board's duty to monitor the firm. The rule arising out of this case contains both a procedural and a substantive aspect. First, absent suspicion of wrongdoing, there is no duty upon the board to install and operate a corporate system to find wrongdoing that the board does not suspect or believe exists. Second, the board must attempt in good faith to ensure that an adequate reporting system is in place so that the board can obtain the necessary information to make informed decisions. One way a board can ensure it has good information is to establish compliance programs, such as policy manuals, employee training, audits, sanctions for violations, and provisions for self-reporting violations to regulators. Directors don't necessarily have to do a perfect job, but they do have to do their job and in order to do their job they must be informed. However, as we have seen above, once a board of directors takes action to inform itself, the decisions of the board are typically protected. Typically, provided directors do not have information that something improper is occurring and there is a good system in place for corporate information, the directors are not liable for failing to monitor. Once there is some suspicion of wrongdoing, the directors have a *greater* obligation to monitor.

There is some question as to what the applicable standard is to evaluate whether or not directors have adequately informed themselves. Recent cases suggest that, absent a showing of bad faith, a director will not be liable for failure to exercise oversight (". . .only a sustained or systematic failure of the board to exercise oversight—such as an utter failure to attempt to assure a reasonable information and reporting system exists—will establish the lack of good faith that is a necessary condition to liability." *In re Caremark Int'l Inc. Derivative Litigation,* 698 A.2d 959 at 971). However, other cases suggest that once a director is aware of wrongdoing, if the director fails to take adequate action, that failure is evaluated under a gross negligence standard. Of course if the directors do take action, that action should be protected by the business judgment rule.

In re Caremark Intern. Inc. Derivative Litigation

698 A.2d 959 (Del. 1996)

ALLEN, Chancellor:

Pending is a motion pursuant to Chancery Rule 23.1 to approve as fair and reasonable a proposed settlement of a consolidated derivative action on behalf of Caremark International, Inc. ("Caremark"). The suit involves claims that the members of Caremark's board of directors (the "Board") breached their fiduciary duty of care to Caremark in connection with alleged violations by Caremark employees of federal and state laws and regulations applicable to health care providers. As a result of the alleged violations, Caremark was subject to an extensive four year investigation by the United States Department of Health and Human Services and the Department of Justice. In 1994 Caremark was charged in an indictment with multiple felonies. It thereafter entered into a number of agreements with the Department of Justice and others. Those agreements included a plea agreement in which Caremark pleaded guilty to a single felony of mail fraud and agreed to pay civil and criminal fines. Subsequently, Caremark agreed to make reimbursements to various private and public parties. In all, the payments that Caremark has been required to make total approximately $250 million.

This suit was filed in 1994, purporting to seek on behalf of the company recovery of these losses from the individual defendants who constitute the board of directors of Caremark. The parties now propose that it be settled and, after notice to Caremark shareholders, a hearing on the fairness of the proposal was held on August 16, 1996.

. . . .The ultimate issue then is whether the proposed settlement appears to be fair to the corporation and its absent shareholders. In this effort the court does not determine contested facts, but evaluates the claims and defenses on the discovery record to achieve a sense of the relative strengths of the parties' positions. . . .

Legally, evaluation of the central claim made entails consideration of the legal standard governing a board of directors' obligation to supervise or monitor corporate performance. For the reasons set forth below I conclude, in light of the discovery record, that there is a very low probability that it would be determined that the directors of Caremark breached any duty to appropriately monitor and supervise the enterprise. Indeed the record tends to show an active consideration by Caremark management and its Board of the Caremark structures and programs that ultimately led to the company's indictment and to the large financial losses incurred in the settlement of those claims. It does not tend to show knowing or intentional violation of law. Neither the fact that the Board, although advised by lawyers and accountants, did not accurately predict the severe consequences to the company that would ultimately follow from the deployment by the company of the strategies and practices that ultimately led to this liability, nor the scale of the liability, gives rise to an inference of breach of any duty imposed by corporation law upon the directors of Caremark.

I. BACKGROUND

. . . . Caremark, a Delaware corporation with its headquarters in Northbrook, Illinois, was created in November 1992 when it was spun-off from Baxter International, Inc. ("Baxter") and became a publicly held company listed on the New York Stock Exchange. The business practices that created the problem pre-dated the spin-off. During the relevant period Caremark was involved in two main health care business segments, providing patient care and managed care services. . . .

A. Events Prior to the Government Investigation

A substantial part of the revenues generated by Caremark's businesses is derived from third party payments, insurers, and Medicare and Medicaid reimbursement programs. The latter source of payments are subject to the terms of the Anti-Referral Payments Law ("ARPL") which prohibits health care providers from paying any form of remuneration to induce the referral of Medicare or Medicaid patients. From its inception, Caremark entered into a variety of agreements with hospitals, physicians, and health care providers for advice and services, as well as distribution agreements with drug manufacturers, as had its predecessor prior to 1992. Specifically, Caremark did have a practice of entering into contracts for services (*e.g.,* consultation agreements and research grants) with physicians at least some of whom prescribed or recommended services or products that Caremark provided to Medicare recipients and other patients. Such contracts were not prohibited by the ARPL but they obviously raised a possibility of unlawful "kickbacks."

As early as 1989, Caremark's predecessor issued an internal "Guide to Contractual Relationships" ("Guide") to govern its employees in entering into contracts with physicians and hospitals. The Guide tended to be reviewed annually by lawyers and updated. Each version of the Guide stated as Caremark's and its predecessor's policy that no payments would be made in exchange for or to induce patient referrals. But what one might deem a prohibited *quid pro quo* was not always clear. Due to a scarcity of court decisions interpreting the ARPL, however, Caremark repeatedly publicly stated that there was uncertainty concerning Caremark's interpretation of the law.

* * * *

B. Government Investigation and Related Litigation

In August 1991, the HHS Office of the Inspector General ("OIG") initiated an investigation of Caremark's predecessor. Caremark's predecessor was served with a subpoena requiring the production of documents, including contracts between Caremark's predecessor and physicians (Quality Service Agreements ("QSAs")). Under the QSAs, Caremark's predecessor appears to have paid physicians fees for monitoring patients under Caremark's predecessor's care, including Medicare and Medicaid recipients. Sometimes apparently those monitoring patients were referring physicians, which raised ARPL concerns.

In March 1992, the Department of Justice ("DOJ") joined the OIG investigation and separate investigations were commenced by several additional federal and state agencies.

C. Caremark's Response to the Investigation

During the relevant period, Caremark had approximately 7,000 employees and ninety branch operations. It had a decentralized management structure. By May 1991, however, Caremark asserts that it had begun making attempts to centralize its management structure in order to increase supervision over its branch operations.

The first action taken by management, as a result of the initiation of the OIG investigation, was an announcement that as of October 1, 1991, Caremark's predecessor would no longer pay management fees to physicians for services to Medicare and Medicaid patients. . . .

During this period, Caremark's Board took several additional steps consistent with an effort to assure compliance with company policies concerning the ARPL and the contractual forms in the Guide. In April 1992, Caremark published a fourth revised version of its Guide apparently designed to assure that its agreements either complied with the ARPL and regulations or excluded Medicare and Medicaid patients altogether. In addition, in September 1992, Caremark instituted a policy requiring its regional officers, Zone Presidents, to approve each contractual relationship entered into by Caremark with a physician.

Although there is evidence that inside and outside counsel had advised Caremark's directors that their contracts were in accord with the law, Caremark recognized that some uncertainty respecting the correct interpretation of the law existed. . . .

Throughout the period of the government investigations, Caremark had an internal audit plan designed to assure compliance with business and ethics policies. In addition, Caremark employed Price Waterhouse as its outside auditor. On February 8, 1993, the Ethics Committee of Caremark's Board received and reviewed an outside auditors report by Price Waterhouse which concluded that there were no material weaknesses in Caremark's control structure. Despite the positive findings of Price Waterhouse, however, on April 20, 1993, the Audit & Ethics Committee adopted a new internal audit charter requiring a comprehensive review of compliance policies and the compilation of an employee ethics handbook concerning such policies.

The Board appears to have been informed about this project and other efforts to assure compliance with the law. For example, Caremark's management reported to the Board that Caremark's sales force was receiving an ongoing education regarding the ARPL and the proper use of Caremark's form contracts which had been approved by in-house counsel. On July 27, 1993, the new ethics manual, expressly prohibiting payments in exchange for referrals and requiring employees to report all illegal conduct to a toll free confidential ethics hotline, was approved and allegedly disseminated. The record suggests that Caremark continued these policies in subsequent years, causing employees to be given revised versions of the ethics manual and requiring them to participate in training sessions concerning compliance with the law.

During 1993, Caremark took several additional steps which appear to have been aimed at increasing management supervision. These steps included new policies requiring local branch managers to secure home office approval for all disbursements under agreements with health care providers and to certify compliance with the ethics program. In addition, the chief financial officer was appointed to serve as Caremark's compliance officer. In 1994, a fifth revised Guide was published.

D. Federal Indictments Against Caremark and Officers

On August 4, 1994, a federal grand jury in Minnesota issued a 47 page indictment charging Caremark, two of its officers (not the firm's chief officer), an individual who had been a sales employee of Genentech, Inc., and David R. Brown, a physician practicing in Minneapolis, with violating the ARPL over a lengthy period. According to the indictment, over $1.1 million had been paid to Brown to induce him to distribute Protropin, a human growth hormone drug marketed by Caremark. The substantial payments involved started, according to the allegations of the indictment, in 1986 and continued through 1993. Some payments were "in the guise of research grants," Ind. P20, and others were "consulting agreements", Ind. P19. The indictment charged, for example, that Dr. Brown performed virtually none of the consulting functions described in his 1991 agreement with Caremark, but was nevertheless neither required to return the money he had received nor precluded from receiving future funding from Caremark. In addition the indictment charged that Brown received from Caremark payments of staff and office expenses, including telephone answering services and fax rental expenses.

In reaction to the Minnesota Indictment and the subsequent filing of this and other derivative actions in 1994, the Board met and was informed by management that the investigation had resulted in an indictment; .... Management reiterated the grounds for its view that the contracts were in compliance with law.

Subsequently, five stockholder derivative actions were filed in this court and consolidated into this action. The original complaint, dated August 5, 1994, alleged, in relevant part, that Caremark's directors breached their duty of care by failing adequately to supervise the conduct of Caremark employees, or institute corrective measures, thereby exposing Caremark to fines and liability.

* * * *

E. Settlement Negotiations

* * * *

Caremark began settlement negotiations with federal and state government entities in May 1995. In return for a guilty plea to a single count of mail fraud by the corporation, the payment of a criminal fine, the payment of substantial civil damages, and cooperation with further federal investigations on matters relating to the OIG investigation, the government entities agreed to negotiate a settlement that would permit Caremark to continue participating in Medicare and Medicaid programs. On June 15, 1995, the Board approved a settlement ("Government Settlement Agreement") with the DOJ, OIG, U.S. Veterans Administration, U.S. Federal Employee Health Benefits Program, federal Civilian Health and Medical Program of the Uniformed Services, and related state agencies in all fifty states and the District of Columbia.[10] No senior officers or directors were charged with wrongdoing in the Government Settlement Agreement or in any of the prior indictments. In fact, as part of the sentencing in the Ohio action on June 19, 1995, the United States stipulated that *no senior executive of Caremark participated in, condoned, or was willfully ignorant of wrongdoing in connection with the home infusion business practices.*

* * * *

[10] The agreement, covering allegations since 1986, required a Caremark subsidiary to enter a guilty plea to two counts of mail fraud, and required Caremark to pay $29 million in criminal fines, $129.9 million relating to civil claims concerning payment practices, $3.5 million for alleged violations of the Controlled Substances Act, and $2 million, in the form of a donation, to a grant program set up by the Ryan White Comprehensive AIDS Resources Emergency Act. Caremark also agreed to enter into a compliance agreement with the HHS.

F. The Proposed Settlement of this Litigation

In relevant part the terms upon which these claims asserted are proposed to be settled are as follows:

1. That Caremark, undertakes that it and its employees, and agents not pay any form of compensation to a third party in exchange for the referral of a patient to a Caremark facility or service or the prescription of drugs marketed or distributed by Caremark for which reimbursement may be sought from Medicare, Medicaid, or a similar state reimbursement program;
2. That Caremark, undertakes for itself and its employees, and agents not to pay to or split fees with physicians, joint ventures, any business combination in which Caremark maintains a direct financial interest, or other health care providers with whom Caremark has a financial relationship or interest, in exchange for the referral of a patient to a Caremark facility or service or the prescription of drugs marketed or distributed by Caremark for which reimbursement may be sought from Medicare, Medicaid, or a similar state reimbursement program;
3. That the full Board shall discuss all relevant material changes in government health care regulations and their effect on relationships with health care providers on a semi-annual basis;
4. That Caremark's officers will remove all personnel from health care facilities or hospitals who have been placed in such facility for the purpose of providing remuneration in exchange for a patient referral for which reimbursement may be sought from Medicare, Medicaid, or a similar state reimbursement program;
5. That every patient will receive written disclosure of any financial relationship between Caremark and the health care professional or provider who made the referral;
6. That the Board will establish a Compliance and Ethics Committee of four directors, two of which will be non-management directors, to meet at least four times a year to effectuate these policies and monitor business segment compliance with the ARPL, and to report to the Board semi-annually concerning compliance by each business segment; and

7. That corporate officers responsible for business segments shall serve as compliance officers who must report semi-annually to the Compliance and Ethics Committee and, with the assistance of outside counsel, review existing contracts and get advanced approval of any new contract forms.

II. LEGAL PRINCIPLES

* * * *

B. Directors' Duties To Monitor Corporate Operations

The complaint charges the director defendants with breach of their duty of attention or care in connection with the on-going operation of the corporation's business. The claim is that the directors allowed a situation to develop and continue which exposed the corporation to enormous legal liability and that in so doing they violated a duty to be active monitors of corporate performance. The complaint thus does not charge either director self-dealing or the more difficult loyalty-type problems arising from cases of suspect director motivation, such as entrenchment or sale of control contexts. The theory here advanced is possibly the most difficult theory in corporation law upon which a plaintiff might hope to win a judgment. . . .

1. *Potential liability for directoral decisions:* Director liability for a breach of the duty to exercise appropriate attention may, in theory, arise in two distinct contexts. First, such liability may be said to follow *from a board decision* that results in a loss because that decision was ill advised or "negligent". Second, liability to the corporation for a loss may be said to arise from an *unconsidered failure of the board to act* in circumstances in which due attention would, arguably, have prevented the loss. [*Citation omitted.*] The first class of cases will typically be subject to review under the director-protective business judgment rule, assuming the decision made was the product of *a process* that *either* deliberately considered in good faith or was otherwise rational. [*Citation omitted.*] What should be understood, but may not widely be understood by courts or commentators who are not often required to face such questions, is that compliance with a director's duty of care can never appropriately be judicially determined by reference to *the content of the board decision* that leads to a corporate loss, apart from consideration of the good faith *or* rationality of the process employed. That is, whether a judge or jury considering the matter after the fact, believes a decision substantively wrong, or degrees of wrong

> extending through "stupid" to "egregious" or "irrational", provides no ground for director liability, so long as the court determines that the process employed was either rational or employed in *a good faith* effort to advance corporate interests. To employ a different rule—one that permitted an "objective" evaluation of the decision—would expose directors to substantive second guessing by ill-equipped judges or juries, which would, in the long-run, be injurious to investor interests. Thus, the business judgment rule is process oriented and informed by a deep respect for all *good faith* board decisions.

Indeed, one wonders on what moral basis might shareholders attack a *good faith* business decision of a director as "unreasonable" or "irrational". Where a director *in fact exercises a good faith effort to be informed and to exercise appropriate judgment,* he or she should be deemed to satisfy fully the duty of attention. If the shareholders thought themselves entitled to some other quality of judgment than such a director produces in the good faith exercise of the powers of office, then the shareholders should have elected other directors.

* * * *

> 2. *Liability for failure to monitor:* The second class of cases in which director liability for inattention is theoretically possible entail circumstances in which a loss eventuates not from a decision but, from unconsidered inaction. Most of the decisions that a corporation, acting through its human agents, makes are, of course, not the subject of director attention. Legally, the board itself will be required only to authorize the most significant corporate acts or transactions: mergers, changes in capital structure, fundamental changes in business, appointment and compensation of the CEO, etc. As the facts of this case graphically demonstrate, ordinary business decisions that are made by officers and employees deeper in the interior of the organization can, however, vitally affect the welfare of the corporation and its ability to achieve its various strategic and financial goals. . . .

Modernly this question has been given special importance by an increasing tendency, especially under federal law, to employ the criminal law to assure corporate compliance with external legal requirements, including environmental, financial, employee and product safety as well as assorted other health and safety regulations. In 1991, pursuant to the Sentencing Reform Act of 1984, the United States Sentencing Commission adopted Organizational Sentencing Guidelines which impact importantly on the prospective effect these criminal sanctions might have on business corporations. The Guidelines set forth a uniform sentencing structure for organizations to be sentenced for violation of federal criminal statutes and provide for penalties that equal or often massively exceed those previously imposed on corporations. The Guidelines offer powerful incentives for corporations today to have in place compliance programs to detect violations of law, promptly to report violations to appropriate public officials when discovered, and to take prompt, voluntary remedial efforts.

In 1963, the Delaware Supreme Court in *Graham v. Allis-Chalmers Mfg. Co.,* addressed the question of potential liability of board members for losses experienced by the corporation as a result of the corporation having violated the anti-trust laws of the United States. There was no claim in that case that the directors knew about the behavior of subordinate employees of the corporation that had resulted in the liability. Rather, as in this case, the claim asserted was that the directors *ought to have known* of it and if they had known they would have been under a duty to bring the corporation into compliance with the law and thus save the corporation from the loss. The Delaware Supreme Court concluded that, under the facts as they appeared, there was no basis to find that the directors had breached a duty to be informed of the ongoing operations of the firm. In notably colorful terms, the court stated that "absent cause for suspicion there is no duty upon the directors to install and operate a corporate system of espionage to ferret out wrongdoing which they have no reason to suspect exists." The Court found that there were no grounds for suspicion in that case and, thus, concluded that the directors were blamelessly unaware of the conduct leading to the corporate liability.

How does one generalize this holding today? Can it be said today that, absent some ground giving rise to suspicion of violation of law, that corporate directors have no duty to assure that a corporate information gathering and reporting systems exists which represents a good faith attempt to provide senior management and the Board with information respecting material acts, events or conditions within the corporation, including compliance with applicable statutes and regulations? I certainly do not believe so. I doubt that such a broad generalization of the *Graham* holding would have been accepted by the Supreme Court in 1963. The case can be more narrowly interpreted as standing for the proposition that, absent grounds to suspect deception, neither corporate boards nor senior officers can be charged with wrongdoing simply for assuming the integrity of employees and the honesty of their dealings on the company's behalf. . . .

A broader interpretation of *Graham v. Allis-Chalmers*—that it means that a corporate board has no responsibility to assure that appropriate information and reporting systems are established by management—would not, in any event, be accepted by the Delaware Supreme Court in 1996, in my opinion. In stating the basis for this view, I start with the recognition that in recent years the Delaware Supreme Court has made it clear—especially in its jurisprudence concerning takeovers, from *Smith v. Van Gorkom* through *Paramount Communications v. QVC* the seriousness with which the corporation law views the role of the corporate board. Secondly, I note the elementary fact that relevant and timely *information* is an essential predicate for satisfaction of the board's supervisory and monitoring role under Section 141 of the Delaware General Corporation Law. Thirdly, I note the potential impact of the federal organizational sentencing guidelines on any business organization. Any rational person attempting in good faith to meet an organizational governance responsibility would be bound to take into account this development and the enhanced penalties and the opportunities for reduced sanctions that it offers.

In light of these developments, it would, in my opinion, be a mistake to conclude that our Supreme Court's statement in *Graham* concerning "espionage" means that corporate boards may satisfy their obligation to be reasonably informed concerning the corporation, without assuring themselves that information and reporting systems exist in the organization that are reasonably designed to provide to senior management and to the board itself timely, accurate information sufficient to allow management and the board, each within its scope, to reach informed judgments concerning both the corporation's compliance with law and its business performance.

Obviously the level of detail that is appropriate for such an information system is a question of business judgment. And obviously too, no rationally designed information and reporting system will remove the possibility that the corporation will violate laws or regulations, or that senior officers or directors may nevertheless sometimes be misled or otherwise fail reasonably to detect acts material to the corporation's compliance with the law. But it is important that the board exercise a good faith judgment that the corporation's information and reporting system is in concept and design adequate to assure the board that appropriate information will come to its attention in a timely manner as a matter of ordinary operations, so that it may satisfy its responsibility.

Thus, I am of the view that a director's obligation includes a duty to attempt in good faith to assure that a corporate information and reporting system, which the board concludes is adequate, exists, and that failure to do so under some circumstances may, in theory at least, render a director liable for losses caused by non-compliance with applicable legal standards. I now turn to an analysis of the claims asserted with this concept of the directors duty of care, as a duty satisfied in part by assurance of adequate information flows to the board, in mind.

III. ANALYSIS OF THIRD AMENDED COMPLAINT AND SETTLEMENT

A. The Claims

On balance . . . I conclude that this settlement is fair and reasonable. In light of the fact that the Caremark Board already has a functioning committee charged with overseeing corporate compliance, the changes in corporate practice that are presented as consideration for the settlement do not impress one as very significant. Nonetheless, that consideration appears fully adequate to support dismissal of the derivative claims of director fault asserted, because those claims find no substantial evidentiary support in the record and quite likely were susceptible to a motion to dismiss in all events.

In order to show that the Caremark directors breached their duty of care by failing adequately to control Caremark's employees, plaintiffs would have to show either (1) that the directors knew or (2) should have known that violations of law were occurring and, in either event, (3) that the directors took no steps in a good faith effort to prevent or remedy that situation, and (4) that such failure proximately resulted in the losses complained of, although under *Cede & Co. v. Technicolor, Inc.,* Del.Supr., 636 A.2d 956 (1994) this last element may be thought to constitute an affirmative defense.

> 1. *Knowing violation for statute:* Concerning the possibility that the Caremark directors knew of violations of law, none of the documents submitted for review, nor any of the deposition transcripts appear to provide evidence of it. . . . [T]he Board appears to have been informed by experts that the company's practices while contestable, were lawful. There is no evidence that reliance on such reports was not reasonable. Thus, this case presents no occasion to apply a principle to the effect that knowingly causing the corporation to violate a criminal statute constitutes a breach of a director's fiduciary duty. [*Citations omitted.*] It is not clear that the Board knew the detail found, for example, in the indictments arising from the Company's payments. But, of course, the duty to act in good faith to be informed cannot be thought to require directors to possess detailed information about all aspects of the operation of the enterprise. Such a

requirement would simple be inconsistent with the scale and scope of efficient organization size in this technological age.

2. *Failure to monitor:* . . . I turn to a consideration of the other potential avenue to director liability that the pleadings take: director inattention or "negligence". Generally where a claim of directorial liability for corporate loss is predicated upon ignorance of liability creating activities within the corporation, as in *Graham* or in this case, in my opinion only a sustained or systematic failure of the board to exercise oversight—such as an utter failure to attempt to assure a reasonable information and reporting system exists—will establish the lack of good faith that is a necessary condition to liability. . . .

Here the record supplies essentially no evidence that the director defendants were guilty of a sustained failure to exercise their oversight function. To the contrary, . . . the corporation's information systems appear to have represented a good faith attempt to be informed of relevant facts. If the directors did not know the specifics of the activities that lead to the indictments, they cannot be faulted.

The liability that eventuated in this instance was huge. But the fact that it resulted from a violation of criminal law alone does not create a breach of fiduciary duty by directors. The record at this stage does not support the conclusion that the defendants either lacked good faith in the exercise of their monitoring responsibilities or conscientiously permitted a known violation of law by the corporation to occur. . . .

* * * *

I am today entering an order consistent with the foregoing.

NOTES AND QUESTIONS

1. In 2015 Volkswagen AG was caught manipulating emissions in mandated testing for diesel vehicles sold in the U.S. market. A substantial number of Volkswagen diesel cars were sold in America with a "defeat device" installed in the cars. A defeat device referred to software that was installed in diesel engines of certain Volkswagen cars that could detect when the cars were being tested, and changed the car's emission performance accordingly to improve results. Between fines, recalls, buybacks, settlements, and other payments, Volkswagen agreed to pay up to $25 billion because of the scandal. Using the standard articulated in the Caremark case above, please explain the circumstances under

which directors on Volkswagen's board of directors might incur liability for the company's actions.

2. In 2016 Wells Fargo was fined $185 million arising out of a scandal uncovered by a *Los Angeles Times* 2013 investigation, revealing that, over the course of many years and without the permission of customers, bank employees had opened approximately 1.5 million unauthorized deposit accounts and issued more than 500,000 unauthorized credit card applications. Subsequent investigations alleged that the bank had also set up renters insurance and life insurance policies for customers who never asked for them and charged business clients inflated foreign transaction fees. Wells Fargo also had to pay $142 million to settle a substantial portion of the class-action law suits against it. Many of the law suits against the bank claimed that the fraudulent behavior arose from employee efforts to meet aggressive sales targets. Other workers claimed that there were "retaliated against" for reporting unauthorized accounts. Even if there is little evidence that the Wells Fargo board of directors had actual knowledge of the ongoing and, apparently widespread behavior, at what point does the obligation to have an adequate reporting system require that some affirmative action be taken with respect to any reporting system in place? Does the possibility that the unlawful behavior might have been motivated by compensation incentives approved by the bank, create additional obligations? If Wells Fargo were to face a subsequent scandal involving employee behavior, in what ways might the board's potential liability be different?

SECTION IV: The Obligation for Fiduciaries to Act in Good Faith

The duty of care requires that each member of the board of directors, when discharging the duties of a director, shall act: (1) in good faith and (2) in a manner the director *reasonably believes* to be in the best interests of the corporation. Model Business Corporations Act § 830(a).

American Law Institute, *Principles of Corporate Governance*

Analysis and Recommendations

§ 4.01

(a) A director or officer has a duty to the corporation to perform the director's or officer's functions in good faith, in a manner that he or she *reasonably* believes to be in the best interests of the corporation, and with the care that an ordinarily prudent person would reasonably be expected to exercise in a like position and under similar circumstances. This Subsection (a) is subject to the provisions of Subsection (c) (the business judgment rule) where applicable.

(1) The duty in Subsection (a) includes the obligation to make, or cause to be made, an inquiry when, but only when, the circumstances would alert a reasonable director or officer to the need therefor. The extent of such inquiry shall be such as the director or officer reasonably believes to be necessary.

(2) In performing any of his or her functions (including oversight functions), a director or officer is entitled to rely on materials and persons in accordance with §§ 4.02 and 4.03 (reliance on directors, officers, employees, experts, other persons, and committees of the board).

Delaware courts do not currently view the requirement that fiduciaries act in good faith as a separate duty that is independent of the duty of care. Nevertheless, this requirement of good faith provides a basic standard, without which the protections of the business judgment rule will not apply. Furthermore, good faith provides a standard to evaluate whether the failure of a board of directors to act might result in culpability.

In re the Walt Disney Company Derivative Litigation

906 A.2d 27 (Del. 2006)

JACOBS, J.:

In August 1995, Michael Ovitz ("Ovitz") and The Walt Disney Company ("Disney" or the "Company") entered into an employment agreement under which Ovitz would serve as President of Disney for five years. In December 1996, only fourteen months after he commenced employment, Ovitz was terminated without cause, resulting in a severance payout to Ovitz valued at approximately $130 million.

In January 1997, several Disney shareholders brought derivative actions in the Court of Chancery, on behalf of Disney, against Ovitz and the directors of Disney who served at the time of the events complained of (the "Disney defendants"). The plaintiffs claimed that the $130 million severance payout was the product of fiduciary duty and contractual breaches by Ovitz, and breaches of fiduciary duty by the Disney defendants, and a waste of assets. . . . In August 2005, the Chancellor handed down a well-crafted 174 page Opinion and Order, determining that "the director defendants did not breach their fiduciary duties or commit waste." The Court entered judgment in favor of all defendants on all claims alleged in the amended complaint.

. . . . We conclude, for the reasons that follow, that the Chancellor's factual findings and legal rulings were correct and not erroneous in any respect. . . .

I. THE FACTS

. . . . The critical events flow from what turned out to be an unfortunate hiring decision at Disney, a company that for over half a century has been one of America's leading film and entertainment enterprises.

In 1994 Disney lost in a tragic helicopter crash its President and Chief Operating Officer, Frank Wells, who together with Michael Eisner, Disney's Chairman and Chief Executive Officer, had enjoyed remarkable success at the Company's helm. Eisner temporarily assumed Disney's presidency, but only three months later, heart disease required Eisner to undergo quadruple bypass surgery. Those two events persuaded Eisner and Disney's board of directors that the time had come to identify a successor to Eisner.

Eisner's prime candidate for the position was Michael Ovitz, who was the leading partner and one of the founders of Creative Artists Agency ("CAA"), the premier talent agency whose business model had reshaped the entire industry. By 1995, CAA had 550 employees and a roster of about 1400 of Hollywood's top actors, directors, writers, and musicians. That roster generated about $150 million in annual revenues and an annual income of over $20 million for Ovitz, who was regarded as one of the most powerful figures in Hollywood.

Eisner and Ovitz had enjoyed a social and professional relationship that spanned nearly 25 years. Although in the past the two men had casually discussed possibly working together, in 1995, when Ovitz began negotiations to leave CAA and join Music Corporation of America ("MCA"), Eisner became seriously interested in recruiting Ovitz to join Disney. Eisner shared that desire with Disney's board members on an individual basis.[4]

---

[4] The Disney board of directors at that time and at the time the Ovitz Employment Agreement was approved (the "old board") consisted of Eisner, Roy E. Disney, Stanley P. Gold, Sanford M. Litvack, Richard A. Nunis, Sidney Poitier, Irwin E. Russell, Robert A.M. Stern, E. Cardon Walker, Raymond L. Watson, Gary L. Wilson, Reveta F. Bowers, Ignacio E. Lozano, Jr., George J. Mitchell, and Stephen F. Bollenbach. The board of directors at the time Ovitz was terminated as President of Disney (the "new board") consisted of the persons listed above (other than Bollenbach), plus Leo J. O'Donovan and Thomas S. Murphy. Neither O'Donovan nor Murphy served on the old board.

A. Negotiation Of The Ovitz Employment Agreement

Eisner and Irwin Russell, who was a Disney director and chairman of the compensation committee, first approached Ovitz about joining Disney. Their initial negotiations were unproductive, however, because at that time MCA had made Ovitz an offer that Disney could not match. The MCA-Ovitz negotiations eventually fell apart, and Ovitz returned to CAA in mid-1995. Business continued as usual, until Ovitz discovered that Ron Meyer, his close friend and the number two executive at CAA, was leaving CAA to join MCA. That news devastated Ovitz, who concluded that to remain with the company he and Meyer had built together was no longer palatable. At that point Ovitz became receptive to the idea of joining Disney. Eisner learned of these developments and re-commenced negotiations with Ovitz in earnest. By mid-July 1995, those negotiations were in full swing.

. . . . [D]uring the negotiations Ovitz came to believe that he and Eisner would run Disney, and would work together in a relation akin to that of junior and senior partner. Unfortunately, Ovitz's belief was mistaken, as Eisner had a radically different view of what their respective roles at Disney should be.

Russell assumed the lead in negotiating the financial terms of the Ovitz employment contract. In the course of negotiations, Russell learned from Ovitz's attorney, Bob Goldman, that Ovitz owned 55% of CAA and earned approximately $20 to $25 million a year from that company. From the beginning Ovitz made it clear that he would not give up his 55% interest in CAA without "downside protection." Considerable negotiation then ensued over downside protection issues. During the summer of 1995, the parties agreed to a draft version of Ovitz's employment agreement (the "OEA") modeled after Eisner's and the late Mr. Wells' employment contracts. As described by the Chancellor, the draft agreement included the following terms:

> Under the proposed OEA, Ovitz would receive a five-year contract with two tranches of options. The first tranche consisted of three million options vesting in equal parts in the third, fourth, and fifth years, and if the value of those options at the end of the five years had not appreciated to $50 million, Disney would make up the difference. The second tranche consisted of two million options that would vest immediately if Disney and Ovitz opted to renew the contract.
>
> The proposed OEA sought to protect both parties in the event that Ovitz's employment ended prematurely, and provided that absent

defined causes, neither party could terminate the agreement without penalty. If Ovitz, for example, walked away, for any reason other than those permitted under the OEA, he would forfeit any benefits remaining under the OEA and could be enjoined from working for a competitor. Likewise, if Disney fired Ovitz for any reason other than gross negligence or malfeasance, Ovitz would be entitled to a non-fault payment (Non-Fault Termination or "NFT"), which consisted of his remaining salary, $7.5 million a year for unaccrued bonuses, the immediate vesting of his first tranche of options and a $10 million cash out payment for the second tranche of options.

As the basic terms of the OEA were crystallizing, Russell prepared and gave Ovitz and Eisner a "case study" to explain those terms. In that study, Russell also expressed his concern that the negotiated terms represented an extraordinary level of executive compensation. Russell acknowledged, however, that Ovitz was an "exceptional corporate executive" and "highly successful and unique entrepreneur" who merited "downside protection and upside opportunity." Both would be required to enable Ovitz to adjust to the reduced cash compensation he would receive from a public company, in contrast to the greater cash distributions and other perquisites more typically available from a privately held business. But, Russell did caution that Ovitz's salary would be at the top level for any corporate officer and significantly above that of the Disney CEO. Moreover, the stock options granted under the OEA would exceed the standards applied within Disney and corporate America and would "raise very strong criticism." Russell shared this original case study only with Eisner and Ovitz. He also recommended another, additional study of this issue.

To assist in evaluating the financial terms of the OEA, Russell recruited Graef Crystal, an executive compensation consultant, and Raymond Watson, a member of Disney's compensation committee and a past Disney board chairman who had helped structure Wells' and Eisner's compensation packages. . . .

On August 10, Russell, Watson and Crystal met. They discussed and generated a set of values using different and various inputs and assumptions, accounting for different numbers of options, vesting periods, and potential proceeds of option exercises at various times and prices. After discussing their conclusions, they agreed that Crystal would memorialize his findings and fax them to Russell. Two days later, Crystal faxed to Russell a memorandum concluding that the OEA would provide Ovitz with approximately $23.6 million per year for the first five years, or $23.9 million a year over seven years if Ovitz exercised a two year renewal option. Those sums, Crystal opined, would approximate Ovitz's current annual compensation at CAA.

During a telephone conference that same evening, Russell, Watson and Crystal discussed Crystal's memorandum and its assumptions. . . . But, rather than address the points Russell highlighted, Crystal faxed to Russell a new letter that expressed Crystal's concern about the OEA's $50 million option appreciation guarantee. Crystal's concern, based on his understanding of the current draft of the OEA, was that Ovitz could hold the first tranche of options, wait out the five-year term, collect the $50 million guarantee, and then exercise the in-the-money options and receive an additional windfall. Crystal was philosophically opposed to a pay package that would give Ovitz the best of both worlds—low risk and high return.

Addressing Crystal's concerns, Russell made clear that the guarantee would not function as Crystal believed it might. Crystal then revised his original letter, adjusting the value of the OEA (assuming a two year renewal) to $24.1 million per year. Up to that point, only three Disney directors—Eisner, Russell and Watson—knew the status of the negotiations with Ovitz and the terms of the draft OEA.

While Russell, Watson and Crystal were finalizing their analysis of the OEA, Eisner and Ovitz reached a separate agreement. Eisner told Ovitz that: (1) the number of options would be reduced from a single grant of five million to two separate grants, the first being three million options for the first five years and the second consisting of two million more options if the contract was renewed; and (2) Ovitz would join Disney only as President, not as a co-CEO with Eisner. After deliberating, Ovitz accepted those terms, and that evening Ovitz, Eisner, Sid Bass and their families celebrated Ovitz's decision to join Disney.

Unfortunately, the celebratory mood was premature. The next day, August 13, Eisner met with Ovitz, Russell, Sanford Litvack (an Executive Vice President and Disney's General Counsel), and Stephen Bollenbach (Disney's Chief Financial Officer) to discuss the decision to hire Ovitz. Litvack and Bollenbach were unhappy with that decision, and voiced concerns that Ovitz would disrupt the cohesion that existed between Eisner, Litvack and Bollenbach. Litvack and Bollenbach were emphatic that they would not report to Ovitz, but would continue to report to Eisner. Despite Ovitz's concern about his "shrinking authority" as Disney's future President, Eisner was able to provide sufficient reassurance so that ultimately Ovitz acceded to Litvack's and Bollenbach's terms.

On August 14, Eisner and Ovitz signed a letter agreement (the "OLA"), which outlined the basic terms of Ovitz's employment, and stated that the agreement (which would ultimately be embodied in a formal contract) was subject to approval by Disney's compensation committee and board of directors. . . . . [Russell, Watson and Eisner, then contacted the other Disney directors] to inform them of the impending new hire, and to explain [Eisner's] friendship with Ovitz and Ovitz's qualifications.

That same day, a press release made the news of Ovitz's hiring public. The reaction was extremely positive: Disney was applauded for the decision, and Disney's stock price rose 4.4 % in a single day, thereby increasing Disney's market capitalization by over $1 billion.

* * * *

On September 26, 1995, the Disney compensation committee (which consisted of Messrs. Russell, Watson, Poitier and Lozano) met for one hour to consider, among other agenda items, the proposed terms of the OEA. A term sheet was distributed at the meeting, although a draft of the OEA was not. The topics discussed were historical comparables, such as Eisner's and Wells' option grants, and also the factors that Russell, Watson and Crystal had considered in setting the size of the option grants and the termination provisions of the contract. Watson testified that he provided the compensation committee with the spreadsheet analysis that he had performed in August, and discussed his findings with the committee. . . . After Russell's and Watson's presentations, Litvack also responded to substantive questions. At trial Poitier and Lozano testified that they believed they had received sufficient information from Russell's and Watson's presentations to exercise their judgment in the best interests of the Company. The committee voted unanimously to approve the OEA terms, subject to "reasonable further negotiations within the framework of the terms and conditions" described in the OEA.

Immediately after the compensation committee meeting, the Disney board met in executive session. . . . [and] voted unanimously to elect Ovitz as President.

* * * *

B. Ovitz's Performance as President of Disney

Ovitz's tenure as President of the Walt Disney Company officially began on October 1, 1995, the date that the OEA was executed. When Ovitz took office, the initial reaction was optimistic, and Ovitz did make some positive contributions while serving as President of the Company. By the fall of 1996, however, it had become clear that Ovitz was "a poor fit with his fellow executives." By then the Disney directors were discussing that the disconnect between Ovitz and the Company was likely irreparable and that Ovitz would have to be terminated.

* * * *

Although the plaintiffs attempted to show that Ovitz acted improperly (*i.e.*, with gross negligence or malfeasance) while in office, the Chancellor found that the trial record did not support those accusations. . . . [The Chancellor rejected the plaintiffs' claims that Ovitz was insubordinate, a "habitual liar" and that Ovitz had violated the Company's policies relating to expenses and to reporting gifts he received while President of Disney.]

* * * *

Nonetheless, Ovitz's relationship with the Disney executives did continue to deteriorate through September 1996. In mid-September, Litvack, with Eisner's approval, told Ovitz that he was not working out at Disney and that he should start looking for a graceful exit from Disney and a new job. Litvack reported this conversation to Eisner, who sent Litvack back to Ovitz to make it clear that Eisner no longer wanted Ovitz at Disney and that Ovitz should seriously consider other opportunities, including one then developing at Sony. Ovitz responded by telling Litvack that he was not leaving and that if Eisner wanted him to leave Disney, Eisner could tell him that to his face.

On September 30, 1996, the Disney board met. During an executive session of that meeting, and in small group discussions where Ovitz was not present, Eisner told the other board members of the continuing problems with Ovitz's performance.

Those interchanges set the stage for Ovitz's eventual termination as Disney's President.

C. Ovitz's Termination at Disney

After the discussions between Litvack and Ovitz, Eisner and Ovitz met several times. During those meetings they discussed Ovitz's future, including Ovitz's employment prospects at Sony. Eisner believed that because Ovitz had a good, longstanding relationship with many Sony senior executives, Sony would be willing to take Ovitz in "trade" from Disney. Eisner favored such a trade, which would not only remove Ovitz from Disney, but also would relieve Disney of any obligation to pay Ovitz under the OEA. . . . Those negotiations did not prove fruitful, however. . . .

In response to this unwelcome news, Eisner wrote (but never sent) a letter to Ovitz on November 11, in which Eisner attempted to make it clear that Ovitz was no longer welcome at Disney. Instead of sending that letter, Eisner met with Ovitz personally on November 13, and discussed much of what the letter contained. Eisner left that meeting believing that "Ovitz just would not listen to what he was trying to tell him and instead, Ovitz insisted that he would stay at Disney, going so far as to state that he would chain himself to his desk."

During this period Eisner was also working with Litvack to explore whether they could terminate Ovitz under the OEA for cause. If so, Disney would not owe Ovitz the NFT payment. From the very beginning, Litvack advised Eisner that he did not believe there was cause to terminate Ovitz under the OEA. Litvack's advice never changed.

At the end of November 1996, Eisner again asked Litvack if Disney had cause to fire Ovitz and thereby avoid the costly NFT payment. Litvack proceeded to examine that issue more carefully. He studied the OEA, refreshed himself on the meaning of "gross negligence" and "malfeasance," and reviewed all the facts concerning Ovitz's performance of which he was aware. Litvack also consulted Val Cohen, co-head of Disney's litigation department and Joseph Santaniello, in Disney's legal department. Cohen and Santaniello both concurred in Litvack's conclusion that no basis existed to terminate Ovitz for cause. . . . Although the Chancellor was critical of Litvack and Eisner for lacking sufficient documentation to support his conclusion and the work they did to arrive at that conclusion, the Court found that Eisner and Litvack "did in fact make a concerted effort to determine if Ovitz could be terminated for cause, and that despite these efforts, they were unable to manufacture the desired result."

Litvack also believed that it would be inappropriate, unethical and a bad idea to attempt to coerce Ovitz (by threatening a for-cause termination) into negotiating for a smaller NFT package than the OEA provided. The reason was that when pressed by Ovitz's attorneys, Disney would have to admit that in fact there was no cause, which could subject Disney to a wrongful termination lawsuit. Litvack believed that attempting to avoid legitimate contractual obligations would harm Disney's reputation as an honest business partner and would affect its future business dealings.

* * * *

On December 11, Eisner met with Ovitz to agree on the wording of a press release to announce the termination, and to inform Ovitz that he would not receive any of the additional items that he requested. By that time it had already been decided that Ovitz would be terminated without cause and that he would receive his contractual NFT payment, but nothing more. Eisner and Ovitz agreed that neither Ovitz nor Disney would disparage each other in the press, and that the separation was to be undertaken with dignity and respect for both sides. After his December 11 meeting with Eisner, Ovitz never returned to Disney.

* * * *

II. SUMMARY OF APPELLANTS' CLAIMS OF ERROR

* * * *

The appellants' claims of error are most easily analyzed in two separate groupings: (1) the claims against the Disney defendants and (2) the claims against Ovitz. The first category encompasses the claims that the Disney defendants breached their fiduciary duties to act with due care and in good faith by (1) approving the OEA, and specifically, its NFT provisions; and (2) approving the NFT severance payment to Ovitz upon his termination—a payment that is also claimed to constitute corporate waste. It is notable that the appellants do not contend that the Disney defendants are directly liable as a consequence of those fiduciary duty breaches. Rather, appellants' core argument is indirect, i.e., that those breaches of fiduciary duty deprive the Disney defendants of the protection of business judgment review, and require them to shoulder the burden of establishing that their acts were entirely fair to Disney. . . .

* * * *

IV. THE CLAIMS AGAINST THE DISNEY DEFENDANTS

We next turn to the claims of error that relate to the Disney defendants. Those claims are subdivisible into two groups: (A) claims arising out of the approval of the OEA and of Ovitz's election as President; and (B) claims arising out of the NFT severance payment to Ovitz upon his termination. . . .

A. Claims Arising from the Approval of the OEA and Ovitz's Election as President

. . . [T]he appellants' core argument in the trial court was that the Disney defendants' approval of the OEA and election of Ovitz as President were not entitled to business judgment rule protection, because those actions were either grossly negligent or not performed in good faith. . . .

* * * *

1. *The Due Care Determinations*

. . . . The appellants claim that the Chancellor erred by: (1) treating as distinct questions whether the plaintiffs had established by a preponderance of the evidence either gross negligence or a lack of good faith; (2) ruling that the old board was not required to approve the OEA; (3) determining whether the old board had breached its duty of care on a director-by-director basis rather than collectively; (4) concluding that the compensation committee members did not breach their duty of care in approving the NFT provisions of the OEA; and (5) holding that the remaining members of the old board (*i.e.,* the directors who were not members of the compensation committee) had not breached their duty of care in electing Ovitz as Disney's President.

* * * *

(a) TREATING DUE CARE AND BAD FAITH AS SEPARATE GROUNDS FOR DENYING BUSINESS JUDGMENT RULE REVIEW

This argument is best understood against the backdrop of the presumptions that cloak director action being reviewed under the business judgment standard. Our law presumes that "in making a business decision the directors of a corporation acted on an informed basis, in good faith, and in the honest belief that the action taken was in the best interests of the company." Those presumptions can be rebutted if the plaintiff shows that the directors breached their fiduciary duty of care or of loyalty or acted in bad faith. If that is shown, the burden then shifts to the director defendants to demonstrate that the challenged act or transaction was entirely fair to the corporation and its shareholders.

Because no duty of loyalty claim was asserted against the Disney defendants, the only way to rebut the business judgment rule presumptions would be to show that the Disney defendants had either breached their duty of care or had not acted in good faith. At trial, the plaintiff-appellants attempted to establish both grounds, but the Chancellor determined that the plaintiffs had failed to prove either.

* * * *

(b) RULING THAT THE FULL DISNEY BOARD WAS NOT REQUIRED TO CONSIDER AND APPROVE THE OEA

The appellants next challenge the Court of Chancery's determination that the full Disney board was not required to consider and approve the OEA, because the Company's governing instruments allocated that decision to the compensation committee. This challenge also cannot survive scrutiny.

* * * *

The Delaware General Corporation Law (DGCL) expressly empowers a board of directors to appoint committees and to delegate to them a broad range of responsibilities, which may include setting executive compensation. Nothing in the DGCL mandates that the entire board must make those decisions. At Disney, the responsibility to consider and approve executive compensation was allocated to the compensation committee, as distinguished from the full board.

* * * *

(d) HOLDING THAT THE COMPENSATION COMMITTEE MEMBERS DID NOT FAIL TO EXERCISE DUE CARE IN APPROVING THE OEA

The appellants next challenge the Chancellor's determination that although the compensation committee's decision-making process fell far short of corporate governance "best practices," the committee members breached no duty of care in considering and approving the NFT terms of the OEA. That conclusion is reversible error, the appellants claim, because the record establishes that the compensation committee members did not properly inform themselves of the material facts and, hence, were grossly negligent in approving the NFT provisions of the OEA.

* * * *

In our view, a helpful approach is to compare what actually happened here to what would have occurred had the committee followed a "best practices" (or "best case") scenario, from a process standpoint. In a "best case" scenario, all committee members would have received, before or at the committee's first meeting on September 26, 1995, a spreadsheet or similar document prepared by (or with the assistance of) a compensation expert (in this case, Graef Crystal). Making different, alternative assumptions, the spreadsheet would disclose the amounts that Ovitz could receive under the OEA in each circumstance that might foreseeably arise. One variable in that matrix of possibilities would be the cost to Disney of a non-fault termination for each of the five years of the initial term of the OEA. The contents of the spreadsheet would be explained to the committee members, either by the expert who prepared it or by a fellow committee member similarly knowledgeable about the subject. That spreadsheet, which ultimately would become an exhibit to the minutes of the compensation committee meeting, would form the basis of the committee's deliberations and decision.

Had that scenario been followed, there would be no dispute (and no basis for litigation) over what information was furnished to the committee members or when it was furnished. Regrettably, the committee's informational and decisionmaking process used here was not so tidy. That is one reason why the Chancellor found that although the committee's process did not fall below the level required for a proper exercise of due care, it did fall short of what best practices would have counseled.

The Disney compensation committee met twice: on September 26 and October 16, 1995. The minutes of the September 26 meeting reflect that the committee approved the terms of the OEA (at that time embodied in the form of a letter agreement), except for the option grants, which were not approved until October 16—after the Disney stock incentive plan had been amended to provide for those options. At the September 26 meeting, the compensation committee considered a "term sheet" which, in summarizing the material terms of the OEA, relevantly disclosed that in the event of a non-fault termination, Ovitz would receive: (i) the present value of his salary ($1 million per year) for the balance of the contract term, (ii) the present value of his annual bonus payments (computed at $7.5 million) for the balance of the contract term, (iii) a $10 million termination fee, and (iv) the acceleration of his options for 3 million shares, which would become immediately exercisable at market price.

Thus, the compensation committee knew that in the event of an NFT, Ovitz's severance payment alone could be in the range of $40 million cash, plus the value of the accelerated options. Because the actual payout to Ovitz was approximately $130 million, of which roughly $38.5 million was cash, the value of the options at the time of the NFT payout would have been about $91.5 million. Thus, the issue may be framed as whether the compensation committee members knew, at the time they approved the OEA, that the value of the option component of the severance package could reach the $92 million order of magnitude if they terminated Ovitz without cause after one year. The evidentiary record shows that the committee members were so informed.

On this question the documentation is far less than what best practices would have dictated. There is no exhibit to the minutes that discloses, in a single document, the estimated value of the accelerated options in the event of an NFT termination after one year. The information imparted to the committee members on that subject is, however, supported by other evidence, most notably the trial testimony of various witnesses about spreadsheets that were prepared for the compensation committee meetings.

The compensation committee members derived their information about the potential magnitude of an NFT payout from two sources. The first was the value of the "benchmark" options previously granted to Eisner and Wells and the valuations by Watson of the proposed Ovitz options. Ovitz's options were set at 75% of parity with the options previously granted to Eisner and to Frank Wells. Because the compensation committee had established those earlier benchmark option grants to Eisner and Wells and were aware of their value, a simple mathematical calculation would have informed them of the potential value range of Ovitz's options. Also, in August and September 1995, Watson and Russell met with Graef Crystal to determine (among other things) the value of the potential Ovitz options, assuming different scenarios. Crystal valued the options under the Black-Scholes method, while Watson used a different valuation metric. Watson recorded his calculations and the resulting values on a set of spreadsheets that reflected what option profits Ovitz might receive, based upon a range of different assumptions about stock market price increases. Those spreadsheets were shared with, and explained to, the committee members at the September meeting.

The committee's second source of information was the amount of "downside protection" that Ovitz was demanding. Ovitz required financial protection from the risk of leaving a very lucrative and secure position at CAA, of which he was a controlling partner, to join a publicly held corporation to which Ovitz was a stranger, and that had a very different culture and an environment which prevented him from completely controlling his destiny. The committee members knew that by leaving CAA and coming to Disney, Ovitz would be sacrificing "booked" CAA commissions of $150 to $200 million—an amount that Ovitz demanded as protection against the risk that his employment relationship with Disney might not work out. Ovitz wanted at least $50 million of that compensation to take the form of an "up-front" signing bonus. Had the $50 million bonus been paid, the size of the option grant would have been lower. Because it was contrary to Disney policy, the compensation committee rejected the up-front signing bonus demand, and elected instead to compensate Ovitz at the "back end," by awarding him options that would be phased in over the five-year term of the OEA.

It is on this record that the Chancellor found that the compensation committee was informed of the material facts relating to an NFT payout. If measured in terms of the documentation that would have been generated if "best practices" had been followed, that record leaves much to be desired. The Chancellor acknowledged that, and so do we. But, the Chancellor also found that despite its imperfections, the evidentiary record was sufficient to support the conclusion that the compensation committee had adequately informed itself of the potential magnitude of the entire severance package, including the options, that Ovitz would receive in the event of an early NFT.

The OEA was specifically structured to compensate Ovitz for walking away from $150 million to $200 million of anticipated commissions from CAA over the five-year OEA contract term. This meant that if Ovitz was terminated without cause, the earlier in the contract term the termination occurred the larger the severance amount would be to replace the lost commissions. Indeed, because Ovitz was terminated after only one year, the total amount of his severance payment (about $130 million) closely approximated the lower end of the range of Ovitz's forfeited commissions ($150 million), less the compensation Ovitz received during his first and only year as Disney's President. Accordingly, the Court of Chancery had a sufficient evidentiary basis in the record from which to find that, at the time they approved the OEA, the compensation committee members were adequately informed of the potential magnitude of an early NFT severance payout.

* * * *

(e) HOLDING THAT THE REMAINING DISNEY DIRECTORS DID NOT FAIL TO EXERCISE DUE CARE IN APPROVING THE HIRING OF OVITZ AS THE PRESIDENT OF DISNEY

The appellants' final claim in this category is that the Court of Chancery erroneously held that the remaining members of the old Disney board had not breached their duty of care in electing Ovitz as President of Disney. . . .

The appellants argue that the Disney directors breached their duty of care by failing to inform themselves of all material information reasonably available with respect to Ovitz's employment agreement. . . . The only properly reviewable action of the entire board was its decision to elect Ovitz as Disney's President. In that context the sole issue, as the Chancellor properly held, is "whether [the remaining members of the old board] properly exercised their business judgment and acted in accordance with their fiduciary duties when they elected Ovitz to the Company's presidency." The Chancellor determined that in electing Ovitz, the directors were informed of all information reasonably available and, thus, were not grossly negligent. We agree.

The Chancellor found and the record shows the following: well in advance of the September 26, 1995 board meeting the directors were fully aware that the Company needed—especially in light of Wells' death and Eisner's medical problems—to hire a "number two" executive and potential successor to Eisner. There had been many discussions about that need and about potential candidates who could fill that role even before Eisner decided to try to recruit Ovitz. Before the September 26 board meeting Eisner had individually discussed with each director the possibility of hiring Ovitz, and Ovitz's background and qualifications. The directors thus knew of Ovitz's skills, reputation and experience, all of which they believed would be highly valuable to the Company. The directors also knew that to accept a position at Disney, Ovitz would have to walk away from a very successful business—a reality that would lead a reasonable person to believe that Ovitz would likely succeed in similar pursuits elsewhere in the industry. The directors also knew of the public's highly positive reaction to the Ovitz announcement, and that Eisner and senior management had supported the Ovitz hiring. Indeed, Eisner, who had long desired to bring Ovitz within the Disney fold, consistently vouched for Ovitz's qualifications and told the directors that he could work well with Ovitz.

The board was also informed of the key terms of the OEA (including Ovitz's salary, bonus and options). Russell reported this information to them at the September 26, 1995 executive session, which was attended by Eisner and all non-executive directors. Russell also reported on the compensation committee meeting that had immediately preceded the executive session. And, both Russell and Watson responded to questions from the board. Relying upon the compensation committee's approval of the OEA and the other information furnished to them, the Disney directors, after further deliberating, unanimously elected Ovitz as President.

Based upon this record, we uphold the Chancellor's conclusion that, when electing Ovitz to the Disney presidency the remaining Disney directors were fully informed of all material facts, and that the appellants failed to establish any lack of due care on the directors' part.

2. *The Good Faith Determinations*

The Court of Chancery held that the business judgment rule presumptions protected the decisions of the compensation committee and the remaining Disney directors, not only because they had acted with due care but also because they had not acted in bad faith. That latter ruling, the appellants claim, was reversible error because the Chancellor formulated and then applied an incorrect definition of bad faith.

In its Opinion the Court of Chancery defined bad faith as follows:

> Upon long and careful consideration, I am of the opinion that the concept of *intentional dereliction of duty*, a *conscious disregard for one's responsibilities*, is an appropriate (although not the only) standard for determining whether fiduciaries have acted in good faith. Deliberate indifference and inaction *in the face of a duty to act* is, in my mind, conduct that is clearly disloyal to the corporation. It is the epitome of faithless conduct.

* * * *

. . .This case . . . is one in which the duty to act in good faith has played a prominent role, yet to date is not a well-developed area of our corporate fiduciary law. Although the good faith concept has recently been the subject of considerable scholarly writing, which includes articles focused on this specific case, the duty to act in good faith is, up to this point relatively uncharted. Because of the increased recognition of the importance of good faith, some conceptual guidance to the corporate community may be helpful. . . .

The precise question is whether the Chancellor's articulated standard for bad faith corporate fiduciary conduct—intentional dereliction of duty, a conscious disregard for one's responsibilities—is legally correct. In approaching that question, we note that the Chancellor characterized that definition as "an appropriate (*although not the only*) standard for determining whether fiduciaries have acted in good faith." That observation is accurate and helpful, because as a matter of simple logic, at least three different categories of fiduciary behavior are candidates for the "bad faith" pejorative label.

The first category involves so-called "subjective bad faith," that is, fiduciary conduct motivated by an actual intent to do harm. That such conduct constitutes classic, quintessential bad faith is a proposition so well accepted in the liturgy of fiduciary law that it borders on axiomatic. We need not dwell further on this category, because no such conduct is claimed to have occurred, or did occur, in this case.

The second category of conduct, which is at the opposite end of the spectrum, involves lack of due care—that is, fiduciary action taken solely by reason of gross negligence and without any malevolent intent. In this case, appellants assert claims of gross negligence to establish breaches not only of director due care but also of the directors' duty to act in good faith. Although the Chancellor found, and we agree, that the appellants failed to establish gross negligence, to afford guidance we address the issue of whether gross negligence (including a failure to inform one's self of available material facts), without more, can also constitute bad faith. The answer is clearly no.

From a broad philosophical standpoint, that question is more complex than would appear, if only because (as the Chancellor and others have observed) "issues of good faith are (to a certain degree) inseparably and necessarily intertwined with the duties of care and loyalty. . . ." But, in the pragmatic, conduct-regulating legal realm which calls for more precise conceptual line drawing, the answer is that grossly negligent conduct, without more, does not and cannot constitute a breach of the fiduciary duty to act in good faith. The conduct that is the subject of due care may overlap with the conduct that comes within the rubric of good faith in a psychological sense, but from a legal standpoint those duties are and must remain quite distinct. Both our legislative history and our common law jurisprudence distinguish sharply between the duties to exercise due care and to act in good faith, and highly significant consequences flow from that distinction.

The Delaware General Assembly has addressed the distinction between bad faith and a failure to exercise due care (*i.e.*, gross negligence) in two separate contexts. The first is Section 102(b)(7) of the DGCL, which authorizes Delaware corporations, by a provision in the certificate of incorporation, to exculpate their directors from monetary damage liability for a breach of the duty of care. That exculpatory provision affords significant protection to directors of Delaware corporations. The statute carves out several exceptions, however, including most relevantly, "for acts or omissions not in good faith. . . ." Thus, a corporation can exculpate its directors from monetary liability for a breach of the duty of care, but not for conduct that is not in good faith. . . .

* * * *

That leaves the third category of fiduciary conduct, which falls in between the first two categories of (1) conduct motivated by subjective bad intent and (2) conduct resulting from gross negligence. This third category is what the Chancellor's definition of bad faith—intentional dereliction of duty, a conscious disregard for one's responsibilities—is intended to capture. The question is whether such misconduct is properly treated as a non-exculpable, non-indemnifiable violation of the fiduciary duty to act in good faith. In our view it must be, for at least two reasons.

First, the universe of fiduciary misconduct is not limited to either disloyalty in the classic sense (*i.e.*, preferring the adverse self-interest of the fiduciary or of a related person to the interest of the corporation) or gross negligence. Cases have arisen where corporate directors have no conflicting self-interest in a decision, yet engage in misconduct that is more culpable than simple inattention or failure to be informed of all facts material to the decision. To protect the interests of the corporation and its shareholders, fiduciary conduct of this kind, which does not involve disloyalty (as traditionally defined) but is qualitatively more culpable than gross negligence, should be proscribed. A vehicle is needed to address such violations doctrinally, and that doctrinal vehicle is the duty to act in good faith. The Chancellor implicitly so recognized in his Opinion, where he identified different examples of bad faith as follows:

> The good faith required of a corporate fiduciary includes not simply the duties of care and loyalty, in the narrow sense that I have discussed them above, but all actions required by a true faithfulness and devotion to the interests of the corporation and its shareholders. A failure to act in good faith may be shown, for instance, where the fiduciary intentionally acts with a purpose other than that of advancing the best interests of the corporation, where the fiduciary acts with the intent to violate applicable positive law, or where the fiduciary intentionally fails to act in the face of a known duty to act, demonstrating a conscious disregard for his duties. There may be other examples of bad faith yet to be proven or alleged, but these three are the most salient.

Those articulated examples of bad faith are not new to our jurisprudence. Indeed, they echo pronouncements our courts have made throughout the decades.

Second, the legislature has also recognized this intermediate category of fiduciary misconduct, which ranks between conduct involving subjective bad faith and gross negligence. Section 102(b)(7)(ii) of the DGCL expressly denies money damage exculpation for "acts or omissions not in good faith or which involve intentional misconduct or a knowing violation of law." By its very terms that provision distinguishes between "intentional misconduct" and a "knowing violation of law" (both examples of subjective bad faith) on the one hand, and "acts . . . not in good faith," on the other. Because the statute exculpates directors only for conduct amounting to gross negligence, the statutory denial of exculpation for "acts . . . not in good faith" must encompass the intermediate category of misconduct captured by the Chancellor's definition of bad faith.

For these reasons, we uphold the Court of Chancery's definition as a legally appropriate, although not the exclusive, definition of fiduciary bad faith. We need go no further. To engage in an effort to craft (in the Court's words) "a definitive and categorical definition of the universe of acts that would constitute bad faith"[112] would be unwise and is unnecessary to dispose of the issues presented on this appeal.

Having sustained the Chancellor's finding that the Disney directors acted in good faith when approving the OEA and electing Ovitz as President, we next address the claims arising out of the decision to pay Ovitz the amount called for by the NFT provisions of the OEA.

B. Claims Arising From The Payment of the NFT Severance Payout to Ovitz

The appellants advance three alternative claims . . . whose overall thrust is that even if the OEA approval was legally valid, the NFT severance payout to Ovitz pursuant to the OEA was not. Specifically, the appellants contend that: (1) only the full Disney board with the concurrence of the compensation committee—but not Eisner alone—was authorized to terminate Ovitz; (2) because Ovitz could have been terminated for cause, Litvack and Eisner acted without due care and in bad faith in reaching the contrary conclusion; and (3) the business judgment rule presumptions did not protect the new Disney board's acquiescence in the NFT payout, because the new board was not entitled to rely upon Eisner's and Litvack's contrary advice. Appellants urge that in rejecting these claims the Court of Chancery committed reversible error. We disagree.

1. *Was Action by the New Board Required to Terminate Ovitz as the President of Disney?*

The Chancellor determined that although the board as constituted upon Ovitz's termination (the "new board") had the authority to terminate Ovitz, neither that board nor the compensation committee was required to act, because Eisner also had, and properly exercised, that authority. The new board, the Chancellor found, was not required to terminate Ovitz under the company's internal documents. Without such a duty to act, the new board's failure to vote on the termination could not give rise to a breach of the duty of care or the duty to act in good faith. . .

---

112 . . .For the same reason, we do not reach or otherwise address the issue of whether the fiduciary duty to act in good faith is a duty that, like the duties of care and loyalty, can serve as an independent basis for imposing liability upon corporate officers and directors. That issue is not before us on this appeal.

* * * *

Here, the extrinsic evidence clearly supports the conclusion that the board and Eisner understood that Eisner, as Board Chairman/CEO had concurrent power with the board to terminate Ovitz as President. In that regard, the Chancellor credited the testimony of new board members that Eisner, as Chairman and CEO, was empowered to terminate Ovitz without board approval or intervention; and also Litvack's testimony that during his tenure as general counsel, many Company officers were terminated and the board never once took action in connection with their terminations. Because Eisner possessed, and exercised, the power to terminate Ovitz unilaterally, we find that the Chancellor correctly concluded that the new board was not required to act in connection with that termination, and, therefore, the board did not violate any fiduciary duty to act with due care or in good faith.

* * * *

2. *In Concluding that Ovitz Could Not Be Terminated for Cause, Did Litvack or Eisner Breach Any Fiduciary Duty?*

It is undisputed that Litvack and Eisner (based on Litvack's advice) both concluded that if Ovitz was to be terminated, it could only be without cause, because no basis existed to terminate Ovitz for cause. . . . . [T]he Chancellor determined independently, as a matter of fact and law, that (1) Ovitz had not engaged in any conduct as President that constituted gross negligence or malfeasance—the standard for an NFT under the OEA; and (2) in arriving at that same conclusion in 1996, Litvack and Eisner did not breach their fiduciary duty of care or their duty to act in good faith.

* * * *

Despite their inability to show factual or legal error in the Chancellor's determination that Ovitz could not be terminated for cause, appellants contend that Litvack and Eisner breached their fiduciary duty to exercise due care and to act in good faith in reaching that same conclusion. The Court of Chancery scrutinized the record to determine independently whether, in reaching their conclusion, Litvack and Eisner had separately exercised due care and acted in good faith. The Court determined that they had properly discharged both duties. Appellants' attack upon that determination lacks merit, because it is also without basis in the factual record.

* * * *

With respect to Eisner, the Chancellor found that faced with a situation where he was unable to work well with Ovitz, who required close and constant supervision, Eisner had three options: 1) keep Ovitz as President and continue trying to make things work; 2) keep Ovitz at Disney, but in a role other than as President; or 3) terminate Ovitz. The first option was unacceptable, and the second would have entitled Ovitz to the NFT, or at the very least would have resulted in a costly lawsuit to determine whether Ovitz was so entitled. After an unsuccessful effort to "trade" Ovitz to Sony, that left only the third option, which was to terminate Ovitz and pay the NFT. The Chancellor found that in choosing this alternative, Eisner had breached no duty and had exercised his business judgment. . . .

* * * *

. . . .Even though the Chancellor found much to criticize in Eisner's "imperial CEO" style of governance, nothing has been shown to overturn the factual basis for the Court's conclusion that, in the end, Eisner's conduct satisfied the standards required of him as a fiduciary.

3. *Were the Remaining Directors Entitled to Rely Upon Eisner's and Litvack's Advice that Ovitz Could Not Be Fired For Cause?*

The appellants' third claim of error challenges the Chancellor's conclusion that the remaining new board members could rely upon Litvack's and Eisner's advice that Ovitz could be terminated only without cause. The short answer to that challenge is that, for the reasons previously discussed, the advice the remaining directors received and relied upon was accurate. Moreover, the directors' reliance on that advice was found to be in good faith.

* * * *

V. THE WASTE CLAIM

The appellants' final claim is that even if the approval of the OEA was protected by the business judgment rule presumptions, the payment of the severance amount to Ovitz constituted waste. This claim is rooted in the doctrine that a plaintiff who fails to rebut the business judgment rule presumptions is not entitled to any remedy unless the transaction constitutes waste. . . .

To recover on a claim of corporate waste, the plaintiffs must shoulder the burden of proving that the exchange was "so one sided that no business person of ordinary, sound judgment could conclude that the corporation has received adequate consideration." A claim of waste will arise only in the rare, "unconscionable case where directors irrationally squander or give away corporate assets." This onerous standard for waste is a corollary of the proposition that where business judgment presumptions are applicable, the board's decision will be upheld unless it cannot be "attributed to any rational business purpose."

The claim that the payment of the NFT amount to Ovitz, without more, constituted waste is meritless on its face, because at the time the NFT amounts were paid, Disney was contractually obligated to pay them. The payment of a contractually obligated amount cannot constitute waste, unless the contractual obligation is itself wasteful. Accordingly, the proper focus of a waste analysis must be whether the amounts required to be paid in the event of an NFT were wasteful *ex ante*.

* * * *

. . . [Appellants allege that] the OEA gave Ovitz every incentive to leave the Company before serving out the full term of his contract. The appellants urge that although the OEA may have induced Ovitz to join Disney as President, no contractual safeguards were in place to retain him in that position. In essence, appellants claim that the NFT provisions of the OEA created an irrational incentive for Ovitz to get himself fired.

That claim does not come close to satisfying the high hurdle required to establish waste. The approval of the NFT provisions in the OEA had a rational business purpose: to induce Ovitz to leave CAA, at what would otherwise be a considerable cost to him, in order to join Disney. . . . To suggest that at the time he entered into the OEA Ovitz would engineer an early departure at the cost of his extraordinary reputation in the entertainment industry and his historical friendship with Eisner, is not only fanciful but also without proof in the record. Indeed, the Chancellor found that it was "patently unreasonable to assume that Ovitz intended to perform just poorly enough to be fired quickly, but not so poorly that he could be terminated for cause."

We agree. Because the appellants have failed to show that the approval of the NFT terms of the OEA was not a rational business decision, their waste claim must fail. . . .

QUESTIONS

1. Michael Ovitz seems to have received an extraordinarily generous compensation package. What was the business justification for agreeing to such a package?

2. While the Court found the practices of the Disney board to have been "not so tidy," it did not find them culpable. If you were representing Disney, what steps would you have advised the Disney board of directors take in order to strengthen the directors' ability to defeat a legal challenge to their decision to hire Ovitz with such a generous compensation package?

3. If you were representing Disney, how would you have advised Michael Eisner with respect to the decision on whether to terminate Ovitz "for cause" or "without cause"?

Delaware General Corporation Law

- ***Del. Code Ann. tit. 8 § 102(b)***

  (7) A provision eliminating or limiting the personal liability of a director to the corporation or its stockholders for monetary damages for breach of fiduciary duty as a director, provided that such provision shall not eliminate or limit the liability of a director: (i) For any breach of the director's duty of loyalty to the corporation or its stockholders; (ii) *for acts or omissions not in good faith* or which involve intentional misconduct or a knowing violation of law. (*Emphasis added.*)

- ***Del. Code Ann. tit. 8 § 145***

  (a) A corporation shall have power to indemnify any [. . .]director, officer, employee or agent of the corporation[. . .] if the person acted in good faith and in a manner the person reasonably believed to be in or not opposed to the best interests of the corporation, and, with respect to any criminal action or proceeding, had no reasonable cause to believe the person's conduct was unlawful. (Emphasis added.)

  (b) A corporation shall have power to indemnify any person who was or is a party or is threatened to be made a party to any threatened, pending or completed action or suit by or in the right of the corporation to procure a judgment in its favor by reason of the fact that the person is or was a director, officer, employee or agent of the corporation, or is or was serving at the request of the corporation as a director[or] officer [. . .] *if the person acted in good faith and in a manner the person reasonably believed to be in or not opposed to the best interests of the corporation*. . . (*Emphasis added.*)

In the *Stone v. Ritter* case that follows, the Delaware Court clarified its position with respect to a director's obligations to act in good faith with respect to the corporation.

Stone v. Ritter

911 A.2d 362 (Del. 2006)

HOLLAND, J.:

This is an appeal from a final judgment of the Court of Chancery dismissing a derivative complaint against fifteen present and former directors of AmSouth Bancorporation ("AmSouth"), a Delaware corporation. . . .

The Court of Chancery characterized the allegations in the derivative complaint as a "classic *Caremark* claim," a claim that derives its name from *In re Caremark Int'l Deriv. Litig.*[1] In *Caremark*, the Court of Chancery recognized that: "[g]enerally where a claim of directorial liability for corporate loss is predicated upon ignorance of liability creating activities within the corporation . . . only a sustained or systematic failure of the board to exercise oversight—such as an utter failure to attempt to assure a reasonable information and reporting system exists—will establish the lack of good faith that is a necessary condition to liability."[2]

In this appeal, the plaintiffs acknowledge that the directors neither "knew [n]or should have known that violations of law were occurring," *i.e.*, that there were no "red flags" before the directors. Nevertheless, the plaintiffs argue that the Court of Chancery erred by dismissing the derivative complaint which alleged that "the defendants had utterly failed to implement any sort of statutorily required monitoring, reporting or information controls that would have enabled them to learn of problems requiring their attention.". . . .

* * * *

---

1 *In re Caremark Int'l Inc. Deriv. Litig., 698 A.2d 959 (Del. Ch. 1996).*

2 *In re Caremark Int'l Inc. Deriv. Litig., 698 A.2d at 971. . . .*

This derivative action is brought on AmSouth's behalf by William and Sandra Stone, who . . . owned AmSouth common stock. . . . During the relevant period, AmSouth's wholly-owned subsidiary, AmSouth Bank, operated about 600 commercial banking branches in six states throughout the southeastern United States and employed more than 11,600 people.

In 2004, AmSouth and Amsouth Bank paid $40 million in fines and $10 million in civil penalties to resolve government and regulatory investigations pertaining principally to the failure by bank employees to file "Suspicious Activity Reports" ("SARs"), as required by the federal Bank Secrecy Act ("BSA") and various anti-money-laundering ("AML") regulations. Those investigations were conducted by the United States Attorney's Office for the Southern District of Mississippi ("USAO"), the Federal Reserve, FinCEN and the Alabama Banking Department. No fines or penalties were imposed on AmSouth's directors, and no other regulatory action was taken against them.

The government investigations arose originally from an unlawful "Ponzi" scheme operated by Louis D. Hamric, II and Victor G. Nance. In August 2000, Hamric, then a licensed attorney, and Nance, then a registered investment advisor with Mutual of New York, contacted an AmSouth branch bank in Tennessee to arrange for custodial trust accounts to be created for "investors" in a "business venture." That venture (Hamric and Nance represented) involved the construction of medical clinics overseas. In reality, Nance had convinced more than forty of his clients to invest in promissory notes bearing high rates of return, by misrepresenting the nature and the risk of that investment. Relying on similar misrepresentations by Hamric and Nance, the AmSouth branch employees in Tennessee agreed to provide custodial accounts for the investors and to distribute monthly interest payments to each account upon receipt of a check from Hamric and instructions from Nance.

The Hamric-Nance scheme was discovered in March 2002, when the investors did not receive their monthly interest payments. . . . Hamric and Nance were indicted on federal money-laundering charges, and both pled guilty.

. . . . On October 12, 2004, AmSouth and the USAO entered into a Deferred Prosecution Agreement ("DPA") in which AmSouth agreed: first, to the filing by USAO of a one-count Information in the United States District Court for the Southern District of Mississippi, charging AmSouth with failing to file SARs; and second, to pay a $40 million fine. In conjunction with the DPA, the USAO issued a "Statement of Facts," which noted that although in 2000 "at least one" AmSouth employee suspected that Hamric was involved in a possibly illegal scheme, AmSouth failed to file SARs in a timely manner. In neither the

Statement of Facts nor anywhere else did the USAO ascribe any blame to the Board or to any individual director.

On October 12, 2004, the Federal Reserve and the Alabama Banking Department concurrently issued a Cease and Desist Order against AmSouth, requiring it, for the first time, to improve its BSA/AML program. That Cease and Desist Order required AmSouth to (among other things) engage an independent consultant "to conduct a comprehensive review of the Bank's AML Compliance program and make recommendations, as appropriate, for new policies and procedures to be implemented by the Bank." KPMG Forensic Services ("KPMG") performed the role of independent consultant and issued its report on December 10, 2004 (the "KPMG Report").

Also on October 12, 2004, FinCEN and the Federal Reserve jointly assessed a $10 million civil penalty against AmSouth for operating an inadequate anti-money-laundering program and for failing to file SARs. . . . Among FinCEN's specific determinations were its conclusions that "AmSouth's [AML compliance] program lacked adequate board and management oversight," and that "reporting to management for the purposes of monitoring and oversight of compliance activities was materially deficient." AmSouth neither admitted nor denied FinCEN's determinations in this or any other forum.

Demand Futility and Director Independence

* * * *

In this appeal, the plaintiffs concede that "[t]he standards for determining demand futility in the absence of a business decision" are set forth in *Rales v. Blasband.* To excuse demand under *Rales,* "a court must determine whether or not the particularized factual allegations of a derivative stockholder complaint create a reasonable doubt that, as of the time the complaint is filed, the board of directors could have properly exercised its independent and disinterested business judgment in responding to a demand." . . . .

Critical to this demand excused argument is the fact that the directors' potential personal liability depends upon whether or not their conduct can be exculpated by the section 102(b)(7) provision contained in the AmSouth certificate of incorporation. Such a provision can exculpate directors from monetary liability for a breach of the duty of care, but not for conduct that is not in good faith or a breach of the duty of loyalty. The standard for assessing a director's potential personal liability for failing to act in good faith in discharging his or her oversight responsibilities has evolved beginning with our decision in

Graham v. Allis-Chalmers Manufacturing Company,[15] through the Court of Chancery's Caremark decision to our most recent decision in *Disney.*[16] A brief discussion of that evolution will help illuminate the standard that we adopt in this case.

Graham and Caremark

Graham was a derivative action brought against the directors of Allis-Chalmers for failure to prevent violations of federal anti-trust laws by Allis-Chalmers employees. There was no claim that the Allis-Chalmers directors knew of the employees' conduct that resulted in the corporation's liability. Rather, the plaintiffs claimed that the Allis-Chalmers directors *should have known* of the illegal conduct by the corporation's employees. In *Graham*, this Court held that "*absent cause for suspicion* there is no duty upon the directors to install and operate a corporate system of espionage to ferret out wrongdoing which they have no reason to suspect exists."

In *Caremark*, ...[t]he plaintiffs claimed that the Caremark directors should have known that certain officers and employees of Caremark were involved in violations of the federal Anti-Referral Payments Law. That law prohibits health care providers from paying any form of remuneration to induce the referral of Medicare or Medicaid patients. . . .

[I]n *Caremark,* the Court of Chancery narrowly construed our holding in *Graham* "as standing for the proposition that, absent grounds to suspect deception, neither corporate boards nor senior officers can be charged with wrongdoing simply for assuming the integrity of employees and the honesty of their dealings on the company's behalf." The *Caremark* Court opined it would be a "mistake" to interpret this Court's decision in *Graham* to mean that:

> corporate boards may satisfy their obligation to be reasonably informed concerning the corporation, without assuring themselves that information and reporting systems exist in the organization that are reasonably designed to provide to senior management and to the board itself timely, accurate information sufficient to allow management and the board, each within its scope, to reach informed judgments concerning both the corporation's compliance with law and its business performance.

---

15 *Graham v. Allis-Chalmers Mfg. Co.,* 41 Del. Ch. 78, 188 A.2d 125 (Del. 1963).

16 *In re Walt Disney Co. Deriv. Litig., 906 A.2d 27 (Del. 2006).*

. . . . The Court of Chancery then formulated the following standard for assessing the liability of directors where the directors are unaware of employee misconduct that results in the corporation being held liable:

> Generally where a claim of directorial liability for corporate loss is predicated upon ignorance of liability creating activities within the corporation, as in *Graham* or in this case, . . . only a sustained or systematic failure of the board to exercise oversight—such as an utter failure to attempt to assure a reasonable information and reporting system exists—will establish the lack of good faith that is a necessary condition to liability.

Caremark Standard Approved

As evidenced by the language quoted above, the *Caremark* standard for so-called "oversight" liability draws heavily upon the concept of director failure to act in good faith. That is consistent with the definition(s) of bad faith recently approved by this Court in its recent *Disney* decision, where we held that a failure to act in good faith requires conduct that is qualitatively different from, and more culpable than, the conduct giving rise to a violation of the fiduciary duty of care (i.e., gross negligence). In *Disney,* we identified the following examples of conduct that would establish a failure to act in good faith:

> A failure to act in good faith may be shown, for instance, where the fiduciary intentionally acts with a purpose other than that of advancing the best interests of the corporation, where the fiduciary acts with the intent to violate applicable positive law, or where the fiduciary intentionally fails to act in the face of a known duty to act, demonstrating a conscious disregard for his duties. There may be other examples of bad faith yet to be proven or alleged, but these three are the most salient.

The third of these examples describes, and is fully consistent with, the lack of good faith conduct that the *Caremark* court held was a "necessary condition" for director oversight liability, i.e., "a sustained or systematic failure of the board to exercise oversight—such as an utter failure to attempt to assure a reasonable information and reporting system exists . . . ."

Indeed, our opinion in *Disney* cited *Caremark* with approval for that proposition. Accordingly, the Court of Chancery applied the correct standard in assessing whether demand was excused in this case where failure to exercise oversight was the basis or theory of the plaintiffs' claim for relief.

It is important, in this context, to clarify a doctrinal issue that is critical to understanding fiduciary liability under *Caremark* as we construe that case. The phraseology used in *Caremark* and that we employ here—describing the lack of good faith as a "necessary condition to liability"—is deliberate. The purpose of that formulation is to communicate that a failure to act in good faith is not conduct that results, *ipso facto,* in the direct imposition of fiduciary liability. The failure to act in good faith may result in liability because the requirement to act in good faith "is a subsidiary element[,]" i.e., a condition, "of the fundamental duty of loyalty." It follows that because a showing of bad faith conduct, in the sense described in *Disney* and *Caremark,* is essential to establish director oversight liability, the fiduciary duty violated by that conduct is the duty of loyalty.

This view of a failure to act in good faith results in two additional doctrinal consequences. First, although good faith may be described colloquially as part of a "triad" of fiduciary duties that includes the duties of care and loyalty, the obligation to act in good faith does not establish an independent fiduciary duty that stands on the same footing as the duties of care and loyalty. Only the latter two duties, where violated, may directly result in liability, whereas a failure to act in good faith may do so, but indirectly. The second doctrinal consequence is that the fiduciary duty of loyalty is not limited to cases involving a financial or other cognizable fiduciary conflict of interest. It also encompasses cases where the fiduciary fails to act in good faith. As the Court of Chancery aptly put it in *Guttman,* "[a] director cannot act loyally towards the corporation unless she acts in the good faith belief that her actions are in the corporation's best interest."

We hold that *Caremark* articulates the necessary conditions predicate for director oversight liability: (a) the directors utterly failed to implement any reporting or information system or controls; or (b) having implemented such a system or controls, consciously failed to monitor or oversee its operations thus disabling themselves from being informed of risks or problems requiring their attention. In either case, imposition of liability requires a showing that the directors knew that they were not discharging their fiduciary obligations. Where directors fail to act in the face of a known duty to act, thereby demonstrating a conscious disregard for their responsibilities, they breach their duty of loyalty by failing to discharge that fiduciary obligation in good faith.

* * * *

Reasonable Reporting System Existed

The KPMG Report evaluated the various components of AmSouth's longstanding BSA/AML compliance program. The KPMG Report reflects that

AmSouth's Board dedicated considerable resources to the BSA/AML compliance program and put into place numerous procedures and systems to attempt to ensure compliance. According to KPMG, the program's various components exhibited between a low and high degree of compliance with applicable laws and regulations.

The KPMG Report describes the numerous AmSouth employees, departments and committees established by the Board to oversee AmSouth's compliance with the BSA and to report violations to management and the Board:

> **BSA Officer.** Since 1998, AmSouth has had a "BSA Officer" "responsible for all BSA/AML-related matters including employee training, general communications, CTR reporting and SAR reporting," and "presenting AML policy and program changes to the board of directors, the managers at the various lines of business, and participants in the annual training of security and audit personnel[;]"
>
> **BSA/AML Compliance Department.** AmSouth has had for years a BSA/AML Compliance Department, headed by the BSA Officer and comprised of nineteen professionals, including a BSA/AML Compliance Manager and a Compliance Reporting Manager;
>
> **Corporate Security Department.** AmSouth's Corporate Security Department has been at all relevant times responsible for the detection and reporting of suspicious activity as it relates to fraudulent activity, and William Burch, the head of Corporate Security, has been with AmSouth since 1998 and served in the U.S. Secret Service from 1969 to 1998; and
>
> **Suspicious Activity Oversight Committee.** Since 2001, the "Suspicious Activity Oversight Committee" and its predecessor, the "AML Committee," have actively overseen AmSouth's BSA/AML compliance program. The Suspicious Activity Oversight Committee's mission has for years been to "oversee the policy, procedure, and process issues affecting the Corporate Security and BSA/AML Compliance Programs, to ensure that an effective program exists at AmSouth to deter, detect, and report money laundering, suspicious activity and other fraudulent activity."

The KPMG Report reflects that the directors not only discharged their oversight responsibility to establish an information and reporting system, but also proved that the system was designed to permit the directors to periodically monitor AmSouth's compliance with BSA and AML regulations. For example, as KPMG noted in 2004, AmSouth's designated BSA Officer "has made annual high-level presentations to the Board of Directors in each of the last five years." Further, the Board's Audit and Community Responsibility Committee (the "Audit Committee") oversaw AmSouth's BSA/AML compliance program on a quarterly basis. The KPMG Report states that "the BSA Officer presents BSA/AML training to the Board of Directors annually," and the "Corporate Security training is also presented to the Board of Directors."

The KPMG Report shows that AmSouth's Board at various times enacted written policies and procedures designed to ensure compliance with the BSA and AML regulations. For example, the Board adopted an amended bank-wide "BSA/AML Policy" on July 17, 2003—four months before AmSouth became aware that it was the target of a government investigation. That policy was produced to plaintiffs in response to their demand to inspect AmSouth's books and records pursuant to section 220 and is included in plaintiffs' appendix. Among other things, the July 17, 2003, BSA/AML Policy directs all AmSouth employees to immediately report suspicious transactions or activity to the BSA/AML Compliance Department or Corporate Security.

Complaint Properly Dismissed

. . . . Delaware courts have recognized that "[m]ost of the decisions that a corporation, acting through its human agents, makes are, of course, not the subject of director attention." Consequently, a claim that directors are subject to personal liability for employee failures is "possibly the most difficult theory in corporation law upon which a plaintiff might hope to win a judgment."

* * * *

The KPMG Report—which the plaintiffs explicitly incorporated by reference into their derivative complaint—refutes the assertion that the directors "never took the necessary steps . . . to ensure that a reasonable BSA compliance and reporting system existed." KPMG's findings reflect that the Board received and approved relevant policies and procedures, delegated to certain employees and departments the responsibility for filing SARs and monitoring compliance, and exercised oversight by relying on periodic reports from them. Although there ultimately may have been failures by employees to report deficiencies to the Board, there is no basis for an oversight claim seeking to hold the directors personally liable for such failures by the employees.

With the benefit of hindsight, the plaintiffs' complaint seeks to equate a bad outcome with bad faith. The lacuna in the plaintiffs' argument is a failure to recognize that the directors' good faith exercise of oversight responsibility may not invariably prevent employees from violating criminal laws, or from causing the corporation to incur significant financial liability, or both,. . . . In the absence of red flags, good faith in the context of oversight must be measured by the directors' actions "to assure a reasonable information and reporting system exists" and not by second-guessing after the occurrence of employee conduct that results in an unintended adverse outcome. Accordingly, we hold that the Court of Chancery properly applied *Caremark* and dismissed the plaintiffs' derivative complaint for failure to excuse demand by alleging particularized facts that created reason to doubt whether the directors had acted in good faith in exercising their oversight responsibilities.

Conclusion

The judgment of the Court of Chancery is affirmed.

QUESTIONS

1. Following *Stone v. Ritter,* how should an action taken by a director in bad faith be evaluated?

2. Consider a situation in which a disgruntled director approves a transaction for a Delaware corporation with a foreign government, thinking the transaction will harm the corporation, but makes a mistake in calculating the exchange rate, and, as a result, the Delaware corporation enters into a hugely successful transaction. Would that director incur liability under *Stone v. Ritter*?

CHAPTER FIVE

Duty of Loyalty

AS YOU GAIN EXPERIENCE working at the firm, you begin to acquire your own clients. One day you are referred a client named Bill. Bill is a director for a major toy company called Yots, Inc. Yots, Inc. manufactures and distributes a wide range of toys for boys and girls. Bill comes into your office and relates the following events.

Experiencing Assignment 7: Go Grammar

FACTS:

Bill has three children who all go to Smart Kids Elementary School. One night at a party for Smart Kids Elementary School parents, Bill was speaking with his daughter's English teacher, Tina. Tina asked Bill about the toy business, and Bill told her about the newest Yots' toys, which include toys that focus on destructive play, "fashion" play and imaginative play. After they had been talking for a little while, Tina said:

"To be perfectly honest Bill, I am not so big on toys. I think they distract from homework. I actually invented a learning activity called "Go Grammar" as an alternative activity for kids. Go Grammar is a learning activity that helps kids improve their grammar and learn about parts of speech like nouns, verbs and adjectives. It also teaches more complex rules like prepositions and the subjunctive. It is also very engaging and the kids I have shown it to really like it. One of the features of Go Grammar is that when kids "pass" a level, by taking a test online, they receive "rewards." Unfortunately, I do not know how to sell or market the program."

Bill then said to Tina, "I know all about that; I can help you."

Bill and Tina have already had several meetings. Bill has agreed to invest $250,000 and to help Tina build her business in exchange for 40% of the *Go Grammar* business. Bill and Tina plan to offer the *Go Grammar* program as a book paired with an online learning website. There will also be a smartphone application. In the name of supporting education, Bill has arranged with major corporations to provide $5.00 gift certificates to participants in the *Go Grammar* program as participants "pass" each grammar level. Bill has already obtained agreements to provide these certificates from companies like Apple, Best Buy, and Toys "R" Us. Each of these companies has agreed to provide over $1 million in gift certificates for free, since all of these companies want to contribute to education.

Two weeks before the official launch of *Go Grammar,* the Yots, Inc. Board of Directors heard about Bill's activities. The chairman of the Yots, Inc.'s Board has asked Bill to appear at the next board meeting and explain why Bill did not bring the *Go Grammar* opportunity to Yots and to discuss whether Yots is entitled to some or all of Bill's interest in the *Go Grammar* business. Bill is very upset, and he has come to you for advice. In addition to the above information, Bill tells you that Yots does not sell educational products, but it does have an electronic division and sells online games.

ASSIGNMENT:

Bill would like you to write a memo evaluating his position. In the memo he would like you to discuss the strengths and weaknesses of his position as well as whether there is anything he can do to strengthen his position. Also, Bill would like you to outline no more than five "bullet points" that will help when he speaks to the Yots, Inc. Board of Directors. (Note that a bullet point is usually one sentence, but, even if it is more than one sentence, it is not more than one idea. Also, less than five "points" is fine, but more is not.) Remember, that neither Bill, nor most of Yots Inc.'s Board members are lawyers. They will not be impressed by legal jargon or case citations.

Your memo to Bill should include the following warning:

"CONFIDENTIAL ATTORNEY CLIENT COMMUNICATION: This memo contains legally privileged and/or confidential information. If you are not the intended recipient, or the employee or agent responsible for delivery of this memo to the intended recipient, you are hereby notified that any disclosure, dissemination, distribution, copying or the taking of any action in reliance on the contents of this memo is strictly prohibited."

The body of the memo, which does not include the heading or the above warning, but does include the bullet points, may not exceed 900 words.

However, if the memo is less than 650 words, you will receive one additional point on the assignment.

This Assignment does not need to be completed, and should not be completed, until the end of the section. However, as you study the cases and other materials that follow, it might be helpful to do so with a view toward providing assistance to Bill. Some of the materials in the chapter will relate more than others to the issues facing Bill. However, the materials are designed to build your understanding of the fiduciary duty issues that arise in a partnership and assist you in addressing Bill's concerns and putting them in context. Please keep Bill's issues and the questions presented by the assignment in mind while reading the materials that follow.

SECTION I: Duty of Loyalty in General

The duty of loyalty requires that fiduciaries (such as officers and directors) put the interests of the corporation ahead of their own interests. The duty of loyalty is implicated when a director is involved in a situation in which there is a conflict of interest, meaning that there is some aspect of the situation that creates a personal benefit for the fiduciary. A conflict of interest exists when the director knows, at the time he is asked to take action with regard to a potential transaction, that he or a person related to him (1) is a party to the transaction or (2) has a beneficial financial interest in the transaction, and then exercises his influence to the detriment of the corporation. Model Business Corporations Act § 8.60.

Some typical situations that create conflicts of interest include: "self-dealing" (when a fiduciary for the corporation enters into a transaction with himself or herself or with an entity in which he or she (or a family member) has a substantial financial interest); taking a "corporate opportunity" (when a fiduciary for the corporation misappropriates an opportunity that belongs to the corporation); executive compensation (when the executives whose compensation is at issue are also on the board of directors that votes to determine their compensation); and other situations in which a fiduciary's personal financial interests are, at least potentially, in conflict with the financial interests of the corporation.

Even if a transaction does present a conflict of interest, it may be "cleansed" if the transaction in question is approved by a vote of a majority of the fully informed, disinterested directors; ratified by the informed shareholders; or shown to have been "intrinsically fair" to the corporation.

A. Conflicts of Interest

Delaware General Corporation Law

. . . Subchapter IV. Directors and Officers

* * * *

§ 144. Interested directors; quorum.

(a) No contract or transaction between a corporation and 1 or more of its directors or officers, or between a corporation and any other corporation, partnership, association, or other organization in which 1 or more of its directors or officers, are directors or officers, or have a financial interest, shall be void or voidable solely for this reason, or solely because the director or officer is present at or participates in the meeting of the board or committee which authorizes the contract or transaction, or solely because any such director's or officer's votes are counted for such purpose, if:

(1) The material facts as to the director's or officer's relationship or interest and as to the contract or transaction are disclosed or are known to the board of directors or the committee, and the board or committee in good faith authorizes the contract or transaction by the affirmative votes of a majority of the disinterested directors, even though the disinterested directors be less than a quorum; or

(2) The material facts as to the director's or officer's relationship or interest and as to the contract or transaction are disclosed or are known to the stockholders entitled to vote thereon, and the contract or transaction is specifically approved in good faith by vote of the stockholders; or

(3) The contract or transaction is fair as to the corporation as of the time it is authorized, approved or ratified, by the board of directors, a committee or the stockholders.

(b) Common or interested directors may be counted in determining the presence of a quorum at a meeting of the board of directors or of a committee which authorizes the contract or transaction.

The several cases that follow each involve an alleged violation of the duty of loyalty. As you read through the cases, ask yourself:

- Is there a true conflict of interest?
- Is there the appearance of a conflict of interest?
- Has the fiduciary (or fiduciaries) breached a duty to put the corporation's interests ahead of their own interests?
- If so, how has the corporation been injured?
- How would you have counseled the parties participating in the alleged breach of duty had they come to you for advice before taking action?

Bayer v. Beran

49 N.Y.S.2d 2 (N.Y. Sup. 1944)

SHIENTAG, J.:

* * * *

To encourage freedom of action on the part of directors, or to put it another way, to discourage interference with the exercise of their free and independent judgment, there has grown up what is known as the 'business judgment rule'. [*Citations omitted.*] 'Questions of policy of management, expediency of contracts or action, adequacy of consideration, lawful appropriation of corporate funds to advance corporate interests, are left solely to their honest and unselfish decision, for their powers therein are without limitation and free from restraint, and the exercise of them for the common and general interests of the corporation may not be questioned, although the results show that what they did was unwise or inexpedient.' *Pollitz v. Wabash R. Co.,* 207 N.Y. 113, 124, 100 N.E. 721, 724. Indeed, although the concept of 'responsibility' is firmly fixed in the law, it is only in a most unusual and extraordinary case that directors are held liable for negligence in the absence of fraud, or improper motive, or personal interest.

The 'business judgment rule', however, yields to the rule of undivided loyalty. This great rule of law is designed 'to avoid the possibility of fraud and to avoid the temptation of self-interest.' [*Citations omitted.*] It is 'designed to obliterate all divided loyalties which may creep into a fiduciary relation * * *.' [*Citation omitted.*] 'Included within its scope is every situation in which a trustee chooses to deal with another in such close relation with the trustee that possible advantage to such other person might influence, consciously or unconsciously, the judgment of the trustee * * *.' Lehman, Ch. J., in *Albright v. Jefferson County National Bank,* 292 N.Y. 31, 39, 53 N.E.2d 753, 756. The dealings of a director with the corporation for which he is the fiduciary are therefore viewed 'with jealousy by the courts.' *Globe Woolen Co. v. Utica Gas & Electric Co.,* 224 N.Y. 483, 121 N.E. 378, 380. Such personal transactions of directors with their corporations, such transactions as may tend to produce a conflict between self-interest and fiduciary obligation, are, when challenged, examined with the most scrupulous care, and if there is any evidence of improvidence or oppression, any indication of unfairness or undue advantage, the transactions will be voided. [*Citations omitted.*] 'Their dealings with the corporation are subjected to rigorous scrutiny and where any of their contracts or engagements with the corporation are challenged the burden is on the director not only to prove the good faith of the transaction but also to show its inherent fairness from the viewpoint of the corporation and those interested therein.' *Pepper v. Litton,* 308 U.S. 295, 306, 60 S. Ct. 238, 245, 84 L. Ed. 281.

* * * *

The first, or 'advertising', cause of action charges the directors with negligence, waste and improvidence in embarking the corporation [Celanese Corporation of America] upon a radio advertising program beginning in 1942 and costing about $1,000,000 a year. It is further charged that they were negligent in selecting the type of program and in renewing the radio contract for 1943. More serious than these allegations is the charge that the directors were motivated by a noncorporate purpose in causing the radio program to be undertaken and in expending large sums of money therefor. It is claimed that this radio advertising was for the benefit of Miss Jean Tennyson, one of the singers on the program, who in private life is Mrs. Camille Dreyfus, the wife of the president of the company and one of its directors; that it was undertaken to 'further, foster and subsidize her career'; to 'furnish a vehicle' for her talents.

Eliminating for the moment the part played by Miss Tennyson in the radio advertising campaign, it is clear that the character of the advertising, the amount to be expended therefor, and the manner in which it should be used, are all matters of business judgment and rest peculiarly within the discretion of the board of directors. Under the authorities previously cited, it is not, generally speaking, the function of a court of equity to review these matters or even to consider them. Had the wife of the president of the company not been involved, the advertising cause of action could have been disposed of summarily. Her connection with the program, however, makes it necessary to go into the facts in some detail.

Before 1942 the company had not resorted to radio advertising. While it had never maintained a fixed advertising budget, the company had, through its advertising department, spent substantial sums of money for advertising purposes. In 1941, for example, the advertising expense was $683,000, as against net sales for that year of $62,277,000 and net profits (before taxes) of $13,972,000. The advertising was at all times directed towards the creation of a consumer preference which would compel or induce the various trade elements linking the corporation to the consumer to label the corporation's products so that the consumer would know he was buying the material he wanted. The company had always claimed that its products, which it had called or labeled 'Celanese', were different from rayon, chemically and physically; that its products had qualities, special and unique, which made them superior to rayon. The company had never called or designated its products as rayon.

As far back as ten years ago, a radio program was considered, but it did not seem attractive. In 1937, the Federal Trade Commission promulgated a rule, the effect of which was to require all celanese products to be designated and labeled rayon. The name 'Celanese' could no longer be used alone. The products had to be called or labeled 'rayon' or 'celanese rayon'. This gave the directors much concern. As one of them expressed it, 'When we were compelled to put our product under the same umbrella with rayon rather than being left outside as a separate product, a thermo-plastic such as nylon is, we believed we were being treated in an unfair manner and that it was up to us, however, to do the best we could to circumvent the situation in which we found ourselves. * * * All manner of things were considered but there seemed only one thing we could do. We could either multiply our current advertising and our method of advertising in the same mediums we had been using, or we could go into radio'.

The directors, in considering the matter informally, but not collectively as a board, decided towards the end of 1941 to resort to the radio and to have the company go on the air with a dignified program of fine music, the kind of program which they felt would be in keeping with what they believed to be the beauty and superior quality of their products. The radio program was not adopted on the spur of the moment or at the whim of the directors. They acted after studies reported to them, made by the advertising department, beginning in 1939. A radio consultant was employed to advise as to time and station. An advertising agency of national repute was engaged to take charge of the formulation and production of the program. It was decided to expend about

$1,000,000 a year, but the commitments were to be subject to cancellation every thirteen weeks, so that the maximum obligation of the company would be not more than $250,000.

So far, there is nothing on which to base any claim of breach of fiduciary duty. Some care, diligence and prudence were exercised by these directors before they committed the company to the radio program. It was for the directors to determine whether they would resort to radio advertising; it was for them to conclude how much to spend; it was for them to decide the kind of program they would use. It would be an unwarranted act of interference for any court to attempt to substitute its judgment on these points for that of the directors, honestly arrived at. The expenditure was not reckless or unconscionable. Indeed, it bore a fair relationship to the total amount of net sales and to the earnings of the company. . . . That a program of classical and semiclassical music was selected, rather than a variety program, or a news commentator program, furnishes no ground for legal complaint. True, variety programs have a wider popular appeal than do musicals, but it would be a very sad thing if the former were the only kind of radio programs to be used. Some of the largest industrial concerns in the country have recognized this and have maintained fine musical programs on the radio for many years.

Now we have to take up an unfortunate incident, one which cannot be viewed with the complacency displayed by some of the directors of the company. This is not a closely held family corporation. The Doctors Dreyfus and their families own about 135,000 shares of common stock, the other directors about 10,000 shares out of a total outstanding issue of 1,376,500 shares. Some of these other directors were originally employed by Dr. Camille Dreyfus, the president of the company. His wife, to whom he has been married for about twelve years, is known professionally as Miss Jean Tennyson and is a singer of wide experience.

Dr. Dreyfus, as was natural, consulted his wife about the proposed radio program; he also asked the advertising agency, that had been retained, to confer with her about it. She suggested the names of the artists, all stars of the Metropolitan Opera Company, and the name of the conductor, prominent in his field. She also offered her own services as a paid artist. All of her suggestions as to personnel were adopted by the advertising agency. While the record shows Miss Tennyson to be a competent singer, there is nothing to indicate that she was indispensable or essential to the success of the program. She received $500 an evening. It would be far-fetched to suggest that the directors caused the company to incur large expenditures for radio advertising to enable the president's wife to make $24,000 in 1942 and $20,500 in 1943.

Of course it is not improper to appoint relatives of officers or directors to responsible positions in a company. But where a close relative of the chief executive officer of a corporation, and one of its dominant directors, takes a position closely associated with a new and expensive field of activity, the motives of the directors are likely to be questioned. The board would be placed in a position where selfish, personal interests might be in conflict with the duty it owed to the corporation. That being so, the entire transaction, if challenged in the courts, must be subjected to the most rigorous scrutiny to determine whether the action of the directors was intended or calculated 'to subserve some outside purpose, regardless of the consequences to the company, and in a manner inconsistent with its interests.' [*Citations omitted.*]

After such careful scrutiny I have concluded that, up to the present, there has been no breach of fiduciary duty on the part of the directors. The president undoubtedly knew that his wife might be one of the paid artists on the program. The other directors did not know this until they had approved the campaign of radio advertising and the general type of radio program. The evidence fails to show that the program was designed to foster or subsidize 'the career of Miss Tennyson as an artist' or to 'furnish a vehicle for her talents'. That her participation in the program may have enhanced her prestige as a singer is no ground for subjecting the directors to liability, as long as the advertising served a legitimate and a useful corporate purpose and the company received the full benefit thereof.

The musical quality of 'Celanese Hour' has not been challenged, nor does the record contain anything reflecting on Miss Tennyson's competence as an artist. There is nothing in the testimony to show that some other soprano would have enhanced the artistic quality of the program or its advertising appeal. There is no suggestion that the present program is inefficient or that its cost is disproportionate to what a program of that character reasonably entails. Miss Tennyson's contract with the advertising agency retained by the directors was on a standard form, negotiated through her professional agent. Her compensation, as well as that of the other artists, was in conformity with that paid for comparable work. She received less than any of the other artists on the program. Although she appeared with a greater regularity than any other singer, she received no undue prominence, no special build-up. Indeed, all of the artists were subordinated to the advertisement of the company and of its products. The company was featured. It appears also that the popularity of the program has increased since it was inaugurated.

It is clear, therefore, that the directors have not been guilty of any breach of fiduciary duty, in embarking upon the program of radio advertising and in renewing it. It is unfortunate that they have allowed themselves to be placed in a position where their motives concerning future decisions on radio advertising may be impugned. . . .

It is urged that the expenditures were illegal because the radio advertising program was not taken up at any formal meeting of the board of directors, and no resolution approving it was adopted by the board or by the executive committee. The general rule is that directors acting separately and not collectively as a board cannot bind the corporation. There are two reasons for this: first, that collective procedure is necessary in order that action may be deliberately taken after an opportunity for discussion and an interchange of views; and second, that directors are the agents of the stockholders and are given by law no power to act except as a board. [*Citations omitted.*] Liability may not, however, be imposed on directors because they failed to approve the radio program by resolution at a board meeting.

It is desirable to follow the regular procedure, prescribed by law, which is something more than what has, at times, thoughtlessly been termed red tape. Long experience has demonstrated the necessity for doing this in order to safeguard the interests of all concerned, particularly where, as here, the company has over 1,375,000 shares outstanding in the hands of the public, of which about 10% are held by the officers and directors.

But the failure to observe the formal requirements is by no means fatal. [*Citations omitted.*] The directorate of this company is composed largely of its executive officers. It is a close, working directorate. Its members are in daily association with one another and their full time is devoted to the business of the company with which they have been connected for many years. In this respect it differs from the boards of many corporations of comparable size, where the directorate is made up of men of varied interests who meet only at stated, and somewhat infrequent, intervals.

The same informal practice followed in this transaction had been the customary procedure of the directors in acting on corporate projects of equal and greater magnitude. All of the members of the executive committee were available for daily consultation and they discussed and approved the plan for radio advertising. While a greater degree of formality should undoubtedly be exercised in the future, it is only just and proper to point out that these directors, with all their loose procedure, have done very well for the corporation. Under their administration the company has thrived and prospered. . . .

The expenditures for radio advertising, although made without resolution at a formal meeting of the board, were approved and authorized by the members individually, and may in no sense be considered to have been ultra vires. The resolution adopted by the board on July 6, 1943, with all of the directors present, except two who were resident England, while expressly ratifying only the renewal of the broadcasting contract, may be deemed a ratification of all prior action taken in connection with the radio advertising. When this resolution was adopted, the Celanese Hour had been on the air to the knowledge of all the directors for eighteen months. Moreover, acceptance and retention of the benefits of the radio advertising, with full knowledge thereof, was as complete a ratification as would have resulted from any formal all-inclusive resolution. [*Citations omitted.*]

* * * *

On the entire case, the directors acted in the free exercise of their honest business judgment and their conduct in the transactions challenged did not constitute negligence, waste or improvidence. The complaint is accordingly dismissed on the merits. . . .

Cookies Food Products, Inc. v. Lakes Warehouse Distributing, Inc.

430 N.W.2d 447 (Iowa 1988)

NEUMAN, J.:

This is a shareholders' derivative suit brought by the minority shareholders of a closely held Iowa corporation specializing in barbeque sauce, Cookies Food Products, Inc. (Cookies). The target of the lawsuit is the majority shareholder, Duane "Speed" Herrig and two of his family-owned corporations, Lakes Warehouse Distributing, Inc. (Lakes) and Speed's Automotive Co., Inc. (Speed's). Plaintiffs alleged that Herrig, by acquiring control of Cookies and executing self-dealing contracts, breached his fiduciary duty to the company and fraudulently misappropriated and converted corporate funds. . . . Trial to the court resulted in a verdict for the defendants, the district court finding that Herrig's actions benefited, rather than harmed, Cookies. We affirm.

* * * *

L.D. Cook of Storm Lake, Iowa, founded Cookies in 1975 to produce and distribute his original barbeque sauce. Searching for a plant site in a community that would provide financial backing, Cook met with business leaders in seventeen Iowa communities, outlining his plans to build a growth-oriented company. He selected Wall Lake, Iowa, persuading thirty-five members of that community, including Herrig and the plaintiffs, to purchase Cookies stock. All of the investors hoped Cookies would improve the local job market and tax base. The record reveals that it has done just that.

Early sales of the product, however, were dismal. After the first year's operation, Cookies was in dire financial straits. At that time, Herrig was one of thirty-five shareholders and held only two hundred shares. He was also the owner of an auto parts business, Speed's Automotive, and Lakes Warehouse Distributing, Inc., a company that distributed auto parts from Speed's. Cookies' board of directors approached Herrig with the idea of distributing the company's products. It authorized Herrig to purchase Cookies' sauce for twenty percent under wholesale price, which he could then resell at full wholesale price. Under this arrangement, Herrig began to market and distribute the sauce to his auto parts customers and to grocery outlets from Lakes' trucks as they traversed the regular delivery routes for Speed's Automotive.

In May 1977, Cookies formalized this arrangement by executing an exclusive distribution agreement with Lakes. Pursuant to this agreement, Cookies was responsible only for preparing the product; Lakes, for its part, assumed all costs of warehousing, marketing, sales, delivery, promotion, and advertising. Cookies retained the right to fix the sales price of its products and agreed to pay Lakes thirty percent of its gross sales for these services.

Cookies' sales have soared under the exclusive distributorship contract with Lakes. Gross sales in 1976, the year prior to the agreement, totaled only $20,000, less than half of Cookies' expenses that year. In 1977, however, sales jumped five-fold, then doubled in 1978, and have continued to show phenomenal growth every year thereafter. By 1985, when this suit was commenced, annual sales reached $2,400,000.

As sales increased, Cookies' board of directors amended and extended the original distributorship agreement. In 1979, the board amended the original agreement to give Lakes an additional two percent of gross sales to cover freight costs for the ever-expanding market for Cookies' sauce. In 1980, the board extended the amended agreement through 1984 to allow Herrig to make long-term advertising commitments. Recognizing the role that Herrig's personal strengths played in the success of their joint endeavor, the board also amended the agreement that year to allow Cookies to cancel the agreement with Lakes if Herrig died or disposed of the corporation's stock.

In 1981, L.D. Cook, the majority shareholder up to this time, decided to sell his interest in Cookies. He first offered the directors an opportunity to buy his stock, but the board declined to purchase any of his 8100 shares. Herrig then offered Cook and all other shareholders $10 per share for their stock, which was twice the original price. Because of the overwhelming response to these offers, Herrig had purchased enough Cookies stock by January 1982 to become the majority shareholder. His investment of $140,000 represented fifty-three percent of the 28,700 outstanding shares. . . .

Shortly after Herrig acquired majority control he replaced four of the five members of the Cookies' board with members he selected. This restructuring of authority, following on the heels of an unsuccessful attempt by certain stockholders to prevent Herrig from acquiring majority status, solidified a division of opinion within the shareholder ranks. Subsequent changes made in the corporation under Herrig's leadership formed the basis for this lawsuit.

First, under Herrig's leadership, Cookies' board has extended the term of the exclusive distributorship agreement with Lakes and expanded the scope of services for which it compensates Herrig and his companies. In April 1982, when a sales increase of twenty-five percent over the previous year required Cookies to seek additional short-term storage for the peak summer season, the board accepted Herrig's proposal to compensate Lakes at the "going rate" for use of its nearby storage facilities. The board decided to use Lakes' storage facilities because building and staffing its own facilities would have been more expensive. Later, in July 1982, the new board approved an extension of the exclusive distributorship agreement. Notably, this agreement was identical to the 1980 extension that the former board had approved while four of the plaintiffs in this action were directors.

Second, Herrig moved from his role as director and distributor to take on an additional role in product development. This created a dispute over a royalty Herrig began to receive. Herrig's role in product development began in 1982 when Cookies diversified its product line to include taco sauce. Herrig developed the recipe because he recognized that taco sauce, while requiring many of the same ingredients needed in barbeque sauce, is less expensive to produce. Further, since consumer demand for taco sauce is more consistent throughout the year than the demand for barbeque sauce, this new product line proved to be a profitable method for increasing year-round utilization of production facilities and staff. In August 1982, Cookies' board approved a royalty fee to be paid to Herrig for this taco sauce recipe. This royalty plan was similar to royalties the board paid to L.D. Cook for the barbeque sauce recipe. That plan gives Cook three percent of the gross sales of barbeque sauce; Herrig receives a flat rate per case. Although Herrig's rate is equivalent to a sales percentage slightly higher than what Cook receives, it yields greater profit to Cookies because this new product line is cheaper to produce.

Third, since 1982 Cookies' board has twice approved additional compensation for Herrig. In January 1983, the board authorized payment of a $1000 per month "consultant fee" in lieu of salary, because accelerated sales required Herrig to spend extra time managing the company. Averaging eighty-hour work weeks, Herrig devoted approximately fifteen percent of his time to Cookies and eighty percent to Lakes business. In August, 1983, the board authorized another increase in Herrig's compensation. Further, at the suggestion of a Cookies director who also served as an accountant for Cookies, Lakes, and Speed's, the Cookies board amended the exclusive distributorship agreement to allow Lakes an additional two percent of gross sales as a promotion allowance to expand the market for Cookies products outside of Iowa. As a direct result of this action, by 1986 Cookies regularly shipped products to several states throughout the country.

As we have previously noted, however, Cookies' growth and success has not pleased all its shareholders. The discontent is motivated by two factors that have effectively precluded shareholders from sharing in Cookies' financial success, the fact that Cookies is a closely held corporation, and the fact that it has not paid dividends. Because Cookies' stock is not publicly traded, shareholders have no ready access to buyers for their stock at current values that reflect the company's success. Without dividends, the shareholders have no ready method of realizing a return on their investment in the company. This is not to say that Cookies has improperly refused to pay dividends. The evidence reveals that Cookies would have violated the terms of its loan with the Small Business Administration had it declared dividends before repaying that debt. That SBA loan was not repaid until the month before the plaintiffs filed this action.

Unsatisified with the status quo, a group of minority shareholders commenced this equitable action in 1985. Based on the facts we have detailed, the plaintiffs claimed that the sums paid Herrig and his companies have grossly exceeded the value of the services rendered, thereby substantially reducing corporate profits and shareholder equity. Through the exclusive distributorship agreements, taco sauce royalty, warehousing fees, and consultant fee, plaintiffs claimed that Herrig breached his fiduciary duties to the corporation and its shareholders because he allegedly negotiated for these arrangements without fully disclosing the benefit he would gain.

* * * *

The [district] court concluded that Herrig had breached no duties owed to Cookies or to its minority shareholders, and found that Herrig's compensation was fair and reasonable for each of the four challenged categories of service.

* * * *

II. Fiduciary Duties.

Herrig, as an officer and director of Cookies, owes a fiduciary duty to the company and its shareholders. [*Citations omitted.*] Herrig concedes that Iowa law imposed the same fiduciary responsibilities based on his status as majority stockholder. [*Citations omitted.*] Conversely, before acquiring majority control in February 1982, Herrig owed no fiducuary duty to Cookies or plaintiffs. [*Citations omitted.*] Therefore, Herrig's conduct is subject to scrutiny only from the time he began to exercise control of Cookies.

* * * *

Appellants make no claim that Herrig breached his duty of care by entering self-dealing transactions or accepting compensation for services performed in accordance with the agreements previously described. Instead, appellants claim that Herrig violated his duty of loyalty to Cookies. That duty derives from "the prohibition against self-dealing that inheres in the fiduciary relationship." *Norlin,* 744 F.2d at 264. As a fiduciary, one may not secure for oneself a business opportunity that "in fairness belongs to the corporation." *Rowen v. LeMars Mut. Ins. Co. of Iowa,* 282 N.W.2d 639, 660 (Iowa 1979).

* * * *

Against this common law backdrop, the legislature enacted section 496A.34, quoted here in pertinent part, that establishes three sets of circumstances under which a director may engage in self-dealing without clearly violating the duty of loyalty:

> No contract or other transaction between a corporation and one or more of its directors or any other corporation, firm, association or entity in which one or more of its directors are directors or officers or are financially interested, shall be either void or voidable because of such relationship or interest . . . if any of the following occur:

1. The fact of such relationship or interest is disclosed or known to the board of directors or committee which authorizes, approves, or ratifies the contract or transaction . . . without counting the votes . . . of such interested director.
2. The fact of such relationship or interest is disclosed or known to the shareholders entitled to vote [on the transaction] and they authorize . . . such contract or transaction by vote or written consent.
3. The contract or transaction is fair and reasonable to the corporation.

Some commentators have supported the view that satisfaction of any one of the foregoing statutory alternatives, in and of itself, would prove that a director has fully met the duty of loyalty. [*Citations omitted.*] We are obliged, however, to interpret statutes in conformity with the common law wherever statutory language does not directly negate it. [*Citations omitted.*] Because the common law and section 496A.34 require directors to show "good faith, honesty, and fairness" in self-dealing, we are persuaded that satisfaction of any one of these three alternatives under the statute would merely preclude us from rendering the transaction void or voidable *outright* solely on the basis "of such [director's] relationship or interest." Iowa Code § 496A.34; . . . To the contrary, we are convinced that the legislature did not intend by this statute to enable a court, in a shareholder's derivative suit, to rubber stamp any transaction to which a board of directors or the shareholders of a corporation have consented. Such an interpretation would invite those who stand to gain from such transactions to engage in improprieties to obtain consent. We thus require directors who engage in self-dealing to establish the additional element that they have acted in good faith, honesty, and fairness. . . .

III. Burden of Proof.

* * * *

Appellants correctly assert that the business judgment rule governs only where a director is shown not to have a self interest in the transaction at issue. [*Citations omitted.*] When self-dealing is demonstrated, "the duty of loyalty supersedes the duty of care, and the burden shifts to the director . . . to 'prove that the transaction was fair and reasonable to the corporation.' " *Norlin,* 744 F.2d at 265 (citations omitted). . . . [T]he plaintiffs first made out a prima facie showing that Herrig had engaged in self-dealing with Cookies. Defendants then presented witnesses and exhibits to prove that Herrig's actions in these challenged transactions were done in good faith and with honesty and fairness toward Cookies. The plaintiffs countered with rebuttal testimony and exhibits. The mere fact that the district court credited Herrig and his evidence instead of accepting plaintiffs' contrary proof does not establish that the court improperly allocated the burden of proof. The assignment of error is without merit.

IV. Standard of Law.

. . . . The crux of appellants' claim is that the court should have focused on the fair market value of Herrig's services to Cookies rather than on the success Cookies achieved as a result of Herrig's actions.

We agree with appellants' contention that corporate profitability should not be the sole criteria by which to test the fairness and reasonableness of Herrig's fees. . . . [H]owever, we cannot agree with appellants' assertion that Herrig's services were either unfairly priced or inconsistent with Cookies corporate interest.

There can be no serious dispute that the four agreements in issue—for exclusive distributorship, taco sauce royalty, warehousing, and consulting fees—have all benefited Cookies, as demonstrated by its financial success. Even if we assume Cookies could have procured similar services from other vendors at lower costs, we are not convinced that Herrig's fees were therefore unreasonable or exorbitant. Like the district court, we are not persuaded by appellants' expert testimony that Cookies' sales and profits would have been the same under agreements with other vendors. As Cookies' board noted prior to Herrig's takeover, he was the driving force in the corporation's success. Even plaintiffs' expert acknowledged that Herrig has done the work of at least five people—production supervisor, advertising specialist, warehouseman, broker, and salesman. While eschewing the lack of internal control, for accounting purposes, that such centralized authority may produce, the expert conceded that Herrig may in fact be underpaid for all he has accomplished. We believe the board properly considered this source of Cookies' success when it entered these transactions, as did the district court when it reviewed them.

* * * *

While both Iowa's statutes and case law impose a duty of disclosure on interested directors who engage in self-dealing, neither has delineated what information must be disclosed, or to whom. [*Citations omitted.*] While these cases strongly encourage directors to make the fullest possible disclosure of pertinent facts to persons responsible for making informed decisions, they also suggest the court must look to the particular facts of each case to determine whether a director has violated the duty of disclosure.

Examining Herrig's conduct under this duty of disclosure, we find no support for plaintiffs' assertion that Herrig owed the minority shareholders a duty to disclose *any* information before the board executed the exclusive distributorship, royalty, warehousing, or consultant fee agreements. These actions comprise management activity, and our statutes place the duty of managing the affairs of the corporation on the board of directors, not the shareholders. *See* Iowa Code § 496A.34 (1987). Because the shareholders had no role in making decisions concerning these agreements, we hold that Herrig owed these share-holders no duty to disclose facts concerning any aspect of these agreements before the board entered or extended them. . . .

. . . [T]he record before us aptly demonstrates that all members of Cookies' board were well aware of Herrig's dual ownership in Lakes and Speed's. We are unaware of any authority supporting plaintiffs' contention that Herrig was obligated to disclose to Cookies' board or shareholders the extent of his profits resulting from these distribution and warehousing agreements; nevertheless, the exclusive distribution agreement with Lakes authorized the board to ascertain that information had it so desired. Appellants cannot reasonably claim that Herrig owed Cookies a duty to render such services at no profit to himself or his companies. Having found that the compensation he received from these agreements was fair and reasonable, we are convinced that Herrig furnished sufficient pertinent information to Cookies' board to enable it to make prudent decisions concerning the contracts.

* * * *

AFFIRMED.

All Justices concur except Schultz, J., who dissents.

SCHULTZ, J. (dissenting)

My quarrel with the majority opinion is not with its interpretation of the law, but with its application of the law to the facts. I would reverse the trial court's holding.

* * * *

In the present case, Herrig gained control of the corporation by buying a majority of the stock. His first act was to replace all of the board of directors except one, an employee of the company. From that time on, he engaged in a course of self-dealing and refused to cooperate or comply with the requests of the minority stockholders. He renewed his exclusive distributing contract, increased commissions for freight and advertising expenses, additional storage cost and his own salary, plus paid himself a royalty for taco sauce and instigated a consultation fee for himself. It was Herrig's burden to demonstrate that all of his self-dealing transactions were fair to the company.

Much of Herrig's evidence concerned the tremendous success of the company. I believe that the trial court and the majority opinion have been so enthralled by the success of the company that they have failed to examine whether these matters of self-dealing were fair to the stockholders. While much credit is due to Herrig for the success of the company, this does not mean that these transactions were fair to the company.

I believe that Herrig failed on his burden of proof by what he did not show. He did not produce evidence of the local going rate for distribution contracts or storage fees outside of a very limited amount of self-serving testimony. He simply did not show the fair market value of his services or expense for freight, advertising and storage cost. He did not show that his taco sauce royalty was fair. This was his burden. He cannot succeed on it by merely showing the success of the company.

The shareholders, on the other hand . . . have put forth convincing testimony that Herrig has been grossly over compensated for his services based on their fair market value. Appellant's expert witness, a CPA, performed an analysis to show what the company would have earned if it had hired a $65,000 a year executive officer, paid a marketing supervisor and an advertising agency a commission of five percent of the sales each, built a new warehouse and hired a warehouseman. It was compared with what the company actually did make under Herrig's management. . . . In 1985 alone, the company's income would have doubled what it actually made were these changes made. The evidence clearly shows that the fair market value of those services is considerably less than what Herrig actually has been paid.

Similarly, appellant's food broker expert witness testified that for $110,865, what the CPA analysis stated was the fair market value for brokerage services, his company would have provided all of the services that Herrig had performed. The company actually paid $730,637 for the services, a difference of $620,000 in one year.

. . . I believe the majority was dazzled by the tales of Herrig's efforts and Cookies' success in these difficult economic times. In the process, however, it is forgotten that Herrig owes a fiduciary duty to the corporation to deal fairly and reasonably with it in his self-dealing transactions. Herrig is not entitled to skim off the majority of the profits through self-dealing transactions unless they are fair to the minority stockholders. At trial, he failed to prove how his charges were in line with what the company could have gotten on the open market. Because I cannot ignore this inequity to the company and its shareholders, I must respectfully dissent.

Benihana of Tokyo, Inc. v. Benihana, Inc.

906 A.2d 114 (Del. 2006)

BERGER, J:

In this appeal, we consider whether Benihana, Inc. was authorized to issue $20 million in preferred stock and whether Benihana's board of directors acted properly in approving the transaction. . . .

Rocky Aoki founded Benihana of Tokyo, Inc. (BOT), and its subsidiary, Benihana, which own and operate Benihana restaurants in the United States and other countries. Aoki owned 100% of BOT until 1998, when he pled guilty to insider trading charges. In order to avoid licensing problems created by his status as a convicted felon, Aoki transferred his stock to the Benihana Protective Trust. The trustees of the Trust were Aoki's three children (Kana Aoki Nootenboom, Kyle Aoki and Kevin Aoki) and Darwin Dornbush (who was then the family's attorney, a Benihana director, and, effectively, the company's general counsel).

Benihana, a Delaware corporation, has two classes of common stock. There are approximately 6 million shares of Class A common stock outstanding. Each share has 1/10 vote and the holders of Class A common are entitled to elect 25% of the directors. There are approximately 3 million shares of Common stock outstanding. Each share of Common has one vote and the holders of Common stock are entitled to elect the remaining 75% of Benihana's directors. Before the transaction at issue, BOT owned 50.9% of the Common stock and 2% of the Class A stock. . . .

In 2003, shortly after Aoki married Keiko Aoki, conflicts arose between Aoki and his children. In August, the children were upset to learn that Aoki had changed his will to give Keiko control over BOT. Joel Schwartz, Benihana's president and chief executive officer, also was concerned about this change in control. He discussed the situation with Dornbush, and they briefly considered various options, including the issuance of sufficient Class A stock to trigger a provision in the certificate of incorporation that would allow the Common and Class A to vote together for 75% of the directors.

The Aoki family's turmoil came at a time when Benihana also was facing challenges. Many of its restaurants were old and outmoded. Benihana hired WD Partners to evaluate its facilities and to plan and design appropriate renovations. The resulting Construction and Renovation Plan anticipated that the project would take at least five years and cost $56 million or more. Wachovia offered to provide Benihana a $60 million line of credit for the Construction and Renovation Plan, but the restrictions Wachovia imposed made it unlikely that Benihana would be able to borrow the full amount. Because the Wachovia line of credit did not assure that Benihana would have the capital it needed, the company retained Morgan Joseph & Co. to develop other financing options.

On January 9, 2004, after evaluating Benihana's financial situation and needs, Fred Joseph, of Morgan Joseph, met with Schwartz, Dornbush and John E. Abdo, the board's executive committee. Joseph expressed concern that Benihana would not have sufficient available capital to complete the Construction and Renovation Plan and pursue appropriate acquisitions. Benihana was conservatively leveraged, and Joseph discussed various financing alternatives, including bank debt, high yield debt, convertible debt or preferred stock, equity and sale/leaseback options.

The full board met with Joseph on January 29, 2004. He reviewed all the financing alternatives that he had discussed with the executive committee, and recommended that Benihana issue convertible preferred stock. Joseph explained that the preferred stock would provide the funds needed for the Construction and Renovation Plan and also put the company in a better negotiating position if it sought additional financing from Wachovia.

Joseph gave the directors a board book, marked "Confidential," containing an analysis of the proposed stock issuance (the Transaction). The book included, among others, the following anticipated terms: (i) issuance of $20,000,000 of preferred stock, convertible into Common stock; (ii) dividend of 6% +/– 0.5%; (iii) conversion premium of 20% +/– 2.5%; (iv) buyer's approval required for material corporate transactions; and (v) one to two board seats to the buyer. At trial, Joseph testified that the terms had been chosen by looking at comparable stock issuances and analyzing the Morgan Joseph proposal under a theoretical model.

The board met again on February 17, 2004, to review the terms of the Transaction. The directors discussed Benihana's preferences and Joseph predicted what a buyer likely would expect or require. . . . . [T]he board understood that the preferred terms were akin to a "wish list."

Shortly after the February meeting, Abdo contacted Joseph and told him that BFC Financial Corporation was interested in buying the new convertible stock.[5] In April 2005, Joseph sent BFC a private placement memorandum. Abdo negotiated with Joseph for several weeks.[6] They agreed to the Transaction on the following basic terms: (i) $20 million issuance in two tranches of $10 million each, with the second tranche to be issued one to three years after the first; (ii) BFC obtained one seat on the board, and one additional seat if Benihana failed to pay dividends for two consecutive quarters; (iii) BFC obtained preemptive rights on any new voting securities; (iv) 5% dividend; (v) 15% conversion premium; (vi) BFC had the right to force Benihana to redeem the preferred stock in full after ten years; and (vii) the stock would have immediate "as if converted" voting rights. Joseph testified that he was satisfied with the negotiations, as he had obtained what he wanted with respect to the most important points.

On April 22, 2004, Abdo sent a memorandum to Dornbush, Schwartz and Joseph, listing the agreed terms of the Transaction. He did not send the memorandum to any other members of the Benihana board. Schwartz did tell Becker, Sturges, Sano, and possibly Pine that BFC was the potential buyer. At its next meeting, held on May 6, 2004, the entire board was officially informed of BFC's involvement in the Transaction. Abdo made a presentation on behalf of BFC and then left the meeting. Joseph distributed an updated board book, which explained that Abdo had approached Morgan Joseph on behalf of BFC, and included the negotiated terms. The trial court found that the board was not informed that Abdo had negotiated the deal on behalf of BFC. But the board did know that Abdo was a principal of BFC. After discussion, the board reviewed and approved the Transaction, subject to the receipt of a fairness opinion.

On May 18, 2004, after he learned that Morgan Joseph was providing a fairness opinion, Schwartz publicly announced the stock issuance. Two days later, Aoki's counsel sent a letter asking the board to abandon the Transaction and pursue other, more favorable, financing alternatives. The letter expressed concern about the directors' conflicts, the dilutive effect of the stock issuance, and its "questionable legality." Schwartz gave copies of the letter to the directors at the May 20 board meeting, and Dornbush advised that he did not believe that Aoki's concerns had merit. Joseph and another Morgan Joseph representative

---

[5] BFC, a publicly traded Florida corporation, is a holding company for several investments. Abdo is a director and vice chairman. He owns 30% of BFC's stock.

[6] At the outset of the negotiations, Joseph agreed not to shop the Transaction to any other potential investor for a limited period of time.

then joined the meeting by telephone and opined that the Transaction was fair from a financial point of view. The board then approved the Transaction.

During the following two weeks, Benihana received three alternative financing proposals. Schwartz asked Becker, Pine and Sturges to act as an independent committee and review the first offer. The committee decided that the offer was inferior and not worth pursuing. Morgan Joseph agreed with that assessment. Schwartz referred the next two proposals to Morgan Joseph, with the same result.

On June 8, 2004, Benihana and BFC executed the Stock Purchase Agreement. On June 11, 2004, the board met and approved resolutions ratifying the execution of the Stock Purchase Agreement and authorizing the stock issuance. Schwartz then reported on the three alternative proposals that had been rejected by the ad hoc committee and Morgan Joseph. On July 2, 2004, BOT filed this action against all of Benihana's directors, except Kevin Aoki, alleging breaches of fiduciary duties; and against BFC, alleging that it aided and abetted the fiduciary violations. Three months later, as the parties were filing their pre-trial briefs, the board again reviewed the Transaction. After considering the allegations in the amended complaint, the board voted once more to approve it. . . .

* * * *

Even if the Benihana board had the power to issue the disputed stock, BOT maintains that the trial court erred in finding that it acted properly in approving the Transaction. Specifically, BOT argues that the Court of Chancery erred: (1) by applying 8 Del. C. § 144(a)(1), because the board did not know all material facts before it approved the Transaction; (2) by applying the business judgment rule, because Abdo breached his fiduciary duties; and (3) by finding that the board's primary purpose in approving the Transaction was not to dilute BOT's voting power.

A. Section 144(a)(1) Approval

Section 144 of the Delaware General Corporation Law provides a safe harbor for interested transactions, like this one, if "[t]he material facts as to the director's . . . relationship or interest and as to the contract or transaction are disclosed or are known to the board of directors . . . and the board . . . in good faith authorizes the contract or transaction by the affirmative votes of a majority of the disinterested directors. . . ." After approval by disinterested directors, courts review the interested transaction under the business judgment rule, which "is a presumption that in making a business decision, the directors of a corporation acted on an informed basis, in good faith and in the honest belief that the action taken was in the best interest of the company."

BOT argues that § 144(a)(1) is inapplicable because, when they approved the Transaction, the disinterested directors did not know that Abdo had negotiated the terms for BFC. Abdo's role as negotiator is material, according to BOT, because Abdo had been given the confidential term sheet prepared by Joseph and knew which of those terms Benihana was prepared to give up during negotiations. We agree that the board needed to know about Abdo's involvement in order to make an informed decision. The record clearly establishes, however, that the board possessed that material information when it approved the Transaction on May 6, 2004 and May 20, 2004.

Shortly before the May 6 meeting, Schwartz told Becker, Sturges and Sano that BFC was the proposed buyer. Then, at the meeting, Abdo made the presentation on behalf of BFC. Joseph's board book also explained that Abdo had made the initial contact that precipitated the negotiations. The board members knew that Abdo is a director, vice-chairman, and one of two people who control BFC. Thus, although no one ever said, "Abdo negotiated this deal for BFC," the directors understood that he was BFC's representative in the Transaction. As Pine testified, "whoever actually did the negotiating, [Abdo] as a principal would have to agree to it. So whether he sat in the room and negotiated it or he sat somewhere else and was brought the results of someone else's negotiation, he was the ultimate decision-maker." 15 Accordingly, we conclude that the disinterested directors possessed all the material information on Abdo's interest in the Transaction, and their approval at the May 6 and May 20 board meetings satisfies § 144(a)(1).

B. Abdo's alleged fiduciary violation

BOT next argues that the Court of Chancery should have reviewed the Transaction under an entire fairness standard because Abdo breached his duty of loyalty when he used Benihana's confidential information to negotiate on behalf of BFC. This argument starts with a flawed premise. The record does not support BOT's contention that Abdo used any confidential information against Benihana. Even without Joseph's comments at the February 17 board meeting, Abdo knew the terms a buyer could expect to obtain in a deal like this. Moreover, as the trial court found, "the negotiations involved give and take on a number of points" and Benihana "ended up where [it] wanted to be" for the most important terms. Abdo did not set the terms of the deal; he did not deceive the board; and he did not dominate or control the other directors' approval of the Transaction. In short, the record does not support the claim that Abdo breached his duty of loyalty.

C. Dilution of BOT's voting power

Finally, BOT argues that the board's primary purpose in approving the Transaction was to dilute BOT's voting control. BOT points out that Schwartz was concerned about BOT's control in 2003 and even discussed with Dornbush the possibility of issuing a huge number of Class A shares. Then, despite the availability of other financing options, the board decided on a stock issuance, and agreed to give BFC "as if converted" voting rights. According to BOT, the trial court overlooked this powerful evidence of the board's improper purpose.

It is settled law that, "corporate action . . . may not be taken for the sole or primary purpose of entrenchment." Here, however, the trial court found that "the primary purpose of the . . . Transaction was to provide what the directors subjectively believed to be the best financing vehicle available for securing the necessary funds to pursue the agreed upon Construction and Renovation Plan for the Benihana restaurants." . . . .

Conclusion

Based on the foregoing, the judgment of the Court of Chancery is affirmed.

Marciano v. Nakash

535 A.2d 400 (Del. 1987)

WALSH, J.:

This is an appeal from a decision of the Court of Chancery which validated a claim in liquidation of Gasoline, Ltd. ("Gasoline"), a Delaware corporation, placed in custodial status pursuant to 8 Del. C. § 226 by reason of a deadlock among its board of directors. Fifty percent of Gasoline is owned by Ari, Joe, and Ralph Nakash (the "Nakashes") and fifty percent by Georges, Maurice, Armand and Paul Marciano (the "Marcianos"). The Vice Chancellor ruled that $2.5 million in loans made by the Nakashes faction to Gasoline were valid and enforceable debts of the corporation, notwithstanding their origin in self-dealing transactions. The Marcianos argue that the disputed debt is voidable as a matter of law but, in any event, the Nakashes failed to meet their burden of establishing full fairness. We conclude that the Vice Chancellor applied the proper standard for review of self-dealing transactions and the finding of full fairness is supported by the record. Accordingly, we affirm.

I

The factual basis underlying the contested loans was fully developed in the Court of Chancery. The liquidation proceeding marked the end of a joint venture launched in 1984 by the Marcianos and the Nakashes to market designer jeans and sportswear. Through a solely owned corporation called Guess? Inc. ("Guess"), the California based Marcianos had been engaged in the design and distribution of stylized jeans for several years. In 1983 they decided to form a separate division to market copies of Guess creations in a broader retail market. In order to secure financing and broaden market exposure the Marcianos entered into negotiations with the New York based Nakash brothers, the owners of Jordache Enterprises, Inc. a leading manufacturer of jeans. Ultimately, it was agreed that the Nakashes would receive fifty percent of the stock of Guess for a consideration of $4.7 million. As a result, the three Nakash brothers joined three of the Marcianos on the Guess board of directors.

Similarly, when Gasoline was formed, stock ownership and board composition was shared equally by the two families. Although corporate control and direction were equally divided, from an operational standpoint Gasoline functioned in New York under the Nakashes' operational guidance while the parent, Guess, continued under the primary attention of the Marcianos. Differences between the two factions quickly surfaced with resulting deadlocks at the director level of both Guess and Gasoline. The Marcianos filed an action, partly derivative, against Guess and the Nakashes in California followed by the Delaware proceeding in which the Marcianos sought the appointment of a custodian for Gasoline in addition to asserting derivative claims for diversion of corporate opportunities and assets arising out of the Nakashes' operation of Gasoline. Ultimately, the derivative aspect of the Delaware action was stayed in favor of the California proceedings and the Court of Chancery, after a court-ordered shareholder's meeting failed to resolve the director deadlock, appointed a custodian whose power was limited to resolving deadlocks on the Gasoline board.

The custodial arrangement failed to resolve the underlying policy differences between the two factions and neither group appeared willing to invest additional funds or provide guarantees to permit Gasoline to function as a viable commercial enterprise. In early 1987 the custodian advised the Court of Chancery that because of a lack of financing Gasoline had no prospects of continuation and recommended liquidation. A court-approved plan of liquidation authorized the custodian to sell the assets of Gasoline (with both the Marcianos and the Nakashes permitted to bid), pay all valid debts of the corporation and distribute the net proceeds to the shareholders. The determination of those debts, in particular the loan claims asserted by the Nakashes, was sharply disputed in the Court of Chancery and is the focus of this appeal.

. . . . Prior to March, 1986, Gasoline had secured the necessary financing to support its inventory purchases from the Israel Discount Bank in New York. The bank advanced funds at one percent above prime rate secured by Gasoline's accounts receivable and the Nakashes' personal guarantee. Although requested to do so, the Marcianos were unwilling to participate in loan guarantees because of their dissatisfaction with the Nakashes' management. In response, the Nakashes withdrew their guarantees causing the Israel Discount Bank to terminate its outstanding loan of $1.6 million.

Without consulting the Marcianos, the Nakashes advanced approximately $2.3 million of their personal funds to Gasoline to enable the corporation to pay outstanding bills and acquire inventory. In June, 1986, the Nakashes arranged for U.F. Factors, an entity owned by them, to assume their personal loans and become Gasoline's lender. U.F. Factors charged interest at one percent over prime to which the Nakashes added one percent for their personal guarantees of the U.F. Factors loan. As of April 24, 1987, Gasoline's debt to U.F. Factors amounted to $2,575,000 of which $25,000 represented the Nakashes' guarantee fee. . . .

In November, 1986, the Nakashes had replaced the U.F. Factors loan, secured by a series of promissory notes executed by Gasoline, with a line of credit collateralized by Gasoline's assets including trademarks and copyrights. This action took place without the knowledge or consent of the custodian and was subsequently rescinded by the Nakashes. At the time of the court-ordered sale of assets, the Nakashes and their entities were general creditors of Gasoline. If allowed in full the Nakashes' claim will exhaust Gasoline's assets, leaving nothing for its shareholders.[1]

The parties agree that the loans made by the Nakashes to Gasoline were interested transactions. The Nakashes as officers of Gasoline executed the various documents which supported the loans and at the same time guaranteed those loans extended through their wholly owned entities. It is also not disputed that, given the control deadlock, the questioned transactions did not receive majority approval of Gasoline's directors or shareholders. The Marcianos argue

---

[1] The Nakashes used their $2.5 million claim as the basis for their liquidation bid ($1,000,101) for Gasoline's non-cash assets.

that the loan transaction is voidable at the option of the corporation notwithstanding its fairness or the good faith of its participants. A review of this contention, rejected by the Court of Chancery, requires analysis of the concept of director self-dealing under Delaware law.

II

It is a long-established principle of Delaware corporate law that the fiduciary relationship between directors and the corporation imposes fundamental limitations on the extent to which a director may benefit from dealings with the corporation he serves. *Guth v. Loft, Inc., Del. Supr.,* 23 Del. Ch. 255, 5 A.2d 503 (1939). Thus, the "voting [for] and taking" of compensation may be deemed "constructively fraudulent" in the absence of shareholder ratification, or statutory or bylaw authorization. *Cahall v. Lofland, Del. Ch.,* 12 Del. Ch. 299, 114 A. 224, 232 (1921). . . .

* * * *

The principle of per se voidability for interested transactions, which is sometimes characterized as the common law rule, was significantly ameliorated by the 1967 enactment of Section 144 of the Delaware General Corporation Law. The Marcianos argue that section 144(a) provides the only basis for immunizing self-interested transactions and since none of the statute's component tests are satisfied the stricture of the common law per se rule applies. The Vice Chancellor agreed that the disputed loans did not withstand a section 144(a) analysis but ruled that the common law rule did not invalidate transactions determined to be intrinsically fair. We agree that section 144(a) does not provide the only validation standard for interested transactions.

It overstates the common law rule to conclude that relationship, alone, is the controlling factor in interested transactions. . . .

In other Delaware cases, decided before the enactment of section 144, interested director transactions were deemed voidable only after an examination of the fairness of a particular transaction *vis-a-vis* the nonparticipating shareholders and a determination of whether the disputed conduct received the approval of a noninterested majority of directors or shareholders. [*Citations omitted*].

The Marcianos view compliance with section 144 as the sole basis for avoiding the per se rule of voidability. The Court of Chancery rejected this contention and we agree that it is not consonant with Delaware corporate law. . . .

If section 144 validation of interested director transactions is not deemed exclusive, as *Fliegler* [*v. Lawrence*, 361 A.2d 218 (Del. Supr. 1976)] clearly holds, the continued viability of the intrinsic fairness test is mandated not only by fact situations, such as here present, where shareholder deadlock prevents ratification but also where shareholder control by interested directors precludes independent review. Indeed, if an independent committee of the board, contemplated by section 144(a)(1) is unavailable, the sole forum for demonstrating intrinsic fairness may be a judicial one. *See Merritt v. Colonial Foods, Inc., Del. Ch.,* 505 A.2d 757, 764 (1986). In such situations the intrinsic fairness test furnishes the substantive standard against which the evidential burden of the interested directors is applied. It is this burden which was addressed by this Court in *Weinberger v. UOP, Inc., Del. Supr.,* 457 A.2d 701 (1983):

> When directors of a Delaware corporation are on both sides of a transaction, they are required to demonstrate their utmost good faith and the most scrupulous inherent fairness of the bargain.
>
> * * * *
>
> The requirement of fairness is unflinching in its demand that where one stands on both sides of a transaction, he has the burden of establishing its entire fairness, sufficient to pass the test of careful scrutiny by the courts.

Id. at 710.

This case illustrates the limitation inherent in viewing section 144 as the touchstone for testing interested director transactions. Because of the shareholder deadlock, even if the Nakashes had attempted to invoke section 144, it was realistically unavailable. The ratification process contemplated by section 144 presupposes the functioning of corporate constituencies capable of providing assents. Just as the statute cannot "sanction unfairness" neither can it invalidate fairness if, upon judicial review, the transaction withstands close scrutiny of its intrinsic elements.

III

On the issue of intrinsic fairness, the Court of Chancery concluded that the "U.F. Factors loans compared favorably with the terms available from unrelated lenders" and that the need for external financing had been clearly demonstrated. . . .

. . . . It suffices to note that throughout 1985 and 1986, Gasoline was able to function only through cash advances from, and loans obtained by, the

Nakashes, first through the Israel Discount Bank and later through U.F. Factors. During this period the evidence reflects the continued threat of bank overdrafts and inability to pay for purchases, particularly imported finished goods.

A finding of fairness is particularly appropriate in this case because the evidence indicates that the loans were made by the Nakashes with the *bona fide* intention of assisting Gasoline's efforts to remain in business. Directors who advance funds to a corporation in such circumstances do not forfeit their claims as creditors merely because of relationship. *New York Stock Exchange v. Pickard & Co., Inc., Del. Ch.,* 296 A.2d 143, 149 (1972). Further, in arranging for the loan, the interested directors were not depriving the corporation of a business opportunity but were instead providing a benefit for the corporation which was unavailable elsewhere.

* * * *

IV

Apart from the question of whether the corporation was disadvantaged by the terms of the loan transactions, the Marcianos contend, as a separate basis for disallowance of the loans, that the Nakashes were guilty of unfair dealing. The Marcianos' argument of unfair dealing is constructed upon the dual test of fairness for interested director transaction fashioned by this Court in *Weinberger,* 457 A.2d 701. Although the Vice Chancellor expressed doubt that the *Weinberger* standard is applicable to interested loan transactions, the Court concluded, that in any event, the unfair dealing claim would survive liquidation and be assertable in the ongoing derivative actions.

We agree with the Vice Chancellor that a *Weinberger* "fair dealing" analysis is not applicable in this case. . . .

* * * *

We hold, therefore, that the Court of Chancery properly applied the intrinsic fairness test in determining the validity of the interested director transactions and its finding of full fairness is clearly supported by the record. Accordingly, the decision is AFFIRMED.

NOTE ON AIDING AND ABETTING

There are cases that have found a defendant may be liable in the breach of a fiduciary duty, even though the defendant itself is not a fiduciary. For example, a defendant may be held liable for aiding and abetting a breach of the duty of loyalty, even though the defendant did not owe the plaintiff an independent fiduciary duty. *American Master Lease LLC v. Idanta Partners, Ltd.*, 225 Cal. App. 4th 1451 (2014). In this case the court distinguished the liability that might arise from aiding and abetting a breach of fiduciary duty from the liability that would arise under a claim of civil conspiracy to breach that duty. In a claim for aiding and abetting, the focus is on "... whether a defendant knowingly gave 'substantial assistance' to someone who performed wrongful conduct, not on whether the defendant agreed to join the wrongful conduct." *Id.*, citing *Berg & Berg Enterprises, LLC v. Sherwood Partners, Inc.* 131 Cal.App.4th 802 (2005). The court quoted *Neilson v. Union Bank of California, N.A.* (290 F.Supp.2d 1101 (2003)), to explain that, unlike conspiracy, "... the act of aiding and abetting is distinct from the primary violation; liability attaches because the aider and abettor behaves in a manner that enables the primary violator to commit the underlying tort. ... Because aiders and abettors do not agree to commit, and are not held liable as joint tortfeasors for committing, the underlying tort, it is not necessary that they owe plaintiff the same duty as the primary violator." Finally, the court emphasized that causation is an essential element of an aiding and abetting claim, i.e., the plaintiff must show that the aider and abettor provided assistance that was a substantial factor in causing the harm suffered." *Id.* at 1176.

SECTION II: The Corporate Opportunity Doctrine

An important limitation that arises under the duty of loyalty is known as the "Corporate Opportunity Doctrine." The Corporate Opportunity Doctrine is not a separate duty. Rather, it is a subset of the duty of loyalty. In fact, most issues that arise under this doctrine could be addressed by a traditional duty of loyalty analysis. Instead, however, specific rules have developed to deal with these specific types of problems. The Corporate Opportunity Doctrine stands for the principal that a fiduciary (an officer or director) of a corporation may not take, for personal gain, an opportunity (like a business venture or a new opportunity or discovery) in which the firm has a property right, and use it for his or her own advantage without first offering it to the corporation.

The Corporate Opportunity Doctrine generally applies to a corporation's officers and board members (but not its shareholders, unless those shareholders also hold another position with the firm) as well as certain other individuals who have a fiduciary (or fiduciary-like) relationship with the corporation (such as a lawyer or a consultant). Note that agents have similar duties to their principals that would cover the corporation's employees as well, but under agency law, not corporate law. We have also encountered some of the principles that arise under this doctrine in partnership law. (*See Meinhard v. Salmon, supra.*)

There are several definitions of a corporate opportunity that have developed over the years. Most states use some type of hybrid test that typically includes a blend of other distinct tests. Almost all tests include some question of whether the opportunity is something that is consistent with the corporation's current, or anticipated future, business, and whether it is something that the corporation has the financial resources to pursue. An early definition of a corporate opportunity was something in which the corporation had an "interest," an "expectancy" or a "necessity." An "interest" is something in which the corporation has a preexisting contractual right. An "expectancy" is something to which the corporation did not necessarily have a legal right, but, given the other contractual dealings of the corporation, there was a reasonable expectancy that the opportunity would be offered to the corporation (e.g., a lease renewal). A "necessity" is something that the corporation needs in order to stay in business (e.g., certain raw materials necessary to manufacture a product).

Line of Business Test and Fairness Test

Because the above definitions were relatively narrow, an additional test developed known as the "line of business" test. The line of business test was articulated in the 1939 case of *Guth v. Loft,* in which the court explained that a corporate opportunity would include activities "as to which . . . [the corporation] has fundamental knowledge, practical experience and ability to pursue, which, logically and naturally, . . . [are] adaptable to its business [taking into account the corporation's] . . . financial position, . . . reasonable needs and aspirations for expansion. . . ." *Guth v. Loft,* 5 A.2d 503, 514 (Del. 1939). The idea behind this test is that if the opportunity falls within the corporation's business or its prospective business, it should still be deemed to be a corporate opportunity. A corporate opportunity under this test includes not just where the business is right now and what it is doing right now, but also where the firm is headed in the future. Most hybrid tests include the "line of business" concept and some aspect of the interest, expectancy, and necessity tests.

Some states (although not California or Delaware) employ a "fairness test" to evaluate whether something is a corporate opportunity. Under the fairness test, one would need to determine whether the officer or director taking the opportunity would violate *standards of what is fair and equitable by corporate standards.*

Common Defenses

There are also a variety of defenses to a determination that something is a corporate opportunity. In other words, even if an opportunity would fall under one of the above "tests," it might still be found not to qualify as a corporate opportunity if a valid defense is present. As a result, someone who takes the opportunity would not be liable if they can show that the corporation was not able to take advantage of the opportunity, so it was not truly a "corporate opportunity."

One common defense is the "incapacity" defense. The incapacity defense applies in circumstances in which a corporation is not able to take advantage of an opportunity. A corporation might be subject to this defense if it could not take advantage of the opportunity because of legal restrictions such as antitrust laws, contractual restrictions in a loan agreement, or if the corporation is in bankruptcy and thus subject to restrictions on its business dealings. A corporation might also not have been able to take advantage of an opportunity because of practical restrictions—for example, if the corporation did not have the financial resources to purchase a particular opportunity; if the holder of the opportunity refused to deal with the corporation; or if the corporation lacked the skills to engage in the opportunity. The incapacity defense would also apply if a corporation's charter prohibited it from engaging in an activity involved in the opportunity.

Another common defense, known as the "source" defense, arises when an opportunity is presented to someone, not because of their corporate position, but because of their personal skills, attributes or expertise. In such circumstances, an opportunity which otherwise might qualify as a corporate opportunity might be deemed not to be because the opportunity is determined to belong to the individual, not to the corporation.

Any time a corporate opportunity exists, a person bound by the doctrine who wishes to take advantage of the opportunity must fully disclose the opportunity and his or her interest in the opportunity to the board of directors. The board of directors has, what amounts to, a right of first refusal, on the opportunity. If the board properly rejects the opportunity, following a full disclosure, the individual may take the opportunity for him or herself. Note that in order for a disclosure to be effective, one may not just casually inquire whether the firm is interested in the opportunity. The opportunity AND the person's interest in taking the opportunity must both be disclosed. If the board does not properly reject the opportunity, and the individual takes the opportunity, that "breach" might still be "cleansed" by disclosure to, and approval by, the shareholders or by showing that the transaction was fair.

A violation of the corporate opportunity doctrine is subject to various equitable remedies, such as constructive trust, so that the benefits that are received in violation of the doctrine are held "in trust" for the corporation. Of course, any violation may also be subject to damages.

Note that there is not liability (at least under the corporate opportunity doctrine) for possessing or knowing about a corporate opportunity. However, one could imagine a situation in which failure to exercise an opportunity on behalf of the corporation, or failure to inform the corporation about a desirable opportunity, might constitute a violation of the duty of care or the duty of loyalty, depending upon the specific facts.

Northeast Harbor Golf Club v. Harris

661 A.2d 1146, 1995 Me. LEXIS 158 (Me. 1995)

ROBERTS, J.:

Northeast Harbor Golf Club, Inc., appeals from a judgment entered in the Superior Court (Hancock County, Atwood, J.) following a nonjury trial. The Club maintains that the trial court erred in finding that Nancy Harris did not breach her fiduciary duty as president of the Club by purchasing and developing property abutting the golf course. Because we today adopt principles different from those applied by the trial court in determining that Harris's activities did not constitute a breach of the corporate opportunity doctrine, we vacate the judgment.

I. The Facts

Nancy Harris was the president of the Northeast Harbor Golf Club, a Maine corporation, from 1971 until she was asked to resign in 1990. The Club also had a board of directors that was responsible for making or approving significant policy decisions. The Club's only major asset was a golf course in Mount Desert. During Harris's tenure as president, the board occasionally discussed the possibility of developing some of the Club's real estate in order to raise money. Although Harris was generally in favor of tasteful development, the board always "shied away" from that type of activity.

In 1979, Robert Suminsby informed Harris that he was the listing broker for the Gilpin property, which comprised three noncontiguous parcels located among the fairways of the golf course. The property included an unused right-of-way on which the Club's parking lot and clubhouse were located. It was also encumbered by an easement in favor of the Club allowing foot traffic from the green of one hole to the next tee. Suminsby testified that he contacted Harris because she was the president of the Club and he believed that the Club would be interested in buying the property in order to prevent development.

Harris immediately agreed to purchase the Gilpin property in her own name for the asking price of $45,000. She did not disclose her plans to purchase the property to the Club's board prior to the purchase. She informed the board at its annual August meeting that she had purchased the property, that she intended to hold it in her own name, and that the Club would be "protected." The board took no action in response to the Harris purchase. She testified that at the time of the purchase she had no plans to develop the property and that no such plans took shape until 1988.

In 1984, while playing golf with the postmaster of Northeast Harbor, Harris learned that a parcel of land owned by the heirs of the Smallidge family might be available for purchase. The Smallidge parcel was surrounded on three sides by the golf course and on the fourth side by a house lot. It had no access to the road. With the ultimate goal of acquiring the property, Harris instructed her lawyer to locate the Smallidge heirs. Harris testified that she told a number of individual board members about her attempt to acquire the Smallidge parcel. At a board meeting in August 1985, Harris formally disclosed to the board that she had purchased the Smallidge property.[1] The minutes of that meeting show that she told the board she had no present plans to develop the Smallidge parcel. Harris testified that at the time of the purchase of the Smallidge property she nonetheless thought it might be nice to have some houses there. Again, the board took no formal action as a result of Harris's purchase. Harris acquired the Smallidge property from ten heirs, paying a total of $60,000. In 1990, Harris paid $275,000 for the lot and building separating the Smallidge parcel from the road in order to gain access to the otherwise landlocked parcel.

The trial court expressly found that the Club would have been unable to purchase either the Gilpin or Smallidge properties for itself, relying on testimony that the Club continually experienced financial difficulties, operated annually at a deficit, and depended on contributions from the directors to pay its bills. On the other hand, there was evidence that the Club had occasionally engaged in successful fund-raising, including a two-year period shortly after the Gilpin

1 In fact, it appears that Harris did not take title to the property until October 26, 1985. She had only signed a purchase and sale agreement at the time of the August board meeting.

purchase during which the Club raised $115,000. The Club had $90,000 in a capital investment fund at the time of the Smallidge purchase.

. . . . At the time the Club filed this suit, the property was divided into 11 lots, some owned by Harris and others by her children who are also defendants in this case. Harris estimated the value of all the real estate at the time of the trial to be $1,550,000.

In 1988, Harris, who was still president of the Club, and her children began the process of obtaining approval for a five-lot subdivision known as Bushwood on the lower Gilpin property. Even when the board learned of the proposed subdivision, a majority failed to take any action. . . .

After Harris's plans to develop Bushwood became apparent, the board grew increasingly divided concerning the propriety of development near the golf course. At least two directors, Henri Agnese and Nick Ludington, testified that they trusted Harris to act in the best interests of the Club and that they had no problem with the development plans for Bushwood. Other directors disagreed.

In particular, John Schafer, a Washington, D.C., lawyer and long-time member of the board, took issue with Harris's conduct. He testified that he had relied on Harris's representations at the time she acquired the properties that she would not develop them. According to Schafer, matters came to a head in August 1990 when a number of directors concluded that Harris's development plans irreconcilably conflicted with the Club's interests. As a result, Schafer and two other directors asked Harris to resign as president. In April 1991, after a substantial change in the board's membership, the board authorized the instant lawsuit against Harris for the breach of her fiduciary duty to act in the best interests of the corporation. The board simultaneously resolved that the proposed housing development was contrary to the best interests of the corporation.

The Club filed a complaint against Harris, her sons John and Shepard, and her daughter-in-law Melissa Harris. As amended, the complaint alleged that during her term as president Harris breached her fiduciary duty by purchasing the lots without providing notice and an opportunity for the Club to purchase the property and by subdividing the lots for future development. The Club sought an injunction to prevent development and also sought to impose a constructive trust on the property in question for the benefit of the Club.

The trial court found that Harris had not usurped a corporate opportunity because the acquisition of real estate was not in the Club's line of business. Moreover, it found that the corporation lacked the financial ability to purchase the real estate at issue. Finally, the court placed great emphasis on Harris's good faith. It noted her long and dedicated history of service to the Club, her personal oversight of the Club's growth, and her frequent financial contributions to the Club. The court found that her development activities were "generally . . . compatible with the corporation's business." This appeal followed.

II. The Corporate Opportunity Doctrine

Corporate officers and directors bear a duty of loyalty to the corporations they serve. As Justice Cardozo explained the fiduciary duty in *Meinhard v. Salmon,* 249 N.Y. 458, 164 N.E. 545, 546 (N.Y. 1928):

> A trustee is held to something stricter than the morals of the marketplace. Not honesty alone, but the punctilio of an honor the most sensitive, is then the standard of behavior. As to this there has developed a tradition that is unbending and inveterate.

Maine has embraced this "unbending and inveterate" tradition. Corporate fiduciaries in Maine must discharge their duties in good faith with a view toward furthering the interests of the corporation. They must disclose and not withhold relevant information concerning any potential conflict of interest with the corporation, and they must refrain from using their position, influence, or knowledge of the affairs of the corporation to gain personal advantage. See *Rosenthal v. Rosenthal,* 543 A.2d 348, 352 (Me. 1988); 13–A M.R.S.A. § 716 (Supp. 1994).

Despite the general acceptance of the proposition that corporate fiduciaries owe a duty of loyalty to their corporations, there has been much confusion about the specific extent of that duty when, as here, it is contended that a fiduciary takes for herself a corporate opportunity. . . .

Various courts have embraced different versions of the corporate opportunity doctrine. The test applied by the trial court and embraced by Harris is generally known as the "line of business" test. The seminal case applying the line of business test is *Guth v. Loft, Inc.,* 23 Del. Ch. 255, 5 A.2d 503 (Del. 1939). In Guth, the Delaware Supreme Court adopted an intensely factual test stated in general terms as follows:

> If there is presented to a corporate officer or director a business opportunity which the corporation is financially able to undertake, is, from its nature, in the line of the corporation's business and is of practical advantage to it, is one in which the corporation has an interest or a reasonable expectancy, and, by embracing the

> opportunity, the self-interest of the officer or director will be brought into conflict with that of his corporation, the law will not permit him to seize the opportunity for himself.

Id. at 511. The "real issue" under this test is whether the opportunity "was so closely associated with the existing business activities . . . as to bring the transaction within that class of cases where the acquisition of the property would throw the corporate officer purchasing it into competition with his company." *Id.* at 513. The Delaware court described that inquiry as "a factual question to be decided by reasonable inferences from objective facts." *Id.*

The line of business test suffers from some significant weaknesses. First, the question whether a particular activity is within a corporation's line of business is conceptually difficult to answer. The facts of the instant case demonstrate that difficulty. The Club is in the business of running a golf course. It is not in the business of developing real estate. In the traditional sense, therefore, the trial court correctly observed that the opportunity in this case was not a corporate opportunity within the meaning of the Guth test. Nevertheless, the record would support a finding that the Club had made the policy judgment that development of surrounding real estate was detrimental to the best interests of the Club. The acquisition of land adjacent to the golf course for the purpose of preventing future development would have enhanced the ability of the Club to implement that policy. The record also shows that the Club had occasionally considered reversing that policy and expanding its operations to include the development of surrounding real estate. Harris's activities effectively foreclosed the Club from pursuing that option with respect to prime locations adjacent to the golf course.

Second, the Guth test includes as an element the financial ability of the corporation to take advantage of the opportunity. The court in this case relied on the Club's supposed financial incapacity as a basis for excusing Harris's conduct. Often, the injection of financial ability into the equation will unduly favor the inside director or executive who has command of the facts relating to the finances of the corporation. Reliance on financial ability will also act as a disincentive to corporate executives to solve corporate financing and other problems. In addition, the Club could have prevented development without spending $275,000 to acquire the property Harris needed to obtain access to the road.

The Massachusetts Supreme Judicial Court adopted a different test in *Durfee v. Durfee & Canning, Inc.,* 323 Mass. 187, 80 N.E.2d 522 (Mass. 1948). The

Durfee test has since come to be known as the "fairness test." According to Durfee, the

> true basis of governing doctrine rests on the unfairness in the particular circumstances of a director, whose relation to the corporation is fiduciary, taking advantage of an opportunity [for her personal profit] when the interest of the corporation justly call[s] for protection. This calls for application of ethical standards of what is fair and equitable . . . in particular sets of facts.

Id. at 529 (*quoting Ballantine on Corporations* 204–05 (rev. ed. 1946)). As with the Guth test, the Durfee test calls for a broad-ranging, intensely factual inquiry. The Durfee test suffers even more than the Guth test from a lack of principled content. It provides little or no practical guidance to the corporate officer or director seeking to measure her obligations.

The Minnesota Supreme Court elected "to combine the 'line of business' test with the 'fairness' test." *Miller v. Miller, 301 Minn.* 207, 222 N.W.2d 71, 81 (Minn. 1974). It engaged in a two-step analysis, first determining whether a particular opportunity was within the corporation's line of business, then scrutinizing "the equitable considerations existing prior to, at the time of, and following the officer's acquisition." *Id.* . . . In fact, the test adopted in Miller merely piles the uncertainty and vagueness of the fairness test on top of the weaknesses in the line of business test.

Despite the weaknesses of each of these approaches to the corporate opportunity doctrine, they nonetheless rest on a single fundamental policy. At bottom, the corporate opportunity doctrine recognizes that a corporate fiduciary should not serve both corporate and personal interests at the same time. As we observed in *Camden Land Co. v. Lewis,* 101 Me. 78, 97, 63 A. 523, 531 (1905), corporate fiduciaries "owe their whole duty to the corporation, and they are not to be permitted to act when duty conflicts with interest. They cannot serve themselves and the corporation at the same time." The various formulations of the test are merely attempts to moderate the potentially harsh consequences of strict adherence to that policy. It is important to preserve some ability for corporate fiduciaries to pursue personal business interests that present no real threat to their duty of loyalty.

III. The American Law Institute Approach

In an attempt to protect the duty of loyalty while at the same time providing long-needed clarity and guidance for corporate decision-makers, the American Law Institute has offered the most recently developed version of the corporate opportunity doctrine. PRINCIPLES OF CORPORATE GOVERNANCE § 5.05 (May 13, 1992), provides as follows:

§ 505 Taking of Corporate Opportunities by Directors or Senior Executives

(a) *General Rule.* A director [§ 1.13] or senior executive [§ 1.33] may not take advantage of a corporate opportunity unless:

(1) The director or senior executive first offers the corporate opportunity to the corporation and makes disclosure concerning the conflict of interest [§ 1.14(a)] and the corporate opportunity [§ 1.14(b)];

(2) The corporate opportunity is rejected by the corporation; and

(3) Either:

(A) The rejection of the opportunity is fair to the corporation;

(B) The opportunity is rejected in advance, following such disclosure, by disinterested directors [§ 1.15], or, in the case of a senior executive who is not a director, by a disinterested superior, in a manner that satisfies the standards of the business judgment rule [§ 4.01(c)]; or

(C) The rejection is authorized in advance or ratified, following such disclosure, by disinterested shareholders [§ 1.16], and the rejection is not equivalent to a waste of corporate assets [§ 1.42].

(b) *Definition of a Corporate Opportunity.* For purposes of this Section, a corporate opportunity means:

(1) Any opportunity to engage in a business activity of which a director or senior executive becomes aware, either:

(A) In connection with the performance of functions as a director or senior executive, or under circumstances that should reasonably lead the director or senior executive to believe that the person offering the opportunity expects it to be offered to the corporation; or

(B) Through the use of corporate information or property, if the resulting opportunity is one that the director or senior executive should reasonably be expected to believe would be of interest to the corporation; or

(2) Any opportunity to engage in a business activity of which a senior executive becomes aware and knows is closely related to a business in which the corporation is engaged or expects to engage.

(c) *Burden of Proof* A party who challenges the taking of a corporate opportunity has the burden of proof, except that if such party establishes that the requirements of Subsection (a)(3)(B) or (C) are not met, the director or the senior executive has the burden of proving that the rejection and the taking of the opportunity were fair to the corporation.

(d) *Ratification of Defective Disclosure.* A good faith but defective disclosure of the facts concerning the corporate opportunity may be cured if at any time (but no later than a reasonable time after suit is filed challenging the taking of the corporate opportunity) the original rejection of the corporate opportunity is ratified, following the required disclosure, by the board, the shareholders, or the corporate decisionmaker who initially approved the rejection of the corporate opportunity, or such decisionmaker's successor.

(e) *Special Rule Concerning Delayed Offering of Corporate Opportunities.* Relief based solely on failure to first offer an opportunity to the corporation under Subsection (a)(1) is not available if: (1) such failure resulted from a good faith belief that the business activity did not constitute a corporate opportunity, and (2) not later than a reasonable time after suit is filed challenging the taking of the corporate opportunity, the corporate opportunity is to the extent possible offered to the corporation and rejected in a manner that satisfies the standards of Subsection (a).

The central feature of the ALI test is the strict requirement of full disclosure prior to taking advantage of any corporate opportunity. *Id.*, § 5.05(a)(1). "If the opportunity is not offered to the corporation, the director or senior executive will not have satisfied § 5.05(a)." *Id.*, cmt. to § 5.05(a). The corporation must then formally reject the opportunity. *Id.*, § 505(a)(2). The ALI test is discussed at length and ultimately applied by the Oregon Supreme Court in *Klinicki v. Lundgren,* 298 Ore. 662, 695 P.2d 906 (Or. 1985). As Klinicki describes the test, "full disclosure to the appropriate corporate body is . . . an absolute condition precedent to the validity of any forthcoming rejection as well as to the availability to the director or principal senior executive of the defense of fairness." *Id.* at 920. A "good faith but defective disclosure" by the corporate officer may be ratified after the fact only by an affirmative vote of the disinterested directors or shareholders. PRINCIPLES OF CORPORATE GOVERNANCE § 5.05(d).

The ALI test defines "corporate opportunity" broadly. It includes opportunities "closely related to a business in which the corporation is engaged." *Id.*, § 5.05(b). It also encompasses any opportunities that accrue to the fiduciary as a result of her position within the corporation. *Id.* This concept is most clearly illustrated by the testimony of Suminsby, the listing broker for the Gilpin property, which, if believed by the factfinder, would support a finding that the Gilpin property was offered to Harris specifically in her capacity as president of the Club. If the factfinder reached that conclusion, then at least the opportunity to acquire the Gilpin property would be a corporate opportunity. The state of the record concerning the Smallidge purchase precludes us from intimating any opinion whether that too would be a corporate opportunity.

Under the ALI standard, once the Club shows that the opportunity is a corporate opportunity, it must show either that Harris did not offer the opportunity to the Club or that the Club did not reject it properly. If the Club shows that the board did not reject the opportunity by a vote of the disinterested directors after full disclosure, then Harris may defend her actions on the basis that the taking of the opportunity was fair to the corporation. *Id.*, § 5.05(c). If Harris failed to offer the opportunity at all, however, then she may not defend on the basis that the failure to offer the opportunity was fair. *Id.*, cmt. to § 5.05(c).

. . . We . . . follow the ALI test. The disclosure-oriented approach provides a clear procedure whereby a corporate officer may insulate herself through prompt and complete disclosure from the possibility of a legal challenge. The requirement of disclosure recognizes the paramount importance of the corporate fiduciary's duty of loyalty. At the same time it protects the fiduciary's ability pursuant to the proper procedure to pursue her own business ventures free from the possibility of a lawsuit.

* * * *

IV. Conclusion

The question remains how our adoption of the rule affects the result in the instant case. The trial court made a number of factual findings based on an extensive record. The court made those findings, however, in the light of legal principles that are different from the principles that we today announce. Similarly, the parties did not have the opportunity to develop the record in this case with knowledge of the applicable legal standard. In these circumstances, fairness requires that we remand the case for further proceedings. Those further proceedings may include, at the trial court's discretion, the taking of further evidence.

The entry is:

Judgment vacated.

Remanded for further proceedings consistent with the opinion herein.

All concurring.

NOTES AND QUESTIONS

1. Would it have made a difference if, under the same circumstances, Ms. Harris had the opportunity to purchase a golf course property in Vermont?

2. What if the property had been an abandoned gold mine 10 miles away, and Ms. Harris believed there was still millions of dollars of gold in the mine AND her suspicions proved correct?

3. Following remand, the court found that both purchases were corporate opportunities and that Ms. Harris had breached her fiduciary duty to the Club by taking those opportunities for herself and not offering them first to the Club. However, the court also found that the Club's action against Ms. Harris was barred by the statute of limitations.

4. If Ms. Harris had approached you prior to either of the purchases that led to this case and asked for your legal advice on how she might buy the property, but not violate the corporate opportunity doctrine, what advice might you could give her?

Broz v. Cellular Info. Systems, Inc.

673 A.2d 148 (Del. 1996)

VEASEY, C.J.:

In this appeal, we consider the application of the doctrine of corporate opportunity. The Court of Chancery decided that the defendant, a corporate director, breached his fiduciary duty by not formally presenting to the corporation an opportunity which had come to the director individually and independent of the director's relationship with the corporation. Here the opportunity was not one in which the corporation in its current mode had an interest or which it had the financial ability to acquire, but, under the unique circumstances here, that mode was subject to change by virtue of the impending acquisition of the corporation by another entity.

We conclude that, although a corporate director may be shielded from liability by offering to the corporation an opportunity which has come to the director independently and individually, the failure of the director to present the opportunity does not necessarily result in the improper usurpation of a corporate opportunity. . . .

I. THE CONTENTIONS OF THE PARTIES AND THE DECISION BELOW

Robert F. Broz ("Broz") is the President and sole stockholder of RFB Cellular, Inc. ("RFBC"), a Delaware corporation engaged in the business of providing cellular telephone service in the Midwestern United States. At the time of the conduct at issue in this appeal, Broz was also a member of the board of directors of plaintiff below-appellee, Cellular Information Systems, Inc. ("CIS"). CIS is a publicly held Delaware corporation and a competitor of RFBC.

The conduct before the Court involves the purchase by Broz of a cellular telephone service license for the benefit of RFBC. The license in question, known as the Michigan-2 Rural Service Area Cellular License ("Michigan-2"), is issued by the Federal Communications Commission ("FCC") and entitles its holder to provide cellular telephone service to a portion of northern Michigan. CIS . . .[is], contending that the purchase of this license by Broz constituted a usurpation of a corporate opportunity properly belonging to CIS, irrespective of whether or not CIS was interested in the Michigan-2 opportunity at the time it was offered to Broz.

The principal basis for the contention of CIS is that PriCellular, Inc. ("PriCellular"), another cellular communications company which was contemporaneously engaged in an acquisition of CIS, was interested in the Michigan-2 opportunity. CIS contends that, in determining whether the Michigan-2 opportunity rightfully belonged to CIS, Broz was required to consider the interests of PriCellular insofar as those interests would come into alignment with those of CIS as a result of PriCellular's acquisition plans.

* * * *

II. FACTS

Broz has been the President and sole stockholder of RFBC since 1992. RFBC owns and operates an FCC license area, known as the Michigan-4 Rural Service Area Cellular License ("Michigan-4"). The license entitles RFBC to provide cellular telephone service to a portion of rural Michigan. Although Broz' efforts have been devoted primarily to the business operations of RFBC, he also served as an outside director of CIS at the time of the events at issue in this case. CIS was at all times fully aware of Broz' relationship with RFBC and the obligations incumbent upon him by virtue of that relationship.

In April of 1994, Mackinac Cellular Corp. ("Mackinac") sought to divest itself of Michigan-2 the license area immediately adjacent to Michigan-4. To this end, Mackinac contacted Daniels & Associates ("Daniels") and arranged for the brokerage firm to seek potential purchasers for Michigan-2. In compiling a list of prospects, Daniels included RFBC as a likely candidate. In May of 1994, David Rhodes, a representative of Daniels, contacted Broz and broached the subject of RFBC's possible acquisition of Michigan-2. . . .

Michigan-2 was not, however, offered to CIS. Apparently, Daniels did not consider CIS to be a viable purchaser for Michigan-2 in light of CIS' recent financial difficulties. The record shows that, at the time Michigan-2 was offered to Broz, CIS had recently emerged from lengthy and contentious Chapter 11 proceedings. . . .

During the period from early 1992 until the time of CIS' emergence from bankruptcy in 1994, CIS divested itself of some fifteen separate cellular license systems.[2] CIS contracted to sell four additional license areas on May 27, 1994, leaving CIS with only five remaining license areas, all of which were outside of the Midwest.

On June 13, 1994, following a meeting of the CIS board, Broz spoke with CIS' Chief Executive Officer, Richard Treibick ("Treibick"), concerning his interest in acquiring Michigan-2. Treibick communicated to Broz that CIS was not interested in Michigan-2. Treibick further stated that he had been made aware of the Michigan-2 opportunity prior to the conversation with Broz, and that any offer to acquire Michigan-2 was rejected. After the commencement of the PriCellular tender offer, in August of 1994, Broz contacted another CIS director, Peter Schiff ("Schiff"), to discuss the possible acquisition of Michigan-2 by RFBC. Schiff, like Treibick, indicated that CIS had neither the wherewithal nor the inclination to purchase Michigan-2. In late September of 1994, Broz also

[2] Of these fifteen licenses, three were sold to subsidiaries of PriCellular. . . .

contacted Stanley Bloch ("Bloch"), a director and counsel for CIS, to request that Bloch represent RFBC in its dealings with Mackinac. Bloch agreed to represent RFBC, and, like Schiff and Treibick, expressed his belief that CIS was not at all interested in the transaction. Ultimately, all the CIS directors testified at trial that, had Broz inquired at that time, they each would have expressed the opinion that CIS was not interested in Michigan-2.[5]

On June 28, 1994, following various overtures from PriCellular concerning an acquisition of CIS six CIS directors 6 entered into agreements with PriCellular to sell their shares in CIS at a price of $2.00 per share. These agreements were contingent upon, *inter alia,* the consummation of a PriCellular tender offer for all CIS shares at the same price. . . . .

. . . . Financing difficulties ultimately caused PriCellular to delay the closing date of the tender offer from September 16, 1994 until October 14, 1994 and then again until November 9, 1994.

On August 6, September 6 and September 21, 1994, Broz submitted written offers to Mackinac for the purchase of Michigan-2. During this time period, PriCellular also began negotiations with Mackinac to arrange an option for the purchase of Michigan-2. PriCellular's interest in Michigan-2 was fully disclosed to CIS' chief executive, Treibick, who did not express any interest in Michigan-2, and was actually incredulous that PriCellular would want to acquire the license. Nevertheless, CIS was fully aware that PriCellular and Broz were bidding for Michigan-2 and did not interpose CIS in this bidding war.

In late September of 1994, PriCellular reached agreement with Mackinac on an option to purchase Michigan-2. The exercise price of the option agreement was set at $6.7 million, with the option remaining in force until December 15, 1994. . . . The agreement further provided that Mackinac was free to sell Michigan-2 to any party who was willing to exceed the exercise price of the Mackinac-PriCellular option contract by at least $500,000. On November 14, 1994, Broz agreed to pay Mackinac $7.2 million for the Michigan-2 license, thereby meeting the terms of the option agreement. An asset purchase agreement was thereafter executed by Mackinac and RFBC.

---

[5] We assume arguendo that informal contacts and individual opinions of board members are not a substitute for a formal process of presenting an opportunity to a board of directors. Nevertheless, in our view such a formal process was not necessary under the circumstances of this case in order for Broz to avoid liability. These contacts with individual board members do however, tend to show that Broz was not acting surreptitiously or in bad faith.

Nine days later, on November 23, 1994, PriCellular completed its financing and closed its tender offer for CIS. Prior to that point, PriCellular owned no equity interest in CIS. . . .

* * * *

IV. APPLICATION OF THE CORPORATE OPPORTUNITY DOCTRINE

The doctrine of corporate opportunity represents but one species of the broad fiduciary duties assumed by a corporate director or officer. A corporate fiduciary agrees to place the interests of the corporation before his or her own in appropriate circumstances. . .

The corporate opportunity doctrine, as delineated by *Guth* [*v. Loft*] and its progeny, holds that a corporate officer or director may not take a business opportunity for his own if: (1) the corporation is financially able to exploit the opportunity; (2) the opportunity is within the corporation's line of business; (3) the corporation has an interest or expectancy in the opportunity; and (4) by taking the opportunity for his own, the corporate fiduciary will thereby be placed in a position inimicable to his duties to the corporation. The Court in Guth also derived a corollary which states that a director or officer may take a corporate opportunity if: (1) the opportunity is presented to the director or officer in his individual and not his corporate capacity; (2) the opportunity is not essential to the corporation; (3) the corporation holds no interest or expectancy in the opportunity; and (4) the director or officer has not wrongfully employed the resources of the corporation in pursuing or exploiting the opportunity. *Guth, 5 A.2d at 509.*

. . . . In the instant case, we find that the facts do not support the conclusion that Broz misappropriated a corporate opportunity.

We note at the outset that Broz became aware of the Michigan-2 opportunity in his individual and not his corporate capacity. . . . In fact, it is clear from the record that Mackinac did not consider CIS a viable candidate for the acquisition of Michigan-2. Accordingly, Mackinac did not offer the property to CIS. In this factual posture, many of the fundamental concerns undergirding the law of corporate opportunity are not present (*e.g.,* misappropriation of the corporation's proprietary information). The burden imposed upon Broz to show adherence to his fiduciary duties to CIS is thus lessened to some extent. . . . Nevertheless, this fact is not dispositive. . . .

We turn now to an analysis of the factors relied on by the trial court. First, we find that CIS was not financially capable of exploiting the Michigan-2 opportunity. Although the Court of Chancery concluded otherwise, we hold that this finding was not supported by the evidence. [*Citation omitted.*] The record shows that [h]aving recently emerged from lengthy and contentious bankruptcy proceedings, CIS was not in a position to commit capital to the acquisition of new assets. Further, the loan agreement entered into by CIS and its creditors severely limited the discretion of CIS as to the acquisition of new assets and substantially restricted the ability of CIS to incur new debt.

* * * *

[W]hile it may be said with some certainty that the Michigan-2 opportunity was within CIS' line of business, it is not equally clear that CIS had a cognizable interest or expectancy in the license. Under the third factor laid down by this Court in *Guth,* for an opportunity to be deemed to belong to the fiduciary's corporation, the corporation must have an interest or expectancy in that opportunity. . . . At the time the opportunity was presented, CIS was actively engaged in the process of divesting its cellular license holdings. CIS' articulated business plan did not involve any new acquisitions. Further, as indicated by the testimony of the entire CIS board, the Michigan-2 license would not have been of interest to CIS even absent CIS' financial difficulties and CIS' then current desire to liquidate its cellular license holdings. Thus, CIS had no interest or expectancy in the Michigan-2 opportunity. . . .

Finally, the corporate opportunity doctrine is implicated only in cases where the fiduciary's seizure of an opportunity results in a conflict between the fiduciary's duties to the corporation and the self-interest of the director . . . . In the instant case, Broz' interest in acquiring and profiting from Michigan-2 created no duties that were inimicable to his obligations to CIS. . . . Broz, however, comported himself in a manner that was wholly in accord with his obligations to CIS. Broz took care not to usurp any opportunity which CIS was willing and able to pursue. Broz sought only to compete with an outside entity, PriCellular, for acquisition of an opportunity which both sought to possess. Broz was not obligated to refrain from competition with PriCellular. . . .

A. Presentation to the Board:

In concluding that Broz had usurped a corporate opportunity, the Court of Chancery placed great emphasis on the fact that Broz had not formally presented the matter to the CIS board. . . . In so holding, the trial court erroneously grafted a new requirement onto the law of corporate opportunity, *viz.,* the requirement of formal presentation under circumstances where the corporation does not have an interest, expectancy or financial ability.

The teaching of *Guth* and its progeny is that the director or officer must analyze the situation *ex ante* to determine whether the opportunity is one rightfully belonging to the corporation. If the director or officer believes, based on one of the factors articulated above, that the corporation is not entitled to the opportunity, then he may take it for himself. Of course, presenting the opportunity to the board creates a kind of "safe harbor" for the director, which removes the specter of a *post hoc* judicial determination that the director or officer has improperly usurped a corporate opportunity. . . .

* * * *

Thus, we hold that Broz was not required to make formal presentation of the Michigan-2 opportunity to the CIS board prior to taking the opportunity for his own. . . .

* * * *

Broz was under no duty to consider the interests of PriCellular when he chose to purchase Michigan-2. . . . At the time Broz purchased Michigan-2, PriCellular had not yet acquired CIS. Any plans to do so would still have been wholly speculative. Accordingly, Broz was not required to consider the contingent and uncertain plans of PriCellular in reaching his determination of how to proceed.

* * * *

Broz, as an active participant in the cellular telephone industry, was entitled to proceed in his own economic interest in the absence of any countervailing duty. The right of a director or officer to engage in business affairs outside of his or her fiduciary capacity would be illusory if these individuals were required to consider every potential, future occurrence in determining whether a particular business strategy would implicate fiduciary duty concerns. In order for a director to engage meaningfully in business unrelated to his or her corporate role, the director must be allowed to make decisions based on the situation as it exists at the time a given opportunity is presented. Absent such a rule, the corporate fiduciary would be constrained to refrain from exploiting any opportunity for fear of liability based on the occurrence of subsequent events. This state of affairs would unduly restrict officers and directors and would be antithetical to certainty in corporation law.

VI. CONCLUSION

. . . .

Therefore, we hold that Broz did not breach his fiduciary duties to CIS. . . .

QUESTIONS

1. The Delaware General Corporation Law provides that:

> Every corporation created under this chapter shall have power to: . . . . [r]enounce, in its certificate of incorporation or by action of its board of directors, any interest or expectancy of the corporation in, or in being offered an opportunity to participate in, specified business opportunities or specified classes or categories of business opportunities that are presented to the corporation or 1 or more of its officers, directors or stockholders.
>
> *DGCL Subchapter II,* § 122. Specific Powers

Consider under what circumstances it might be appropriate to make use of the foregoing provision when representing a corporation or an investor in a corporation.

2. Is a provision allowing directors to take advantage of corporate opportunities without first offering those opportunities to the corporation ever in the corporation's best interest?

3. If so, under what circumstances?

In re eBay, Inc. Shareholders Litigation

2004 Del. Ch. LEXIS 4 (Del. Ch. 2004)

Shareholders of eBay, Inc. filed these consolidated derivative actions against certain eBay directors and officers for usurping corporate opportunities. Plaintiffs allege that eBay's investment banking advisor, Goldman Sachs Group, engaged in "spinning," a practice that involves allocating shares of lucrative initial public offerings of stock to favored clients. In effect, the plaintiff shareholders allege that Goldman Sachs bribed certain eBay insiders, using the currency of highly profitable investment opportunities-opportunities that should have been offered to, or provided for the benefit of, eBay rather than the favored insiders. Plaintiffs accuse Goldman Sachs of aiding and abetting the corporate insiders breach of their fiduciary duty of loyalty to eBay.

The individual eBay defendants, as well as Goldman Sachs, have moved to dismiss these consolidated actions for failure to state a claim. . . .

I. BACKGROUND FACTS

The facts, as alleged in the complaint, are straightforward. In 1995, defendants Pierre M. Omidyar and Jeffrey Skoll founded nominal defendant eBay, a Delaware corporation, as a sole proprietorship. eBay is a pioneer in online trading platforms, providing a virtual auction community for buyers and sellers to list items for sale and to bid on items of interest. In 1998, eBay retained Goldman Sachs and other investment banks to underwrite an initial public offering of common stock. Goldman Sachs was the lead underwriter. The stock was priced at $18 per share. Goldman Sachs purchased about 1.2 million shares. Shares of eBay stock became immensely valuable during 1998 and 1999, rising to $175 per share in early April 1999. Around that time, eBay made a secondary offering, issuing 6.5 million shares of common stock at $170 per share for a total of $1.1 billion. Goldman Sachs again served as lead underwriter. Goldman Sachs was asked in 2001 to serve as eBay's financial advisor in connection with an acquisition by eBay of PayPal, Inc. For these services, eBay has paid Goldman Sachs over $8 million.

During this same time period, Goldman Sachs "rewarded" the individual defendants by allocating to them thousands of IPO shares, managed by Goldman Sachs, at the initial offering price. Because the IPO market during this particular period of time was extremely active, prices of initial stock offerings often doubled or tripled in a single day. Investors who were well. connected, either to Goldman Sachs or to similarly situated investment banks serving as IPO underwriters, were able to flip these investments into instant profit by selling the equities in a few days or even in a few hours after they were initially purchased.

The essential allegation of the complaint is that Goldman Sachs provided these IPO share allocations to the individual defendants to show appreciation for eBay's business and to enhance Goldman Sachs' chances of obtaining future eBay business. In addition to co-founding eBay, defendant Omidyar has been eBay's CEO, CFO and President. He is eBay's largest stockholder, owning more than 23% of the company's equity. Goldman Sachs allocated Omidyar shares in at least forty IPOs at the initial offering price. Omidyar resold these securities in the public market for millions of dollars in profit. Defendant Whitman owns

3.3% of eBay stock and has been President, CEO and a director since early 1998. Whitman also has been a director of Goldman Sachs since 2001. Goldman Sachs allocated Whitman shares in over a 100 IPOs at the initial offering price. Whitman sold these equities in the open market and reaped millions of dollars in profit. Defendant Skoll, in addition to co-founding eBay, has served in various positions at the company, including Vice-President of Strategic Planning and Analysis and President. He served as an eBay director from December 1996 to March 1998. Skoll is eBay's second largest stockholder, owning about 13% of the company. Goldman Sachs has allocated Skoll shares in at least 75 IPOs at the initial offering price, which Skoll promptly resold on the open market, allowing him to realize millions of dollars in profit. Finally, defendant Robert C. Kagle has served as an eBay director since June 1997. Goldman Sachs allocated Kagle shares in at least 25 IPOs at the initial offering price. Kagle promptly resold these equities, and recorded millions of dollars in profit.

II. ANALYSIS

* * * *

B. Corporate Opportunity

Plaintiffs have stated a claim that defendants usurped a corporate opportunity of eBay. Defendants insist that Goldman Sachs' IPO allocations to eBay's insider directors were "collateral investments opportunities" that arose by virtue of the inside directors status as wealthy individuals. They argue that this is not a corporate opportunity within the corporation's line of business or an opportunity in which the corporation had an interest or expectancy. These arguments are unavailing.

First, no one disputes that eBay financially was able to exploit the opportunities in question. Second, eBay was in the business of investing in securities. The complaint alleges that eBay "consistently invested a portion of its cash on hand in marketable securities." According to eBay's 1999 10-K, for example, eBay had more than $550 million invested in equity and debt securities. eBay invested more than $181 million in "short-term investments" and $373 million in "long-term investments." Thus, investing was "a line of business" of eBay. Third, the facts alleged in the complaint suggest that investing was integral to eBay's cash management strategies and a significant part of its business. Finally, it is no answer to say, as do defendants, that IPOs are risky investments. It is undisputed that eBay was never given an opportunity to turn down the IPO allocations as too risky.

Defendants also argue that to view the IPO allocations in question as corporate opportunities will mean that every advantageous investment opportunity that comes to an officer or director will be considered a corporate opportunity. On the contrary, the allegations in the complaint in this case indicate that unique, below-market price investment opportunities were offered by Goldman Sachs to the insider defendants as financial inducements to maintain and secure corporate business. This was not an instance where a broker offered advice to a director about an investment in a marketable security. The conduct challenged here involved a large investment bank that regularly did business with a company steering highly lucrative IPO allocations to select insider directors and officers at that company, allegedly both to reward them for past business and to induce them to direct future business to that investment bank. This is a far cry from the defendants' characterization of the conduct in question as merely "a broker's investment recommendations" to a wealthy client.

Nor can one seriously argue that this conduct did not place the insider defendants in a position of conflict with their duties to the corporation. One can realistically characterize these IPO allocations as a form of commercial discount or rebate for past or future investment banking services. Viewed pragmatically, it is easy to understand how steering such commercial rebates to certain insider directors places those directors in an obvious conflict between their self-interest and the corporation's interest. . . .

Finally, even if one assumes that IPO allocations like those in question here do not constitute a corporate opportunity, a cognizable claim is nevertheless stated on the common law ground that an agent is under a duty to account for profits obtained personally in connection with transactions related to his or her company. The complaint gives rise to a reasonable inference that the insider directors accepted a commission or gratuity that rightfully belonged to eBay but that was improperly diverted to them. Even if this conduct does not run afoul of the corporate opportunity doctrine, it may still constitute a breach of the fiduciary duty of loyalty. Thus, even if one does not consider Goldman Sachs' IPO allocations to these corporate insiders-allocations that generated millions of dollars in profit-to be a corporate opportunity, the defendant directors were nevertheless not free to accept this consideration from a company, Goldman Sachs, that was doing significant business with eBay and that arguably intended the consideration as an inducement to maintaining the business relationship in the future.

* * * *

III. CONCLUSION

For all of the above reasons, I deny the defendants' motions to dismiss the complaint in this consolidated action.

SECTION III: Dominant Shareholders and the Duty of Loyalty

Typically, fiduciary duties do not apply to a corporation's shareholders. They usually apply only to a corporation's "fiduciaries," which include its directors, officers and certain agents. An "ordinary" shareholder of a corporation does not have duties to her fellow shareholders. She can vote in an irresponsible manner. She can vote selfishly for a transaction that will benefit her, even if she knows that it will be bad for the long-term interests of other shareholders. However, this absence of responsibility changes if a shareholder is a "dominant" shareholder. Because a dominant shareholder has more influence over the corporation and over the board of directors, there are certain instances when dominant shareholders are bound by certain fiduciary duties. These duties arise only with respect to certain "duty of loyalty" transactions. The rationale behind imposing additional duties on transactions in which a dominant shareholder has a conflict or a financial interest is that if a shareholder has a large enough ownership interest to "control" the board of directors, any transactions that involve that shareholder being treated in a different way than the other shareholders are suspect.

Most courts do not allow an interested transaction with a dominant shareholder to be cleansed by a vote of the board of directors since, typically, the board of directors has been selected by that same shareholder. Typically, the transaction will be subject to scrutiny and evaluated as to whether the transaction was in the best interests of the corporation. In Delaware, this analysis will involve an evaluation of whether the transaction was "intrinsically fair," unless a merger is involved, in which case "entire" fairness (a showing, discussed *supra*, that the procedures associated with the transaction as well as the price of the transaction was fair) is required. However, in recent years, Delaware courts have allowed certain transactions (such as freeze out mergers) involving a dominant shareholder to be "cleansed" when a corporation can show both the approval of an independent, well-functioning special committee AND a fully informed and uncoerced approving vote of the majority of the minority shareholders. *Kahn v. M & F Worldwide Corp.*, 88 A.3d 635 (Del. 2014). In such instances, Delaware courts will apply the business judgement rule to review the transaction, rather than subject the transaction to entire fairness scrutiny. Such transactions and the use of special committees to obtain the business judgment rule standard are addressed in Chapter 10, *infra.*

In some situations even the determination of whether an individual or entity is a "dominant" shareholder can be a difficult question. The question turns upon whether, given the nature of the corporation and the holdings of the other shareholders, the holdings of a particular shareholder are sufficient for that shareholder to exert control over the corporation. In other words, the assessment of shareholder "dominance" is context dependent. If one shareholder has 25% of a corporation's outstanding stock, that shareholder is not dominant if another shareholder has 75%. However, if one shareholder has 25% of a corporation's stock and all of the other shareholders each hold 1% (or less), the shareholder with 25% might very well be "dominant." Many dominant shareholder cases (such as *Sinclair Oil Corp. v. Levien* which follows) involve a situation in which, rather than an individual being a dominant shareholder, there is a corporate parent company playing the role of the dominant shareholder. In these situations, issues arise because the parent company does not own 100% of the subsidiary, so the subsidiary is not "wholly owned." If the parent owns more than 50% of the subsidiary, the subsidiary is "majority controlled." If not, the subsidiary is "minority controlled." Either way, if the parent has control, it is a dominant or controlling shareholder and subject to the increased duties to the "minority" shareholders discussed in this section.

Sinclair Oil Corp. v. Levien

280 A.2d 717 (Del. 1971)

WOLOCOTT, C.J.:

This is an appeal by the defendant, Sinclair Oil Corporation (hereafter Sinclair), from an order of the *Court of Chancery,* 261 A.2d 911 in a derivative action requiring Sinclair to account for damages sustained by its subsidiary, Sinclair Venezuelan Oil Company (hereafter Sinven), organized by Sinclair for the purpose of operating in Venezuela, as a result of dividends paid by Sinven, the denial to Sinven of industrial development, and a breach of contract between Sinclair's wholly-owned subsidiary, Sinclair International Oil Company, and Sinven.

Sinclair, operating primarily as a holding company, is in the business of exploring for oil and of producing and marketing crude oil and oil products. At all times relevant to this litigation, it owned about 97% of Sinven's stock. The plaintiff owns about 3000 of 120,000 publicly held shares of Sinven. Sinven, incorporated in 1922, has been engaged in petroleum operations primarily in Venezuela and since 1959 has operated exclusively in Venezuela.

Sinclair nominates all members of Sinven's board of directors. The Chancellor found as a fact that the directors were not independent of Sinclair. Almost without exception, they were officers, directors, or employees of corporations in the Sinclair complex. By reason of Sinclair's domination, it is clear that Sinclair owed Sinven a fiduciary duty. [*Citations omitted.*] . . .

The Chancellor held that because of Sinclair's fiduciary duty and its control over Sinven, its relationship with Sinven must meet the test of intrinsic fairness. The standard of intrinsic fairness involves both a high degree of fairness and a shift in the burden of proof. Under this standard the burden is on Sinclair to prove, subject to careful judicial scrutiny, that its transactions with Sinven were objectively fair. [*Citations omitted*].

Sinclair argues that the transactions between it and Sinven should be tested, not by the test of intrinsic fairness with the accompanying shift of the burden of proof, but by the business judgment rule . . . . A board of directors enjoys a presumption of sound business judgment, and its decisions will not be disturbed if they can be attributed to any rational business purpose. A court under such circumstances will not substitute its own notions of what is or is not sound business judgment.

We think, however, that Sinclair's argument in this respect is misconceived. When the situation involves a parent and a subsidiary, with the parent controlling the transaction and fixing the terms, the test of intrinsic fairness, with its resulting shifting of the burden of proof, is applied. [*Citations omitted.*] The basic situation for the application of the rule is the one in which the parent has received a benefit to the exclusion and at the expense of the subsidiary.

* * * *

A parent does indeed owe a fiduciary duty to its subsidiary when there are parent-subsidiary dealings. However, this alone will not evoke the intrinsic fairness standard. This standard will be applied only when the fiduciary duty is accompanied by self-dealing—the situation when a parent is on both sides of a transaction with its subsidiary. Self-dealing occurs when the parent, by virtue of its domination of the subsidiary, causes the subsidiary to act in such a way that the parent receives something from the subsidiary to the exclusion of, and detriment to, the minority stockholders of the subsidiary.

We turn now to the facts. The plaintiff argues that, from 1960 through 1966, Sinclair caused Sinven to pay out such excessive dividends that the industrial development of Sinven was effectively prevented, and it became in reality a corporation in dissolution.

From 1960 through 1966, Sinven paid out $108,000,000 in dividends ($38,000,000 in excess of Sinven's earnings during the same period). The Chancellor held that Sinclair caused these dividends to be paid during a period when it had a need for large amounts of cash. Although the dividends paid exceeded earnings, the plaintiff concedes that the payments were made in compliance with 8 Del.C. § 170, authorizing payment of dividends out of surplus or net profits. However, the plaintiff attacks these dividends on the ground that they resulted from an improper motive—Sinclair's need for cash. The Chancellor, applying the intrinsic fairness standard, held that Sinclair did not sustain its burden of proving that its transactions were intrinsically fair to the minority stockholders of Sinven. . . .

Sinclair contends that it is improper to apply the intrinsic fairness standard to dividend payments even when the board which voted for the dividends is completely dominated. In support of this contention, Sinclair relies heavily on *American District Telegraph Co. [ADT] v. Grinnell Corp.*, (N.Y.Sup.Ct.1969) aff'd. 33 A.D.2d 769, 306 N.Y.S.2d 209 (1969). Plaintiffs were minority stockholders of ADT, a subsidiary of Grinnell. The plaintiffs alleged that Grinnell, realizing that it would soon have to sell its ADT stock because of a pending anti-trust action, caused ADT to pay excessive dividends. Because the dividend payments conformed with applicable statutory law, and the plaintiffs could not prove an abuse of discretion, the court ruled that the complaint did not state a cause of action. . . .

We do not accept the argument that the intrinsic fairness test can never be applied to a dividend declaration by a dominated board, although a dividend declaration by a dominated board will not inevitably demand the application of the intrinsic fairness standard. [*Citations omitted.*] If such a dividend is in essence self-dealing by the parent, then the intrinsic fairness standard is the proper standard. For example, suppose a parent dominates a subsidiary and its board of directors. The subsidiary has outstanding two classes of stock, X and Y. Class X is owned by the parent and Class Y is owned by minority stockholders of the subsidiary. If the subsidiary, at the direction of the parent, declares a dividend on its Class X stock only, this might well be self-dealing by the parent. It would be receiving something from the subsidiary to the exclusion of and detrimental to its minority stockholders. This self-dealing, coupled with the parents' fiduciary duty, would make intrinsic fairness the proper standard by which to evaluate the dividend payments.

Consequently it must be determined whether the dividend payments by Sinven were, in essence, self-dealing by Sinclair. The dividends resulted in great sums of money being transferred from Sinven to Sinclair. However, a proportionate share of this money was received by the minority shareholders of Sinven. Sinclair received nothing from Sinven to the exclusion of its minority stockholders. As such, these dividends were not self-dealing. We hold therefore that the Chancellor erred in applying the intrinsic fairness test as to these dividend payments. The business judgment standard should have been applied.

We conclude that the facts demonstrate that the dividend payments complied with the business judgment standard and with 8 Del.C. § 170. The motives for causing the declaration of dividends are immaterial unless the plaintiff can show that the dividend payments resulted from improper motives and amounted to waste. The plaintiff contends only that the dividend payments drained Sinven of cash to such an extent that it was prevented from expanding.

The plaintiff proved no business opportunities which came to Sinven independently and which Sinclair either took to itself or denied to Sinven. As a matter of fact, with two minor exceptions which resulted in losses, all of Sinven's operations have been conducted in Venezuela, and Sinclair had a policy of exploiting its oil properties located in different countries by subsidiaries located in the particular countries.

From 1960 to 1966 Sinclair purchased or developed oil fields in Alaska, Canada, Paraguay, and other places around the world. The plaintiff contends that these were all opportunities which could have been taken by Sinven. . . . .

However, the plaintiff could point to no opportunities which came to Sinven. Therefore, Sinclair usurped no business opportunity belonging to Sinven. Since Sinclair received nothing from Sinven to the exclusion of and detriment to Sinven's minority stockholders, there was no self-dealing. Therefore, business judgment is the proper standard by which to evaluate Sinclair's expansion policies.

Since there is no proof of self-dealing on the part of Sinclair, it follows that the expansion policy of Sinclair and the methods used to achieve the desired result must, as far as Sinclair's treatment of Sinven is concerned, be tested by the standards of the business judgment rule. Accordingly, Sinclair's decision, absent fraud or gross overreaching, to achieve expansion through the medium of its subsidiaries, other than Sinven, must be upheld.

Even if Sinclair was wrong in developing these opportunities as it did, the question arises, with which subsidiaries should these opportunities have been shared? No evidence indicates a unique need or ability of Sinven to develop these opportunities. The decision of which subsidiaries would be used to implement Sinclair's expansion policy was one of business judgment with which a court will not interfere absent a showing of gross and palpable overreaching. [*Citation omitted.*] No such showing has been made here.

Next, Sinclair argues that the Chancellor committed error when he held it liable to Sinven for breach of contract.

In 1961 Sinclair created Sinclair International Oil Company (hereafter International), a wholly owned subsidiary used for the purpose of coordinating all of Sinclair's foreign operations. All crude purchases by Sinclair were made thereafter through International.

On September 28, 1961, Sinclair caused Sinven to contract with International whereby Sinven agreed to sell all of its crude oil and refined products to International at specified prices. The contract provided for minimum and maximum quantities and prices. The plaintiff contends that Sinclair caused this contract to be breached in two respects. Although the contract called for payment on receipt, International's payments lagged as much as 30 days after receipt. Also, the contract required International to purchase at least a fixed minimum amount of crude and refined products from Sinven. International did not comply with this requirement.

Clearly, Sinclair's act of contracting with its dominated subsidiary was self-dealing. Under the contract Sinclair received the products produced by Sinven, and of course the minority shareholders of Sinven were not able to share in the receipt of these products. If the contract was breached, then Sinclair received these products to the detriment of Sinven's minority shareholders. We agree with the Chancellor's finding that the contract was breached by Sinclair, both as to the time of payments and the amounts purchased.

Although a parent need not bind itself by a contract with its dominated subsidiary, Sinclair chose to operate in this manner. As Sinclair has received the benefits of this contract, so must it comply with the contractual duties.

Under the intrinsic fairness standard, Sinclair must prove that its causing Sinven not to enforce the contract was intrinsically fair to the minority shareholders of Sinven. Sinclair has failed to meet this burden. Late payments were clearly breaches for which Sinven should have sought and received adequate damages. As to the quantities purchased, Sinclair argues that it purchased all the products produced by Sinven. This, however, does not satisfy the standard of intrinsic fairness. Sinclair has failed to prove that Sinven could not possibly have produced or someway have obtained the contract minimums. As such, Sinclair must account on this claim.

* * * *

We will therefore reverse that part of the Chancellor's order that requires Sinclair to account to Sinven for damages sustained as a result of dividends paid between 1960 and 1966, and by reason of the denial to Sinven of expansion during that period. We will affirm the remaining portion of that order and remand the cause for further proceedings.

QUESTIONS

1. Recall that in the *Dodge v. Ford Motor Co.* case, *supra,* the Dodge brothers sought to compel Ford to issue a dividend. In the *Sinclair* case, the plaintiffs complained that dividends were issued by Sinven in violation of its duty to satisfy Sinclair Oil's need for cash. Do you think the court in the *Sinclair* case would have agreed with Ford or with the Dodges?

2. Does the *Sinclair* case stand for the proposition that a dominant shareholder must "renounce" all thought of self (as Judge Cardozo suggests that partners must do in *Meinhard v. Salmon, supra*), or are there instances in which a dominant shareholder may act more "selfishly" even if its actions are not in the best interests of the minority shareholders?

Zahn v. Transamerica Corporation

162 F.2d 36 (3d Cir. 1947)

BIGGS, J.:

Zahn, a holder of Class A common stock of Axton-Fisher Tobacco Company, a corporation of Kentucky, sued Transamerica Corporation, a Delaware company, on his own behalf and on behalf of all stockholders similarly situated, in the District Court of the United States for the District of Delaware. His complaint as amended asserts that Transamerica caused Axton-Fisher to redeem its Class A stock at $80.80 per share on July 1, 1943, instead of permitting the Class A stockholders to participate in the assets on the liquidation of their company in June, 1944. He alleges in brief that if the Class A stockholders had been allowed to participate in the assets on liquidation of Axton-Fisher and had received their respective shares of the assets, he and the other Class A stockholders would have received $240 per share instead of $80.80. Zahn takes the position that he has two separate causes of action, one based on the Class A shares which were not turned back to the company for redemption; another based on the shares which were redeemed. He prayed the court below to direct Transamerica to pay over to the shareholders who had not surrendered their stock the liquidation value and to pay over to those shareholders who had surrendered their stock the liquidation value less $80.80. . . .

The facts follow as appear from the pleadings, which recite provisions of Axton-Fisher's charter. Prior to April 30, 1943, Axton-Fisher had authorized and outstanding three classes of stock, designated respectively as preferred stock, Class A stock and Class B stock. Each share of preferred stock had a par value of $100 and was entitled to cumulative dividends at the rate of $6 per annum and possessed a liquidation value of $105 plus accrued dividends. The Class A stock, specifically described in the charter as a 'common' stock, was entitled to an annual cumulative dividend of $3.20 per share. If further funds were made available by action of the board of directors by way of dividends, the Class A stock and the Class B stock were entitled to share equally therein. Upon liquidation of the company and the payment of the sums required by the preferred stock, the Class A stock was entitled to share with the Class B stock in the distribution of the remaining assets, but the Class A stock was entitled to receive twice as much per share as the Class B stock.[2]

Each share of Class A stock was convertible at the option of the shareholder into one share of Class B stock. All or any of the shares of Class A stock were callable by the corporation at any quarterly dividend date upon sixty days' notice to the shareholders, at $60 per share with accrued dividends.[3] The

---

2 The charter provides as follows:

'In the event of the dissolution, liquidation, merger or consolidation of the corporation, or sale of substantially all its assets, whether voluntary or involuntary, there shall be paid to the holders of the preferred stock then outstanding $105 per share, together with all unpaid accrued dividends thereon, before any sum shall be paid to or any assets distributed among the holders of the Class A common stock and/or the holders of the Class B common stock. After such payment to the holders of the preferred stock, and all unpaid accrued dividends on the Class A common stock shall have been paid, then all remaining assets and funds of the corporation shall be divided among and paid to the holders of the Class A common stock and to the holders of the Class B common stock in the ratio of 2 to 1; that is to say, there shall be paid upon each share of Class A common stock twice the amount paid upon each share of Class B common stock, in any such event.'

3 The charter provides as follows:

voting rights were vested in the Class B stock but if there were four successive defaults in the payment of quarterly dividends, the class or classes of stock as to which such defaults occurred gained voting rights equal share for share with the Class B stock. By reason of this provision the Class A stock had possessed equal voting rights with the Class B stock since on or about January 1, 1937.

On or about May 16, 1941, Transamerica purchased 80,160 shares of Axton-Fisher's Class B common stock. This was about 71.5% of the outstanding Class B stock and about 46.7% of the total voting stocks of Axton-Fisher. By August 15, 1942, Transamerica owned 5,332 shares of Class A stock and 82,610 shares of Class B stock. By March 31, 1943, the amount of Class A stock of Axton-Fisher owned by Transamerica had grown to 30,168 shares or about 66 ⅔ % of the total amount of this stock outstanding, and the amount of Class B stock owned by Transamerica had increased to 90,768 shares or about 80% of the total outstanding. . . . Since May 16, 1941, Transamerica had control of and had dominated the management, directorate, financial policies, business and affairs of Axton-Fisher. Since the date last stated Transamerica had elected a majority of the board of directors of Axton-Fisher. These individuals are in large part officers or agents of Transamerica.

In the fall of 1942 and in the spring of 1943 Axton-Fisher possessed as its principal asset leaf tobacco which had cost it about $6,361,981. This asset was carried on Axton-Fisher's books in that amount. The value of leaf tobacco had risen sharply and, to quote the words of the complaint, 'unbeknown to the public holders of * * * Class A common stock of Axton-Fisher, but known to Transamerica, the market value of * * * (the) tobacco had, in March and April of 1943, attained the huge sum of about $20,000,000.'

The complaint then alleges the gist of the plaintiff's grievance, viz., that Transamerica, knowing of the great value of the tobacco which Axton-Fisher possessed, conceived a plan to appropriate the value of the tobacco to itself by redeeming the Class A stock at the price of $60 a share plus accrued dividends, the redemption being made to appear as if 'incident to the continuance of the business of Axton-Fisher as a going concern,' and thereafter, the redemption of

---

'The whole or any part of the Class A common stock of the corporation at the option of the Board of Directors, may be redeemed on any quarterly dividend payment date by paying therefor in cash Sixty dollars ($60.00) per share and all unpaid and accrued dividends thereon at the date fixed for such redemption, upon sending by mail to the registered holders of the Class A common stock at least sixty (60) days' notice of the exercise of such option. If at any time the Board of Directors shall determine to redeem less than the whole amount of Class A common stock then outstanding, the particular stock to be so redeemed shall be determined in such manner as the Board of Directors shall prescribe; provided, however, that no holder of Class A common stock shall be preferred over any other holder of such stock.'

the Class A stock being completed, to liquidate Axton-Fisher; that this would result, after the disbursal of the sum required to be paid to the preferred stock, in Transamerica gaining for itself most of the value of the warehouse tobacco. The complaint further alleges that in pursuit of this plan Transamerica, by a resolution of the Board of Directors of Axton-Fisher on April 30, 1943, called the Class A stock at $60 and, selling a large part of the tobacco to Phillip-Morris Company, Ltd., Inc., together with substantially all of the other assets of Axton-Fisher, thereafter liquidated Axton-Fisher, paid off the preferred stock and pocketed the balance of the proceeds of the sale. Warehouse receipts representing the remainder of the tobacco were distributed to the Class B stockholders.

Assuming as we must that the allegations of the complaint are true, it will be observed that agents or representatives of Transamerica constituted Axton-Fisher's board of directors at the times of the happening of the events complained of, and that Transamerica was Axton-Fisher's principal and controlling stockholder at such times. . .

* * * *

The circumstances of the case at bar are sui generis and we can find no Kentucky decision squarely in point. In our opinion, however, the law of Kentucky imposes upon the directors of a corporation or upon those who are in charge of its affairs by virtue of majority stock ownership or otherwise the same fiduciary relationship in respect to the corporation and to its stockholders as is imposed generally by the laws of Kentucky's sister States or which was imposed by federal law prior to *Erie R. Co. v. Tompkins,* 304 U.S. 64, 58 S. Ct. 817, 82 L. Ed. 1188, 114 A.L.R. 1487.

The tenor of the federal decisions in respect to the general fiduciary duty of those in control of a corporation is unmistakable. The Supreme Court in *Southern Pacific Co. v. Bogert,* 250 U.S. 483, 487, 488, 39 S. Ct. 533, 535, 63 L. Ed. 1099, said: 'The rule of corporation law and of equity invoked is well settled and has been often applied. The majority has the right to control; but when it does so, it occupies a fiduciary relation toward the minority, as much so as the corporation itself or its officers and directors.' . . . .

* * * *

It is appropriate to emphasize at this point that the right to call the Class A stock for redemption was confided by the charter of Axton-Fisher to the directors and not to the stockholders of that corporation. We must also re-emphasize . . . . that there is a radical difference when a stockholder is voting strictly as a stockholder and when voting as a director; that when voting as a stockholder he may have the legal right to vote with a view of his own benefits and to represent himself only; but that when he votes as a director he represents all the stockholders in the capacity of a trustee for them and cannot use his office as a director for his personal benefit at the expense of the stockholders.

Two theories are presented on one of which the case at bar must be decided: One, vigorously asserted by Transamerica and based on its interpretation of the decision in the Taylor case, is that the board of directors of Axton-Fisher, whether or not dominated by Transamerica, the principal Class B stockholder, at any time and for any purpose, might call the Class A stock for redemption; the other, asserted with equal vigor by Zahn, is that the board of directors of Axton-Fisher as fiduciaries were not entitled to favor Transamerica, the Class B stockholder, by employing the redemption provisions of the charter for its benefit.

. . . .The Court [in another Kentucky case] took the position on that record that the directors at any time might call the Class A stock for redemption and that the redemption provision of the charter was written as much for the benefit of the Class B as for the Class A stock. It is argued by Transamerica very persuasively that what the Court of Appeals of Kentucky held was that when the Class A stock received its allocation of $60 a share plus accrued dividends it received its full due and that the directors had the right at any time to eliminate Class A stock from the corporate setup for the benefit of the Class B stock. It does not appear from the opinion of the Court of Appeals of Kentucky whether or not the subsequent liquidation of Axton-Fisher was brought to the attention of the Court. But it is clear from the pleading that the subsequent liquidation was not an issue in the case. . . . We think that it is the settled law of Kentucky that directors may not declare or withhold the declaration of dividends for the purpose of personal profit or, by analogy, take any corporate action for such a purpose.

The difficulty in accepting Transamerica's contentions in the case at bar is that the directors of Axton-Fisher, if the allegations of the complaint be accepted as true, were the instruments of Transamerica, were directors voting in favor of their special interest, that of Transamerica, could not and did not exercise an independent judgment in calling the Class A stock, but made the call for the purpose of profiting their true principal, Transamerica. In short a puppet-puppeteer relationship existed between the directors of Axton-Fisher and Transamerica.

The act of the board of directors in calling the Class A stock, an act which could have been legally consummated by a disinterested board of directors, was here effected at the direction of the principal Class B stockholder in order to profit it. Such a call is voidable in equity at the instance of a stockholder injured thereby. It must be pointed out that under the allegations of the complaint there was no reason for the redemption of the Class A stock to be followed by the liquidation of Axton-Fisher except to enable the Class B stock to profit at the expense of the Class A stock. As has been hereinbefore stated the function of the call was confided to the board of directors by the charter and was not vested by the charter in the stockholders of any class. It was the intention of the framers of Axton-Fisher's charter to require the board of directors to act disinterestedly if that body called the Class A stock, and to make the call with a due regard for its fiduciary obligations. If the allegations of the complaint be proved, it follows that the directors of Axton-Fisher, the instruments of Transamerica, have been derelict in that duty. Liability which flows from the dereliction must be imposed upon Transamerica which, under the allegations of the complaint, constituted the board of Axton-Fisher and controlled it.

. . . .[W]hether the law of Delaware be applicable to determine the extent of the breach of fiduciary duty, or that of Kentucky or of New York, there will be found to be no substantial difference.

. . . .In our opinion, if the allegations of the complaint be proved, Zahn may maintain his cause of action to recover from Transamerica the value of the stock retained by him as that shall be represented by its aliquot share of the proceeds of Axton-Fisher on dissolution. . . .

* * * *

Fliegler v. Lawrence

361 A.2d 218 (Del. 1976)

MCNEILLY, J.:

In this shareholder derivative action brought on behalf of Agau Mines, Inc., a Delaware corporation, (Agau) against its officers and directors and United States Antimony Corporation, a Montana corporation (USAC), we are asked to decide whether the individual defendants, in their capacity as directors and officers of both corporations, wrongfully usurped a corporate opportunity belonging to Agau, and whether all defendants wrongfully profited by causing Agau to exercise an option to purchase that opportunity. The Court of Chancery found in favor of the defendants on both issues. . . .

I

In November, 1969, defendant, John C. Lawrence (then president of Agau, a publicly held corporation engaged in a dualphased gold and silver exploratory venture) in his individual capacity, acquired certain antimony properties under a lease option for $60,000. Lawrence offered to transfer the properties, which were then "a raw prospect", to Agau, but after consulting with other members of Agau's board of directors, he and they agreed that the corporation's legal and financial position would not permit acquisition and development of the properties at that time. Thus, it was decided to transfer the properties to USAC, (a closely held corporation formed just for this purpose and a majority of whose stock was owned by the individual defendants) where capital necessary for development of the properties could be raised without risk to Agau through the sale of USAC stock; it was also decided to grant Agau a long-term option to acquire USAC if the properties proved to be of commercial value.

In January, 1970, the option agreement was executed by Agau and USAC. Upon its exercise and approval by Agau shareholders, Agau was to deliver 800,000 shares of its restricted investment stock for all authorized and issued shares of USAC. The exchange was calculated on the basis of reimbursement to USAC and its shareholders for their costs in developing the properties to a point where it could be ascertained if they had commercial value. Such costs were anticipated to range from $250,000. to $500,000. . . .

In July, 1970, the Agau board resolved to exercise the option, an action which was approved by majority vote of the shareholders in October, 1970. Subsequently, plaintiff instituted this suit on behalf of Agau to recover the 800,000 shares and for an accounting.

II

The Vice-Chancellor determined that the chance to acquire the antimony claims was a corporate opportunity which should have been (and was) offered to Agau, but because the corporation was not in a position, either financially or legally, to accept the opportunity at that time, the individual defendants were entitled to acquire it for themselves after Agau rejected it.

* * * *

III

Plaintiff contends that because the individual defendants personally profited through the use of Agau's resources, *viz.*, personnel (primarily Lawrence) to develop the USAC properties . . ., they must be compelled to account to Agau for that profit. This argument pre-supposes that defendants did in fact so misuse corporate assets; however, the record reveals substantial evidence to support the Vice-Chancellor's conclusion that there was no misuse of either Agau personnel or warrants. . . .and plaintiff did not prove that alleged use of Agau's personnel and equipment was detrimental to the corporation.

Nevertheless, our inquiry cannot stop here, for it is clear that the individual defendants stood on both sides of the transaction in implementing and fixing the terms of the option agreement. Accordingly, the burden is upon them to demonstrate its intrinsic fairness [*Citations omitted.*] We agree with the Vice-Chancellor that the record reveals no bad faith on the part of the individual defendants. But that is not determinative. The issue is where the 800,000 restricted investment shares of Agau stock, objectively, was a fair price for Agau to pay for USAC as a wholly-owned subsidiary.

A.

Preliminarily, defendants argue that they have been relieved of the burden of proving fairness by reason of shareholder ratification of the Board's decision to exercise the option. They rely on 8 Del.C. § 144(a)(2) and *Gottlieb v. Heyden Chemical Corp., Del.Supr.,* 33 Del.Ch. 177, 91 A.2d 57 (1952).

In *Gottlieb*, this Court stated that shareholder ratification of an "interested transaction", although less than unanimous, shifts the burden of proof to an objecting shareholder to demonstrate that the terms are so unequal as to amount to a gift or waste of corporate assets. . . . The Court explained:

> "[The] entire atmosphere is freshened and a new set of rules invoked where formal approval has been given by a majority of independent, fully informed [shareholders]." 91 A.2d at 59.

The purported ratification by the Agau shareholders would not affect the burden of proof in this case because the majority of shares voted in favor of exercising the option were cast by defendants in their capacity as Agau shareholders. Only about one-third of the "disinterested" shareholders voted, and we cannot assume that such non-voting shareholders either approved or disapproved. Under these circumstances, we cannot say that "the entire atmosphere has been freshened" and that departure from the objective fairness test is permissible. [*Citations omitted.*] In short, defendants have not established factually a basis for applying *Gottlieb*.

Nor do we believe the Legislature intended a contrary policy and rule to prevail by enacting 8 Del.C. § 144, which provides, in part:

essentially, that a controlling interest be transferred only by means of an offer to all stockholders, i.e., a tender offer. This would be contrary to existing law and if so radical a change is to be effected it would best be done by the Legislature.

Perlman v. Feldmann

219 F.2d 173 (2d Cir. 1955), cert. denied, 349 U.S. 952 (1955)

CLARK, C.J.:

This is a derivative action brought by minority stockholders of Newport Steel Corporation to compel accounting for, and restitution of, allegedly illegal gains which accrued to defendants as a result of the sale in August, 1950, of their controlling interest in the corporation. The principal defendant, C. Russell Feldmann, who represented and acted for the others, members of his family,[1] was at that time not only the dominant stockholder, but also the chairman of the board of directors and the president of the corporation. Newport, an Indiana corporation, operated mills for the production of steel sheets for sale to manufacturers of steel products, first at Newport, Kentucky, and later also at other places in Kentucky and Ohio. The buyers, a syndicate organized as Wilport Company, a Delaware corporation, consisted of end-users of steel who were interested in securing a source of supply in a market becoming ever tighter in the Korean War. Plaintiffs contend that the consideration paid for the stock included compensation for the sale of a corporate asset, a power held in trust for the corporation by Feldmann as its fiduciary. This power was the ability to control the allocation of the corporate product in a time of short supply, through control of the board of directors; and it was effectively transferred in this sale by having Feldmann procure the resignation of his own board and the election of Wilport's nominees immediately upon consummation of the sale.

. . . . Plaintiffs argue here, as they did in the court below, that in the situation here disclosed the vendors must account to the non-participating minority stockholders for that share of their profit which is attributable to the sale of the corporate power. Judge Hincks denied the validity of the premise, holding that the rights involved in the sale were only those normally incident to the possession of a controlling block of shares, with which a dominant stockholder, in the absence of fraud or foreseeable looting, was entitled to deal according to

---

[1] The stock was not held personally by Feldmann in his own name, but was held by the members of his family and by personal corporations. The aggregate of stock thus had amounted to 33% of the outstanding Newport stock and gave working control to the holder. The actual sale included 55,552 additional shares held by friends and associates of Feldmann, so that a total of 37% of the Newport stock was transferred.

his own best interests. Furthermore, he held that plaintiffs had failed to satisfy their burden of proving that the sales price was not a fair price for the stock per se. . . .

. . . Newport was a relative newcomer in the steel industry with predominantly old installations which were in the process of being supplemented by more modern facilities. Except in times of extreme shortage Newport was not in a position to compete profitably with other steel mills for customers not in its immediate geographical area. Wilport, the purchasing syndicate, consisted of geographically remote end-users of steel who were interested in buying more steel from Newport than they had been able to obtain during recent periods of tight supply. The price of $20 per share was found by Judge Hincks to be a fair one for a control block of stock, although the over-the-counter market price had not exceeded $12 and the book value per share was $17.03. But this finding was limited by Judge Hincks' statement that "what value the block would have had if shorn of its appurtenant power to control distribution of the corporate product, the evidence does not show." It was also conditioned by his earlier ruling that the burden was on plaintiffs to prove a lesser value for the stock.

Both as director and as dominant stockholder, Feldmann stood in a fiduciary relationship to the corporation and to the minority stockholders as beneficiaries thereof. . . . Directors of a corporation are its agents, and they are governed by the rules of law applicable to other agents, and, as between themselves and their principal, the rules relating to honesty and fair dealing in the management of the affairs of their principal are applicable. They must not, in any degree, allow their official conduct to be swayed by their private interest, which must yield to official duty. . . .

In Indiana, then, as elsewhere, the responsibility of the fiduciary is not limited to a proper regard for the tangible balance sheet assets of the corporation, but includes the dedication of his uncorrupted business judgment for the sole benefit of the corporation, in any dealings which may adversely affect it. *Young v. Higbee Co.,* 324 U.S. 204, 65 S. Ct. 594, 89 L. Ed. 890; *Irving Trust Co. v. Deutsch, 2 Cir.,* 73 F.2d 121, certiorari denied 294 U.S. 708, 55 S. Ct. 405, 79 L. Ed. 1243; *Seagrave Corp. v. Mount, 6 Cir.,* 212 F.2d 389; *Meinhard v. Salmon,* 249 N.Y. 458, 164 N.E. 545, 62 A.L.R. 1; *Commonwealth Title Ins. & Trust Co. v. Seltzer,* 227 Pa. 410, 76 A. 77. Although the Indiana case is particularly relevant to Feldmann as a director, the same rule should apply to his fiduciary duties as majority stockholder, for in that capacity he chooses and controls the directors, and thus is held to have assumed their liability. Pepper v. Litton, *supra,*

308 U.S. 295, 60 S. Ct. 238. This, therefore, is the standard to which Feldmann was by law required to conform in his activities here under scrutiny.

It is true, as defendants have been at pains to point out, that this is not the ordinary case of breach of fiduciary duty. We have here no fraud, no misuse of confidential information, no outright looting of a helpless corporation. But on the other hand, we do not find compliance with that high standard which we have just stated and which we and other courts have come to expect and demand of corporate fiduciaries. In the often-quoted words of Judge Cardozo: "Many forms of conduct permissible in a workaday world for those acting at arm's length, are forbidden to those bound by fiduciary ties. A trustee is held to something stricter than the morals of the market place. Not honesty alone, but the punctilio of an honor the most sensitive, is then the standard of behavior. As to this there has developed a tradition that is unbending and inveterate. Uncompromising rigidity has been the attitude of courts of equity when petitioned to undermine the rule of undivided loyalty by the "disintegrating erosion" of particular exceptions." *Meinhard v. Salmon, supra,* 249 N.Y. 458, 464, 164 N.E. 545, 546, 62 A.L.R. 1. The actions of defendants in siphoning off for personal gain corporate advantages to be derived from a favorable market situation do not betoken the necessary undivided loyalty owed by the fiduciary to his principal.

The corporate opportunities of whose misappropriation the minority stockholders complain need not have been an absolute certainty in order to support this action against Feldmann. If there was possibility of corporate gain, they are entitled to recover. . . . [I]n Irving Trust Co. v. Deutsch, *supra*, 2 Cir., 73 F.2d 121, 124, an accounting was required of corporate directors who bought stock for themselves for corporate use, even though there was an affirmative showing that the corporation did not have the finances itself to acquire the stock. . . .

. . . . In the past Newport had used and profited by its market leverage by operation of what the industry had come to call the "Feldmann Plan." This consisted of securing interest-free advances from prospective purchasers of steel in return for firm commitments to them from future production. The funds thus acquired were used to finance improvements in existing plants and to acquire new installations. In the summer of 1950 Newport had been negotiating for cold-rolling facilities which it needed for a more fully integrated operation and a more marketable product, and Feldmann plan funds might well have been used toward this end.

Further, as plaintiffs alternatively suggest, Newport might have used the period of short supply to build up patronage in the geographical area in which it could compete profitably even when steel was more abundant. Either of these opportunities was Newport's, to be used to its advantage only. Only if defendants had been able to negate completely any possibility of gain by Newport could they have prevailed. . . . [Defendants, as] fiduciaries always have the burden of proof in establishing the fairness of their dealings with trust property. . . .

Defendants seek to categorize the corporate opportunities which might have accrued to Newport as too unethical to warrant further consideration. It is true that reputable steel producers were not participating in the gray market brought about by the Korean War and were refraining from advancing their prices, although to do so would not have been illegal. But Feldmann plan transactions were not considered within this self-imposed interdiction; the trial court found that around the time of the Feldmann sale Jones & Laughlin Steel Corporation, Republic Steel Company, and Pittsburgh Steel Corporation were all participating in such arrangements. In any event, it ill becomes the defendants to disparage as unethical the market advantages from which they themselves reaped rich benefits.

We do not mean to suggest that a majority stockholder cannot dispose of his controlling block of stock to outsiders without having to account to his corporation for profits or even never do this with impunity when the buyer is an interested customer, actual or potential, for the corporation's product. But when the sale necessarily results in a sacrifice of this element of corporate good will and consequent unusual profit to the fiduciary who has caused the sacrifice, he should account for his gains. So in a time of market shortage, where a call on a corporation's product commands an unusually large premium, in one form or another, we think it sound law that a fiduciary may not appropriate to himself the value of this premium. Such personal gain at the expense of his coventurers seems particularly reprehensible when made by the trusted president and director of his company. In this case the violation of duty seems to be all the clearer because of this triple role in which Feldmann appears, though we are unwilling to say, and are not to be understood as saying, that we should accept a lesser obligation for any one of his roles alone.

Hence to the extent that the price received by Feldmann and his codefendants included such a bonus, he is accountable to the minority stockholders who sue here. [*Citation omitted.*] And plaintiffs, as they contend, are entitled to a recovery in their own right, instead of in right of the corporation (as in the usual derivative actions), since neither Wilport nor their successors in interest should share in any judgment which may be rendered. . . .

* * * *

SWAN, J. (dissenting)

With the general principles enunciated in the majority opinion as to the duties of fiduciaries I am, of course, in thorough accord. But, as Mr. Justice Frankfurter stated in *Securities and Exchange Comm. v. Chenery Corp.,* 318 U.S. 80, 85, 63 S. Ct. 454, 458, 87 L. Ed. 626, "to say that a man is a fiduciary only begins analysis; it gives direction to further inquiry. To whom is he a fiduciary? What obligations does he owe as a fiduciary? In what respect has he failed to discharge these obligations?" My brothers' opinion does not specify precisely what fiduciary duty Feldmann is held to have violated or whether it was a duty imposed upon him as the dominant stockholder or as a director of Newport. Without such specification I think that both the legal profession and the business world will find the decision confusing and will be unable to foretell the extent of its impact upon customary practices in the sale of stock.

The power to control the management of a corporation, that is, to elect directors to manage its affairs, is an inseparable incident to the ownership of a majority of its stock, or sometimes, as in the present instance, to the ownership of enough shares, less than a majority, to control an election. Concededly a majority or dominant shareholder is ordinarily privileged to sell his stock at the best price obtainable from the purchaser. In so doing he acts on his own behalf, not as an agent of the corporation. If he knows or has reason to believe that the purchaser intends to exercise to the detriment of the corporation the power of management acquired by the purchase, such knowledge or reasonable suspicion will terminate the dominant shareholder's privilege to sell and will create a duty not to transfer the power of management to such purchaser. The duty seems to me to resemble the obligation which everyone is under not to assist another to commit a tort rather than the obligation of a fiduciary. But whatever the nature of the duty, a violation of it will subject the violator to liability for damages sustained by the corporation. Judge Hincks found that Feldmann had no reason to think that Wilport would use the power of management it would acquire by the purchase to injure Newport, and that there was no proof that it ever was so used. Feldmann did know, it is true, that the reason Wilport wanted the stock was to put in a board of directors who would be likely to permit Wilport's members to purchase more of Newport's steel than they might otherwise be able to get. But there is nothing illegal in a dominant shareholder purchasing from his own corporation at the same prices it offers to other customers. That is what the members of Wilport did, and there is no proof that Newport suffered any detriment therefrom.

My brothers say that "the consideration paid for the stock included compensation for the sale of a corporate asset", which they describe as "the ability to control the allocation of the corporate product in a time of short supply, through control of the board of directors; and it was effectively transferred in this sale by having Feldmann procure the resignation of his own board and the election of Wilport's nominees immediately upon consummation of the sale." The implications of this are not clear to me. If it means that when market of a corporation's product to wish to of a corporation's product to which to buy a controlling block of stock in order to be able to purchase part of the corporation's output at the same mill list prices as are offered to other customers, the dominant stockholder is under a fiduciary duty not to sell his stock, I cannot agree. For reasons already stated, in my opinion Feldmann was not proved to be under any fiduciary duty as a stockholder not to sell the stock he controlled.

Feldmann was also a director of Newport. Perhaps the quoted statement means that as a director he violated his fiduciary duty in voting to elect Wilport's nominees to fill the vacancies created by the resignations of the former directors of Newport. As a director Feldmann was under a fiduciary duty to use an honest judgment in acting on the corporation's behalf. A director is privileged to resign, but so long as he remains a director he must be faithful to his fiduciary duties and must not make a personal gain from performing them. Consequently, if the price paid for Feldmann's stock included a payment for voting to elect the new directors, he must account to the corporation for such payment, even though he honestly believed that the men he voted to elect were well qualified to serve as directors. He can not take pay for performing his fiduciary duty. . . .

Judge Hincks went into the matter of valuation of the stock with his customary care and thoroughness. He made no error of law in applying the principles relating to valuation of stock. Concededly a controlling block of stock has greater sale value than a small lot. While the spread between $10 per share for small lots and $20 per share for the controlling block seems rather extraordinarily wide, the $20 valuation was supported by the expert testimony of Dr. Badger, whom the district judge said he could not find to be wrong. I see no justification for upsetting the valuation as clearly erroneous. Nor can I agree with my brothers that the $20 valuation "was limited" by the last sentence in finding 120. The controlling block could not by any possibility be shorn of its appurtenant power to elect directors and through them to control distribution of the corporate product. It is this "appurtenant power" which gives a controlling block its value as such block. What evidence could be adduced to show the value of the block "if shorn" of such appurtenant power, I cannot conceive, for it cannot be shorn of it.

The opinion also asserts that the burden of proving a lesser value that $20 per share was not upon the plaintiffs but the burden was upon the defendants to prove that the stock was worth that value. Assuming that this might be true as to the defendants who were directors of Newport, they did show it, unless finding 120 be set aside. Furthermore, not all the defendants were directors; upon what theory the plaintiffs should be relieved from the burden of proof as to defendants who were not directors, the opinion does not explain.

The final conclusion of my brothers is that the plaintiffs are entitled to recover in their own right instead of in the right of the corporation. This appears to be completely inconsistent with the theory advanced at the outset of the opinion, namely, that the price of the stock "included compensation for the sale of a corporate asset." If a corporate asset was sold, surely the corporation should recover the compensation received for it by the defendants. . . .

I would affirm the judgment on appeal.

NOTES AND QUESTIONS

1. *Perlman v. Feldmann* does not represent a typical result in a sale of control case. The decision might even be explained by unique external factors, such as the Korean War. Nevertheless, the decision represents an example of a decision preventing a shareholder from retaining a control premium. How would you explain this decision to a client seeking to avoid a similar result?

2. How might you advise a client to proceed when selling a dominant interest in a corporation for a premium?

3. Allowing a dominant shareholder to collect a control premium that she is not required to "share," enables that shareholder to retain a gain that is not available to the corporation's minority shareholder(s). If you were in a position to determine the rules governing control premiums would you preserve the current treatment, which allows dominant shareholders to keep control premiums, or would you treat control premiums as a form of "corporate opportunity" that had to be allocated, *pro rata,* among all of the corporation's Shareholders?

4. Consider the Discussion Problem that follows:

Discussion Problem:

Your beloved elderly Aunt Tilly owns 33% of Big Woods Camp, Inc. ("BWCI"). BWCI has operated a camp in the mountains for over 50 years. The camp makes a reasonable profit and has brought happiness to countless individuals who either attended summer camp at BWCI or were part of the many other groups who rent the property throughout the remainder of the year. Aunt Tilly is retired, and she depends on the dividends from BWCI to pay her living and medical expenses. Aunt Tilly's brother, Joe, used to own 77% of Big Woods Camp, Inc., but Joe died a few years ago, and Joe's 77% of BWCI passed to Joe's greedy grandson, Lou Cypher. At Joe's death, the total value of BWCI was appraised at $6 million.

Lou recently informed Aunt Tilly that he has made arrangements to sell his stock in BWCI to the Maleficent Mining Company for $9 million. Maleficent Mining Company is going to close the BWCI camp and set up mining operations on the BWCI property. Lou also informed Aunt Tilly that Maleficent Mining Company has no interest in buying Aunt Tilly's shares in BWCI and that it plans to stop paying dividends for the foreseeable future. Aunt Tilly comes to you for advice and wants to know if she can stop the sale to Maleficent Mining Company. If she cannot, she would like to know if she can either require Maleficent Mining Company to buy her shares as well, or require Lou to share some of the proceeds from his sale of the BWCI stock. Please assess Aunt Tilly's position and whether any of the foregoing approaches are likely to be successful.

CHAPTER SIX

Shareholder Voting, Rights and Remedies, and Access to Information

ONE SATURDAY, WHILE YOU ARE at a local farmers' market, enjoying the day, you receive a text message from a partner in your firm's environmental law group. The partner asks you to come into his office that afternoon. When you get to the office, the partner tells you about a client who needs assistance right away.

Experiencing Assignment 8: Build a Better Tomorrow

FACTS:

The firm represents an environmentally friendly mutual fund called the Build a Better Tomorrow Fund ("BBTF"). The fund manages assets worth approximately $1 billion and will only invest in companies that engage in environmentally friendly practices, use renewable energy, employ efficient production methods, and/or engage in the development of technologies that might address current challenges to the environment. BBTF also does not invest in companies that have committed serious or repeated environmental offenses.

BBTF is run by Reed Cycle. Reed has just discovered that one of BBTF's portfolio companies, Solar Systems, Inc. ("SSI"), a publicly traded company, is selling "solar powered" toys that actually run on batteries. Reed tells you that SSI makes and sells consumer products that purportedly use solar power. SSI has a toy division that sells "solar" toys, which are marketed as using solar energy and being "environmental toys." The toys account for 15% of SSI's sales. It turns out that, for some of the toys SSI sells, the solar charging panel on the toy does not provide sufficient energy to properly operate the toy, and SSI has determined that correcting this problem would make the toy too expensive. SSI's solution is to use solar charging for a component of the toy. For example, the solar panel on the SSI toy cars does not create enough energy to race the cars, and kids like cars that go fast. So, SSI includes batteries and uses the solar panel merely to illuminate the name of the toy car. Reed has spoken with SSI, but SSI refuses to change these products or remove the claim that the toys "use" solar energy. SSI explains that the cars do "use" solar energy; they are just battery powered as well. Reed feels that such practices violate the spirit of SSI's stated goals. Each SSI toy package contains the statements: "Solar Toys for Girls and Boys" and "SSI—making a better world for our children." Reed has also discovered that many of the SSI toys are produced in an overseas factory that has very bad working conditions and is creating pollution in the province in which the factory is located.

Because Reed likes other aspects of the SSI business and does not want to sell the BBTF investment in SSI, Reed would like to try to get SSI to engage in "better" and more environmentally friendly practices. It turns out that the SSI annual meeting of shareholders is approximately five months away, and Reed would like to use that meeting to make his point.

ASSIGNMENT:

Reed would like you to draft a Shareholder Proposal, to be included with the SSI proxy materials for the upcoming annual meeting, that address SSI's "bad" practices in its toy division and the need for SSI to adopt more environmentally friendly practices with respect to the toys it produces and sells, consistent with SSI's slogans. BBTF has an investment of $500,000 in SSI and has held that investment, continuously, for 2 ½ years. BBTF has never made a shareholder proposal before, but it thinks this is a good place to start. If SSI does not correct what seems to be a practice that is not environmentally friendly, BBTF will probably sell its shares in SSI.

Please draft a Shareholder Proposal designed to withstand a challenge from the SSI board under Section 14a–8 of the Securities Exchange Act of 1934, and provide Reed with a brief assessment of whether BBTF might seek reimbursement for the costs associated with the Proposal.

This Assignment does not need to be completed, and should not be completed, until the end of the section. However, as you study the cases and other materials that follow, it might be helpful to do so with a view toward providing assistance to BBTF in drafting an effective Shareholder Proposal. Some of the materials in the section will relate more than others to the specific issues involved in BBTF's proposal. However, the materials are designed to build your understanding of the issues that arise when a shareholder wants to have a Proposal included in a corporation's proxy materials and assist you in addressing BBTF's concerns and putting them in context. Please keep the issues involved in drafting the BBTF Shareholder Proposal and the questions presented by the assignment in mind while reading the materials that follow.

SECTION I: Shareholders and the Rights Associated with Ownership

While it is important to understand the internal structure and operation of a corporation, there are also several issues that arise relating to the rights, privileges and preferences of shareholders in that firm. Shareholders, unless they are also directors, officers or employees, are not involved in the management of the corporation. Therefore, there are not typically fiduciary duties associated with the role of shareholder. (While, as discussed earlier, there are such duties in the case of a dominant shareholder, these duties arise because of the dominant shareholder's potential ability to exert control over the corporation irrespective of whether they also hold a position on the board of directors.) Because shareholders do not typically exercise control in their shareholder role, their voting decisions are not regulated. This means that most shareholders may vote on an uninformed, foolish or even a selfish basis. This lack of control also underlies the rationale for shareholders' limited liability. However, in exchange, shareholders may not control the management of the corporation from the shareholders' role. Consistent with this limited role, there are restrictions on the subject matter about which shareholders have input, relating to the corporation, and there are limits on the matters which are appropriate to submit to shareholders for a vote.

Shareholders vote on major transactions, elect board members, and can vote on various resolutions that are typically not binding on the board. A good way to understand this division is to remember that shareholders get to decide who will operate the corporation, but may not operate the corporation themselves.

A. Shareholder Ownership Rights

When an individual (or entity) owns any portion of a corporation, that ownership interest is represented in shares of stock. The stock of a corporation may be divided into as many shares as the owner(s) desire. There may be one share of stock, representing the entire ownership (100%) of a corporation, or there may be millions of shares. When a corporation is formed, the Articles of Incorporation set forth how many shares of stock are authorized and whether there is more than one "class" of stock. If there is only one class of stock, that class is typically known as "common" stock. Common stock typically has the right to vote AND the right to receive dividends, if any. Common stock also represents a claim on any assets remaining in the corporation once all creditors have been paid and any obligations which might exist on other classes of stock, if any, have been satisfied. This right to claim that which is left is known as a "residual claim," and the shareholders holding such a right may be characterized as "residual claimants."

The rights associated with a share of common stock usually fall into one of two categories: economic rights and voting rights. In fact, both economic and voting rights must exist, in some form, in the ownership structure of the corporation. While in most corporations, economic rights and voting rights both reside in the corporation's common stock, there is no requirement that these rights be present in the same class of stock. In fact a corporation may have multiple classes of stock with each class possessing different rights, privileges and preferences. Recall the *Benihana of Tokyo, Inc.,* case *supra* (where the company had both common stock and preferred stock, each with different rights) and the *Transamerica case, supra,* in which Axton-Fisher Tobacco Company had two classes of common stock (Class A and Class B) and one class of preferred stock. (Control structures involving multiple classes of stock are also discussed in the next chapter.)

B. Shareholder Economic Rights

Regardless of how many shares (or classes) of stock a corporation has authorized, economic rights accompany and are determined based on the shares that are issued and outstanding (i.e., shares that are actually owned by shareholders at any given point in time). Assuming there are no other classes of stock in a particular corporation, the shareholders of the common stock may determine their percentage of the total economic rights by looking at the number of shares they hold compared to the total number of shares which are issued and outstanding. If a shareholder holds 10 shares, and there are a total of 200 shares issued and outstanding (all of the same class of shares), then that shareholder is entitled to receive 5% of dividends paid to shareholders and 5% of any money which is paid to shareholders upon the liquidation of the corporation.

C. Shareholder Voting Rights

Shareholders do not manage the corporation. The Board of Directors is charged with the responsibility of management. However, shareholders vote to elect directors, and that power to elect directors is critical to the control over the corporation. Shareholders vote on other matters as well, such as whether to grant approval of certain significant transactions outside of the corporation's ordinary course of business that would involve a fundamental change to the corporation (such as merger, sale of all the assets, corporate dissolution and amending the Articles of Incorporation or the Bylaws). Shareholders also have the power to vote on resolutions and shareholder proposals.

As addressed in the materials below, resolutions may take two different forms: (i) resolutions which are proposed by a corporation's management such as a resolution to ratify an option plan, or an action taken by the Board of Directors; or (ii) proposals which are made by the shareholders, requesting or advising that the Board take certain action.

D. How Do Shareholders Vote?

Shareholder voting can take place at any meeting of the shareholders. A shareholder's percentage ownership of a corporation typically determines how much voting power that shareholder has and how much control that shareholder can exercise over the corporation. Percentage based voting is referred to as "*pro rata,*" meaning that shareholders vote in proportion to their holdings. (Note that directors serving on the Board do NOT vote on a pro rata basis. Directors vote on a "*per capita*" basis, or per person, so each Board member receives one vote.) A shareholder usually may vote all of the shares owned by that shareholder on a particular matter.

Typically a simple majority (greater than 50%) vote is required to take an action, and shareholders are entitled to one vote for each share they hold. However, sometimes a corporation's organizational documents, such as the Articles of Incorporation or the Bylaws, may provide for different voting structures or different numbers of affirmative votes required to approve a matter. If a percentage greater than a simple majority is required to take some action, that greater percentage is called a "super majority." Super majorities may be required for all votes, only for votes on specific matters, or not at all. It depends on the governing documents of the corporation. In addition, sometimes different classes of stock will have different voting rights. For example, certain classes of stock may hold greater voting rights than other classes, or may be entitled to elect a certain number of the directors on the board.

Shareholders who hold stock on a certain date, known as the "record date," are entitled to vote in shareholder elections, immediately following that date. The record date is established by the board of directors (typically a few weeks before a scheduled shareholder vote), and it determines which shareholders are entitled to vote at a particular shareholder meeting or on a particular proposal, even if they sell their shares after the record date.

E. Cumulative Voting

Cumulative voting is an alternative to traditional voting used to give minority shareholders a greater opportunity to select a director to a corporation's Board. In a traditional voting structure the majority shareholder (or shareholders) would be able to appoint all of the directors on the Board. In cumulative voting, shareholders are entitled to spread out their votes, or to "accumulate" all their votes, to select one or two directors on a "slate" with a much larger number of candidates, to maximize a minority shareholder's impact and to increase the chance for them to elect a director to the Board. In some states, such as California, cumulative voting is required, except in publicly held corporations. In other states this structure is optional. (The *Ringling Bros.-Barnum & Bailey Combined Shows v. Ringling* case, *infra,* provides a good example of the application of cumulative voting.)

SECTION II: Proxies and Proxy Rules

A. What Is a Proxy?

Often a shareholder is not able to attend a meeting, but would still like to vote on a matter. In these instances, the shareholder may give a proxy to someone else to vote that shareholder's shares. A proxy is a written (or these days it might be an electronic) document which is given to someone else, allowing them (or instructing them) to vote on a person's behalf. In the corporate context a proxy refers to the right to vote a person's shares, but the term could apply to any vote. The person who is given the proxy to vote is called the "proxy holder." Proxies may give the holder discretion or no discretion in that they may provide specific instructions on how the shares are to be voted, or they may leave the discretion of how to vote to the proxy holder. Proxies may also be revocable or, in certain circumstances, "irrevocable."

Proxies are often important because in order to have a meeting of the shareholders of a corporation, a quorum is required. A quorum is a minimum number of people, voters or votes (in this case shareholders), who must be present at a meeting in order to make the meeting valid. Quorum requirements are usually established by statute, but may be modified, subject to statutory limits, in a corporation's Bylaws. A typical quorum requirement for a shareholder vote would be fifty percent of the votes, plus one. Note that because shareholders vote based upon percentages, it is the number of shares that is relevant and not the number of shareholders. Because so few shareholders actually attend annual meetings (at least of large corporations), without the use of proxies the corporation's shareholders would be unable to vote because the quorum requirements would not be met. Therefore, a corporation's management will often solicit proxies from its shareholders prior to a meeting in order to meet the quorum requirements and have a valid election.

B. Proxy Rules

There are several rules governing the entire proxy process (the "Proxy Rules") which are addressed in Regulation 14A, adopted under of the Securities Exchange Act of 1934 (the "1934 Act"). The Proxy Rules regulate the manner and means by which proxies may be obtained or solicited. In order to understand these rules one must understand the term "solicitation" which includes: any request for a proxy; any request to execute, not to execute, or to revoke a proxy; and furnishing a form of proxy *or other communication,* reasonably calculated to result in the procurement, withholding or revocation of a proxy. Courts have found that even communications which may "constitute a step in a chain of communications designed to accomplish such a result" may also constitute a "solicitation." *Long Island Lighting Co. v. Barbash,* 779 F.2d 793, 796 (2d Cir.1985).

Prior to the time that any person makes a "solicitation," the person being solicited must first receive, or have received, a "proxy statement." Rule 14a–3 *et seq.*, also regulates the form, content and filing requirements for Proxy Statements. These rules, which prohibit materially misleading statements, are intended, among other things, to provide for adequate disclosure for shareholders before their proxies are solicited.

There are also several exceptions to what constitutes a solicitation. These exceptions are important since only communications with shareholders which constitute "solicitations" under the Proxy Rules are regulated. Communications which are not "solicitations" are not subject to the Proxy Rules. Exceptions to "solicitations" include: public statements or speeches or advertisements stating how a shareholder intends to vote and the reasoning behind that vote; solicitations by someone (other than, among many other exceptions, an affiliate of the corporation or a party in interest) who does not intend to act on another's behalf; any solicitation made to 10 or fewer persons, provided it is not made by the corporation; and advice to any person with whom the person furnishing the advice (the "advisor") has a business relationship (provided that the advisor does not have certain other interests or undisclosed connections to the corporation which would amount to a conflict of interest). The SEC recently proposed Rules pursuant to the JOBS Act which would also exempt general solicitations and advertising to "accredited investors" participating in a securities offering made under Rule 506 (Rule 506 is an exemption to the rules that requires the registration of securities offerings).

Long Island Lighting Co. v. Barbash

779 F.2d 793 (2d Cir. 1985)

CARDAMONE, C.J.:

A Long Island utility furnishing that area with power has scheduled a stockholders meeting for Thursday December 12, 1985. It has been embroiled in public controversy over its construction of the Shoreham Nuclear Power Plant and adverse publicity intensified recently because of extended loss of service to customers arising from damages to the transmission system caused by Hurricane Gloria.

In this setting, the company, believing that several groups had begun to solicit proxies during October in anticipation of the upcoming stockholders meeting, brought suit to enjoin them. . . .

Long Island Lighting Company (LILCO) brings this expedited appeal . . . to enjoin defendants' alleged violations of § 14(a) of the Securities Exchange Act of 1934 and Rules 14a–9, 17 C.F.R. § 240.14a–9 and 14a–11, 17 C.F.R. 240.14a–11, promulgated under that statute, that govern proxy solicitations. The complaint alleges that defendants have committed such violations by publishing a false and misleading advertisement in connection with a special meeting of LILCO's shareholders scheduled for the purpose of electing a new LILCO Board of Directors. For the reasons explained below, this matter is remanded to the district court.

I

Plaintiff LILCO is a New York electric company serving Nassau and Suffolk Counties on Long Island, New York. Its common and preferred stocks are registered in accordance with Section 12(b) of the Securities Exchange Act and are traded on the New York Stock Exchange. Defendant John W. Matthews was an unsuccessful candidate for Nassau County Executive in the election held November 5, 1985. During the campaign he strongly opposed LILCO and its operation of the Shoreham Nuclear Power Plant. As an owner of 100 shares of

LILCO's preferred stock and a manager of an additional 100 shares of common stock held by his company, Island Insulation Corp., Matthews initiated a proxy contest for the purpose of electing a majority of LILCO's Board of Directors. The stated purpose of the other defendants, the Citizens Committee [the Steering Committee of Citizens to Replace], is to replace LILCO with a municipally owned utility company. The Citizens Committee was formed prior to this litigation, in order to challenge LILCO's construction of the Shoreham atomic energy plant, its service and its rates.

LILCO filed its complaint on October 21, 1985 alleging that defendants published a materially false and misleading advertisement in *Newsday*, a Long Island newspaper, and ran false and misleading radio advertisements throughout the New York area. The ads criticized LILCO's management and encouraged citizens to replace LILCO with a state-run company. The complaint sought an injunction against further alleged solicitation of LILCO shareholders until the claimed false and misleading statements had been corrected . . . .

* * * *

II

LILCO argues first, that in view of the necessity in every case to determine whether a communication constitutes a "solicitation" under the proxy rates, the district court abused its discretion by limiting LILCO's opportunity for discovery. Second, LILCO asserts that the district court erroneously held that communications to shareholders through general and indirect publications can in no circumstances constitute "solicitations" under the proxy rules. Finally, LILCO contests the district court's view that this construction of the proxy rules is necessary to render them compatible with the *First Amendment.*

* * * *

B. Rules Governing Proxy Solicitation

In our view the district court further erred in holding that the proxy rules cannot cover communications appearing in publications of general circulation and that are indirectly addressed to shareholders. Regulation 14(a) of the Securities Exchange Act governs the solicitation of proxies with respect to the securities of publicly held companies, with enumerated exceptions set forth in the rules. . . . Proxy rules promulgated by the Securities Exchange Commission (SEC) regulate as proxy solicitations:

(1) any request for a proxy whether or not accompanied by or included in a form of proxy;

(2) any request to execute or not to execute, or to revoke, a proxy; or

(3) the furnishing of a form of proxy or other communications to security holders under circumstances reasonably calculated to result in the procurement, withholding or revocation of a proxy.

Rule 14a–1, 17 C.F.R. § 240.14a–1

These rules apply not only to direct requests to furnish, revoke or withhold proxies, but also to communications which may indirectly accomplish such a result or constitute a step in a chain of communications designed ultimately to accomplish such a result. *Securities and Exchange Commission v. Okin,* 132 F.2d 784, 786 (2d Cir. 1943) (letter to shareholders was within the scope of the proxy rules where it was alleged that it was "a step in a campaign whose purpose it was to get [defendant] elected an officer of the company; it was to pave the way for an out-and-out solicitation later.")

The question in every case is whether the challenged communication, seen in the totality of circumstances, is "reasonably calculated" to influence the shareholders' votes. *[Citation omitted.]* Determination of the purpose of the communication depends upon the nature of the communication and the circumstances under which it was distributed. *Brown v. Chicago, Rock Island & Pacific* R.R., 328 F.2d 122 (7th Cir. 1964). . . .

Deciding whether a communication is a proxy solicitation does not depend upon whether it is "targeted directly" at shareholders. *See* Rule 14a–6(g), 17 C.F.R. § 240.14a–6(g) (requiring that solicitations in the form of "speeches, press releases, and television scripts" be filed with the SEC). As the SEC correctly notes in its amicus brief, it would "permit easy evasion of the proxy rules" to exempt all general and indirect communications to shareholders, and this is true whether or not the communication purports to address matters of "public interest." *See Medical Comm. for Human Rights v. SEC,* 139 U.S. App. D.C. 226, 432 F.2d 659 (D.C. Cir. 1970) (applying proxy rules to shareholder's proposal to prohibit company from manufacturing napalm during the Vietnam War). The SEC's authority to regulate proxy solicitations has traditionally extended into matters of public interest.

C. First Amendment Concerns

The extent to which the activities of the defendants amount to a solicitation of the proxies of shareholders of LILCO may determine whether or not their actions are protected by the *First Amendment.* Therefore, it is unnecessary to express an opinion on any claim of privilege under the *First Amendment* until there has been a determination of the "solicitation" issue as a result of further proceedings in the district court.

III

Because discovery here was so abbreviated and the district court's determination was predicated on a mistaken notion of what constitutes a proxy solicitation and on the relationship between the proxy rules and the *First Amendment,* the case must be remanded to the district court. . . .

DISSENT BY: WINTER

WINTER, C.J., dissenting:

In order to avoid a serious *first amendment* issue, I would construe the federal regulations governing the solicitation of proxies as inapplicable to the newspaper advertisement in question. *See Lowe v. Securities and Exchange Commission,* 472 U.S. 181, 105 S. Ct. 2557, 86 L. Ed. 2d 130 (1985). Further discovery would then be unnecessary, and I therefore respectfully dissent.

* * * *

II

The content of the Committee's advertisement is of critical importance. First, it is on its face addressed solely to the public. Second, it makes no mention either of proxies or of the shareholders' meeting demanded by Matthews. Third, the issues the ad addresses are quintessentially matters of public political debate, namely, whether a public power authority would provide cheaper electricity than LILCO. Claims of LILCO mismanagement are discussed solely in the context of their effect on its customers. Finally, the ad was published in the middle of an election campaign in which LILCO's future was an issue.

On these facts, therefore, LILCO's claim raises a constitutional issue of the first magnitude. It asks nothing less than that a federal court act as a censor, empowered to determine the truth or falsity of the ad's claims about the merits of public power and to enjoin further advocacy containing false claims. We need not resolve this constitutional issue, however.

Where advertisements are critical of corporate conduct but are facially directed solely to the public, in no way mention the exercise of proxies, and debate only matters of conceded public concern, I would construe federal proxy regulation as inapplicable, whatever the motive of those who purchase them. This position, which is strongly suggested by relevant case law, *see infra,* maximizes public debate, avoids embroiling the federal judiciary in determining the rightness or wrongness of conflicting positions on public policy, and does not significantly impede achievement of Congress' goal that shareholders exercise proxy rights on the basis of accurate information.

It is of course true that LILCO shareholders may be concerned about public allegations of mismanagement on LILCO's part. However, shareholders are most unlikely to be misled into thinking that advertisements of this kind, particularly when purchased in the name of a committee so obviously disinterested in the return on investment to LILCO's shareholders, are either necessarily accurate or authoritative sources of information about LILCO's management. Such advertisements, which in no way suggest internal reforms shareholders might bring about through the exercise of their proxies, are sheer political advocacy and would be so recognized by any reasonable shareholder.

To be sure, the fact that a corporation has become a target of political advocacy might well justify unease among shareholders. No one seriously asserts, however, that the right to criticize corporate behavior as a matter of public concern diminishes as shareholders' meetings become imminent.

* * * *

C. Proxy Fights

Sometimes different groups within a corporation will have different positions on how the shareholders should vote. In addition, there are sometimes challenges to the existing management of a corporation, and situations may arise in which different, competing groups of potential directors are battling for control of a corporation. In those instances, the outcome will often depend on which group has collected the most proxies. For this reason, a battle to obtain control of a corporation through a vote of the shareholders is referred to as a "proxy fight."

Proxy fights are one way a group might attempt to take control of a company (as opposed to "tender offers" or "acquisitions," discussed below). Proxy fights often occur when a group that wants to gain control, known as the "insurgent group," tries to become elected to the board and oust existing management, known as the "incumbent directors," by soliciting proxies from a large enough number of shareholders to elect its (the insurgent group's) own representatives to the Board of Directors. Of course there are several rules which govern the process of soliciting and obtaining proxies for a corporate election. Many of these rules are set forth in Rule 14(a) promulgated under the 1934 Act. For example, Rule 14a–7 provides that when an insurgent group wants to contact shareholders and provide material related to the contested vote, either: (i) management may mail the insurgent group's material to the shareholders directly and charge the group for the cost; or (ii) management can give the insurgent group a copy of the shareholder list and let the insurgent group distribute its own materials. As one can imagine, management typically prefers to control contact with its shareholders, so there is often an additional dispute about providing an insurgent group with access to a shareholder list that includes shareholder contact information.

Recovering Costs Associated with Obtaining Proxies in a Battle for Control

Once the proxy battle is over and one side has won and the other has lost, the parties often turn to the issue of getting their costs reimbursed. The rules might vary from state to state, but, in general, there are different rules which govern the reimbursement of costs for insurgents and for incumbents. When the incumbent directors expend money to defend their positions from an insurgent effort to oust them, as long as the expenses are *not excessive and not illegal,* there is not typically a problem with the group reimbursing themselves from company assets once they are victorious. The issues relating to reimbursement of costs arising in a proxy battle are discussed in the *Rosenfeld v. Fairchild Engine & Airplane Corp.* case, below.

Rosenfeld v. Fairchild Engine & Airplane Corp.

128 N.E.2d 291 (N.Y. 1955)

FROESSEL, J.:

In a stockholder's derivative action brought by plaintiff, an attorney, who owns 25 out of the company's over 2,300,000 shares, he seeks to compel the return of $261,522, paid out of the corporate treasury to reimburse both sides in a proxy contest for their expenses. The Appellate Division has unanimously affirmed a judgment of an Official Referee dismissing plaintiff's complaint on the merits, and we agree. . . .

Of the amount in controversy $106,000 were spent out of corporate funds by the old board of directors while still in office in defense of their position in said contest; $28,000 were paid to the old board by the new board after the change of management following the proxy contest, to compensate the former directors for such of the remaining expenses of their unsuccessful defense as the new board found was fair and reasonable; payment of $127,000, representing reimbursement of expenses to members of the prevailing group, was expressly ratified by a 16 to 1 majority vote of the stockholders.

The essential facts are not in dispute. . . . The Appellate Division found that the difference between plaintiff's group and the old board "went deep into the policies of the company", and that among these Ward's [employment] contract was one of the "main points of contention". . . .

By way of contrast with the findings here, in *Lawyers' Adv. Co. v. Consolidated Ry. Lighting & Refrig. Co.* (187 N.Y. 395), which was an action to recover for the cost of publishing newspaper notices not authorized by the board of directors, it was expressly found that the proxy contest there involved was "by one faction in its contest with another for the control of the corporation * * * a contest for the perpetuation of their offices and control" (p. 399). We there said by way of *dicta* that under *such* circumstances the publication of certain notices on behalf of the management faction was not a corporate expenditure which the directors had the power to authorize.

Other jurisdictions and our own lower courts have held that management may look to the corporate treasury for the reasonable expenses of soliciting proxies to defend its position in a bona fide policy contest. [*Citations omitted.*]

It should be noted that plaintiff does not argue that the aforementioned sums were fraudulently extracted from the corporation; indeed, his counsel conceded that "the charges were fair and reasonable", but denied "they were legal charges which may be reimbursed for". This is therefore not a case where a stockholder challenges specific items, which, on examination, the trial court may find unwarranted, excessive or otherwise improper. . . .

If directors of a corporation may not in good faith incur reasonable and proper expenses in soliciting proxies in these days of giant corporations with vast numbers of stockholders, the corporate business might be seriously interfered with because of stockholder indifference and the difficulty of procuring a quorum, where there is no contest. In the event of a proxy contest, if the directors may not freely answer the challenges of outside groups and in good faith defend their actions with respect to corporate policy for the information of the stockholders, they and the corporation may be at the mercy of persons seeking to wrest control for their own purposes, so long as such persons have ample funds to conduct a proxy contest. The test is clear. When the directors act in good faith in a contest over policy, they have the right to incur reasonable and proper expenses for solicitation of proxies and in defense of their corporate policies, and are not obliged to sit idly by. The courts are entirely competent to pass upon their *bona fides* in any given case, as well as the nature of their expenditures when duly challenged.

It is also our view that the members of the so-called new group could be reimbursed by the corporation for their expenditures in this contest by affirmative vote of the stockholders. With regard to these ultimately successful contestants, as the Appellate Division below has noted, there was, of course, "no duty * * * to set forth the facts, with corresponding obligation of the corporation to pay for such expense". However, where a majority of the stockholders chose—in this case by a vote of 16 to 1—to reimburse the successful contestants for achieving the very end sought and voted for by them as owners of the corporation, we see no reason to deny the effect of their ratification nor to hold the corporate body powerless to determine how its own moneys shall be spent.

The rule then which we adopt is simply this: In a contest over policy, as compared to a purely personal power contest, corporate directors have the right to make reasonable and proper expenditures, subject to the scrutiny of the courts when duly challenged, from the corporate treasury for the purpose of persuading the stockholders of the correctness of their position and soliciting their support for policies which the directors believe, in all good faith, are in the best interests of the corporation. The stockholders, moreover, have the right to reimburse successful contestants for the reasonable and bona fide expenses incurred by them in any such policy contest, subject to like court scrutiny. That is not to say, however, that corporate directors can, under any circumstances, disport themselves in a proxy contest with the corporation's moneys to an unlimited extent. Where it is established that such moneys have been spent for personal power, individual gain or private advantage, and not in the belief that such expenditures are in the best interests of the stockholders and the corporation, or where the fairness and reasonableness of the amounts allegedly expended are duly and successfully challenged, the courts will not hesitate to disallow them.

The judgment of the Appellate Division should be affirmed, without costs.

* * * *

SECTION III: Shareholder Proposals

A. Rule 14a–8

Rule 14a–8 of the 1934 Act allows qualifying shareholders to submit certain proposals to their fellow shareholders for a vote by having these proposals placed on the company's proxy statement to the shareholders. Since the company already bears the expenses associated with its proxy statement, Rule 14a–8 allows the shareholder's proposal to be included with the company's proxy statement at no additional cost to the shareholder. The biggest question that arises in this area (and therefore, the question most frequently asked of students) is what criteria need to be satisfied in order for a shareholder proposal to "qualify" to be included in the proxy statement. Realize that shareholders (even through a proposal) do not get to "control" the Board of Directors. The proposals must relate to certain areas over which the shareholders have control. In order to satisfy the requirement that a proposal be within an area which is a proper subject for action by the shareholders, most proposals are worded as recommendations, rather than mandates and are nonbinding in nature. Often a company will seek to exclude a shareholder proposal from its proxy materials. Shareholder proposals may be excluded if the proposal meets one of the many grounds for exclusion contained in Rule 14a–8. In order to exclude a proposal, a company will typically submit a request for a "no-action letter" with the Securities and Exchange Commission (the "SEC"). In such a request, the company will provide the grounds that it believes exist to exclude a shareholder proposal and ask whether the SEC staff would recommend an enforcement action against the company if it excluded the proposal on those grounds. No-action letters are neither binding, nor required, but they are a device frequently used in such circumstances. No-action letters are also not binding on the courts. In *AFSCME v. AIG, Inc.* (462 F.3d 121 (2d Cir. 2006)) the SEC, at AIG's request, had issued a no-action letter saying that AIG could exclude a shareholder proposal by the American Federation of State, County & Municipal Employees from the AIG corporate proxy materials. Notwithstanding the no-action letter, the court held that AIG could not exclude the proposal.

There are both procedural and substantive requirements under Rule 14a–8 which must be met for a shareholder proposal to be included in a company's proxy materials. The procedural requirements include:

- In order to be eligible to submit a proposal a shareholder must hold $2,000 in market value of the company's stock (or 1% of the company's voting stock), and have held it, continuously, for the 12 months preceding the proposal;

- A shareholder may not submit more than one proposal for each shareholder's meeting;
- A proposal may not exceed 500 words;
- Most proposals must be submitted to the company at least 120 days before the company's proxy statement is released; and
- Either the shareholder or the shareholder's "qualified representative" must attend the meeting at which the proposal is to be considered.

The substantive requirements for a shareholder proposal include:

- The topic of the proposal must be a proper subject for actions by shareholders under state law of the state in which the corporation is organized;
- The proposal may not, if implemented, cause the company to violate any law;
- The proposal may not address a personal grievance or special interest which is not applicable to the other shareholders;
- If the proposal relates to the company's operations, those operations must involve at least 5% of the company's assets, net earnings, or gross sales OR the operations must otherwise be "significantly related to the company's business." (Proposals will be included notwithstanding their failure to reach the specified economic threshold IF a significant relationship to the company's business is demonstrated on the face of the resolution or in the supporting material);
- The proposal must not violate the Proxy Rules (such as those prohibiting materially misleading statements);
- The proposal cannot be beyond the company's power to implement (such as a vote requiring the world to adopt a universal currency);
- The proposal may not address management functions, such as the company's ordinary business operations;
- The proposal may not relate to specific amounts of cash or stock dividends; and

- The proposal may not directly conflict with one of the company's own proposals that is being submitted at the same meeting.
- In addition, if the proposal was previously submitted within the last 5 years and did not receive the required percentage of votes, it may be excluded by the company. (If more than 10% of the shareholders voted in favor of the previously submitted proposal, it will not be excluded on these grounds. If fewer than 10% of the shareholders voted in favor of the previously submitted proposal, the rules become more complex.)

Lovenheim v. Iroquois Brands, Ltd.

618 F. Supp. 554 (D.C. 1985)

EASCH, J.:

I. BACKGROUND

This matter is now before the Court on plaintiff's motion for preliminary injunction.

Plaintiff Peter C. Lovenheim, owner of two hundred shares of common stock in Iroquois Brands, Ltd. (hereinafter "Iroquois/Delaware"), seeks to bar Iroquois/Delaware from excluding from the proxy materials being sent to all shareholders in preparation for an upcoming shareholder meeting information concerning a proposed resolution he intends to offer at the meeting. Mr. Lovenheim's proposed resolution relates to the procedure used to force-feed geese for production of pate de foie gras in France,[2] a type of pate imported by Iroquois/Delaware. Specifically, his resolution calls upon the Directors of Iroquois/Delaware to:

---

2 Paté de foie gras is made from the liver of geese. According to Mr. Lovenheim's affidavit, force-feeding is frequently used in order to expand the liver and thereby produce a larger quantity of pate. Mr. Lovenheim's affidavit also contains a description of the force-feeding process:

> *Force-feeding usually begins when the geese are four months old. On some farms where feeding is mechanized, the bird's body and wings are placed in a metal brace and its neck is stretched. Through a funnel inserted 10–12 inches down the throat of the goose, a machine pumps up to 400 grams of corn-based mash into its stomach. An elastic band around the goose's throat prevents regurgitation. When feeding is manual, a handler uses a funnel and stick to force the mash down. . . .*

Plaintiff contends that such force-feeding is a form of cruelty to animals. . . .

> *Plaintiff has offered no evidence that force-feeding is used by Iroquois/Delaware's supplier in producing the pate imported by Iroquois/Delaware. However his proposal calls upon the committee he seeks to create to investigate this question.*

> form a committee to study the methods by which its French supplier produces pate de foie gras, and report to the shareholders its findings and opinions, based on expert consultation, on whether this production method causes undue distress, pain or suffering to the animals involved and, if so, whether further distribution of this product should be discontinued until a more humane production method is developed. . . .

Mr. Lovenheim's right to compel Iroquois/Delaware to insert information concerning his proposal in the proxy materials turns on the applicability of section 14(a) of the Securities Exchange Act of 1934 . . . ("the Exchange Act"), and the shareholder proposal rule promulgated by the Securities and Exchange Commission ("SEC"), Rule 14a–8. That rule states in pertinent part:

> If any security holder of an issuer notifies the issuer of his intention to present a proposal for action at a forthcoming meeting of the issuer's security holders, the issuer shall set forth the proposal in its proxy statement and identify it in its form of proxy and provide means by which security holders [presenting a proposal may present in the proxy statement a statement of not more than 200* words in support of the proposal].

Iroquois/Delaware has refused to allow information concerning Mr. Lovenheim's proposal to be included in proxy materials being sent in connection with the next annual shareholders meeting. In doing so, Iroquois/Delaware relies on an exception to the general requirement of Rule 14a–8, Rule 14a–8(c)(5). That exception provides that an issuer of securities "may omit a proposal and any statement in support thereof" from its proxy statement and form of proxy:

> if the proposal relates to operations which account for less than 5 percent of the issuer's total assets at the end of its most recent fiscal year, and for less than 5 percent of its net earnings and gross sales for its most recent fiscal year, and is not otherwise significantly related to the issuer's business.

Rule 14a–8(c)(5). . . .

* * * *

* [The current word limit under Rule 14a–8 is 500 words.—*Eds.*]

C. Applicability of Rule 14a–8(c)(5) Exception

. . . [T]he likelihood of plaintiff's prevailing in this litigation turns primarily on the applicability to plaintiff's proposal of the exception to the shareholder proposal rule contained in Rule 14a–8(c)(5).

Iroquois/Delaware's reliance on the argument that this exception applies is based on the following information contained in the affidavit of its president: Iroquois/Delaware has annual revenues of $141 million with $6 million in annual profits and $78 million in assets. In contrast, its pate de foie gras sales were just $79,000 last year, representing a net loss on pate sales of $3,121. Iroquois/Delaware has only $34,000 in assets related to pate. Thus none of the company's net earnings and less than .05 percent of its assets are implicated by plaintiff's proposal. McCaffrey Affidavit para. 6. These levels are obviously far below the five percent threshold set forth in the first portion of the exception claimed by Iroquois/Delaware.

Plaintiff does not contest that his proposed resolution relates to a matter of little economic significance to Iroquois/Delaware. Nevertheless he contends that the Rule 14a–8(c)(5) exception is not applicable as it cannot be said that his proposal "is not otherwise significantly related to the issuer's business" as is required by the final portion of that exception. In other words, plaintiff's argument that Rule 14a–8 does not permit omission of his proposal rests on the assertion that the rule and statute on which it is based do not permit omission merely because a proposal is not economically significant where a proposal has "ethical or social significance.[8]"

Iroquois/Delaware challenges plaintiff's view that ethical and social proposals cannot be excluded even if they do not meet the economic or five percent test. Instead, Iroquois/Delaware views the exception solely in economic terms as permitting omission of any proposals relating to a de minimis share of assets and profits. Iroquois/Delaware asserts that since corporations are economic entities, only an economic test is appropriate.

---

[8] The assertion that the proposal is significant in an ethical and social sense relies on plaintiff's argument that "the very availability of a market for products that may be obtained through the inhumane force-feeding of geese cannot help but contribute to the continuation of such treatment." Plaintiff's brief characterizes the humane treatment of animals as among the foundations of western culture and cites in support of this view the Seven Laws of Noah, an animal protection statute enacted by the Massachusetts Bay Colony in 1641, numerous federal statutes enacted since 1877, and animal protection laws existing in all fifty states and the District of Columbia. An additional indication of the significance of plaintiff's proposal is the support of such leading organizations in the field of animal care as the American Society for the Prevention of Cruelty to Animals and The Humane Society of the United States for measures aimed at discontinuing use of force-feeding. . . .

The Court would note that the applicability of the Rule 14a–8(c)(5) exception to Mr. Lovenheim's proposal represents a close question given the lack of clarity in the exception itself. In effect, plaintiff relies on the word "otherwise," suggesting that it indicates the drafters of the rule intended that other noneconomic tests of significance be used. Iroquois/Delaware relies on the fact that the rule examines other significance in relation to the issuer's business. Because of the apparent ambiguity of the rule, the Court considers the history of the shareholder proposal rule in determining the proper interpretation of the most recent version of that rule.

Prior to 1983, paragraph 14a–8(c)(5) excluded proposals "not significantly related to the issuer's business" but did not contain an objective economic significance test such as the five percent of sales, assets, and earnings specified in the first part of the current version. Although a series of SEC decisions through 1976 allowing issuers to exclude proposals challenging compliance with the Arab economic boycott of Israel allowed exclusion if the issuer did less than one percent of their business with Arab countries or Israel, the Commission stated later in 1976 that it did "not believe that subparagraph (c) (5) should be hinged solely on the economic relativity of a proposal." [*Citation omitted.*] Thus the Commission required inclusion "in many situations in which the related business comprised less than one percent" of the company's revenues, profits or assets "where the proposal has raised *policy questions* important enough to be considered 'significantly related' to the issuer's business.[11]"

As indicated above, the 1983 revision adopted the five percent test of economic significance in an effort to create a more objective standard. Nevertheless, in adopting this standard, the Commission stated that proposals will be includable notwithstanding their "failure to reach the specified economic thresholds if a significant relationship to the issuer's business is demonstrated on the face of the resolution or supporting statement." [*Citation omitted.*] Thus it seems clear based on the history of the rule that "the meaning of 'significantly related' is not *limited* to economic significance." [*Citation omitted.*]

The only decision in this Circuit cited by the parties relating to the scope of section 14 and the shareholder proposal rule is *Medical Committee for Human Rights v. SEC,* 139 U.S. App. D.C. 226, 432 F.2d 659 (D.C. Cir. 1970). That case concerned an effort by shareholders of Dow Chemical Company to advise other

---

11 . . . For example, "proposals requesting the cessation of further development, planning and construction of nuclear power plants and proposals requesting shareholders be informed as to all aspects of the company's business in European communist countries have been included in this way." . . . .

shareholders of their proposal directed at prohibiting Dow's production of napalm. Dow had relied on the counterpart of the 14a–8(c) (5) exemption then in effect to exclude the proposal from proxy materials and the SEC accepted Dow's position without elaborating on its basis for doing so. In remanding the matter back to the SEC for the Commission to provide the basis for its decision, *id.* at 682, the Court noted what it termed "substantial questions" as to whether an interpretation of the shareholder proposal rule "which permitted omission of [a] proposal as one motivated primarily by *general* political or social concerns would conflict with the congressional intent underlying section 14(a) of the [Exchange] Act." 432 F.2d at 680 (emphasis in original).

Iroquois/Delaware attempts to distinguish *Medical Committee for Human Rights* as a case where a company sought to exclude a proposal that, unlike Mr. Lovenheim's proposal, was economically significant merely because the motivation of the proponents was political. The argument is not without appeal given the fact that the *Medical Committee* Court was confronted with a regulation that contained no reference to economic significance. [*Citation omitted.*] Yet the *Medical Committee* decision contains language suggesting that the Court assumed napalm was not economically significant to Dow. . . .

This Court . . . . cannot ignore the history of the rule which reveals no decision by the Commission to limit the determination to the economic criteria relied on by Iroquois/Delaware. The Court therefore holds that in light of the ethical and social significance of plaintiff's proposal and the fact that it implicates significant levels of sales, plaintiff has shown a likelihood of prevailing on the merits with regard to the issue of whether his proposal is "otherwise significantly related" to Iroquois/Delaware's business.[16]

III. Other Factors Bearing on Injunctive Relief

* * * *

C. Public Interest

Plaintiff contends that the public interest represented in the Exchange Act is served by granting injunctive relief and allowing all shareholders to make an informed vote on the proposal. In contrast, Iroquois/Delaware submits that an injunction would be contrary to the "public interest in permitting businesses to function free from harassment, and in preventing proxy statements from

[16] The result would, of course, be different if plaintiff's proposal was ethically significant in the abstract but had no meaningful relationship to the business of Iroquois/Delaware as Iroquois/Delaware was not engaged in the business of importing pate de foie gras.

becoming cluttered." Given the "overriding" public interest embodied in section 14(a) and the shareholder proposal rule in assuring shareholders the right to control the important decisions which affect corporations, *Medical Committee*, 432 F.2d at 680–81, the Court finds that granting the preliminary injunction would be consistent with the public interest.

IV. CONCLUSION

For the reasons discussed above, the Court concludes that plaintiff's motion for preliminary injunction should be granted.

CA, Inc. v. AFSCME Employees Pension Plan

953 A.2d 227 (Del. 2008)

JACOBS, J.:

This proceeding arises from a certification by the United States Securities and Exchange Commission (the "SEC"), to this Court, of two questions of law pursuant to Article IV, Section 11(8) of the Delaware Constitution and Supreme Court Rule 41. . . .

I. FACTS

CA is a Delaware corporation whose board of directors consists of twelve persons, all of whom sit for reelection each year. CA's annual meeting of stockholders is scheduled to be held on September 9, 2008. . . .

AFSCME, a CA stockholder, is associated with the American Federation of State, County and Municipal Employees. On March 13, 2008, AFSCME submitted a proposed stockholder bylaw (the "Bylaw" or "proposed Bylaw") for inclusion in the Company's proxy materials for its 2008 annual meeting of stockholders. The Bylaw, if adopted by CA stockholders, would amend the Company's bylaws to provide as follows:

> RESOLVED, that pursuant to section 109 of the Delaware General Corporation Law and Article IX of the bylaws of CA, Inc., stockholders of CA hereby amend the bylaws to add the following Section 14 to Article II:
>
> The board of directors shall cause the corporation to reimburse a stockholder or group of stockholders (together, the "Nominator") for reasonable expenses ("Expenses") incurred in connection with nominating one or more candidates in a contested election of directors to the corporation's board of directors, including, without

> limitation, printing, mailing, legal, solicitation, travel, advertising and public relations expenses, so long as (a) the election of fewer than 50% of the directors to be elected is contested in the election, (b) one or more candidates nominated by the Nominator are elected to the corporation's board of directors, (c) stockholders are not permitted to cumulate their votes for directors, and (d) the election occurred, and the Expenses were incurred, after this bylaw's adoption. The amount paid to a Nominator under this bylaw in respect of a contested election shall not exceed the amount expended by the corporation in connection with such election.

* * * *

It is undisputed that the decision whether to reimburse election expenses is presently vested in the discretion of CA's board of directors, subject to their fiduciary duties and applicable Delaware law.

On April 18, 2008, CA notified the SEC's Division of Corporation Finance (the "Division") of its intention to exclude the proposed Bylaw from its 2008 proxy materials. The Company requested from the Division a "no-action letter" stating that the Division would not recommend any enforcement action to the SEC if CA excluded the AFSCME proposal.

* * * *

To obtain guidance, the SEC, at the Division's request, certified two questions of Delaware law to this Court. Given the short timeframe for the filing of CA's proxy materials, we concluded that "there are important and urgent reasons for an immediate determination of the questions certified," and accepted those questions for review on July 1, 2008.

II. THE CERTIFIED QUESTIONS

The two questions certified to us by the SEC are as follows:

1. Is the AFSCME Proposal a proper subject for action by shareholders as a matter of Delaware law?
2. Would the AFSCME Proposal, if adopted, cause CA to violate any Delaware law to which it is subject?

* * * *

III. THE FIRST QUESTION

A. Preliminary Comments

The first question presented is whether the Bylaw is a proper subject for shareholder action, more precisely, whether the Bylaw may be proposed and enacted by shareholders without the concurrence of the Company's board of directors. Before proceeding further, we make some preliminary comments in an effort to delineate a framework within which to begin our analysis.

First, the DGCL empowers both the board of directors and the shareholders of a Delaware corporation to adopt, amend or repeal the corporation's bylaws. 8 Del. C. § 109(a) relevantly provides that:

> After a corporation has received any payment for any of its stock, the power to adopt, amend or repeal bylaws shall be in the stockholders entitled to vote. . .; provided, however, any corporation may, in its certificate of incorporation, confer the power to adopt, amend or repeal bylaws upon the directors. . . . The fact that such power has been so conferred upon the directors. . . shall not divest the stockholders. . ., of the power, nor limit their power to adopt, amend or repeal bylaws.

Pursuant to Section 109(a), CA's Certificate of Incorporation confers the power to adopt, amend or repeal the bylaws upon the Company's board of directors. Because the statute commands that conferral "shall not divest the stockholders ... of... nor limit" their power, both the board and the shareholders of CA, independently and concurrently, possess the power to adopt, amend and repeal the bylaws.

Second, the vesting of that concurrent power in both the board and the shareholders raises the issue of whether the stockholders' power is coextensive with that of the board, and vice versa. . . . [T]he DGCL has not allocated to the board and the shareholders the identical, coextensive power to adopt, amend and repeal the bylaws. Therefore, how that power is allocated between those two decision-making bodies requires an analysis that is more complex.

. . . Section 109(a) vests in the shareholders a power to adopt, amend or repeal bylaws that is legally sacrosanct, i.e., the power cannot be non-consensually eliminated or limited by anyone other than the legislature itself. If viewed in isolation, Section 109(a) could be read to make the board's and the shareholders' power to adopt, amend or repeal bylaws identical and coextensive, but Section 109(a) does not exist in a vacuum. It must be read together with 8 Del. C. § 141(a), which pertinently provides that:

> The business and affairs of every corporation organized under this chapter shall be managed by or under the direction of a board of directors, except as may be otherwise provided in this chapter or in its certificate of incorporation.

No such broad management power is statutorily allocated to the shareholders. Indeed, it is well-established that stockholders of a corporation subject to the DGCL may not directly manage the business and affairs of the corporation, at least without specific authorization in either the statute or the certificate of incorporation. Therefore, the shareholders' statutory power to adopt, amend or repeal bylaws is not coextensive with the board's concurrent power and is limited by the board's management prerogatives under Section 141(a).[7]

Third, it follows that, to decide whether the Bylaw proposed by AFSCME is a proper subject for shareholder action under Delaware law, we must first determine: (1) the scope or reach of the shareholders' power to adopt, alter or repeal the bylaws of a Delaware corporation, and then (2) whether the Bylaw at issue here falls within that permissible scope. Where, as here, the proposed bylaw is one that limits director authority, that is an elusively difficult task. . . .

B. Analysis

1.

Two other provisions of the DGCL, *8 Del.* C. §§ 109(b) and 102(b)(1), bear importantly on the first question and form the basis of contentions advanced by each side.

* * * *

AFSCME relies heavily upon the language of Section 109(b), which permits the bylaws of a corporation to contain "any provision. . . relating to the. . . rights or powers of its stockholders [and] directors. . . ." The Bylaw, AFSCME argues, "relates to" the right of the stockholders meaningfully to participate in the process of electing directors, a right that necessarily "includes the right to nominate an opposing slate."

---

[7] Because the board's managerial authority under Section 141(a) is a cardinal precept of the DGCL, we do not construe Section 109 as an "except[ion]. . . otherwise specified in th[e] [DGCL]" to Section 141(a). Rather, the shareholders' statutory power to adopt, amend or repeal bylaws under Section 109 cannot be "inconsistent with law," including Section 141(a).

CA argues, in response, that Section 109(b) is not dispositive, because it cannot be read in isolation from, and without regard to, Section 102(b)(1). CA's argument runs as follows: the Bylaw would limit the substantive decision-making authority of CA's board to decide whether or not to expend corporate funds for a particular purpose, here, reimbursing director election expenses. Section 102(b)(1) contemplates that any provision that limits the broad statutory power of the directors must be contained in the certificate of incorporation. Therefore, the proposed Bylaw can only be in CA's Certificate of Incorporation, as distinguished from its bylaws. Accordingly, the proposed bylaw falls outside the universe of permissible bylaws authorized by Section 109(b).

Implicit in CA's argument is the premise that *any* bylaw that in any respect might be viewed as limiting or restricting the power of the board of directors automatically falls outside the scope of permissible bylaws. That simply cannot be. That reasoning, taken to its logical extreme, would result in eliminating altogether the shareholders' statutory right to adopt, amend or repeal bylaws. Bylaws, by their very nature, set down rules and procedures that bind a corporation's board and its shareholders. In that sense, most, if not all, bylaws could be said to limit the otherwise unlimited discretionary power of the board. Yet Section 109(a) carves out an area of shareholder power to adopt, amend or repeal bylaws that is expressly inviolate.[13] Therefore, to argue that the Bylaw at issue here limits the board's power to manage the business and affairs of the Company only begins, but cannot end, the analysis needed to decide whether the Bylaw is a proper subject for shareholder action. The question left unanswered is what is the scope of shareholder action that Section 109(b) permits yet does not improperly intrude upon the directors' power to manage corporation's business and affairs under Section 141(a).

* * * *

2.

It is well-established Delaware law that a proper function of bylaws is not to mandate how the board should decide specific substantive business decisions, but rather, to define the process and procedures by which those decisions are made. As the Court of Chancery has noted:

---

[13] Section 109(a), to reiterate, provides that the fact that the certificate of incorporation confers upon the directors the power to adopt, amend or repeal bylaws "shall not divest the stockholders . . . of the power. . ., nor limit their power to adopt, amend or repeal bylaws."

> Traditionally, the bylaws have been the corporate instrument used to set forth the rules by which the corporate board conducts its business. . . .

. . . .Such purely procedural bylaws do not improperly encroach upon the board's managerial authority under Section 141(a).

The process-creating function of bylaws provides a starting point to address the Bylaw at issue. It enables us to frame the issue in terms of whether the Bylaw is one that establishes or regulates a process for substantive director decision-making, or one that mandates the decision itself. Not surprisingly, the parties sharply divide on that question. We conclude that the Bylaw, even though infelicitously couched as a substantive-sounding mandate to expend corporate funds, has both the intent and the effect of regulating the process for electing directors of CA. Therefore, we determine that the Bylaw is a proper subject for shareholder action, and set forth our reasoning below.

Although CA concedes that "restrictive procedural bylaws (such as those requiring the presence of all directors and unanimous board consent to take action) are acceptable," it points out that even facially procedural bylaws can unduly intrude upon board authority. The Bylaw being proposed here is unduly intrusive, CA claims, because, by mandating reimbursement of a stockholder's proxy expenses, it limits the board's broad discretionary authority to decide whether to grant reimbursement at all. CA further claims that because (in defined circumstances) the Bylaw mandates the expenditure of corporate funds, its subject matter is necessarily substantive, not process-oriented, and, therefore falls outside the scope of what Section 109(b) permits.

Because the Bylaw is couched as a command to reimburse ("The board of directors shall cause the corporation to reimburse a stockholder"), it lends itself to CA's criticism. But the Bylaw's wording, although relevant, is not dispositive of whether or not it is process-related. The Bylaw could easily have been worded differently, to emphasize its process, as distinguished from its mandatory payment, component. By saying this we do not mean to suggest that this Bylaw's reimbursement component can be ignored. What we do suggest is that a bylaw that requires the expenditure of corporate funds does not, for that reason alone, become automatically deprived of its process-related character. A hypothetical example illustrates the point. Suppose that the directors of a corporation live in different states and at a considerable distance from the corporation's headquarters. Suppose also that the shareholders enact a bylaw that requires all meetings of directors to take place in person at the corporation's headquarters. Such a bylaw would be clearly process-related, yet it cannot be supposed that the shareholders would lack the power to adopt the bylaw because it would require the corporation to expend its funds to reimburse the directors' travel expenses. Whether or not a bylaw is process-related must necessarily be determined in light of its context and purpose.

The context of the Bylaw at issue here is the process for electing directors—a subject in which shareholders of Delaware corporations have a legitimate and protected interest. The purpose of the Bylaw is to promote the integrity of that electoral process by facilitating the nomination of director candidates by stockholders or groups of stockholders. Generally, and under the current framework for electing directors in contested elections, only board-sponsored nominees for election are reimbursed for their election expenses. Dissident candidates are not, unless they succeed in replacing at least a majority of the entire board. The Bylaw would encourage the nomination of non-management board candidates by promising reimbursement of the nominating stockholders' proxy expenses if one or more of its candidates are elected. In that the shareholders also have a legitimate interest, because the Bylaw would facilitate the exercise of their right to participate in selecting the contestants. . . .

The shareholders of a Delaware corporation have the right "to participate in selecting the contestants" for election to the board. The shareholders are entitled to facilitate the exercise of that right by proposing a bylaw that would encourage candidates other than board-sponsored nominees to stand for election. The Bylaw would accomplish that by committing the corporation to reimburse the election expenses of shareholders whose candidates are successfully elected. That the implementation of that proposal would require the expenditure of corporate funds will not, in and of itself, make such a bylaw an improper subject matter for shareholder action. Accordingly, we answer the first question certified to us in the affirmative.

. . . .[W]e turn to the second certified question, which is whether the proposed Bylaw, if adopted, would cause CA to violate any Delaware law to which it is subject.

IV. THE SECOND QUESTION

In answering the first question, we have already determined that the Bylaw does not facially violate any provision of the DGCL or of CA's Certificate of Incorporation. The question thus becomes whether the Bylaw would violate any common law rule or precept. . . . Therefore, in response to the second question, we must necessarily consider any possible circumstance under which a board of directors might be required to act. Under at least one such hypothetical, the board of directors would breach their fiduciary duties if they complied with the Bylaw. Accordingly, we conclude that the Bylaw, as drafted, would violate the prohibition, which our decisions have derived from Section 141(a), against contractual arrangements that commit the board of directors to a course of action that would preclude them from fully discharging their fiduciary duties to the corporation and its shareholders.

This Court has previously invalidated contracts that would require a board to act or not act in such a fashion that would limit the exercise of their fiduciary duties. In *Paramount Communications, Inc. v. QVC Network, Inc.,* we invalidated a "no shop" provision of a merger agreement with a favored bidder (Viacom) that prevented the directors of the target company (Paramount) from communicating with a competing bidder (QVC) the terms of its competing bid in an effort to obtain the highest available value for shareholders. . . .

Similarly, in *Quickturn Design Systems, Inc. v. Shapiro,* the directors of the target company (Quickturn) adopted a "poison pill" rights plan that contained a so-called "delayed redemption provision" as a defense against a hostile takeover bid, as part of which the bidder (Mentor Graphics) intended to wage a proxy contest to replace the target company board. The delayed redemption provision was intended to deter that effort, by preventing any newly elected board from redeeming the poison pill for six months. This Court invalidated that provision, because it would "impermissibly deprive any newly elected board of both its statutory authority to manage the corporation under *8 Del. C.* § 141(a) and its concomitant fiduciary duty pursuant to that statutory mandate." We held that:

> One of the most basic tenets of Delaware corporate law is that the board of directors has the ultimate responsibility for managing the business and affairs of a corporation. [. . .] The Quickturn certificate of incorporation contains no provision purporting to limit the authority of the board in any way. The Delayed Redemption Provision, however, would prevent a newly elected board of directors from *completely* discharging its fundamental management duties to the corporation and its stockholders for six months. While the Delayed Redemption Provision limits the board of directors' authority in only one respect, the suspension of the Rights Plan, it nonetheless restricts the board's power in an area of fundamental importance to the shareholders—negotiating a possible sale of the corporation. Therefore, we hold that the Delayed Redemption Provision is invalid under Section 141(a), which confers upon any newly elected board of

directors *full* power to manage and direct the business and affairs of a Delaware corporation. [*Citations omitted.*]

Both *QVC* and *Quickturn* involved binding contractual arrangements that the board of directors had voluntarily imposed upon themselves. This case involves a binding bylaw that the shareholders seek to impose involuntarily on the directors in the specific area of election expense reimbursement. Although this case is distinguishable in that respect, the distinction is one without a difference. The reason is that the internal governance contract—which here takes the form of a bylaw—is one that would also prevent the directors from exercising their full managerial power in circumstances where their fiduciary duties would otherwise require them to deny reimbursement to a dissident slate. That this limitation would be imposed by a majority vote of the shareholders rather than by the directors themselves, does not, in our view, legally matter.[32]

* * * *

[T]he Bylaw, as written, [is] invalid: the Bylaw mandates reimbursement of election expenses in circumstances that a proper application of fiduciary principles could preclude. That such circumstances could arise is not far fetched. Under Delaware law, a board may expend corporate funds to reimburse proxy expenses "[w]here the controversy is concerned with a question of policy as distinguished from personnel o[r] management." But in a situation where the proxy contest is motivated by personal or petty concerns, or to promote interests that do not further, or are adverse to, those of the corporation, the board's fiduciary duty could compel that reimbursement be denied altogether.[34]

It is in this respect that the proposed Bylaw, as written, would violate Delaware law if enacted by CA's shareholders. As presently drafted, the Bylaw would afford CA's directors full discretion to determine what *amount* of reimbursement is appropriate, because the directors would be obligated to grant only the "reasonable" expenses of a successful short slate. Unfortunately, that does not go far enough, because the Bylaw contains no language or provision that would reserve to CA's directors their full power to exercise their fiduciary duty to decide whether or not it would be appropriate, in a specific case, to award reimbursement at all.

---

32 Only if the Bylaw provision were enacted as an amendment to CA's Certificate of Incorporation would that distinction be dispositive. *See 8 Del. C.* § 102 (b)(1) and § 242.

34 Such a circumstance could arise, for example, if a shareholder group affiliated with a competitor of the company were to cause the election of a minority slate of candidates committed to using their director positions to obtain, and then communicate, valuable proprietary strategic or product information to the competitor.

* * * *

In arriving at this conclusion, we express no view on whether the Bylaw as currently drafted, would create a better governance scheme from a policy standpoint. We decide only what is, and is not, legally permitted under the DGCL. That statute, as currently drafted, is the expression of policy as decreed by the Delaware legislature. Those who believe that CA's shareholders should be permitted to make the proposed Bylaw as drafted part of CA's governance scheme, have two alternatives. They may seek to amend the Certificate of Incorporation to include the substance of the Bylaw; *or* they may seek recourse from the Delaware General Assembly.

Accordingly, we answer the second question certified to us in the affirmative. . . .

QUESTIONS

1. The court in the preceding case determined that the amendment of the Bylaws was a proper matter for shareholder action. However, the bylaw, as drafted, was problematic because it impacted the CA directors' ability to "exercise their full fiduciary duty." What point was the court making?

2. If the proposed bylaw were to be adopted, could you suggest amendments to the CA charter that might protect the board of directors from claims that they had violated their fiduciary duty?

B. The Dodd-Frank Act, Director Nominations and "Say on Pay"

Under the authority of the Dodd-Frank Act of 2010, the SEC had adopted rules that purported to provide shareholders with increased input about the directors elected to a company's board. The rules were adopted to address the concern that shareholders of publicly traded companies do not have the right to nominate directors and typically could only vote on a "slate" of directors proposed by the Board of Directors. The SEC's new rule 14a–11 of the 1934 Act applied to public companies, and would have allowed certain shareholders (those who have owned at least 3% of the outstanding shares of that corporation for a continuous three-year period) to nominate a director for inclusion on the "slate" of directors using the corporation's proxy solicitation materials. The SEC placed limitations on the number of nominees that may be proposed by shareholders and any nominee had to meet certain standards of independence that apply to directors generally. However Rule 14a–11 was vacated in *Bus. Roundtable and Chamber of Commerce of the United States of America v. S.E.C.* (647 F.3d 1144, 396 U.S. App. D.C. 259 (D.C. Cir. 2011)) because the court found that the SEC "acted arbitrarily and capriciously here because it neglected its statutory responsibility to determine the likely economic consequences of Rule 14a–11 and to connect those consequences to efficiency, competition, and capital formation." *Id.* at 263. The court also noted that, when the SEC adopted Rule 14a–11, it simultaneously amended *Rule 14a–8* to prevent companies from excluding from their proxy materials shareholder proposals to establish a procedure for shareholders to nominate directors. *Id. at 268.* Since Rule 14a–8 was not challenged in the case, its status is unclear. Furthermore, efforts continue to enable shareholders to have a greater ability to nominate directors. It is unclear whether the SEC will revise and re-issue rules or if other changes will take place or if these efforts will be successful.

The Dodd-Frank Act also resulted in the SEC's adoption Rule 14a–21(a), which requires publicly held companies to provide shareholders with an advisory "say on pay" vote (at least once every three years) on the compensation of a company's senior executives. Section 14A(a)(1) of the 1934 Act and Rule 14a–21(a) adopted thereunder requires that public companies must provide "a separate shareholder advisory vote in proxy statements to approve the compensation of their named executive officers. . ." Although such a vote is required every three years, and although the new rules also provide that the companies must have shareholders vote on how frequently the "Say on Pay" votes should occur and whether the vote should occur every year, every two years, or every three years, most companies, thus far, have adopted an annual frequency for these votes. Note that these votes are "advisory" and are not binding on the company. (Recent legislative efforts to modify or even eliminate certain provisions of the Dodd-Frank Act have left the say on pay provisions in tact.)

The SEC has also provided sample language for the Say on Pay resolution which would satisfy the SEC requirements. The sample language is:

> "RESOLVED, that the compensation paid to the company's named executive officers, as disclosed pursuant to Item 402 of Regulation S-K, including the Compensation Discussion and Analysis, compensation tables and narrative discussion is hereby APPROVED."

SECTION IV: Shareholder Inspection Rights

Shareholders also have rights to inspect corporate records. The rules typically provide that a shareholder with some minimum ownership stake in the corporation has a right to inspect certain records. For a variety of very legitimate reasons, shareholders may want to communicate directly with other shareholders and/or may need access to corporate records beyond just shareholder lists. However, other concerns must be balanced against a legitimate interest in shareholder lists and corporate records.

These "other concerns" include the fact that some shareholders want access to information for improper purposes, and corporations have an interest in protecting certain information. Furthermore, the corporation's shareholders do not want to wind up on mailing lists and receive solicitations to purchase products or services just because they happen to be shareholders in a corporation.

The evaluation of whether a request for information constitutes a proper or improper purpose is further complicated by the fact that it is not merely the purpose of the shareholder that matters, but the type of record to which the shareholder seeks access. In many states, such as Delaware, depending upon the type of records being sought, the burden of proof will shift, requiring either that the corporation show an improper purpose or the shareholder seeking access to records must show a proper purpose. If the shareholder wants to obtain a list of shareholder names, the burden of proof is on the corporation to show that the shareholder does NOT have a proper purpose. However, if the shareholder wants to obtain corporate records, the burden of proof is usually on the shareholder to show that the shareholder has a proper purpose. One court explained a denial of access to a shareholder by distinguishing between a proper purpose that involves *any economic benefit to the shareholders of the company* and an improper purpose that was to persuade the company to adopt the shareholder's social and political concerns. *See State Ex Rel. Pillsbury-Honeywell, Inc.,* below.

Shareholders should have a right to information because they are entitled to know about, and to be involved with, their investments. However, this right is subject to certain limitations. The requirement that a proper purpose accompany requests for information is designed to prevent one shareholder exercising his rights from negatively impacting the corporation. Another way to view these limitations is that they are an effort to balance a shareholder's right to information with the rights of the other shareholders in the corporation.

The several cases that follow provide a variety of instances in which shareholders sought to obtain records or information from the companies in which they held stock. Since these analyses are often heavily fact dependent a number of cases are provided. In each of the following imagine that you are the attorney for the shareholder. Try to envision how you would have strategically positioned your client to obtain the information sought and what arguments you might have made. Then imagine that you represent the company and think how you would have represented the company in defending against such an action. You might also consider whether in certain instances you would have advised your client to acquiesce.

Saito v. McKesson HBOC, Inc.

806 A.2d 113 (Del. 2002)

BERGER, J.:

In this appeal, we consider the limitations on a stockholder's statutory right to inspect corporate books and records. The statute, 8 *Del. C.* § 220, enables stockholders to investigate matters "reasonably related to [their] interest as [stockholders]" including, among other things, possible corporate wrongdoing. It does not open the door to the wide ranging discovery that would be available in support of litigation. For this statutory tool to be meaningful, however, it cannot be read narrowly to deprive a stockholder of necessary documents solely because the documents were prepared by third parties or because the documents predate the stockholder's first investment in the corporation. A stockholder who demands inspection for a proper purpose should be given access to all of the documents in the corporation's possession, custody or control, that are necessary to satisfy that proper purpose. Thus, where a § 220 claim is based on alleged corporate wrongdoing, and assuming the allegation is meritorious, the stockholder should be given enough information to effectively address the problem, either through derivative litigation or through direct contact with the corporation's directors and/or stockholders.

Factual and Procedural Background

On October 17, 1998, McKesson Corporation entered into a stock-for-stock merger agreement with HBO & Company ("HBOC"). On October 20, 1998, appellant, Noel Saito, purchased McKesson stock. The merger was consummated in January 1999 and the combined company was renamed McKesson HBOC, Incorporated. HBOC continued its separate corporate existence as a wholly-owned subsidiary of McKesson HBOC.

Starting in April and continuing through July 1999, McKesson HBOC announced a series of financial restatements triggered by its year-end audit process. During that four month period, McKesson HBOC reduced its revenues by $ 327.4 million for the three prior fiscal years. The restatements all were attributed to HBOC accounting irregularities. The first announcement precipitated several lawsuits, including a derivative action pending in the Court of Chancery, captioned *Ash v. McCall,* Civil Action No. 17132. Saito was one of four plaintiffs in the *Ash* complaint, which alleged that: (i) McKesson's directors breached their duty of care by failing to discover the HBOC accounting irregularities before the merger; (ii) McKesson's directors committed corporate waste by entering into the merger with HBOC; (iii) HBOC's directors breached their fiduciary duties by failing to monitor the company's compliance with financial reporting requirements prior to the merger; and (iv) McKesson HBOC's directors failed in the same respect during the three months following the merger. Although the Court of Chancery granted defendants' motion to dismiss the complaint, the dismissal was without prejudice as to the pre-merger and post-merger oversight claims.

In its decision on the motion to dismiss, the Court of Chancery specifically suggested that Saito and the other plaintiffs "use the 'tools at hand,' most prominently § 220 books and records actions, to obtain information necessary to sue derivatively." Saito was the only *Ash* plaintiff to follow that advice. The stated purpose of Saito's demand was:

> (1) to further investigate breaches of fiduciary duties by the boards of directors of HBO & Co., Inc., McKesson, Inc., and/or McKesson HBOC, Inc. related to their oversight of their respective company's accounting procedures and financial reporting; (2) to investigate potential claims against advisors engaged by McKesson, Inc. and HBO & Co., Inc. to the acquisition of HBO & Co., Inc. by McKesson, Inc.; and (3) to gather information relating to the above in order to supplement the complaint in *Ash v. McCall,* et al., . . . in accordance with the September 15, 2000 Opinion of the Court of Chancery. Saito demanded access to eleven categories of documents, including those relating to Arthur Andersen's pre-merger review and verification of HBOC's financial condition; communications between or among HBOC, McKesson, and their investment bankers and accountants concerning HBOC's accounting practices; and discussions among members of the Boards of Directors of HBOC, McKesson, and/or McKesson HBOC concerning reports published

in April 1997 and thereafter about HBOC's accounting practices or financial condition.

After trial, the Court of Chancery found that Saito stated a proper purpose for the inspection of books and records—to ferret out possible wrongdoing in connection with the merger of HBOC and McKesson. . . .

DISCUSSION

Stockholders of Delaware corporations enjoy a qualified common law and statutory right to inspect the corporation's books and records. . . . The common law right is codified in 8 *Del. C.* § 220, which provides in relevant part:

> (b) Any stockholder . . . shall, upon written demand under oath stating the purpose thereof, have the right . . . to inspect for any proper purpose the corporation's stock ledger, a list of its stockholders, and its other books and records, and to make copies or extracts therefrom. A proper purpose shall mean a purpose reasonably related to such person's interest as a stockholder. Once a stockholder establishes a proper purpose under § 220, the right to relief will not be defeated by the fact that the stockholder may have secondary purposes that are improper. The scope of a stockholder's inspection, however, is limited to those books and records that are necessary and essential to accomplish the stated, proper purpose.

After trial, the Court of Chancery found "credible evidence of possible wrongdoing," which satisfied Saito's burden of establishing a proper purpose for the inspection of corporate books and records. But the Court of Chancery limited Saito's access to relevant documents in three respects. First, it held that, since Saito would not have standing to bring an action challenging actions that occurred before he purchased McKesson stock, Saito could not obtain documents created before October 20, 1998. Second, the court concluded that Saito was not entitled to documents relating to possible wrongdoing by the financial advisors to the merging companies. Third, the court denied Saito access to any HBOC documents, since Saito never was a stockholder of HBOC. We will consider each of these rulings in turn.

A. The Standing Limitation

By statute, stockholders who bring derivative suits must allege that they were stockholders of the corporation "at the time of the transaction of which such stockholder complains. . . ." The Court of Chancery decided that this limitation on Saito's ability to maintain a derivative suit controlled the scope of his inspection rights. As a result, the court held that Saito was "effectively limited to examining conduct of McKesson and McKesson HBOC's boards *following* the negotiation and public announcement of the merger agreement."

Although we recognize that there may be some interplay between the two statutes, we do not read § 327 as defining the temporal scope of a stockholder's inspection rights under § 220. The books and records statute requires that a stockholder's purpose be one that is "reasonably related" to his or her interest as a stockholder. The standing statute, § 327, bars a stockholder from bringing a derivative action unless the stockholder owned the corporation's stock at the time of the alleged wrong. If a stockholder wanted to investigate alleged wrongdoing that substantially predated his or her stock ownership, there could be a question as to whether the stockholder's purpose was reasonably related to his or her interest as a stockholder, especially if the stockholder's only purpose was to institute derivative litigation. But stockholders may use information about corporate mismanagement in other ways, as well. They may seek an audience with the board to discuss proposed reforms or, failing in that, they may prepare a stockholder resolution for the next annual meeting, or mount a proxy fight to elect new directors. None of those activities would be prohibited by § 327.

Even where a stockholder's only purpose is to gather information for a derivative suit, the date of his or her stock purchase should not be used as an automatic "cut-off" date in a § 220 action. First, the potential derivative claim may involve a continuing wrong that both predates and postdates the stockholder's purchase date. In such a case, books and records from the inception of the alleged wrongdoing could be necessary and essential to the stockholder's purpose. Second, the alleged post-purchase date wrongs may have their foundation in events that transpired earlier. In this case, for example, Saito wants to investigate McKesson's apparent failure to learn of HBOC's accounting irregularities until months after the merger was consummated. Due diligence documents generated before the merger agreement was signed may be essential to that investigation. In sum, the date on which a stockholder first acquired the corporation's stock does not control the scope of records available under § 220. If activities that occurred before the purchase date are "reasonably related" to the stockholder's interest as a stockholder, then the stockholder should be given access to records necessary to an understanding of those activities.[10]

---

[10] . . . a Section 220 proceeding does not open the door to wide ranging discovery. See *Brehm v. Eisner,* 746 A.2d 244, 266–67 (Del. 2000) (Plaintiffs "bear the burden of showing a proper purpose and [must] make specific and discrete identification, with rifled precision. . .[to] establish that each category

B. The Financial Advisors' Documents

The Court of Chancery denied Saito access to documents in McKesson-HBOC's possession that the corporation obtained from financial and accounting advisors, on the ground that Saito could not use § 220 to develop potential claims against third parties. On appeal, Saito argues that he is seeking third party documents for the same reason he is seeking McKesson HBOC documents—to investigate possible wrongdoing by McKesson and McKesson HBOC. Since the trial court found that to be a proper purpose, Saito argues that he should not be precluded from seeing documents that are necessary to his purpose, and in McKesson HBOC's possession, simply because the documents were prepared by third party advisors.

We agree that, generally, the source of the documents in a corporation's possession should not control a stockholder's right to inspection under § 220. It is not entirely clear, however, that the trial court restricted Saito's access on that basis. The Court of Chancery decided that Saito's interest in pursuing claims against McKesson HBOC's advisors was not a proper purpose. It recognized that a secondary improper purpose usually is irrelevant if the stockholder establishes his need for the same documents to support a proper purpose. But the court apparently concluded that the categories of third party documents that Saito demanded did not support the proper purpose of investigating possible wrongdoing by McKesson and McKesson HBOC.

We cannot determine from the present record whether the Court of Chancery intended to exclude all third party documents, but such a blanket exclusion would be improper. The source of the documents and the manner in which they were obtained by the corporation have little or no bearing on a stockholder's inspection rights. The issue is whether the documents are necessary and essential to satisfy the stockholder's proper purpose. In this case, Saito wants to investigate possible wrongdoing relating to McKesson and McKesson HBOC's failure to discover HBOC's accounting irregularities. Since McKesson and McKesson HBOC relied on financial and accounting advisors to evaluate HBOC's financial condition and reporting, those advisors' reports and correspondence would be critical to Saito's investigation.

---

of books and records is essential to the accomplishment of their articulated purpose. . ."); *Security First Corp. v. U.S. Die Casting and Dev. Co.,* 687 A.2d 563, 568, 570 (Del. 1977) ("mere curiosity or desire for a fishing expedition" is insufficient.).

C. HBOC Documents

Finally, the Court of Chancery held that Saito was not entitled to any HBOC documents because he was not a stockholder of HBOC before or after the merger. Although Saito is a stockholder of HBOC's parent, McKesson HBOC, stockholders of a parent corporation are not entitled to inspect a subsidiary's books and records, "absent a showing of a fraud or that a subsidiary is in fact the mere alter ego of the parent. . . ." The Court of Chancery found no basis to disregard HBOC's separate existence and, therefore, denied access to its records.

We reaffirm this settled principle, which applies to those HBOC books and records that were never provided to McKesson or McKesson HBOC. But it does not apply to relevant documents that HBOC gave to McKesson before the merger, or to McKesson HBOC after the merger. We assume that HBOC provided financial and accounting information to its proposed merger partner and, later, to its parent company. As with the third party advisors' documents, Saito would need access to relevant HBOC documents in order to understand what his company's directors knew and why they failed to recognize HBOC's accounting irregularities.

Conclusion

Based on the foregoing, the decision of the Court of Chancery is AFFIRMED in part and REVERSED in part, and action in this matter is REMANDED for further accordance with this decision. Jurisdiction is not retained.

NOTES AND QUESTIONS

1. Section 220(c) of the Delaware General Corporation Law provides that:

. . . . Where the stockholder seeks to inspect the corporation's books and records, *other than its stock ledger or list of stockholders,* such stockholder shall first establish that:

(1) Such stockholder is a stockholder;

(2) Such stockholder has complied with this section respecting the form and manner of making demand for inspection of such documents; and

(3) *The inspection such stockholder seeks is for a proper purpose.*

> Where the stockholder seeks to inspect the corporation's stock ledger or list of stockholders and establishes that such stockholder is a stockholder and has complied with this section respecting the form and manner of making demand for inspection of such documents, *the burden of proof shall be upon the corporation to establish that the inspection such stockholder seeks is for an improper purpose*. . . . (emphasis added.)

2. Does this distinction that shifts the burden, depending upon the information sought, seem appropriate or arbitrary?

3. What might be the distinction between a proper and an improper purposes?

4. Consider your answers in the context of the *Seinfeld* case that follows.

Seinfeld v. Verizon Communications, Inc.

909 A.2d 117 (Del. 2006)

HOLLAND, J.:

The plaintiff-appellant, Frank D. Seinfeld ("Seinfeld"), brought suit under section 220 of the Delaware General Corporation Law to compel the defendant-appellee, Verizon Communications, Inc. ("Verizon"), to produce, for his inspection, its books and records related to the compensation of Verizon's three highest corporate officers from 2000 to 2002. Seinfeld claimed that their executive compensation, individually and collectively, was excessive and wasteful. On cross-motions for summary judgment, the Court of Chancery applied well-established Delaware law and held that Seinfeld had not met his evidentiary burden to demonstrate a proper purpose to justify the inspection of Verizon's records. The settled law of Delaware required Seinfeld to present some evidence that established a credible basis from which the Court of Chancery could infer there were legitimate issues of possible waste, mismanagement or wrongdoing that warranted further investigation. . . .

We reaffirm the well-established law of Delaware that stockholders seeking inspection under section 220 must present "some evidence" to suggest a "credible basis" from which a court can infer that mismanagement, waste or wrongdoing may have occurred. The "credible basis" standard achieves an appropriate balance between providing stockholders who can offer some evidence of possible wrongdoing with access to corporate records and safeguarding the right of the corporation to deny requests for inspections that are based only upon suspicion or curiosity. Accordingly, the judgment of the Court of Chancery must be affirmed.

Facts

Seinfeld asserts that he is the beneficial owner of approximately 3,884 shares of Verizon, held in street name through a brokerage firm. His stated purpose for seeking Verizon's books and records was to investigate mismanagement and corporate waste regarding the executive compensations of Ivan G. Seidenberg, Lawrence T. Babbio, Jr. and Charles R. Lee. Seinfeld alleges that the three executives were all performing in the same job and were paid amounts, including stock options, above the compensation provided for in their employment contracts. Seinfeld's section 220 claim for inspection is further premised on various computations he performed which indicate that the three executives' compensation totaled $205 million over three years and was, therefore, excessive, given their responsibilities to the corporation.

During his deposition, Seinfeld acknowledged he had no factual support for his claim that mismanagement had taken place. He admitted that the three executives did not perform any duplicative work. Seinfeld conceded he had no factual basis to allege the executives "did not earn" the amounts paid to them under their respective employment agreements. Seinfeld also admitted "there is a possibility" that the $205 million executive compensation amount he calculated was wrong.

The issue before us is quite narrow: should a stockholder seeking inspection under section 220 be entitled to relief without being required to show some evidence to suggest a credible basis for wrongdoing? We conclude that the answer must be no.

Stockholder Inspection Rights

Delaware corporate law provides for a separation of legal control and ownership. The legal responsibility to manage the business of the corporation for the benefit of the stockholder owners is conferred on the board of directors by statute. The common law imposes fiduciary duties upon the directors of Delaware corporations to constrain their conduct when discharging that statutory responsibility.

Stockholders' rights to inspect the corporation's books and records were recognized at common law because "[a]s a matter of self-protection, the stockholder was entitled to know how his agents were conducting the affairs of the corporation of which he or she was a part owner." The qualified inspection rights that originated at common law are now codified in Title 8, section 220 of the Delaware Code, which provides, in part:

> (b) Any stockholder, in person or by attorney or other agent, shall, upon written demand under oath stating the purpose thereof, have the right during the usual hours for business to inspect for any proper purpose.

Section 220 provides stockholders of Delaware corporations with a "powerful right." By properly asserting that right under section 220, stockholders are able to obtain information that can be used in a variety of contexts. Stockholders may use information about corporate mismanagement, waste or wrongdoing in several ways. For example, they may: institute derivative litigation; "seek an audience with the board [of directors] to discuss proposed reform or, failing in that, they may prepare a stockholder resolution for the next annual meeting, or mount a proxy fight to elect new directors."

Inspection Litigation Increases

. . . .Today . . . stockholders who have concerns about corporate governance are increasingly making a broad array of section 220 demands. The rise in books and records litigation is directly attributable to this Court's encouragement of stockholders, who can show a proper purpose, to use the "tools at hand" to obtain the necessary information before filing a derivative action. Section 220 is now recognized as "an important part of the corporate governance landscape."

Seinfeld Denied Inspection

The Court of Chancery determined that Seinfeld's deposition testimony established only that he was concerned about the large amount of compensation paid to the three executives. That court concluded that Seinfeld offered "no evidence from which [it] could evaluate whether there is a reasonable ground for suspicion that the executive's compensation rises to the level of waste." It also concluded that Seinfeld did not "submit any evidence showing that the executives were not entitled to [the stock] options." The Court of Chancery properly noted that a disagreement with the business judgment of Verizon's board of directors or its compensation committee is not evidence of wrongdoing and did not satisfy Seinfeld's burden under section 220.

* * * *

Credible Basis From Some Evidence

In a section 220 action, a stockholder has the burden of proof to demonstrate a proper purpose by a preponderance of the evidence. It is well established that a stockholder's desire to investigate wrongdoing or mismanagement is a "proper purpose." Such investigations are proper, because where the allegations of mismanagement prove meritorious, investigation furthers the interest of all stockholders and should increase stockholder return.

The evolution of Delaware's jurisprudence in section 220 actions reflects judicial efforts to maintain a proper balance between the rights of shareholders to obtain information based upon credible allegations of corporation mismanagement and the rights of directors to manage the business of the corporation without undue interference from stockholders. . . .

* * * *

Standard Achieves Balance

Investigations of meritorious allegations of possible mismanagement, waste or wrongdoing, benefit the corporation, but investigations that are "indiscriminate fishing expeditions" do not. "At some point, the costs of generating more information fall short of the benefits of having more information. At that point, compelling production of information would be wealth-reducing, and so shareholders would not want it produced." Accordingly, this Court has held that an inspection to investigate possible wrongdoing where there is no "credible basis," is a license for "fishing expeditions" and thus adverse to the interests of the corporation. . . .

A stockholder is "not required to prove by a preponderance of the evidence that waste and [mis]management are actually occurring." Stockholders need only show, by a preponderance of the evidence, a credible basis from which the Court of Chancery can infer there is possible mismanagement that would warrant further investigation—a showing that "may ultimately fall well short of demonstrating that anything wrong occurred." That "threshold may be satisfied by a credible showing, through documents, logic, testimony or otherwise, that there are legitimate issues of wrongdoing."

Although the threshold for a stockholder in a section 220 proceeding is not insubstantial, the "credible basis" standard sets the lowest possible burden of proof. The only way to reduce the burden of proof further would be to eliminate any requirement that a stockholder show *some evidence* of possible wrongdoing. That would be tantamount to permitting inspection based on the "mere suspicion" standard that Seinfeld advances in this appeal. However, such a standard has been repeatedly rejected as a basis to justify the enterprise cost of an inspection.

* * * *

Requiring stockholders to establish a "credible basis" for the Court of Chancery to infer possible wrongdoing by presenting "some evidence" has not impeded stockholder inspections. . . . . [T]here are a myriad of cases where stockholders have successfully presented "some evidence" to establish a "credible basis" to infer possible mismanagement and thus received some narrowly tailored right of inspection.

We remain convinced that the rights of stockholders and the interests of the corporation in a section 220 proceeding are properly balanced by requiring a stockholder to show "some evidence of *possible* mismanagement as would warrant further investigation." The "credible basis" standard maximizes stockholder value by limiting the range of permitted stockholder inspections to those that might have merit. . . .

Conclusion

The judgment of the Court of Chancery is affirmed.

State ex rel. Pillsbury v. Honeywell, Inc.

191 N.W.2d 406 (Minn. 1971)

KELLY, J.:

Petitioner appeals from an order and judgment of the district court denying all relief prayed for in a petition for writ of mandamus to compel respondent, Honeywell, Inc., (Honeywell) to produce its original shareholder ledger, current shareholder ledger, and all corporate records dealing with weapons and munitions manufacture. We must affirm.

* * * *

Petitioner attended a meeting on July 3, 1969, of a group involved in what was known as the "Honeywell Project." Participants in the project believed that American involvement in Vietnam was wrong, that a substantial portion of Honeywell's production consisted of munitions used in that war, and that Honeywell should stop this production of munitions. Petitioner had long opposed the Vietnam war, but it was at the July 3rd meeting that he first learned of Honeywell's involvement. He was shocked at the knowledge that Honeywell had a large government contract to produce antipersonnel fragmentation bombs. Upset because of knowledge that such bombs were produced in his own community by a company which he had known and respected, petitioner determined to stop Honeywell's munitions production.

On July 14, 1969, petitioner ordered his fiscal agent to purchase 100 shares of Honeywell. He admits that the sole purpose of the purchase was to give himself a voice in Honeywell's affairs so he could persuade Honeywell to cease producing munitions. Apparently not aware of that purpose, petitioner's agent registered the stock in the name of a Pillsbury family nominee—Quad & Co. Upon discovering the nature of the registration, petitioner bought one share of Honeywell in his own name on August 11, 1969. In his deposition testimony petitioner made clear the reason for his purchase of Honeywell's shares:

> "Q. * * * [D]o I understand that you requested Mr. Lacey to buy these 100 shares of Honeywell in order to follow up on the desire you had to bring to Honeywell management and to stockholders these theses that you have told us about here today?
>
> "A. Yes. That was my motivation."

The "theses" referred to are petitioner's beliefs concerning the propriety of producing munitions for the Vietnam war.

* * * *

Prior to the instigation of this suit, petitioner submitted two formal demands to Honeywell requesting that it produce its original shareholder ledger, current shareholder ledger, and all corporate records dealing with weapons and munitions manufacture. Honeywell refused.

* * * *

In the deposition petitioner outlined his beliefs concerning the Vietnam war and his purpose for his involvement with Honeywell. He expressed his desire to communicate with other shareholders in the hope of altering Honeywell's board of directors and thereby changing its policy. To this end, he testified, business records are necessary to insure accuracy.

A hearing was held on January 8, 1970, during which Honeywell introduced the deposition, conceded all material facts stated therein, and argued that petitioner was not entitled to any relief as a matter of law. Petitioner asked that alternative writs of mandamus issue for all the relief requested in his petition. On April 8, 1970, the trial court dismissed the petition, holding that the relief requested was for an improper and indefinite purpose. Petitioner contends in this appeal that the dismissal was in error.

1. Honeywell is a Delaware corporation doing business in Minnesota. Both petitioner and Honeywell spent considerable effort in arguing whether Delaware or Minnesota law applies. The trial court, applying Delaware law, determined that the outcome of the case rested upon whether or not petitioner has a proper purpose germane to his interest as a shareholder. . . .

Under the Delaware statute the shareholder must prove a proper purpose to inspect corporate records other than shareholder lists. [*Citations omitted.*] . . . .

2. The trial court ordered judgment for Honeywell, ruling that petitioner had not demonstrated a proper purpose germane to his interest as a stockholder. Petitioner contends that a stockholder who disagrees with management has an absolute right to inspect corporate records for purposes of soliciting proxies. He would have this court rule that such solicitation is per se a "proper purpose." Honeywell argues that a "proper purpose" contemplates concern with investment return. We agree with Honeywell.

This court has had several occasions to rule on the propriety of shareholders' demands for inspection of corporate books and records. . . . . While inspection will not be permitted for purposes of curiosity, speculation, or vexation, adverseness to management and a desire to gain control of the corporation for economic benefit does not indicate an improper purpose.

Several courts agree with petitioner's contention that a mere desire to communicate with other shareholders is, per se, a proper purpose. [*Citations omitted.*] This would seem to confer an almost absolute right to inspection. We believe that a better rule would allow inspections only if the shareholder has a proper purpose for such communication. This rule was applied in McMahon v. Dispatch Printing Co. 101 N.J.L. 470, 129 A. 425 (1925), where inspection was denied because the shareholder's objective was to discredit politically the president of the company, who was also the New Jersey secretary of state.

The act of inspecting a corporation's shareholder ledger and business records must be viewed in its proper perspective. In terms of the corporate norm, inspection is merely the act of the concerned owner checking on what is in part his property. In the context of the large firm, inspection can be more akin to a weapon in corporate warfare. The effectiveness of the weapon is considerable:

"Considering the huge size of many modern corporations and the necessarily complicated nature of their bookkeeping, it is plain that to permit their thousands of stockholders to roam at will through their records would render impossible not only any attempt to keep their records efficiently, but the proper carrying on of their businesses." *Cooke v. Outland*, 265 N.C. 601, 611, 144 S.E. 2d 835, 842 (1965).

* * * *

Petitioner's standing as a shareholder is quite tenuous. He only owns one share in his own name, bought for the purposes of this suit. . . .

Petitioner had utterly no interest in the affairs of Honeywell before he learned of Honeywell's production of fragmentation bombs. Immediately after obtaining this knowledge, he purchased stock in Honeywell for the sole purpose of asserting ownership privileges in an effort to force Honeywell to cease such production. We agree with the court in *Chas. A. Day & Co. v. Booth*, 123 Maine 443, 447, 123 A. 557, 558 (1924) that "where it is shown that such stockholding is only colorable, or solely for the purpose of maintaining proceedings of this kind, [we] fail to see how the petitioner can be said to be a person interested, entitled as of right to inspect * * *." But for his opposition to Honeywell's policy, petitioner probably would not have bought Honeywell stock, would not be interested in Honeywell's profits and would not desire to communicate with Honeywell's shareholders. His avowed purpose in buying Honeywell stock was to place himself in a position to try to impress his opinions favoring a reordering of priorities upon Honeywell management and its other shareholders. Such a motivation can hardly be deemed a proper purpose germane to his economic interest as a shareholder.

3. The fact that petitioner alleged a proper purpose in his petition will not necessarily compel a right to inspection. "A mere statement in a petition alleging a proper purpose is not sufficient. The facts in each case may be examined." *Sawers v. American Phenolic Corp.* 404 Ill. 440, 449, 89 N.E. 2d 374, 379 (1949). Neither is inspection mandated by the recitation of proper purpose in petitioner's testimony. Conversely, a company cannot defeat inspection by merely alleging an improper purpose. From the deposition, the trial court concluded that petitioner had already formed strong opinions on the immorality and the social

> and economic wastefulness of war long before he bought stock in Honeywell. His sole motivation was to change Honeywell's course of business because that course was incompatible with his political views. If unsuccessful, petitioner indicated that he would sell the Honeywell stock.

We do not mean to imply that a shareholder with a bona fide investment interest could not bring this suit if motivated by concern with the long- or short-term economic effects on Honeywell resulting from the production of war munitions. Similarly, this suit might be appropriate when a shareholder has a bona fide concern about the adverse effects of abstention from profitable war contracts on his investment in Honeywell.

In the instant case, however, the trial court, in effect, has found from all the facts that petitioner was not interested in even the long-term well-being of Honeywell or the enhancement of the value of his shares. His sole purpose was to persuade the company to adopt his social and political concerns, irrespective of any economic benefit to himself or Honeywell. This purpose on the part of one buying into the corporation does not entitle the petitioner to inspect Honeywell's books and records.

> 4. Petitioner argues that he wishes to inspect the stockholder ledger in order that he may correspond with other shareholders with the hope of electing to the board one or more directors who represent his particular viewpoint. . . .

While a plan to elect one or more directors is specific and the election of directors normally would be a proper purpose, here the purpose was not germane to petitioner's or Honeywell's economic interest. Instead, the plan was designed to further petitioner's political and social beliefs. Since the requisite propriety of purpose germane to his or Honeywell's economic interest is not present, the allegation that petitioner seeks to elect a new board of directors is insufficient to compel inspection. * * * The order of the trial court denying the writ of mandamus is affirmed.

QUESTIONS

1. Why do you think the result in this case was different from the result in the *Lovenheim v. Iroquois Brands, Ltd.* case, above?

2. Is there a different standard of the "proper purpose" for a shareholder proposal than for access to information?

3. If Pillsbury were your client, what advice could you have given him that might have made his efforts more successful?

SECTION V: Shareholder Suits

Experiencing Assignment 9: Quarterback Blues

One day, while working on a transactional matter, you receive an e-mail from a senior partner in the firm's litigation department. The partner explains that one of the firm's clients, Athletic Products Corporation ("APC"), is involved in a derivative lawsuit that has been brought by one of APC's shareholders. APC would like your firm to bring a motion to dismiss the suit. The partner (who is a bit rusty on the rules surrounding derivative lawsuits) wants you to provide some basis from a corporate law perspective upon which the suit might be dismissed. The partner knows that you do not typically litigate matters and does not need you to investigate other foundations that might exist for dismissal. You only need to concern yourself with the rules that govern derivative lawsuits. The partner relates the following facts:

FACTS:

APC is a publicly traded, Delaware corporation that sells athletic products internationally. One very successful APC product is its baseball mitts. The derivative suit against APC and its directors is actually being brought by a corporation called Mitt Manufacturer, Inc. ("MMI"). MMI is, and has been, an APC shareholder for many years and, for many years, has also served as the biggest manufacturer of APC baseball mitts. However, MMI was recently replaced as an APC manufacturer by another company called Touchdown Enterprises ("TE"). Touchdown Enterprises is owned by Tom Touchdown, the CEO and chairman of the Board of Directors of APC.

Approximately three years ago, APC's CEO was retiring after founding the company and running it for 30 years. The APC Board of Directors consisted of seven directors, all of whom were former athletes. Tom Touchdown had been one of the best quarterbacks ever to play professional football. Unfortunately, Tom had never run a company and did not have formal business training. Nevertheless, the APC Board, after discussing Tom's strengths and weaknesses, decided that anyone who could quarterback a team to several Super Bowl victories would be great at "quarterbacking" APC. The Board hired Tom as

APC's CEO, and Tom was elected as chairman of the Board of Directors, replacing the retiring APC founder. In connection with this new position, Tom was given a pay package worth approximately $15 million a year. The package was much larger than that of most CEOs of comparable companies but only a little more than the pay package of APC's retiring former CEO. As it turns out, Tom was not a bad CEO. He let APC continue to operate as it had for many years and let the managers of the various APC divisions run their divisions. After Tom had been with APC for two years, two seats on the Board opened up, and they were filled, at Tom's suggestion, with two of Tom's former teammates.

Six months ago, Tom came to the Board with a proposal. Tom said that he owned a manufacturing company called Touchdown Enterprises. He thought that MMI was making too much profit on its contract with APC. Tom suggested that APC terminate its contract with MMI and pay MMI liquidated damages, provided for in the contract, of $5 million. Then APC should enter into a 10-year agreement with TE to produce APC baseball mitts. Tom explained that this would reduce APC's costs by approximately $2 million each year. Tom disclosed to the board his financial interest in TE, and that if the contract were granted to TE, Tom would make several million dollars. Tom acknowledges that he had a conflict and did not attend the board meeting at which this transaction was decided. APC approved the termination of the MMI contract, and the new 10-year contract with TE.

Following the transactions described above MMI brought a derivative suit against APC and its entire Board of Directors in which MMI claimed that the APC directors breached their fiduciary duties to the APC shareholders. The suit alleges that the termination of the MMI agreement and the transaction with TE involved a conflict of interest and was not properly cleansed, and that, even if the APC directors could be characterized as "disinterested," the transaction constituted waste in that TE made inferior products to MMI, and MMI believes that this will result in reduced sales for TE. Furthermore, MMI alleged that, because of the "hero worship" the Board felt for Tom, the APC board was incapable of properly evaluating the transaction and would "rubber stamp" any proposal made by Tom. MMI also alleged that the APC board would also never vote against any proposal Tom made because of the directors' need to prove that they had made a good decision in hiring Tom and giving him such a generous contract. Because MMI named the entire Board in its suit, and alleged that the APC Board would agree to anything that Tom proposed, MMI did not make "demand" on the APC Board prior to bringing its derivative lawsuit.

ASSIGNMENT:

The litigation partner asks you to prepare a brief outline of the grounds (relating to derivative lawsuits) on which APC might seek to have the MMI suit dismissed. The partner asks that you include any particularly strong arguments that you would advance to argue for dismissal. (In addition, you should acknowledge any *particularly strong* counter-arguments that MMI is likely to make.) The partner requests that you not include any arguments that lack a strong foundation because APC wants to maintain credibility with the court. Although you probably do not need reminding, the partner reminds you that a motion to dismiss is not the appropriate forum to litigate the substance of the allegations. So, you should not include arguments about why APC would prevail in a trial on the merits with respect to the breach of fiduciary duty allegations. The partner is only interested in instances in which MMI failed to state a claim, failed to follow the rules and requirements necessary to bring a derivative lawsuit or other arguments that would result in the dismissal of the MMI suit. The partner informs you that Delaware law will apply and that, at this point, formal case citations are not necessary. The partner just wants to understand the rules about derivative lawsuits and whether APC has a chance of getting the MMI suit dismissed. The partner would like your information to be as succinct as possible, but under no circumstances should your assessment exceed two pages.

This Assignment does not need to be completed, and should not be completed, until the end of this section. However, as you study the cases and other materials that follow, it might be helpful to do so with a view toward providing assistance to APC. Some of the materials in the chapter will relate more than others to the issues facing APC. However, the materials are designed to build your understanding of the issues that arise in evaluating a derivative action and assist you in addressing APC's concerns and putting them in context. Please keep APC's issues and the questions presented by the assignment in mind while reading the materials that follow.

A. Direct or Derivative Actions

When a shareholder has a complaint regarding a corporation in which she holds stock, there are two types of actions that she may bring: a direct action or a derivative action. In a ***direct*** action, the shareholder makes a claim in her own name against the corporation, or against a director or officer of the corporation, for a wrong that was done directly to her. In other words, the wrong must have impacted the shareholder directly. Direct actions are often brought as class actions if the wrong complained of affects many shareholders. In such instances, the shareholder sues as a representative of a "class" of similarly situated shareholders who have suffered from the same wrong. Such suits are still "direct." (A direct class action suit (under Federal law) would be governed by the provisions of Federal Rule of Civil Procedure 23.)

In a shareholder ***derivative*** action, the complained of wrong has damaged the corporation and, as a result of the harm to the corporation, negatively impacts the shareholder. In instances in which the wrong has hurt the corporation and the corporation has failed to act, the shareholder might be able to bring a suit compelling the corporation to take action against the perpetrator of the wrong. A derivative action is a suit in equity against the corporation to force the corporation to sue a third party. When bringing a derivative action, a shareholder actually brings two suits. The shareholder simultaneously sues the corporation and the party (which may be an officer, a director, or an outside third party) against whom the shareholder is asserting the corporation has a claim. The nature of a derivative suit is the shareholder suing to force the corporation to take some action to address *some harm to the corporation.*

Because of the many different rights and requirements associated with each type of shareholder suit (direct and derivative), the parties will often dispute which type of suit is appropriate. In order to understand why the parties would care about which type of suit (direct or derivative) was brought, it is important to understand some of the differences between them. For example, only shareholders can bring derivative suits (not creditors). Because a derivative lawsuit arises out of a "wrong" done to the corporation, any remedy or recovery goes to the corporation, not to the shareholder bringing the lawsuit. On the other hand, since a direct lawsuit arises out of a "wrong" done to the shareholder, the shareholder bringing the direct lawsuit may collect damages. In derivative lawsuits, the court may require the corporation to pay the shareholder's attorney fees, provided that the suit results in a monetary recovery or a substantial nonmonetary benefit to the corporation. However, there are many more procedural "hurdles" to meet in bringing a derivative suit than there are in bringing a direct suit.

There are additional requirements that must be satisfied before a shareholder may bring a derivative lawsuit. These requirements vary from state to state. However, most states have some "contemporaneous ownership" requirement. A shareholder seeking to bring a derivative lawsuit typically must have been a shareholder at the time of the injury claimed and at the time that the suit is brought. Some states also require that the shareholder remain a shareholder through the court's decision. Other states allow for exceptions to this requirement if certain circumstances are shown (such as no similar action has been brought by other interested parties, the plaintiff acquired shares prior to any public disclosure, a showing that the suit could prevent a defendant from profiting from the willful breach of a fiduciary duty, and no unjust enrichment to the corporation).

Tooley v. Donaldson, Lufkin, & Jenrette, Inc.

845 A.2d 1031 (Del. 2004)

VEASEY, C.J.:

Plaintiff-stockholders brought a purported class action in the Court of Chancery, alleging that the members of the board of directors of their corporation breached their fiduciary duties by agreeing to a 22-day delay in closing a proposed merger. Plaintiffs contend that the delay harmed them due to the lost time-value of the cash paid for their shares. The Court of Chancery granted the defendants' motion to dismiss on the sole ground that the claims were, "at most," claims of the corporation being asserted derivatively. They were, thus, held not to be direct claims of the stockholders, individually. Thereupon, the Court held that the plaintiffs lost their standing to bring this action when they tendered their shares in connection with the merger.

Although the trial court's legal analysis of whether the complaint alleges a direct or derivative claim reflects some concepts in our prior jurisprudence, we believe those concepts are not helpful and should be regarded as erroneous. We set forth in this Opinion the law to be applied henceforth in determining whether a stockholder's claim is derivative or direct. That issue must turn *solely* on the following questions: (1) who suffered the alleged harm (the corporation or the suing stockholders, individually); and (2) who would receive the benefit of any recovery or other remedy (the corporation or the stockholders, individually)?

To the extent we have concluded that the trial court's analysis of the direct vs. derivative dichotomy should be regarded as erroneous, we view the error as harmless in this case because the complaint does not set forth *any* claim upon which relief can be granted. In its opinion, the Court of Chancery properly found on the facts pleaded that the plaintiffs have no separate contractual right to the alleged lost time-value of money arising out of extensions in the closing of a tender offer. These extensions were made in connection with a merger where the plaintiffs' right to any payment of the merger consideration had not ripened at the time the extensions were granted. No other individual right of these stockholders having been asserted in the complaint, it was correctly dismissed.

In affirming the judgment of the trial court as having correctly dismissed the complaint, we reverse only its dismissal with prejudice. We remand this action to the Court of Chancery with directions to amend its order of dismissal to provide that: (a) the action is dismissed for failure to state a claim upon which relief can be granted; and (b) that the dismissal is without prejudice. . . .

Facts

Patrick Tooley and Kevin Lewis are former minority stockholders of Donaldson, Lufkin & Jenrette, Inc. (DLJ), a Delaware corporation engaged in investment banking. DLJ was acquired by Credit Suisse Group (Credit Suisse) in the Fall of 2000. Before that acquisition, AXA Financial, Inc.(AXA), which owned 71% of DLJ stock, controlled DLJ. Pursuant to a stockholder agreement between AXA and Credit Suisse, AXA agreed to exchange with Credit Suisse its DLJ stockholdings for a mix of stock and cash. The consideration received by AXA consisted primarily of stock. Cash made up one-third of the purchase price. Credit Suisse intended to acquire the remaining minority interests of publicly-held DLJ stock through a cash tender offer, followed by a merger of DLJ into a Credit Suisse subsidiary.

The tender offer price was set at $90 per share in cash. The tender offer was to expire 20 days after its commencement. The merger agreement, however, authorized two types of extensions. First, Credit Suisse could unilaterally extend the tender offer if certain conditions were not met, such as SEC regulatory approvals or certain payment obligations. Alternatively, DLJ and Credit Suisse could agree to postpone acceptance by Credit Suisse of DLJ stock tendered by the minority stockholders.

Credit Suisse availed itself of both types of extensions to postpone the closing of the tender offer. The tender offer was initially set to expire on October 5, 2000, but Credit Suisse invoked the five-day unilateral extension provided in the agreement. Later, by agreement between DLJ and Credit Suisse, it postponed the merger a second time so that it was then set to close on November 2, 2000.

Plaintiffs challenge the second extension that resulted in a 22-day delay. They contend that this delay was not properly authorized and harmed minority stockholders while improperly benefitting AXA. They claim damages representing the time-value of money lost through the delay.

The Decision of the Court of Chancery

. . . . The ruling before us on appeal is that the plaintiffs' claim is derivative, purportedly brought on behalf of DLJ. The Court of Chancery, relying upon our confusing jurisprudence on the direct/derivative dichotomy, based its dismissal on the following ground: "Because this delay affected all DLJ shareholders equally, plaintiffs' injury was not a special injury, and this action is, thus, a derivative action, at most."

Plaintiffs argue that they have suffered a "special injury" because they had an alleged contractual right to receive the merger consideration of $90 per share without suffering the 22-day delay arising out of the extensions under the merger agreement. But the trial court's opinion convincingly demonstrates that plaintiffs had no such contractual right that had ripened at the time the extensions were entered into. . . . Moreover, no other individual right of these stockholder-plaintiffs was alleged to have been violated by the extensions.

That conclusion could have ended the case because it portended a definitive ruling that plaintiffs have no claim whatsoever on the facts alleged. But the defendants chose to argue, and the trial court chose to decide, the standing issue, which is predicated on an assertion that this claim is a derivative one asserted on behalf of the corporation, DLJ.

. . . . The trial court's analysis was hindered, however, because it focused on the confusing concept of "special injury" as the test for determining whether a claim is derivative or direct. . . .

In our view, the concept of "special injury" that appears in some Supreme Court and Court of Chancery cases is not helpful to a proper analytical distinction between direct and derivative actions. We now disapprove the use of the concept of "special injury" as a tool in that analysis.

The Proper Analysis to Distinguish Between Direct and Derivative Actions

The analysis must be based solely on the following questions: Who suffered the alleged harm—the corporation or the suing stockholder individually—and who would receive the benefit of the recovery or other remedy? This simple analysis is well imbedded in our jurisprudence, but some cases have complicated it by injection of the amorphous and confusing concept of "special injury."

> The Chancellor, in the very recent *Agostino* case [*Agostino v. Hicks,* 845 A.2d 1110 (Del. Ch., 2004)], correctly points this out and strongly suggests that we should disavow the concept of "special injury." In a scholarly analysis of this area of the law, he also suggests that the

inquiry should be whether the stockholder has demonstrated that he or she has suffered an injury that is not dependent on an injury to the corporation. In the context of a claim for breach of fiduciary duty, the Chancellor articulated the inquiry as follows: "Looking at the body of the complaint and considering the nature of the wrong alleged and the relief requested, has the plaintiff demonstrated that he or she can prevail without showing an injury to the corporation?[9]" We believe that this approach is helpful in analyzing the first prong of the analysis: what person or entity has suffered the alleged harm? The second prong of the analysis should logically follow.

A Brief History of Our Jurisprudence

The derivative suit has been generally described as "one of the most interesting and ingenious of accountability mechanisms for large formal organizations." It enables a stockholder to bring suit on behalf of the corporation for harm done to the corporation. Because a derivative suit is being brought on behalf of the corporation, the recovery, if any, must go to the corporation. A stockholder who is directly injured, however, does retain the right to bring an individual action for injuries affecting his or her legal rights as a stockholder. Such a claim is distinct from an injury caused to the corporation alone. In such individual suits, the recovery or other relief flows directly to the stockholders, not to the corporation.

Determining whether an action is derivative or direct is sometimes difficult and has many legal consequences, some of which may have an expensive impact on the parties to the action. For example, if an action is derivative, the plaintiffs are then required to comply with the requirements of Court of Chancery Rule 23.1, that the stockholder: (a) retain ownership of the shares throughout the litigation; (b) make presuit demand on the board; and (c) obtain court approval of any settlement. Further, the recovery, if any, flows only to the corporation. The decision whether a suit is direct or derivative may be outcome-

[9] . . .The Chancellor further explains that the focus should be on the person or entity to whom the relevant duty is owed. . . . As noted in *Agostino*, *id.*, this test is similar to that articulated by the American Law Institute (ALI), a test that we cited with approval in *Grimes v. Donald*, 673 A.2d 1207 (Del. 1996). The ALI test is as follows:

> A direct action may be brought in the name and right of a holder to redress an injury sustained by, or enforce a duty owed to, the holder. An action in which the holder can prevail without showing an injury or breach of duty to the corporation should be treated as a direct action that may be maintained by the holder in an individual capacity.

2 American Law Institute, Principles of Corporate Governance: Analysis and Recommendations § 7.01(b) at 17.

determinative. Therefore, it is necessary that a standard to distinguish such actions be clear, simple and consistently articulated and applied by our courts.

* * * *

In *Bokat v. Getty Oil Co.,* a stockholder of a subsidiary brought suit against the director of the parent corporation for causing the subsidiary to invest its resources wastefully, resulting in a loss to the subsidiary. The claim in *Bokat* was essentially for mismanagement of corporate assets. Therefore, the Court held that any recovery must be sought on behalf of the corporation, and the claim was, thus, found to be derivative.

* * * *

In *Kramer v. Western Pacific Industries, Inc.,* this Court found to be derivative a stockholder's challenge to corporate transactions that occurred six months immediately preceding a buy-out merger. The stockholders challenged the decision by the board of directors to grant stock options and golden parachutes to management. The stockholders argued that the claim was direct because their share of the proceeds from the buy-out sale was reduced by the resources used to pay for the options and golden parachutes. Once again, our analysis was that to bring a direct action, the stockholder must allege something other than an injury resulting from a wrong to the corporation. We interpreted *Elster* to require the court to determine the nature of the action based on the "nature of the wrong alleged" and the relief that could result. That was, and is, the correct test. The claim in *Kramer* was essentially for mismanagement of corporate assets. Therefore, we found the claims to be derivative. That was the correct outcome.

In *Grimes v. Donald,* [673 A.2d 1207, 1213 (Del. 1996).] we sought to distinguish between direct and derivative actions in the context of employment agreements granted to certain officers that allegedly caused the board to abdicate its authority. Relying on the *Elster and Kramer* precedents that the court must look to the nature of the wrong and to whom the relief will go,[23] we concluded that the plaintiff was not seeking to recover any damages for injury to the corporation. Rather, the plaintiff was seeking a declaration of the invalidity of the agreements on the ground that the board had abdicated its responsibility to the stockholders. Thus, based on the relief requested, we affirmed the judgment of the Court of Chancery that the plaintiff was entitled to pursue a direct action.

---

[23] *Elster v. American Airlines, Inc.,* 100 A.2d 219, 221–23; *Kramer,* 546 A.2d at 351. *See also* John W. Welch, *Shareholder Individual and Derivative Actions: Underlying Rationales and the Closely Held Corporation,* 9 J. Corp. L. 147, 160 (1984) (stating that courts should analyze the rights involved to determine whether the action is direct or derivative).

Grimes was followed by *Parnes v. Bally Entertainment Corp.*, which held, among other things, that the injury to the stockholders must be "independent of any injury to the corporation.[25]" As the Chancellor correctly noted in *Agostino,* neither *Grimes* nor *Parnes* applies the purported "special injury" test.

. . . .The proper analysis has been and should remain that stated in *Grimes*, *Kramer* and *Parnes*. That is, a court should look to the nature of the wrong and to whom the relief should go. The stockholder's claimed direct injury must be independent of any alleged injury to the corporation. The stockholder must demonstrate that the duty breached was owed to the stockholder and that he or she can prevail without showing an injury to the corporation.

Standard to Be Applied in This Case

In this case it cannot be concluded that the complaint alleges a derivative claim. There is no derivative claim asserting injury to the corporate entity. There is no relief that would go the corporation. Accordingly, there is no basis to hold that the complaint states a derivative claim.

But, it does not necessarily follow that the complaint states a direct, individual claim. While the complaint purports to set forth a direct claim, in reality, it states no claim at all. The trial court analyzed the complaint and correctly concluded that it does not claim that the plaintiffs have any rights that have been injured. Their rights have not yet ripened. The contractual claim is nonexistent until it is ripe, and that claim will not be ripe until the terms of the merger are fulfilled, including the extensions of the closing at issue here. Therefore, there is no direct claim stated in the complaint before us.

Accordingly, the complaint was properly dismissed. But, due to the reliance on the concept of "special injury" by the Court of Chancery, the ground set forth for the dismissal is erroneous, there being no derivative claim. That error is harmless, however, because, in our view, there is no direct claim either.

Conclusion

* * * *

We affirm the judgment of the Court of Chancery dismissing the complaint, although on a different ground from that decided by the Court of Chancery. We reverse the dismissal with prejudice and remand this matter to the Court of Chancery to amend the order of dismissal: (a) to state that the

25 722 A.2d 1243, 1245 (Del. 1999).

complaint is dismissed on the ground that it does not state a claim upon which relief can be granted; and (b) that the dismissal is without prejudice.

* * * *

Eisenberg v. The Flying Tiger Line, Inc.

451 F.2d 267 (2d Cir. 1971)

KAUFMAN, C.J.:

Max Eisenberg, a resident of New York, "as stockholder of The Flying Tiger Line, Inc. [Flying Tiger], on behalf of himself and all other stockholders of said corporation similarly situated" commenced this action in the Supreme Court of the State of New York to enjoin the effectuation of a plan of reorganization and merger. Flying Tiger, a Delaware corporation with its principal place of business in California, removed the action to the District Court for the Eastern District of New York.

Flying Tiger pleaded several affirmative defenses and moved for an order to require Eisenberg to comply with New York Business Corporation Law § 627 (McKinney's Consol.Laws, c. 4 1963), which requires a plaintiff suing derivatively on behalf of a corporation to post security for the corporation's costs. Judge Travia granted the motion without opinion and afforded Eisenberg thirty days to post security in the sum of $35,000. Eisenberg did not comply, his action was dismissed and he appeals. We find Eisenberg's cause of action to be personal and not derivative within the meaning of § 627. We therefore reverse the dismissal.

In this action, Eisenberg is seeking to overturn a reorganization and merger which Flying Tiger effected in 1969. He charges that a series of corporate maneuvers were intended to dilute his voting rights. In order to achieve this end, he alleges, Flying Tiger in July 1969 organized a wholly owned Delaware subsidiary, the Flying Tiger Corporation ("FTC"). In August, FTC in turn organized a wholly owned subsidiary, FTL Air Freight Corporation ("FTL"). The three Delaware corporations then entered into a plan of reorganization, subject to stockholder approval, by which Flying Tiger merged into FTL and only FTL survived. A proxy statement dated August 11 was sent to stockholders, who approved the plan by the necessary two-thirds vote at the stockholders' meeting held on September 15.

Upon consummation of this merger Flying Tiger ceased as the operating company, FTL took over operations and Flying Tiger shares were converted into an identical number of FTC shares. Thereafter, FTL changed its name to "Flying Tiger Line, Inc.," for the obvious purpose of continuing without disruption the business previously conducted by Flying Tiger. The approximately 4,500,000 shares of the company traded on the New York and Pacific Coast stock exchanges are now those of the holding company, FTC, rather than those of the operating company, Flying Tiger. The effect of the merger is that business operations are now confined to a wholly owned subsidiary of a holding company whose stockholders are the former stockholders of Flying Tiger.

It is of passing interest that Eisenberg contends that the end result of this complex plan was to deprive minority stockholders of any vote or any influence over the affairs of the newly spawned company. Flying Tiger insists the plan was devised to bring about diversification without interference from the Civil Aeronautics Board, which closely regulates air carriers, and to better use available tax benefits. Even if any of these motives prove to be relevant, the alleged illegality is not relevant to the questions before this court. We are called on to decide, assuming Eisenberg's complaint is sufficient on its face, only whether he should have been required to post security for costs as a condition to prosecuting his action.

To resolve this question we look first to *Cohen v. Beneficial Industrial Loan Corp.,* 337 U.S. 541, 69 S. Ct. 1221, 93 L. Ed. 1528 (1949), which instructs that a federal court with diversity jurisdiction must apply a state statute providing security for costs if the state court would require the security in similar circumstances. *Cohen* teaches that the applicability of costs security statutes cannot be determined upon a simplistic determination whether substantive or procedural law will govern. . . . But, this Court still must determine whether to apply the New York costs security statute, Business Corporation Law § 627, or, as Eisenberg contends, Delaware law, which has no such requirement. New York clearly has indicated that § 627 will be applied in its courts whether or not New York substantive law controls the merits of the case. . . . Since New York courts would invoke its own law on security for costs rather than Delaware's, we are required to do the same. [*Citation omitted.*]

Eisenberg argues, however, that New York courts would refuse to invoke § 627 in the instant case because the section applies exclusively to derivative actions specified in Business Corporation Law § 626. He urges that his class action is representative and not derivative.

We are told that if the gravamen of the complaint is injury to the corporation the suit is derivative, but "if the injury is one to the plaintiff as a stockholder and to him individually and not to the corporation," the suit is individual in nature and may take the form of a representative class action. 13 Fletcher, Private Corporation § 5911 (1970 Rev.Vol.). This generalization is of little use in our case which is one of those "borderline cases which are more or less troublesome to classify." *Id.* The essence of Eisenberg's claimed injury is that the reorganization has deprived him and fellow stockholders of their right to vote on the operating company affairs and that this right in no sense ever belonged to Flying Tiger itself. This right, he says, belonged to the stockholders *per se*. Flying Tiger notes, however, that the stockholders were harmed, if at all, only because their company was dissolved, and their vote can be restored only if that company is revived. It insists, therefore, that stockholders are affected only secondarily or derivatively because we must first breathe life back into their dissolved corporation before the stockholders can be helped.

Despite a leading New York case which would seem at first glance to support Flying Tiger's position, we find that its contention misses the mark by a wide margin in its failure to distinguish between derivative and non-derivative class actions. In *Gordon v. Elliman,* 306 N.Y. 456, 119 N.E.2d 331 (1954), by a vote of 4 to 3, the Court of Appeals took an expansive view of the coverage of § 627's predecessor, General Corporation Law § 61–b. The majority held that an action to compel the payment of a dividend was derivative in nature and security for costs could be required. The test formulated by the majority was "whether the object of the lawsuit is to recover upon a chose in action belonging directly to the stockholders, or whether it is to compel the performance of corporate acts which good faith requires the directors to take in order to perform a duty which they owe to the corporation, and through it, to its stockholders." [*Citation omitted.*] Pursuant to this test it is argued that, if Flying Tiger's directors had a duty not to merge the corporation, that duty was owed to the corporation and only derivatively to its stockholders. Both the 4–1 Appellate Division and the 4–3 Court of Appeals opinions evoked the quick and unanimous condemnation of commentators. Moreover, this test, "which appears to sweep away the distinction between a representative and a derivative action," in effect classifying all stockholder class actions as derivative, has been limited strictly to its facts by lower New York courts. *Lazar v. Knolls Cooperative Section No. 2, Inc.,* 205 Misc. 748, 130 N.Y.S.2d 407, 410 (Sup.Ct.1954). [*Citations omitted.*] In *Lazar,* a stockholder sought to force directors to call a stockholders' meeting. The court stated security for costs could not be required where a plaintiff

> "does not challenge acts of the management on behalf of the corporation. He challenges the right of the present management to

> exclude him and other stockholders from proper participation in the affairs of the corporation. He claims that the defendants are interfering with the plaintiff's rights and privileges as stockholders."

130 N.Y.S. at 410, 205 Misc. at 752. In substance, this is a similar to what Eisenberg challenges here.

The legislature also was concerned with the sweeping breadth of *Gordon.* In the recodification of corporate statutes completed in 1963, it added three words to the definition of derivative suits contained in § 626. Suits are now derivative only if brought in the right of a corporation to procure a judgment "in its favor." This was to "forestall any such pronouncement in the future as that made by the Court of Appeals in Gordon v. Elliman." . . . .

Other New York cases which have distinguished between derivative and representative actions are of some interest. . . . [A]ctions to compel the dissolution of a corporation have been held representative, since the corporation could not possibly benefit therefrom. [*Citations omitted.*] *Lennan v. Blakeley,* 80 N.Y.S.2d 288 (Sup.Ct.1948), teaches that an action by preferred stockholders against directors is not derivative. And *Lehrman v. Godchaux Sugars, Inc., supra,* discloses that an action by a stockholder complaining that a proposed recapitalization would unfairly benefit holders of another class of stock was representative. . . . Professor Moore instructs that "where a shareholder sues on behalf of himself and all others similarly situated to * * * enjoin a proposed merger or consolidation * * * he is not enforcing a derivative right; he is, by an appropriate type of class suit enforcing a right common to all the shareholders which runs against the corporation."

Eisenberg's position is even stronger than it would be in the ordinary merger case. In routine merger circumstances the stockholders retain a voice in the operation of the company, albeit a corporation other than their original choice. Here, however, the reorganization deprived him and other minority stockholders of any voice in the affairs of their previously existing operating company.

It is thus clear to us that *Gordon* is factually distinguishable from the instant case. Moreover, a close analysis of other New York cases, the amendment to § 626 and the major treatises, lead us to conclude that *Gordon* has lost its viability as stating a broad principle of law.

* * * *

Perhaps the strongest string in Eisenberg's bow is one he helped to fashion when he made an investment some forty years ago in Central Zone Property

Corp. In 1952 that New York corporation obtained stockholder approval to transfer its assets to a new Delaware corporation in return for the new company's stock. The stock was to be held by trustees in a voting trust, and the former stockholders received voting trust certificates. Eisenberg complained that this effectively deprived him of a voice in the operation of his company which would be run in the future by the trustees of the voting trust. The Court of Appeals agreed that New York law did not permit such a reorganization. *Eisenberg v. Central Zone Property Corp.,* 203 Misc. 59, 116 N.Y.S.2d 154, aff'd, 306 N.Y. 58, 115 N.E.2d 652 (1953). Although we have emphasized that we do not reach the merits of Eisenberg's present complaint, it is of some interest that security for costs was neither sought nor was it discussed in the *Central Zone* opinions, even though Eisenberg did not own five percent of the shares of the corporation. It was clear to all that the allegations of the complaint, quite similar in character to the instant one, stated a representative cause of action. We cannot conceive that the question of security for costs was not considered by the able counsel for the corporation or by the court, particularly since *Gordon* had been decided in the Appellate Division less than one year before the *Central Zone* decision in the Court of Appeals and extensive commentaries had already appeared. We believe Eisenberg's action should not have been dismissed for failure to post security pursuant to § 627.

Reversed.

B. The Demand Requirement

Since the very nature of a derivative suit is that the claim belongs to the corporation, most states require that the shareholder approach the board of directors and demand that the board pursue litigation before the shareholder is allowed to bring a derivate suit in the name of the corporation. However, if demand is made on the board and the board determines not to bring the suit, then that decision is usually protected by the business judgment rule. As a result, plaintiffs usually seek to avoid making "demand" on the board of directors. In fact, there are circumstances in which the "demand requirement" is excused, and no demand need be made on the board.

Demand is excused when asking the board to bring a suit would be "futile." In order to determine when demand would be futile, one must examine the applicable case law. Each state will have slightly different standards. In the *Aronson v. Lewis* (473 A.2d 805 (Del. 1984)) case below, the Delaware standard is articulated. In Delaware, one must show that there is reasonable doubt that the majority of the directors are disinterested AND independent. Demand is also excused if the board is not independent, typically because it is controlled by the individual who is the focus of the underlying suit. Alternatively, the plaintiff could show that there is a reasonable doubt that the challenged transaction was a valid exercise of business judgment. (If the plaintiff can show that the transaction would not be subject to the protection of the business judgment rule (e.g. *conflict of interest, fraud, waste, procedural challenge,* etc.), then an exception to the demand requirement might apply.) *Id.*

Aronson v. Lewis

473 A.2d 805 (Del. 1984)

MOORE, J.:

In the wake of *Zapata Corp. v. Maldonado,* Del. Supr., 430 A.2d 779 (1981), this Court left a crucial issue unanswered: when is a stockholder's demand upon a board of directors, to redress an alleged wrong to the corporation, excused as futile prior to the filing of a derivative suit? We granted this interlocutory appeal to the defendants, Meyers Parking System, Inc. (Meyers), a Delaware corporation, and its directors, to review the Court of Chancery's denial of their motion to dismiss this action, pursuant to Chancery Rule 23.1, for the plaintiff's failure to make such a demand or otherwise demonstrate its futility. The Vice Chancellor ruled that plaintiff's allegations raised a "reasonable inference" that the directors' action was unprotected by the business judgment rule. Thus, the board could not have impartially considered and acted upon the demand. . . .

We cannot agree with this formulation of the concept of demand futility. In our view demand can only be excused where facts are alleged with particularity which create a reasonable doubt that the directors' action was entitled to the protections of the business judgment rule. Because the plaintiff failed to make a demand, and to allege facts with particularity indicating that such demand would be futile, we reverse the Court of Chancery and remand with instructions that plaintiff be granted leave to amend the complaint.

I.

The issues of demand futility rest upon the allegations of the complaint. The plaintiff, Harry Lewis, is a stockholder of Meyers. The defendants are Meyers and its ten directors, some of whom are also company officers.

In 1979, Prudential Building Maintenance Corp. (Prudential) spun off its shares of Meyers to Prudential's stockholders. Prior thereto Meyers was a wholly owned subsidiary of Prudential. Meyers provides parking lot facilities and related services throughout the country. Its stock is actively traded over-the-counter.

This suit challenges certain transactions between Meyers and one of its directors, Leo Fink, who owns 47% of its outstanding stock. Plaintiff claims that these transactions were approved only because Fink personally selected each director and officer of Meyers.

Prior to January 1, 1981, Fink had an employment agreement with Prudential which provided that upon retirement he was to become a consultant to that company for ten years. This provision became operable when Fink retired in April 1980. Thereafter, Meyers agreed with Prudential to share Fink's consulting services and reimburse Prudential for 25% of the fees paid Fink. Under this arrangement Meyers paid Prudential $48,332 in 1980 and $45,832 in 1981.

On January 1, 1981, the defendants approved an employment agreement between Meyers and Fink for a five year term with provision for automatic renewal each year thereafter, indefinitely. Meyers agreed to pay Fink $150,000 per year, plus a bonus of 5% of its pre-tax profits over $2,400,000. Fink could terminate the contract at any time, but Meyers could do so only upon six months' notice. At termination, Fink was to become a consultant to Meyers and be paid $150,000 per year for the first three years, $125,000 for the next three years, and $100,000 thereafter for life. Death benefits were also included. Fink agreed to devote his best efforts and substantially his entire business time to advancing Meyers' interests. The agreement also provided that Fink's compensation was not to be affected by any inability to perform services on Meyers' behalf. Fink was 75 years old when his employment agreement with Meyers was approved by the directors. There is no claim that he was, or is, in poor health.

Additionally, the Meyers board approved and made interest-free loans to Fink totalling [sic] $225,000. These loans were unpaid and outstanding as of August 1982 when the complaint was filed. At oral argument defendants' counsel represented that these loans had been repaid in full.

The complaint charges that these transactions had "no valid business purpose", and were a "waste of corporate assets" because the amounts to be paid are "grossly excessive", that Fink performs "no or little services", and because of his "advanced age" cannot be "expected to perform any such services". The plaintiff also charges that the existence of the Prudential consulting agreement with Fink prevents him from providing his "best efforts" on Meyers' behalf. Finally, it is alleged that the loans to Fink were in reality "additional compensation" without any "consideration" or "benefit" to Meyers.

The complaint alleged that no demand had been made on the Meyers board because:

> 13. . . . such attempt would be futile for the following reasons:
>
> (a) All of the directors in office are named as defendants herein and they have participated in, expressly approved and/or acquiesced in, and are personally liable for, the wrongs complained of herein.
>
> (b) Defendant Fink, having selected each director, controls and dominates every member of the Board and every officer of Meyers.
>
> (c) Institution of this action by present directors would require the defendant-directors to sue themselves, thereby placing the conduct of this action in hostile hands and preventing its effective prosecution.

. . .The relief sought included the cancellation of the Meyers-Fink employment contract and an accounting by the directors, including Fink, for all damages sustained by Meyers and for all profits derived by the directors and Fink.

Defendants moved to dismiss for plaintiff's failure to make demand on the Meyers board prior to suit, or to allege with factual particularity why demand is excused.

* * * *

IV.

A.

A cardinal precept of the General Corporation Law of the State of Delaware is that directors, rather than shareholders, manage the business and affairs of the corporation. 8 *Del. C.* § 141(a). Section 141(a) states in pertinent part:

> "The *business and affairs* of a corporation organized under this chapter *shall be managed by or under the direction* of a board of directors except as may be otherwise provided in this chapter or in its certificate of incorporation."

8 Del. C. § 141(a) (Emphasis added). The existence and exercise of this power carries with it certain fundamental fiduciary obligations to the corporation and its shareholders. *Loft, Inc. v. Guth,* Del. Ch., 23 Del. Ch. 138, 2 A.2d 225 (1938), *aff'd,* Del. Supr., 23 Del. Ch. 255, 5 A.2d 503 (1939). Moreover, a stockholder is not powerless to challenge director action which results in harm to the corporation. The machinery of corporate democracy and the derivative suit are potent tools to redress the conduct of a torpid or unfaithful management. The derivative action developed in equity to enable shareholders to sue in the corporation's name where those in control of the company refused to assert a claim belonging to it. The nature of the action is two-fold. First, it is the equivalent of a suit by the shareholders to compel the corporation to sue. Second, it is a suit by the corporation, asserted by the shareholders on its behalf, against those liable to it.

By its very nature the derivative action impinges on the managerial freedom of directors. Hence, the demand requirement of Chancery Rule 23.1 exists at the threshold, first to insure that a stockholder exhausts his intercorporate remedies, and then to provide a safeguard against strike suits. Thus, by promoting this form of alternate dispute resolution, rather than immediate recourse to litigation, the demand requirement is a recognition of the fundamental precept that directors manage the business and affairs of corporations.

In our view the entire question of demand futility is inextricably bound to issues of business judgment and the standards of that doctrine's applicability. The business judgment rule is an acknowledgment of the managerial prerogatives of Delaware directors under Section 141(a). See *Zapata Corp. v. Maldonado,* 430 A.2d at 782. It is a presumption that in making a business decision the directors of a corporation acted on an informed basis, in good faith and in the honest belief that the action taken was in the best interests of the company. [*Citations omitted.*] Absent an abuse of discretion, that judgment will be respected by the courts. The burden is on the party challenging the decision to establish facts rebutting the presumption. [*Citation omitted.*]

The function of the business judgment rule is of paramount significance in the context of a derivative action. It comes into play in several ways—in addressing a demand, in the determination of demand futility, in efforts by independent disinterested directors to dismiss the action as inimical to the corporation's best interests, and generally, as a defense to the merits of the suit. However, in each of these circumstances there are certain common principles governing the application and operation of the rule.

First, its protections can only be claimed by disinterested directors whose conduct otherwise meets the tests of business judgment. From the standpoint of interest, this means that directors can neither appear on both sides of a transaction nor expect to derive any personal financial benefit from it in the sense of self-dealing, as opposed to a benefit which devolves upon the corporation or all stockholders generally. *Sinclair Oil Corp. v. Levien,* Del. Supr., 280 A.2d 717, 720 (1971); *Cheff v. Mathes,* Del. Supr., 41 Del. Ch. 494, 199 A.2d 548, 554 (1964); *David J. Greene & Co. v. Dunhill International, Inc.,* Del. Ch., 249 A.2d 427, 430 (1968). See also 8 *Del. C.* § 144. Thus, if such director interest is present, and the transaction is not approved by a majority consisting of the disinterested directors, then the business judgment rule has no application whatever in determining demand futility. See 8 *Del. C.* § 144(a)(1).

Second, to invoke the rule's protection directors have a duty to inform themselves, prior to making a business decision, of all material information reasonably available to them. Having become so informed, they must then act with requisite care in the discharge of their duties. While the Delaware cases use a variety of terms to describe the applicable standard of care, our analysis satisfies us that under the business judgment rule director liability is predicated upon concepts of gross negligence. [*Citations omitted.*]

However, it should be noted that the business judgment rule operates only in the context of director action. Technically speaking, it has no role where directors have either abdicated their functions, or absent a conscious decision, failed to act. But it also follows that under applicable principles, a conscious decision to refrain from acting may nonetheless be a valid exercise of business judgment and enjoy the protections of the rule.

* * * *

Delaware courts have addressed the issue of demand futility on several earlier occasions. [*Citations omitted.*] The rule emerging from these decisions is that where officers and directors are under an influence which sterilizes their discretion, they cannot be considered proper persons to conduct litigation on behalf of the corporation. Thus, demand would be futile. *See, e.g., McKee v. Rogers,* Del. Ch., 18 Del. Ch. 81, 156 A. 191, 192 (1931) (holding that where a defendant controlled the board of directors, "it is manifest then that there can be no expectation that the corporation would sue him, and if it did, it can hardly be said that the prosecution of the suit would be entrusted to proper hands"). *But see, e.g., Fleer v. Frank H. Fleer Corp.,* Del. Ch., 14 Del. Ch. 277, 125 A. 411, 415 (1924) ("where the demand if made would be directed to the particular individuals who themselves are the alleged wrongdoers and who therefore would be invited to sue themselves, the rule is settled that a demand and refusal is not requisite"); *Miller v. Loft, Inc.,* Del. Ch., 17 Del. Ch. 301, 153 A. 861, 862 (1931) ("if by reason of hostile interest or guilty participation in the wrongs complained of, the directors cannot be expected to institute suit, . . . no demand upon them to institute suit is requisite").

However, those cases cannot be taken to mean that any board approval of a challenged transaction automatically connotes "hostile interest" and "guilty participation" by directors, or some other form of sterilizing influence upon them. Were that so, the demand requirements of our law would be meaningless, leaving the clear mandate of Chancery Rule 23.1 devoid of its purpose and substance.

The trial court correctly recognized that demand futility is inextricably bound to issues of business judgment, but stated the test to be based on allegations of fact, which, if true, "show that there is a reasonable inference" the business judgment rule is not applicable for purposes of a pre-suit demand. . . .

The problem with this formulation is the concept of reasonable inferences to be drawn against a board of directors based on allegations in a complaint. As is clear from this case, and the conclusory allegations upon which the Vice Chancellor relied, demand futility becomes virtually automatic under such a test. Bearing in mind the presumptions with which director action is cloaked, we believe that the matter must be approached in a more balanced way.

Our view is that in determining demand futility the Court of Chancery in the proper exercise of its discretion must decide whether, under the particularized facts alleged, a reasonable doubt is created that: (1) the directors are disinterested and independent and (2) the challenged transaction was otherwise the product of a valid exercise of business judgment. Hence, the Court of Chancery must make two inquiries, one into the independence and disinterestedness of the directors and the other into the substantive nature of the challenged transaction and the board's approval thereof. As to the latter inquiry the court does not assume that the transaction is a wrong to the corporation requiring corrective steps by the board. Rather, the alleged wrong is substantively reviewed against the factual background alleged in the complaint. As to the former inquiry, directorial independence and disinterestedness, the court reviews the factual allegations to decide whether they raise a reasonable doubt, as a threshold matter, that the protections of the business judgment rule are available to the board. Certainly, if this is an "interested" director transaction, such that the business judgment rule is inapplicable to the board majority approving the transaction, then the inquiry ceases. In that event futility of demand has been established by any objective or subjective standard. [*Citations omitted.*] This includes situations involving self-dealing directors. [*Citations omitted.*]

However, the mere threat of personal liability for approving a questioned transaction, standing alone, is insufficient to challenge either the independence or disinterestedness of directors, although in rare cases a transaction may be so egregious on its face that board approval cannot meet the test of business judgment, and a substantial likelihood of director liability therefore exists. [*Citations omitted.*] In sum the entire review is factual in nature. The Court of Chancery in the exercise of its sound discretion must be satisfied that a plaintiff has alleged facts with particularity which, taken as true, support a reasonable doubt that the challenged transaction was the product of a valid exercise of business judgment. Only in that context is demand excused.

B.

Having outlined the legal framework within which these issues are to be determined, we consider plaintiff's claims of futility here: Fink's domination and control of the directors, board approval of the Fink-Meyers employment agreement, and board hostility to the plaintiff's derivative action due to the directors' status as defendants.

Plaintiff's claim that Fink dominates and controls the Meyers' board is based on: (1) Fink's 47% ownership of Meyers' outstanding stock, and (2) that he "personally selected" each Meyers director. Plaintiff also alleges that mere approval of the employment agreement illustrates Fink's domination and control of the board. In addition, plaintiff argued on appeal that 47% stock ownership, though less than a majority, constituted control given the large number of shares outstanding, 1,245,745.

Such contentions do not support any claim under Delaware law that these directors lack independence. In *Kaplan v. Centex Corp.,* Del. Ch., 284 A. 2d 119 (1971), the Court of Chancery stated that "stock ownership alone, at least when it amounts to less than a majority, is not sufficient proof of domination or control." *Id.* at 123. Moreover, in the demand context even proof of majority ownership of a company does not strip the directors of the presumptions of independence, and that their acts have been taken in good faith and in the best interests of the corporation. There must be coupled with the allegation of control such facts as would demonstrate that through personal or other relationships the directors are beholden to the controlling person. . . .

The requirement of director independence inheres in the conception and rationale of the business judgment rule. The presumption of propriety that flows from an exercise of business judgment is based in part on this unyielding precept. Independence means that a director's decision is based on the corporate merits of the subject before the board rather than extraneous considerations or influences. While directors may confer, debate, and resolve their differences through compromise, or by reasonable reliance upon the expertise of their colleagues and other qualified persons, the end result, nonetheless, must be that each director has brought his or her own informed business judgment to bear with specificity upon the corporate merits of the issues without regard for or succumbing to influences which convert an otherwise valid business decision into a faithless act.

Thus, it is not enough to charge that a director was nominated by or elected at the behest of those controlling the outcome of a corporate election. That is the usual way a person becomes a corporate director. It is the care, attention and sense of individual responsibility to the performance of one's duties, not the method of election, that generally touches on independence.

We conclude that in the demand-futile context a plaintiff charging domination and control of one or more directors must allege particularized facts manifesting "a direction of corporate conduct in such a way as to comport with the wishes or interests of the corporation (or persons) doing the controlling." *Kaplan*, 284 A.2d at 123. The shorthand shibboleth of "dominated and controlled directors" is insufficient. . . .[W]e stress that the plaintiff need only allege specific facts; he need not plead evidence. . . .

Here, plaintiff has not alleged any facts sufficient to support a claim of control. The personal-selection-of-directors allegation stands alone, unsupported. At best it is a conclusion devoid of factual support. The causal link between Fink's control and approval of the employment agreement is alluded to, but nowhere specified. The director's approval, alone, does not establish control, even in the face of Fink's 47% stock ownership. *See Kaplan v. Centex Corp.,* 284 A.2d at 122, 123. The claim that Fink is unlikely to perform any services under the agreement, because of his age, and his conflicting consultant work with Prudential, adds nothing to the control claim. Therefore, we cannot conclude that the complaint factually particularizes any circumstances of control and domination to overcome the presumption of board independence, and thus render the demand futile.

C.

Turning to the board's approval of the Meyers-Fink employment agreement, plaintiff's argument is simple: all of the Meyers directors are named defendants, because they approved the wasteful agreement; if plaintiff prevails on the merits all the directors will be jointly and severally liable; therefore, the directors' interest in avoiding personal liability automatically and absolutely disqualifies them from passing on a shareholder's demand.

Such allegations are conclusory at best. In Delaware mere directorial approval of a transaction, absent particularized facts supporting a breach of fiduciary duty claim, or otherwise establishing the lack of independence or disinterestedness of a majority of the directors, is insufficient to excuse demand. Here, plaintiff's suit is premised on the notion that the Meyers-Fink employment agreement was a waste of corporate assets. So, the argument goes, by approving such waste the directors now face potential personal liability, thereby rendering futile any demand on them to bring suit. Unfortunately, plaintiff's claim falls in its initial premise. The complaint does not allege particularized facts indicating that the agreement is a waste of corporate assets. Indeed, the complaint as now drafted may not even state a cause of action, given the directors' broad corporate power to fix the compensation of officers.

In essence, the plaintiff alleged a lack of consideration flowing from Fink to Meyers, since the employment agreement provided that compensation was not contingent on Fink's ability to perform any services. The bare assertion that Fink performed "little or no services" was plaintiff's conclusion based solely on Fink's age and the *existence* of the Fink-Prudential employment agreement. As for Meyers' loans to Fink, beyond the bare allegation that they were made, the complaint does not allege facts indicating the wastefulness of such arrangements. Again, the mere existence of such loans, given the broad corporate powers conferred by Delaware law, does not even state a claim.

* * * *

D.

Plaintiff's final argument is the incantation that demand is excused because the directors otherwise would have to sue themselves, thereby placing the conduct of the litigation in hostile hands and preventing its effective prosecution. This bootstrap argument has been made to and dismissed by other courts. [*Citations omitted.*] Its acceptance would effectively abrogate Rule 23.1 and weaken the managerial power of directors. Unless facts are alleged with particularity to overcome the presumptions of independence and a proper exercise of business judgment, in which case the directors could not be expected to sue themselves, a bare claim of this sort raises no legally cognizable issue under Delaware corporate law.

V.

In sum, we conclude that the plaintiff has failed to allege facts with particularity indicating that the Meyers directors were tainted by interest, lacked independence, or took action contrary to Meyers' best interests in order to create a reasonable doubt as to the applicability of the business judgment rule. Only in the presence of such a reasonable doubt may a demand be deemed futile. Hence, we reverse the Court of Chancery's denial of the motion to dismiss, and remand with instructions that plaintiff be granted leave to amend his complaint to bring it into compliance with Rule 23.1 based on the principles we have announced today.

* * * *

REVERSED AND REMANDED.

NOTES

1. The standards relating to demand futility were also addressed in *Stone v. Ritter, supra.* The section from *Stone v. Ritter*, 911 A.2d 362 (Del. 2006), discussing demand futility is reprinted below:

> Demand Futility and Director Independence
>
> It is a fundamental principle of the Delaware General Corporation Law that "[t]he business and affairs of every corporation organized under this chapter shall be managed by or under the direction of a board of directors . . . ."[6] Thus, "by its very nature [a] derivative action impinges on the managerial freedom of directors."[7] Therefore, the right of a stockholder to prosecute a derivative suit is limited to situations where either the stockholder has demanded the directors pursue a corporate claim and the directors have wrongfully refused to do so, or where demand is excused because the directors are incapable of making an impartial decision regarding whether to

---

6 *Del. Code Ann. tit. 8, 141(a) (2006). See Rales v. Blasband,* 634 A.2d 927, 932 (Del. 1993).

7 *Pogostin v. Rice,* 480 A.2d 619, 624 (Del. 1984).

> institute such litigation.[8] Court of Chancery Rule 23.1, accordingly, requires that the complaint in a derivative action "allege with particularity the efforts, if any, made by the plaintiff to obtain the action the plaintiff desires from the directors [or] the reasons for the plaintiff's failure to obtain the action or for not making the effort."[9]
>
> In this appeal, the plaintiffs concede that "[t]he standards for determining demand futility in the absence of a business decision" are set forth in *Rales v. Blasband*.[10] To excuse demand under Rales, "a court must determine whether or not the particularized factual allegations of a derivative stockholder complaint create a reasonable doubt that, as of the time the complaint is filed, the board of directors could have properly exercised its independent and disinterested business judgment in responding to a demand."[11] The plaintiffs attempt to satisfy the *Rales* test in this proceeding by asserting that the incumbent defendant directors "face a substantial likelihood of liability" that renders them "personally interested in the outcome of the decision on whether to pursue the claims asserted in the complaint," and are therefore not disinterested or independent.
>
> Critical to this demand excused argument is the fact that the directors' potential personal liability depends upon whether or not their conduct can be exculpated by the section 102(b)(7) provision contained in the AmSouth certificate of incorporation.[13] Such a provision can exculpate directors from monetary liability for a breach of the duty of care, but not for conduct that is not in good faith or a breach of the duty of loyalty.

Id. at 366–7.

In ***Beam v. Stewart***, 845 A.2d 1040 (Del. 2004): the Delaware Supreme Court considered a derivative lawsuit brought by a shareholder against Martha Stewart and five other members of the Martha Stewart Living Omnimedia, Inc.

---

8 *Aronson v. Lewis,* 473 A.2d 805, 811 (Del. 1984), *overruled on other grounds by Brehm v. Eisner,* 746 A.2d 244 (Del. 2000).

9 Ch. Ct. R. 23.1. Allegations of demand futility under Rule 23.1 "must comply with stringent requirements of factual particularity that differ substantially from the permissive notice pleadings governed solely by Chancery Rule 8(a)." *Brehm v. Eisner,* 746 A.2d at 254.

10 *Rales v. Blasband,* 634 A.2d 927 (Del. 1993).

11 *Id. at 934.*

13 *Del. Code Ann. tit. 8, 102(b)(7) (2006).*

("MSO") Board of Directors, alleging that Stewart had breached her fiduciary duties of loyalty and care by illegally selling ImClone stock in December of 2001 and that the financial future of MSO was jeopardized by the mishandling of the media attention that followed. The plaintiff, Beam, failed to make demand on the MSO Board, prior to bringing the suit, and the Court of Chancery dismissed the claims under Rule 23.1 finding that the plaintiff had failed to demonstrate demand futility. In upholding the lower court's decision, Chief Justice Veasey provided additional insight on the issue of director independence:

> . . . .*Demand Futility and Director Independence*
>
> This Court reviews *de novo* a decision of the Court of Chancery to dismiss a derivative suit under Rule 23.1. . . . The Court should draw all reasonable inferences in the plaintiff's favor. Such reasonable inferences must logically flow from particularized facts alleged by the plaintiff. "Conclusory allegations are not considered as expressly pleaded facts or factual inferences." [*White v. Panic,* 783 A.2d 543, 549 (Del. 2001).] Likewise, inferences that are not objectively reasonable cannot be drawn in the plaintiff's favor.
>
> Under the first prong of Aronson, a stockholder may not pursue a derivative suit to assert a claim of the corporation unless: (a) she has first demanded that the directors pursue the corporate claim and they have wrongfully refused to do so; or (b) such demand is excused because the directors are deemed incapable of making an impartial decision regarding the pursuit of the litigation. The issue in this case is the quantum of doubt about a director's independence that is "reasonable" in order to excuse a presuit demand. . . .
>
> The key principle upon which this area of our jurisprudence is based is that the directors are entitled to a presumption that they were faithful to their fiduciary duties. In the context of presuit demand, the burden is upon the plaintiff in a derivative action to overcome that presumption. The Court must determine whether a plaintiff has alleged particularized facts creating a reasonable doubt of a director's independence to rebut the presumption at the pleading stage. If the Court determines that the pleaded facts create a reasonable doubt that a majority of the board could have acted independently in responding to the demand, the presumption is rebutted for pleading purposes and demand will be excused as futile.

A director will be considered unable to act objectively with respect to a presuit demand if he or she is interested in the outcome of the litigation or is otherwise not independent.[20] A director's interest may be shown by demonstrating a potential personal benefit or detriment to the director as a result of the decision. "In such circumstances, a director cannot be expected to exercise his or her independent business judgment without being influenced by the . . .personal consequences resulting from the decision." The primary basis upon which a director's independence must be measured is whether the director's decision is based on the corporate merits of the subject before the board, rather than extraneous considerations or influences. This broad statement of the law requires an analysis of whether the director is disinterested in the underlying transaction and, even if disinterested, whether the director is otherwise independent. More precisely in the context of the present case, the independence inquiry requires us to determine whether there is a reasonable doubt that any one of these three directors is capable of objectively making a business decision to assert or not assert a corporate claim against Stewart.

Independence Is a Contextual Inquiry

Independence is a fact-specific determination made in the context of a particular case. The court must make that determination by answering the inquiries: independent from whom and independent for what purpose? To excuse presuit demand in this case, the plaintiff has the burden to plead particularized facts that create a reasonable doubt sufficient to rebut the presumption that either Moore, Seligman or Martinez was independent of defendant Stewart.*

---

[20] *See Grimes v. Donald,* 673 A.2d 1207, 1216 (Del. 1996) ("The basis for claiming excusal would normally be that: (1) a majority of the board has a material financial or familial interest; (2) a majority of the board is incapable of acting independently for some other reason such as domination or control; or (3) the underlying transaction is not the product of a valid exercise of business judgment." (footnotes omitted)); see also *In re eBay, Inc. S'Holders Litig.*, C.A. No. 19988-NC, 2004 Del. Ch. LEXIS 4 (Del. Ch. Feb. 11, 2004) (demand was excused where futility analysis turned not on personal relationship but on allegations that compensation to non-interested directors in the form of not-yet-vested stock options created a reasonable doubt of their independence for presuit pleading purposes; although allegations were made of "personal ties," the analysis addressed only the financial ties and whether that raised the pleading inference that the non-interested directors were beholden to the interested directors).

* [The court had already determined that two members of the MSO, six member board, Stewart and Patrick, were not disinterested or independent for purposes of considering a presuit demand and one member, Ubben was presumed to be independent. Therefore, if even one of these other three

In order to show lack of independence, the complaint of a stockholder-plaintiff must create a reasonable doubt that a director is not so "beholden" to an interested director (in this case Stewart) that his or her "discretion would be sterilized." . . . .

Personal Friendship

A variety of motivations, including friendship, may influence the demand futility inquiry. But, to render a director unable to consider demand, a relationship must be of a bias-producing nature. Allegations of mere personal friendship or a mere outside business relationship, standing alone, are insufficient to raise a reasonable-doubt about a director's independence. In this connection, we adopt as our own the Chancellor's analysis in this case:

> Some professional or personal friendships, which may border on or even exceed familial loyalty and closeness, may raise a reasonable doubt whether a director can appropriately consider demand. This is particularly true when the allegations raise serious questions of either civil or criminal liability of such a close friend. Not all friendships, or even most of them, rise to this level and the Court cannot make a reasonable inference that a particular friendship does so without specific factual allegations to support such a conclusion.

The facts alleged by Beam regarding the relationships between Stewart and these other members of MSO's board of directors largely boil down to a "structural bias" argument, which presupposes that the professional and social relationships that naturally develop among members of a board impede independent decisionmaking. . . .

In the present case, the plaintiff attempted to plead affinity beyond mere friendship between Stewart and the other directors, but her attempt is not sufficient to demonstrate demand futility. Even if the alleged friendships may have preceded the directors' membership on MSO's board and did not necessarily arise out of that membership, these relationships are of the same nature as those giving rise to the structural bias argument.

Allegations that Stewart and the other directors moved in the same social circles, attended the same weddings, developed business

---

board members were shown not to be independent, that would mean that a majority of the MSO board was not independent, and demand would be excused.—*Eds.*]

relationships before joining the board, and described each other as "friends," even when coupled with Stewart's 94% voting power, are insufficient, without more, to rebut the presumption of independence. They do not provide a sufficient basis from which reasonably to infer that Martinez, Moore and Seligman may have been beholden to Stewart. Whether they arise before board membership or later as a result of collegial relationships among the board of directors, such affinities—standing alone—will not render presuit demand futile.

The Court of Chancery in the first instance, and this Court on appeal, must review the complaint on a case-by-case basis to determine whether it states with particularity facts indicating that a relationship—whether it preceded or followed board membership—is so close that the director's independence may reasonably be doubted. This doubt might arise either because of financial ties, familial affinity, a particularly close or intimate personal or business affinity or because of evidence that in the past the relationship caused the director to act non-independently vis a vis an interested director. No such allegations are made here. Mere allegations that they move in the same business and social circles, or a characterization that they are close friends, is not enough to negate independence for demand excusal purposes.

That is not to say that personal friendship is always irrelevant to the independence calculus. But, for presuit demand purposes, friendship must be accompanied by substantially more in the nature of serious allegations that would lead to a reasonable doubt as to a director's independence. That a much stronger relationship is necessary to overcome the presumption of independence at the demand futility stage becomes especially compelling when one considers the risks that directors would take by protecting their social acquaintances in the face of allegations that those friends engaged in misconduct. To create a reasonable doubt about an outside director's independence, a plaintiff must plead facts that would support the inference that because of the nature of a relationship or additional circumstances other than the interested director's stock ownership or voting power, the non-interested director would be more willing to risk his or her reputation than risk the relationship with the interested director. . . .

Id. at 1048–1052

Be aware that the test for the futility of demand relates to a board of directors' ability to make an unbiased decision at the time the suit is brought. It does not evaluate the composition of the board at the time of the action that is the subject of the suit. It evaluates the board's ability to evaluate the lawsuit at the time it is being brought. As a result, if there has been significant change in the composition of the board between the time of the alleged wrong and the time the complaint is brought, it might be difficult to satisfy this test.

If the shareholder makes demand on the board, even if demand is excused, then the futility argument is forfeited, and the board then has the right to hear the demand and to dismiss the claim. That dismissal would typically be subject to protection under the Business Judgment Rule. If demand is NOT excused, then the board (or a majority of disinterested directors) may, subject to the Business Judgment Rule, dismiss the action.

C. Special Litigation Committees

In recent years, corporations have appointed "special litigation committees" to evaluate derivative litigation. A special litigation committee is a committee of disinterested board members and some outsiders that evaluate the lawsuit. The idea behind the "committee" is that, even if the board is not in a position to evaluate the litigation from an unbiased perspective, it can still appoint a committee of unbiased members to evaluate whether the litigation is in the best interests of the corporation. Based upon the recommendation of the special litigation committee, the board can still move to dismiss a derivative action, and, assuming that the special litigation committee is disinterested, that dismissal would be subject to the protection of the Business Judgment Rule.

A shareholder who is dissatisfied with the special litigation committee might be able to attack the special litigation committee's judgment on limited grounds. The shareholder might argue that the special litigation committee's judgment was not proper because the decision was procedurally defective. (In other words, the special litigation used an improper or ineffective method to investigate the case.) Usually the special litigation committee's substantive interpretation is protected by the business judgment rule. A shareholder might also argue that the special litigation committee failed to act independently, in good faith, and with a reasonable investigation. This requirement means that even a determination by the special litigation committee that dismissal is appropriate may be attacked unless the corporation can show that the committee acted independently, with the requisite investigation, and in good faith. A successful example of such an assertion is seen in the *In Re Oracle Corp. Derivative Litigation* case found at the end of this chapter. Even this test will be construed differently in different states. Some states, such as New York, are more deferential to special litigation committees. Other states might require stricter scrutiny of the committee. A small number of states, which includes Delaware, have an additional requirement that the court exercise its own business judgment in evaluating the decision to dismiss.

Zapata Corporation v. Maldonado

430 A.2d 779 (Del. 1981)

QUILLEN, J.:

This is an interlocutory appeal from an order entered on April 9, 1980, by the Court of Chancery denying appellant-defendant Zapata Corporation's (Zapata) alternative motions to dismiss the complaint or for summary judgment. . . .

In June, 1975, William Maldonado, a stockholder of Zapata, instituted a derivative action in the Court of Chancery on behalf of Zapata against ten officers and/or directors of Zapata, alleging, essentially, breaches of fiduciary duty. Maldonado did not first demand that the board bring this action, stating instead such demand's futility because all directors were named as defendants and allegedly participated in the acts specified. . . .

By June, 1979, four of the defendant-directors were no longer on the board, and the remaining directors appointed two new outside directors to the board. The board then created an "Independent Investigation Committee" (Committee), composed solely of the two new directors, to investigate Maldonado's actions, as well as a similar derivative action then pending in Texas, and to determine whether the corporation should continue any or all of the litigation. The Committee's determination was stated to be "final, . . . not . . . subject to review by the Board of Directors and . . . in all respects . . . binding upon the Corporation."

Following an investigation, the Committee concluded, in September, 1979, that each action should "be dismissed forthwith as their continued maintenance is inimical to the Company's best interests . . . ." Consequently, Zapata moved for dismissal or summary judgment. . . .

* * * *

We limit our review in this interlocutory appeal to whether the Committee has the power to cause the present action to be dismissed.

. . . . Directors of Delaware corporations derive their managerial decision making power, which encompasses decisions whether to initiate, or refrain from entering, litigation, from 8 *Del.C.* § 141 (a).[6] This statute is the fount of directorial powers. The "business judgment" rule is a judicial creation that presumes propriety, under certain circumstances, in a board's decision. Viewed defensively, it does not create authority. In this sense the "business judgment" rule is not relevant in corporate decision making until after a decision is made. It is generally used as a defense to an attack on the decision's soundness. The board's managerial decision making power, however, comes from § 141(a). The judicial creation and legislative grant are related because the "business judgment" rule evolved to give recognition and deference to directors' business expertise when exercising their managerial power under § 141(a).

In the case before us, although the corporation's decision to move to dismiss or for summary judgment was, literally, a decision resulting from an exercise of the directors' (as delegated to the Committee) business judgment, the question of "business judgment", in a defensive sense, would not become relevant until and unless the decision to seek termination of the derivative lawsuit was attacked as improper. . . . .

[T]he focus in this case is on the power to speak for the corporation as to whether the lawsuit should be continued or terminated. As we see it, this issue in the current appellate posture of this case has three aspects: the conclusions of the Court below concerning the continuing right of a stockholder to maintain a derivative action; the corporate power under Delaware law of an authorized board committee to cause dismissal of litigation instituted for the benefit of the corporation; and the role of the Court of Chancery in resolving conflicts between the stockholder and the committee.

Accordingly, we turn first to the Court of Chancery's conclusions concerning the right of a plaintiff stockholder in a derivative action. We find that its determination that a stockholder, once demand is made and refused, possesses an independent, individual right to continue a derivative suit for

[6] 8 *Del.C.* § 141(a) states:

"The business and affairs of every corporation organized under this chapter shall be managed by or under the direction of a board of directors, except as may be otherwise provided in this chapter or in its certificate of incorporation. If any such provision is made in the certificate of incorporation, the powers and duties conferred or imposed upon the board of directors by this chapter shall be exercised or performed to such extent and by such person or persons as shall be provided in the certificate of incorporation."

breaches of fiduciary duty over objection by the corporation, *Maldonado,* 413 A.2d at 1262–63, as an absolute rule, is erroneous. The Court of Chancery relied principally upon *Sohland v. Baker,* Del.Supr., 15 Del. Ch. 431, 141 A. 277 (1927), for this statement of the Delaware rule. . . . *Sohland* is sound law. But *Sohland* cannot be fairly read as supporting the broad proposition which evolved in the opinion below.

In *Sohland,* the complaining stockholder was allowed to file the derivative action in equity after making demand and after the board refused to bring the lawsuit. But the question before us relates to the power of the corporation by motion to terminate a lawsuit properly commenced by a stockholder without prior demand. No Delaware statute or case cited to us directly determines this new question and we do not think that *Sohland* addresses it by implication.

The language in *Sohland* relied on by the Vice Chancellor negates the contention that the case stands for the broad rule of stockholder right which evolved below. This Court therein stated that "a stockholder *may sue* in his own name for the purpose of enforcing corporate rights . . . in a proper case if the corporation on the demand of the stockholder refuses to bring suit." 141 A. at 281 (emphasis added). The Court also stated that "whether ("(t)he right of a stockholder to *file a bill* to litigate corporate rights") exists necessarily depends on the facts of each particular case." 141 A. at 282 (emphasis added). Thus, the precise language only supports the stockholder's right to initiate the lawsuit. It does not support an absolute right to continue to control it.

Additionally, the issue and context in *Sohland* are simply different from this case. Baker, a stockholder, suing on behalf of Bankers' Mortgage Co., sought cancellation of stock issued to Sohland, a director of Bankers', in a transaction participated in by a "great majority" of Bankers' board. Before instituting his suit, Baker requested the board to assert the cause of action. The board refused. Interestingly, though, on the same day the board refused, it authorized payment of Baker's attorneys fees so that he could pursue the claim; one director actually escorted Baker to the attorneys suggested by the board. At this chronological point, Sohland had resigned from the board, and it was he, not the board, who was protesting Baker's ability to bring suit. In sum, despite the board's refusal to bring suit, it is clear that the board supported Baker in his efforts. It is not surprising then that he was allowed to proceed as the corporation's representative "for the prevention of injustice", because "the corporation itself refused to litigate an apparent corporate right." 141 A. at 282.

Moreover, *McKee v. Rogers,* Del.Ch., 18 Del. Ch. 81, 156 A. 191 (1931), stated "as a general rule" that "a stockholder cannot be permitted . . . to invade the discretionary field committed to the judgment of the directors and sue in the corporation's behalf when the managing body refuses. This rule is a well settled one." 156 A. at 193.

The *McKee* rule, of course, should not be read so broadly that the board's refusal will be determinative in every instance. Board members, owing a well-established fiduciary duty to the corporation, will not be allowed to cause a derivative suit to be dismissed when it would be a breach of their fiduciary duty. Generally disputes pertaining to control of the suit arise in two contexts.

Consistent with the purpose of requiring a demand, a board decision to cause a derivative suit to be dismissed as detrimental to the company, after demand has been made and refused, will be respected unless it was wrongful.[10] [*Citations omitted.*] A claim of a wrongful decision not to sue is thus the first exception and the first context of dispute. Absent a wrongful refusal, the stockholder in such a situation simply lacks legal managerial power. . . .

But it cannot be implied that, absent a wrongful board refusal, a stockholder can never have an individual right to initiate an action. For, as is stated in *McKee,* a "well settled" exception exists to the general rule.

> "(A) stockholder may sue in equity in his derivative right to assert a cause of action in behalf of the corporation, *without prior demand* upon the directors to sue, when it is apparent that a demand would be futile, that the officers are under an influence that sterilizes discretion and could not be proper persons to conduct the litigation."

156 A. at 193 (emphasis added). This exception, the second context for dispute, is consistent with the Court of Chancery's statement below, that "the stockholders' individual right to bring the action does not ripen, however, . . . unless he can show a demand to be futile.". . . .

These comments in *McKee* and in the opinion below make obvious sense. A demand, when required and refused (if not wrongful), terminates a stockholder's legal ability to initiate a derivative action. But where demand is properly excused, the stockholder does possess the ability to initiate the action on his corporation's behalf.

---

[10] In other words, when stockholders, after making demand and having their suit rejected, attack the board's decision as improper, the board's decision falls under the "business judgment" rule and will be respected if the requirements of the rule are met. . . . That situation should be distinguished from the instant case, where demand was not made, and the *power* of the board to seek a dismissal, due to disqualification, presents a threshold issue. . . . We recognize that the two contexts can overlap in practice.

These conclusions, however, do not determine the question before us. . . . We see no inherent reason why the "two phases" of a derivative suit, the stockholder's suit to compel the corporation to sue and the corporation's suit . . ., should automatically result in the placement in the hands of the litigating stockholder sole control of the corporate right throughout the litigation. To the contrary, it seems to us that such an inflexible rule would recognize the interest of one person or group to the exclusion of all others within the corporate entity. Thus, we reject the view of the Vice Chancellor as to the first aspect of the issue on appeal.

The question to be decided becomes: When, if at all, should an authorized board committee be permitted to cause litigation, properly initiated by a derivative stockholder in his own right, to be dismissed? As noted above, a board has the power to choose not to pursue litigation when demand is made upon it, so long as the decision is not wrongful. If the board determines that a suit would be detrimental to the company, the board's determination prevails. Even when demand is excusable, circumstances may arise when continuation of the litigation would not be in the corporation's best interests. Our inquiry is whether, under such circumstances, there is a permissible procedure under § 141(a) by which a corporation can rid itself of detrimental litigation. If there is not, a single stockholder in an extreme case might control the destiny of the entire corporation. This concern was bluntly expressed by the Ninth Circuit in *Lewis v. Anderson,* 9th Cir., 615 F.2d 778, 783 (1979), *cert. denied,* 449 U.S. 869, 101 S. Ct. 206, 66 L. Ed. 2d 89 (1980): "To allow one shareholder to incapacitate an entire board of directors merely by leveling charges against them gives too much leverage to dissident shareholders." But, when examining the means, including the committee mechanism examined in this case, potentials for abuse must be recognized. This takes us to the second and third aspects of the issue on appeal.

Before we pass to equitable considerations as to the mechanism at issue here, it must be clear that an independent committee possesses the corporate power to seek the termination of a derivative suit. Section 141(c) allows a board to delegate all of its authority to a committee. Accordingly, a committee with properly delegated authority would have the power to move for dismissal or summary judgment if the entire board did.

Even though demand was not made in this case and the initial decision of whether to litigate was not placed before the board, Zapata's board, it seems to us, retained all of its corporate power concerning litigation decisions. If Maldonado had made demand on the board in this case, it could have refused to bring suit. Maldonado could then have asserted that the decision not to sue was wrongful and, if correct, would have been allowed to maintain the suit. The board, however, never would have lost its statutory managerial authority. The demand requirement itself evidences that the managerial power is retained by the board. When a derivative plaintiff is allowed to bring suit after a wrongful refusal, the board's authority to choose whether to pursue the litigation is not challenged although its conclusion—reached through the exercise of that authority—is not respected since it is wrongful. Similarly, Rule 23.1, by excusing demand in certain instances, does not strip the board of its corporate power. It merely saves the plaintiff the expense and delay of making a futile demand resulting in a probable tainted exercise of that authority in a refusal by the board or in giving control of litigation to the opposing side. But the board entity remains empowered under § 141(a) to make decisions regarding corporate litigation. The problem is one of member disqualification, not the absence of power in the board.

The corporate power inquiry then focuses on whether the board, tainted by the self-interest of a majority of its members, can legally delegate its authority to a committee of two disinterested directors. We find our statute clearly requires an affirmative answer to this question. As has been noted, under an express provision of the statute, § 141(c), a committee can exercise all of the authority of the board to the extent provided in the resolution of the board. Moreover, at lest by analogy to our statutory section on interested directors, 8 *Del.C.* § 141, it seems clear that the Delaware statute is designed to permit disinterested directors to act for the board. . . .

We do not think that the interest taint of the board majority is per se a legal bar to the delegation of the board's power to an independent committee composed of disinterested board members. The committee can properly act for the corporation to move to dismiss derivative litigation that is believed to be detrimental to the corporation's best interest.

Our focus now switches to the Court of Chancery which is faced with a stockholder assertion that a derivative suit, properly instituted, should continue for the benefit of the corporation and a corporate assertion, properly made by a board committee acting with board authority, that the same derivative suit should be dismissed as inimical to the best interests of the corporation.

At the risk of stating the obvious, the problem is relatively simple. If, on the one hand, corporations can consistently wrest bona fide derivative actions away from well-meaning derivative plaintiffs through the use of the committee mechanism, the derivative suit will lose much, if not all, of its generally-recognized effectiveness as an intra-corporate means of policing boards of directors. [*Citation omitted.*] If, on the other hand, corporations are unable to rid themselves of meritless or harmful litigation and strike suits, the derivative action, created to benefit the corporation, will produce the opposite, unintended result. . . . It thus appears desirable to us to find a balancing point where bona fide stockholder power to bring corporate causes of action cannot be unfairly trampled on by the board of directors, but the corporation can rid itself of detrimental litigation.

As we noted, the question has been treated by other courts as one of the "business judgment" of the board committee. If a "committee, composed of independent and disinterested directors, conducted a proper review of the matters before it, considered a variety of factors and reached, in good faith, a business judgment that (the) action was not in the best interest of (the corporation)", the action must be dismissed. [*Citation omitted.*] The issues become solely independence, good faith, and reasonable investigation. The ultimate conclusion of the committee, under that view, is not subject to judicial review.

We are not satisfied, however, that acceptance of the "business judgment" rationale at this stage of derivative litigation is a proper balancing point. While we admit an analogy with a normal case respecting board judgment, it seems to us that there is sufficient risk in the realities of a situation like the one presented in this case to justify caution beyond adherence to the theory of business judgment.

The context here is a suit against directors where demand on the board is excused. We think some tribute must be paid to the fact that the lawsuit was properly initiated. It is not a board refusal case. Moreover, this complaint was filed in June of 1975 and, while the parties undoubtedly would take differing views on the degree of litigation activity, we have to be concerned about the creation of an "Independent Investigation Committee" four years later, after the election of two new outside directors. Situations could develop where such motions could be filed after years of vigorous litigation for reasons unconnected with the merits of the lawsuit.

Moreover, notwithstanding our conviction that Delaware law entrusts the corporate power to a properly authorized committee, we must be mindful that directors are passing judgment on fellow directors in the same corporation and fellow directors, in this instance, who designated them to serve both as directors and committee members. The question naturally arises whether a "there but for the grace of God go I" empathy might not play a role. And the further question arises whether inquiry as to independence, good faith and reasonable investigation is sufficient safeguard against abuse, perhaps subconscious abuse.

* * * *

Whether the Court of Chancery will be persuaded by the exercise of a committee power resulting in a summary motion for dismissal of a derivative action, where a demand has not been initially made, should rest, in our judgment, in the independent discretion of the Court of Chancery. We thus steer a middle course between those cases which yield to the independent business judgment of a board committee and this case as determined below which would yield to unbridled plaintiff stockholder control. In pursuit of the course, we recognize that "the final substantive judgment whether a particular lawsuit should be maintained requires a balance of many factors—ethical, commercial, promotional, public relations, employee relations, fiscal as well as legal." *Maldonado v. Flynn, supra,* 485 F. Supp. at 285. But we are content that such factors are not "beyond the judicial reach" of the Court of Chancery which regularly and competently deals with fiduciary relationships, disposition of trust property, approval of settlements and scores of similar problems. We recognize the danger of judicial overreaching but the alternatives seem to us to be outweighed by the fresh view of a judicial outsider. Moreover, if we failed to balance all the interests involved, we would in the name of practicality and judicial economy foreclose a judicial decision on the merits. At this point, we are not convinced that is necessary or desirable.

After an objective and thorough investigation of a derivative suit, an independent committee may cause its corporation to file a pretrial motion to dismiss in the Court of Chancery. The basis of the motion is the best interests of the corporation, as determined by the committee. The motion should include a thorough written record of the investigation and its findings and recommendations. Under appropriate Court supervision, akin to proceedings on summary judgment, each side should have an opportunity to make a record on the motion. As to the limited issues presented by the motion noted below, the moving party should be prepared to meet the normal burden under Rule 56 that there is no genuine issue as to any material fact and that the moving party is entitled to dismiss as a matter of law. The Court should apply a two-step test to the motion.

First, the Court should inquire into the independence and good faith of the committee and the bases supporting its conclusions. Limited discovery may be ordered to facilitate such inquiries. The corporation should have the burden of proving independence, good faith and a reasonable investigation, rather than presuming independence, good faith and reasonableness.[17] If the Court determines either that the committee is not independent or has not shown reasonable bases for its conclusions, or, if the Court is not satisfied for other reasons relating to the process, including but not limited to the good faith of the committee, the Court shall deny the corporation's motion. If, however, the Court is satisfied under Rule 56 standards that the committee was independent and showed reasonable bases for good faith findings and recommendations, the Court may proceed, in its discretion, to the next step.

The second step provides, we believe, the essential key in striking the balance between legitimate corporate claims as expressed in a derivative stockholder suit and a corporation's best interests as expressed by an independent investigating committee. The Court should determine, applying its own independent business judgment, whether the motion should be granted. This means, of course, that instances could arise where a committee can establish its independence and sound bases for its good faith decisions and still have the corporation's motion denied. The second step is intended to thwart instances where corporate actions meet the criteria of step one, but the result does not appear to satisfy its spirit, or where corporate actions would simply prematurely terminate a stockholder grievance deserving of further consideration in the corporation's interest. The Court of Chancery of course must carefully consider and weigh how compelling the corporate interest in dismissal is when faced with a non-frivolous lawsuit. The Court of Chancery should, when appropriate, give special consideration to matters of law and public policy in addition to the corporation's best interests.

If the Court's independent business judgment is satisfied, the Court may proceed to grant the motion, subject, of course, to any equitable terms or conditions the Court finds necessary or desirable.

The interlocutory order of the Court of Chancery is reversed and the cause is remanded for further proceedings consistent with this opinion.

---

17 Compare *Auerbach v. Bennett*, 47 N.Y.2d 619, 419 N.Y.S.2d 920, 928–29, 393 N.E.2d 994 (1979). Our approach here is analogous to and consistent with the Delaware approach to "interested director" transactions, where the directors, once the transaction is attacked, have the burden of establishing its "intrinsic fairness" to a court's careful scrutiny. . . .

In re Oracle Corp. Derivative Litigation

824 A.2d 917 (Del. Ch. 2003)

STRINE, V.C.:

In this opinion, I address the motion of the special litigation committee ("SLC") of Oracle Corporation to terminate this action, "the Delaware Derivative Action," and other such actions pending in the name of Oracle against certain Oracle directors and officers. These actions allege that these Oracle directors engaged in insider trading while in possession of material, non-public information showing that Oracle would not meet the earnings guidance it gave to the market for the third quarter of Oracle's fiscal year 2001. The SLC bears the burden of persuasion on this motion and must convince me that there is no material issue of fact calling into doubt its independence. This requirement is set forth in *Zapata Corp. v. Maldonado* and its progeny.

The question of independence "turns on whether a director is, *for any substantial reason,* incapable of making a decision with only the best interests of the corporation in mind." That is, the independence test ultimately "focus[es] on impartiality and objectivity." In this case, the SLC has failed to demonstrate that no material factual question exists regarding its independence. . . .

* * * *

I. Factual Background

A. Summary of the Plaintiffs' Allegations

The Delaware Derivative Complaint centers on alleged insider trading by four members of Oracle's board of directors—Lawrence Ellison, Jeffrey Henley, Donald Lucas, and Michael Boskin (collectively, the "Trading Defendants"). Each of the Trading Defendants had a very different role at Oracle.

Ellison is Oracle's Chairman, Chief Executive Officer, and its largest stockholder, owning nearly twenty-five percent of Oracle's voting shares. . . .Ellison is one of the wealthiest men in America. By virtue of his managerial position, Ellison has regular access to a great deal of information about how Oracle is performing on a week-to-week basis.

Henley is Oracle's Chief Financial Officer, Executive Vice President, and a director of the corporation. Like Ellison, Henley has his finger on the pulse of Oracle's performance constantly.

Lucas is a director who chairs Oracle's Executive Committee and its Finance and Audit Committee. . . .

Boskin is a director, Chairman of the Compensation Committee, and a member of the Finance and Audit Committee. . .

According to the plaintiffs, each of these Trading Defendants possessed material, non-public information demonstrating that Oracle would fail to meet the earnings and revenue guidance it had provided to the market in December 2000.

* * * *

Into early to mid-February, Oracle allegedly continued to assure the market that it would meet its December guidance. Then, on March 1, 2001, the company announced that rather than posting 12 cents per share in quarterly earnings and 25% license revenue growth as projected, the company's earnings for the quarter would be 10 cents per share and license revenue growth only 6%. The stock market reacted swiftly and negatively to this news, with Oracle's share price dropping as low as $ 15.75 before closing at $ 16.88—a 21% decline in one day. These prices were well below the above $ 30 per share prices at which the Trading Defendants sold in January 2001.

* * * *

B. The Plaintiffs' Claims in the Delaware Derivative Action

The plaintiffs make two central claims in their amended complaint in the Delaware Derivative Action. First, the plaintiffs allege that the Trading Defendants breached their duty of loyalty by misappropriating inside information and using it as the basis for trading decisions. . . . [by arguing that] the Trading Defendants were aware (or at least possessed information that should have made them aware) that the company would miss its December guidance by a wide margin and used that information to their advantage in selling at artificially inflated prices.

Second, as to the other defendants—who are the members of the Oracle board who did not trade—the plaintiffs allege a *Caremark* violation, in the sense that the board's indifference to the deviation between the company's December guidance and reality was so extreme as to constitute subjective bad faith.

* * * *

D. The Formation of the Special Litigation Committee

On February 1, 2002, Oracle formed the SLC in order to investigate the Delaware Derivative Action and to determine whether Oracle should press the claims raised by the plaintiffs, settle the case, or terminate it. Soon after its formation, the SLC's charge was broadened to give it the same mandate as to all the pending derivative actions, wherever they were filed.

The SLC was granted full authority to decide these matters without the need for approval by the other members of the Oracle board.

E. The Members of the Special Litigation Committee

Two Oracle board members were named to the SLC. Both of them joined the Oracle board on October 15, 2001, more than a half a year after Oracle's 3Q FY 2001 closed. The SLC members also share something else: both are tenured professors at Stanford University.

Professor Hector Garcia-Molina is Chairman of the Computer Science Department at Stanford. . . .

The other SLC member, Professor Joseph Grundfest, is the W.A. Franke Professor of Law and Business at Stanford University. . . .

For their services, the SLC members were paid $ 250 an hour, a rate below that which they could command for other activities, such as consulting or expert witness testimony. Nonetheless, during the course of their work, the SLC members became concerned that (arguably scandal-driven) developments in the evolving area of corporate governance as well as the decision in *Telxon v. Meyerson,* might render the amount of their compensation so high as to be an argument against their independence. Therefore, Garcia-Molina and Grundfest agreed to give up any SLC-related compensation if their compensation was deemed by this court to impair their impartiality.

F. The SLC Members Are Recruited to the Board

The SLC members were recruited to the board primarily by defendant Lucas, with help from defendant Boskin. . . . Before deciding to join the Oracle board, Grundfest, in particular, did a good deal of due diligence. His review included reading publicly available information, among other things, the then-current complaint in the Federal Class Action.

Grundfest then met with defendants Ellison and Henley, among others, and asked them some questions about the Federal Class Action. . . . Grundfest testified that this did not mean that he had concluded that the claims in the Federal Class Action had no merit, only that Ellison's and Henley's explanations of their conduct were plausible. Grundfest did, however, conclude that these were reputable businessmen with whom he felt comfortable serving as a fellow director. . . .

G. The SLC's Advisors

The most important advisors retained by the SLC were its counsel from Simpson Thacher & Bartlett LLP. Simpson Thacher had not performed material amounts of legal work for Oracle or any of the individual defendants before its engagement, and the plaintiffs have not challenged its independence.

National Economic Research Advisors ("NERA") was retained by the SLC to perform some analytical work. The plaintiffs have not challenged NERA's independence.

H. The SLC's Investigation and Report

The SLC's investigation was, by any objective measure, extensive. The SLC reviewed an enormous amount of paper and electronic records. SLC counsel interviewed seventy witnesses, some of them twice. SLC members participated in several key interviews, including the interviews of the Trading Defendants.

* * * *

During the course of the investigation, the SLC met with its counsel thirty-five times for a total of eighty hours. In addition to that, the SLC members, particularly Professor Grundfest, devoted many more hours to the investigation.

In the end, the SLC produced an extremely lengthy Report totaling 1,110 pages (excluding appendices and exhibits) that concluded that Oracle should not pursue the plaintiffs' claims against the Trading Defendants or any of the other Oracle directors. . . .

* * * *

[T]he SLC concluded that even a hypothetical Oracle executive who possessed all information regarding the company's performance in December and January of 3Q FY 2001 would not have possessed material, non-public information that the company would fail to meet the earnings and revenue guidance it provided the market in December. Although there were hints of potential weakness in Oracle's revenue growth, especially starting in mid-January 2001, there was no reliable information indicating that the company would fall short of the mark, and certainly not to the extent that it eventually did.

* * * *

II. The SLC Moves to Terminate

Consistent with its Report, the SLC moved to terminate this litigation. The plaintiffs were granted discovery focusing on three primary topics: the independence of the SLC, the good faith of its investigative efforts, and the reasonableness of the bases for its conclusion that the lawsuit should be terminated. Additionally, the plaintiffs received a large volume of documents comprising the materials that the SLC relied upon in preparing its Report.

III. The Applicable Procedural Standard

In order to prevail on its motion to terminate the Delaware Derivative Action, the SLC must persuade me that: (1) its members were independent; (2) that they acted in good faith; and (3) that they had reasonable bases for their recommendations. If the SLC meets that burden, I am free to grant its motion or may, in my discretion, undertake my own examination of whether Oracle should terminate and permit the suit to proceed if I, in my oxymoronic judicial "business judgment," conclude that procession is in the best interests of the company. This two-step analysis comes, of course, from *Zapata.*

* * * *

IV. Is the SLC Independent?

A. The Facts Disclosed in the Report

In its Report, the SLC took the position that its members were independent. In support of that position, the Report noted several factors including:

- the fact that neither Grundfest nor Garcia-Molina received compensation from Oracle other than as directors;
- the fact that neither Grundfest nor Garcia-Molina were on the Oracle board at the time of the alleged wrongdoing;
- the fact that both Grundfest and Garcia-Molina were willing to return their compensation as SLC members if necessary to preserve their status as independent;
- the absence of any other material ties between Oracle, the Trading Defendants, and any of the other defendants, on the one hand, and Grundfest and Garcia-Molina, on the other; and
- the absence of any material ties between Oracle, the Trading Defendants, and any of the other defendants, on the one hand, and the SLC's advisors, on the other.

Noticeably absent from the SLC Report was any disclosure of several significant ties between Oracle or the Trading Defendants and Stanford

University, the university that employs both members of the SLC. In the Report, it was only disclosed that:

- defendant Boskin was a Stanford professor;
- the SLC members were aware that Lucas had made certain donations to Stanford; and
- among the contributions was a donation of $ 50,000 worth of stock that Lucas donated to Stanford Law School after Grundfest delivered a speech to a venture capital fund meeting in response to Lucas's request. It happens that Lucas's son is a partner in the fund and that approximately half the donation was allocated for use by Grundfest in his personal research.

B. The "Stanford" Facts that Emerged During Discovery

In view of the modesty of these disclosed ties, it was with some shock that a series of other ties among Stanford, Oracle, and the Trading Defendants emerged during discovery. Although the plaintiffs have embellished these ties considerably beyond what is reasonable, the plain facts are a striking departure from the picture presented in the Report.

* * * *

. . .I begin to discuss the specific ties that allegedly compromise the SLC's independence, beginning with those involving Professor Boskin.

1. Boskin

Defendant Michael J. Boskin is the T.M. Friedman Professor of Economics at Stanford University. During the Administration of President George H.W. Bush, Boskin occupied the coveted and important position of Chairman of the President's Council of Economic Advisors. He returned to Stanford after this government service, continuing a teaching career there that had begun many years earlier.

During the 1970s, Boskin taught Grundfest when Grundfest was a Ph.D. candidate. Although Boskin was not Grundfest's advisor and although they do not socialize, the two have remained in contact over the years, speaking occasionally about matters of public policy.

* * * *

2. Lucas

As noted in the SLC Report, the SLC members admitted knowing that Lucas was a contributor to Stanford. They also acknowledged that he had donated $ 50,000 to Stanford Law School in appreciation for Grundfest having given a speech at his request. About half of the proceeds were allocated for use by Grundfest in his research.

But Lucas's ties with Stanford are far, far richer than the SLC Report lets on. To begin, Lucas is a Stanford alumnus, having obtained both his undergraduate and graduate degrees there. By any measure, he has been a very loyal alumnus.

In showing that this is so, I start with a matter of some jousting between the SLC and the plaintiffs. Lucas's brother, Richard, died of cancer and by way of his will established a foundation. Lucas became Chairman of the Foundation and serves as a director along with his son, a couple of other family members, and some non-family members. A principal object of the Foundation's beneficence has been Stanford. The Richard M. Lucas Foundation has given $ 11.7 million to Stanford since its 1981 founding. Among its notable contributions, the Foundation funded the establishment of the Richard M. Lucas Center for Magnetic Resonance Spectroscopy and Imaging at Stanford's Medical School. Donald Lucas was a founding member and lead director of the Center.

* * * *

Lucas's connections with Stanford as a contributor go beyond the Foundation, however. From his own personal funds, Lucas has contributed $ 4.1 million to Stanford, a substantial percentage of which has been donated within the last half-decade. . . .

From these undisputed facts, it is inarguable that Lucas is a very important alumnus of Stanford and a generous contributor to not one, but two, parts of Stanford important to Grundfest: the Law School and SIEPR. . . . [Stanford Institute for Economic Policy Research].

There can be little doubt that Ellison is a major figure in the community in which Stanford is located. The so-called Silicon Valley has generated many success stories, among the greatest of which is that of Oracle and its leader, Ellison. One of the wealthiest men in America, Ellison is a major figure in the nation's increasingly important information technology industry. Given his wealth, Ellison is also in a position to make—and, in fact, he has made—major charitable contributions.

* * * *

Stanford has . . . been the beneficiary of grants from the Ellison Medical Foundation—to the tune of nearly $10 million in paid or pledged funds. . . .

During the time Ellison has been CEO of Oracle, the company itself has also made over $ 300,000 in donations to Stanford. . . .

Taken together, these facts suggest that Ellison (when considered as an individual and as the key executive and major stockholder of Oracle) had, at the very least, been involved in several endeavors of value to Stanford.

* * * *

In order to buttress the argument that Stanford did not feel beholden to him, Ellison shared with the court the (otherwise private) fact that one of his children had applied to Stanford in October 2000 and was not admitted. If Stanford felt comfortable rejecting Ellison's child, the SLC contends, why should the SLC members hesitate before recommending that Oracle press insider trading-based fiduciary duty claims against Ellison?

But the fact remains that Ellison was still talking very publicly and seriously about the possibility of endowing a graduate interdisciplinary studies program at Stanford during the summer *after* his child was rejected from Stanford's undergraduate program.

C. The SLC's Argument

The SLC contends that even together, these facts regarding the ties among Oracle, the Trading Defendants, Stanford, and the SLC members do not impair the SLC's independence. In so arguing, the SLC places great weight on the fact that none of the Trading Defendants have the practical ability to deprive either Grundfest or Garcia-Molina of their current positions at Stanford. Nor, given their tenure, does Stanford itself have any practical ability to punish them for taking action adverse to Boskin, Lucas, or Ellison—each of whom, as we have seen, has contributed (in one way or another) great value to Stanford as an institution. . . .

In so arguing, the SLC focuses on the language of previous opinions of this court and the Delaware Supreme Court that indicates that a director is not independent only if he is dominated and controlled by an interested party, such as a Trading Defendant. The SLC also emphasizes that much of our jurisprudence on independence focuses on economically consequential relationships between the allegedly interested party and the directors who allegedly cannot act independently of that director. Put another way, much of our law focuses the bias inquiry on whether there are economically material ties between the interested party and the director whose impartiality is questioned, treating the possible effect on one's personal wealth as the key to the independence inquiry. Putting a point on this, the SLC cites certain decisions of Delaware courts concluding that directors who are personal friends of an interested party were not, by virtue of those personal ties, to be labeled non-independent.

* * * *

E. The Court's Analysis of the SLC's Independence

Having framed the competing views of the parties, it is now time to decide.

I begin with an important reminder: the SLC bears the burden of proving its independence. It must convince me.

* * * *

. . .Delaware law should not be based on a reductionist view of human nature that simplifies human motivations on the lines of the least sophisticated notions of the law and economics movement. *Homo sapiens* is not merely *homo economicus*. We may be thankful that an array of other motivations exist that influence human behavior; not all are any better than greed or avarice, think of envy, to name just one. But also think of motives like love, friendship, and collegiality, think of those among us who direct their behavior as best they can on a guiding creed or set of moral values.

Nor should our law ignore the social nature of humans. To be direct, corporate directors are generally the sort of people deeply enmeshed in social institutions. Such institutions have norms, expectations that, explicitly and implicitly, influence and channel the behavior of those who participate in their operation. Some things are "just not done," or only at a cost, which might not be so severe as a loss of position, but may involve a loss of standing in the institution. In being appropriately sensitive to this factor, our law also cannot assume—absent some proof of the point—that corporate directors are, as a general matter, persons of unusual social bravery, who operate heedless to the inhibitions that social norms generate for ordinary folk.

For all these reasons, this court has previously held that the Delaware Supreme Court's teachings on independence can be summarized thusly:

> At bottom, the question of independence turns on whether a director is, *for any substantial reason,* incapable of making a decision with only the best interests of the corporation in mind. That is, the Supreme Court cases ultimately focus on impartiality and objectivity.

* * * *

1. The Contextual Nature of the Independence Inquiry Under Delaware Law

In examining whether the SLC has met its burden to demonstrate that there is no material dispute of fact regarding its independence, the court must bear in mind the function of special litigation committees under our jurisprudence. . . .

Special litigation committees are permitted as a last chance for a corporation to control a derivative claim in circumstances when a majority of its directors cannot impartially consider a demand. By vesting the power of the board to determine what to do with the suit in a committee of independent directors, a corporation may retain control over whether the suit will proceed, so long as the committee meets the standard set forth in *Zapata.*

In evaluating the independence of a special litigation committee, this court must take into account the extraordinary importance and difficulty of such a committee's responsibility. It is, I daresay, easier to say no to a friend, relative, colleague, or boss who seeks assent for an act (*e.g.,* a transaction) that has not yet occurred than it would be to cause a corporation to sue that person.

* * * *

Thus, in assessing the independence of the Oracle SLC, I necessarily examine the question of whether the SLC can independently make the difficult decision entrusted to it: to determine whether the Trading Defendants should face suit for insider trading-based allegations of breach of fiduciary duty. An affirmative answer by the SLC to that question would have potentially huge negative consequences for the Trading Defendants, not only by exposing them to the possibility of a large damage award but also by subjecting them to great reputational harm. To have Professors Grundfest and Garcia-Molina declare that Oracle should press insider trading claims against the Trading Defendants would have been, to put it mildly, "news." Relatedly, it is reasonable to think that an SLC determination that the Trading Defendants had likely engaged in insider trading would have been accompanied by a recommendation that they step down as fiduciaries until their ultimate culpability was decided. . . .

* * * *

2. The SLC Has Not Met Its Burden to Demonstrate the Absence of a Material Dispute of Fact About Its Independence

. . . I conclude that the SLC has not met its burden to show the absence of a material factual question about its independence. I find this to be the case because the ties among the SLC, the Trading Defendants, and Stanford are so substantial that they cause reasonable doubt about the SLC's ability to impartially consider whether the Trading Defendants should face suit.

* * * *

In so concluding, I necessarily draw on a general sense of human nature. It may be that Grundfest is a very special person who is capable of putting these kinds of things totally aside. But the SLC has not provided evidence that that is the case. In this respect, it is critical to note that I do not infer that Grundfest would be less likely to recommend suit against Boskin than someone without these ties. Human nature being what it is, it is entirely possible that Grundfest would in fact be tougher on Boskin than he would on someone with whom he did not have such connections. The inference I draw is subtly, but importantly, different. What I infer is that a person in Grundfest's position would find it difficult to assess Boskin's conduct without pondering his own association with Boskin and their mutual affiliations. Although these connections might produce bias in either a tougher or laxer direction, the key inference is that these connections would be on the mind of a person in Grundfest's position, putting him in the position of either causing serious legal action to be brought against a person with whom he shares several connections (an awkward thing) or not doing so (and risking being seen as having engaged in favoritism toward his old professor and SIEPR colleague).

The same concerns also exist as to Lucas. For Grundfest to vote to accuse Lucas of insider trading would require him to accuse SIEPR's Advisory Board Chair and major benefactor of serious wrongdoing—of conduct that violates federal securities laws. Such action would also require Grundfest to make charges against a man who recently donated $50,000 to Stanford Law School after Grundfest made a speech at his request.

And, for both Grundfest and Garcia-Molina, service on the SLC demanded that they consider whether an extremely generous and influential Stanford alumnus should be sued by Oracle for insider trading. Although they were not responsible for fundraising, as sophisticated professors they undoubtedly are aware of how important large contributors are to Stanford, and they share in the benefits that come from serving at a university with a rich endowment. A reasonable professor giving any thought to the matter would obviously consider the effect his decision might have on the University's relationship with Lucas, it being (one hopes) sensible to infer that a professor of reasonable collegiality and loyalty cares about the well-being of the institution he serves.

In so concluding, I give little weight to the SLC's argument that it was unaware of just how substantial Lucas's beneficence to Stanford has been. I do so for two key reasons. Initially, it undermines, rather than inspires, confidence that the SLC did not examine the Trading Defendants' ties to Stanford more closely in preparing its Report. . . .

. . . there were too many visible manifestations of Lucas's status as a major contributor for me to conclude that Grundfest, at the very least, did not understand Lucas to be an extremely generous benefactor of Stanford. . . . Combined with the other obvious indicia of Lucas's large contributor status (including the $ 50,000 donation Lucas made to Stanford Law School to thank Grundfest for giving a speech) and Lucas's obviously keen interest in his alma mater, Grundfest would have had to be extremely insensitive to his own working environment not to have considered Lucas an extremely generous alumni benefactor of Stanford, and at SIEPR and the Law School in particular.

Garcia-Molina is in a somewhat better position to disclaim knowledge of how generous an alumnus Lucas had been. Even so, the scope of Lucas's activities and their easy discoverability gives me doubt that he did not know of the relative magnitude of Lucas's generosity to Stanford. Furthermore, Grundfest comprised half of the SLC and was its most active member. His non-independence is sufficient alone to require a denial of the SLC's motion.

* * * *

Nor has the SLC convinced me that tenured faculty are indifferent to large contributors to their institutions, such that a tenured faculty member would not be worried about writing a report finding that a suit by the corporation should proceed against a large contributor and that there was credible evidence that he had engaged in illegal insider trading. The idea that faculty members would not be concerned that action of that kind might offend a large contributor who a university administrator or fellow faculty colleague . . . had taken the time to cultivate strikes me as implausible and as resting on an narrow-minded understanding of the way that collegiality works in institutional settings.

In view of the ties involving Boskin and Lucas alone, I would conclude that the SLC has failed to meet its burden on the independence question. The tantalizing facts about Ellison merely reinforce this conclusion. The SLC, of course, argues that Ellison is not a large benefactor of Stanford personally, that Stanford has demonstrated its independence of him by rejecting his child for admission, and that, in any event, the SLC was ignorant of any negotiations between Ellison and Stanford about a large contribution. For these reasons, the SLC says, its ability to act independently of Ellison is clear.

I find differently. The notion that anyone in Palo Alto can accuse Ellison of insider trading without harboring some fear of social awkwardness seems a stretch. That being said, I do not mean to imply that the mere fact that Ellison is worth tens of billions of dollars and is the key force behind a very important social institution in Silicon Valley disqualifies all persons who live there from being independent of him. Rather, it is merely an acknowledgement of the simple fact that accusing such a significant person in that community of such serious wrongdoing is no small thing.

. . . .Ellison was publicly considering making extremely large contributions to Stanford. Although the SLC denies knowledge of these public statements, Gmndfest claims to have done a fair amount of research before joining the board, giving me doubt that he was not somewhat aware of the possibility that Ellison might bestow large blessings on Stanford.

* * * *

Before closing, it is necessary to address two concerns. The first is the undeniable awkwardness of opinions like this one. By finding that there exists too much doubt about the SLC's independence for the SLC to meet its *Zapata* burden, I make no finding about the subjective good faith of the SLC members, both of whom are distinguished academics at one of this nation's most prestigious institutions of higher learning. Nothing in this record leads me to conclude that either of the SLC members acted out of any conscious desire to favor the Trading Defendants or to do anything other than discharge their duties with fidelity. But that is not the purpose of the independence inquiry.

That inquiry recognizes that persons of integrity and reputation can be compromised in their ability to act without bias when they must make a decision adverse to others with whom they share material affiliations. To conclude that the Oracle SLC was not independent is not a conclusion that the two accomplished professors who comprise it are not persons of good faith and moral probity, it is solely to conclude that they were not situated to act with the required degree of impartiality. *Zapata* requires independence to ensure that stockholders do not have to rely upon special litigation committee members who must put aside personal considerations that are ordinarily influential in daily behavior in making the already difficult decision to accuse fellow directors of serious wrongdoing.

* * * *

The SLC's motion to terminate is DENIED. IT IS SO ORDERED.

NOTES AND QUESTIONS

1. Given the standards set forth in the preceding case of what circumstances suffice to make an individual serving on a special litigation committee "interested," how would you advise a client to select individuals to serve on such a committee?

2. In *Beam v. Martha Stewart,* discussed *supra,* the court specifically commented on the *Oracle* case:

> *A Word About the Oracle Case*
>
> . . . .*Oracle* involved the issue of the independence of the Special Litigation Committee (SLC) appointed by the Oracle board to determine whether or not the corporation should cause the dismissal of a corporate claim by stockholder-plaintiffs against directors. The Court of Chancery undertook a searching inquiry of the relationships between the members of the SLC and Stanford University in the context of the financial support of Stanford by the corporation and its management. The Vice Chancellor concluded, after considering the SLC Report and the discovery record, that those relationships were too close for purposes of the SLC analysis of independence.
>
> An SLC is a unique creature that was introduced into Delaware law by *Zapata v. Maldonado* in 1981. The SLC procedure is a method sometimes employed where presuit demand has already been excused and the SLC is vested with the full power of the board to conduct an extensive investigation into the merits of the corporate claim with a view toward determining whether—in the SLC's business judgment—the corporate claim should be pursued. Unlike the demand-excusal context, where the board is presumed to be independent, the SLC has the burden of establishing its own independence by a yardstick that must be "like Caesar's wife"-"above reproach." Moreover, unlike the presuit demand context, the SLC analysis contemplates not only a shift in the burden of persuasion but

> also the availability of discovery into various issues, including independence.
>
> We need not decide whether the substantive standard of independence in an SLC case differs from that in a presuit demand case. As a practical matter, the procedural distinction relating to the diametrically-opposed burdens and the availability of discovery into independence may be outcome-determinative on the issue of independence. Moreover, because the members of an SLC are vested with enormous power to seek dismissal of a derivative suit brought against their director-colleagues in a setting where presuit demand is already excused, the Court of Chancery must exercise careful oversight of the bona fides of the SLC and its process.
>
> Aside from the procedural distinctions, the Stanford connections in *Oracle* are factually distinct from the relationships present here.

Id. at 1054–55.

3. What does that court mean by: "As a practical matter, the procedural distinction relating to the diametrically-opposed burdens and the availability of discovery into independence may be outcome-determinative on the issue of independence?"

4. Should the broad standard of what constitutes "interest" seen in *Oracle* be used in all instances when evaluating whether a director is interested or disinterested or only in the context of evaluating the independence of a special litigation committee?

CHAPTER SEVEN

Control Issues in Corporations

AS YOU GAIN EXPERIENCE AS a business attorney, the complexity of the projects you are given increases. One day a senior partner asks you into her office and tells you that she has received an inquiry from Dell O'Ware, the president of a small business called Sweet Treats, Inc. ("STI"), a potential new client. The matter is too small for the partner (who handles multi-million dollar transactions) to handle, but she suggests that you might want to "run with it" and that STI might develop into a good client for you. The partner tells you that she will be available if you have questions, but she would like you to take on this matter as your own. You contact Dell and set up a meeting. At this meeting, Dell relates the following facts:

Experiencing Assignment 10: Sweet Treats, Inc.

FACTS:

Andy, Brittney, Carol and Dell all work for STI and are the sole owners of STI. STI's board of directors has four seats and is elected through cumulative voting. Andy, Brittney, Carol and Dell each own 25% of STI and each serve as one of the four STI directors.

STI is a Massachusetts corporation which creates new and unusual types of candy and sells the candy to regional stores. The company hopes to expand and sell its candy on a national basis in two years. The business has done well and each of the owners is employed by the company and receives a salary of $100,000 a year. This salary is high but not unreasonable, given that the company had sales of $2 million and profits (after salaries were paid) of $500,000 last year. The company has never paid dividends, and all profits are reinvested in growing the company. Unfortunately, over the last year, Andy has become more and more difficult to work with. Every day, he comes to work wearing bright red clothing from head to toe. He has decided to only communicate with people through song lyrics, so he sings in all communications. He also frequently brings a terrible-smelling lunch to work.

Andy is STI's Chief Technology Officer ("CTO") and handles the company's website and information technology needs, so he does not interact with customers or the candy. He does a perfectly fine job, but no one wants to be around him.

None of the owners have employment contracts. Brittney, Carol and Dell come to you and explain that they would like to fire Andy from his position as CTO, hire someone to replace Andy and continue to grow the business. Any replacement for Andy would probably require a salary of $75,000 a year. (Note that replacements for Brittney, Carol or Dell could also be hired at respective salaries of $75,000 per year.)

Andy, Brittney, Carol and Dell are also all parties to an STI Shareholders', Agreement, the relevant portion of which provides that the STI stock of any shareholder who ceases to be employed by STI for any reason for a period of 6 months or more, may be repurchased by the company, provided that such repurchase is consummated within one year of the termination of that shareholder's employment with STI. Any such repurchase must be made at a price equal to the fair market value of such shares at the time of such termination. If the parties cannot agree on the fair market value of the shares to be repurchased, then the price is to be determined by appraisal.

ASSIGNMENT:

Dell asks you to design a course of action for STI to follow to remove Andy in order to minimize the potential liability of STI and of Brittney, Carol and Dell. Make sure to include affirmative steps that you think the board should take and also any actions that you want to make sure the board does NOT take. Be sure to advise the STI board of directors of the potential liabilities they may face in taking this course of action. If you are missing information and need to make assumptions, please state your assumptions clearly. STI does not have significant resources to pay for extensive legal work, so Dell asks that you please limit your response to 1,000 words.

This Assignment does not need to be completed, and should not be completed, until the end of this Chapter. However, as you study the cases and other materials that follow, it might be helpful to do so with a view toward providing assistance to STI. Some of the materials in the chapter will relate more than others to the issues facing STI. The materials are designed to build your understanding of the issues that arise in working with closely held corporations and in dealing with the rights of shareholders as well as some of the potential limits on shareholders' efforts to wield control. The materials are also designed to assist you in addressing STI's concerns and putting them in context. Please keep STI's issues and the questions presented by the assignment in mind while reading the materials that follow.

SECTION I: Issues of Control

Corporations are often differentiated based upon whether a corporation's stock is publicly traded or privately held. The former are often referred to as "public" companies; the latter as "closely held" or "close" corporations. Although all corporations have boards of directors, officers, and shareholders, the distinction between public and closely held corporations relates to the number of shareholders and the market for the corporation's stock. In a public company the stock is often owned by thousands of shareholders, most of whom do not know each other. The stock of the corporation (or at least one class of stock) has been registered with the SEC and may be bought or sold on one of the public exchanges, such as the New York Stock Exchange or NASDAQ. A closely held corporation's stock is typically held by a relative few number of shareholders. Its shares are not publicly traded and sales of stock take place in private transactions, typically requiring an exemption from the registration requirements of the Securities Act of 1933. Closely held corporations are often also referred to as "private companies" and often have shareholders who also serve on the board of directors and hold positions as officers as well.

While control can become an issue in all corporations, this issue is often different in closely held corporations. In public companies battles for control can take the form of proxy fights or tender offers. These battles, which typically take place on a large scale, are primarily related to the size of the company and the vast number of the shareholders, most of whom seek to play no role in the management of the corporation. In closely held corporations the struggle for control often focuses on a shareholder's ability to control votes, often through agreements or the structure of the business.

One reason why these issues are different in a closely held corporation is that the shareholders often serve on the board of directors and as the officers. Often control represents the ability to determine and pay salaries in these corporations. In addition, the employees/shareholders of these corporations will often prefer to pay salaries instead of dividends to avoid double taxation. Since there is no public market for the stock of a closely held corporation and often no (or limited) dividends, control provides an individual or a group of individuals with access to income from the "value" of the closely held corporation.

The board of directors selects the employees/officers and determines how much salary they will make. If a shareholder is not an employee, then that shareholder would only receive funds from the corporation in the form of dividends. However, the board of directors determines how much, if any, dividends will be paid. Therefore, control of the board of directors results in the ability to control (within reason, recall the holding in *Ford v. Dodge, supra*) the payment of money to shareholders; whether those shareholders are hired as employees; and once hired, how much salary they will receive. Of course, these decisions are limited by fiduciary duties, but they are also protected, in many instances, by the Business Judgment Rule. The individuals elected to the board of directors are usually determined by a majority of the shareholders. Therefore, if one shareholder owns a relatively small percentage of a corporation's stock and someone else owns a majority of the corporation's stock, the shareholder holding a minority of the shares does not have the ability (at least under ordinary voting rules) to require that he or she be elected to the board of directors, selected as an officer, employed by the corporation or that dividends be paid.

A. Stock Ownership and a Shareholder's Right to Vote

Typically, stock ownership consists of both economic and voting rights. However, while state law typically requires that at least one class of ownership have residual economic rights in the corporation and one class of ownership have voting rights, these rights do not need to reside in the same class of stock. When a shareholder has control in a corporation, it means that the shareholder has the ability to elect a sufficient number of directors to control the board of directors. In other words, control is wielded through a shareholder's ability to vote his or her shares. Since control is dependent upon a shareholder's voting rights, the ability to issue non-voting shares enables a corporation to issue significant economic rights in a corporation to a class of shareholders, while retaining control for another class of "management" shareholders. Virtually all states provide that corporations may issue non-voting shares of stock.

In recent years many high profile public companies have received attention as a result of their utilization of voting structures that provide a disproportionate allocation of control to a shareholder or shareholder group. Some of the high profile companies with an allocation of control that is different from economic rights include: Facebook, Google, Dreamworks, Groupon, Ford Motor Company, Broadcom, Comcast, Appolo Group, The Hershey Company and

The New York Times Company. The IRRC study, from which excerpts are provided below, discusses some of the issues present in these types of structures:

Controlled Companies in the Standard & Poor's 1500: *A Ten Year Performance and Risk Review*

Published by: IRRC Institute (Investor Responsibility Research Center Institute), ISS (Institutional Shareholder Services Inc.), October, 2012

. . .At most U.S. firms, ownership is dispersedly—held and voting power is proportionate to capital at risk. At a minority of firms, however, a significant amount of the vote is controlled by one party through a sizeable ownership stake or, alternately, through a multiclass capital structure created specifically to allow voting power to be disproportionate to capital commitment. These controlling parties often include company founders and/or insiders whose interests may or may not conflict with those of unaffiliated shareholders. The issue of control has received much attention since the initial public offerings of LinkedIn Corp., Zynga Inc., Groupon Inc., and Facebook Inc. . . . A common feature of these firms is a capital structure that allows founders to control a majority of the voting stock while holding a comparatively small portion of their firm's economic value. Supporters of these structures claim that control of a firm's voting power enables management to govern with minimal outside interference and focus on long-term business growth, ultimately delivering shareholders higher returns in exchange for control rights. Detractors, however, claim that control mechanisms misalign interest between affiliated and external shareholders and allow insiders to operate without the normal accountability mechanisms. . . .

Control Mechanisms

There are two primary control mechanisms in the study group: multiclass capital structures with unequal voting rights . . . and ownership of 30 percent or more of [a] single class of capital stock by a person or group. . . . The study group does not include pyramidal ownership structures, which are more commonly found in non-U.S. markets.

Multiclass Capital Structures

Multiclass capital structures with unequal voting rights permit control of a firm through one or more classes of stock that entitle their holder(s) to enhanced voting rights relative to economic ownership. While this mechanism takes many forms, the two most common are those with super-voting shares, which carry more votes per share than other classes of voting stock (or entitle holders of a class to a fixed percentage of the total vote), and those which allow holders of one class to elect a fixed number or percentage (usually a majority) of board members. Firms that employ both of these features in their capital structure and those whose outside shareholders hold mostly non-voting shares are categorized in the latter group.

Super-Voting Shares

For [some] controlled companies, the control mechanism is a multiclass capital structure that includes at least one class of super-voting shares but does not provide exclusive rights to elect a certain number or percentage of board members. Most . . . of these firms have two classes of stock including one class of super-voting shares. . . . The number of votes carried by each share of super-voting stock is fixed at [most] firms; in most cases [that were part of the study], super-voting shares entitle their holder to 10 votes per share compared to one vote for other classes. At Interactive Brokers Group, Inc. and Ford Motor Co., the number of votes attached to each share of super-voting stock is adjusted by a formula to reflect insiders' right to cast a certain percentage of the total voting power. Most firms with super-voting shares adopt this form of capital structure prior to their initial public offering. Some firms restrict ownership of super-voting shares to insiders or require that such shares convert to common stock upon transfer to a non-controlling party. Notable exceptions are Berkshire Hathaway and Urstadt Biddle Properties Inc., which created new classes of common stock in 1996 and 1998, respectively. These firms' founders had held considerable ownership stakes in their respective companies prior to creating these new classes of stock, which carry inferior voting rights relative to economic ownership. Neither of these companies has ownership restrictions on the original class of shares. However, subsequent share issuances at these firms have been mostly in the form of the newer classes of stock, which has enabled their founders to maintain a significant level of voting power over time. At these firms, the controlling shareholders are generally company founders, their relatives, and/or their descendents [sic]. For example, at Tootsie Roll Industries, the controlling shareholders are CEO Melvin Gordon and his wife Helen, who serves as the company's COO and is the daughter of a former executive of the firm who established a controlling stake in the firm subsequent to its initial public offering.

While super-voting shares can magnify a relatively small ownership stake, at [some of the] controlled firms with super-voting shares, the controlling party owns at least 30 percent but less than a majority of the voting power. Other study companies were observed to have multiclass capital structures with unequal voting rights but no controlling shareholder. In these cases, the super-voting shares were widely dispersed or did not constitute a significant percentage of the total voting power.

Enhanced or Exclusive Director Election Rights

At [some] controlled companies . . ., holders of at least one class of stock are entitled to elect a fixed number or percentage of board members. The voting rights at these firms vary: at [some] firms, holders of each class of stock vote separately for director nominees while at [other controlled] companies, holders of all classes vote together on certain nominees but not others. . . . [Some of the controlled companies studied] have classes of non-voting shares including [some] where the non-voting stock is a majority of the aggregate number of shares outstanding. At [some] firms, there are classes of stock with both super-voting shares and the exclusive right to elect a majority of the board. [Some] companies have classes of stock with limited voting rights, including Scripps Networks Interactive, Inc. and its former parent, The E.W. Scripps Co., where outside shareholders are entitled to elect a minority of directors but may not vote on other items. Further, Molex Inc. has non-voting shares as well as a mostly insider-held class of stock with exclusive rights to vote on matters other than director elections. At [a few] companies—Brady Corp., EZCORP Inc., Eaton Vance Corp., Apollo Group., and Federated Investors, Inc.—all of the voting shares are closely held by insiders and there is no public market for any class of stock other than non-voting shares. At [another] company, International Speedway Corp., descendents [sic] of the company's founder control a majority of the class of stock with super-voting rights. Non-affiliated shareholders of these firms are effectively relegated to the status of silent partners.

Firms in this group share many characteristics with those with super-voting shares. Most are controlled by founders, their families, and/or their descendents [sic] and the control mechanisms generally date back to each firm's initial public offering or spinoff from a parent company. It appears that only at International Speedway Corp. was the structure created following the company's initial public offering.

* * * *

The conventional argument for control companies is that control allows management to invest for the long-term, without regard to short-term pressures that may incent non-control companies to skimp on sensible investment in areas such as research and development, new product initiatives, etc. Somewhat counter-intuitively, non-controlled companies outperformed over a 10-year period, while controlled companies outperformed over shorter (1- 3- and 5-year) time frames.

* * * *

B. Control and the Potential for Deadlock

While some efforts to obtain control over a corporation, discussed above, involve the issuance of non-voting stock, other corporations have been known to issue stock that has "super-voting" rights, even if those rights are accompanied by significantly reduced economic rights. (*See e.g., Stroh v. Blackhawk Holding Corp.* 48 Ill2d. 471, 272 N.E.2s 1 (1971).) Often such an issuance is utilized to assure or to allocate control, but in the *Lehrman v. Cohen* case that follows, the corporation issued stock with no economic rights, merely with the goal of avoiding the potential of a deadlock. Of course, if the person to whom control is allocated primarily sides with one shareholder or shareholder group, then the shares granted to prevent a deadlock also have the function of giving that shareholder control.

Lehrman v. Cohen

43 Del. Ch. 222, 222 A.2d 800 (Del. 1966)

HERRMANN, J.:

The primary problem presented on this appeal involves the applicability of the Delaware Voting Trust Statute [8 Del.C. § 218]. Other questions involve the legality of stock having voting power but no dividend or liquidation rights except repayment of par value, and an alleged unlawful delegation of directorial duties and powers.

These are the material facts:

Giant Food Inc. (hereinafter the "Company") was incorporated in Delaware in 1935 by the defendant N. M. Cohen and Samuel Lehrman, deceased father of the plaintiff Jacob Lehrman. From its inception, the Company was controlled by the Cohen and Lehrman families, each of which owned equal quantities of the voting stock, designated Class AC (held by the Cohen family) and Class AL (held by the Lehrman family) common stock. The two classes of stock have cumulative voting rights and each is entitled to elect two members of the Company's four-member board of directors.

Over the years, as may have been expected, there were differences of opinion between the Cohen and Lehrman families as to operating policies of the Company. Samuel Lehrman died in 1949; each of his children inherited part of his stock in the Company; but a dispute arose among the children regarding an *inter vivos* gift of certain shares made to the plaintiff by his father shortly before his death. To eliminate the Lehrman family dispute and its possible disruption of the affairs of the Company, an arrangement was made which settled the dispute and permitted the plaintiff to acquire all of the outstanding Class AL stock, thereby vesting in him voting power equal to that held by the Cohen family. The arrangement involved repurchase by the Company of the stock held by the plaintiff's brothers and sister, their relinquishment of any claim to the stock gift, and an equalizing surrender of certain stock by the Cohens to the Company for retirement. An essential part of the arrangement, upon the insistence of the Cohens, was the establishment of a fifth directorship to obviate the risk of deadlock which would have continued if the equal division of voting power between AL and AC stock were continued.

To implement the arrangement, on December 31, 1949, the Company's certificate of incorporation was amended, *inter alia,* to create a third class of voting stock, designated Class AD common stock, entitled to elect the fifth director. Article Fourth of the amendment to the certificate of incorporation provided for the issuance of one share of Class AD stock, having a par value of $10. and the following rights and powers:

"The holder of Class AD common stock shall be entitled to all of the rights and privileges pertaining to common stock without any limitations, prohibitions, restrictions or qualifications except that the holder of said Class AD stock shall not be entitled to receive any dividends declared and paid by the corporation, shall not be entitled to share in the distribution of assets of the corporation upon liquidation or dissolution either partial or final, except to the extent of the par value of said Class AD common stock, and in the election of Directors shall have the right to vote for and elect one of the five Directors hereinafter provided for.

"The corporation shall have the right, at any time, to redeem and call in the Class AD stock by paying to the holder thereof the par value of said stock, provided however, that such redemption or call shall be authorized and directed by the affirmative vote of four of the five Directors hereinafter provided for."[2]

---

[2] Article Fourth of the amendment also co-related the Class AL and the Class AC stock as follows:

By resolution of the board of directors, the share of Class AD stock was issued forthwith to the defendant Joseph B. Danzansky, who had served as counsel to the Company since 1944. All corporate action regarding the creation and the issuance of the Class AD stock was accomplished by the unanimous vote of the AC and AL stockholders and of the board of directors. In April 1950, pursuant to the arrangement, Danzansky voted his share of AD stock to elect himself as the Company's fifth director; and he served as such until the institution of this action in 1964. During that entire period, the AC and AL stock have been voted to elect two directors each. From 1950 through 1964, Danzansky regularly attended board meetings, raised and discussed general items of business, and voted on all issues as they came before the board. He was not obliged to break any deadlock among the directors prior to October 1, 1964 because no such deadlock arose before that date.

Beginning in December 1959, 200,000 shares of non-voting common stock of the Company were sold in a public issue for over $3,000,000. Each prospectus published in connection with the public issue contained the following statement:

"Common Stock AD is not a participating stock, and the only purpose for the provision and issuance of such stock is to prevent a deadlock in case the Directors elected by the Common Stock AC and the Directors elected by the Common Stock AL cannot reach an agreement."? Similarly, a letter on behalf of the Company to the Commissioner of Internal Revenue, dated July 15, 1959, contained the following statement:

"As can be seen from the enclosed certified copy of the stock provisions of the certificate of Incorporation, as amended, the Class AD common stock is not a participating stock, the only purpose for the provision and issuance of such a stock being to prevent a deadlock in case the AC and AL Directors cannot reach an agreement."

From the outset and until October 1, 1964, the defendant N. M. Cohen was president of the Company. On that date, a resolution was adopted at the Company's annual stockholders' meeting to give Danzansky a fifteen year

---

"The holders of Class AL common stock shall be entitled to all of the rights and privileges pertaining to common stock without any limitations, prohibitions, restrictions, or qualifications except that the holder or holders of said Class AL common stock, in the election of Directors, shall have the right to vote for and elect two of the five Directors hereinafter provided for.

"The holders of Class AC common stock shall be entitled to all of the rights and privileges pertaining to common stock without any limitations, prohibitions, restrictions, or qualifications except that the holder or holders of said Class AC common stock, in the election of Directors, shall have the right to vote for and elect two of the five Directors hereinafter provided for."

executive employment contract at an annual salary of $67,600., and options for 25,000 shares of the non-voting common stock of the Company. The AC and AD stock were voted in favor and the AL stock was voted against the resolution. At a directors meeting held the same day, Danzansky was elected president of the Company by a 3–2 vote, the two AL directors voting in opposition. On December 11, 1964, Danzansky resigned as director and voted his share of AD stock to elect as the fifth director, Millard F. West, Jr., a former AL director and investment banker whose firm was one of the underwriters of the public issue of the Company's stock. The newly constituted board ratified the election of Danzansky as president; and, on January 27, 1965, after the commencement of this action and after a review and report by a committee consisting of the new AD director and one AL director, Danzansky's employment contract was approved and adopted with certain modifications.

The plaintiff brought this action on December 11, 1964, basing it upon two claims: The First Claim charges that the creation, issuance, and voting of the one share of Class AD stock resulted in an arrangement illegal under the law of this State for the reasons hereinafter set forth. The Second Claim, addressed to the events of October 1, 1964, charges that the election of Danzansky as president of the Company and his employment contract violated the terms of the 1959 deadlock-breaking arrangement, as made between the holders of the AC and AL stock, and constituted breaches of contract and fiduciary duty. . . .

I.

The plaintiff's primary contention is that the Class AD stock arrangement is, in substance and effect, a voting trust; that, as such, it is illegal because [it is] not limited to a ten year period as required by the Voting Trust Statute. The defendants deny that the AD stock arrangement constitutes a disguised voting trust; but they concede that if it is, the arrangement is illegal for violation of the Statute. Thus, issue is clearly joined on the point.

The criteria of a voting trust under our decisions have been summarized by this Court in *Abercrombie v. Davies,* 36 Del.Ch. 371, 130 A.2d 338 (1957). The tests there set forth, accepted by both sides of this cause as being applicable, are as follows: (1) the rights of the stock are separated from the other attributes of ownership; (2) the voting rights granted are intended to be irrevocable for a definite period of time; and (3) the principal purpose of the grant of voting rights is to acquire voting control of the corporation.

* * * *

The AD arrangement did not separate the voting rights of the AC or the AL stock from the other attributes of ownership of those classes of stock. Each AC and AL stockholder retains complete control over the voting of his stock; each can vote his stock directly; no AL or AC stockholder is divested of his right to vote his stock as he sees fit; no AL or AC stock can be voted against the shareholder's wishes; and the AL and AC stock continued to elect two directors each.

The AD stock arrangement, as we view it, became a part of the capitalization of the Company. The fact that there is but a single share, or that the par value is nominal, is of no legal significance; the one share and the $10. par value might have been multiplied many times over, with the same consequence. It is true that the creation of the separate class of AD stock may have diluted the voting *power* which had previously existed in the AC and AL stock—the usual consequence when additional voting stock is created—but the creation of the new class did not divest and separate the voting *rights* which remain vested in each AC and AL shareholder, together with the other attributes of the ownership of that stock. The fallacy of the plaintiff's position lies in his premise that since the voting power of the AC and AL stock was reduced by the creation of the AD stock, the percentage of reduction became the *res* of a voting trust. In any recapitalization involving the creation of additional voting stock, the voting power of the previously existing stock is diminished; but a voting trust is not necessarily the result.

Since the holders of the Class AC and Class AL stock of the Company did not separate the voting rights from the other attributes of ownership of those classes when they created the Class AD stock, the first *Abercrombie* test of a voting trust is not met.

. . . Having held that the AC and AL stockholders have not divested themselves of their voting rights, although they may have diluted their voting powers, we do not reach the remaining *Abercrombie* tests, both of which assume the divestiture of voting rights.

* * * *

We hold, therefore, that the Class AD stock arrangement is not controlled by the Voting Trust Statute.

II.

The plaintiff's second point is that even if the Class AD stock arrangement is not a voting trust in substance and effect, the AD stock is illegal, nevertheless, because the creation of a class of stock having voting rights only, and lacking any substantial participating proprietary interest in the corporation, violates the public policy of this State as declared in *§ 218*.

The fallacy of this argument is twofold: First, it is more accurate to say that what the law has disfavored, and what the public policy underlying the Voting Trust Statute means to control, is the separation of the vote from the stock—not from the stock ownership. [*Citations omitted.*] Clearly, the AD stock arrangement is not violative of that public policy. Secondly, there is nothing in *§ 218*, either expressed or implied, which requires that all stock of a Delaware corporation must have both voting rights and proprietary interests. Indeed, public policy to the contrary seems clearly expressed by *8 Del.C. § 151(a)* which authorizes, in very broad terms, such voting powers and participating rights as may be stated in the certificate of incorporation. Non-voting stock is specifically authorized by *§ 151(a);* and in the light thereof, consistency does not permit the conclusion, urged by the plaintiff, that the present public policy of this State condemns the separation of voting rights from beneficial stock ownership.[5] [*Citations omitted.*]

We conclude that the plaintiff's contention in this regard cannot withstand the force and effect of *§ 151(a)*. In our view, that Statute permits the creation of stock having voting rights only, as well as stock having property rights only. The voting powers and the participating rights of the Class AD stock being specified in the Company's certificate of incorporation, we are of the opinion that the Class AD stock is legal by virtue of *§ 151(a)*.

* * * *

III.

The plaintiff advances yet another reason for invalidating the AD stock. The essence of this argument is that the only function of that class of stock is to break directorial deadlocks; that the issuance of the AD stock is merely a

---

[5] *8 Del.C. § 151(a)* provides:

"*§ 151.* Classes and series of stock; rights, etc.

"(a) Every corporation may issue one or more classes of stock or one or more series of stock within any class thereof, any or all of which classes may be of stock with par value or stock without par value, with such voting powers, full or limited, or without voting powers and in such series and with such designations, preferences and relative, participating, optional or other special rights, and qualifications, limitations or restrictions thereof, as shall be stated and expressed in the certificate of incorporation or of any amendment thereto, or in the resolution or resolutions providing for the issue of such stock adopted by the board of directors pursuant to authority expressly vested in it by the provisions of the certificate of incorporation or of any amendment thereto. * * *."

technical device to permit that result; that, as such, it is illegal because it permits the AC and AL directors of the Company to delegate their statutory duties to the AD director as an arbitrator.

We see nothing inherently wrong or contrary to the public policy of this State, as plaintiff seems to suggest, about a device, otherwise lawful, designed by the stockholders of a corporation to break deadlocks of directors. The plaintiff says in this connection, that if public policy sanctioned such devise, our General Corporation Law would provide for it. The fallacy of this argument lies in the assumption that legislative silence is a dependable indicator of public policy. [*Citations omitted.*] We know of no reason. either under our statutes or our decisions, which would prevent the stockholders of a Delaware corporation from protecting themselves and their corporation, by a plan otherwise lawful, against the paralyzing and often fatal consequences of a stalemate in the directorate of the corporation. We hold, therefore, that the AD stock arrangement had a proper purpose.

As to the means adopted for the accomplishment of that purpose, we find the AD stock arrangement valid by virtue of § 141(a) of the Delaware Corporation Law which provides:

"The business of every corporation organized under the provisions of this chapter shall be managed by a board of directors, except as hereinafter or in its certificate of incorporation otherwise provided."

The AD stock arrangement was created by the unanimous action of the stockholders of the Company by amendment to the certificate of incorporation. The stockholders thereby provided how the business of the corporation is to be managed, as is their privilege and right under § 141(a). It was this stockholder action which delegated to the AD director whatever powers and duties he possesses; they were not delegated to him by his fellow directors, either out of their own powers and duties, or otherwise.

It is settled, of course, as a general principle, that directors may not delegate their duty to manage the corporate enterprise. *Adams v. Clearance Corporation,* 35 Del. 459, 121 A.2d 302 (1956). But there is no conflict with that principle where, as here, the delegation of duty, if any, is made not by the directors but by stockholder action under § 141(a), via the certificate of incorporation.

In our judgment, therefore, the AD stock arrangement is not invalid on the ground that it permits the AC and AL directors of the Company to delegate their statutory duties to the AD director.

On this point, the plaintiff relies mainly upon the Chancery Court decision in *Abercrombie v. Davies,* 35 Del.Ch. 599, 611, 123 A.2d 893 (1956). There, in considering an agreement requiring all eight directors to submit a disputed question to an arbitrator if seven were unable to agree, the Chancery Court stated that legal sanction may not be accorded to an agreement, at least when made by less than all the stockholders, which takes from the board of directors the power of determining substantial management policy. The plaintiff's reliance is misplaced, because, inter alia, the *Abercrombie* arrangement was not created by the certificate of incorporation, within the authority of § 141(a). The plaintiff also relies in this connection upon *Field v. Carlisle Corp.,* 31 Del.Ch. 227, 68 A.2d 817 (1949) and *Adams v. Clearance Corp.,* 35 Del.Ch. 459, 121 A.2d 302 (1956). The *Field* case is not in point because it involved delegation of authority by the directors themselves, rather than, as here, by the stockholders speaking through the certificate of incorporation. The *Adams* case is of no aid to the plaintiff's position because there, too, the certificate of incorporation was not involved in the delegation of directorial duties asserted.

* * * *

Finding no error in the judgment below, it is affirmed.

NOTES AND QUESTIONS

1. Why would a deadlock of the board of directors have been a problem?

2. Is it possible that, if an action cannot be agreed upon, then it should not be taken?

3. If you are representing a company with an evenly split board of directors that has the potential for a deadlock, how would you advise them to resolve deadlocks?

4. If an evenly split board of directors wanted to select an individual to serve as the "tie-breaking vote" in the event of a deadlock, how would you suggest such person be selected?

5. Note that § 14.30 of the Model Business Corporations Act provides that a court "may dissolve a corporation. . . . in a proceeding by a shareholder if it is established that . . . the directors are deadlocked in the management of the corporate affairs, the shareholders are unable to break the deadlock, and irreparable injury to the corporation is threatened or being suffered, or the

business and affairs of the corporation can no longer be conducted to the advantage of the shareholders generally, because of the deadlock. . . ."

C. Devices for Allocating Control Among Shareholders

Because of the importance of, and value in, the control of a corporation, several devices (other than the variations in the corporation's organizational structure discussed above) to allocate control among shareholders have developed. However, in order to understand these devices, and their limitations, one must keep in mind that the importance of control arises out of the potential access to income (and other corporate resources), and the way control and devices to exercise control are moderated by fiduciary duties. Most control devices are designed to provide a shareholder or a group of shareholders with sufficient votes to determine or impact certain important decisions in a corporation. Some of the most common devices include: Voting Trusts; Vote Pooling Agreements; Shareholders Agreements; and Irrevocable Proxies.

A *Voting Trust* is a device whereby two or more shareholders place their shares in "trust." The trust has a trustee who is responsible for voting the shares. The trust is typically governed by a trust agreement, which determines how long the trust will last and how the shares will be voted. For example, the trust agreement may provide that the shares are voted in accordance with one person's determination, by a vote of the parties, by one person one year and another person the next year, or even by a flip of a coin. The advantage of a voting trust is that a voting trust contains a mechanism to assure compliance since the trustee holds and votes the shares. Voting trusts also avoid the problems of deadlocks among shareholders. However, shareholders might be uncomfortable with turning over possession of their shares to a trustee and with the loss of control that accompanies relinquishing possession. Also, there is often a limit (usually determined by state law) on the number of years for which a voting trust might exist. This limit is typically 10 years in most states, but may vary from state to state. Finally, it is important to remember that voting trusts relate to the election of directors to the corporation's Board, not to how those directors will vote. Director votes may not be controlled by a voting trust.

A *Vote Pooling Agreement* is a device that is similar to a voting trust. However, there is no trustee, and the shareholders do not typically relinquish control over their shares (although the agreement may delegate control to an individual who has a relatively small ownership percentage). A vote pooling agreement is an agreement between, or among, two or more shareholders which states that the parties' shares will be voted in a certain way, based upon some criteria. As in the case of a voting trust, the criteria in a vote pooling agreement can range from a vote among the parties to the agreement, to the determination of a "neutral" party, to the flip of a coin. Vote pooling agreements are very flexible and may be used in a variety of situations. These agreements may cover all shareholder votes or only certain votes, such as the election of directors. Unlike voting trusts, Vote pooling agreements may be for an unlimited period of time or for a defined period. They may also cover a portion of a shareholder's shares or all of a shareholder's shares.

Shareholders Agreements deal with a wide variety of matters relating to the corporation. Some of these matters might involve issues unrelated to control of the corporation, such as transferability restrictions or the corporation's rights to repurchase stock upon the occurrence of certain events. However, shareholders agreements might also be used to handle matters relating to voting and/or control. Note that a vote pooling agreement might also be called a "Shareholders Agreement." Typically, a shareholders agreement covers a broad range of topics beyond those that would be handled in a vote pooling agreement, but a vote pooling agreement might be contained in a shareholders agreement, *even if it is not labeled as such,* and an agreement that deals only with vote pooling might be called a shareholders agreement. The name is less significant than the substance of the agreement. Shareholders agreements might also address specific matters, such as who will be appointed to the board of directors or which groups will have the right to select certain seats on the corporation's board of directors.

Irrevocable Proxies are discussed in a broader context in the materials relating to shareholder voting. However, in the context of control, irrevocable proxies are used in a similar way to other voting arrangements with one important difference: a proxy is typically given to one entity or individual to enable that individual to have control. So, unlike a voting trust or a vote pooling agreement through which two or more people work together to exercise collective control, a proxy usually involves one (or more) shareholders handing over their votes to a third party to increase that third party's control. A proxy is typically revocable. In order to make a proxy irrevocable, it must be "*coupled with an interest.*" An "interest" may be a job with the corporation, a loan made to corporation, or some other interest in the firm. A proxy does not become irrevocable merely because it is coupled with an interest. The parties must intend for the proxy to be irrevocable and may only make it so if it is coupled with an interest. The proxy may be "irrevocable" for as long as the interest lasts.

Consider the potential use of the various devices in the fact pattern that arises in the following case.

Ringling Bros.-Barnum & Bailey Combined Shows v. Ringling

29 Del. Ch. 610, 53 A.2d 441 (Del. 1947)

PEARSON, J.:

The Court of Chancery was called upon to review an attempted election of directors at the 1946 annual stockholders meeting of the corporate defendant. The pivotal questions concern an agreement between two of the three present stockholders, and particularly the effect of this agreement with relation to the exercise of voting rights by these two stockholders. At the time of the meeting, the corporation had outstanding 1000 shares of capital stock held as follows: 315 by petitioner Edith Conway Ringling; 315 by defendant Aubrey B. Ringling Haley (individually or as executrix and legatee of a deceased husband); and 370 by defendant John Ringling North. The purpose of the meeting was to elect the entire board of seven directors. The shares could be voted cumulatively. Mrs. Ringling asserts that by virtue of the operation of an agreement between her and Mrs. Haley, the latter was bound to vote her shares for an adjournment of the meeting, or in the alternative, for a certain slate of directors. Mrs. Haley contends that she was not so bound for reason that the agreement was invalid, or at least revocable.

The two ladies entered into the agreement in 1941. . . . The agreement recites that each party was the owner "subject only to possible claims of creditors of the estates of Charles Ringling and Richard Ringling, respectively" (deceased husbands of the parties), of 300 shares of the capital stock of the defendant corporation; that in 1938 these shares had been deposited under a voting trust agreement which would terminate in 1947, or earlier, upon the elimination of certain liability of the corporation; that each party also owned 15 shares individually; that the parties had "entered into an agreement in April 1934 providing for joint action by them in matters affecting their ownership of stock and interest in" the corporate defendant; that the parties desired "to continue to act jointly in all matters relating to their stock ownership or interest in" the corporate defendant (and the other corporation). The agreement then provides as follows:

> "Now, Therefore, in consideration of the mutual covenants and agreements hereinafter contained the parties hereto agree as follows:

"1. Neither party will sell any shares of stock or any voting trust certificates in either of said corporations to any other person whosoever, without first making a written offer to the other party hereto of all of the shares or voting trust certificates proposed to be sold, for the same price and upon the same terms and conditions as in such proposed sale, and allowing such other party a time of not less than 180 days from the date of such written offer within which to accept same.

"2. In exercising any voting rights to which either party may be entitled by virtue of ownership of stock or voting trust certificates held by them in either of said corporation, each party will consult and confer with the other and the parties will act jointly in exercising such voting rights in accordance with such agreement as they may reach with respect to any matter calling for the exercise of such voting rights.

"3. In the event the parties fail to agree with respect to any matter covered by paragraph 2 above, the question in disagreement shall be submitted for arbitration to Karl D. Loos, of Washington, D. C. as arbitrator and his decision thereon shall be binding upon the parties hereto. Such arbitration shall be exercised to the end of assuring for the respective corporations good management and such participating therein by the members of the Ringling family as the experience, capacity and ability of each may warrant. The parties may at any time by written agreement designate any other individual to act as arbitrator in lieu of said Loos.

"4. Each of the parties hereto will enter into and execute such voting trust agreement or agreements and such other instruments as, from time to time they may deem advisable and as they may be advised by counsel are appropriate to effectuate the purposes and objects of this agreement.

"5. This agreement shall be in effect from the date hereof and shall continue in effect for a period of ten years unless sooner terminated by mutual agreement in writing by the parties hereto.

* * * *

The Mr. Loos mentioned in the agreement is an attorney and has represented both parties since 1937, and, before and after the voting trust was terminated in late 1942, advised them with respect to the exercise of their voting rights. At the annual meetings in 1943 and the two following years, the parties voted their shares in accordance with mutual understandings arrived at as a result of discussions. In each of these years, they elected five of the seven directors. Mrs. Ringling and Mrs. Haley each had sufficient votes, independently of the other, to elect two of the seven directors. By both voting for an additional candidate, they could be sure of his election regardless of how Mr. North, the remaining stockholder, might vote.[1]

Some weeks before the 1946 meeting, they discussed with Mr. Loos the matter of voting for directors. They were in accord that Mrs. Ringling should cast sufficient votes to elect herself and her son; and that Mrs. Haley should elect herself and her husband; but they did not agree upon a fifth director. The day before the meeting, the discussions were continued, Mrs. Haley being represented by her husband since she could not be present because of illness. In a conversation with Mr. Loos, Mr. Haley indicated that he would make a motion for an adjournment of the meeting for sixty days, in order to give the ladies additional time to come to an agreement about their voting. On the morning of the meeting, however, he stated that because of something Mrs. Ringling had done, he would not consent to a postponement. Mrs. Ringling then made a demand upon Mr. Loos to act under the third paragraph of the agreement "to arbitrate the disagreement" between her and Mrs. Haley in connection with the manner in which the stock of the two ladies should be voted. At the opening of the meeting, Mr. Loos read the written demand and stated that he determined and directed that the stock of both ladies be voted for an adjournment of sixty days. Mrs. Ringling then made a motion for adjournment and voted for it. Mr. Haley, as proxy for his wife, and Mr. North voted against the motion. Mrs. Ringling (herself or through her attorney, it is immaterial which,) objected to the voting of Mrs. Haley's stock in any manner other than in accordance with Mr. Loos' direction. The chairman ruled that the stock could not be voted contrary to such direction, and declared the motion for adjournment had carried.

---

[1] Each lady was entitled to cast 2205 votes (since each had the cumulative voting rights of 315 shares, and there were 7 vacancies in the directorate). The sum of the votes of both is 4410, which is sufficient to allow 882 votes for each of 5 persons. Mr. North, holding 370 shares, was entitled to cast 2590 votes, which obviously cannot be divided so as to give to more than two candidates as many as 882 votes each. It will be observed that in order for Mrs. Ringling and Mrs. Haley to be sure to elect five directors (regardless of how Mr. North might vote) they must act together in the sense that their combined votes must be divided among five different candidates and at least one of the five must be voted for by both Mrs. Ringling and Mrs. Haley.

Nevertheless, the meeting proceeded to the election of directors. Mrs. Ringling stated that she would continue in the meeting "but without prejudice to her position with respect to the voting of the stock and the fact that adjournment had not been taken." Mr. Loos directed Mrs. Ringling to cast her votes

- 882 for Mrs. Ringling,
- 882 for her son, Robert, and
- 441 for a Mr. Dunn, who had been a member of the board for several years.

She complied. Mr. Loos directed that Mrs. Haley's votes be cast

- 882 for Mrs. Haley,
- 882 for Mr. Haley, and
- 441 for Mr. Dunn.

Instead of complying, Mr. Haley attempted to vote his wife's shares

- 1103 for Mrs. Haley, and
- 1102 for Mr. Haley.

Mr. North voted his shares

- 864 for a Mr. Woods,
- 863 for a Mr. Griffin, and
- 863 for Mr. North.

The chairman ruled that the five candidates proposed by Mr. Loos, together with Messrs. Woods and North, were elected. The Haley-North group disputed this ruling insofar as it declared the election of Mr. Dunn; and insisted that Mr. Griffin, instead, had been elected. A directors' meeting followed in which Mrs. Ringling participated after stating that she would do so "without prejudice to her position that the stockholders' meeting had been adjourned and that the directors' meeting was not properly held." Mr. Dunn and Mr. Griffin, although each was challenged by an opposing faction, attempted to join in voting as directors for different slates of officers. Soon after the meeting, Mrs. Ringling instituted this proceeding.

The Vice-Chancellor determined that the agreement to vote in accordance with the direction of Mr. Loos was valid as a "stock pooling agreement" with lawful objects and purposes, and that it was not in violation of any public policy of this state. He held that where the arbitrator acts under the agreement and one party refuses to comply with his direction, "the Agreement constitutes the willing party * * * an implied agent possessing the irrevocable proxy of the recalcitrant party for the purpose of casting the particular vote." It was ordered that a new election be held before a master, with the direction that the master should recognize and give effect to the agreement if its terms were properly invoked.

Before taking up defendants' objections to the agreement, let us analyze particularly what it attempts to provide with respect to voting, including what functions and powers it attempts to repose in Mr. Loos, the "arbitrator". The agreement recites that the parties desired "to continue to act jointly in all matters relating to their stock ownership or interest in" the corporation. The parties agreed to consult and confer with each other in exercising their voting rights and to act jointly—that is, concertedly; unitedly; towards unified courses of action—in accordance with such agreement as they might reach. Thus, so long as the parties agree for whom or for what their shares shall be voted, the agreement provides no function for the arbitrator. His role is limited to situations where the parties fail to agree upon a course of action. In such cases, the agreement directs that "the question in disagreement shall be submitted for arbitration" to Mr. Loos "as arbitrator and his decision thereon shall be binding upon the parties." These provisions are designed to operate in aid of what appears to be a primary purpose of the parties, "to act jointly" in exercising their voting rights, by providing a means for fixing a course of action whenever they themselves might reach a stalemate.

Should the agreement be interpreted as attempting to empower the arbitrator to carry his directions into effect? Certainly there is no express delegation or grant of power to do so, either by authorizing him to vote the shares or to compel either party to vote them in accordance with his directions. The agreement expresses no other function of the arbitrator than that of deciding questions in disagreement which prevent the effectuation of the purpose "to act jointly." The power to enforce a decision does not seem a necessary or usual incident of such a function. Mr. Loos is not a party to the agreement. It does not contemplate the transfer of any shares or interest in shares to him, or that he should undertake any duties which the parties might compel him to perform. They provided that they might designate any other individual to act instead of Mr. Loos. The agreement does not attempt to make the arbitrator a trustee of an express trust. What the arbitrator is to do is for the benefit of the parties, not for his own benefit. Whether the parties accept or reject his decision is no concern of his, so far as the agreement or the surrounding circumstances reveal. We think the parties sought to bind each other, but to be bound only to each other, and not to empower the arbitrator to enforce decisions he might make.

From this conclusion, it follows necessarily that no decision of the arbitrator could ever be enforced if both parties to the agreement were unwilling that it be enforced, for the obvious reason that there would be no one to enforce it. Under the agreement, something more is required after the arbitrator has given his decision in order that it should become compulsory; at least one of the parties must determine that such decision shall be carried into effect. Thus, any "control" of the voting of the shares, which is reposed in the arbitrator, is substantially limited in action under the agreement in that it is subject to the overriding power of the parties themselves.

The agreement does not describe the undertaking of each party with respect to a decision of the arbitrator other than to provide that it "shall be binding upon the parties". It seems to us that this language, considered with relation to its context and the situations to which it is applicable, means that each party promised the other to exercise her own voting rights in accordance with the arbitrator's decision. The agreement is silent about any exercise of the voting rights of one party by the other. The language with reference to situations where the parties arrive at an understanding as to voting plainly suggests "action" by each, and "exercising" voting rights by each, rather than by one for the other. There is no intimation that this method should be different where the arbitrator's decision is to be carried into effect. Assuming that a power in each party to exercise the voting rights of the other might be a relatively more effective or convenient means of enforcing a decision of the arbitrator than would be available without the power, this would not justify implying a delegation of the power in the absence of some indication that the parties bargained for that means. The method of voting actually employed by the parties tends to show that they did not construe the agreement as creating powers to vote each other's shares; for at meetings prior to 1946 each party apparently exercised her own voting rights, and at the 1946 meeting, Mrs. Ringling, who wished to enforce the agreement, did not attempt to cast a ballot in exercise of any voting rights of Mrs. Haley. We do not find enough in the agreement or in the circumstances to justify a construction that either party was empowered to exercise voting rights of the other.

Having examined what the parties sought to provide by the agreement, we come now to defendants' contention that the voting provisions are illegal and revocable. They say that the courts of this state have definitely established the doctrine "that there can be no agreement, or any device whatsoever, by which the voting power of stock of a Delaware corporation may be irrevocably separated from the ownership of the stock, except by an agreement which complies with Section 18" of the Corporation Law, Rev. Code 1935, § 2050, and except by a proxy coupled with an interest. . . . The statute reads, in part, as follows:

> "Sec. 18. Fiduciary Stockholders; Voting Power of; Voting Trusts:—Persons holding stock in a fiduciary capacity shall be entitled to vote the shares so held, and persons whose stock is pledged shall be entitled to vote, unless in the transfer by the pledgor on the books of the corporation he shall have expressly empowered the pledgee to vote thereon, in which case only the pledgee, or his proxy may represent said stock and vote thereon.
>
> "One or more stockholders may by agreement in writing deposit capital stock of an original issue with or transfer capital stock to any person or persons, or corporation or corporations authorized to act as trustee, for the purpose of vesting in said person or persons, corporation or corporations, who may be designated Voting Trustee or Voting Trustees, the right to vote thereon for any period of time determined by such agreement, not exceeding ten years, upon the terms and conditions stated in such agreement. Such agreement may contain any other lawful provisions not inconsistent with said purpose. * * * Said Voting Trustees may vote upon the stock so issued or transferred during the period in such agreement specified; stock standing in the names of such Voting Trustees may be voted either in person or by proxy, and in voting said stock, such Voting Trustees shall incur no responsibility as stockholder, trustee or otherwise, except for their own individual malfeasance."[2]

In our view, neither the cases nor the statute sustain the rule for which the defendants contend. Their sweeping formulation would impugn well-recognized means by which a shareholder may effectively confer his voting rights upon others while retaining various other rights. For example, defendants' rule would apparently not permit holders of voting stock to confer upon stockholders of another class, by the device of an amendment of the certificate of incorporation, the exclusive right to vote during periods when dividends are not paid on stock

[2] Omitted portions of the section provide requirements for the filing of a copy of the agreement in the principal Delaware office of the corporation for the issuance of certificates of stock to the voting trustees, for the voting of stock where there are more than one voting trustee, and for the extension of the agreement for additional periods, not exceeding ten years each.

of the latter class. The broad prohibitory meaning which defendants find in Section 18 seems inconsistent with their concession that proxies coupled with an interest may be irrevocable, for the statute contains nothing about such proxies. The statute authorizes, among other things, the deposit or transfer of stock in trust for a specified purpose, namely, "vesting" in the transferee "the right to vote thereon" for a limited period; and prescribes numerous requirements in this connection. Accordingly, it seems reasonable to infer that to establish the relationship and accomplish the purpose which the statute authorizes, its requirements must be complied with. But the statute does not purport to deal with agreements whereby shareholders attempt to bind each other as to how they shall vote their shares. Various forms of such pooling agreements, as they are sometimes called, have been held valid and have been distinguished from voting trusts. [*Citations omitted.*] We think the particular agreement before us does not violate Section 18 or constitute an attempted evasion of its requirements, and is not illegal for any other reason. Generally speaking, a shareholder may exercise wide liberality of judgment in the matter of voting, and it is not objectionable that his motives may be for personal profit, or determined by whims or caprice, so long as he violates no duty owed his fellow shareholders. *Heil v. Standard G. & E. Co.,* 17 Del. Ch. 214, 151 A. 303. The ownership of voting stock imposes no legal duty to vote at all. A group of shareholders may, without impropriety, vote their respective shares so as to obtain advantages of concerted action. They may lawfully contract with each other to vote in the future in such way as they, or a majority of their group, from time to time determine. . . . .Reasonable provisions for cases of failure of the group to reach a determination because of an even division in their ranks seem unobjectionable. The provision here for submission to the arbitrator is plainly designed as a deadlock-breaking measure, and the arbitrator's decision cannot be enforced unless at least one of the parties (entitled to cast one-half of their combined votes) is willing that it be enforced. We find the provision reasonable. It does not appear that the agreement enables the parties to take any unlawful advantage of the outside shareholder, or of any other person. It offends no rule of law or public policy of this state of which we are aware.

Legal consideration for the promises of each party is supplied by the mutual promises of the other party. The undertaking to vote in accordance with the arbitrator's decision is a valid contract. The good faith of the arbitrator's action has not been challenged and, indeed, the record indicates that no such challenge could be supported. Accordingly, the failure of Mrs. Haley to exercise her voting rights in accordance with his decision was a breach of her contract. It is no extenuation of the breach that her votes were cast for two of the three candidates directed by the arbitrator. His directions to her were part of a single plan or course of action for the voting of the shares of both parties to the agreement, calculated to utilize an advantage of joint action by them which would bring about the election of an additional director. The actual voting of Mrs. Haley's shares frustrates that plan to such an extent that it should not be treated as a partial performance of her contract.

Throughout their argument, defendants make much of the fact that all votes cast at the meeting were by the registered shareholders. The Court of Chancery may, in a review of an election, reject votes of a registered shareholder where his voting of them is found to be in violation of rights of another person. [*Citations omitted.*] It seems to us that upon the application of Mrs. Ringling, the injured party, the votes representing Mrs. Haley's shares should not be counted. Since no infirmity in Mr. North's voting has been demonstrated, his right to recognition of what he did at the meeting should be considered in granting any relief to Mrs. Ringling; for her rights arose under a contract to which Mr. North was not a party. With this in mind, we have concluded that the election should not be declared invalid, but that effect should be given to a rejection of the votes representing Mrs. Haley's shares. No other relief seems appropriate in this proceeding. Mr. North's vote against the motion for adjournment was sufficient to defeat it. With respect to the election of directors, the return of the inspectors should be corrected to show a rejection of Mrs. Haley's votes, and to declare the election of the six persons for whom Mr. North and Mrs. Ringling voted.

This leaves one vacancy in the directorate. The question of what to do about such a vacancy was not considered by the court below and has not been argued here. For this reason, and because an election of directors at the 1947 annual meeting (which presumably will be held in the near future) may make a determination of the question unimportant, we shall not decide it on this appeal. If a decision of the point appears important to the parties, any of them may apply to raise it in the Court of Chancery, after the mandate of this court is received there.

An order should be entered directing a modification of the order of the Court of Chancery in accordance with this opinion.

QUESTIONS

1. If the Haleys had come to you prior the initial vote and said their objective was to remove Robert and elect John North as president, could you have designed an easier (and less controversial) way to accomplish that goal?

2. When the original Vote Pooling Agreement was drafted, were there additional steps that Mr. Loos could have taken to facilitate the enforcement of the Agreement?

3. What would have been different if the Haleys and Ringlings had used a Voting Trust instead?

4. Why do you think this was not done?

SECTION II: Limitations on Control Arrangements

The preceding section explored a number of devices that shareholders may implement to allocate or wield control. However, as discussed in earlier chapters a corporation's directors have different fiduciary duties than do a corporation's shareholders. Because a corporation's directors have fiduciary obligations to all of the shareholders, there are limitations upon the agreements that these directors may make. Directors need to be free to act in the best interests of the corporation and in accordance with their fiduciary obligations, not bound to act in accordance with an agreement to a few interested parties. The following cases explore the limitations on control arrangements that may be made as they apply to directors and to the actions that an individual acting in his or her capacity as a director might take.

McQuade v. Stoneham

263 N.Y. 323, 189 N.E. 234 (N.Y. 1934)

POUND, CH J.:

The action is brought to compel specific performance of an agreement between the parties, entered into to secure the control of National Exhibition Company, also called the Baseball Club (New York Nationals or "Giants"). This was one of Stoneham's enterprises which used the New York polo grounds for its home games. McGraw was manager of the Giants. McQuade was at the time the contract was entered into a City Magistrate. He resigned December 8, 1930.

Defendant Stoneham became the owner of 1,306 shares, or a majority of the stock of National Exhibition Company. Plaintiff and defendant McGraw each purchased seventy shares of his stock. Plaintiff paid Stoneham $50,338.10 for the stock he purchased. As a part of the transaction the agreement in question was entered into. It was dated May 21, 1919. Some of its pertinent provisions are

> "VIII. The parties hereto will use their best endeavors for the purpose of continuing as directors of said Company and as officers thereof the following:
>
> **Directors:**
>
> Charles A. Stoneham,
>
> John J. McGraw,
>
> Francis X. McQuade,
>
> with the right to the party of the first part [Stoneham] to name all additional directors as he sees fit:
>
> **Officers:**
>
> Charles A. Stoneham, President,
>
> John J. McGraw, Vice-President,
>
> Francis X. McQuade, Treasurer.
>
> "IX. No salaries are to be paid to any of the above officers or directors, except as follows:
>
> | | |
> |---|---|
> | President | $45,000 |
> | Vice-President | $7,500 |
> | Treasurer | $7,500 |
>
> X. There shall be no change in said salaries, no change in the amount of capital, or the number of shares, no change or amendment of the by-laws of the corporation or any matters regarding the policy of the business of the corporation or any matters which may in anywise affect, endanger or interfere with the rights of minority stockholders, excepting upon the mutual and unanimous consent of all of the parties hereto.
>
> * * * *

"XIV. This agreement shall continue and remain in force so long as the parties or any of them or the representative of any, own the stock referred to in this agreement, to wit, the party of the first part, 1,166 shares, the party of the second part 70 shares and the party of the third part 70 shares, except as may otherwise appear by this agreement * * *."

In pursuance of this contract Stoneham became president and McGraw vice-president of the corporation. McQuade became treasurer. In June, 1925, his salary was increased to $10,000 a year. He continued to act until May 2, 1928, when Leo J. Bondy was elected to succeed him. The board of directors consisted of seven men. The four outside of the parties hereto were selected by Stoneham and he had complete control over them. At the meeting of May 2, 1928, Stoneham and McGraw refrained from voting, McQuade voted for himself and the other four voted for Bondy. Defendants did not keep their agreement with McQuade to use their best efforts to continue him as treasurer. On the contrary, he was dropped with their entire acquiescence. At the next stockholders' meeting he was dropped as a director although they might have elected him.

The courts below have refused to order the reinstatement of McQuade, but have given him damages for wrongful discharge, with a right to sue for future damages.

The cause for dropping McQuade was due to the falling out of friends. McQuade and Stoneham had disagreed. The trial court has found in substance that their numerous quarrels and disputes did not affect the orderly and efficient administration of the business of the corporation; that plaintiff was removed because he had antagonized the dominant Stoneham by persisting in challenging his power over the corporate treasury and for no misconduct on his part. The court also finds that plaintiff was removed by Stoneham for protecting the corporation and its minority stockholders. We will assume that Stoneham put him out when he might have retained him, merely in order to get rid of him.

Defendants say that the contract in suit was void because the directors held their office charged with the duty to act for the corporation according to their best judgment and that any contract which compels a director to vote to keep any particular person in office and at a stated salary is illegal. Directors are the exclusive executive representatives of the corporation, charged with administration of its internal affairs and the management and use of its assets. They manage the business of the corporation. (Gen. Corp. Law; Cons. Laws, ch. 23, § 27.) "An agreement to continue a man as president is dependent upon his continued loyalty to the interests of the corporation." (*Fells v. Katz*, 256 N. Y. 67, 72.) So much is undisputed.

Plaintiff contends that the converse of this proposition is true and that an agreement among directors to continue a man as an officer of a corporation is not to be broken so long as such officer is loyal to the interests of the corporation and that, as plaintiff has been found loyal to the corporation, the agreement of defendants is enforceable.

Although it has been held that an agreement among stockholders whereby it is attempted to divest the directors of their power to discharge an unfaithful employee of the corporation is illegal as against public policy (*Fells v. Katz, supra*), it must be equally true that the stockholders may not, by agreement among themselves, control the directors in the exercise of the judgment vested in them by virtue of their office to elect officers and fix salaries. Their motives may not be questioned so long as their acts are legal. The bad faith or the improper motives of the parties does not change the rule. (*Manson v. Curtis,* 223 N. Y. 313, 324.) Directors may not by agreements entered into as stockholders abrogate their independent judgment. [*Citations omitted.*]

Stockholders may, of course, combine to elect directors. That rule is well settled. As Holmes, Ch. J., pointedly said (*Brightman v. Bates,* 175 Mass. 105, 111): "If stockholders want to make their power felt, they must unite. There is no reason why a majority should not agree to keep together." The power to unite is, however, limited to the election of directors and is not extended to contracts whereby limitations are placed on the power of directors to manage the business of the corporation by the selection of agents at defined salaries.

The minority shareholders whose interests McQuade says he has been punished for protecting, are not, aside from himself, complaining about his discharge. He is not acting for the corporation or for them in this action. It is impossible to see how the corporation has been injured by the substitution of Bondy as treasurer in place of McQuade. As McQuade represents himself in this action and seeks redress for his own wrongs, "we prefer to listen to [the corporation and the minority stockholders] before any decision as to their wrongs." (*Faulds v. Yates,* 57 Ill. 416, 421.)

It is urged that we should pay heed to the morals and manners of the market place to sustain this agreement and that we should hold that its violation gives rise to a cause of action for damages rather than base our decision on any outworn notions of public policy. Public policy is a dangerous guide in determining the validity of a contract and courts should not interfere lightly with the freedom of competent parties to make their own contracts. We do not close our eyes to the fact that such agreements, tacitly or openly arrived at, are not uncommon, especially in close corporations where the stockholders are doing business for convenience under a corporate organization. We know that majority stockholders, united in voting trusts, effectively manage the business of a corporation by choosing trustworthy directors to reflect their policies in the corporate management. Nor are we unmindful that McQuade has, so the court has found, been shabbily treated as a purchaser of stock from Stoneham. We have said: "A trustee is held to something stricter than the morals of the market place" (*Meinhard v. Salmon,* 249 N. Y. 458, 464), but Stoneham and McGraw were not trustees for McQuade as an individual. Their duty was to the corporation and its stockholders, to be exercised according to their unrestricted lawful judgment. They were under no legal obligation to deal righteously with McQuade if it was against public policy to do so.

The courts do not enforce mere moral obligations, nor legal ones either, unless someone seeks to establish rights which may be waived by custom and for convenience. We are constrained by authority to hold that a contract is illegal and void so far as it precludes the board of directors, at the risk of incurring legal liability, from changing officers, salaries or policies or retaining individuals in office, except by consent of the contracting parties. On the whole, such a holding is probably preferable to one which would open the courts to pass on the motives of directors in the lawful exercise of their trust.

A further reason for reversal exists. At the time the contract was made the plaintiff was a City Magistrate. . . .

The Inferior Criminal Courts Act (Laws of 1910, ch. 659, as amd.) provides that no "city magistrate shall engage in any other business, profession or hold any other public office or shall serve as the representative of any political party for any assembly, aldermanic, senatorial or congressional district in the executive committee or other governing body of any political party organization or political party association. No city magistrate shall engage in any other business or profession or act as referee, or receiver, but each of said justices and magistrates shall devote his whole time and capacity, so far as the public interest demands, to the duties of his office. * * *" (§ 161, Laws 1933, ch. 746, formerly § 102 as amended, Laws 1915, ch. 531). . . . .

* * * *

Until the date when the defendants repudiated the agreement, its performance constituted a violation of the statute. Even though we should assume that the contract was not illegal in purpose at its inception, it created a combination which resulted in a succession of illegal acts. The defendants cannot be held in damages for refusal to continue such a combination. The plaintiff can recover no compensation for loss of opportunity to perform services forbidden by law. . . .

The judgment of the Appellate Division and that of the Trial Term should be reversed and the complaint dismissed, with costs in all courts.

QUESTIONS

1. Are there other steps that McQuade could have taken to protect his "promised" position?

2. How would you advise someone in McQuade's position to proceed before he made the $50,338.10 stock purchase?

Clark v. Dodge

269 N.Y. 410, 199 N.E. 641 (N.Y. 1936)

CROUCH, J.:

The action is for the specific performance of a contract between the plaintiff Clark and the defendant Dodge, relating to the affairs of the two defendant corporations. . . .

Those facts, briefly stated, are as follows: The two corporate defendants are New Jersey corporations manufacturing medicinal preparations by secret formulae. The main office, factory and assets of both corporations are located in the State of New York. In 1921, and at all times since, Clark owned twenty-five per cent and Dodge seventy-five per cent of the stock of each corporation. Dodge took no active part in the business, although he was a director and, through ownership of their qualifying shares, controlled the other directors of both corporations. He was the president of Bell & Company, Inc., and nominally general manager of Hollings-Smith Company, Inc. The plaintiff Clark was a director and held the offices of treasurer and general manager of Bell & Company, Inc., and also had charge of the major portion of the business of Hollings-Smith Company, Inc. The formulae and methods of manufacture of the medicinal preparations were known to him alone. Under date of February 15, 1921, Dodge and Clark, the sole owners of the stock of both corporations, entered into a written agreement under seal, which after reciting the stock ownership of both parties, the desire of Dodge that Clark should continue in the efficient management and control of the business of Bell & Company, Inc., so long as he should "remain faithful, efficient and competent to so manage and control the said business;" and his further desire that Clark should not be the sole custodian of a specified formula but should share his knowledge thereof and of the method of manufacture with a son of Dodge, provided, in substance, as follows: That Dodge during his lifetime and, after his death, a trustee to be appointed by his will, would so vote his stock and so vote as a director that the plaintiff (a) should continue to be a director of Bell & Company, Inc. and (b) should continue as its general manager so long as he should be "faithful, efficient and competent;" (c) should during his life receive one-fourth of the net income of the corporations either by way of salary or dividends; and (d) that no unreasonable or incommensurate salaries should be paid to other officers or agents which would so reduce the net income as materially to affect Clark's profits. Clark on his part agreed to disclose the specified formula to the son and to instruct him in the details and methods of manufacture; and further, at the end of his life to bequeath his stock—if no issue survived him—to the wife and children of Dodge.

It was further provided that the provisions in regard to the division of net profits and the regulation of salaries should also apply to the Hollings-Smith Company.

The complaint alleges due performance of the contract by Clark and breach thereof by Dodge in that he has failed to use his stock control to continue Clark as a director and as general manager, and has prevented Clark from receiving his proportion of the income, while taking his own, by causing the employment of incompetent persons at excessive salaries, and otherwise.

The relief sought is reinstatement as director and general manager and an accounting by Dodge and by the corporations for waste and for the proportion of net income due plaintiff, with an injunction against further violations.

The only question which need be discussed is whether the contract is illegal as against public policy within the decision in *McQuade v. Stoneham* (263 N. Y. 323), upon the authority of which the complaint was dismissed by the Appellate Division.

"The business of a corporation shall be managed by its board of directors." (General Corporation Law . . . § 27.) That is the statutory norm. Are we committed by the *McQuade* case to the doctrine that there may be no variation, however slight or innocuous, from that norm, where salaries or policies or the retention of individuals in office are concerned? There is ample authority supporting that doctrine [*Citations omitted.*], and something may be said for it, since it furnishes a simple, if arbitrary, test. Apart from its practical administrative convenience, the reasons upon which it is said to rest are more or less nebulous. Public policy, the intention of the Legislature, detriment to the corporation, are phrases which in this connection mean little. Possible harm to *bona fide* purchasers of stock or to creditors or to stockholding minorities have more substance; but such harms are absent in many instances. If the enforcement of a particular contract damages nobody—not even, in any perceptible degree, the public—one sees no reason for holding it illegal, even though it impinges slightly upon the broad provision of section 27. Damage suffered or threatened is a logical and practical test, and has come to be the one generally adopted by the courts. [*Citations omitted.*] Where the directors are the sole stockholders, there seems to be no objection to enforcing an agreement among them to vote for certain people as officers. There is no direct decision to that effect in this court, yet there are strong indications that such a rule has long been recognized. The opinion in *Manson v. Curtis (*223 N. Y. 313, 325) closed its discussion by saying: "The rule that all the stockholders by their universal consent may do as they choose with the corporate concerns and assets, provided the interests of creditors are not affected, because they are the complete owners of the corporation, cannot be invoked here." That was because all the stockholders were not parties to the agreement there in question. So, where the public was not affected, "the parties in interest, might, by their original agreement of incorporation, limit their respective rights and powers," even where there was a conflicting statutory standard. (*Ripin v. U. S. Woven Label Co.,* 205 N. Y. 442, 448.) . . . . The rule recognized in *Manson v. Curtis,* and quoted above, was thus stated by Blackmar, J., in *Kassel v. Empire Tinware Co.* (178 App. Div. 176, 180): "As the parties to the action are the complete owners of the corporation, there is no reason why the exercise of the power and discretion of the directors cannot be controlled by valid agreement between themselves, provided that the interests of creditors are not affected."

* * * *

Except for the broad dicta in the *McQuade* opinion, we think there can be no doubt that the agreement here in question was legal and that the complaint states a cause of action. There was no attempt to sterilize the board of directors, as in the *Manson and McQuade* cases. The only restrictions on Dodge were (a) that as a stockholder he should vote for Clark as a director—a perfectly legal contract; (b) that as director he should continue Clark as general manager, so long as he proved faithful, efficient and competent—an agreement which could harm nobody; (c) that Clark should always receive as salary or dividends one-fourth of the "net income." For the purposes of this motion, it is only just to construe that phrase as meaning whatever was left for distribution after the directors had in good faith set aside whatever they deemed wise; (d) that no salaries to other officers should be paid, unreasonable in amount or incommensurate with services rendered—a beneficial and not a harmful agreement.

If there was any invasion of the powers of the directorate under that agreement, it is so slight as to be negligible; and certainly there is no damage suffered by or threatened to any body. The broad statements in the *McQuade* opinion, applicable to the facts there, should be confined to those facts.

The judgment of the Appellate Division should be reversed and the order of the Special Term affirmed, with costs in this court and in the Appellate Division.

As discussed above, shareholders may generally agree on how they will vote as shareholders. However, while shareholders may agree that they will elect each other to the board of directors, they may not agree that, once they are on the board, they will elect each other as officers. An agreement among directors to elect one another as officers is typically not enforceable. Decisions made by directors must be made consistent with a director's fiduciary duties to act in the best interests of the corporation and of all of its shareholders, not consistent with contractual obligations to certain shareholders.

However, there are some exceptions to this principle which would allow otherwise unenforceable agreements (or provisions in agreements) among shareholders to be enforceable. Typically, shareholders may agree how they will vote on certain matters as directors (such as dividends or the election of officers) if ALL of the shareholders have entered into the agreement. This is sometimes known as a "shareholder unanimity exception." There are also cases in some states as seen in the *Galler* case below, which hold that, even if all of the shareholders are not parties to the agreement, the agreement is still enforceable, provided that certain conditions are met.

Galler v. Galler

32 Ill. 2d 16, 203 N.E.2d 577 (Ill. 1964)

UNDERWOOD, J.:

Plaintiff, Emma Galler, sued in equity for an accounting and for specific performance of an agreement made in July, 1955, between plaintiff and her husband, of one part, and defendants, Isadore A. Galler and his wife, Rose, of the other. . . .

There is no substantial dispute as to the facts in this case. From 1919 to 1924, Benjamin and Isadore Galler, brothers, were equal partners in the Galler Drug Company, a wholesale drug concern. In 1924 the business was incorporated under the Illinois Business Corporation Act, each owning one half of the outstanding 220 shares of stock. In 1945 each contracted to sell 6 shares to an employee, Rosenberg, at a price of $10,500 for each block of 6 shares, payable within 10 years. They guaranteed to repurchase the shares if Rosenberg's employment were terminated, and further agreed that if they sold their shares, Rosenberg would receive the same price per share as that paid for the brothers' shares. Rosenberg was still indebted for the 12 shares in July, 1955, and continued to make payments on account even after Benjamin Galler died in 1957 and after the institution of this action by Emma Galler in 1959. Rosenberg was not involved in this litigation either as a party or as a witness, and in July of 1961, prior to the time that the master in chancery hearings were concluded, defendants Isadore and Rose Galler purchased the 12 shares from Rosenberg. A supplemental complaint was filed by the plaintiff, Emma Galler, asserting an equitable right to have 6 of the 12 shares transferred to her and offering to pay the defendants one half of the amount that the defendants paid Rosenberg. The parties have stipulated that pending disposition of the instant case, these shares will not be voted or transferred. For approximately one year prior to the entry of the decree by the chancellor in July of 1962, there were no outstanding minority shareholder interests.

In March, 1954, Benjamin and Isadore, on the advice of their accountant, decided to enter into an agreement for the financial protection of their immediate families and to assure their families, after the death of either brother, equal control of the corporation. In June, 1954, while the agreement was in the process of preparation by an attorney-associate of the accountant, Benjamin suffered a heart attack. Although he resumed his business duties some months later, he was again stricken in February, 1955, and thereafter was unable to return to work. During his brother's illness, Isadore asked the accountant to have the shareholders' agreement put in final form in order to protect Benjamin's wife, and this was done by another attorney employed in the accountant's office. On a Saturday night in July, 1955, the accountant brought the agreement to Benjamin's home, and 6 copies of it were executed there by the two brothers and their wives. The accountant then collected all signed copies of the agreement and informed the parties that he was taking them for safe keeping. Between the execution of the agreement in July, 1955, and Benjamin's death in December, 1957, the agreement was not modified. . . . Because of the state of Benjamin's health, nothing further was said to him by any of the parties concerning the agreement. It appears from the evidence that some months after the agreement was signed, the defendants Isadore and Rose Galler and their son, the defendant, Aaron Galler, sought to have the agreements destroyed. The evidence is undisputed that defendants had decided prior to Benjamin's death they would not honor the agreement, but never disclosed their intention to plaintiff or her husband.

On July 21, 1956, Benjamin executed an instrument creating a trust naming his wife as trustee. The trust covered, among other things, the 104 shares of Galler Drug Company stock and the stock certificates were endorsed by Benjamin and delivered to Emma. When Emma presented the certificates to defendants for transfer into her name as trustee, they sought to have Emma abandon the 1955 agreement or enter into some kind of a noninterference agreement as a price for the transfer of the shares. Finally, in September, 1956, after Emma had refused to abandon the shareholders' agreement, she did agree to permit defendant Aaron to become president for one year and agreed that she would not interfere with the business during that year. The stock was then reissued in her name as trustee. During the year 1957 while Benjamin was still alive, Emma tried many times to arrange a meeting with Isadore to discuss business matters but he refused to see her.

Shortly after Benjamin's death, Emma went to the office and demanded the terms of the 1955 agreement be carried out. Isadore told her that anything she had to say could be said to Aaron, who then told her that his father would not abide by the agreement. He offered a modification of the agreement by proposing the salary continuation payment but without her becoming a director. When Emma refused to modify the agreement and sought enforcement of its terms, defendants refused and this suit followed.

During the last few years of Benjamin's life both brothers drew an annual salary of $42,000. Aaron, whose salary was $15,000 as manager of the warehouse prior to September, 1956, has since the time that Emma agreed to his acting as president drawn an annual salary of $20,000. In 1957, 1958, and 1959 a $40,000 annual dividend was paid. Plaintiff has received her proportionate share of the dividend.

The July, 1955, agreement in question here, entered into between Benjamin, Emma, Isadore and Rose, recites that Benjamin and Isadore each own 47 1/2% of the issued and outstanding shares of the Galler Drug Company, an Illinois corporation, and that Benjamin and Isadore desired to provide income for the support and maintenance of their immediate families. No reference is made to the shares then being purchased by Rosenberg. The essential features of the contested portions of the agreement are substantially as set forth in the opinion of the Appellate Court: (2) that the bylaws of the corporation will be amended to provide for a board of four directors; that the necessary quorum shall be three directors; and that no directors' meeting shall be held without giving ten days notice to all directors. (3) The shareholders will cast their votes for the above named persons (Isadore, Rose, Benjamin and Emma) as directors at said special meeting and at any other meeting held for the purpose of electing directors. (4, 5) In the event of the death of either brother his wife shall have the right to nominate a director in place of the decedent. (6) Certain annual dividends will be declared by the corporation. The dividend shall be $50,000 payable out of the accumulated earned surplus in excess of $500,000. If 50% of the annual net profits after taxes exceeds the minimum $50,000, then the directors shall have discretion to declare a dividend up to 50% of the annual net profits. If the net profits are less than $50,000, nevertheless the minimum $50,000 annual dividend shall be declared, providing the $500,000 surplus is maintained. Earned surplus is defined. (9) The certificates evidencing the said shares of Benjamin Galler and Isadore Galler shall bear a legend that the shares are subject to the terms of this agreement. (10) A salary continuation agreement shall be entered into by the corporation which shall authorize the corporation upon the death of Benjamin Galler or Isadore Galler, or both, to pay a sum equal to twice the salary of such officer, payable monthly over a five-year period. Said sum shall be paid to the widow during her widowhood, but should be paid to such widow's children if the widow remarries within the five-year period. . . . In the event either Benjamin or Isadore decides to sell his shares he is required to offer them first to the remaining shareholders and then to the corporation at book value, according each six months to accept the offer.

The Appellate Court found the 1955 agreement void because "the undue duration, stated purpose and substantial disregard of the provisions of the Corporation Act outweigh any considerations which might call for divisibility" and held that "the public policy of this state demands voiding this entire agreement".

While the conduct of defendants towards plaintiff was clearly inequitable, the basically controlling factor is the absence of an adverse effect upon a minority interest, together with the absence of public detriment. . . .

Faulds v. Yates, 57 Ill. 416, decided by this court in 1870, established the general rule that the owners of the majority of the stock of a corporation have the right to select the agents for the management of the corporation. This court observed *(57 Ill. 416, 421):* "It is strange that a man can not, for honest purposes, unite with others in the protection and security of his property and rights without liability to the charge of fraud and inequity".

* * * *

Again, in 1913, this court in *Venner v. Chicago City Railway Co.* 258 Ill. 523, 539, followed the *Faulds* case and said: "There is no statute of this State which prohibits a trust of the stock of a corporation for the purpose of controlling its management. There is no rule of public policy in this State which prohibits the combination of the owners of the majority of the stock of a corporation for the purpose of controlling the corporation. On the contrary, it has been expressly held that a contract by the owners of more than one-half of the shares of stock of a corporation to elect the directors of the corporation so as to secure the management of its property, to ballot among themselves for directors and officers if they could not agree, to cast their vote as a unit as the majority should decide so as to control the election, and not to buy or sell stock except for their joint benefit is not dishonest, violative of the rights of others or in contravention of public policy (*Faulds v. Yates,* 57 Ill. 416.)

* * * *

At this juncture it should be emphasized that we deal here with a so-called close corporation. Various attempts at definition of the close corporation have been made. . . . For our purposes, a close corporation is one in which the stock is held in a few hands, or in a few families, and wherein it is not at all, or only rarely, dealt in by buying or selling. [*Citations omitted.*] Moreover, it should be recognized that shareholder agreements similar to that in question here are often, as a practical consideration, quite necessary for the protection of those financially interested in the close corporation. While the shareholder of a public-issue corporation may readily sell his shares on the open market should management fail to use, in his opinion, sound business judgment, his counterpart of the close corporation often has a large total of his entire capital invested in the business and has no ready market for his shares should he desire to sell. He feels, understandably, that he is more than a mere investor and that his voice should be heard concerning all corporate activity. Without a shareholder agreement, specifically enforceable by the courts, insuring him a modicum of control, a large minority shareholder might find himself at the mercy of an oppressive or unknowledgeable majority. Moreover, as in the case at bar, the shareholders of a close corporation are often also the directors and officers thereof. With substantial shareholding interests abiding in each member of the board of directors, it is often quite impossible to secure, as in the large public-issue corporation, independent board judgment free from personal motivations concerning corporate policy. For these and other reasons too voluminous to enumerate here, often the only sound basis for protection is afforded by a lengthy, detailed shareholder agreement securing the rights and obligations of all concerned. . . .

As the preceding review of the applicable decisions of this court points out, there has been a definite, albeit inarticulate, trend toward eventual judicial treatment of the close corporation as *sui generis*. Several shareholder-director agreements that have technically "violated" the letter of the Business Corporation Act have nevertheless been upheld in the light of the existing practical circumstances, *i.e.,* no apparent public injury, no apparent injury to a minority interest, and no apparent prejudice to creditors. However, we have thus far not attempted to limit these decisions as applicable only to close corporations and have seemingly implied that general considerations regarding judicial supervision of all corporate behavior apply.

* * * *

It is . . . necessary, we feel, to discuss the instant case with the problems peculiar to the close corporation particularly in mind.

It would admittedly facilitate judicial supervision of corporate behavior if a strict adherence to the provisions of the Business Corporation Act were required in all cases without regard to the practical exigencies peculiar to the close corporation. [*Citations omitted.*] However, courts have long ago quite realistically, we feel, relaxed their attitudes concerning statutory compliance when dealing with close corporate behavior, permitting "slight deviations" from corporate "norms" in order to give legal efficacy to common business practice. See, *e.g., Clark v. Dodge,* 269 N.Y. 410, 199 N.E. 641; [*Citations omitted.*] This attitude is illustrated by the following language in *Clark v. Dodge:* "Public policy, the intention of the Legislature, detriment to the corporation, are phrases which in this connection [the court was discussing a shareholder-director agreement whereby the directors pledged themselves to vote for certain people as officers of the corporation] mean little. Possible harm to bona fide purchasers of stock or to creditors or to stockholding minorities have more substance; but such harms are absent in many instances. If the enforcement of a particular contract damages nobody—not even, in any perceptible degree, the public—one sees no reason for holding it illegal, even though it impinges slightly on the broad provisions of [the relevant statute providing that the business of a corporation shall be managed by its board of directors.]. Damage suffered or threatened is a logical and practical test, and has come to be the one generally adopted by the courts. See 28 Columbia L. Rev. 366, 372." *Clark v. Dodge,* 199 N.E. 641, 642.

Again, "As the parties to the action are the complete owners of the corporation, there is no reason why the exercise of the power and discretion of the directors cannot be controlled by valid agreement between themselves, provided that the interests of creditors are not affected." *Clark v. Dodge,* 119 N.E. 641, 643, quoting from *Kassel v. Empire Tinware Co.* 178 App. Div. 176, 180, 164 N.Y.S. 1033, 1035.

Numerous helpful textual statements and law review articles dealing with the judicial treatment of the close corporation have been pointed out by counsel. One article concludes with the following: "New needs compel fresh formulation of corporate 'norms'. There is no reason why mature men should not be able to adapt the statutory form to the structure they want, so long as they do not endanger other stockholders, creditors, or the public, or violate a clearly mandatory provision of the corporation laws. In a typical close corporation the stockholders' agreement is usually the result of careful deliberation among all initial investors. In the large public-issue corporation, on the other hand, the 'agreement' represented by the corporate charter is not consciously agreed to by the investors; they have no voice in its formulation, and very few ever read the certificate of incorporation. Preservation of the corporate norms may there be necessary for the protection of the public investors." Hornstein, "Stockholders' Agreements in the Closely Held Corporation", 59 Yale L. Journal, 1040, 1056.

This court has recognized, albeit *sub silentio,* the significant conceptual differences between the close corporation and its public-issue counterpart in, among other cases, *Kantzler v. Bensinger,* 214 Ill. 589, where an agreement quite similar to the one under attack here was upheld. Where, as in *Kantzler* and here, no injury to a minority interest appears, no fraud or apparent injury to the public or creditors is present, and no clearly prohibitory statutory language is violated, we can see no valid reason for precluding the parties from reaching any arrangements concerning the management of the corporation which are agreeable to all.

[T]he courts can no longer fail to expressly distinguish between the close and public-issue corporation when confronted with problems relating to either. What we do here is to illuminate this problem . . . in the context of a particular fact situation. To do less would be to shirk our responsibility, to do more would, perhaps be to invade the province of the legislative branch.

We now, in the light of the foregoing, turn to specific provisions of the 1955 agreement.

The Appellate Court correctly found many of the contractual provisions free from serious objection, and we need not prolong this opinion with a discussion of them here. That court did, however, find difficulties in the stated purpose of the agreement as it relates to its duration, the election of certain persons to specific offices for a number of years, the requirement for the mandatory declaration of stated dividends (which the Appellate Court held invalid), and the salary continuation agreement.

Since the question as to the duration of the agreement is a principal source of controversy, we shall consider it first. The parties provided no specific termination date, and while the agreement concludes with a paragraph that its terms "shall be binding upon and shall inure to the benefits of" the legal representatives, heirs and assigns of the parties, this clause is, we believe, intended to be operative only as long as one of the parties is living. It further provides that it shall be so construed as to carry out its purposes, and we believe these must be determined from a consideration of the agreement as a whole. Thus viewed, a fair construction is that its purposes were accomplished at the death of the survivor of the parties. While these life spans are not precisely ascertainable, and the Appellate Court noted Emma Galler's life expectancy at her husband's death was 26.9 years, we are aware of no statutory or public policy provision against stockholder's agreements which would invalidate this agreement on that ground. *(Thompson v. Thompson Carnation Co.*, 279 Ill. 54.). . . . That the policy against agreements in which stock ownership and voting rights are separated . . . is inapplicable to voting control agreements was emphasized in *Thompson* wherein a control agreement was upheld as not attempting to separate ownership and voting power. While limiting voting trusts in 1947 to a maximum duration of 10 years, the legislature has indicated no similar policy regarding straight voting agreements although these have been common since prior to 1870. In view of the history of decisions of this court generally upholding, in the absence of fraud or prejudice to minority interests or public policy, the right of stockholders to agree among themselves as to the manner in which their stock will be voted, we do not regard the period of time within which this agreement may remain effective as rendering the agreement unenforceable.

The clause that provides for the election of certain persons to specified offices for a period of years likewise does not require invalidation. In *Kantzler v. Bensinger,* 214 Ill. 589, this court upheld an agreement entered into by all the stockholders providing that certain parties would be elected to the offices of the corporation for a fixed period. In *Faulds v. Yates,* 57 Ill. 416, we upheld a similar agreement among the majority stockholders of a corporation, notwithstanding the existence of a minority which was not before the court complaining thereof. [*Citations omitted.*]

We turn next to a consideration of the effect of the stated purpose of the agreement upon its validity. The pertinent provision is: "The said Benjamin A. Galler and Isadore A. Galler desire to provide income for the support and maintenance of their immediate families." Obviously, there is no evil inherent in a contract entered into for the reason that the persons originating the terms desired to so arrange their property as to provide post-death support for those dependent upon them. Nor does the fact that the subject property is corporate stock alter the situation so long as there exists no detriment to minority stock interests, creditors or other public injury. It is, however, contended by defendants that the methods provided by the agreement for implementation of the stated purpose are, as a whole, violative of the Business Corporation Act [*Citations omitted.*] to such an extent as to render it void *in toto.*

The terms of the dividend agreement require a minimum annual dividend of $50,000, but this duty is limited by the subsequent provision that it shall be operative only so long as an earned surplus of $500,000 is maintained. It may be noted that in 1958, the year prior to commencement of this litigation, the corporation's net earnings after taxes amounted to $202,759 while its earned surplus was $1,543,270, and this was increased in 1958 to $1,680,079 while earnings were $172,964. The minimum earned surplus requirement is designed for the protection of the corporation and its creditors, and we take no exception to the contractual dividend requirements as thus restricted. [*Citation omitted.*]

The salary continuation agreement is a common feature, in one form or another, of corporate executive employment. It requires that the widow should receive a total benefit, payable monthly over a five-year period, aggregating twice the amount paid her deceased husband in one year. This requirement was likewise limited for the protection of the corporation by being contingent upon the payments being income tax-deductible by the corporation. The charge made in those cases which have considered the validity of payments to the widow of an officer and shareholder in a corporation is that a gift of its property by a noncharitable corporation is in violation of the rights of its shareholders and *ultra vires.* Since there are no shareholders here other than the parties to the contract, this objection is not here applicable, and its effect, as limited, upon the corporation is not so prejudicial as to require its invalidation.

* * * *

We hold defendants must account for all monies received by them from the corporation since September 25, 1956, in excess of that theretofore authorized.

Accordingly, the judgment of the Appellate Court is reversed, except insofar as it relates to fees, and is, as to them affirmed. The cause is remanded to the circuit court of Cook County with directions to proceed in accordance herewith.

Affirmed in part and reversed in part, and remanded with directions.

The following case contains a discussion of the enforceability (and limitations) of certain agreements among shareholders; it is also a strong example of the significant consequences that might follow from a failure to adhere to such agreements.

Ramos v. Estrada

10 Cal. Rptr. 2d 833, 8 Cal. App. 4th 1070 (Cal. App. 2 Dist. 1992)

GILBERT, J.:

Defendants Tila and Angel Estrada appeal a judgment which states they breached a written corporate shareholder voting agreement. We hold that a corporate shareholders' voting agreement may be valid even though the corporation is not technically a close corporation. We affirm.

FACTS

Plaintiffs Leopoldo Ramos et al. formed Broadcast Corporation for the purpose of obtaining a Federal Communications Commission (FCC) construction permit to build a Spanish language television station in Ventura County.

Ramos and his wife held 50 percent of Broadcast Corp. stock. The remaining 50 percent was issued in equal amounts to five other couples. The Estradas were one of the couples who purchased a 10 percent interest in Broadcast Corp. Tila Estrada became president of Broadcast Corp., sometimes known as the "Broadcast Group."

In 1986, Broadcast Corp. merged with a competing applicant group, Ventura 41 Television Associates (Ventura 41), to form Costa del Oro Television, Inc. (Television Inc.). The merger agreement authorized the issuance of 10,002 shares of Television Inc. voting stock.

Initially, Television Inc. was to issue 5,000 shares to Broadcast Corp. and 5,000 to Ventura 41. Each group would have the right to elect half of an eight-member board of directors. The two remaining outstanding shares were to be issued to Broadcast Corp. after the television station had operated at full power for six months. Television Inc.'s board would then increase to nine members, five of whom would be elected by Broadcast Corp.

The merger agreement contained restrictions on the transfer of stock and required each group to adopt internal shareholder agreements to carry out the merger agreement. With FCC approval, Broadcast Corp. and Ventura 41 modified their agreement to permit stock in Television Inc. to be issued directly to the respective owners of the merged entities instead of to the entities themselves. Ventura 41 sought this change so that Television Inc. would be treated as a Subchapter S corporation for tax purposes. In part, Broadcast Group agreed to this change in exchange for approval by Ventura 41 of the agreement at issue here, which is known as the June Broadcast Agreement. Among other things, the June Broadcast Agreement provides for block voting for directors by the Broadcast Group shareholders according to their ownership.

In January 1987, Broadcast Group executed a written shareholder agreement, known as the January Broadcast Agreement, to govern the voting and transfer of Broadcast Corp. shares in Television Inc. stock. At a later date, Broadcast Group drafted a written schedule showing the valuation of shares transferred pursuant to the January Broadcast Agreement. It set the price for purchase and sale of shares as their investment cost plus 8 percent per annum.

In June 1987, the shareholders of Broadcast Group executed a Master Shareholder Agreement. This agreement was designed to implement the Merger Agreement. It permits direct shareholder ownership of stock and governs various voting and transfer provisions. It requires that shareholder votes be made in the manner voted by the majority of the shareholders.

Members of Broadcast Group subscribed for shares of Television Inc. in their respective proportion of ownership pursuant to written subscription agreements attached to the Master Shareholder Agreement. The Ventura 41 group acted similarly.

Television Inc. issued stock to these subscribers in December 1987, and they elected an eight-member board. They also elected Leopoldo Ramos president, and Tila Estrada as one of the directors.

At a special directors' meeting held on October 8, 1988, Tila Estrada voted with the Ventura 41 group block to remove Ramos as president and to replace him with Walter Ulloa, a member of Ventura 41. She also joined Ventura 41 in voting to remove Romualdo Ochoa, a Broadcast Group member, as secretary and to replace him with herself.

Under the June Broadcast Agreement and the Merger Agreement, each of the groups were required to vote for the directors upon whom a majority of each respective group had agreed. The terms of that agreement expressly state that failure to adhere to the agreement constitutes an election by the shareholder to sell his or her shares pursuant to buy/sell provisions of the agreement.* The agreement also calls for specific enforcement of such buy/sell provisions.

On October 15, 1988, the Broadcast Group noticed another meeting to decide how its members would vote their shares for directors at the annual meeting. All members attended except the Estradas. The group agreed to nominate another slate of directors which did not include either of the Estradas. The Estradas were notified of the results of this meeting.

The Estradas unilaterally declared the June Broadcast Agreement null and void as of October 15, 1988, in a letter dictated for them by Paul Zevnik, the attorney for Ventura 41. Tila Estrada refused to recognize the October 15 vote of the majority of the Broadcast Group to replace her as a director of Television Inc. Ramos et al. sued the Estradas for breach of the June Broadcast Agreement, among other things.

The court ruled that the Estradas materially breached the valid June Broadcast Agreement, and it ordered their shares sold in accordance with the specific enforcement provisions of the June Broadcast Agreement. The court restrained the Estradas from voting their shares other than as provided in the June Broadcast Agreement.

---

* [Eds. The agreement seems to have adopted the earlier measure for price, providing for the sale of shares of those who breach the agreement at their investment cost plus 8 percent per annum.]

DISCUSSION

The Estradas contend that the June Broadcast Agreement is void because it constitutes an expired proxy which the Estradas validly revoked.

* * * *

Corporations Code section 178 defines a proxy to be "a written authorization signed . . . by a shareholder . . . *giving another person or persons* power to vote with respect to the shares of such shareholder." (Italics added.)

Section 7.1 of the June Broadcast Agreement details the voting arrangement among the shareholders. It states, in pertinent part: "The Stockholders agree that they shall consult with each other prior *to voting their shares* in the Company. They shall attempt in good faith to reach a consensus as to the outcome of any such vote. In the case of a vote for directors, they agree that no director shall be selected who is not acceptable to at least one member (*i.e.,* spousal unit) of each of Group A and Group B. (See P 1.2(b)(1) above [which states that: 'The Stockholders shall be divided into two groups, Group "A" being composed of Leopoldo Ramos and Cecilia Morris, and Group "B" being composed of all the other Stockholders.'].) In the case of all *votes of Stockholders* they agree that, following consultation and compliance with the other provisions of this paragraph, *they will all vote their stock in the manner voted by a majority* of the Stockholders." (Second italics in original.)

No proxies are created by this agreement. The agreement has the characteristics of a shareholders' voting agreement expressly authorized by section 706, subdivision (a) for close corporations. [*Citations omitted.*] Although the articles of incorporation do not contain the talismanic statement that "This corporation is a close corporation," the arrangements of this corporation, and in particular this voting agreement, are strikingly similar to ones authorized by the code for close corporations.

Section 706, subdivision (a) states, in pertinent part: "an agreement between two or more shareholders of a close corporation, if in writing and signed by the parties thereto, may provide that in exercising any voting rights the shares held by them shall be voted as provided by the agreement, or as the parties may agree or as determined in accordance with a procedure agreed upon by them . . . ."

Here, the members of this corporation executed a written agreement providing that they shall try to reach a consensus on all votes and that they shall consult with one another and vote their own stock in accordance with the majority of the stockholders. They entered into this agreement because they "mutually desire[d]" to limit the transferability of their stock to ensure "the Company does not pass into the control of persons whose interests might be incompatible with the interests of the Company and of the Stockholders, establishing their mutual rights and obligations in the event of death, and establishing a mechanism for determining how the Stockholders' voting rights in the Company shall be exercised . . . ."

Even though this corporation does not qualify as a close corporation, this agreement is valid and binding on the Estradas. Section 706, subdivision (d) states: "This section shall not invalidate any voting or other agreement among shareholders . . . which agreement . . . is not otherwise illegal."

The legislative committee comment regarding section 706, subdivision (d) states that "[t]his subdivision is intended to preserve any agreements which would be upheld under court decisions *even though they do not comply with one or more of the requirements of this section, including voting agreements of corporations other than close corporations.*" (West's Ann. Corp. Code, § 706 (1990) p. 330, italics added.)

The California Practice Guide indicates that such "pooling" agreements are valid not only for close corporations, but also "among any number of shareholders of other corporations as well." (Friedman, *Cal. Practice Guide: Corporations* (The Rutter Group 1992) P 3:159.2, p. 3–31.)

* * * *

The instant agreement is valid, enforceable and supported by consideration. It states, in pertinent part, that the stockholders entered into the agreement for the purposes of "limiting the transferability of . . . stock in the Company, ensuring that the Company does not pass into the control of persons whose interests might be incompatible with the interests of the Company and of the Stockholders, establishing their mutual rights and obligations in the event of death, and establishing a mechanism for determining how the Stockholders' voting rights . . . shall be exercised . . . ."

Section 7.2 of the agreement states that "[t]he Stockholders understand and acknowledge that the purpose of the foregoing arrangement is to preserve their relative voting power in the Company . . . . Accordingly, in the event that a Stockholder fails to abide by this arrangement for whatever reason, that failure shall constitute on [*sic*] irrevocable election by the Stockholder to sell his stock in the Company, triggering the same rights of purchase provided in Article IV above."

The agreement calls for enforcement by specific performance of its terms because the stock is not readily marketable. Section 709, subdivision (c) expressly permits enforcement of shareholder voting agreements by such equitable remedies. It states, in pertinent part: "The court may determine the person entitled to the office of director or may order a new election to be held or appointment to be made, may determine the validity, effectiveness and construction of voting agreements . . . and the right of persons to vote and may direct such other relief as may be just and proper."

The Estradas contend that the forced sale provision is unconscionable and oppressive. They portray themselves as naive, small-town business people who were forced to sign an adhesion agreement without reviewing its contents.

Substantial evidence supports the findings that Tila Estrada has been a licensed real estate broker. She is an astute businesswoman experienced with contracts concerning real property. The consent and signatures of the Estradas to the agreement were not procured by fraud, duress or other wrongful conduct of Ramos. The Estradas read and discussed with other members of Broadcast Group, and with their own counsel, the voting, buy/sell and other provisions of the agreement and the January Broadcast Agreement, as well as various drafts of these documents, and they freely signed these agreements.

On direct examination . . . Tila Estrada admitted she owns and operates a real estate brokerage business; she regularly reviews a broad variety of real estate documents; she and her husband own and manage investment property; and she has considered herself "to be an astute business woman" since 1985. Tila Estrada also has been a participant and owner in another application before the FCC, for an FM radio station, before the instant suit was filed.

Ms. Estrada stated she got copies "of all the drafts and all the Shareholders Agreements." She discussed these agreements with other members of Broadcast Group and with its counsel, Mr. Howard Weiss.

The June Broadcast Agreement, including its voting and buy/sell provisions, was unanimously executed after the Estradas had a full and fair opportunity to consider it in its entirety. As the trial court found, the buy out provisions at issue here are valid, favored by courts and enforceable by specific performance. (And see 3 Marsh, *supra,* at § 22.14, p. 1867; see generally *Vannucci v. Pedrini* (1932) 217 Cal. 138, 144–145 [17 P.2d 706], on the right of those who are the original incorporators to enter into a corporate agreement requiring limitations on shareholder actions so as to preserve control of the corporation as set forth in their executed agreements.)

The Estradas breached the agreement by their written repudiation of it. Their breach constituted an election to sell their Television Inc. shares in accordance with the terms of the buy/sell provisions in the agreement. This election does not constitute a forfeiture—they violated the agreement voluntarily, aware of the consequences of their acts and they are provided full compensation, per their agreement. The judgment is affirmed. Costs to Ramos.

QUESTIONS

1. Was Tila Estrada's vote to remove Ramos as President and replace him with Ulloa a breach of the June Broadcast Agreement?

2. If not, what was the breach?

3. Why would the Estradas have violated the Agreement, if the consequences were so severe?

4. If you represented the Estradas what advice would you have given them, if the goal was to "get out of" the June Broadcast Agreement?

A. Allocations of Control in a Corporation's Governing Documents

The cases in the preceding section involve agreements that have been used to address control issues. However, there are other devices that might be used to address some of the same issues. Sometimes corporations will alter the standard voting requirements dictated by the general corporation law to require a "super majority" vote for the approval of certain matters. The term super majority merely means some percentage greater than a simple majority (i.e., greater than 50%). Also, a super majority requirement might only apply to certain votes. For example, a corporation might include a provision in its bylaws, requiring that any vote involving the sale of land owned by the corporation requires an affirmative vote of 75%. Often, such requirements are included in a corporation's bylaws, but they may also be included in its Articles (or Certificate) of Incorporation. Super majority provisions may be used to apply to votes by the board of directors or votes of the shareholders.

Another use of super majority provisions is the protection of minority shareholders. Super majority provisions are not used to give control to minority shareholders. Rather, they might provide minority shareholders with a "veto" right, enabling them to block actions which otherwise might have been approved. For example if a minority shareholder owns 40% of a corporation and another shareholder owns 60%, the dominant shareholder would typically have the power to control the corporation and make all of the decisions. However, if instead, all decisions made in that same corporation required approval of a super majority of 66%, then no action could be taken unless both shareholders agreed. While such a structure does substantially increase the risk of deadlocks, it also provides the minority shareholder with protections that he would not otherwise have. Consider the *Sutton v. Sutton* case that follows and ask yourself whether you think a super majority provision was a good device for Abraham Sutton to include in the Bag Bazaar Ltd.'s certificate of incorporation.

Sutton v. Sutton

84 N.Y.2d 37, 637 N.E.2d 260 (N.Y. 1984)

SIMONS, J.:

In this CPLR article 78 proceeding, petitioners seek (1) a declaration that an amendment to the certificate of incorporation of Bag Bazaar, Ltd. is valid and (2) to compel respondent David S. Sutton, as a director of the corporation, to sign and deliver a certificate of amendment to petitioners for filing. Respondent has refused to execute the certificate, contending it is not valid because the amendment had the support of only 70% of the shareholders when the certificate of incorporation required unanimous approval. The appeal requires an interpretation of section 616 (b) of the Business Corporation Law which states that supermajority provisions in a certificate of incorporation may be amended by a two-thirds vote unless the certificate "specifically" provides otherwise.

Petitioners contend that notwithstanding the general unanimity provision contained in Bag Bazaar's certificate, a two-thirds vote amend is sufficient under this statute unless the certificate explicitly provides unanimous consent is required to amend the supermajority provision. As they see it, prior to a 1962 statutory amendment, which added the word "specifically", a general requirement of a unanimous vote for any amendment of the certificate—i.e., a provision like the one here—would be read to apply to the supermajority provision. Thus, they reason that the Legislature, by adding the word "specifically" in the 1962 amendment, intended to require an amendment provision explicitly directed at the procedure for changing a supermajority provision. The Appellate Division disagreed and held that the provision in Bag Bazaar's certificate of incorporation was sufficiently specific and that the amendment was not valid because it lacked unanimous shareholder approval . . . We now affirm.

In 1963, the certificate of incorporation of Bag Bazaar, Ltd. was amended to provide that "[t]he unanimous vote or consent of the holders of all the issued and outstanding shares of Common Stock of the corporation shall be necessary for the transaction of any business . . . of the corporation, including amendment to the certificate of incorporation". At that time the business was run by Abraham Sutton and none of the parties to this litigation was a shareholder. In 1971 Abraham's brother, respondent David S. Sutton, purchased 30 shares. Two years later Abraham's son, petitioner Solomon A. Sutton, joined the business and subsequently acquired 30 shares. On Abraham's death, in 1987, his widow, petitioner Yvette Sutton, inherited Abraham's remaining 40 shares. Thus, petitioners now own 70% of the outstanding shares of the corporation and respondent and his wife own 30 shares. Petitioner Solomon A. Sutton serves as one of the two directors of the company and respondent David S. Sutton as the other.

The corporation was run without incident for nearly 30 years under Abraham's leadership. After he relinquished control of the company, however, disputes arose between Solomon and David Sutton concerning the management of the corporation. These disputes culminated in an April 1992 shareholders' meeting, where petitioners voted their 70% of the shares in favor of a resolution to strike the unanimity provision, while respondent's 30% of the shares voted against the resolution.

Respondent, as a director of the corporation, refused to sign a certificate of amendment reflecting the deletion of the unanimity provision, thereby preventing the amendment from taking effect. Accordingly, petitioners commenced this proceeding and moved for judgment declaring the resolution valid and enforceable and compelling respondent to sign the certificate of amendment. . . .

To support their position on this appeal, petitioners contend that the Legislature added the word "specifically" to section 616 (b) because it recognized that a unanimity provision gives minority shareholders the ability to deadlock any and all corporate action. The amendment was intended to minimize deadlocks by permitting a two-thirds majority of the shareholders to alter or delete the unanimity requirement unless the certificate of incorporation explicitly stated otherwise. Respondent maintains that "specifically" was added to the statute to clarify that if more than a two-thirds vote was required to amend a unanimity provision, the certificate should state exactly what greater percentage is needed. They maintain that this certificate satisfied that requirement by declaring that a unanimous vote was required for *any* amendment.

The history of Business Corporation Law § 616 (b) begins with *Benintendi v. Kenton Hotel* (294 NY 112), where this Court invalidated a unanimity provision adopted by unanimous shareholder vote. We reasoned that such a provision was antithetical to the basic concept of corporate governance by majority rule and contrary to public policy *(id.,* at 118–119). In 1948, the Legislature abrogated *Benintendi* by enacting section 9 of the Stock Corporation Law, which authorized unanimity provisions when approved by a unanimous vote [*Citation omitted.*] The effect of section 9 was to require unanimous shareholder consent to either add or amend a unanimity provision. . . . In 1951, this section was amended to allow adoption or change of a supermajority provision by a two-thirds or greater vote. A unanimous vote was still required, however, where the certificate called for a unanimous vote; where the unanimity provision itself required such a vote; or where the unanimity provision was adopted prior to the effective date of the 1951 amendment [*Citation omitted.*]

In 1961, the Business Corporation Law was adopted to replace the Stock Corporation Law, and section 9 was substantially reenacted as Business Corporation Law § 616 (b) and § 709 (b). However, in 1962, prior to the 1963 effective date of the Business Corporation Law, a series of changes were made, including the addition of the word "specifically" in section 616 (b). As finally enacted, section 616 (b) provides that "[a]n amendment of the certificate of incorporation which changes or strikes out a [supermajority] provision . . . shall be authorized at a meeting of shareholders by vote of the holders of two-thirds of all outstanding shares entitled to vote thereon, or of such greater proportion of shares . . . as may be provided *specifically* in the certificate of incorporation" (emphasis added). According to the Legislative Study Committee the word "specifically" was one of a number of "technical" amendments added to the chapter to clarify existing language and avoid minor inconsistencies. It was not intended to effect a substantive change in the law (Mem of Joint Legis Comm To Study Revision of Corp Laws, Bill Jacket, L 1962, ch 834, at 86).

Thus, nothing in the legislative history or the statute itself suggests the necessity for a discrete paragraph addressed solely to the supermajority provision and explicitly declaring the vote required for its amendment. The history reveals that Stock Corporation Law § 9 stated that a provision in the certificate of incorporation requiring unanimous consent could only be amended by unanimous consent and this provision was substantially reenacted in the

Business Corporation Law.* Inasmuch as the Legislature did not intend the "technical" revisions added before the effective date of the Business Corporation Law to change the existing law substantively, the present statute should be construed as section 9 of the Stock Corporation Law was. Unanimity was required under the prior law to amend a unanimity provision, such as this one, and the addition of the word "specifically" merely provides that a two-thirds majority may now amend a unanimity provision unless the certificate requires a greater percentage.

The provision in Bag Bazaar's certificate is unambiguous: it requires unanimous shareholder consent for the transaction of "any business . . . including amendment to the certificate of incorporation." To read section 616 (b) as requiring more to address amendment of the supermajority provision would be unnecessarily restrictive in light of the legislative history. The certificate need only clearly state what vote, if greater than two thirds, is required to amend a unanimity provision. The certificate of Bag Bazaar, Ltd. does so.

* * * *

Finally, petitioners note that unless section 616 (b) is read as requiring an explicit certificate provision governing the amendment of unanimity provisions, majority shareholders will be unable to conduct the business of a corporation in the face of opposition from the minority. But as respondent notes, there is nothing inherently unfair or improper about a voluntary organization's consensual decision to assure protection for minority shareholders, and shareholders are not without remedies where deadlocks do arise *(see generally, Business Corporation Law § 1104).*

Accordingly, the order of the Appellate Division should be affirmed, with costs. . . .

QUESTIONS

1. Do you think the super majority provision in the Sutton case achieved its objective?

---

* While the 1951 amendments to that section allowed a unanimity provision to be amended by a two-thirds vote in certain instances, petitioners acknowledge that the provision at issue here would have required unanimous shareholder consent to amend, despite the 1951 amendment.

2. If Abraham Sutton had come into your office and asked for help in creating a voting structure for Bag Bazaar Ltd., to function when he was no longer running the company, what might you have suggested?

3. How much should a business attorney consider "family dynamics" in creating such a structure?

SECTION III: Freeze Outs and the Abuse of Control

While directors and officers have fiduciary duties to the corporation, ordinary shareholders typically do not owe such duties either to the corporation or to the other shareholders. However, as seen in the earlier materials on fiduciary duties, in certain situations in which a dominant (or controlling) shareholder is present, there are some limitations on this principle, resulting in some limits on dominant shareholders with respect to actions that involve self-dealing. In closely held corporations there are some additional issues that arise with respect to shareholders because of the potential for "freeze outs."

A common form of freeze out occurs when the majority shareholder (or block of shareholders) earns a return at the expense of the other shareholders, often by channeling corporate funds to the officer "salaries" of the controlling shareholder(s) and depriving the other shareholder(s) of the opportunity to share in funds paid out by the company. In this context, a freeze out involves a situation in which a minority shareholder is blocked from holding a paid position with the corporation, such as a position as an officer or an employee, by the majority shareholder (or a block of shareholders wielding control). Such actions are often accompanied by a failure or refusal by the corporation to pay dividends.

Freeze outs are handled differently in different jurisdictions. In Delaware the fiduciary duty of a dominant shareholder is frequently applied to freeze out situations. Most courts will treat a group of shareholders acting together (who collectively hold a dominant/controlling ownership position in the corporation) as a dominant shareholder. The fiduciary duty limits on a dominant shareholder would, therefore, prevent a shareholder (or group of shareholders) from taking all of the benefits of ownership of the corporation for himself, herself or itself. In general, controlling shareholders may not take all of the money in a corporation and distribute it to themselves without engaging in a conflict of interest and violating the duty of loyalty. Directors, even if they are also shareholders, always have fiduciary duties to ALL of the shareholders. On the other hand, minority shareholders know that they are in a non-controlling position. A minority shareholder is charged with the knowledge that, a minority shareholder (absent some control device (discussed above)) does not have the power to force the other shareholder(s) to elect that minority shareholder to the board of directors or to hire him or her as an officer. On the other hand, a controlling shareholder often does have the power to be elected president of the corporation by other directors and to be paid a salary (provided, of course that the salary satisfies "fairness standards"). In such a situation, it is unlikely that a minority shareholder could show a violation of any fiduciary duties.

Other jurisdictions, such as Massachusetts, apply a partnership-like analysis to closely held corporations. Courts in these jurisdictions often find that there are some fiduciary duties among shareholders in a closely held corporation reminiscent of certain duties seen in partnerships. In general, the courts in these jurisdictions have taken the position that shareholders in closely held corporations owe each other a duty of good faith. In the *Wilkes v. Springside Nursing Home, Inc.* case below, the court established a "test" to evaluate the conduct of shareholders in freeze out situations.

Wilkes v. Springside Nursing Home, Inc.

370 Mass. 842, 353 N.E.2d 657 (Mass. 1976)

HENNESSEY, C.J.:

On August 5, 1971, the plaintiff (Wilkes) filed a bill in equity for declaratory judgment in the Probate Court for Berkshire County, naming as defendants T. Edward Quinn (Quinn), Leon L. Riche (Riche), the First Agricultural National Bank of Berkshire County and Frank Sutherland MacShane as executors under the will of Lawrence R. Connor (Connor), and the Springside Nursing Home, Inc. (Springside or the corporation). Wilkes alleged that he, Quinn, Riche and Dr. Hubert A. Pipkin (Pipkin) entered into a partnership agreement in 1951, prior to the incorporation of Springside, which agreement was breached in 1967 when Wilkes's salary was terminated and he was voted out as an officer and director of the corporation. . . .

On appeal, Wilkes argued in the alternative that (1) he should recover damages for breach of the alleged partnership agreement; and (2) he should recover damages because the defendants, as majority stockholders in Springside, breached their fiduciary duty to him as a minority stockholder by their action in February and March, 1967.

* * * *

A summary of the pertinent facts as found by the master is set out in the following pages. . . .

In 1951 Wilkes acquired an option to purchase a building and lot located on the corner of Springside Avenue and North Street in Pittsfield, Massachusetts, the building having previously housed the Hillcrest Hospital. Though Wilkes was principally engaged in the roofing and siding business, he had gained a reputation locally for profitable dealings in real estate. Riche, an acquaintance of Wilkes, learned of the option, and interested Quinn (who was known to Wilkes through membership on the draft board in Pittsfield) and Pipkin (an acquaintance of both Wilkes and Riche) in joining Wilkes in his investment. The four men met and decided to participate jointly in the purchase of the building and lot as a real estate investment which, they believed, had good profit potential on resale or rental.

The parties later determined that the property would have its greatest potential for profit if it were operated by them as a nursing home. Wilkes consulted his attorney, who advised him that if the four men were to operate the contemplated nursing home as planned, they would be partners and would be liable for any debts incurred by the partnership and by each other. On the attorney's suggestion, and after consultation among themselves, ownership of the property was vested in Springside, a corporation organized under Massachusetts law.

Each of the four men invested $1,000 and subscribed to ten shares of $100 par value stock in Springside.[6] At the time of incorporation it was understood by all of the parties that each would be a director of Springside and each would participate actively in the management and decision making involved in operating the corporation.[7] It was, further, the understanding and intention of all the parties that, corporate resources permitting, each would receive money from the corporation in equal amounts as long as each assumed an active and ongoing responsibility for carrying a portion of the burdens necessary to operate the business.

[6] On May 2, 1955, and again on December 23, 1958, each of the four original investors paid for and was issued additional shares of $100 par value stock, eventually bringing the total number of shares owned by each to 115.

[7] Wilkes testified before the master that, when the corporate officers were elected, all four men "were . . . guaranteed directorships." Riche's understanding of the parties' intentions was that they all wanted to play a part in the management of the corporation and wanted to have some "say" in the risks involved; that, to this end, they all would be directors; and that "unless you [were] a director and officer you could not participate in the decisions of [the] enterprise."

The work involved in establishing and operating a nursing home was roughly apportioned, and each of the four men undertook his respective tasks.[8] Initially, Riche was elected president of Springside, Wilkes was elected treasurer, and Quinn was elected clerk.[9] Each of the four was listed in the articles of organization as a director of the corporation.

At some time in 1952, it became apparent that the operational income and cash flow from the business were sufficient to permit the four stockholders to draw money from the corporation on a regular basis. Each of the four original parties initially received $35 a week from the corporation. As time went on the weekly return to each was increased until, in 1955, it totalled $100.

In 1959, after a long illness, Pipkin sold his shares in the corporation to Connor, who was known to Wilkes, Riche and Quinn through past transactions with Springside in his capacity as president of the First Agricultural National Bank of Berkshire County. Connor received a weekly stipend from the corporation equal to that received by Wilkes, Riche and Quinn. He was elected a director of the corporation but never held any other office. He was assigned no specific area of responsibility in the operation of the nursing home but did participate in business discussions and decisions as a director and served additionally as financial adviser to the corporation.

In 1965 the stockholders decided to sell a portion of the corporate property to Quinn who, in addition to being a stockholder in Springside, possessed an interest in another corporation which desired to operate a rest home on the property. Wilkes was successful in prevailing on the other stockholders of Springside to procure a higher sale price for the property than Quinn apparently anticipated paying or desired to pay. After the sale was consummated, the relationship between Quinn and Wilkes began to deteriorate.

The bad blood between Quinn and Wilkes affected the attitudes of both Riche and Connor. As a consequence of the strained relations among the parties, Wilkes, in January of 1967, gave notice of his intention to sell his shares for an amount based on an appraisal of their value. In February of 1967 a directors' meeting was held and the board exercised its right to establish the salaries of its

---

[8] Wilkes took charge of the repair, upkeep and maintenance of the physical plant and grounds; Riche assumed supervision over the kitchen facilities and dietary and food aspects of the home; Pipkin was to make himself available if and when medical problems arose; and Quinn dealt with the personnel and administrative aspects of the nursing home, serving informally as a managing director. Quinn further coordinated the activities of the other parties and served as a communication link among them when matters had to be discussed and decisions had to be made without a formal meeting.

[9] Riche held the office of president from 1951 to 1963; Quinn served as president from 1963 on, as clerk from 1951 to 1967, and as treasurer from 1967 on; Wilkes was treasurer from 1951 to 1967.

officers and employees.[10] A schedule of payments was established whereby Quinn was to receive a substantial weekly increase and Riche and Connor were to continue receiving $100 a week. Wilkes, however, was left off the list of those to whom a salary was to be paid. The directors also set the annual meeting of the stockholders for March, 1967.

At the annual meeting in March, Wilkes was not reelected as a director, nor was he reelected as an officer of the corporation. He was further informed that neither his services nor his presence at the nursing home was wanted by his associates.

The meetings of the directors and stockholders in early 1967, the master found, were used as a vehicle to force Wilkes out of active participation in the management and operation of the corporation and to cut off all corporate payments to him. Though the board of directors had the power to dismiss any officers or employees for misconduct or neglect of duties, there was no indication in the minutes of the board of directors' meeting of February, 1967, that the failure to establish a salary for Wilkes was based on either ground. The severance of Wilkes from the payroll resulted not from misconduct or neglect of duties, but because of the personal desire of Quinn, Riche and Connor to prevent him from continuing to receive money from the corporation. Despite a continuing deterioration in his personal relationship with his associates, Wilkes had consistently endeavored to carry on his responsibilities to the corporation in the same satisfactory manner and with the same degree of competence he had previously shown. Wilkes was at all times willing to carry on his responsibilities and participation if permitted so to do and provided that he receive his weekly stipend.

1. We turn to Wilkes's claim for damages based on a breach of fiduciary duty owed to him by the other participants in this venture. In light of the theory underlying this claim, we do not consider it vital to our approach to this case whether the claim is governed by partnership law or the law applicable to business corporations. This is so because, as all the parties agree, Springside was at all times relevant to this action, a close corporation as we have recently defined such an entity in *Donahue v. Rodd Electrotype Co. of New England, Inc.,* 367 Mass. 578, 585–586 (1975).

---

[10] The by-laws of the corporation provided that the directors, subject to the approval of the stockholders, had the power to fix the salaries of all officers and employees. This power, however, up until February, 1967, had not been exercised formally; all payments made to the four participants in the venture had resulted from the informal but unanimous approval of all the parties concerned.

In *Donahue,* we held that "stockholders in the close corporation owe one another substantially the same fiduciary duty in the operation of the enterprise that partners owe to one another." *Id.* at 593 (footnotes omitted). As determined in previous decisions of this court, the standard of duty owed by partners to one another is one of "utmost good faith and loyalty." *Cardullo v. Landau,* 329 Mass. 5, 8 (1952), and cases cited. [*Citations omitted.*] Thus, we concluded in *Donahue,* with regard to "their actions relative to the operations of the enterprise and the effects of that operation on the rights and investments of other stockholders," "[s]tockholders in close corporations must discharge their management and stockholder responsibilities in conformity with this strict good faith standard. They may not act out of avarice, expediency or self-interest in derogation of their duty of loyalty to the other stockholders and to the corporation." 367 Mass. at 593 n.18.

In the *Donahue* case we recognized that one peculiar aspect of close corporations was the opportunity afforded to majority stockholders to oppress, disadvantage or "freeze out" minority stockholders. In *Donahue* itself, for example, the majority refused the minority an equal opportunity to sell a ratable number of shares to the corporation at the same price available to the majority. The net result of this refusal, we said, was that the minority could be forced to "sell out at less than fair value," 367 Mass. at 592, since there is by definition no ready market for minority stock in a close corporation.

"Freeze outs," however, may be accomplished by the use of other devices. One such device which has proved to be particularly effective in accomplishing the purpose of the majority is to deprive minority stockholders of corporate offices and of employment with the corporation. F.H. O'Neal, "Squeeze-Outs" of Minority Shareholders 59, 78–79 (1975). [*Citation omitted.*] This "freeze-out" technique has been successful because courts fairly consistently have been disinclined to interfere in those facets of internal corporate operations, such as the selection and retention or dismissal of officers, directors and employees, which essentially involve management decisions subject to the principle of majority control. [*Citations omitted.*] As one authoritative source has said, "[M]any courts apparently feel that there is a legitimate sphere in which the controlling [directors or] shareholders can act in their own interest even if the minority suffers." [*Citation omitted.*]

The denial of employment to the minority at the hands of the majority is especially pernicious in some instances. A guaranty of employment with the corporation may have been one of the "basic reason[s] why a minority owner has invested capital in the firm." Symposium—The Close Corporation, 52 Nw.

U.L. Rev. 345, 392 (1957). [*Citations omitted.*] The minority stockholder typically depends on his salary as the principal return on his investment, since the "earnings of a close corporation . . . are distributed in major part in salaries, bonuses and retirement benefits." [*Citation omitted.*] Other noneconomic interests of the minority stockholder are likewise injuriously affected by barring him from corporate office. . . . In sum, by terminating a minority stockholder's employment or by severing him from a position as an officer or director, the majority effectively frustrate the minority stockholder's purposes in entering on the corporate venture and also deny him an equal return on his investment.[13]

The *Donahue* decision acknowledged, as a "natural outgrowth" of the case law of this Commonwealth, a strict obligation on the part of majority stockholders in a close corporation to deal with the minority with the utmost good faith and loyalty. On its face, this strict standard is applicable in the instant case. The distinction between the majority action in *Donahue* and the majority action in this case is more one of form than of substance. Nevertheless, we are concerned that untempered application of the strict good faith standard enunciated in *Donahue* to cases such as the one before us will result in the imposition of limitations on legitimate action by the controlling group in a close corporation which will unduly hamper its effectiveness in managing the corporation in the best interests of all concerned. The majority, concededly, have certain rights to what has been termed "selfish ownership" in the corporation which should be balanced against the concept of their fiduciary obligation to the minority. [*Citations omitted.*]

Therefore, when minority stockholders in a close corporation bring suit against the majority alleging a breach of the strict good faith duty owed to them by the majority, we must carefully analyze the action taken by the controlling stockholders in the individual case. It must be asked whether the controlling group can demonstrate a legitimate business purpose for its action. [*Citations omitted.*] In asking this question, we acknowledge the fact that the controlling group in a close corporation must have some room to maneuver in establishing the business policy of the corporation. It must have a large measure of discretion, for example, in declaring or withholding dividends, deciding whether to merge or consolidate, establishing the salaries of corporate officers, dismissing directors with or without cause, and hiring and firing corporate employees.

---

13 We note here that the master found that Springside never declared or paid a dividend to its stockholders.

When an asserted business purpose for their action is advanced by the majority, however, we think it is open to minority stockholders to demonstrate that the same legitimate objective could have been achieved through an alternative course of action less harmful to the minority's interest. [*Citations omitted.*] If called on to settle a dispute, our courts must weigh the legitimate business purpose, if any, against the practicability of a less harmful alternative.

Applying this approach to the instant case it is apparent that the majority stockholders in Springside have not shown a legitimate business purpose for severing Wilkes from the payroll of the corporation or for refusing to reelect him as a salaried officer and director. The master's subsidiary findings relating to the purpose of the meetings of the directors and stockholders in February and March, 1967, are supported by the evidence. There was no showing of misconduct on Wilkes's part as a director, officer or employee of the corporation which would lead us to approve the majority action as a legitimate response to the disruptive nature of an undesirable individual bent on injuring or destroying the corporation. On the contrary, it appears that Wilkes had always accomplished his assigned share of the duties competently, and that he had never indicated an unwillingness to continue to do so.

It is an inescapable conclusion from all the evidence that the action of the majority stockholders here was a designed "freeze out" for which no legitimate business purpose has been suggested. Furthermore, we may infer that a design to pressure Wilkes into selling his shares to the corporation at a price below their value well may have been at the heart of the majority's plan.[14]

In the context of this case, several factors bear directly on the duty owed to Wilkes by his associates. At a minimum, the duty of utmost good faith and loyalty would demand that the majority consider that their action was in disregard of a long-standing policy of the stockholders that each would be a director of the corporation and that employment with the corporation would go hand in hand with stock ownership; that Wilkes was one of the four originators of the nursing home venture; and that Wilkes, like the others, had invested his capital and time for more than fifteen years with the expectation that he would continue to participate in corporate decisions. Most important is the plain fact that the cutting off of Wilkes's salary, together with the fact that the corporation never declared a dividend (see note 13 *supra*), assured that Wilkes would receive no return at all from the corporation.

---

[14] This inference arises from the fact that Connor, acting on behalf of the three controlling stockholders, offered to purchase Wilkes's shares for a price Connor admittedly would not have accepted for his own shares.

2. The question of Wilkes's damages at the hands of the majority has not been thoroughly explored on the record before us. Wilkes, in his original complaint, sought damages in the amount of the $100 a week he believed he was entitled to from the time his salary was terminated up until the time this action was commenced. However, the record shows that, after Wilkes was severed from the corporate payroll, the schedule of salaries and payments made to the other stockholders varied from time to time. In addition, the duties assumed by the other stockholders after Wilkes was deprived of his share of the corporate earnings appear to have changed in significant respects. Any resolution of this question must take into account whether the corporation was dissolved during the pendency of this litigation.

. . . . The case is remanded to the Probate Court for Berkshire County for further proceedings concerning the issue of damages. Thereafter a judgment shall be entered declaring that Quinn, Riche and Connor breached their fiduciary duty to Wilkes as a minority stockholder in Springside, and awarding money damages therefor. Wilkes shall be allowed to recover from Riche, the estate of T. Edward Quinn and the estate of Lawrence R. Connor, ratably, according to the inequitable enrichment of each, the salary he would have received had he remained an officer and director of Springside. In considering the issue of damages the judge on remand shall take into account the extent to which any remaining corporate funds of Springside may be diverted to satisfy Wilkes's claim.

So ordered.

It is important to keep in mind that it is not just the actions or circumstances that are relevant in evaluating a "freeze out" situation; it is also the intent behind the actions and circumstances. The frozen out shareholder must be able to show a breach of duty and that the majority group is diverting the profits of the corporation to themselves to the exclusion of the frozen out shareholder and, therefore, depriving the frozen out shareholder of his or her rightful return on his or her investment.

It is also important to remember that freeze outs are not always actionable. A shareholder who holds a minority (non-controlling) position in a corporation must know that being frozen out is a possibility. This possibility does not have to do with the shareholder's expectations about how he, she or it will be treated by the majority, just with the mathematical realities of the situations. The majority controls most (or all) of the corporation's decisions. To the extent those decisions are made by the corporation's board of directors, they are regulated by fiduciary duties. However, these duties do not encompass many of the situations in which a shareholder would be frozen out. Although many states, including Delaware, do not follow *Wilkes*, even without the additional scrutiny *Wilkes* might place on the behavior of controlling shareholders in closely held corporations, a dominant or controlling shareholder (or even a group of shareholder's acting in concert to control a corporation) is still subject to certain fiduciary duties. As discussed in Chapter 5, *supra*, these fiduciary duties placed on a dominant shareholder would prevent self-dealing which would include actions by a dominant shareholder to take the profits of the corporation for herself and deny those profits to the minority shareholder(s). On the other hand, this duty is subject to a fairness analysis. So, if a dominant shareholder pays herself a reasonable salary and does not pay dividends, it is often hard for the minority shareholder to show that such action would not satisfy a fairness test.

For example, in *Nixon v. Blackwell,* 626 A.2d 1366 (Del. 1993) the Delaware Supreme Court found that defendant directors had not breached their fiduciary duties in setting up an employee stock ownership plan that benefitted the employee stockholders but not the non-employee stockholder plaintiffs. The defendants in that case had also purchased "key man life insurance policies to provide liquidity for the defendants and other corporate employees to enable them to sell their stock while providing no comparable liquidity for minority stockholders." (*Id.* at 1370.) Despite the fact that the defendants (who were directors, employees and stockholders) were receiving benefits from the corporation that were not being provided to the non-employee stockholders, the court found that the defendants met their burden of establishing the entire fairness of their dealings with the non-employee stockholders. The court noted that the non-employee stockholders were "entitled to be treated fairly but not necessarily to be treated equally." (*Id.* at 1379.)

Of course, in a situation in which the dominant shareholders pay themselves salaries well in excess of a reasonable salary, leaving no funds to distribute to the minority shareholder(s), then it would be much easier to show that the duty of loyalty had been violated. Ultimately, these different approaches will still result in a similar outcome in a substantial number of cases. In the Delaware approach, the restrictions on dominant shareholders and the fiduciary duties of Directors will still prevent many of the actions which would be barred by the *Wilkes* approach, applying a duty of good faith to shareholders. These cases are very dependent on the specific facts and often turn on whether "fair" salaries are being paid and whether the controlling group can show a legitimate business purpose.

As discussed above, sometimes courts have "unusual" constructs of what might constitute "control" in a given situation. Consider the case that follows and think about how it might impact the advice you would give to a client who held a minority position in a corporation, but who also held veto rights over certain corporate actions.

Smith v. Atl. Props., Inc.

12 Mass. App. Ct. 201, 422 N.E.2d 798 (Mass. App. Ct. 1981)

CUTTER, J.:

In December, 1951, Dr. Louis E. Wolfson agreed to purchase land in Norwood for $350,000, with an initial cash payment of $50,000 and a mortgage note of $300,000 payable in thirty-three months. Dr. Wolfson offered a quarter interest each in the land to Mr. Paul T. Smith, Mr. Abraham Zimble, and William H. Burke. Each paid to Dr. Wolfson $12,500, one quarter of the initial payment. Mr. Smith, an attorney, organized the defendant corporation (Atlantic) in 1951 to operate the real estate. Each of the four subscribers received twenty-five shares of stock. Mr. Smith included, both in the corporation's articles of organization and in its by-laws, a provision reading, "No election, appointment or resolution by the Stockholders and no election, appointment, resolution, purchase, sale, lease, contract, contribution, compensation, proceeding or act by the Board of Directors or by any officer or officers shall be valid or binding upon the corporation until effected, passed, approved or ratified by an affirmative vote of eighty (80%) per cent of the capital stock issued outstanding and entitled to vote." This provision (hereafter referred to as the 80% provision) was included at Dr. Wolfson's request and had the effect of giving to any one of the four original shareholders a veto in corporate decisions.

Atlantic purchased the Norwood land. Some of the land and other assets were sold for about $220,000. Atlantic retained twenty-eight acres on which stood about twenty old brick or wood mill-type structures, which required expensive and constant repairs. After the first year, Atlantic became profitable and showed a profit every year prior to 1969, ranging from a low of $7,683 in 1953 to a high of $44,358 in 1954. The mortgage was paid by 1958 and Atlantic has incurred no long-term debt thereafter. Salaries of about $25,000 were paid only in 1959 and 1960. Dividends in the total amount of $10,000 each were paid in 1964 and 1970. By 1961, Atlantic had about $172,000 in retained earnings, more than half in cash.

For various reasons, which need not be stated in detail, disagreements and ill will soon arose between Dr. Wolfson, on the one hand, and the other stockholders as a group.[3] Dr. Wolfson wished to see Atlantic's earnings devoted to repairs and possibly some improvements in its existing buildings and adjacent facilities. The other stockholders desired the declaration of dividends. Dr. Wolfson fairly steadily refused to vote for any dividends. Although it was pointed out to him that failure to declare dividends might result in the imposition by the Internal Revenue Service of a penalty under the Internal Revenue Code, I.R.C. § 531 et seq. (relating to unreasonable accumulation of corporate earnings and profits), Dr. Wolfson persisted in his refusal to declare dividends. The other shareholders did agree over the years to making at least the most urgent repairs to Atlantic's buildings, but did not agree to make all repairs and improvements which were recommended in a 1962 report by an engineering firm retained by Atlantic to make a complete estimate of all repairs and improvements which might be beneficial.

The fears of an Internal Revenue Service assessment of a penalty tax were soon realized. Penalty assessments were made in 1962, 1963, and 1964. These were settled by Dr. Wolfson for $11,767.71 in taxes and interest. Despite this settlement, Dr. Wolfson continued his opposition to declaring dividends. The record does not indicate that he developed any specific and definitive schedule or plan for a series of necessary or desirable repairs and improvements to Atlantic's properties. At least none was proposed which would have had a reasonable chance of satisfying the Internal Revenue Service that expenditures for such repairs and improvements constituted "reasonable needs of the business," I.R.C. § 534(c), a term which includes (see I.R.C. § 537) "the reasonably anticipated needs of the business." Predictably, despite further warnings by Dr. Wolfson's shareholder colleagues, the Internal Revenue Service assessed further penalty taxes for the years 1965, 1966, 1967, and 1968. These taxes were upheld by the United States Tax Court in *Atlantic Properties, Inc. v. Commissioner,* 62 T.C. 644 (1974), and on appeal in 519 F.2d 1233 (1st Cir. 1975). . . . An examination of these decisions makes it apparent that Atlantic has incurred substantial penalty taxes and legal expense largely because of Dr. Wolfson's refusal to vote for the declaration of sufficient dividends to avoid the

[3] At least one cause of ill will on Dr. Wolfson's part may have been the refusal of the other shareholders to consent to his transferring his shares in Atlantic to the Louis E. Wolfson Foundation, a charitable foundation created by Dr. Wolfson.

penalty, a refusal which was (in the Tax Court and upon appeal) attributed in some measure to a tax avoidance purpose on Dr. Wolfson's part.

On January 30, 1967, the shareholders, other than Dr. Wolfson, initiated this proceeding in the Superior Court, later supplemented to reflect developments after the original complaint. The plaintiffs sought a court determination of the dividends to be paid by Atlantic, the removal of Dr. Wolfson as a director, and an order that Atlantic be reimbursed by him for the penalty taxes assessed against it and related expenses. The case was tried before a judge of the Superior Court (jury waived) in September and October, 1979.

The trial judge made findings (but in more detail) of essentially the facts outlined above and concluded that Dr. "Wolfson's obstinate refusal to vote in favor of . . . dividends was . . . caused more by his dislike for other stockholders and his desire to avoid additional tax payments than . . . by any genuine desire to undertake a program for improving . . . [Atlantic] property." . . . . She also ordered the directors of Atlantic to declare "a reasonable dividend at the earliest practical date and reasonable dividends annually thereafter consistent with good business practice." In addition, the trial judge directed that jurisdiction of the case be retained in the Superior Court "for a period of five years to [e]nsure compliance." Judgment was entered pursuant to the trial judge's order. . . .

1. The trial judge, in deciding that Dr. Wolfson had committed a breach of his fiduciary duty to other stockholders, relied greatly on broad language in *Donahue v. Rodd Electrotype Co.,* 367 Mass. 578, 586–597 (1975), in which the Supreme Judicial Court afforded to a minority stockholder in a close corporation equality of treatment (with members of a controlling group of shareholders) in the matter of the redemption of shares. The court (at 592–593) relied on the resemblance of a close corporation to a partnership and held that "stockholders in the close corporation owe one another substantially the same fiduciary duty in the operation of the enterprise that partners owe to one another" (footnotes omitted). That standard of duty, the court said, was the "utmost good faith and loyalty." The court went on to say that such stockholders "may not act out of avarice, expediency or self-interest in derogation of their duty of loyalty to the other stockholders and to the corporation." Similar principles were stated in *Wilkes v. Springside Nursing Home, Inc.,* 370 Mass. 842, 848–852 (1976), but with some modifications . . . of the sweeping language of the *Donahue* case. [*Citations omitted.*]

In the *Donahue case, 367 Mass. at 593 n.17,* the court recognized that cases may arise in which, in a close corporation, majority stockholders may ask protection from a minority stockholder. Such an instance arises in the present case because Dr. Wolfson has been able to exercise a veto concerning corporate action on dividends by the 80% provision (in Atlantic's articles of organization and by-laws) already quoted. The 80% provision may have substantially the effect of reversing the usual roles of the majority and the minority shareholders. The minority, under that provision, becomes an ad hoc controlling interest.[6]

It does not appear to be argued that this 80% provision is not authorized by G. L. c. 156B (inserted by St. 1964, c. 723, § 1). . . . Chapter 156B was intended to provide desirable flexibility in corporate arrangements. The provision is only one of several methods which have been devised to protect minority shareholders in close corporations from being oppressed by their colleagues and, if the device is used reasonably, there may be no strong public policy considerations against its use. . . . In the present case, Dr. Wolfson testified that he requested the inclusion of the 80% provision "in case the people [the other shareholders] whom I knew, but not very well, ganged up on me." The possibilities of shareholder disagreement on policy made the provision seem a sensible precaution.[8] A question is presented, however, concerning the extent to which such a veto power possessed by a minority stockholder may be exercised as its holder may wish, without a violation of the "fiduciary duty" referred to in the *Donahue case, 367 Mass. at 593,* as modified in the *Wilkes* case. [*Citation omitted.*]

The decided cases in Massachusetts do little to answer this question. The most pertinent guidance is probably found in the *Wilkes* case . . . essentially to the effect that in any judicial intervention in such a situation there must be a weighing of the business interests advanced as reasons for their action (a) by the majority or controlling group and (b) by the rival persons or group. . . .

---

6 The majority shareholders, in the event of a deadlock, at least may seek dissolution of the corporation if forty percent of the voting power can be mustered, whereas a single stockholder with only twenty-five percent of the stock may not do so. See *G. L. c. 156B, § 99(b),* as amended by St. 1969, c. 392, § 23.

8 Dr. Wolfson himself had discovered the business opportunity which led to the formation of Atlantic, had made the initial $50,000 payment which made possible the Norwood land purchase, and had given the other shareholders an opportunity to share with him in what looked like a probably profitable enterprise. It was reasonably foreseeable that there might be differences of opinion between Dr. Wolfson, a man with substantial income likely to be in a high income tax bracket, and less affluent shareholders on such matters of policy as dividend declarations, salaries, and investment in improvements in the property. The other shareholders, two of whom were attorneys, should have known that it was as open to Dr. Wolfson reasonably to exercise the veto provided to him by the 80% provision in favor of a policy of reinvestment of earnings in Atlantic's properties, which would probably avoid taxes and increase the value of the corporate assets, as it was for them (possessed of the same veto) to use reasonably their voting power in favor of a more generous dividend and salary policy.

2. With respect to the past damage to Atlantic caused by Dr. Wolfson's refusal to vote in favor of any dividends, the trial judge was justified in finding that his conduct went beyond what was reasonable. The other stockholders shared to some extent responsibility for what occurred by failing to accept Dr. Wolfson's proposals with much sympathy, but the inaction on dividends seems the principal cause of the tax penalties. Dr. Wolfson had been warned of the dangers of an assessment under the Internal Revenue Code, I.R.C. § 531 et seq. He had refused to vote dividends in any amount adequate to minimize that danger and had failed to bring forward, within the relevant taxable years, a convincing, definitive program of appropriate improvements which could withstand scrutiny by the Internal Revenue Service. Whatever may have been the reason for Dr. Wolfson's refusal to declare dividends (and even if in any particular year he may have gained slight, if any, tax advantage from withholding dividends) we think that he recklessly ran serious and unjustified risks of precisely the penalty taxes eventually assessed, risks which were inconsistent with any reasonable interpretation of a duty of "utmost good faith and loyalty." The trial judge (despite the fact that the other shareholders helped to create the voting deadlock and despite the novelty of the situation) was justified in charging Dr. Wolfson with the out-of-pocket expenditure incurred by Atlantic for the penalty taxes and related counsel fees of the tax cases.

* * * *

5. The judgment is affirmed so far as it (par. 1) orders payments into Atlantic's treasury by Dr. Wolfson. . . . The trial judge's denial of the plaintiff's motion to be allowed counsel fees is affirmed. Costs of this appeal are to be paid from the assets of Atlantic.

So ordered.

QUESTIONS

1. Do you think the court reached the right decision in the preceding case?

2. How would you have advised Dr. Wolfson to protect his rights if you had been advising him in structuring Atlantic?

3. How would you have advised Dr. Wolfson about the actions he took that led to the conflict that resulted in the preceding case?

4. Do you think this case might have had a different result if it were decided under Delaware law? Why?

SECTION IV: Oppression of Minority Shareholders, Dissolution, Buyout and Other Remedies

The Wilkes case, above, suggests that one remedy in the case of a freeze out "for which no legitimate business purpose" exists, is to pay damages equivalent to what the frozen out shareholder would have received had he not been frozen out. However, there are instances in which a minority shareholder is improperly excluded from a business and he or she might seek a stronger remedy. Section 14.30(a)(2) of the Model Business Corporations Act provides grounds for judicial dissolution upon the request of a shareholder:

§ 14.30 Grounds for Judicial Dissolution

(a) The [Court] may dissolve a corporation:

* * * *

(2) in a proceeding by a shareholder if it is established that:

. . . . (ii) the directors or those in control of the corporation have acted, are acting, or will act in a manner that is illegal, oppressive, or fraudulent;

Section 14.34 of the Model Business Corporations Act provides a means to avoid dissolution in a proceeding under section 14.30(2) by allowing the corporation or the shareholders of a corporation to purchase all of the shares owned by the shareholder petitioning for dissolution at the fair value of the shares.

Many states have enacted liberal involuntary dissolution provisions similar to, or based upon, these Model Business Corporations Act provisions, which enable a minority shareholder to request that a court dissolve a corporation (or force a buyout) in instances of "oppressive conduct" by the majority or controlling shareholder(s). The following cases represent a few instances of courts' consideration of the criteria under which judges should utilize the powers granted under such statutes and of courts' abilities to fashion remedies under such statutes.

Matter of Kemp & Beatley, Inc.

64 N.Y.2d 63, 484 N.Y.S.2d 799, 473 N.E.2d 1173 (1984).

COOKE. C.J.:

When the majority shareholders of a close corporation award *de facto* dividends to all shareholders except a class of minority shareholders, such a policy may constitute "oppressive actions" and serve as a basis for an order made pursuant to section 1104–a of the Business Corporation Law dissolving the corporation. In the instant matter, there is sufficient evidence to support the lower courts' conclusion that the majority shareholders had altered a long-standing policy to distribute corporate earnings on the basis of stock ownership, as against petitioners only. Moreover, the courts did not abuse their discretion by concluding that dissolution was the only means by which petitioners could gain a fair return on their investment.

I

The business concern of Kemp & Beatley, incorporated under the laws of New York, designs and manufactures table linens and sundry tabletop items. The company's stock consists of 1,500 outstanding shares held by eight shareholders. Petitioner Dissin had been employed by the company for 42 years when, in June 1979, he resigned. Prior to resignation, Dissin served as vice-president and a director of Kemp & Beatley. Over the course of his employment, Dissin had acquired stock in the company and currently owns 200 shares.

Petitioner Gardstein, like Dissin, had been a long-time employee of the company. Hired in 1944, Gardstein was for the next 35 years involved in various aspects of the business including material procurement, product design, and plant management. His employment was terminated by the company in December 1980. He currently owns 105 shares of Kemp & Beatley stock.

Apparent unhappiness surrounded petitioners' leaving the employ of the company. Of particular concern was that they no longer received any distribution of the company's earnings. Petitioners considered themselves to be "frozen out" of the company; whereas it had been their experience when with the company to receive a distribution of the company's earnings according to their stockholdings, in the form of either dividends or extra compensation, that distribution was no longer forthcoming.

Gardstein and Dissin, together holding 20.33% of the company's outstanding stock, commenced the instant proceeding in June 1981, seeking dissolution of Kemp & Beatley pursuant to section 1104–a of the Business

Corporation Law. Their petition alleged "fraudulent and oppressive" conduct by the company's board of directors such as to render petitioners' stock "a virtually worthless asset." Supreme Court referred the matter for a hearing, which was held in March 1982.

Upon considering the testimony of petitioners and the principals of Kemp & Beatley, the referee concluded that "the corporate management has by its policies effectively rendered petitioners' shares worthless, and * * * the only way petitioners can expect any return is by dissolution". Petitioners were found to have invested capital in the company expecting, among other things, to receive dividends or "bonuses" based upon their stock holdings. Also found was the company's "established buy-out policy" by which it would purchase the stock of employee shareholders upon their leaving its employ.

The involuntary-dissolution statute (*Business Corporation Law, § 1104–a*) permits dissolution when a corporation's controlling faction is found guilty of "oppressive action" toward the complaining shareholders. The referee considered oppression to arise when "those in control" of the corporation "have acted in such a manner as to defeat those expectations of the minority stockholders which formed the basis of [their] participation in the venture." The expectations of petitioners that they would not be arbitrarily excluded from gaining a return on their investment and that their stock would be purchased by the corporation upon termination of employment, were deemed defeated by prevailing corporate policies. Dissolution was recommended in the referee's report, subject to giving respondent corporation an opportunity to purchase petitioners' stock.

Supreme Court confirmed the referee's report. It, too, concluded that due to the corporation's new dividend policy petitioners had been prevented from receiving any return on their investments. Liquidation of the corporate assets was found the only means by which petitioners would receive a fair return. The court considered judicial dissolution of a corporation to be "a serious and severe remedy." Consequently, the order of dissolution was conditioned upon the corporation's being permitted to purchase petitioners' stock. The Appellate Division affirmed, without opinion.

At issue in this appeal is the scope of section 1104–a of the Business Corporation Law. Specifically, this court must determine whether the provision for involuntary dissolution when the "directors or those in control of the corporation have been guilty of * * * oppressive actions toward the complaining shareholders" was properly applied in the circumstances of this case. We hold that it was, and therefore affirm.

II

Judicially ordered dissolution of a corporation at the behest of minority interests is a remedy of relatively recent vintage in New York. . . .

Minority shareholders were granted standing in the absence of statutory authority to seek dissolution of corporations when controlling shareholders engaged in certain egregious conduct (see *Leibert v. Clapp,* 13 NY2d 313; *Fontheim v. Walker,* 282 App Div 373, affd no opn 306 NY 926). Predicated on the majority shareholders' fiduciary obligation to treat all shareholders fairly and equally, to preserve corporate assets, and to fulfill their responsibilities of corporate management with "scrupulous good faith," the courts' equitable power can be invoked when "it appears that the directors and majority shareholders 'have so palpably breached the fiduciary duty they owe to the minority shareholders that they are disqualified from exercising the exclusive discretion and the dissolution power given to them by statute.' " (*Leibert v. Clapp,* 13 NY2d, at p 317, *supra,* quoting Hoffman, New Horizons for the Close Corporation, 28 Brooklyn L Rev 1, 14.) True to the ancient principle that equity jurisdiction will not lie when there exists a remedy at law [*Citations omitted.*], the courts have not entertained a minority's petition in equity when their rights and interests could be adequately protected in a legal action, such as by a shareholder's derivative suit. [*Citations omitted.*]

Supplementing this principle of judicially ordered equitable dissolution of a corporation, the Legislature has shown a special solicitude toward the rights of minority shareholders of closely held corporations by enacting section 1104–a of the Business Corporation Law. That statute provides a mechanism for the holders of at least 20% of the outstanding shares of a corporation whose stock is not traded on a securities market to petition for its dissolution "under special circumstances" (see *Business Corporation Law, § 1104–a, subd [a]*). The circumstances that give rise to dissolution fall into two general classifications: mistreatment of complaining shareholders (subd [a], par [1]), or misappropriation of corporate assets (subd [a], par [2]) by controlling shareholders, directors or officers.

Section 1104–a (subd [a], par [1]) describes three types of proscribed activity: "illegal", "fraudulent", and "oppressive" conduct. The first two terms are familiar words that are commonly understood at law. The last, however, does not enjoy the same certainty gained through long usage. As no definition is provided by the statute, it falls upon the courts to provide guidance. [*Citations omitted.*]

The statutory concept of "oppressive actions" can, perhaps, best be understood by examining the characteristics of close corporations and the Legislature's general purpose in creating this involuntary-dissolution statute. It is widely understood that, in addition to supplying capital to a contemplated or ongoing enterprise and expecting a fair and equal return, parties comprising the ownership of a close corporation may expect to be actively involved in its management and operation. [*Citations omitted.*] The small ownership cluster seeks to "contribute their capital, skills, experience and labor" toward the corporate enterprise. [*Citations omitted.*]

As a leading commentator in the field has observed: "Unlike the typical shareholder in a publicly held corporation, who may be simply an investor or a speculator and cares nothing for the responsibilities of management, the shareholder in a close corporation is a co-owner of the business and wants the privileges and powers that go with ownership. His participation in that particular corporation is often his principal or sole source of income. As a matter of fact, providing employment for himself may have been the principal reason why he participated in organizing the corporation. He may or may not anticipate an ultimate profit from the sale of his interest, but he normally draws very little from the corporation as dividends. In his capacity as an officer or employee of the corporation, he looks to his salary for the principal return on his capital investment, because earnings of a close corporation, as is well known, are distributed in major part in salaries, bonuses and retirement benefits." (O'Neal, Close Corporations [2d ed], § 1.07, at pp 21–22 [n omitted].)

Shareholders enjoy flexibility in memorializing these expectations through agreements setting forth each party's rights and obligations in corporate governance (see, generally, Kessler, Shareholder-Managed Close Corporation Under the New York Business Corporation Law, 43 Fordham L Rev 197; Davidian, *op. cit.,* 56 St John's L Rev 24, 29–30, and nn 21–22). In the absence of such an agreement, however, ultimate decision-making power respecting corporate policy will be reposed in the holders of a majority interest in the corporation (see, e.g., *Business Corporation Law, §§ 614, 708).* A wielding of this power by any group controlling a corporation may serve to destroy a stockholder's vital interests and expectations.

As the stock of closely held corporations generally is not readily salable, a minority shareholder at odds with management policies may be without either a voice in protecting his or her interests or any reasonable means of withdrawing his or her investment. This predicament may fairly be considered the legislative concern underlying the provision at issue in this case; inclusion of the criteria that the corporation's stock not be traded on securities markets and that the complaining shareholder be subject to oppressive actions supports this conclusion.

Defining oppressive conduct as distinct from illegality in the present context has been considered in other forums. The question has been resolved by considering oppressive actions to refer to conduct that substantially defeats the "reasonable expectations" held by minority shareholders in committing their capital to the particular enterprise. [*Citations omitted.*] This concept is consistent with the apparent purpose underlying the provision under review. A shareholder who reasonably expected that ownership in the corporation would entitle him or her to a job, a share of corporate earnings, a place in corporate management, or some other form of security, would be oppressed in a very real sense when others in the corporation seek to defeat those expectations and there exists no effective means of salvaging the investment.

Given the nature of close corporations and the remedial purpose of the statute, this court holds that utilizing a complaining shareholder's "reasonable expectations" as a means of identifying and measuring conduct alleged to be oppressive is appropriate. A court considering a petition alleging oppressive conduct must investigate what the majority shareholders knew, or should have known, to be the petitioner's expectations in entering the particular enterprise. Majority conduct should not be deemed oppressive simply because the petitioner's subjective hopes and desires in joining the venture are not fulfilled. Disappointment alone should not necessarily be equated with oppression.

Rather, oppression should be deemed to arise only when the majority conduct substantially defeats expectations that, objectively viewed, were both reasonable under the circumstances and were central to the petitioner's decision to join the venture. It would be inappropriate, however, for us in this case to delineate the contours of the courts' consideration in determining whether directors have been guilty of oppressive conduct. As in other areas of the law, much will depend on the circumstances in the individual case.

The appropriateness of an order of dissolution is in every case vested in the sound discretion of the court considering the application (see *Business Corporation Law, § 1111, subd [a]*). Under the terms of this statute, courts are instructed to consider both whether "liquidation of the corporation is the only feasible means" to protect the complaining shareholder's expectation of a fair return on his or her investment and whether dissolution "is reasonably necessary" to protect "the rights or interests of any substantial number of shareholders" not limited to those complaining (*Business Corporation Law,*

§ 1104–a, subd [b], pars [1], [2]). Implicit in this direction is that once oppressive conduct is found, consideration must be given to the totality of circumstances surrounding the current state of corporate affairs and relations to determine whether some remedy short of or other than dissolution constitutes a feasible means of satisfying both the petitioner's expectations and the rights and interests of any other substantial group of shareholders (see, also, *Business Corporation Law, § 1111, subd [b],* par [1]).

By invoking the statute, a petitioner has manifested his or her belief that dissolution may be the only appropriate remedy. Assuming the petitioner has set forth a prima facie case of oppressive conduct, it should be incumbent upon the parties seeking to forestall dissolution to demonstrate to the court the existence of an adequate, alternative remedy. . . . A court has broad latitude in fashioning alternative relief, but when fulfillment of the oppressed petitioner's expectations by these means is doubtful, such as when there has been a complete deterioration of relations between the parties, a court should not hesitate to order dissolution. Every order of dissolution, however, must be conditioned upon permitting any shareholder of the corporation to elect to purchase the complaining shareholder's stock at fair value (see *Business Corporation Law, § 1118*).

One further observation is in order. The purpose of this involuntary dissolution statute is to provide protection to the minority shareholder whose reasonable expectations in undertaking the venture have been frustrated and who has no adequate means of recovering his or her investment. It would be contrary to this remedial purpose to permit its use by minority shareholders as merely a coercive tool. [*Citations omitted.*] Therefore, the minority shareholder whose own acts, made in bad faith and undertaken with a view toward forcing an involuntary dissolution, give rise to the complained-of oppression should be given no quarter in the statutory protection. . . .

III

There was sufficient evidence presented at the hearing to support the conclusion that Kemp & Beatley had a long-standing policy of awarding *de facto* dividends based on stock ownership in the form of "extra compensation bonuses." Petitioners, both of whom had extensive experience in the management of the company, testified to this effect. Moreover, both related that receipt of this compensation, whether as true dividends or disguised as "extra compensation", was a known incident to ownership of the company's stock understood by all of the company's principals. Finally, there was uncontroverted proof that this policy was changed either shortly before or shortly after petitioners' employment ended. Extra compensation was still awarded by the company. The only difference was that stock ownership was no longer a basis for the payments; it was asserted that the basis became services rendered to the corporation. It was not unreasonable for the fact finder to have determined that this change in policy amounted to nothing less than an attempt to exclude petitioners from gaining any return on their investment through the mere recharacterization of distributions of corporate income. Under the circumstances of this case, there was no error in determining that this conduct constituted oppressive action within the meaning of section 1104–a of the Business Corporation Law.

Nor may it be said that Supreme Court abused its discretion in ordering Kemp & Beatley's dissolution, subject to an opportunity for a buy-out of petitioners' shares. After the referee had found that the controlling faction of the company was, in effect, attempting to "squeeze-out" petitioners by offering them no return on their investment and increasing other executive compensation, respondents, in opposing the report's confirmation, attempted only to controvert the factual basis of the report. They suggested no feasible, alternative remedy to the forced dissolution. In light of an apparent deterioration in relations between petitioners and the governing shareholders of Kemp & Beatley, it was not unreasonable for the court to have determined that a forced buy-out of petitioners' shares or liquidation of the corporation's assets was the only means by which petitioners could be guaranteed a fair return on their investments.

Accordingly, the order of the Appellate Division should be modified, with costs to petitioners-respondents, by affirming the substantive determination of that court but extending the time for exercising the option to purchase petitioners-respondents' shares to 30 days following this court's determination. . . .

Meiselman v. Meiselman

309 N.C. 279, 307 S.E.2d 551 (N.C. 1983)

FRYE, J.:

In this appeal, we must determine whether Michael Meiselman, a minority shareholder with a substantial percentage of the outstanding stock in a group of family-owned close corporations, is entitled to relief under N.C.G.S. § 55–125(a)(4) and N.C.G.S. § 55–125.1, the statutes granting trial courts the authority to order dissolution or another more appropriate remedy when "reasonably necessary" for the protection of the "rights or interests" of the complaining shareholder. . . . We must also determine whether the trial court erred in concluding that Ira Meiselman, Michael's brother, committed "no actionable breach of fiduciary responsibility" as an officer or director of the defendant corporations through his sole ownership of the stock in a corporation holding a management contract with one of the family corporations. . . .

I.

Michael Meiselman, the plaintiff and complaining minority shareholder in this action, and Ira Meiselman, one of the defendants in this action, are brothers. Michael, the older of the two, was born in 1932 and has never married. Ira was born ten years later. He is married and has two children. The two men are the only surviving children of Mr. H. B. Meiselman, who immigrated to the United States from Austria in 1913. Over the years, Mr. Meiselman accumulated substantial wealth through his development of several family business enterprises. Specifically, Mr. Meiselman invested in and developed movie theaters and real estate. Several of the enterprises were merged into Eastern Federal Corporation [hereinafter referred to as Eastern Federal], a close corporation, most of the stock of which is owned by Ira and Michael. In addition, there are seven other corporations which, together with Eastern Federal, comprise the Meiselman family business and are the corporate defendants in this case.

Beginning in 1951, Mr. Meiselman started a series of *inter vivos* transfers of corporate stock in the various corporations which, generally speaking, he divided equally between his two sons. However, in March 1971 Mr. Meiselman transferred 83,072 shares of stock in Eastern Federal to Ira, while Michael received only 1,966 shares in the corporation. . . .

The effect, then, of these transfers of stock from Mr. Meiselman to his two sons was to give Ira, the younger son, majority shareholder status in Eastern Federal while relegating Michael, the older son, to the position of minority shareholder. In addition, Ira owns a controlling interest in all of the other family corporations except General Shopping Centers, Inc., the corporation in which he and Michael hold an equal number of shares.

. . . . The book value of all of the corporations was $11,168,778 as of 31 December 1978. The book value of Michael's shares in all of the corporations. . . $3,330,303 as of that date.

As is true of many close corporations, the two shareholders—Michael and Ira—were employed by the family corporations. Michael began working for the family business in 1956 and Ira began nine years later in 1965. . . . [B]oth sides agree that from 1973 until 1979 Michael was employed by the family business. It is also clear that Ira fired Michael in September 1979, less than one month after Michael filed suit against Ira in connection with Ira's sole ownership of the stock in a corporation which held a management contract with Eastern Federal.

In the certified letter Ira sent to Michael informing Michael that he was being fired, Ira also notified his brother that his car insurance, his hospital insurance and his life insurance policies were all being terminated. In addition, Ira asked his brother in that same letter to return his "Air Travel credit card" and "any other corporate cards you might have as any further use of them is not authorized." Ira then sent his brother a second certified letter demanding payment within ten days to Eastern Federal of Michael's note of $61,500 plus interest of $2,028.66 and the balance of Michael's open account, $19,000. Furthermore, Lawrence A. Poston, Vice President and Treasurer of Eastern Federal stated that the effect of the letter terminating Michael's employment "also was to terminate Michael's participation in the profit-sharing trust."

In his deposition, Ira essentially admitted that he fired his brother in response to the lawsuit Michael had brought challenging Ira's sole ownership of Republic Management Corporation [hereinafter referred to as Republic], the corporation with which Eastern Federal had contracted to provide management services. However, Ira indicated that Michael's loss of employment was only an incidental effect of his termination of the employment contract between the two corporations, a corporate decision he felt was justified in light of the threat of continuing litigation on this matter. Ira stated that "[t]he purpose and the effect of the letter [terminating Michael's employment] were principally to advise [Michael] that we were terminating the arrangement between Eastern Federal and Republic and, correspondingly, that it would alter, affect, or eliminate his source of compensation as applied to Republic."

* * * *

According to Ira, ... Republic was "nothing more than a tool" through which the administrative costs incurred in operating the various Meiselman business units—including over 30 theaters—were apportioned.

As noted above, Republic agreed to perform . . . management services as a result of a contract entered into between it and Eastern Federal. Specifically, Republic agreed to perform the management services in exchange for 5.5

percent of Eastern Federal's theater admissions and concession sales. Although Republic paid Michael an annual salary from 1973 until he was fired in 1979, Michael did not own any of the stock in the management corporation; Ira owned all of it. Although Republic earned profits some years while losing money in others, the net result was that it had retained earnings of over $65,000, earnings which only Ira as sole shareholder in Republic would enjoy and in which Michael claims he is entitled to share. It is this ownership to which Michael objects and upon which he bases his shareholder's derivative claim that Ira has breached the fiduciary duty he owes to the corporate defendants.

We turn now to an examination of the tenor of the relationship existing between Michael and Ira. In his brief, Ira contends "[t]he Record on Appeal reflects no bitterness and hostility between Michael and Ira, other than that which Michael generated after Mr. Meiselman's death in an effort to secure a redistribution of his father's patrimony." Further, he contends that "Michael was never denied participation in the management of the corporate defendants," that, on the contrary, Michael "voluntarily limited his participation in their affairs."

On the other hand, Michael vehemently denies Ira's characterization of their relationship and of his participation in the management of the corporations. In his deposition, Michael stated that his job has been "out in the field," and that when he had a recommendation to make he was, for the most part, to report it to his brother. Michael indicated that he was allowed to participate in the management of Eastern Federal in this manner apparently until the corporation entered into the management contract with Republic at issue here. Michael characterized this alleged change in his participation of the management of Eastern Federal as follows:

> My brother had the majority of stock in Eastern Federal Corporation before this management contract. As to whether he had the final say in the control of Eastern Federal Corporation, that is the point. He might have been the final say, but when Republic Management started, I lost all say-so because he wouldn't listen to anybody.

In addition, Michael contends that, among other things, he has not been "allowed to even come up to the office and have [sic] been discouraged in getting the full details as to what they [the companies] borrow"; that Ira "will not let me walk in the office where the film buyer is and talk to him, not even [to] help"; that "theaters are being sold without my knowledge and theaters are being built without my knowledge"; and that "my brother solely and without my consent, not only develops but closes, sells, does anything he wants with all of the properties." Finally, Michael claims that although he previously worked 60 to 70 hours a week, he has been "discouraged systematically over a number of years to where I cannot exert the time and effort that I want to."

In examining the record, we are struck by the tone of Ira's comments when referring to his dealings with his brother. Indeed, many of his statements indicate that although Michael may not have been actively prevented from entering the corporate offices, his participation in the decision-making carried on within those offices was less than welcome. For example, in testifying that Michael has never been barred from the home offices of the company, Ira stated that Michael "has exercised the privilege of going there on frequent occasions, *unannounced*, whenever he felt like it." (Emphasis added.) He also stated that "[w]e have never failed, *when he is entitled to notice*, to give him adequate notice of stockholders' meetings." (Emphasis added.) Furthermore, in a letter to Michael's lawyer concerning, among other things, the possibility of Michael's serving on the boards of directors of the family enterprises, Ira's lawyer stated that, "[w]e have no desire to see the productive efforts of the boards be affected by possibly allowing them to function as a forum for airing personal hurts and slights; and we all recognize that the course of business activity for the companies is not going to be altered by Michael's representation."

* * * *

Perhaps most indicative of the tenor of the relationship between the two brothers is Ira's comment that "[y]es, it is my position in this case that my brother, Michael, suffers as stated there [in defendant's brief] from crippling mental disorders and that was a reason that my father put me in control of the family corporations." Apparently in support of his allegations that his brother suffers from "crippling mental disorders," Ira presented evidence of an argument Michael had with his father which took place about 20 years ago during which Mr. Meiselman castigated Michael for having a non-Jewish woman at a family function. In addition, Ira testified to another fight which occurred between himself and Michael after he had failed to invite Michael to a football game to which all of the males in the family traditionally had been invited.

Finally, it appears the history of this litigation itself indicates a breakdown of the personal relationship between Michael and Ira. In June 1978, about two months after their father's death, Michael and Ira began negotiations in an effort to work out their differences. Over one year later, in August 1979, Michael filed suit. He was fired the next month. In short, this litigation and the tensions inherent in such activity have been going on for over four years now.

We turn now to the history of this litigation as it developed in the courts. In his amended complaint, Michael asked that the trial court "dissolve the Corporate Defendants under the provisions of G.S. 55–125(a) or, in the alternative, order such other relief under the provisions of G.S. 55–125.1 as the Court may deem just and equitable" because such relief is "reasonably necessary" for the protection of Michael's "rights and interests." Before this Court, Michael is requesting relief specifically under N.C.G.S. § 55–125.1(a)(4), a buy-out at fair value of Michael's interest in the corporate defendants. He is not seeking dissolution.

With respect to the derivative claim he brought asserting that Ira had breached the fiduciary duty he owes to the corporate defendants through his sole ownership of the stock in Republic, Michael asked that the "profits wrongfully diverted from the Corporate Defendants into Republic Management Corporation" be recovered.

* * * *

II.

We note at the outset that the enterprises with which we are dealing are close corporations, not publicly held corporations. This distinction is crucial because the two types of corporations are functionally quite different. Indeed, the commentators all appear to agree that "[c]lose corporations are often little more than incorporated partnerships." [*Citations omitted.*]

* * * *

Professor O'Neal, perhaps the foremost authority on close corporations, points out that many close corporations are companies based on personal relationships that give rise to certain "reasonable expectations" on the part of those acquiring an interest in the close corporation. Those "reasonable expectations" include, for example, the parties' expectation that they will participate in the management of the business or be employed by the company. O'Neal, *Close Corporations: Existing Legislation and Recommended Reform,* 33 Bus. Law 873, 885 (1978). . . .

Thus, when personal relations among the participants in a close corporation break down, the "reasonable expectations" the participants had, for example, an expectation that their employment would be secure, or that they would enjoy meaningful participation in the management of the business—become difficult if not impossible to fulfill. In other words, when the personal relationships among the participants break down, the majority shareholder, because of his greater voting power, is in a position to terminate the minority shareholder's employment and to exclude him from participation in management decisions.

Some may argue that the minority shareholder should have bargained for greater protection before agreeing to accept his minority shareholder position in a close corporation. However, the practical realities of this particular business situation oftentimes do not allow for such negotiations. . . . In his article, *Special Characteristics, Problems, and Needs of the Close Corporation,* 1969 U. Ill. L.F. 1 (1969), Professor Hetherington, another recognized authority in this field, explains the situation as follows:

> . . . the circumstances under which a party takes a minority stock position in a close corporation vary widely. Many involve situations where the minority party, because of lack of awareness of the risks, or because of the weakness of his bargaining position, fails to negotiate for protection. Probably a common instance of this kind occurs where an employee or an outsider is given an opportunity to buy stock in a close corporation wholly or substantially owned by a single stockholder or a small group of associates, often a family. Typically, the controlling individual or group retains a substantial majority position. The opportunity to buy into the business is highly valued by the recipient; his enthusiasm and weak bargaining position make it unlikely almost to a certainty that he will ask for—let alone insist upon—protection for his position as a minority stockholder. Purchases of stock in such situations are likely to be arranged without either party consulting a lawyer. The result is the assumption of a minority stock position without, or with only limited, appreciation of the risks involved.

Id. at 17–18 (footnote omitted).

In short, then, the "minority shareholder who acquired his shares to secure his position with the firm may have lacked sufficient bargaining power to force the majority to agree to terms which would enable him to protect his interests." Comment, *Dissolution Under the California Corporations Code, supra,* at 603–04. Indeed, as one commentator notes, "close corporations are often formed by friends or family members who simply may not believe that disagreements could ever arise." *Id.* Furthermore, when a minority shareholder receives his shares in a close corporation from another in the form of a gift or inheritance, as did plaintiff here, the minority shareholder never had the opportunity to negotiate for any sort of protection with respect to the "reasonable expectations" he had or hoped to enjoy in the close corporation.

Unfortunately, when dissension develops in such a situation, as Professor O'Neal notes, "American courts traditionally have been reluctant to interfere in the internal affairs of corporations . . . ." F. O'Neal, *Oppression of Minority Shareholders* § 9.04, at 582 (1975). This reluctance, as applied to a minority shareholder holding an interest in a close corporation, places the minority shareholder in a remediless situation. As Professor O'Neal points out, when the personal relationship among the participants in a close corporation breaks down, the minority shareholder has neither the power to dissolve the business unit at will, as does a partner in a partnership, nor does he have the "way out" which is open to a shareholder in a publicly held corporation, the opportunity to sell his shares on the open market. 2 F. O'Neal, *Close Corporations* § 9.02. Thus, the illiquidity of a minority shareholder's interest in a close corporation renders him vulnerable to exploitation by the majority shareholders. . . . Professor Hetherington succinctly outlines in one of his articles the uniquely vulnerable position a minority shareholder occupies in a close corporation:

> The right of the majority to control the enterprise achieves a meaning and has an impact in close corporations that it has in no other major form of business organization under our law. Only in the close corporation does the power to manage carry with it the de facto power to allocate the benefits of ownership arbitrarily among the shareholders and to discriminate against a minority whose investment is imprisoned in the enterprise. The essential basis of this power in the close corporation is the inability of those so excluded from the benefits of proprietorship to withdraw their investment at will. The power to withdraw one's capital from a publicly held corporation or from a partnership is unqualified in the sense that the participant's right is not dependent upon misconduct by the management or upon the occurrence of any other event. The shareholder or partner can withdraw his capital for any or no reason.

Hetherington, *supra*, at 21.

* * * *

Apparently in response to these commentators' uniform calls for reform in this area of corporate law, many state legislatures have enacted statutes giving the tribunals in their states the power to grant relief to minority shareholders under more liberal circumstances.

* * * *

In helping to establish this growing trend toward enactment of more liberal grounds under which dissolution will be granted to a complaining shareholder, the legislature in this State enacted in 1955 N.C.G.S. § 55–125(a)(4), the statute granting superior court judges the "power to liquidate the assets and business of a corporation in an action by a shareholder when it is established" that "[l]iquidation is reasonably necessary for the protection of the rights or interests of the complaining shareholder." Two other states have similar statutes—California and New York. Cal. Corp. Code § 1800(b)(5) (West 1977) (formerly § 4651(f)); N. Y. Bus. Corp. Law § 1104–a(b)(2) (McKinney Cum. Supp. 1983).

* * * *

In short, then, it appears that these new statutory schemes which permit involuntary dissolution of corporations pursuant to actions brought by minority shareholders—and which "virtually every state has"—"represent a concerted effort and recognition by the states that the perpetual existence of the corporate structure at common law is ill-suited to the functional realities of the closely held corporation." [*Citation omitted.*] However, it is important to recognize that the statutes in question apply to *all* corporations, not just "close" corporations. Of course, "the rights or interests of the complaining shareholder" will vary according to the circumstances, including the circumstance of the nature of the corporation, whether public or a close corporation. Likewise, whether liquidation (or some alternate form of relief) "is reasonably necessary for the protection of" those "rights or interests" will also depend, to a great extent, on whether the corporation is a public corporation or a close corporation.

III.

* * * *

The basic question at issue is what standard we should adopt to determine whether a minority shareholder is entitled to dissolution or other relief. The statutes require a standard in which all of the circumstances surrounding the parties are considered in deciding whether relief should be granted and, if so, the nature and method of such relief.

When a shareholder brings suit seeking relief under N.C.G.S. § 55–125(a)(4) and N.C.G.S. § 55–125.1, he has the burden of proving that his "rights or interests" as a shareholder are being contravened. However, once the shareholder has established this, the trial court, in deciding whether to grant relief, "must exercise its equitable discretion, and consider the actual benefit and injury to [all of] the shareholders resulting from dissolution" or other possible relief. *Henry George & Sons, Inc. v. Cooper-George, Inc., Wash.*, 632 P. 2d 512, 516 (1981). "The question is essentially one for resolution through the familiar balancing process and flexible remedial resources of courts of equity." *Id.* To hold otherwise would allow a plaintiff to demand at will dissolution of a corporation or a forced buy out of his shares or other relief at the expense of the corporation and without regard to the rights and interests of the other shareholders.

Michael, as the complaining shareholder in this case, brought an action under N.C.G.S. § 55–125(a), the statutory provision which articulates four situations, one of which must be "established" before a Superior Court Judge has the power to liquidate a corporation in an action brought by a shareholder. Specifically, N.C.G.S. § 55–125(a) provides as follows:

The superior court shall have power to liquidate the assets and business of a corporation in an action by a shareholder when it is established that:

(1) The directors are deadlocked in the management of the corporate affairs and the shareholders are unable to break the deadlock, so that the business can no longer be conducted to the advantage of all the shareholders; or

(2) The shareholders are deadlocked in voting power, otherwise than by virtue of special provisions or arrangements designed to create veto power among the shareholders, and for that reason have been unable at two consecutive annual meetings to elect successors to directors whose terms had expired; or

(3) All of the present shareholders are parties to, or are transferees or subscribers of shares with actual notice of a written agreement, whether embodied in the charter or separate therefrom, entitling the complaining shareholder to liquidation or dissolution of the corporation at will or upon the occurrence of some event which has subsequently occurred; or

(4) Liquidation is reasonably necessary for the protection of the rights or interests of the complaining shareholder.

Michael alleged that he was entitled to relief under subsection (4); in effect, he is claiming that liquidation is "reasonably necessary" for the protection of his "rights or interests." However, before it can be determined whether, in any given case, it has been "established" that liquidation is "reasonably necessary" to protect the complaining shareholder's "rights or interest," the particular "rights or interests" of the complaining shareholder must be articulated. . . . [T]he "rights or interests" which Michael has in these family-run, close corporations must be determined with reference to the specific facts in this case. In so doing, we hold that a complaining shareholder's "rights or interests" in a close corporation include the "reasonable expectations" the complaining shareholder has in the corporation. These "reasonable expectations" are to be ascertained by examining the entire history of the participants' relationship. That history will include the "reasonable expectations" created at the inception of the participants' relationship; those "reasonable expectations" as altered over time; and the "reasonable expectations" which develop as the participants engage in a course of dealing in conducting the affairs of the corporation. The interests and views of the other participants must be considered in determining "reasonable expectations." The key is "*reasonable*." In order for plaintiff's expectations to be reasonable, they must be known to or assumed by the other shareholders and concurred in by them. Privately held expectations which are not made known to the other participants are not "reasonable." . . . .

In short, then, the "rights or interests" of a shareholder in any given case will not necessarily be the same "rights or interests" of any other shareholder.

* * * *

After articulating the "rights or interests" of the complaining shareholder, the trial court is then to determine if liquidation is "reasonably necessary" for the protection of those "rights or interests."

* * * *

Thus, when an action is brought under N.C.G.S. § 55–125(a)(4), the trial court is to examine all of the following possibilities: (1) whether . . . *liquidation* is reasonably necessary; . . . whether . . . *any other "alternative" relief* is more appropriate than dissolution . . . As noted, N.C.G.S. § 55–125.1(b) provides that the trial court has the authority to grant any other alternative relief whenever such relief, *but not dissolution,* is appropriate. It is clear, then, that when N.C.G.S. § 55–125(a)(4) and 55–125.1(b) are read in conjunction, it must only be "established" under N.C.G.S. § 55–125(a)(4) that *relief of some kind,* and not just liquidation, is "reasonably necessary" for the protection of the complaining shareholder's "rights or interests." To interpret N.C.G.S. § 55–125(a)(4) as providing that relief can be given only when *liquidation* is "reasonably necessary" for the protection of the complaining shareholder's "rights or interests" would, in effect, fail to recognize the existence of N.C.G.S. § 55–125.1(b) to the extent that it grants trial courts the power to order alternative relief where relief of some kind *but not dissolution* is appropriate.

In sum, therefore, we hold that under N.C.G.S. § 55–125(a)(4) a trial court is: (1) to define the "rights or interests" the complaining shareholder has in the corporation; and (2) to determine whether some form of relief is "reasonably necessary" for the protection of those "rights or interests." For plaintiff to obtain relief under the expectations' analysis, he must prove that (1) he had one or more substantial reasonable expectations known or assumed by the other participants; (2) the expectation has been frustrated; (3) the frustration was without fault of plaintiff and was in large part beyond his control; and (4) under all of the circumstances of the case, plaintiff is entitled to some form of equitable relief.

IV.

We will now review the "rights or interests" each party contends Michael has in the family corporations. Michael suggests in his brief that the "rights or interests" he has as a shareholder in these close corporations include "rights or interests" in secure employment, fringe benefits which flow from his association with the corporations, and meaningful participation in the management of the family business. . . .

While it may be true that a shareholder in, for example, a publicly held corporation may have "rights or interests" defined as defendants argue, a shareholder's rights in a closely held corporation may not necessarily be so narrowly defined. In short, we hold that the shareholder in this case—one who owns stock worth well over $3,000,000 and which accounts for a 30 to 40 percent ownership in these closely held, family-run corporations worth well over $11,000,000 and who also has been employed by the corporations, provided with fringe benefits, and, to some extent, allowed to participate in management decisions—has "rights or interests" more broadly defined than defendants contend. Put another way, Michael's "reasonable expectations" are not as limited as defendants contend.

Again, we note that N.C.G.S. § 55–125(a)(4) speaks in terms of the "rights or interests" of "*the complaining shareholder.*" Thus, those "rights or interests" must be defined with reference to the "rights or interests" the complaining shareholder has under the facts of the particular case—the "reasonable expectations" the participants' relationship has generated. Indeed, the legislature would not have had reason to enact N.C.G.S. § 55–125 (a)(4) if "rights or interests" were to always comprise only the traditional shareholder rights: other statutes already address the traditional rights and remedies to which shareholders have been entitled. *See e.g.,* N.C.G.S. § 55–62(a) (notice of shareholder's meetings); N.C.G.S. § 55–67(c) (right to cumulative voting); N.C.G.S. § 55–37(a)(4) and N.C.G.S. § 55–38(b) (right to examine books and records); and N.C.G.S. § 55–50(1) and (m) (right to compel payment of dividends).

Our task at this juncture, then, is to determine, in light of each party's contentions and the analysis articulated above that is to be applied to suits brought under N.C.G.S. § 55–125(a)(4), whether the trial court made appropriate findings of fact. Specifically, we must determine whether the trial court defined the "rights or interests" Michael does have in these family-run corporations, and whether it determined that some form of relief is "reasonably necessary" to protect those particular "rights or interests."

* * * *

Because the trial court's findings of fact failed to address the "rights or interests" Michael has in these family corporations, we must remand the case to the trial court for an evidentiary hearing to resolve this issue. On remand, after hearing the evidence, the trial court is to: (1) articulate specifically Michael's "rights or interests"—his "reasonable expectations"—in the corporate defendants; and (2) determine if these "rights or interests" are in need of protection, and, thus, that relief of some sort should be granted. In addition, the trial court is to prescribe the form of relief which the evidence indicates is most appropriate, should it find that relief is warranted. In remanding this case for an evidentiary hearing and new findings, we need not address the issue of whether the trial court abused its discretion in refusing to grant relief to Michael.

V.

Michael also contends that Ira breached the fiduciary duty he owes as a director and officer of the corporate defendants through his sole ownership of the stock in Republic, the corporation with which Eastern Federal contracted to provide management services. Michael concedes that the trial court was correct when it found that the management contract between Republic and Eastern Federal was just and reasonable at the time it was executed. He states that he has "never complained about Republic management itself nor about the management contract." It is only Ira's sole ownership of the stock in Republic to which he objects.

In essence, then, Michael is claiming that Ira breached his fiduciary duty to the corporate defendants by usurping a corporate opportunity which belonged to them—the opportunity to buy the stock of Republic.

* * * *

[We] . . . remand this case to the Court of Appeals to be remanded to the trial court for further findings. In making its findings, the trial court must determine whether the opportunity to purchase the stock in Republic rightfully belonged to the corporate defendants rather than to Ira personally. In so doing, the trial court will examine the facts and decide if the corporate defendants would have had an interest or expectancy in purchasing all of the shares of stock in a corporation whose sole function appears to be the management of the Meiselman family business. It also is to determine whether Ira's acquisition of all of the stock in this type of corporation is an activity functionally related to those of the corporate defendants. Under either approach, the trial court may find that Ira usurped a business opportunity which rightfully belonged to the corporate defendants.

VI.

In sum, therefore, we hold that the order of the trial court denying plaintiff's claim for relief under N.C.G.S. § 55–125(a)(4) and N.C.G.S. § 55–125.1 must be vacated. . . . The case is remanded to the Court of Appeals for remand to the Superior Court, Mecklenburg County, for further proceedings consistent with this opinion.

Modified, affirmed and remanded.

* * * *

CONCUR BY: MARTIN

JUSTICE MARTIN concurring in the result.

Except as herein set forth, I concur in the majority opinion. . . .

In determining whether plaintiff's expectations have been frustrated, the actions of all the participants, including plaintiff, must be considered. The majority fails to address this aspect of the case. In *Exadaktilos v. Cinnaminson Realty Co.,* 167 N.J. Super. 141, 400 A. 2d 554 (1979), aff'd, 173 N.J. Super. 559, 414 A. 2d 994 (1980), plaintiff acquired a twenty percent interest in a corporation that operated a restaurant. He expected to learn the restaurant business and participate in management. Unfortunately, he did not get along with the other employees and stockholders and was fired for what the court viewed as "unsatisfactory performance." In deciding plaintiff's claim for relief, the court considered the propriety of the actions by the controlling shareholders. The court found that the opportunity had been offered plaintiff and it was lost through *no fault* of the defendants. In weighing plaintiff's claim against the disruptive effects the grant of relief would have upon the business, the court found it appropriate to consider the actions of all parties in determining the cause of the frustration of plaintiff's expectations.

* * * *

Another factor to be considered by the court in determining whether to grant relief is whether the minority shareholder has diligently pursued all of the other available statutory means for the protection of his rights and that after doing so "[l]iquidation [or alternative relief under N.C.G.S. 55–125.1] is reasonably necessary for the protection of [his] rights or interests . . . ." N.C. Gen. Stat. § 55–125(a)(4) (1982). [*Citation omitted.*] The majority shareholders and the corporation should not be subject to dissolution, the most drastic form of relief available, where other statutory rights may provide an adequate remedy for the minority shareholder. This is in accord with the general rule that equitable relief will not ordinarily be granted when plaintiff has an adequate remedy at law. [*Citation omitted.*] Such statutory rights include, e.g., the minority's right to attempt to gain representation on the board of directors under N.C.G.S. 55–25 and the right to compel the payment of dividends under N.C.G.S. 55–50.

In determining whether to grant equitable relief under N.C.G.S. 55–125.1, the trial court must consider all the circumstances of the case. If it is determined that plaintiff's rights or interests require protection because of plaintiff's own conduct, it would be improper to grant equitable relief. . . .

The court should also consider what effect the granting of relief will have upon the corporation and other shareholders. Will it interfere with the corporation's ability to attract financing for its business? Will it interfere with its ability to attract additional capital? Will it require burdensome financing upon the corporation or the shareholders? Will it interfere with the rights of creditors? If a buy-out of plaintiff's shares is forced upon the company, it may be far from painless. If it is determined that the granting of relief will be unduly burdensome to the corporation or other shareholders, the trial court should consider this in determining whether to grant relief and, if so, whether this should affect the purchase price or value attached to plaintiff's shares or the method of payment. * * *

. . . I cannot agree that merely because plaintiff's expectations were not fulfilled it necessarily follows that the majority stockholders were guilty of oppression.

* * * *

QUESTIONS

1. Do you think that, upon remand the Eastern Federal Corporation and the other Meiselman family corporations should be dissolved?

2. Should Michael be able to force a buyout of his shares?

3. When Mr. Meiselman (the father) left majority ownership of the family businesses to Ira, what do you think he hoped would happen?

4. If you were representing Mr. Meiselman, how would you have advised him to structure the ownership and control of the business?

5. How would you have advised Ira, if he had come to you before firing Michael?

6. Do you agree more with the Massachusetts/North Carolina line of cases, that takes additional steps to protect minority shareholders, or the Delaware approach seen in *Sinclair Oil Corp. v. Levien* and *Nixon v. Blackwell, supra,* that creates limitations on the actions that might be taken by a dominant shareholder, but does not inquire into the breadth of the "rights and interests" of a shareholder in a close corporation?

SECTION V: Employee or Shareholder

Many "freeze out" cases involve a shareholder's claim that he should be allowed to be an employee and receive a salary since that is the only way funds are distributed by the corporation. Often these cases will turn on an assessment of whether the individual is (a) a shareholder whose right to employment is a byproduct of his position as a shareholder or (b) an employee who happened to obtain shares as a result of employment. At-will employees who just happen to be shareholders do not usually have the fiduciary duties, discussed above, protecting their rights to employment. On the other hand, most employee/shareholder situations can often be avoided if there is an employment agreement present. In many such situations, courts will rely on the employment agreement to determine the rights of the employee/shareholder, rather than more abstract applications of fiduciary duties. In many situations, controlling shareholders have used employment agreements to their advantage to secure their rights to terminate the employment of an employee who is also a minority shareholder. The cases that follow highlight instances in which the rights of an employee and the rights of a shareholder intersect and, sometimes, conflict with each other.

Gallagher v. Lambert

74 N.Y.2d 562, 549 N.E.2d 136, 549 N.Y.S.2d 945 (N.Y. 1989)

BELLACOSA, J.:

Plaintiff Gallagher purchased stock in the defendant close corporation with which he was employed. The purchase of his 8.5% interest was subject to a mandatory buy-back provision: if the employment ended for any reason before January 31, 1985, the stock would return to the corporation for book value. The corporation fired plaintiff prior to the fulcrum date, after which the buy-back price would have been higher.

* * * *

Gallagher was employed by defendant Eastdil Realty as a mortgage broker from 1968 to 1973. Three years later, in 1976, he returned to the company as a broker, officer and director, serving additionally as president and chief executive officer of defendant's wholly owned subsidiary, Eastdil Advisors, Inc. Gallagher was at all times an employee at will. Still later, in 1981, Eastdil offered all its executive employees an opportunity to purchase stock subject to a mandatory buy-back provision, which provided that upon "voluntary resignation or other termination" prior to January 31, 1985, an employee would be required to return the stock for book value. After that date, the formula for the buy-back price was keyed to the company's earnings. Plaintiff accepted the offer and its terms.

On January 10, 1985, Gallagher was fired by Eastdil Realty. He did not and does not now contest the firing. But he demanded payment for his shares calculated on the post-January 31, 1985 buy-back formula. Eastdil refused and Gallagher sued, asserting eight causes of action. Only three claims, based on an alleged breach of fiduciary duty of good faith and fair dealing, are before us. . . .

The parties negotiated a written contract containing a common and plain buy-back provision. Plaintiff got what he bargained for—book value for his minority shares if his employment in the corporation ended before January 31, 1985. There being no basis presented for the courts to interfere with the operation and consequences of this agreement between the parties, the order of the Appellate Division granting summary judgment to defendants, dismissing the first three causes of action, should be affirmed. . .

Earlier this year, in *Ingle v. Glamore Motor Sales* (73 NY2d 183), we expressly refrained from deciding the precise issue presented by this case. There, the challenge was directed to the at-will discharge from employment and was predicated on a claimed fiduciary obligation flowing from the shareholder relationship. Relying principally on *Sabetay v. Sterling Drug (69 NY2d 329, 335–336)* and *Murphy v. American Home Prods. Corp.* (58 NY2d 293, 300), we held that "[a] minority shareholder in a close corporation, by that status alone, who contractually agrees to the repurchase of his shares upon termination of his employment for any reason, *acquires no right from the corporation or majority shareholders against at-will discharge." (Ingle v. Glamore Motor Sales,* 73 NY2d, *supra,* at 188 [emphasis added].) However, we cautioned that "[it] is necessary * * * to appreciate and keep distinct the duty a corporation owes to a minority shareholder *as a shareholder* from any duty it might owe him as an *employee." (Id.,* at 188.)

The causes before us on this appeal are based on an alleged departure from a fiduciary duty of fair dealing existing independently of the employment and arising from the plaintiff's simultaneous relationship as a minority shareholder in the corporation. Plaintiff claims entitlement to the higher price based on a breach flowing from Eastdil's premature "bad faith" termination of his at-will employment because, he asserts, the sole purpose of the firing at that time was to acquire the stock at a contractually and temporally measured lower buy-back price formula.

The claim seeking a higher price for the shares cannot be neatly divorced, as the dissent urges, from the employment because the buy-back provision links them together as to timing and consequences. Plaintiff not only agreed to the particular buy-back formula, he helped write it and he reviewed it with his attorney during the negotiation process, before signing the agreement and purchasing the minority interest. These provisions, which require an employee shareholder to sell back stock upon severance from corporate employment, are designed to ensure that ownership of all of the stock, especially of a close corporation, stays within the control of the remaining corporate owners-employees; that is, those who will continue to contribute to its successes or failures. [*Citations omitted.*] These agreements define the scope of the relevant fiduciary duty and supply certainty of obligation to each side. They should not be undone simply upon an allegation of unfairness. This would destroy their very purpose, which is to provide a certain formula by which to value stock in the future. . . .

Gallagher accepted the offer to become a minority stockholder, but only for the period during which he remained an employee. The buy-back price formula was designed for the benefit of both parties precisely so that they could know their respective rights on certain dates and avoid costly and lengthy litigation on the "fair value" issue. . . . Permitting these causes to survive would open the door to litigation on both the value of the stock and the date of termination, and hinder the employer from fulfilling its contractual rights under the agreement. This would frustrate the agreement and would be disruptive of the settled principles governing like agreements where parties contract between themselves in advance so that there may be reliance, predictability and definitiveness between themselves on such matters. There being no dispute that the employer had the unfettered discretion to fire plaintiff at any time, we should not redefine the precise measuring device and scope of the agreement. Defendant agreed to abide by these terms and thus fulfilled its fiduciary duty in that respect.

The dissenting opinion uses a number of rhetorical characterizations about the defendant and about what we are deciding or avoiding to decide, none of which, we believe, require response, because our holding and rationale rest on the application of fundamental contractual principles to the plain terms in the parties' own stock repurchase agreement.

Accordingly, the order of the Appellate Division should be affirmed, with costs, and the certified question answered in the affirmative.

DISSENT

KAYE, J. (dissenting).

* * * *

Here, plaintiff *does* question the duty the corporation owes him as a shareholder. He *does* contend that the corporation undervalued his shares and that it did not offer a fair price for his equity interest. Indeed, that is the only question he raises; he does not challenge defendant's absolute right to terminate his employment.

* * * *

III.

Gallagher alleges that defendants had no bona fide, business-related reason to terminate his employment when they did—assertions we must accept as true on this summary judgment motion. He charges that defendants fired him for the sole purpose of recapturing his shares at an unfairly low price and redistributing them among themselves.

These claims put in issue an aspect of the employee-shareholder relationship that we have not previously considered in our at-will employment cases. Plaintiff claims that defendants, the holders of a majority of the corporate stock, breached distinctly different duties to him by manipulating his termination so as to deprive him of the opportunity to reap the benefits of a "golden handcuffs" agreement, and for no other reason than to effect repurchase of his shares at less than their fair value. In short, plaintiff claims defendants breached two duties related to each other but conceptually unrelated to his at-will employment status: (1) a duty of good faith in the performance of the shareholders' agreement, and (2) a fiduciary obligation owed to him as a minority shareholder by the controlling shareholders to refrain from purely self-aggrandizing conduct. Neither claim is foreclosed by plaintiff's status as an at-will employee.

If plaintiff were a minority shareholder, but not an employee, defendants would be barred from acting selfishly and opportunistically, for no corporate purpose, as he alleges they did. The controlling stockholders in a close corporation stand, in relation to minority owners, in the same fiduciary position as corporate directors generally, and are held "to the extreme measure of candor, unselfishness and good faith."

* * * *

Directors and majority shareholders may not act "for the aggrandizement or undue advantage of the fiduciary to the exclusion or detriment of the [minority] stockholders." (*Alpert v. 28 Williams St. Corp.,* 63 NY2d 557, 569 [citing cases].) Nor is it considered a legitimate corporate interest if the sole purpose is reduction of the number of profit-sharers, or ultimately "to increase the individual wealth of the remaining shareholders" (*id.,* at 573). Yet that is precisely what we must assume defendants' motive was, and this court now sanctions such conduct.

* * * *

Moreover, defendants' interpretation denies that defendants themselves had any duty of good faith in connection with the shareholders' agreement. We have said that "there is an implied covenant that neither party shall do anything which will have the effect of destroying or injuring the right of the other party to receive the fruits of the contract, which means that in every contract there exists an implied covenant of good faith and fair dealing." (*Kirke La Shelle Co. v. Armstrong Co.,* 263 NY 79, 87.) This general rule does not apply to at-will employment relationships, as "it would be incongruous to say that an inference may be drawn that the employer impliedly agreed to a provision which would be destructive of his right of termination." (*Murphy v. American Home Prods. Corp.,* 58 NY2d 293, 304–305.) It does not follow, however, that there can be no covenant of good faith implicit in the shareholders' agreement that gives rise to obligations surviving termination of the employment relationship.

* * * *

IV.

Denial of summary judgment would deprive defendants of no legitimate expectation or right, contractual or otherwise. Under the law, they remain free to terminate plaintiff's employment as agreed; they remain free to buy back his stock at book value as agreed—so long as there is a corporate purpose for their conduct. What controlling shareholders cannot do to a minority shareholder is take action against him solely for the self-aggrandizing, opportunistic purpose of themselves acquiring his shares at the low price, and they cannot do this because in the law it means something to be a shareholder, particularly a minority shareholder.

Because the majority gives no credence whatever to plaintiff's independent status as a shareholder, and because the majority now needlessly extends the at-will employment doctrine yet another notch, to diminish the long-recognized duties owed minority shareholders, I must dissent.

QUESTIONS

1. If you were Gallagher's attorney, would you have advised him to sign the Agreement?

2. What if Gallagher's employment was contingent on entering into the Agreement?

3. If Eastdil had acknowledged that it was firing Gallagher solely to prevent him from reaching the date at which the buy-back price for his stock would increase, would that change the outcome of this case?

4. If Eastdil were your client, could you suggest any additional provisions to add to the Agreement, to strengthen Eastdil's position in subsequent cases like this?

Jordan v. Duff & Phelps, Inc.

815 F.2d 429 (7th Cir. 1987)

EASTERBROOK, C.J.:

Flamm v. Eberstadt, 814 F.2d 1169 (7th Cir. 1987), holds that a corporation need not disclose, to investors trading in the stock market, ongoing negotiations for a merger. A public corporation may keep silent until the firms reach agreement in principle on the price and structure of the deal. [*Citations omitted.*] Things are otherwise for closely held corporations. *Michaels v. Michaels,* 767 F.2d 1185, 1194–97 (7th Cir. 1985), holds that a closely held firm must disclose material information to investors from whom it purchases stock, and that a decision to seek another firm with which to merge may be the sort of material information that must be disclosed to the investor selling his shares, even though the firm has not reached agreement in principle on the price and structure of a deal. [*Citations omitted.*]

The treatment of public and private corporations is different because of the potential effects of disclosure. Often negotiations must be conducted in secrecy to increase their prospects of success. . . . A close corporation may disclose to an investor without alerting the public at large, however, so that disclosure does not injure investors as a whole. . . . It need disclose the existence of the decision to sell (and the status of negotiations) only to the person whose stock is to be acquired. The face-to-face negotiations allow the investor to elicit the information he requires, see *Michaels,* 767 F.2d at 1196, *and Hamilton v. Harrington,* 807 F.2d 102, 106–07 & n.5 (7th Cir. 1986), while permitting the firm to extract promises of confidentiality that safeguard the negotiations.

This case contains two wrinkles. First, it involves the acquisition of a closely held corporation by a public corporation. Second, the investor in the closely held corporation was an employee, and he was offered shares to cement his loyalty to the firm; yet he quit (and was compelled by a shareholders' agreement to sell his shares) for reasons unrelated to the value of the stock. . . .

I

The case is here following a grant of summary judgment for the defendants. . . .

Duff and Phelps, Inc., evaluates the risk and worth of firms and their securities. It sells credit ratings, investment research, and financial consulting services to both the firms under scrutiny and potential investors in them. Jordan started work at Duff & Phelps in May 1977 and was viewed as a successful securities analyst. In 1981 the firm offered Jordan the opportunity to buy some stock. By November 1983 Jordan had purchased 188 of the 20,100 shares outstanding. He was making installment payments on another 62 shares. Forty people other than Jordan held stock in Duff & Phelps.

Jordan purchased his stock at its "book value" (the accounting net worth of Duff & Phelps, divided by the number of shares outstanding). Before selling him any stock, Duff & Phelps required Jordan to sign a "Stock Restriction and Purchase Agreement" (the Agreement). This provided in part:

> Upon the termination of any employment with the Corporation . . . for any reason, including resignation, discharge, death, disability or retirement, the individual whose employment is terminated or his estate shall sell to the Corporation, and the Corporation shall buy, all Shares of the Corporation then owned by such individual or his estate. The price to be paid for such Shares shall be equal to the adjusted book value (as hereinafter defined) of the Shares on the December 31 which coincides with, or immediately precedes, the date of termination of such individual's employment.

Duff & Phelps enforced this restriction with but a single exception. During 1983 the board of directors of Duff & Phelps adopted a resolution—of which Jordan did not learn until 1984—allowing employees fired by the firm to keep their stock for five years. The resolution followed the discharge of Carol Franchik, with whom Claire Hansen, the (married) chairman of the board, had been having an affair. When Franchik threatened suit, the board allowed her to keep her stock.

While Jordan was accumulating stock, Hansen, the chairman of the board, was exploring the possibility of selling the firm. Between May and August 1983 Hansen and Francis Jeffries, another officer of Duff & Phelps, negotiated with Security Pacific Corp., a bank holding company. The negotiators reached agreement on a merger, in which Duff & Phelps would be valued at $50 million, but a higher official within Security Pacific vetoed the deal on August 11, 1983. As of that date, Duff & Phelps had no irons in the fire.

Jordan, however, was conducting a search of his own—for a new job. Jordan's family lived near Chicago, the headquarters of Duff & Phelps, and Jordan's wife did not get along with Jordan's mother. The strain between the two occasionally left his wife in tears. He asked Duff & Phelps about the possibility of a transfer to the firm's only branch office, in Cleveland, but the firm did not need Jordan's services there. Concluding that it was time to choose between his job and his wife, Jordan chose his wife and started looking for employment far away from Chicago. His search took him to Houston, where Underwood Neuhaus & Co., a broker-dealer in securities, offered him a job at a salary ($110,000 per year) substantially greater than his compensation ($67,000) at Duff & Phelps. Jordan took the offer on the spot during an interview in Houston, but Underwood would have allowed Jordan to withdraw this oral acceptance.

On November 16, 1983, Jordan told Hansen that he was going to resign and accept employment with Underwood. Jordan did not ask Hansen about potential mergers; Hansen did not volunteer anything. Jordan delivered a letter of resignation, which Duff & Phelps accepted the same day. By mutual agreement, Jordan worked the rest of the year for Duff & Phelps even though his loyalties had shifted. He did this so that he could receive the book value of the stock as of December 31, 1983—for under the Agreement a departure in November would have meant valuation as of December 31, 1982. Jordan delivered his certificates on December 30, 1983, and the firm mailed him a check for $23,225, the book value (at $123.54 per share) of the 188 shares of stock. Jordan surrendered, as worthless under the circumstances, the right to buy the remaining 62 shares.

Before Jordan cashed the check, however, he was startled by the announcement on January 10, 1984, of a merger between Duff & Phelps and a subsidiary of Security Pacific. Under the terms of the merger Duff & Phelps would be valued at $50 million. If Jordan had been an employee on January 10, had quickly paid for the other 62 shares, and the merger had closed that day, he would have received $452,000 in cash and the opportunity to obtain as much as $194,000 more in "earn out" (a percentage of Duff & Phelps's profits to be paid to the former investors—an arrangement that keeps the employees' interest in the firm keen and reduces the buyer's risk if profits fall short). Jordan refused to cash the check and demanded his stock back; Duff & Phelps told him to get lost. He filed this suit in March 1984, asking for damages measured by the value his stock would have had under the terms of the acquisition.

The public announcement on January 10 explained that the boards of the two firms had reached an agreement in principle on January 6. The definitive agreement was signed on March 23. Because Security Pacific is a bank holding company, the acquisition required the approval of the Board of Governors of the Federal Reserve. The Fed granted approval, but with a condition so onerous that the firms abandoned the transaction. The Fed objected to Security Pacific's acquisition of Duff & Phelps's credit rating business. 71 Fed. Res. Bull. 118 (1985). The agreement was formally cancelled on January 9, 1985. Duff & Phelps quickly asked the district court to dismiss Jordan's suit, on the ground that he could not establish damages. Jordan responded by amending his complaint, with Judge Hart's permission, to ask for rescission rather than damages.

Throughout 1985 Duff & Phelps continued looking for a partner; finding none, it decided to dance with itself. The firm's management formed an "Employee Stock Ownership Trust", which was able to borrow $40 million against the security of the firm's assets and business. The Trust acquired Duff & Phelps through a new firm, Duff Research, Inc. This transaction occurred in December 1985. The employees at the time, together with Carol Franchik, received cash, notes, and beneficial interests in the Trust. Jordan asserts that the package was worth almost $2000 per share, or $497,000 if he had held 250 shares in December 1985.

* * * *

II

Michaels holds that close corporations that purchase their own stock must disclose to the sellers all information that meets the standard of "materiality" set out in *TSC Industries, Inc. v. Northway, Inc.,* 426 U.S. 438, 449, 48 L. Ed. 2d 757, 96 S. Ct. 2126 (1976). *See Michaels,* 767 F.2d at 1194–97. . . . A jury would be free under *Michaels* to conclude that the board's decision of November 14 to seek a buyer for Duff & Phelps—coupled with the fact that at least one putative buyer thought Duff & Phelps worth $50 million, which casts an important light on the prospect of a profitable conclusion to the search—was "material" under the standard of *TSC Industries.* That is, there is a "substantial likelihood that, under all the circumstances, the omitted fact would have assumed actual significance in the deliberations of the reasonable shareholder" and "would have been viewed by the reasonable investor as having significantly altered the 'total mix' of information made available." *426 U.S. at 449* (footnote omitted)

Duff & Phelps replies that *Michaels* is inapplicable. The district court agreed, but we do not. The rationale for the price-and-structure rule, which we adopted in *Flamm,* is that firms may need secrecy to obtain the best price. *Flamm,* slip op. 11–15. To tell one stockholder of a publicly traded firm is to tell all, letting the cat out of the bag. Security Pacific therefore was entitled to be mum about its plans and to insist that Duff & Phelps also keep matters secret. But a whisper in Jordan's ear would not have revealed anything to the public. Hansen and other members of the executive committee of Duff & Phelps's board already knew about the negotiations, and apparently Hansen had been whispering in Franchik's ear. Because it is possible to inform shareholders of closely held firms about ongoing negotiations without informing the public—because indeed the firm need tell only the few investors from whom it buys stock during the negotiations—*Michaels* rather than Flamm supplies the definition of materiality here.

A jury could find that the information withheld on November 16 is "material". A jury also could find that December 30, rather than November 16, is the date of the "sale" of the stock. If December 30 is the date of sale, the information withheld then was "material" under *Michaels* and *TSC Industries* as a matter of law. By then the negotiating teams for Duff & Phelps and Security Pacific had negotiated the price and structure of the deal. . . . So there are two linked materiality questions for the jury: whether the information withheld on November 16 was material, and whether the sale took place on November 16 or December 30.

Duff & Phelps insists that nothing after November 16 matters. A person who sells stock through a broker has several business days to deliver the certificates; the sale is nonetheless final—with price and disclosure obligations fixed forever—on the date of the deal rather than the date of delivery. Duff & Phelps treats the letter of resignation on November 16 as an irrevocable sale with deferred delivery. Yet if the "sale" occurred on November 16, then under the Agreement the stock would have been valued as of December 31, 1982. That Duff & Phelps valued the stock as of December 31, 1983, may persuade a jury that it treated the "sale" as made on that date. Moreover, Jordan insists that other employees were allowed to withdraw their resignations, and that he could have done so as late as December 31—if, say, his wife and his mother had reconciled. A cabinet officer who resigns (and has the resignation accepted by the President) is out of office and cannot stick around without being nominated and confirmed again; but private parties may decide to give less finality to resignations. The terms on which resignations may be withdrawn may be implicit parts of the relations between Duff & Phelps and its employees, and Jordan is entitled to an opportunity to demonstrate that he could have remained at the firm. If he can prove this, then December 30 rather than November 16 is the date on which the materiality of the firm's omissions must be assessed.

All of this supposes that Duff & Phelps had a duty to disclose anything to Jordan. Most people are free to buy and sell stock on the basis of valuable private knowledge without informing their trading partners. Strangers transact in markets all the time using private information that might be called "material" and, unless one has a duty to disclose, both may keep their counsel. *Dirks v. SEC,* 463 U.S. 646, 653–64, 77 L. Ed. 2d 911, 103 S. Ct. 3255 (1983); *Chiarella v. United States,* 445 U.S. 222, 227–35, 63 L. Ed. 2d 348, 100 S. Ct. 1108 (1980). . . . The ability to make profits from the possession of information is the principal spur to create the information, which the parties and the market as a whole may find valuable. The absence of a duty to disclose may not justify a lie about a material fact, but Duff & Phelps did not lie to Jordan. It simply remained silent when Jordan quit and tendered the stock, and it offered the payment required by the Agreement. Duff & Phelps maintains that it was entitled to be silent, as Dirks could trade in silence and tip off his friends, even though it could not have lied in response to the questions Jordan should (in retrospect) have asked but did not.

This argument is unavailing on the facts as we know them. The "duty" in question is the fiduciary duty of corporate law. Close corporations buying their own stock, like knowledgeable insiders of closely held firms buying from outsiders, have a fiduciary duty to disclose material facts. *Kohler* and *Michaels* rest on this duty, as do some of the earliest cases of trading by insiders on material information. The "special facts" doctrine developed by several courts at the turn of the century is based on the principle that insiders in closely held firms may not buy stock from outsiders in person-to-person transactions without informing them of new events that substantially affect the value of the stock. . . .

Because the fiduciary duty is a standby or off-the-rack guess about what parties would agree to if they dickered about the subject explicitly, parties may contract with greater specificity for other arrangements. It is a violation of duty to steal from the corporate treasury; it is not a violation to write oneself a check that the board has approved as a bonus. We may assume that duties concerning the timing of disclosure by an otherwise-silent firm also may be the subject of contract. Section 29 (a) of the Securities Exchange Act of 1934, 15 U.S.C. § 78cc (a), forbids waivers of the provisions of the Act, and here the critical provision is § 10 (b), 15 U.S.C. § 78j (b), and the SEC's Rule 10b–5. . . . But a provision must be applicable to be "waived", and the existence of a requirement to speak is a condition of the application of § 10 (b) to a person's silence during a securities trade. The obligation to break silence is itself based on state law, see *Dirks, Chiarella,* and *Barker,* and so may be redefined to the extent state law permits. See, e.g., *Toledo Trust Co. v. Nye,* 588 F.2d 202, 206 (6th Cir. 1978) (there is no liability under the securities laws for failing to disclose information that has been made irrelevant by contract, in *Nye* a contract allowing someone to purchase shares at a formula price on a date certain). But we need not decide how far contracts can redefine obligations to disclose. Jordan was an employee at will; he signed no contract.

The stock was designed to bind Duff & Phelps's employees loyally to the firm. The buy-sell agreement tied ownership to employment. Understandably Duff & Phelps did not want a viper in its nest, a disgruntled employee remaining only in the hope of appreciation of his stock. So there could have been reason to divorce the employment decision from the value of the stock. Perhaps it would have been rational for each employee to agree with Duff & Phelps to look to salary alone in deciding whether to stay. A contractual agreement that the firm had no duty to disclose would have uncoupled the investment decision from the employment decision, leaving whoever was in the firm on the day of a merger to receive a surprise appreciation. Some might lose by leaving early; some might reap a windfall by buying just before the announcement; all might think it wise to have as little as possible said in the interim.

Yet an explicit agreement to make all employment decisions in ignorance of the value of the stock might not have been in the interests of the firm or its employees. Duff & Phelps was trying to purchase loyalty by offering stock to its principal employees. The package of compensation contained salary and the prospect of appreciation of the stock. Perhaps it paid a lower salary than, say, Underwood Neuhaus & Co., because its package contained a higher component of gain from anticipated appreciation in the stock. It is therefore unwarranted to say that the implicit understanding between Jordan and Duff & Phelps should be treated as if it had such a no-duty clause; we are not confident that this is the clause firms and their employees regularly would prefer. . . .

The course of dealing between Jordan and Duff & Phelps suggests that the firm did not demand that employees decide whether to stay or go without regard to the value of the stock. It apparently informed Jordan what the book value was expected to be on December 31, 1983, so that Jordan could decide whether to leave in November (receiving the value as of December 31, 1982) or stay for another six weeks. The firm did not demand that Jordan depart as soon as it learned he had switched loyalties; it allowed employees to time their departures to obtain the maximum advantage from their stock. The Agreement did not ensure that employees disregard the value of the stock when deciding what to do, and neither did the usual practice at Duff & Phelps. So the possibility that a firm could negotiate around the fiduciary duty does not assist Duff & Phelps; it did not obtain such an agreement, express or implied.

The closest Duff & Phelps came is the provision in the Agreement fixing the price of the stock at book value. Yet although the Agreement fixed the price to be paid those who quit, it did not establish the terms on which anyone would leave. Thus cases such as *Toledo Trust and St. Louis Union Trust Co. v. Merrill Lynch,*

Pierce, Fenner & Smith, Inc., 562 F.2d 1040 (8th Cir. 1977), do not assist Duff & Phelps. These cases dealt with agreements calling for valuation at a formula price on a fixed date. In *St. Louis Union Trust* the date was the death of the employee, the formula was book value. The court of appeals held that there was no need to pay the employee's estate a different price, just because a few weeks later Merrill Lynch went public at a higher price. The employee presumably did not take the possibility of a merger into account in deciding whether to die, and the formula price made "disclosure" irrelevant. *Toledo Trust,* too, discussed a buyback triggered by death. . . . Jordan, though, exercised choice about the date on which the formula would be triggered. He could have remained at Duff & Phelps; his decision to depart was affected by his wife's distress, his salary, his working conditions, the enjoyment he received from the job, and the value of his stock. The departure of such an employee is an investment decision as much as it is an employment decision. It is not fanciful to suppose that Mrs. Jordan would have found her mother in law a whole lot more tolerable if she had known that Jordan's stock might shortly be worth 20 times book value.

The securities acts apply to investment decisions, even those made indirectly or bound up with other decisions, such as employment or entrepreneurship. . . . The position of this court that § 10 (b) and cognate provisions of the securities laws were designed exclusively to protect passive investors . . . was rejected in *Landreth and, e.g., United States v. Naftalin,* 441 U.S. 768, 775–77, 60 L. Ed. 2d 624, 99 S. Ct. 2077 (1979). There must be an "investment" decision, to be sure. . .; but Jordan unavoidably made one. That he took the value of stock into account is evident from the timing of his departure. A few thousand dollars' increase in book value led the Jordans to stay in Chicago an extra six weeks. How long would they have stayed for the prospect of another $620,000?

Our dissenting colleague concludes that all of this is beside the point because Hansen could have said, on receiving Jordan's letter on November 16: "In a few weeks we will pull off a merger that would have made your stock 20 times more valuable. It's a shame you so foolishly resigned. But even if you hadn't resigned, we would have fired you, the better to engross the profits of the merger for ourselves. So long, sucker." This would have been permissible, under our colleague's interpretation, because Jordan was an employee at will and therefore could have been fired at any time, even the day before the merger, for any reason—including the desire to deprive Jordan of a share of the profits. The ability to fire Jordan enabled the firm to "call" his shares, at book value, on whim. On this view, it is foolish to say that Duff & Phelps had a duty to disclose, because disclosure would have been no use to Jordan. (Perhaps this is really an argument about "causation" rather than "duty", but the terminology is unimportant.) But Duff & Phelps itself does not press this argument, and in civil litigation an appellate court ought not put words in a party's mouth and use them as the grounds on which to decide. . . . The district court has not had an opportunity to address such a claim, and Jordan has not been asked to respond to it. Perhaps Duff & Phelps does not want to establish a reputation for shoddy dealing; as our dissenting brother observes, a firm's desire to preserve its reputation is a powerful inducement to treat its contractual partners well. To attribute to a litigant an argument that it will take every possible advantage is to assume that the party wishes to dissipate its reputation, and the assumption is unwarranted.

More than that, a person's status as an employee "at will" does not imply that the employer may discharge him for every reason. Illinois, where Jordan was employed, has placed some limits on the discharge of at-will employees. . . . We do not disparage the utility of at-will contracts; this very panel recently recognized the value of informal (meaning not legally binding) employment relations. . . . But employment at will is still a contractual relation, one in which a particular duration ("at will") is implied in the absence of a contrary expression. . . . The silence of the parties may make it necessary to imply other terms—those we are confident the parties would have bargained for if they had signed a written agreement. One term implied in every written contract and therefore, we suppose, every unwritten one, is that neither party will try to take opportunistic advantage of the other. "The fundamental function of contract law (and recognized as such at least since Hobbes's day) is to deter people from behaving opportunistically toward their contracting parties, in order to encourage the optimal timing of economic activity and to make costly self-protective measures unnecessary." Richard A. Posner, *Economic Analysis of Law 81* (3d ed. 1986). [*Citations omitted.*]

Employment creates occasions for opportunism. A firm may fire an employee the day before his pension vests, or a salesman the day before a large commission becomes payable. Cases of this sort may present difficult questions about the reasons for the decision (was it opportunism, or was it a decline in the employee's performance?). The difficulties of separating opportunistic conduct from honest differences of opinion about an employee's performance on the job may lead firms and their employees to transact on terms that keep such disputes out of court—which employment at will usually does. But no one . . . doubts that an *avowedly* opportunistic discharge is a breach of contract, although the employment is at-will. . . . The element of good faith dealing implied in a contract "is not an enforceable legal duty to be nice or to behave decently in a general way." [*Citation omitted.*] It is not a version of the Golden Rule, to regard the interests of one's contracting partner the same way you regard your own. An employer may be thoughtless, nasty, and mistaken. Avowedly opportunistic conduct has been treated differently, however.

The stock component in Jordan's package induced him to stick around and work well. Such an inducement is effective only if the employee reaps the rewards of success as well as the penalties of failure. We do not suppose for a second that if Jordan had not resigned on November 16, the firm could have fired him on January 9 with a little note saying: "Dear Mr. Jordan: There will be a lucrative merger tomorrow. You have been a wonderful employee, but in order to keep the proceeds of the merger for ourselves, we are letting you go, effective this instant. Here is the $23,000 for your shares." Had the firm fired Jordan for this stated reason, it would have broken an implied pledge to avoid opportunistic conduct. . . . . Jordan's employment at will, the essential ingredient of our colleague's argument that Jordan waived the duty to disclose, does not establish that the firm had no duties concerning the stock.

The timing of the sale and the materiality of the information Duff & Phelps withheld on November 16 are for the jury to determine. Our dissenting colleague stresses that businesses would be shocked to learn that they must disclose valuable corporate information to fickle employees. If disclosure is unthinkable, however, Jordan may have trouble establishing that Duff & Phelps acted with intent to defraud, a necessary element of a case under *Rule 10b–5*. . . .

III

Jordan's complaint, as amended, asks for rescission of the sale of stock.

* * * *

Rescission entails the undoing of the deal, the return of the parties to the position they occupied before. Jordan quit on December 31, 1983, and moved to Houston. His employment was a quid pro quo for ownership of the stock. It is too late to restore his employment for 1984–86, and he has not offered to go back to work at Duff & Phelps if he wins the case. We therefore need not discuss whether a district court could force Duff & Phelps to take him back. Jordan is entitled only to damages, as his initial complaint requested. . . .

But what might the damages be? Judge Leinenweber held that there are none, as a matter of law, because the merger with Security Pacific fell through.

Doubtless the news of the deal with Security Pacific was the reason Jordan filed this suit. Yet the rationale of finding a securities violation—if there was one, a qualification we will not repeat—is that Jordan sold his stock in ignorance of facts that would have established a higher value. The relevance of the fact does not depend on how things turn out. Just as a lie that overstates a firm's prospects is a violation even if, against all odds, every fantasy comes true, *Escott v. BarChris Construction Corp.,* 283 F. Supp. 643, 669–70, 675 (S.D.N.Y. 1968), so a failure to disclose an important beneficent event is a violation even if things later go sour. The news, here that some firm was willing to pay $50 million for Duff & Phelps in an arms' length transaction, allows investors to assess the worth of the stock. If one deal for $50 million falls through, another may be possible at a similar price. Investors will either hold the stock or demand a price that reflects the value of that information. The conclusion that because the first deal collapsed there are no damages must reflect a belief that if the firm was not worth $50 million, then it was worth only $2.5 million (its book value). That is implausible. Security Pacific was willing to pay $50 million because, it concluded, Duff & Phelps was worth that much. If it was worth that much to Security Pacific, it was worth that much to someone else. Some value may be produced by interactions unique to Security Pacific, but there is no reason to think that Security Pacific would pay the investors of Duff & Phelps for the elements of value Security Pacific brought to the deal. The price of an asset usually is what the second-highest bidder will pay. So if Security Pacific bid $50 million, it believed that someone else would pay that much too (or that Duff & Phelps would hold out as part of a risky gaming strategy); otherwise Security Pacific would have bid less. The end of Security Pacific's bid—for reasons unrelated to a reassessment of the value of Duff & Phelps—therefore does not show that Jordan was uninjured. And less than a year later Duff & Phelps sold the firm to a trust (which is to say, to the syndicate of banks that loaned the money to the trust) for about $40 million.

The sticky problem is not whether Jordan can show some damages in principle but whether he can establish causation. . . . Because of the Agreement, employment and ownership of the shares were tied. Jordan could sell his stock in two ways: by leaving the firm and receiving book value, or by holding the stock until a merger or LBO and receiving the offered price. Even if the stock was worth more than book value, Jordan could not receive that price without holding on. So it seems that to recover, Jordan must establish that on learning of the negotiations with Security Pacific he would have dropped plans to go to Houston, and that even after the disappointment of the Fed's action that scuttled the deal with Security Pacific Jordan would have stuck around until the end of 1985, finally receiving the payment from the LBO. Judge Hart denied defendants' motion for summary judgment, holding that causation is a question for the jury. We think that right. Because a reasonable investor would not conclude that the withdrawal of one bid implies that there will be no others—and because Jordan would have known of the board's decision to sell the firm—a jury would be entitled to conclude that Jordan would have stuck around. Difficulties with a mother in law are a strain, but families bear strains greater than that for the prospect of financial gain.

* * * *

[A lengthy discussion of potential measures of damages is omitted.]

REVERSED AND REMANDED.

* * * *

DISSENT

POSNER, CIRCUIT JUDGE, dissenting.

A corporate employee at will quit, owning shares that he had agreed to sell back to the corporation at book value. The agreement was explicit that his status as a shareholder conferred no job rights on him. Nevertheless the court holds that the corporation had, as a matter of law, a duty, enforceable by proceedings under *Rule 10b–5* of the Securities Exchange Act, to volunteer to the employee information about the corporation's prospects that might have led him to change his mind about quitting, although as an employee at will he had no right to change his mind. I disagree with this holding. The terms of the stockholder agreement show that there was no duty of disclosure, and since there was no duty there was no violation of *Rule 10b–5.*

The plaintiff, a young man named Jordan, had gone to work for Duff and Phelps as a financial analyst. He had no employment contract; he was an employee at will. [*Citations omitted.*] As a junior executive he was permitted to buy modest quantities of stock in the company, which was (and is) closely held. He agreed that if he left the company, whether voluntarily or involuntarily, he would sell back his stock at its book value on the December 31 preceding or coinciding with the end of his employment.

After working for Duff and Phelps for six and a half years Jordan had accumulated about one percent of the company's stock. His stock had a book value on December 31, 1983, of $23,000 (I round all dollar figures to the nearest $1,000). Earlier in 1983 Jordan had decided to leave Chicago because his mother, who also lived in Chicago, didn't get along with his wife. After Duff and Phelps declined to move him to its only other office (Cleveland), he began to explore the possibility of leaving the firm. On November 11, 1983, he accepted a job in Houston, Texas, at a substantially higher salary than his salary at Duff and Phelps ($110,000 versus $67,000). On November 14 he told Hansen, the chief executive officer of Duff and Phelps, that he was quitting, and on November 16 handed him a letter of resignation. At Jordan's request, Hansen agreed that the resignation would not take effect till the end of the year, so that Jordan would get a higher price for his stock. Both men believed that the book value of the stock would be higher on December 31, 1983, than it had been on December 31, 1982, the relevant date if Jordan's resignation took effect before the end of the year.

Hansen did not reveal to Jordan that in the summer he and Jeffries (the other principal officer of Duff and Phelps) had negotiated with some executives at Security Pacific Corporation to sell Duff and Phelps to Security Pacific for $50 million; that had the deal gone through Jordan's stock would have been worth $640,000 rather than $23,000; that the deal had been nixed in August by higher levels of Security Pacific's management; but that the episode had so encouraged Hansen that at a meeting of the board of directors of Duff and Phelps on November 14 (just before Jordan came to him with the news that he was leaving) he had sought and obtained authority to make active efforts to sell the company.

Negotiations between Duff and Phelps and Security Pacific resumed in December. On December 30, Jordan, who knew nothing of the negotiations, delivered his shares to Duff and Phelps, as his agreement with the company required him to do. The resumed negotiations were successful, and resulted in an announcement in January (1984) that Security Pacific would buy Duff and Phelps for $50 million, contingent on regulatory approval. Shortly afterward Duff and Phelps sent Jordan a check for $23,000 in payment for his stock. Rather than cash the check Jordan brought this suit, seeking damages equal to the value of his stock if he hadn't quit Duff and Phelps and if the deal with Security Pacific went through. It didn't go through. It collapsed the following January when the Federal Reserve Board refused to approve it except on conditions that Security Pacific found too onerous. Jordan amended his complaint, dropping the claim for damages and asking instead for rescission of the sale of his stock to Duff and Phelps. Almost a year later, Duff and Phelps reorganized, and its shareholders exchanged their stock for a combination of cash, notes, and pension rights that Jordan believes to be worth about $40 million.

Rule 10b–5 forbids "fraud or deceit" in the sale or purchase of corporate securities. Jordan does not argue that Duff and Phelps made any misleading statements. He makes nothing of the fact that when he told Hansen he was quitting, Hansen said that the firm had a good potential for growth and that Jordan's shares would rise in value if he stayed. The target of the complaint is not misrepresentation or even misleading half-truths; it is Hansen's omission to tell Jordan that he should think twice about quitting since the company might soon be sold at a price that would increase the value of Jordan's stock almost 30-fold. The statement that Hansen failed to make may have been material, since it might have caused Jordan to change his mind about resigning. I say "may have been material" rather than "was material" because Hansen need not have allowed Jordan to change his mind about resigning. But I shall pass this point and assume materiality, in order to reach the more fundamental question, which is duty. "One who fails to disclose material information prior to the consummation of a transaction commits fraud only when he is under a duty to do so." *Chiarella v. United States,* 445 U.S. 222, 228, 63 L. Ed. 2d 348, 100 S. Ct. 1108 (1980).

We should ask why liability for failing to disclose, as distinct from liability for outright misrepresentation, depends on proof of duty. The reason is that information is a valuable commodity, and its production is discouraged if the producer must share it with the whole world. Hence an inventor is not required to blurt out his secrets, and a skilled investor is not required to disclose the results of his research and insights before he is able to profit from them. [*Citations omitted.*] But one who makes a contract, express or implied, to disclose information to another acts wrongfully if he then withholds the information. The question is whether Duff and Phelps made an undertaking, and therefore assumed a duty, to disclose to any stockholding employee who announced his resignation information regarding the prospects for a profitable sale of the company.

My brethren find such a duty implicit in the fiduciary relationship between a closely held corporation and its shareholders. By this approach, what should be the beginning of analysis becomes its end. A publicly held corporation is a fiduciary of its shareholders, too; yet if Duff and Phelps had been publicly held it would have had no duty to tell Jordan about the company's prospects of being sold. This is the "price and structure" rule, which this circuit adopted in *Flamm v. Eberstadt,* 814 F.2d 1169 (7th Cir. 1987)—rightly so, in my opinion. Thus the mere existence of a fiduciary relationship between a corporation and its shareholders does not require disclosure of material information to the shareholders. A further inquiry is necessary, and here must focus on the particulars of Jordan's relationship with Duff and Phelps.

The cases do not establish an automatic duty to disclose, even on the part of closely held corporations, though they are not sheltered by the "price and structure" rule. . . . *Michaels v. Michaels,* 767 F.2d 1185, 1192–93, 1197–98 (7th Cir. 1985), did find a duty, and it is the case most like the present one factually, because it involved a shareholder who, like Jordan, was also an employee. But his status as a shareholder, unlike Jordan's, was not contingent on his remaining an employee. The contingent nature of Jordan's status as a shareholder has a twofold significance. First, it raises a question about the applicability of the majority's rule requiring disclosure "in the course of negotiating to purchase stock." One may doubt whether there was any real negotiation in this case, for once Jordan resigned he was contractually obligated to sell back his stock at a predetermined price. Second, and more important, the contingent nature of Jordan's status as a shareholder negates the existence of a right to be informed and hence a duty to disclose. This point is central to my dissent and has now to be explained.

Jordan's deal with Duff and Phelps required him to surrender his stock at book value if he left the company. It didn't matter whether he quit or was fired, retired or died; the agreement is explicit on these matters. My brethren hypothesize "implicit parts of the relations between Duff & Phelps and its employees." But those relations are totally defined by (1) the absence of an employment contract, which made Jordan an employee at will; (2) the shareholder agreement, which has no "implicit parts" that bear on Duff and Phelps' duty to Jordan, and explicitly ties his rights as a shareholder to his status as an employee at will; (3) a provision in the stock purchase agreement between Jordan and Duff and Phelps (signed at the same time as the shareholder agreement) that "nothing herein contained shall confer on the Employee any right to be continued in the employment of the Corporation." There is no occasion to speculate about "the implicit understanding" between Jordan and Duff and Phelps. The parties left nothing to the judicial imagination. The effect of the shareholder and stock purchase agreements (which for simplicity I shall treat as a single "stockholder agreement"), against a background of employment at will, was to strip Jordan of any contractual protection against what happened to him, and indeed against worse that might have happened to him. Duff and Phelps points out that it would not have had to let Jordan withdraw his resignation had he gotten wind of the negotiations with Security Pacific and wanted to withdraw it. On November 14 Hansen could have said to Jordan, "I accept your resignation effective today; we hope to sell Duff and Phelps for $50 million but have no desire to see you participate in the resulting bonanza. You will receive the paltry book value of your shares as of December 31, 1982." The "nothing herein contained" provision in the stockholder agreement shows that this tactic is permitted. Equally, on November 14, at the board meeting before Hansen knew that Jordan wanted to quit, the board could have decided to fire Jordan in order to increase the value of the deal with Security Pacific to the remaining shareholders.

These possibilities eliminate any inference that the stockholder agreement obligated Duff and Phelps to inform Jordan about the company's prospects. Under the agreement, if Duff and Phelps didn't want to give him the benefit of the information all it had to do to escape any possible liability was to give Jordan the information and then fire him.

* * * *

My brethren correctly observe that, "Because the fiduciary duty is a standby or off-the-rack guess about what parties would agree to if they dickered about the subject explicitly, parties may contract with greater specificity for other arrangements." But, they add, "we need not decide how far contracts can redefine obligations to disclose. Jordan was an employee at will; he signed no contract." It is true that he signed no contract of employment, but he signed a stockholder agreement that defined his rights as a shareholder "with greater specificity." The agreement entitled Duff and Phelps to terminate Jordan as shareholder, subject only to a duty to buy back his shares at book value. The arrangement that resulted (call it "shareholder at will") is incompatible with an inference that Duff and Phelps undertook to keep him abreast of developments affecting the value of the firm.

* * * *

Since receipt of the information would have conferred no right on Jordan to benefit from the information, how can the parties be thought to have intended Duff and Phelps to have an enforceable duty to disclose the information to him? There is no duty to give shareholders information that they have no right to benefit from. [*Citations omitted.*] By signing the stockholder agreement Jordan gave Duff and Phelps in effect an option (as in *Nye*) to buy back his stock at any time at a fixed price. The grant of the option denied Jordan the right to profit from any information that the company might have about its prospects but prefer not to give him. If Hansen had known of the rule of law that my brethren adopt today, he could have avoided liability simply by telling

Jordan that, come what may, December 30 would be Jordan's last day working for Duff and Phelps. Failure to disclose would be immaterial because Jordan could not act on the disclosure. Only because Hansen failed to make Jordan's resignation effective immediately (a generous gesture, which we have given Hansen cause to regret), as he could have done without violating any contractual obligation, is he held to have violated a duty of disclosure.

The case would be different if Jordan had had an employment contract or if he had had the right to retain his stock after ceasing to be an employee. Then a right to information about the prospects of the company would have been meaningful. Such a right is not meaningful when the employee has no right to act on it. That was Jordan's position. The company could have told him everything yet still have prevented him from benefiting from the information, by firing him.

Was Jordan a fool to have become a shareholder of Duff and Phelps on such disadvantageous terms as I believe he agreed to? (If so, that might be a reason for doubting whether those were the real terms.) He was not. Few business executives in this country have contractual entitlements to earnings, bonuses, or even retention of their jobs. They would rather take their chances on their employer's good will and interest in reputation, and on their own bargaining power and value to the firm, than pay for contract rights that are difficult and costly to enforce. [*Citations omitted.*] If Jordan had had greater rights as a shareholder he would have had a lower salary; when he went to work for a new employer in Houston and received no stock rights he got a higher salary.

I go further: Jordan was protected by Duff and Phelps' own self-interest from being exploited. The principal asset of a service company such as Duff and Phelps is good will. It is a product largely of its employees' efforts and skills. If Jordan were a particularly valuable employee, so that the firm would be worth less without him, Hansen, desiring as he did to sell the firm for the highest possible price, would have told him about the prospects for selling the company. If Jordan was not a particularly valuable employee—if his departure would not reduce the value of the firm—there was no reason why he should participate in the profits from the sale of the firm, unless perhaps he had once been a particularly valuable employee but had ceased to be so. That possibility might, but did not, lead him to negotiate for an employment contract, or for stock rights that would outlast his employment. By the type of agreement that he made with Duff and Phelps, Jordan gambled that he was and would continue to be such a good employee that he would be encouraged to stay long enough to profit from the firm's growth. The relationship that the parties created aligned their respective self-interests better than the legal protections that the court devises today.

My brethren are well aware that Duff and Phelps faced market constraints against exploiting its employee shareholders, but seem to believe that this implies that the company also assumed contractual duties. Businessmen, however, are less enthusiastic about contractual duties than lawyers are, . . . so it is incorrect to infer from the existence of market constraints against exploitation that the parties also imposed a contractual duty against exploitation. Contractual obligation is a source of uncertainty and cost, and is therefore an expensive way of backstopping market forces. That is why employment at will is such a common form of employment relationship. It is strange to infer that firms invariably assume a legal obligation not to do what is not in their self-interest to do, and stranger to suppose—in the face of an explicit disclaimer—that by "allow[ing] employees to time their departures to obtain the maximum advantage from their stock," Duff and Phelps obligated itself to allow them to do this.

Having earlier in its opinion tried to get mileage out of the fact that Jordan "signed no [employment] contract," the majority later tries to get additional mileage from the observation that employment at will is a "contractual relation." This is the kind of legal half-truth that should make us thankful that our opinions are not subject to *Rule 10b–5*. Employment at will is a voluntary relationship, and thus contractual in the sense in which the word contract is used in the expression "freedom of contract." And the relationship can provide a framework for contracting: if Duff and Phelps had not paid Jordan his agreed-on wage after he had earned it, he could have sued the company for breach of contract. But the only element of employment at will that is relevant to this case is that employment at will is terminable at will, meaning that the employer can fire the employee without worrying about legal sanctions and likewise the employee can quit without worrying about them. Freedom of contract includes freedom not to contract.

* * * *

The inroads that the majority opinion makes on freedom of contract are not justified by its quotation from my academic writings concerning the purpose of contract law (which presupposes an agreement that the parties regard as legally enforceable) or by the possibility that corporations will exploit their junior executives, which may well be the least urgent problem facing our nation. The majority's statement that "one term implied in every written contract and therefore, we suppose, every unwritten one, is that neither party will try to take opportunistic advantage of the other" confuses the underlying rationale of contract law with the actual requirements of that law, and is anyway irrelevant since the parties decided not to subject the relevant parts of their relationship to the law of contracts and not to give Jordan any contractual protections against being fired. There was no "implied pledge to avoid opportunistic conduct" any more than there were "implicit parts of the relations" giving rise to contractual obligations.

* * * *

QUESTIONS

1. Following this case, how would you advise a corporate client in preliminary merger talks to handle the resignation of an employee who also held stock in the corporation?

2. How might Judges Easterbrook and Posner have ruled in the *Gallagher* case that precedes this one?

SECTION VI: Contractual Protections for Minority Shareholders

Experiencing Assignment 11: Growth, Inc.

Based upon your excellent work on the STI matter [the Assignment at the beginning of this chapter], you have been referred another client. You learn that the new client, Growth, Inc., has not yet been formed. It is being started by three individuals named Bill, Carl and Diane. Bill calls you (based on the recommendation of his good friend Brittney who works at STI) and provides you with the following background information. You schedule a meeting for the following week.

FACTS:

Growth, Inc., will manufacture, sell and distribute a "revolutionary" lawn care product that will keep grass healthy and green all year round. Once Growth Inc. is formed, Bill, Carl and Diane are each going to invest $50,000, quit their jobs and work for the company, full-time.

Bill has years of experience in the home care/improvement industry. He has worked in senior management for major corporations and also has marketing expertise. Carl has years of experience in research and development with advanced degrees in biology and a specialization in horticultural. Diane has years of experience in product development and a strong software engineering background. She also has an MBA.

Bill, Carl and Diane have been advised that it is wise to enter into a Shareholders Agreement before starting a business. They would like your assistance and guidance with various provisions. They would like to meet with you to discuss creating an agreement that meets the needs of Growth Inc. and the needs of each of the three founders. In addition, Bill has emailed you a few specific questions.

> *Dear Legal Advisor:*
>
> *Before our meeting next week, I just wanted you to be aware of a few of my concerns. I am sure that Carl and Diane will have additional and/or similar concerns, but I thought these might help focus our discussion.*
>
> *What happens if I need money and want to sell my stock (or a portion of my stock) to someone else?*
>
> *If I am injured or if I die, will my family be able to share in the value of the business that I have helped build?*
>
> *What happens if Carl, Diane and I disagree?*
>
> *Can I be fired?*
>
> *Are there specific issues that we want to make sure we address in the agreement that I haven't already mentioned?*
>
> *Thank you for your time,*
>
> *Bill*

ASSIGNMENT:

Please prepare an outline for your meeting with Bill, Carl and Diane. Your outline should be brief, but it should include suggestions for Bill, Carl and Diane that address Bill's questions. You should assume that Bill, Carl and Diane recognize that you cannot determine for them the exact provisions that they might want to include in a Shareholder Agreement. Rather, they would like suggestions of provisions that might address their concerns. They also do not want you to draft any specific provisions. They just want your suggestions and an explanation of the issues that the provisions you suggest might address.

This Assignment does not need to be completed, and should not be completed, until the end of this section. However, as you study the materials case that follow, it might be helpful to do so with a view toward providing assistance to Bill, Carl and Diane. Please keep Bill's questions and the issues that you might want to include in a Shareholder Agreement in mind while reading the *Frandsen v. Jensen-Sundquist Agency, Inc.* case that follows.

A. Shareholder Agreements

A minority shareholder, who is concerned about being frozen out, has very limited options. In most closely held corporations there is no market for shares in the corporation. There is even less of a market for shares in a corporation held by someone who is already, or could be, frozen out. Shareholders facing this situation might be able to acquire some level of protection through agreement or through provisions placed in the corporation's governing documents. Some of the options for minority shareholders fearing a freeze out or concerned about protecting themselves against freeze outs might include: a shareholder agreement protecting the minority shareholder's right to be on the board of directors and/or (if all the other shareholders agree) to be an officer; an employment agreement, assuring the minority shareholder of a certain position with the corporation and a salary; a buyout agreement (or a shareholder agreement containing buy out provisions), entitling the minority shareholder to force the company to buy his or her shares under certain circumstances, such as a freeze out; a contractual right for the minority shareholder to require the dissolution of the corporation; and/or mandatory dividend requirements. (Provisions requiring that certain dividends be paid might be included in the corporation's Articles of Incorporation.)

The following case presents just one example of protections that are sometimes instituted by a minority shareholder and of the efforts a majority shareholder might sometimes take in order to avoid those protections.

Frandsen v. Jensen-Sundquist Agency, Inc.

802 F.2d 941 (7th Cir. 1986)

POSNER, C.J.:

The appeals in this diversity suit require us to consider issues of Wisconsin contract and tort law in the setting of a dispute over the rights of a minority shareholder in a closely held corporation. The facts are as follows. In 1975 Walter Jensen owned all the stock of Jensen-Sundquist Agency, Inc., a holding company whose principal asset was a majority of the stock of the First Bank of Grantsburg; Jensen-Sundquist also owned a small insurance company. That year Jensen sold 52 percent of his stock in the holding company to members of his family—the "majority bloc," as we shall call them and the interest they acquired; 8 percent to Dennis Frandsen, a substantial businessman who was not a member of Jensen's family and who paid Jensen $97,000 for the stock; and the rest, in smaller chunks, to other non-family members. By a stockholder agreement drafted by Jensen and a lawyer representing the bank and Jensen's family, the majority bloc agreed "that should they at any time offer to sell their stock in Jensen-Sundquist, Inc., . . . they will first offer their stock to (Frandsen and six other shareholders who had negotiated for this provision) at the same price as may be offered to (the majority bloc) . . . and . . . they will not sell their stock to any other person, firm, or organization without first offering said stock" to these minority shareholders "at the same price and upon the same terms." The majority bloc also agreed not to "sell any of their shares to anyone without at the same time offering to purchase all the shares of" these minority shareholders "at the same price." Thus if the majority bloc offered to sell its shares it had to give Frandsen a right to buy the shares at the offer price. If Frandsen declined, the second protective provision came into play: the majority bloc had to offer to buy his shares at the same price at which it sold its own shares.

In 1984 the president of Jensen-Sundquist began discussions with First Wisconsin Corporation, Wisconsin's largest bank holding company, looking to the acquisition by First Wisconsin of First Bank of Grantsburg, Jensen-Sundquist's principal property. A price of $88 per share of stock in the First Bank of Grantsburg was agreed to in principle. The acquisition was to be effected (we simplify slightly) by First Wisconsin's buying Jensen-Sundquist for cash, followed by a merger of First Bank of Grantsburg into a bank subsidiary of First Wisconsin. Each stockholder of Jensen-Sundquist would receive $62 per share, which would translate into $88 per share of the bank. (The reasons that the share values were not the same were that there were more holding company shares than bank shares and that the holding company had another asset besides the bank—the insurance company.) Jensen-Sundquist asked each of the minority shareholders to sign a waiver of any rights he "may have" in the transaction, rights arising from the stockholder agreement, but advised each shareholder that in counsel's opinion the shareholder had no rights other than to receive $62 per share.

Each of the minority shareholders except Frandsen signed or was expected to sign the waiver. Frandsen not only refused to sign but announced that he was exercising his right of first refusal and would buy the majority bloc's shares at $62 a share. (He also offered to buy out the other minority shareholders.) The majority did not want to sell its shares to him—Frandsen says because the president of Jensen-Sundquist, who was also the chairman of the board of First Bank of Grantsburg and a member of the majority bloc, was afraid he would lose his job if Frandsen took over. The deal was restructured. Jensen-Sundquist agreed to sell its shares in First Bank of Grantsburg to First Wisconsin at $88 a share and then liquidate, so that in the end all the stockholders would end up with cash plus the insurance company and First Wisconsin would end up with the bank, which was all it had ever wanted out of the deal. All this was done over Frandsen's protest. he then brought this suit against the majority bloc, charging breach of the stockholder agreement, and against First Wisconsin, charging tortious interference with his contract rights. The district judge granted summary judgment for the defendants and Frandsen appeals.

* * * *

The case would be easy if the transaction had been structured from the start as a simple acquisition by First Wisconsin of First Bank of Grantsburg from Jensen-Sundquist. Nothing in the stockholder agreement suggests that any minority shareholder has the right to block the sale by Jensen-Sundquist of any of its assets, including its principal asset, a controlling interest in First Bank of Grantsburg. The right of first refusal is a right to buy the shares of the majority bloc in Jensen-Sundquist if they are offered for sale, and there would be no offer of sale if Jensen-Sundquist simply sold some or for that matter all of its assets and became an investment company instead of a bank holding company. Nor did the contract entitle Frandsen to insist that the deal be configured so as to trigger his right of first refusal. [*Citations omitted.*]

The case is a little harder because the transaction was originally configured as a purchase of the holding company rather than just of the bank, an asset of the holding company. . . . And Frandsen points out that under the stockholder agreement his right of first refusal was triggered by an *offer*, so that the fact the offer was later withdrawn would not affect his right of first refusal if he had already tried to exercise it—and he had tried, before the defendants reconfigured the transaction. But the point is academic, because we agree with the district judge that there never was an offer within the scope of the agreement. The part of the agreement that grants a right of first refusal refers to an offer to sell "their stock," and to a sale of "their stock," and the "their" refers to the majority shareholders. They never offered to sell their stock to First Wisconsin. First Wisconsin was not interested in becoming a majority shareholder of Jensen-

Sundquist, in owning an insurance company, and in dealing with Frandsen and the other minority shareholders. It just wanted the bank.

What is more, a sale of stock was never contemplated, again for the reason that First Wisconsin was not interested in becoming a shareholder of Jensen-Sundquist. The transaction originally contemplated was a merger of Jensen-Sundquist into First Wisconsin. In a merger, as the word implies, the acquired firm disappears as a distinct legal entity. [*Citations omitted.*] In effect, the shareholders of the merged firm yield up all of the assets of the firm, receiving either cash or securities in exchange, and the firm dissolves. [*Citations omitted.*] In this case the shareholders would have received cash. Their shares would have disappeared but not by sale, for in a merger the shares of the acquired firm are not bought, they are extinguished. There would have been no Jensen-Sundquist after the merger, and no shareholders in Jensen-Sundquist.

The distinction between a sale of shares and a merger is such a familiar one in the business world that it is unbelievable that so experienced a businessman as Frandsen would have overlooked it. It is true that he was not represented by a lawyer in connection with the stockholder agreement, but when an experienced businessman deliberately eschews legal assistance in making a contract he cannot by doing so obtain a legal advantage over a represented party should a dispute arise.

Nor are we persuaded by Frandsen's argument that if interpreted literally the stockholder agreement gave him no right of first refusal worthy of the name. It is true that under that interpretation if as happened the majority bloc did not want to sell out to him, all it had to do was find a merger partner. But these alternatives are not identical in all but from, as he argues. The majority bloc was only 52 percent. If the majority wanted to sell its stock to someone who wanted a controlling interest in the company rather than the company itself or an asset of the company such as the First Bank of Grantsburg, it had to offer its shares to Frandsen first (and to the other six minority shareholders who had a right of first refusal—what would have happened if all had exercised their right we need not speculate about). If it wanted to bypass Frandsen it had to find someone willing to buy not just its shares, but the company.

Most important, Frandsen may have been concerned not with a sale of the company itself at a price agreeable to a majority and therefore likely to be attractive to him as well, but with a sale of the majority bloc that would leave him a minority shareholder in a company owned by strangers. The lot of a minority shareholder in a closely held company is not an enviable one, even in the best of circumstances. A majority coalition may gang up on him. And he may not have the usual recourse of a victimized minority shareholder—to sell out. For there may be no market for his shares, except the very people who have ganged up on him. See Easterbrook & Fischel, *Close Corporations and Agency Costs,* 38 Stan. L. Rev. 271 (1986); William A. Gregory, *Stock Transfer Restrictions in Close Corporations,* 1978 So. Ill. U. L.J. 477. Frandsen may just have wanted to protect himself against being put at the mercy of a new and perhaps hostile majority bloc. The right of first refusal was one protection against this danger.

Against this Frandsen argues that the right of first refusal must have had an additional purpose, for otherwise it would merely have duplicated the second protective provision in the stockholder agreement, which guaranteed that the majority bloc if it sold its shares would offer to buy his shares at the same price. It is true that this provision protected Frandsen against finding himself a minority shareholder in a company controlled by persons other than the members of the original majority bloc, but it did so at the price of forcing him to leave the company. The right of first refusal enabled him to remain in the company by buying out the majority bloc at the same price that the bloc was willing to sell its shares to others. It thus gave him additional protection. It did not give him protection against a sale of the company itself but this does not make the agreement incoherent or unclear, for his only concern may have been with the possibility of finding himself confronted with a new majority bloc, and that is the only possibility he may have thought it important to negotiate with reference to.

We note in this connection that Frandsen himself had once taken over a bank by paying a premium to a majority of shareholders and then, after he acquired control in this way, buying out the minority shareholders at a lower price. Evidently he wanted to make sure that no one did this to him in Jensen-Sundquist by buying the majority bloc and then making life uncomfortable for him and the other minority shareholders so that they would sell their shares on the cheap. The stockholder agreement that he negotiated with Jensen was well designed to protect him against a maneuver that he had practiced himself. The defendants' efforts to get Frandsen to sign a waiver do not as he argues establish a practical construction of the stockholder agreement as entitling him to exercise his right of first refusal in the event of a proposed merger. A waiver is like a quitclaim deed: the signer waives whatever rights he may have, but does not warrant that he has any rights to waive.

Frandsen's principal argument is that the word "sell" is sufficiently ambiguous to embrace a disposition that has the same practical effect as a sale of the majority bloc's shares. This may be; *Wilson v. Whinery,* 37 Wash. App. 24,

28–29, 678 P.2d 354, 357 (1984), held that a transfer of all beneficial use of parcel B, "thereby granting (the transferee) substantial control over parcel B," was a sale of B for purposes of a right of first refusal triggered by such a sale. But our main point has been that a sale of the majority bloc's shares is not the same thing as a sale of either all or some of the holding company's assets. The sale of assets does not result in substituting a new majority bloc, and that is the possibility at which the protective provisions are aimed. This appears with sufficient clarity, moreover, to justify the district judge's refusal to go outside the text of the contract to find its meaning.

Any lingering doubts of the propriety of this course are dispelled by the rule that rights of first refusal are to be interpreted narrowly. [*Citations omitted.*] This may seem to be one of those fusty "canons of construction" that invite ridicule because they have no basis and contradict each other and are advanced simply as rhetorical flourishes to embellish decisions reached on other, more practical grounds. [*Citations omitted.*] But actually it makes some sense. The effect of a right of first refusal is to add a party to a transaction, for the right is triggered by an offer of sale, and the effect is therefore to inject the holder of the right into the sale transaction. Adding a party to a transaction increases the costs of transacting exponentially; the formula for the number of links required to connect up all the members of an n-member set is n(n–1)/2, meaning that, for example, increasing the number of parties to a transaction from three to four increases the number of required linkages from three to six. Certainly the claim of a right of first refusal complicated the transaction here! If all the costs of the more complicated transaction were borne by the parties, it would hardly be a matter of social concern. But some of the costs are borne by the taxpayers who support the court system, and the courts are not enthusiastic about this, and have decided not to be hospitable to such rights. The right is enforceable but only if the contract clearly confers it.

* * * *

The district judge correctly dismissed all of Frandsen's claims.

AFFIRMED.

NOTES AND QUESTIONS

1. Why do you think the Jensen family sold its stock in the business to "non-family" members?

2. Why would they have given Frandsen and the other shareholders a right of first refusal?

3. The portion of the agreement in which the "majority bloc" agreed not to "sell any of their shares to anyone without at the same time offering to purchase all the shares of" the minority shareholders "at the same price" is commonly known as a "tag along" right. Why would such a right be important to a minority shareholder?

4. Why would a purchaser wish to buy only a portion of the stock of a corporation?

5. Shareholder agreements might involve a variety of provisions and protections. Some of the management and control provisions that might be included in such an agreement are discussed case above. The *Frandsen* case presents examples of a right of first refusal provision and a "tag along" provision. Other provisions commonly included in shareholder agreements might include: (1) the right to repurchase a shareholder's stock if that shareholder is no longer "employed" by the company; (2) the right to repurchase a shareholder's stock upon the shareholder's death or disability; (3) the requirement that in any divorce a shareholder repurchase any ownership interest that might be held by his or her spouse; (4) the right to require all shareholders to approve a sale of the company if a majority of the shareholders approve the sale (sometimes called a "drag along" right); (5) a buy-sell agreement (allowing one shareholder to establish a value for the company and then force the other shareholders to elect to either buy his shares at that price or sell him their shares at that price); (6) additional restrictions on transfer (including providing for certain "approved" transfers that might not be subject to those restrictions or to rights of first refusal or tag along rights); and (7) non-compete provisions (even some states that restrict the use of non-compete clauses will allow owners of a business to agree to not compete with that business for a reasonable period of time after leaving the business).

CHAPTER EIGHT

Securities Laws

ONE DAY YOU ARE SITTING in your office working on a term sheet for your client, Bayou Corporation ("BC"), a publicly traded company. BC is a major manufacturer, distributor and retail seller of furniture products in the U.S. and is planning to acquire one of its competitors, Byeme, Inc. ("BI"). BI is also publicly traded, but it is a much smaller company. BC has a market capitalization of approximately $1 billion, while BI has a market capitalization of $100 million. There have been rumors that BC is going to acquire a competitor, but these rumors have never been publicly confirmed. The term sheet on which you are working involves BC acquiring BI in a friendly merger for $115 million in a combination of cash and BC stock. While you are working, you get an e-mail marked "URGENT" from the president of BC, Sally Short.

Experiencing Assignment 12: Publicity Problems

FACTS:

A reporter has approached Sally and told her that a very respected securities analyst is going to downgrade BC's stock. This downgrade is based upon the fact that BC makes and sells wooden furniture but not plastic or metal. A large percentage of BC's furniture is imported from China. The analyst has determined that a shift in consumer demand, regulatory restrictions, tariffs and investigations (currently going on) into imports of Chinese furniture have the potential to significantly increase the costs of BC's products. All of these are actual risk factors of which BC is aware, and some or all of them are likely to occur. In fact, they form the basis for BC's desire to acquire BI. BI products are, primarily, made in the U.S. and are made of plastic, metal or other materials. They will fill the gap in BC's product line and will be a good defense against shifts in the market.

The reporter has asked Sally to comment on whether the rumors of BC looking for an acquisition target are true; whether that target is BI; and whether

BC has comments about the analyst's report. Unfortunately, a BC senior vice president, Charlie Chatterbox, who knows about the merger plans, has already commented to the reporter, saying: "I don't know of any specific merger plans. Don't you think I would know if we had an agreement to acquire BI?" Since the terms of the merger have not quite been finalized, Charlie's comments are technically true, but you are about to finalize the terms that should create the final agreement in the next few days, maybe weeks. Unfortunately, if the analyst's downgrade comes out without comment from BC, Sally believes that BC's stock price will drop significantly, making it much harder to complete the transaction with BI. However, Sally is also concerned about securities laws restrictions and an agreement between BI and BC to keep the merger discussions confidential.

ASSIGNMENT:

The partner in your firm dealing with this matter has just had back surgery (a result of spending too many years sitting at his desk), and is completely unavailable for the next few days. Sally needs a response in a few hours. Please give Sally your advice about how she should respond to the reporter, and, if you determine it is appropriate, draft a brief response to the reporter. In addition, please tell Sally of the risks with respect to the securities laws for any course of action you recommend.

This Assignment does not need to be completed, and should not be completed, until the end of the section. However, as you study the cases and other materials that follow, it might be helpful to do so with a view toward providing counsel to Sally and BC. Some of the materials in the chapter will relate more than others to the issues facing BC. However, the materials are designed to build your understanding of the securities law issues that arise in evaluating public disclosures or omissions relating to a corporation's securities and assist you in addressing Sally's concerns and putting them in context. Please keep these issues and the questions presented by the assignment in mind while reading the materials that follow.

SECTION I: Securities Laws

The securities laws in the United States are detailed and complex. In fact, there is an entire law school course focused only on these laws. However, any class on business associations should provide an introduction to these laws and highlight certain securities rules and regulations since securities represent and define the ownership structure of the corporation. Securities laws set forth parameters by which directors and officers must conduct themselves when the corporation's securities are involved. The basic areas of focus in a business associations course often involve anti-fraud legislation in or arising under, the Securities Act of 1933 and the Securities Exchange Act of 1934 (referred to as the "1933 Act" and the "1934 Act," respectively). A primary effort of these securities laws is to promote full disclosure and prevent "fraud." In order for these laws to apply to a given situation, a "security" must be involved. This might seem like a simple matter. However, because the securities laws provide such powerful tools, it becomes a critical question to determine when they apply. As a result there has been a lot of litigation over just what constitutes a "security."

A. What Is a Security?

There are certain specific "instruments," such as shares of stock, which are almost always considered to be securities. However, there are other situations in which an instrument, contract, scheme or structure needs to be evaluated to determine if it indeed qualifies as a "security." In general, unless an instrument is already considered to be a security (such as stock), the circumstances surrounding the transaction must be evaluated. A typical transaction involving a security is one in which an investment is made with another person, or entity, from which the investor expects to profit, based on the efforts of others.

Section 2(1) of the 1933 Act lists two broad categories of instruments which qualify as a security. There are specific instruments that automatically (or almost automatically) qualify as a security in one category and some general "catchall" definitions in the other category. Some of the specific instruments include stock, notes, bonds, debentures, options, and voting trust certificates. The general definitions of a security also include more general terms that classify certain categories of financial instruments as securities, such as "*evidence of indebtedness*" and "*investment contracts*."

Finally, the securities definition in the 1933 Act includes any instrument that is "commonly known as a 'security.' " In addition, the case law "clarifies" that the items listed are considered securities under § 2(1) of the 1933 Act, *unless* context requires otherwise. When trying to identify if a scheme, contract or instrument qualifies as a "security," one might look for the presence of some the following features which are characteristics of typical securities: the right to receive dividends contingent upon an apportionment of profits; negotiability; the ability to be pledged or hypothecated; voting rights which accompany an instrument and correspond to the number of shares (or other form of interest) owned; and/or the ability to appreciate in value.

In evaluating an instrument, context is important and could lead a court to find something is or is not a security. Often, when an instrument is not included on the list of specific instruments, someone will argue that it falls into one of the general categories, often the "investment contract" category. In order to evaluate if something is an investment contract there are four requirements (known as the "*Howey Test,*" *S.E.C. v. W.J. Howey, Co.,* 328 U.S. 293, 298–99, 90 L. Ed. 1244, 66 S. Ct. 1100 (1946)). First, there must be a contract, transaction, or scheme through which a person invests money (or any other consideration). Second, the investment must be made into a common enterprise (either with "horizontal commonality" in which the investment is made with others or, in some circuits, but not all, with "vertical commonality" in which the investment is made with a promoter who is working to make money for the investor). Third, there must be an expectation of profits (or some other financial benefits). Fourth, the profits must come "solely" from the efforts of others. This "efforts of others" clause is intended to include the requirement that the investor NOT participate in the operation of the investment opportunity. To expect profit (or financial benefit) based on the efforts of others means that the investor is depending upon the work, skill, expertise and/or efforts of people other than him or herself to produce the profitable result. However, most courts interpret the word "solely," in this context, to mean "primarily."

Securities and Exchange Commission v. Life Partners, Inc.

87 F.3d 536 (D.C. Cir. 1996)

GINSBURG, C.J.:

A viatical settlement is an investment contract pursuant to which an investor acquires an interest in the life insurance policy of a terminally ill person—typically an AIDS victim—at a discount of 20 to 40 percent, depending upon the insured's life expectancy. When the insured dies, the investor receives the benefit of the insurance. The investor's profit is the difference between the discounted purchase price paid to the insured and the death benefit collected from the insurer, less transaction costs, premiums paid, and other administrative expenses.

Life Partners, Inc., under the direction of its former president and current chairman Brian Pardo, arranges these transactions and performs certain post-transaction administrative services. The SEC contends that the fractional interests marketed by LPI are securities, and that LPI violated the Securities Act of 1933 and the Securities Exchange Act of 1934 by selling them without first complying with the registration and other requirements of those Acts. The district court agreed and preliminarily enjoined LPI from making further sales.

* * * *

We agree with the district court that viatical settlements are not exempt from the securities laws as insurance contracts. Contrary to the district court, however, we conclude that LPI's contracts are not securities subject to the federal securities laws because the profits from their purchase do not derive predominantly from the efforts of a party or parties other than the investors.

I. Background

* * * *

LPI sells fractional interests in insurance policies to retail investors, who may pay as little as $650 and buy as little as 3% of the benefits of a policy. In order to reach its customers, LPI uses some 500 commissioned "licensees," mostly independent financial planners. For its efforts, LPI's net compensation is roughly 10% of the purchase price after payment of referral and other fees.

* * * *

Both LPI's program for individual investors and its IRA program have gone through three iterations during the course of this litigation. In each, LPI performed or performs a number of pre-purchase functions: Specifically, even before assembling the investors, LPI evaluates the insured's medical condition, reviews his insurance policy, negotiates the purchase price, and prepares the legal documents. The difference among the three versions is that LPI performs ever fewer (and ultimately no) post-purchase functions.

In Version I, the program that was the subject of the district court's August 1995 order, LPI or Pardo could appear, and continue to appear after the investors had purchased their interests, in an insurance company's records as the owner of a policy; LPI insists, however, that this practice was adopted not because LPI had any continuing entrepreneurial role to play but only at the urging of the insurance companies for their administrative convenience; the investor was at all times the legal owner. Also, once an investor acquired an interest in a policy he could avail himself of LPI's on-going administrative services, which included monitoring the insured's health, assuring that the policy did not lapse, converting a group policy into an individual policy where required, and arranging for resale of the investor's interest when so requested and feasible.

Sterling Trust Company, an independent escrow agent acting for LPI, actually performed most of these post-purchase administrative functions. When the purchase closed, Sterling collected its own fee and that of LPI, escrowed funds for expected premium payments, and delivered the balance to the seller. Thereafter Sterling held the policy, held and disbursed all funds, ensured that all paperwork was in order, and filed the death claim. If an investor designated Sterling as the beneficiary, then Sterling also collected and distributed the death benefits. LPI had no continuing economic interest in the transaction after receipt of its fee upon the sale to the investor.

Between the district court's August 1995 and January 1996 orders, LPI implemented revised procedures in an unsuccessful effort to meet the objections raised by the SEC and upheld by the court. In this Version II, neither LPI nor Pardo appeared as the owner of record of the insurance policy; instead, the investors were at all times the owners of record and thus had a direct contractual relationship with the insurance company. . . .

Finally, in yet a further attempt to allay the concerns of the SEC and of the district court, LPI in February 1996 unveiled Version III. Pardo would resign as president of LPI in favor of Mike Posey, the former president of Sterling. More important, LPI declared that it would no longer provide any post-purchase services to purchasers either directly or indirectly (*i.e.,* through an agent such as Sterling). All such services would become the sole responsibility of the investor; Sterling would still be available to provide services as the agent of the investor if the investor elected to contract with Sterling for that purpose. The district court rejected this proposal in its March 1996 order.

II. Analysis

We take up first LPI's opening argument that viatical settlements are insurance contracts and therefore entitled to an exemption from the 1933 Act. Finding that argument wanting, we proceed to consider whether the fractional interests promoted by LPI are "securities" within the meaning of that Act using the three-part test prescribed in *SEC v. W.J. Howey Co.,* 328 U.S. 293, 90 L. Ed. 1244, 66 S. Ct. 1100 (1946), in which each investor acquired an individual parcel of citrus fruit acreage together with a portion of the profits arising from the promoter's management of the citrus grove. . . . The Supreme Court held in *Howey* that an investment contract is a security if the investors (1) expect profits from (2) a common enterprise that (3) depends upon the efforts of others. . . . Because LPI's contracts fail the third element of this test, we hold that they are not securities. . . .

* * * *

B. The Three-Part Test of Howey

We turn next to the question whether the LPI contracts are properly characterized as securities within the terms of the 1933 Act. That determination is controlled by the Supreme Court's decision in *Howey* which, as stated above, holds that an investment contract is a security subject to the Act if investors purchase with (1) an expectation of profits arising from (2) a common enterprise that (3) depends upon the efforts of others. . . . To the extent practical we examine each component of the test separately.

1. *Expectation of Profits*

* * * *

. . . LPI maintains that under *United Housing Foundation, Inc. v. Forman,* 421 U.S. 837, 852, 44 L. Ed. 2d 621, 95 S. Ct. 2051 (1975), profits must be derived from "either capital appreciation resulting from the development of the initial investment . . . or a participation in earnings resulting from the use of the investors' funds," neither of which obtains with respect to viatical contracts.

* * * *

The Court's general principle we think, is only that the expected profits must, in conformity with ordinary usage, be in the form of a financial return on the investment, not in the form of consumption. This principle distinguishes between buying a note secured by a car and buying the car itself.

The asset acquired by an LPI investor is a claim on future death benefits. The buyer is obviously purchasing not for consumption—unmatured claims cannot be currently consumed—but rather for the prospect of a return on his investment. As we read the *Forman* gloss on *Howey,* that is enough to satisfy the requirement that the investment be made in the expectation of profits.

2. *Common Enterprise*

The second element of the *Howey* test for a security is that there be a "common enterprise." So-called horizontal commonality—defined by the pooling of investment funds, shared profits, and shared losses—is ordinarily sufficient to satisfy the common enterprise requirement. . . . Here, LPI brings together multiple investors and aggregates their funds to purchase the death benefits of an insurance policy. If the insured dies in a relatively short time, then the investors realize profits; if the insured lives a relatively long time, then the investors may lose money or at best fail to realize the return they had envisioned;

i.e., they experience a loss of the return they could otherwise have realized in some alternative investment of equivalent risk. Any profits or losses from an LPI contract accrue to all of the investors in that contract; *i.e.,* it is not possible for one investor to realize a gain or loss without each other investor gaining or losing proportionately, based upon the amount that he invested. In that sense, the outcomes are shared among the investors; the sum that each receives is a predetermined portion of the aggregate death benefit.

LPI claims, however, that there is no pooling and therefore no shared profits or losses because each investor acquires his own interest in the policy. Moreover, there is no requirement that the entire policy be purchased. It seems to us that the pooling issue reduces to the question whether there is a threshold percentage of a policy that must be sold before an investor can be assured that his purchase of a smaller percentage interest will be consummated. If not, then each investor's acquisition is independent of all the other investors' acquisitions and LPI is correct in asserting that there is no pooling. On the other hand, if LPI must have investors ready to buy some minimum percentage of the policy before the transaction will occur, then the investment is contingent upon a pooling of capital.

When we raised this point at oral argument, the SEC contended that inter-dependency among investors was not necessary to a determination that their funds are pooled; the test, according to the Commission, is whether the funds are "commingled." In this context, however, commingling in itself is but an administrative detail; it is the inter-dependency of the investors that transforms the transaction substantively into a pooled investment. (Indeed, if the investments are inter-dependent, it would not matter if LPI scrupulously avoided commingling the investors' funds—for example, by passing their checks directly to the seller at the closing.) . . . . Many of the post-purchase administrative functions (*e.g.,* monitoring the insured's health, collecting the death benefit) involve costs that are seemingly invariant to the number of investors or the percentage of a policy that has been sold. Neither LPI nor the investors would be anxious to spread these costs over contracts representing much less than the full value of a policy.

Therefore, we think that pooling is in practice an essential ingredient of the LPI program; that is, any individual investor would find that the profitability if not the completion of his or her purchase depends upon the completion of the larger deal. Because LPI's viatical settlements entail this implicit form of pooling, and because any profits or losses accrue to all investors (in proportion to the amount invested), we conclude that all three elements of horizontal commonality—pooling, profit sharing, and loss sharing—attend the purchase of a fractional interest through LPI. (We need not reach, therefore, the SEC's alternate contention that the LPI program entails "strict vertical commonality"—another formulation of the common enterprise test recognized in some circuits. . .)

* * * *

3. *Profits Derived Predominantly from the Efforts of Others*

The final requirement of the *Howey* test for an investment to be deemed a security is that the profits expected by the investor be derived from the efforts of others. In this connection, the SEC suggests that investors in LPI's viatical settlements are essentially passive; their profits, the Commission argues, depend predominantly upon the efforts of LPI, which provides pre-purchase expertise in identifying existing policyholders and, together with Sterling, provides post-purchase management of the investment. Meanwhile, LPI argues that its pre-purchase functions are wholly irrelevant and that the post-purchase functions, by whomever performed, should not count because they are only ministerial. On this view, once the transaction closes, the investors do not look to the efforts of others for their profits because the only variable affecting profits is the timing of the insured's death, which is outside of LPI's and Sterling's control.

By its terms *Howey* requires that profits be generated "solely" from the efforts of others. . . . Although the lower courts have given the Supreme Court's definition of a security broader sweep by requiring that profits be generated only "predominantly" from the efforts of others [*Citations omitted.*], they have never suggested that purely ministerial or clerical functions are by themselves sufficient; indeed, quite the opposite is true. *See, e.g., SEC v. Koscot Interplanetary, Inc.*, 497 F.2d 473, 483 (5th Cir. 1974); *SEC v. Glenn W. Turner Enterprises, Inc.*, 474 F.2d 476, 482 (9th Cir. 1973) (efforts of others must be "undeniably significant ones, those essential managerial efforts which affect the failure or success of the enterprise"). Because post-purchase entrepreneurial activities are the "efforts of others" most obviously relevant to the question whether a promoter is selling a "security," we turn first to the distinction between those post-purchase functions that are entrepreneurial and those that are ministerial. . . .

Ministerial versus entrepreneurial functions, post-purchase. In Version I of its program, LPI and not the investor could appear as the owner of record of the insurance policy. LPI's ownership gave it the ability, post-purchase, to change the party designated as the beneficiary of the policy, indeed to substitute itself as beneficiary. That ability tied the fortunes of the investors more closely to those of LPI in the sense that it made the investors dependent upon LPI's continuing to deal honestly with them, at least to the extent of not wrongfully dropping them as beneficiaries.

This does not, however, establish an association between the profits of the investors and the "efforts" of LPI. Nothing that LPI could do by virtue of its record ownership had any effect whatsoever upon the near-exclusive determinant of the investors' rate of return, namely how long the insured survives. . . . Such a possibility provides no basis upon which to distinguish securities from non-securities. The promoter's "efforts" not to engage in criminal or tortious behavior, or not to breach its contract are not the sort of entrepreneurial exertions that the *Howey* Court had in mind when it referred to profits arising from "the efforts of others."

In Version II LPI no longer appeared as the record owner of a policy, but LPI and Sterling continued to offer the following post-purchase services: holding the policy, monitoring the insured's health, paying premiums, converting a group policy into an individual policy where required, filing the death claim, collecting and distributing the death benefit (if requested), and assisting an investor who might wish to resell his interest. LPI characterizes these functions as clerical and routine in nature, not managerial or entrepreneurial, and therefore unimportant to the source of investor expectations; in sum, anyone including the investor himself could supply these services. The district court seemed to agree with LPI about the character if not the significance of most post-purchase services, for it described them as "often ministerial in nature."

The Commission disputes the district court's characterization of post-purchase services as ministerial, but attempts to portray only one service in particular as entrepreneurial: we refer to the secondary market that LPI purportedly makes. By establishing a resale market, according to the SEC, LPI links the profitability of the investments it sells to the success of its own efforts. We find this argument unconvincing for several reasons. . . .

LPI's promise of help in arranging for the resale of a policy is not an adequate basis upon which to conclude that the fortunes of the investors are tied to the efforts of the company, much less that their profits derive "predominantly" from those efforts.

In Version III LPI provides no post-purchase services. All such services are the sole responsibility of the investors, who may purchase them from

Sterling or not, as they choose. The district court minimized the significance of this choice, stating that "it is neither realistic nor feasible for multiple investors, who are strangers to each other, to perform post-purchase tasks without relying on the knowledge and expertise of a third party [and] the third party in this case will almost certainly be Sterling." Even if we accept this assessment, it does not alter our analysis. As we have seen, none of Sterling's post-purchase services can meaningfully affect the profitability of the investment. It is therefore of no moment whether Sterling performs those services usually or always, or whether it does so as the agent of LPI or as the agent of the investor.

In sum, the SEC has not identified any significant non-ministerial service that LPI or Sterling performs for investors once they have purchased their fractional interests in a viatical settlement. Nor do we find that any of the ministerial functions have a material impact upon the profits of the investors. Therefore, we turn to the question whether LPI's pre-purchase services count as "the efforts of others" under the *Howey* test.

Entrepreneurial functions, pre-purchase. LPI's assertion that its pre-purchase efforts are irrelevant receives strong, albeit implicit, support from the Ninth Circuit decision in *Noa v. Key Futures, Inc.,* 638 F.2d 77 (1980) *(per curiam).* In that case, which involved investments in silver bars, the court observed that the promoter made pre-purchase efforts to identify the investment and to locate prospective investors; offered to store the silver bars at no charge for a year after purchase and to repurchase them at the published spot price at any time without charging a brokerage fee. The court concluded, however, that these services were only minimally related to the profitability of the investment: "Once the purchase . . . was made, the profits to the investor depended upon the fluctuations of the silver market, not the managerial efforts of [the promoter]." *Id.* at 79–80.

* * * *

. . . . The Commission reminds us that the Supreme Court did not draw a bright line distinction in *Howey* between pre- and post-purchase efforts, and notes that LPI may continue to perform some functions, such as preparing the preliminary agreement and evaluating the insured's policy and medical file, right up to the closing of the transaction. Therefore it would be hypertechnical, according to the Commission, to discount the importance of LPI's pre-purchase entrepreneurial functions simply because they occur before the moment of closing.

Absent compelling legal support for the Commission's theory—and the Commission actually furnishes no support at all—we cannot agree that the time of sale is an artificial dividing line. It is a legal construct but a significant one. If the investor's profits depend thereafter predominantly upon the promoter's efforts, then the investor may benefit from the disclosure and other requirements of the federal securities laws. But if the value of the promoter's efforts has already been impounded into the promoter's fees or into the purchase price of the investment, and if neither the promoter nor anyone else is expected to make further efforts that will affect the outcome of the investment, then the need for federal securities regulation is greatly diminished. While, to be sure, coverage under the 1933 Act might increase the quantity (and perhaps the quality) of information available to the investor prior to the closing, "the securities laws [are not] a broad federal remedy for all fraud." *Marine Bank v. Weaver,* 455 U.S. 551, 556, 71 L. Ed. 2d 409, 102 S. Ct. 1220 (1982). They are concerned only with securities fraud, and the question before us is the threshold question whether a fractional interest in a viatical settlement is a security. To answer that question we look for "an investment in a common venture" with profits "derived from the entrepreneurial or managerial efforts of others." *Forman,* 421 U.S. at 852.

* * * *

While we doubt that pre-purchase services should ever count for much, for present purposes we need only agree with the district court that pre-purchase services cannot by themselves suffice to make the profits of an investment arise predominantly from the efforts of others, and that ministerial functions should receive a good deal less weight than entrepreneurial activities. . . .

In this case it is the length of the insured's life that is of overwhelming importance to the value of the viatical settlements marketed by LPI. As a result, the SEC is unable to show that the promoter's efforts have a predominant influence upon investors' profits; and because all three elements of the *Howey* test must be satisfied before an investment is characterized as a security. . ., we must conclude that the viatical settlements marketed by LPI are not securities.

* * * *

Accordingly, this case is remanded to the district court with instructions to vacate the three injunctions entered against LPI in August 1995, January 1996, and March 1996.

So ordered.

Securities and Exchange Commission v. Edwards

540 U.S. 389, 124 S. Ct. 892, 157 L. Ed. 2d 813 (2004)

JUSTICE O'CONNOR delivered the opinion of the Court.

"Opportunity doesn't always knock . . . sometimes it rings." App. 113 (ETS Payphones promotional brochure). And sometimes it hangs up. So it did for the 10,000 people who invested a total of $300 million in the payphone sale-and-leaseback arrangements touted by respondent under that slogan. The Securities and Exchange Commission (SEC) argues that the arrangements were investment contracts, and thus were subject to regulation under the federal securities laws. In this case, we must decide whether a moneymaking scheme is excluded from the term "investment contract" simply because the scheme offered a contractual entitlement to a fixed, rather than a variable, return.

I

Respondent Charles Edwards was the chairman, chief executive officer, and sole shareholder of ETS Payphones, Inc. (ETS). ETS, acting partly through a subsidiary also controlled by respondent, sold payphones to the public via independent distributors. The payphones were offered packaged with a site lease, a 5-year leaseback and management agreement, and a buyback agreement. All but a tiny fraction of purchasers chose this package, although other management options were offered. The purchase price for the payphone packages was approximately $7,000. Under the leaseback and management agreement, purchasers received $82 per month, a 14% annual return. Purchasers were not involved in the day-to-day operation of the payphones they owned. ETS selected the site for the phone, installed the equipment, arranged for connection and long-distance service, collected coin revenues, and maintained and repaired the phones. Under the buyback agreement, ETS promised to refund the full purchase price of the package at the end of the lease or within 180 days of a purchaser's request.

In its marketing materials and on its Web site [sic], ETS trumpeted the "incomparable pay phone" as "an exciting business opportunity," in which recent deregulation had "open[ed] the door for profits for individual pay phone owners and operators." According to ETS, "[v]ery few business opportunities can offer the potential for ongoing revenue generation that is available in today's pay telephone industry." . . . .

The payphones did not generate enough revenue for ETS to make the payments required by the leaseback agreements, so the company depended on funds from new investors to meet its obligations. In September 2000, ETS filed for bankruptcy protection. The SEC brought this civil enforcement action the same month. It alleged that respondent and ETS had violated the registration requirements of §§ 5(a) and (c) of the Securities Act of 1933. . ., the antifraud provisions of both § 17(a) of the Securities Act of 1933 . . . and § 10(b) of the Securities Exchange Act of 1934. . ., and Rule 10b–5 thereunder. . . . The District Court concluded that the payphone sale-and-leaseback arrangement was an investment contract within the meaning of, and therefore was subject to, the federal securities laws. . . . The Court of Appeals reversed. . . . . It held that respondent's scheme was not an investment contract, on two grounds. First, it read this Court's opinions to require that an investment contract offer either capital appreciation or a participation in the earnings of the enterprise, and thus to exclude schemes, such as respondent's, offering a fixed rate of return. . . . Second, it held that our opinions' requirement that the return on the investment be "derived solely from the efforts of others" was not satisfied when the purchasers had a contractual entitlement to the return. . . . We conclude that it erred on both grounds.

II

"Congress' purpose in enacting the securities laws was to regulate i*nvestments,* in whatever form they are made and by whatever name they are called." *Reves v. Ernst & Young,* 494 U.S. 56, 61, 108 L. Ed. 2d 47, 110 S. Ct. 945 (1990). To that end, it enacted a broad definition of "security," sufficient "to encompass virtually any instrument that might be sold as an investment." *Ibid.* Section 2(a)(1) of the 1933 Act, 15 U.S.C. § 77b(a)(1), and § 3(a)(10) of the 1934 Act, 15 U.S.C. § 78c(a)(10), in slightly different formulations which we have treated as essentially identical in meaning. . ., define "security" to include "any note, stock, treasury stock, security future, bond, debenture, . . . investment contract, . . . [or any] instrument commonly known as a 'security'." "Investment contract" is not itself defined.

The test for whether a particular scheme is an investment contract was established in our decision in *SEC v. W. J. Howey Co.,* 328 U.S. 293, 90 L. Ed. 1244, 66 S. Ct. 1100 (1946). We look to "whether the scheme involves an investment of money in a common enterprise with profits to come solely from the efforts of others" . . . . This definition "embodies a flexible rather than a static principle, one that is capable of adaptation to meet the countless and variable schemes devised by those who seek the use of the money of others on the promise of profits." *Id.,* at 299, 90 L. Ed. 1244, 66 S. Ct. 1100.

In reaching that result, we first observed that when Congress included "investment contract" in the definition of security, it "was using a term the meaning of which had been crystallized" by the state courts' interpretation of their "blue sky" laws. . . . (Those laws were the precursors to federal securities regulation and were so named, it seems, because they were "aimed at promoters who 'would sell building lots in the blue sky in fee simple.' " 1 L. Loss & J. Seligman, Securities Regulation 36, 31–43 (3d ed. 1998) (quoting Mulvey, Blue Sky Law, 36 Can. L. Times 37 (1916)).) The state courts had defined an investment contract as "a contract or scheme for 'the placing of capital or laying out of money in a way intended to secure income or profit from its employment,' " and had "uniformly applied" that definition to "a variety of situations where individuals were led to invest money in a common enterprise with the expectation that they would earn a profit solely through the efforts of the promoter or [a third party]." *Howey, supra,* 328 U.S. 293 at 298. . . . Thus, when we held that "profits" must "come solely from the efforts of others," we were speaking of the profits that investors seek on their investment, not the profits of the scheme in which they invest. We used "profits" in the sense of income or return, to include, for example, dividends, other periodic payments, or the increased value of the investment.

There is no reason to distinguish between promises of fixed returns and promises of variable returns for purposes of the test, so understood. In both cases, the investing public is attracted by representations of investment income, as purchasers were in this case by ETS' invitation to " 'watch the profits add up.' " . . . . Moreover, investments pitched as low-risk (such as those offering a "guaranteed" fixed return) are particularly attractive to individuals more vulnerable to investment fraud, including older and less sophisticated investors. . . . . Under the reading respondent advances, unscrupulous marketers of investments could evade the securities laws by picking a rate of return to promise. We will not read into the securities laws a limitation not compelled by the language that would so undermine the laws' purposes.

Respondent protests that including investment schemes promising a fixed return among investment contracts conflicts with our precedent. We disagree. No distinction between fixed and variable returns was drawn in the blue sky law cases that the *Howey* Court used, in formulating the test, as its evidence of Congress' understanding of the term. . . . Indeed, two of those cases involved an investment contract in which a fixed return was promised. *People v. White,* 124 Cal. App. 548, 550–551, 12 P.2d 1078, 1079 (1932) (agreement between defendant and investors stated that investor would give defendant $5,000, and would receive $7,500 from defendant one year later); *Stevens v. Liberty Packing Corp.,* 111 N. J. Eq. 61, 62–63, 161 A. 193, 193–194 (1932) ("ironclad contract" offered by defendant to investors entitled investors to $56 per year for 10 years on initial investment of $175, ostensibly in sale and leaseback of breeding rabbits).

None of our post-*Howey* decisions is to the contrary. . . .

* * * *

Given that respondent's position is supported neither by the purposes of the securities laws nor by our precedents, it is no surprise that the SEC has consistently taken the opposite position, and maintained that a promise of a fixed return does not preclude a scheme from being an investment contract. . . .

The Eleventh Circuit's perfunctory alternative holding, that respondent's scheme falls outside the definition because purchasers had a contractual entitlement to a return, is incorrect and inconsistent with our precedent. We are considering investment *contracts*. The fact that investors have bargained for a return on their investment does not mean that the return is not also expected to come solely from the efforts of others. Any other conclusion would conflict with our holding that an investment contract was offered in *Howey* itself. 328 U.S. 293 at 295–296, 90 L. Ed. 1244, 66 S. Ct. 1100 (service contract entitled investors to allocation of net profits).

We hold that an investment scheme promising a fixed rate of return can be an "investment contract" and thus a "security" subject to the federal securities laws. The judgment of the United States Court of Appeals for the Eleventh Circuit is reversed, and the case is remanded for further proceedings consistent with this opinion.

It is so ordered.

NOTES AND QUESTIONS

1. Why should it be so critical whether something is a "security?" If the securities laws are intended to protect investors, why shouldn't they apply to all investments?

2. Kickstarter is an internet website that enables businesses and other projects to raise funds. The site allows "project creators" to set funding goals and a deadline. Then "backers" pledge money to a project. The backers typically are entitled to a "reward" such as a copy of the book that is written or a product

that a business is manufacturing or developing. Backers do not own a percentage of the businesses they support, and the money that backers provide is not called an "investment." If you represented Kickstarter before they launched this website and you were asked whether such activities designed to raise money for business projects would be deemed to be "securities" and subject to the securities laws, what would you advise your client, and why?

NOTE ON INITIAL COIN OFFERINGS

Recently, a number of technology startups, many of which are involved in the realm of digital-currency, have created and sold digital tokens or new digital currencies to raise money through an "Initial Coin Offering" or "ICO" to fund the firm's operations. These ICO tokens or currencies are purchased with Bitcoin (which is itself a cryptocurrency) or using Ethereum (which is a digital-currency platform that standardizes the coding for creating digital tokens). Some ICOs offer tokens that may be used within a firm's online platform, service or marketplace; other offerings resemble shares in an investment fund. (*See* Paul Vigna, *What's an Intiail Coin Offering? ICOs Explained in 11 Questions*, The Wall Street Journal, Oct. 2, 2017.) Digital coin offerings were recently banned in China and South Korea. There have been many questions about whether ICOs should be regulated in the United States and whether they involve the sale of a security. In July of 2017 the SEC provided some clarification that the *Howey* test would be applied to evaluate whether the digital tokens offered in an ICO meet the definition of a security. The SEC report indicated that the answer would involve a fact specific inquiry and would depend on the economic realities and circumstances of the ICO being reviewed. Securities and Exchange Commission, Release No. 81207/July 25, 2017. On March 4, 2018 the SEC charged two co-founders of a purported financial services start-up with orchestrating a fraudulent ICO that raised more than $32 million from thousands of investors last year. On March 6, 2018, Praetorian Group filed with the SEC to register a $75 million ICO as a security offering in what will be (if accepted) the first registered ICO. The registration describes Praetorian Group as a "Cryptocurrency Real Estate Investment Vehicle." It seems that future ICOs are likely to be subject to oversight by the SEC and additional regulation.

B. Securities in Partnerships and Limited Liability Companies

The preceding cases illustrate that not all investments are securities. However, it is equally important to note the broad application of the definition of a security to investment contracts and other business arrangements. It is important to understand these broader definitions of what is a security in order to evaluate how they might apply in the context of other, non-corporate, entities, such as partnerships and LLCs. An example of an investment that is not a security might be an investment in a general partnership. Since all of the partners have the right to be involved in management, it is rare that a partnership interest would be considered a security, since the "profits from the efforts of others" aspect of the *Howey* test is not met. Conversely, a typical interest of a limited partner in a limited partnership is a security since limited partners typically do not participate in management, and therefore, the requirements of the *Howey* test are usually met. The evaluation of how this test might be applied in an LLC is more complicated, particularly because an LLC may be "member-managed" or "manager-managed." While there might be a temptation to treat manager-managed LLC interests as securities and interests in member-managed LLCs as not meeting the test, such a construct would over-simplify the question. Because LLCs have great flexibility to define the role of their members, regardless of the management designation, it is important to evaluate the actual structure of the LLC in order to evaluate whether the members are expecting to profit from the efforts of others. Consider the following case.

Robinson v. Glynn

349 F.3d 166 (4th Cir. 2003)

WILKINSON, C.J.:

Plaintiff James Robinson filed suit against Thomas Glynn, Glynn Scientific, Inc., and GeoPhone Company, LLC, alleging that Glynn committed federal securities fraud when he sold Robinson a partial interest in Geophone Company. The district court found that Robinson's membership interest in GeoPhone was not a security within the meaning of the federal securities laws, and it dismissed Robinson's securities fraud claim. Because Robinson was an active and knowledgeable executive at GeoPhone, rather than a mere passive investor in the company, we affirm. To do otherwise would unjustifiably expand the scope of the federal securities laws by treating an ordinary commercial venture as an investment contract.

I.

. . . In 1995, Glynn organized GeoPhone Corporation to develop and commercially market the GeoPhone telecommunications system. The GeoPhone system was designed around a signal processing technology, Convolutional Ambiguity Multiple Access (CAMA), that Glynn purportedly designed. Glynn was GeoPhone Corporation's majority shareholder and chairman. In September 1995, GeoPhone Corporation became a limited liability company, GeoPhone Company, LLC. . . .

In March 1995, Glynn and his associates contacted James Robinson, a businessman with no prior telecommunications experience, in an effort to raise capital for GeoPhone. Over the next several months, Glynn met and corresponded with Robinson, attempting to convince Robinson to invest in GeoPhone. Glynn described to Robinson the CAMA technology, its centrality to the GeoPhone system, and Geo-Phone's business plan. In July 1995, Robinson agreed to loan Glynn $1 million so that Glynn could perform a field test of the GeoPhone system and the CAMA technology.

In addition to Robinson's loan, in August 1995 Robinson and Glynn executed a "Letter of Intent," in which Robinson pledged to invest up to $25 million in GeoPhone, LLC if the field test indicated that CAMA worked in the GeoPhone system. Robinson's $25 million investment was to be comprised of his initial $1 million loan, an immediate $14 million investment upon successful completion of the field test, and a later $10 million investment. In October 1995, engineers hired by Glynn performed the field test, but, apparently with Glynn's knowledge, they did not use CAMA in the test. Nevertheless, Glynn allegedly told Robinson that the field test had been a success.

Consistent with the Letter of Intent, in December 1995 Robinson and Glynn executed an "Agreement to Purchase Membership Interests in GeoPhone" (APMIG). Under the APMIG, Robinson agreed to convert his $1 million loan and his $14 million investment into equity and subsequently to invest the additional $10 million. Robinson and Glynn also entered into an "Amended and Restated GeoPhone Operating Agreement" (ARGOA), which detailed the capital contribution, share ownership, and management structure of GeoPhone.

Pursuant to the ARGOA, Robinson received 33,333 of GeoPhone's 133,333 shares. On the back of the share certificates that Robinson received, the restrictive legend referred to the certificates as "shares" and "securities." It also specified that the certificates were exempt from registration under the *Securities*

Act of 1933, and stated that the certificates could not be transferred without proper registration under the federal and state securities laws.

In addition, the ARGOA established a seven-person board of managers that was authorized to manage GeoPhone's affairs. Two of the managers were to be appointed by Robinson with the remaining five appointed by Glynn and his brother. Finally, the ARGOA vested management of GeoPhone in Robinson and Glynn based on each member's ownership share. Robinson was named GeoPhone's treasurer, and he was appointed to the board of managers and the company's executive committee. Glynn served as GeoPhone's chairman and was intimately involved in the company's operations and technical development.

Trouble first surfaced only a few months later in April 1996, when Robinson sued Glynn in Maryland state court. Robinson alleged breach of fiduciary duty, fraud, and conversion, all due to Glynn's purported mismanagement of GeoPhone funds. In October 1997, Robinson and Glynn settled the state court action, and as part of the settlement in November 1997 they entered into a "Membership Interest Purchase Agreement" (MIPA). Under the MIPA, Robinson purchased all of Glynn's shares in GeoPhone.

Yet in 1998 Robinson allegedly learned for the first time that the CAMA technology had never been implemented in the GeoPhone system—not even in the field test that had provided the basis for Robinson's investment. Robinson then filed suit in federal court, claiming violation of the federal securities laws, specifically § 10(b) of the Securities Exchange Act of 1934 and Rule 10b–5. The district court, however, granted summary judgment to Glynn, because it found that Robinson's membership interest in GeoPhone, LLC did not constitute a security under the federal securities laws. Robinson now challenges the district court's dismissal of his federal securities law claim.

II.

In order to establish a claim under *Rule 10b–5,* Robinson must prove fraud in connection with the purchase of securities. [*Citations omitted.*] The Securities Act of 1933, 15 U.S.C. § 77b(a)(1), and the Securities Exchange Act of 1934 define a "security" broadly as "any note, stock, treasury stock, security future, bond, debenture, . . .investment contract, . . . or, in general, any interest or instrument commonly known as a 'security.' " In this case, Robinson claims that his membership interest in GeoPhone, a limited liability company (LLC), qualifies as either an "investment contract" or "stock" under the Securities Acts.

A.

The district court determined that Robinson's interest in GeoPhone was not an investment contract, a question of law that we review de novo. The Supreme Court has defined an investment contract as "a contract, transaction or scheme whereby a person invests his money in a common enterprise and is led to expect profits solely from the efforts of the promoter or a third party." *S.E.C. v. W.J. Howey, Co.,* 328 U.S. 293, 298–99, 90 L. Ed. 1244, 66 S. Ct. 1100 (1946). The parties agree that Robinson invested his money in a common enterprise with an expectation of profits. Their disagreement concerns whether Robinson expected profits "solely from the efforts" of others, most notably Glynn.

Since *Howey,* however, the Supreme Court has endorsed relaxation of the requirement that an investor rely only on others' efforts, by omitting the word "solely" from its restatements of the *Howey* test. [*Citations omitted.*] And neither our court nor our sister circuits have required that an investor like Robinson expect profits "solely" from the efforts of others. [*Citations omitted.*] Requiring investors to rely wholly on the efforts of others would exclude from the protection of the securities laws any agreement that involved even slight efforts from investors themselves. [*Citations omitted.*] It would also exclude any agreement that offered investors control in theory, but denied it to them in fact. Agreements do not annul the securities laws by retaining nominal powers for investors unable to exercise them. [*Citations omitted.*]

What matters more than the form of an investment scheme is the "economic reality" that it represents. [*Citations omitted.*] The question is whether an investor, as a result of the investment agreement itself or the factual circumstances that surround it, is left unable to exercise meaningful control over his investment. [*Citations omitted.*] Elevating substance over form in this way ensures that the term "investment contract" embodies "a flexible rather than a static principle, one that is capable of adaptation to meet the countless and variable schemes devised by those who seek the use of the money of others on the promise of profits." *Howey,* 328 U.S. at 299.

B.

In looking at the powers accorded Robinson under GeoPhone's operating agreement, as well as Robinson's activity as an executive at GeoPhone, it is clear that Robinson was no passive investor heavily dependent on the efforts of others like Glynn. Under the ARGOA, management authority for GeoPhone resided in a board of managers. Robinson not only had the power to appoint two of the board members, but he himself assumed one of the board seats and was named as the board's vice-chairman. The board, in turn, delegated extensive responsibility to a four-person executive committee of which Robinson was also a member.

In addition, Robinson served as GeoPhone's Treasurer. Among his powers were the ability to select external financial and legal consultants; to consult with GeoPhone's Chief Financial Officer on all financial matters relating to the company; to review status reports from the President and other officers; and to assemble the executive committee in order to discuss variations from GeoPhone's operating plan. Beyond even these fairly extensive powers, the ARGOA forbade GeoPhone from either incurring any indebtedness outside the normal course of business without Robinson's approval or diluting his interest in GeoPhone without first consulting him. In short, Robinson carefully negotiated for a level of control "antithetical to the notion of member passivity" required to find an investment contract under the federal securities laws. *Keith v. Black Diamond Advisors, Inc.,* 48 F. Supp. 2d 326, 333 (S.D.N.Y. 1999).

None of this, of course, establishes that Robinson could entirely direct the affairs of GeoPhone. He controlled neither the board nor the executive committee, and he lacked the technological expertise of Glynn and others at the company. But Robinson was not interested in sole managerial control of GeoPhone; he was interested instead in sufficient managerial control to ensure that other managers like Glynn could neither harm nor dilute his investment. . .

Robinson argues, however, that his lack of technological expertise relative to Glynn prevented him from meaningfully exercising his rights. . . . To the extent that Robinson needed assistance in understanding any particular aspect of the CAMA technology, nothing prevented him from seeking it from outside parties or others at GeoPhone. . . .

Indeed, the record amply supports the district court's conclusion that Robinson exercised his management rights despite his lack of technical expertise. For instance, Robinson reviewed GeoPhone's technology and financial records, as well as weekly status reports from GeoPhone's President, Chief Operating Officer, and Chief Financial Officer covering numerous aspects of GeoPhone's operation. He disapproved disbursements and proposed licenses of the GeoPhone technology. Robinson even expressed to the board of managers problems he perceived with GeoPhone, including the company's technological development, its management, and marketability. In the end, Robinson generally asserts that he lacked technical sophistication, without explaining in any detail what was beyond his ken or why it left him powerless to exercise his management rights.

* * * *

Finally, Robinson argues that he and Glynn considered his interest in GeoPhone a security, based on language in the APMIG, in the ARGOA, and on the back of Robinson's GeoPhone certificates. For instance, the restrictive legend on the back of Robinson's certificates refers to the certificates as "shares" and "securities." While this may be persuasive evidence that Robinson and Glynn believed the securities laws to apply, it does not indicate that their understanding was well-founded. Just as agreements cannot evade the securities laws by reserving powers to members unable to exercise them, neither can agreements invoke those same laws simply by labelling commercial ventures as securities. It is the "economic reality" of a particular instrument, rather than the label attached to it, that ultimately determines whether it falls within the reach of the securities laws. *See Great Rivers Coop. v. Farmland Indus., Inc.,* 198 F.3d 685, 701 (8th Cir. 1999). The "economic reality" here is that Robinson was not a passive investor relying on the efforts of others, but a knowledgeable executive actively protecting his interest and position in the company.

III.

Robinson further claims that his membership interest in GeoPhone was not only an "investment contract" within the meaning of the federal securities laws, but "stock" as well.[3] Congress intended catch-all terms like "investment contract" to encompass the range of novel and unusual instruments whose economic realities invite application of the securities laws; but the term "stock" refers to a narrower set of instruments with a common name and characteristics. *See Landreth Timber Co. v. Landreth,* 471 U.S. 681, 686, 85 L. Ed. 2d 692, 105 S. Ct. 2297 (1985). Thus the securities laws apply "when an instrument is both called 'stock' and bears stock's usual characteristics." Yet Robinson's membership interest was neither denominated stock by the parties, nor did it possess all the usual characteristics of stock.

The characteristics typically associated with common stock are (i) the right to receive dividends contingent upon an apportionment of profits; (ii) negotiability; (iii) the ability to be pledged or hypothecated; (iv) the conferring of voting rights in proportion to the number of shares owned; and (v) the

[3] The Securities Acts define a "security" as "any note, stock, treasury stock, security future, bond, debenture, . . .,investment contract, . . ., or, in general, any interest or instrument commonly known as a 'security.' " 15 U.S.C. §§ 77b(a)(1) & 78c(a)(10).

capacity to appreciate in value. *See id.* Robinson's membership interest in GeoPhone lacked several of these characteristics. [*Citations omitted.*]

First, as is common with interests in LLCs, GeoPhone's members did not share in the profits in proportion to the number of their shares. [*Citations omitted.*] Pursuant to the ARGOA, Robinson was to receive 100 percent of GeoPhone's net profits up to a certain amount, only after which were funds to be distributed pro rata to the members in proportion to their relative shares.

Second, like interests in LLCs more generally, Robinson's membership interests were not freely negotiable. [*Citations omitted.*] According to the ARGOA, Robinson could only transfer his interests if he first offered other members the opportunity to purchase his interests on similar terms. Moreover, unlike with stock (except some stock in close corporations), anyone to whom Robinson or other members transferred their interests would not have thereby acquired any of the control or management rights that normally attend a stock transfer. . . .

Similarly, Robinson could pledge his interest, but the pledgee would acquire only distribution rights and not control rights. . . . As for the apportionment of voting rights, the parties dispute whether voting rights were conferred in proportion to members' interests in Geo-Phone. Even resolving this dispute in Robinson's favor, it remains clear that Robinson's membership interest lacked the ordinary attributes of stock.

Finally, from the very beginning Robinson and Glynn consistently viewed Robinson's investment as a "membership interest," and never as "stock." The purchase and operating agreements that Robinson and Glynn executed, as well as the agreement in which Robinson bought out Glynn's interest in GeoPhone, all termed Robinson's investment as a "membership interest" rather than "stock." Even the shares that Robinson received as a result of his investments declared Robinson the holder of "membership interests in GeoPhone Company, L.L.C., within the meaning of the Delaware Limited Liability Company Act." Robinson thus cannot argue that he was misled into believing that his membership interests were stock whose purchases were governed by the securities laws. *See Landreth,* 471 U.S. at 687, 693 (finding that calling instruments "stock" justifiably leads purchasers to believe that the federal securities laws apply). And it would do violence to the statutory language of the securities laws to include within the term "stock" an instrument that was neither labelled stock nor like stock.

IV.

The parties have vigorously urged us to rule broadly in this case, asking that we generally classify interests in limited liability companies, or LLCs, as investment contracts (Robinson's view) or nonsecurities (Glynn's view). LLCs are particularly difficult to categorize under the securities laws, however, because they are hybrid business entities that combine features of corporations, general partnerships, and limited partnerships. [*Citations omitted.*] As their name indicates, LLCs can limit the liability of their members, which may mean that LLC members are more likely to be passive investors who need the protection of the securities laws. [*Citations omitted.*] However, LLC members are also able to actively participate in management without piercing the veil of their liability, which would suggest that LLC members are more likely than limited partners or corporate shareholders to be active investors not in need of the securities statutes. [*Citations omitted.*]

Precisely because LLCs lack standardized membership rights or organizational structures, they can assume an almost unlimited variety of forms. It becomes, then, exceedingly difficult to declare that LLCs, whatever their form, either possess or lack the economic characteristics associated with investment contracts. Even drawing firm lines between member-managed and manager-managed LLCs threatens impermissibly to elevate form over substance. Certainly the members in a member-managed LLC will often have powers too significant to be considered passive investors under the securities laws. And yet even members in a member-managed LLC may be unable as a practical matter to exercise any meaningful control, perhaps because they are too numerous, inexperienced, or geographically disparate. [*Citations omitted.*] By the same token, while interests in manager-managed LLCs may often be securities, their members need not necessarily be reliant on the efforts on their managers. [*Citations omitted.*]. We decline, therefore, the parties' invitation for a broader holding. On the facts of this case, it is clear that Robinson did not lack the ability to meaningfully exercise the rights granted him under GeoPhone's operating agreement. To the contrary, Robinson had a significant say in GeoPhone's management. If Robinson, despite his own managerial efforts, was misled by Glynn about his investment, his remedy belongs to another forum. The federal securities laws were not intended to be a substitute for state fraud and breach of contract actions. . . .

SECTION II: Rule 10b–5: Fraud Under the Federal Securities Laws

Rule 10b–5 is probably the most important (or at least the most utilized) piece of antifraud securities legislation. Rule 10b–5 may be used both by the SEC and by private individuals in pursuing fraud claims. (Rule 10b–5 is also used to restrict insider trading actions as will be seen in Chapter 9, *infra.*) A critical aspect of Rule 10b–5 is that it creates potential liability for anyone who makes a misleading representation or omission that is connected with the purchase or sale of a security. This potential liability can arise when someone buys or sells a security, even if she does not buy it from or sell it to, the person who makes the misleading statement. Rule 10b–5 has also been used to create a private right of action in areas in which Congress has been silent. In other words, this is not just a provision that the SEC can use to pursue those who make misrepresentations. This Rule can be used by individuals as well.

Section 10(b) of the Securities Exchange Act of 1934 provides that:

> It shall be unlawful for any person, directly or indirectly, by the use of any means or instrumentality of interstate commerce or of the mails, or of any facility of any national securities exchange—. . .
>
> (b) To use or employ, in connection with the purchase or sale of any security registered on a national securities exchange or any security not so registered,. . . any manipulative or deceptive device or contrivance **in contravention of such rules and regulations as the Commission may prescribe** as necessary or appropriate in the public interest or for the protection of investors. [emphasis added.]

Notice that this provision requires the SEC to make "rules and regulations" to which § 10(b) will apply. In following this requirement the SEC adopted Rule 10b–5 which states:

> It shall be unlawful for any person, directly or indirectly, by the use of any means or instrumentality of interstate commerce, or of the mails or of any facility of any national securities exchange,
>
> (a) To employ any device, scheme, or artifice to defraud,
>
> (b) To make any untrue statement of a material fact or to omit to state a material fact necessary in order to make the statements made, in the light of the circumstances under which they were made, not misleading, or

(c) To engage in any act, practice, or course of business which operates or would operate as a fraud or deceit upon any person, in connection with the purchase or sale of any security.

A. Claims Made Under Rule 10b–5: Standing

It is important to recognize that the question under a Rule 10b–5 claim is not whether a wrong has been committed. It is whether a wrong has been committed which satisfies the elements of Rule 10b–5. There are several requirements that must be met in order to bring a claim under Rule 10b–5. However, even before a would-be plaintiff might be able to make a substantive claim under 10b–5, that potential plaintiff would first need to meet certain basic "standing" requirements. Section 10(b) has an interstate commerce jurisdictional requirement. This requirement means that the statute (§ 10(b)) only applies if the fraud involved the use of "means or instrumentality of interstate commerce, or mail or a facility of a national securities exchange." Intrastate activities are not regulated by § 10(b). So, if none of these interstate activities occur, there may be fraud, but Rule 10b–5 will not apply.

Also, even if the facts meet the jurisdictional requirements, the plaintiff must show that the activity involves a "security." (See the discussion in the preceding Section. The determination of whether an activity constitutes a security for purposes for Rule 10b–5, can often dictate whether or not there will be liability for the participants in that activity.) Note that Rule 10b–5 applies to any security, not just securities in a public corporation; it applies to closely-held corporations (even though they are private companies generally not subject to many of the reporting provisions of the 1934 Act) as well as transactions in government securities; it also applies to option traders who purchase stock options because an option contract confers the right to buy or sell shares of a particular stock at a specific price on or before the expiration date of the contract. *See Deutschman v. Beneficial Corp.,* 841 F.2d 502 (3d Cir. 1988).

Furthermore, even if the facts meet the jurisdictional requirements and the "security" requirement, the activity also must involve a purchase or sale of securities. If an individual or the corporation makes a false or misleading statement, BUT there is no associated purchase or sale of stock arising out of that false or misleading statement, there is no liability. For example, if the plaintiff decides *not* to sell or *not* to buy because of a misrepresentation or an omission, he may be damaged, but he does not have a claim under 10b–5. *See Blue Chip Stamps v. Manor Drug Stores,* 421 U.S. 723 (1975). However, the fraud need only *touch and concern* the transaction. While there is not a well-established definition of "touch and concern," even a tenuous connection between the "fraud" and the transaction will probably suffice.

Blue Chip Stamps v. Manor Drug Stores, 421 U.S. 723 (1975): Following a civil antitrust action and a consent decree, the Blue Chip Stamp Co. ("Blue Chip") had agreed to merge into a newly formed corporation and offer a substantial number of shares of common stock in that new corporation to retailers who had used the stamp service in the past but were not shareholders in the company. This offering took place in 1968.

> . . .The reorganization plan was carried out, the offering was registered with the SEC as required by the 1933 Act, and a prospectus was distributed to all offerees as required by § 5 of that Act. . . Somewhat more than 50% of the offered units were actually purchased. In 1970, two years after the offering, respondent, a former user of the stamp service and therefore an offeree of the 1968 offering, filed this suit in the United States District Court. . . .
>
> Respondent's complaint alleged, *inter alia,* that the prospectus prepared and distributed by Blue Chip in connection with the offering was materially misleading in its overly pessimistic appraisal of Blue Chip's status and future prospects. It alleged that Blue Chip intentionally made the prospectus overly pessimistic in order to discourage respondent and other members of the allegedly large class whom it represents from accepting what was intended to be a bargain offer, so that the rejected shares might later be offered to the public at a higher price. The complaint alleged that class members because of and in reliance on the false and misleading prospectus failed to purchase the offered units. Respondent therefore sought on behalf of the alleged class some $21,400,000 in damages representing the lost opportunity to purchase the units; the right to purchase the previously rejected units at the 1968 price; and in addition, it sought some $25,000,000 in exemplary damages.

Id. at 725.

In denying plaintiffs' claim the Court adopted the rule from *Birnbaum v. Newport Steel Corp.,* 193 F.2d 461 (2d Cir.), *cert. denied* 343 U.S. 956 (1952) that there was not a private cause of action for money damages under Rule 10b–5 for a party who had neither purchased nor sold any securities. The Court went on to note:

> The panel which decided *Birnbaum* consisted of Chief Judge Swan and Judges Learned Hand and Augustus Hand. . . Since both § 10(b) and Rule 10b–5 proscribed only fraud "in connection with the purchase or sale" of securities, and since the history of § 10(b) revealed no congressional intention to extend a private civil remedy for money damages to other than defrauded purchasers or sellers of securities, in contrast to the express civil remedy provided by § 16(b) of the 1934 Act, the court concluded that the plaintiff class in a Rule 10b–5 action was limited to actual purchasers and sellers. 193 F. 2d, at 463–464.

Id. at 731.

> Three principal classes of potential plaintiffs are presently barred by the *Birnbaum* rule. First are potential purchasers of shares, either in a new offering or on the Nation's post-distribution trading markets, who allege that they decided not to purchase because of an unduly gloomy representation or the omission of favorable material which made the issuer appear to be a less favorable investment vehicle than it actually was. Second are actual shareholders in the issuer who allege that they decided not to sell their shares because of an unduly rosy representation or a failure to disclose unfavorable material. Third are shareholders, creditors, and perhaps others related to an issuer who suffered loss in the value of their investment due to corporate or insider activities in connection with the purchase or sale of securities which violate Rule 10b–5. It has been held that shareholder members of the second and third of these classes may frequently be able to circumvent the Birnbaum limitation through bringing a derivative action on behalf of the corporate issuer if the latter is itself a purchaser or seller of securities. . . . But the first of these classes, of which respondent is a member, cannot claim the benefit of such a rule.
>
> * * * *
>
> There has been widespread recognition that litigation under Rule 10b–5 presents a danger of vexatiousness different in degree and in kind from that which accompanies litigation in general. . . .
>
> Judge Friendly in commenting on another aspect of Rule 10b–5 litigation has referred to the possibility that unduly expansive imposition of civil liability "will lead to large judgments, payable in the last analysis by innocent investors, for the benefit of speculators and

> their lawyers. . . ." *SEC v. Texas Gulf Sulphur Co.,* 401 F. 2d 833, 867 (CA2 1968) (concurring opinion). . . .
>
> We believe that the concern expressed for the danger of vexatious litigation which could result from a widely expanded class of plaintiffs under Rule 10b–5 is founded in something more substantial than the common complaint of the many defendants who would prefer avoiding lawsuits entirely to either settling them or trying them. . . .

Id. at 737–40

* * * *

> Thus we conclude that what may be called considerations of policy, which we are free to weigh in deciding this case, are by no means entirely on one side of the scale. Taken together with the precedential support for the *Birnbaum* rule over a period of more than 20 years, and the consistency of that rule with what we can glean from the intent of Congress, they lead us to conclude that it is a sound rule and should be followed. . . .

Id. at 749

B. Rule 10b–5 Elements

Once the jurisdictional requirements of Rule 10b–5 have been met, and there is a purchase or sale of a security, in order to show a violation of Rule 10b–5, one must still show that the statutory elements have been met. This requirement is met by showing that the defendant: (a) employed a device, scheme, or artifice to defraud **AND** (b) either (i) made an untrue statement of a material fact; (ii) omitted, or failed to state, a material fact necessary in order to make the statements made, in light of the circumstances under which they were made, not misleading; or (iii) omitted a material fact that the defendant had a duty to disclose **OR** (c) engaged in "any act, practice, or course of business which operated or would operate as a fraud or deceit upon any person . . . in connection with that purchase or sale of a security."

A party bringing a suit under 10b–5 must show that the defendant exhibited each of the following in order to satisfy the statutory requirements: (1) An *untrue or misleading statement or omission;* (2) *Scienter* (intent); (3) *Materiality;* (4) *Reliance;* **AND** (5) *Causation* (proximate cause or "loss causation").

1. Untrue or Misleading Statement or Omission

In order to incur liability under Rule 10b–5, a defendant had to have made a false or misleading statement or omitted information that made a statement false or misleading. In situations in which liability is based on the omission of a material fact, rather than a misrepresentation, there can only be liability if there was a duty to disclose that fact.

Elkind v. Liggett & Myers, Inc. [Part I]

635 F.2d 156 (2d Cir. 1980)

MANSFIELD, J.:

This case presents a number of issues arising out of what has become a form of corporate brinkmanship-non-public disclosure of business-related information to financial analysts. The action is a class suit by Arnold B. Elkind on behalf of certain purchasers (more fully described below) of the stock of Liggett & Myers, Inc. (Liggett) against it. They seek damages for alleged failure of its officers to disclose certain material information with respect to its earnings and operations and for their alleged wrongful tipping of inside information to certain persons who then sold Liggett shares on the open market.

* * * *

Liggett is a diversified company, with traditional business in the tobacco industry supplemented by acquisitions in such industries as liquor (Paddington Corp., importer of J&B Scotch), pet food (Allen Products Co. and Perk Foods Co., manufacturer of Alpo dog food), cereal, watchbands, cleansers and rugs. Its common stock is listed on the New York Stock Exchange.

In 1969 Liggett officers concluded that the company's stock was underpriced, due in part to lack of appreciation in the financial community for the breadth of its market activity. To cure this perceived deficiency, Liggett initiated an "analyst program," hiring a public relations firm and encouraging closer contact between analysts and company management. This included meetings with analysts at which Liggett officials discussed operations. Liggett also reviewed and commented on reports which the analysts were preparing, to correct errors and other misunderstandings.

Liggett had a record year in 1971. . . . On March 22, Liggett issued a press release reporting that sales of the non-tobacco lines had continued to increase in the first two months, but noting that current stockpiling of J&B Scotch by customers (in anticipation of a price increase) could affect sales. On May 3, 1972, the company released its first quarter figures, showing earnings of $1.00 per share (compared to $.81 in the first quarter of 1971).

This quarterly operations report led to considerable optimism in the financial community over Liggett's prospects. Management did nothing to deflate the enthusiasm. A number of reports containing predictions that 1972 earnings would increase about 10% over 1971 earnings were reviewed by officials of Liggett during the first five months of 1972. While company personnel corrected factual errors in these reports, they did not comment (or made noncommittal or evasive comments) on the earnings projections. . . . At group meetings with analysts in February and March, management indicated that it was making "good progress" with certain products and that it was "well-positioned" to take advantage of industry trends. At the end of March, Liggett successfully made a public offering of $50 million of debentures. At an April 25 stockholders' meeting, Liggett's Executive Vice President expressed general optimism that the company was continuing to make good progress. On May 3, the first quarter earnings were released. At a May 16 meeting with analysts in New York, officials reiterated their vague but quieting pronouncements.[1] Similar

---

[1] Since, as the chronology below will indicate, this meeting took place one day after Liggett management became aware that the month of April had been a bad one for the company, the remarks made at the meeting merit scrutiny. The Director of Corporate Marketing, Samuel White, and the president of the Cigarette and Tobacco Division, Kenneth McAllister, each gave a speech focusing on the first quarter performance.

White discussed market trends, commenting on Liggett's position in light of those trends. He began,

> "As you know, our non-tobacco operations have been successful, and all of our diversified consumer product lines had sales increases in the first quarter."

With respect to the liquor industry, he said,

> "The increase in sales of our alcoholic beverages (particularly J&B Scotch) was unusually high in the first quarter, due to anticipated increases in imported liquor prices. . . . We expect J&B to continue to solidify its position as the number one Scotch in 1972, but it is difficult to say how the stock piling in the last three quarters might affect sales the rest of the year, as the Scotch market continues to grow."

He expressed hope for future improvement in the pet food line, and concern over weak performance of the company's carpet subsidiary, saying,

> "we cannot predict how Mercury will do for the rest of the year, but over the long term, Mercury has good potential, as the carpet industry is expected to resume the growth trend of the 60's, based on a sharp increase in housing starts last year. . . ."

Finally, he summarized:

> "We are optimistic that most of our divisions will continue to make good progress. They are well-positioned in their respective industries, are growing, and can be expected to contribute significantly to our future growth."

McAllister spoke of the tobacco industry, explaining that operations had been disappointing during the last year, and that "we can not realistically look for anything better than moderate improvement for the year 1972."

comments, to the effect that 1972 was expected to be a "good year," were voiced at a June 5 presentation in London.[2]

Despite the company's outward appearance of strength, Liggett's management was less sanguine intramurally. Internal budget projections called for only a two percent increase in earnings in 1972. In April and May, a full compilation of updated figures was ordered, and new projections were presented to the Board of Directors on May 15, April was marked by a sharp decline, with earnings of only $.03 per share (compared to $.30 the previous April). The 1972 earnings projection was revised downward from $4.30 to $3.95 per share. . . . At meetings with analysts during this period, Liggett officials took a more negative tone, emphasizing, for example, various cost pressures. There was no public disclosure of the adverse financial developments at this time. Beginning in late June, 1972, the price of Liggett's common stock steadily declined.

On July 17, preliminary earnings data for June and six-month totals became available to the Board of Directors. June earnings were $.20 per share (compared to $.44 in June 1971). The first half earnings for 1972 were approximately $1.46 per share, down from $1.82 the previous year. The Board decided to issue a press release the following day. That release, issued at about 2:15 P.M. on July 18, disclosed the preliminary earnings figures and attributed the decline to shortcomings in all of Liggett's product lines.

* * * *

1. Obligation to Disclose

Plaintiff asserts that Liggett's practice of reviewing and correcting draft reports regarding the company's operations gave rise to a duty to disclose that its own internal forecasts were less exuberant, and to "correct" the investment

---

[2] At the London meeting, Samuel White made remarks substantially the same as his remarks at the May 16 meeting in New York, emphasizing market trends and making no specific or implied representations about short-term performance of Liggett, except as to first quarter figures. McAllister repeated his comments from the previous meeting as well.

Chief financial officer Ralph Moore discussed the performance of its stock and its bond issuance, then added:

> "As you know, Gentlemen, the practice of making sales and earnings forecasts is somewhat more prevalent in the U.K. than in the United States. Liggett & Myers has traditionally been conservative in this respect and we refrain from making sales and earnings predictions. However, we expect another good year in 1972, and we expect to continue to make good progress thereafter."

Plaintiff contends that this representation that the company expected "another good year" in 1972 was tantamount to predicting a significant increase in earnings, despite the fact that, as will be seen below, the company had by then become aware that the month of April had been a bad one (although the first quarter had been very good) and that the internal budget prediction of earnings had been lowered to $3.95 per share for 1972.

community's expectations. The district court held itself bound to reject this claim by *Electronic Specialty Co. v. International Controls Corp., supra.* In that case, arising under § 14(e) of the 1934 Act (as amended in 1968) the plaintiff argued that the defendant, which was preparing to make a tender offer, was under a duty to correct erroneous factual statements in a Wall Street Journal column of which it may have had knowledge but was not the source. We ruled that "(w)hile a company may choose to correct a misstatement in the press not attributable to it, . . . we find nothing in the securities legislation requiring it to do so." 409 F.2d at 949 (*citation omitted*).

While we readily agree that Electronic Specialty is the law of this circuit and that its rule is equally applicable in a suit relying on § 10(b) and Rule 10b–5, the controversy before us is whether Liggett sufficiently entangled itself with the analysts' forecasts to render those predictions "attributable to it," thus removing it from the conduct held protected in Electronic Specialty. We have no doubt that a company may so involve itself in the preparation of reports and projections by outsiders as to assume a duty to correct material errors in those projections. This may occur when officials of the company have, by their activity, made an implied representation that the information they have reviewed is true or at least in accordance with the company's views. [*Citations omitted.*]

After reviewing the facts of this case, however, we find no reason to reverse as clearly erroneous the district court's finding that Liggett did not place its imprimatur, expressly or impliedly, on the analysts' projections. The company did examine and comment on a number of reports, but its policy was to refrain from comment on earnings forecasts. . . . Nor has plaintiff demonstrated that Liggett left uncorrected any factual statements which it knew or believed to be erroneous.[11] Thus, Liggett assumed no duty to disclose its own forecasts or to warn the analysts (and the public) that their optimistic view was not shared by the company.

While we find no liability for non-disclosure in this aspect of the present case, it bears noting that corporate pre-release review of the reports of analysts is a risky activity, fraught with danger. Management must navigate carefully between the "Scylla" of misleading stockholders and the public by implied approval of reviewed analyses and the "Charybdis" of tipping material inside information by correcting statements which it knows to be erroneous. A

[11] A number of commentators have suggested, contrary to Electronic Specialty, the existence of a corporate duty under certain circumstances to correct erroneous information in the marketplace even though the corporation was not the source of that information and has not created the appearance of confirming its accuracy. . . . None of these writers, however, goes so far as to suggest a duty to "correct" projections which differ substantially from the company's internal projections.

company which undertakes to correct errors in reports presented to it for review may find itself forced to choose between raising no objection to a statement which, because it is contradicted by internal information, may be misleading and making that information public at a time when corporate interests would best be served by confidentiality. Management thus risks sacrificing a measure of its autonomy by engaging in this type of program. Since Liggett had not undertaken to pass on earnings forecasts, however, it did not violate any duty to correct these figures.

* * * *

Plaintiff's second argument on appeal is that Liggett's officers intentionally engaged in misleading behavior by their repeated assertions that 1972 was expected to be a good year, knowing that the listening analysts might understand this to confirm their predictions of a 10% increase in earnings, when in fact Liggett expected a less bountiful harvest and had figures showing that the company had fared poorly in April. The district court found this claim to be substantially a restatement of the "duty to disclose" claim which it had rejected, and held that "plaintiff has failed to prove that Liggett made misrepresentations about its financial condition." 472 F. Supp. at 126–27.

The record, particularly the passage quoted in note 2, *supra*, raises the possibility that management was indulging in Delphic pronouncements intended to give the false impression that all was well without stating any untrue facts. The misleading character of a statement is not changed by its vagueness or ambiguity. Liability may follow where management intentionally fosters a mistaken belief concerning a material fact, such as its evaluation of the company's progress and earnings prospects in the current year.

In the present case, the disputed question is whether the statements of Liggett officials to the analyst groups carried an implication that the company viewed the forecasts of the analysts as attainable. If so, the management's statements were material, and (if accompanied by scienter) they were certainly improper. If false, they were deceptive and misleading; if true, they may have constituted non-public disclosure of inside information. In determining how these undisputed statements were intended and likely to be taken by the assembled listeners, we must accord considerable deference to the trial judge, who heard testimony from both the management speakers and those who heard them, as well as from expert witnesses. Evaluation of the context of the statements, the atmosphere of the meetings and standard practices in meetings of this sort, all relevant in this inquiry, is primarily the responsibility of the trier of fact. We cannot conclude as a matter of law that comments such as "we expect another good year in 1972" were likely to confirm the optimistic projections then in circulation or to lead the sophisticated and experienced listeners astray, compare *SEC v. Bausch & Lomb, Inc.,* 565 F.2d 8, 16 (2d Cir. 1977), or that they misrepresented the views of management at the time. We therefore affirm the dismissal of plaintiff's claim alleging misleading conduct.

* * * *

[The Court went on to determine that Liggett's chief financial officer had "tipped" a financial analyst in violation of Rule 10b–5 and then went on to determine the appropriate measure of damages. The discussion of damages set forth in Chapter 9, infra, on Insider Trading.—Eds.]

---

2. *Scienter (Intent or Knowledge of Wrongdoing)*

In a 10b–5 action, the defendant must have acted with an intent to deceive, manipulate, or defraud; negligence alone does NOT suffice. *Ernst & Ernst v. Hochfelder* 425 U.S. 185, 96 S. Ct. 1375, 47 L. Ed. 2d 668 (1976). In *Ernst & Ernst,* an accounting firm had been retained by a small brokerage firm to perform periodic audits of the brokerage firm's books and records. Respondents were customers of the brokerage firm who had invested in a fraudulent securities scheme perpetrated by the president of the brokerage firm. This fraud came to light when Nay, the brokerage firm's president, committed suicide, leaving a note that described the brokerage firm as bankrupt and the accounts as "spurious." Respondents then filed an action for damages against Ernst & Ernst under Rule 10b–5 based on a theory of negligent nonfeasance. Respondents specifically disclaimed the existence of fraud or intentional misconduct on the part of Ernst & Ernst, and the District Court concluded that there was no genuine issue of material fact with respect to whether Ernst & Ernst had conducted its audits in accordance with generally accepted auditing standards.

The Supreme Court held that the Respondents could not bring a private claim for damages "in the absence of any allegation of 'scienter' " which required an intent to deceive, manipulate or defraud by the defendant. The Court went on to explain: "Section 10(b) makes unlawful the use or employment of 'any manipulative or deceptive device or contrivance' in contravention of Commission rules. The words 'manipulative or deceptive' used in conjunction with 'device or contrivance' strongly suggest that § 10(b) was intended to proscribe knowing or intentional misconduct." *Id.* at 197.

The Court in *Hochfelder* did not address the questions of whether a showing of scienter is required in an injunctive action or whether recklessness satisfies the requirement of scienter. Subsequent decisions have determined that scienter is required in an injunctive action (*Aaron v. SEC,* 446 U.S. 680, 100 S. Ct. 1945, 64 L. E2 2d 611 (1980)). However, especially following the passage by Congress of the Private Securities Litigation Reform Act in 1995, there has been a split among the circuits regarding what, if any standard of recklessness will suffice. Most agree that "deliberate" or "severe" recklessness will meet the scienter requirement, but there is disagreement about what constitutes adequate proof of deliberate recklessness.

3. Materiality

The defendant's misrepresentation or omission must have been material, meaning a reasonable investor would likely consider the misstatement or omission to be important in deciding whether to buy or sell. (Note that this standard is about the *reasonable investor*—not the eccentric investor.)

Basic Inc. v. Levinson

485 U.S. 224, 108 S. Ct. 978 (1988)

JUSTICE BLACKMUN delivered the opinion of the Court.

This case requires us to apply the materiality requirement of § 10(b) of the Securities Exchange Act of 1934 . . . in the content of preliminary corporate merger discussions. . .

I

Prior to December 20, 1978, Basic Incorporated was a publicly traded company primarily engaged in the business of manufacturing chemical refractories for the steel industry. As early as 1965 or 1966, Combustion Engineering, Inc., a company producing mostly alumina-based refractories, expressed some interest in acquiring Basic, but was deterred from pursuing this inclination seriously because of antitrust concerns it then entertained. In 1976, however, regulatory action opened the way to a renewal of Combustion's interest. The "Strategic Plan," dated October 25, 1976, for Combustion's Industrial Products Group included the objective: "Acquire Basic Inc. $30 million."

Beginning in September 1976, Combustion representatives had meetings and telephone conversations with Basic officers and directors, including petitioners here, concerning the possibility of a merger. During 1977 and 1978, Basic made three public statements denying that it was engaged in merger negotiations.[4] On December 18, 1978, Basic asked the New York Stock Exchange to suspend trading in its shares and issued a release stating that it had been "approached" by another company concerning a merger. On December 19, Basic's board endorsed Combustion's offer of $46 per share for its common stock, and on the following day publicly announced its approval of Combustion's tender offer for all outstanding shares.

Respondents are former Basic shareholders who sold their stock after Basic's first public statement of October 21, 1977, and before the suspension of trading in December 1978. Respondents brought a class action against Basic and its directors, asserting that the defendants issued three false or misleading public statements and thereby were in violation of § 10(b) of the 1934 Act and of Rule 10b–5. Respondents alleged that they were injured by selling Basic shares at artificially depressed prices in a market affected by petitioners' misleading statements and in reliance thereon.

The District Court adopted a presumption of reliance by members of the plaintiff class upon petitioners public statements that enabled the court to conclude that common questions of fact or law predominated over particular questions pertaining to individual plaintiffs. [*Citation omitted.*] The District Court therefore certified respondents' class. On the merits, however, the District Court granted summary judgment for the defendants. It held that, as a matter of law, any misstatements were immaterial: there were no negotiations ongoing at the time of the first statement, and although negotiations were taking place when the second and third statements were issued, those negotiations were not

---

4 On October 21, 1977, after heavy trading and a new high in Basic stock, the following news item appeared in the Cleveland Plain Dealer:

> "[Basic] President Max Muller said the company knew no reason for the stock's activity and that no negotiations were under way with any company for a merger. He said Flintkote recently denied Wall Street rumors that it would make a tender offer of $25 a share for control of the Cleveland-based maker of refractories for the steel industry.". . .

On September 25, 1978, in reply to an inquiry from the New York Stock Exchange, Basic issued a release concerning increased activity in its stock and stated that

> "management is unaware of any present or pending company development that would result in the abnormally heavy trading activity and price fluctuation in company shares that have been experienced in the past few days.". . .

On November 6, 1978, Basic issued to its shareholders a "Nine Months Report 1978." This Report stated:

> "With regard to the stock market activity in the Company's shares we remain unaware of any present or pending developments which would account for the high volume of trading and price fluctuations in recent months,". . .

"destined, with reasonable certainty, to become a merger agreement in principle."

The United States Court of Appeals for the Sixth Circuit affirmed the class certification, but reversed the District Court's summary judgment, and remanded the case. 786 F. 2d 741 (1986). The court reasoned that while petitioners were under no general duty to disclose their discussions with Combustion, any statement the company voluntarily released could not be " 'so incomplete as to mislead.' " [*Citations omitted.*] In the Court of Appeals' view, Basic's statements that no negotiations were taking place, and that it knew of no corporate developments to account for the heavy trading activity, were misleading. With respect to materiality, the court rejected the argument that preliminary merger discussions are immaterial as a matter of law, and held that "once a statement is made denying the existence of any discussions, even discussions that might not have been material in absence of the denial are material because they make the statement made untrue." 786 F. 2d, at 749.

The Court of Appeals joined a number of other circuits in accepting the "fraud-on-the-market theory" to create a rebuttable presumption that respondents relied on petitioners' material misrepresentations, noting that without the presumption it would be impractical to certify a class under Fed. Rule Civ. Proc. 23(b)(3). [*Citation omitted.*]

We granted certiorari, 484 U.S. 1083 (1987), to resolve the split . . . among the Courts of Appeals as to the standard of materiality applicable to preliminary merger discussions, and to determine whether the courts below properly applied a presumption of reliance in certifying the class, rather than requiring each class member to show direct reliance on Basic's statements.

II

The 1934 Act was designed to protect investors against manipulation of stock prices. . . .

Judicial interpretation and application, legislative acquiescence, and the passage of time have removed any doubt that a private cause of action exists for a violation of § 10(b) and Rule 10b–5, and constitutes an essential tool for enforcement of the 1934 Act's requirements. [*Citations omitted.*]

The Court previously has addressed various positive and common-law requirements for a violation of § 10(b) or of Rule 10b–5. [*Citations omitted.*] The Court also explicitly has defined a standard of materiality under the securities laws, see *TSC Industries, Inc. v. Northway, Inc.,* 426 U.S. 438 (1976), concluding in the proxy-solicitation context that "an omitted fact is material if there is a substantial likelihood that a reasonable shareholder would consider it important in deciding how to vote." *Id.,* at 449. Acknowledging that certain information concerning corporate developments could well be of "dubious significance," the Court was careful not to set too low a standard of materiality; it was concerned that a minimal standard might bring an overabundance of information within its reach, and lead management "simply to bury the shareholders in an avalanche of trivial information—a result that is hardly conducive to informed decisionmaking." It further explained that to fulfill the materiality requirement "there must be a substantial likelihood that the disclosure of the omitted fact would have been viewed by the reasonable investor as having significantly altered the 'total mix' of information made available." *Id.,* at 449. We now expressly adopt the TSC Industries standard of materiality for the § 10(b) and Rule 10b–5 context.

III

The application of this materiality standard to preliminary merger discussions is not self-evident. Where the impact of the corporate development on the target's fortune is certain and clear, the TSC Industries materiality definition admits straightforward application. Where, on the other hand, the event is contingent or speculative in nature, it is difficult to ascertain whether the "reasonable investor" would have considered the omitted information significant at the time. Merger negotiations, because of the ever-present possibility that the contemplated transaction will not be effectuated, fall into the latter category.

A

Petitioners urge upon us a Third Circuit test for resolving this difficulty. Under this approach, preliminary merger discussions do not become material until "agreement-in-principle" as to the price and structure of the transaction has been reached between the would-be merger partners. [*Citations omitted.*] By definition, then, information concerning any negotiations not yet at the agreement-in-principle stage could be withheld or even misrepresented without a violation of Rule 10b–5.

* * * *

None of . . . [the] policy-based rationales, however, purports to explain why drawing the line at agreement-in-principle reflects the significance of the information upon the investor's decision. . . . The role of the materiality requirement is not to "attribute to investors a child-like simplicity, an inability to grasp the probabilistic significance of negotiations," *Flamm v. Eberstadt,* 814 F. 2d, at 1175, but to filter out essentially useless information that a reasonable investor would not consider significant, even as part of a larger "mix" of factors to consider in making his investment decision. *TSC Industries, Inc. v. Northway, Inc.,* 426 U. S., at 448–449.

The . . . importance of secrecy during the early stages of merger discussions, also seems irrelevant to an assessment whether their existence is significant to the trading decision of a reasonable investor. . . .

We need not ascertain, however, whether secrecy necessarily maximizes shareholder wealth. . . . We face here the narrow question whether information concerning the existence and status of preliminary merger discussions is significant to the reasonable investor's trading decision. Arguments based on the premise that some disclosure would be "premature" in a sense are more properly considered under the rubric of an issuer's duty to disclose. The "secrecy" rationale is simply inapposite to the definition of materiality.

The final justification offered in support of the agreement-in-principle test seems to be directed solely at the comfort of corporate managers. A bright-line rule indeed is easier to follow than a standard that requires the exercise of judgment in the light of all the circumstances. But ease of application alone is not an excuse for ignoring the purposes of the securities acts and Congress' policy decisions. . . . After much study, the Advisory Committee on Corporate Disclosure cautioned the SEC against administratively confining materiality to a rigid formula. Courts also would do well to heed this advice.

We therefore find no valid justification for artificially excluding from the definition of materiality information concerning merger discussions, which would otherwise be considered significant to the trading decision of a reasonable investor, merely because agreement-in-principle as to price and structure has not yet been reached by the parties or their representatives.

* * * *

C

Even before this Court's decision in TSC Industries, the Second Circuit had explained the role of the materiality requirement of Rule 10b–5, with respect to contingent or speculative information or events, in a manner that gave that term meaning that is independent of the other provisions of the Rule. Under such circumstances, materiality "will depend at any given time upon a balancing of both the indicated probability that the event will occur and the anticipated magnitude of the event in light of the totality of the company activity." *SEC v. Texas Gulf Sulphur Co.,* 401 F. 2d, at 849. . . .

In a subsequent decision, the late Judge Friendly, writing for a Second Circuit panel, applied the *Texas Gulf Sulphur* probability/magnitude approach in the specific context of preliminary merger negotiations. After acknowledging that materiality is something to be determined on the basis of the particular facts of each case, he stated:

> "Since a merger in which it is bought out is the most important event that can occur in a small corporation's life, to wit, its death, we think that inside information, as regards a merger of this sort, can become material at an earlier stage than would be the case as regards lesser transactions—and this even though the mortality rate of mergers in such formative stages is doubtless high."

SEC v. Geon Industries, Inc., 531 F. 2d 39, 47–48 (1976). We agree with that analysis.

Whether merger discussions in any particular case are material therefore depends on the facts. Generally, in order to assess the probability that the event will occur, a factfinder will need to look to indicia of interest in the transaction at the highest corporate levels. Without attempting to catalog all such possible factors, we note by way of example that board resolutions, instructions to investment bankers, and actual negotiations between principals or their intermediaries may serve as indicia of interest. To assess the magnitude of the transaction to the issuer of the securities allegedly manipulated, a factfinder will need to consider such facts as the size of the two corporate entities and of the potential premiums over market value. No particular event or factor short of closing the transaction need be either necessary or sufficient by itself to render merger discussions material.[17]

As we clarify today, materiality depends on the significance the reasonable investor would place on the withheld or misrepresented information. The fact-

---

[17] To be actionable, of course, a statement must also be misleading. Silence, absent a duty to disclose, is not misleading under Rule 10b–5. "No comment" statements are generally the functional equivalent of silence. . . .

It has been suggested that given current market practices, a "no comment" statement is tantamount to an admission that merger discussions are underway. See *Flamm v. Eberstadt,* 814 F. 2d, at 1178. That may well hold true to the extent that issuers adopt a policy of truthfully denying merger rumors when no discussions are underway, and of issuing "no comment" statements when they are in the midst of negotiations. There are, of course, other statement policies firms could adopt; we need not now advise issuers as to what kind of practice to follow, within the range permitted by law. . . .

specific inquiry we endorse here is consistent with the approach a number of courts have taken in assessing the materiality of merger negotiations. Because the standard of materiality we have adopted differs from that used by both courts below, we remand the case for reconsideration of the question whether a grant of summary judgment is appropriate on this record.

IV

A

We turn to the question of reliance and the fraud-on-the-market theory. Succinctly put:

> "The fraud on the market theory is based on the hypothesis that, in an open and developed securities market, the price of a company's stock is determined by the available material information regarding the company and its business. . . . Misleading statements will therefore defraud purchasers of stock even if the purchasers do not directly rely on the misstatements. . . . The causal connection between the defendants' fraud and the plaintiffs' purchase of stock in such a case is no less significant than in a case of direct reliance on misrepresentations." *Peil v. Speiser,* 806 F. 2d 1154, 1160–1161 (CA3 1986).

Our task, of course, is not to assess the general validity of the theory, but to consider whether it was proper for the courts below to apply a rebuttable presumption of reliance, supported in part by the fraud-on-the-market theory. . . .

This case required resolution of several common questions of law and fact concerning the falsity or misleading nature of the three public statements made by Basic, the presence or absence of scienter, and the materiality of the misrepresentations, if any. In their amended complaint, the named plaintiffs alleged that in reliance on Basic's statements they sold their shares of Basic stock in the depressed market created by petitioners. [*Citations omitted.*] Requiring proof of individualized reliance from each member of the proposed plaintiff class effectively would have prevented respondents from proceeding with a class action, since individual issues then would have overwhelmed the common ones. . . .

Petitioners and their amici complain that the fraud-on-the-market theory effectively eliminates the requirement that a plaintiff asserting a claim under Rule 10b–5 prove reliance. They note that reliance is and long has been an element of common-law fraud [*Citations omitted.*] and argue that because the analogous express right of action includes a reliance requirement . . . so too must an action implied under § 10(b).

We agree that reliance is an element of a Rule 10b–5 cause of action. [*Citations omitted.*] Reliance provides the requisite causal connection between a defendant's misrepresentation and a plaintiff's injury. [*Citations omitted.*] There is, however, more than one way to demonstrate the causal connection. Indeed, we previously have dispensed with a requirement of positive proof of reliance, where a duty to disclose material information had been breached, concluding that the necessary nexus between the plaintiffs' injury and the defendant's wrongful conduct had been established. See *Affiliated Ute Citizens v. United States,* 406 U.S., at 153–154. . . .

The modern securities markets, literally involving millions of shares changing hands daily, differ from the face-to-face transactions contemplated by early fraud cases, and our understanding of *Rule 10b–5's* reliance requirement must encompass these differences.

> "In face-to-face transactions, the inquiry into an investor's reliance upon information is into the subjective pricing of that information by that investor. With the presence of a market, the market is interposed between seller and buyer and, ideally, transmits information to the investor in the processed form of a market price. Thus the market is performing a substantial part of the valuation process performed by the investor in a face-to-face transaction. The market is acting as the unpaid agent of the investor, informing him that given all the information available to it, the value of the stock is worth the market price." *In re LTV Securities Litigation,* 88 F.R.D. 134, 143 (ND Tex. 1980). . . .

B

Presumptions typically serve to assist courts in managing circumstances in which direct proof, for one reason or another, is rendered difficult. [*Citations omitted.*] The courts below accepted a presumption, created by the fraud-on-the-market theory and subject to rebuttal by petitioners, that persons who had traded Basic shares had done so in reliance on the integrity of the price set by the market, but because of petitioners' material misrepresentations that price had been fraudulently depressed. Requiring a plaintiff to show a speculative state of facts, i.e., how he would have acted if omitted material information had been disclosed . . . or if the misrepresentation had not been made, . . . would place an unnecessarily unrealistic evidentiary burden on the Rule 10b–5 plaintiff who has traded on an impersonal market. . .

Arising out of considerations of fairness, public policy, and probability, as well as judicial economy, presumptions are also useful devices for allocating the burdens of proof between parties. . . . The presumption of reliance employed in this case is consistent with, and, by facilitating Rule 10b–5 litigation, supports, the congressional policy embodied in the 1934 Act. . . .

The presumption is also supported by common sense and probability. Recent empirical studies have tended to confirm Congress' premise that the market price of shares traded on well-developed markets reflects all publicly available information, and, hence, any material misrepresentations. It has been noted that "it is hard to imagine that there ever is a buyer or seller who does not rely on market integrity. Who would knowingly roll the dice in a crooked crap game?" *Schlanger v. Four-Phase Systems Inc.,* 555 F. Supp. 535, 538 (SDNY 1982). Indeed, nearly every court that has considered the proposition has concluded that where materially misleading statements have been disseminated into an impersonal, well-developed market for securities, the reliance of individual plaintiffs on the integrity of the market price may be presumed. Commentators generally have applauded the adoption of one variation or another of the fraud-on-the-market theory. An investor who buys or sells stock at the price set by the market does so in reliance on the integrity of that price. Because most publicly available information is reflected in market price, an investor's reliance on any public material misrepresentations, therefore, may be presumed for purposes of a Rule 10b–5 action.

C

The Court of Appeals found that petitioners "made public material misrepresentations and [respondents] sold Basic stock in an impersonal, efficient market. Thus the class, as defined by the district court, has established the threshold facts for proving their loss." 786 F.2d, at 751. The court acknowledged that petitioners may rebut proof of the elements giving rise to the presumption, or show that the misrepresentation in fact did not lead to a distortion of price or that an individual plaintiff traded or would have traded despite his knowing the statement was false.

Any showing that severs the link between the alleged misrepresentation and either the price received (or paid) by the plaintiff, or his decision to trade at a fair market price, will be sufficient to rebut the presumption of reliance. For example, if petitioners could show that the "market makers" were privy to the truth about the merger discussions here with Combustion, and thus that the market price would not have been affected by their misrepresentations, the causal connection could be broken: the basis for finding that the fraud had been transmitted through market price would be gone. Similarly, if, despite petitioners' allegedly fraudulent attempt to manipulate market price, news of the merger discussions credibly entered the market and dissipated the effects of the misstatements, those who traded Basic shares after the corrective statements would have no direct or indirect connection with the fraud. Petitioners also could rebut the presumption of reliance as to plaintiffs who would have divested themselves of their Basic shares without relying on the integrity of the market. For example, a plaintiff who believed that Basic's statements were false and that Basic was indeed engaged in merger discussions, and who consequently believed that Basic stock was artificially underpriced, but sold his shares nevertheless because of other unrelated concerns, e.g., potential antitrust problems, or political pressures to divest from shares of certain businesses, could not be said to have relied on the integrity of a price he knew had been manipulated.

V

* * * *

The judgment of the Court of Appeals is vacated and the case is remanded to that court for further proceedings consistent with this opinion.

It is so ordered.

THE CHIEF JUSTICE, JUSTICE SCALIA, and JUSTICE KENNEDY took no part in the consideration or decision of this case.

DISSENT

JUSTICE WHITE, with whom JUSTICE O'CONNOR joins, concurring in part and dissenting in part.

I join Parts I–III of the Court's opinion, as I agree that the standard of materiality we set forth in *TSC Industries, Inc. v. Northway, Inc.,* 426 U. S. 438, 449 (1976), should be applied to actions under § 10(b) and Rule 10b–5. But I dissent from the remainder of the Court's holding because I do not agree that the "fraud-on-the-market" theory should be applied in this case.

I

[T]he fraud-on-the-market theory is a mere babe. Yet today, the Court embraces this theory with the sweeping confidence usually reserved for more mature legal doctrines. In so doing, I fear that the Court's decision may have many adverse, unintended effects as it is applied and interpreted in the years to come.

A

At the outset, I note that there are portions of the Court's fraud-on-the-market holding with which I am in agreement. Most importantly, the Court rejects the version of that theory, heretofore adopted by some courts, which equates "causation" with "reliance," and permits recovery by a plaintiff who claims merely to have been harmed by a material misrepresentation which altered a market price, notwithstanding proof that the plaintiff did not in any way rely on that price. . . . I agree with the Court that if Rule 10b–5's reliance requirement is to be left with any content at all, the fraud-on-the-market presumption must be capable of being rebutted by a showing that a plaintiff did not "rely" on the market price. For example, a plaintiff who decides, months in advance of an alleged misrepresentation, to purchase a stock; one who buys or sells a stock for reasons unrelated to its price; one who actually sells a stock "short" days before the misrepresentation is made—surely none of these people can state a valid claim under Rule 10b–5. . . .

* * * *

B

But even as the Court attempts to limit the fraud-on-the-market theory it endorses today, the pitfalls in its approach are revealed by previous uses by the lower courts of the broader versions of the theory. Confusion and contradiction in court rulings are inevitable when traditional legal analysis is replaced with economic theorization by the federal courts.

In general, the case law developed in this Court with respect to § 10(b) and Rule 10b–5 has been based on doctrines with which we, as judges, are familiar: common-law doctrines of fraud and deceit. . . . The federal courts have proved adept at developing an evolving jurisprudence of Rule 10b–5 in such a manner. But with no staff economists, no experts schooled in the "efficient-capital-market hypothesis," no ability to test the validity of empirical market studies, we are not well equipped to embrace novel constructions of a statute based on contemporary microeconomic theory.

* * * *

For while the economists' theories which underpin the fraud-on-the-market presumption may have the appeal of mathematical exactitude and scientific certainty, they are—in the end—nothing more than theories which may or may not prove accurate upon further consideration. Even the most earnest advocates of economic analysis of the law recognize this. . . . Thus, while the majority states that, for purposes of reaching its result it need only make modest assumptions about the way in which "market professionals generally" do their jobs, and how the conduct of market professionals affects stock prices. . ., I doubt that we are in much of a position to assess which theories aptly describe the functioning of the securities industry.

Consequently, I cannot join the Court in its effort to reconfigure the securities laws, based on recent economic theories, to better fit what it perceives to be the new realities of financial markets. I would leave this task to others more equipped for the job than we.

C

At the bottom of the Court's conclusion that the fraud-on-the-market theory sustains a presumption of reliance is the assumption that individuals rely "on the integrity of the market price" when buying or selling stock in "impersonal, well-developed market[s] for securities." . . . . [I]n adopting a "presumption of reliance," the Court also assumes that buyers and sellers rely—not just on the market price—but on the "integrity" of that price. It is this aspect of the fraud-on-the-market hypothesis which most mystifies me.

. . . But the meaning of this phrase ["integrity of the market price"] eludes me, for it implicitly suggests that stocks have some "true value" that is measurable by a standard other than their market price. While the Scholastics of Medieval times professed a means to make such a valuation of a commodity's "worth," I doubt that the federal courts of our day are similarly equipped.

Even if securities had some "value"—knowable and distinct from the market price of a stock—investors do not always share the Court's presumption that a stock's price is a "reflection of [this] value." Indeed, "many investors purchase or sell stock because they believe the price inaccurately reflects the corporation's worth." . . . .

I do not propose that the law retreat from the many protections that § 10(b) and Rule 10b–5, as interpreted in our prior cases, provide to investors. But any extension of these laws, to approach something closer to an investor insurance scheme, should come from Congress, and not from the courts.

* * * *

III

Finally, the particular facts of this case make it an exceedingly poor candidate for the Court's fraud-on-the-market theory, and illustrate the illogic achieved by that theory's application in many cases.

Respondents here are a class of sellers who sold Basic stock between October, 1977 and December 1978, a fourteen-month period. At the time the class period began, Basic's stock was trading at $20 a share (at the time, an all-time high); the last members of the class to sell their Basic stock got a price of just over $30 a share. It is indisputable that virtually every member of the class made money from his or her sale of Basic stock.

The oddities of applying the fraud-on-the-market theory in this case are manifest. First, there are the facts that the plaintiffs are sellers and the class period is so lengthy—both are virtually without precedent in prior fraud-on-the-market cases. For reasons I discuss in the margin, I think these two facts render this case less apt to application of the fraud-on-the-market hypothesis.

Second, there is the fact that in this case, there is no evidence that petitioner's officials made the troublesome misstatements for the purpose of manipulating stock prices, or with any intent to engage in underhanded trading of Basic stock. Indeed, during the class period, petitioners do not appear to have purchased or sold any Basic stock whatsoever. . . . And it is difficult to square liability in this case with § 10(b)'s express provision that it prohibits fraud "in connection with the purchase or sale of any security." [*Citations omitted.*]

Third, there are the peculiarities of what kinds of investors will be able to recover in this case. As I read the District Court's class certification order, there are potentially many persons who did not purchase Basic stock until after the first false statement (October 1977), but who nonetheless will be able to recover under the Court's fraud-on-the-market theory. Thus, it is possible that a person who heard the first corporate misstatement and disbelieved it—i.e., someone who purchased Basic stock thinking that petitioners' statement was false—may still be included in the plaintiff-class on remand. How a person who undertook such a speculative stock-investing strategy—and made $10 a share doing so (if he bought on October 22, 1977, and sold on December 15, 1978)—can say that he was "defrauded" by virtue of his reliance on the "integrity" of the market price is beyond me. . . .

Indeed, the facts of this case lead a casual observer to the almost inescapable conclusion that many of those who bought or sold Basic stock during the period in question flatly disbelieved the statements which are alleged to have been "materially misleading." Despite three statements denying that merger negotiations were underway, Basic stock hit record-high after record-high during the 14-month class period. It seems quite possible that, like Casca's knowing disbelief of Caesear's "thrice refusal" of the Crown, clever investors were skeptical of petitioners' three denials that merger talks were going on. Yet such investors, the savviest of the savvy, will be able to recover under the Court's opinion, as long as they now claim that they believed in the "integrity of the market price" when they sold their stock (between September and December, 1978). Thus, persons who bought after hearing and relying on the falsity of petitioner's statements may be able to prevail and recover money damages on remand.

And who will pay the judgments won in such actions? I suspect that all too often the majority's rule will "lead to large judgments, payable in the last analysis by innocent investors, for the benefit of speculators and their lawyers." . . . . Yet such a bitter harvest is likely to be the reaped from the seeds sewn by the Court's decision today.

IV

In sum, I think the court's embracement of the fraud-on-the-market theory represents a departure in securities law that we are ill-suited to commence—and even less equipped to control as it proceeds. As a result, I must respectfully dissent.

NOTE ON THE MATERIALITY OF A CONTINGENT EVENT

The preceding case involves a situation in which a determination must be made about whether something that *might* happen (a contingent event) is material. In order to evaluate a contingent event, the probability/magnitude test (sometimes called "the *Basic* Test") should be used. In this test one must evaluate the probability that an event will happen and the importance of the event, if it does happen. There are four possible results when looking at the probability and magnitude of an event occurring:

1. A contingent event could have both a high probability of occurring and high magnitude (i.e., significance or importance) if it does occur. If so, it is material.

2. Conversely, a contingent event could have both a low probability of occurring and a low magnitude if it does occur. If so, it would not be material.

3. Even an event which has a high probability of occurring, but a low magnitude if it does occur, is not material since it is unlikely that something of little importance or significance would impact a company's stock price.

4. The most difficult situation to evaluate involves a contingent event that has a low to moderate probability of occurring but high magnitude if it does. Whether a contingent event in this category is "material" is ultimately a question of fact.

---

4. Reliance

If a plaintiff brings a private action, there must also be a showing that he or she actually AND justifiably relied on the defendant's misrepresentation. (Sometimes reliance is referred to as "transaction causation," *Abell v. Potomac Ins. Co.*, 858 F.2d 1104, 1118 (5th Cir. 1988).) Reliance is critical to a claim because it establishes a causal connection between the misstatement made and the damage suffered by the plaintiff. If a plaintiff did not rely on a misstatement, then how could the plaintiff have been damaged by it? Reliance must also be reasonable. *List v. Fashion Park, Inc.,* 340 F.2d 457, 462 (2d Cir. 1965). While it is clear how a party may show that they "relied" on an untrue statement, it is, of course, difficult to show reliance upon a statement that was not made.

Reliance on Omissions

There are some situations in which the company or an officer of the company has a duty to speak but does not. If an event of large significance occurs, a company would typically have an obligation to disclose that event. The company's failure to disclose that event would be considered an omission. However, how does a plaintiff show that he or she "relied" on something that was not said? The answer is that, given the duty to disclose, a person is entitled to rely that appropriate disclosures will be made. In effect, one may rely on silence as a "statement" that there is no material information *that the company is required to disclose,* which has not been disclosed. Therefore, in the case of an omission, reliance is presumed, but this is a rebuttable presumption. *Affiliated Ute Citizens v. United States,* 406 U.S. 128, 153–54 (1972).

Reliance and Fraud-on-the-Market

There are several cases involving affirmative misrepresentations (usually involving a large group of people), in which the plaintiffs cannot show that they each relied on the misstatements. It is around this situation that the doctrine of "fraud on the market" has arisen. (*See* Section IV of the *Basic* case, *supra.*) The fraud on the market theory was developed as a way to show how a large group of people could have relied on a misstatement. The fraud on the market theory creates a rebuttable presumption that, even if the plaintiff was unaware of the misstatement, there was still reliance on the integrity of the market price and, thus, the case may proceed.

As discussed in the *West* case, below, fraud on the market is invoked when there is a *public affirmative misrepresentation* AND *the market is an efficient market* (e.g. the stock market). It does NOT apply in private transactions. Behind the fraud on the market theory is the concept that, BECAUSE a large number of sophisticated analysts at a large number of firms read and evaluate public statements about a corporation and make substantial decisions for their firms to buy or sell stock based on statements, those purchases or sales (because collectively, they are so large) affect the price of the stock. As a result, any misrepresentation is priced into the market and thus, affects the price at which the unsophisticated investor buys and sells stock, even if that unsophisticated investor did not hear, read or rely on the actual misrepresentation. The practical impact of this theory is often to eliminate the reliance requirement in these cases. If the defendant in such cases wants to avoid liability, the defendant needs to rebut the theory by showing that the misrepresentation did NOT affect the market price. Fraud-on-the-market relies on the notion that information is taken into account by the market and the market operates efficiently given that information.

West v. Prudential Securities, Inc.

282 F.3d 935 (7th Cir. 2002)

EASTERBROOK, C.J.:

According to the complaint in this securities-fraud action, James Hofman, a stockbroker working for Prudential Securities, told 11 of his customers that Jefferson Savings Bancorp was "certain" to be acquired, at a big premium, in the near future. Hofman continued making this statement for seven months (repeating it to some clients); it was a lie, for no acquisition was impending. And if the statement had been the truth, then Hofman was inviting unlawful trading on the basis of material non-public information. He is a securities offender coming or going, s*ee Bateman Eichler, Hill Richards, Inc. v. Berner,* 472 U.S. 299, 86 L. Ed. 2d 215, 105 S. Ct. 2622 (1985), as are any customers who traded on what they thought to be confidential information—if Hofman said what the plaintiffs allege, a subject still to be determined. What we must decide is whether the action may proceed, not on behalf of those who received Hofman's "news" in person but on behalf of everyone who bought Jefferson stock during the months when Hofman was misbehaving. The district judge certified such a class, invoking the fraud-on-the-market doctrine of *Basic, Inc. v. Levinson,* 485 U.S. 224, 241–49, 99 L. Ed. 2d 194, 108 S. Ct. 978 (1988). Prudential asks us to entertain an interlocutory appeal under Fed. R. Civ. P. 23(f). For two reasons, this is an appropriate case for such an appeal, which we now accept. . . .

First, the district court's order marks a substantial extension of the fraud-on-the-market approach. Basic held that "because most publicly available information is reflected in market price, an investor's reliance on any public material misrepresentations, therefore, may be presumed for purposes of a Rule 10b–5 action." 485 U.S. at 247. The theme of Basic and other fraud-on-the-market decisions is that public information reaches professional investors, whose evaluations of that information and trades quickly influence securities prices. But Hofman did not release information to the public, and his clients thought that they were receiving and acting on non-public information; its value (if any) lay precisely in the fact that other traders did not know the news. No newspaper or other organ of general circulation reported that Jefferson was soon to be acquired. As plaintiffs summarize their position, their "argument in a nutshell is that it is unimportant for purposes of the fraud-on-the-market doctrine whether the information was 'publicly available' in the . . . sense that . . . the information was disseminated through a press release, or prospectus or other written format". Yet extending the fraud-on-the-market doctrine in this way requires not only a departure from Basic but also a novelty in fraud cases as a class—as another court of appeals remarked only recently in another securities suit, oral frauds have not been allowed to proceed as class actions, for the details of the deceit differ from victim to victim, and the nature of the loss also may be statement-specific. . . .

Second, very few securities class actions are litigated to conclusion, so review of this novel and important legal issue may be possible only through the Rule 23(f) device. What is more, some scholars believe that the settlements in securities cases reflect high risk of catastrophic loss, which together with imperfect alignment of managers' and investors' interests leads defendants to pay substantial sums even when the plaintiffs have weak positions. [*Citations omitted.*] The strength of this effect has been debated, see Joel Seligman, *The Merits Do Matter,* 108 Harv. L. Rev. 438 (1994), but its existence is established.

The effect of a class certification in inducing settlement to curtail the risk of large awards provides a powerful reason to take an interlocutory appeal.

* * * *

Causation is the shortcoming in this class certification. Basic describes a mechanism by which public information affects stock prices, and thus may affect traders who did not know about that information. Professional investors monitor news about many firms; good news implies higher dividends and other benefits, which induces these investors to value the stock more highly, and they continue buying until the gains are exhausted. With many professional investors alert to news, markets are efficient in the sense that they rapidly adjust to all public information; if some of this information is false, the price will reach an incorrect level, staying there until the truth emerges. This approach has the support of financial economics as well as the imprimatur of the Justices: few propositions in economics are better established than the quick adjustment of securities prices to public information. [*Citations omitted.*]

No similar mechanism explains how prices would respond to non-public information, such as statements made by Hofman to a handful of his clients. These do not come to the attention of professional investors or money managers, so the price-adjustment mechanism just described does not operate. Sometimes full-time market watchers can infer important news from the identity of a trader (when the corporation's CEO goes on a buying spree, this implies good news) or from the sheer volume of trades (an unprecedented buying volume may suggest that a bidder is accumulating stock in anticipation of a tender offer), but neither the identity of Hofman's customers nor the volume of their trades would have conveyed information to the market in this fashion. No one these days accepts the strongest version of the efficient capital market hypothesis, under which non-public information automatically affects prices. That version is empirically false: the public announcement of news (good and bad) has big effects on stock prices, which could not happen if prices already incorporated the effect of non-public information. Thus it is hard to see how Hofman's non-public statements could have caused changes in the price of Jefferson Savings stock. Basic founded the fraud-on-the-market doctrine on a causal mechanism with both theoretical and empirical power; for non-public information there is nothing comparable.

The district court did not identify any causal link between non-public information and securities prices, let alone show that the link is as strong as the one deemed sufficient (by a bare majority) in Basic (only four of the six Justices who participated in that case endorsed the fraud-on-the-market doctrine).

Instead the judge observed that each side has the support of a reputable financial economist (Michael J. Barclay for the plaintiffs, Charles C. Cox for the defendant) and thought the clash enough by itself to support class certification and a trial on the merits. That amounts to a delegation of judicial power to the plaintiffs, who can obtain class certification just by hiring a competent expert. A district judge may not duck hard questions by observing that each side has some support, or that considerations relevant to class certification also may affect the decision on the merits. Tough questions must be faced and squarely decided, if necessary by holding evidentiary hearings and choosing between competing perspectives. [*Citations omitted.*]

Because the record here does not demonstrate that non-public information affected the price of Jefferson Savings' stock, a remand is unnecessary. What the plaintiffs have going for them is that Jefferson's stock did rise in price (by about $5, or 20% of its trading price) during the months when Hofman was touting an impending acquisition, plus a model of demand-pull price increases offered by their expert. Barclay started with a model devised by another economist, in which trades themselves convey information to the market and thus affect price. *See* Joel Hasbrouck, *Measuring the Information Content of Stock Trades*, 46 J. Fin. 179 (1991). Hasbrouck's model assumes that some trades are by informed traders and some by uninformed traders, and that the market may be able to draw inferences about which is which. The model has not been verified empirically. Barclay approached the issue differently, assuming that all trades affect prices by raising demand even if no trader is well informed—as if there were an economic market in "Jefferson Savings stock" as there is in dill pickles or fluffy towels. Hofman's tips raised the demand for Jefferson Savings stock and curtailed the supply (for the tippees were less likely to sell their own shares); that combination of effects raised the stock's price. Yet investors do not want Jefferson Savings stock (as if they sought to paper their walls with beautiful certificates); they want monetary returns (at given risk levels), returns that are available from many financial instruments. One fundamental attribute of efficient markets is that information, not demand in the abstract, determines stock prices. [*Citations omitted.*] There are so many substitutes for any one firm's stock that the effective demand curve is horizontal. It may shift up or down with new information but is not sloped like the demand curve for physical products. That is why institutional purchases (which can be large in relation to normal trading volume) do not elevate prices, while relatively small trades by insiders can have substantial effects; the latter trades convey information, and the former do not. Barclay, who took the view that the market for Jefferson Savings securities is efficient, did not explain why he departed from the normal understanding that information rather than raw demand determines securities prices.

Data may upset theory, and if Barclay had demonstrated that demand by itself elevates securities prices, then the courts would be required to attend closely. What Barclay did is inquire whether the price of Jefferson Savings stock rose during the period of additional demand by Hofman's customers. He gave an affirmative answer and stopped. Yet it is not possible to prove a relation between demand and price without considering other potential reasons. Was there perhaps some truthful Jefferson-specific information released to the market at the time? Did Jefferson perhaps move with the market? It rose relative to a basket of all financial institutions, but (according to Cox's report) not relative to a portfolio of Midwestern financial intermediaries. Several Missouri banks and thrifts similar to Jefferson Savings were acquired during the months in question, and these transactions conveyed some information about the probability of a deal involving Jefferson Savings. If the price of Jefferson Savings was doing just what one would have expected in the presence of this changing probability of acquisition, and the absence of any Hofman-induced trades, then the causal link between Hofman's statements and price has not been made out. By failing to test for and exclude other potential sources of price movement, Barclay undercut the power of the inference that he advanced.

Indeed, Barclay's report calls into question his belief that the market for Jefferson Savings stock is efficient, the foundation of the fraud-on-the-market doctrine. In an efficient market, how could one ignorant outsider's lie cause a long-term rise in price? Professional investors would notice the inexplicable rise and either investigate for themselves (discovering the truth) or sell short immediately, driving the price back down. In an efficient market, a lie told by someone with nothing to back up the statement (no professional would have thought Hofman a person "in the know") will self-destruct long before eight months have passed. Hofman asserted that an acquisition was imminent. That statement might gull people for a month, but after two or three months have passed the lack of a merger or tender offer puts the lie to the assertion; professional investors then draw more astute inferences and the price effect disappears. That this did not occur implies either that Jefferson Savings was not closely followed by professional investors (and that the market therefore does not satisfy Basic's efficiency requirement) or that something other than Hofman's statements explains these price changes.

The record thus does not support extension of the fraud-on-the-market doctrine to the non-public statements Hofman is alleged to have made about Jefferson Savings Bancorp. . . .

Reversed.

NOTES AND QUESTIONS

1. Defendants may rebut the applicability of the fraud on the market theory to a particular transaction by showing that: the misrepresentation did not affect market price; the defendants issued corrective statements which were also priced into the market; the plaintiffs would have bought or sold anyway, even with full disclosure; or the plaintiff did not rely on the integrity of the market.

2. If you were representing a defendant to a 10b–5 action who was defending against allegations that there had been a fraud on the market, how might you go about showing that the statement did not affect the market price?

3. What does it mean to "rely on the integrity of the market" and why should it matter?

4. Note that not all states recognize fraud on the market as a valid legal theory that will take the place of reliance.

---

5. Causation

Causation is also known as "proximate cause" or "loss causation." To satisfy this requirement, it is not enough to show that the misrepresentation caused the transaction (*see* reliance above), the plaintiff also needs to show that the misrepresentation or omission caused the loss itself. Furthermore, as will be seen in the *Dura Pharmaceuticals, Inc. v. Broudo* case which follows, the Supreme Court has held that a plaintiff making a securities fraud claim must do more than merely allege that the price of the security in question was inflated because of the misrepresentation. The plaintiff must allege and prove the "traditional elements of causation and loss." When reading the case that follows, consider how an attorney for the plaintiff in such a case might go about proving these elements and what actions an attorney for the defendant might take in an effort to refute such claims of causation.

Dura Pharmaceuticals, Inc. v. Broudo

544 U.S. 336, 125 S. Ct. 1627, 161 L. Ed. 2d 577 (2005)

BREYER, J., delivered the opinion for a unanimous Court.

A private plaintiff who claims securities fraud must prove that the defendant's fraud caused an economic loss. . . . We consider a Ninth Circuit holding that a plaintiff can satisfy this requirement—a requirement that courts call "loss causation"—simply by alleging in the complaint and subsequently establishing that "the price" of the security "*on the date of purchase* was inflated because of the misrepresentation." 339 F.3d 933, 938 (2003) (internal quotation marks omitted). In our view, the Ninth Circuit is wrong, both in respect to what a plaintiff must prove and in respect to what the plaintiffs' complaint here must allege.

I

Respondents are individuals who bought stock in Dura Pharmaceuticals, Inc., on the public securities market between April 15, 1997, and February 24, 1998. They have brought this securities fraud class action against Dura and some of its managers and directors (hereinafter Dura) in federal court. In respect to the question before us, their detailed amended . . . complaint makes substantially the following allegations:

(1) Before and during the purchase period, Dura (or its officials) made false statements concerning both Dura's drug profits and future Food and Drug Administration (FDA) approval of a new asthmatic spray device. See, *e.g.,* App. 45a, 55a, 89a.

(2) In respect to drug profits, Dura falsely claimed that it expected that its drug sales would prove profitable. See, *e.g., id.,* at 66a–69a.

(3) In respect to the asthmatic spray device, Dura falsely claimed that it expected the FDA would soon grant its approval. See, *e.g., id.,* at 89a–90a, 103a–104a.

(4) On the last day of the purchase period, February 24, 1998, Dura announced that its earnings would be lower than expected, principally due to slow drug sales. *Id.,* at 51a.

(5) The next day Dura's shares lost almost half their value (falling from about $39 per share to about $21). *Ibid.*

(6) About eight months later (in November 1998), Dura announced that the FDA would not approve Dura's new asthmatic spray device. *Id.,* at 110a.

(7) The next day Dura's share price temporarily fell but almost fully recovered within one week. *Id.,* at 156a.

Most importantly, the complaint says the following (and nothing significantly more than the following) about economic losses attributable to the spray device misstatement: "*In reliance on the integrity of the market, [the plaintiffs] . . . paid artificially inflated prices for Dura securities" and the plaintiffs suffered "damage[s]" thereby*. *Id.,* at 139a (emphasis added).

The District Court dismissed the complaint. In respect to the plaintiffs' drug-profitability claim, it held that the complaint failed adequately to allege an appropriate state of mind, *i.e.,* that defendants had acted knowingly, or the like. In respect to the plaintiffs' spray device claim, it held that the complaint failed adequately to allege "loss causation."

The Court of Appeals for the Ninth Circuit reversed. In the portion of the court's decision now before us—the portion that concerns the spray device claim—the Circuit held that the complaint adequately alleged "loss causation." The Circuit wrote that "plaintiffs establish loss causation if they have shown that the price *on the date of purchase* was inflated because of the misrepresentation." 339 F.3d at 938 (emphasis in original; internal quotation marks and citation omitted). It added that "the injury occurs at the time of the transaction." *Ibid.* Since the complaint pleaded "that the price at the time of purchase was overstated," and it sufficiently identified the cause, its allegations were legally sufficient. *Ibid.*

Because the Ninth Circuit's views about loss causation differ from those of other Circuits that have considered this issue, we granted Dura's petition for certiorari. [*Citations omitted.*] We now reverse.

II

Private federal securities fraud actions are based upon federal securities statutes and their implementing regulations. Section 10(b) of the Securities Exchange Act of 1934 forbids (1) the "use or employ[ment] . . . of any . . . deceptive device," (2) "in connection with the purchase or sale of any security," and (3) "in contravention of" Securities and Exchange Commission "rules and regulations." . . . Commission Rule 10b–5 forbids, among other things, the making of any "untrue statement of a material fact" or the omission of any material fact "necessary in order to make the statements made . . . not misleading." . . .

The courts have implied from these statutes and Rule a private damages action, which resembles, but is not identical to, common-law tort actions for deceit and misrepresentation. See, *e.g., Blue Chip Stamps v. Manor Drug Stores,* 421 U.S. 723, 730, 744, 44 L. Ed. 2d 539, 95 S. Ct. 1917 (1975); *Ernst & Ernst v. Hochfelder,* 425 U.S. 185, 196, 47 L. Ed. 2d 668, 96 S. Ct. 1375 (1976). And Congress has imposed statutory requirements on that private action. *E.g.,* 15 U S C § 78u–4(b)(4) [15 U S C S § 78u–4(b)(4)].

In cases involving publicly traded securities and purchases or sales in public securities markets, the action's basic elements include:

(1) *a material misrepresentation (or omission),* see *Basic Inc. v. Levinson,* 485 U.S. 224, 231–232, 99 L. Ed. 2d 194, 108 S. Ct. 978 (1988);

(2) *scienter, i.e., a wrongful state of mind,* see *Ernst & Ernst, supra,* at 197, 199, 47 L. Ed. 2d 668, 96 S. Ct. 1375;

(3) *a connection with the purchase or sale of a security,* see *Blue Chip Stamps, supra,* at 730–731, 44 L. Ed. 2d 539, 95 S. Ct. 1917;

(4) *reliance,* often referred to in cases involving public securities markets (fraud-on-the-market cases) as "transaction causation," see *Basic, supra,* at 248–249, 99 L. Ed. 2d 194, 108 S. Ct. 978 (nonconclusively presuming that the price of a publicly traded share reflects a material misrepresentation and that plaintiffs have relied upon that misrepresentation as long as they would not have bought the share in its absence);

(5) *economic loss,* 15 U S C § 78u–4(b)(4) [15 U S C S § 78u–4(b)(4)]; and

(6) "*loss causation,*" *i.e.,* a causal connection between the material misrepresentation and the loss, *ibid.;* cf. T. Hazen, Law of Securities Regulation §§ 12.11[1], [3] (5th ed. 2005).

Dura argues that the complaint's allegations are inadequate in respect to these last two elements.

A

We begin with the Ninth Circuit's basic reason for finding the complaint adequate, namely, that at the end of the day plaintiffs need only "establish," *i.e.,* prove, that "the price *on the date of purchase* was inflated because of the misrepresentation." 339 F.3d at 938 (internal quotation marks and citation omitted). In our view, this statement of the law is wrong. Normally, in cases such as this one (*i.e.,* fraud-on-the-market cases), an inflated purchase price will not itself constitute or proximately cause the relevant economic loss.

For one thing, as a matter of pure logic, at the moment the transaction takes place, the plaintiff has suffered no loss; the inflated purchase payment is offset by ownership of a share that *at that instant* possesses equivalent value. Moreover, the logical link between the inflated share purchase price and any later economic loss is not invariably strong. Shares are normally purchased with an eye toward a later sale. But if, say, the purchaser sells the shares quickly before the relevant truth begins to leak out, the misrepresentation will not have led to any loss. If the purchaser sells later after the truth makes its way into the marketplace, an initially inflated purchase price *might* mean a later loss. But that is far from inevitably so. When the purchaser subsequently resells such shares, even at a lower price, that lower price may reflect, not the earlier misrepresentation, but changed economic circumstances, changed investor expectations, new industry-specific or firm-specific facts, conditions, or other events, which taken separately or together account for some or all of that lower price. (The same is true in respect to a claim that a share's higher price is lower than it would otherwise have been—a claim we do not consider here.) Other things being equal, the longer the time between purchase and sale, the more likely that this is so, *i.e.,* the more likely that other factors caused the loss.

Given the tangle of factors affecting price, the most logic alone permits us to say is that the higher purchase price will *sometimes* play a role in bringing about a future loss. It may prove to be a necessary condition of any such loss, and in that sense one might say that the inflated purchase price suggests that the misrepresentation (using language the Ninth Circuit used) "touches upon" a later economic loss. *Ibid.* But, even if that is so, it is insufficient. To "touch upon" a loss is not to *cause* a loss, and it is the latter that the law requires. . . .

For another thing, the Ninth Circuit's holding lacks support in precedent. Judicially implied private securities fraud actions resemble in many (but not all) respects common-law deceit and misrepresentation actions. [*Citations omitted.*] The common law of deceit subjects a person who "fraudulently" makes a "misrepresentation" to liability "for pecuniary loss caused" to one who justifiably relies upon that misrepresentation. [*Citations omitted.*] And the common law has long insisted that a plaintiff in such a case show not only that had he known the truth he would not have acted but also that he suffered actual economic loss. See, *e.g., Pasley v. Freeman,* 3 T.R. 51, 65, 100 Eng. Rep. 450, 457

(1789) (if "no injury is occasioned by the lie, it is not actionable: but if it be attended with a damage, it then becomes the subject of an action"). . . .

Given the common-law roots of the securities fraud action (and the common-law requirement that a plaintiff show actual damages), it is not surprising that other Courts of Appeals have rejected the Ninth Circuit's "inflated purchase price" approach to proving causation and loss. [*Citations omitted.*] Indeed, the Restatement of Torts, in setting forth the judicial consensus, says that a person who "misrepresents the financial condition of a corporation in order to sell its stock" becomes liable to a relying purchaser "for the loss" the purchaser sustains "when the facts . . . become generally known" and "as a result" share value "depreciate[s]." § 548A, Comment b, at 107. Treatise writers, too, have emphasized the need to prove proximate causation. Prosser and Keeton § 110, at 767 (losses do "not afford any basis for recovery" if "brought about by business conditions or other factors").

We cannot reconcile the Ninth Circuit's "inflated purchase price" approach with these views of other courts. And the uniqueness of its perspective argues against the validity of its approach in a case like this one where we consider the contours of a judicially implied cause of action with roots in the common law.

Finally, the Ninth Circuit's approach overlooks an important securities law objective. The securities statutes seek to maintain public confidence in the marketplace. [*Citation omitted.*] They do so by deterring fraud, in part, through the availability of private securities fraud actions. [*Citation omitted.*] But the statutes make these latter actions available, not to provide investors with broad insurance against market losses, but to protect them against those economic losses that misrepresentations actually cause. Cf. *Basic,* 485 U.S., at 252, 99 L. Ed. 2d 194, 108 S. Ct. 978 (White, J., joined by O'Connor, J., concurring in part and dissenting in part) ("[A]llowing recovery in the face of affirmative evidence of nonreliance—would effectively convert Rule 10b–5 into a scheme of investor's insurance. There is no support in the Securities Exchange Act, the Rule, or our cases for such a result" (internal quotation marks and citations omitted)).

The statutory provision at issue here and the paragraphs that precede it emphasize this last mentioned objective. Private Securities Litigation Reform Act of 1995, 109 Stat 737. The statute insists that securities fraud complaints "specify" each misleading statement; that they set forth the facts "on which [a] belief" that a statement is misleading was "formed"; and that they "state with particularity facts giving rise to a strong inference that the defendant acted with the required state of mind." [*Citation omitted.*] And the statute expressly imposes on plaintiffs "the burden of proving" that the defendant's misrepresentations "caused the loss for which the plaintiff seeks to recover." [*Citation omitted.*]

The statute thereby makes clear Congress' intent to permit private securities fraud actions for recovery where, but only where, plaintiffs adequately allege and prove the traditional elements of causation and loss. By way of contrast, the Ninth Circuit's approach would allow recovery where a misrepresentation leads to an inflated purchase price but nonetheless does not proximately cause any economic loss. That is to say, it would permit recovery where these two traditional elements in fact are missing.

In sum, we find the Ninth Circuit's approach inconsistent with the law's requirement that a plaintiff prove that the defendant's misrepresentation (or other fraudulent conduct) proximately caused the plaintiff's economic loss. We need not, and do not, consider other proximate cause or loss-related questions.

B

Our holding about plaintiffs' need to *prove* proximate causation and economic loss leads us also to conclude that the plaintiffs' complaint here failed adequately to *allege* these requirements. We concede that the Federal Rules of Civil Procedure require only "a short and plain statement of the claim showing that the pleader is entitled to relief." Fed. Rule Civ. Proc. 8(a)(2). And we assume, at least for argument's sake, that neither the Rules nor the securities statutes impose any special further requirement in respect to the pleading of proximate causation or economic loss. But, even so, the "short and plain statement" must provide the defendant with "fair notice of what the plaintiff's claim is and the grounds upon which it rests." *Conley v. Gibson,* 355 U.S. 41, 47, 2 L. Ed. 2d 80, 78 S. Ct. 99 (1957). The complaint before us fails this simple test.

As we have pointed out, the plaintiffs' lengthy complaint contains only one statement that we can fairly read as describing the loss caused by the defendants' "spray device" misrepresentations. That statement says that the plaintiffs "paid artificially inflated prices for Dura's securities" and suffered "damage[s]." . . . The statement implies that the plaintiffs' loss consisted of the "artificially inflated" purchase "prices." The complaint's failure to claim that Dura['s] share price fell significantly after the truth became known suggests that the plaintiffs considered the allegation of purchase price inflation alone sufficient. The complaint contains nothing that suggests otherwise.

For reasons set forth in Part II-A, *supra,* however, the "artificially inflated purchase price" is not itself a relevant economic loss. And the complaint nowhere else provides the defendants with notice of what the relevant economic loss might be or of what the causal connection might be between that loss and the misrepresentation concerning Dura's "spray device."

We concede that ordinary pleading rules are not meant to impose a great burden upon a plaintiff. [*Citation omitted.*] But it should not prove burdensome for a plaintiff who has suffered an economic loss to provide a defendant with some indication of the loss and the causal connection that the plaintiff has in mind. At the same time, allowing a plaintiff to forgo giving any indication of the economic loss and proximate cause that the plaintiff has in mind would bring about harm of the very sort the statutes seek to avoid. Cf. H. R. Conf. Rep. No. 104–369, p 31 (1995) (criticizing "abusive" practices including "the routine filing of lawsuits . . . with only [a] faint hope that the discovery process might lead eventually to some plausible cause of action"). It would permit a plaintiff "with a largely groundless claim to simply take up the time of a number of other people, with the right to do so representing an *in terrorem* increment of the settlement value, rather than a reasonably founded hope that the [discovery] process will reveal relevant evidence." *Blue Chip Stamps,* 421 U.S., at 741, 44 L. Ed. 2d 539, 95 S. Ct. 1917. Such a rule would tend to transform a private securities action into a partial downside insurance policy. [*Citations omitted.*]

For these reasons, we find the plaintiffs' complaint legally insufficient. We reverse the judgment of the Ninth Circuit, and we remand the case for further proceedings consistent with this opinion.

It is so ordered.

C. Damages in a 10b–5 Claim

Assuming the elements of a 10b–5 claim are satisfied, the defendant is liable for damages. Damages in a 10b–5 action may take the form of: (1) out-of-pocket damages (which would involve a determination of the difference between the price actually paid or received and the price that should have been paid without the 10b–5 violation); (2) restitution (also known as "disgorgement," which would involve the defendant turning over the profit derived from the fraud to the plaintiff); (3) rescission (which could involve the return of the price paid or the securities sold by the plaintiff, or the difference between the original sale price and the subsequent sale price by the defendant); and (4) benefit of the bargain damages (which might only arise in limited circumstances in which there is a difference between the value received and the value promised, which may be established with reasonable certainty). Note that any measure of damages might also include consequential damages under circumstances provided they can be shown with sufficient certainty. Remember that the plaintiff must also have standing and be able to show injury/damages. Punitive damages are not available under Rule 10b–5 in a private cause of action. However, the SEC may seek treble damages and claims under many states' laws may seek punitive damages.

In a claim made under Rule 10b–5, for out-of-pocket damages, the plaintiffs are entitled to receive the difference between the price of the stock and its value on the date of the transaction, if the truth were known, measured by what a reasonable investor would have paid if she had known the facts. In other words, the calculation of damages is based upon the loss (or the decrease in profits) caused by the misstatement, not the purchase price minus the sale price. Of course, it can be quite difficult to measure the "value" of a security under hypothetical conditions, and there has been a great deal of litigation about how to determine such a value with accuracy. Note that the Private Securities Litigation Reform Act limits damages in such actions that are based upon reference to the "market price of a security" to the difference between the price paid and the "mean trading price" for the 90-day period following the date on which the information correcting the misstatement or omission that is the basis for the action is disseminated to the market.

D. Claims Not Covered by Rule 10b–5

Rule 10b–5 is NOT about correcting every wrong—it is about full disclosure. Once a full and fair disclosure is made, the fairness of the transaction is a not an issue under federal law. In such instances the appropriate remedy must be sought under state law.

Furthermore, in order to support a claim under Rule 10b–5, the disclosure at issue must touch and concern the purchase or sale of stock.

Santa Fe Industries, Inc. v. Green

430 U.S. 462, 97 S. Ct. 1292 (1977)

JUSTICE WHITE delivered the opinion of the court,

* * * *

In 1936, petitioner Santa Fe Industries, Inc. (Santa Fe), acquired control of 60% of the stock of Kirby Lumber Corp. (Kirby), a Delaware corporation. Through a series of purchases over the succeeding years, Santa Fe increased its control of Kirby's stock to 95%; the purchase prices during the period 1968–1973 ranged from $65 to $92.50 per share. In 1974, wishing to acquire 100%

ownership of Kirby, Santa Fe availed itself of § 253 of the Delaware Corporation Law, known as the "short-form merger" statute. Section 253 permits a parent corporation owning at least 90% of the stock of a subsidiary to merge with that subsidiary, upon approval by the parent's board of directors, and to make payment in cash for the shares of the minority stockholders. The statute does not require the consent of, or advance notice to, the minority stockholders. However, notice of the merger must be given within 10 days after its effective date, and any stockholder who is dissatisfied with the terms of the merger may petition the Delaware Court of Chancery for a decree ordering the surviving corporation to pay him the fair value of his shares, as determined by a court-appointed appraiser subject to review by the court. [*Citations omitted.*]

Santa Fe obtained independent appraisals of the physical assets of Kirby—land, timber, buildings, and machinery—and of Kirby's oil, gas, and mineral interests. These appraisals, together with other financial information, were submitted to Morgan Stanley & Co. (Morgan Stanley), an investment banking firm retained to appraise the fair market value of Kirby stock. Kirby's physical assets were appraised at $320 million (amounting to $640 for each of the 500,000 shares); Kirby's stock was valued by Morgan Stanley at $125 per share. Under the terms of the merger, minority stockholders were offered $150 per share.

The provisions of the short-form merger statute were fully complied with. The minority stockholders of Kirby were notified the day after the merger became effective and were advised of their right to obtain an appraisal in Delaware court if dissatisfied with the offer of $150 per share. They also received an information statement containing, in addition to the relevant financial data about Kirby, the appraisals of the value of Kirby's assets and the Morgan Stanley appraisal concluding that the fair market value of the stock was $125 per share.

Respondents, minority stockholders of Kirby, objected to the terms of the merger, but did not pursue their appraisal remedy in the Delaware Court of Chancery. Instead, they brought this action in federal court on behalf of the corporation and other minority stockholders, seeking to set aside the merger or to recover what they claimed to be the fair value of their shares. The amended complaint asserted that, based on the fair market value of Kirby's physical assets as revealed by the appraisal included in the information statement sent to minority shareholders, Kirby's stock was worth at least $772 per share. The complaint alleged further that the merger took place without prior notice to minority stockholders; that the purpose of the merger was to appropriate the difference between the "conceded pro rata value of the physical assets," App. 103a, and the offer of $150 per share—to "freez[e] out the minority stockholders at a wholly inadequate price,". . .; and that Santa Fe, knowing the appraised value of the physical assets, obtained a "fraudulent appraisal" of the stock from Morgan Stanley and offered $25 above that appraisal "in order to lull the minority stockholders into erroneously believing that [Santa Fe was] generous." . . . This course of conduct was alleged to be "a violation of Rule 10b–5 because defendants employed a 'device, scheme, or artifice to defraud' and engaged in an 'act, practice or course of business which operates or would operate as a fraud or deceit upon any person, in connection with the purchase or sale of any security.' " Morgan Stanley assertedly participated in the fraud as an accessory by submitting its appraisal of $125 per share although knowing the appraised value of the physical assets.

The District Court dismissed the complaint for failure to state a claim upon which relief could be granted. 391 F. Supp. 849 (SDNY 1975). As the District Court understood the complaint, respondents' case rested on two distinct grounds. First, federal law was assertedly violated because the merger was for the sole purpose of eliminating the minority from the company, therefore lacking any justifiable business purpose, and because the merger was undertaken without prior notice to the minority shareholders. Second, the low valuation placed on the shares in the cash-exchange offer was itself said to be a fraud actionable under Rule 10b–5. In rejecting the first ground for recovery, the District Court reasoned that Delaware law required neither a business purpose for a short-form merger nor prior notice to the minority shareholders who the statute contemplated would be removed from the company, and that Rule 10b–5 did not override these provisions of state corporate law by independently placing a duty on the majority not to merge without prior notice and without a justifiable business purpose.

As for the claim that actionable fraud inhered in the allegedly gross undervaluation of the minority shares, the District Court observed that respondents valued their shares at a minimum of $772 per share, "basing this figure on the *pro rata* value of Kirby's physical assets." Accepting this valuation for purposes of the motion to dismiss, the District Court further noted that, as revealed by the complaint, the physical asset appraisal, along with other information relevant to Morgan Stanley's valuation of the shares, had been included with the information statement sent to respondents within the time required by state law. It thought that if "full and fair disclosure is made, transactions eliminating minority interests are beyond the purview of Rule 10b–5," and concluded that the "complaint fail[ed] to allege an omission, misstatement or fraudulent course of conduct that would have impeded a shareholder's judgment of the value of the offer." The complaint therefore failed to state a claim and was dismissed.

A divided Court of Appeals for the Second Circuit reversed. . . . As to the first aspect of the case, the Court of Appeals did not disturb the District Court's conclusion that the complaint did not allege a material misrepresentation or nondisclosure with respect to the value of the stock; and the court declined to rule that a claim of gross undervaluation itself would suffice to make out a Rule 10b–5 case. With respect to the second aspect of the case, however, the court fundamentally disagreed with the District Court as to the reach and coverage of Rule 10b–5. The Court of Appeals' view was that, although the Rule plainly reached material misrepresentations and nondisclosures in connection with the purchase or sale of securities, neither misrepresentation nor nondisclosure was a necessary element of a Rule 10b–5 action; the Rule reached "breaches of fiduciary duty by a majority against minority shareholders without any charge of misrepresentation or lack of disclosure.

* * * *

II

Section 10(b) of the 1934 Act makes it "unlawful for any person. . . to use or employ. . . any manipulative or deceptive device or contrivance in contravention of [Securities and Exchange Commission rules]"; Rule 10b–5, promulgated by the SEC under § 10(b), prohibits, in addition to nondisclosure and misrepresentation, any "artifice to defraud" or any act "which operates or would operate as a fraud or deceit." . . . The Court of Appeals' approach to the interpretation of Rule 10b–5 is inconsistent with that taken by the Court last Term in *Ernst & Ernst v. Hochfelder,* 425 U.S. 185 (1976).

[*Ernst & Ernst v. Hochfelder,* 425 U.S. 185] makes clear that in deciding whether a complaint states a cause of action for "fraud" under Rule 10b–5, "we turn first to the language of § 10(b), for '[t]he starting point in every case involving construction of a statute is the language itself.' " . . . .

To the extent that the Court of Appeals would rely on the use of the term "fraud" in Rule 10b–5 to bring within the ambit of the Rule all breaches of fiduciary duty in connection with a securities transaction, its interpretation would, like the interpretation rejected by the Court in *Ernst & Ernst,* "add a gloss to the operative language of the statute quite different from its commonly accepted meaning." *Id.,* at 199.

* * * *

The language of § 10(b) gives no indication that Congress meant to prohibit any conduct not involving manipulation or deception. Nor have we been cited to any evidence in the legislative history that would support a departure from the language of the statute. "When a statute speaks so specifically in terms of manipulation and deception,. . . and when its history reflects no more expansive intent, we are quite unwilling to extend the scope of the statute. . . ." *Id.,* at 214. Thus the claim of fraud and fiduciary breach in this complaint states a cause of action under any part of Rule 10b–5 only if the conduct alleged can be fairly viewed as "manipulative or deceptive" within the meaning of the statute.

III

It is our judgment that the transaction, if carried out as alleged in the complaint, was neither deceptive nor manipulative and therefore did not violate either § 10(b) of the Act or Rule 10b–5.

As we have indicated, the case comes to us on the premise that the complaint failed to allege a material misrepresentation or material failure to disclose. The finding of the District Court, undisturbed by the Court of Appeals, was that there was no "omission" or "misstatement" in the information statement accompanying the notice of merger. On the basis of the information provided, minority shareholders could either accept the price offered or reject it and seek an appraisal in the Delaware Court of Chancery. Their choice was fairly presented, and they were furnished with all relevant information on which to base their decision.

We therefore find inapposite the cases relied upon by respondents and the court below, in which the breaches of fiduciary duty held violative of Rule 10b–5 included some element of deception. Those cases forcefully reflect the principle that "[§] 10(b) must be read flexibly, not technically and restrictively" and that the statute provides a cause of action for any plaintiff who "suffer[s] an injury as a result of deceptive practices touching its sale [or purchase] of securities. . . ." *Superintendent of Insurance v. Bankers Life & Cas. Co.,* 404 U.S. 6, 12–13 (1971). But the cases do not support the proposition, adopted by the Court of Appeals below and urged by respondents here, that a breach of fiduciary duty by majority stockholders, without any deception, misrepresentation, or nondisclosure, violates the statute and the Rule.

It is also readily apparent that the conduct alleged in the complaint was not "manipulative" within the meaning of the statute. "Manipulation" is "virtually a term of art when used in connection with securities markets." *Ernst & Ernst,*

425 U.S., at 199. The term refers generally to practices, such as wash sales, matched orders, or rigged prices, that are intended to mislead investors by artificially affecting market activity. [*Citations omitted.*]. . . Section 10(b)'s general prohibition of practices deemed by the SEC to be "manipulative"—in this technical sense of artificially affecting market activity in order to mislead investors—is fully consistent with the fundamental purpose of the 1934 Act " 'to substitute a philosophy of full disclosure for the philosophy of *caveat emptor. . . .*' " *Affiliated Ute Citizens v. United States,* 406 U.S. 128, 151 (1972), quoting *SEC v. Capital Gains Research Bureau,* 375 U.S. 180, 186 (1963). Indeed, nondisclosure is usually essential to the success of a manipulative scheme. No doubt Congress meant to prohibit the full range of ingenious devices that might be used to manipulate securities prices. But we do not think it would have chosen this "term of art" if it had meant to bring within the scope of § 10(b) instances of corporate mismanagement such as this, in which the essence of the complaint is that shareholders were treated unfairly by a fiduciary.

IV

The language of the statute is, we think, "sufficiently clear in its context" to be dispositive here, *Ernst & Ernst,* at 201; but even if it were not, there are additional considerations that weigh heavily against permitting a cause of action under Rule 10b–5 for the breach of corporate fiduciary duty alleged in this complaint. Congress did not expressly provide a private cause of action for violations of § 10(b). Although we have recognized an implied cause of action under that section in some circumstances, [*Citation omitted.*] we have also recognized that a private cause of action under the antifraud provisions of the Securities Exchange Act should not be implied where it is "unnecessary to ensure the fulfillment of Congress' purposes" in adopting the Act. [*Citations omitted.*] As we noted earlier, the Court repeatedly has described the "fundamental purpose" of the Act as implementing a "philosophy of full disclosure"; once full and fair disclosure has occurred, the fairness of the terms of the transaction is at most a tangential concern of the statute. [*Citations omitted.*] As in *Cort v. Ash,* 422 U.S. 66, 80 (1975), we are reluctant to recognize a cause of action here to serve what is "at best a subsidiary purpose" of the federal legislation.

A second factor in determining whether Congress intended to create a federal cause of action in these circumstances is "whether 'the cause of action [is] one traditionally relegated to state law. . . .' " [*Citations omitted.*] The Delaware Legislature has supplied minority shareholders with a cause of action in the Delaware Court of Chancery to recover the fair value of shares allegedly undervalued in a short-form merger. Of course, the existence of a particular state-law remedy is not dispositive of the question whether Congress meant to provide a similar federal remedy, but as in *Cort and Piper,* we conclude that "it is entirely appropriate in this instance to relegate respondent and others in his situation to whatever remedy is created by state law." 422 U.S., at 84. . .

The reasoning behind a holding that the complaint in this case alleged fraud under Rule 10b–5 could not be easily contained. It is difficult to imagine how a court could distinguish, for purposes of Rule 10b–5 fraud, between a majority stockholder's use of a short-form merger to eliminate the minority at an unfair price and the use of some other device, such as a long-form merger, tender offer, or liquidation, to achieve the same result; or indeed how a court could distinguish the alleged abuses in these going private transactions from other types of fiduciary self-dealing involving transactions in securities. The result would be to bring within the Rule a wide variety of corporate conduct traditionally left to state regulation. In addition to posing a "danger of vexatious litigation which could result from a widely expanded class of plaintiffs under Rule 10b–5," [*Citation omitted.*] this extension of the federal securities laws would overlap and quite possibly interfere with state corporate law. Federal courts applying a "federal fiduciary principle" under Rule 10b–5 could be expected to depart from state fiduciary standards at least to the extent necessary to ensure uniformity within the federal system. Absent a clear indication of congressional intent, we are reluctant to federalize the substantial portion of the law of corporations that deals with transactions in securities, particularly where established state policies of corporate regulation would be overridden. As the Court stated in *Court v. Ash:* "Corporations are creatures of state law, and investors commit their funds to corporate directors on the understanding that, except where federal law *expressly* requires certain responsibilities of directors with respect to stockholders, state law will govern the internal affairs of the corporation." 422 U.S., at 84 (emphasis added).

We thus adhere to the position that "Congress by § 10(b) did not seek to regulate transactions which constitute no more than internal corporate mismanagement." *Superintendent of Insurance v. Bankers Life & Cas. Co.,* 404 U.S., at 12. There may well be a need for uniform federal fiduciary standards to govern mergers such as that challenged in this complaint. But those standards should not be supplied by judicial extension of § 10(b) and Rule 10b–5 to "cover the corporate universe."

The judgment of the Court of Appeals is reversed, and the case is remanded for further proceedings consistent with this opinion.

So ordered.

SECTION III: The Sarbanes-Oxley Act

The Sarbanes-Oxley Act of 2002 ("SOX") was passed in an effort to increase disclosure by, and oversight of, publicly traded companies in the wake of the Enron scandal. While SOX is filled with regulations, there are a few that often arise in the introductory study of business organizations. One example includes the requirement that a publicly traded company's president or CEO, as well as its Chief Financial Officer must sign its financial statements, verifying that these officers have each reviewed the statements, the statements are accurate, and that the signatory takes responsibility for what is in the statements. Another SOX requirement is that public companies may not make personal loans to their officers or directors and must adopt a "code of ethics" for their respective CEOs and various financial officers.

SOX also places additional responsibilities on attorneys who are aware of their clients' violations of securities laws or fiduciary duty transgressions. SOX requires that attorneys who represent publicly held companies report these violations to the company's CEO. Section 307 of SOX, which contains these provisions, is more fully summarized below.

Sarbanes-Oxley Act Summaries of Key Provisions

Section 302: Summary

The chief executive officer and the chief financial officer shall certify in each annual or quarterly financial reports filed under the 1934 Act, that (among other things):

- The signing officers have reviewed the report;
- The report does not contain any material untrue statements or material omission or be considered misleading;
- The financial statements and related information fairly present the financial condition and the results in all material respects;
- The signing officers are responsible for internal controls and have evaluated these internal controls within the previous ninety days and have reported on their findings;

- A list of all deficiencies in the internal controls and information on any fraud that involves employees who are involved with internal activities has been disclosed to the firm's auditors and the board of directors audit committee; and
- Any significant changes in internal controls or related factors that could have a negative impact on the internal controls.
- Companies may not attempt to avoid these requirements by reincorporating their activities or transferring their activities outside of the United States.

Section 307: Summary

Rules of Professional Responsibility for Attorneys.

The SEC was instructed to issue rules, in the public interest and for the protection of investors, setting forth minimum standards of professional conduct for attorneys representing issuers.

These rules require attorneys to report evidence of a material violation of securities law or breach of fiduciary duty or similar violation by the company or any agent thereof, to the chief legal counsel or the chief executive officer of the company (or the equivalent thereof); and require an attorney, if the chief legal counsel or the chief executive officer of the company does not respond appropriately to the evidence, to report the evidence to the audit committee, another committee of independent directors, or the full board of directors. If the company does not take appropriate action, then the attorney must withdraw from the representation. The rules also allow an attorney, ". . . without the consent of an issuer client, to reveal confidential information related to his or her representation to the extent the attorney reasonably believes necessary (1) to prevent the issuer from committing a material violation likely to cause substantial financial injury to the financial interests or property of the issuer or investors; (2) to prevent the issuer from committing an illegal act; or (3) to rectify the consequences of a material violation or illegal act in which the attorney's services have been used."

Section 401: Summary

Financial information included in any report filed with the SEC pursuant to the securities law as well as any public disclosure or press release, must be presented in a manner that does not contain untrue statements or omit to state material information. The financial statements published or filed by a firm subject to the 1934 Act shall also include all material off-balance sheet liabilities, obligations or transactions.

Section 404: Summary

Reporting companies are required to include information in their annual reports concerning the scope and adequacy of their internal control structure and procedures for financial reporting. The report must also include a statement assessing the effectiveness of such internal controls and procedures.

If a company in the preceding paragraph has outstanding equity with a market value in excess of $75 million, the registered accounting firm that prepares the companies audit report shall, in the same report, "attest to and report on the assessment made by the management. . . ." on the effectiveness of the internal control structure and procedures for financial reporting.

Section 409: Summary

". . . Each issuer reporting under section 13(a) or 15(d) shall disclose to the public on a rapid and current basis such additional information concerning material changes in the financial condition or operations of the issuer, in plain English, which may include trend and qualitative information and graphic presentations, as the Commission determines, by rule, is necessary or useful for the protection of investors and in the public interest."

Section 802: Summary

This section imposes penalties of fines and/or up to 20 years imprisonment for altering, destroying, mutilating, concealing, altering, falsifying, or making a false entry in, any record, documents or tangible objects with the intent to impede, obstruct or influence a legal investigation. This section also imposes penalties of fines and/or imprisonment up to 10 years on any accountant who knowingly and willfully violates the requirements by failing to maintain all audit or review papers for a period of 5 years.

SECTION IV: Initial Public Offerings and Registration

Various provisions of the securities laws apply to different types of transactions. Often, several different provisions will apply to the same transaction. One example of this is the regulation of securities registrations. In order for a security to be sold to the public, it must either be registered or have an exemption from registration. Section 12 of the 1934 Act provides that "It shall be unlawful for any member, broker, or dealer to effect any transaction in any security (other than an exempted security) on a national securities exchange unless a registration is effective as to such security for such exchange in accordance with the provisions of this title and the rules and regulations thereunder. . . ." There are many exemptions to registration, and many private offerings proceed under those exemptions. However, if no exemption is available, then the company issuing the securities (aka the "issuer") must "register" the securities. When a company's stock is registered, the company is usually described as "publicly traded." However, what is really meant is that at least one class of the company's stock is publicly traded. It is possible for a company to have some of its securities be publicly traded and others not.

A. The Initial Public Offering

When a company first registers its stock to be sold to the public, it is called an "initial public offering" or "IPO." A company's IPO represents a transition from being a "private" or closely held company to a "public" company. There are many reasons why a company would want to go public. Often a company's IPO can create a way for early investors in a company to sell that investment and reap the value the business has created. Since the shares of a public company are traded on a public exchange, being public also creates a "currency" for the company, in that the company's stock has value (due to its liquidity) that it might not have as a private company. The company can reward its employees with stock options that have a tangible and immediate value, and it can use its stock to raise money or to acquire other companies. When a company sells stock in an IPO, that company is often referred to as the "issuer." The "offering" typically represents new shares that are being issued by the company to be sold to the public. There are instances where shares of existing shareholders are also sold to the public as part of the IPO, however, such sales are usually discouraged, because they send a negative message to new potential investors that existing investors do not have confidence in the company. The offering typically represents 10–15% of the shares of the issuer. It does not represent all of the outstanding stock of the issuer.

In order to execute an IPO there are a number of steps that must be taken, and the entire process is subject to a substantial number of regulations well beyond the scope of this book. However, the following is a brief summary of the process:

Securing an Investment Bank

When a company "goes public," the first step is usually selecting an investment bank or banks to manage the public offering. The investment bank acts as the "underwriter" for the offering. This means that the investment bank facilitates and funds the sale of the company's offered shares. In most large IPOs the underwriter assures the company that it will buy all the shares the company offers on the day of the IPO at the IPO price, minus the firm's commission (typically 5–7% of the amount raised in the offering). This shifts the burden of selling the shares from the company to the investment bankers. Because one investment bank does not usually want to take on the risk of underwriting an entire offering alone, it will typically "invite" other investment banks to join in an underwriting group. Each member of the group commits to purchasing a portion of the offering from the issuer. The group appoints a managing underwriter to act on behalf of the group. (Note that in smaller and more speculative offerings, the underwriter will not provide a firm commitment to purchase the shares of the issuer and will only agree to use its "best efforts" to sell as many shares as possible to investors.)

The Pre-Filing Period

When a company decides to conduct a public offering (usually marked by selecting an investment bank) a "quiet" period begins, during which Section 5(c) of the 1933 Act prohibits any activity that would be considered an "offering" of the issuer's non-exempt securities during this period. The quiet period extends until the registration statement is filed. During the quiet period, there are strict rules about what information may be released to the public by the company. The rules also prohibit any offer, including any oral offer and any solicitation of an offer, of the company's securities, unless it is exempted by a special rule. During this period, any public disclosure or dissemination of information that is not exempt and that tends to create interest in the offering is referred to as "gun-jumping." Gun-jumping can result in a right to rescind and/or can allow the SEC to delay the offering.

The Registration Statement

The issuer, the investment bank, the company's lawyers, the underwriter's lawyers and accountants will all participate in preparing an S-1 registration, often called the "registration statement" or the "prospectus," which describes the "offering." The preparation of the S-1 is usually managed by the company's attorneys. The registration statement is a disclosure document and is filed with the SEC. In addition to the description of the offering and the use of proceeds, the company is required to provide a comprehensive disclosure of the company in the S-1, including business operations, management of the company, financial condition, risks associated with the business, and three years of financial statements (except in the case of smaller reporting companies for which only two years is required). Some of the specific regulations governing registration statements arising under Section 12 of the 1934 Act and Section 11 of the 1933 Act are discussed below. Once the S-1 is completed and signed, it is filed with the SEC. Note that filings are also required in the states in which the company intends to offer its securities and with FINRA (the Financial Industry Regulatory Authority).

The SEC reviews the S-1 and provides comments, which often require amending the registration statement, with the goal of having the S-1 provide a full and fair disclosure that does not contain misstatements or omissions of material facts. (Note that the SEC's evaluation does not provide assurances, or even findings that the data provided in the S-1 is accurate or complete.) The filing starts a "waiting period," or "cooling-off" period, during which the company and its underwriters are restricted by the information that may be released. However, during this period some "offers" and "indications of interest in," but not "sales" of, the issuer's securities are permitted. The waiting period continues until the "effective date" of the registration statement, which is determined by the SEC.

Real World Example: *The Problem with Executives. . .*

Unfortunately, there are occasionally business executives who either do not fully understand, or do not feel bound by, the restrictions of the securities laws. For example:

A few days after Groupon Inc., filed its registration statement for its IPO, Bloomberg News published a statement by Eric Lefkofsky,

Groupon's co-founder and Executive Chairman. Lefkofsky was quoted as saying that Groupon was going to be "wildly profitable." Such a statement violates the rules by promoting the offering and, at least if taken literally, assures investors that an investment in Groupon Inc.'s stock will make them money. As a result, Groupon had to file an amended registration statement. The amended statement included the following language:

> "The reported statement does not accurately or completely reflect Mr. Lefkofsky's views and should not be considered by prospective investors in isolation or at all."
>
> "We have in the past and may continue to receive, a high degree of media coverage, including coverage that is not directly attributable to statements made by our officers and employees, incorrectly reports on statements made by our officers or employees, or is misleading as a result of omitting to state information provided by us or our officers or employees."
>
> "You should rely only on the information contained in this prospectus in determining whether to purchase our shares."

In 2004, Google's founders Larry Page and Sergey Brin gave an interview to Playboy magazine during Google's quiet period, prompting an SEC inquiry.

Potential Investors—The Road Show

While the investment banks underwriting the IPO typically "commit" to purchasing the issuer's offered shares, these underwriters do so with the intent of selling those shares on the day of the IPO to institutional clients. To accomplish this, once the S-1 has been filed, the investment bankers and executives of the issuer will arrange a number of brief meetings with a large number of potential institutional investors as part of a "road show" to discuss the company, its plans and to give the institutions an opportunity to ask questions of the issuer's CEO and top management. The company still has a number of limitations about its activities during this period. Only certain types of oral offers and a limited group of written offers may be made during the waiting period.

The goal of the road show is to line up investors willing to buy some of the stock being offered by the company as part of its IPO. If interested, the institutions will "subscribe" to the offering. However, because sales of the securities are not permitted before the effective date, these subscriptions are non-binding. Because the exact price of the shares is not determined until the day of the IPO, the institutions subscribe for a requested number of shares, without knowing the exact cost. The institutions are not obligated to purchase any of the issuer's shares until the price is set and the registration becomes effective. Nevertheless, when the underwriters are confident (based upon these investors' subscriptions or "indications of interest") that the underwriters can sell all of the shares for the offering, the deal closes.

Setting the Price and Conducting the Offering

The last step is the "pricing" of the offering. The investment bankers (who have previously set a range within which the price per share at which the stock will be offered) set an exact price, usually the night before the offering. When the offering goes "live" on the effective date, the underwriters purchase the shares from the issuer for the IPO price, minus the underwriter's commission. The underwriters then, immediately, sell those shares, at the IPO price, to the institutional investors who have subscribed for the shares (assuming the subscribers decide to buy once they are informed of the IPO price). If any institutional investor withdraws their bid, the investment bank will continue to own the shares. The investment bank may, then, choose to either hold the shares or to sell them to someone else. Once the investment bankers have sold the shares and "credited" them to their clients' accounts, the shares are "released" for trading. The stock, now owned by these investors, is "traded" and may be sold on the public market on which it was registered, usually NASDAQ or the New York Stock Exchange. Some investors will sell or "flip" their shares immediately. Others may decide to hold their shares. The price of the stock is then determined by the market.

B. More on Registration Statement Requirements

As mentioned above, the process through which a company goes public involves the preparation of a registration statement, which is approved by the SEC and provided to potential investors who might want to buy the stock that is being offered. The registration statement is intended to be a comprehensive description of the offering and to include any risks or other information that an investor might want to know before investing. Section 12(b)(1) of the 1934 Act sets forth a list of some of the information that is required to be included in a registration statement. While the list is not comprehensive, it provides a useful insight in to the type, scope and breadth of information that is required when a company is making comprehensive disclosures:

1934 Act, Section 12

. . .

(b) A security may be registered on a national securities exchange by the issuer filing an application with the exchange (and filing with the Commission such duplicate originals thereof as the Commission may require), which application shall contain—

1. Such information, in such detail, as to the issuer and any person directly or indirectly controlling or controlled by, or under direct or indirect common control with, the issuer, and any guarantor of the security as to principal or interest or both, as the Commission may by rules and regulations require, as necessary or appropriate in the public interest or for the protection of investors, in respect of the following:

   A. the organization, financial structure, and nature of the business;

   B. the terms, position, rights, and privileges of the different classes of securities outstanding;

   C. the terms on which their securities are to be, and during the preceding three years have been, offered to the public or otherwise;

   D. the directors, officers, and underwriters, and each security holder of record holding more than 10 per centum of any class of any equity security of the issuer (other than an exempted security), their remuneration and their interests in the securities of, and their material contracts with, the issuer and any person directly or indirectly controlling or controlled by, or under direct or indirect common control with, the issuer;

   E. remuneration to others than directors and officers exceeding $20,000 per annum;

   F. bonus and profit-sharing arrangements;

   G. management and service contracts;

   H. options existing or to be created in respect of their securities;

I. material contracts, not made in the ordinary course of business, which are to be executed in whole or in part at or after the filing of the application or which were made not more than two years before such filing, and every material patent or contract for a material patent right shall be deemed a material contract;

J. balance sheets for not more than the three preceding fiscal years, certified if required by the rules and regulations of the Commission by a registered public accounting firm;

K. profit and loss statements for not more than the three preceding fiscal years, certified if required by the rules and regulations of the Commission by a registered public accounting firm; and

L. any further financial statements which the Commission may deem necessary or appropriate for the protection of investors.

1933 Act, Section 11

Section 11 of the 1933 Act also regulates registration statements and creates responsibilities for anyone who signs the registration statement, officers of the issuer, experts who assisted in the preparation of the registration statement, and underwriters promoting the offering. Under Section 11, issuers of securities have strict liability for anything misleading (whether because of an omission or misstatement) in the registration statement. However, others connected to the registration statement have a defense of due diligence. That due diligence defense typically requires reading the registration statement and investigating the registration statement to make sure that the statements and assertions contained in that statement are true. Under a due diligence defense (when available), if something in the registration statement turned out to be false, in order to avoid liability, the defendant in question would need to show that he or she did not know that it was false and should not have known it was false.

A registration statement may be divided into two portions: the "expertised" portion and the "non-expertised" portion. In the expertised portion, accountants and auditors (i.e., the "experts") have gone through the statement and confirmed the information. The experts must conduct a *reasonable investigation* and have reasonable grounds to believe, and in fact believe, that the statements in this expertised portion of the registration statement are true. Non-experts must only show that they had no reason to believe, and, in fact, did not believe that the statements in the expertised portion were misleading.

With regard to the "non-expertised" portions, the experts (who, by definition, did not work on these portions) have no liability. The non-experts must conduct a *reasonable investigation* and have reasonable grounds to believe, and, in fact believe, that the statements in this non-expertised portion of the registration statement are true. The standard of care applied to these tests is the care that a reasonable person would exercise if his or her money were at stake.

SECTION V: Exempt Offerings

If an issuer wants to raise money without registration, then that issuer must have an exemption from registration.

A. Private Placements

Various aspects of the offering will determine if it is exempt from registration. These include factors such as the size of the offering and how much money is being raised. (Note, there are exemptions for certain offerings under $1 million and $5 million.) Other factors include the number of units offered, how many shares are available and what percentage of the company total ownership (i.e., "the pie") that constitutes. Another factor is the manner of the offering and how people hear about the transaction because the rules restrict advertising to and solicitations of, the general public. Additionally, the number of offerees affects the analysis. The focus of this factor is NOT on how many people actually invest, but how many are offered the opportunity to invest. This must be a limited number. Note that not all offerees are considered the same. For purposes of determining whether an exemption is available, different offerees are often treated differently. Some exemptions do not "count" certain sophisticated investors, known as "Accredited Investors," as part of the number of offerees. An individual accredited investor typically has a net worth, not including the investor's house, over $1 million or income over $200,000 for the prior few years. There are different standards for corporations seeking accredited investor status. It is also important to show that an offeree has had access to information from and about the issuer.

If a transaction is "exempt," the process of raising money for the corporation conducting the exempt transaction is often referred to as a "private placement." Most private placements are conducted under Regulation D or Section 4(2) of the 1933 Act. While private placements are exempt from Section

11 of the 1933 Act, they are still subject to Section 10(b)(5) of the 1934 Act as well as to other provisions of the Securities Acts. In addition to satisfying federal law requirements, securities transactions must also meet the requirements of any state in which they are offered. These state rules are known as "blue sky" laws and may vary from state to state. (If a securities transaction takes place entirely within one state, it is often exempt from federal registration requirements under an "intrastate" exemption.)

B. Crowdfunding Exemption

A provision in the Jumpstart Our Business Startups (or "JOBS") Act legislation of 2012 (amended in 2017 to adjust for inflation), created a "crowdfunding" exemption (which has been included in the 1933 Act as a new Section 4(6)), allowing entrepreneurs and small businesses to raise up to $1,070,000* from a large number of investors, even if those investors are not "accredited." The concept of *crowdfunding* which has been facilitated, if not created, by the Internet, is that many investors will put up a small amount of money to provide investment to a business or even an idea. Under this provision in the JOBS Act, companies could raise up to $1,070,000 from investors during any 12 month period, without registering the transaction with the SEC. The JOBS Act limits individual contributions made during any 12 month period, pursuant to this exemption to (i) the greater of $2,200 or 5 percent of an investor's net worth or annual income for investors whose net worth OR annual income is less than $107,000; or (ii) the greater of 10 percent of an investor's net worth or annual income for investors whose net worth or annual income is greater than $107,000. However, the amount invested by any individual under this exemption may not exceed $107,000. Any money raised through this exemption must be raised through a broker or funding portal.**

---

* The original amount was $1 million. The numbers that follow have all been adjusted for inflation by the SEC. ($107,000 was originally $100,000 and $2,200 was originally $2,000.)

** The term "funding portal" means any person acting as an intermediary in a transaction involving the offer or sale of securities for the account of others, solely pursuant to Section 4(6) of the 1933 Act, that does not—

(A) offer investment advice or recommendations;

(B) solicit purchases, sales, or offers to buy the securities offered or displayed on its website or portal;

(C) compensate employees, agents, or other persons for such solicitation or based on the sale of securities displayed or referenced on its website or portal;

(D) hold, manage, possess, or otherwise handle investor funds or securities; or

(E) engage in such other activities as the SEC, by rule, determines appropriate.

See Section 304(b) JOBS Act.

One of the stated purposes of the JOBS Act is to diminish the regulatory burden of raising capital. The process of raising money and complying with the multitude of securities regulations can be prohibitively expensive for a small company raising a relatively small amount of money. The crowdfunding exemption is one instance of the effort to facilitate efforts by start-up businesses that might not have access to traditional sources of capital. The crowdfunding legislation endeavors to make it easier for a small company to raise money through Internet portals and social media, without the overwhelming cost and burden of regulatory compliance that would be present when raising millions of dollars through more traditional avenues. Of course, even transactions that raise capital through an exemption to the securities laws requiring registration are still subject to the investor protections of other securities laws such as Rule 10b–5, discussed *supra* in this Chapter.

CHAPTER NINE

Insider Trading

A PARTNER IN YOUR FIRM, who handles white-collar criminal cases, is scheduled to meet with a potential new client regarding an insider trading matter. The potential client is a well-known celebrity who is interviewing several potential firms. As part of the interview process, the client is asking that each firm prepare a response to a hypothetical fact pattern. While your firm does not usually participate in such "beauty contests," the firm feels that this matter would increase the firm's profile in this area and would be great for business. The partner asks that you "take the first crack" at the response. The fact pattern contains the following instructions:

Experiencing Assignment 13: Martha Stewart

Dear Potential Attorney,

The following fact pattern is taken from the events surrounding the insider trading case involving Martha Stewart (*United States v. Stewart,* 433 F.3d 273 (2d Cir. 2003)). I am not as well-known as Martha Stewart; however, I feel my case raises similar issues, and I would like to know how you would have handled that case before we discuss the actual facts of my case.

FACTS:

Peter Bacanovic was a stock broker at Merrill Lynch. His clients included Martha Stewart, CEO of Martha Stewart Living Omnimedia, Inc., ImClone CEO Sam Waksal, and Waksal's daughter Aliza. ImClone, a biotechnology company, had been doing quite well on public anticipation of FDA approval for its cancer-treating drug, "Erbitux." Stewart held 3,928 shares of ImClone stock.

During the last week of December 2001, Bacanovic was vacationing in Florida. Douglas Faneuil, a Merrill Lynch client associate and Bacanovic's assistant, was covering Bacanovic's desk while Bacanovic was away. On December 26, 2001, Waksal privately learned that the FDA had decided to refuse to file ImClone's biologics license application for Erbitux. On the morning of December 27, 2001, Faneuil received several phone calls on Bacanovic's line from Sam Waksal's daughters, Aliza Waksal and Elana Waksal Posner, and from Waksal's accountant, Alan Goldberg. Prior to the opening of the market, Aliza Waksal placed a market order to sell all of her approximately 40,000 shares of ImClone, which Faneuil executed. Shortly thereafter, Faneuil received a call from Alan Goldberg directing him to sell all of Sam Waksal's ImClone shares immediately. Faneuil advised Goldberg that he was unable to do so because of SEC rules restricting Waksal's trading of his company's shares. Goldberg informed Faneuil that, pursuant to facsimile instructions from Waksal that were dated December 26th (but not received at Merrill Lynch until December 27th), he was to transfer Waksal's entire holding of approximately 80,000 ImClone shares to the account of his daughter Aliza and sell it from there. Faneuil confirmed—with both Bacanovic and Merrill Lynch compliance personnel—his understanding that the proposed transaction was not permissible. Faneuil spoke with Goldberg five or six times by phone that day, and the transfer between accounts took place the following day, December 28th. Faneuil also received two calls that morning from Elana Waksal Posner regarding the sale of her ImClone shares; she expressed disappointment that the price was "already going down."

Faneuil kept Bacanovic apprised of the details of the calls from the Waksal family by telephone. In the midst of one of their conversations, Faneuil heard Bacanovic say suddenly, "Oh, my God, get Martha [Stewart] on the phone." With Bacanovic on the line, Faneuil placed a call to Stewart's New York office. Bacanovic left a message after being told by Stewart's assistant, Ann Armstrong, that Stewart was traveling. Armstrong logged the message as follows: "Peter Bacanovic thinks ImClone is going to start trading downward." In a follow-up call, Bacanovic instructed Faneuil to "tell [Stewart] what's going on" when she returned the call. Faneuil recalled that Bacanovic expressly confirmed that Faneuil was to advise Stewart of Waksal's efforts to sell his ImClone stock, a communication that Faneuil knew would violate Merrill Lynch's client confidentiality policy.

At 1:18 p.m. Bacanovic sent an e-mail to Faneuil inquiring as to whether any news had "come out" regarding ImClone; Faneuil responded that there had been nothing yet. Shortly thereafter, Stewart called her office and was informed by Armstrong of Bacanovic's message. Armstrong transferred the call to Bacanovic's office, where Faneuil answered, "Merrill Lynch, Peter Bacanovic's office." It is unclear whether Faneuil identified himself to Stewart. Faneuil told Stewart that, although there had been no news release from ImClone, Bacanovic thought she would "like to act on the information that Sam Waksal was trying to sell all of his shares," at least those he held in Merrill Lynch accounts. Stewart asked Faneuil for a price quote and directed him to sell all of the ImClone shares that remained in her portfolio.

Stewart then placed a call to Sam Waksal, reaching his secretary Emily Perret. Stewart asked Perret if she knew what was going on with ImClone and told Perret to find Waksal. Perret informed Stewart that Waksal was not in the office, and she noted the call on Waksal's messages sheet for December 27, 2001 as follows:

> "1:43 Martha Stewart, something is going on with ImClone and she wants to know what. She is on her way to Mexico and she is staying at Los Vantanos [*sic*]."

Back in New York, Stewart's ImClone sell order was executed at an average price of $58.43 per share, yielding proceeds of approximately $230,000. Pursuant to Stewart's instructions, Faneuil sent an e-mail to her personal account confirming the trade. Faneuil also informed Bacanovic that, after hearing that Waksal was trying to sell all of his ImClone shares, Stewart sold her own shares. The next day, ImClone announced that the FDA had rejected approval for its cancer treatment drug. On the next day of trading, ImClone's stock price dropped 18 percent. By selling before the announcement, Stewart avoided losses of approximately $45,000.

Several days later, while Stewart and Mariana Pasternak were speaking in Mexico, their discussion turned to the New Year's plans of various friends, and Pasternak inquired about Sam Waksal. Among other things, Stewart told Pasternak about the decline in ImClone's stock price, Waksal's efforts to sell his holdings, and her own sale. Pasternak later testified that she was either told by Stewart or was left with the impression that it was "nice to have brokers who tell you those things," and she acknowledged knowing that Bacanovic was Stewart's broker.

ASSIGNMENT:

The SEC charged Martha Stewart with violating Rule 10b–5. Imagine that you had been hired by Martha Stewart to defend her on the 10b–5 claim, and before any case against her was even filed, you had the opportunity to meet with attorneys from the SEC and try to convince them that they did not have a good 10b–5 case against Stewart. Please draft the arguments that you would make to the SEC in such a meeting. Please limit your arguments to those relating to the 10b–5 claim, not to any other (non-legal) rationales. You can assume that the

SEC is familiar with all of the relevant cases, so you do not need to summarize case fact patterns.

Please keep your arguments clear and concise, and under no circumstances should your response exceed 1000 words.

This Assignment does not need to be completed, and should not be completed, until the end of this chapter. However, as you study the cases and other materials that follow, it might be helpful to do so with a view toward how you would impress the potential client by providing (albeit hypothetical) assistance to Ms. Stewart. Some of the materials in the chapter will relate more than others to the issues facing Martha Stewart. However, the materials are designed to build your understanding of the insider trading issues that arise in such a case and assist you in putting them in context. Please keep the issues faced by Martha Stewart in this problem and the questions presented by the assignment in mind while reading the materials that follow.

* * * *In preparing this assignment you may use any of the cases and materials in this book, but you may not research or review any of the pleadings, cases, articles or other materials relating to the Martha Stewart case itself.* * * *

SECTION I: Insider Trading—Background and History

The prohibition of insider trading of securities involves the concept that those with access to nonpublic information should not have an advantage over those from whom they buy, or to whom they sell, securities. There is a fair amount of debate over whether this restriction makes sense from an economic policy perspective. Not everyone is against insider trading. Some feel that it creates more efficient markets. Milton Friedman, an extremely respected economist once explained, "You should want more insider trading, not less. You want to give the people most likely to have knowledge about deficiencies of the company an incentive to make the public aware of that." However, such policy debates are outside of the focus of this book.

This chapter will focus on some of the significant restrictions on the purchase or sale of securities by a person who is in possession of material nonpublic information. Before examining these restrictions, it is important to note that the insider trading prohibitions do NOT create a blanket prohibition on such trading. Most observers agree that the stock market becomes more efficient when the public is aware of the strengths and weaknesses of publicly traded firms. Analysts make their livings by gathering such information about these firms and making assessments about a firm's prospects. The law does not want to discourage such activities. Most agree that good research should be rewarded. The insider trading rules, therefore, focus on the way in which information is discovered, not merely whether someone has information that is not known to the public. The key to understanding insider trading is realizing that the law only goes so far in restricting trading on "inside" information. In understanding the applicable restrictions, it might be useful to focus on WHEN the law prohibits trades while in possession of inside information, rather than whether the law prohibits such trades.

A. State Laws Regulating Insider Trading

Prior to the passage of the 1933 Act and the 1934 Act, insider trading was regulated by state securities laws. Although Federal securities laws have not preempted this area, the state laws are not frequently used, and their development has not been significant. One reason for the lack of use of state securities laws with respect to insider trading transactions is that these laws primarily regulate face-to-face transactions. Since most stock transactions take place over an exchange with an unknown person, there are few incidents when these state laws would apply. It is also important to remember that state securities laws (and for that matter Federal securities laws) involve a specialized area that focuses on wrongdoing involved in a specific type of transaction. The securities laws developed because of the difficulty in proving a fraud claim and the importance of public confidence in the securities markets. Even though there was already a cause of action to address fraud, lawmakers felt that it was important to have "stricter" regulations of the securities markets. However, in instances of true deception and wrongdoing, plaintiffs will often have a state law claim for fraud in addition to any claim they might possess arising out of a violation of the securities laws.

Among states there is a wide range of positions taken in the cases involving insider trading. There are three different "standards" or "rules." The "majority rule" seen in the *Goodwin v. Agassiz* case below, takes the position that, except in instances involving fraud, officers and directors of a corporation may trade in the corporation's stock, without disclosing material information.

Goodwin v. Agassiz, 283 Mass. 358, 186 N.E. 659 (1933): In the *Goodwin* case, Agasiz and MacNaughton, officers and directors of the Cliff Mining Company, purchased shares in the company's stock on the Boston Stock Exchange, based on nonpublic information derived from a geologist's report, indicating that valuable copper deposits were located on land owned by the company. (Agasiz and MacNaughton did not want the information disclosed publicly since such a disclosure would increase the price of other land nearby or adjacent to the land where the suspected copper deposits lay, and Agasiz and MacNaughton intended to secure options to purchase that land for another copper company in which they were both officers.) The plaintiff had seen an article about the closing of exploratory operations by the Cliff Mining Company and immediately sold his shares in the company. (It does not appear that defendants were responsible for this article.) The plaintiff did not know about the geologist's theory or about Agasiz and MacNaughton's intention to test that theory and would not have sold his stock if he had known of it. The plaintiff sued and alleged that Agassiz and MacNaughton had a fiduciary duty to disclose the nonpublic information before purchasing his stock. The Massachusetts Supreme Judicial Court held that directors and officers did not have such a duty, at least when the identity of the buyers and sellers of the stock in question was not known to the parties.

The holding in *Goodwin* was sometimes applied to face-to-face transactions and became the majority rule. Ironically, while this rule is still called the "majority rule," it is no longer the rule in a majority of states, although it is still the law in several states.

The "Special Circumstances Rule" (adopted in *Strong v. Repide,* 213 U.S. 419, 29 S. Ct. 521, 53 L. Ed. 853 (1909)) creates certain exceptions to the majority rule, taking the position that a corporation's officers or directors have a duty to disclose information before they trade with *shareholders of the corporation* when certain "special circumstances" are present, such as when the information is highly material; the officer or director conceals his or her identity or engages in some other act of fraud or deceit; or the officer or director is trading with an especially vulnerable person, such as an elderly widow with no financial understanding. Finally, the "minority rule" (sometimes known as the "Kansas rule") takes the position that the corporation's officers and directors (i.e., the insiders) do have a duty to disclose material information whenever buying from a shareholder, at least in face-to-face transactions.

The state law rules are based on the duties of "insiders" to the shareholders. There are many law professors (but not all) who would assert that these restrictions, to the extent they apply, would only apply to an insider's purchase from an existing shareholder, not an insider's sale of stock to someone who was not a shareholder at the time of the transaction. However, this distinction does not apply to suits brought under the Federal securities laws.

State Law Claims for Trades on National Exchanges

It is worth mentioning that there are state law cases that deal with transactions that take place on national exchanges and are not face-to-face. However, in the vast majority of these cases, state courts have not found a breach of duty on the part of the insider and, therefore, have not found liability. There are a few cases that suggest that, under certain special circumstances, there might be liability for the insider for such trades. Additional issues that arise in the context of state law claims related to trades made on nonpublic information belonging to a corporation are addressed at the end of this Chapter.

SECTION II: Rule 10b–5 and Traditional Insider Trading

A. Disclose or Abstain

The vast majority of current insider trading restrictions arise under Rule 10b–5. Insider trading involves a very specific violation under Rule 10b–5 in which someone "deceives" by omission. The "omission" is that the person is in possession of material, nonpublic information which, if known, would impact the price of the security. The securities laws try to prevent these situations by restricting the ability of someone in possession of such information to use it to profit from trading.

However, one of the most important facts to understand about the insider trading laws is that these laws do NOT prohibit the use of all nonpublic information. Early cases appeared to consider restricting the use of all inside information. This approach (sometimes characterized as a blanket duty to "disclose or abstain" from trading while in possession of material nonpublic information) was developed in *In re Cady, Roberts & Co.,* 40 S.E.C. 907 (1961) and *Securities and Exchange Commission v. Texas Gulf Sulphur Co.,* 401 F.2d 833 (2d Cir. 1968). However, subsequent cases (as we will see) take a more limited approach based upon the language of the statute.

Securities and Exchange Commission v. Texas Gulf Sulphur Co.

401 F.2d 833 (2d Cir. 1968)

WATERMAN, C.J.:

This action was commenced in the United States District Court for the Southern District of New York by the Securities and Exchange Commission (the SEC) . . . against Texas Gulf Sulphur Company (TGS) and several of its officers, directors and employees, to enjoin certain conduct by TGS and the individual defendants said to violate Section 10(b) of the Act . . . and to compel the rescission by the individual defendants of securities transactions assertedly conducted contrary to law.

* * * *

THE FACTUAL SETTING

This action derives from the exploratory activities of TGS begun in 1957 on the Canadian Shield in eastern Canada. In March of 1959, aerial geophysical surveys were conducted over more than 15,000 square miles of this area by a group led by defendant Mollison, a mining engineer and a Vice President of TGS. The group included defendant Holyk, TGS's chief geologist, defendant Clayton, an electrical engineer and geophysicist, and defendant Darke, a geologist. These operations resulted in the detection of numerous anomalies, i.e., extraordinary variations in the conductivity of rocks, one of which was on the Kidd 55 segment of land located near Timmins, Ontario.

On October 29 and 30, 1963, Clayton conducted a ground geophysical survey on the northeast portion of the Kidd 55 segment which confirmed the presence of an anomaly and indicated the necessity of diamond core drilling for further evaluation. Drilling of the initial hole, K-55-1, at the strongest part of the anomaly was commenced on November 8 and terminated on November 12 at a depth of 655 feet. Visual estimates by Holyk of the core of K-55-1 indicated an average copper content of 1.15% and an average zinc content of 8.64% over a length of 599 feet. This visual estimate convinced TGS that it was desirable to acquire the remainder of the Kidd 55 segment, and in order to facilitate this acquisition TGS President Stephens instructed the exploration group to keep the results of K-55-1 confidential and undisclosed even as to other officers, directors, and employees of TGS. The hole was concealed and a barren core was intentionally drilled off the anomaly. Meanwhile, the core of K-55-1 had been shipped to Utah for chemical assay which, when received in early December, revealed an average mineral content of 1.18% copper, 8.26% zinc, and 3.94% ounces of silver per ton over a length of 602 feet. These results were so remarkable that neither Clayton, an experienced geophysicist, nor four other TGS expert witnesses, had ever seen or heard of a comparable initial exploratory drill hole in a base metal deposit. So, the trial court concluded, "There is no doubt that the drill core of K-55-1 was unusually good and that it excited the interest and speculation of those who knew about it." [*Citation omitted.*]. . .

During this period, from November 12, 1963 when K-55-1 was completed, to March 31, 1964 when drilling was resumed, certain of the individual defendants . . . purchased TGS stock or calls [options] thereon. . . .

On February 20, 1964, also during this period, TGS issued stock options to 26 of its officers and employees whose salaries exceeded a specified amount, five of whom were the individual defendants Stephens, Fogarty, Mollison, Holyk, and Kline. Of these, only Kline was unaware of the detailed results of K-55-1, but he, too, knew that a hole containing favorable bodies of copper and zinc ore had been drilled in Timmins. At this time, neither the TGS Stock Option Committee nor its Board of Directors had been informed of the results of K-55-1, presumably because of the pending land acquisition program which required confidentiality. All of the foregoing defendants accepted the options granted them.

* * * *

On April 8 TGS began with a second drill rig to drill another hole, K-55-6, 300 feet easterly of K-55-1. . . . On April 10, a third drill rig commenced drilling yet another hole. . . . By the evening of April 10 in this hole, too, substantial copper mineralization had been encountered over the last 42 feet of its 97-foot length.

Meanwhile, rumors that a major ore strike was in the making had been circulating throughout Canada. On the morning of Saturday, April 11, Stephens at his home in Greenwich, Conn. read in the New York Herald Tribune and in the New York Times unauthorized reports of the TGS drilling which seemed to infer a rich strike from the fact that the drill cores had been flown to the United States for chemical assay. Stephens immediately contacted Fogarty at his home in Rye, N.Y., who in turn telephoned and later that day visited Mollison at Mollison's home in Greenwich to obtain a current report and evaluation of the drilling progress. The following morning, Sunday, Fogarty again telephoned Mollison, inquiring whether Mollison had any further information and told him to return to Timmins with Holyk, the TGS Chief Geologist, as soon as possible "to move things along." With the aid of one Carroll, a public relations consultant, Fogarty drafted a press release designed to quell the rumors, which release, after having been channeled through Stephens and Huntington, a TGS attorney, was issued at 3:00 P.M. on Sunday, April 12, and which appeared in the morning newspapers of general circulation on Monday, April 13. It read in pertinent part as follows:

> NEW YORK, April 12—The following statement was made today by Dr. Charles F. Fogarty, executive vice president of Texas Gulf Sulphur Company, in regard to the company's drilling operations near Timmins, Ontario, Canada. Dr. Fogarty said:
>
> "During the past few days, the exploration activities of Texas Gulf Sulphur in the area of Timmins, Ontario, have been widely reported in the press, coupled with rumors of a substantial copper discovery there. These reports exaggerate the scale of operations, and mention plans and statistics of size and grade of ore that are without factual basis and have evidently originated by speculation of people not connected with TGS.
>
> "The facts are as follows. TGS has been exploring in the Timmins area for six years as part of its overall search in Canada and elsewhere for various minerals—lead, copper, zinc, etc. During the course of this work, in Timmins as well as in Eastern Canada, TGS has conducted exploration entirely on its own, without the participation by others. Numerous prospects have been investigated by geophysical means and a large number of selected ones have been core-drilled. These cores are sent to the United States for assay and detailed examination as a matter of routine and on advice of expert Canadian legal counsel. No inferences as to grade can be drawn from this procedure.
>
> "Most of the areas drilled in Eastern Canada have revealed either barren pyrite or graphite without value; a few have resulted in discoveries of small or marginal sulphide ore bodies.
>
> "Recent drilling on one property near Timmins has led to preliminary indications that more drilling would be required for proper evaluation of this prospect. The drilling done to date has not been conclusive, but the statements made by many outside quarters are unreliable and include information and figures that are not available to TGS.

> "The work done to date has not been sufficient to reach definite conclusions and any statement as to size and grade of ore would be premature and possibly misleading. When we have progressed to the point where reasonable and logical conclusions can be made, TGS will issue a definite statement to its stockholders and to the public in order to clarify the Timmins project."

* * * *

The release purported to give the Timmins drilling results as of the release date, April 12. From Mollison Fogarty had been told of the developments through 7:00 P.M. on April 10, and of the remarkable discoveries made up to that time, detailed supra, which discoveries, according to the calculations of the experts who testified for the SEC at the hearing, demonstrated that TGS had already discovered 6.2 to 8.3 million tons of proven ore having gross assay values from $26 to $29 per ton. TGS experts, on the other hand, denied at the hearing that proven or probable ore could have been calculated on April 11 or 12 because there was then no assurance of continuity in the mineralized zone.

The evidence as to the effect of this release on the investing public was equivocal and less than abundant. On April 13 the New York Herald Tribune in an article head-noted "Copper Rumor Deflated" quoted from the TGS release of April 12 and backtracked from its original April 11 report of a major strike but nevertheless inferred from the TGS release that "recent mineral exploratory activity near Timmins, Ontario, has provided preliminary favorable results, sufficient at least to require a step-up in drilling operations." Some witnesses who testified at the hearing stated that they found the release encouraging. On the other hand, a Canadian mining security specialist, Roche, stated that "earlier in the week [before April 16] we had a Dow Jones saying that they [TGS] didn't have anything basically" and a TGS stock specialist for the Midwest Stock Exchange became concerned about his long position in the stock after reading the release. The trial court stated only that "While, in retrospect, the press release may appear gloomy or incomplete, this does not make it misleading or deceptive on the basis of the facts then known." [*Citation omitted.*]

* * * *

While drilling activity ensued to completion, TGC officials were taking steps toward ultimate disclosure of the discovery. On April 13, a previously-invited reporter for *The Northern Miner*, a Canadian mining industry journal, visited the drillsite, interviewed Mollison, Holyk and Darke, and prepared an article which confirmed a 10 million ton ore strike. This report, after having been submitted to Mollison and returned to the reporter unamended on April 15, was published in the April 16 issue. A statement relative to the extent of the discovery, in substantial part drafted by Mollison, was given to the Ontario Minister of Mines for release to the Canadian media. Mollison and Holyk expected it to be released over the airways at 11 P.M. on April 15th, but, for undisclosed reasons, it was not released until 9:40 A.M. on the 16th. An official detailed statement, announcing a strike of at least 25 million tons of ore, based on the drilling data set forth above, was read to representatives of American financial media from 10:00 A.M. to 10:10 or 10:15 A.M. on April 16, and appeared over Merrill Lynch's private wire at 10:29 A.M. and, somewhat later than expected, over the Dow Jones ticker tape at 10:54 A.M.

Between the time the first press release was issued on April 12 and the dissemination of the TGS official announcement on the morning of April 16, the only defendants before us on appeal who engaged in market activity were Clayton and Crawford and TGS director Coates. Clayton ordered 200 shares of TGS stock through his Canadian broker on April 15 and the order was executed that day over the Midwest Stock Exchange. Crawford ordered 300 shares at midnight on the 15th and another 300 shares at 8:30 A.M. the next day, and these orders were executed over the Midwest Exchange in Chicago at its opening on April 16. Coates left the TGS press conference and called his broker son-in-law Haemisegger shortly before 10:20 A.M. on the 16th and ordered 2,000 shares of TGS for family trust accounts of which Coates was a trustee but not a beneficiary; Haemisegger executed this order over the New York and Midwest Exchanges, and he and his customers purchased 1500 additional shares.

During the period of drilling in Timmins, the market price of TGS stock fluctuated but steadily gained overall. On Friday, November 8, when the drilling began, the stock closed at 173/8; on Friday, November 15, after K-55-1 had been completed, it closed at 18. After a slight decline to 163/8 by Friday, November 22, the price rose to 207/8 by December 13, when the chemical assay results of K-55-1 were received, and closed at a high of 24 1/8 on February 21, the day after the stock options had been issued. It had reached a price of 26 by March 31, after the land acquisition program had been completed and drilling had been resumed, and continued to ascend to 301/8 by the close of trading on April 10, at which time the drilling progress up to then was evaluated for the April 12th press release. On April 13, the day on which the April 12 release was disseminated, TGS opened at 301/8, rose immediately to a high of 32 and gradually tapered off to close at 30 7/8. It closed at 301/4 the next day, and at 293/8 on April 15. On April 16, the day of the official announcement of the

Timmins discovery, the price climbed to a high of 37 and closed at 363/8. By May 15, TGS stock was selling at 581/4.

I. The Individual Defendants

A. Introductory

Rule 10b–5 on which this action is predicated, provides:

> It shall be unlawful for any person, directly or indirectly, by the use of any means or instrumentality of interstate commerce, or of the mails, or of any facility of any national securities exchange,
>
> (1) to employ any device, scheme, or artifice to defraud,
>
> (2) to make any untrue statement of a material fact or to omit to state a material fact necessary in order to make the statements made, in the light of the circumstances under which they were made, not misleading, or
>
> (3) to engage in any act, practice, or course of business which operates or would operate as a fraud or deceit upon any person, in connection with the purchase or sale of any security.

Rule 10b–5 was promulgated pursuant to the grant of authority given the SEC by Congress in Section 10(b) of the Securities Exchange Act of 1934 (15 U.S.C. § 78j(b). By that Act Congress purposed to prevent inequitable and unfair practices and to insure fairness in securities transactions generally, whether conducted face-to-face, over the counter, or on exchanges, . . . the Rule is based in policy on the justifiable expectation of the securities marketplace that all investors trading on impersonal exchanges have relatively equal access to material information. . . [*Citations omitted.*] The essence of the Rule is that anyone who, trading for his own account in the securities of a corporation has "access, directly or indirectly, to information intended to be available only for a corporate purpose and not for the personal benefit of anyone" may not take "advantage of such information knowing it is unavailable to those with whom he is dealing," i.e., the investing public. *In re Cady, Roberts & Co.,* 40 SEC 907, 912 (1961). Insiders, as directors or management officers are, of course, by this Rule, precluded from so unfairly dealing, but the Rule is also applicable to one possessing the information who may not be strictly termed an "insider" within the meaning of Sec. 16(b) of the Act. . . . Thus, anyone in possession of material inside information must either disclose it to the investing public, or, if he is disabled from disclosing it in order to protect a corporate confidence, or he chooses not to do so, must abstain from trading in or recommending the securities concerned while such inside information remains undisclosed. So, it is here no justification for insider activity that disclosure was forbidden by the legitimate corporate objective of acquiring options to purchase the land surrounding the exploration site; if the information was, as the SEC contends, material, its possessors should have kept out of the market until disclosure was accomplished. . . .

B. Material Inside Information

An insider is not, of course, always foreclosed from investing in his own company merely because he may be more familiar with company operations than are outside investors. An insider's duty to disclose information or his duty to abstain from dealing in his company's securities arises only in "those situations which are essentially extraordinary in nature and which are reasonably certain to have a substantial effect on the market price of the security if [the extraordinary situation is] disclosed." [*Citation omitted.*]

Nor is an insider obligated to confer upon outside investors the benefit of his superior financial or other expert analysis by disclosing his educated guesses or predictions. . . .

This is not to suggest, however, as did the trial court, that "the test of materiality must necessarily be a conservative one, particularly since many actions under Section 10(b) are brought on the basis of hindsight," . . . in the sense that the materiality of facts is to be assessed solely by measuring the effect the knowledge of the facts would have upon prudent or conservative investors. As we stated in List v. Fashion Park. . . . "The basic test of materiality * * * is whether a *reasonable* man would attach importance * * * in determining his choice of action in the transaction in question. [*Citation omitted.*] This, of course, encompasses any fact "* * * which in reasonable and objective contemplation *might* affect the value of the corporation's stock or securities * * *." *List v. Fashion Park, Inc., supra* at 462. . . . (Emphasis supplied.) Such a fact is a material fact and must be effectively disclosed to the investing public prior to the commencement of insider trading in the corporation's securities. The speculators and chartists of Wall and Bay Streets are also "reasonable" investors entitled to the same legal protection afforded conservative traders. Thus, material facts include not only information disclosing the earnings and distributions of a company but also those facts which affect the probable future of the company and those which may affect the desire of investors to buy, sell, or hold the company's securities.

In each case, then, whether facts are material within Rule 10b–5 when the facts relate to a particular event . . . will depend at any given time upon a balancing of both the indicated probability that the event will occur and the anticipated magnitude of the event in light of the totality of the company activity. Here, notwithstanding the trial court's conclusion that the results of the first drill core, K-55-1, were "too 'remote' * * * to have had any significant impact on the market, i.e., to be deemed material," knowledge of the possibility, which surely was more than marginal, of the existence of a mine of the vast magnitude indicated by the remarkably rich drill core located rather close to the surface (suggesting mineability by the less expensive openpit method) within the confines of a large anomaly (suggesting an extensive region of mineralization) might well have affected the price of TGS stock and would certainly have been an important fact to a reasonable, if speculative, investor in deciding whether he should buy, sell, or hold. After all, this first drill core was "unusually good and * * * excited the interest and speculation of those who knew about it." 258 F. Supp. at 282.

Our disagreement with the district judge on the issue does not, then, go to his findings of basic fact, as to which the "clearly erroneous" rule would apply, but to his understanding of the legal standard applicable to them. [*Citation omitted.*] Our survey of the facts found below conclusively establishes that knowledge of the results of the discovery hole, K-55-1, would have been important to a reasonable investor and might have affected the price of the stock.[12] On April 16, *The Northern Miner*, a trade publication in wide circulation among mining stock specialists, called K-55-1, the discovery hole, "one of the most impressive drill holes completed in modern times." . . .

Finally, a major factor in determining whether the K-55-1 discovery was a material fact is the importance attached to the drilling results by those who knew about it. In view of other unrelated recent developments favorably affecting TGS, participation by an informed person in a regular stock-purchase program, or even sporadic trading by an informed person, might lend only nominal support to the inference of the materiality of the K-55-1 discovery; nevertheless,

---

[12] We do not suggest that material facts must be disclosed immediately; the timing of disclosure is a matter for the business judgment of the corporate officers entrusted with the management of the corporation within the affirmative disclosure requirements promulgated by the exchanges and by the SEC. Here, a valuable corporate purpose was served by delaying the publication of the K-55-1 discovery. We do intend to convey, however, that where a corporate purpose is thus served by withholding the news of a material fact, those persons who are thus quite properly true to their corporate trust must not during the period of non-disclosure deal personally in the corporation's securities or give to outsiders confidential information not generally available to all the corporations' stockholders and to the public at large.

the timing by those who knew of it of their stock purchases and their purchases of *short-term* calls—purchases in some cases by individuals who had never before purchased calls or even TGS stock—virtually compels the inference that the insiders were influenced by the drilling results. . . .

Our decision to expand the limited protection afforded outside investors by the trial court's narrow definition of materiality is not at all shaken by fears that the elimination of insider trading benefits will deplete the ranks of capable corporate managers by taking away an incentive to accept such employment. Such benefits, in essence, are forms of secret corporate compensation . . . derived at the expense of the uninformed investing public and not at the expense of the corporation which receives the sole benefit from insider incentives. Moreover, adequate incentives for corporate officers may be provided by properly administered stock options and employee purchase plans of which there are many in existence. . . .

The core of Rule 10b–5 is the implementation of the Congressional purpose that all investors should have equal access to the rewards of participation in securities transactions. It was the intent of Congress that all members of the investing public should be subject to identical market risks,—which market risks include, of course the risk that one's evaluative capacity or one's capital available to put at risk may exceed another's capacity or capital. The insiders here were not trading on an equal footing with the outside investors. . . . Such inequities based upon unequal access to knowledge should not be shrugged off as inevitable in our way of life, or, in view of the congressional concern in the area, remain uncorrected.

We hold, therefore, that all transactions in TGS stock or calls by individuals apprised of the drilling results of K-55-1 were made in violation of Rule 10b–5. Inasmuch as the visual evaluation of that drill core (a generally reliable estimate though less accurate than a chemical assay) constituted material information, those advised of the results of the visual evaluation as well as those informed of the chemical assay traded in violation of law. . . .

B. The Development of Traditional Insider Trading Theory

As the case law evolved, the Supreme Court limited restrictions on the use of nonpublic information to certain situations, primarily those in which the use of the nonpublic information could be traced to a breach of some fiduciary duty. The result of these rules leaves some uses of "inside" information actionable, and other uses, not actionable. Therefore, it is important to understand the structure, so that the issues may be properly evaluated.

The restrictions arising under Rule 10b–5 prohibit "insiders" at a company from trading in the company's stock if those insiders are in possession of material, nonpublic information. Under traditional insider trading, there needs to be a breach of the duty of loyalty by the insider (or temporary insider). An insider is someone who, by virtue of his or her position with the company, has a duty (or temporary fiduciary duties) to the company's shareholders. Whether there was a breach of that duty is measured by whether the insider received a personal benefit. This is the only breach that matters for traditional insider trading under Rule 10b–5. This benefit is typically a financial benefit that is gained by trading in the company's securities. However, the gain could also arise from a sale of the information to others. Absent a fiduciary duty to the shareholders, there is no violation of Rule 10b–5 for trading on inside information under traditional insider trading theory.

It is important to understand that insiders (and constructive insiders, defined below) actually have a duty to disclose or abstain, meaning that, unless they disclose the information to the public, they must refrain from trading in the corporation's stock while they are in possession of material, nonpublic information. Note that insiders are not prevented from *possessing* material, nonpublic information. They just may not trade on that information. If they want to trade in the corporation's stock, then they must disclose the information. However, in the real world, the rule really becomes "abstain" since most corporate officers and directors are prevented from disclosure by their other duties to the corporation.

Note that there is no requirement of reliance or causation in insider trading cases, just scienter and materiality. Insider trading problems fall into two categories: Traditional Insider Trading and Misappropriation. The basic analysis of a traditional insider trading situation under Rule 10b–5 involves a determination of whether the defendant traded based upon material nonpublic information and whether that defendant was an insider or a "constructive insider."

C. Limits on Traditional Insider Trading

It is important to be aware that traditional insider trading only covers actions that start with the breach of duty of an insider (or constructive insider). This limitation means that there are many situations in which people might trade on material, nonpublic information that would not constitute a violation of Rule

10b–5. For example, the traditional insider trading doctrine would not apply if an insider at Company A used nonpublic, material information about a new Company A product (which would impact Company B) to trade in the stock of Company B, because the Company A insider does not owe any duty to the Company B shareholders. While the Company A insider's behavior might be regulated by other rules or regulations, the action is not a violation of the traditional insider trading rules.

D. Tipper-Tippee Liability

There are, of course, several ways to profit from inside information. The traditional insider trading analysis involves a situation in which an insider actually trades on that information. However, individuals might also share inside information with others. The dissemination of inside (material, nonpublic) information also has consequences. The insider trading rules limit the dissemination of material, nonpublic information ("tipping") by someone in possession of that information (the "tipper") and prohibit the use of that information by the recipient (the "tippee"). However, tipper/tippee liability must also be based upon a breach of duty and, with regard to the tippee, knowledge of that breach of duty.

Dirks v. Securities and Exchange Commission

463 U.S. 646 (1983)

JUSTICE POWELL delivered the opinion of the Court.

Petitioner Raymond Dirks received material nonpublic information from "insiders" of a corporation with which he had no connection. He disclosed this information to investors who relied on it in trading in the shares of the corporation. The question is whether Dirks violated the antifraud provisions of the federal securities laws by this disclosure.

I

In 1973, Dirks was an officer of a New York broker-dealer firm who specialized in providing investment analysis of insurance company securities to institutional investors. On March 6, Dirks received information from Ronald Secrist, a former officer of Equity Funding of America. Secrist alleged that the assets of Equity Funding, a diversified corporation primarily engaged in selling life insurance and mutual funds, were vastly overstated as the result of fraudulent corporate practices. Secrist also stated that various regulatory agencies had failed to act on similar charges made by Equity Funding employees. He urged Dirks to verify the fraud and disclose it publicly.

Dirks decided to investigate the allegations. He visited Equity Funding's headquarters in Los Angeles and interviewed several officers and employees of the corporation. The senior management denied any wrongdoing, but certain corporation employees corroborated the charges of fraud. Neither Dirks nor his firm owned or traded any Equity Funding stock, but throughout his investigation he openly discussed the information he had obtained with a number of clients and investors. Some of these persons sold their holdings of Equity Funding securities, including five investment advisers who liquidated holdings of more than $16 million.

While Dirks was in Los Angeles, he was in touch regularly with William Blundell, the Wall Street Journal's Los Angeles bureau chief. Dirks urged Blundell to write a story on the fraud allegations. Blundell did not believe, however, that such a massive fraud could go undetected and declined to write the story. He feared that publishing such damaging hearsay might be libelous.

During the 2-week period in which Dirks pursued his investigation and spread word of Secrist's charges, the price of Equity Funding stock fell from $26 per share to less than $15 per share. This led the New York Stock Exchange to halt trading on March 27. Shortly thereafter California insurance authorities impounded Equity Funding's records and uncovered evidence of the fraud. Only then did the Securities and Exchange Commission (SEC) file a complaint against Equity Funding and only then, on April 2, did the Wall Street Journal publish a front-page story based largely on information assembled by Dirks. Equity Funding immediately went into receivership.

The SEC began an investigation into Dirks' role in the exposure of the fraud. After a hearing by an Administrative Law Judge, the SEC found that Dirks had aided and abetted violations of § 17(a) of the Securities Act of 1933, . . . § 10(b) of the Securities Exchange Act of 1934 . . . and SEC Rule 10b–5, . . . by repeating the allegations of fraud to members of the investment community who later sold their Equity Funding stock. The SEC concluded: "Where 'tippees'—regardless of their motivation or occupation—come into possession of material 'corporate information that they know is confidential and know or should know came from a corporate insider,' they must either publicly disclose that information or refrain from trading." [*Citation omitted.*] Recognizing, however, that Dirks "played an important role in bringing [Equity Funding's] massive fraud to light," . . . the SEC only censured him.

* * * *

In view of the importance to the SEC and to the securities industry of the question presented by this case, we granted a writ of certiorari. [*Citation omitted.*] We now reverse.

II

In the seminal case of *In re Cady, Roberts & Co.,* 40 S.E.C. 907 (1961), the SEC recognized that the common law in some jurisdictions imposes on "corporate 'insiders,' particularly officers, directors, or controlling stockholders" an "affirmative duty of disclosure . . . when dealing in securities." *Id.,* at 911, and n. 13. The SEC found that not only did breach of this common-law duty also establish the elements of a Rule 10b–5 violation, but that individuals other than corporate insiders could be obligated either to disclose material nonpublic information before trading or to abstain from trading altogether. *Id.,* at 912. *In Chiarella,* we accepted the two elements set out in *Cady, Roberts* for establishing a Rule 10b–5 violation: "(i) the existence of a relationship affording access to inside information intended to be available only for a corporate purpose, and (ii) the unfairness of allowing a corporate insider to take advantage of that information by trading without disclosure." 445 U.S., at 227. In examining whether Chiarella had an obligation to disclose or abstain, the Court found that there is no general duty to disclose before trading on material nonpublic information, and held that "a duty to disclose under § 10(b) does not arise from the mere possession of nonpublic market information." *Id.,* at 235. Such a duty arises rather from the existence of a fiduciary relationship. *See id.,* at 227–235.

Not "all breaches of fiduciary duty in connection with a securities transaction," however, come within the ambit of Rule 10b–5. *Santa Fe Industries, Inc. v. Green,* 430 U.S. 462, 472 (1977). There must also be "manipulation or deception." *Id.,* at 473. In an inside-trading case this fraud derives from the "inherent unfairness involved where one takes advantage" of "information intended to be available only for a corporate purpose and not for the personal benefit of anyone." [*Citation omitted.*] Thus, an insider will be liable under Rule 10b–5 for inside trading only where he fails to disclose material nonpublic information before trading on it and thus makes "secret profits." *Cady, Roberts, supra,* at 916, n. 31.

III

We were explicit in *Chiarella* in saying that there can be no duty to disclose where the person who has traded on inside information "was not [the corporation's] agent, . . . was not a fiduciary, [or] was not a person in whom the sellers [of the securities] had placed their trust and confidence." 445 U.S., at 232. Not to require such a fiduciary relationship, we recognized, would "[depart] radically from the established doctrine that duty arises from a specific relationship between two parties" and would amount to "recognizing a general duty between all participants in market transactions to forgo actions based on material, nonpublic information." *Id.,* at 232, 233. This requirement of a specific relationship between the shareholders and the individual trading on inside information has created analytical difficulties for the SEC and courts in policing tippees who trade on inside information. Unlike insiders who have independent fiduciary duties to both the corporation and its shareholders, the typical tippee has no such relationships.[14] In view of this absence, it has been unclear how a tippee acquires the *Cady, Roberts* duty to refrain from trading on inside information.

A

The SEC's position, as stated in its opinion in this case, is that a tippee "inherits" the *Cady, Roberts* obligation to shareholders whenever he receives inside information from an insider. . . .

This view differs little from the view that we rejected as inconsistent with congressional intent in *Chiarella*. . . . Here, the SEC maintains that anyone who knowingly receives nonpublic material information from an insider has a fiduciary duty to disclose before trading.

In effect, the SEC's theory of tippee liability in both cases appears rooted in the idea that the antifraud provisions require equal information among all traders. This conflicts with the principle set forth in *Chiarella* that only some persons, under some circumstances, will be barred from trading while in possession of material nonpublic information. . . .

Imposing a duty to disclose or abstain solely because a person knowingly receives material nonpublic information from an insider and trades on it could have an inhibiting influence on the role of market analysts, which the SEC itself

[14] Under certain circumstances, such as where corporate information is revealed legitimately to an underwriter, accountant, lawyer, or consultant working for the corporation, these outsiders may become fiduciaries of the shareholders. The basis for recognizing this fiduciary duty is not simply that such persons acquired nonpublic corporate information, but rather that they have entered into a special confidential relationship in the conduct of the business of the enterprise and are given access to information solely for corporate purposes. . . . For such a duty to be imposed, however, the corporation must expect the outsider to keep the disclosed nonpublic information confidential, and the relationship at least must imply such a duty.

recognizes is necessary to the preservation of a healthy market.[17] It is commonplace for analysts to "ferret out and analyze information," 21 S. E. C. Docket, at 1406,[18] and this often is done by meeting with and questioning corporate officers and others who are insiders. And information that the analysts obtain normally may be the basis for judgments as to the market worth of a corporation's securities. The analyst's judgment in this respect is made available in market letters or otherwise to clients of the firm. It is the nature of this type of information, and indeed of the markets themselves, that such information cannot be made simultaneously available to all of the corporation's stockholders or the public generally.

B

The conclusion that recipients of inside information do not invariably acquire a duty to disclose or abstain does not mean that such tippees always are free to trade on the information. The need for a ban on some tippee trading is clear. Not only are insiders forbidden by their fiduciary relationship from personally using undisclosed corporate information to their advantage, but they also may not give such information to an outsider for the same improper purpose of exploiting the information for their personal gain. . . .

Thus, some tippees must assume an insider's duty to the shareholders not because they receive inside information, but rather because it has been made available to them *improperly*. And for Rule 10b–5 purposes, the insider's disclosure is improper only where it would violate his *Cady, Roberts* duty. Thus, a tippee assumes a fiduciary duty to the shareholders of a corporation not to trade on material nonpublic information only when the insider has breached his fiduciary duty to the shareholders by disclosing the information to the tippee and the tippee knows or should know that there has been a breach. . . . Tipping

---

[17] . . . The SEC asserts that analysts remain free to obtain from management corporate information for purposes of "filling in the 'interstices in analysis'. . . ."[*Citation omitted.*] But this rule is inherently imprecise, and imprecision prevents parties from ordering their actions in accord with legal requirements. Unless the parties have some guidance as to where the line is between permissible and impermissible disclosures and uses, neither corporate insiders nor analysts can be sure when the line is crossed. . . .

[18] On its facts, this case is the unusual one. Dirks is an analyst in a broker-dealer firm, and he did interview management in the course of his investigation. He uncovered, however, startling information that required no analysis or exercise of judgment as to its market relevance. Nonetheless, the principle at issue here extends beyond these facts. The SEC's rule—applicable without regard to any breach by an insider—could have serious ramifications on reporting by analysts of investment views.

. . . Dirks' careful investigation brought to light a massive fraud at the corporation. And until the Equity Funding fraud was exposed, the information in the trading market was grossly inaccurate. But for Dirks' efforts, the fraud might well have gone undetected longer.

thus properly is viewed only as a means of indirectly violating the *Cady, Roberts* disclose-or-abstain rule.

C

In determining whether a tippee is under an obligation to disclose or abstain, it thus is necessary to determine whether the insider's "tip" constituted a breach of the insider's fiduciary duty. All disclosures of confidential corporate information are not inconsistent with the duty insiders owe to shareholders. In contrast to the extraordinary facts of this case, the more typical situation in which there will be a question whether disclosure violates the insider's *Cady, Roberts* duty is when insiders disclose information to analysts. . . . In some situations, the insider will act consistently with his fiduciary duty to shareholders, and yet release of the information may affect the market. For example, it may not be clear—either to the corporate insider or to the recipient analyst—whether the information will be viewed as material nonpublic information. Corporate officials may mistakenly think the information already has been disclosed or that it is not material enough to affect the market. Whether disclosure is a breach of duty therefore depends in large part on the purpose of the disclosure. This standard was identified by the SEC itself in *Cady, Roberts:* a purpose of the securities laws was to eliminate "use of inside information for personal advantage." [*Citation omitted.*] Thus, the test is whether the insider personally will benefit, directly or indirectly, from his disclosure. Absent some personal gain, there has been no breach of duty to stockholders. And absent a breach by the insider, there is no derivative breach. . . .

. . . In determining whether the insider's purpose in making a particular disclosure is fraudulent, the SEC and the courts are not required to read the parties' minds. Scienter in some cases is relevant in determining whether the tipper has violated his *Cady, Roberts* duty. But to determine whether the disclosure itself "[deceives], [manipulates], or [defrauds]" shareholders, . . . the initial inquiry is whether there has been a breach of duty by the insider. This requires courts to focus on objective criteria, i. e., whether the insider receives a direct or indirect personal benefit from the disclosure, such as a pecuniary gain or a reputational benefit that will translate into future earnings. . . . There are objective facts and circumstances that often justify such an inference. For example, there may be a relationship between the insider and the recipient that suggests a *quid pro quo* from the latter, or an intention to benefit the particular recipient. The elements of fiduciary duty and exploitation of nonpublic information also exist when an insider makes a gift of confidential information to a trading relative or friend. The tip and trade resemble trading by the insider himself followed by a gift of the profits to the recipient.

Determining whether an insider personally benefits from a particular disclosure, a question of fact, will not always be easy for courts. But it is essential, we think, to have a guiding principle for those whose daily activities must be limited and instructed by the SEC's inside-trading rules, and we believe that there must be a breach of the insider's fiduciary duty before the tippee inherits the duty to disclose or abstain. . . .

IV

Under the inside-trading and tipping rules set forth above, we find that there was no actionable violation by Dirks. It is undisputed that Dirks himself was a stranger to Equity Funding, with no pre-existing fiduciary duty to its shareholders. He took no action, directly or indirectly, that induced the shareholders or officers of Equity Funding to repose trust or confidence in him. There was no expectation by Dirks' sources that he would keep their information in confidence. Nor did Dirks misappropriate or illegally obtain the information about Equity Funding. Unless the insiders breached their *Cady, Roberts* duty to shareholders in disclosing the nonpublic information to Dirks, he breached no duty when he passed it on to investors as well as to the Wall Street Journal.

It is clear that neither Secrist nor the other Equity Funding employees violated their *Cady, Roberts* duty to the corporation's shareholders by providing information to Dirks. The tippers received no monetary or personal benefit for revealing Equity Funding's secrets, nor was their purpose to make a gift of valuable information to Dirks. As the facts of this case clearly indicate, the tippers were motivated by a desire to expose the fraud. . . . In the absence of a breach of duty to shareholders by the insiders, there was no derivative breach by Dirks. . . .

V

We conclude that Dirks, in the circumstances of this case, had no duty to abstain from use of the inside information that he obtained. The judgment of the Court of Appeals therefore is

Reversed.

NOTES AND QUESTIONS

1. Under the standards of liability articulated in *Dirks,* an insider is only liable for tipping if he or she violated a fiduciary duty of loyalty by providing the tip. The law measures whether the duty of loyalty was violated by asking if the insider (or constructive insider) received a "personal benefit" by providing the information to another person (i.e., tipping). However, sometimes it is difficult to determine what constitutes a personal benefit. You might ask yourself how broadly this term might be construed. Imagine a scenario in which your client is approached by a friend who says: "I know things have been tough for you financially. Here is a tip; buy stock in my company. No one knows this yet, but we are about to announce a new product, and the stock is going to go up as soon as we make the announcement. I know this, because I am a senior officer in charge of the team working on the product. I don't want anything for this tip. I just want to help you out." Your client wants to know if he may buy the stock. Has your client's friend obtained a personal benefit?

2. Most of the cases following *Dirks* have construed the personal benefit test quite broadly. For example, in *SEC v. Sargent,* 229 F.2d 68 (1st Cir. 2000), the court determined that the tipper, Dennis Shepard, received a "personal benefit" by providing his friend and dentist with confidential information about a tender offer "to effect a reconciliation with his friend and to maintain a useful networking contact." *Id.* at 77.

3. However, in *SEC v. Switzer,* 590 F. Supp. 756 (W.D. Okla. 1984), Barry Switzer, who was at the time the football coach for the University of Oklahoma, was at his son's track meet and overheard the CEO and a director of Phoenix Resources, Co. ("Phoenix"), George Platt, discussing with his wife, Mrs. Platt, material, nonpublic information about Phoenix. Switzer was laying down in the stands behind the Platts "sunbathing" at the time, waiting for his son's next event. The Platts were not aware that Switzer was there. Switzer overheard the discussion about liquidating Phoenix, bought stock and profited. The court found that "The information that Switzer heard at the track meet about Phoenix was overheard and was not the result of an intentional disclosure by G. Platt," *id.* at 762, nor was the disclosure made by Platt for an improper purpose. "Platt did not personally benefit, directly or indirectly, monetarily or otherwise from the inadvertent disclosure." *Id.* at 766. Therefore, because Platt had not breached a fiduciary duty to Phoenix, there could be no tippee liability for Switzer. So Switzer, as well as some of his friends with whom Switzer had shared the information, was allowed to keep his substantial profits.

NOTE ON SALMAN V. UNITED STATES

The Supreme Court recently affirmed that the personal benefit test should be construed broadly. In *Salman v. United States*, 137 S. Ct. 420 (2016), the Supreme Court, applying *Dirks*, held that the personal benefit test is met if a fiduciary makes a gift of confidential information to a friend or family member, even though no tangible benefit is received by the fiduciary. In *Salman*, Maher Kara, an employee at the investment bank Citigroup, shared inside information he learned in his capacity as a fiduciary with his brother, Michael, knowing Michael planned to use this information to make trades. Maher did not receive any money or property for this information. He shared the information with Michael to "appease" him, and to "help him" and to "fulfil[l] whatever needs he had." Unbeknownst to Maher, Michael shared the inside information with Michael's friend (and Maher's brother-in-law), Bassam Salman, who was told by Michael that the information came from Maher. Salman used this information to trade, earning over $1.5 million in profits (that he split with another relative who executed trades on Salman's behalf). Maher and Michael pleaded guilty. Salman was indicted for securities fraud, and appealed to the Supreme Court, arguing that a gift of confidential information alone is insufficient to establish the personal benefit required for liability, and that a tipper does not personally benefit unless the tipper's goal in disclosing information is to obtain money, property or something of tangible value. (Of course, if the tipper is not liable for the disclosure, then the tippee would not be liable for trading on the information.) Salman's argument was consistent with the Second Circuit's interpretation of the requirements for a gift to satisfy the personal benefit test set forth in in *United States v. Newman*, 773 F.3d 438 (2d Cir. 2014). Salman argued that the Second Circuit's interpretation required that in order for a tipper to incur liability for disclosing inside information, that tipper had to receive a tangible personal benefit. The Supreme Court disagreed, explaining that the Court was adhering to the principles discussed in *Dirks*, specifically that when a fiduciary gives inside information to a trading relative or friend, "the tipper benefits personally because giving a gift of trading information is the same thing as trading by the tipper followed by a gift of the proceeds" (*Salman*, 137 S. Ct. at 428), and therefore, the personal benefit requirement was met.

The defendant in *Salman* also argued that if the personal benefit test is met when a fiduciary merely makes a gift of confidential information to a friend or family member, without any further benefit, then the test is unconstitutionally vague. The Court, however, held that the *Dirks* gift-giving standard "created a simple and clear "guiding principle" for determining tippee liability." The Court acknowledged that this standard could give rise to future cases in which "some factual circumstances assessing liability for gift giving will be difficult[,]" but "[t]hat alone cannot render 'shapeless' a federal criminal prohibition, for even clear rules 'produce close cases.' " *Id.*, at 428–429.

More on Tipper-Tippee Liability

Under *Dirks,* a tippee's liability is based completely on the tipper's liability. If the tipper has no liability, then the tippee cannot have liability. The tippee can "inherit" the tipper's fiduciary duty to the shareholders of the corporation not to trade on material, nonpublic information only when the tipper tips in violation of a fiduciary duty, and only if the tippee knows or should know that the tip was a breach of the tipper's duty. (Note that knowledge that the tipper breached a duty means knowledge about the facts that would lead a court to determine a duty had been breached. For example, if an insider provides a tip in exchange for money, the tippee only needs to know that the insider tipped for money, not that tipping for money constitutes a breach of fiduciary duty. This is a situation in which ignorance of the facts might be a defense, but ignorance of the law is not.)

This existence of tipper/tippee liability requires that, even after following the traditional insider trading analysis to evaluate trades made by an insider, one must go on to another line of analysis, regardless of whether or not the defendant entered into a personal trade, in order to determine if the insider also has "tipper" liability. Furthermore, any tippee who knowingly receives material, nonpublic information, arising out of an insider's breach of duty, can also be liable as a tipper if that individual passes that information along to others in exchange for a personal benefit. Note that an individual may be liable both as a tipper and as a tippee.

This analysis may be carried forward to a chain of subsequent tippees. In each instance, in order to measure if a tipper is liable, one must determine if that tipper knew or should have known about the insider's (or constructive insider's) breach of duty and whether the subsequent tipper received a personal benefit. If so, then the subsequent tipper is also liable for trades made on any inside information he or she provides. In order to determine if the subsequent tippee is liable, one must determine whether the subsequent tippee knew or should have known about the original insider's breach of duty. Each subsequent tippee in the chain will be liable if he or she knew or should have known that the insider breached a duty. It is not relevant for the subsequent tippee's liability if other tippers in the chain received a personal benefit. Even if the subsequent tippee knew or should have known about the original insider's (or constructive insider's) breach of duty, if no trade has been made, then there is no liability.

E. Damages in Insider Trading

Typically, damages in an insider trading action involve restitution or disgorgement of profits. (See the *Texas Gulf Sulphur* case, *supra.*) The *Elkind* case below (the first part of which is in the preceding chapter on Securities Laws) contains a thorough discussion of damages that might be available under Rule 10b–5 and their application in the context of insider tipping involved in that case. The approach to determine (and limit) damages discussed in the *Elkind* case was codified in the Insider Trading and Securities Fraud Enforcement Act of 1988 which added Section 20A to the 1934 Act. Subsection (a) provides liability for a person who buys or sells a security while in possession of "material, nonpublic information" to any contemporaneous seller or buyer of that security. However, subsection (b)(1) of § 20A provides that "The total amount of damages imposed . . . shall not exceed the profit gained or loss avoided in the transaction or transactions that are the subject of the violation."

Elkind v. Liggett & Myers, Inc. [Part II]

635 F.2d 156 (2d Cir. 1980)

MANSFIELD, J.:

[The first portion of this case in which the Court determines that the defendant Liggett's actions that preceded the release of its disappointing earnings figures on July 18, 1972 did not constitute "misleading" is set forth in the previous chapter. This portion of the case considers the improper tipping of information by Liggett's chief financial officer and the damages that follow therefrom.—*Eds.*]

* * * *

Liggett is a diversified company, with traditional business in the tobacco industry supplemented by acquisitions in such industries as liquor (Paddington Corp., importer of J&B Scotch), pet food (Allen Products Co. and Perk Foods Co., manufacturer of Alpo dog food), cereal, watchbands, cleansers and rugs. Its common stock is listed on the New York Stock Exchange.

* * * *

On July 17, preliminary [disappointing] earnings data for June and six-month totals became available to the Board of Directors. . . . The Board decided to issue a press release the following day. That release, issued at about 2:15 P.M. on July 18, disclosed the preliminary earnings figures and attributed the decline to shortcomings in all of Liggett's product lines.

The district court found two "tips" of material inside information in the days before the July 18 press release. . . . [The Court determined that the first tip, known as the "July 10 tip," was not material and was not made with the requisite scienter to incur liability under Rule 10b–5.]

The second "tip" occurred on July 17, one day before the preliminary earnings figures for the first half were released. Analyst Robert Cummins of Loeb Rhoades & Co. questioned Ralph Moore, Liggett's chief financial officer, about the recent decline in price of Liggett's common stock, as well as performance of the various subsidiaries. According to Cummins' deposition, he asked Moore whether there was a good possibility that earnings would be down, and received an affirmative ("grudging") response. Moore added that this information was confidential. Cummins sent a wire to his firm, and spoke with a stockholder who promptly sold 1,800 shares of Liggett stock on behalf of his customers.

* * * *

3. Tipping Liability

The knowing use by corporate insiders of nonpublic information for their own benefit or that of "tippees" by trading in corporate securities amounts to a violation of Rule 10b–5, *SEC v. Texas Gulf Sulphur Co.,* 401 F.2d 833 (2d Cir. 1968) (en banc), cert. denied, 394 U.S. 976, 89 S. Ct. 1454, 22 L. Ed. 2d 756 (1969); *In re Cady, Roberts & Co.,* 40 S.E.C. 907 (1961), which may give rise to a suit for damages by uninformed outsiders who trade during a period of tippee trading. *Shapiro v. Merrill Lynch, Pierce, Fenner & Smith,* 495 F.2d 228 (2d Cir. 1974). *See Chiarella v. United States,* 445 U.S. 222, 100 S. Ct. 1108, 63 L. Ed. 2d 348 (1980).

The duty imposed on a company and its officers is an alternative one: they must disclose material inside information either to no outsiders or to all outsiders equally. As with any claim under Rule 10b–5, scienter must be proven. *Ernst & Ernst v. Hochfelder,* 425 U.S. 185, 96 S. Ct. 1375, 47 L. Ed. 2d 668 (1976). However, if there is no trading by tippees (or those to whom the tippees convey their information), there can be no damages for tipping under § 10(b). [*Citations omitted.*] Trades by tippees are attributed to the tipper. [*Citations omitted.*] Tippee trading, therefore, is the primary and essential element of the offense. The investor otherwise has no right to confidential undisclosed data from the company's files even though it might, if disclosed, influence his investment decision.

The corporate officer dealing with financial analysts inevitably finds himself in a precarious position, which we have analogized to "a fencing match conducted on a tightrope." *SEC v. Bausch & Lomb, Inc.,* 565 F.2d 8, 9 (2d Cir. 1977). A skilled analyst with knowledge of the company and the industry may piece seemingly inconsequential data together with public information into a mosaic which reveals material nonpublic information. Whenever managers and analysts meet elsewhere than in public, there is a risk that the analysts will emerge with knowledge of material information which is not publicly available.

Despite the risks attendant upon these contacts, the SEC and the stock exchanges as well as some commentators have taken the view that meetings and discussions with analysts serve an important function in collecting, evaluating and disseminating corporate information for public use. The reconciliation of this outlook with the SEC's mandate that material facts may be disclosed to investors, provided they are made available to all (through filings with the SEC) and not merely to analysts, has led to a case-by-case approach. *SEC v. Bausch & Lomb, Inc., supra,* 565 F.2d at 10.

The prerequisites of tipping liability, in addition to the revelation of nonpublic information about a company to someone who then takes advantage of this superior knowledge by trading in the company's stock, are that the tipped information must be material, and that the tipper-defendant must have acted with scienter.

(a) Materiality. We discussed the meaning of "materiality" in the Bausch & Lomb case, *supra,* reiterating the language of Texas Gulf Sulphur that the disclosed information must be "reasonably certain to have a substantial effect on the market price of the security." 565 F.2d at 15. We further applied the Supreme Court's definition of materiality from *TSC Industries, Inc. v. Northway, Inc.,* 426 U.S. 438, 449, 96 S. Ct. 2126, 2132, 48 L. Ed. 2d 757 (1976):

> "What the standard (of materiality) does contemplate is a showing of a substantial likelihood that, under all the circumstances, the omitted fact would have assumed actual significance in the deliberations of the reasonable shareholder. Put another way, there must be a substantial likelihood that the disclosure of the omitted fact would have been

viewed by the reasonable investor as having significantly altered the "total mix' of information made available."

Thus a relevant question in determining materiality in a case of alleged tipping to analysts is whether the tipped information, if divulged to the public, would have been likely to affect the decision of potential buyers and sellers.

* * * *

The July 17 tip, however, was sufficiently directed to the matter of earnings to sustain the district court's finding of materiality. According to the deposition of Robert Cummins, the tippee, he inquired whether there was a "possibility" that earnings for the second quarter would be down, and received an affirmative response. He then inquired whether this was a "good possibility," and was again told yes. He was asked to keep the information confidential. Cummins then sent off a wire . . . stating that second quarter earnings, and probably first half earnings as well, would be lower than the previous year's totals.

While there is considerable room for doubt concerning the materiality of this disclosure, particularly in view of the lack of specificity . . . there are sufficient indicia of materiality to support the district court's conclusion. The request by Moore (Liggett's chief financial officer) that Cummins not repeat what he had been told added to the impression that the earnings were worse than those following the stock expected them to be. Moreover, 1,800 shares were sold by a stockbroker on behalf of his customers, after speaking with Cummins by telephone. The stockbroker was left with the impression that "the second quarter was going to be very poor," which he considered significant enough to prompt the sale. We therefore conclude that the July 17 tip was one of material inside information.

* * * *

. . . The tip of July 17 . . . was material and made with scienter. We turn, then, to the computation of damages.

4. Damages

This case presents a question of measurement of damages which we have previously deferred, believing that damages are best addressed in a concrete setting. [*Citations omitted.*] We ruled in Shapiro that defendants selling on inside information would be liable to those who bought on the open market and sustained "substantial losses" during the period of insider trading.

The district court looked to the measure of damages used in cases where a buyer was induced to purchase a company's stock by materially misleading statements or omissions. In such cases of fraud by a fiduciary intended to induce others to buy or sell stock the accepted measure of damages is the "out-of-pocket" measure. This consists of the difference between the price paid and the "value" of the stock when brought (or when the buyer committed himself to buy, if earlier).[25] Except in rare face-to-face transactions, however, uninformed traders on an open, impersonal market are not induced by representations on the part of the tipper or tippee to buy or sell. Usually they are wholly unacquainted with and uninfluenced by the tippee's misconduct. They trade independently and voluntarily but without the benefit of information known to the trading tippee.

In determining what is the appropriate measure of damages to be awarded to the outside uninformed investor as the result of tippee-trading through use of information that is not equally available to all investors is must be remembered that investors who trade in a stock on the open market have no absolute right to know inside information.[26] They are, however, entitled to an honest market in which those with whom they trade have no confidential corporate information. *See SEC v. Texas Gulf Sulphur Co., supra,* 401 F.2d at 848, 851–02.

* * * *

It is the combination of the tip and the tippee's trading that poses the evil against which the open market investor must be protected. [*Citations omitted.*] The reason for the "disclose or abstain" rule is the unfairness in permitting an insider to trade for his own account on the basis of material inside information not available to others. The tipping of material information is a violation of the fiduciary's duty but no injury occurs until the information is used by the tippee. The entry into the market of a tippee with superior knowledge poses the threat that if he trades on the basis of the inside information he may profit at the expense of investors who are disadvantaged by lack of the inside information. For this both the tipper and the tippee are liable. See *SEC v. Texas Gulf Sulphur Co.,* 312 F. Supp. 77, 95 (S.D.N.Y. 1970), *aff'd.,* 446 F.2d 1301, 1308 (2d Cir. 1971). If the insider chooses not to trade, on the other hand, no injury may be

[25] Some cases have suggested the availability as an alternative measure of damages of a modified rescissionary measure, consisting of the difference between the price the defrauded party paid and the price at the time he learned or should have learned the true state of affairs. The theory of this measure is to restore the plaintiff to the position where he would have been had he not been fraudulently induced to trade. . . . The soundness of this measure has been vigorously disputed in the case of open market trading. . . . Since the district court did not apply this modified rescissionary measure, we need not pass on it here.

[26] . . . Indeed, the tipper will often lack the authority to make public disclosure, which is a matter for the business judgment. . . .

claimed by the outside investor, since the public has no right to the undisclosed information.

Recognizing the foregoing, we in Shapiro suggested that the district court must be accorded flexibility in assessing damages, after considering

> "the extent of the selling defendants' trading in Douglas stock, whether such trading effectively impaired the integrity of the market, . . . what profits or other benefits were realized by defendants (and) what expenses were incurred and what losses were sustained by plaintiffs. . . . Moreover, we do not foreclose the possibility that an analysis by the district court of the nature and character of the Rule 10b–5 violations committed may require limiting the extent of liability imposed on either class of defendants." 495 F.2d at 242.

We thus gave heed to the guidance provided by the Supreme Court in *Affiliated Ute Citizens v. United States,* 406 U.S. 128, 151, 92 S. Ct. 1456, 1471, 31 L. Ed. 2d 741 (1972), to the effect that "Congress intended securities legislation enacted for the purpose of avoiding frauds to be construed 'not technically and restrictively, but flexibly to effectuate its remedial purposes.' " *Id.* . . .

Within the flexible framework thus authorized for determining what amounts should be recoverable by the uninformed trader from the tipper and tippee trader, several measures are possible. First, there is the traditional out-of-pocket measure used by the district court in this case. For several reasons this measure appears to be inappropriate. In the first place, as we have noted, it is directed toward compensating a person for losses directly traceable to the defendant's fraud upon him. No such fraud or inducement may be attributed to a tipper or tippee trading on an impersonal market. Aside from this the measure poses serious proof problems that may often be insurmountable in a tippee-trading case. The "value" of the stock traded during the period of nondisclosure of the tipped information (i. e., the price at which the market would have valued the stock if there had been a disclosure) is hypothetical. Expert testimony regarding that "value" may, as the district court found in the present case, be entirely speculative. This has led some courts to conclude that the drop in price of the stock after actual disclosure and after allowing a period of time to elapse for the market to absorb the news may sometimes approximate the drop which would have occurred earlier had the tip been disclosed. [*Citation omitted.*] The court below adopted this approach of using post-public disclosure market price as *nunc pro tunc* evidence of the "value" of the stock during the period of non-disclosure.

Whatever may be the reasonableness of the *nunc pro tunc* "value" method of calculating damages in other contexts, it has serious vulnerabilities here. It rests on the fundamental assumptions (1) that the tipped information is substantially the same as that later disclosed publicly, and (2) that one can determine how the market would have reacted to the public release of the tipped information at an earlier time by its reaction to that information at a later, proximate time. This theory depends on the parity of the "tip" and the "disclosure." When they differ, the basis of the damage calculation evaporates. One could not reasonably estimate how the public would have reacted to the news that the Titanic was near an iceberg from how it reacted to news that the ship had struck an iceberg and sunk. In the present case, the July 10 tip that preliminary earnings would be released in a week is not comparable to the later release of the estimated earnings figures on July 18. Nor was the July 17 tipped information that there was a good possibility that earnings would be down comparable to the next day's release of the estimated earnings figures.

An equally compelling reason for rejecting the theory is its potential for imposition of Draconian, exorbitant damages, out of all proportion to the wrong committed, lining the pockets of all interim investors and their counsel at the expense of innocent corporate stockholders. . . .

An alternative measure would be to permit recovery of damages caused by erosion of the market price of the security that is traceable to the tippee's wrongful trading, i.e., to compensate the uninformed investor for the loss in market value that he suffered as a direct result of the tippee's conduct. Under this measure an innocent trader who bought Liggett shares at or after a tippee sold on the basis of inside information would recover any decline in value of his shares caused by the tippee's trading. Assuming the impact of the tippee's trading on the market is measurable, this approach has the advantage of limiting the plaintiffs to the amount of damage actually caused in fact by the defendant's wrongdoing and avoiding windfall recoveries by investors at the expense of stockholders other than the tippee trader, which could happen in the present action against Liggett. The rationale is that if the market price is not affected by the tippee's trading, the uninformed investor is in the same position as he would have been had the insider abstained from trading. In such event the equilibrium of the market has not been disturbed and the outside investor has not been harmed by the informational imbalance. Only where the market has been contaminated by the wrongful conduct would damages be recoverable.

This causation-in-fact approach has some disadvantages. It allows no recovery for the tippee's violation of his duty to disclose the inside information before trading. Had he fulfilled this duty, others, including holders of the stock, could then have traded on an equal informational basis. Another disadvantage of such a measure lies in the difficult of not impossible burden it would impose on the uninformed trader of proving the time when and extent to which the integrity of the market was affected by the tippee's conduct. . . . Moreover, even assuming market erosion caused by this trading to be provable and that the uninformed investor could show that it continued after his purchase, there remains the question of whether the plaintiff would not be precluded from recovery on the ground that any post-purchase decline in market price attributable to the tippee's trading would not be injury to him as a purchaser, i. e., "in connection with the purchase and sale of securities," but injury to him as a stockholder due to a breach of fiduciary duty by the company's officers, which is not actionable under § 10(b) of the 1934 Act or Rule 10b–5 promulgated thereunder. [*Citations omitted.*] For these reasons, we reject this strict direct market-repercussion theory of damages.

A third alternative is (1) to allow any uninformed investor, where a reasonable investor would either have delayed his purchase or not purchased at all if he had had the benefit of the tipped information, to recover any post-purchase decline in market value of his shares up to a reasonable time after he learns of the tipped information or after there is a public disclosure of it but (2) limit his recovery to the amount gained by the tippee as a result of his selling at the earlier date rather than delaying his sale until the parties could trade on an equal informational basis. Under this measure if the tippee sold 5,000 shares at $50 per share on the basis of inside information and the stock thereafter declined to $40 per share within a reasonable time after public disclosure, an uninformed purchaser, buying shares during the interim (e.g., at $45 per share) would recover the difference between his purchase price and the amount at which he could have sold the shares on an equal informational basis (i. e., the market price within a reasonable time after public disclosure of the tip), subject to a limit of $50,000, which is the amount gained by the tippee as a result of his trading on the inside information rather than on an equal basis. Should the intervening buyers, because of the volume and price of their purchases, claim more than the tippee's gain, their recovery (limited to that gain) would be shared pro rata.

This third alternative, which may be described as the disgorgement measure, has in substance been recommended by the American Law Institute. . . . It offers several advantages. To the extent that it makes the tipper and tippees liable up to the amount gained by their misconduct, it should deter tipping of inside information and tippee-trading. On the other hand, by limiting the total recovery to the tippee's gain, the measure bars windfall recoveries of exorbitant amounts bearing no relation to the seriousness of the misconduct. It also avoids the extraordinary difficulties faced in trying to prove traditional out-of-pocket damages based on the true "value" of the shares purchased or damages claimed by reason of market erosion attributable to tippee trading. A plaintiff would simply be required to prove (1) the time, amount, and price per share of his purchase, (2) that a reasonable investor would not have paid as high a price or made the purchase at all if he had had the information in the tippee's possession, and (3) the price to which the security had declined by the time he learned the tipped information or at a reasonable time after it became public, whichever event first occurred. He would then have a claim and, up to the limits of the tippee's gain, could recover the decline in market value of his shares before the information became public or known to him. In most cases the damages recoverable under the disgorgement measure would be roughly commensurate to the actual harm caused by the tippee's wrongful conduct. In a case where the tippee sold only a few shares, for instance, the likelihood of his conduct causing any substantial injury to intervening investors buying without benefit of his confidential information would be small. If, on the other hand, the tippee sold large amounts of stock, realizing substantial profits, the likelihood of injury to intervening uninformed purchasers would be greater and the amount of potential recovery thereby proportionately enlarged.

We recognize that there cannot be any perfect measure of damages caused by tippee-trading. The disgorgement measure, like others we have described, does have some disadvantages. It modifies the principle that ordinarily gain to the wrongdoer should not be a prerequisite to liability for violation of Rule 10b–5. [*Citations omitted.*] It partially duplicates disgorgement remedies available in proceedings by the SEC or others. Under some market conditions such as where the market price is depressed by wholly unrelated causes, the tippee might be vulnerable to heavy damages, permitting some plaintiffs to recover undeserved windfalls. In some instances the total claims could exceed the wrongdoer's gain, limiting each claimant to a pro rata share of the gain. In other situations, after deducting the cost of recovery, including attorneys' fees, the remainder might be inadequate to make a class action worthwhile. However, as between the various alternatives we are persuaded, after weighing the pros and cons, that the disgorgement measure, despite some disadvantages, offers the most equitable resolution of the difficult problems created by conflicting interests.

In the present case the sole Rule 10b–5 violation was the tippee-trading of 1,800 Liggett shares on the afternoon of July 17, 1972. Since the actual preliminary Liggett earnings were released publicly at 2:15 P.M. on July 18 and were effectively disseminated in a Wall Street Journal article published on the morning of July 19, the only outside purchasers who might conceivably have been damaged by the insider-trading were those who bought Liggett shares between the afternoon of July 17 and the opening of the market on July 19. Thereafter all purchasers bought on an equal informational footing, and any outside purchaser who bought on July 17 and 18 was able to decide within a reasonable time after the July 18–19 publicity whether to hold or sell his shares in the light of the publicly-released news regarding Liggett's less favorable earnings.

The market price of Liggett stock opened on July 17, 1972, at $555/8, and remained at substantially the same price on that date, closing at $551/4. By the close of the market on July 18 the price declined to $521/2 per share. Applying the disgorgement measure, any member of the plaintiff class who bought Liggett shares during the period from the afternoon of July 17 to the close of the market on July 18 and met the reasonable investor requirement would be entitled to claim a pro rata portion of the tippee's gain, based on the difference between their purchase price and the price to which the market price declined within a reasonable time after the morning of July 19. By the close of the market on July 19 the market price had declined to $463/8 per share. The total recovery thus would be limited to the gain realized by the tippee from the inside information, i. e., 1,800 shares multiplied by approximately $9.35 per share.[29]

. . . The award of damages is . . . reversed and the case is remanded for a determination of damages recoverable for tippee-trading based on the July 17, 1972, tip, to be measured in accordance with the foregoing. . . .

QUESTIONS

1. The court provides that any member of the plaintiff class who bought Leggett shares during the period in question is entitled to a "pro rata" portion

[29] Since, as previously pointed out, the tipped information was not as adverse as the bad news ultimately disclosed, the defendants could plausibly argue that the tippee's gain (and therefore the limit of plaintiffs' recovery) should be only the difference between the price at which he sold and the hypothetical price to which the stock would have declined if the tip had been disclosed. While that approach would make sense if a tippee were held liable for the out-of-pocket losses of all plaintiffs, we think that when only a disgorgement measure of damages is used, a tippee who trades is liable for the entire difference between the price at which he sold and the price the stock reached after the tip became known. By trading on tipped information, the tippee takes the risk that by the time the tip is disclosed the market price may reflect disclosure of information more adverse than the tip and other adverse market conditions.

of the tippee's gain. If there were a means to determine the actual party who bought their shares from the defendant, should that party be entitled to recover and not those individuals who were not "lucky" enough to buy their shares during the "right" time period?

2. Would the plaintiff want the class of plaintiffs to be large or small?

3. Who would bring a suit if the recovery was most likely limited to relatively small sum?

SECTION III: The Misappropriation Theory

A. Liability Under the Misappropriation Theory

Misappropriation as a theory of liability developed over time. Prior to the *O'Hagan* case (which follows), in order to find liability, one needed to show that the defendant breached a duty (or in the case of tippee liability, that the information arose out of a breach of duty) *to the company in whose stock the defendant had traded. See Chiarella v. United States,* 445 U.S. 222 (1980). The misappropriation theory broadened liability to extend to those who had breached a duty to the source of the information. Instead of asking about a breach of a fiduciary duty to the company, the misappropriation theory asks about duties to the source of the information and about whether the defendant breached (or knew about a breach of) a duty arising out of a relationship of trust and confidence to the source of the information.

United States v. O'Hagan

521 U.S. 642 (1997)

JUSTICE GINSBURG delivered the opinion of the Court.

This case concerns the interpretation and enforcement of § 10(b) and § 14(e) of the Securities Exchange Act of 1934, and rules made by the Securities and Exchange Commission pursuant to these provisions, Rule 10b–5 and Rule 14e–3(a). . . . In particular, we address and resolve these issues: (1) Is a person who trades in securities for personal profit, using confidential information misappropriated in breach of a fiduciary duty to the source of the information, guilty of violating § 10(b) and Rule 10b–5? (2) Did the Commission exceed its rulemaking authority by adopting Rule 14e–3(a), which proscribes trading on undisclosed information in the tender offer setting, even in the absence of a duty to disclose? Our answer to the first question is yes, and to the second question, viewed in the context of this case, no.

I

Respondent James Herman O'Hagan was a partner in the law firm of Dorsey & Whitney in Minneapolis, Minnesota. In July 1988, Grand Metropolitan PLC (Grand Met), a company based in London, England, retained Dorsey & Whitney as local counsel to represent Grand Met regarding a potential tender offer for the common stock of the Pillsbury Company, headquartered in Minneapolis. Both Grand Met and Dorsey & Whitney took precautions to protect the confidentiality of Grand Met's tender offer plans. O'Hagan did no work on the Grand Met representation. Dorsey & Whitney withdrew from representing Grand Met on September 9, 1988. Less than a month later, on October 4, 1988, Grand Met publicly announced its tender offer for Pillsbury stock.

On August 18, 1988, while Dorsey & Whitney was still representing Grand Met, O'Hagan began purchasing call options for Pillsbury stock. Each option gave him the right to purchase 100 shares of Pillsbury stock by a specified date in September 1988. Later in August and in September, O'Hagan made additional purchases of Pillsbury call options. By the end of September, he owned 2,500 unexpired Pillsbury options, apparently more than any other individual investor. O'Hagan also purchased, in September 1988, some 5,000 shares of Pillsbury common stock, at a price just under $39 per share. When Grand Met announced its tender offer in October, the price of Pillsbury stock rose to nearly $60 per share. O'Hagan then sold his Pillsbury call options and common stock, making a profit of more than $4.3 million.

The Securities and Exchange Commission (SEC or Commission) initiated an investigation into O'Hagan's transactions, culminating in a 57-count indictment. The indictment alleged that O'Hagan defrauded his law firm and its client, Grand Met, by using for his own trading purposes material, nonpublic information regarding Grand Met's planned tender offer. According to the indictment, O'Hagan used the profits he gained through this trading to conceal his previous embezzlement and conversion of unrelated client trust funds. O'Hagan was charged with 20 counts of mail fraud, . . . 17 counts of securities fraud, in violation of § 10(b) of the Securities Exchange Act of 1934 and SEC Rule 10b–5; 17 counts of fraudulent trading in connection with a tender offer, in violation of § 14(e) of the Exchange Act, and SEC Rule 14e–3(a); and 3 counts of violating federal money laundering statutes. A jury convicted O'Hagan on all 57 counts, and he was sentenced to a 41-month term of imprisonment.

A divided panel of the Court of Appeals for the Eighth Circuit reversed all of O'Hagan's convictions. . . . [The Court of Appeals ruled that] [l]iability under § 10(b) and Rule 10b–5, the Eighth Circuit held, may not be grounded on the "misappropriation theory" of securities fraud on which the prosecution relied. [*Citation omitted.*] The Court of Appeals also held that Rule 14e–3(a)—which prohibits trading while in possession of material, nonpublic information relating to a tender offer—exceeds the SEC's § 14(e) rulemaking authority because the rule contains no breach of fiduciary duty requirement. . . .

Decisions of the Courts of Appeals are in conflict on the propriety of the misappropriation theory under § 10(b) and Rule 10b–5, and on the legitimacy of Rule 14e–3(a) under § 14(e). We granted certiorari, and now reverse the Eighth Circuit's judgment.

II

. . . We hold, in accord with several other Courts of Appeals, that criminal liability under § 10(b) may be predicated on the misappropriation theory.

A

* * * *

Under the "traditional" or "classical theory" of insider trading liability, § 10(b) and Rule 10b–5 are violated when a corporate insider trades in the securities of his corporation on the basis of material, nonpublic information. Trading on such information qualifies as a "deceptive device" under § 10(b), we have affirmed, because "a relationship of trust and confidence [exists] between the shareholders of a corporation and those insiders who have obtained confidential information by reason of their position with that corporation." *Chiarella v. United States,* 445 U.S. 222, 228, 63 L. Ed. 2d 348, 100 S. Ct. 1108 (1980). That relationship, we recognized, "gives rise to a duty to disclose [or to abstain from trading] because of the 'necessity of preventing a corporate insider from . . . taking unfair advantage of . . . uninformed . . . stockholders.' " *Id.,* at 228–229 (citation omitted). The classical theory applies not only to officers, directors, and other permanent insiders of a corporation, but also to attorneys, accountants, consultants, and others who temporarily become fiduciaries of a corporation. *See Dirks v. SEC,* 463 U.S. 646, 655, n.14 (1983).

The "misappropriation theory" holds that a person commits fraud "in connection with" a securities transaction, and thereby violates § 10(b) and Rule

10b–5, when he misappropriates confidential information for securities trading purposes, in breach of a duty owed to the source of the information. Under this theory, a fiduciary's undisclosed, self-serving use of a principal's information to purchase or sell securities, in breach of a duty of loyalty and confidentiality, defrauds the principal of the exclusive use of that information. In lieu of premising liability on a fiduciary relationship between company insider and purchaser or seller of the company's stock, the misappropriation theory premises liability on a fiduciary-turned-trader's deception of those who entrusted him with access to confidential information.

The two theories are complementary. . . . The classical theory targets a corporate insider's breach of duty to shareholders with whom the insider transacts; the misappropriation theory outlaws trading on the basis of nonpublic information by a corporate "outsider" in breach of a duty owed not to a trading party, but to the source of the information. The misappropriation theory is thus designed to "protect the integrity of the securities markets against abuses by 'outsiders' to a corporation who have access to confidential information that will affect the corporation's security price when revealed, but who owe no fiduciary or other duty to that corporation's shareholders." [*Citation omitted.*]

In this case, the indictment alleged that O'Hagan, in breach of a duty of trust and confidence he owed to his law firm, Dorsey & Whitney, and to its client, Grand Met, traded on the basis of nonpublic information regarding Grand Met's planned tender offer for Pillsbury common stock. This conduct, the Government charged, constituted a fraudulent device in connection with the purchase and sale of securities.[5]

B

We agree with the Government that misappropriation, as just defined, satisfies § 10(b)'s requirement that chargeable conduct involve a "deceptive device or contrivance" used "in connection with" the purchase or sale of securities. We observe, first, that misappropriators, as the Government describes them, deal in deception. A fiduciary who "[pretends] loyalty to the principal

[5] The Government could not have prosecuted O'Hagan under the classical theory, for O'Hagan was not an "insider" of Pillsbury, the corporation in whose stock he traded. Although an "outsider" with respect to Pillsbury, O'Hagan had an intimate association with, and was found to have traded on confidential information from, Dorsey & Whitney, counsel to tender offeror Grand Met. Under the misappropriation theory, O'Hagan's securities trading does not escape Exchange Act sanction, as it would under the dissent's reasoning, simply because he was associated with, and gained nonpublic information from, the bidder, rather than the target.

while secretly converting the principal's information for personal gain," [*Citation omitted.*] "dupes" or defrauds the principal. . . .

* * * *

Deception through nondisclosure is central to the theory of liability for which the Government seeks recognition. As counsel for the Government stated in explanation of the theory at oral argument: "To satisfy the common law rule that a trustee may not use the property that [has] been entrusted [to] him, there would have to be consent. To satisfy the requirement of the Securities Act that there be no deception, there would only have to be disclosure." . . .[6]

The misappropriation theory advanced by the Government is consistent with *Santa Fe Industries, Inc. v. Green,* 430 U.S. 462 (1977), a decision underscoring that § 10(b) is not an all-purpose breach of fiduciary duty ban; rather, it trains on conduct involving manipulation or deception. [*Citation omitted.*] In contrast to the Government's allegations in this case, in *Santa Fe Industries,* all pertinent facts were disclosed by the persons charged with violating § 10(b) and Rule 10b–5. . .; therefore, there was no deception through nondisclosure to which liability under those provisions could attach. . . . Similarly, full disclosure forecloses liability under the misappropriation theory: Because the deception essential to the misappropriation theory involves feigning fidelity to the source of information, if the fiduciary discloses to the source that he plans to trade on the nonpublic information, there is no "deceptive device" and thus no § 10(b) violation—although the fiduciary-turned-trader may remain liable under state law for breach of a duty of loyalty.[7]

We turn next to the § 10(b) requirement that the misappropriator's deceptive use of information be "in connection with the purchase or sale of [a] security." This element is satisfied because the fiduciary's fraud is consummated, not when the fiduciary gains the confidential information, but when, without disclosure to his principal, he uses the information to purchase or sell securities. The securities transaction and the breach of duty thus coincide. This is so even though the person or entity defrauded is not the other party to the trade, but is, instead, the source of the nonpublic information. [*Citation omitted.*] A

---

[6] Under the misappropriation theory urged in this case, the disclosure obligation runs to the source of the information, here, Dorsey & Whitney and Grand Met. Chief Justice Burger, dissenting in *Chiarella*, advanced a broader reading of § 10(b) and Rule 10b–5; the disclosure obligation, as he envisioned it, ran to those with whom the misappropriator trades. . . . The Government does not propose that we adopt a misappropriation theory of that breadth.

[7] Where, however, a person trading on the basis of material, nonpublic information owes a duty of loyalty and confidentiality to two entities or persons—for example, a law firm and its client—but makes disclosure to only one, the trader may still be liable under the misappropriation theory.

misappropriator who trades on the basis of material, nonpublic information, in short, gains his advantageous market position through deception; he deceives the source of the information and simultaneously harms members of the investing public. . . .

* * * *

The misappropriation theory comports with § 10(b)'s language, which requires deception "in connection with the purchase or sale of any security," not deception of an identifiable purchaser or seller. . . . Although informational disparity is inevitable in the securities markets, investors likely would hesitate to venture their capital in a market where trading based on misappropriated nonpublic information is unchecked by law. An investor's informational disadvantage vis-a-vis a misappropriator with material, nonpublic information stems from contrivance, not luck; it is a disadvantage that cannot be overcome with research or skill. *See* Brudney, Insiders, Outsiders, and Informational Advantages Under the Federal Securities Laws, 93 Harv. L. Rev. 322, 356 (1979) ("If the market is thought to be systematically populated with . . . transactors [trading on the basis of misappropriated information] some investors will refrain from dealing altogether, and others will incur costs to avoid dealing with such transactors or corruptly to overcome their unerodable informational advantages."). . .

In sum, considering the inhibiting impact on market participation of trading on misappropriated information, and the congressional purposes underlying § 10(b), it makes scant sense to hold a lawyer like O'Hagan a § 10(b) violator if he works for a law firm representing the target of a tender offer, but not if he works for a law firm representing the bidder. The text of the statute requires no such result.[9] The misappropriation at issue here was properly made the subject of a § 10(b) charge because it meets the statutory requirement that there be "deceptive" conduct "in connection with" securities transactions. . . .

* * * *

---

[9] As noted earlier, however, the textual requirement of deception precludes § 10(b) liability when a person trading on the basis of nonpublic information has disclosed his trading plans to, or obtained authorization from, the principal—even though such conduct may affect the securities markets in the same manner as the conduct reached by the misappropriation theory. Contrary to the dissent's suggestion, the fact that § 10(b) is only a partial antidote to the problems it was designed to alleviate does not call into question its prohibition of conduct that falls within its textual proscription. Moreover, once a disloyal agent discloses his imminent breach of duty, his principal may seek appropriate equitable relief under state law. Furthermore, in the context of a tender offer, the principal who authorizes an agent's trading on confidential information may, in the Commission's view, incur liability for an Exchange Act violation under Rule 14e–3(a).

"reasonably designed to prevent . . . acts and practices [that] are fraudulent." [*Citation omitted.*]

Because Congress has authorized the Commission, in § 14(e), to prescribe legislative rules, we owe the Commission's judgment "more than mere deference or weight." *Batterton v. Francis,* 432 U.S. 416, 424–426 (1977). Therefore, in determining whether Rule 14e–3(a)'s "disclose or abstain from trading" requirement is reasonably designed to prevent fraudulent acts, we must accord the Commission's assessment "controlling weight unless [it is] arbitrary, capricious, or manifestly contrary to the statute." *Chevron U.S.A. Inc. v. Natural Resources Defense Council, Inc.,* 467 U.S. 837, 844 (1984). In this case, we conclude, the Commission's assessment is none of these. . . .

* * * *

In sum, it is a fair assumption that trading on the basis of material, nonpublic information will often involve a breach of a duty of confidentiality to the bidder or target company or their representatives. The SEC, cognizant of the proof problem that could enable sophisticated traders to escape responsibility, placed in Rule 14e–3(a) a "disclose or abstain from trading" command that does not require specific proof of a breach of fiduciary duty. That prescription, we are satisfied, applied to this case, is a "means reasonably designed to prevent" fraudulent trading on material, nonpublic information in the tender offer context ". . . [Rule 14e–3(a)] retains a close nexus between the prohibited conduct and the statutory aims."). . . . Therefore, insofar as it serves to prevent the type of misappropriation charged against O'Hagan, Rule 14e–3(a) is a proper exercise of the Commission's prophylactic power under § 14(e).

* * * *

The judgment of the Court of Appeals for the Eighth Circuit is reversed, and the case is remanded for further proceedings consistent with this opinion.

It is so ordered.

NOTES AND QUESTIONS

1. How broadly should this duty of trust and confidence be construed?

2. Should it extend to employees? In *Carpenter v. United States,* 484 U.S. 19 (1987), ten years before the *O'Hagan* case, an evenly divided Supreme Court, while not adopting the misappropriation theory, nevertheless affirmed a conviction of an employee, R. Foster Winans, of the *Wall Street Journal* under

Rule 10b–5 in which the Second Circuit Court of Appeals had ruled that Winans had fraudulently misappropriated "property." The facts and the lower courts' reasoning are excerpted below:

> In 1981, Winans became a reporter for the Wall Street Journal (the Journal) and in the summer of 1982 became one of the two writers of a daily column, "Heard on the Street." That column discussed selected stocks or groups of stocks, giving positive and negative information about those stocks and taking "a point of view with respect to investment in the stocks that it reviews." . . . Winans regularly interviewed corporate executives to put together interesting perspectives on the stocks that would be highlighted in upcoming columns, but, at least for the columns at issue here, none contained corporate inside information or any "hold for release" information. . . . Because of the "Heard" column's perceived quality and integrity, it had the potential of affecting the price of the stocks which it examined. The District Court concluded on the basis of testimony presented at trial that the "Heard" column "does have an impact on the market, difficult though it may be to quantify in any particular case." . . .
>
> The official policy and practice at the Journal was that prior to publication, the contents of the column were the Journal's confidential information. Despite the rule, with which Winans was familiar, he entered into a scheme in October 1983 with Peter Brant and petitioner Felis, both connected with the Kidder Peabody brokerage firm in New York City, to give them advance information as to the timing and contents of the "Heard" column. This permitted Brant and Felis and another conspirator, David Clark, a client of Brant, to buy or sell based on the probable impact of the column on the market. Profits were to be shared. The conspirators agreed that the scheme would not affect the journalistic purity of the "Heard" column, and the District Court did not find that the contents of any of the articles were altered to further the profit potential of petitioners' stock-trading scheme. . . . Over a 4-month period, the brokers made prepublication trades on the basis of information given them by Winans about the contents of some 27 "Heard" columns. The net profits from these trades were about $690,000.
>
> * * * *

> The District Court found, and the Court of Appeals agreed, that Winans had knowingly breached a duty of confidentiality by misappropriating prepublication information regarding the timing and contents of the "Heard" column, information that had been gained in the course of his employment under the understanding that it would not be revealed in advance of publication and that if it were, he would report it to his employer. It was this appropriation of confidential information that underlay both the securities laws and mail and wire fraud counts. With respect to the § 10(b) charges, the courts below held that the deliberate breach of Winans' duty of confidentiality and concealment of the scheme was a fraud and deceit on the Journal. Although the victim of the fraud, the Journal, was not a buyer or seller of the stocks traded in or otherwise a market participant, the fraud was nevertheless considered to be "in connection with" a purchase or sale of securities within the meaning of the statute and the rule. The courts reasoned that the scheme's sole purpose was to buy and sell securities at a profit based on advance information of the column's contents.

Id. at 22–24.

B. Misappropriation Analysis and the Duty of Trust and Confidence

The questions asked to evaluate an insider trading violation under the misappropriation theory are very similar to those asked to evaluate a violation under traditional insider trading. The rule under misappropriation theory is that a person commits fraud in a securities transaction when he or she "misappropriates" material, nonpublic information in breach of a duty (typically a duty of trust and confidence) owed to the source of the information, AND does not disclose his intentions to trade to the source of the information, AND trades on that information. Note that the breach of duty is not just a fiduciary duty owed to the company whose stock is traded; rather it is a breach of a duty owed to the source of the information.

In a misappropriation analysis, one is still looking for a breach of duty to the owner of nonpublic information, and in the tipper/tippee analysis under the misappropriation theory, one still asks whether the tippee knew (or should he have known) about the breach of duty. The tipper/tippee analysis under the misappropriation theory is very similar to tipper/tippee analysis under traditional insider trading. However, liability under the misappropriation theory can be broader because it is not just about the insider's conduct. In traditional insider trading, if there is no breach of duty by the insider, there can be no violation by the tippee, but in evaluating whether there might be misappropriation liability, one needs to ask if anyone along the chain of information dissemination breached a fiduciary duty or a duty arising out of a relationship of trust and confidence ("RETAC"). If a tippee knows or should know about a prior breach in the chain of that duty, then the tippee can be held liable for his or her trades. Because a breach of duty can arise at any point in the chain of information dissemination, a determination must be made whether a duty of confidentiality has been violated in any RETAC as information passes along a chain of tippers and tippees. (Most would argue that a breach of duty by the tipper is still measured by whether the person breaching the duty received a personal benefit. *See SEC v. Yun*, 327 F.3d 1263 (2003).) However, there are courts that have taken the position that there is no need to "make an affirmative showing of benefit in cases of misappropriation." *See SEC v. Sargent*, 229 F.3d 68, 77 (1st Cir. 2000); *see also SEC v. Willis*, 777 F. Supp. 1165 (S.D.N.Y. 1991) (in which a psychiatrist traded on nonpublic information learned from a patient in the course of therapy) and *SEC v. Musella*, 748 F. Supp. 1028 (S.D.N.Y. 1989).

One important aspect to note is that the duty to the source of the information may arise out of a traditional fiduciary relationship or out of a relationship of trust and confidence similar in nature to those characterized by traditional fiduciary duties. In other words, the analysis involves asking if there was a breach of a fiduciary duty or a similar duty arising out of a RETAC. In *United States v. Chestman*, 947 F.2d 551 (2d Cir. 1991), the president of the Waldbaum grocery store chain told his sister, Shirley, about the pending acquisition of the company; Shirley told her daughter, Susan, who in turn told her husband, Keith. Keith shared the information with his broker, Chestman, who traded on the information. The SEC brought charges against Chestman and argued that a duty of trust and confidence existed between Susan and Keith as husband and wife. Chestman was convicted, but the Second Circuit reversed the conviction, finding that no fiduciary relationship existed between husband and wife without some additional element. The court explained that "a fiduciary duty cannot be imposed unilaterally by entrusting a person with confidential information," even if that person is a family member. *Id.* at 567. A relationship of trust and confidence giving rise to such a duty "must be the functional equivalent of a fiduciary relationship." *Id.* at 568.

In an effort to expand the reach of the misappropriation doctrine, and effectively overrule *Chestman*, the SEC adopted Rule 10b5–2, which provides a non-exhaustive list of examples of relationships of trust and confidence for the purpose of misappropriation. Rule 10b5–2 provides that a duty of trust and confidence exists in the following circumstances (among others):

(1) Whenever a person agrees to maintain information in confidence;

(2) Whenever the person communicating the material, nonpublic information and the person to whom it is communicated have a history, pattern, or practice of sharing confidences, such that the recipient of the information knows or reasonably should know that the person communicating the material nonpublic information expects that the recipient will maintain its confidentiality; or

(3) Whenever a person receives or obtains material, nonpublic information from his or her spouse, parent, child, or sibling; provided, however, that the person receiving or obtaining the information may demonstrate that no duty of trust or confidence existed with respect to the information by establishing that he or she neither knew nor reasonably should have known that the person who was the source of the information expected that the person would keep the information confidential, because of the parties' history, pattern, or practice of sharing and maintaining confidences, and because there was no agreement or understanding to maintain the confidentiality of the information.

Following the adoption of Rule 10b5–2, the duties owed between a husband and wife were again considered in the *SEC v. Yun* case, which follows.

Securities and Exchange Commission v. Yun

327 F.3d 1263 (11th Cir. 2003)

TJOFLAT, C.J.:

This is an insider trading case, brought by the Securities and Exchange Commission ("SEC") under section 10(b) of the Securities Exchange Act of 1934 ("Exchange Act"), 15 U.S.C. § 78j(b), and (SEC) Rule 10b–5, 17 C.F.R. § 240. 10b–5, against Donna Yun and Jerry Burch. Answering special verdicts, a jury found that the defendants had "violated Section 10(b)" under the "misappropriation theory" of liability. Acting on those verdicts, the district court entered judgment against the defendants, holding them "jointly liable" for $269,000, the profits generated by the prohibited trading. . . .

Yun and Burch now appeal, contending that the district court erred in denying their motions for judgment as a matter of law. . . .

I.

A.

Donna Yun is married to David Yun, the president of Scholastic Book Fairs, Inc., a subsidiary of Scholastic Corporation ("Scholastic"), a publisher and distributor of children's books whose stock is quoted on the NASDAQ National Market System and whose option contracts are traded on the Chicago Board Options Exchange. On January 27, 1997, David attended a senior management retreat at which Scholastic's chief financial officer revealed that the company would post a loss for the current quarter, and that before the quarter ended, the company would make a public announcement revising its earnings forecast downward. He cautioned the assembled executives not to sell any of their Scholastic holdings until after the announcement, which would likely result in a decline in the market price of Scholastic shares, and warned them to keep the matter confidential. Approximately two weeks later, on February 13, Scholastic's chief financial officer informed David that the negative earnings announcement would be made on February 20.

Over the weekend of February 15–16, David and Donna discussed a statement of assets that he had provided her in connection with their negotiation of a post-nuptial division of assets. David explained to Donna that he had assigned a $55 value to his Scholastic options listed on the asset statement, even though Scholastic's stock was then trading at $65 per share, because he believed that the price of the shares would drop following Scholastic's February 20 earnings announcement. He also told her not to disclose this information to anyone else, and she agreed to keep the information confidential.

The following Tuesday, February 18, Donna went to her place of work—a real estate office located in a nearby housing development. The office was a small sales trailer, approximately eleven by thirteen feet, that Donna shared with other real estate agents, including Jerry Burch. During the late morning or early afternoon, Donna telephoned Sam Weiss—the attorney assisting her in negotiating the post-nuptial division of assets—from her office to discuss David's statement of assets. While she was speaking to Weiss, Burch entered the office to gather materials for a real estate client. Standing three to four feet from Donna, Burch heard her tell Weiss what David had said about Scholastic's impending earnings announcement and that David expected the price of the company's shares to fall. As he testified at trial, Burch did not learn enough from what he overheard to feel "comfortable" trading in Scholastic's stock.

That evening, Donna and Burch attended a real estate awards banquet at the Isleworth Country Club. Donna, Burch, and another agent, Maryann Hartmann, carpooled to the reception. All three stayed at the reception for three hours and left together.

The next morning Burch called his broker and requested authority to purchase put options in Scholastic. When the broker advised Burch that he knew of no new information indicating the price of Scholastic stock would decline, Burch stated that based on information he had obtained at a cocktail party, he nonetheless wanted to purchase the put options. The broker warned Burch of the risks of trading in options, and cautioned him about insider trading prohibitions. Despite these warnings, between the afternoon of February 19 and midday on February 20, Burch purchased $19,750 in Scholastic put options, which was equal to two-thirds of his total income for the previous year and nearly half the value of his entire investment portfolio.

After the stock market closed on February 20, Scholastic announced that its earnings would be well below the analysts' expectations. When the market opened the next day, the price of Scholastic shares had dropped approximately 40 percent to $36 per share. Burch then sold his Scholastic puts, realizing a profit of $269,000—a 1,300 percent return on his investment. . . . In a one-count complaint, the SEC alleged that Donna and Burch had violated section 10(b) of the Exchange Act and Rule 10b–5. . . .

B.

There are two theories of insider trading liability: the "classical theory" and the "misappropriation theory." The classical theory imposes liability on corporate "insiders" who trade on the basis of confidential information obtained by reason of their position with the corporation. The liability is based on the notion that a corporate insider breaches "a . . . [duty] of trust and confidence" to the shareholders of his corporation. *United States v. O'Hagan,* 521 U.S. 642, 652, 117, 138 L. Ed. 2d 724, 117 S. Ct. 2199 (1997). The misappropriation theory, on the other hand, imposes liability on "outsiders" who trade on the basis of confidential information obtained by reason of their relationship with the person possessing such information, usually an insider. The liability under the latter theory is based on the notion that the outsider breaches "a duty of loyalty and confidentiality" to the person who shared the confidential information with him. . . .

. . . To establish liability, . . . all the SEC needs to show is that the tipper received a "benefit," directly or indirectly, from his disclosure.

This is a tipper-tippee case. The SEC prosecuted it under the "misappropriation theory" of insider trading liability. Its complaint alleged that Donna was an outsider who had a fiduciary relationship with David, and that she breached that duty when she divulged to Burch confidential information, which David had given her, "for her direct and/or indirect benefit because of her business relationship and friendship with . . . Burch." Under these circumstances, the complaint alleged, Donna was liable under section 10(b) of the Exchange Act and Rule 10b–5 to disgorge the profits Burch realized from the put options trades. Because Burch knew of Donna's breach of her fiduciary duty to David, but nonetheless traded on the confidential information she gave him, he, too, was liable under § 10(b) and Rule 10b–5.

* * * *

II.

A.

In assessing the district court's ruling on appellants' motions for judgment as a matter of law, we first consider whether Donna owed David a duty of loyalty and confidentiality not to disclose the revised earnings information he had received in confidence.

As stated *supra,* to prevail in an insider trading case, the SEC must establish that the misappropriator breached a duty of loyalty and confidentiality owed to the source of the confidential information. Certain business relationships, such as attorney-client or employer-employee, clearly provide the requisite duty of loyalty and confidentiality. On the other hand, it is unsettled whether non-business relationships, such as husband and wife, provide the duty of loyalty and confidentiality necessary to satisfy the misappropriation theory. The leading case on when a duty of loyalty and confidentiality exists in the context of family members—the case relied on by the parties and the district court for the elements of a confidential relationship—is *United States v. Chestman,* 947 F.2d 551 (2d Cir. 1991) (en banc).

In a divided en banc decision, the Second Circuit held that marriage alone does not create a relationship of loyalty and confidentiality. *Id.* at 568. Either an "express agreement of confidentiality" or the "functional equivalent" of a "fiduciary relationship" must exist between the spouses for a court to find a confidential relationship for purposes of § 10(b) and Rule 10b–5 liability. Since the spouses had not entered into a confidentiality agreement, the court turned its focus to determining what constitutes a fiduciary relationship or its functional equivalent. "At the heart of the fiduciary relationship," the court declared, "lies reliance, and de facto control and dominance." *Id.* at 568 (citations and internal quotation marks omitted). Having so concluded, the court explained that the functional equivalent of a fiduciary relationship "must share these qualities." *Id.* at 569. Applying the requisite qualities of reliance, control, and dominance to the husband and wife relationship at hand, the *Chestman* majority held that no fiduciary relationship or its functional equivalent existed. The spouses' sharing and maintaining of "generic confidences" in the past was insufficient to establish the functional equivalent of a fiduciary relationship. *Id.* at 571. Accordingly, the court decided that the defendants were not subject to sanctions for insider trading violations.

A lengthy dissent by Judge Winter, joined by four judges, took issue with the narrowness in which the majority would find a relationship of loyalty and confidentiality amongst family members, pointing out that under the majority's approach, the disclosure of sensitive corporate information essentially could be "avoided only by family members extracting formal, express promises of confidentiality." *Id.* at 580. Such an approach, in the view of the dissent, was "unrealistic in that it expects family members to behave like strangers toward each other." *Id.* Moreover, the normal reluctance to recognize obligations based on family relationships—the concern that intra-family litigation would exacerbate strained relationships and weaken the sense of mutual obligation underlying family relationships—was inapplicable in insider trading cases because the suits are brought by the government. *See id.* at 580. Given the circumstances of the case, the dissent concluded that a confidential relationship existed between the husband and wife which gave rise to a duty of loyalty and confidentiality on his part not to disclose the sensitive information.

We are inclined to accept the dissent's view that the *Chestman* decision too narrowly defined the circumstances in which a duty of loyalty and confidentiality is created between husband and wife. We think that the majority, by insisting on either an express agreement of confidentiality or a strictly defined fiduciary-like relationship, ignored the many instances in which a spouse has a reasonable expectation of confidentiality. In our view, a spouse who trades in breach of a reasonable and legitimate expectation of confidentiality held by the other spouse sufficiently subjects the former to insider trading liability. If the SEC can prove that the husband and wife had a history or practice of sharing business confidences, and those confidences generally were maintained by the spouse receiving the information, then in most instances the conveying spouse would have a reasonable expectation of confidentiality such that the breach of the expectation would suffice to yield insider trading liability. Of course, a breach of an agreement to maintain business confidences would also suffice.

For purposes of this case, then, the existence of a duty of loyalty and confidentiality turns on whether David Yun granted his wife, Donna, access to confidential information in reasonable reliance on a promise that she would safeguard the information. *See SEC v. Sargent,* 229 F.3d 68, 75 (1st Cir. 2000) ("The misappropriation theory premises liability on a fiduciary-turned-trader's deception of those who entrusted him with access to confidential information.") (citing *O'Hagan,* 521 U.S. at 652, 117 S. Ct. at 2199). If the SEC presented evidence that David and Donna had a history or pattern of sharing business confidences, which were generally kept, then Donna could have been found by the jury to have breached a duty of loyalty and confidentiality by disclosing to Burch the information regarding Scholastic's upcoming earnings announcement. Similarly, if the SEC presented evidence that Donna had agreed in this particular instance to keep the information confidential, then Donna could have been found to have committed the necessary breach of a duty of loyalty and confidentiality.

We conclude that the SEC provided sufficient evidence both that an agreement of confidentiality and a history or pattern of sharing and keeping of business confidences existed between David and Donna Yun such that David could have reasonably expected Donna to keep confidential what he told her about Scholastic's pending announcement. First, the SEC presented evidence that Donna explicitly accepted the duty to keep in confidence the business information she received. She testified that she considered the information confidential because, "David always told me, anything that he talks to me in regards to the company is confidential and can't go past he or I." That she fully understood and agreed to the understanding of confidentiality is further manifested by the fact that she declined to disclose any information about David's company to her attorney until she had "absolute certainty that there was confidentiality with everything [she] was sharing with him." Second, both David and Donna testified that David repeatedly shared confidential information about Scholastic with Donna, including information regarding its sales goals. This certainly qualified as a history or pattern of sharing business confidences.

Overall, the SEC presented evidence upon which a jury could find that a duty of loyalty and confidentiality existed between David and Donna Yun; the SEC therefore established the first element of a "misappropriation theory" claim.

B.

Having reached this conclusion, we turn to the question of whether the evidence was sufficient to show that Donna breached her duty to David. According to the allegations of the complaint, the answer to this question depends on whether Donna deliberately communicated the confidential information to Burch "for her direct and/or indirect benefit because of her business relationship and friendship with . . . Burch." The SEC contends—contrary to the position it assumed in its complaint—that it did not have to prove that Donna divulged the information for her own benefit; all it had to show was that Donna acted with "severe recklessness." According to the SEC, the "intent to benefit" element only applies in cases brought under the classical theory of liability; the element has no application in cases brought under the misappropriation theory of liability. In other words, whether Donna expected to benefit from the disclosure of the confidential information is irrelevant.

. . . Several district courts have addressed the issue, though, with some requiring an expected benefit and others holding that no showing of an expected benefit is necessary. None of these courts, however, gave the issue more than perfunctory thought. After considering the policies underpinning the insider trading rules, we are led to the conclusion that the SEC must prove that a misappropriator expected to benefit from the tip.

* * * *

. . . The SEC's approach essentially would allow the SEC and the courts to ignore precedent involving the classical theory of liability whenever the SEC brings its actions under a misappropriation theory, and vice versa. . . .

First, we note that there is no reason to distinguish between a tippee who receives confidential information from an insider (under the classical theory) and a tippee who receives such information from an outsider (under the misappropriation theory). In either case, the tippee is under notice that he has received confidential information through an improper breach of a duty of loyalty and confidentiality. And should the tippee nonetheless trade on the confidential information, his potential liability would not vary according to the theory—classical or misappropriation—under which the case is prosecuted. . . .

Given that the position of a tippee is the same whether his tipper is an insider or an outsider, it makes "scant sense" for the elements the SEC must prove to establish a § 10(b) and Rule 10b–5 violation depend on the theory under which the SEC chooses to litigate the case. *See id.* at 659, 117 S. Ct. at 2210–11. The tippee's liability should be determined under the same principles. And for better or worse, the Supreme Court has required that the only way to taint a tippee with liability for insider trading is to find a co-venture with the fiduciary, and that co-venture exists only if the tipper intends to benefit. To equalize the position of tippees under both theories of liability, therefore, it is necessary to require an outsider who tips to have intended to benefit by his tip.

Requiring an intent to benefit regardless of the theory of insider trading liability also serves to equalize the positions of tippers. Since under both theories of liability the tipper is breaching a duty of loyalty and confidentiality by disclosing confidential information, and since the harm to marketplace traders is identical under either breach, it again makes "scant sense" to impose liability more readily on a tipping outsider who breaches a duty to a source of information than on a tipping insider who breaches a duty to corporate shareholders.

* * * *

We also think the SEC's position is inconsistent with the principle "that § 10(b) is not an all-purpose breach of fiduciary duty ban." *O'Hagan,* 521 U.S. at 655, 117 S. Ct. at 2209 (citing *Santa Fe Indus., Inc. v. Green,* 430 U.S. 462, 97 S. Ct. 1292, 51 L. Ed. 2d 480 (1977)). Section 10(b) "trains on conduct involving manipulation or deception." *Id.* This manipulation or deception, i.e., fraud, "is consummated . . . when, . . . [the fiduciary] uses the information to purchase or sell securities" and thereby "gain no-risk profits"; if the information is put to an "other" use, no breach has occurred for purposes of the securities laws. *Id.* at 656, 117 S. Ct. at 2209. In other words, § 10(b) "does not catch all conceivable forms of fraud involving confidential information; rather, it catches fraudulent means of capitalizing on such information through securities transactions." *Id.* . . .

Our conclusion that the SEC must establish that all tippers, both insider and outsiders, intend to benefit from their disclosure of confidential information is amply supported by language in *O'Hagan.* There, the Court observed that an outsider who "pretends loyalty to the principal while secretly converting the principal's information for *personal gain* dupes or defrauds the principal. *Id.* at 653–54, 117 S. Ct. at 2208 (emphasis added) (internal quotation marks and alteration omitted). Likewise, an outsider "who trades on the basis of material, nonpublic information, in short, gains his advantageous market position through deception." *Id.* at 656, 117 S. Ct. at 2209 (emphasis added). In the same vein: "The misappropriation theory targets information of a sort that misappropriators ordinarily *capitalize* upon to *gain no-risk profits* through the purchase or sale of securities. . . . [The theory] catches fraudulent means of *capitalizing* on such information *through securities transactions." Id.* (emphasis added). Finally, it is a fiduciary's "*self-serving use* of a principal's information *to purchase or sell securities*" that constitutes a breach of duty of loyalty and confidentiality. *Id.* at 652, 117 S. Ct. at 2207 (emphasis added).

All of the above quoted language from *O'Hagan* explicitly states or implicitly assumes that a misappropriator must gain personally from his trading on the confidential information. If we were to hold that a misappropriator who tips—rather than trades—is liable even though he intends no personal benefit from his tip, then we would impose liability more readily for tipping than trading. Such a result would be absurd, and would undermine the Supreme Court's rationale for imposing the benefit requirement in the first place: the desire to ensure that a tip rises to the level of a trade. *See Dirks,* 436 U.S. at 664, 103 S. Ct. at 3266 ("The tip and trade resemble trading by the insider himself followed by a gift of the profits to the recipient."). The better approach, in our view, is to follow *Dirks* and ensure that an outsider who tips must have done so with the intent of benefitting from the tippee's trading.

Finally, and perhaps most importantly, the need for an identical approach to determining tipper and tippee liability under the two theories becomes evident when one realizes that nearly all violations under the classical theory of insider trading can be alternatively characterized as misappropriations. [*Citation omitted.*] To allow the SEC to avoid establishing the personal benefit element simply by proceeding under the misappropriation theory instead of the classical theory would essentially render *Dirks* a dead letter in this circuit. Such an effect would be unwarranted, particularly in light of the fact that *O'Hagan* incorporated its principals with, rather than overruled, *Dirks.*

Requiring an intent to benefit in both classical and misappropriation theory cases equalizes the positions of tippers and tippees and is also consistent with Supreme Court precedent. Perhaps the simplest way to view potential insider trading liability is as follows: (1) an insider who trades is liable; (2) an insider who tips (rather than trades) is liable if he intends to benefit from the disclosure; (3) an outsider who trades is liable; (4) an outsider who tips (rather than trades) is liable if he intends to benefit from the disclosure.

* * * *

In this case, the SEC presented evidence that the two appellants were "friendly," worked together for several years, and split commissions on various real estate transactions over the years. This evidence is sufficient for a jury reasonably to conclude that Donna expected to benefit from her tip to Burch by maintaining a good relationship between a friend and frequent partner in real estate deals. *See Sargent,* 229 F.2d at 77 (finding evidence of personal benefit when the tipper passed on information "to effect a reconciliation with his friend and to maintain a useful networking contact"). Accordingly, the SEC has sufficiently established the second element of a misappropriation theory claim—a breach of a duty of loyalty and confidentiality.

* * * *

IV.

In conclusion, we AFFIRM the district court's decisions denying appellants' motions for judgment as a matter of law. Because we find prejudicial error in the district court's instruction on the elements of the misappropriation theory of liability, we VACATE the court's judgment and REMAND the case for a new trial.

SO ORDERED.

In the *SEC v. Cuban* case below, the court considers the question of the circumstances in which a confidential relationship exists and the distinction between an obligation to keep information confidential and a promise to not trade on that information.

Securities and Exchange Commission v. Cuban

620 F.3d 551 (5th Cir. 2010)

HIGGINBOTHAM, C.J.:

This case raises questions of the scope of liability under the misappropriation theory of insider trading. Taking a different view from our able district court brother of the allegations of the complaint, we are persuaded that the case should not have been dismissed under Fed. R. Civ. P. 9(b) and 12 and must proceed to discovery.

Mark Cuban is a well known entrepreneur and current owner of the Dallas Mavericks and Landmark theaters, among other businesses. The SEC brought this suit against Cuban alleging he violated Section 17(a) of the Securities Act of

1933, Section 10(b) of the Securities Exchange Act of 1934, and Rule 10b–5 by trading in Mamma.com stock in breach of his duty to the CEO and Mamma.com—amounting to insider trading under the misappropriation theory of liability. The core allegation is that Cuban received confidential information from the CEO of Mamma.com, a Canadian search engine company in which Cuban was a large minority stakeholder, agreed to keep the information confidential, and acknowledged he could not trade on the information. The SEC alleges that, armed with the inside information regarding a private investment of public equity (PIPE) offering, Cuban sold his stake in the company in an effort to avoid losses from the inevitable fall in Mamma.com's share price when the offering was announced.

Cuban moved to dismiss the action under Rule 9(b) and 12(b)(6). The district court found that, at most, the complaint alleged an agreement to keep the information confidential, but did not include an agreement not to trade. Finding a simple confidentiality agreement to be insufficient to create a duty to disclose or abstain from trading under the securities laws, the court granted Cuban's motion to dismiss. The SEC appeals, arguing that a confidentiality agreement creates a duty to disclose or abstain and that, regardless, the confidentiality agreement alleged in the complaint also contained an agreement not to trade on the information and that agreement would create such a duty.

* * * *

. . . The misappropriation theory . . . holds that a person violates section 10(b) "when he misappropriates confidential information for securities trading purposes, in breach of a duty owed to the source of the information." The Supreme Court first adopted this theory in *United States v. O'Hagan*. There, a lawyer traded the securities of a company his client was targeting for a takeover. O'Hagan could not be liable under the classical theory as he owed no duty to the shareholders of the target company. Nevertheless, the court found O'Hagan violated section 10(b). The Court held that in trading the target company's securities, *O'Hagan* misappropriated the confidential information regarding the planned corporate takeover, breaching "a duty of trust and confidence" he owed to his law firm and client. Trading on such information "involves feigning fidelity to the source of information and thus utilizes a 'deceptive device' as required by section 10(b)." The Court stated that while there is "no general duty between all participants in market transactions to forgo actions based on material nonpublic information," the breach of a duty to the source of the information is sufficient to give rise to insider trading liability.

While *O'Hagan* did not set the contours of a relationship of "trust and confidence" giving rise to the duty to disclose or abstain and misappropriation liability, we are tasked to determine whether Cuban had such a relationship with Mamma.com. The SEC seeks to rely on Rule 10b5–2(b)(1), which states that a person has "a duty of trust and confidence" for purposes of misappropriation liability when that person "agrees to maintain information in confidence." In dismissing the case, the district court read the complaint to allege that Cuban agreed not to disclose any confidential information but did not agree not to trade, that such a confidentiality agreement was insufficient to create a duty to disclose or abstain from trading under the misappropriation theory, and that the SEC overstepped its authority under section 10(b) in issuing Rule 10b5–2(b)(1). We differ from the district court in reading the complaint and need not reach the latter issues.

The complaint alleges that, in March 2004, Cuban acquired 600,000 shares, a 6.3% stake, of Mamma.com. Later that spring, Mamma.com decided to raise capital through a PIPE offering* on the advice of the investment bank Merriman Curhan Ford & Co. At the end of June, at Merriman's suggestion, Mamma.com decided to invite Cuban to participate in the PIPE offering. . . .

After getting in touch with Cuban on June 28, Mamma.com's CEO told Cuban he had confidential information for him and Cuban agreed to keep whatever information the CEO shared confidential. The CEO then told Cuban about the PIPE offering. Cuban became very upset "and said, among other things, that he did not like PIPEs because they dilute the existing shareholders." "At the end of the call, Cuban told the CEO 'Well, now I'm screwed. I can't sell.' "

The CEO told the company's executive chairman about the conversation with Cuban. The executive chairman sent an e-mail to the other Mamma.com board members updating them on the PIPE offering. The executive chairman included:

> Today, after much discussion, [the CEO] spoke to Mark Cuban about this equity raise and whether or not he would be interested in participating. As anticipated he initially 'flew off the handle' and said he would sell his shares (recognizing that he was not able to do

---

* [" 'PIPE' stands for 'private investment in public equity.' In a PIPE offering, investors commit to purchase a certain number of restricted shares from a company at a specified price. The company agrees, in turn, to file a resale registration statement so that the investors can resell the shares to the public. To the extent that they increase the supply of a company's stock in the market, PIPE offerings can potentially dilute the value of existing shares.' " (http://www.sec.gov/answers/pipeofferings.htm). —*Eds*]

> anything until we announce the equity) but then asked to see the terms and conditions which we have arranged for him to receive from one of the participating investor groups with which he has dealt in the past.

The CEO then sent Cuban a follow up e-mail, writing " '[i]f you want more details about the private placement please contact . . . [Merriman].' "

Cuban called the Merriman representative and they spoke for eight minutes. "During that call, the salesman supplied Cuban with additional confidential details about the PIPE. In response to Cuban's questions, the salesman told him that the PIPE was being sold at a discount to the market price and that the offering included other incentives for the PIPE investors." It is a plausible inference that Cuban learned the off-market prices available to him and other PIPE participants.

With that information and one minute after speaking with the Merriman representative, Cuban called his broker and instructed him to sell his entire stake in the company. Cuban sold 10,000 shares during the evening of June 28, 2004, and the remainder during regular trading the next day.

* * * *

After the markets closed on June 29, Mamma.com announced the PIPE offering. The next day, Mamma.com's stock price fell 8.5% and continued to decline over the next week, eventually closing down 39% from the June 29 closing price. By selling his shares when he did, Cuban avoided over $750,000 in losses. Cuban notified the SEC that he had sold his stake in the company and publicly stated that he sold his shares because Mamma.com "was conducting a PIPE, which issued shares at a discount to the prevailing market price and also would have caused his ownership position to be diluted."

In reading the complaint to allege only an agreement of confidentiality, the court held that Cuban's statement that he was "screwed" because he "[could not] sell" "appears to express his belief, at least at that time, that it would be illegal for him to sell his Mamma.com shares based on the information the CEO provided." But the court stated that this statement "cannot reasonably be understood as an agreement not to sell based on the information." The court found "the complaint asserts no facts that reasonably suggest that the CEO intended to obtain from Cuban an agreement to refrain from trading on the information as opposed to an agreement merely to keep it confidential." Finally, the court stated that "the CEO's expectation that Cuban would not sell was also insufficient" to allege any further agreement.

Reading the complaint in the light most favorable to the SEC, we reach a different conclusion. In isolation, the statement "Well, now I'm screwed. I can't sell" can plausibly be read to express Cuban's view that learning the confidences regarding the PIPE forbade his selling his stock before the offering but to express no agreement not to do so. However, after Cuban expressed the view that he could not sell to the CEO, he gained access to the confidences of the PIPE offering. According to the complaint's recounting of the executive chairman's e-mail to the board, during his short conversation with the CEO regarding the planned PIPE offering, Cuban requested the terms and conditions of the offering. Based on this request, the CEO sent Cuban a follow up e-mail providing the contact information for Merriman. Cuban called the salesman, who told Cuban "that the PIPE was being sold at a discount to the market price and that the offering included other incentives for the PIPE investors." Only after Cuban reached out to obtain this additional information, following the statement of his understanding that he could not sell, did Cuban contact his broker and sell his stake in the company.

The allegations, taken in their entirety, provide more than a plausible basis to find that the understanding between the CEO and Cuban was that he was not to trade, that it was more than a simple confidentiality agreement. By contacting the sales representative to obtain the pricing information, Cuban was able to evaluate his potential losses or gains from his decision to either participate or refrain from participating in the PIPE offering. It is at least plausible that each of the parties understood, if only implicitly, that Mamma.com would only provide the terms and conditions of the offering to Cuban for the purpose of evaluating whether he would participate in the offering, and that Cuban could not use the information for his own personal benefit. It would require additional facts that have not been put before us for us to conclude that the parties could not plausibly have reached this shared understanding. Under Cuban's reading, he was allowed to trade on the information but prohibited from telling others—in effect providing him an exclusive license to trade on the material nonpublic information. Perhaps this was the understanding, or perhaps Cuban mislead the CEO regarding the timing of his sale in order to obtain a confidential look at the details of the PIPE. We say only that on this factually sparse record, it is at least equally plausible that all sides understood there was to be no trading before the PIPE. That both Cuban and the CEO expressed the belief that Cuban could not trade appears to reinforce the plausibility of this reading.

the Offeror, the target company (i.e., the issuer of the securities sought by the Offeror), or an officer, director, agent, employee or constructive insider of the Offeror or the target company; and (4) the Recipient purchases or sells (or causes to be purchased or sold) securities of the target company or the Offeror at any time prior to the public announcement of the tender offer, without first disclosing the information (along with its source) to the person with whom the recipient is trading. Even if the foregoing elements are present, the Recipient will incur liability if, and only if, the Offeror has commenced or has taken substantial steps toward commencement of a bid for the target company (e.g. passage of a resolution about the tender offer by the Offeror's board of directors, formulation of a tender offer plan, arrangement of financing to pay for all or a portion of the tender offer and/or preparation of tender offer documents and materials).

It is important to note the there is no breach of duty or "deception" required for liability under Rule 14e–3. If someone meets the above test and trades, that person is liable. There is no need for separate standards for tippees under the rule, since the standard is the same. There is also tipper liability under Rule 14e–3 for any person who meets the above criteria and communicates this information to others, if it is reasonably foreseeable that they (the others) will proceed to violate the rule. However, there is a defense for a tipper who acts in good faith and communicates information about the tender offer to the Offeror or to appropriate agents of the Offeror or to the target company or to appropriate agents of the target company. There is an exemption under Rule 14e–3 for the Offeror and for any party (i.e., a shareholder of the target company) who tenders shares in conjunction with the tender offer. So, Rule 14e–3 would not prevent the Offeror from trading in shares of the target company, even before the tender offer was announced.

D. The Expansion of the Misappropriation Theory

Notwithstanding the admonition in *Yun*, regarding the expansion of the misappropriation theory, there have been different efforts to expand the reach of the ban on trading of nonpublic information. One such expansion was seen in the passage of the Stop Trading on Congressional Knowledge Act of 2012 (the "STOCK Act"). The STOCK Act amended the 1934 Act to include members and employees of Congress and "affirmed" a duty of trust and confidence for members of Congress, judicial officers and other public employees with respect to information derived from that person's position. As a result, the misappropriation doctrine will now apply to trades made by government officials and employees based on nonpublic information, even if that information was obtained in the performance of their job and not through a breach of duty.

In recent years, there has also been at least some effort to expand the misappropriation theory beyond the requirement that there be a breach of a more traditional duty that is fiduciary in nature or based on a relationship of trust and confidence. While the *Dorozhko* decision below has been met with some criticism, it provides an example of such efforts.

Securities and Exchange Commission v. Dorozhko

574 F.3d 42 (2d Cir. 2009)

JOSE A. CABRANES, C.J.:

We are asked to consider whether, in a civil enforcement lawsuit brought by the United States Securities and Exchange Commission ("SEC") under Section 10(b) of the Securities Exchange Act of 1934 ("Section 10(b)"), computer hacking may be "deceptive" where the hacker did not breach a fiduciary duty in fraudulently obtaining material, nonpublic information used in connection with the purchase or sale of securities. For the reasons stated herein, we answer the question in the affirmative.

BACKGROUND

In early October 2007, defendant Oleksandr Dorozhko, a Ukranian national and resident, opened an online trading account with Interactive Brokers LLC ("Interactive Brokers") and deposited $ 42,500 into that account. At about the same time, IMS Health, Inc. ("IMS") announced that it would release its third-quarter earnings during an analyst conference call scheduled for October 17, 2007 at 5 p.m.—that is, after the close of the securities markets in New York City. IMS had hired Thomson Financial, Inc. ("Thomson") to provide investor relations and web-hosting services, which included managing the online release of IMS's earnings reports.

Beginning at 8:06 a.m. on October 17, and continuing several times during the morning and early afternoon, an anonymous computer hacker attempted to gain access to the IMS earnings report by hacking into a secure server at Thomson prior to the report's official release. At 2:15 p.m.—minutes after Thomson actually received the IMS data—that hacker successfully located and downloaded the IMS data from Thomson's secure server.

Beginning at 2:52 p.m., defendant—who had not previously used his Interactive Brokers account to trade—purchased $ 41,670.90 worth of IMS "put" options that would expire on October 25 and 30, 2007.[1] These purchases represented approximately 90% of all purchases of "put" options for IMS stock for the six weeks prior to October 17. In purchasing these options, which the SEC describes as "extremely risky," defendant was betting that IMS's stock price would decline precipitously (within a two-day expiration period) and significantly (by greater than 20%). . . .

At 4:33 p.m.—slightly ahead of the analyst call—IMS announced that its earnings per share were 28% below "Street" expectations, *i.e.,* the expectations of many Wall Street analysts. When the market opened the next morning, October 18, at 9:30 a.m., IMS's stock price sank approximately 28% almost immediately—from $ 29.56 to $ 21.20 per share. Within six minutes of the market opening, defendant had sold all of his IMS options, realizing a net profit of $ 286,456.59 overnight.

Interactive Brokers noticed the irregular trading activity and referred the matter to the SEC, which now alleges that defendant was the hacker. . . .

On January 8, 2008, in a thoughtful and careful opinion, the District Court denied the SEC's request for a preliminary injunction [which would have frozen the proceeds of the "put" option] because the SEC had not shown a likelihood of success. Specifically, the District Court ruled that computer hacking was not "deceptive" within the meaning of Section 10(b) as defined by the Supreme Court. According to the District Court, "a breach of a fiduciary duty of disclosure is a required element of any 'deceptive' device under § 10b.". . . The District Court reasoned that since defendant was a corporate outsider with no special relationship to IMS or Thomson, he owed no fiduciary duty to either. Although computer hacking might be fraudulent and might violate a number of federal and state criminal statutes, the District Court concluded that this behavior did not violate Section 10(b) without an accompanying breach of a fiduciary duty.

This appeal followed. On appeal, the SEC maintains its theory that the fraud in this case consists of defendant's alleged computer hacking, which involves various misrepresentations. The SEC does not argue that defendant breached any fiduciary duties as part of his scheme. In this critical regard, we recognize that the SEC's claim against defendant—a corporate outsider who

1 A "put" is "[a]n option that conveys to its holder the right, but not the obligation, to sell a specific asset at a predetermined price until a certain date. . . . Investors purchase puts in order to take advantage of a decline in the price of the asset." David L. Scott, *Wall Street Words* 295 (2003).

owed no fiduciary duties to the source of the information—is not based on either of the two generally accepted theories of insider trading. *See United States v. Cusimano,* 123 F.3d 83, 87 (2d Cir. 1997) (distinguishing "the traditional theory of insider trading, under which a corporate insider trades in the securities of his own corporation on the basis of material, nonpublic information," from "the misappropriation theory, [under which] § 10(b) and Rule 10b–5 are violated whenever a person trades while in knowing possession of material, nonpublic information that has been gained in violation of a fiduciary duty to its source"). The SEC's claim is nonetheless based on a claim of fraud, and we turn our attention to whether this fraud is "deceptive" within the meaning of Section 10(b).

DISCUSSION

* * * *

"Deceptive Device"

"Section 10(b) prohibits the use or employ, in connection with the purchase or sale of any security . . ., [of] any manipulative or deceptive device or contrivance in contravention of such rules and regulations as the [SEC] may prescribe." 15 U.S.C. § 78j (b). The instant case requires us to decide whether the "device" in this case—computer hacking—could be "deceptive."

* * * *

The District Court determined that the Supreme Court has interpreted the "deceptive" element of Section 10(b) to require a breach of a fiduciary duty. . . . The District Court reached this conclusion by relying principally on three Supreme Court opinions: *Chiarella v. United States,* 445 U.S. 222, 100 S. Ct. 1108, 63 L. Ed. 2d 348 (1980), *United States v. O'Hagan,* 521 U.S. 642, 117 S. Ct. 2199, 138 L. Ed. 2d 724 (1997), *and SEC v. Zandford,* 535 U.S. 813, 122 S. Ct. 1899, 153 L. Ed. 2d 1 (2002). We consider each of these cases in turn.

In *Chiarella,* the defendant was employed by a financial printer and used information passing through his office to trade securities offered by acquiring and target companies. In a criminal prosecution, the government alleged that the defendant committed fraud by not disclosing to the market that he was trading on the basis of material, nonpublic information. The Supreme Court held that defendant's "silence," or nondisclosure, was not fraud because he was under no obligation to disclose his knowledge of inside information. "When an allegation of fraud is based upon nondisclosure, there can be no fraud absent a duty to speak. We hold that a duty to disclose under § 10(b) does not arise from the mere possession of nonpublic market information." 445 U.S. at 235; *see also United States v. Chestman,* 947 F.2d 551, 575 (2d Cir. 1991) (Winter, J., concurring in part and dissenting in part) (stating that, after *Chiarella,* "silence cannot constitute a fraud absent a duty to speak owed to those who are injured"). Justice Blackmun, joined by Justice Marshall, dissented. In their view, stealing information from an employer was fraudulent within the meaning of Section 10(b) because the statute was designed as a "catchall" provision to protect investors from unknown risks. *Id.* at 246 (Blackmun, *J.,* dissenting). . . .

In *O'Hagan,* the defendant was an attorney who traded in securities based on material, nonpublic information regarding his firm's clients. As in *Chiarella,* the government alleged that the defendant had committed fraud through "silence" because the defendant had a duty to disclose to the source of the information (his client) that he would trade on the information. The Supreme Court agreed, noting that "[d]eception through nondisclosure is central to the theory of liability for which the Government seeks recognition." 521 U.S. at 654. "[I]f the fiduciary discloses to the source that he plans to trade on the nonpublic information, there is no 'deceptive device' and thus no § 10(b) violation—although the fiduciary-turned-trader may remain liable under state law for breach of a duty of loyalty." *Id.* at 655.

In *Zandford,* the defendant was a securities broker who traded under a client's account and transferred the proceeds to his own account. The Fourth Circuit held that the defendant's fraud was not "in connection with" the purchase or sale of a security because it was mere theft that happened to involve securities, rather than true securities fraud. The Supreme Court reversed in a unanimous opinion, observing that Section 10(b) "should be construed not technically and restrictively, but flexibly to effectuate its remedial purposes." 535 U.S. at 819. Although the Court warned that not "every common-law fraud that happens to involve securities [is] a violation of § 10(b)," *id.* at 820, the defendant's scheme was a single plan to deceive, rather than a series of independent frauds, and was therefore "in connection with" the purchase or sale of a security, *id.* at 825. In a final footnote, the Court offered the following observation: "[I]f the broker told his client he was stealing the client's assets, that breach of fiduciary duty might be in connection with a sale of securities, but it would not involve a deceptive device or fraud." 535 U.S. at 825 n.4. In the instant case, the District Court interpreted the *Zandford* footnote as an "explicit acknowledg[ment] that Zandford would not be liable under § 10(b) if he *had* disclosed to Wood that he was planning to steal his money.". . .

The District Court concluded that in *Chiarella, O'Hagan, and Zandford,* the Supreme Court developed a requirement that any "deceptive device" requires a breach of a fiduciary duty. In applying that interpretation to the instant case, the District Court ruled that "[a]lthough [defendant] may have broken the law, he is not liable in a civil action under § 10(b) because he owed no fiduciary or similar duty either to the source of his information or to those he transacted with in the market." . . .

In our view, none of the Supreme Court opinions relied upon by the District Court—much less the sum of all three opinions—establishes a fiduciary-duty requirement as an element of every violation of Section 10(b). In *Chiarella, O'Hagan, and Zandford,* the theory of fraud was silence or nondisclosure, not an affirmative misrepresentation. The Supreme Court held that remaining silent was actionable only where there was a duty to speak, arising from a fiduciary relationship. In *Chiarella,* the Supreme Court held that there was no deception in an employee's silence because he did not have duty to speak. *See* 445 U.S. at 226 ("This case concerns the legal effect of the petitioner's *silence.*" (emphasis added)); *see also id.* at 227–28 ("At common law, misrepresentation made for the purpose of inducing reliance upon the false statement is fraudulent. But *one who fails to disclose* material information prior to the consummation of a transaction commits fraud only when he is under a duty to do so." (emphasis added)). In *O'Hagan,* an attorney who traded on client secrets had a fiduciary duty to inform his firm that he was trading on the basis of the confidential information. *See* 521 U.S. at 653 (noting that a "breach of a duty of trust and confidence . . . to his law firm" was conduct that "satisfies § 10(b)'s requirement that chargeable conduct involve a 'deceptive device or contrivance' "); *see also id.* at 654 ("Deception through *nondisclosure* is central to the theory of liability for which the Government seeks recognition." (emphasis added)). Even in *Zandford,* which dealt principally with the statutory requirement that a deceptive device be used "in connection with" the purchase or sale of a security, the defendant's fraud consisted of not telling his brokerage client—to whom he owed a fiduciary duty—that he was stealing assets from the account. *See* 535 U.S. at 822 ("[Defendant's brokerage clients] were injured as investors through [defendant's] deceptions, which deprived them of any compensation for the sale of their valuable securities."); *see also id.* at 823 ("[A]ny distinction between omissions and misrepresentations is illusory in the context of a broker who has a fiduciary duty to her clients.").

Chiarella, O'Hagan, and Zandford all stand for the proposition that nondisclosure in breach of a fiduciary duty "satisfies § 10(b)'s requirement . . .

[of] a 'deceptive device or contrivance,' " *O'Hagan,* 521 U.S. at 653. However, what is sufficient is not always what is necessary, and none of the Supreme Court opinions considered by the District Court *require* a fiduciary relationship as an element of an actionable securities claim under Section 10(b). While *Chiarella, O'Hagan,* and *Zandford* all dealt with fraud *qua* silence, an affirmative misrepresentation is a distinct species of fraud. Even if a person does not have a fiduciary duty to "disclose or abstain from trading," there is nonetheless an affirmative obligation in commercial dealings not to mislead. . . .

In this case, the SEC has not alleged that defendant fraudulently remained silent in the face of a "duty to disclose or abstain" from trading. Rather, the SEC argues that defendant affirmatively misrepresented himself in order to gain access to material, nonpublic information, which he then used to trade. We are aware of no precedent of the Supreme Court or our Court that forecloses or prohibits the SEC's straightforward theory of fraud.[6] Absent a controlling precedent that "deceptive" has a more limited meaning than its ordinary meaning, we see no reason to complicate the enforcement of Section 10(b) by divining new requirements. In reaching this conclusion, we are mindful of the Supreme Court's oft-repeated instruction that Section 10(b) "should be construed not technically and restrictively, but flexibly to effectuate its remedial purposes." *Zandford,* 535 U.S. at 819 (internal quotation marks omitted).[7] Accordingly, we adopt the SEC's proposed interpretation of *Chiarella* and its progeny: "misrepresentations are fraudulent, but . . . silence is fraudulent only if there is a duty to disclose." . . .

Having denied the SEC's application for a preliminary injunction freezing defendant's trading account on the basis of a perceived fiduciary duty requirement stemming from the *Chiarella* line of insider trading cases, the District Court did not decide whether the ordinary meaning of "deceptive" covers the computer hacking in this case—or, indeed, whether the computer hacking in this case involved any misrepresentation at all. Defendant invites us

---

6 The District Court found it "noteworthy" that in the over seventy years since the enactment of the Securities Exchange Act of 1934, "no federal court has *ever* held that those who steal material nonpublic information and then trade on it violate § 10(b)," even though "traditional theft (*e.g.* breaking into an investment bank and stealing documents) is hardly a new phenomenon, and involves similar elements for purposes of our analysis here." . . . The District Court suggested that "hacking and trading" schemes have been and ought to be prosecuted under "any number of federal and/or state criminal statutes," rather than through civil enforcement actions. . . .

7 We are further counseled by the observations of Judge Augustus N. Hand, who reasoned over fifty years ago that had Congress intended to impose a fiduciary-duty requirement on Section 10(b) liability, it would have said so. *See Birnbaum v. Newport Steel Corp.,* 193 F.2d 461, 464 (2d Cir. 1952) (A. Hand, J.). . . .

to remand both questions so that the District Court may decide in the first instance.

In its ordinary meaning, "deceptive" covers a wide spectrum of conduct involving cheating or trading in falsehoods. [*Citations omitted.*] In light of this ordinary meaning, it is not at all surprising that Rule 10b–5 equates "deceit" with "fraud." *See* 17 C.F.R. § 240.10b–5 (prohibiting "any untrue statement of a material fact . . . or . . . *any act, practice, or course of business* which operates or would operate as a *fraud or deceit* upon any person, in connection with the purchase or sale of any security" (emphases added)). Indeed, we have previously observed that the conduct prohibited by Section 10(b) and Rule 10b–5 "irreducibly entails some act that gives the victim a false impression." *United States v. Finnerty,* 533 F.3d 143, 148 (2d Cir. 2008).

The District Court—summarizing the SEC's allegations—described the computer hacking in this case as "employ[ing] electronic means to trick, circumvent, or bypass computer security in order to gain unauthorized access to computer systems, networks, and information . . . and to steal such data." . . . On appeal, the SEC adds a further gloss, arguing that, in general, "[computer h]ackers either (1) 'engage in false identification and masquerade as another user['] . . . or (2) 'exploit a weakness in [an electronic] code within a program to cause the program to malfunction in a way that grants the user greater privileges.' " . . . In our view, misrepresenting one's identity in order to gain access to information that is otherwise off limits, and then stealing that information is plainly "deceptive" within the ordinary meaning of the word. It is unclear, however, that exploiting a weakness in an electronic code to gain unauthorized access is "deceptive," rather than being mere theft. Accordingly, depending on how the hacker gained access, it seems to us entirely possible that computer hacking could be, by definition, a "deceptive device or contrivance" that is prohibited by Section 10(b) and Rule 10b–5.

However, we are hesitant to move from this general principle to a particular application without the benefit of the District Court's views as to whether the computer hacking in this case—as opposed to computer hacking in general—was "deceptive." . . . Having established that the SEC need not demonstrate a breach of fiduciary duty, we now remand to the District Court to consider, in the first instance, whether the computer hacking in this case involved a fraudulent misrepresentation that was "deceptive" within the ordinary meaning of Section 10(b). . . .

CONCLUSION

For the foregoing reasons, the District Court's January 8, 2008 order denying the SEC's motion for a preliminary injunction is VACATED. The cause is REMANDED for further proceedings consistent with this opinion.

NOTES AND QUESTIONS

1. Do you agree with the court's analysis that the breach of a fiduciary duty or duty of trust and confidence should not be required in insider trading cases?

2. Does all crime involve "deception"?

3. If so, who was deceived in the *Dorozhko* case? Was it Thomson's computer system?

4. Recognize that the question is not whether Dorozhko should be punished; the question is whether Congress provided for punishment under § 10(b) of the 1934 Act.

SECTION IV: Regulation FD

A. The Adoption of Regulation FD

In 2000 the SEC adopted Regulation FD. Regulation FD was intended to prevent the "selective disclosure" of information by publicly traded companies. Regulation FD provides that when an issuer discloses material, nonpublic information to certain individuals or entities—generally, securities market professionals, such as stock analysts, or holders of the issuer's securities who may well trade on the basis of the information—the issuer must make public disclosure of that information. (SEC Website, Fair Disclosure, Regulation FD)

Rule 100 of Regulation FD sets forth the basic rule regarding selective disclosure.

> 17 C.F.R. § 243.100 General rule regarding selective disclosure.
>
> (a) Whenever an issuer, or any person acting on its behalf, discloses any material nonpublic information regarding that issuer or its securities to any person described in paragraph (b)(1) of this section [in general, securities market professionals or holders of the issuer's securities who might buy or sell the issuer's securities

on the basis of the information], the issuer shall make public disclosure of that information as provided in § 243.101(e):

(1) Simultaneously, in the case of an intentional disclosure; and

(2) Promptly, in the case of a non-intentional disclosure.

The restrictions of § 243.100(a) do not apply to disclosures made:

(i) To a person who owes a duty of trust or confidence to the issuer (such as an attorney, investment banker, or accountant);

(ii) To a person who expressly agrees to maintain the disclosed information in confidence; or

(iii) In connection with a securities offering registered under the 1933 Act. . . .

Id.

When the SEC adopted Regulation FD, it explained that it had become increasingly concerned about "the selective disclosure by issuers of material nonpublic information." The SEC related its reasoning as follows:

> We believe that the practice of selective disclosure leads to a loss of investor confidence in the integrity of our capital markets. Investors who see a security's price change dramatically and only later are given access to the information responsible for that move rightly question whether they are on a level playing field with market insiders.
>
> Issuer selective disclosure bears a close resemblance in this regard to ordinary "tipping" and insider trading. In both cases, a privileged few gain an informational edge—and the ability to use that edge to profit—from their superior access to corporate insiders, rather than from their skill, acumen, or diligence. Likewise, selective disclosure has an adverse impact on market integrity that is similar to the adverse impact from illegal insider trading: investors lose confidence in the fairness of the markets when they know that other participants may exploit "unerodable informational advantages" derived not from hard work or insights, but from their access to corporate insiders. The economic effects of the two practices are essentially the same. Yet, as a result of judicial interpretations, tipping and insider trading can be severely punished under the antifraud provisions of the federal securities laws, whereas the status of issuer selective disclosure has been considerably less clear.

SEC Release: *Final Rule: Selective Disclosure and Insider Trading,* August 15, 2000. Effective Date: October 23, 2000. [Release Nos. 33–7881; 34–43154; IC–24599, File No. S7–31–99] ("SEC Release on Selective Disclosure").

Regulation FD has been somewhat controversial. There are many who feel that companies have curtailed discussions with analysts rather than risk a violation of Regulation FD, so that the impact of the regulation has been to prevent disclosures to securities analysts who would then disseminate the information to the public. As a result, critics feel that the regulation has resulted in less disclosure in the name of creating a more level playing field.

B. Public Disclosure

Regulation FD requires "public disclosure" in accordance with Rule 101(e) which provides:

(e) ***Public disclosure.***

(1) Except as provided in paragraph (e)(2) of this section, an issuer shall make the "public disclosure" of information required by § 243.100(a) by furnishing to or filing with the Commission a Form 8-K . . . disclosing that information.

(2) An issuer shall be exempt from the requirement to furnish or file a Form 8-K if it instead disseminates the information through another method (or combination of methods) of disclosure that is reasonably designed to provide broad, non-exclusionary distribution of the information to the public.

17 C.F.R. § 243.101(e)

With respect to methods (other than filing Form 8-K) through which distribution of information might be made to the public, the SEC also has explained that, "technological developments have made it much easier for issuers to disseminate information broadly. Whereas issuers once may have had to rely on analysts to serve as information intermediaries, issuers now can use a variety of methods to communicate directly with the market. In addition to press releases, these methods include, among others, Internet webcasting and teleconferencing. Accordingly, technological limitations no longer provide an excuse for abiding the threats to market integrity that selective disclosure represents." SEC Release on Selective Disclosure.

Case Study: Netflix and the Facebook "Disclosure"

Following a disclosure by Reed Hastings, the CEO of Netflix, Inc., on Hasting's Facebook page, that Netflix had achieved a substantial milestone, the SEC conducted an investigation relating to a potential violation of Regulation FD. The following are excerpts from the *Report of Investigation Pursuant to Section 21(a) of the Securities Exchange Act of 1934: Netflix, Inc., and Reed Hastings*, Release No. 69279 (Apr. 2, 2013).

* * * *

> Facts:
>
> . . . On July 3, 2012, just before 11:00 a.m. Eastern time, Hastings posted the following message on his personal Facebook page:
>
> > Congrats to Ted Sarados, and his amazing content licensing team. Netflix monthly viewing exceeded 1 billion hours for the first time ever in June. When House of Cards and Arrested Development debut, we'll blow these records away. Keep going, Ted, we need even more!
>
> This announcement represented a nearly 50% increase in streaming hours from Netflix's January 25, 2012 announcement that it had streamed 2 billion hours over the preceding three-month quarter.
>
> Prior to his post, Hastings did not receive input from Netflix's chief financial officer, the legal department, or investor relations department. Netflix did not file with or furnish to the Commission a Current Report on Form 8-K, issue a press release through its standard distribution channels, or otherwise announce the streaming milestone. Also on July 3, 2012, and after the Facebook post, Netflix issued a press release announcing the date of its second quarter 2012 earnings release but did not mention Hastings's Facebook post. Netflix's stock continued a rise that began when the market opened on July 3, increasing from $70.45 at the time of Hastings's Facebook post to $81.72 at the close of the following trading day.
>
> The announcement of the streaming milestone reached the securities market incrementally. The post was picked up by a technology-focused blog about an hour later and by a handful of news outlets within two hours. Approximately an hour after the post, Netflix sent it to several reporters, but did not disseminate it to the

broader mailing list normally used for corporate press releases. After the markets closed early at 1:00 p.m., several articles in the mainstream financial press picked up the story. Research analysts also wrote about the streaming milestone, describing the metric as a positive measure of customer engagement, indicative of a reduction in the rate Netflix is losing customers, or "churn," and possibly suggesting that quarterly subscriber numbers would be at the high end of guidance.

Facebook members can subscribe to Hastings's Facebook page, which had over 200,000 subscribers at the time of the post, including equity research analysts associated with registered broker-dealers, shareholders, reporters, and bloggers. Neither Hastings nor Netflix had previously used Hastings's Facebook page to announce company metrics. Nor had they taken any steps to make the investing public aware that Hastings's personal Facebook page might be used as a medium for communicating information about Netflix. . . .

The SEC Report included the following guidance:

* * * *

A. Disclosures Triggering Regulation FD

Regulation FD applies when an issuer discloses material, nonpublic information to certain enumerated persons, including shareholders and securities professionals. It prohibits selective disclosure "[w]henever an issuer, or any person acting on its behalf, discloses any material nonpublic information regarding that issuer *to any person* described in paragraph (b)(1) of this section." Although the Regulation FD Adopting Release highlights the Commission's special concerns about selective disclosure of information to favored analysts or investors, the identification of the enumerated persons within Regulation FD is inclusive, and the prohibition does not turn on an intent or motive of favoritism. Nor does the rule suggest that disclosure of material, nonpublic information to a broader group that includes both enumerated and non-enumerated persons but that still falls short of a public disclosure negates the applicability of Regulation FD. On the contrary, the rule makes clear that public disclosure of material, nonpublic information must be made in a manner that conforms with Regulation FD whenever such information is disclosed to any group that includes one or more enumerated persons.

Accordingly, we emphasize for issuers that all disclosures to groups that include an enumerated person should be analyzed for compliance with Regulation FD. Specifically, if an issuer makes a disclosure to an enumerated person, including to a broader group of recipients through a social media channel, the issuer must consider whether that disclosure implicates Regulation FD. This would include determining whether the disclosure includes material, nonpublic information. Further, if the issuer were to elect not to file a Form 8-K, the issuer would need to consider whether the information was being disseminated in a manner "reasonably designed to provide broad, non-exclusionary distribution of the information to the public."

B. Broad, Non-Exclusionary Distribution of Information to the Public

Our 2008 Guidance was directed primarily at the use of corporate web sites for the disclosure of material, nonpublic information. Like web sites, corporate social media pages are created, populated, and updated by the issuer. The 2008 Guidance, furthermore, specifically identified "push" technologies, such as e-mail alerts and RSS feeds and "interactive" communication tools, such as blogs, which could enable the automatic electronic dissemination of information to subscribers. Today's evolving social media channels are an extension of these concepts, whereby information can be disseminated to those with access. Thus, the 2008 Guidance continues to provide a relevant framework for applying Regulation FD to evolving social media channels of distribution.

Specifically, in light of the direct and immediate communication from issuers to investors that is now possible through social media channels, such as Facebook and Twitter, we expect issuers to examine rigorously the factors indicating whether a particular channel is a "recognized channel of distribution" for communicating with their investors. We emphasize for issuers that the steps taken to alert the market about which forms of communication a company intends to use for the dissemination of material, nonpublic information, including the social media channels that may be used and the types of information that may be disclosed through these channels, are critical to the fair and efficient disclosure of information. Without such notice, the investing public would be forced to keep pace with a changing and expanding universe of potential disclosure channels, a virtually impossible task.

Providing appropriate notice to investors of the specific channels a company will use for the dissemination of material, nonpublic information is a sensible and expedient solution. It is not expected that this step would limit the channels of communication a company could use after appropriate notice or the opportunity for a company and investors to benefit from technological innovation and changes in communications practices. The 2008 Guidance encourages issuers to consider including in periodic reports and press releases the corporate web site address and disclosures that the company routinely posts important information on that web site. Similarly, disclosures on corporate web sites identifying the specific social media channels a company intends to use for the dissemination of material nonpublic information would give investors and the markets the opportunity to take the steps necessary to be in a position to receive important disclosures—e.g., subscribing, joining, registering, or reviewing that particular channel. These are some, but certainly not all, of the methods a company could use, with minimal burden, to enable evolving social media channels of corporate disclosure to be used as recognized channels of distribution in compliance with Regulation FD and the 2008 Guidance.

Although every case must be evaluated on its own facts, disclosure of material, nonpublic information on the personal social media site of an individual corporate officer, without advance notice to investors that the site may be used for this purpose, is unlikely to qualify as a method "reasonably designed to provide broad, non-exclusionary distribution of the information to the public" within the meaning of Regulation FD. This is true even if the individual in question has a large number of subscribers, friends, or other social media contacts, such that the information is likely to reach a broader audience over time. Personal social media sites of individuals employed by a public company would not ordinarily be assumed to be channels through which the company would disclose material corporate information. Without adequate notice that such a site may be used for this purpose, investors would not have an opportunity to access this information or, in some cases, would not know of that opportunity, at the same time as other investors.

V. Conclusion

There has been a rapid proliferation of social media channels for corporate communication since the issuance of the Commission's 2008 Guidance. An increasing number of public companies are using social media to communicate with their shareholders and the investing public. We appreciate the value and prevalence of social media channels in contemporary market communications, and the Commission supports companies seeking new ways to communicate and engage with shareholders and the market. This Report is not aimed at inhibiting corporate communication through evolving social media channels. To the contrary, we seek to remind issuers that disclosures to persons enumerated in Regulation FD, even if made through evolving social media channels, must still be analyzed for compliance with Regulation FD. Moreover, we emphasize that the Commission's 2008 Guidance, though largely focused on the use of web sites, is equally applicable to current and evolving social media channels of corporate communication. The 2008 Guidance explained that issuers must take steps sufficient to alert investors and the market to the channels it will use for the dissemination of material, nonpublic information. We believe that adherence to this guidance will help, with minimal burden, to assure compliance with Regulation FD and the fair and efficient operation of the market.

By the Commission.

QUESTIONS

1. Given the provisions of the report, how would you counsel the CEO of a publicly traded company who wanted to generate excitement for its products and interest in its stock by posting information to followers through various social media channels?

2. What if your client, a publicly traded company, was a provider of social media?

3. Could that company disseminate information to the "public" through its own social media and refuse to use other forms of social media?

SECTION V: Short Swing Profits, Section 16(b)

A. Section 16(b) in General

Section 16(b) of the 1934 Act was created by Congress before it was clear that Section 10(b) was going to apply to insider trading. Section 16(b) is intended to recapture any profits made by a corporation's "insiders" within a six-month period of time. Because the rule only applies to profits that arise with a six-month period of time, this rule is also referred to as covering "short swing profits." Because the rule is so rigid, it does produce some odd results. It captures many "innocent" trades that, if some analysis were applied, would be unlikely to raise any issue and does not capture many trades that a regulatory body might seek to prevent. Section 16(b) of the 1934 Act provides that:

> Section 16—Directors, Officers, and Principal Stockholders
>
> . . .b. Profits from purchase and sale of security within six months
>
> For the purpose of preventing the unfair use of information which may have been obtained by such beneficial owner, director, or officer by reason of his relationship to the issuer, any profit realized by him from any purchase and sale, or any sale and purchase, of any equity security of such issuer (other than an exempted security) . . . involving any such equity security within any period of less than six months, unless such security or security-based swap agreement was acquired in good faith in connection with a debt previously contracted, shall inure to and be recoverable by the issuer, irrespective of any intention on the part of such beneficial owner, director, or officer in entering into such transaction of holding the security or security-based swap agreement purchased or of not repurchasing the security or security-based swap agreement sold for a period exceeding six months. . . . This subsection shall not be construed to cover any transaction where such beneficial owner was not such both at the time of the purchase and sale, or the sale and purchase, of the security . . . involved, or any transaction or transactions which the Commission by rules and regulations may exempt as not comprehended within the purpose of this subsection. 15 U.S.C. § 78p(b)

Section 16(b) applies to: "Every person who is directly or indirectly the beneficial owner of more than 10 percent of any class of any equity security (other than an exempted security) which is registered pursuant to section 12 [of the 1934 Act], or who is a director or an officer of the issuer of such security. . . ."

Section 16(b) covers transactions only in the securities of Reporting Companies (defined below) and applies to any officer, director or beneficial owner (an "insider") who buys or sells equity securities in that company within a six-month period. It does not matter whether the insider purchases first and then sells or sells first and then subsequently buys. Any profit that the insider makes in such a transaction must be paid to the company. Section 16(b) applies to all "insiders." Section 16(b) applies to someone who was an officer or a director of the corporation *either* at the time of the purchase *OR* at the time of the sale. *Feder v. Martin Marietta Corp.*, 406 F.2d 260 (2d Cir. 1969). However, it only applies to shareholders who beneficially (directly or indirectly) hold more than 10% of the corporation's equity securities *both* at the time of the purchase *and* at the time of the sale in question. See *Adler v. Klawans*, 267 F.2d 840, 845 (2d Cir. 1959) (explaining that "officers and directors have more ready access to the intimate business secrets of corporations and factors which can affect the real and ultimately the market value of stock. . . . [and] can usually stimulate more directly actions which affect stock values").

Section 16(b) applies only to companies that are required to register under the 1934 Act. Companies with more than $10 million in assets and more than 500 shareholders of record ("Reporting Companies") are required to register with the SEC and are subject to certain reporting and other requirements. In contrast to Section 10(b), Section 16(b) does not apply to closely held corporations; it only covers transactions in a company's stock or convertible debt.

Section 16(b) does not include provisions relating to any tipping liability; there is no evaluation of whether a duty was breached, and there is no misappropriation. Note, however, that it would be possible for an insider to violate both Section 16(b) and Rule 10b–5 with the same transaction.

B. Computation of Damages

Any insider who violates section 16(b) is liable for damages. Section 16(b) enables a company to recover any profit made by an insider within a six-month period. In evaluating the profit, the insider does not get to identify specific shares that were bought and sold. Any transaction in a company's securities by the insider may be matched with any other transaction in those securities by the same insider (provided that the transactions occurred within a six-month window) to determine the maximum profit. However, Section 16(b) does not include any transactions made by shareholders (who were not also officers or directors) when they were not holders of 10% or more of the company's equity securities. That maximum profit is what is recoverable from the insider. Section 16(b) also allows a shareholder of the company to sue derivatively on behalf of a company to recover the profit if the company does not bring or diligently prosecute a Section 16(b) claim. The following case examines the method by which damages are calculated under Section 16(b) and some of the limitations that can arise from its rigid structure.

Gratz v. Claughton

187 F.2d 46 (2d Cir.), *cert. denied,* 341 U.S. 920 (1951)

HAND, C.J.:

This is an appeal by the defendant, Claughton, from a judgment against him, entered upon the report of a master, in an action by a shareholder of the Missouri-Kansas-Texas Railroad Company under Sec. 16(b) of the Securities Exchange Act of 1934.

* * * *

There remains the question of the computation of profits, which we dealt with in *Smolowe v. Delendo Corporation, supra,* [136 F.2d 231 (2d Cir. 1943)] Section 16(b) declares that 'any profit realized * * * from any purchase and sale, or any sale and purchase * * * within any period of less than six months * * * shall inure to and be recoverable by the issuer': the corporation. It is plain that this presupposes some matching of (1) purchases against sales, or of (2) sales against purchases, and that there must therefore be some principle upon which both the minuend—the sale price—and the subtrahend—the purchase price—can be determined. At first blush it might seem that the statute limited the recovery to profits derived from transactions in the same shares; as, for example, that a dealer's profit upon the sale of any given number of shares was to be measured by subtracting what he paid for those shares from what he got upon a sale of the same certificate. However, as we observed in *Smolowe v. Delendo Corporation* . . . that would allow an easy avoidance of the statute; in order to speculate freely an officer, director, or 'beneficial owner' need only hold a substantial block of shares for more than six months. If, for example, on January 1st, he had 10,000 shares which he had bought before October 1st, he could buy 1,000 shares on February 1st and sell 1,000 shares at a profit on April 1st, making delivery out of certificates from the 10,000 shares purchased before October 1st. After the two transactions his position would be what it had been on January 1st save that in two months he had made a profitable turn in 1,000 shares—exactly the evil against which the statute is directed. Moreover, there is an added reason for this interpretation, if one be needed. In the case of a sale followed by a purchase it is impossible to identify any purchase with any previous sale; one would have to confine such transactions to the practically non-existent occasions when the proceeds of the sale were used to purchase. Thus it appears, regardless of anything said during the passage of the bill through Congress and of the different forms it took, that the Act does not demand—that the same shares should be sold which were bought. This accords with the fungible nature of shares of stock. Indeed, if we translate the transaction into sales and purchases, or purchases and sales, of gallons of oil in a single tank, or of bushels of wheat in a single bin, it at once appears that the ascertainment of the particular shares bought or sold must be wholly irrelevant.

Although for these reasons it appears that the transactions—sales and purchases, or purchases and sales—are not to be matched by identifying the shares dealt in, we are no nearer than before to finding an answer as to how transactions shall be matched; all that so far appeared, is that the matching is to be between contracts of sale and contracts of purchase, or vice versa. On the other hand it is manifest that the intent of the fiduciary cannot be the test; first, because he generally has no ascertainable intent; and second, because that would open the door even more widely to the evil in question. The statute does not allow the fiduciary to minimize his profits, any more than to set off his losses against them. We can therefore find no principle by which to select any two transactions which are to be matched; and, so far as we can see, we are forced to one of two alternatives: to match any given purchase, taken as subtrahend, in such a way as to reduce profits to their lowest possible amount, or in such a way as to increase them to the greatest possible amount. The master adopted the second course, following what he supposed to be the doctrine of *Smolowe v. Delendo Corporation, supra*. . . . We think that he was right for the following reasons.

The question is in substance the same as when a trustee's account is to be surcharged, for, as we have said, the statute makes the fiduciary a constructive trustee for any profits he may make. It is true that on the beneficiary in an accounting rests the burden of proof of a surcharge, although the fiduciary has the burden of establishing any credits. Since the plaintiff was seeking to surcharge the defendant we will therefore assume that it rested upon her to show how the transactions are to be matched; and, that, if there were nothing more, since she cannot do so, she must be content to have them matched in the way that shows the least profit. Obviously that cannot be the right answer, for the reasons we have given; and perhaps the fact that it cannot be, is reason enough for adopting the alternative. But there is another ground for reaching the same result. As we have said, the statute makes all such dealings unlawful, and makes the fiduciary accountable to the corporation. Although it is impossible in the case at bar to compute the defendant's profits, except that they must fall between two limits—the minimum and the maximum-the cause of this uncertainty is the number of transactions within six months: that is, the number of defendant's derelictions. The situation falls within the doctrine which has been law since the days of the 'Chimney Sweeper's Jewel Case,' that when damages are at some unascertainable amount below an upper limit and when the uncertainty arises from the defendant's wrong, the upper limit will be taken as the proper amount.

This results in looking for six months both before and after any sale, and not for three months only, as the defendant insists. If one is seeking an equation of purchase and sale, one may take any sale as the minuend and look back for six months for a purchase at less price to match against it. On the other hand, if one is looking for an equation of sale and purchase, one may take the same sale and look forward for six months for any purchase at a lower price. Although obviously no transaction can figure in more than one equation, with that exception we can see no escape from what we have just said. It is true that this means that no director, officer, or 'beneficial owner' may safely buy and sell, or sell and buy, shares of stock in the company except at intervals of six months. Whether that is too drastic a means of meeting the evil, we have not to decide; it is enough that we can find no other way to administer the statute. Therefore, not only will be follow *Smolowe v. Delendo Corporation* . . . as a precent [sic]; but as *res integra* and after independent analysis we reassert its doctrine. . . . The crushing liabilities which Sec. 16(b) may impose are apparent from this action in which the judgment was for over $ 300,000; it should certainly serve as a warning, and may prove a deterrent.

Judgment affirmed.

QUESTIONS AND NOTES

1. Do you agree with the court's formulation that liability under Section 16(b) should be determined in such a way to calculate the maximum profit?

2. Would you apply this measure even if it differed from a defendant's actual profit?

3. The reason the court called the computation of damages a "crushing liability" is that, it turns out, the defendant, Gratz, suffered a net loss of $400,000 on his trading in the company's stock, yet he was charged under Section 16(b) for a $300,000 profit. How could this be? Consider a senior officer in a Company A, who, in month 1, buys one share of stock in Company A for $10. At the end of month 1, he sells the share of stock for $8. He now has a loss of $2. At the beginning of month 3, the same officer buys one more share of Company A's stock for $5. However, the price of Company A's stock continues to decline, and the officer sells that share for $3 at the end of month 3 for another loss of $2. The officer would calculate that he had two, $2 losses for a total of $4 in losses. However, under Section 16(b), the officer's sale of stock at the end of month 1 for $8 and his purchase of stock at the beginning of month 3 for $5, would be matched, and the officer would be liable for $3 in damages. Hence the use of the term "crushing."

4. Heidi is a director of Short Swing, Inc., a publicly traded company. For many years, Heidi owned 500 shares of Short Swing, Inc. stock, which she had purchased in August of 2007 for $30 per share and a total of $15,000. In 2008 the price of Short Swing Inc.'s stock fell dramatically, but, after some time, the price began to increase toward its former levels. On December 1, 2012, Short Swing, Inc.'s share price had climbed back up to $29.80 per share, and Heidi sold her 500 shares at a small loss, for $29.80 per share, for a total of $14,900. In early 2013 the price of Short Swing, Inc. stock dropped again, and on April 1, 2013, Heidi calls you, her attorney, for advice. Heidi wants to purchase another 500 shares of Short Swing, Inc. stock at the current price of $10 per share. She thinks that $10 a share is a great deal. Heidi knows about Section 16(b) but thinks she is "fine" since her prior purchase and sale did not result in a profit. She also tells you that she has already completed her 2012 tax return on which she reported the capital loss of $100 associated with the recent sale of the 500 shares, which she has matched with her purchase of the original 500 shares of Short Swing, Inc. stock. She is calling you to just make sure that there is no problem under Section 16(b). What advice should you give Heidi about her potential liability under Section 16(b)?

C. Determination of "Beneficial Owner" Status

As the application of Section 16(b) evolved, it was clear how the rule applied to officers and directors, but unclear how the rule applied to shareholders owning 10% or more of a company's stock. Unlike the rule for officers and directors, who were covered by Section 16(b) if they were an officer or director either at the time of purchase or at the time of sale, shareholders were covered only if they held 10% or more of a company's stock, both at the time of purchase and at the time of sale. This rule left itself open to great manipulation. For example, could a shareholder, holding over 10% of the company's stock, comply with the letter of the law by selling just enough stock to reduce his holdings to 9.9% (which would be subject to Section 16(b)) and then sell the remaining 9.9% "free" from the application of Section 16(b)? That was the question considered by the Court in the *Reliance Electric Co. v. Emerson Electric Co.* case, which follows.

Reliance Electric Co. v. Emerson Electric Co.

404 U.S. 418 (1972)

JUSTICE STEWART delivered the opinion of the Court.

Section 16(b) of the Securities Exchange Act of 1934, 48 Stat. 896, 15 U.S.C. § 78p(b), provides, among other things, that a corporation may recover for itself the profits realized by an owner of more than 10% of its shares from a purchase and sale of its stock within any six-month period, provided that the owner held more than 10% "both at the time of the purchase and sale." In this case, the respondent, the owner of 13.2% of a corporation's shares, disposed of its entire holdings in two sales, both of them within six months of purchase. The first sale reduced the respondent's holdings to 9.96%, and the second disposed of the remainder. The question presented is whether the profits derived from the second sale are recoverable by the Corporation under § 16(b). We hold that they are not.

I

On June 16, 1967, the respondent, Emerson Electric Co., acquired 13.2% of the outstanding common stock of Dodge Manufacturing Co., pursuant to a tender offer made in an unsuccessful attempt to take over Dodge. The purchase price for this stock was $63 per share. Shortly thereafter, the shareholders of Dodge approved a merger with the petitioner, Reliance Electric Co. Faced with the certain failure of any further attempt to take over Dodge, and with the prospect of being forced to exchange its Dodge shares for stock in the merged corporation in the near future, Emerson, following a plan outlined by its general counsel, decided to dispose of enough shares to bring its holdings below 10%, in order to immunize the disposal of the remainder of its shares from liability under § 16 (b). Pursuant to counsel's recommendation, Emerson on August 28 sold 37,000 shares of Dodge common stock to a brokerage house at $68 per share. This sale reduced Emerson's holdings in Dodge to 9.96% of the outstanding common stock. The remaining shares were then sold to Dodge at $69 per share on September 11.

After a demand on it by Reliance for the profits realized on both sales, Emerson filed this action seeking a declaratory judgment as to its liability under § 16(b). Emerson first claimed that it was not liable at all, because it was not a 10% owner at the time of the *purchase* of the Dodge shares. The District Court disagreed, holding that a purchase of stock falls within § 16(b) where the purchaser becomes a 10% owner by virtue of the purchase. The Court of Appeals affirmed this holding, and Emerson did not cross-petition for certiorari. Thus that question is not before us.

Emerson alternatively argued to the District Court that, assuming it was a 10% stockholder at the time of the purchase, it was liable only for the profits on the August 28 sale of 37,000 shares, because after that time it was no longer a 10% owner within the meaning of § 16(b). After trial on the issue of liability alone, the District Court held Emerson liable for the entire amount of its profits. The court found that Emerson's sales of Dodge stock were "effected pursuant to a single predetermined plan of disposition with the overall intent and purpose of avoiding Section 16(b) liability," and construed the term "time of . . . sale" to include "the entire period during which a series of related transactions take place pursuant to a plan by which a 10% beneficial owner disposes of his stock holdings" 306 F. Supp. 588, 592.

On an interlocutory appeal under 28 U.S.C. § 1292(b), the Court of Appeals upheld the finding that Emerson "split" its sale of Dodge stock simply in order to avoid most of its potential liability under § 16 (b), but it held this fact irrelevant under the statute so long as the two sales are "not legally tied to each other and [are] made at different times to different buyers . . . ." 434 F.2d 918, 926. Accordingly, the Court of Appeals reversed the District Court's judgment as to Emerson's liability for its profits on the September 11 sale, and remanded for a determination of the amount of Emerson's liability on the August 28 sale. Reliance filed a petition for certiorari, which we granted in order to consider an unresolved question under an important federal statute. 401 U.S. 1008.

II

The history and purpose of § 16(b) have been exhaustively reviewed by federal courts on several occasions since its enactment in 1934. [*Citations omitted.*] Those courts have recognized that the only method Congress deemed effective to curb the evils of insider trading was a flat rule taking the profits out of a class of transactions in which the possibility of abuse was believed to be intolerably great. As one court observed:

> "In order to achieve its goals, Congress chose a relatively arbitrary rule capable of easy administration. The objective standard of Section 16(b) imposes strict liability upon substantially all transactions occurring within the statutory time period, regardless of the intent of the insider or the existence of actual speculation. This approach maximized the ability of the rule to eradicate speculative abuses by reducing difficulties in proof. Such arbitrary and sweeping coverage was deemed necessary to insure the optimum prophylactic effect." *Bershad v. McDonough,* 428 F.2d 693, 696.

Thus Congress did not reach every transaction in which an investor actually relies on inside information. A person avoids liability if he does not meet the statutory definition of an "insider," or if he sells more than six months after purchase. Liability cannot be imposed simply because the investor structured his transaction with the intent of avoiding liability under § 16(b). The question is, rather, whether the method used to "avoid" liability is one permitted by the statute.

Among the "objective standards" contained in § 16(b) is the requirement that a 10% owner be such "both at the time of the purchase and sale . . . of the security involved." Read literally, this language clearly contemplates that a statutory insider might sell enough shares to bring his holdings below 10%, and later—but still within six months—sell additional shares free from liability under the statute. Indeed, commentators on the securities laws have recommended this exact procedure for a 10% owner who, like Emerson, wishes to dispose of his holdings within six months of their purchase.

Under the approach urged by Reliance, and adopted by the District Court, the apparent immunity of profits derived from Emerson's second sale is lost where the two sales, though independent in every other respect, are "interrelated parts of a single plan." 306 F. Supp., at 592. But a "plan" to sell that is conceived within six months of purchase clearly would not fall within § 16(b) if the sale were made after the six months had expired, and we see no basis in the statute for a different result where the 10% requirement is involved rather than the six-month limitation. . . .

The preceding case resolved that Section 16(b) applies only to transactions by shareholders when they actually hold 10% or more of a company's stock. However, this did not stop others from questioning when a 10% shareholder becomes a 10% shareholder. The question resolved in *Foremost-McKesson, Inc. v. Provident Securities Co.*, below, is whether the purchase which carries the shareholder over the 10% threshold "counts" as a purchase for the purposes of Section 16(b).

Foremost-McKesson, Inc. v. Provident Securities Co.

423 U.S. 232 (1976)

JUSTICE POWELL delivered the opinion of the Court.

This case presents an unresolved issue under § 16(b) of the Securities Exchange Act of 1934 (Act). That section of the Act was designed to prevent a corporate director or officer or "the beneficial owner of more than 10 per centum" of a corporation from profiteering through short-swing securities transactions on the basis of inside information. It provides that a corporation may capture for itself the profits realized on a purchase and sale, or sale and purchase, of its securities within six months by a director, officer, or beneficial owner. Section 16(b)'s last sentence, however, provides that it "shall not be construed to cover any transaction where such beneficial owner was not such both at the time of the purchase and sale, or the sale and purchase, of the security involved. . . ." The question presented here is whether a person purchasing securities that put his holdings above the 10% level is a beneficial owner "at the time of the purchase" so that he must account for profits realized on a sale of those securities within six months. The United States Court of Appeals for the Ninth Circuit answered this question in the negative. 506 F.2d 601 (1974). We affirm.

I

Respondent, Provident Securities Co., was a personal holding company. In 1968 Provident decided tentatively to liquidate and dissolve, and it engaged an agent to find a purchaser for its assets. Petitioner, Foremost-McKesson, Inc., emerged as a potential purchaser, but extensive negotiations were required to resolve a disagreement over the nature of the consideration Foremost would pay. Provident wanted cash in order to facilitate its dissolution, while Foremost wanted to pay with its own securities.

Eventually a compromise was reached, and Provident and Foremost executed a purchase agreement embodying their deal on September 25, 1969. The agreement provided that Foremost would buy two-thirds of Provident's assets for $4.25 million in cash and $49.75 million in Foremost convertible subordinated debentures. The agreement further provided that Foremost would register under the Securities Act of 1933 $25 million in principal amount of the debentures and would participate in an underwriting agreement by which those debentures would be sold to the public. At the closing on October 15, 1969, Foremost delivered to Provident the cash and a $40 million debenture which was subsequently exchanged for two debentures in the principal amounts of $25 million and $15 million. Foremost also delivered a $2.5 million debenture to an escrow agent on the closing date. On October 20 Foremost delivered to Provident a $7.25 million debenture representing the balance of the purchase price. These debentures were immediately convertible into more than 10% of Foremost's outstanding common stock.

On October 21 Provident, Foremost, and a group of underwriters executed an underwriting agreement to be closed on October 28. The agreement provided for sale to the underwriters of the $25 million debenture. On October 24 Provident distributed the $15 million and $7.25 million debentures to its stockholders, reducing the amount of Foremost common into which the company's holdings were convertible to less than 10%. On October 28 the closing under the underwriting agreement was accomplished. Provident thereafter distributed the cash proceeds of the debenture sale to its stockholders and dissolved.

Provident's holdings in Foremost debentures as of October 20 were large enough to make it a beneficial owner of Foremost within the meaning of § 16.[5] Having acquired and disposed of these securities within six months, Provident faced the prospect of a suit by Foremost to recover any profits realized on the sale of the debenture to the underwriters. Provident therefore sued for a declaration that it was not liable to Foremost under § 16(b). The District Court granted summary judgment for Provident, and the Court of Appeals affirmed.

Provident's principal argument below for nonliability was based on *Kern County Land Co. v. Occidental Corp.,* 411 U.S. 582 (1973). There we held that an "unorthodox transaction" in securities that did not present the possibility of

---

[5] A beneficial owner is one who owns more than 10% of an "equity security" registered pursuant to § 12 of the Act. . . . The owner of debentures convertible into more than 10% of a corporation's registered common stock is a beneficial owner within the meaning of the Act. . . . Foremost's common stock was registered; thus Provident's holdings made it a beneficial owner.

speculative abuse of inside information was not a "sale" within the meaning of § 16(b). Provident contended that its reluctant acceptance of Foremost debentures in exchange for its assets was an "unorthodox transaction" not presenting the possibility of speculative abuse and therefore was not a "purchase" within the meaning of § 16(b). Although the District Court's pre-*Kern County* opinion had adopted this type of analysis, 331 F. Supp. 787 (N.D. Cal. 1971), the Court of Appeals rejected it, reasoning that Provident's acquisition of the debentures was not "unorthodox" and that the circumstances did not preclude the possibility of speculative abuse. 506 F. 2d, at 604–605.

* * * *

II

The meaning of the exemptive provision has been disputed since § 16 (b) was first enacted. The discussion has focused on the application of the provision to a purchase-sale sequence, the principal disagreement being whether "at the time of the purchase" means "before the purchase" or "immediately after the purchase." The difference in construction is determinative of a beneficial owner's liability in cases such as Provident's where such owner sells within six months of purchase the securities the acquisition of which made him a beneficial owner. The commentators divided immediately over which construction Congress intended, and they remain divided. The Courts of Appeals also are in disagreement over the issue.

* * * *

III

A

The general purpose of Congress in enacting § 16(b) is well known. See *Kern County Land Co.,* 411 U.S., at 591–592; *Reliance Electric Co.,* 404 U.S., at 422, and the authorities cited therein. Congress recognized that insiders may have access to information about their corporations not available to the rest of the investing public. By trading on this information, these persons could reap profits at the expense of less well informed investors. In § 16(b) Congress sought to "curb the evils of insider trading [by] . . . taking the profits out of a class of transactions in which the possibility of abuse was believed to be intolerably great." *Reliance Electric Co., supra,* at 422. It accomplished this by defining directors, officers, and beneficial owners as those presumed to have access to inside information and enacting a flat rule that a corporation could recover the profits these insiders made on a pair of security transactions within six months.

purchase or sale of equity securities is involuntary (for example required by a preexisting contractual arrangement) and the specific facts of the situation do not create the possibility of "speculative abuse of inside information." (An example of this might be a situation that existed in the *Kern* case, in which the 10% shareholder, because it was at odds with the company, was extremely unlikely to, and did not, have access to any confidential information or input regarding the timing of the transaction.)

SECTION VI: Derivative State Law Claims Based on the Use of Inside Information

The state law claims for insider trading discussed at the beginning of this chapter typically involve direct suits against officers and directors. However, there have been cases in which a shareholder brought a derivative suit against a director and officer for trading in the corporation's stock based on nonpublic information. One such suit required the defendants to disgorge to the corporation the profits made on these sales. *Diamond v. Oreamuno*, 248 N.E.2d 910 (N.Y. 1969). However, several jurisdictions would find that allowing such a recovery in all such cases is too broad, and instead require that the insider's actions have been contrary to the corporation's interests or that the actions have harmed the corporation in some way before a derivative suit to disgorge profits would be allowed to succeed. For example, if the insider were to purchase stock in a company that he knew the corporation was intending to acquire and his purchases of that stock raised the price that the corporation had to pay, there would be a harm to the corporation AND a breach of the insider's duty. The corporation would have a claim against the insider, and, if the corporation refused to bring that claim, it could probably be brought in a derivative action.

Freeman v. Decio

584 F.2d 186 (7th Cir. 1978)

WOOD, JR., C.J.:

The principal question presented by this case is whether under Indiana law the plaintiff may sustain a derivative action against certain officers and directors of the Skyline Corporation for allegedly trading in the stock of the corporation on the basis of material inside information. . . . Alternatively, the court held that the plaintiff had failed to state a cause of action in that Indiana law has never recognized a right in a corporation to recover profits from insider trading and is not likely to follow the lead of the New York Court of Appeals in *Diamond v. Oreamuno,* 24 N.Y.2d 494, 301 N.Y.S.2d 78, 248 N.E.2d 910 (1969), in creating such a cause of action. We affirm. . . .

Plaintiff-appellant Marcia Freeman is a stockholder of the Skyline Corporation, a major producer of mobile homes and recreational vehicles. Skyline is a publicly owned corporation whose stock is traded on the New York Stock Exchange (NYSE). Defendant Arthur J. Decio is the largest shareholder of Skyline, the chairman of its board of directors, and until September 25, 1972, was also the president of the company. . . .

Throughout the 1960's and into 1972 Skyline experienced continual growth in sales and earnings. At the end of fiscal 1971 the company was able to report to its shareholders that over the previous five years sales had increased at a 40% Average compound rate and that net income had grown at a 64% Rate. This enormous success was reflected in increases in the price of Skyline stock. By April of 1972 Skyline common had reached a high of $ 72.00 per share. . . . Then, on December 22, 1972, Skyline reported that earnings for the quarter ending November 30, 1972, declined from $ 4,569,007 to $ 3,713,545 compared to the comparable period of the preceding year, rather than increasing substantially as they had done in the past. The NYSE immediately suspended trading in the stock. Trading was resumed on December 26 at $ 34.00 per share, down $ 13.50 from the preannouncement price. This represented a drop in value of almost 30%.

Plaintiff alleges that the defendants sold Skyline stock on the basis of material inside information during two distinct periods. Firstly, it is alleged that the financial results reported by Skyline for the quarters ending May 31 and August 31, 1972, significantly understated material costs and overstated earnings. It is further alleged that Decio, Kaufman and Mandell made various sales of Skyline stock totalling nearly $ 10 million during the quarters in question, knowing that earnings were overstated. Secondly, plaintiff asserts that during the quarter ending November 30 and up to December 22, 1972, Decio and Mandell made gifts and sales of Skyline stock totalling nearly $ 4 million while knowing that reported earnings for the November 30 quarter would decline. . . .

* * * *

I.

Diamond v. Oreamuno and Indiana Law

Both parties agree that there is no Indiana precedent directly dealing with the question of whether a corporation may recover the profits of corporate officials who trade in the corporation's securities on the basis of inside information. However, the plaintiff suggests that were the question to be presented to the Indiana courts, they would adopt the holding of the New York Court of Appeals in *Diamond v. Oreamuno,* 24 N.Y.2d 494, 301 N.Y.S.2d 78, 248 N.E.2d 910 (1969). There . . . the court held that the officers and directors of a corporation breached their fiduciary duties owed to the corporation by trading in its stock on the basis of material nonpublic information acquired by virtue of their official positions and that they should account to the corporation for their profits from those transactions. Since Diamond was decided, few courts have had an opportunity to consider the problem there presented. In fact, only one case has been brought to our attention which raised the question of whether Diamond would be followed in another jurisdiction. In *Schein v. Chasen,* 478 F.2d 817 (2d Cir. 1973) . . . the Second Circuit . . . not only tacitly concluded that Florida would adopt Diamond, but that the Diamond cause of action should be extended so as to permit recovery of the profits of non-insiders who traded in the corporation's stock on the basis of inside information received as tips from insiders. . . . That court not only stated that it would not "give the unprecedented expansive reading to Diamond sought by appellants" but that, furthermore, it did not "choose to adopt the innovative ruling of the New York Court of Appeals in Diamond (itself)." 313 So.2d 739, 746 (Fla. 1975). Thus, the question here is whether the Indiana courts are more likely to follow the New York Court of Appeals or to join the Florida Supreme Court in refusing to undertake such a change from existing law.

It appears that from a policy point of view it is widely accepted that insider trading should be deterred because it is unfair to other investors who do not enjoy the benefits of access to inside information. The goal is not one of equality of possession of information since some traders will always be better "informed" than others by dint of greater expenditures of time and resources, greater experience, or greater analytical abilities but rather equality of access to information. . . .

Yet, a growing body of commentary suggests that pursuit of this goal of "market egalitarianism" may be costly. In addition to the costs associated with enforcement of the laws prohibiting insider trading, there may be a loss in the efficiency of the securities markets in their capital allocation function. The basic insight of economic analysis here is that securities prices act as signals helping to route capital to its most productive uses and that insider trading helps assure that those prices will reflect the best information available (i.e., inside information) as to where the best opportunities lie. However, even when confronted with the possibility of a trade-off between fairness and economic efficiency, most authorities appear to find that the balance tips in favor of discouraging insider trading.

* * * *

The SEC has also used its full panoply of powers to police insider trading through enforcement actions and civil actions. The agency has relied, Inter alia, on Section 17(a) of the 1933 Act, Section 15(c)(1) of the 1934 Act, and Rule 10b–5. The relief obtained has included not only injunctions and suspension orders, but also disgorgement of profits earned in insider trading.

Lastly, the "victims" of insider trading may recover damages from the insiders in many instances. Absent fraud, the traditional common law approach has been to permit officers and directors of corporations to trade in their corporation's securities free from liability to other traders for failing to disclose inside information. However, there has been a movement towards the imposition of a common law duty to disclose in a number of jurisdictions, at least where the insider is dealing with an existing stockholder. A few jurisdictions now require disclosure where certain "special facts" exist, and some even impose a strict fiduciary duty on the insider Vis-a-vis the selling shareholder. But the most important remedies available to those injured by insider trading are found in the federal securities laws and in particular Rule 10b–5. Judicial development of a private right of action under that rule has led to significant relaxation of many of the elements of common law fraud, including privity, reliance, and the distinction between misrepresentation and non-disclosure. The rule has proven a favorite vehicle for damage suits against insiders for failing to disclose material information while trading in their corporation's stock. . . . Lastly, persons injured by insider trading may be able to take advantage of the liability sections of state securities laws. A number of states, including Indiana, have enacted laws containing antifraud provisions modeled on Rule 10b–5. . . .

Yet, the New York Court of Appeals in Diamond found the existing remedies for controlling insider trading to be inadequate. Although the court felt that the device of a class action under the federal securities laws held out hope of a more effective remedy in the future, it concluded that "the desirability of creating an effective common-law remedy is manifest." 301 N.Y.S.2d at 85, 248

N.E.2d at 915. It went on to do so by engineering an innovative extension of the law governing the relation between a corporation and its officers and directors. The court held that corporate officials who deal in their corporation's securities on the basis of nonpublic information gained by virtue of their inside position commit a breach of their fiduciary duties to the corporation. This holding represents a departure from the traditional common law approach, which was that a corporate insider did not ordinarily violate his fiduciary duty to the corporation by dealing in the corporation's stock, unless the corporation was thereby harmed.

The Diamond court relied heavily on the Delaware case of *Brophy v. Cities Service Co.,* 31 Del. Ch. 241, 70 A.2d 5 (1949), the most significant departure from the traditional common law approach prior to Diamond itself. There, the confidential secretary to a director of a corporation purchased a number of shares of the company's stock after finding out that the corporation was about to enter the market to make purchases of its stock itself, and then sold at a profit after the corporation began its purchases. The Delaware Court of Chancery upheld the complaint in a derivative action on behalf of the corporation to recover those profits. The court stated that the employee occupied a position of trust and confidence toward his employer and that public policy would not permit him to abuse that relation for his own profit, regardless of whether or not the employer suffered a loss.

* * * *

There are a number of difficulties with the Diamond court's ruling. Perhaps the thorniest problem was posed by the defendants' objection that whatever the ethical status of insider trading, there is no injury to the corporation which can serve as a basis for recognizing a right of recovery in favor of the latter. The Court of Appeals' response to this argument was two-fold, suggesting first that no harm to the corporation need be shown and second that it might well be inferred that the insiders' activities did in fact cause some harm to the corporation. . . .

Some might see the Diamond court's decision as resting on a broad, strict-trust notion of the fiduciary duty owed to the corporation: no director is to receive any profit, beyond what he receives from the corporation, solely because of his position. Although, once accepted, this basis for the Diamond rule would obviate the need for finding a potential for injury to the corporation, it is not at all clear that current corporation law contemplates such an extensive notion of fiduciary duty. It is customary to view the Diamond result as resting on a characterization of inside information as a corporate asset. The lack of necessity for looking for an injury to the corporation is then justified by the traditional "no inquiry" rule with respect to profits made by trustees from assets belonging to the trust Res. However, to start from the premise that all inside information should be considered a corporate asset may presuppose an answer to the inquiry at hand. It might be better to ask whether there is any potential loss to the corporation from the use of such information in insider trading before deciding to characterize the inside information as an asset with respect to which the insider owes the corporation a duty of loyalty (as opposed to a duty of care). This approach would be in keeping with the modern view of another area of application of the duty of loyalty the corporate opportunity doctrine. Thus, while courts will require a director or officer to automatically account to the corporation for diversion of a corporate opportunity to personal use, they will first inquire to see whether there was a possibility of a loss to the corporation i.e., whether the corporation was in a position to potentially avail itself of the opportunity before deciding that a corporate opportunity in fact existed. Similarly, when scrutinizing transactions between a director or officer and the corporation under the light of the duty of loyalty, most courts now inquire as to whether there was any injury to the corporation, i. e., whether the transaction was fair and in good faith, before permitting the latter to avoid the transaction. An analogous question might be posed with respect to the Diamond court's unjust enrichment analysis: is it proper to conclude that an insider has been unjustly enriched Vis-a-vis the corporation (as compared to other traders in the market) when there is no way that the corporation could have used the information to its own profit, just because the insider's trading was made possible by virtue of his corporate position?

Not all information generated in the course of carrying on a business fits snugly into the corporate asset mold. Information in the form of trade secrets, customer lists, etc., can easily be categorized as a valuable or potentially valuable corporate "possession," in that it can be directly used by the corporation to its own economic advantage. However, most information involved in insider trading is not of this ilk, e. g., knowledge of an impending merger, a decline in earnings, etc. If the corporation were to attempt to exploit such nonpublic information by dealing in its own securities, it would open itself up to potential liability under federal and state securities laws, just as do the insiders when they engage in insider trading. This is not to say that the corporation does not have any interests with regard to such information. It may have an interest in either preventing the information from becoming public or in regulating the timing of disclosure. However, insider trading does not entail the disclosure of inside information, but rather its use in a manner in which the corporation itself is prohibited from exploiting it.

Yet, the Diamond court concluded that it might well be inferred that insider trading causes some harm to the corporation. . . . It must be conceded that the unfairness that is the basis of the widespread disapproval of insider trading is borne primarily by participants in the securities markets, rather than by the corporation itself. By comparison, the harm to corporate goodwill posited by the Diamond court pales in significance. At this point, the existence of such an indirect injury must be considered speculative, as there is no actual evidence of such a reaction. Furthermore, it is less than clear to us that the nature of this harm would form an adequate basis for an action for an accounting based on a breach of the insiders' duty of loyalty, as opposed to an action for damages based on a breach of the duty of care. The injury hypothesized by the Diamond court seems little different from the harm to the corporation that might be inferred whenever a responsible corporate official commits an illegal or unethical act using a corporate asset. Absent is the element of loss of opportunity or potential susceptibility to outside influence that generally is present when a corporate fiduciary is required to account to the corporation.

The Brophy case is capable of being distinguished on this basis. Although the court there did not openly rely on the existence of a potential harm to the corporation, such a harm was possible. Since the corporation was about to begin buying its own shares in the market, by purchasing stock for his own account the insider placed himself in direct competition with the corporation. To the degree that his purchases might have caused the stock price to rise, the corporation was directly injured in that it had to pay more for its purchases. . . .

A second problem presented by the recognition of a cause of action in favor of the corporation is that of potential double liability. The Diamond court thought that this problem would seldom arise, since it thought it unlikely that a damage suit would be brought by investors where the insiders traded on impersonal exchanges. . . . The Second Circuit also gave consideration to the possibility of double liability in *Schein v. Chasen,* 478 F.2d at 824–25, but concluded that double liability could be avoided by methods such as that employed in *SEC v. Texas Gulf Sulphur Co.,* 312 F. Supp. 77, 93 (S.D.N.Y.1970), where the defendants' disgorged profits were placed in a fund subject first to the claims of injured investors, with the residue payable to the corporation. The efficacy of the Diamond court's suggestion of resort to an interpleader action is open to question. . . .

Since the Diamond court's action was motivated in large part by its perception of the inadequacy of existing remedies for insider trading, it is noteworthy that over the decade since Diamond was decided, the 10b–5 class action has made substantial advances toward becoming the kind of effective remedy for insider trading that the court of appeals hoped that it might become. Most importantly, recovery of damages from insiders has been allowed by, or on the behalf of, market investors even when the insiders dealt only through impersonal stock exchanges, although this is not yet a well-settled area of the law. In spite of other recent developments indicating that such class actions will not become as easy to maintain as some plaintiffs had perhaps hoped, it is clear that the remedies for insider trading under the federal securities laws now constitute a more effective deterrent than they did when Diamond was decided.

[H]aving carefully examined the decision of the New York Court of Appeals in Diamond, we are of the opinion that although the court sought to ground its ruling in accepted principles of corporate common law, that decision can best be understood as an example of judicial securities regulation. Although the question is a close one, we believe that were the issue to be presented to the Indiana courts at the present time, they would most likely join the Florida Supreme Court in refusing to adopt the New York court's innovative ruling.

* * * *

The judgment of the district court is AFFIRMED.

QUESTIONS

1. Do you agree with the view that inside information is an asset of the corporation?

2. If so, could a corporation allow its employees to trade on that information as a "perk"?

3. If there is no "harm" to the corporation, should its fiduciaries be prohibited from using nonpublic information to make a profit? (Consider the Delaware Supreme Court's analysis in the *Kahn* case, below.)

Kahn v. Kolberg Kravis Roberts & Co., L.P.

23 A.3d 831 (Del. 2011)

STEELE, C. J.:

The Appellants in this derivative action, Linda Kahn and Alan Spiegal, who are shareholders of Primedia, Inc., appeal the Court of Chancery's decision granting the Primedia Special Litigation Committee's Motion to Dismiss claims arising out of a series of alleged violations of fiduciary duty by defendants, Kohlberg, Kravis, Roberts & Co., Primedia, Inc., and other Primedia officers and directors. Because we do not agree with the Court of Chancery's interpretation of a *Brophy* claim as explained in *Pfeiffer*, we must reverse the Court of Chancery's judgment of dismissal and remand the case for further proceedings consistent with this Opinion.

I. FACTS AND PROCEDURAL HISTORY

* * * *

B. The Facts

On December 19, 2001, Primedia's board of directors approved a plan for Primedia to acquire up to $100 million dollars of its preferred shares, at 50% to 60% of redemption value, in exchange for common stock. As of December 19, 2001, KKR controlled approximately 60% of Primedia's outstanding stock and had three of its designees on Primedia's board. At the May 16, 2002 board meeting, Primedia's directors authorized an additional $100 million in buybacks of its preferred shares. On May 21, 2002, Primedia's KKR directors authored an advisory memo to KKR's Investment Committee and Portfolio Committee containing an update on Primedia's second quarter performance and advocating the purchase of Primedia's preferred shares. The May 21st memo contained nonpublic information about Primedia.

At some point in 2002, KKR sought from the Primedia board of directors permission for KKR to purchase Primedia's preferred shares, as long as Primedia was not purchasing those shares in the market. On July 2, 2002, Primedia director (and General Counsel) Beverley Chell circulated the unanimous written consent to the disinterested directors. After receiving advice from outside counsel, Chell circulated the written consent to Primedia's entire board on July 8, 2002. The written consent stated, in part, that KKR's purchase of up to $50 million in Primedia preferred stock was acceptable and not a usurpation of corporate opportunity. The board purportedly executed the written consent on July 8, 2002, without any serious deliberations. The record is unclear when the written consent actually became effective, because the original version's signature page bore no date and at least one signature was not received until July 12, 2002. On July 3, 2002, KKR formed ABRA III LLC as an investment vehicle to purchase Primedia's preferred shares, and ABRA began purchasing preferred shares on July 8, 2002. Between July 8 and November 5, 2002, KKR (through ABRA) purchased over $75 million of Primedia's preferred stock, an amount that exceeded the $50 million limit allowed by the written consent.

On September 26, 2002, Primedia's board of directors met and approved the sale of one of its biggest assets, the American Baby Group, for approximately $115 million in cash. Primedia did not publicly disclose the American Baby Group sale until November 4, 2002. Between September 26 and November 4, 2002, KKR spent $39 million to acquire Primedia's preferred stock. On November 5, 2002, Primedia's board of directors decided to explore repurchasing Primedia preferred shares. ABRA made its last purchase of Primedia's preferred shares on November 5, 2002.

C. The Procedural History

* * * *

On March 16, 2010, plaintiffs filed a Third Amended Complaint, which included the *Brophy* claim [*Brophy v. Cities Serv. Co.,* 31 Del. Ch. 241, 70 A.2d 5 (Del. Ch. 1949)] that KKR possessed material, nonpublic information. This latest complaint alleged that KKR knew that: (1) Primedia's earnings would be better than previously forecasted to the market, and (2) the Company anticipated at some point redeeming its outstanding preferred stock and KKR traded on this information during the period July 8 to November 5, 2002.

On June 14, 2010, the Court of Chancery heard oral argument and, ruling from the bench, granted the SLC's Motion to Dismiss. Kahn now appeals from that judgment. First, Kahn argues that the Court of Chancery erroneously held that disgorgement was not an available remedy for its *Brophy* claims, consistent with *Pfeiffer's* holding. [*Pfeiffer v. Toll,* 989 A.2d 683 (Del. Ch. 2010)]. . . .

II. ANALYSIS

* * * *

B. *Brophy* Does Not Require an Element of Harm to the Corporation Before Disgorgement is an Available Remedy and to the Extent *Pfeiffer* Conflicts With This Holding, It is Wrong.

We review a trial judge's legal conclusions *de novo*. . . .

* * * *

. . .The Court of Chancery's function under *Zapata's* second prong is to "strik[e] a balance between 'legitimate corporate claims' as expressed in the derivative shareholder suit and the corporation's best interest as ascertained by the Special Litigation Committee." Here, the Vice Chancellor started from "the proposition that there is a *Brophy* claim that would blow by a motion to dismiss on failure to state a claim." Then the Vice Chancellor held that under the law, as explained in *Pfeiffer v. Toll,* disgorgement is not an available remedy for most of the Brophy claims. But, P*feiffer's* holding—which requires a plaintiff to show that the corporation suffered actual harm before bringing a Brophy claim—is not a correct statement of our law. To the extent *Pfeiffer v. Toll* conflicts with our current interpretation of *Brophy v. Cities Service Co., Pfeiffer* cannot be Delaware law.

In the venerable case of *Brophy v. Cities Service Co.,* one of the defendants was an employee who had acquired inside information that the corporate plaintiff was about to enter the market and purchase its own shares. Using this confidential information, the employee, who was not an officer, bought a large block of shares and, after the corporation's purchases had caused the price to rise, resold them at a profit. Because the employee defendant occupied a position of trust and confidence within the plaintiff corporation, the court found his relationship analogous to that of a fiduciary. The employee defendant argued that the plaintiff had failed to state a claim because "it [did] not appear that the corporation suffered any loss through his purchase of its stock." The Court of Chancery expressly rejected that argument, stating that:

> In equity, when the breach of confidential relation by an employee is relied on and an accounting for any resulting profit is sought, loss to the corporation need not be charged in the complaint. . . . Public policy will not permit an employee occupying a position of trust and confidence toward his employer to abuse that

relation to his own profit, regardless of whether his employer suffers a loss.

Thus, actual harm to the corporation is not required for a plaintiff to state a claim under *Brophy*. In *Brophy,* the court relied on the principles of restitution and equity, citing the Restatement of the Law of Restitution § 200, comment a, for the proposition that a fiduciary cannot use confidential corporate information for his own benefit. As the court recognized in *Brophy,* it is inequitable to permit the fiduciary to profit from using confidential corporate information. Even if the corporation did not suffer actual harm, equity requires disgorgement of that profit.

This Court has cited *Brophy* approvingly when discussing how the duty of loyalty governs the misuse of confidential corporate information by fiduciaries.[26] In I*n re Oracle Corp. Deriv. Litig.,* [*In re Oracle Corp.,* 867 A.2d 904 (Del. Ch. 2004), aff'd, 872 A.2d 960 (Del. 2005)] we affirmed the Court of Chancery's articulation of the elements essential for a plaintiff to prevail on a *Brophy* claim. The plaintiff must show that: "1) the corporate fiduciary possessed material, nonpublic company information; and 2) the corporate fiduciary used that information improperly by making trades because she was motivated, in whole or in part, by the substance of that information."

In *Pfeiffer v. Toll,* the plaintiff stockholder brought a derivative action against the defendants, who were eight members of the Toll Brothers' board of directors, to recover damages suffered by the company from their alleged insider trading. Pfeiffer claimed that the defendants sold significant amounts of Toll Brothers stock from December 2004 through September 2005 while in

26 *See Oberly v. Kirby,* 592 A.2d 445, 463 (Del. 1991) ("[T]he absence of specific damage to a beneficiary is not the sole test for determining disloyalty by one occupying a fiduciary position. It is an act of disloyalty for a fiduciary to profit personally from the use of information secured in a confidential relationship, even if such profit or advantage is not gained at the expense of the fiduciary. The result is nonetheless one of unjust enrichment which will not be countenanced by a Court of Equity."); *Mills Acquisition Co. v. Macmillan, Inc.,* 559 A.2d 1261, 1283 (Del. 1989) (citing *Brophy* as supporting duty of fair dealing by "those who are privy to material information obtained in the course of representing corporate interests" and holding that "[a]t a minimum, this rule dictates that fiduciaries, corporate or otherwise, may not use superior information or knowledge to mislead others in the performance of their own fiduciary obligations"); *Weinberger v. UOP, Inc.,* 457 A.2d 701, 711 (Del. 1983) ("[O]ne possessing superior knowledge may not mislead any stockholder by use of corporate information to which the latter is not privy. Delaware has long imposed this duty even upon persons who are not corporate officers or directors, but who nonetheless are privy to matters of interest or significance to their company."); *Singer v. Magnavox Co.,* 380 A.2d 969, 977 (Del. 1977) (citing *Brophy* as one of many precedents enforcing the "fiduciary obligation of honesty, loyalty, good faith and fairness"), overruled on other grounds by *Weinberger,* 457 A.2d at 715. *See also Adams v. Jankouskas,* 452 A.2d 148, 152 (Del. 1982) (citing *Brophy* as authority for imposing constructive trust "when a defendant's fraudulent, unfair or unconscionable conduct causes him to be unjustly enriched at the expense of another to whom he owed some duty").

possession of material, nonpublic information about Toll Brothers' future prospects. Specifically, Toll Brothers was projecting 20% growth in net income for 2006 and 2007, and its stock price more than doubled from December 2004 to July 2005. During this same period, the director defendants allegedly sold 14 million shares of stock for over $615 million. Based on those sales, which were inconsistent with past trading patterns and were suspicious in their timing and amount, Pfeiffer asserted a derivative claim for breach of fiduciary duty under *Brophy*.

The defendants moved to dismiss the complaint, arguing, among other things, that *Brophy* is an outdated precedent in light of the federal securities laws, which govern insider trading claims. While on one hand upholding *Brophy* as good law, the Court of Chancery concluded that "[t]he purpose of a *Brophy* claim is to remedy harm to the corporation." By focusing on that harm, it "disposes of the defendants' contentions that Brophy is a misguided vehicle for recovering the same trading losses that are addressed by the federal securities laws . . . [and] the contention that *Brophy* grants a remedy without underlying harm." Next, the Vice Chancellor concluded that the harm to the corporation "is generally not measured by insider trading gains or reciprocal losses." Citing to this Court's precedent on two occasions, the Vice Chancellor found that Delaware law "does not provide a class-wide remedy for market based-harm" and "interpreting *Brophy* as a basis for recovering those measures of damages would conflict with [those holdings]." Moreover, the court found that "disgorgement of insider trading profits . . . is also not the appropriate measure of damages because insiders who trade on an impersonal market typically are not engaging in the type of self-dealing transaction to which a disgorgement remedy historically applies." The court also held that market trading "typically does not involve the usurpation of a corporate opportunity, where disgorgement has been the preferred remedy."

To that end, the Vice Chancellor concluded that in the context of a *Brophy* claim, disgorgement is "theoretically available" in two circumstances: (1) "when a fiduciary engages directly in actual fraud and benefits from trading on the basis of the fraudulent information;" and (2) "if the insider used confidential corporate information to compete directly with the corporation." *Brophy*, in the Vice Chancellor's view, was an example of the second circumstance where disgorgement is an appropriate remedy. But, in most circumstances a corporation would only be able to recover for "actual harm causally related (in both the actual and proximate sense) to the breach of the duty of loyalty"—for example "costs and expenses for regulatory proceedings and internal investigations, fees paid to counsel and other professionals, fines paid to regulators, and judgments in litigation."

We decline to adopt *Pfeiffer's* thoughtful, but unduly narrow, interpretation of *Brophy* and its progeny. We also disagree with the *Pfeiffer* court's conclusion that the purpose of *Brophy* is to "remedy harm to the corporation." In fact, *Brophy* explicitly held that the corporation did not need to suffer an actual loss for there to be a viable claim. Importantly, *Brophy* focused on preventing a fiduciary wrongdoer from being unjustly enriched. Moreover, we have found no cases requiring that the corporation suffer actual harm for a plaintiff to bring a *Brophy* claim. To read *Brophy* as applying only where the corporation has suffered actual harm improperly limits its holding.

We decline to adopt *Pfeiffer's* interpretation that would limit the disgorgement remedy to a usurpation of corporate opportunity or cases where the insider used confidential corporate information to compete directly with the corporation. *Brophy* was not premised on either of those rationales. Rather, *Brophy* focused on the public policy of preventing unjust enrichment based on the misuse of confidential corporate information. Just as the *Brophy* court relied on the seminal decision in *Guth v. Loft,* we also rely on the *Guth* court's rationale in this case, and refuse to restrict disgorgement in *Brophy* cases as *Pfeiffer* suggests.

> The rule, inveterate and uncompromising in its rigidity, does not rest upon the narrow ground of injury or damage to the corporation resulting from a betrayal of confidence, but upon a broader foundation of a wise public policy that, for the purpose of removing all temptation, extinguishes all possibility of profit flowing from a breach of the confidence imposed by the fiduciary relation.

Given *Guth's* eloquent articulation of Delaware's public policy and the fact that "Delaware law dictates that the scope of recovery for a breach of the duty of loyalty is not to be determined narrowly," we find no reasonable public policy ground to restrict the scope of disgorgement remedy in *Brophy* cases—irrespective of arguably parallel remedies grounded in federal securities law.

* * * *

2. Zapata's Second Prong

We cannot ascertain from the present record whether the Vice Chancellor analyzed the SLC's Motion to Dismiss without improperly relying on *Pfeiffer.* Although the SLC did not rely on *Pfeiffer's* holding in its motion to dismiss, it did argue lack of cognizable harm during oral argument to the Vice Chancellor. The

SLC argued that materiality, scienter, timeliness, and indemnification obligations were independent grounds for dismissal. Nevertheless, we cannot determine whether the Vice Chancellor relied on the materiality or scienter elements because he did not discuss either element in the bench ruling. For instance, we are unable to determine whether the Vice Chancellor's comment, "I start from the proposition that there is a *Brophy* claim here that would blow by a motion to dismiss on failure to state a claim," implicitly suggests he thought the information was sufficiently material but dismissed the claim because of his reliance on *Pfeiffer.* Absent a more focused analysis in the record, we must therefore reverse and remand. On remand, the Vice Chancellor should analyze the claim without any assumption that an element of harm to the corporation must exist before a disgorgement equitable remedy is available.

III. CONCLUSION

The judgment of the Court of Chancery is REVERSED and the action is REMANDED for proceedings consistent with this Opinion.

CHAPTER TEN

Mergers, Acquisitions and Takeovers

WHILE SITTING IN YOUR OFFICE, a senior partner from the firm's Trusts & Estates department asks you to come into her office to discuss a matter. One of the partner's clients, Jacob Elder, has a substantial investment in a company called, Mattress Moguls, Inc. ("MMI"). MMI is about to merge with another company and Jacob is concerned that he is going to be forced to sell his stock at an unfairly low price. The partner relates to you the following facts:

Experiencing Assignment 14: Mattress Moguls, Inc.

FACTS:

MMI is a publicly traded, Delaware corporation. It is one of the largest mattress companies in the world. MMI manufactures mattresses and sells them in retail locations, nationwide and, through licensees, worldwide. Last year MMI had revenues of approximately $1 billion. Approximately 65% of MMI is owned by Private Equity Palace ("PEP"), a large and well-known, private equity group. It seems that PEP is planning to take the company private and merge it into a wholly owned subsidiary. PEP has had MMI appraised at a value of $1.25 billion and plans to provide the MMI minority shareholders with their pro rata share of that amount. Jacob owns 1% of MMI so his share of the proceeds will be approximately $12.5 million. However, Jacob suspects that PEP is buying MMI because it has plans to extract even more value. He thinks that PEP plans to leverage MMI, pay itself a substantial sum in connection with the merger and then resell MMI for $2 to $2.5 billion in three years. Jacob, apparently, has been informed that there is a confidential MMI business plan that explains this strategy. However, Jacob has never seen the plan. In fact, other than a "long legal document" about the terms of the deal, Jacob does not have much information about the deal or PEP's plans for MMI. Jacob also believes that PEP does not need to buy out the minority shareholders. He thinks PEP's only reason for getting rid of the minority shareholders is to make more money when it sells MMI in three years.

The partner wants you to provide Jacob with advice so Jacob can decide how he will vote on the MMI deal. Jacob wants to compare what will happen if he accepts the deal with what might happen if he votes against the deal and sues the MMI board for a breach of fiduciary duty. He also wants to know if there is a chance that he and the other minority shareholders can block the deal. Jacob understands that you have neither the ability, nor the appropriate information, to develop any financial models that might help you determine the value of the deal or whether the price being offered to the minority shareholders is fair. He only wants to understand his legal rights and options, and be better able to evaluate whether he might be able to block the MMI merger or obtain a better deal if he votes against the merger and pursues his rights through legal action.

ASSIGNMENT:

The partner has scheduled a meeting with you and Jacob tomorrow, but, before the meeting, the partner would like to see a somewhat detailed outline of what you plan to tell Jacob. Please prepare the outline. The partner tells you that Jacob hates large legal bills and long-winded lawyers. So, he asks that you keep your presentation brief and just outline the important issues.

This Assignment does not need to be completed, and should not be completed, until the end of the following Section. However, as you study the cases and other materials that follow, it might be helpful to do so with a view toward providing assistance to Jacob. Some of the materials in the Section will relate more than others to the issues facing Jacob. However, the materials are designed to build your understanding of the issues that arise in the context of a merger transaction and assist you in addressing Jacob's concerns and putting them in context. Please keep Jacob's issues and the questions presented by the assignment in mind while reading the materials that follow.

SECTION I: Mergers and Acquisitions

While the comprehensive topic of mergers and acquisitions can cover an entire course, there are some fundamental principles and concepts involving mergers and acquisitions which should be addressed in a comprehensive study of business associations. This is true because many of the most fundamental issues in corporate law arise in the context of a merger or an acquisition. In addition there are some variations in how certain fiduciary duty principles are applied in the context of a merger or an acquisition, which are necessary to grasp in order to complete one's introduction to the subject matter.

A. Potential Structures in a Merger or Acquisition

A merger occurs when two companies come together to form one company. If one of the two original companies survives then the process is called a merger. If the combination results in a new company, then the process is called a "consolidation." Mergers and consolidations are accomplished through a statutory process in which the firms formally merge or consolidate through state law filings. Section 11.02 of the Model Business Corporations Act provides:

§ 11.02 Merger

(a) One or more domestic business corporations may merge with one or more domestic or foreign business corporations or eligible entities pursuant to a plan of merger, or two or more foreign business corporations or domestic or foreign eligible entities may merge into a new domestic business corporation to be created in the merger in the manner provided in this chapter.

* * * *

(c) The plan of merger must include:

(1) the name of each domestic or foreign business corporation or eligible entity that will merge and the name of the domestic or foreign business corporation or eligible entity that will be the survivor of the merger;

(2) the terms and conditions of the merger;

(3) the manner and basis of converting the shares of each merging domestic or foreign business corporation and eligible interests of each merging domestic or foreign eligible entity into shares or other securities, eligible interests, obligations, rights to acquire shares, other securities or eligible interests, cash, other property, or any combination of the foregoing;

(4) the articles of incorporation . . . to be created by the merger, or if a new domestic or foreign business . . . is not to be created by the merger, any amendments to the survivor's articles of incorporation or organic documents; and

(5) any other provisions required by the laws under which any party to the merger is organized or by which it is governed, or by the articles of incorporation or organic document of any such party.

There are also other structures that may be used when firms combine. Each structure will have its own advantages and disadvantages. There are three basic ways that companies may combine:

- ***Statutory Merger or Consolidation:*** A statutory merger involves a combination in accordance with applicable state law. (The above provisions from the Model Business Corporations Act § 11.02 are examples of provisions that might be included in a state's corporate merger statues.)
- ***Sale of Assets:*** An asset sale occurs when one company purchases all (or substantially all) of the assets of another company.
- ***Sale of Stock:*** A stock sale involves the purchase of the stock of one company by another entity or individual.

Technically, only a statutory merger is actually a "merger" or a "consolidation," and a sale of stock or assets is actually an "*acquisition.*" However, often the technical definition of merger is not used, and the general term "merger" is used to describe any combination of firms. There are a variety of ways to structure mergers and acquisitions; however, the structure is almost always determined by the underlying tax issues. While the specific tax issues that arise in a merger or acquisition are the subjects of a course in corporate taxation, it is important to be aware of their significance. In all the above combinations there is an exchange of ownership for value. This value (or "consideration") may consist of stock, assets, cash or some combination thereof.

In the most basic of mergers one company is identified as the "Acquirer" while the other is identified as the "Target." Even when the companies merging are of relatively equal size, it is useful to use these terms to understand the mechanics of how a merger takes place. In a simple merger or consolidation, there is only one company at the end of the process. In contrast, even in a simple sale of stock (*e.g.* when Corporation A purchases all of the outstanding stock of Corporation B), there are often two companies that remain following the sale. In a typical transaction the Acquirer would pay the Target (or the Target's shareholders) either cash or stock (or a combination of cash and stock) in exchange for assets or stock, depending upon the nature of the transaction. (Note that in some mergers a portion of the consideration might also include a promise to pay money (i.e., cash) in the future in the form of a promissory note or some other "debt" instrument.)

Voting

A shareholder vote is almost always required of the Target's shareholders in a merger, consolidation or acquisition. This is because the transaction usually represents a fundamental transaction for the Target company, and shareholders have the right to have a voice in such transactions. In general, the management of a company would prefer to avoid shareholder votes because these votes can use up corporate time and resources. However, of greater concern is that the shareholders might vote "no" or that an insufficient number of shareholders would vote "yes." (Recall, there are rules about quorums and percentage of votes required.) If the transaction requires shareholder approval and does not receive it, the transaction cannot move forward. While most merger, consolidation or acquisition transactions will require the approval of the Target's shareholders, a more difficult question is whether the merger or acquisition will require a vote of the Acquirer's shareholders.

Appraisal Rights

Appraisal rights entitle shareholders of some corporations involved in a merger or consolidation (and in some states corporations involved in the sale of stock or substantially all of their assets) to certain rights if those shareholders "dissent" from the transaction. These dissenting shareholders are entitled to receive a different amount of compensation for the transaction. Rather than receive the consideration which they would have received in the transaction, shareholders who exercise their appraisal rights are entitled to have the "fair value" of their interest in the firm determined by a court (using an appraisal method which often includes financial analysts and/or investment bankers), and receive that amount instead. The "fair value" determined by appraisal could be more or less than the consideration paid in the transaction. *See Cede & Co. v. Technicolor, Inc.* (discussed in Chapter 4, *supra*) in which, after approximately 10 years of litigation, Cinerama's interest in Technicolor, Inc. was appraised at $21.60 per share, less than the $23 per share Cinerama would have received had it voted for the merger. In a recent case, the Delaware Supreme Court suggested that, while there was no definitive formula for determining fair value and that the court had discretion to consider "all relevant factors," the deal price will often prove the "most reliable evidence of fair value," at least when that deal price arises out of a robust and conflict-free process. *DFC Global Corporation v. Muirfield Value Partners, L.P.* No. 518, 2016 (Del. Aug. 1, 2017).

If too large a number of shareholders seek appraisal of their interests, the transaction will not proceed. If the transaction does proceed, many dissenting shareholders might prefer to accept the merger compensation rather than seek to pursue their appraisal rights because the litigation is often expensive, and it can take a substantial period of time to receive the "fair value," during which time the dissenting shareholder's stock is typically not liquid. Delaware and several other states do not provide an appraisal remedy if the shares involved are publicly traded since, at least in theory, those shares may be sold for fair value on the open market before the deal is finalized. *See e.g.* Delaware General Corporation Law § 262(b)(1) which contains a provision known as a "market-out" exception, providing that, subject to certain exceptions, appraisal rights are not available "for the shares of any class or series of stock, which . . . [is] . . . listed on a national securities exchange . . . ." Section 262 of the Delaware General Corporation Law was recently amended to provide additional limitations on the appraisal process. One portion of the amendment seeks to place significant limitations on *de minimis* appraisal claims and provides that in the case of corporations listed on a national securities exchange that might not be subject to the market-out exception of § 262(b)(1), the Court shall dismiss appraisal proceedings as to all holders of shares who are otherwise entitled to appraisal rights unless: (1) the total number of shares entitled to appraisal exceeds 1% of the outstanding shares of the class or series eligible for appraisal; (2) the value of the consideration provided in the merger or consolidation for such total number of shares exceeds $1 million; *or* (3) the merger was a statutory short-form merger (discussed *infra*). Another provision in the amendment provides a corporation subject to an appraisal proceeding with a way to prevent the accrual of statutory interest by prepaying all or a portion of the amount it may owe to a shareholder seeking appraisal.

Statutory Merger

In a statutory merger two firms combine to form one firm. In either a merger or a consolidation, the new company holds both the assets *and* the liabilities, of both firms. A merger transaction must be approved by the shareholders of both companies. Shareholders who do not approve the transaction (dissenters) are typically (with some exceptions) entitled to appraisal rights, unless both companies are publicly traded.

In traditional mergers the two companies negotiate the relative percentage ownership that each respective company's shareholders will hold in the new firm. Typically, the consideration paid to the Target's shareholders is stock in the surviving firm. However, it is permissible to pay the shareholders with other consideration. In a merger/consolidation the consideration passes to the

Target's shareholders, provided they are not dissenting and opting to exercise their appraisal rights.

Sale of Assets

In a sale of assets, the Acquirer corporation gives the Target corporation either stock or cash (or some combination of cash and stock) in exchange for the Target corporation's assets.

Following the sale, the Target usually has few or no assets, other than the consideration paid by the Acquirer. In a sale of assets, the Target must usually make its creditors aware of the sale so that the creditors may make a claim against the consideration being paid for the Target's assets. Once the Target's creditors have been paid and the Target has received the balance of the consideration paid by the Acquirer, the Target may then issue a liquidating dividend to its shareholders. If the liquidating dividend is cash, then the Target shareholders take the cash and their ownership interest is terminated. If any of the consideration paid by the Acquirer corporation was paid in stock of the Acquirer, then the Target shareholders will receive that stock when the Target is liquidated and become shareholders in the Acquirer corporation. A sale of assets, especially if the Target has a substantial number of assets, can be a more complicated process than a statutory merger because, among other requirements, a sale of assets will require the transfer of ownership of each specific asset of the Target that is being sold, and the title to these different assets (such as real property versus personal property versus intellectual property) will often have different mechanisms of transfer.

In a sale of assets, the shareholders of the Target corporation are entitled to vote on a sale of all, or substantially all, the assets. (There might be some debate as to what constitutes "substantially all" of the assets, but generally sales in excess of 75% of the assets will qualify.) In Delaware, the shareholders of the Acquirer corporation are not entitled to vote on such transactions, but some other states do allow shareholders in the Acquirer corporation to vote on transactions involving the sale (albeit from the Acquirer's perspective the purchase) of substantially all of the Target's assets. Although Delaware does not provide dissenting shareholders in the Target corporation with appraisal rights in a sale of assets transaction some other states do provide such right. In contrast, dissenting shareholders in the Acquirer corporation are not entitled to appraisal rights in asset sales. At least in theory, the Acquiring corporation will obtain the Target corporation's assets but not its liabilities. However, students should be aware that there are certain circumstances in which an increasing number of rules and legal doctrines can create successor liability for the Acquirer, making it more difficult, but not impossible to avoid prior liabilities.

Sale of Stock

A sale of stock is very similar to a sale of assets, however, in a sale of stock, the Target corporation provides stock instead of assets. As a result, the Target corporation becomes a subsidiary of the Acquirer corporation, so there are two "surviving" corporations instead of one.

Typically, in a sale of stock the consideration from the Acquirer is paid to the Target's shareholders in exchange for their ownership interest in the Target. Like a sale of assets, the Target corporation's shareholders will be entitled to vote and to have appraisal rights, and the Acquirer corporation's shareholders will only have these rights in a few states. However, the treatment of the liabilities of the Target corporation is different in a sale of stock than it is in a sale of assets. Because the Target corporation survives, so do its liabilities. However, those liabilities will likely be limited to the assets of the Target corporation. So, unless a creditor can pierce the corporate veil of the Target corporation or make a claim of some improper distribution to the Acquirer corporation, there should be some protection for the Acquirer corporation from the liabilities of Target corporation.

Triangular Mergers

The above forms merely represent the simplest forms of such transactions. Firms often enter into more complex transactions for a variety of reasons. One hybrid form of acquisition is known as the triangular merger (or a reverse triangular merger). In this structure, the Acquiring corporation firm forms a subsidiary. The subsidiary is funded with cash and/or stock that will serve as the consideration for the eventual merger. Then the subsidiary is merged with the Target. So, Target becomes a subsidiary of the Acquirer, and the shareholders of the Target corporation get stock and/or cash. If the Target corporation's shareholders receive some of the Acquirer's stock as part of the transaction, then they become shareholders in the Acquirer. When this structure is used, if the subsidiary of the Acquirer corporation survives, then it is called a "Triangular Merger." If the Target Corporation survives, then it is called a "Reverse Triangular Merger."

Triangular mergers represent an effort to capture the benefits of both a statutory merger and a sale of stock. Since the Acquirer corporation is typically the sole shareholder of its subsidiary, the Acquirer corporation's board of directors makes all decisions about the merger. The Acquirer corporation's shareholders neither vote nor receive appraisal rights since they are one step removed from the transaction. Of course, the Target corporation's shareholders still get to vote and receive appraisal rights, as provided by applicable state law. With regard to liability, as in a sale of stock, the Target corporation remains a wholly owned subsidiary of the Acquirer corporation. As a result, unless the Acquirer subsequently merges the Target subsidiary into the Acquirer, any liabilities of the Target would not become liabilities of the Acquirer, unless a creditor can pierce the Target corporation's corporate veil or make a claim of some improper distribution to the Acquirer corporation.

B. The De Facto Merger Doctrine

One of the big debates that can arise over the form of a business combination is about how much the form of the transaction should matter. Shareholders are often angry and frustrated when a company manipulates the form of the transaction to avoid a shareholder vote or to avoid appraisal rights. The *de facto* merger doctrine involves focusing on the substance of the transaction, rather than the form. The doctrine is applied in the following case.

Farris v. Glen Alden Corporation

393 Pa. 427, 143 A.2d 25 (Pa. 1958)

COHEN, J.:

We are required to determine on this appeal whether, as a result of a "Reorganization Agreements" executed by the officers of Glen Alden Corporation and List Industries Corporation, and approved by the shareholders of the former company, the rights and remedies of a dissenting shareholder accrue to the plaintiff.

Glen Alden is a Pennsylvania corporation engaged principally in the mining of anthracite coal and lately in the manufacture of air conditioning units and firefighting equipment. In recent years the company's operating revenue has declined substantially, and in fact, its coal operations have resulted in tax loss carry overs of approximately $14,000,000. In October 1957, List, a Delaware holding company owning interests in motion picture theaters, textile companies and real estate, and to a lesser extent, in oil and gas operations, warehouses and aluminum piston manufacturing, purchased through a wholly owned subsidiary

38.5% of Glen Alden's outstanding stock.[1] This acquisition enabled List to place three of its directors on the Glen Alden board.

On March 20, 1958, the two corporations entered into a "reorganization agreement," subject to stockholder approval, which contemplated the following actions:

1. Glen Alden is to acquire all of the assets of List, excepting a small amount of cash reserved for the payment of List's expenses in connection with the transaction. These assets include over $8,000,000 in cash held chiefly in the treasuries of List's wholly owned subsidiaries.

2. In consideration of the transfer, Glen Alden is to issue 3,621,703 shares of stock to List. List in turn is to distribute the stock to its shareholders at a ratio of five shares of Glen Alden stock for each six shares of List stock. . . .

3. Further, Glen Alden is to assume all of List's liabilities including a $5,000,000 note incurred by List in order to purchase Glen Alden stock in 1957, outstanding stock options, incentive stock options plans, and pension obligations.

4. Glen Alden is to change its corporate name from Glen Alden Corporation to List Alden Corporation.

5. The present directors of both corporations are to become directors of List Alden.

6. List is to be dissolved and List Alden is to then carry on the operations of both former corporations.

Two days after the agreement was executed notice of the annual meeting of Glen Alden to be held on April 11, 1958, was mailed to the shareholders together with a proxy statement analyzing the reorganization agreement and recommending its approval as well as approval of certain amendments to Glen Alden's articles of incorporation and bylaws necessary to implement the agreement. At this meeting the holders of a majority of the outstanding shares (not including those owned by List), voted in favor of a resolution approving the reorganization agreement.

On the day of the shareholders' meeting, plaintiff, a shareholder of Glen Alden, filed a complaint in equity against the corporation and its officers seeking

1 Of the purchase price of $8,719,109, $5,000,000 was borrowed.

to enjoin them temporarily until final hearing, and perpetually thereafter, from executing and carrying out the agreement.

The gravamen of the complaint was that the notice of the annual shareholders' meeting did not conform to the requirements of the Business Corporation Law in three respects: (1) It did not give notice to the shareholders that the true intent and purpose of the meeting was to effect a merger or consolidation of Glen Alden and List; (2) It failed to give notice to the shareholders of their right to dissent to the plan of merger or consolidation and claim fair value for their shares, and (3) It did not contain copies of the text of certain sections of the Business Corporation Law as required.[3]

By reason of these omissions, plaintiff contended that the approval of the reorganization agreement by the shareholders at the annual meeting was invalid and unless the carrying out of the plan were enjoined, he would suffer irreparable loss by being deprived of substantial property rights.

The defendants answered admitting the material allegations of fact in the complaint but denying that they gave rise to a cause of action because the transaction complained of was a purchase of corporate assets as to which shareholders had no rights of dissent or appraisal. For these reasons the defendants then moved for judgment on the pleadings.[5]

The court below concluded that the reorganization agreement entered into between the two corporations was a plan for a *de facto* merger, and that therefore the failure of the notice of the annual meeting to conform to the pertinent requirements of the merger provisions of the Business Corporation Law rendered the notice defective and all proceedings in furtherance of the agreement void. Wherefore, the court entered a final decree denying defendants' motion for judgment on the pleadings, entering judgment upon plaintiff's complaint and granting the injunctive relief therein sought. This appeal followed.

When use of the corporate form of business organization first became widespread, it was relatively easy for courts to define a "merger" or a "sale of

---

[3] The proxy statement included the following declaration: "Appraisal Rights.

In the opinion of counsel, the shareholders of neither Glen Alden nor List Industries will have any rights of appraisal or similar rights of dissenters with respect to any matter to be acted upon at their respective meetings."

[5] Counsel for the defendants concedes that if the corporation is required to pay the dissenting shareholders the appraised fair value of their shares, the resultant drain of cash would prevent Glen Alden from carrying out the agreement. On the other hand, plaintiff contends that if the shareholders had been told of their rights as dissenters, rather than specifically advised that they had no such rights, the resolution approving the reorganization agreement would have been defeated.

assets" and to label a particular transaction as one or the other. [*Citations omitted.*] But prompted by the desire to avoid the impact of adverse, and to obtain the benefits of favorable, government regulations, particularly federal tax laws, new accounting and legal techniques were developed by lawyers and accountants which interwove the elements characteristic of each, thereby creating hybrid forms of corporate amalgamation. Thus, it is no longer helpful to consider an individual transaction in the abstract and solely by reference to the various elements therein determine whether it is a "merger" or a "sale". Instead, to determine properly the nature of a corporate transaction, we must refer not only to all the provisions of the agreement, but also to the consequences of the transaction and to the purposes of the provisions of the corporation law said to be applicable. We shall apply this principle to the instant case.

Section 908A of the Pennsylvania Business Corporation Law provides: "If any shareholder of a domestic corporation which becomes a party to a plan of merger or consolidation shall object to such plan of merger or consolidation . . . such shareholder shall be entitled to . . . [the fair value of his shares upon surrender of the share certificate or certificates representing his shares]." [*Citations omitted.*]

This provision had its origin in the early decision of this Court in *Lauman v. The Lebanon Valley R.R. Co.,* 30 Pa. 42 (1858). There a shareholder who objected to the consolidation of his company with another was held to have a right in the absence of statute to treat the consolidation as a dissolution of his company and to receive the value of his shares upon their surrender.

The rationale of the *Lauman* case, and of the present section of the Business Corporation Law based thereon, is that when a corporation combines with another so as to lose its essential nature and alter the original fundamental relationships of the shareholders among themselves and to the corporation, a shareholder who does not wish to continue his membership therein may treat his membership in the original corporation as terminated and have the value of his shares paid to him. [*Citations omitted.*]

Does the combination outlined in the present "reorganization" agreement so fundamentally change the corporate character of Glen Alden and the interest of the plaintiff as a shareholder therein, that to refuse him the rights and remedies of a dissenting shareholder would in reality force him to give up his stock in one corporation and against his will accept shares in another? If so, the combination is a merger within the meaning of section 908A of the corporation law. [*Citations omitted.*]

If the reorganization agreement were consummated plaintiff would find that the "List Alden" resulting from the amalgamation would be quite a different corporation than the "Glen Alden" in which he is now a shareholder. Instead of continuing primarily as a coal mining company, Glen Alden would be transformed, after amendment of its articles of incorporation, into a diversified holding company whose interests would range from motion picture theaters to textile companies. Plaintiff would find himself a member of a company with assets of $169,000,000 and a long-term debt of $38,000,000 in lieu of a company one-half the size and with but one-seventh the long-term debt.

While the administration of the operations, and properties of Glen Alden as well List would be in the hands of management common to both companies, since all executives of List would be retained in List Alden, the control of Glen Alden would pass to the directors of List; for List would hold eleven of the seventeen directorships on the new board of directors.

As an aftermath of the transaction plaintiff's proportionate interest in Glen Alden would have been reduced to only two-fifths of what it presently is because of the issuance of an additional 3,621,703 shares to List which would not be subject to pre-emptive rights. In fact, ownership of Glen Alden would pass to the stockholders of List who would hold 76.5% of the outstanding shares as compared with but 23.5% retained by the present Glen Alden shareholders.

Perhaps the most important consequence to the plaintiff, if he were denied the right to have his shares redeemed at their fair value, would be the serious financial loss suffered upon consummation of the agreement. While the present book value of his stock is $38 a share after combination it would be worth only $21 a share. In contrast, the shareholders of List who presently hold stock with a total book value of $33,000,000 or $7.50 a share, would receive stock with a book value of $76,000,000, or $21 a share.

Under these circumstances it may well be said that if the proposed combination is allowed to take place without right of dissent, plaintiff would have his stock in Glen Alden taken away from him and the stock of a new company thrust upon him in its place. He would be projected against his will into a new enterprise under terms not of his own choosing. It was to protect dissident shareholders against just such a result that this Court one hundred years ago in the *Lauman* case, and the legislature thereafter in section 908A, granted the right of dissent. And it is to accord that protection to the plaintiff that we conclude that the combination proposed in the case at hand is a merger within the intendment of section 908A.

Nevertheless, defendants contend that the 1957 amendments to sections 311 and 908 of the corporation law preclude us from reaching this result and require the entry of judgment in their favor. Subsection F of section 311 dealing with the voluntary transfer of corporate assets provides: "The shareholders of a business corporation which acquires by sale, lease or exchange all or substantially all of the property of another corporation by the issuance of stock, securities or otherwise shall not be entitled to the rights and remedies of dissenting shareholders . . . ." [*Citations omitted.*]

And the amendment to section 908 reads as follows: "The right of dissenting shareholders . . . shall not apply to the purchase by a corporation of assets whether or not the consideration therefor be money or property, real or personal, including shares or bonds or other evidences of indebtedness of such corporation. The shareholders of such corporation shall have no right to dissent from any such purchase." [*Citations omitted.*]

Defendants view these amendments as abridging the right of shareholders to dissent to a transaction between two corporations which involves a transfer of assets for a consideration even though the transfer has all the legal incidents of a merger. They claim that only if the merger is accomplished in accordance with the prescribed statutory procedure does the right of dissent accrue. In support of this position they cite to us the comment on the amendments by the Committee on Corporation Law of the Pennsylvania Bar Association, the committee which originally drafted these provisions. The comment states that the provisions were intended to overrule cases which granted shareholders the right to dissent to a sale of assets when accompanied by the legal incidents of a merger. *See* 62 Ann. Rep. Pa. Bar Ass'n. 277, 284 (1957).[7] Whatever may have been the intent of the *committee,* there is no evidence to indicate that the *legislature* intended the 1957 amendments to have the effect contended for. But furthermore, the language of these two provisions does not support the opinion

7 "The amendment to Section 311 expressly provides that a sale, lease or exchange of substantially all corporate assets in connection with its liquidation or dissolution is subject to the provisions of Article XI of the Act, and that no consent or authorization of shareholders other than what is required by Article XI is necessary. The recent decision in *Marks v. Autocar* Co., U.S.D.C.E.D. Pa., Civil Action No. 16075, is to the contrary. This amendment, together with the proposed amendment to Section 1104 expressly permitting the directors in liquidating the corporation to sell only such assets as may be required to pay its debts and distribute any assets remaining among shareholders (Section 1108B now so provides in the case of receivers) have the effect of overruling *Marks v. Autocar Co.* . . . which permits a shareholder dissenting from such a sale to obtain the fair value of his shares. The Marks case relied substantially on *Bloch v. Baldwin Locomotive Works, 75 D. & C. 24,* also believed to be an undesirable decision. That case permitted a holder of stock of a corporation which purchased for stock all the assets of another corporation to obtain the fair value of his shares. That case is also in effect overruled by the new Sections 311F and 908C." . . .

of the committee and is inapt to achieve any such purpose. The amendments of 1957 do not provide that a transaction between two corporations which has the effect of a merger but which includes a transfer of assets for consideration is to be exempt from the protective provisions of sections 908A and 515. They provide only that the shareholders of a corporation which acquires the property or purchases the assets of another corporation, *without more,* are not entitled to the right to dissent from the transaction. So, as in the present case, when as part of a transaction between two corporations, one corporation dissolves, its liabilities are assumed by the survivor, its executives and directors take over the management and control of the survivor, and, as consideration for the transfer, its stockholders acquire a majority of the shares of stock of the survivor, then the transaction is no longer simply a purchase of assets or acquisition of property to which sections 311F and 908C apply, but a merger governed by section 908A of the corporation law. To divest shareholders of their right of dissent under such circumstances would require express language which is absent from the 1957 amendments.

Even were we to assume that the combination provided for in the reorganization agreement is a "sale of assets" to which section 908A does not apply, it would avail the defendants nothing; we will not blind our eyes to the realities of the transaction. Despite the designation of the parties and the form employed, Glen Alden does not in fact acquire List, rather, List acquires Glen Alden, [*Citations omitted.*], and under section 311D[8] the right of dissent would remain with the shareholders of Glen Alden.

We hold that the combination contemplated by the reorganization agreement, although consummated by contract rather than in accordance with the statutory procedure, is a merger within the protective purview of sections 908A and 515 of the corporation law. The shareholders of Glen Alden should have been notified accordingly and advised of their statutory rights of dissent and appraisal. The failure of the corporate officers to take these steps renders the stockholder approval of the agreement at the 1958 shareholders' meeting invalid. The lower court did not err in enjoining the officers and directors of Glen Alden from carrying out this agreement.

---

[8] "If any shareholder of a business corporation which sells, leases or exchanges all or substantially all of its property and assets otherwise than (1) in the usual and regular course of its business, (2) for the purpose of relocating its business, or (3) in connection with its dissolution and liquidation, shall object to such sale, lease or exchange and comply with the provisions of section 515 of this act, such shareholder shall be entitled to the rights and remedies of dissenting shareholders as therein provided." Act of July 11, 1957, P.L. 711, 15 P.S. § 2852–311D.

Delaware and a majority of jurisdictions do not recognize the *de facto* merger doctrine. (In fact, even Pennsylvania no longer recognizes the doctrine.) The cases from these jurisdictions generally take the position that states have different processes to achieve the same results and, as long as the process used is legal, courts should not recast the transactions, as that would only increase uncertainty and litigation. *See* the *Hariton v. Arco Electronics, Inc.* case that follows.

Hariton v. Arco Electronics, Inc.

41 Del. Ch. 74, 188 A.2d 123 (Del. 1963)

SOUTHERLAND, C. J.:

This case involves a sale of assets under *§ 271* of the corporation law, 8 Del. C. It presents for decision the question presented, but not decided, in *Heilbrunn v. Sun Chemical Corporation, 38 Del. Ch. 321, 150 A.2d 755*. It may be stated as follows:

A sale of assets is effected under *§ 271* in consideration of shares of stock of the purchasing corporation. The agreement of sale embodies also a plan to dissolve the selling corporation and distribute the shares so received to the stockholders of the seller, so as to accomplish the same result as would be accomplished by a merger of the seller into the purchaser. Is the sale legal?

The facts are these:

The defendant Arco and Loral Electronics Corporation, a New York corporation, are both engaged, in somewhat different forms, in the electronic equipment business. In the summer of 1961 they negotiated for an amalgamation of the companies. As of October 27, 1961, they entered into a "Reorganization Agreement and Plan." The provisions of this Plan pertinent here are in substance as follows:

1. Arco agrees to sell all its assets to Loral in consideration (*inter alia*) of the issuance to it of 283,000 shares of Loral.
2. Arco agrees to call a stockholders meeting for the purpose of approving the Plan and the voluntary dissolution.
3. Arco agrees to distribute to its stockholders all the Loral shares received by it as a part of the complete liquidation of Arco.

At the Arco meeting all the stockholders voting (about 80%) approved the Plan. It was thereafter consummated.

Plaintiff, a stockholder who did not vote at the meeting, sued to enjoin the consummation of the Plan on the grounds (1) that it was illegal, and (2) that it was unfair. The second ground was abandoned. Affidavits and documentary evidence were filed, and defendant moved for summary judgment and dismissal of the complaint. The Vice Chancellor granted the motion and plaintiff appeals.

The question before us we have stated above. Plaintiff's argument that the sale is illegal runs as follows:

The several steps taken here accomplish the same result as a merger of Arco into Loral. In a "true" sale of assets, the stockholder of the seller retains the right to elect whether the selling company shall continue as a holding company. Moreover, the stockholder of the selling company is forced to accept an investment in a new enterprise without the right of appraisal granted under the merger statute. *§ 271* cannot therefore be legally combined with a dissolution proceeding under *§ 275* and a consequent distribution of the purchaser's stock. Such a proceeding is a misuse of the power granted under *§ 271*, and a *de facto* merger results.

The foregoing is a brief summary of plaintiff's contention.

Plaintiff's contention that this sale has achieved the same result as a merger is plainly correct. The same contention was made to us in *Heilbrunn v. Sun Chemical Corporation,* 38 Del. Ch. 321, 150 A.2d 755. Accepting it as correct, we noted that this result is made possible by the overlapping scope of the merger statute and section 271, mentioned in *Sterling v. Mayflower Hotel Corporation,* 33 Del. Ch. 293, 93 A.2d 107, 38 A.L.R.2d 425. We also adverted to the increased use, in connection with corporate reorganization plans, of *§ 271* instead of the merger statute. Further, we observed that no Delaware case has held such procedure to be improper, and that two cases appear to assume its legality. . . .

We now hold that the reorganization here accomplished through § 271 and a mandatory plan of dissolution and distribution is legal. This is so because the sale-of-assets statute and the merger statute are independent of each other. They are, so to speak, of equal dignity, and the framers of a reorganization plan may resort to either type of corporate mechanics to achieve the desired end. This is not an anomalous result in our corporation law. As the Vice Chancellor pointed out, the elimination of accrued dividends, though forbidden under a charter amendment . . . may be accomplished by a merger. [*Citation omitted.*]

In *Langfelder v. Universal Laboratories, D.C.,* 68 F. Supp. 209, Judge Leahy commented upon "the general theory of the Delaware Corporation Law that action taken pursuant to the authority of the various sections of that law constitute acts of independent legal significance and their validity is not dependent on other sections of the Act." 68 F. Supp. at 211, footnote.

In support of his contentions of a *de facto* merger plaintiff cites *Finch v. Warrior Cement Corporation,* 16 Del. Ch. 44, 141 A. 54, and *Drug Inc. v. Hunt,* 35 Del. (5 Harr.) 339, 168 A. 87. They are patently inapplicable. Each involved a disregard of the statutory provisions governing sales of assets. Here it is admitted that the provisions of the statute were fully complied with.

Plaintiff concedes, as we read his brief, that if the several steps taken in this case had been taken separately they would have been legal. That is, he concedes that a sale of assets, followed by a separate proceeding to dissolve and distribute, would be legal, even though the same result would follow. This concession exposes the weakness of his contention. To attempt to make any such distinction between sales under *§ 271* would be to create uncertainty in the law and invite litigation.

We are in accord with the Vice Chancellor's ruling, and the judgment below is affirmed.

NOTES AND QUESTIONS

1. The preceding two cases highlight a frequently litigated issue regarding form versus substance, which often involves a debate of the difference between the language of a statute and the intent behind that statute. Regardless of which construct you prefer, a good attorney must be able to make both arguments. Can you think of other examples in the preceding materials when you have encountered a rule that applied form over substance and another instance in which the substance of activities was given more weight than form?

2. Consider how the transactions in the preceding cases were structured to achieve a certain result given the needs of the client. If the form of a transaction may be manipulated to circumvent statutory protections for shareholders, do those protections have any value?

3. How would you advise a client who was purchasing stock in a corporation and wanted to have a vote before the company was sold?

C. Freeze Out Mergers

Freeze out mergers (also sometimes called "cash-out" or "squeeze-out" mergers) are a process by which, in some states, a majority shareholder (or shareholders) may force the minority shareholders to sell their stock in a merger with, or acquisition by, an entity owned by the majority shareholder(s), enabling the majority shareholder(s) to acquire 100% control of the company. These transactions are often used following a tender offer in order to eliminate shareholders who did not tender their shares. A freeze out merger is also used when a controlling shareholder or group of shareholders wants to own all of the company. Sometimes these transactions are also the final stage in a process known as "taking a company private"—a process through which a publicly traded company becomes a closely held, "private" company. These transactions are usually structured as triangular mergers in which the controlling shareholder creates a subsidiary, and the subsidiary enters into a statutory merger with the Target company in which the acquiring shareholder has a controlling interest.

These transactions, of course, involve a conflict of interest. In most cases, the standard for reviewing a merger transaction involving a controlling shareholder with a conflict of interest has been is "entire fairness" (discussed in Chapters 5 and 6, *supra*). The entire fairness standard requires that the transaction must be accomplished by both a fair process and at a fair price. This standard means that as long as the majority shareholder effectuates the freeze out merger at a fair price and by a fair process, then the merger may proceed. Factors that courts might consider in evaluating whether a freeze out merger meets the test of entire fairness might include determining: whether an independent committee was appointed to negotiate on behalf of the minority shareholders; whether that committee was, in fact, independent, and whether there is evidence that it had true bargaining power; whether the price paid to the minority shareholders reflected the value of the minority shareholders' stock as a percentage of the value of the entire firm or whether it was based upon a "minority discount"; whether a thorough and complete "fairness opinion" was prepared; and whether the transaction was approved by a majority of the minority shareholders. Many of these elements are discussed in evaluating the fairness of the cash-out merger in the *Weinberger v. UOP, Inc.* case that follows.

Initially, the burden of proving that a merger transaction involving a controlling shareholder was entirely fair lies with the director defendants. However, this burden may be shifted from the defendant to the plaintiff when a transaction with a controlling shareholder (or any transaction involving a conflict of interest such as an uncleansed transaction with corporation officers or directors) is approved by a properly-functioning independent special committee ***or*** by a majority of the non-controlling/disinterested shareholders. Furthermore, Delaware courts recently have provided a mechanism for directors to obtain the benefit of the business judgment rule in a controlling stockholder merger, provided that the transaction has been both: (i) negotiated and approved by a special committee of independent directors fully empowered to say no, ***and*** (ii) approved by an uncoerced, fully informed vote of a majority of the minority shareholders. *In re MFW Shareholders Litigation*, 67 A.3d 496 (Del. Ch. 2013). The *MFW Shareholders Litigation* case (which immediately follows the *Weinberger* case below) provides an in-depth assessment by the Delaware Court of Chancery of a going-private transaction involving a controlling shareholder and includes a detailed discussion of the important features that are necessary for a special committee and a shareholder vote to obtain the business judgment rule standard of review.

Weinberger v. UOP, Inc.

457 A.2d 701 (Del. 1983)

MOORE, J.:

This post-trial appeal was reheard en banc from a decision of the Court of Chancery. It was brought by the class action plaintiff below, a former shareholder of UOP, Inc., who challenged the elimination of UOP's minority shareholders by a cash-out merger between UOP and its majority owner, The Signal Companies, Inc. . . . The present Chancellor held that the terms of the merger were fair to the plaintiff and the other minority shareholders of UOP. Accordingly, he entered judgment in favor of the defendants.

Numerous points were raised by the parties, but we address only the following questions presented by the trial court's opinion:

1) The plaintiff's duty to plead sufficient facts demonstrating the unfairness of the challenged merger;

2) The burden of proof upon the parties where the merger has been approved by the purportedly informed vote of a majority of the minority shareholders;

3) The fairness of the merger in terms of adequacy of the defendants' disclosures to the minority shareholders;

4) The fairness of the merger in terms of adequacy of the price paid for the minority shares and the remedy appropriate to that issue; and

5) The continued force and effect of *Singer v. Magnavox Co.,* Del. Supr., 380 A.2d 969, 980 (1977), and its progeny.

In ruling for the defendants, the Chancellor re-stated his earlier conclusion that the plaintiff in a suit challenging a cash-out merger must allege specific acts of fraud, misrepresentation, or other items of misconduct to demonstrate the unfairness of the merger terms to the minority. We approve this rule and affirm it.

The Chancellor also held that even though the ultimate burden of proof is on the majority shareholder to show by a preponderance of the evidence that the transaction is fair, it is first the burden of the plaintiff attacking the merger to demonstrate some basis for invoking the fairness obligation. We agree with that principle. However, where corporate action has been approved by an informed vote of a majority of the minority shareholders, we conclude that the burden entirely shifts to the plaintiff to show that the transaction was unfair to the minority. [*Citation omitted.*] But in all this, the burden clearly remains on those relying on the vote to show that they completely disclosed all material facts relevant to the transaction.

Here, the record does not support a conclusion that the minority stockholder vote was an informed one. Material information, necessary to acquaint those shareholders with the bargaining positions of Signal and UOP, was withheld under circumstances amounting to a breach of fiduciary duty. We therefore conclude that this merger does not meet the test of fairness, at least as we address that concept, and no burden thus shifted to the plaintiff by reason of the minority shareholder vote. Accordingly, we reverse and remand for further proceedings consistent herewith.

In considering the nature of the remedy available under our law to minority shareholders in a cash-out merger, we believe that it is, and hereafter should be, an appraisal under 8 Del. C. § 262 as hereinafter construed. . . . But to give full effect to section 262 within the framework of the General Corporation Law we adopt a more liberal, less rigid and stylized, approach to the valuation process than has heretofore been permitted by our courts. While the present state of these proceedings does not admit the plaintiff to the appraisal remedy per se, the practical effect of the remedy we do grant him will be co-extensive with the liberalized valuation and appraisal methods we herein approve for cases coming after this decision.

Our treatment of these matters has necessarily led us to a reconsideration of the business purpose rule announced in the trilogy of *Singer v. Magnavox Co., supra; Tanzer v. International General Industries, Inc.,* Del. Supr., 379 A.2d 1121 (1977); *and Roland International Corp. v. Najjar,* Del. Supr., 407 A.2d 1032 (1979). For the reasons hereafter set forth we consider that the business purpose requirement of these cases is no longer the law of Delaware.

I.

* * * *

Signal is a diversified, technically based company operating through various subsidiaries. Its stock is publicly traded on the New York, Philadelphia and Pacific Stock Exchanges. UOP, formerly known as Universal Oil Products Company, was a diversified industrial company engaged in various lines of business, including petroleum and petro-chemical services and related products, construction, fabricated metal products, transportation equipment products, chemicals and plastics, and other products and services including land development, lumber products and waste disposal. Its stock was publicly held and listed on the New York Stock Exchange.

In 1974 Signal sold one of its wholly-owned subsidiaries for $420,000,000 in cash. [*Citation omitted.*] While looking to invest this cash surplus, Signal became interested in UOP as a possible acquisition. Friendly negotiations ensued, and Signal proposed to acquire a controlling interest in UOP at a price of $19 per share. UOP's representatives sought $25 per share. In the arm's length bargaining that followed, an understanding was reached whereby Signal agreed to purchase from UOP 1,500,000 shares of UOP's authorized but unissued stock at $21 per share.

This purchase was contingent upon Signal making a successful cash tender offer for 4,300,000 publicly held shares of UOP, also at a price of $21 per share. This combined method of acquisition permitted Signal to acquire 5,800,000 shares of stock, representing 50.5% of UOP's outstanding shares. The UOP board of directors advised the company's shareholders that it had no objection to Signal's tender offer at that price. Immediately before the announcement of the tender offer, UOP's common stock had been trading on the New York Stock Exchange at a fraction under $14 per share.

The negotiations between Signal and UOP occurred during April 1975, and the resulting tender offer was greatly oversubscribed. However, Signal limited its total purchase of the tendered shares so that, when coupled with the stock bought from UOP, it had achieved its goal of becoming a 50.5% shareholder of UOP.

Although UOP's board consisted of thirteen directors, Signal nominated and elected only six. Of these, five were either directors or employees of Signal. The sixth, a partner in the banking firm of Lazard Freres & Co., had been one of Signal's representatives in the negotiations and bargaining with UOP concerning the tender offer and purchase price of the UOP shares.

However, the president and chief executive officer of UOP retired during 1975, and Signal caused him to be replaced by James V. Crawford, a long-time employee and senior executive vice president of one of Signal's wholly-owned subsidiaries. Crawford succeeded his predecessor on UOP's board of directors and also was made a director of Signal.

By the end of 1977 Signal basically was unsuccessful in finding other suitable investment candidates for its excess cash, and by February 1978 considered that it had no other realistic acquisitions available to it on a friendly basis. Once again its attention turned to UOP.

The trial court found that at the instigation of certain Signal management personnel, including William W. Walkup, its board chairman, and Forrest N. Shumway, its president, a feasibility study was made concerning the possible acquisition of the balance of UOP's outstanding shares. This study was performed by two Signal officers, Charles S. Arledge, vice president (director of planning), and Andrew J. Chitiea, senior vice president (chief financial officer). Messrs. Walkup, Shumway, Arledge and Chitiea were all directors of UOP in addition to their membership on the Signal board.

Arledge and Chitiea concluded that it would be a good investment for Signal to acquire the remaining 49.5% of UOP shares at any price up to $24 each. Their report was discussed between Walkup and Shumway who, along with Arledge, Chitiea and Brewster L. Arms, internal counsel for Signal, constituted Signal's senior management. In particular, they talked about the proper price to be paid if the acquisition was pursued, purportedly keeping in mind that as UOP's majority shareholder, Signal owed a fiduciary responsibility to both its own stockholders as well as to UOP's minority. It was ultimately agreed that a meeting of Signal's Executive Committee would be called to propose that Signal acquire the remaining outstanding stock of UOP through a cash-out merger in the range of $20 to $21 per share.

The Executive Committee meeting was set for February 28, 1978. As a courtesy, UOP's president, Crawford, was invited to attend, although he was not a member of Signal's executive committee. On his arrival, and prior to the meeting, Crawford was asked to meet privately with Walkup and Shumway. He was then told of Signal's plan to acquire full ownership of UOP and was asked for his reaction to the proposed price range of $20 to $21 per share. Crawford said he thought such a price would be "generous", and that it was certainly one which should be submitted to UOP's minority shareholders for their ultimate consideration. He stated, however, that Signal's 100% ownership could cause internal problems at UOP. He believed that employees would have to be given some assurance of their future place in a fully-owned Signal subsidiary. Otherwise, he feared the departure of essential personnel. Also, many of UOP's key employees had stock option incentive programs which would be wiped out by a merger. Crawford therefore urged that some adjustment would have to be made, such as providing a comparable incentive in Signal's shares, if after the merger he was to maintain his quality of personnel and efficiency at UOP.

Thus, Crawford voiced no objection to the $20 to $21 price range, nor did he suggest that Signal should consider paying more than $21 per share for the minority interests. Later, at the Executive Committee meeting the same factors were discussed, with Crawford repeating the position he earlier took with Walkup and Shumway. Also considered was the 1975 tender offer and the fact that it had been greatly oversubscribed at $21 per share. . . .

Thus, it was the consensus that a price of $20 to $21 per share would be fair to both Signal and the minority shareholders of UOP. Signal's executive committee authorized its management "to negotiate" with UOP "for a cash acquisition of the minority ownership in UOP, Inc., with the intention of presenting a proposal to [Signal's] board of directors . . . on March 6, 1978". Immediately after this February 28, 1978 meeting, Signal issued a press release stating:

> The Signal Companies, Inc. and UOP, Inc. are conducting negotiations for the acquisition for cash by Signal of the 49.5 per cent of UOP which it does not presently own. . . .
>
> Price and other terms of the proposed transaction have not yet been finalized and would be subject to approval of the boards of

directors of Signal and UOP, scheduled to meet early next week, the stockholders of UOP and certain federal agencies.

The announcement also referred to the fact that the closing price of UOP's common stock on that day was $14.50 per share.

Two days later, on March 2, 1978, Signal issued a second press release stating that its management would recommend a price in the range of $20 to $21 per share for UOP's 49.5% minority interest. . . .

Between Tuesday, February 28, 1978 and Monday, March 6, 1978, a total of four business days, Crawford spoke by telephone with all of UOP's non-Signal, i.e., outside, directors. Also during that period, Crawford retained Lehman Brothers to render a fairness opinion as to the price offered the minority for its stock. He gave two reasons for this choice. First, the time schedule between the announcement and the board meetings was short (by then only three business days) and since Lehman Brothers had been acting as UOP's investment banker for many years, Crawford felt that it would be in the best position to respond on such brief notice. Second, James W. Glanville, a long-time director of UOP and a partner in Lehman Brothers, had acted as a financial advisor to UOP for many years. Crawford believed that Glanville's familiarity with UOP, as a member of its board, would also be of assistance in enabling Lehman Brothers to render a fairness opinion within the existing time constraints.

Crawford telephoned Glanville, who gave his assurance that Lehman Brothers had no conflicts that would prevent it from accepting the task. Glanville's immediate personal reaction was that a price of $20 to $21 would certainly be fair, since it represented almost a 50% premium over UOP's market price. Glanville sought a $250,000 fee for Lehman Brothers' services, but Crawford thought this too much. After further discussions Glanville finally agreed that Lehman Brothers would render its fairness opinion for $150,000.

During this period Crawford also had several telephone contacts with Signal officials. In only one of them, however, was the price of the shares discussed. In a conversation with Walkup, Crawford advised that as a result of his communications with UOP's non-Signal directors, it was his feeling that the price would have to be the top of the proposed range, or $21 per share, if the approval of UOP's outside directors was to be obtained. But again, he did not seek any price higher than $21.

Glanville assembled a three-man Lehman Brothers team to do the work on the fairness opinion. These persons examined relevant documents and information concerning UOP, including its annual reports and its Securities and Exchange Commission filings from 1973 through 1976, as well as its audited financial statements for 1977, its interim reports to shareholders, and its recent and historical market prices and trading volumes. In addition, on Friday, March 3, 1978, two members of the Lehman Brothers team flew to UOP's headquarters in Des Plaines, Illinois, to perform a "due diligence" visit, during the course of which they interviewed Crawford as well as UOP's general counsel, its chief financial officer, and other key executives and personnel.

As a result, the Lehman Brothers team concluded that "the price of either $20 or $21 would be a fair price for the remaining shares of UOP". They telephoned this impression to Glanville, who was spending the weekend in Vermont.

On Monday morning, March 6, 1978, Glanville and the senior member of the Lehman Brothers team flew to Des Plaines to attend the scheduled UOP directors meeting. Glanville looked over the assembled information during the flight. The two had with them the draft of a "fairness opinion letter" in which the price had been left blank. Either during or immediately prior to the directors' meeting, the two-page "fairness opinion letter" was typed in final form and the price of $21 per share was inserted.

On March 6, 1978, both the Signal and UOP boards were convened to consider the proposed merger. Telephone communications were maintained between the two meetings. Walkup, Signal's board chairman, and also a UOP director, attended UOP's meeting with Crawford in order to present Signal's position and answer any questions that UOP's non-Signal directors might have. Arledge and Chitiea, along with Signal's other designees on UOP's board, participated by conference telephone. . . .

First, Signal's board unanimously adopted a resolution authorizing Signal to propose to UOP a cash merger of $21 per share as outlined in a certain merger agreement and other supporting documents. This proposal required that the merger be approved by a majority of UOP's outstanding minority shares voting at the stockholders meeting at which the merger would be considered, and that the minority shares voting in favor of the merger, when coupled with Signal's 50.5% interest would have to comprise at least two-thirds of all UOP shares. Otherwise the proposed merger would be deemed disapproved.

UOP's board then considered the proposal. Copies of the agreement were delivered to the directors in attendance, and other copies had been forwarded earlier to the directors participating by telephone. They also had before them

UOP financial data for 1974–1977, UOP's most recent financial statements, market price information, and budget projections for 1978. In addition they had Lehman Brothers' hurriedly prepared fairness opinion letter finding the price of $21 to be fair. Glanville, the Lehman Brothers partner, and UOP director, commented on the information that had gone into preparation of the letter.

Signal also suggests that the Arledge-Chitiea feasibility study, indicating that a price of up to $24 per share would be a "good investment" for Signal, was discussed at the UOP directors' meeting. The Chancellor made no such finding, and our independent review of the record, detailed *infra,* satisfies us by a preponderance of the evidence that there was no discussion of this document at UOP's board meeting. Furthermore, it is clear beyond peradventure that nothing in that report was ever disclosed to UOP's minority shareholders prior to their approval of the merger.

After consideration of Signal's proposal, Walkup and Crawford left the meeting to permit a free and uninhibited exchange between UOP's non-Signal directors. Upon their return a resolution to accept Signal's offer was then proposed and adopted. While Signal's men on UOP's board participated in various aspects of the meeting, they abstained from voting. However, the minutes show that each of them "if voting would have voted yes".

On March 7, 1978, UOP sent a letter to its shareholders advising them of the action taken by UOP's board with respect to Signal's offer. This document pointed out, among other things, that on February 28, 1978 "both companies had announced negotiations were being conducted".

Despite the swift board action of the two companies, the merger was not submitted to UOP's shareholders until their annual meeting on May 26, 1978. In the notice of that meeting and proxy statement sent to shareholders in May, UOP's management and board urged that the merger be approved. The proxy statement also advised:

> The price was determined after *discussions* between James V. Crawford, a director of Signal and Chief Executive Officer of UOP, and officers of Signal which took place during meetings on February 28, 1978, and in the course of several subsequent telephone conversations. (Emphasis added.)

In the original draft of the proxy statement the word "negotiations" had been used rather than "discussions". However, when the Securities and Exchange Commission sought details of the "negotiations" as part of its review of these materials, the term was deleted and the word "discussions" was substituted. The proxy statement indicated that the vote of UOP's board in approving the merger had been unanimous. It also advised the shareholders that Lehman Brothers had given its opinion that the merger price of $21 per share was fair to UOP's minority. However, it did not disclose the hurried method by which this conclusion was reached.

As of the record date of UOP's annual meeting, there were 11,488,302 shares of UOP common stock outstanding, 5,688,302 of which were owned by the minority. At the meeting only 56%, or 3,208,652, of the minority shares were voted. Of these, 2,953,812, or 51.9% of the total minority, voted for the merger, and 254,840 voted against it. When Signal's stock was added to the minority shares voting in favor, a total of 76.2% of UOP's outstanding shares approved the merger while only 2.2% opposed it.

By its terms the merger became effective on May 26, 1978, and each share of UOP's stock held by the minority was automatically converted into a right to receive $21 cash.

II.

A.

A primary issue mandating reversal is the preparation by two UOP directors, Arledge and Chitiea, of their feasibility study for the exclusive use and benefit of Signal. This document was of obvious significance to both Signal and UOP. Using UOP data, it described the advantages to Signal of ousting the minority at a price range of $21–$24 per share. Mr. Arledge, one of the authors, outlined the benefits to Signal [The parentheses indicate . . . handwritten comments of Mr. Arledge]:

Purpose Of The Merger

1) Provides an outstanding investment opportunity for Signal—(Better than any recent acquisition we have seen.)

2) Increases Signal's earnings.

3) Facilitates the flow of resources between Signal and its subsidiaries—(Big factor—works both ways.)

4) Provides cost savings potential for Signal and UOP.

5) Improves the percentage of Signal's 'operating earnings' as opposed to 'holding company earnings'.

6) Simplifies the understanding of Signal.

7) Facilitates technological exchange among Signal's subsidiaries.

8) Eliminates potential conflicts of interest.

Having written those words, solely for the use of Signal, it is clear from the record that neither Arledge nor Chitiea shared this report with their fellow directors of UOP. We are satisfied that no one else did either. This conduct hardly meets the fiduciary standards applicable to such a transaction. While Mr. Walkup, Signal's chairman of the board and a UOP director, attended the March 6, 1978 UOP board meeting and testified at trial that he had discussed the Arledge-Chitiea report with the UOP directors at this meeting, the record does not support this assertion. Perhaps it is the result of some confusion on Mr. Walkup's part. In any event Mr. Shumway, Signal's president, testified that he made sure the Signal outside directors had this report prior to the March 6, 1978 Signal board meeting, but he did not testify that the Arledge-Chitiea report was also sent to UOP's outside directors.

Mr. Crawford, UOP's president, could not recall that any documents, other than a draft of the merger agreement, were sent to UOP's directors before the March 6, 1978 UOP meeting. Mr. Chitiea, an author of the report, testified that it was made available to Signal's directors, but to his knowledge it was not circulated to the outside directors of UOP. He specifically testified that he "didn't share" that information with the outside directors of UOP with whom he served.

* * * *

Actually, it appears that a three-page summary of figures was given to all UOP directors. Its first page is identical to one page of the Arledge-Chitiea report, but this dealt with nothing more than a justification of the $21 price. Significantly, the contents of this three-page summary are what the minutes reflect Mr. Walkup told the UOP board. However, nothing contained in either the minutes or this three-page summary reflects Signal's study regarding the $24 price.

The Arledge-Chitiea report speaks for itself in supporting the Chancellor's finding that a price of up to $24 was a "good investment" for Signal. It shows that a return on the investment at $21 would be 15.7% versus 15.5% at $24 per share. This was a difference of only two-tenths of one percent, while it meant over $17,000,000 to the minority. Under such circumstances, paying UOP's minority shareholders $24 would have had relatively little long-term effect on Signal, and the Chancellor's findings concerning the benefit to Signal, even at a price of $24, were obviously correct. *Levitt v. Bouvier, Del. Supr., 287 A.2d 671, 673 (1972).*

Certainly, this was a matter of material significance to UOP and its shareholders. Since the study was prepared by two UOP directors, using UOP information for the exclusive benefit of Signal, and nothing whatever was done to disclose it to the outside UOP directors or the minority shareholders, a question of breach of fiduciary duty arises. This problem occurs because there were common Signal-UOP directors participating, at least to some extent, in the UOP board's decision-making processes without full disclosure of the conflicts they faced.[7]

B.

In assessing this situation, the Court of Chancery was required to:

> examine what information defendants had and to measure it against what they gave to the minority stockholders, in a context in which 'complete candor' is required. In other words, the limited function of the Court was to determine whether defendants had disclosed all information in their possession germane to the transaction in issue. And by 'germane' we mean, for present purposes, information such as a reasonable shareholder would consider important in deciding whether to sell or retain stock.
>
> * * *
>
> . . . Completeness, not adequacy, is both the norm and the mandate under present circumstances.

Lynch v. Vickers Energy Corp., Del. Supr., 383 A.2d 278, 281 (1977) *(Lynch I).*

This is merely stating in another way the long-existing principle of Delaware law that these Signal designated directors on UOP's board still owed UOP and its shareholders an uncompromising duty of loyalty. The classic language of *Guth v. Loft, Inc.,* Del. Supr., 23 Del. Ch. 255, 5 A.2d 503, 510 (1939), requires no embellishment:

---

[7] Although perfection is not possible, or expected, the result here could have been entirely different if UOP had appointed an independent negotiating committee of its outside directors to deal with Signal at arm's length. . . . Since fairness in this context can be equated to conduct by a theoretical, wholly independent, board of directors acting upon the matter before them, it is unfortunate that this course apparently was neither considered nor pursued. . . . Particularly in a parent-subsidiary context, a showing that the action taken was as though each of the contending parties had in fact exerted its bargaining power against the other at arm's length is strong evidence that the transaction meets the test of fairness. . . .

> A public policy, existing through the years, and derived from a profound knowledge of human characteristics and motives, has established a rule that demands of a corporate officer or director, peremptorily and inexorably, the most scrupulous observance of his duty, not only affirmatively to protect the interests of the corporation committed to his charge, but also to refrain from doing anything that would work injury to the corporation, or to deprive it of profit or advantage which his skill and ability might properly bring to it, or to enable it to make in the reasonable and lawful exercise of its powers. The rule that requires an undivided and unselfish loyalty to the corporation demands that there shall be no conflict between duty and self-interest.

Given the absence of any attempt to structure this transaction on an arm's length basis, Signal cannot escape the effects of the conflicts it faced, particularly when its designees on UOP's board did not totally abstain from participation in the matter. There is no "safe harbor" for such divided loyalties in Delaware. When directors of a Delaware corporation are on both sides of a transaction, they are required to demonstrate their utmost good faith and the most scrupulous inherent fairness of the bargain. [*Citation omitted.*] The requirement of fairness is unflinching in its demand that where one stands on both sides of a transaction, he has the burden of establishing its entire fairness, sufficient to pass the test of careful scrutiny by the courts. [*Citations omitted.*]

There is no dilution of this obligation where one holds dual or multiple directorships, as in a parent-subsidiary context. [*Citation omitted.*] Thus, individuals who act in a dual capacity as directors of two corporations, one of whom is parent and the other subsidiary, owe the same duty of good management to both corporations, and in the absence of an independent negotiating structure (see note 7, *supra*), or the directors' total abstention from any participation in the matter, this duty is to be exercised in light of what is best for both companies. [*Citation omitted.*] The record demonstrates that Signal has not met this obligation.

C.

The concept of fairness has two basic aspects: fair dealing and fair price. The former embraces questions of when the transaction was timed, how it was initiated, structured, negotiated, disclosed to the directors, and how the approvals of the directors and the stockholders were obtained. The latter aspect of fairness relates to the economic and financial considerations of the proposed merger, including all relevant factors: assets, market value, earnings, future prospects, and any other elements that affect the intrinsic or inherent value of a company's stock. [*Citations omitted.*] However, the test for fairness is not a bifurcated one as between fair dealing and price. All aspects of the issue must be examined as a whole since the question is one of entire fairness. However, in a non-fraudulent transaction we recognize that price may be the preponderant consideration outweighing other features of the merger. Here, we address the two basic aspects of fairness separately because we find reversible error as to both.

D.

Part of fair dealing is the obvious duty of candor required by *Lynch I, supra.* Moreover, one possessing superior knowledge may not mislead any stockholder by use of corporate information to which the latter is not privy. [*Citation omitted.*] Delaware has long imposed this duty even upon persons who are not corporate officers or directors, but who nonetheless are privy to matters of interest or significance to their company. *Brophy v. Cities Service Co.,* Del. Ch., 31 Del. Ch. 241, 70 A.2d 5, 7 (1949). With the well-established Delaware law on the subject, and the Court of Chancery's findings of fact here, it is inevitable that the obvious conflicts posed by Arledge and Chitiea's preparation of their "feasibility study", derived from UOP information, for the sole use and benefit of Signal, cannot pass muster.

The Arledge-Chitiea report is but one aspect of the element of fair dealing. How did this merger evolve? It is clear that it was entirely initiated by Signal. The serious time constraints under which the principals acted were all set by Signal. It had not found a suitable outlet for its excess cash and considered UOP a desirable investment, particularly since it was now in a position to acquire the whole company for itself. For whatever reasons, and they were only Signal's, the entire transaction was presented to and approved by UOP's board within four business days. Standing alone, this is not necessarily indicative of any lack of fairness by a majority shareholder. It was what occurred, or more properly, what did not occur, during this brief period that makes the time constraints imposed by Signal relevant to the issue of fairness.

The structure of the transaction, again, was Signal's doing. So far as negotiations were concerned, it is clear that they were modest at best. Crawford, Signal's man at UOP, never really talked price with Signal, except to accede to its management's statements on the subject, and to convey to Signal the UOP outside directors' view that as between the $20–$21 range under consideration, it would have to be $21. The latter is not a surprising outcome, but hardly arm's length negotiations. Only the protection of benefits for UOP's key employees and the issue of Lehman Brothers' fee approached any concept of bargaining.

As we have noted, the matter of disclosure to the UOP directors was wholly flawed by the conflicts of interest raised by the Arledge-Chitiea report. All of those conflicts were resolved by Signal in its own favor without divulging any aspect of them to UOP.

This cannot but undermine a conclusion that this merger meets any reasonable test of fairness. The outside UOP directors lacked one material piece of information generated by two of their colleagues, but shared only with Signal. True, the UOP board had the Lehman Brothers' fairness opinion, but that firm has been blamed by the plaintiff for the hurried task it performed, when more properly the responsibility for this lies with Signal. There was no disclosure of the circumstances surrounding the rather cursory preparation of the Lehman Brothers' fairness opinion. Instead, the impression was given UOP's minority that a careful study had been made, when in fact speed was the hallmark, and Mr. Glanville, Lehman's partner in charge of the matter, and also a UOP director, having spent the weekend in Vermont, brought a draft of the "fairness opinion letter" to the UOP directors' meeting on March 6, 1978 with the price left blank. We can only conclude from the record that the rush imposed on Lehman Brothers by Signal's timetable contributed to the difficulties under which this investment banking firm attempted to perform its responsibilities. Yet, none of this was disclosed to UOP's minority.

Finally, the minority stockholders were denied the critical information that Signal considered a price of $24 to be a good investment. Since this would have meant over $17,000,000 more to the minority, we cannot conclude that the shareholder vote was an informed one. Under the circumstances, an approval by a majority of the minority was meaningless. [*Citations omitted.*]

Given these particulars and the Delaware law on the subject, the record does not establish that this transaction satisfies any reasonable concept of fair dealing, and the Chancellor's findings in that regard must be reversed.

E.

Turning to the matter of price, plaintiff also challenges its fairness. His evidence was that on the date the merger was approved the stock was worth at least $26 per share. In support, he offered the testimony of a chartered investment analyst who used two basic approaches to valuation: a comparative analysis of the premium paid over market in ten other tender offer-merger combinations, and a discounted cash flow analysis.

In this breach of fiduciary duty case, the Chancellor perceived that the approach to valuation was the same as that in an appraisal proceeding. Consistent with precedent, he rejected plaintiff's method of proof and accepted defendants' evidence of value as being in accord with practice under prior case law. This means that the so-called "Delaware block" or weighted average method was employed wherein the elements of value, i.e., assets, market price, earnings, etc., were assigned a particular weight and the resulting amounts added to determine the value per share. This procedure has been in use for decades. [*Citations omitted.*] However, to the extent it excludes other generally accepted techniques used in the financial community and the courts, it is now clearly outmoded. It is time we recognize this in appraisal and other stock valuation proceedings and bring our law current on the subject.

. . . . We believe that a more liberal approach [for determining the value of a company's stock] must include proof of value by any techniques or methods which are generally considered acceptable in the financial community and otherwise admissible in court, subject only to our interpretation of 8 Del. C. § 262(h), *infra. See also* D.R.E. 702–05. This will obviate the very structured and mechanistic procedure that has heretofore governed such matters. . . .

Fair price obviously requires consideration of all relevant factors involving the value of a company. This has long been the law of Delaware as stated in *Tri-Continental Corp.,* 74 A.2d at 72:

> The basic concept of value under the appraisal statute is that the stockholder is entitled to be paid for that which has been taken from him, viz., his proportionate interest in a going concern. By value of the stockholder's proportionate interest in the corporate enterprise is meant the true or intrinsic value of his stock which has been taken by the merger. In determining what figure represents this true or intrinsic value, the appraiser and the courts must take into consideration all factors and elements which reasonably might enter into the fixing of value. Thus, market value, asset value, dividends, earning prospects, the nature of the enterprise and any other facts which were known or which could be ascertained as of the date of merger and which throw any light on *future prospects* of the merged corporation are not only pertinent to an inquiry as to the value of the dissenting stockholders' interest, but must be *considered* by the agency fixing the value. (Emphasis added.)

This is not only in accord with the realities of present day affairs, but it is thoroughly consonant with the purpose and intent of our statutory law. . . .

It is significant that section 262 now mandates the determination of "fair" value based upon "all relevant factors". Only the speculative elements of value that may arise from the "accomplishment or expectation" of the merger are excluded. We take this to be a very narrow exception to the appraisal process, designed to eliminate use of *pro forma* data and projections of a speculative variety relating to the completion of a merger. But elements of future value, including the nature of the enterprise, which are known or susceptible of proof as of the date of the merger and not the product of speculation, may be considered. When the trial court deems it appropriate, fair value also includes any damages, resulting from the taking, which the stockholders sustain as a class. If that was not the case, then the obligation to consider "all relevant factors" in the valuation process would be eroded. We are supported in this view not only by *Tri-Continental Corp.,* 74 A.2d at 72, but also by the evolutionary amendments to section 262.

* * * *

Although the Chancellor received the plaintiff's evidence, his opinion indicates that the use of it was precluded because of past Delaware practice. While we do not suggest a monetary result one way or the other, we do think the plaintiff's evidence should be part of the factual mix and weighed as such. Until the $21 price is measured on remand by the valuation standards mandated by Delaware law, there can be no finding at the present stage of these proceedings that the price is fair. Given the lack of any candid disclosure of the material facts surrounding establishment of the $21 price, the majority of the minority vote, approving the merger, is meaningless.

The plaintiff has not sought an appraisal, but rescissory damages of the type contemplated by *Lynch v. Vickers Energy Corp.,* Del. Supr., 429 A.2d 497, 505–06 (1981) *(Lynch II).* In view of the approach to valuation that we announce today, we see no basis in our law for *Lynch II's* exclusive monetary formula for relief. On remand the plaintiff will be permitted to test the fairness of the $21 price by the standards we herein establish, in conformity with the principle applicable to an appraisal—that fair value be determined by taking "into account all relevant factors" . . . . In our view this includes the elements of rescissory damages if the Chancellor considers them susceptible of proof and a remedy appropriate to all the issues of fairness before him. To the extent that *Lynch II,* 429 A.2d at 505–06, purports to limit the Chancellor's discretion to a single remedial formula for monetary damages in a cash-out merger, it is overruled.

While a plaintiff's monetary remedy ordinarily should be confined to the more liberalized appraisal proceeding herein established, we do not intend any limitation on the historic powers of the Chancellor to grant such other relief as the facts of a particular case may dictate. The appraisal remedy we approve may not be adequate in certain cases, particularly where fraud, misrepresentation, self-dealing, deliberate waste of corporate assets, or gross and palpable overreaching are involved. [*Citation omitted.*] Under such circumstances, the Chancellor's powers are complete to fashion any form of equitable and monetary relief as may be appropriate, including rescissory damages. Since it is apparent that this long completed transaction is too involved to undo, and in view of the Chancellor's discretion, the award, if any, should be in the form of monetary damages based upon entire fairness standards, i.e., fair dealing and fair price.

. . . . [T]he provisions of 8 Del. C. § 262, as herein construed, respecting the scope of an appraisal and the means for perfecting the same, shall govern the financial remedy available to minority shareholders in a cash-out merger. . . .

III.

Finally, we address the matter of business purpose. The defendants contend that the purpose of this merger was not a proper subject of inquiry by the trial court. The plaintiff says that no valid purpose existed—the entire transaction was a mere subterfuge designed to eliminate the minority. The Chancellor ruled otherwise, but in so doing he clearly circumscribed the thrust and effect of *Singer*. *Weinberger v. UOP,* 426 A.2d at 1342–43, 1348–50. This has led to the thoroughly sound observation that the business purpose test "may be . . . virtually interpreted out of existence, as it was in *Weinberger*".

The requirement of a business purpose is new to our law of mergers and was a departure from prior case law. [*Citation omitted.*]

In view of the fairness test which has long been applicable to parent-subsidiary mergers, . . . the expanded appraisal remedy now available to shareholders, and the broad discretion of the Chancellor to fashion such relief as the facts of a given case may dictate, we do not believe that any additional meaningful protection is afforded minority shareholders by the business purpose requirement of the trilogy of *Singer, Tanzer, Najjar,* and their progeny. Accordingly, such requirement shall no longer be of any force or effect.

The judgment of the Court of Chancery, finding both the circumstances of the merger and the price paid the minority shareholders to be fair, is reversed.

The matter is remanded for further proceedings consistent herewith. Upon remand the plaintiff's post-trial motion to enlarge the class should be granted.

REVERSED AND REMANDED.

NOTES AND QUESTIONS

1. The *Weinberger* case represented significant changes in the Delaware approach to evaluating "freeze out" mergers. It increased the factors that could be considered by a court in determining the fair price to which minority shareholders are entitled. It eliminated the requirement of a valid business purpose, and it broadened the understanding of "fair dealing," requiring that minority shareholders have appropriate disclosures and adequate time to consider the offer.

2. Why would such expansive "fairness" be required if the minority shareholders were receiving a fair price and can be outvoted by the majority shareholder?

3. How would you evaluate a freeze out merger that required approval of 75% of the shareholders when the corporation had a majority shareholder holding 55% of the corporation's stock?

4. Of course, different states have different requirements for such mergers. For example, New York requires the approval of a super majority of the shareholders; California will only allow a majority shareholder to "cash-out" the minority in a "short form merger" in which the majority shareholder must own at least 90% of the corporation and the transaction must be approved by the California Commissioner of Corporations.

In re MFW Shareholders Litigation

67 A.3d 496 (Del. Ch. 2013)

STRINE, Chancellor:

I. *Introduction*

This case presents a novel question of law. Here, MacAndrews & Forbes—a holding company whose equity is solely owned by defendant Ronald Perelman—owned 43% of M & F Worldwide ("MFW"). MacAndrews & Forbes offered to purchase the rest of the corporation's equity in a going private merger for $24 per share. But upfront, MacAndrews & Forbes said it would not proceed with any going private transaction that was not approved: (i) by an independent special committee; and (ii) by a vote of a majority of the stockholders unaffiliated with the controlling stockholder (who, for simplicity's sake, are termed the "minority"). A special committee was formed, which picked its own legal and financial advisors. The committee met eight times during the course of three months and negotiated with MacAndrews & Forbes, eventually getting it to raise its bid by $1 per share, to $25 per share. The merger was then approved by an affirmative vote of the majority of the minority MFW stockholders, with 65% of them approving the merger.

MacAndrews & Forbes, Perelman, and the other directors of MFW were, of course, sued by stockholders alleging that the merger was unfair. After initially seeking a preliminary injunction hearing in advance of the merger vote with agreement from the defendants and receiving a good deal of expedited discovery, the plaintiffs changed direction and dropped their injunction motion in favor of seeking a post-closing damages remedy for breach of fiduciary duty.

The defendants have moved for summary judgment as to that claim. The defendants argue that there is no material issue of fact that the MFW special committee was comprised of independent directors, had the right to and did engage qualified legal and financial advisors to inform itself whether a going private merger was in the best interests of MFW's minority stockholders, was fully empowered to negotiate with Perelman over the terms of his offer and to say no definitively if it did not believe the ultimate terms were fair to the MFW minority stockholders, and after an extensive period of deliberation and negotiations, approved a merger agreement with Perelman. The defendants further argue that there is no dispute of fact that a majority of the minority stockholders supported the merger upon full disclosure and without coercion. Because, the defendants say, the merger was conditioned up front on two key procedural protections that, together, replicate an arm's-length merger—the employment of an active, unconflicted negotiating agent free to turn down the transaction and a requirement that any transaction negotiated by that agent be approved by the disinterested stockholders—they contend that the judicial standard of review should be the business judgment rule. Under that rule, the court is precluded from inquiring into the substantive fairness of the merger, and must dismiss the challenge to the merger unless the merger's terms were so disparate that no rational person acting in good faith could have thought the merger was fair to the minority. On this record, the defendants say, it is clear that the merger, which occurred at a price that was a 47% premium to the stock price before Perelman's offer was made, cannot be deemed waste, a conclusion confirmed by the majority-of-the-minority vote itself.

In other words, the defendants argue that the effect of using both protective devices is to make the form of the going private transaction analogous to that of a third-party merger under Section 251 of the Delaware General Corporation Law. The approval of a special committee in a going private transaction is akin to that of the approval of the board in a third-party transaction, and the approval of the noncontrolling stockholders replicates the approval of all the stockholders.

The question of what standard of review should apply to a going private merger conditioned upfront by the controlling stockholder on approval by both a properly empowered, independent committee and an informed, uncoerced majority-of-the-minority vote has been a subject of debate for decades now. For various reasons, the question has never been put directly to this court or, more important, to our Supreme Court.

This is in part due to uncertainty arising from a question that has been answered. Almost twenty years ago, in *Kahn v. Lynch*, our Supreme Court held that the approval by either a special committee or the majority of the noncontrolling stockholders of a merger with a buying controlling stockholder would shift the burden of proof under the entire fairness standard from the defendant to the plaintiff. Although *Lynch* did not involve a merger conditioned by a controlling stockholder on both procedural protections, statements in the decision could be, and were, read as suggesting that a controlling stockholder who consented to both procedural protections for the minority would receive no extra legal credit for doing so, and that regardless of employing both procedural protections, the merger would be subject to review under the entire fairness standard.

Uncertainty about the answer to a question that had not been put to our Supreme Court thus left controllers with an incentive system all of us who were adolescents (or are now parents or grandparents of adolescents) can understand. Assume you have a teenager with math and English assignments due Monday morning. If you tell the teenager that she can go to the movies Saturday night if she completes her math or English homework Saturday morning, she is unlikely to do both assignments Saturday morning. She is likely to do only that which is necessary to get to go to the movies—i.e., complete one of the assignments—leaving her parents and siblings to endure her stressful last-minute scramble to finish the other Sunday night.

For controlling stockholders who knew that they would get a burden shift if they did one of the procedural protections, but who did not know if they would get any additional benefit for taking the certain business risk of assenting to an additional and potent procedural protection for the minority stockholders, the incentive to use both procedural devices and thus replicate the key elements of the arm's-length merger process was therefore minimal to downright discouraging.

Because of these and other incentives, the underlying question has never been squarely presented to our courts, and lawyers, investment bankers, managers, stockholders, and scholars have wondered what would be the effect on the standard of review of using both of these procedural devices. In this decision, Perelman and his codefendants ask this court to answer that question by arguing that because the merger proposal that led to the merger challenged here was conditioned from the time of its proposal on both procedural protections, the business judgment rule standard applies and requires a grant of summary judgment against the plaintiffs' claims.

In this decision, the court answers the question the defendants ask, but only after assuring itself that an answer is in fact necessary. For that answer to be necessary, certain conditions have to exist.

First, it has to be clear that the procedural protections employed qualify to be given cleansing credit under the business judgment rule. For example, if the MFW special committee was not comprised of directors who qualify as independent under our law, the defendants would not be entitled to summary judgment under their own argument. Likewise, if the majority-of-the-minority vote were tainted by a disclosure violation or coercion, the defendants' motion would fail.

The court therefore analyzes whether the defendants are correct that the MFW special committee and the majority-of-the-minority vote qualify as cleansing devices under our law. As to the special committee, the court concludes that the special committee does qualify because there is no triable issue of fact regarding (i) the independence of the special committee, (ii) its ability to employ financial and legal advisors and its exercise of that ability, and (iii) its empowerment to negotiate the merger and definitively to say no to the transaction. The special committee met on eight occasions and there are no grounds for the plaintiffs to allege that the committee did not fulfill its duty of care. As to the majority-of-the-minority vote, the plaintiffs admit that it was a fully informed vote, as they fail to point to any failure of disclosure. Nor is there any evidence of coercion of the electorate.

Second, the court has to satisfy itself that our Supreme Court has not already answered the question. If our Supreme Court has done so, this court is bound by that answer, which may only be altered by the Supreme Court itself or by legislative action. Therefore, the court considers whether the plaintiffs are correct in saying that the Supreme Court has held, as a matter of law, that a controlling stockholder merger conditioned up front on special committee negotiation and approval, and an informed, uncoerced majority-of-the-minority vote must be reviewed under the entire fairness standard, rather than the business judgment rule standard. Although admitting that there is language in prior Supreme Court decisions that can be read as indicating that there are no circumstances when a merger with a controlling stockholder can escape fairness review, the court concludes that this language does not constitute a holding of our Supreme Court as to a question it was never afforded the opportunity to answer. In no prior case was our Supreme Court given the chance to determine whether a controlling stockholder merger conditioned on both independent committee approval and a majority-of-the-minority vote should receive the protection of the business judgment rule. . . . After reading the prior authority again, the court concludes that the question remains open and that this court must give its own answer in the first instance, while giving important weight to the reasoning of our Supreme Court in its prior jurisprudence.

After resolving these two predicate issues, the court answers the important question asked by the defendants in the affirmative. Although rational minds may differ on the subject, the court concludes that when a controlling stockholder merger has, from the time of the controller's first overture, been subject to (i) negotiation and approval by a special committee of independent directors fully empowered to say no, and (ii) approval by an uncoerced, fully informed vote of a majority of the minority investors, the business judgment rule standard of review applies. This conclusion is consistent with the central tradition of Delaware law, which defers to the informed decisions of impartial directors, especially when those decisions have been approved by the disinterested stockholders on full information and without coercion. Not only that, the adoption of this rule will be of benefit to minority stockholders because it will provide a strong incentive for controlling stockholders to accord minority investors the transactional structure that respected scholars believe will provide them the best protection, a structure where stockholders get the benefits of independent, empowered negotiating agents to bargain for the best price and say no if the agents believe the deal is not advisable for any proper reason, plus the critical ability to determine for themselves whether to accept any deal that their negotiating agents recommend to them. A transactional structure with both these protections is fundamentally different from one with only one protection. A special committee alone ensures only that there is a bargaining agent who can negotiate price and address the collective action problem facing stockholders, but it does not provide stockholders any chance to protect themselves. A majority-of-the-minority vote provides stockholders a chance to vote on a merger proposed by a controller-dominated board, but with no chance to have an independent bargaining agent work on their behalf to negotiate the merger price, and determine whether it is a favorable one that the bargaining agent commends to the minority stockholders for acceptance at a vote. These protections are therefore incomplete and not substitutes, but are complementary and effective in tandem.

Not only that, a controller's promise that it will not proceed unless the special committee assents ensures that the committee will not be bypassed by the controller through the intrinsically more coercive setting of a tender offer. It was this threat of bypass that was of principal concern in *Lynch* and cast doubt on the special committee's ability to operate effectively. Precisely because the controller can only get business judgment rule treatment if it foregoes the chance to go directly to stockholders, any potential for coercion is minimized. Indeed, given the high-profile promise the controller has to make not to proceed without the committee's approval, any retributive action would be difficult to conceal, and the potent tools entrusted to our courts to protect stockholders against violations of the duty of loyalty would be available to police retributive action. As important, market realities provide no rational basis for concluding that stockholders will not vote against a merger they do not favor. Stockholders, especially institutional investors who dominate market holdings, regularly vote against management on many issues, and do not hesitate to sue, or to speak up. Thus, when such stockholders are given a free opportunity to vote no on a merger negotiated by a special committee, and a majority of them choose to support the merger, it promises more cost than benefit to investors generally in terms of the impact on the overall cost of capital to have a standard of review other than the business judgment rule. That is especially the case because stockholders who vote no, and do not wish to accept the merger consideration in a going private transaction despite the other stockholders' decision to support the merger, will typically have the right to seek appraisal.

In addition, if the approach taken were applied consistently to the equitable review of going private transactions proposed by controllers through tender offers, an across-the-board incentive would be created to provide minority stockholders with the best procedural protections in all going private transactions. Whether proceeding by a merger or a tender offer, a controlling stockholder would recognize that it would face entire fairness review unless it agreed not to proceed without the approval of an independent negotiator with the power to say no, and without the uncoerced, fully informed consent of a majority of the minority. This approach is consistent with *Lynch* and its progeny, as a controller who employed only one of the procedural protections would continue to get burden-shifting credit within the entire fairness rubric, but could not escape an ultimate judicial inquiry into substantive fairness. Importantly, by also providing transactional planners with a basis to structure transactions from the beginning in a manner that, if properly implemented, qualifies for the business judgment rule, the benefit-to-cost ratio of litigation challenging controlling stockholders for investors in Delaware corporations will improve, as suits will not have settlement value simply because there is no feasible way for defendants to get them dismissed on the pleadings.

This approach promises minority stockholders a great deal in terms of increasing the prevalence of employing both fairness-enhancing protections in more transactions—most notably, by giving investors a more constant chance to protect themselves at the ballot box through more prevalent majority-of-the-minority voting conditions. It also seems to come at very little cost, owing to the lack of evidence that entire fairness review in cases where both procedural protections are employed adds any real value that justifies the clear costs to diversified investors that such litigation imposes. Thus, respected scholars deeply concerned about the well-being of minority stockholders support this approach as beneficial for minority stockholders. For the same reason, the court embraces it, and therefore grants the defendants' motion for summary judgment.

II. *The Structure Of This Decision*

Consistent with the introduction, this opinion will first address whether, under the undisputed facts of record, the defendants are correct that the MFW special committee and the majority-of-the minority provision qualify as cleansing devices under Delaware's approach to the business judgment rule. After addressing that issue, the court then considers whether our Supreme Court has answered the question of what judicial standard of review applies to a merger with a controlling stockholder conditioned upfront on a promise that no transaction will proceed without (i) special committee approval, and (ii) the affirmative vote of a majority of the minority stockholders. Finally, having concluded that the question has not been answered by our Supreme Court, this court answers the question itself.

In keeping with this structure, therefore, the court begins by discussing the undisputed facts that are relevant to deciding the legal issues raised by the pending motion for summary judgment, applying the familiar procedural standard. That motion seeks summary judgment on the ground that the two procedural devices in question qualify as cleansing devices and, taken together, warrant application of the business judgment rule. Because the merger's terms are indisputably ones that a rational person could think fair to the minority stockholders, the defendants say that summary judgment is warranted.

For their part, the plaintiffs argue that there are material questions of fact regarding the independence of the special committee. The plaintiffs also raise debatable issues of valuation, similar to those that are typically addressed in an appraisal or in the part of entire fairness analysis dealing with the substantive fairness of a merger price. Most important, however, the plaintiffs argue that regardless of whether the MFW special committee and the majority-of-the-minority vote qualify as cleansing devices, this court must still hold a trial and determine for itself whether the merger was entirely fair. At best, the defendants are entitled to a shift in the burden of persuasion on that point at trial under the preponderance of the evidence standard. But that slight tilt is all, the plaintiffs say, that is permitted under prior precedent.

III. *The Procedural Devices Used To Protect The Minority Are Entitled To Cleansing Effect Under Delaware's Traditional Approach To The Business Judgment Rule*

Determining whether the defendants are entitled to judgment that, as a matter of law, the MFW special committee and the majority-of-the-minority vote condition should be given cleansing effect, necessitates a discussion of how the merger came about.

A. *MacAndrews & Forbes Proposes To Take MFW Private*

MFW is a holding company incorporated in Delaware. Before the merger that is the subject of this dispute, MFW was 43.4% owned by MacAndrews & Forbes, which is entirely owned by Ron Perelman. MFW had four business segments. Three of these were owned through a holding company, Harland Clarke Holding Corporation ("HCHC"). These are the Harland Clarke Corporation ("Harland"), which printed bank checks; Harland Clarke Financial Solutions, which provided technology products and services to financial services companies; and Scantron Corporation, which manufactured scanning equipment used for educational and other purposes. The fourth segment, which was not part of HCHC, was Mafco Worldwide Corporation, a manufacturer of licorice flavorings.

The MFW board had thirteen members. The members were Ron Perelman, Barry Schwartz, William Bevins, Bruce Slovin, Charles Dawson, Stephen Taub, John Keane, Theo Folz, Philip Beekman, Martha Byorum, Viet Dinh, Paul Meister, and Carl Webb. Perelman, Schwartz, and Bevins had roles at both MFW and MacAndrews & Forbes. Perelman was the Chairman of MFW, and the Chairman and CEO of MacAndrews & Forbes; Schwartz was the President and CEO of MFW, and the Vice Chairman and Chief Administrative Officer of MacAndrews & Forbes; and Bevins was a Vice President at MacAndrews & Forbes.

In May 2011, Perelman began to explore the possibility of taking MFW private. At that time, MFW's stock price traded in the $20 to $24 range. MacAndrews & Forbes engaged the bank Moelis & Company to advise it. Moelis prepared valuations based on projections that had been supplied to lenders by MFW in April and May 2011. Moelis valued MFW at between $10 and $32 a share.

On June 10, 2011, MFW's shares closed on the New York Stock Exchange at $16.96. The next business day, June 13, 2011, Schwartz sent a proposal to the MFW board to buy the remaining shares for $24 in cash. The proposal stated, in relevant part:

> The proposed transaction would be subject to the approval of the Board of Directors of the Company [i.e., MFW] and the negotiation and execution of mutually acceptable definitive transaction documents. It is our expectation that the Board of Directors will appoint a special committee of independent directors to consider our proposal and make a recommendation to the Board of Directors. We will not move forward with the transaction unless it is approved by such a special committee. In addition, the transaction will be subject to a non-waivable condition requiring the approval of a majority of the shares of the Company not owned by M & F or its affiliates. . . .
>
> . . . In considering this proposal, you should know that in our capacity as a stockholder of the Company we are interested only in acquiring the shares of the Company not already owned by us and that in such capacity we have no interest in selling any of the shares owned by us in the Company nor would we expect, in our capacity as a stockholder, to vote in favor of any alternative sale, merger or similar transaction

> involving the Company. If the special committee does not recommend or the public stockholders of the Company do not approve the proposed transaction, such determination would not adversely affect our future relationship with the Company and we would intend to remain as a long-term stockholder.
>
> . . . .
>
> In connection with this proposal, we have engaged Moelis & Company as our financial advisor and Skadden, Arps, Slate, Meagher & Flom LLP as our legal advisor, and we encourage the special committee to retain its own legal and financial advisors to assist it in its review.

MacAndrews & Forbes filed this letter with the SEC and issued a press release containing substantially the same information.

B. *The MFW Board Forms A Special Committee Of Independent Directors To Consider The Offer*

The MFW board met the following day to consider the proposal. At the meeting, Schwartz presented the offer on behalf of MacAndrews & Forbes. Schwartz and Bevins, as the two directors present who were also on the MacAndrews & Forbes board, then recused themselves from the meeting, as did Dawson, the CEO of HCHC, who had previously expressed support for the offer. The independent directors then invited counsel from Willkie Farr & Gallagher, which had recently represented a special committee of MFW's independent directors in relation to a potential acquisition of a subsidiary of MacAndrews & Forbes, to join the meeting. The independent directors decided to form a special committee, and resolved further that:

> [T]he Special Committee is empowered to: (i) make such investigation of the Proposal as the Special Committee deems appropriate; (ii) evaluate the terms of the Proposal; (iii) negotiate with Holdings [i.e., MacAndrews & Forbes] and its representatives any element of the Proposal; (iv) negotiate the terms of any definitive agreement with respect to the Proposal (it being understood that the execution thereof shall be subject to the approval of the Board); (v) report to the Board its recommendations and conclusions with respect to the Proposal, including a determination and recommendation as to whether the Proposal is fair and in the best interests of the stockholders of the Company other than Holdings and its affiliates and should be

approved by the Board; and (vi) determine to elect not to pursue the Proposal. . . .

> . . . .
>
> . . . [T]he Board shall not approve the Proposal without a prior favorable recommendation of the Special Committee. . . .
>
> . . . [T]he Special Committee [is] empowered to retain and employ legal counsel, a financial advisor, and such other agents as the Special Committee shall deem necessary or desirable in connection with these matters. . . .
>
> The special committee consisted of Byorum, Dinh, Meister (the chair), Slovin, and Webb. The following day, Slovin recused himself because, although the board had determined that he qualified as an independent director under the rules of the New York Stock Exchange, he had "some current relationships that could raise questions about his independence for purposes of serving on the special committee."

C. *The Special Committee Was Empowered To Negotiate And Veto The Transaction*

It is undisputed that the special committee was empowered to hire its own legal and financial advisors. Besides hiring Willkie Farr as its legal advisor, the special committee engaged Evercore Partners as its financial advisor.

It is also undisputed that the special committee was empowered not simply to "evaluate" the offer, . . . but to negotiate with MacAndrews & Forbes over the terms of its offer to buy out the noncontrolling stockholders. Critically, this negotiating power was accompanied by the clear authority to say no definitively to MacAndrews & Forbes. Thus, unlike in some prior situations that the court will discuss, MacAndrews & Forbes promised that it would not proceed with any going private proposal that did not have the support of the special committee. Therefore, the MFW committee did not have to fear that if it bargained too hard, MacAndrews & Forbes could bypass the committee and make a tender offer directly to the minority stockholders. Rather, the special committee was fully empowered to say no and make that decision stick.

Although the special committee had the authority to negotiate and say no, it did not have the practical authority to market MFW to other buyers. In its announcement, MacAndrews & Forbes plainly stated that it was not interested in selling its 43% stake. Under Delaware law, MacAndrews & Forbes had no duty to sell its block, which was large enough, as a practical matter, to preclude any other buyer from succeeding unless it decided to become a seller. And absent MacAndrews & Forbes declaring that it was open to selling, it was unlikely that any potentially interested party would incur the costs and risks of exploring a purchase of MFW. This does not mean, however, that the MFW special committee did not have the leeway to get advice from its financial advisor about the strategic options available to MFW, including the potential interest that other buyers might have if MacAndrews & Forbes was willing to sell. The record is undisputed that the special committee did consider, with the help of its financial advisor, whether there were other buyers who might be interested in purchasing MFW, and whether there were other strategic options, such as asset divestitures, that might generate more value for minority stockholders than a sale of their stock to MacAndrews & Forbes.

For purposes of this motion, therefore, there is undisputed evidence that the special committee could and did hire qualified legal and financial advisors; that the special committee could definitely say no; that the special committee could and did study a full range of financial information to inform itself, including by evaluating other options that might be open to MFW; and that the special committee could and, as we shall see, did negotiate with MacAndrews & Forbes over the terms of its offer.

D. *The Independence Of The Special Committee*

One of the plaintiffs' major arguments against summary judgment is that the MFW special committee was not comprised of directors who meet the definition of independence under our law. Although the plaintiffs concede the independence of the special committee's chairman (Meister), they challenge the independence of each of the other three members, contending that various business and social ties between these members and MacAndrews & Forbes render them beholden to MacAndrews & Forbes and its controller Perelman, or at least create a permissible inference that that is so, thus defeating a key premise of the defendants' summary judgment motion.

To evaluate the parties' competing positions, the court applies settled authority of our Supreme Court. Under Delaware law, there is a presumption that directors are independent. To show that a director is not independent, a plaintiff must demonstrate that the director is "beholden" to the controlling party "or so under [the controller's] influence that [the director's] discretion would be sterilized." Our law is clear that mere allegations that directors are friendly with, travel in the same social circles, or have past business relationships with the proponent of a transaction or the person they are investigating, are not enough to rebut the presumption of independence. Rather, the Supreme Court has made clear that a plaintiff seeking to show that a director was not independent must meet a materiality standard, under which the court must conclude that the director in question's material ties to the person whose proposal or actions she is evaluating are sufficiently substantial that she cannot objectively fulfill her fiduciary duties. Consistent with the overarching requirement that any disqualifying tie be material, the simple fact that there are some financial ties between the interested party and the director is not disqualifying. Rather, the question is whether those ties are material, in the sense that the alleged ties could have affected the impartiality of the director. . . . .

* * * * [*Discussion of allegations regarding the independence of the members of the special committee is omitted. Eds.*]

For all these reasons, therefore, the MFW special committee was, as a matter of law, comprised entirely of independent directors.

E. *There Is No Dispute Of Fact That The MFW Special Committee Satisfied Its Duty Of Care*

The plaintiffs do not make any attempt to show that the MFW special committee failed to meet its duty of care, in the sense of making an informed decision regarding the terms on which it would be advantageous for the minority stockholders to sell their shares to MacAndrews & Forbes. At its first meeting, the special committee interviewed four financial advisors, before hiring Evercore Partners. Such an interview process not only lets the client consider a number of qualified advisors and, one hopes, therefore get better financial terms from the winner because the winner knows it has competition. The process has another utility, which is that each of the pitching firms present "pitch books" relevant to the potential engagement, and give the committee a chance to hear preliminary thoughts from a variety of well qualified financial advisors, a process that therefore helps the committee begin to get fully grounded in the relevant economic factors.

From the outset, the special committee and Evercore had projections that had been prepared by MFW's business segments in April and May 2011. Early in its process, Evercore and the special committee requested MFW to produce new projections that reflected the management's most up-to-date, and presumably most accurate, thinking. Mafco, the licorice business, told Evercore that all of its projections would remain the same. Harland Clarke updated its projections. On July 22, Evercore received new projections from HCHC, which incorporated the updated projections from Harland Clarke, and Evercore constructed a valuation model based on them.

The updated projections forecast EBITDA for MFW of $491 million in 2015, as opposed to $535 million under the original projections. On August 10, Evercore produced a range of valuations for MFW, based on the updated projections, of $15 to $45 per share. Evercore valued MFW using a variety of accepted methods, including a DCF model, which generated a range of fair value of $22 to $38 per share, and a premiums paid analysis, with a resulting value range of $22 to $45. MacAndrews & Forbes's $24 offer fell within the range of values produced by each of Evercore's valuation techniques.

The special committee asked Evercore to analyze how the possible sale of Harland to a rival check printing company might affect the valuation. Evercore produced this analysis a week later, at the next meeting of the special committee, on August 17. Evercore opined that such a sale would not produce a higher valuation for the company. The special committee rejected the $24 proposal, and countered at $30 a share. MacAndrews & Forbes was disappointed by this counteroffer. On September 9, 2011, MacAndrews & Forbes rejected the special committee's $30 counteroffer, and reiterated its $24 offer. Meister informed Schwartz that he would not recommend the $24 to the special committee. Schwartz then obtained approval from Perelman to make a "best and final" offer of $25 a share. At their eighth, and final, meeting, on September 10, 2011, Evercore opined that the price was fair, and the special committee unanimously decided to accept the offer.

The MFW board then discussed the offer. Perelman, Schwartz, and Bevins, the three directors affiliated with MacAndrews & Forbes, and Dawson and Taub, the CEOs of HCHC and Mafco, recused themselves. The remaining eight directors voted unanimously to recommend the offer to the stockholders.

In their briefs, the plaintiffs make a number of arguments in which they question the business judgment of the special committee, in terms of issues such as whether the special committee could have extracted another higher bid from MacAndrews & Forbes if it had said no to the $25 per share offer, and whether the special committee was too conservative in valuing MFW's future prospects. These are the sorts of questions that can be asked about any business negotiation, and that are, of course, the core of an appraisal proceeding and relevant when a court has to make a determination itself about the financial fairness of a merger transaction under the entire fairness standard.

What is not in question is that the plaintiffs do not point to any evidence indicating that the independent members of the special committee did not meet their duty of care in evaluating, negotiating and ultimately agreeing to a merger at $25 per share. The record is clear that the special committee met frequently and was presented with a rich body of financial information relevant to whether and at what price a going private transaction was advisable, and thus there is no triable issue of fact as to its satisfaction of its duty of care. Because the special committee was comprised entirely of independent directors, there is no basis to infer that they did not attempt in good faith to obtain the most favorable price they could secure for the minority or believe they had done so.

F. *A Fully Informed, Uncoerced Majority Of The Minority Votes To Support The Merger*

On November 18, 2011, the stockholders were provided with a proxy statement containing the history of the merger and recommending that they vote in favor of the transaction. The proxy statement made clear, among other things, that the special committee had countered at $30 per share, but only was able to get a final offer of $25 per share. The proxy statement indicated that the MFW business divisions discussed with Evercore whether the initial projections that Evercore received reflected management's latest thinking, and that plainly stated that the new projections were lower. The proxy also gave the five separate ranges for the value of MFW's stock that Evercore had produced with different analyses.

When the votes were counted on December 21, 2011, stockholders representing 65% of the shares not owned by MacAndrews & Forbes voted to accept the offer. The merger closed that same day.

Under settled authority, the uncoerced, fully informed vote of disinterested stockholders is entitled to substantial weight under our law. Traditionally, such a vote on a third-party merger would, in itself, be sufficient to invoke the business judgment standard of review. In the controlling stockholder merger context, it is settled that an uncoerced, informed majority-of-the-minority vote, without any other procedural protection, is itself sufficient to shift the burden of persuasion to the plaintiff under the entire fairness standard.

Here, therefore, it is clear that as a matter of law, the majority-of-the-minority vote condition qualifies as a cleansing device under traditional Delaware corporate law principles. The consequences of these determinations for the resolution of this motion are important. Absent both of the procedural protections qualifying as a cleansing device, there would be no reason to answer the ultimate question the defendants pose, because that question depends on both of the protections having sufficient integrity to invoke the business judgment standard.

The court concludes here that there is no triable issue of fact regarding the operation of these devices. For the reasons stated, the plaintiffs themselves do not dispute that that majority-of-the-minority vote was fully informed and uncoerced, because they fail to allege any failure of disclosure or any act of coercion.

As to the special committee, the court has rejected the plaintiffs' challenge to the independence of the committee membership. The court also finds, as a matter of law, that there is no issue that the special committee was sufficiently empowered to hire its own advisors, inform itself, negotiate, and to definitively say no. Lastly, there is no triable issue of fact regarding whether the special committee fulfilled its duty of care.

These conditions are sufficient, under a traditional approach, to be effective in influencing the intensity of review, and as to a conflict transaction not involving a controlling stockholder, to invoke the business judgment rule standard of review.

The court gives the committee such effect here. In doing so, the court eschews determining that the special committee was "effective" in a more colloquial sense. Although prior cases can potentially be read as requiring an assessment of whether a special committee was effective in the sense of being substantively good at its appointed task, such a precondition is fundamentally inconsistent with the application of the business judgment rule standard of review. For a court to determine whether a special committee was effective in obtaining a good economic outcome involves the sort of second-guessing that the business judgment rule precludes. When a committee is structurally independent, has a sufficient mandate and cannot be bypassed, and fulfills its duty of care, it should be given standard-shifting effect. Any other approach as a matter of fact involves the application of a form of entire fairness review or at least the type of heightened reasonableness scrutiny required under the *Unocal* or *Revlon* standards, i.e., standards that intentionally involve judges in reviewing director behavior in a manner not permitted under the business judgment rule. Furthermore, adhering to this approach is consistent with a close reading of prior cases. In many of the cases where special committees were not given cleansing effect, the reason was not that the court second-guessed tactical decisions made by a concededly independent committee with a sufficient mandate to protect the minority investors. Rather, it was precisely because the special committee lacked one of these essential attributes that the committee was not given weight. For example, in *Lynch*, the committee's effectiveness was undermined because the controller made plain that if the committee did not consensually agree to a transaction, the controller would end-run the committee and go to the stockholders with a tender offer, a form of transaction that is generally considered intrinsically more coercive than one preceded by a merger vote. Likewise, in *Tremont* [*Kahn v. Tremont Corp.*, 694 A.2d 422 (Del. 1997)], the committee was ineffective because two of the three directors breached their duty of care by "abdicat[ing] their responsibility" in favor of the chair, who had been lucratively employed as a consultant by the controller and did not come close to the standard of independence required of what was for practical purposes a one-person committee.

To the extent that the fundamental rule is that a special committee should be given standard-influencing effect if it replicates arm's-length bargaining, that test is met if the committee is independent, can hire its own advisors, has a sufficient mandate to negotiate and the power to say no, and meets its duty of care. Under that approach, the MFW special committee qualifies.

G. *There Is No Triable Issue Of Fact That The Merger Was A Transaction That A Rational Person Could Believe Was Favorable To MFW's Minority Stockholders*

If the business judgment rule standard of review applies, the claims against the defendants must be dismissed unless no rational person could have believed that the merger was favorable to MFW's minority stockholders. Although the plaintiffs raise arguments as to why the merger should have been at a higher price, these arguments, and the scant facts supporting them, do not raise a triable issue of fact under the business judgment rule. The merger was effected at a 47% premium to the closing price before MacAndrews & Forbes's offer. A financial advisor for the special committee found that the price was fair in light of various analyses, including a DCF analysis, which mirrors the valuation standard applicable in an appraisal case. MFW's businesses faced long-term challenges, particularly its check-printing business, Harland Clarke, which faced serious pricing pressure as its primary contract was put out to bid by the grantor and a seemingly irrevocable long-term decline in its industry because of global trends to eliminate as many checks as possible and conduct all transactions online. After disclosure of the material facts, 65% of the minority stockholders decided for themselves that the price was favorable.

The plaintiffs' argument that many of these stockholders were arbitrageurs who had bought from longer-term stockholders and whose views should be discounted has a fundamental logical problem. The fact that long-term MFW stockholders sold at a price that was substantially higher than the market price when MacAndrews & Forbes made its offer but less than $25 per share merger price does not suggest that the price was one that long-term stockholders viewed as unfavorable. Rather, it suggests the opposite. The value of most stocks is highly debatable. What is not debatable here is that a rational mind could have believed the merger price fair, and that is what is relevant under the business judgment rule, which precludes judicial second-guessing when that is the case.

* * * *

V. *The Business Judgment Rule Governs And Summary Judgment Is Granted*

This case thus presents, for the first time, the question of what should be the correct standard of review for mergers between a controlling stockholder and its subsidiary, when the merger is conditioned on the approval of both an independent, adequately empowered special committee that fulfills its duty of care, and the uncoerced, informed vote of a majority of the minority stockholders.

In prior cases, this court has outlined the development of the case law in this area, as have distinguished scholars, and there is no need to repeat that recitation. The core legal question is framed by the parties' contending positions. For their part, the defendants say that it would be beneficial systemically to minority stockholders to review transactions structured with both procedural protections under the business judgment rule. Absent an incentive to do so, the defendants argue that controlling stockholders will not agree upfront to both protections, thus denying minority stockholders access to the transaction structure most protective of their interests—one that gives them the benefit of an active and empowered bargaining agent to negotiate price and to say no, plus the ability to freely decide for themselves on full information whether to accept any deal approved by that agent. This structure is not common now because controlling stockholders have no incentive under the law to agree to it, and such an incentive is needed because it involves the controller ceding potent power to the independent directors and minority stockholders. The defendants argue that the benefits of their preferred approach are considerable, and that the costs are negligible because there is little utility to having an expensive, judicially intensive standard of review when stockholders can protect themselves by voting no if they do not like the recommendation of a fully empowered independent committee that exercised due care. In support of that argument, the defendants can cite to empirical evidence showing that the absence of a legally recognized transaction structure that can invoke the business judgment rule standard of review has resulted not in litigation that generates tangible positive results for minority stockholders in the form of additional money in their pockets, but in litigation that is settled for fees because there is no practical way of getting the case dismissed at the pleading stage and the costs of discovery and entanglement in multiyear litigation exceed the costs of paying attorneys' fees. Finally, the defendants note that Delaware law on controlling stockholder going private transactions is now inconsistent, with the intrinsically more coercive route of using a tender offer to accomplish a going private transaction escaping the full force of equitable review, when a similarly structured merger where a less coercive chance to say no exists would not.[144]

In response, the plaintiffs argue that a requirement that every controlling stockholder transaction be subject to fairness review is good for minority stockholders. The plaintiffs, rather surprisingly, argue that giving stockholders the protection of a majority-of-the-minority vote in addition to a special committee adds little value because, in their view, stockholders will always vote for a good premium deal, and long-term stockholders will sell out to arbitrageurs in advance of the vote, leaving the minority vote in the hands of stockholders who will invariably vote for the deal. That said, the plaintiffs conceded in their briefing that minority stockholders would benefit if more controlling stockholders would use a structure that gave minority stockholders an independent bargaining and veto agent as well as a majority-of-the-minority vote. But they contend that the cost of not having an invariable judicial inquiry into fairness outweighs that benefit.

After considering these arguments, the court concludes that the rule of equitable common law that best protects minority investors is one that encourages controlling stockholders to accord the minority this potent combination of procedural protections.

---

144 Compare *In re Siliconix Inc. S'holders Litig.*, 2001 WL 716787 (Del.Ch. June 21, 2001), with *Lynch I*, 638 A.2d 1110. The implication of the Supreme Court's decision in *Solomon v. Pathe* and cases following it, such as *Siliconix*, is that a going private transaction proposed by a controller by the tender offer method is not subject to equitable review. *Solomon v. Pathe Commc'ns Corp.*, 672 A.2d 35 (1996). Although this implication has been affected by later cases such [as] *Pure and Cox*, it remains the case that it is not certain that a controlling stockholder owes the same equitable obligations when it seeks to acquire the rest of a corporation's equity by a tender offer, rather than by a statutory merger. See Gilson & Gordon, *Controlling Shareholders*, at 796–832; Subramanian, *Fixing Freezeouts*, at 11–22.

There are several reasons for this conclusion. The court begins with a Delaware tradition. Under Delaware law, it has long been thought beneficial to investors for courts, which are not experts in business, to defer to the disinterested decisions of directors, who are expert, and stockholders, whose money is at stake. Thus, when no fiduciary has a personal self-interest adverse to that of the company and its other stockholders, the fiduciary is well-informed, and there is no statutory requirement for a vote, the business judgment rule standard of review applies and precludes judicial second-guessing so long as the board's decision "can be attributed to any rational business purpose." Outside the controlling stockholder merger context, it has long been the law that even when a transaction is an interested one but not requiring a stockholder vote, Delaware law has invoked the protections of the business judgment rule when the transaction was approved by disinterested directors acting with due care.

This tradition of respecting the value of impartial decisionmaking [*sic*] by disinterested fiduciaries was maintained even when Delaware confronted the takeover boom that started in the late 1970s. The innovative standards that emerged in *Unocal* and *Revlon* required more judicially intensive review, but gave heavy credit for empowering the independent elements of the board. And when arm's-length cash mergers were approved by fully informed, uncoerced votes of the disinterested stockholders, the business judgment rule standard of review was applied to any class-action claim for monetary relief based on the inadequacy of the merger price.

But tradition should admittedly not persist if it lacks current value. If providing an incentive for a disinterested bargaining agent and a disinterested approval vote are of no utility to minority investors, it would not make sense to shape a rule that encourages their use.

But even the plaintiffs here admit that this transactional structure is the optimal one for minority stockholders. They just claim that there is some magical way to have it spread that involves no cost. That is not so, however. Absent doing something that is in fact inconsistent with binding precedent—requiring controlling stockholders to use both protections in order to get any credit under the entire fairness standard—there is no way to create an incentive for the use of both protections other than to give controllers who grant both protections to the minority the benefit of business judgment rule review.

A choice about our common law of corporations must therefore be made, and the court is persuaded that what is optimal for the protection of stockholders and the creation of wealth through the corporate form is adopting a form of the rule the defendants advocate. By giving controlling stockholders the opportunity to have a going private transaction reviewed under the business judgment rule, a strong incentive is created to give minority stockholders much broader access to the transactional structure that is most likely to effectively protect their interests. In fact, this incentive may make this structure the common one, which would be highly beneficial to minority stockholders. That structure, it is important to note, is critically different than a structure that uses only one of the procedural protections. The "or" structure does not replicate the protections of a third-party merger under the DGCL approval process, because it only requires that one, and not both, of the statutory requirements of director and stockholder approval be accomplished by impartial decisionmakers.155 The "both" structure, by contrast, replicates the arm's-length merger steps of the DGCL by "requir[ing] two independent approvals, which it is fair to say serve independent integrity-enforcing functions."

When these two protections are established up-front, a potent tool to extract good value for the minority is established. From inception, the controlling stockholder knows that it cannot bypass the special committee's ability to say no. And, the controlling stockholder knows it cannot dangle a majority-of-the-minority vote before the special committee late in the process as a deal-closer rather than having to make a price move. From inception, the controller has had to accept that any deal agreed to by the special committee will also have to be supported by a majority of the minority stockholders. That understanding also affects the incentives of the special committee in an important way. The special committee will understand that those for whom it is bargaining will get a chance to express whether they think the special committee did a good or poor job. Although it is possible that there are independent directors who have little regard for their duties or for being perceived by their company's stockholders (and the larger network of institutional investors) as being effective at protecting public stockholders, the court thinks they are likely to be exceptional, and certainly our Supreme Court's jurisprudence does not embrace such a skeptical view. The Supreme Court has held that independent directors are presumed to be motivated to do their duty with fidelity, like most other people, and has also observed that directors have a more self-protective interest in retaining their reputations as faithful, diligent fiduciaries. The requirement that a majority of the minority approve the special committee's recommendation enhances both motivations, because most directors will want to procure a deal that their minority stockholders think is a favorable one, and virtually all will not want to suffer the reputational embarrassment of repudiation at the ballot box. That is especially so in a market where many independent directors serve on several boards, and where institutional investors and their voting advisors, such as ISS and Glass Lewis, have computer-aided memory banks available to remind them of the past record of directors when considering whether to vote for them or withhold votes at annual meetings of companies on whose boards they serve.

The premise that independent directors with the right incentives can play an effective role on behalf of minority investors is one shared by respected scholars sincerely concerned with protecting minority investors from unfair treatment by controlling stockholders. Their scholarship and empirical evidence indicates that special committees have played a valuable role in generating outcomes for minority investors in going private transactions that compare favorably with the premiums received in third-party merger transactions.

But, like these scholars, the court is aware that even impartial directors acting in good faith and with due care can sometimes come out with an outcome that minority investors themselves do not find favorable. Conditioning the going private transaction's consummation on a majority-of-the-minority vote deals with this problem in two important and distinct ways. The first was just described. Because a special committee in this structure knows from the get-go that its work will be subject to disapproval by the minority stockholders, the special committee has a strong incentive to get a deal that will gain their approval. And, critically, so does another key party: the controlling stockholder itself, which will want to close the deal, having sunk substantial costs into the process.

But the second is equally important. If, despite these incentives, the special committee approves a transaction that the minority investors do not like, the minority investors get to vote it down, on a full information base and without coercion. In the *Unitrin* case [*Unitrin v. American General Corp.*, 651 A.2d 1361 (Del. Supr. 1995)] nearly a generation ago, our Supreme Court noted the prevalence of institutional investors in the target company's stockholder base in concluding that a proxy contest centering on the price of a takeover offer was viable, despite insiders having increased their stock ownership to 28%, stating that "[i]nstitutions are more likely than other shareholders to vote at all [and] more likely to vote against manager proposals." Market developments in the score of years since have made it far easier, not harder, for stockholders to protect themselves. With the development of the internet, there is more public information than ever about various commentators', analysts', institutional investors', journalists' and others' views about the wisdom of transactions. Likewise, the internet facilitates campaigns to defeat management recommendations. Not only that, institutional investor holdings have only grown since 1994, making it easier for a blocking position of minority investors to be assembled. Perhaps most important, it is difficult to look at the past generation of experience and conclude that stockholders are reluctant to express positions contrary to those espoused by company management. Stockholders have been effective in using their voting rights to adopt precatory proposals that have resulted in a sharp increase in so-called majority voting policies and a sharp decrease in structural takeover defenses. Stockholders have mounted more proxy fights, and, as important, wielded the threat of a proxy fight or a "withhold vote" campaign to secure changes in both corporate policies and the composition of corporate boards. Stockholders have voted against mergers they did not find favorable, or forced increases in price. Nor has timidity characterized stockholder behavior in companies with large blockholders or even majority stockholders; such companies still face stockholder activism in various forms, and are frequently the subject of lawsuits if stockholders suspect wrongdoing.

As our Supreme Court has recognized more than once, the application of fiduciary duty principles must be influenced by current corporate practices. Given the evident and growing power of modern stockholders, there seems to be little basis to doubt the fairness-assuring effectiveness of an upfront majority-of-the-minority vote condition when that condition is combined, as it was here, by a promise that the controller would not proceed with a transaction without both the approval of the special committee and the approval of a majority of the minority. Although one of the rationales identified in *Lynch* for fairness review of a going private merger with only one of the protections was that minority stockholders might be too afraid in any circumstance to vote freely, that rationale was one advanced in the context of a deal structure where the minority was expressly faced with a situation where a controller informed the special committee that it would put a lower priced offer directly to the stockholders in the intrinsically more coercive form of a tender offer. One of the things two very distinguished but very different corporate governance experts—Lucian Bebchuk and Marty Lipton—agree upon is that a tender offer, particularly one where there is the possibility that a non-tendering stockholder will be left as part of a stub minority or receive an even lower value than if she tenders, is intrinsically more coercive than a merger vote where a stockholder can vote no and still get the merger consideration if the other stockholders vote in sufficient numbers to approve the deal. The "both" structure limits coercion like this because the controller cannot end run the special committee in this way, and thus addresses the rationale advanced in *Lynch*.

So does another element of the structure. *Lynch* suggested that minority stockholders might be inhibited from voting freely because the controller could engage in retribution. The upfront promise not to bypass the special committee or the majority-of-the-minority condition limits the potential for any retributive going private effort. A controller who violated this promise would face withering scrutiny from stockholders. As important, the past generation has demonstrated, time and again, the willingness of the Delaware Supreme Court to uphold strong medicine against violations of the duty of loyalty, and even to reverse this court when it failed to deliver a remedy the Supreme Court viewed as sufficient. Given the increasing concentration of institutional investors and the demonstrated willingness of stockholders to vote against management's recommended course of actions, the potency of remedies available under our law, and statutory protections that prevent controlling stockholders from discriminating against minority stockholders and thus require them to engage in nihilism if they wish to try to starve minority investors who are probably more diversified than themselves and thus less dependent on the cash flows from the controlled company, there seems no rational reason to conclude that a majority-of-the-minority condition employed in the manner described will not provide an extremely valuable, fairness-assuring protection to minority investors. Again, distinguished scholars known for being skeptical of managerial authority in the M & A arena agree, and support using the business judgment rule standard of review when a going private merger is conditioned upfront on both the negotiation and approval of an empowered independent committee and an uncoerced, fully informed majority-of-the-minority vote. And to their credit, the plaintiffs themselves do not argue that minority stockholders will vote against a going private transaction because of fear of retribution, they just believe that most investors like a premium and will tend to vote for a deal that delivers one and that many long-term investors will sell out when they can obtain most of the premium without waiting for the ultimate vote.175 But that argument is not one that suggests that the voting decision is not voluntary, it is simply an editorial about the motives of investors and does not contradict the premise that a majority-of-the-minority condition gives minority investors a free and voluntary opportunity to decide what is fair for themselves.

Of course, as with any choice in making common law, there are costs. The loss from invoking the business judgment rule standard of review is whatever residual value it provides to minority investors to have the potential for a judicial review of fairness even in cases where a going private transaction has been conditioned upfront on the approval of a special committee comprised of independent directors with the absolute authority to say no and a majority-of-the-minority vote, that special committee has met its duty of care and negotiated and approved a deal, and the deal is approved by the minority stockholders on fair disclosures and without coercion. The difficulty for the plaintiffs is that what evidence exists suggests that the systemic benefits of the possibility of such review in cases like this are slim to non-existent. Indeed, the evidence that the possibility of such review provides real benefits to stockholders even in cases where a special committee is the only procedural protection is very slim at best, and there is a good case to be made that it is negative overall. The lack of demonstrable benefit is contrasted with the clear evidence of costs, because, absent the ability of defendants to bring an effective motion to dismiss, every case has settlement value, not for merits reasons, but because the cost of paying an attorneys' fee to settle litigation and obtain a release without having to pay the minority stockholders in excess of the price agreed to by the special committee exceeds the cost in terms of dollars and time consumed of going through the discovery process under a standard of review in which a substantive review of financial fairness is supposedly inescapable. This incentive structure has therefore resulted in frequent payouts of attorneys' fees but without anything close to a corresponding record of settlements or litigation results where the minority stockholders got more than the special committee had already secured. In fact, it is easier to find a case where a special committee got more than the price at which plaintiffs were willing to settle than it is to find the opposite. And it is unavoidable that it is investors themselves who are injured if the litigation system does not function with a rational benefit-to-cost ratio. Ultimately, litigation costs are borne by investors in the form of higher D & O insurance fees and other costs of capital to issuers that reduce the return to diversified investors. If those costs are not justified in a particular context by larger benefits, stockholders are hurt, not aided. Relatedly and as important, if no credit is given for the use of both procedural protections in tandem, minority investors will be denied access to the transactional structure that gives them the most power to protect themselves. Without any clear benefit to controllers for the clear costs of agreeing upfront to a majority-of-the-minority condition—a condition that controllers know creates uncertainty for their ability to consummate a deal and that puts pressure on them to put more money on the table—those conditions are now much less common than special committees, and when used are often done as part of a late stage deal-closing exercise in lieu of price moves. Under an approach where the business judgment rule standard is available if a controller uses a majority-of-the-minority condition upfront, minority investors will have an incentive for this potent fairness protection to become the market standard and to be able more consistently to protect themselves in the most cost-effective way, at the ballot box.

Nor are the litigation rights of minority investors unimportant even under this structure. The business judgment rule is only invoked if: (i) the controller conditions the procession of the transaction on the approval of both a special committee and a majority of the minority stockholders; (ii) the special committee is independent; (iii) the special committee is empowered to freely select its own advisors and to say no definitively; (iv) the special committee meets its duty of care; (v) the vote of the minority is informed; and (vi) there is no coercion of the minority. A plaintiff that can plead facts supporting a rational inference that any of those conditions did not exist could state a claim and go on to receive discovery. If, after discovery, triable issues of fact remain about any of those conditions, the plaintiff can go to trial and if those conditions are not found to exist by the court, the court will conduct a substantive fairness review. And any minority stockholder who voted no on a going private merger where appraisal is available, which is frequently the case, may also exercise her appraisal rights. Although appraisal is not a cost-free remedy, institutional ownership concentration has made it an increasingly effective one, and there are obvious examples of where it has been used effectively.

Importantly, this incentive structure can be made even more effective as an efficient and powerful way of ensuring fair treatment of the minority in going private transactions. In the area of takeover defense, Delaware jurisprudence has not varied the power or equitable duties of directors because an acquirer has made an acquisition bid directly to stockholders through a tender offer not requiring director action to be consummated. Rather, our Supreme Court has made clear that the directors have the duty to respond to any takeover they believe threatens the corporation and its stockholders by reasonable means, regardless of the form of the offer. In the going private area, it is not clear that a controlling stockholder who proceeds by the more coercive route of a tender offer is subject to the same equitable duties as a controller that proceeds in the manner less coercive to the minority stockholders, a merger. That is so even though stockholders would seem to need the protection of independent directors more when responding to a self-interested offer by a controller than in reacting to a third party's tender offer. As this court has pointed out, if the equitable duties of controlling stockholders seeking to acquire the rest of the controlled company's shares were consistent, regardless of transactional method, a sensible, across-the-board incentive system would be created to ensure fair treatment of minority stockholders.

When all these factors are considered, the court believes that the approach most consistent with Delaware's corporate law tradition is the one best for investors in Delaware corporations, which is the application of the business judgment rule. That approach will provide a strong incentive for the wide employment of a transactional structure highly beneficial to minority investors, a benefit that seems to far exceed any cost to investors, given the conditions a controller must meet in order to qualify for business judgment rule protection. Obviously, rational minds can disagree about this question, and our Supreme Court will be able to bring its own judgment to bear if the plaintiffs appeal. But, this court determines that on the conditions employed in connection with MacAndrews & Forbes's acquisition by merger of MFW, the business judgment rule applies and summary judgment is therefore entered for the defendants on all counts.

IT IS SO ORDERED.

NOTES AND QUESTIONS

1. In *Cinerama, Inc. v. Technicolor*, the Delaware Supreme Court noted, "Because the effect of the proper invocation of the business judgment rule is so powerful and the standard of entire fairness so exacting, the determination of the appropriate standard of judicial review frequently is determinative of the outcome of [the] litigation." *Cinerama, Inc. v. Technicolor*, 663 A.2d 1156, 1163 n.8 (Del. 1994). What does the Court mean by "determinative of the outcome"?

2. Would a shift of the burden of proof from the defendants to the plaintiff to show entire fairness also be determinative of the outcome?

3. A proper special committee must be both "well-formed" and "well-functioning." The *In re Southern Peru Copper Corp. Shareholder Derivative Litigation* case (52 A.3d 761, 763–65 (Del. Ch. 2011), *aff'd sub nom. Ams. Mining Corp. v. Theriault*, 51 A.3d 1213 (Del. 2012)) discusses a situation in which shareholders brought a suit against defendants for self-dealing by a controlling shareholder. In that case the court found that the special committee that the corporation created to review the transaction was not well-run, and therefore, reviewed the case under the entire fairness standard, with the defendant bearing the burden of proof. What features would be characteristic of a well-formed, well-functioning special committee?

4. Consider the stringent standards of independence for the members of a special litigation committee articulated in the *Oracle* case *supra* and whether those

standards might also apply to the standards for a "well-formed" special committee evaluating a transaction with a dominant shareholder.

D. Statutory Short Form Mergers

A statutory short form merger is a device that is authorized by state law. In many states (such as California as mentioned above) a majority shareholder (or group of shareholders) may perform a cash-out merger without shareholder approval, provided the majority shareholder holds a certain significant percentage of the corporation's outstanding stock. The exact requirements (including the exact percentage required) are determined by state law, but 90% is the required percentage in both Delaware and California and represents the typical requirement for such transactions. *See e.g.* DGCL §§ 253 and 267.

Short form mergers are often used following tender offers in order to eliminate any remaining minority shareholders. Because the process is simpler and easier than a non-short form, cash-out merger, the goal of many tender offers (in which 100% ownership is desired) is to acquire a percentage of the corporation sufficient to complete a statutory short form merger.

Alternatively, if the Acquirer in a two step merger, involving a tender offer is unable to acquire the 90% threshold of ownership required to consummate a statutory short form merger, there is, at least in Delaware, still a chance that an acquirer, who holds at least a majority of the Target corporation's outstanding stock in the tender offer, can affect the second step of the merger without a shareholder vote. In 2013 Delaware adopted (and amended in 2014), section 251(h) of the DGCL, which offers an option between the majority vote requirement of a long form merger and the 90% ownership threshold of a statutory short form merger. Subject to certain requirements, after completing the first step of a two-step negotiated acquisition process of a publicly held company and holding a majority of the Target's outstanding stock, Section 251(h) allows an acquirer, acting pursuant to a merger agreement that permits the merger to be effected pursuant to § 251(h), to complete the second step of the two-step merger without a vote of the Target corporation's remaining shareholders. In a two-step merger the Target corporation and the Acquirer enter in a negotiated merger agreement, pursuant to which the Acquirer launches a tender or exchange offer for all of the outstanding stock (subject to some exceptions) of the Target (i.e., the first step). Following this first step, as long as certain requirements are met, a majority shareholder can achieve results similar to a statutory short form merger even though that shareholder does not hold

90% of the corporation's outstanding stock. Section 251(h) eliminates the expense of instituting a shareholder vote, significantly increases the speed with which the second step (and the resulting payout of the Target corporation's shareholders) may be completed, and provides for additional financing options for the Acquirer by increasing the certainty that, following a successful tender offer, the merger transaction will be consummated rapidly and without costly objection. In addition, Delaware courts have held: that when a Target corporation's uncoerced, fully informed shareholders tender a majority of the corporation's outstanding shares pursuant to a tender offer made under § 251(h), they are accepting that tender offer; that their acceptance has the same cleansing effect as a vote in favor of that merger; and that, therefore, the transaction is subject to review under the business judgment rule. *In re Volcano Corp. Stockholder Litig.*, 143 A.3d 727, 738 (Del. Ch. 2016).

SECTION II: Hostile Acquisitions

Experiencing Assignment 15: Heavenly Chocolates, Inc., II

You continue to work at your firm and to gain respect based upon the high quality of your work. One day, you receive a call from an old client, Olive Sweetz. You recall that Olive is the president of Heavenly Chocolates, Inc. ("HCI"). Several years ago you assisted HCI in evaluating its obligations in the purchase of a chocolate plantation to secure a good source of high quality chocolate. You also recall that HCI is dedicated to producing high quality chocolate. The company operates based upon a core philosophy that HCI customers have refined tastes and appreciate the care and quality that goes into HCI's chocolate products.

FACTS:

Olive informs you that a few days ago HCI received notice that Junk Food Junction Corp. ("JFJ") has launched a tender offer for HCI stock and is trying to take over HCI. JFJ is a mass producer of low quality chocolate and a publicly traded company. Olive tells you that JFJ has always envied HCI's Caribbean plantation. She also tells you that the HCI board believes that JFJ just wants to use the HCI name but lower the quality of the HCI products to exploit customers. In order to avoid being taken over, Olive and the rest of the HCI board have come up with the plan that HCI should launch its own tender offer for JFJ's stock (the "HCI Plan"). The HCI Plan is to take over JFJ, improve the quality of JFJ's products and take advantage of JFJ's broad distribution network to increase the market for HCI products. HCI would need to borrow substantial capital in order to implement its bid for JFJ, and this borrowing could jeopardize HCI's financial stability in the future. Assume that the entire HCI board would approve the HCI Plan.

ASSIGNMENT:

Olive acknowledges that the HCI Plan is aggressive. She would like you explain how the HCI Plan to acquire JFJ would be evaluated if it were challenged and, since the HCI has not yet formally approved the HCI Plan, what steps HCI could take to strengthen its position in any such challenge. Olive and the HCI directors do not want case citations. They want to understand the best procedures to follow, the risks involved and the legal standards by which their actions might be judged.

This Assignment does not need to be completed, and should not be completed, until the end of the chapter. However, as you study the cases and other materials that follow, it might be helpful to do so with a view toward providing assistance to the HCI directors. Some of the materials in the chapter will relate more than others to the issues facing HCI. However, the materials are designed to build your understanding of the issues that arise in evaluating actions taken by a corporation's board of directors in the context of a takeover battle, and assist you in addressing HCI's concerns and putting them in context. Please keep HCI's issues and the questions presented by the assignment in mind while reading the materials that follow.

A. Hostile Acquisitions in General

A merger or a negotiated acquisition is a consensual process. Both firms' board of directors must agree in order for the transaction to proceed. However, there are situations in which one firm or individual wants to acquire another, and the board of directors of the Target firm does not want to be acquired or does not want to be acquired by that particular person or firm. In these instances, the would-be Acquirer can take steps, other than the consensual processes discussed earlier, to acquire the firm. The process of excluding a Target's board from the Acquirer's efforts to acquire control of a company is generally referred to as a "hostile takeover" attempt. A hostile takeover involves an effort to acquire sufficient shares to control the Target's board of directors (often through a tender offer), and then replacing the Target's directors with the

Acquirer's own slate of directors. This process is often followed by some form of statutory merger of the acquired Target entity into a subsidiary entity, controlled by the Acquirer and may or may not involve cashing out the remaining shareholders.

Though these processes, to varying degrees, may be utilized in "friendly" circumstances as well, there are three main approaches that might be used to circumvent the Target's board of directors:

> **Tender Offers:** a tender offer involves a public offer, usually made to all the shareholders of the Target corporation, in which the Offeror offers to buy all (or a certain percentage of) the Target's shares at a specific price.
>
> **Direct Share Purchases:** direct purchases involve direct purchases of stock by the potential Acquirer in the public markets or through privately negotiated transactions with a limited number of the Target's shareholders.
>
> **Proxy Contests:** proxy contests (discussed in Chapter 6, *supra*) involve a battle for control of the Target's board of directors through the shareholder voting process.

B. Tender Offers

There are many rules governing tender offers. We have already seen Rule 14e–3 with respect to insider trading and tender offers, but there are many more. The most significant rules arise out of the Williams Act (1968), which amended the 1934 Act to add provisions relating to tender offers. These provisions are found in sections 13(d), 13(e), 14(d) and 14(e) of the 1934 Act. Some of the significant provisions included in Section 13(d) of the 1934 Act include requirements that a person disclose: (i) when that person acquires (directly or indirectly) more than 5% of a registered company's shares; (ii) whether that person's intended purpose in acquiring those shares is to acquire control and/or to sell, liquidate or make a fundamental change to the Target company; (iii) the identity of the person acquiring the shares; (iv) the number of shares which are beneficially owned; and (v) any contracts, arrangements or understandings that person has with anyone else with respect to any securities of the Target company.

Any person who commences a tender offer (often referred to as the "Bidder") in an effort to acquire more than 5% of a company, must also comply with the extensive rules and regulations arising under sections 14(d) and 14(e) of the 1934 Act. Bidders must provide a great deal of information, which must include full and fair disclosure of all aspects of the tender offer, including all of the disclosures required under section 13(d) with respect to the tender offer. There are also specific ways in which a tender offer must be delivered to the Target company's shareholders. The Bidder must also make a public announcement that includes the Bidder's identity, the Target's identity, the amount of shares sought and the price at which the Bidder is offering to buy those shares. When this disclosure is provided, the Target company is required to respond.

Cheff v. Mathes

41 Del. Ch. 494, 199 A.2d 548 (Del. 1964)

CAREY, J.:

This is an appeal from the decision of the Vice-Chancellor in a derivative suit holding certain directors of Holland Furnace Company liable for loss allegedly resulting from improper use of corporate funds to purchase shares of the company. Because a meaningful decision upon review turns upon a complete understanding of the factual background, a somewhat detailed summary of the evidence is required.

Holland Furnace Company, a corporation of the State of Delaware, manufactures warm air furnaces, air conditioning equipment, and other home heating equipment. At the time of the relevant transactions, the board of directors was composed of the seven individual defendants. Mr. Cheff had been Holland's Chief Executive Officer since 1933, received an annual salary of $77,400, and personally owned 6,000 shares of the company. He was also a director. Mrs. Cheff, the wife of Mr. Cheff, was a daughter of the founder of Holland and had served as a director since 1922. She personally owned 5,804 shares of Holland and owned 47.9 percent of Hazelbank United Interest, Inc. Hazelbank is an investment vehicle for Mrs. Cheff and members of the Cheff-Landwehr family group, which owned 164,950 shares of the 883,585 outstanding shares of Holland. As a director, Mrs. Cheff received a compensation of $200.00 for each monthly board meeting, whether or not she attended the meeting.

The third director, Edgar P. Landwehr, is the nephew of Mrs. Cheff and personally owned 24,010 shares of Holland and 8.6 percent of the outstanding shares of Hazelbank. He received no compensation from Holland other than the monthly director's fee.

Robert H. Trenkamp is an attorney who first represented Holland in 1946. In May 1953, he became a director of Holland and acted as general counsel for the company. During the period in question, he received no retainer from the company, but did receive substantial sums for legal services rendered the company. Apart from the above-described payments, he received no compensation from Holland other than the monthly director's fee. He owned 200 shares of Holland Furnace stock. Although he owned no shares of Hazelbank, at the time relevant to this controversy, he was serving as a director and counsel of Hazelbank.

John D. Ames was then a partner in the Chicago investment firm of Bacon, Whipple & Co. and joined the board at the request of Mr. Cheff. During the periods in question, his stock ownership varied between ownership of no shares to ownership of 300 shares. He was considered by the other members of the Holland board to be the financial advisor to the board. He received no compensation from Holland other than the normal director's fee.

Mr. Ralph G. Boalt was the Vice President of J. R. Watkins Company, a manufacturer and distributor of cosmetics. In 1953, at the request of Mr. Cheff, he became a member of the board of directors. Apart from the normal director's fee, he received no compensation from Holland for his services.

Mr. George Spatta was the President of Clark Equipment Company, a large manufacturer of earth moving equipment. In 1951, at the request of Mr. Cheff, he joined the board of directors of Holland. Apart from the normal director's fee, he received no compensation from the company.

The board of directors of Hazelbank included the five principal shareholders: Mrs. Cheff; Leona Kolb, who was Mrs. Cheff's daughter; Mr. Landwehr; Mrs. Bowles, who was Mr. Landwehr's sister; Mrs. Putnam, who was also Mr. Landwehr's sister; Mr. Trenkamp; and Mr. William DeLong, an accountant.

Prior to the events in question, Holland employed approximately 8500 persons and maintained 400 branch sales offices located in 43 states. The volume of sales had declined from over $41,000,000 in 1948 to less than $32,000,000 in 1956. Defendants contend that the decline in earnings is attributable to the artificial post-war demand generated in the 1946–1948 period. In order to stabilize the condition of the company, the sales department apparently was reorganized and certain unprofitable branch offices were closed. By 1957 this reorganization had been completed and the management was convinced that the changes were manifesting beneficial results. The practice of the company was to directly employ the retail salesman, and the management considered that practice—unique in the furnace business—to be a vital factor in the company's success.

During the first five months of 1957, the monthly trading volume of Holland's stock on the New York Stock Exchange ranged between 10,300 shares to 24,200 shares. In the last week of June 1957, however, the trading increased to 37,800 shares, with a corresponding increase in the market price. In June of 1957, Mr. Cheff met with Mr. Arnold H. Maremont, who was President of Maremont Automotive Products, Inc. and Chairman of the boards of Motor Products Corporation and Allied Paper Corporation. Mr. Cheff testified, on deposition, that Maremont generally inquired about the feasibility of merger between Motor Products and Holland. Mr. Cheff testified that, in view of the difference in sales practices between the two companies, he informed Mr. Maremont that a merger did not seem feasible. In reply, Mr. Maremont stated that, in the light of Mr. Cheff's decision, he had no further interest in Holland nor did he wish to buy any of the stock of Holland.

None of the members of the board apparently connected the interest of Mr. Maremont with the increased activity of Holland stock. However, Mr. Trenkamp and Mr. Staal, the Treasurer of Holland, unsuccessfully made an informal investigation in order to ascertain the identity of the purchaser or purchasers. The mystery was resolved, however, when Maremont called Ames in July of 1957 to inform the latter that Maremont then owned 55,000 shares of Holland stock. At this juncture, no requests for change in corporate policy were made, and Maremont made no demand to be made a member of the board of Holland.

Ames reported the above information to the board at its July 30, 1957 meeting. Because of the position now occupied by Maremont, the board elected to investigate the financial and business history of Maremont and corporations controlled by him. Apart from the documentary evidence produced by this investigation, which will be considered infra, Staal testified, on deposition, that "leading bank officials" had indicated that Maremont "had been a participant, or had attempted to be, in the liquidation of a number of companies." Staal specifically mentioned only one individual giving such advice, the Vice President of the First National Bank of Chicago. Mr. Cheff testified, at trial, of Maremont's alleged participation in liquidation activities. Mr. Cheff testified that: "Throughout the whole of the Kalamazoo-Battle Creek area, and Detroit too, where I spent considerable time, he is well known and not highly regarded by any stretch." This information was communicated to the board.

On August 23, 1957, at the request of Maremont, a meeting was held between Mr. Maremont and Cheff. At this meeting, Cheff was informed that Motor Products then owned approximately 100,000 shares of Holland stock. Maremont then made a demand that he be named to the board of directors, but Cheff refused to consider it. Since considerable controversy has been generated by Maremont's alleged threat to liquidate the company or substantially alter the sales force of Holland, we believe it desirable to set forth the testimony of Cheff on this point: "Now we have 8500 men, direct employees, so the problem is entirely different. He indicated immediately that he had no interest in that type of distribution, that he didn't think it was modern, that he felt furnaces could be sold as he sold mufflers, through half a dozen salesmen in a wholesale way."

Testimony was introduced by the defendants tending to show that substantial unrest was present among the employees of Holland as a result of the threat of Maremont to seek control of Holland. Thus, Mr. Cheff testified that the field organization was considering leaving in large numbers because of a fear of the consequences of a Maremont acquisition; he further testified that approximately "25 of our key men" were lost as the result of the unrest engendered by the Maremont proposal. Staal, corroborating Cheff's version, stated that a number of branch managers approached him for reassurances that Maremont was not going to be allowed to successfully gain control. Moreover, at approximately this time, the company was furnished with a Dun and Bradstreet report, which indicated the practice of Maremont to achieve quick profits by sales or liquidations of companies acquired by him. The defendants were also supplied with an income statement of Motor Products, Inc., showing a loss of $336,121.00 for the period in 1957.

On August 30, 1957, the board was informed by Cheff of Maremont's demand to be placed upon the board and of Maremont's belief that the retail sales organization of Holland was obsolete. The board was also informed of the results of the investigation by Cheff and Staal. Predicated upon this information, the board authorized the purchase of company stock on the market with corporate funds, ostensibly for use in a stock option plan.

Subsequent to this meeting, substantial numbers of shares were purchased and, in addition, Mrs. Cheff made alternate personal purchases of Holland stock. As a result of purchases by Maremont, Holland and Mrs. Cheff, the market price rose. On September 13, 1957, Maremont wrote to each of the directors of Holland and requested a broad engineering survey to be made for the benefit of all stockholders. During September, Motor Products released its annual report, which indicated that the investment in Holland was "special situation" as opposed to the normal policy of placing the funds of Motor Products into "an active company". On September 4th, Maremont proposed to sell his current holdings of Holland to the corporation for $14.00 a share. However, because of delay in responding to this offer, Maremont withdrew the offer. At this time, Mrs. Cheff was obviously quite concerned over the prospect of a Maremont acquisition, and had stated her willingness to expend her personal resources to prevent it.

On September 30, 1957, Motor Products Corporation, by letter to Mrs. Bowles, made a buy-sell offer to Hazelbank. At the Hazelbank meeting of October 3, 1957, Mrs. Bowles presented the letter to the board. The board took no action, but referred the proposal to its finance committee. Although Mrs. Bowles and Mrs. Putnam were opposed to any acquisition of Holland stock by Hazelbank, Mr. Landwehr conceded that a majority of the board were in favor of the purchase. Despite this fact, the finance committee elected to refer the offer to the Holland board on the grounds that it was the primary concern of Holland.

Thereafter, Mr. Trenkamp arranged for a meeting with Maremont, which occurred on October 14–15, 1957, in Chicago. Prior to this meeting, Trenkamp was aware of the intentions of Hazelbank and Mrs. Cheff to purchase all or portions of the stock then owned by Motor Products if Holland did not so act. As a result of the meeting, there was a tentative agreement on the part of Motor Products to sell its 155,000 shares at $14.40 per share. On October 23, 1957, at a special meeting of the Holland board, the purchase was considered. All directors, except Spatta, were present. The dangers allegedly posed by Maremont were again reviewed by the board. Trenkamp and Mrs. Cheff agree that the latter informed the board that either she or Hazelbank would purchase part or all of the block of Holland stock owned by Motor Products if the Holland board did not so act. The board was also informed that in order for the corporation to finance the purchase, substantial sums would have to be borrowed from commercial lending institutions. A resolution authorizing the purchase of 155,000 shares from Motor Products was adopted by the board. The price paid was in excess of the market price prevailing at the time, and the book value of the stock was approximately $20.00 as compared to approximately $14.00 for the net quick asset value. The transaction was subsequently consummated. The stock option plan mentioned in the minutes has never been implemented. In 1959, Holland stock reached a high of $15.25 a share.

On February 6, 1958, plaintiffs, owners of 60 shares of Holland stock, filed a derivative suit in the court below naming all of the individual directors of

Holland, Holland itself and Motor Products Corporation as defendants. The complaint alleged that all of the purchases of stock by Holland in 1957 were for the purpose of insuring the perpetuation of control by the incumbent directors. . . .

After trial, the Vice Chancellor found the following facts: (a) Holland directly sells to retail consumers by means of numerous branch offices. There were no intermediate dealers. (b) Immediately prior to the complained-of transactions, the sales and earnings of Holland had declined and its marketing practices were under investigation by the Federal Trade Commission. (c) Mr. Cheff and Trenkamp had received substantial sums as Chief Executive and attorney of the company, respectively. (d) Maremont, on August 23rd, 1957, demanded a place on the board. (e) At the October 14th meeting between Trenkamp, Staal and Maremont, Trenkamp and Staal were authorized to speak for Hazelbank and Mrs. Cheff as well as Holland. Only Mr. Cheff, Mrs. Cheff, Mr. Landwehr, and Mr. Trenkamp clearly understood, prior to the October 23rd meeting, that either Hazelbank or Mrs. Cheff would have utilized their funds to purchase the Holland stock if Holland had not acted. (g) There was no real threat posed by Maremont and no substantial evidence of intention by Maremont to liquidate Holland. (h) Any employee unrest could have been caused by factors other than Maremont's intrusion and "only one important employee was shown to have left, and his motive for leaving is not clear." . . . The Court rejected the stock option plan as a meaningful rationale for the purchase from Maremont or the prior open market purchases.

The Court then found that the actual purpose behind the purchase was the desire to perpetuate control, but because of its finding that only the four above-named directors knew of the "alternative", the remaining directors were exonerated.

* * * *

Under the provisions of 8 Del. C. § 160, a corporation is granted statutory power to purchase and sell shares of its own stock. Such a right, as embodied in the statute, has long been recognized in this State. See *In re International Radiator Co.,* 10 Del. Ch. 358, 92 A. 255. The charge here is not one of violation of statute, but the allegation is that the true motives behind such purchases were improperly centered upon perpetuation of control. In an analogous field courts have sustained the use of proxy funds to inform stockholders of management's views upon the policy questions inherent in an election to a board of directors, but have not sanctioned the use of corporate funds to advance the selfish desires of directors to perpetuate themselves in office. [*Citations omitted.*] Similarly, if the actions of the board were motivated by a sincere belief that the buying out of the dissident stockholder was necessary to maintain what the board believed to be proper business practices, the board will not be held liable for such decision, even though hindsight indicates the decision was not the wisest course. *See Kors v. Carey,* Del. Ch., 158 A.2d 136. On the other hand, if the board has acted solely or primarily because of the desire to perpetuate themselves in office, the use of corporate funds for such purposes is improper. [*Citations omitted.*]

Our first problem is the allocation of the burden of proof to show the presence or lack of good faith on the part of the board in authorizing the purchase of shares. Initially, the decision of the board of directors in authorizing a purchase was presumed to be in good faith and could be overturned only by a conclusive showing by plaintiffs of fraud or other misconduct. [*Citations omitted.*] In Kors, cited supra, the court merely indicated that the directors are presumed to act in good faith and the burden of proof to show to the contrary falls upon the plaintiff. However, in *Bennett v. Propp, supra,* we stated:

> "We must bear in mind the inherent danger in the purchase of shares with corporate funds to remove a threat to corporate policy when a threat to control is involved. The directors are of necessity confronted with a conflict of interest, and an objective decision is difficult. * * * Hence, in our opinion, the burden should be on the directors to justify such a purchase as one primarily in the corporate interest." ([*Bennet v. Propp, Del.,*] 41 Del. Ch. 14, 187 A.2d 405, at page 409).

* * * *

To say that the burden of proof is upon the defendants is not to indicate, however, that the directors have the same "self-dealing interest" as is present, for example, when a director sells property to the corporation. The only clear pecuniary interest shown on the record was held by Mr. Cheff, as an executive of the corporation, and Trenkamp, as its attorney. The mere fact that some of the other directors were substantial shareholders does not create a personal pecuniary interest in the decisions made by the board of directors, since all shareholders would presumably share the benefit flowing to the substantial shareholder. See *Smith v. Good Music Station, Inc.,* 36 Del. Ch. 262, 129 A.2d 242. Accordingly, these directors other than Trenkamp and Cheff, while called upon to justify their actions, will not be held to the same standard of proof required of those directors having personal and pecuniary interest in the transaction.

As noted above, the Vice Chancellor found that the stock option plan, mentioned in the minutes as a justification for the purchases, was not a motivating reason for the purchases. This finding we accept, since there is evidence to support it; in fact, Trenkamp admitted that the stock option plan was not the motivating reason. The minutes of October 23, 1957 dealing with the purchase from Maremont do not, in fact, mention the option plan as a reason for the purchase. While the minutes of the October 1, 1957 meeting only indicated the stock option plan as the motivating reason, the defendants are not bound by such statements and may supplement the minutes by oral testimony to show that the motivating reason was genuine fear of an acquisition by Maremont. See *Bennett v. Propp,* cited *supra.*

Plaintiffs urge that the sale price was unfair in view of the fact that the price was in excess of that prevailing on the open market. However, as conceded by all parties, a substantial block of stock will normally sell at a higher price than that prevailing on the open market, the increment being attributable to a "control premium". Plaintiffs argue that it is inappropriate to require the defendant corporation to pay a control premium, since control is meaningless to an acquisition by a corporation of its own shares. However, it is elementary that a holder of a substantial number of shares would expect to receive the control premium as part of his selling price, and if the corporation desired to obtain the stock, it is unreasonable to expect that the corporation could avoid paying what any other purchaser would be required to pay for the stock. In any event, the financial expert produced by defendant at trial indicated that the price paid was fair and there was no rebuttal. Ames, the financial man on the board, was strongly of the opinion that the purchase was a good deal for the corporation. The Vice Chancellor made no finding as to the fairness of the price other than to indicate the obvious fact that the market price was increasing as a result of open market purchases by Maremont, Mrs. Cheff and Holland.

The question then presented is whether or not defendants satisfied the burden of proof of showing reasonable grounds to believe a danger to corporate policy and effectiveness existed by the presence of the Maremont stock ownership. It is important to remember that the directors satisfy their burden by showing good faith and reasonable investigation; the directors will not be penalized for an honest mistake of judgment, if the judgment appeared reasonable at the time the decision was made. [*Citations omitted.*]

In holding that employee unrest could as well be attributed to a condition of Holland's business affairs as to the possibility of Maremont's intrusion, the Vice Chancellor must have had in mind one or both of two matters: (1) the pending proceedings before the Federal Trade Commission concerning certain sales practices of Holland; (2) the decrease in sales and profits during the preceding several years. Any other possible reason would be pure speculation. In the first place, the adverse decision of the F.T.C. was not announced until *after* the complained-of transaction. Secondly, the evidence clearly shows that the downward trend of sales and profits had reversed itself, presumably because of the reorganization which had then been completed. Thirdly, everyone who testified on the point said that the unrest was due to the possible threat presented by Maremont's purchases of stock. There was, in fact, no *testimony* whatever of any connection between the unrest and either the F.T.C. proceedings or the business picture.

The Vice Chancellor found that there was no substantial evidence of a liquidation posed by Maremont. This holding overlooks an important contention. The fear of the defendants, according to their testimony, was not limited to the possibility of liquidation; it included the alternate possibility of a material change in Holland's sales policies, which the board considered vital to its future success. The *unrebutted* testimony before the court indicated: (1) Maremont had deceived Cheff as to his original intentions, since his open market purchases were contemporaneous with his disclaimer of interest in Holland; (2) Maremont had given Cheff some reason to believe that he intended to eliminate the retail sales force of Holland; (3) Maremont demanded a place on the board; (4) Maremont substantially increased his purchases after having been refused a place on the board; (5) the directors had good reason to believe that unrest among key employees had been engendered by the Maremont threat; (6) the board had received advice from Dun and Bradstreet indicating the past liquidation or quick sale activities of Motor Products; (7) the board had received professional advice from the firm of Merrill Lynch, Fenner & Beane, who recommended that the purchase from Motor Products be carried out; (8) the board had received competent advice that the corporation was over-capitalized; (9) Staal and Cheff had made informal personal investigations from contacts in the business and financial community and had reported to the board of the alleged poor reputation of Maremont. The board was within its rights in relying upon that investigation, since 8 Del. C. § 141 (f) allows the directors to reasonably rely upon a report provided by corporate officers. [*Citations omitted.*]

Accordingly, we are of the opinion that the evidence presented in the court below leads inevitably to the conclusion that the board of directors, based upon direct investigation, receipt of professional advice, and personal observations of the contradictory action of Maremont and his explanation of corporate purpose, believed, with justification, that there was a reasonable threat to the continued existence of Holland, or at least existence in its present form, by the plan of Maremont to continue building up his stock holdings. We find no evidence in the record sufficient to justify a contrary conclusion. The opinion of the Vice Chancellor that employee unrest may have been engendered by other factors or that the board had no grounds to suspect Maremont is not supported in any manner by the evidence.

As noted above, the Vice-Chancellor found that the purpose of the acquisition was the improper desire to maintain control, but, at the same time, he exonerated those individual directors whom he believed to be unaware of the possibility of using non-corporate funds to accomplish this purpose. Such a decision is inconsistent with his finding that the motive was improper, within the rule enunciated in Bennett. If the actions were in fact improper because of a desire to maintain control, then the presence or absence of a non-corporate alternative is irrelevant, as corporate funds may not be used to advance an improper purpose even if there is no non-corporate alternative available. Conversely, if the actions were proper because of a decision by the board made in good faith that the corporate interest was served thereby, they are not rendered improper by the fact that some individual directors were willing to advance personal funds if the corporation did not. It is conceivable that the Vice Chancellor considered this feature of the case to be of significance because of his apparent belief that any excess corporate funds should have been used to finance a subsidiary corporation. That action would not have solved the problem of Holland's over-capitalization. In any event, this question was a matter of business judgment, which furnishes no justification for holding the directors personally responsible in this case.

Accordingly, the judgment of the court below is reversed and remanded with instruction to enter judgment for the defendants.

QUESTIONS

1. Why does the court make a distinction between those directors who received compensation from Holland and those who received no such compensation, other than normal director's fees?

2. If you had been asked by Holland's board, would you have advised them to purchase Maremont's shares?

3. Are there other approaches you might have suggested?

C. Fiduciary Duties in Takeover Defenses

One of the fundamental issues that arises with regard to all defenses to, and rejections of, unwanted takeovers is determining the duties of the Target company's directors. While earlier chapters have already examined fiduciary duties in the day-to-day operations of a corporation, the tests to evaluate whether fiduciary duties have been met are different in the context of a hostile takeover. This different approach arises out of two important distinctions. The first is that these transactions involve a fundamental change to the corporation and often represent the potential end of the corporation's existence. The second distinction is that most hostile takeovers represent a threat to the positions of the Target company's senior officers and directors, so their decisions are somewhat suspect and are not afforded the same deference as might occur in a typical application of the Business Judgment Rule.

In order to evaluate the actions taken by the board of directors in the face of a hostile takeover transaction, one must examine both the board's specific actions and its motivations for taking such actions. When a company takes any defensive measures to fight off or to reject a hostile acquisition, the first level of analysis is to determine whether the company's board of directors is comprised of "inside" directors or "outside" directors. Inside directors are directors who are also officers of the company. Because they will lose their jobs if the hostile takeover succeeds, they have a conflict of interest. Therefore, inside directors' actions are subject to scrutiny under the duty of loyalty, not the duty of care. If a defensive action is taken by inside directors, or if their votes are necessary to approve an action, then it must be cleansed by a majority of the disinterested directors or by the shareholders after full disclosure. If the action is not cleansed, then it must be determined to be "fair" to the corporation, otherwise the directors supporting the action may be found to have violated their fiduciary duties and the transaction may be voidable and/or result in liability for those directors approving the action.

Outside directors, those who are neither employees of the Target company nor dependent on their positions with the Target company for their livelihood, are not viewed as having a conflict. However, there is still some additional scrutiny placed on their actions for the reasons stated above. In circumstances in which there are outside directors on the board, even if there are also inside directors, the actions of the board of directors are typically evaluated under a measure known as the *"Unocal"* test, which arises out of the *Unocal Corp. v. Mesa Petroleum Co.* case, which follows.

Unocal Corporation v. Mesa Petroleum Co.

493 A.2d 946 (Del.1985)

MOORE J.:

We confront an issue of first impression in Delaware—the validity of a corporation's self-tender for its own shares which excludes from participation a stockholder making a hostile tender offer for the company's stock.

The Court of Chancery granted a preliminary injunction to the plaintiffs, Mesa Petroleum Co., Mesa Asset Co., Mesa Partners II, and Mesa Eastern, Inc. (collectively "Mesa"),[49] enjoining an exchange offer of the defendant, Unocal Corporation (Unocal) for its own stock. The trial court concluded that a selective exchange offer, excluding Mesa, was legally impermissible. We cannot agree with such a blanket rule. . . .Unocal's board, consisting of a majority of independent directors, acted in good faith, and after reasonable investigation found that Mesa's tender offer was both inadequate and coercive. Under the circumstances the board had both the power and duty to oppose a bid it perceived to be harmful to the corporate enterprise. On this record we are satisfied that the device Unocal adopted is reasonable in relation to the threat posed, and that the board acted in the proper exercise of sound business judgment. We will not substitute our views for those of the board if the latter's decision can be "attributed to any rational business purpose." *Sinclair Oil Corp. v. Levien,* Del. Supr., 280 A.2d 717, 720 (1971). Accordingly, we reverse the decision of the Court of Chancery and order the preliminary injunction vacated.

* * * *

On April 8, 1985, Mesa, the owner of approximately 13% of Unocal's stock, commenced a two-tier "front loaded" cash tender offer for 64 million shares, or approximately 37%, of Unocal's outstanding stock at a price of $54 per share. The "back-end" was designed to eliminate the remaining publicly held shares by an exchange of securities purportedly worth $54 per share. However, pursuant to an order entered by the United States District Court for the Central District of California on April 26, 1985, Mesa issued a supplemental proxy statement to Unocal's stockholders disclosing that the securities offered in the second-step merger would be highly subordinated, and that Unocal's capitalization would differ significantly from its present structure. Unocal has rather aptly termed such securities "junk bonds".

---

[49] T. Boone Pickens, Jr., is President and Chairman of the Board of Mesa Petroleum and President of Mesa Asset and controls the related Mesa entities.

Unocal's board consists of eight independent outside directors and six insiders. It met on April 13, 1985, to consider the Mesa tender offer. Thirteen directors were present, and the meeting lasted nine and one-half hours. The directors were given no agenda or written materials prior to the session. However, detailed presentations were made by legal counsel regarding the board's obligations under both Delaware corporate law and the federal securities laws. The board then received a presentation from Peter Sachs on behalf of Goldman Sachs & Co. (Goldman Sachs) and Dillon, Read & Co. (Dillon Read) discussing the bases for their opinions that the Mesa proposal was wholly inadequate. Mr. Sachs opined that the minimum cash value that could be expected from a sale or orderly liquidation for 100% of Unocal's stock was in excess of $60 per share. In making his presentation, Mr. Sachs showed slides outlining the valuation techniques used by the financial advisors, and others, depicting recent business combinations in the oil and gas industry. The Court of Chancery found that the Sachs presentation was designed to apprise the directors of the scope of the analyses performed rather than the facts and numbers used in reaching the conclusion that Mesa's tender offer price was inadequate.

Mr. Sachs also presented various defensive strategies available to the board if it concluded that Mesa's two-step tender offer was inadequate and should be opposed. One of the devices outlined was a self-tender by Unocal for its own stock with a reasonable price range of $70 to $75 per share. The cost of such a proposal would cause the company to incur $6.1—6.5 billion of additional debt, and a presentation was made informing the board of Unocal's ability to handle it. The directors were told that the primary effect of this obligation would be to reduce exploratory drilling, but that the company would nonetheless remain a viable entity.

The eight outside directors, comprising a clear majority of the thirteen members present, then met separately with Unocal's financial advisors and attorneys. Thereafter, they unanimously agreed to advise the board that it should reject Mesa's tender offer as inadequate, and that Unocal should pursue a self-tender to provide the stockholders with a fairly priced alternative to the Mesa proposal. The board then reconvened and unanimously adopted a resolution rejecting as grossly inadequate Mesa's tender offer. Despite the nine and one-half hour length of the meeting, no formal decision was made on the proposed defensive self-tender.

On April 15, the board met again. . . . Unocal's Vice President of Finance and its Assistant General Counsel made a detailed presentation of the proposed terms of the exchange offer. A price range between $70 and $80 per share was considered, and ultimately the directors agreed upon $72. The board was also advised about the debt securities that would be issued, and the necessity of placing restrictive covenants upon certain corporate activities until the obligations were paid. The board's decisions were made in reliance on the advice of its investment bankers, including the terms and conditions upon which the securities were to be issued. Based upon this advice, and the board's own deliberations, the directors unanimously approved the exchange offer. Their resolution provided that if Mesa acquired 64 million shares of Unocal stock through its own offer (the Mesa Purchase Condition), Unocal would buy the remaining 49% outstanding for an exchange of debt securities having an aggregate par value of $72 per share. The board resolution also stated that the offer would be subject to other conditions that had been described to the board at the meeting, or which were deemed necessary by Unocal's officers, including the exclusion of Mesa from the proposal (the Mesa exclusion). Any such conditions were required to be in accordance with the "purport and intent" of the offer.

Unocal's exchange offer was commenced on April 17, 1985, and Mesa promptly challenged it by filing this suit in the Court of Chancery. On April 22, the Unocal board met again and was advised by Goldman Sachs and Dillon Read to waive the Mesa Purchase Condition as to 50 million shares. This recommendation was in response to a perceived concern of the shareholders that, if shares were tendered to Unocal, no shares would be purchased by either offeror. The directors were also advised that they should tender their own Unocal stock into the exchange offer as a mark of their confidence in it.

Another focus of the board was the Mesa exclusion. Legal counsel advised that under Delaware law Mesa could only be excluded for what the directors reasonably believed to be a valid corporate purpose. The directors' discussion centered on the objective of adequately compensating shareholders at the "back-end" of Mesa's proposal, which the latter would finance with "junk bonds". To include Mesa would defeat that goal, because under the proration aspect of the exchange offer (49%) every Mesa share accepted by Unocal would displace one held by another stockholder. Further, if Mesa were permitted to tender to Unocal, the latter would in effect be financing Mesa's own inadequate proposal.

On April 24, 1985 Unocal issued a supplement to the exchange offer describing the partial waiver of the Mesa Purchase Condition. On May 1, 1985, in another supplement, Unocal extended the withdrawal, proration and expiration dates of its exchange offer to May 17, 1985.

Meanwhile, on April 22, 1985, Mesa amended its complaint in this action to challenge the Mesa exclusion. . . .

On April 29, 1985, the Vice Chancellor temporarily restrained Unocal from proceeding with the exchange offer unless it included Mesa. The trial court recognized that directors could oppose, and attempt to defeat, a hostile takeover which they considered adverse to the best interests of the corporation. However, the Vice Chancellor decided that in a selective purchase of the company's stock, the corporation bears the burden of showing: (1) a valid corporate purpose, and (2) that the transaction was fair to all of the stockholders, including those excluded.

* * * *

II.

The issues we address involve these fundamental questions: Did the Unocal board have the power and duty to oppose a takeover threat it reasonably perceived to be harmful to the corporate enterprise, and if so, is its action here entitled to the protection of the business judgment rule?

* * * *

III.

We begin with the basic issue of the power of a board of directors of a Delaware corporation to adopt a defensive measure of this type. . . . Neither issues of fairness nor business judgment are pertinent without the basic underpinning of a board's legal power to act.

. . . . [I]t is now well established that in the acquisition of its shares a Delaware corporation may deal selectively with its stockholders, provided the directors have not acted out of a sole or primary purpose to entrench themselves in office. [*Citations omitted.*]

* * * *

When a board addresses a pending takeover bid it has an obligation to determine whether the offer is in the best interests of the corporation and its shareholders. In that respect a board's duty is no different from any other responsibility it shoulders, and its decisions should be no less entitled to the respect they otherwise would be accorded in the realm of business judgment. [*Citation omitted.*] There are, however, certain caveats to a proper exercise of this function. Because of the omnipresent specter that a board may be acting primarily in its own interests, rather than those of the corporation and its shareholders, there is an enhanced duty which calls for judicial examination at the threshold before the protections of the business judgment rule may be conferred.

This Court has long recognized that:

> We must bear in mind the inherent danger in the purchase of shares with corporate funds to remove a threat to corporate policy when a threat to control is involved. The directors are of necessity confronted with a conflict of interest, and an objective decision is difficult.

Bennett v. Propp, Del. Supr., 41 Del. Ch. 14, 187 A.2d 405, 409 (1962). In the face of this inherent conflict directors must show that they had reasonable grounds for believing that a danger to corporate policy and effectiveness existed because of another person's stock ownership. *Cheff v. Mathes,* 199 A.2d at 554–55. However, they satisfy that burden "by showing good faith and reasonable investigation. . . ." *Id.* at 555. Furthermore, such proof is materially enhanced, as here, by the approval of a board comprised of a majority of outside independent directors who have acted in accordance with the foregoing standards. *See Aronson v. Lewis,* 473 A.2d at 812, 815; [*Citations omitted.*]

IV.

A.

In the board's exercise of corporate power to forestall a takeover bid our analysis begins with the basic principle that corporate directors have a fiduciary duty to act in the best interests of the corporation's stockholders. *Guth v. Loft, Inc.,* Del. Supr., 23 Del. Ch. 255, 5 A.2d 503, 510 (1939). As we have noted, their duty of care extends to protecting the corporation and its owners from perceived harm whether a threat originates from third parties or other shareholders.[10] But such powers are not absolute. A corporation does not have unbridled discretion to defeat any perceived threat by any Draconian means available.

The restriction placed upon a selective stock repurchase is that the directors may not have acted solely or primarily out of a desire to perpetuate themselves in office. *See Cheff v. Mathes,* 199 A.2d at 556; *Kors v. Carey,* 158 A.2d at 140. Of course, to this is added the further caveat that inequitable action may not be taken under the guise of law. [*Citations omitted.*] The standard of proof established

[10] It has been suggested that a board's response to a takeover threat should be a passive one. Easterbrook & Fischel, *supra*, 36 Bus. Law. at 1750. However, that clearly is not the law of Delaware, and as the proponents of this rule of passivity readily concede, it has not been adopted either by courts or state legislatures. Easterbrook & Fischel, *supra*, 94 Harv. L.Rev. at 1194.

in *Cheff v. Mathes* and discussed *supra* . . ., is designed to ensure that a defensive measure to thwart or impede a takeover is indeed motivated by a good faith concern for the welfare of the corporation and its stockholders, which in all circumstances must be free of any fraud or other misconduct. *Cheff v. Mathes,* 199 A.2d at 554–55. However, this does not end the inquiry.

B.

A further aspect is the element of balance. If a defensive measure is to come within the ambit of the business judgment rule, it must be reasonable in relation to the threat posed. This entails an analysis by the directors of the nature of the takeover bid and its effect on the corporate enterprise. Examples of such concerns may include: inadequacy of the price offered, nature and timing of the offer, questions of illegality, the impact on "constituencies" other than shareholders (i.e., creditors, customers, employees, and perhaps even the community generally), the risk of nonconsummation, and the quality of securities being offered in the exchange. [*Citations omitted.*] While not a controlling factor, it also seems to us that a board may reasonably consider the basic stockholder interests at stake, including those of short term speculators, whose actions may have fueled the coercive aspect of the offer at the expense of the long term investor.[11] Here, the threat posed was viewed by the Unocal board as a grossly inadequate two-tier coercive tender offer coupled with the threat of greenmail.

Specifically, the Unocal directors had concluded that the value of Unocal was substantially above the $54 per share offered in cash at the front end. Furthermore, they determined that the subordinated securities to be exchanged in Mesa's announced squeeze out of the remaining shareholders in the "back-end" merger were "junk bonds" worth far less than $54. It is now well recognized that such offers are a classic coercive measure designed to stampede shareholders into tendering at the first tier, even if the price is inadequate, out of fear of what they will receive at the back end of the transaction. Wholly

[11] There has been much debate respecting such stockholder interests. One rather impressive study indicates that the stock of over 50 percent of target companies, who resisted hostile takeovers, later traded at higher market prices than the rejected offer price, or were acquired after the tender offer was defeated by another company at a price higher than the offer price. . . . Moreover, an update by Kidder Peabody & Company of this study, involving the stock prices of target companies that have defeated hostile tender offers during the period from 1973 to 1982 demonstrates that in a majority of cases the target's shareholders benefited from the defeat. The stock of 81% of the targets studied has, since the tender offer, sold at prices higher than the tender offer price. When adjusted for the time value of money, the figure is 64%. . . . The thesis being that this strongly supports application of the business judgment rule in response to takeover threats. There is, however, a rather vehement contrary view. *See* Easterbrook & Fischel, *supra* 36 Bus. Law. at 1739–1745.

beyond the coercive aspect of an inadequate two-tier tender offer, the threat was posed by a corporate raider with a national reputation as a "greenmailer".[13]

In adopting the selective exchange offer, the board stated that its objective was either to defeat the inadequate Mesa offer or, should the offer still succeed, provide the 49% of its stockholders, who would otherwise be forced to accept "junk bonds", with $72 worth of senior debt. We find that both purposes are valid.

However, such efforts would have been thwarted by Mesa's participation in the exchange offer. First, if Mesa could tender its shares, Unocal would effectively be subsidizing the former's continuing effort to buy Unocal stock at $54 per share. Second, Mesa could not, by definition, fit within the class of shareholders being protected from its own coercive and inadequate tender offer.

Thus, we are satisfied that the selective exchange offer is reasonably related to the threats posed. It is consistent with the principle that "the minority stockholder shall receive the substantial equivalent in value of what he had before." [*Citations omitted.*] This concept of fairness, while stated in the merger context, is also relevant in the area of tender offer law. Thus, the board's decision to offer what it determined to be the fair value of the corporation to the 49% of its shareholders, who would otherwise be forced to accept highly subordinated "junk bonds", is reasonable and consistent with the directors' duty to ensure that the minority stockholders receive equal value for their shares.

V.

Mesa contends that it is unlawful, and the trial court agreed, for a corporation to discriminate in this fashion against one shareholder. It argues correctly that no case has ever sanctioned a device that precludes a raider from sharing in a benefit available to all other stockholders. However, as we have noted earlier, the principle of selective stock repurchases by a Delaware corporation is neither unknown nor unauthorized. [*Citations omitted.*] The only difference is that heretofore the approved transaction was the payment of "greenmail" to a raider or dissident posing a threat to the corporate enterprise. All other stockholders were denied such favored treatment, and given Mesa's past history of greenmail, its claims here are rather ironic.

---

[13] The term "greenmail" refers to the practice of buying out a takeover bidder's stock at a premium that is not available to other shareholders in order to prevent the takeover. The Chancery Court noted that "Mesa has made tremendous profits from its takeover activities although in the past few years it has not been successful in acquiring any of the target companies on an unfriendly basis." Moreover, the trial court specifically found that the actions of the Unocal board were taken in good faith to eliminate both the inadequacies of the tender offer and to forestall the payment of "greenmail".

However, our corporate law is not static. It must grow and develop in response to, indeed in anticipation of, evolving concepts and needs. . . .

[A]s the sophistication of both raiders and targets has developed, a host of other defensive measures to counter such ever mounting threats has evolved and received judicial sanction. These include defensive charter amendments and other devices bearing some rather exotic, but apt, names: Crown Jewel, White Knight, Pac Man, and Golden Parachute. Each has highly selective features, the object of which is to deter or defeat the raider.

Thus, while the exchange offer is a form of selective treatment, given the nature of the threat posed here the response is neither unlawful nor unreasonable. If the board of directors is disinterested, has acted in good faith and with due care, its decision in the absence of an abuse of discretion will be upheld as a proper exercise of business judgment.

To this Mesa responds that the board is not disinterested, because the directors are receiving a benefit from the tender of their own shares, which because of the Mesa exclusion, does not devolve upon *all* stockholders equally. *See Aronson v. Lewis, Del. Supr.,* 473 A.2d 805, 812 (1984). However, Mesa concedes that if the exclusion is valid, then the directors and all other stockholders share the same benefit. The answer of course is that the exclusion is valid, and the directors' participation in the exchange offer does not rise to the level of a disqualifying interest. . . .

* * * *

Mesa contends that the basis of this action is punitive, and solely in response to the exercise of its rights of corporate democracy. Nothing precludes Mesa, as a stockholder, from acting in its own self-interest. . . . However, Mesa, while pursuing its own interests, has acted in a manner which a board consisting of a majority of independent directors has reasonably determined to be contrary to the best interests of Unocal and its other shareholders. In this situation, there is no support in Delaware law for the proposition that, when responding to a perceived harm, a corporation must guarantee a benefit to a stockholder who is deliberately provoking the danger being addressed. . . .

* * * *

VI.

In conclusion, there was directorial power to oppose the Mesa tender offer, and to undertake a selective stock exchange made in good faith and upon a reasonable investigation pursuant to a clear duty to protect the corporate enterprise. Further, the selective stock repurchase plan chosen by Unocal is reasonable in relation to the threat that the board rationally and reasonably believed was posed by Mesa's inadequate and coercive two-tier tender offer. Under those circumstances the board's action is entitled to be measured by the standards of the business judgment rule. Thus, unless it is shown by a preponderance of the evidence that the directors' decisions were primarily based on perpetuating themselves in office, or some other breach of fiduciary duty such as fraud, overreaching, lack of good faith, or being uninformed, a Court will not substitute its judgment for that of the board.

. . . If the stockholders are displeased with the action of their elected representatives, the powers of corporate democracy are at their disposal to turn the board out. [*Citations omitted.*]

With the Court of Chancery's findings that the exchange offer was based on the board's good faith belief that the Mesa offer was inadequate, that the board's action was informed and taken with due care, that Mesa's prior activities justify a reasonable inference that its principle objective was greenmail, and implicitly, that the substance of the offer itself was reasonable and fair to the corporation and its stockholders if Mesa were included, we cannot say that the Unocal directors have acted in such a manner as to have passed an "unintelligent and unadvised judgment". [*Citation omitted.*] The decision of the Court of Chancery is therefore REVERSED, and the preliminary injunction is VACATED.

NOTES AND QUESTIONS

1. The *Unocal* test dictates that when evaluating the actions of the board of directors in taking action against a takeover, the board must show: (i) that it acted in good faith and, after reasonable investigation, concluded that a danger existed to corporate policy and effectiveness; and (ii) that the action taken by the board's response was proportionate (i.e., reasonable in relation to the threat posed). Note that this test represents a shift from the Business Judgment Rule in that the burden is on the board to show there was a "threat." The *Unocal* case also allows for the possibility of evaluating the impact on groups other than shareholders, such as employees, customers and creditors. However, while the impact on other groups may be a consideration, that impact may not be at the expense of the welfare of the company's shareholders.

2. Can you think of circumstances under which the test described in the *Unocal* case might produce a different result than would occur from a typical application of the Business Judgment Rule?

3. Following the *Unocal* decision, the SEC adopted Rule 13e–4(f)(8) under the Williams Act (which, of course, supersedes Delaware State law). Rule 13e–4(f)(8) prohibits discriminatory, self-tender offers like the one made in *Unocal.* Self-tender offers must now be made to all shareholders. Later cases have clarified that, while the defensive measures taken may not be "preclusive" or "coercive," the actions taken may be within a "range of reasonableness," which some believe means that courts will defer to any "reasonable" judgment of the board. (*See Unitrin v. American General Corp.,* 651 A.2d 1361 (Del. 1995).)

4. Even without Rule 13e–4(f)(8), Unocal eventually allowed Mesa to participate in Unocal's self-tender. However, as soon as Mesa tendered its shares, it was sued by a Unocal shareholder. Can you think what securities law statute might create potential liability for Mesa for tendering its shares? (*See Colan v. Mesa Petroleum,* 951 F.2d 1512 (2d Cir. 1991), *cert. denied,* 504 U.S. 911 (1992).)

D. Defensive Tactics and Battles for Control

As seen in the *Unocal* case, companies often attempt to resist hostile takeovers, and do so by utilizing a variety of tactics and strategies, each with different consequences and results. A brief summary of some of the more well-known (and colorful) terms and tactics is included below:

> ***Greenmail***—Greenmail involves a payment made to a potential acquirer to incentivize them to leave the company alone. It usually occurs when a person has started to acquire a significant portion of shares in a Target company and the Target buys those shares back from the acquirer for a price above the shares' market value. (Note that the IRS now taxes any person who receives greenmail at a rate of 50% of the gain received.)
>
> ***White Knight***—A white knight is a "friendly" company that acquires or seeks to acquire a Target company and, in so doing, prevents the Target company from being acquired in a "hostile" takeover. In a typical scenario, the Target company attempts to make a deal with the white knight which will rescue (i.e., acquire) the Target company, and, at least from the perspective of the Target's board, be better for the Target than being acquired by the hostile Bidder.

Poison Pill—A poison pill is, perhaps, one of the most familiar terms used in takeover defenses. While there are several different forms of poison pills, the general concept involves creating a device that multiplies the rights of the Target's shareholders (but not of the would-be Acquirer), so that a person who did acquire the company would find that the increased shareholder "rights" made the takeover so expensive that it would not be feasible. The idea is that an acquirer could not "swallow" the Target company without taking the poison pill, which would destroy the acquisition.

Share Repurchases—Sometimes a company will offer to repurchase its own shares at a premium to thwart a hostile offer. This approach, as well as the use of poison pills, is often called a "scorched Earth policy" because it often involves damaging or weakening the Target company to make it unappealing to the Bidder.

Staggered Board—Sometimes a company will create a staggered board of directors (also known as "classified board") with a large number of directors whose terms expire in different years. For example, a company might have its directors serve for 3-year terms and only re-elect 1/3 of the board each year. This type of structure would mean that it could take several years for a hostile Bidder, even if successful, to elect new directors to replace the existing directors.

Shark repellent—A term that may be used to describe defensive measures which are typically adopted through a company's Articles or Bylaws that make it more difficult to acquire a company without the board of director's consent.

Golden Parachutes—A golden parachute is an extremely lucrative termination package for a company's senior executives, which typically is activated if the executive is terminated or otherwise loses his or her position with the company. These devices are used in other contexts as well, but may also be used to create a disincentive to acquire the Target company.

Pac-man Defense—The "Pac-man" defense is a strategy in which the Target company launches a hostile takeover on the Bidder in an effort to acquire control of the Bidder, rather than let the Bidder acquire control of the Target.

One of the more popular and effective takeover defenses is still a poison pill, sometimes called a "shareholder rights plan" because, although the plans vary in specifics, most create rights for shareholders in an effort to fend off takeover attempts. The rights are typically "activated" when the would-be Acquirer obtains a certain percentage of the Target company's shares over a certain threshold. However, the Acquirer who "activates" the pill is prevented from obtaining/using the rights. As a result, the financial position of the Acquirer is diluted. In the following case, *Moran v. Household International, Inc.*, the Delaware Supreme Court held that a corporation could validly adopt a poison pill, provided the board of directors did not violate the fiduciary duty standards set forth in *Unocal.*

Moran v. Household International, Inc.

500 A.2d 1346 (Del. 1985)

MCNEILLY, J.:

This case presents to this Court for review the most recent defensive mechanism in the arsenal of corporate takeover weaponry—the Preferred Share Purchase Rights Plan ("Rights Plan" or "Plan"). The validity of this mechanism has attracted national attention. *Amici curiae* briefs have been filed in support of appellants by the Security and Exchange Commission ("SEC") and the Investment Company Institute. An *amicus curiae* brief has been filed in support of appellees ("Household") by the United Food and Commercial Workers International Union.

. . .[T]he Court of Chancery upheld the Rights Plan as a legitimate exercise of business judgment by Household. . . . We agree, and therefore, affirm the judgment below.

I

* * * *

On August 14, 1984, the Board of Directors of Household International, Inc. adopted the Rights Plan by a fourteen to two vote. The intricacies of the Rights Plan are contained in a 48-page document entitled "Rights Agreement." Basically, the Plan provides that Household common stockholders are entitled to the issuance of one Right per common share under certain triggering conditions. There are two triggering events that can activate the Rights. The first is the announcement of a tender offer for 30 percent of Household's shares ("30% trigger") and the second is the acquisition of 20 percent of Household's shares by any single entity or group ("20% trigger").

If an announcement of a tender offer for 30 percent of Household's shares is made, the Rights are issued and are immediately exercisable to purchase 1/100 share of new preferred stock for $100 and are redeemable by the Board for $.50 per Right. If 20 percent of Household's shares are acquired by anyone, the Rights are issued and become non-redeemable and are exercisable to purchase 1/100 of a share of preferred. If a Right is not exercised for preferred, and thereafter, a merger or consolidation occurs, the Rights holder can exercise each Right to purchase $200 of the common stock of the tender offeror for $100. This "flip-over" provision of the Rights Plan is at the heart of this controversy.

Household is a diversified holding company with its principal subsidiaries engaged in financial services, transportation and merchandising. HFC, National Car Rental and Vons Grocery are three of its wholly-owned entities.

Household did not adopt its Rights Plan during a battle with a corporate raider, but as a preventive mechanism to ward off future advances. The Vice-Chancellor found that as early as February 1984, Household's management became concerned about the company's vulnerability as a takeover target and began considering amending its charter to render a takeover more difficult. After considering the matter, Household decided not to pursue a fair price amendment.[3]

In the meantime, appellant Moran, one of Household's own Directors and also Chairman of the Dyson-Kissner-Moran Corporation ("D-K-M"), which is the largest single stockholder of Household, began discussions concerning a possible leveraged buy-out of Household by D-K-M. D-K-M's financial studies showed that Household's stock was significantly undervalued in relation to the company's break-up value. It is uncontradicted that Moran's suggestion of a leveraged buy-out never progressed beyond the discussion stage.

Concerned about Household's vulnerability to a raider in light of the current takeover climate, Household secured the services of Wachtell, Lipton, Rosen and Katz ("Wachtell, Lipton") and Goldman, Sachs & Co. ("Goldman, Sachs") to formulate a takeover policy for recommendation to the Household Board at its August 14 meeting. After a July 31 meeting with a Household Board member and a pre-meeting distribution of material on the potential takeover problem and the proposed Rights Plan, the Board met on August 14, 1984.

Representatives of Wachtell, Lipton and Goldman, Sachs attended the August 14 meeting. The minutes reflect that Mr. Lipton explained to the Board

[3] A fair price amendment to a corporate charter generally requires supermajority approval for certain business combinations and sets minimum price criteria for mergers. . . .

> insurgents holding less than 10% stock ownership were able to secure corporate control through a proxy contest or the threat of one.

* * * *

We conclude that there was sufficient evidence at trial to support the Vice-Chancellor's finding that the effect upon proxy contests will be minimal. Evidence at trial established that many proxy contests are won with an insurgent ownership of less than 20%, and that very large holdings are no guarantee of success. There was also testimony that the key variable in proxy contest success is the merit of an insurgent's issues, not the size of his holdings.

IV

Having concluded that the adoption of the Rights Plan was within the authority of the Directors, we now look to whether the Directors have met their burden under the business judgment rule.

The business judgment rule is a "presumption that in making a business decision the directors of a corporation acted on an informed basis, in good faith and in the honest belief that the action taken was in the best interests of the company." *Aronson v. Lewis, Del. Supr.,* 473 A.2d 805, 812 (1984) (citations omitted). Notwithstanding, in *Unocal* we held that when the business judgment rule applies to adoption of a defensive mechanism, the initial burden will lie with the directors. The "directors must show that they had reasonable grounds for believing that a danger to corporate policy and effectiveness existed. . . . They satisfy that burden 'by showing good faith and reasonable investigation. . . .' " [*Citation omitted.*] In addition, the directors must show that the defensive mechanism was "reasonable in relation to the threat posed." [*Citation omitted.*] Moreover, that proof is materially enhanced, as we noted in *Unocal,* where, as here, a majority of the board favoring the proposal consisted of outside independent directors who have acted in accordance with the foregoing standards. [*Citations omitted.*] Then, the burden shifts back to the plaintiffs who have the ultimate burden of persuasion to show a breach of the directors' fiduciary duties. [*Citation omitted.*]

There are no allegations here of any bad faith on the part of the Directors' action in the adoption of the Rights Plan. There is no allegation that the Directors' action was taken for entrenchment purposes. Household has adequately demonstrated, as explained above, that the adoption of the Rights Plan was in reaction to what it perceived to be the threat in the market place of coercive two-tier tender offers. Appellants do contend, however, that the Board did not exercise informed business judgment in its adoption of the Plan.

Appellants contend that the Household Board was uninformed since they were *inter alia,* told the Plan would not inhibit a proxy contest, were not told the plan would preclude all hostile acquisitions of Household, and were told that Delaware counsel opined that the plan was within the business judgment of the Board.

As to the first two contentions, as we explained above, the Rights Plan will not have a severe impact upon proxy contests and it will not preclude all hostile acquisitions of Household. Therefore, the Directors were not misinformed or uninformed on these facts.

Appellants contend the Delaware counsel did not express an opinion on the flip-over provision of the Rights, rather only that the Rights would constitute validly issued and outstanding rights to subscribe to the preferred stock of the company.

To determine whether a business judgment reached by a board of directors was an informed one, we determine whether the directors were grossly negligent. *Smith v. Van Gorkom, Del. Supr.,* 488 A.2d 858, 873 (1985). Upon a review of this record, we conclude the Directors were not grossly negligent. The information supplied to the Board on August 14 provided the essentials of the Plan. The Directors were given beforehand a notebook which included a three-page summary of the Plan along with articles on the current takeover environment. The extended discussion between the Board and representatives of Wachtell, Lipton and Goldman, Sachs before approval of the Plan reflected a full and candid evaluation of the Plan. Moran's expression of his views at the meeting served to place before the Board a knowledgeable critique of the Plan. . . .

In addition, to meet their burden, the Directors must show that the defensive mechanism was "reasonable in relation to the threat posed". The record reflects a concern on the part of the Directors over the increasing frequency in the financial services industry of "boot-strap" and "bust-up" takeovers. The Directors were also concerned that such takeovers may take the form of two-tier offers. In addition, on August 14, the Household Board was aware of Moran's overture on behalf of D-K-M. In sum, the Directors reasonably believed Household was vulnerable to coercive acquisition techniques and adopted a reasonable defensive mechanism to protect itself.

V

In conclusion, the Household Directors receive the benefit of the business judgment rule in their adoption of the Rights Plan.

The Directors adopted the Plan pursuant to statutory authority in 8 Del.C. §§ 141, 151, 157. We reject appellants' contentions that the Rights Plan strips stockholders of their rights to receive tender offers, and that the Rights Plan fundamentally restricts proxy contests.

The Directors adopted the Plan in the good faith belief that it was necessary to protect Household from coercive acquisition techniques. The Board was informed as to the details of the Plan. In addition, Household has demonstrated that the Plan is reasonable in relation to the threat posed. Appellants, on the other hand, have failed to convince us that the Directors breached any fiduciary duty in their adoption of the Rights Plan.

While we conclude for present purposes that the Household Directors are protected by the business judgment rule, that does not end the matter. The ultimate response to an actual takeover bid must be judged by the Directors' actions at that time, and nothing we say here relieves them of their basic fundamental duties to the corporation and its stockholders. [*Citations omitted.*] Their use of the Plan will be evaluated when and if the issue arises.

AFFIRMED.

NOTES AND QUESTIONS

1. In early November of 2012, corporate raider, Carl Icahn, provided filings to the SEC disclosing that he had acquired 9.9% of the outstanding stock of Netflix. Icahn said he invested in Netflix because he believed its stock was undervalued and that the company was well positioned to play a leading role in the media landscape of the future. "All the habits are changing. You're going to have distribution changing the whole entertainment business, and they have the greatest platform," Icahn told the Los Angeles Times (*Los Angeles Times,* November 1, 2012). Icahn also mentioned publicly that Netflix "would make tasty bait" for a tech giant already in the video business such as Microsoft, Apple, Google, Amazon or Verizon. Icahn has a history of trying to exert influence on companies and their board of directors in hopes of either motivating a merger or, in the worst-case scenario, having his stake bought out at a premium.

> In response to Icahn's position in its stock, Netflix announced that its board had adopted a shareholder rights plan, or "poison pill", (the "Plan") just days after Mr. Icahn disclosed he had acquired a 9.9 percent stake. Netflix said the Plan was meant to protect the company and its shareholders from "efforts to obtain control of Netflix that the

> board of directors determines are not in the best interests of Netflix and its stockholders."
>
> Under the Plan, the company issued one right for every common share. Each right enabled a shareholder to buy rights in new preferred shares at the exercise price of $350 per right (the "Rights"). But these Rights could be exercised only if they were "Triggered". The Rights would be Triggered if an investor acquires 10 percent of the company without the approval of the Netflix board. (Institutional investors could acquire up to 20 percent.)
>
> In addition to other features, if the Rights were Triggered and Netflix merged into another company, an acquiring entity merged into Netflix or Netflix sold or transferred more than 50 percent of its assets, cash flow or earning power, then the holder of each Right would be entitled to take certain actions. Upon the occurrence of any of foregoing circumstances, the holder of each Right would be entitled to purchase, for the exercise price of $350, a number of shares of common stock of the person engaging in the transaction having a then-current market value of twice the exercise price ($700 at the $350 exercise price). The acquiring person or entity would not be entitled to exercise these rights, and the Plan expires on Nov. 2, 2015. (*Los Gatos, Calif., Nov. 5, 2012 / PRNewswire*)

In a statement, Icahn said in an SEC filing that "any poison pill without a shareholder vote is an example of poor corporate governance," and that the pill Netflix adopted was "particularly troubling due to its remarkably low and discriminatory 10 percent threshold."

2. Do you agree with Mr. Ichan?

3. How would you argue against the Plan if you represented Mr. Ichan?

4. How would you defend the Plan if you represented Netflix?

5. On November 1, 2012 the Netflix stock price closed at $77.69. Approximately one year later, the Netflix stock price had risen to close at $331.22. Does this change your opinion about the value of the Netflix Plan?

6. During October of 2013, when the Netflix stock price had risen to approximately $323 a share, Mr. Ichan decided to sell more than half of his Neflix holdings. According to Mr. Ichan, his Netflix investment had returned 457 percent, which suggests that Mr. Icahn made a profit of approximately $792

million, just on the shares he sold. He retained 2.67 million shares, representing a 4.5 percent ownership interest in the company.

The Revlon Rule

The *Unocal* test is used to evaluate defensive measures taken by a board of directors to fight a hostile acquisition attempt. However, there is an additional test which is used in circumstances when the board is no longer taking action to preserve the company. In many hostile takeover situations, the Target company attempts to find a "White Knight," a company by which the Target company would prefer to be acquired. In these instances, the Target company often makes a deal with the White Knight to thwart the efforts of the hostile Bidder. However, in these instances courts have held that such actions are no longer "defensive" and are subject to a different level of scrutiny. This level of scrutiny is known as the Revlon Rule since it arose out of the *Revlon, Inc. v. MacAndrews & Forbes Holdings, Inc. case*, which follows.

Revlon, Inc. v. MacAndrews & Forbes Holdings, Inc.

506 A.2d 173 (Del. 1986)

MOORE, J.:

In this battle for corporate control of Revlon, Inc. (Revlon), the Court of Chancery enjoined certain transactions designed to thwart the efforts of Pantry Pride, Inc. (Pantry Pride) to acquire Revlon. The defendants are Revlon, its board of directors, and Forstmann Little & Co. and the latter's affiliated limited partnership (collectively, Forstmann). The injunction barred consummation of an option granted Forstmann to purchase certain Revlon assets (the lock-up option), a promise by Revlon to deal exclusively with Forstmann in the face of a takeover (the no-shop provision), and the payment of a $25 million cancellation fee to Forstmann if the transaction was aborted. The Court of Chancery found that the Revlon directors had breached their duty of care by entering into the foregoing transactions and effectively ending an active auction for the company. The trial court ruled that such arrangements are not illegal *per se* under Delaware law, but that their use under the circumstances here was impermissible. We agree. . . . Additionally, we address for the first time the extent to which a corporation may consider the impact of a takeover threat on constituencies other than shareholders. *See Unocal Corp. v. Mesa Petroleum Co.,* Del. Supr., 493 A.2d 946, 955 (1985).

In our view, lock-ups and related agreements are permitted under Delaware law where their adoption is untainted by director interest or other breaches of fiduciary duty. The actions taken by the Revlon directors, however, did not meet this standard. Moreover, while concern for various corporate constituencies is proper when addressing a takeover threat, that principle is limited by the requirement that there be some rationally related benefit accruing to the stockholders. We find no such benefit here.

* * * *

I.

The somewhat complex maneuvers of the parties necessitate a rather detailed examination of the facts. The prelude to this controversy began in June 1985, when Ronald O. Perelman, chairman of the board and chief executive officer of Pantry Pride, met with his counterpart at Revlon, Michel C. Bergerac, to discuss a friendly acquisition of Revlon by Pantry Pride. Perelman suggested a price in the range of $40–$50 per share, but the meeting ended with Bergerac dismissing those figures as considerably below Revlon's intrinsic value. All subsequent Pantry Pride overtures were rebuffed, perhaps in part based on Mr. Bergerac's strong personal antipathy to Mr. Perelman.

Thus, on August 14, Pantry Pride's board authorized Perelman to acquire Revlon, either through negotiation in the $42–$43 per share range, or by making a hostile tender offer at $45. Perelman then met with Bergerac and outlined Pantry Pride's alternate approaches. Bergerac remained adamantly opposed to such schemes and conditioned any further discussions of the matter on Pantry Pride executing a standstill agreement prohibiting it from acquiring Revlon without the latter's prior approval.

On August 19, the Revlon board met specially to consider the impending threat of a hostile bid by Pantry Pride. At the meeting, Lazard Freres, Revlon's investment banker, advised the directors that $45 per share was a grossly inadequate price for the company. Felix Rohatyn and William Loomis of Lazard Freres explained to the board that Pantry Pride's financial strategy for acquiring Revlon would be through "junk bond" financing followed by a break-up of Revlon and the disposition of its assets. With proper timing, according to the experts, such transactions could produce a return to Pantry Pride of $60 to $70 per share, while a sale of the company as a whole would be in the "mid 50" dollar range. Martin Lipton, special counsel for Revlon, recommended two defensive measures: first, that the company repurchase up to 5 million of its nearly 30 million outstanding shares; and second, that it adopt a Note Purchase Rights Plan. Under this plan, each Revlon shareholder would receive as a dividend one Note Purchase Right (the Rights) for each share of common stock, with the Rights entitling the holder to exchange one common share for a $65 principal Revlon note at 12% interest with a one-year maturity. The Rights would become effective whenever anyone acquired beneficial ownership of 20% or more of Revlon's shares, unless the purchaser acquired all the company's stock for cash at $65 or more per share. In addition, the Rights would not be available to the acquiror, and prior to the 20% triggering event the Revlon board could redeem the rights for 10 cents each. Both proposals were unanimously adopted.

Pantry Pride made its first hostile move on August 23 with a cash tender offer for any and all shares of Revlon at $47.50 per common share and $26.67 per preferred share, subject to (1) Pantry Pride's obtaining financing for the purchase, and (2) the Rights being redeemed, rescinded or voided.

The Revlon board met again on August 26. The directors advised the stockholders to reject the offer. Further defensive measures also were planned. On August 29, Revlon commenced its own offer for up to 10 million shares, exchanging for each share of common stock tendered one Senior Subordinated Note (the Notes) of $47.50 principal at 11.75% interest, due 1995, and one-tenth of a share of $9.00 Cumulative Convertible Exchangeable Preferred Stock valued at $100 per share. . . . Revlon stockholders tendered 87 percent of the outstanding shares (approximately 33 million), and the company accepted the full 10 million shares on a pro rata basis. The new Notes contained covenants which limited Revlon's ability to incur additional debt, sell assets, or pay dividends unless otherwise approved by the "independent" (non-management) members of the board.

At this point, both the Rights and the Note covenants stymied Pantry Pride's attempted takeover. The next move came on September 16, when Pantry Pride announced a new tender offer at $42 per share, conditioned upon receiving at least 90% of the outstanding stock. Pantry Pride also indicated that it would consider buying less than 90%, and at an increased price, if Revlon removed the impeding Rights. While this offer was lower on its face than the earlier $47.50 proposal, Revlon's investment banker, Lazard Freres, described the two bids as essentially equal in view of the completed exchange offer.

The Revlon board held a regularly scheduled meeting on September 24. The directors rejected the latest Pantry Pride offer and authorized management to negotiate with other parties interested in acquiring Revlon. Pantry Pride remained determined in its efforts and continued to make cash bids for the company, offering $50 per share on September 27, and raising its bid to $53 on October 1, and then to $56.25 on October 7.

In the meantime, Revlon's negotiations with Forstmann and the investment group Adler & Shaykin had produced results. The Revlon directors met on October 3 to consider Pantry Pride's $53 bid and to examine possible alternatives to the offer. Both Forstmann and Adler & Shaykin made certain proposals to the board. As a result, the directors unanimously agreed to a leveraged buyout by Forstmann. The terms of this accord were as follows: each stockholder would get $56 cash per share; management would purchase stock in the new company by the exercise of their Revlon "golden parachutes";[5] Forstmann would assume Revlon's $475 million debt incurred by the issuance of the Notes; and Revlon would redeem the Rights and waive the Notes covenants for Forstmann or in connection with any other offer superior to Forstmann's. The board did not actually remove the covenants at the October 3 meeting, because Forstmann then lacked a firm commitment on its financing, but accepted the Forstmann capital structure, and indicated that the outside directors would waive the covenants in due course. Part of Forstmann's plan was to sell Revlon's Norcliff Thayer and Reheis divisions to American Home Products for $335 million. Before the merger, Revlon was to sell its cosmetics and fragrance division to Adler & Shaykin for $905 million. These transactions would facilitate the purchase by Forstmann or any other acquiror of Revlon.

When the merger, and thus the waiver of the Notes covenants, was announced, the market value of these securities began to fall. The Notes, which originally traded near par, around 100, dropped to 87.50 by October 8. One director later reported (at the October 12 meeting) a "deluge" of telephone calls from irate noteholders, and on October 10 the Wall Street Journal reported threats of litigation by these creditors.

Pantry Pride countered with a new proposal on October 7, raising its $53 offer to $56.25, subject to nullification of the Rights, a waiver of the Notes covenants, and the election of three Pantry Pride directors to the Revlon board. On October 9, representatives of Pantry Pride, Forstmann and Revlon conferred in an attempt to negotiate the fate of Revlon, but could not reach agreement. At this meeting Pantry Pride announced that it would engage in

---

[5] In the takeover context "golden parachutes" generally are understood to be termination agreements providing substantial bonuses and other benefits for managers and certain directors upon a change in control of a company.

fractional bidding and top any Forstmann offer by a slightly higher one. It is also significant that Forstmann, to Pantry Pride's exclusion, had been made privy to certain Revlon financial data. Thus, the parties were not negotiating on equal terms.

Again privately armed with Revlon data, Forstmann met on October 11 with Revlon's special counsel and investment banker. On October 12, Forstmann made a new $57.25 per share offer, based on several conditions. The principal demand was a lock-up option to purchase Revlon's Vision Care and National Health Laboratories divisions for $525 million, some $100–$175 million below the value ascribed to them by Lazard Freres, if another acquiror got 40% of Revlon's shares. Revlon also was required to accept a no-shop provision. The Rights and Notes covenants had to be removed as in the October 3 agreement. There would be a $25 million cancellation fee to be placed in escrow, and released to Forstmann if the new agreement terminated or if another acquiror got more than 19.9% of Revlon's stock. Finally, there would be no participation by Revlon management in the merger. In return, Forstmann agreed to support the par value of the Notes, which had faltered in the market, by an exchange of new notes. Forstmann also demanded immediate acceptance of its offer, or it would be withdrawn. The board unanimously approved Forstmann's proposal because: (1) it was for a higher price than the Pantry Pride bid, (2) it protected the noteholders, and (3) Forstmann's financing was firmly in place.[7] The board further agreed to redeem the rights and waive the covenants on the preferred stock in response to any offer above $57 cash per share. The covenants were waived, contingent upon receipt of an investment banking opinion that the Notes would trade near par value once the offer was consummated.

Pantry Pride, which had initially sought injunctive relief from the Rights plan on August 22, filed an amended complaint on October 14 challenging the lock-up, the cancellation fee, and the exercise of the Rights and the Notes covenants. Pantry Pride also sought a temporary restraining order to prevent Revlon from placing any assets in escrow or transferring them to Forstmann. Moreover, on October 22, Pantry Pride again raised its bid, with a cash offer of

---

7 Actually, at this time about $400 million of Forstmann's funding was still subject to two investment banks using their "best efforts" to organize a syndicate to provide the balance. Pantry Pride's entire financing was not firmly committed at this point either, although Pantry Pride represented in an October 11 letter to Lazard Freres that its investment banker, Drexel Burnham Lambert, was highly confident of its ability to raise the balance of $350 million. Drexel Burnham had a firm commitment for this sum by October 18.

$58 per share conditioned upon nullification of the Rights, waiver of the covenants, and an injunction of the Forstmann lock-up.

On October 15, the Court of Chancery prohibited the further transfer of assets, and eight days later enjoined the lock-up, no-shop, and cancellation fee provisions of the agreement. The trial court concluded that the Revlon directors had breached their duty of loyalty by making concessions to Forstmann, out of concern for their liability to the noteholders, rather than maximizing the sale price of the company for the stockholders' benefit. *MacAndrews & Forbes Holdings, Inc. v. Revlon, Inc.,* 501 A.2d at 1249–50.

II.

* * * *

A.

* * * *

. . . [W]hen a board implements anti-takeover measures there arises "the omnipresent specter that a board may be acting primarily in its own interests, rather than those of the corporation and its shareholders . . ." *Unocal Corp. v. Mesa Petroleum Co.,* 493 A.2d at 954. This potential for conflict places upon the directors the burden of proving that they had reasonable grounds for believing there was a danger to corporate policy and effectiveness, a burden satisfied by a showing of good faith and reasonable investigation. *Id.* at 955. In addition, the directors must analyze the nature of the takeover and its effect on the corporation in order to ensure balance—that the responsive action taken is reasonable in relation to the threat posed. *Id.*

B.

The first relevant defensive measure adopted by the Revlon board was the Rights Plan, which would be considered a "poison pill" in the current language of corporate takeovers—a plan by which shareholders receive the right to be bought out by the corporation at a substantial premium on the occurrence of a stated triggering event. *See generally Moran v. Household International, Inc.,* Del. Supr., 500 A.2d 1346 (1985). . . .

The Revlon board approved the Rights Plan in the face of an impending hostile takeover bid by Pantry Pride at $45 per share, a price which Revlon reasonably concluded was grossly inadequate. Lazard Freres had so advised the directors, and had also informed them that Pantry Pride was a small, highly leveraged company bent on a "bust-up" takeover by using "junk bond" financing to buy Revlon cheaply, sell the acquired assets to pay the debts incurred, and retain the profit for itself.[12] In adopting the Plan, the board protected the shareholders from a hostile takeover at a price below the company's intrinsic value, while retaining sufficient flexibility to address any proposal deemed to be in the stockholders' best interests.

To that extent the board acted in good faith and upon reasonable investigation. Under the circumstances it cannot be said that the Rights Plan as employed was unreasonable, considering the threat posed. Indeed, the Plan was a factor in causing Pantry Pride to raise its bids from a low of $42 to an eventual high of $58. At the time of its adoption the Rights Plan afforded a measure of protection consistent with the directors' fiduciary duty in facing a takeover threat perceived as detrimental to corporate interests. *Unocal,* 493 A.2d at 954–55. Far from being a "show-stopper," as the plaintiffs had contended in *Moran,* the measure spurred the bidding to new heights, a proper result of its implementation. *See Moran,* 500 A.2d at 1354, 1356–67.

Although we consider adoption of the Plan to have been valid under the circumstances, its continued usefulness was rendered moot by the directors' actions on October 3 and October 12. At the October 3 meeting the board redeemed the Rights conditioned upon consummation of a merger with Forstmann, but further acknowledged that they would also be redeemed to facilitate any more favorable offer. On October 12, the board unanimously passed a resolution redeeming the Rights in connection with any cash proposal of $57.25 or more per share. Because all the pertinent offers eventually equalled or surpassed that amount, the Rights clearly were no longer any impediment in the contest for Revlon. This mooted any question of their propriety under *Moran or Unocal.*

C.

The second defensive measure adopted by Revlon to thwart a Pantry Pride takeover was the company's own exchange offer for 10 million of its shares. The directors' general broad powers to manage the business and affairs of the corporation are augmented by the specific authority conferred under 8 Del.C. § 160(a), permitting the company to deal in its own stock. [*Citations omitted.*] However, when exercising that power in an effort to forestall a hostile takeover, the board's actions are strictly held to the fiduciary standards outlined in *Unocal.*

12 As we noted in *Moran,* a "bust-up" takeover generally refers to a situation in which one seeks to finance an acquisition by selling off pieces of the acquired company, presumably at a substantial profit. *See Moran,* 500 A.2d at 1349, n. 4.

These standards require the directors to determine the best interests of the corporation and its stockholders, and impose an enhanced duty to abjure any action that is motivated by considerations other than a good faith concern for such interests. *Unocal,* 493 A.2d at 954–55. . . . [*Citations omitted.*]

The Revlon directors concluded that Pantry Pride's $47.50 offer was grossly inadequate. In that regard the board acted in good faith, and on an informed basis, with reasonable grounds to believe that there existed a harmful threat to the corporate enterprise. The adoption of a defensive measure, reasonable in relation to the threat posed, was proper and fully accorded with the powers, duties, and responsibilities conferred upon directors under our law. *Unocal,* 493 A.2d at 954 . . . . [*Citations omitted.*]

D.

However, when Pantry Pride increased its offer to $50 per share, and then to $53, it became apparent to all that the break-up of the company was inevitable. The Revlon board's authorization permitting management to negotiate a merger or buyout with a third party was a recognition that the company was for sale. The duty of the board had thus changed from the preservation of Revlon as a corporate entity to the maximization of the company's value at a sale for the stockholders' benefit. This significantly altered the board's responsibilities under the *Unocal* standards. It no longer faced threats to corporate policy and effectiveness, or to the stockholders' interests, from a grossly inadequate bid. The whole question of defensive measures became moot. The directors' role changed from defenders of the corporate bastion to auctioneers charged with getting the best price for the stockholders at a sale of the company.

III.

This brings us to the lock-up with Forstmann and its emphasis on shoring up the sagging market value of the Notes in the face of threatened litigation by their holders. Such a focus was inconsistent with the changed concept of the directors' responsibilities at this stage of the developments. The impending waiver of the Notes covenants had caused the value of the Notes to fall, and the board was aware of the noteholders' ire as well as their subsequent threats of suit. The directors thus made support of the Notes an integral part of the company's dealings with Forstmann, even though their primary responsibility at this stage was to the equity owners.

The original threat posed by Pantry Pride—the break-up of the company—had become a reality which even the directors embraced. Selective dealing to fend off a hostile but determined bidder was no longer a proper objective. Instead, obtaining the highest price for the benefit of the stockholders should have been the central theme guiding director action. Thus, the Revlon board could not make the requisite showing of good faith by preferring the noteholders and ignoring its duty of loyalty to the shareholders. The rights of the former already were fixed by contract. [*Citations omitted.*] The noteholders required no further protection, and when the Revlon board entered into an auction-ending lock-up agreement with Forstmann on the basis of impermissible considerations at the expense of the shareholders, the directors breached their primary duty of loyalty.

The Revlon board argued that it acted in good faith in protecting the noteholders because *Unocal* permits consideration of other corporate constituencies. Although such considerations may be permissible, there are fundamental limitations upon that prerogative. A board may have regard for various constituencies in discharging its responsibilities, provided there are rationally related benefits accruing to the stockholders. *Unocal,* 493 A.2d at 955. However, such concern for non-stockholder interests is inappropriate when an auction among active bidders is in progress, and the object no longer is to protect or maintain the corporate enterprise but to sell it to the highest bidder.

Revlon also contended that by *Gilbert v. El Paso Co.,* Del. Ch., 490 A.2d 1050, 1054–55 (1984), it had contractual and good faith obligations to consider the noteholders. However, any such duties are limited to the principle that one may not interfere with contractual relationships by improper actions. Here, the rights of the noteholders were fixed by agreement, and there is nothing of substance to suggest that any of those terms were violated. The Notes covenants specifically contemplated a waiver to permit sale of the company at a fair price. The Notes were accepted by the holders on that basis, including the risk of an adverse market effect stemming from a waiver. Thus, nothing remained for Revlon to legitimately protect, and no rationally related benefit thereby accrued to the stockholders. Under such circumstances we must conclude that the merger agreement with Forstmann was unreasonable in relation to the threat posed.

A lock-up is not per se illegal under Delaware law. Its use has been approved in an earlier case. *Thompson v. Enstar Corp.,* Del. Ch., 509 A.2d 578 (1984). Such options can entice other bidders to enter a contest for control of the corporation, creating an auction for the company and maximizing shareholder profit. Current economic conditions in the takeover market are such that a "white knight" like Forstmann might only enter the bidding for the target company if it receives some form of compensation to cover the risks and costs involved. [*Citations omitted.*] However, while those lock-ups which draw bidders into the battle benefit shareholders, similar measures which end an active auction and foreclose further bidding operate to the shareholders' detriment. [*Citations omitted.*]

* * * *

The Forstmann option had a . . . destructive effect on the auction process. Forstmann had already been drawn into the contest on a preferred basis, so the result of the lock-up was not to foster bidding, but to destroy it. The board's stated reasons for approving the transactions were: (1) better financing, (2) noteholder protection, and (3) higher price. As the Court of Chancery found, and we agree, any distinctions between the rival bidders' methods of financing the proposal were nominal at best, and such a consideration has little or no significance in a cash offer for any and all shares. The principal object, contrary to the board's duty of care, appears to have been protection of the noteholders over the shareholders' interests.

While Forstmann's $57.25 offer was objectively higher than Pantry Pride's $56.25 bid, the margin of superiority is less when the Forstmann price is adjusted for the time value of money. In reality, the Revlon board ended the auction in return for very little actual improvement in the final bid. The principal benefit went to the directors, who avoided personal liability to a class of creditors to whom the board owed no further duty under the circumstances. Thus, when a board ends an intense bidding contest on an insubstantial basis, and where a significant by-product of that action is to protect the directors against a perceived threat of personal liability for consequences stemming from the adoption of previous defensive measures, the action cannot withstand the enhanced scrutiny which *Unocal* requires of director conduct. *See Unocal,* 493 A.2d at 954–55.

In addition to the lock-up option, the Court of Chancery enjoined the no-shop provision as part of the attempt to foreclose further bidding by Pantry Pride. [*Citation omitted.*] The no-shop provision, like the lock-up option, while not *per se* illegal, is impermissible under the *Unocal* standards when a board's primary duty becomes that of an auctioneer responsible for selling the company to the highest bidder. The agreement to negotiate only with Forstmann ended rather than intensified the board's involvement in the bidding contest.

It is ironic that the parties even considered a no-shop agreement when Revlon had dealt preferentially, and almost exclusively, with Forstmann throughout the contest. After the directors authorized management to negotiate with other parties, Forstmann was given every negotiating advantage that Pantry Pride had been denied: cooperation from management, access to financial data, and the exclusive opportunity to present merger proposals directly to the board of directors. Favoritism for a white knight to the total exclusion of a hostile bidder might be justifiable when the latter's offer adversely affects shareholder interests, but when bidders make relatively similar offers, or dissolution of the company becomes inevitable, the directors cannot fulfill their enhanced *Unocal* duties by playing favorites with the contending factions. Market forces must be allowed to operate freely to bring the target's shareholders the best price available for their equity. Thus . . .the shareholders' interests necessitated that the board remain free to negotiate in the fulfillment of that duty.

The court below similarly enjoined the payment of the cancellation fee, pending a resolution of the merits, because the fee was part of the overall plan to thwart Pantry Pride's efforts. We find no abuse of discretion in that ruling.

* * * *

V.

In conclusion, the Revlon board was confronted with a situation not uncommon in the current wave of corporate takeovers. A hostile and determined bidder sought the company at a price the board was convinced was inadequate. The initial defensive tactics worked to the benefit of the shareholders, and thus the board was able to sustain its *Unocal* burdens in justifying those measures. However, in granting an asset option lock-up to Forstmann, we must conclude that under all the circumstances the directors allowed considerations other than the maximization of shareholder profit to affect their judgment, and followed a course that ended the auction for Revlon, absent court intervention, to the ultimate detriment of its shareholders. No such defensive measure can be sustained when it represents a breach of the directors' fundamental duty of care. *See Smith v. Van Gorkom, Del. Supr.,* 488 A.2d 858, 874 (1985). In that context the board's action is not entitled to the deference accorded it by the business judgment rule. The measures were properly enjoined. The decision of the Court of Chancery, therefore, is

AFFIRMED.

NOTES AND QUESTIONS

1. The *Revlon* rule dictates that once a breakup of the firm is imminent, the board of directors must maximize the "value" which is received by the shareholders in the transaction. Can you think of a potential takeover scenario in which the highest dollar value for the deal might not be the same as maximizing value to the shareholders?

2. Because many different (albeit reasonable) measures of value may be taken into account, a Target company's board has the ability to evaluate different offers and to select one that truly provides better value to the shareholders, rather than being required to accept the highest bid from a mediocre company.

3. As an attorney advising a potential Bidder for another company, how might you advise your client to structure the offer to provide increased value to the Target?

4. What elements in an offer might decrease its value?

5. The *Revlon* rule applies once breakup of a company becomes imminent. Are there other circumstances in which the rule should apply?

6. If the *Revlon* rule requires a board to maximize value to shareholders, why shouldn't it apply to all mergers and acquisitions? Consider the circumstances in the *Paramount Communications, Inc. v. Time Inc.* case, which follows.

Paramount Communications, Inc. v. Time Inc.

571 A.2d 1140 (Del. 1989)

HORSEY, J.:

Paramount Communications, Inc. ("Paramount") and two other groups of plaintiffs ("Shareholder Plaintiffs"), shareholders of Time Incorporated ("Time"), a Delaware corporation, separately filed suits in the Delaware Court of Chancery seeking a preliminary injunction to halt Time's tender offer for 51% of Warner Communication, Inc.'s ("Warner") outstanding shares at $70 cash per share. The court below consolidated the cases and . . . . refused to enjoin Time's consummation of its tender offer, concluding that the plaintiffs were unlikely to prevail on the merits. . . .

On the same day, plaintiffs filed in this Court an interlocutory appeal, which we accepted on an expedited basis. Pending the appeal, a stay of execution of Time's tender offer was entered for ten days, or until July 24, 1989, at 5:00

p.m. Following briefing and oral argument, on July 24 we concluded that the decision below should be affirmed. We so held in a brief ruling from the bench and a separate Order entered on that date. The effect of our decision was to permit Time to proceed with its tender offer for Warner's outstanding shares. This is the written opinion articulating the reasons for our July 24 bench ruling.

* * * *

Applying our standard of review, we affirm the Chancellor's ultimate finding and conclusion under *Unocal.* We find that Paramount's tender offer was reasonably perceived by Time's board to pose a threat to Time and that the Time board's "response" to that threat was, under the circumstances, reasonable and proportionate. Applying *Unocal,* we reject the argument that the only corporate threat posed by an all-shares, all-cash tender offer is the possibility of inadequate value.

We also find that Time's board did not by entering into its initial merger agreement with Warner come under a *Revlon* duty either to auction the company or to maximize short-term shareholder value, notwithstanding the unequal share exchange. Therefore, the Time board's original plan of merger with Warner was subject only to a business judgment rule analysis. *See Smith v. Van Gorkom, Del. Supr.,* 488 A.2d 858, 873–74 (1985).

I

Time is a Delaware corporation with its principal offices in New York City. Time's traditional business is publication of magazines and books; however, Time also provides pay television programming through its Home Box Office, Inc. and Cinemax subsidiaries. In addition, Time owns and operates cable television franchises through is subsidiary, American Television and Communication Corporation. During the relevant time period, Time's board consisted of sixteen directors. Twelve of the directors were "outside," nonemployee directors. Four of the directors were also officers of the company. . . .

As early as 1983 and 1984, Time's executive board began considering expanding Time's operations into the entertainment industry. In 1987, Time established a special committee of executives to consider and propose corporate strategies for the 1990s. The consensus of the committee was that Time should move ahead in the area of ownership and creation of video programming. This expansion, as the Chancellor noted, was predicated upon two considerations: first, Time's desire to have greater control, in terms of quality and price, over the film products delivered by way of its cable network and franchises; and

3 merger with Warner was entitled to the protection of the business judgment rule. . . .

The Chancellor reached a different conclusion in addressing the Time-Warner transaction as revised three months later. He found that the revised agreement was defense-motivated and designed to avoid the potentially disruptive effect that Paramount's offer would have had on consummation of the proposed merger were it put to a shareholder vote. Thus, the court declined to apply the traditional business judgment rule to the revised transaction and instead analyzed the Time board's June 16 decision under *Unocal.* The court ruled that *Unocal* applied to all director actions taken, following receipt of Paramount's hostile tender offer, that were reasonably determined to be defensive. Clearly that was a correct ruling and no party disputes that ruling.

In *Unocal,* we held that before the business judgment rule is applied to a board's adoption of a defensive measure, the burden will lie with the board to prove (a) reasonable grounds for believing that a danger to corporate policy and effectiveness existed; and (b) that the defensive measures adopted was reasonable in relation to the threat posed. [*Citation omitted.*] Directors satisfy the first part of the *Unocal* test by demonstrating good faith and reasonable investigation. We have repeatedly stated that the refusal to entertain an offer may comport with a valid exercise of a board's business judgment. . . .

Unocal involved a two-tier, highly coercive tender offer. In such a case, the threat is obvious: shareholders may be compelled to tender to avoid being treated adversely in the second stage of the transaction. . . . In subsequent cases the Court of Chancery has suggested that an all-cash, all-shares offer, falling within a range of values that a shareholder might reasonably prefer, cannot constitute a legally recognized "threat" to shareholder interests sufficient to withstand a *Unocal* analysis. [*Citation omitted.*] In those cases, the Court of Chancery determined that whatever threat existed related only to the shareholders and only to price and not to the corporation.

From those decisions by our Court of Chancery, Paramount and the individual plaintiffs extrapolate a rule of law that an all-cash, all-shares offer with values reasonably in the range of acceptable price cannot pose any objective threat to a corporation or its shareholders. Thus, Paramount would have us hold that only if the value of Paramount's offer were determined to be clearly inferior to the value created by management's plan to merge with Warner could the offer be viewed—objectively—as a threat.

Implicit in the plaintiffs' argument is the view that a hostile tender offer can pose only two types of threats: the threat of coercion that results from a two-tier offer promising unequal treatment for nontendering shareholders; and the threat of inadequate value from an all-shares, all-cash offer at a price below what a target board in good faith deems to be the present value of its shares. [*Citation omitted.*] Since Paramount's offer was all-cash, the only conceivable "threat," plaintiffs argue, was inadequate value. We disapprove of such a narrow and rigid construction of *Unocal,* for the reasons which follow.

Plaintiffs' position represents a fundamental misconception of our standard of review under *Unocal* principally because it would involve the court in substituting its judgment as to what is a "better" deal for that of a corporation's board of directors. . . .

The usefulness of *Unocal* as an analytical tool is precisely its flexibility in the face of a variety of fact *scenarios. Unocal* is not intended as an abstract standard; neither is it a structured and mechanistic procedure of appraisal. Thus, we have said that directors may consider, when evaluating the threat posed by a takeover bid, the "inadequacy of the price offered, nature and timing of the offer, questions of illegality, the impact on 'constituencies' other than shareholders, the risk of nonconsummation and the quality of securities being offered in the exchange." . . . . The open-ended analysis mandated by *Unocal* is not intended to lead to a simple mathematical exercise: that is, of comparing the discounted value of Time-Warner's expected trading price at some future date with Paramount's offer and determining which is the higher. Indeed, in our view, precepts underlying the business judgment rule militate against a court's engaging in the process of attempting to appraise and evaluate the relative merits of a long-term versus a short-term investment goal for shareholders. To engage in such an exercise is a distortion of the *Unocal* process and, in particular, the application of the second part of *Unocal's* test, discussed below.

In this case, the Time board reasonably determined that inadequate value was not the only legally cognizable threat that Paramount's all-cash, all-shares offer could present. Time's board concluded that Paramount's eleventh hour offer posed other threats. One concern was that Time shareholders might elect to tender into Paramount's cash offer in ignorance or a mistaken belief of the strategic benefit which a business combination with Warner might produce. Moreover, Time viewed the conditions attached to Paramount's offer as introducing a degree of uncertainty that skewed a comparative analysis. Further, the timing of Paramount's offer to follow issuance of Time's proxy notice was viewed as arguably designed to upset, if not confuse, the Time stockholders' vote. Given this record evidence, we cannot conclude that the Time board's decision of June 6 that Paramount's offer posed a threat to corporate policy and effectiveness was lacking in good faith or dominated by motives of either entrenchment or self-interest.

Paramount also contends that the Time board had not duly investigated Paramount's offer. Therefore, Paramount argues, Time was unable to make an informed decision that the offer posed a threat to Time's corporate policy. Although the Chancellor did not address this issue directly, his findings of fact do detail Time's exploration of the available entertainment companies, including Paramount, before determining that Warner provided the best strategic "fit." In addition, the court found that Time's board rejected Paramount's offer because Paramount did not serve Time's objectives or meet Time's needs. Thus, the record does, in our judgment, demonstrate that Time's board was adequately informed of the potential benefits of a transaction with Paramount. We agree with the Chancellor that the Time board's lengthy pre-June investigation of potential merger candidates, including Paramount, mooted any obligation on Time's part to halt its merger process with Warner to reconsider Paramount. Time's board was under no obligation to negotiate with Paramount. . . .

We turn to the second part of the *Unocal* analysis. The obvious requisite to determining the reasonableness of a defensive action is a clear identification of the nature of the threat. As the Chancellor correctly noted, this "requires an evaluation of the importance of the corporate objective threatened; alternative methods of protecting that objective; impacts of the 'defensive' action, and other relevant factors." [*Citation omitted.*] It is not until both parts of the *Unocal* inquiry have been satisfied that the business judgment rule attaches to defensive actions of a board of directors. . . . As applied to the facts of this case, the question is whether the record evidence supports the Court of Chancery's conclusion that the restructuring of the Time-Warner transaction, including the adoption of several preclusive defensive measures, was a *reasonable response* in relation to a perceived threat.

Paramount argues that, assuming its tender offer posed a threat, Time's response was unreasonable in precluding Time's shareholders from accepting the tender offer or receiving a control premium in the immediately foreseeable future. Once again, the contention stems, we believe, from a fundamental misunderstanding of where the power of corporate governance lies. Delaware law confers the management of the corporate enterprise to the stockholders' duly elected board representatives. . . . The fiduciary duty to manage a corporate enterprise includes the selection of a time frame for achievement of corporate goals. That duty may not be delegated to the stockholders. . . . Directors are not obliged to abandon a deliberately conceived corporate plan for a short-term shareholder profit unless there is clearly no basis to sustain the corporate strategy. . . .

Although the Chancellor blurred somewhat the discrete analyses required under *Unocal,* he did conclude that Time's board reasonably perceived Paramount's offer to be a significant threat to the planned Time-Warner merger and that Time's response was not "overly broad." We have found that even in light of a valid threat, management actions that are coercive in nature or force upon shareholders a management-sponsored alternative to a hostile offer may be struck down as unreasonable and nonproportionate responses. . . .

Here, on the record facts, the Chancellor found that Time's responsive action to Paramount's tender offer was not aimed at "cramming down" on its shareholders a management-sponsored alternative, but rather had as its goal the carrying forward of a pre-existing transaction in an altered form. Thus, the response was reasonably related to the threat. The Chancellor noted that the revised agreement and its accompanying safety devices did not preclude Paramount from making an offer for the combined Time-Warner company or from changing the conditions of its offer so as not to make the offer dependent upon the nullification of the Time-Warner agreement. Thus, the response was proportionate. We affirm the Chancellor's rulings as clearly supported by the record. Finally, we note that although Time was required, as a result of Paramount's hostile offer, to incur a heavy debt to finance its acquisition of Warner, that fact alone does not render the board's decision unreasonable so long as the directors could reasonably perceive the debt load not to be so injurious to the corporation as to jeopardize its well being.

. . .

Conclusion

Applying the test for grant or denial of preliminary injunctive relief, we find plaintiffs failed to establish a reasonable likelihood of ultimate success on the merits. Therefore, we affirm.

QUESTIONS

1. A number of states have adopted anti-takeover statutes (*see* the discussion, following the *CTS Corp. v. Dynamics Corp. of America, infra*) which allow a board

of directors to "consider" the interests of constituencies other than shareholders in making decisions to resist hostile takeovers. Under what circumstances do you think that such legislation would be beneficial?

2. How important was the characterization of this transaction as a merger and not a sale of the company? Consider the following quote from *Revlon:* "However, such concern for non-stockholder interests is inappropriate when an auction among active bidders is in progress, and the object no longer is to protect or maintain the corporate enterprise but to sell it to the highest bidder." *Revlon* 506 A.2d at 182.

A few years later Paramount would again play a role in the *Revlon* rule's evolution. In the next case, a merger between Viacom and Paramount was challenged by QVC on the basis of Chancellor Allen's control argument made in the *Time* case.

Paramount Communications Inc. v. QVC Network Inc.

637 A.2d 34 (Del. 1994)

VEASEY, C.J.:

In this appeal we review an order of the Court of Chancery . . . preliminarily enjoining certain defensive measures designed to facilitate a so-called strategic alliance between Viacom Inc. ("Viacom") and Paramount Communications Inc. ("Paramount") approved by the board of directors of Paramount (the "Paramount Board" or the "Paramount directors") and to thwart an unsolicited, more valuable, tender offer by QVC Network Inc. ("QVC"). In affirming, we hold that the sale of control in this case, which is at the heart of the proposed strategic alliance, implicates enhanced judicial scrutiny of the conduct of the Paramount Board under *Unocal Corp. v. Mesa Petroleum Co.,* Del. Supr. 493 A.2d 946 (1985), and *Revlon, Inc. v. MacAndrews & Forbes Holdings, Inc.,* Del. Supr., 506 A.2d 173 (1986). We further hold that the conduct of the Paramount Board was not reasonable as to process or result.

. . . . This action arises out of a proposed acquisition of Paramount by Viacom through a tender offer followed by a second-step merger (the "Paramount-Viacom transaction"), and a competing unsolicited tender offer by QVC.

* * * *

I. FACTS

* * * *

The majority of Paramount's stock is publicly held by numerous unaffiliated investors. Paramount owns and operates a diverse group of entertainment businesses, including motion picture and television studios, book publishers, professional sports teams and amusement parks.

There are 15 persons serving on the Paramount Board. Four directors are officer-employees of Paramount. . . . Paramount's 11 outside directors are distinguished and experienced business persons who are present or former senior executives of public corporations or financial institutions.

Viacom is a Delaware corporation . . . . controlled by Sumner M. Redstone ("Redstone"), its Chairman and Chief Executive Officer, who owns indirectly approximately 85.2 percent of Viacom's voting Class A stock and approximately 69.2 percent of Viacom's nonvoting Class B stock through National Amusements, Inc. ("NAI"), an entity 91.7 percent owned by Redstone. Viacom has a wide range of entertainment operations, including a number of well-known cable television channels such as MTV, Nickelodeon, Showtime, and The Movie Channel. . . .

QVC is a Delaware corporation. . . . QVC has several large stockholders, including Liberty Media Corporation, Comcast Corporation, Advance Publications, Inc., and Cox Enterprises Inc. Barry Diller ("Diller"), the Chairman and Chief Executive Officer of QVC, is also a substantial stockholder. QVC sells a variety of merchandise through a televised shopping channel. . . .

Beginning in the late 1980s, Paramount investigated the possibility of acquiring or merging with other companies in the entertainment, media, or communications industry. Paramount considered such transactions to be desirable, and perhaps necessary, in order to keep pace with competitors in the rapidly evolving field of entertainment and communications. Consistent with its goal of strategic expansion, Paramount made a tender offer for Time Inc. in 1989, but was ultimately unsuccessful. *See Paramount Communications, Inc. v. Time Inc.,* Del. Supr., 571 A.2d 1140 (1990) ("Time-Warner").

Although Paramount had considered a possible combination of Paramount and Viacom as early as 1990, recent efforts to explore such a transaction began at a dinner meeting between Redstone and Davis [Martin Davis ("Davis") was Paramount's Chairman and CEO.—*Eds.*] . . . . . After several more meetings between Redstone and Davis, serious negotiations began taking place in early July.

It was tentatively agreed that Davis would be the chief executive officer and Redstone would be the controlling stockholder of the combined company, but the parties could not reach agreement on the merger price and the terms of a stock option to be granted to Viacom. With respect to price, Viacom offered a package of cash and stock (primarily Viacom Class B nonvoting stock) with a market value of approximately $61 per share, but Paramount wanted at least $70 per share.

Shortly after negotiations broke down in July 1993, two notable events occurred. First, Davis apparently learned of QVC's potential interest in Paramount, and told Diller over lunch on July 21, 1993, that Paramount was not for sale. Second, the market value of Viacom's Class B nonvoting stock increased from $46.875 on July 6 to $57.25 on August 20. QVC claims (and Viacom disputes) that this price increase was caused by open market purchases of such stock by Redstone or entities controlled by him.

. . . . After a short hiatus, the parties negotiated in earnest in early September, and performed due diligence with the assistance of their financial advisors, Lazard Freres & Co. ("Lazard") for Paramount and Smith Barney for Viacom. On September 9, 1993, the Paramount Board was informed about the status of the negotiations and was provided information by Lazard, including an analysis of the proposed transaction.

On September 12, 1993, the Paramount Board met again and unanimously approved the Original Merger Agreement whereby Paramount would merge with and into Viacom. The terms of the merger provided that each share of Paramount common stock would be converted into 0.10 shares of Viacom Class A voting stock, 0.90 shares of Viacom Class B nonvoting stock, and $9.10 in cash. In addition, the Paramount Board agreed to amend its "poison pill" Rights Agreement to exempt the proposed merger with Viacom. The Original Merger Agreement also contained several provisions designed to make it more difficult for a potential competing bid to succeed. We focus, as did the Court of Chancery, on three of these defensive provisions: a "no-shop" provision (the "No-Shop Provision"), the Termination Fee, and the Stock Option Agreement.

First, under the No-Shop Provision, the Paramount Board agreed that Paramount would not solicit, encourage, discuss, negotiate, or endorse any competing transaction unless: (a) a third party "makes an unsolicited written, bona fide proposal, which is not subject to any material contingencies relating to financing"; and (b) the Paramount Board determines that discussions or negotiations with the third party are necessary for the Paramount Board to comply with its fiduciary duties.

Second, under the Termination Fee provision, Viacom would receive a $100 million termination fee if: (a) Paramount terminated the Original Merger Agreement because of a competing transaction; (b) Paramount's stockholders did not approve the merger; or (c) the Paramount Board recommended a competing transaction.

The third and most significant deterrent device was the Stock Option Agreement, which granted to Viacom an option to purchase approximately 19.9 percent (23,699,000 shares) of Paramount's outstanding common stock at $69.14 per share if any of the triggering events for the Termination Fee occurred. In addition to the customary terms that are normally associated with a stock option, the Stock Option Agreement contained two provisions that were both unusual and highly beneficial to Viacom: (a) Viacom was permitted to pay for the shares with a senior subordinated note of questionable marketability instead of cash, thereby avoiding the need to raise the $1.6 billion purchase price (the "Note Feature"); and (b) Viacom could elect to require Paramount to pay Viacom in cash a sum equal to the difference between the purchase price and the market price of Paramount's stock (the "Put Feature"). Because the Stock Option Agreement was not "capped" to limit its maximum dollar value, it had the potential to reach (and in this case did reach) unreasonable levels.

After the execution of the Original Merger Agreement and the Stock Option Agreement on September 12, 1993, Paramount and Viacom announced their proposed merger. In a number of public statements, the parties indicated that the pending transaction was a virtual certainty. Redstone described it as a "marriage" that would "never be torn asunder" and stated that only a "nuclear attack" could break the deal. Redstone also called Diller and John Malone of Tele-Communications Inc., a major stockholder of QVC, to dissuade them from making a competing bid.

Despite these attempts to discourage a competing bid, Diller sent a letter to Davis on September 20, 1993, proposing a merger in which QVC would acquire Paramount for approximately $80 per share, consisting of 0.893 shares of QVC common stock and $30 in cash. QVC also expressed its eagerness to meet with Paramount to negotiate the details of a transaction. When the Paramount Board met on September 27, it was advised by Davis that the Original Merger Agreement prohibited Paramount from having discussions with QVC (or anyone else) unless certain conditions were satisfied. In particular,

QVC had to supply evidence that its proposal was not subject to financing contingencies. The Paramount Board was also provided information from Lazard describing QVC and its proposal.

On October 5, 1993, QVC provided Paramount with evidence of QVC's financing. The Paramount Board then held another meeting on October 11, and decided to authorize management to meet with QVC. Davis also informed the Paramount Board that Booz-Allen & Hamilton ("Booz-Allen"), a management consulting firm, had been retained to assess, *inter alia,* the incremental earnings potential from a Paramount-Viacom merger and a Paramount-QVC merger. Discussions proceeded slowly, however, due to a delay in Paramount signing a confidentiality agreement. In response to Paramount's request for information, QVC provided two binders of documents to Paramount on October 20.

On October 21, 1993, QVC filed this action and publicly announced an $80 cash tender offer for 51 percent of Paramount's outstanding shares (the "QVC tender offer"). Each remaining share of Paramount common stock would be converted into 1.42857 shares of QVC common stock in a second-step merger. The tender offer was conditioned on, among other things, the invalidation of the Stock Option Agreement, which was worth over $200 million by that point.[5] . . . .

Confronted by QVC's hostile bid, which on its face offered over $10 per share more than the consideration provided by the Original Merger Agreement, Viacom realized that it would need to raise its bid in order to remain competitive. Within hours after QVC's tender offer was announced, Viacom entered into discussions with Paramount concerning a revised transaction. These discussions led to serious negotiations concerning a comprehensive amendment to the original Paramount-Viacom transaction. In effect, the opportunity for a "new deal" with Viacom was at hand for the Paramount Board. With the QVC hostile bid offering greater value to the Paramount stockholders, the Paramount Board had considerable leverage with Viacom.

At a special meeting on October 24, 1993, the Paramount Board approved the Amended Merger Agreement and an amendment to the Stock Option Agreement. The Amended Merger Agreement was, however, essentially the same as the Original Merger Agreement, except that it included a few new provisions. One provision related to an $80 per share cash tender offer by Viacom for 51 percent of Paramount's stock, and another changed the merger

[5] By November 15, 1993, the value of the Stock Option Agreement had increased to nearly $500 million based on the $90 QVC bid. See Court of Chancery Opinion, 635 A.2d at 1271.

consideration so that each share of Paramount would be converted into 0.20408 shares of Viacom Class A voting stock, 1.08317 shares of Viacom Class B nonvoting stock, and 0.20408 shares of a new series of Viacom convertible preferred stock. The Amended Merger Agreement also added a provision giving Paramount the right not to amend its Rights Agreement to exempt Viacom if the Paramount Board determined that such an amendment would be inconsistent with its fiduciary duties because another offer constituted a "better alternative." Finally, the Paramount Board was given the power to terminate the Amended Merger Agreement if it withdrew its recommendation of the Viacom transaction or recommended a competing transaction.

Although the Amended Merger Agreement offered more consideration to the Paramount stockholders and somewhat more flexibility to the Paramount Board than did the Original Merger Agreement, the defensive measures designed to make a competing bid more difficult were not removed or modified. In particular, there is no evidence in the record that Paramount sought to use its newly-acquired leverage to eliminate or modify the No-Shop Provision, the Termination Fee, or the Stock Option Agreement when the subject of amending the Original Merger Agreement was on the table.

* * * *

On November 6, 1993, Viacom unilaterally raised its tender offer price to $85 per share in cash and offered a comparable increase in the value of the securities being proposed in the second-step merger. At a telephonic meeting held later that day, the Paramount Board agreed to recommend Viacom's higher bid to Paramount's stockholders.

QVC responded to Viacom's higher bid on November 12 by increasing its tender offer to $90 per share and by increasing the securities for its second-step merger by a similar amount. . . .

At its meeting on November 15, 1993, the Paramount Board determined that the new QVC offer was not in the best interests of the stockholders. The purported basis for this conclusion was that QVC's bid was excessively conditional. The Paramount Board did not communicate with QVC regarding the status of the conditions because it believed that the No-Shop Provision prevented such communication in the absence of firm financing. Several Paramount directors also testified that they believed the Viacom transaction would be more advantageous to Paramount's future business prospects than a QVC transaction. Although a number of materials were distributed to the Paramount Board describing the Viacom and QVC transactions, the only quantitative analysis of the consideration to be received by the stockholders under each proposal was based on then-current market prices of the securities involved, not on the anticipated value of such securities at the time when the stockholders would receive them.

. . . . November 19, Diller wrote to the Paramount Board to inform it that QVC had obtained financing commitments for its tender offer and that there was no antitrust obstacle to the offer. On November 24, 1993, the Court of Chancery issued its decision granting a preliminary injunction in favor of QVC and the plaintiff stockholders. This appeal followed.

II. APPLICABLE PRINCIPLES OF ESTABLISHED DELAWARE LAW

. . . . Under normal circumstances, neither the courts nor the stockholders should interfere with the managerial decisions of the directors. The business judgment rule embodies the deference to which such decisions are entitled. [*Citation omitted.*]

Nevertheless, there are rare situations which mandate that a court take a more direct and active role in overseeing the decisions made and actions taken by directors. In these situations, a court subjects the directors' conduct to enhanced scrutiny to ensure that it is reasonable.[9] The decisions of this Court have clearly established the circumstances where such enhanced scrutiny will be applied. [*Citations omitted.*] The case at bar implicates two such circumstances:

(1) the approval of a transaction resulting in a sale of control, and (2) the adoption of defensive measures in response to a threat to corporate control.

A. The Significance of a Sale or Change of Control

When a majority of a corporation's voting shares are acquired by a single person or entity, or by a cohesive group acting together, there is a significant diminution in the voting power of those who thereby become minority stockholders. Under the statutory framework of the General Corporation Law, many of the most fundamental corporate changes can be implemented only if they are approved by a majority vote of the stockholders. Such actions include elections of directors, amendments to the certificate of incorporation, mergers, consolidations, sales of all or substantially all of the assets of the corporation, and dissolution. [*Citation omitted.*] Because of the overriding importance of voting

---

[9] Where actual self-interest is present and affects a majority of the directors approving a transaction, a court will apply even more exacting scrutiny to determine whether the transaction is entirely fair to the stockholders.

rights, this Court and the Court of Chancery have consistently acted to protect stockholders from unwarranted interference with such rights.

In the absence of devices protecting the minority stockholders, stockholder votes are likely to become mere formalities where there is a majority stockholder. For example, minority stockholders can be deprived of a continuing equity interest in their corporation by means of a cash-out merger. [*Citation omitted.*] Absent effective protective provisions, minority stockholders must rely for protection solely on the fiduciary duties owed to them by the directors and the majority stockholder, since the minority stockholders have lost the power to influence corporate direction through the ballot. The acquisition of majority status and the consequent privilege of exerting the powers of majority ownership come at a price. That price is usually a control premium which recognizes not only the value of a control block of shares, but also compensates the minority stockholders for their resulting loss of voting power.

In the case before us, the public stockholders (in the aggregate) currently own a majority of Paramount's voting stock. Control of the corporation is not vested in a single person, entity, or group, but vested in the fluid aggregation of unaffiliated stockholders. In the event the Paramount-Viacom transaction is consummated, the public stockholders will receive cash and a minority equity voting position in the surviving corporation. Following such consummation, there will be a controlling stockholder who will have the voting power to: (a) elect directors; (b) cause a break-up of the corporation: (c) merge it with another company; (d) cash-out the public stockholders: (e) amend the certificate of incorporation; (f) sell all or substantially all of the corporate assets; or (g) otherwise alter materially the nature of the corporation and the public stockholders' interests. Irrespective of the present Paramount Board's vision of a long-term strategic alliance with Viacom, the proposed sale of control would provide the new controlling stockholder with the power to alter that vision.

Because of the intended sale of control, the Paramount-Viacom transaction has economic consequences of considerable significance to the Paramount stockholders. Once control has shifted, the current Paramount stockholders will have no leverage in the future to demand another control premium. As a result, the Paramount stockholders are entitled to receive, and should receive, a control premium and/or protective devices of significant value. There being no such protective provisions in the Viacom-Paramount transaction, the Paramount directors had an obligation to take the maximum advantage of the current opportunity to realize for the stockholders the best value reasonably available.

B. The Obligations of Directors in a Sale or Change of Control Transaction

The consequences of a sale of control impose special obligations on the directors of a corporation. In particular, they have the obligation of acting reasonably to seek the transaction offering the best value reasonably available to the stockholders. The courts will apply enhanced scrutiny to ensure that the directors have acted reasonably. . . .

In the sale of control context, the directors must focus on one primary objective—to secure the transaction offering the best value reasonably available for the stockholders—and they must exercise their fiduciary duties to further that end. . . .

* * * *

Barkan [*Barkan v. Amsted Indus., Inc.,* Del. Supr., 567 A.2d 1279, 1286 (1989)] teaches some of the methods by which a board can fulfill its obligation to seek the best value reasonably available to the stockholders. 567 A.2d at 1286–87. These methods are designed to determine the existence and viability of possible alternatives. They include conducting an auction, canvassing the market, etc. Delaware law recognizes that there is "no single blueprint" that directors must follow. [*Citations omitted.*]

In determining which alternative provides the best value for the stockholders, a board of directors is not limited to considering only the amount of cash involved, and is not required to ignore totally its view of the future value of a strategic alliance. [*Citation omitted.*] Instead, the directors should analyze the entire situation and evaluate in a disciplined manner the consideration being offered. Where stock or other non-cash consideration is involved, the board should try to quantify its value, if feasible, to achieve an objective comparison of the alternatives.[14] In addition, the board may assess a variety of practical considerations relating to each alternative including:

> [an offer's] fairness and feasibility; the proposed or actual financing for the offer, and the consequences of that financing; questions of illegality; . . . the risk of non-consummation; . . . the bidder's identity, prior background and other business venture

---

[14] When assessing the value of non-cash consideration, a board should focus on its value as of the date it will be received by the stockholders. Normally, such value will be determined with the assistance of experts using generally accepted methods of valuation.

experiences; and the bidder's business plans for the corporation and their effects on stockholder interests.

Macmillan, 559 A.2d at 1282 n. 29. These considerations are important because the selection of one alternative may permanently foreclose other opportunities. While the assessment of these factors may be complex, the board's goal is straightforward: Having informed themselves of all material information reasonably available, the directors must decide which alternative is most likely to offer the best value reasonably available to the stockholders.

C. Enhanced Judicial Scrutiny of a Sale or Change of Control Transaction

Board action in the circumstances presented here is subject to enhanced scrutiny. Such scrutiny is mandated by: (a) the threatened diminution of the current stockholders' voting power; (b) the fact that an asset belonging to public stockholders (a control premium) is being sold and may never be available again: and (c) the traditional concern of Delaware courts for actions which impair or impede stockholder voting rights. . . .

* * * *

The key features of an enhanced scrutiny test are: (a) a judicial determination regarding the adequacy of the decisionmaking process employed by the directors, including the information on which the directors based their decision; and (b) a judicial examination of the reasonableness of the directors' action in light of the circumstances then existing. The directors have the burden of proving that they were adequately informed and acted reasonably.

Although an enhanced scrutiny test involves a review of the reasonableness of the substantive merits of a board's actions,[17] a court should not ignore the complexity of the directors' task in a sale of control. There are many business and financial considerations implicated in investigating and selecting the best value reasonably available. The board of directors is the corporate decision-making body best equipped to make these judgments. Accordingly, a court applying enhanced judicial scrutiny should be deciding whether the directors made **a reasonable** decision, not **a perfect** decision. If a board selected one of

[17] It is to be remembered that, in cases where the traditional business judgment rule is applicable and the board acted with due care, in good faith, and in the honest belief that they are acting in the best interests of the stockholders (which is not this case), the Court gives great deference to the substance of the directors' decision and will not invalidate the decision, will not examine its reasonableness, and "will not substitute our views for those of the board if the latter's decision can be 'attributed to any rational business purpose.' " *Unocal,* 493 A.2d at 949 (*quoting Sinclair Oil Corp. v. Levien,* Del. Supr., 280 A.2d 717, 720 (1971)). . . .

several reasonable alternatives, a court should not second-guess that choice even though it might have decided otherwise or subsequent events may have cast doubt on the board's determination. Thus, courts will not substitute their business judgment for that of the directors, but will determine if the directors' decision was, on balance, within a range of reasonableness. [*Citations omitted.*]

D. Revlon and Time-Warner Distinguished

The Paramount defendants and Viacom assert that the fiduciary obligations and the enhanced judicial scrutiny discussed above are not implicated in this case in the absence of a "break-up" of the corporation, and that the order granting the preliminary injunction should be reversed. This argument is based on their erroneous interpretation of our decisions in *Revlon* and *Time-Warner.*

In *Revlon,* we reviewed the actions of the board of directors of Revlon, Inc. ("Revlon"), which had rebuffed the overtures of Pantry Pride, Inc. and had instead entered into an agreement with Forstmann Little & Co. ("Forstmann") providing for the acquisition of 100 percent of Revlon's outstanding stock by Forstmann and the subsequent break-up of Revlon. Based on the facts and circumstances present in *Revlon,* we held that "the directors' role changed from defenders of the corporate bastion to auctioneers charged with getting the best price for the stockholders at a sale of the company." 506 A.2d at 182. We further held that "when a board ends an intense bidding contest on an insubstantial basis, . . . [that] action cannot withstand the enhanced scrutiny which *Unocal* requires of director conduct." 506 A.2d at 184.

It is true that one of the circumstances bearing on these holdings was the fact that "the break-up of the company . . . had become a reality which even the directors embraced." 506 A.2d at 182. It does not follow, however, that a "break-up" must be present and "inevitable" before directors are subject to enhanced judicial scrutiny and are required to pursue a transaction that is calculated to produce the best value reasonably available to the stockholders. In fact, we stated in *Revlon* that "when bidders make relatively similar offers, or dissolution of the company becomes inevitable, the directors cannot fulfill their enhanced *Unocal* duties by playing favorites with the contending factions." 506 A.2d at 184 (emphasis added). *Revlon* thus does not hold that an inevitable dissolution or "break-up" is necessary.

The decisions of this Court following *Revlon* reinforced the applicability of enhanced scrutiny and the directors' obligation to seek the best value reasonably available for the stockholders where there is a pending sale of control, regardless of whether or not there is to be a break-up of the corporation.

* * * *

Although [other cases have clearly held that] a change of control imposes on directors the obligation to obtain the best value reasonably available to the stockholders, the Paramount defendants have interpreted our decision in *Time-Warner* as requiring a corporate break-up in order for that obligation to apply. The facts in *Time-Warner,* however, were quite different from the facts of this case, and refute Paramount's position here. In *Time-Warner,* the Chancellor held that there was no change of control in the original stock-for-stock merger between Time and Warner because Time would be owned by a fluid aggregation of unaffiliated stockholders both before and after the merger. . . . Moreover, the transaction actually consummated in *Time-Warner* was not a merger, as originally planned, but a sale of Warner's stock to Time.

In our affirmance of the Court of Chancery's well-reasoned decision, this Court held that "The Chancellor's findings of fact are supported by the record and his **conclusion is correct as a matter of law**." 571 A.2d at 1150 (emphasis added). Nevertheless, the Paramount defendants here have argued that a break-up is a requirement. . . .

The Paramount defendants have misread the holding of *Time-Warner*. . . . The Paramount Board, albeit unintentionally, had "initiated an active bidding process seeking to sell itself" by agreeing to sell control of the corporation to Viacom in circumstances where another potential acquiror (QVC) was equally interested in being a bidder.

The Paramount defendants' position that **both** a change of control **and** a break-up are **required** must be rejected. Such a holding would unduly restrict the application of *Revlon,* is inconsistent with this Court's decisions in *Barkan* and *Macmillan,* and has no basis in policy. There are few events that have a more significant impact on the stockholders than a sale of control or a corporate break-up. Each event represents a fundamental (and perhaps irrevocable) change in the nature of the corporate enterprise from a practical standpoint. It is the significance of **each** of these events that justifies: (a) focusing on the directors' obligation to seek the best value reasonably available to the stockholders; and (b) requiring a close scrutiny of board action which could be contrary to the stockholders' interests.

Accordingly, when a corporation undertakes a transaction which will cause: (a) a change in corporate control; **or** (b) a break-up of the corporate entity, the directors' obligation is to seek the best value reasonably available to the stockholders. This obligation arises because the effect of the Viacom-Paramount transaction, if consummated, is to shift control of Paramount from the public stockholders to a controlling stockholder, Viacom. Neither *Time-Warner* nor any other decision of this Court holds that a "break-up" of the company is essential to give rise to this obligation where there is a sale of control.

III. BREACH OF FIDUCIARY DUTIES BY PARAMOUNT BOARD

We now turn to duties of the Paramount Board under the facts of this case and our conclusions as to the breaches of those duties which warrant injunctive relief.

A. The Specific Obligations of the Paramount Board

Under the facts of this case, the Paramount directors had the obligation: (a) to be diligent and vigilant in examining critically the Paramount-Viacom transaction and the QVC tender offers; (b) to act in good faith; (c) to obtain, and act with due care on, all material information reasonably available, including information necessary to compare the two offers to determine which of these transactions, or an alternative course of action, would provide the best value reasonably available to the stockholders; and (d) to negotiate actively and in good faith with both Viacom and QVC to that end.

Having decided to sell control of the corporation, the Paramount directors were required to evaluate critically whether or not all material aspects of the Paramount-Viacom transaction (separately and in the aggregate) were reasonable and in the best interests of the Paramount stockholders in light of current circumstances, including: the change of control premium, the Stock Option Agreement, the Termination Fee, the coercive nature of both the Viacom and QVC tender offers,[18] the No-Shop Provision, and the proposed disparate use of the Rights Agreement as to the Viacom and QVC tender offers, respectively.

These obligations necessarily implicated various issues, including the questions of whether or not those provisions and other aspects of the Paramount-Viacom transaction (separately and in the aggregate): (a) adversely affected the value provided to the Paramount stockholders; (b) inhibited or encouraged alternative bids; (c) were enforceable contractual obligations in light

---

[18] Both the Viacom and the QVC tender offers were for 51 percent cash and a "back-end" of various securities, the value of each of which depended on the fluctuating value of Viacom and QVC stock at any given time. Thus, both tender offers were two-tiered, front-end loaded, and coercive. Such coercive offers are inherently problematic and should be expected to receive particularly careful analysis by a target board. *See Unocal,* 493 A.2d at 956.

of the directors' fiduciary duties; and (d) in the end would advance or retard the Paramount directors' obligation to secure for the Paramount stockholders the best value reasonably available under the circumstances.

The Paramount defendants contend that they were precluded by certain contractual provisions including the No-Shop Provision, from negotiating with QVC or seeking alternatives. Such provisions, whether or not they are presumptively valid in the abstract, may not validly define or limit the directors' fiduciary duties under Delaware law or prevent the Paramount directors from carrying out their fiduciary duties under Delaware law. To the extent such provisions are inconsistent with those duties, they are invalid and unenforceable. *See Revlon,* 506 A.2d at 184–85.

Since the Paramount directors had already decided to sell control, they had an obligation to continue their search for the best value reasonably available to the stockholders. This continuing obligation included the responsibility, at the October 24 board meeting and thereafter, to evaluate critically both the QVC tender offers and the Paramount-Viacom transaction to determine if: (a) the QVC tender offer was, or would continue to be, conditional; (b) the QVC tender offer could be improved; (c) the Viacom tender offer or other aspects of the Paramount-Viacom transaction could be improved; (d) each of the respective offers would be reasonably likely to come to closure, and under what circumstances; (e) other material information was reasonably available for consideration by the Paramount directors; (f) there were viable and realistic alternative courses of action; and (g) the timing constraints could be managed so the directors could consider these matters carefully and deliberately.

B. The Breaches of Fiduciary Duty by the Paramount Board

The Paramount directors made the decision on September 12, 1993, that, in their judgment, a strategic merger with Viacom on the economic terms of the Original Merger Agreement was in the best interests of Paramount and its stockholders. Those terms provided a modest change of control premium to the stockholders. The directors also decided at that time that it was appropriate to agree to certain defensive measures (the Stock Option Agreement, the Termination Fee, and the No-Shop Provision) insisted upon by Viacom as part of that economic transaction. Those defensive measures, coupled with the sale of control and subsequent disparate treatment of competing bidders, implicated the judicial scrutiny of *Unocal, Revlon, Macmillan,* and their progeny. We conclude that the Paramount directors' process was not reasonable, and the result achieved for the stockholders was not reasonable under the circumstances.

When entering into the Original Merger Agreement, and thereafter, the Paramount Board clearly gave insufficient attention to the potential consequences of the defensive measures demanded by Viacom. The Stock Option Agreement had a number of unusual and potentially "draconian" provisions, including the Note Feature and the Put Feature. Furthermore, the Termination Fee, whether or not unreasonable by itself, clearly made Paramount less attractive to other bidders, when coupled with the Stock Option Agreement. Finally, the No-Shop Provision inhibited the Paramount Board's ability to negotiate with other potential bidders, particularly QVC which had already expressed an interest in Paramount.

Throughout the applicable time period, and especially from the first QVC merger proposal on September 20 through the Paramount Board meeting on November 15, QVC's interest in Paramount provided the **opportunity** for the Paramount Board to seek significantly higher value for the Paramount stockholders than that being offered by Viacom. QVC persistently demonstrated its intention to meet and exceed the Viacom offers, and frequently expressed its willingness to negotiate possible further increases.

The Paramount directors had the opportunity in the October 23–24 time frame, when the Original Merger Agreement was renegotiated, to take appropriate action to modify the improper defensive measures as well as to improve the economic terms of the Paramount-Viacom transaction. Under the circumstances existing at that time, it should have been clear to the Paramount Board that the Stock Option Agreement, coupled with the Termination Fee and the No-Shop Clause, were impeding the realization of the best value reasonably available to the Paramount stockholders. Nevertheless, the Paramount Board made no effort to eliminate or modify these counterproductive devices, and instead continued to cling to its vision of a strategic alliance with Viacom. Moreover, based on advice from the Paramount management, the Paramount directors considered the QVC offer to be "conditional" and asserted that they were precluded by the No-Shop Provision from seeking more information from, or negotiating with, QVC.

By November 12, 1993, the value of the revised QVC offer on its face exceeded that of the Viacom offer by over $1 billion at then current values. This significant disparity of value cannot be justified on the basis of the directors' vision of future strategy, primarily because the change of control would supplant the authority of the current Paramount Board to continue to hold and implement their strategic vision in any meaningful way. Moreover, their uninformed process had deprived their strategic vision of much of its credibility. [*Citations omitted.*]

When the Paramount directors met on November 15 to consider QVC's increased tender offer, they remained prisoners of their own misconceptions and missed opportunities to eliminate the restrictions they had imposed on themselves. Yet, it was not "too late" to reconsider negotiating with QVC. . . . Nevertheless, the Paramount directors remained paralyzed by their uninformed belief that the QVC offer was "illusory." This final opportunity to negotiate on the stockholders' behalf and to fulfill their obligation to seek the best value reasonably available was thereby squandered.

IV. Viacom's Claim Of Vested Contract Rights

Viacom argues that it had certain "vested" contract rights with respect to the No-Shop Provision and the Stock Option Agreement. In effect, Viacom's argument is that the Paramount directors could enter into an agreement in violation of their fiduciary duties and then render Paramount, and ultimately its stockholders, liable for failing to carry out an agreement in violation of those duties. Viacom's protestations about vested rights are without merit. This Court has found that those defensive measures were improperly designed to deter potential bidders, and that such measures do not meet the reasonableness test to which they must be subjected. They are consequently invalid and unenforceable under the facts of this case.

The No-Shop Provision could not validly define or limit the fiduciary duties of the Paramount directors. To the extent that a contract, or a provision thereof, purports to require a board to act or not act in such a fashion as to limit the exercise of fiduciary duties, it is invalid and unenforceable. [*Citations omitted.*] Despite the arguments of Paramount and Viacom to the contrary, the Paramount directors could not contract away their fiduciary obligations. Since the No-Shop Provision was invalid, Viacom never had any vested contract rights in the provision.

As discussed previously, the Stock Option Agreement contained several "draconian" aspects, including the Note Feature and the Put Feature. . . . Under the circumstances of this case, the Stock Option Agreement clearly is invalid. Accordingly, Viacom never had any vested contract rights in that Agreement.

Viacom, a sophisticated party with experienced legal and financial advisors, knew of (and in fact demanded) the unreasonable features of the Stock Option Agreement. It cannot be now heard to argue that it obtained vested contract rights by negotiating and obtaining contractual provisions from a board acting in violation of its fiduciary duties. . . .

V. CONCLUSION

The realization of the best value reasonably available to the stockholders became the Paramount directors' primary obligation under these facts in light of the change of control. That obligation was not satisfied, and the Paramount Board's process was deficient. The directors' initial hope and expectation for a strategic alliance with Viacom was allowed to dominate their decisionmaking process to the point where the arsenal of defensive measures established at the outset was perpetuated (not modified or eliminated) when the situation was dramatically altered. QVC's unsolicited bid presented the opportunity for significantly greater value for the stockholders and enhanced negotiating leverage for the directors. Rather than seizing those opportunities, the Paramount directors chose to wall themselves off from material information which was reasonably available and to hide behind the defensive measures as a rationalization for refusing to negotiate with QVC or seeking other alternatives. Their view of the strategic alliance likewise became an empty rationalization as the opportunities for higher value for the stockholders continued to develop.

* * * *

For the reasons set forth herein, the November 24, 1993, Order of the Court of Chancery has been AFFIRMED, and this matter has been REMANDED for proceedings consistent herewith. . . .

NOTES AND QUESTIONS

1. Do you agree with the court's distinction between the circumstances in the preceding *Paramount v. QVC* case and the *Paramount v. Time* case?

2. How would you advise a client who wanted to acquire another company but was concerned that the announcement of the acquisition would lead to a bidding war?

3. Consider the unsuccessful strategy implemented in *Omnicare, Inc. v. NCS Healthcare, Inc.*, which follows.

Omnicare, Inc. v. NCS Healthcare, Inc.

818 A.2d 914 (Del. 2003)

HOLLAND, J.:

NCS Healthcare, Inc. ("NCS"), a Delaware corporation, was the object of competing acquisition bids, one by Genesis Health Ventures, Inc. ("Genesis"), a Pennsylvania corporation, and the other by Omnicare, Inc. ("Omnicare"), a Delaware corporation. . . .

* * * *

The Parties

The defendant, NCS, is a Delaware corporation headquartered in Beachwood, Ohio. NCS is a leading independent provider of pharmacy services to long-term care institutions including skilled nursing facilities, assisted living facilities and other institutional healthcare facilities. NCS common stock consists of Class A shares and Class B shares. The Class B shares are entitled to ten votes per share and the Class A shares are entitled to one vote per share. The shares are virtually identical in every other respect.

The defendant Jon H. Outcalt is Chairman of the NCS board of directors. Outcalt owns 202,063 shares of NCS Class A common stock and 3,476,086 shares of Class B common stock. The defendant Kevin B. Shaw is President, CEO and a director of NCS. At the time the merger agreement at issue in this dispute was executed with Genesis, Shaw owned 28,905 shares of NCS Class A common stock and 1,141,134 shares of Class B common stock.

The NCS board has two other members, defendants Boake A. Sells and Richard L. Osborne. Sells is a graduate of the Harvard Business School. He was Chairman and CEO at Revco Drugstores in Cleveland, Ohio from 1987 to 1992, when he was replaced by new owners. Sells currently sits on the boards of both public and private companies. Osborne is a full-time professor at the Weatherhead School of Management at Case Western Reserve University. He has been at the university for over thirty years. Osborne currently sits on at least seven corporate boards other than NCS.

The defendant Genesis is a Pennsylvania corporation with its principal place of business in Kennett Square, Pennsylvania. It is a leading provider of healthcare and support services to the elderly. The defendant Geneva Sub, Inc., a wholly owned subsidiary of Genesis, is a Delaware corporation formed by Genesis to acquire NCS.

The plaintiffs in the class action own an unspecified number of shares of NCS Class A common stock. . . .

Omnicare is a Delaware corporation with its principal place of business in Covington, Kentucky. Omnicare is in the institutional pharmacy business, with annual sales in excess of $2.1 billion during its last fiscal year. Omnicare purchased 1000 shares of NCS Class A common stock on July 30, 2002.

* * * *

FACTUAL BACKGROUND

The parties are in substantial agreement regarding the operative facts. They disagree, however, about the legal implications. This recitation of facts is taken primarily from the opinion by the Court of Chancery.

NCS Seeks Restructuring Alternatives

Beginning in late 1999, changes in the timing and level of reimbursements by government and third-party providers adversely affected market conditions in the health care industry. As a result, NCS began to experience greater difficulty in collecting accounts receivables, which led to a precipitous decline in the market value of its stock. NCS common shares that traded above $20 in January 1999 were worth as little as $5 at the end of that year. By early 2001, NCS was in default on approximately $350 million in debt, including $206 million in senior bank debt and $102 million of its 53/4 %Convertible Subordinated Debentures (the "Notes"). After these defaults, NCS common stock traded in a range of $0.09 to $0.50 per share until days before the announcement of the transaction at issue in this case.

NCS began to explore strategic alternatives that might address the problems it was confronting. As part of this effort, in February 2000, NCS retained UBS Warburg, L.L.C. to identify potential acquirers and possible equity investors. UBS Warburg contacted over fifty different entities to solicit their interest in a variety of transactions with NCS. UBS Warburg had marginal success in its efforts. By October 2000, NCS had only received one non-binding indication of interest valued at $190 million, substantially less than the face value of NCS's senior debt. This proposal was reduced by 20% after the offeror conducted its due diligence review.

NCS Financial Deterioration

In December 2000, NCS terminated its relationship with UBS Warburg and retained Brown, Gibbons, Lang & Company as its exclusive financial advisor. During this period, NCS's financial condition continued to deteriorate. In April 2001, NCS received a formal notice of default and acceleration from the trustee for holders of the Notes. As NCS's financial condition worsened, the Noteholders formed a committee to represent their financial interests (the "Ad Hoc Committee"). At about that time, NCS began discussions with various investor groups regarding a restructuring in a "pre-packaged" bankruptcy. NCS did not receive any proposal that it believed provided adequate consideration for its stakeholders. At that time, full recovery for NCS's creditors was a remote prospect, and any recovery for NCS stockholders seemed impossible.

Omnicare's Initial Negotiations

In the summer of 2001, NCS invited Omnicare, Inc. to begin discussions with Brown Gibbons regarding a possible transaction. On July 20, Joel Gemunder, Omnicare's President and CEO, sent Shaw a written proposal to acquire NCS in a bankruptcy sale under Section 363 of the Bankruptcy Code. This proposal was for $225 million subject to satisfactory completion of due diligence. NCS asked Omnicare to execute a confidentiality agreement so that more detailed discussions could take place.

In August 2001, Omnicare increased its bid to $270 million, but still proposed to structure the deal as an asset sale in bankruptcy. Even at $270 million, Omnicare's proposal was substantially lower than the face value of NCS's outstanding debt. It would have provided only a small recovery for Omnicare's Noteholders and no recovery for its stockholders. In October 2001, NCS sent Glen Pollack of Brown Gibbons to meet with Omnicare's financial advisor, Merrill Lynch, to discuss Omnicare's interest in NCS. Omnicare responded that it was not interested in any transaction other than an asset sale in bankruptcy.

There was no further contact between Omnicare and NCS between November 2001 and January 2002. Instead, Omnicare began secret discussions with Judy K. Mencher, a representative of the Ad Hoc Committee. In these discussions, Omnicare continued to pursue a transaction structured as a sale of assets in bankruptcy. In February 2002, the Ad Hoc Committee notified the NCS board that Omnicare had proposed an asset sale in bankruptcy for $313,750,000.

NCS Independent Board Committee

In January 2002, Genesis was contacted by members of the Ad Hoc Committee concerning a possible transaction with NCS. Genesis executed

NCS's standard confidentiality agreement and began a due diligence review. Genesis had recently emerged from bankruptcy because, like NCS, it was suffering from dwindling government reimbursements.

Genesis previously lost a bidding war to Omnicare in a different transaction. This led to bitter feelings between the principals of both companies. More importantly, this bitter experience for Genesis led to its insistence on exclusivity agreements and lock-ups in any potential transaction with NCS.

NCS Financial Improvement

NCS's operating performance was improving by early 2002. As NCS's performance improved, the NCS directors began to believe that it might be possible for NCS to enter into a transaction that would provide some recovery for NCS stockholders' equity. In March 2002, NCS decided to form an independent committee of board members who were neither NCS employees nor major NCS stockholders (the "Independent Committee"). The NCS board thought this was necessary because, due to NCS's precarious financial condition, it felt that fiduciary duties were owed to the enterprise as a whole rather than solely to NCS stockholders.

Sells and Osborne were selected as the members of the committee, and given authority to consider and negotiate possible transactions for NCS. The entire four member NCS board, however, retained authority to approve any transaction. The Independent Committee retained the same legal and financial counsel as the NCS board.

The Independent Committee met for the first time on May 14, 2002. At that meeting Pollack suggested that NCS seek a "stalking-horse merger partner" to obtain the highest possible value in any transaction. The Independent Committee agreed with the suggestion.

Genesis Initial Proposal

Two days later, on May 16, 2002, Scott Berlin of Brown Gibbons, Glen Pollack and Boake Sells met with George Hager, CFO of Genesis, and Michael Walker, who was Genesis's CEO. At that meeting, Genesis made it clear that if it were going to engage in any negotiations with NCS, it would not do so as a "stalking horse." As one of its advisors testified, "We didn't want to be someone who set forth a valuation for NCS which would only result in that valuation . . .being publicly disclosed, and thereby creating an environment where Omnicare felt to maintain its competitive monopolistic positions, that they had to match and exceed that level." Thus, Genesis "wanted a degree of certainty that to the extent [it] was willing to pursue a negotiated merger agreement . . ., [it] would be able to consummate the transaction [it] negotiated and executed."

In June 2002, Genesis proposed a transaction that would take place outside the bankruptcy context. Although it did not provide full recovery for NCS's Noteholders, it provided the possibility that NCS stockholders would be able to recover something for their investment. As discussions continued, the terms proposed by Genesis continued to improve. On June 25, the economic terms of the Genesis proposal included repayment of the NCS senior debt in full, full assumption of trade credit obligations, an exchange offer or direct purchase of the NCS Notes providing NCS Noteholders with a combination of cash and Genesis common stock equal to the par value of the NCS Notes (not including accrued interest), and $20 million in value for the NCS common stock. Structurally, the Genesis proposal continued to include consents from a significant majority of the Noteholders as well as support agreements from stockholders owning a majority of the NCS voting power.

Genesis Exclusivity Agreement

NCS's financial advisors and legal counsel met again with Genesis and its legal counsel on June 26, 2002, to discuss a number of transaction-related issues. At this meeting, Pollack asked Genesis to increase its offer to NCS stockholders. Genesis agreed to consider this request. Thereafter, Pollack and Hager had further conversations. Genesis agreed to offer a total of $24 million in consideration for the NCS common stock, or an additional $4 million, in the form of Genesis common stock.

At the June 26 meeting, Genesis's representatives demanded that, before any further negotiations take place, NCS agree to enter into an exclusivity agreement with it. As Hager from Genesis explained it: "[I] f they wished us to continue to try to move this process to a definitive agreement, that they would need to do it on an exclusive basis with us. We were going to, and already had incurred significant expense, but we would incur additional expenses . . ., both internal and external, to bring this transaction to a definitive signing. We wanted them to work with us on an exclusive basis for a short period of time to see if we could reach agreement." On June 27, 2002, Genesis's legal counsel delivered a draft form of exclusivity agreement for review and consideration by NCS's legal counsel.

The Independent Committee met on July 3, 2002, to consider the proposed exclusivity agreement. Pollack presented a summary of the terms of a possible Genesis merger, which had continued to improve. The then-current Genesis proposal included (1) repayment of the NCS senior debt in full, (2) payment of par value for the Notes (without accrued interest) in the form of a combination of cash and Genesis stock, (3) payment to NCS stockholders in the form of $24 million in Genesis stock, plus (4) the assumption, because the transaction was to be structured as a merger, of additional liabilities to trade and other unsecured creditors.

NCS director Sells testified, Pollack told the Independent Committee at a July 3, 2002 meeting that Genesis wanted the Exclusivity Agreement to be the first step towards a completely locked up transaction that would preclude a higher bid from Omnicare:

> A. [Pollack] explained that Genesis felt that they had suffered at the hands of Omnicare and others. I guess maybe just Omnicare. I don't know much about Genesis [sic] acquisition history. But they had suffered before at the 11: 59: 59 and that they wanted to have a pretty much bulletproof deal or they were not going to go forward.
>
> Q. When you say they suffered at the hands of Omnicare, what do you mean?
>
> A. Well, my expression is that that was related to a deal that was related to me or explained to me that they, Genesis, had tried to acquire, I suppose, an institutional pharmacy, I don't remember the name of it. Thought they had a deal and then at the last minute, Omnicare outbid them for the company in a like 11: 59 kind of thing, and that they were unhappy about that. And once burned, twice shy.

After NCS executed the exclusivity agreement, Genesis provided NCS with a draft merger agreement, a draft Noteholders' support agreement, and draft voting agreements for Outcalt and Shaw, who together held a majority of the voting power of the NCS common stock. Genesis and NCS negotiated the terms of the merger agreement over the next three weeks. During those negotiations, the Independent Committee and the Ad Hoc Committee persuaded Genesis to improve the terms of its merger.

The parties were still negotiating by July 19, and the exclusivity period was automatically extended to July 26. At that point, NCS and Genesis were close to executing a merger agreement and related voting agreements. Genesis proposed a short extension of the exclusivity agreement so a deal could be finalized. On the morning of July 26, 2002, the Independent Committee authorized an extension of the exclusivity period through July 31.

Omnicare Proposes Negotiations

By late July 2002, Omnicare came to believe that NCS was negotiating a transaction, possibly with Genesis or another of Omnicare's competitors, that would potentially present a competitive threat to Omnicare. Omnicare also came to believe, in light of a run-up in the price of NCS common stock, that whatever transaction NCS was negotiating probably included a payment for its stock. . . .

On the afternoon of July 26, 2002, Omnicare faxed to NCS a letter outlining a proposed acquisition. The letter suggested a transaction in which Omnicare would retire NCS's senior and subordinated debt at par plus accrued interest, and pay the NCS stockholders $3 cash for their shares. Omnicare's proposal, however, was expressly conditioned on negotiating a merger agreement, obtaining certain third party consents, and completing its due diligence.

Mencher saw the July 26 Omnicare letter and realized that, while its economic terms were attractive, the "due diligence" condition substantially undercut its strength. In an effort to get a better proposal from Omnicare, Mencher telephoned Gemunder and told him that Omnicare was unlikely to succeed in its bid unless it dropped the "due diligence outs." She explained this was the only way a bid at the last minute would be able to succeed. Gemunder considered Mencher's warning "very real," and followed up with his advisors. They, however, insisted that he retain the due diligence condition "to protect [him] from doing something foolish." Taking this advice to heart, Gemunder decided not to drop the due diligence condition.

Late in the afternoon of July 26, 2002, NCS representatives received voicemail messages from Omnicare asking to discuss the letter. The exclusivity agreement prevented NCS from returning those calls. In relevant part, that agreement precluded NCS from "engaging or participating in any discussions or negotiations with respect to a Competing Transaction or a proposal for one." The July 26 letter from Omnicare met the definition of a "Competing Transaction."

Despite the exclusivity agreement, the Independent Committee met to consider a response to Omnicare. It concluded that discussions with Omnicare about its July 26 letter presented an unacceptable risk that Genesis would abandon merger discussions. The Independent Committee believed that, given Omnicare's past bankruptcy proposals and unwillingness to consider a merger, as well as its decision to negotiate exclusively with the Ad Hoc Committee, the risk of losing the Genesis proposal was too substantial. Nevertheless, the Independent Committee instructed Pollack to use Omnicare's letter to negotiate for improved terms with Genesis.

Genesis Merger Agreement And Voting Agreements

Genesis responded to the NCS request to improve its offer as a result of the Omnicare fax the next day. On July 27, Genesis proposed substantially improved terms. First, it proposed to retire the Notes in accordance with the terms of the indenture, thus eliminating the need for Noteholders to consent to the transaction. This change involved paying all accrued interest plus a small redemption premium. Second, Genesis increased the exchange ratio for NCS common stock to one-tenth of a Genesis common share for each NCS common share, an 80% increase. Third, it agreed to lower the proposed termination fee in the merger agreement from $10 million to $6 million. In return for these concessions, Genesis stipulated that the transaction had to be approved by midnight the next day, July 28, or else Genesis would terminate discussions and withdraw its offer.

The Independent Committee and the NCS board both scheduled meetings for July 28. The committee met first. Although that meeting lasted less than an hour, the Court of Chancery determined the minutes reflect that the directors were fully informed of all material facts relating to the proposed transaction. After concluding that Genesis was sincere in establishing the midnight deadline, the committee voted unanimously to recommend the transaction to the full board.

The full board met thereafter. After receiving similar reports and advice from its legal and financial advisors, the board concluded that "balancing the potential loss of the Genesis deal against the uncertainty of Omnicare's letter, results in the conclusion that the only reasonable alternative for the Board of Directors is to approve the Genesis transaction." The board first voted to authorize the voting agreements with Outcalt and Shaw, for purposes of Section 203 of the Delaware General Corporation Law ("DGCL"). The board was advised by its legal counsel that "under the terms of the merger agreement and because NCS shareholders representing in excess of 50% of the outstanding voting power would be *required* by Genesis to enter into stockholder voting agreements contemporaneously with the signing of the merger agreement, and would agree to vote their shares in favor of the merger agreement, shareholder approval of the merger would be assured even if the NCS Board were to withdraw or change its recommendation. *These facts would prevent NCS from engaging in any alternative or superior transaction in the future.*" (emphasis added).

After listening to a *summary* of the merger terms, the board then resolved that the merger agreement and the transactions contemplated thereby were advisable and fair and in the best interests of all the NCS stakeholders. The NCS board further resolved to recommend the transactions to the stockholders for their approval and adoption. A definitive merger agreement between NCS and Genesis and the stockholder voting agreements were executed later that day. The Court of Chancery held that it was not a *per se* breach of fiduciary duty that the NCS board never read the NCS/Genesis merger agreement word for word.

NCS/Genesis Merger Agreement

Among other things, the NCS/Genesis merger agreement provided the following:

- NCS stockholders would receive 1 share of Genesis common stock in exchange for every 10 shares of NCS common stock held;
- NCS stockholders could exercise appraisal rights under 8 Del. C. § 262;
- NCS would redeem NCS's Notes in accordance with their terms;
- NCS would submit the merger agreement to NCS stockholders regardless of whether the NCS board continued to recommend the merger;
- NCS would not enter into discussions with third parties concerning an alternative acquisition of NCS, or provide non-public information to such parties, unless (1) the third party provided an unsolicited, *bona fide* written proposal documenting the terms of the acquisition; (2) the NCS board believed in good faith that the proposal was or was likely to result in an acquisition on terms superior to those contemplated by the NCS/Genesis merger agreement; and (3) before providing non-public information to that third party, the third party would execute a confidentiality agreement at least as restrictive as the one in place between NCS and Genesis; and
- If the merger agreement were to be terminated, under certain circumstances NCS would be required to pay Genesis a $6

million termination fee and/or Genesis's documented expenses, up to $5 million.

Voting Agreements

Outcalt and Shaw, in their capacity as NCS stockholders, entered into voting agreements with Genesis. NCS was also required to be a party to the voting agreements by Genesis. Those agreements provided, among other things, that:

- Outcalt and Shaw were acting in their capacity as NCS stockholders in executing the agreements, not in their capacity as NCS directors or officers;
- Neither Outcalt nor Shaw would transfer their shares prior to the stockholder vote on the merger agreement;
- Outcalt and Shaw agreed to vote all of their shares in favor of the merger agreement; and
- Outcalt and Shaw granted to Genesis an irrevocable proxy to vote their shares in favor of the merger agreement.
- The voting agreement was specifically enforceable by Genesis.

The merger agreement further provided that if either Outcalt or Shaw breached the terms of the voting agreements, Genesis would be entitled to terminate the merger agreement and potentially receive a $6 million termination fee from NCS. Such a breach was impossible since Section 6 provided that the voting agreements were specifically enforceable by Genesis.

Omnicare's Superior Proposal

On July 29, 2002, hours after the NCS/Genesis transaction was executed, Omnicare faxed a letter to NCS restating its conditional proposal and attaching a draft merger agreement. Later that morning, Omnicare issued a press release publicly disclosing the proposal.

On August 1, 2002, Omnicare filed a lawsuit attempting to enjoin the NCS/Genesis merger, and announced that it intended to launch a tender offer for NCS's shares at a price of $3.50 per share. On August 8, 2002, Omnicare began its tender offer. By letter dated that same day, Omnicare expressed a desire to discuss the terms of the offer with NCS. Omnicare's letter continued to condition its proposal on satisfactory completion of a due diligence investigation of NCS.

On August 8, 2002, and again on August 19, 2002, the NCS Independent Committee and full board of directors met separately to consider the Omnicare tender offer in light of the Genesis merger agreement. NCS's outside legal counsel and NCS's financial advisor attended both meetings. The board was unable to determine that Omnicare's expressions of interest were likely to lead to a "Superior Proposal," as the term was defined in the NCS/Genesis merger agreement. On September 10, 2002, NCS requested and received a waiver from Genesis allowing NCS to enter into discussions with Omnicare without first having to determine that Omnicare's proposal was a "Superior Proposal."

On October 6, 2002, Omnicare irrevocably committed itself to a transaction with NCS. Pursuant to the terms of its proposal, Omnicare agreed to acquire all the outstanding NCS Class A and Class B shares at a price of $3.50 per share in cash. As a result of this irrevocable offer, on October 21, 2002, the NCS board withdrew its recommendation that the stockholders vote in favor of the NCS/Genesis merger agreement. NCS's financial advisor withdrew its fairness opinion of the NCS/Genesis merger agreement as well.

Genesis Rejection Impossible

The Genesis merger agreement permits the NCS directors to furnish non-public information to, or enter into discussions with, "any Person in connection with an unsolicited bona fide written Acquisition Proposal by such person" that the board deems likely to constitute a "Superior Proposal." That provision has absolutely no effect on the Genesis merger agreement. Even if the NCS board "changes, withdraws or modifies" its recommendation, as it did, it must still submit the merger to a stockholder vote.

A subsequent filing with the Securities and Exchange Commission ("SEC") states: "the NCS independent committee and the NCS board of directors have determined to withdraw their recommendations of the Genesis merger agreement and recommend that the NCS stockholders vote against the approval and adoption of the Genesis merger." In that same SEC filing, however, the NCS board explained why the success of the Genesis merger had already been predetermined. "Notwithstanding the foregoing, the NCS independent committee and the NCS board of directors recognize that (1) the existing contractual obligations to Genesis currently prevent NCS from accepting the Omnicare irrevocable merger proposal; and (2) the existence of the voting agreements entered into by Messrs. Outcalt and Shaw, whereby Messrs. Outcalt and Shaw agreed to vote their shares of NCS Class A common stock and NCS Class B common stock in favor of the Genesis merger, ensure NCS stockholder approval of the Genesis merger." This litigation was commenced to prevent the consummation of the inferior Genesis transaction.

LEGAL ANALYSIS

* * * *

Deal Protection Devices Require Enhanced Scrutiny

The dispositive issues in this appeal involve the defensive devices that protected the Genesis merger agreement. The Delaware corporation statute provides that the board's management decision to enter into and recommend a merger transaction can become final only when ownership action is taken by a vote of the stockholders. Thus, the Delaware corporation law expressly provides for a balance of power between boards and stockholders which makes merger transactions a shared enterprise and ownership decision. Consequently, a board of directors' decision to adopt defensive devices to protect a merger agreement may implicate the stockholders' right to effectively vote contrary to the initial recommendation of the board in favor of the transaction.

It is well established that conflicts of interest arise when a board of directors acts to prevent stockholders from effectively exercising their right to vote contrary to the will of the board. The "omnipresent specter" of such conflict may be present whenever a board adopts defensive devices to protect a merger agreement. The stockholders' ability to effectively reject a merger agreement is likely to bear an inversely proportionate relationship to the structural and economic devices that the board has approved to protect the transaction.

* * * *

There are inherent conflicts between a board's interest in protecting a merger transaction it has approved, the stockholders' statutory right to make the final decision to either approve or not approve a merger, and the board's continuing responsibility to effectively exercise its fiduciary duties at all times after the merger agreement is executed. These competing considerations require a threshold determination that board-approved defensive devices protecting a merger transaction are within the limitations of its statutory authority and consistent with the directors' fiduciary duties. Accordingly, in *Paramount v. Time*, we held that the business judgment rule applied to the Time board's original decision to merge with Warner. We further held, however, that defensive devices adopted by the board to protect the original merger transaction must withstand enhanced judicial scrutiny under the *Unocal* standard of review, even when that merger transaction does not result in a change of control.

Enhanced Scrutiny Generally

In *Paramount v. QVC,* this Court identified the key features of an enhanced judicial scrutiny test. The first feature is a "judicial determination regarding the adequacy of the decisionmaking process employed by the directors, including the information on which the directors based their decision." The second feature is "a judicial examination of the reasonableness of the directors' action in light of the circumstances then existing." We also held that "the directors have the burden of proving that they were adequately informed and acted reasonably."

In *QVC,* we explained that the application of an enhanced judicial scrutiny test involves a judicial "review of the reasonableness of the substantive merits of the board's actions." In applying that standard, we held that "a court should not ignore the complexity of the directors' task" in the context in which action was taken. Accordingly, we concluded that a court applying enhanced judicial scrutiny should not decide whether the directors made a perfect decision but instead should decide whether "the directors' decision was, on balance, within a range of reasonableness."

* * * *

A board's decision to protect its decision to enter a merger agreement with defensive devices against uninvited competing transactions that may emerge is analogous to a board's decision to protect against dangers to corporate policy and effectiveness when it adopts defensive measures in a hostile takeover contest. In applying *Unocal's* enhanced judicial scrutiny in assessing a challenge to defensive actions taken by a target corporation's board of directors in a takeover context, this Court held that the board "does not have unbridled discretion to defeat perceived threats by any draconian means available. Similarly, just as a board's statutory power with regard to a merger decision is not absolute, a board does not have unbridled discretion to defeat any perceived threat to a merger by protecting it with any draconian means available.

Since *Unocal,* "this Court has consistently recognized that defensive measures which are either preclusive or coercive are included within the common law definition of draconian." . . . .

Therefore, in applying enhanced judicial scrutiny to defensive devices designed to protect a merger agreement, a court must first determine that those measures are not preclusive or coercive *before* its focus shifts to the "range of reasonableness" in making a proportionality determination. . . .

* * * *

Deal Protection Devices

Defensive devices, as that term is used in this opinion, is a synonym for what are frequently referred to as "deal protection devices." Both terms are used interchangeably to describe any measure or combination of measures that are intended to protect the consummation of a merger transaction. Defensive devices can be economic, structural, or both.

Deal protection devices need not all be in the merger agreement itself. In this case, for example, the Section 251(c) provision in the merger agreement was combined with the separate voting agreements to provide a structural defense for the Genesis merger agreement against any subsequent superior transaction. Genesis made the NCS board's defense of its transaction absolute by insisting on the omission of any effective fiduciary out clause in the NCS merger agreement.

Genesis argues that stockholder voting agreements cannot be construed as deal protection devices taken by a board of directors because stockholders are entitled to vote in their own interest. . . .

In this case, the stockholder voting agreements were inextricably intertwined with the defensive aspects of the Genesis merger agreement. In fact, the voting agreements with Shaw and Outcalt were the linchpin of Genesis' proposed tripartite defense. Therefore, Genesis made the execution of those voting agreements a non-negotiable condition precedent to its execution of the merger agreement. In the case before us, the Court of Chancery held that the acts which locked-up the Genesis transaction were the Section 251(c) provision and "the execution of the *voting agreement* by Outcalt and Shaw."

With the assurance that Outcalt and Shaw would irrevocably agree to exercise their majority voting power in favor of its transaction, Genesis insisted that the merger agreement reflect the other two aspects of its concerted defense, i. e., the inclusion of a Section 251(c) provision and the omission of any effective fiduciary out clause. Those dual aspects of the merger agreement would not have provided Genesis with a complete defense in the absence of the voting agreements with Shaw and Outcalt.

These Deal Protection Devices Unenforceable

In this case, the Court of Chancery correctly held that the NCS directors' decision to adopt defensive devices to *completely* "lock up" the Genesis merger mandated "special scrutiny" under the two-part test set forth in *Unocal.* That conclusion is consistent with our holding in *Paramount v. Time* that "safety devices" adopted to protect a transaction that did not result in a change of control are subject to enhanced judicial scrutiny under a *Unocal* analysis. The record does not, however, support the Court of Chancery's conclusion that the defensive devices adopted by the NCS board to protect the Genesis merger were reasonable and proportionate to the threat that NCS perceived from the potential loss of the Genesis transaction.

Pursuant to the judicial scrutiny required under *Unocal's* two-stage analysis, the NCS directors must first demonstrate "that they had reasonable grounds for believing that a danger to corporate policy and effectiveness existed . . . ." To satisfy that burden, the NCS directors are required to show they acted in good faith after conducting a reasonable investigation. The threat identified by the NCS board was the possibility of losing the Genesis offer and being left with no comparable alternative transaction.

The second stage of the *Unocal* test requires the NCS directors to demonstrate that their defensive response was "reasonable in relation to the threat posed." This inquiry involves a two-step analysis. The NCS directors must first establish that the merger deal protection devices adopted in response to the threat were not "coercive" or "preclusive," and then demonstrate that their response was within a "range of reasonable responses" to the threat perceived. In *Unitrin,* we stated:

- A response is "coercive" if it is aimed at forcing upon stockholders a management-sponsored alternative to a hostile offer.
- A response is "preclusive" if it deprives stockholders of the right to receive all tender offers or precludes a bidder from seeking control by fundamentally restricting proxy contests or otherwise.

This aspect of the *Unocal* standard provides for a disjunctive analysis. If defensive measures are either preclusive or coercive they are draconian and impermissible. In this case, the deal protection devices of the NCS board were *both* preclusive and coercive.

This Court enunciated the standard for determining stockholder coercion in the case of *Williams v. Geier* [671 A.2d 1368 (Del. 1996)]. A stockholder vote may be nullified by wrongful coercion "where the board or some other party takes actions which have the effect of causing the stockholders to vote in favor of the proposed transaction for some reason other than the merits of that transaction." . . . .

Although the minority stockholders were not forced to vote for the Genesis merger, they were required to accept it because it was *a fait accompli.* The record reflects that the defensive devices employed by the NCS board are preclusive and coercive in the sense that they accomplished *a fait accompli.* In this case, despite the fact that the NCS board has withdrawn its recommendation for the Genesis transaction and recommended its rejection by the stockholders, the deal protection devices approved by the NCS board operated in concert to have a preclusive and coercive effect. Those tripartite defensive measures—the Section 251(c) provision, the voting agreements, and the absence of an effective fiduciary out clause—made it "mathematically impossible" and "realistically unattainable" for the Omnicare transaction or any other proposal to succeed, no matter how superior the proposal.

The deal protection devices adopted by the NCS board were designed to coerce the consummation of the Genesis merger and preclude the consideration of any superior transaction. The NCS directors' defensive devices are not within a reasonable range of responses to the perceived threat of losing the Genesis offer because they are preclusive and coercive. Accordingly, we hold that those deal protection devices are unenforceable.

Effective Fiduciary Out Required

The defensive measures that protected the merger transaction are unenforceable not only because they are preclusive and coercive but, alternatively, they are unenforceable because they are invalid as they operate in this case. Given the specifically enforceable irrevocable voting agreements, the provision in the merger agreement requiring the board to submit the transaction for a stockholder vote and the omission of a fiduciary out clause in the merger agreement completely prevented the board from discharging its fiduciary responsibilities to the minority stockholders when Omnicare presented its superior transaction. "To the extent that a [merger] contract, or a provision thereof, purports to require a board to act or not act in such a fashion as to limit the exercise of fiduciary duties, it is invalid and unenforceable."[74]

* * * *

Under the circumstances presented in this case, where a cohesive group of stockholders with majority voting power was irrevocably committed to the merger transaction, "[e]ffective representation of the financial interests of the minority shareholders imposed upon the [NCS board] an affirmative responsibility to protect those minority shareholders' interests." The NCS board could not abdicate its fiduciary duties to the minority by leaving it to the stockholders alone to approve or disapprove the merger agreement because two stockholders had already combined to establish a majority of the voting power that made the outcome of the stockholder vote a foregone conclusion.

* * * *

Taking action that is otherwise legally possible . . . does not *ipso facto* comport with the fiduciary responsibilities of directors in all circumstances. The synopsis to the amendments that resulted in the enactment of Section 251(c) in the Delaware corporation law statute* specifically provides: "the amendments are not intended to address the question of whether such a submission requirement is appropriate in any particular set of factual circumstances." Section 251 provisions, like the no-shop provision examined in QVC, are "presumptively valid in the abstract." Such provisions in a merger agreement may not, however, "validly define or limit the directors' fiduciary duties under Delaware law or prevent the [NCS] directors from carrying out their fiduciary duties under Delaware law."

Genesis admits that when the NCS board agreed to its merger conditions, the NCS board was seeking to assure that the NCS creditors were paid in full and that the NCS stockholders received the highest value available for their

---

[74] *Paramount Communications Inc. v. QVC Network Inc.,* 637 A.2d 34, 51 (Del. 1993) (*citation omitted*). *Restatement (Second) of Contracts* § 193 explicitly provides that a "promise by a fiduciary to violate his fiduciary duty *or a promise that tends to induce such a violation is unenforceable on grounds of public policy.*" The comments to that section indicate that "[d]irectors and other officials of a corporation act in a fiduciary capacity and are subject to the rule stated in this Section." *Restatement (Second) of Contracts* § 193 (1981) (emphasis added).

* [In a footnote to a portion of the opinion that is not presented here, the Court explained: "Section 251(c) was amended in 1998 to allow for the inclusion in a merger agreement of a term requiring that the agreement be put to a vote of stockholders whether or not their directors continue to recommend the transaction. Before this amendment, Section 251 was interpreted as precluding a stockholder vote if the board of directors, after approving the merger agreement but before the stockholder vote, decided no longer to recommend it. *See Smith v. Van Gorkom,* 488 A.2d 858, 887–88 (Del. 1985)." Eds.]

stock. In fact, Genesis defends its "bulletproof" merger agreement on that basis. We hold that the NCS board did not have authority to accede to the Genesis demand for an absolute "lock-up."

The directors of a Delaware corporation have a continuing obligation to discharge their fiduciary responsibilities, as future circumstances develop, after a merger agreement is announced. Genesis anticipated the likelihood of a superior offer after its merger agreement was announced and demanded defensive measures from the NCS board that *completely* protected its transaction. Instead of agreeing to the absolute defense of the Genesis merger from a superior offer, however, the NCS board was required to negotiate a fiduciary out clause to protect the NCS stockholders if the Genesis transaction became an inferior offer. By acceding to Genesis' ultimatum for complete protection *in futuro,* the NCS board disabled itself from exercising its own fiduciary obligations at a time when the board's own judgment is most important, i.e., receipt of a subsequent superior offer.

Any board has authority to give the proponent of a recommended merger agreement reasonable structural and economic defenses, incentives, and fair compensation if the transaction is not completed. To the extent that defensive measures are economic and reasonable, they may become an increased cost to the proponent of any subsequent transaction. Just as defensive measures cannot be draconian, however, they cannot limit or circumscribe the directors' fiduciary duties. Notwithstanding the corporation's insolvent condition, the NCS board had no authority to execute a merger agreement that subsequently prevented it from effectively discharging its ongoing fiduciary responsibilities.

* * * *

The NCS board was required to contract for an effective fiduciary out clause to exercise its continuing fiduciary responsibilities to the minority stockholders.[88] The issues in this appeal do not involve the general validity of either stockholder voting agreements or the authority of directors to insert a Section 251(c) provision in a merger agreement. In this case, the NCS board combined those two otherwise valid actions and caused them to operate in concert as an absolute lock up, in the absence of an effective fiduciary out clause in the Genesis merger agreement.

---

[88] *See Paramount Communications Inc. v. QVC Network Inc.,* 637 A.2d at 42–43. Merger agreements involve an ownership decision and, therefore, cannot become final without stockholder approval. Other contracts do not require a fiduciary out clause because they involve business judgments that are within the exclusive province of the board of directors' power to manage the affairs of the corporation. . . .

In the context of this preclusive and coercive lock up case, the protection of Genesis' contractual expectations must yield to the supervening responsibility of the directors to discharge their fiduciary duties on a continuing basis. The merger agreement and voting agreements, as they were combined to operate in concert in this case, are inconsistent with the NCS directors' fiduciary duties. To that extent, we hold that they are invalid and unenforceable.

* * * *

VEASEY, CHIEF JUSTICE, with whom STEELE, JUSTICE, joins dissenting:

The beauty of the Delaware corporation law, and the reason it has worked so well for stockholders, directors and officers, is that the framework is based on an enabling statute with the Court of Chancery and the Supreme Court applying principles of fiduciary duty in a common law mode on a case-by-case basis. Fiduciary duty cases are inherently fact-intensive and, therefore, unique. This case is unique in two important respects. First, the peculiar facts presented render this case an unlikely candidate for substantial repetition. Second, this is a rare 3–2 split decision of the Supreme Court.

In the present case, we are faced with a merger agreement and controlling stockholders' commitment that assured stockholder approval of the merger before the emergence of a subsequent transaction offering greater value to the stockholders. This does not adequately summarize the unique facts before us, however. Reference is made to the Vice Chancellor's pinion and the factual summary in the Majority Opinion that adopts the Vice Chancellor's findings.

. . . . The Majority adopts a new rule of law that imposes a prohibition on the NCS board's ability to act in concert with controlling stockholders to lock up this merger. The Majority reaches this conclusion by analyzing the challenged deal protection measures as isolated board actions. The Majority concludes that the board owed a duty to the NCS minority stockholders to refrain from acceding to the Genesis demand for an irrevocable lock-up notwithstanding the compelling circumstances confronting the board and the board's disinterested, informed, good faith exercise of its business judgment.

Because we believe this Court must respect the reasoned judgment of the board of directors and give effect to the wishes of the controlling stockholders, we respectfully disagree with the Majority's reasoning that results in a holding that the confluence of board and stockholder action constitutes a breach of fiduciary duty. The essential fact that must always be remembered is that this agreement and the voting commitments of Outcalt and Shaw concluded a lengthy search and intense negotiation process in the context of insolvency and creditor pressure where no other viable bid had emerged. Accordingly, we endorse the Vice Chancellor's well-reasoned analysis that the NCS board's action before the hostile bid emerged was within the bounds of its fiduciary duties under these facts.

. . . . It is now known, of course, after the case is over, that the stockholders of NCS will receive substantially more by tendering their shares into the topping bid of Omnicare than they would have received in the Genesis merger, as a result of the post-agreement Omnicare bid and the injunctive relief ordered by the Majority of this Court. Our jurisprudence cannot, however, be seen as turning on such ex post felicitous results. Rather, the NCS board's good faith decision must be subject to a real-time review of the board action before the NCS-Genesis merger agreement was entered into.

An Analysis of the Process Leading to the Lock-up Reflects a Quintessential, Disinterested and Informed Board Decision Reached in Good Faith

The Majority has adopted the Vice Chancellor's findings and has assumed arguendo that the NCS board fulfilled its duties of care, loyalty, and good faith by entering into the Genesis merger agreement. Indeed, this conclusion is indisputable on this record. The problem is that the Majority has removed from their proper context the contractual merger protection provisions. The lock-ups here cannot be reviewed in a vacuum. A court should review the entire bidding process to determine whether the independent board's actions permitted the directors to inform themselves of their available options and whether they acted in good faith.

Going into negotiations with Genesis, the NCS directors knew that, up until that time, NCS had found only one potential bidder, Omnicare. Omnicare had refused to buy NCS except at a fire sale price through an asset sale in bankruptcy. Omnicare's best proposal at that stage would not have paid off all creditors and would have provided nothing for stockholders. The Noteholders, represented by the Ad Hoc Committee, were willing to oblige Omnicare and force NCS into bankruptcy if Omnicare would pay in full the NCS debt. Through the NCS board's efforts, Genesis expressed interest that became increasingly attractive. Negotiations with Genesis led to an offer paying creditors off and conferring on NCS stockholders $24 million—an amount infinitely superior to the prior Omnicare proposals.

But there was, understandably, a sine qua non. In exchange for offering the NCS stockholders a return on their equity and creditor payment, Genesis demanded certainty that the merger would close. If the NCS board would not have acceded to the Section 251(c) provision, if Outcalt and Shaw had not agreed to the voting agreements and if NCS had insisted on a fiduciary out, there would have been no Genesis deal! Thus, the only value-enhancing transaction available would have disappeared. NCS knew that Omnicare had spoiled a Genesis acquisition in the past, and it is not disputed by the Majority that the NCS directors made a reasoned decision to accept as real the Genesis threat to walk away.

When Omnicare submitted its conditional eleventh-hour bid, the NCS board had to weigh the economic terms of the proposal against the uncertainty of completing a deal with Omnicare. Importantly, because Omnicare's bid was conditioned on its satisfactorily completing its due diligence review of NCS, the NCS board saw this as a crippling condition, as did the Ad Hoc Committee. As a matter of business judgment, the risk of negotiating with Omnicare and losing Genesis at that point outweighed the possible benefits. The lock-up was indisputably a sine qua non to any deal with Genesis.

A lock-up permits a target board and a bidder to "exchange certainties." Certainty itself has value. The acquirer may pay a higher price for the target if the acquirer is assured consummation of the transaction. The target company also benefits from the certainty of completing a transaction with a bidder because losing an acquirer creates the perception that a target is damaged goods, thus reducing its value.

* * * *

While the present case does not involve an attempt to hold on to only one interested bidder, the NCS board was equally concerned about "exchanging certainties" with Genesis. If the creditors decided to force NCS into bankruptcy, which could have happened at any time as NCS was unable to service its obligations, the stockholders would have received nothing. . . .

Situations will arise where business realities demand a lock-up so that wealth-enhancing transactions may go forward. Accordingly, any bright-line rule prohibiting lock-ups could, in circumstances such as these, chill otherwise permissible conduct.

Our Jurisprudence Does Not Compel This Court to Invalidate the Joint Action of the Board and the Controlling Stockholders

The Majority invalidates the NCS board's action by announcing a new rule that represents an extension of our jurisprudence. That new rule can be narrowly stated as follows: A merger agreement entered into after a market search, before any prospect of a topping bid has emerged, which locks up stockholder approval and does not contain a "fiduciary out" provision, is per se invalid when a later significant topping bid emerges. As we have noted, this bright-line, per se rule would apply regardless of (1) the circumstances leading up to the agreement and (2) the fact that stockholders who control voting power had irrevocably committed themselves, *as stockholders,* to vote for the merger. Narrowly stated, this new rule is a judicially-created "third rail" that now becomes one of the given "rules of the game," to be taken into account by the negotiators and drafters of merger agreements. In our view, this new rule is an unwise extension of existing precedent.

Although it is debatable whether *Unocal* applies—and we believe that the better rule in this situation is that the business judgment rule should apply—we will, nevertheless, assume arguendo—as the Vice Chancellor did—that *Unocal* applies. . . . The NCS board's actions—as the Vice Chancellor correctly held—were reasonable in relation to the threat because the Genesis deal was the "only game in town," the NCS directors got the best deal they could from Genesis and—but-for the emergence of Genesis on the scene—there would have been no viable deal.

* * * *

The very measures the Majority cites as "coercive" were approved by Shaw and Outcalt through the lens of their independent assessment of the merits of the transaction. The proper inquiry in this case is whether the NCS board had taken actions that "have the effect of causing the stockholders to vote in favor of the proposed transaction for some reason other than the merits of that transaction." Like the termination fee upheld as a valid liquidated damages clause against a claim of coercion in *Brazen v. Bell Atlantic Corp.,* the deal protection measures at issue here were "an integral part of the merits of the transaction" as the NCS board struggled to secure—and did secure—the only deal available.

Outcalt and Shaw were fully informed stockholders. As the NCS controlling stockholders, they made an informed choice to commit their voting power to the merger. The minority stockholders were deemed to know that when controlling stockholders have 65% of the vote they can approve a merger without the need for the minority votes. Moreover, to the extent a minority stockholder may have felt "coerced" to vote for the merger, which was already a *fait accompli,* it was a meaningless coercion—or no coercion at all—because the controlling votes, those of Outcalt and Shaw, were already "cast." Although the fact that the controlling votes were committed to the merger "precluded" an overriding vote against the merger by the Class A stockholders, the pejorative "preclusive" label applicable in a *Unitrin* fact situation has no application here. Therefore, there was no meaningful minority stockholder voting decision to coerce.

In applying *Unocal* scrutiny, we believe the Majority incorrectly preempted the proportionality inquiry. In our view, the proportionality inquiry must account for the reality that the contractual measures protecting this merger agreement were necessary to obtain the Genesis deal. . . . [I]t is clear to us that the board action to negotiate the best deal reasonably available with the only viable merger partner (Genesis) who could satisfy the creditors and benefit the stockholders, was reasonable in relation to the threat, by any practical yardstick.

An Absolute Lock-up is Not a Per Se Violation of Fiduciary Duty

We respectfully disagree with the Majority's conclusion that the NCS board breached its fiduciary duties to the Class A stockholders by failing to negotiate a "fiduciary out" in the Genesis merger agreement. What is the practical import of a "fiduciary out?" It is a contractual provision, articulated in a manner to be negotiated, that would permit the board of the corporation being acquired to exit without breaching the merger agreement in the event of a superior offer.

In this case, Genesis made it abundantly clear early on that it was willing to negotiate a deal with NCS but only on the condition that it would not be a "stalking horse." Thus, it wanted to be certain that a third party could not use its deal with NCS as a floor against which to begin a bidding war. As a result of this negotiating position, a "fiduciary out" was not acceptable to Genesis. The Majority Opinion holds that such a negotiating position, if implemented in the agreement, is invalid per se where there is an absolute lock-up. We know of no authority in our jurisprudence supporting this new rule, and we believe it is unwise and unwarranted.

* * * *

Conclusion

It is regrettable that the Court is split in this important case. One hopes that the Majority rule announced here—though clearly erroneous in our view—will be interpreted narrowly and will be seen as *sui generis*. By deterring bidders from engaging in negotiations like those present here and requiring that there must always be a fiduciary out, the universe of potential bidders who could reasonably be expected to benefit stockholders could shrink or disappear.

Nevertheless, if the holding is confined to these unique facts, negotiators may be able to navigate around this new hazard.

Accordingly, we respectfully dissent.

[A separate dissent by Justice Steele is omitted.]

QUESTIONS

1. Do you agree with the dissent or the majority?

2. Should a company be able to irrevocably commit to a sale if there might be better offers available?

3. How would you have advised the NCS board of directors if they had wanted to reject the Omnicare offer to pursue a better deal?

4. Given the decision in *Omnicare,* what steps are available to protect an Acquirer that does not want to become a "stalking horse?"

E. Proxy Battles for Control in Hostile Acquisitions

Because poison pills and other defensive measures can be so effective in thwarting a Bidder's tender offer, some Bidders will simultaneously launch proxy battles in an effort to control the board of directors. The strategy behind such maneuvers is that the board often has the power to revoke the poison pill and, thereby, permit the acquisition to proceed. As seen in Chapter 6, *supra,* proxy battles may become quite contentious. In an effort to prevent losing control of a corporation, a board may take quite aggressive measures. While many strong defensive measures are permitted, as seen above, those that might violate fiduciary duties are not. In the *Blasius Industries, Inc. v. Atlas Corp.* case that follows, the court prevents another defensive measure, one that disenfranchises the shareholders.

Blasius Industries, Inc. v. Atlas Corp.

564 A.2d 651 (Del. Ch. 1988)

ALLEN, C.:

[This case involves a contest for control of Atlas Corporation. The directors of Atlas added two new members to its board of directors at a telephonic board meeting on December 31, 1987. The addition of the two board members was in response to efforts by Blasius Industries, Atlas' largest shareholder, holding 9.1% of Atlas, to obtain stockholder consent from the holders of a majority of Atlas' stock that] .... would have increased the board of Atlas from seven to fifteen members and would have elected eight new members nominated by Blasius.

... [This case presents] the question whether a board acts consistently with its fiduciary duty when it acts, in good faith and with appropriate care, for the primary purpose of preventing or impeding an unaffiliated majority of shareholders from expanding the board and electing a new majority. For the reasons that follow, I conclude that, even though defendants here acted on their view of the corporation's interest and not selfishly, their December 31 action constituted an offense to the relationship between corporate directors and shareholders that has traditionally been protected in courts of equity. As a consequence, I conclude that the board action taken on December 31 was invalid and must be voided. . . .

* * * *

I.

Blasius Acquires a 9% Stake in Atlas.

Blasius is a new stockholder of Atlas. It began to accumulate Atlas shares for the first time in July, 1987. On October 29, it filed a Schedule 13D with the Securities Exchange Commission disclosing that, with affiliates, it then owed 9.1% of Atlas' common stock. It stated in that filing that it intended to encourage management of Atlas to consider a restructuring of the Company or other transaction to enhance shareholder values. It also disclosed that Blasius was exploring the feasibility of obtaining control of Atlas, including instituting a tender offer or seeking "appropriate" representation on the Atlas board of directors.

* * * *

The Blasius Proposal of A Leverage Recapitalization Or Sale.

Immediately after filing its 13D on October 29, Blasius' representatives sought a meeting with the Atlas management. . . . Attending that meeting were Messrs. Lubin and Delano for Blasius, and, for Atlas, Messrs. Weaver, Devaney (Atlas' CFO), Masinter (legal counsel and director) and Czajkowski (a representative of Atlas' investment banker, Goldman Sachs).

At that meeting, Messrs. Lubin and Delano suggested that Atlas engage in a leveraged restructuring and distribute cash to shareholders. In such a transaction, which is by this date a commonplace form of transaction, a corporation typically raises cash by sale of assets and significant borrowings and makes a large one time cash distribution to shareholders. The shareholders are typically left with cash and an equity interest in a smaller, more highly leveraged enterprise. . . .

Immediately following the meeting, the Atlas representatives expressed among themselves an initial reaction that the proposal was infeasible. On December 7, Mr. Lubin sent a letter detailing the proposal. In general, it proposed the following: (1) an initial special cash dividend to Atlas' stockholders in an aggregate amount equal to (a) $35 million, (b) the aggregate proceeds to Atlas from the exercise of option warrants and stock options, and (c) the proceeds from the sale or disposal of all of Atlas' operations that are not related to its continuing minerals operations; and (2) a special non-cash dividend to Atlas' stockholders of an aggregate $125 million principal amount of 7% Secured Subordinated Gold-Indexed Debentures. The funds necessary to pay the initial cash dividend were to principally come from (i) a "gold loan" in the amount of $35,625,000, repayable over a three to five year period and secured by 75,000 ounces of gold at a price of $475 per ounce, (ii) the proceeds from the sale of the discontinued Brockton Sole and Plastics and Ready-Mix Concrete businesses, and (iii) a then expected January, 1988 sale of uranium to the Public Service Electric & Gas Company. (DX H.)

Atlas Asks Its Investment Banker to Study the Proposal.

This written proposal was distributed to the Atlas board on December 9 and Goldman Sachs was directed to review and analyze it.

The proposal met with a cool reception from management.

* * * *

The Delivery of Blasius' Consent Statement.

On December 30, 1987, Blasius caused Cede & Co. (the registered owner of its Atlas stock) to deliver to Atlas a signed written consent (1) adopting a precatory resolution recommending that the board develop and implement a restructuring proposal, (2) amending the Atlas bylaws to, among other things, expand the size of the board from seven to fifteen members—the maximum number under Atlas' charter, and (3) electing eight named persons to fill the new directorships. Blasius also filed suit that day in this court seeking a declaration that certain bylaws adopted by the board on September 1, 1987 acted as an unlawful restraint on the shareholders' right, created by Section 228 of our corporation statute, to act through consent without undergoing a meeting.

The reaction was immediate. Mr. Weaver conferred with Mr. Masinter, the Company's outside counsel and a director, who viewed the consent as an attempt to take control of the Company. . . . A telephone meeting was held the next day. At that meeting, the board voted to amend the bylaws to increase the size of the board from seven to nine and appointed John M. Devaney and Harry J. Winters, Jr. to fill those newly created positions. Atlas' Certificate of Incorporation creates staggered terms for directors; the terms to which Messrs. Devaney and Winters were appointed would expire in 1988 and 1990, respectively.

The Motivation of the Incumbent Board In Expanding the Board and Appointing New Members.

In increasing the size of Atlas' board by two and filling the newly created positions, the members of the board realized that they were thereby precluding the holders of a majority of the Company's shares from placing a majority of new directors on the board through Blasius' consent solicitation, should they want to do so. Indeed the evidence establishes that that was the principal motivation in so acting.

The conclusion that, in creating two new board positions on December 31 and electing Messrs. Devaney and Winters to fill those positions the board was principally motivated to prevent or delay the shareholders from possibly placing a majority of new members on the board, is critical to my analysis of the central issue posed by the first filed of the two pending cases. If the board in fact was not so motivated, but rather had taken action completely independently of the consent solicitation, which merely had an incidental impact upon the possible effectuation of any action authorized by the shareholders, it is very unlikely that such action would be subject to judicial nullification. [*Citations omitted.*] The board, as a general matter, is under no fiduciary obligation to suspend its active management of the firm while the consent solicitation process goes forward.

There is testimony in the record to support the proposition that, in acting on December 31, the board was principally motivated simply to implement a plan to expand the Atlas board that preexisted the September, 1987 emergence of Blasius as an active shareholder. I have no doubt that the addition of Mr. Winters, an expert in mining economics, and Mr. Devaney, a financial expert employed by the Company, strengthened the Atlas board and, should anyone ever have reason to review the wisdom of those choices, they would be found to be sensible and prudent. I cannot conclude, however, that the strengthening of the board by the addition of these men was the principal motive for the December 31 action. . . .

* * * *

. . . I conclude that, while the addition of these qualified men would, under other circumstances, be clearly appropriate as an independent step, such a step was in fact taken in order to impede or preclude a majority of the shareholders from effectively adopting the course proposed by Blasius.

* * * *

II.

Plaintiff attacks the December 31 board action as a selfishly motivated effort to protect the incumbent board from a perceived threat to its control of Atlas. Their conduct is said to constitute a violation of the principle, applied in such cases as *Schnell v. Chris Craft Industries,* Del.Supr., 285 A.2d 437 (1971), that directors hold legal powers subjected to a supervening duty to exercise such powers in good faith pursuit of what they reasonably believe to be in the corporation's interest. The December 31 action is also said to have been taken in a grossly negligent manner, since it was designed to preclude the recapitalization from being pursued, and the board had no basis at that time to make a prudent determination about the wisdom of that proposal, nor was there any emergency that required it to act in any respect regarding that proposal before putting itself in a position to do so advisedly.

Defendants, of course, contest every aspect of plaintiffs' claims. They claim the formidable protections of the business judgment rule. [*Citations omitted.*]

They say that, in creating two new board positions and filling them on December 31, they acted without a conflicting interest (since the Blasius proposal did not, in any event, challenge *their* places on the board), they acted with due care (since they well knew the persons they put on the board and did not thereby preclude later consideration of the recapitalization), and they acted in good faith (since they were motivated, they say, to protect the shareholders from the threat of having an impractical, indeed a dangerous, recapitalization program foisted upon them). Accordingly, defendants assert there is no basis to conclude that their December 31 action constituted any violation of the duty of the fidelity that a director owes by reason of his office to the corporation and its shareholders.

Moreover, defendants say that their action was fair, measured and appropriate, in light of the circumstances. Therefore, even should the court conclude that some level of substantive review of it is appropriate under a legal test of fairness, or under the intermediate level of review authorized by *Unocal Corp. v. Mesa Petroleum Co.,* Del.Supr., 493 A.2d 946 (1985), defendants assert that the board's decision must be sustained as valid in both law and equity.

III.

One of the principal thrusts of plaintiffs' argument is that, in acting to appoint two additional persons of their own selection, including an officer of the Company, to the board, defendants were motivated not by any view that Atlas' interest (or those of its shareholders) required that action, but rather they were motivated improperly, by selfish concern to maintain their collective control over the Company. That is, plaintiffs say that the evidence shows there was no policy dispute or issue that really motivated this action, but that asserted policy differences were pretexts for entrenchment for selfish reasons. If this were found to be factually true, one would not need to inquire further. The action taken would constitute a breach of duty. [*Citations omitted.*]

* * * *

While I am satisfied that the evidence is powerful, indeed compelling, that the board was chiefly motivated on December 31 to forestall or preclude the possibility that a majority of shareholders might place on the Atlas board eight new members sympathetic to the Blasius proposal, it is less clear with respect to the more subtle motivational question: whether the existing members of the board did so because they held a good faith belief that such shareholder action would be self-injurious and shareholders needed to be protected from their own judgment.

On balance, I cannot conclude that the board was acting out of a self-interested motive in any important respect on December 31. I conclude rather that the board saw the "threat" of the Blasius recapitalization proposal as posing vital policy differences between itself and Blasius. It acted, I conclude, in a good faith effort to protect its incumbency, not selfishly, but in order to thwart implementation of the recapitalization that it feared, reasonably, would cause great injury to the Company.

The real question the case presents, to my mind, is whether, in these circumstances, the board, even if it *is* acting with subjective good faith (which will typically, if not always, be a contestable or debatable judicial conclusion), may validly act for the principal purpose of preventing the shareholders from electing a majority of new directors. The question thus posed is not one of intentional wrong (or even negligence), but one of authority *as between the fiduciary and the beneficiary* (not simply legal authority, i.e., as between the fiduciary and the world at large).

IV.

It is established in our law that a board may take certain steps—such as the purchase by the corporation of its own stock—that have the effect of defeating a threatened change in corporate control, when those steps are taken advisedly, in good faith pursuit of a corporate interest, and are reasonable in relation to a threat to legitimate corporate interests posed by the proposed change in control. [*Citations omitted.*] Does this rule—that the reasonable exercise of good faith and due care generally validates, in equity, the exercise of legal authority even if the act has an entrenchment effect—apply to action designed for the primary purpose of interfering with the effectiveness of a stockholder vote? Our authorities, as well as sound principles, suggest that the central importance of the franchise to the scheme of corporate governance, requires that, in this setting, that rule not be applied and that closer scrutiny be accorded to such transaction.

1. Why the deferential business judgment rule does not apply to board acts taken for the primary purpose of interfering with a stockholder's vote, even if taken advisedly and in good faith.

A. The Question Of Legitimacy.

The shareholder franchise is the ideological underpinning upon which the legitimacy of directorial power rests. Generally, shareholders have only two protections against perceived inadequate business performance. They may sell their stock (which, if done in sufficient numbers, may so affect security prices as to create an incentive for altered managerial performance), or they may vote to replace incumbent board members.

It has, for a long time, been conventional to dismiss the stockholder vote as a vestige or ritual of little practical importance. It may be that we are now witnessing the emergence of new institutional voices and arrangements that will make the stockholder vote a less predictable affair than it has been. Be that as it may, however, whether the vote is seen functionally as an unimportant formalism, or as an important tool of discipline, it is clear that it is critical to the theory that legitimates the exercise of power by some (directors and officers) over vast aggregations of property that they do not own. Thus, when viewed from a broad, institutional perspective, it can be seen that matters involving the integrity of the shareholder voting process involve consideration not present in any other context in which directors exercise delegated power.

B. *Questions of this type raise issues of the allocation of authority as between the board and the shareholders.*

The distinctive nature of the shareholder franchise context also appears when the matter is viewed from a less generalized, doctrinal point of view. From this point of view, as well, it appears that the ordinary considerations to which the business judgment rule originally responded are simply not present in the shareholder voting context.[2] That is, a decision by the board to act for the primary purpose of preventing the effectiveness of a shareholder vote inevitably involves the question who, as between the principal and the agent, has authority with respect to a matter of internal corporate governance. That, of course, is true in a very specific way in this case which deals with the question who should constitute the board of directors of the corporation, but it will be true in every instance in which an incumbent board seeks to thwart a shareholder majority. A board's decision to act to prevent the shareholders from creating a majority of new board positions and filling them does not involve the exercise of *the corporation's power* over its property, or with respect to *its* rights or obligations; rather, it involves allocation, between shareholders as a class and the board, of effective power with respect to governance of the corporation. This need not be the case with respect to other forms of corporate action that may have an entrenchment effect—such as the stock buybacks present in *Unocal, Cheff or Kors v. Carey*. Action designed principally to interfere with the effectiveness of a vote inevitably involves a conflict between the board and a shareholder majority. Judicial review of such action involves a determination of the legal and equitable

---

2 Delaware courts have long exercised a most sensitive and protective regard for the free and effective exercise of voting rights. This concern suffuses our law, manifesting itself in various settings. For example, the perceived importance of the franchise explains the cases that hold that a director's fiduciary duty requires disclosure to shareholders asked to authorize a transaction of all material information in the corporation's possession, even if the transaction is not a self-dealing one. [*Citations omitted.*]

A similar concern, for credible corporate democracy, underlies those cases that strike down board action that sets or moves an annual meeting date upon a finding that such action was intended to thwart a shareholder group from effectively mounting an election campaign. *See, e.g., Schnell v. Chris Craft, supra;* [*Citations omitted.*]

The cases invalidating stock issued for the primary purpose of diluting the voting power of a control block also reflect the law's concern that a credible form of corporate democracy be maintained. [*Citations omitted.*]

Similarly, a concern for corporate democracy is reflected (1) in our statutory requirement of annual meetings (8 *Del. C.* § 211), and in the cases that aggressively and summarily enforce that right. [*Citations omitted.*]

obligations of an agent towards his principal. This is not, in my opinion, a question that a court may leave to the agent finally to decide so long as he does so honestly and competently; that is, it may not be left to the agent's business judgment.

2. *What rule does apply: per se invalidity of corporate acts intended primarily to thwart effective exercise of the franchise or is there an intermediate standard?*

Plaintiff argues for a rule of *per se* invalidity once a plaintiff has established that a board has acted for the primary purpose of thwarting the exercise of a shareholder vote.

* * * *

A *per se* rule that would strike down, in equity, any board action taken for the primary purpose of interfering with the effectiveness of a corporate vote would have the advantage of relative clarity and predictability. It also has the advantage of most vigorously enforcing the concept of corporate democracy. The disadvantage it brings along is, of course, the disadvantage a *per se* rule always has: it may sweep too broadly.

In two recent cases dealing with shareholder votes, this court struck down board acts done for the primary purpose of impeding the exercise of stockholder voting power. In doing so, a *per se* rule was not applied. Rather, it was said that, in such a case, the board bears the heavy burden of demonstrating a compelling justification for such action.

In *Aprahamian v. HBO & Company,* Del.Ch., 531 A.2d 1204 (1987), the incumbent board had moved the date of the annual meeting on the eve of that meeting when it learned that a dissident stockholder group had or appeared to have in hand proxies representing a majority of the outstanding shares. The court restrained that action and compelled the meeting to occur as noticed, even though the board stated that it had good business reasons to move the meeting date forward, and that that action was recommended by a special committee. The court concluded as follows:

> The corporate election process, if it is to have any validity, must be conducted with scrupulous fairness and without any advantage being conferred or denied to any candidate or slate of candidates. In the interests of corporate democracy, those in charge of the election machinery of a corporation must be held to the highest standards of providing for and conducting corporate elections. The business judgment rule therefore does not confer any presumption of propriety

> on the acts of directors in postponing the annual meeting. Quite to the contrary. When the election machinery appears, at least facially, to have been manipulated those in charge of the election have the burden of persuasion to justify their actions.

Aprahamian, 531 A.2d at 1206–07.

In *Phillips v. Insituform of North America, Inc.,* Del.Ch., 1987 Del. Ch. LEXIS 474, C.A. No. 9173, Allen, C. (Aug. 27, 1987), the court enjoined the voting of certain stock issued for the primary purpose of diluting the voting power of certain control shares. The facts were complex. After discussing *Canada Southern* and *Condec* in light of the more recent, important Supreme Court opinion in *Unocal Corp. v. Mesa Petroleum Company,* it was there concluded as follows:

> One may read *Canada Southern* as creating a black-letter rule prohibiting the issuance of shares for the purpose of diluting a large stockholder's voting power, but one need not do so. It may, as well, be read as a case in which no compelling corporate purpose was presented that might otherwise justify such an unusual course. Such a reading is, in my opinion, somewhat more consistent with the recent *Unocal* case.
>
> * * *
>
> In applying the teachings of these cases, I conclude that no justification has been shown that would arguably make the extraordinary step of issuance of stock for the admitted purpose of impeding the exercise of stockholder rights reasonable in light of the corporate benefit, if any, sought to be obtained. Thus, whether our law creates an unyielding prohibition to the issuance of stock for the primary purpose of depriving a controlling shareholder of control or whether, as *Unocal* suggests to my mind, such an extraordinary step might be justified in some circumstances, the issuance of the Leopold shares was, in my opinion, an unjustified and invalid corporate act.

Phillips v. Insituform of North America, Inc., supra 1987 Del. Ch. LEXIS 474, *26–27. Thus, in *Insituform,* it was unnecessary to decide whether a *per se* rule pertained or not.

In my view, our inability to foresee now all of the future settings in which a board might, in good faith, paternalistically seek to thwart a shareholder vote, counsels against the adoption of a *per se* rule invalidating, in equity, every board action taken for the sole or primary purpose of thwarting a shareholder vote, even though I recognize the transcending significance of the franchise to the claims to legitimacy of our scheme of corporate governance. It may be that some set of facts would justify such extreme action. This, however, is not such a case.

3. *Defendants have demonstrated no sufficient justification for the action of December 31 which was intended to prevent an unaffiliated majority of shareholders from effectively exercising their right to elect eight new directors.*

The board was not faced with a coercive action taken by a powerful shareholder against the interests of a distinct shareholder constituency (such as a public minority). It was presented with a consent solicitation by a 9% shareholder. Moreover, here it had time (and understood that it had time) to inform the shareholders of its views on the merits of the proposal subject to stockholder vote. The only justification that can, in such a situation, be offered for the action taken is that the board knows better than do the shareholders what is in the corporation's best interest. While that premise is no doubt true for any number of matters, it is irrelevant (except insofar as the shareholders wish to be guided by the board's recommendation) when the question is who should comprise the board of directors. The theory of our corporation law confers power upon directors as the agents of the shareholders; it does not create Platonic masters. It may be that the Blasius restructuring proposal was or is unrealistic and would lead to injury to the corporation and its shareholders if pursued. Having heard the evidence, I am inclined to think it was not a sound proposal. The board certainly viewed it that way, and that view, held in good faith, entitled the board to take certain steps to evade the risk it perceived. It could, for example, expend corporate funds to inform shareholders and seek to bring them to a similar point of view. [*Citations omitted.*] But there is a vast difference between expending corporate funds to inform the electorate and exercising power for the primary purpose of foreclosing effective shareholder action. A majority of the shareholders, who were not dominated in any respect, could view the matter differently than did the board. If they do, or did, they are entitled to employ the mechanisms provided by the corporation law and the Atlas certificate of incorporation to advance that view. They are also entitled, in my opinion, to restrain their agents, the board, from acting for the principal purpose of thwarting that action.

I therefore conclude that, even finding the action taken was taken in good faith, it constituted an unintended violation of the duty of loyalty that the board owed to the shareholders. I note parenthetically that the concept of an unintended breach of the duty of loyalty is unusual but not novel. [*Citations omitted.*] That action will, therefore, be set aside by order of this court.

* * * *

QUESTIONS

1. Do you agree that a director could "unintentionally" violate the duty of loyalty?

2. Given the tension between protecting shareholders rights and protecting the corporation against a "harmful" acquisition, what steps could the board have taken?

3. What would you have recommended?

A similar conclusion was reached in the *Hilton v. ITT Corp.* case, which follows. The case involves many of the tactics discussed in this book. In the face of a tender offer and proxy contest from Hilton, ITT's defensive measures included a poison pill, a change in voting rights to require a super majority and a staggered board.

Hilton Hotels Corporation v. ITT

978 F. Supp. 1342 (D. Nev. 1997)

PRO, D.J.:

ORDER RE: INJUNCTIVE AND DECLARATORY RELIEF

Before the Court for consideration is . . . the Motion for Injunctive and Declaratory Relief . . . filed August 26, 1997, on behalf of Hilton Hotels Corporation and HLT Corporation (collectively "Hilton").

* * * *

I. FACTS

On January 27, 1997, Hilton announced a $55.00 per share tender offer for the stock of ITT, and announced plans for a proxy contest at ITT's 1997 annual meeting. This litigation commenced on the same date with the filing of Hilton's Complaint for Injunctive and Declaratory Relief. . . .

On February 11, 1997, ITT formally rejected Hilton's tender offer. ITT proceeded to sell several of its non-core assets and opposed Hilton's takeover attempt before gaming regulatory bodies in Nevada, New Jersey and Mississippi.

When it became apparent that ITT would not conduct its annual meeting in May 1997, as it had customarily done in preceding years, Hilton filed a motion for a mandatory injunction to compel ITT to conduct the annual meeting in

May. On April 21, 1997, this Court denied Hilton's Motion finding that Nevada law and ITT's by-laws did not require that ITT conduct its annual meeting within twelve months of the prior meeting, but rather that ITT had eighteen months within which to do so. [*Citations omitted.*]

On July 15, 1997, ITT announced a Comprehensive Plan which, among other things, proposed to split ITT into three new entities, the largest of which would become ITT Destinations. ITT Destinations would be comprised of the current ITT's hotel and gaming business which account for approximately 93% of ITT's current assets. A second entity, ITT Educational Services, would consist of the current ITT's technical schools, and ITT's European Yellow Pages Division would remain with the current ITT as ITT World Directories.

Most significantly, under the Comprehensive Plan, the board of directors of the new ITT Destinations would be comprised of the members of ITT's current board with one important distinction. The new board would be a "classified" or "staggered" board divided into three classes with each class of directors serving for a term of three years, and with one class to be elected each year. Moreover, a shareholder vote of 80% would be required to remove directors without cause, and 80% shareholder vote would also be required to repeal the classified board provision or the 80% requirement to remove directors without cause.

Additionally, the record fairly supports Hilton's contention that the Comprehensive Plan contains a "poison pill" resulting in a $1.4 billion tax liability which would be triggered if Hilton successfully acquired more than 50% of ITT Destinations and that Hilton would be liable for 90% of the tax bill.

Finally, and critical to this Court's analysis, ITT seeks to implement the Comprehensive Plan prior to ITT's 1997 annual meeting and without obtaining shareholder approval.

II. THE PARTIES' CONTENTIONS AND APPLICABLE LEGAL STANDARDS

* * * *

Shortly after ITT's announcement of its Comprehensive Plan, Hilton announced an amended tender offer of $70.00 per share which was rejected by ITT. On August 26, 1997, Hilton filed its Motion for Injunctive and Declaratory Relief . . . seeking:

1. A preliminary and permanent injunction enjoining ITT from proceeding with its Comprehensive Plan;

2. Declaring that by adopting the Comprehensive Plan, ITT's directors had breached their fiduciary duties to ITT and its shareholders;
3. Declaring that ITT may not implement its Comprehensive Plan without obtaining a shareholder vote; and
4. Requiring ITT to conduct its 1997 annual meeting for the election of directors not later than November 14, 1997.

* * * *

Where, as here, Hilton's Motion seeks mandatory injunctive relief in the sense that a trial on the merits could not practically reverse a preliminary decision enjoining implementation of ITT's Comprehensive Plan until after the 1997 annual meeting, the Motion is subject to heightened scrutiny and the injunction requested should not issue unless the facts and the law clearly favor the party requesting such relief. Hilton, 962 F. Supp. at 1309 (citations omitted). . . .

III. DISCUSSION

This case involves consideration of the powers and duties of the board of directors of a Nevada corporation in responding to a hostile takeover attempt, and the importance of protecting the franchise of the shareholders of the corporation in the process.

Many courts have grappled with legal issues presented by the strategies employed by hostile bidders, such as Hilton, and the concomitant anti-takeover defensive measures utilized by target companies, such as ITT. Coupling an unsolicited tender offer with a proxy contest to replace the incumbent board is a favored strategy of would-be acquirors. A variety of sophisticated defensive measures, including "poison pill" plans have also evolved to frustrate a host of takeover attempts. As a result, "replacing the incumbent directors of the target corporation is viewed as an efficient way to eliminate the target company's ability to utilize these anti-takeover defenses." *Kidsco v. Dinsmore III,* 674 A.2d 483, 490 (Del. Ch. 1995). *See also Unitrin, Inc. v. American Gen. Corp.,* 651 A.2d 1361, 1379 (Del. 1995).

Nevada state case law is virtually silent on the subject. However, provisions of Chapter 78 of the Nevada Revised Statutes ("N.R.S.") speak to the respective rights and duties of directors and officers of corporations, and the rights of corporate stockholders. Nevada's statutory scheme does not, however, provide clear guidance in this case. While N.R.S. § 78.138 addresses several powers of a corporate board in undertaking defensive measures to resist a hostile takeover, nothing in the Nevada statutes, or elsewhere in the law of Nevada, authorizes the incumbent board of a corporation to entrench itself by effectively removing the right of the corporation's shareholders to vote on who may serve on the board of the corporation in which they own a share. Whether a target corporation such as ITT can do so in the face of a hostile takeover attempt by Hilton is the dispositive issue presented in this case.

Where, as here, there is no Nevada statutory or case law on point for an issue of corporate law, this Court finds persuasive authority in Delaware case law. [*Citation omitted.*]

A. Legal Framework for Board Action in Response to a Proxy Contest and Tender Offer.

As this case involves both a tender offer and a proxy contest by Hilton, the proper legal standard is a Unocal/Blasius analysis as articulated in *Stroud v. Grace,* 606 A.2d 75, 92 n.3 (Del. 1992), and *Unitrin,* 651 A.2d 1361 at 1379.

> In assessing a challenge to defensive actions by a target corporation's board of directors in a takeover context, this Court has held that the Court of Chancery should evaluate the board's overall response, including the justification for each contested defensive measure, and the results achieved thereby. Where all of the target board's defensive actions are inextricably related, the principles of Unocal require that such actions be scrutinized collectively as a unitary response to the perceived threat.
>
> *Unitrin,* 651 A.2d at 1386–87 (emphasis supplied).
>
> Where an acquiror launches both a proxy fight and a tender offer, it
>
> "necessarily invoke[s] both Unocal and Blasius" because "both [tests] recognize the inherent conflicts of interest that arise when shareholders are not permitted free exercise of their franchise. . . . In certain circumstances, [the judiciary] must recognize the special import of protecting the shareholders' franchise within Unocal's requirement that any defensive measure be proportionate and 'reasonable in relation to the threat posed.' "
>
> *Unitrin,* 651 A.2d at 1379 (*quoting Stroud,* 606 A.2d 75 at 92 n.3).
>
> A board's unilateral decision to adopt a defensive measure touching "upon issues of control" that purposefully disenfranchises its shareholders is strongly suspect under Unocal, and cannot be sustained without a "compelling justification."

Stroud, 606 A.2d at 92 n.3.

These cases have drawn a distinction between the exercise of two types of corporate power: 1) power over the assets of the corporation and 2) the power relationship between the board (management) and the shareholders. Actions involving the first type of power invoke the business judgment rule, or Unocal if an action is in response to a reasonably perceived threat to the corporation. Actions involving the second power invoke a Blasius analysis. The issues raised in this case require the Court to focus on the power relationship between ITT's board and ITT shareholders, not on the ITT board's actions relating to corporate assets.

Several amicus briefs have been filed on behalf of ITT shareholders, urging that they be allowed to vote on the Comprehensive Plan and the board of directors at the 1997 annual meeting. This Court has found no legal basis mandating a shareholder vote on the adoption of ITT's Comprehensive Plan in its entirety. However, as the Court finds that the Comprehensive Plan would violate the power relationship between ITT's board and ITT's shareholders by impermissibly infringing on the shareholders' right to vote on members of the board of directors, it must be enjoined.

ITT argues that Nevada does not follow Delaware case law since N.R.S. § 78.138 provides that a board, exercising its powers in good faith and with [a] view to the interests of the corporation can resist potential changes in control of a corporation based on the effect to constituencies other than the shareholders. However, the corporate rights provided under N.R.S. § 78.138 are not incompatible with the duties articulated in *Unocal Corp. v. Mesa Petroleum Co.,* 493 A.2d 946 (Del. 1985), *Revlon Inc. v. MacAndrews & Forbes Holdings, Inc.,* 506 A.2d 173 (Del. 1986) and *Blasius Indus. Inc. v. Atlas Corp.,* 564 A.2d 651 (Del. Ch. 1988).

Delaware case law merely clarifies the basic duties established by the Nevada statutes. . . . ITT would have this Court establish that the only duty a board has under Nevada law is a duty of good faith. This Court will not eliminate the principles articulated in Unocal, Blasius and Revlon and the common law duties of care and loyalty without any indication from the Nevada Legislature or the Nevada Supreme Court that that is the legislative intent.

Thus, Delaware precedent establishes that a board has power over the management and assets of a corporation, but that power is not unbridled. That power is limited by the right of shareholders to vote for the members of the board. As articulated in Shoen, this right underlies the concept of corporate democracy. This Court fully endorses the reasoning in Shoen and Blasius regarding the importance of the shareholder franchise to the entire scheme of corporate governance. This Court will, therefore, examine ITT's Comprehensive Plan under the Unocal/Blasius analysis.

Unocal requires the Court to consider the following two questions: 1) Does ITT have reasonable grounds for believing a danger to corporate policy and effectiveness exists? 2) Is the response reasonable in relation to the threat? If it is a defensive measure touching on issues of control, the court must examine whether the board purposefully disenfranchised its shareholders, an action that cannot be sustained without a compelling justification. *Stroud,* 606 A.2d at 92 n.3.

1. The Classified Board for ITT Destinations

The first defensive action this Court will analyze under the Unocal standard is the provision in the Comprehensive Plan for a classified board for ITT Destinations.

a. Reasonable grounds for believing a threat to corporate policy and effectiveness exists.

Nine of ITT's eleven directors are outside directors. Under Unocal, such a majority materially enhances evidence that a hostile offer presents a threat warranting a defensive response. *Unitrin,* 651 A.2d at 1375.

ITT argues strenuously that the Comprehensive Plan is better than Hilton's offer. This is not for the Court to decide, and it is not determinative under its analysis. Under Unocal, a court must first determine if there is a threat to corporate policy and effectiveness. ITT has failed to demonstrate such a threat.

ITT has made no showing that Hilton will pursue a different corporate policy than ITT seeks to implement through its Comprehensive Plan. In fact, over the past few months, ITT has to a large extent adopted Hilton's proposed strategy of how it says it will govern ITT if its slate of directors is elected. There has also been no showing of Hilton's inability or ineffectiveness to run ITT if it does succeed in its takeover attempt. ITT cites to the fact that some Sheraton franchise owners will be unhappy if Hilton enters into certain management contracts, but this is not fundamental or pervasive enough to constitute a "threat" to ITT's corporate policy or effectiveness.

The ITT board has also failed to meet its burden of showing "good faith and reasonable investigation" of a threat to corporate policy or effectiveness which would meet the burden placed on the board under the first prong of the Unocal test. Since Hilton's tender offer was announced, the ITT board has not met with Hilton to discuss the offer. Moreover, the overwhelming majority of ITT's evidence of good faith relates to its approval of the Comprehensive Plan, not to the inadequacy of Hilton's offer.

The sole "threat" ITT points to is that Hilton's offer of $70 a share is inadequate, primarily because this price does not contain a control premium. However, at the August 14, 1997, ITT board meeting, Goldman Sachs told the ITT board that the market valued ITT's plan at $62 to $64 dollars a share. This contradicts ITT's argument that there is no control premium over market price contained in Hilton's offer. That ITT itself was offering to buy back roughly 26% of its stock at $70 a share does not nullify this fact.

The only attempt ITT has made to satisfy the first prong of the Unocal analysis is to argue that Hilton's price is inadequate. However, while inadequacy of an offer is a legally cognizable threat, *Paramount Communications, Inc. v. Time, Inc.,* 571 A.2d 1140, 1153 (Del. 1990), ITT has shown no real harm to corporate policy or effectiveness. The facts in Unocal illustrate this point well. Unocal involved a tender offer with a back-end offer of junk bonds. [*Citation omitted.*] Junk bond financing could reasonably harm the future policy and effectiveness of a company. As ITT itself is offering only $70 a share, and the Comprehensive Plan involves greatly increasing the leveraging of ITT, its claim that Hilton's offer of $70 a share is a threat to policy or effectiveness is unpersuasive. In light of these facts, the alleged inadequacy of Hilton's offer is not a severe threat to ITT. Under the proportionality requirement, the nature of Hilton's threat will set the parameters for the range of permissible defensive tactics under the second prong of the Unocal test. *Unitrin,* 651 A.2d 1361 at 1384.

b. ITT's Response was Preclusive

Assuming Hilton's offer constitutes a cognizable threat under Unocal, ITT's response cannot be preclusive or coercive, and it must be within the range of reasonableness. As articulated in Unitrin, a board cannot "cramm down" on shareholders a management sponsored alternative. [*Citation omitted.*] The installation of a classified board for ITT Destinations, a company which will encompass 93% of the current ITT's assets and 87% of its revenues, is clearly preclusive and coercive under Unitrin. The classified board provision for ITT Destinations will preclude current ITT shareholders from exercising a right they currently possess—to determine the membership of the board of ITT. At the very minimum, ITT shareholders will have no choice but to accept the Comprehensive Plan and a majority of ITT's incumbent board members for another year. Therefore, the Comprehensive Plan is preclusive.

c. The Primary Purpose of the Comprehensive Plan is to Interfere with Shareholder Franchise

ITT's response to Hilton's tender offer touches upon issues of control, and this Court must determine whether the response purposefully disenfranchises ITT's shareholders. If so, under the analysis of Stroud and Unitrin, it is not a reasonable response unless a "compelling justification" exists. It is important to note that in Blasius, the board did something that normally would be entirely permissible under Delaware law and its own by-laws: it expanded the board from seven to nine individuals. It did this in the face of a hostile takeover by a company financed through "junk bonds" and two individuals who sought to substantially "cash out" many of the target corporation's assets. [*Citation omitted.*] Still, while the board in Blasius had a good faith reason to act as it did, and it acted with appropriate care, the board could not lawfully prevent the shareholders from electing a majority of new directors.

Blasius' factual scenario is strikingly similar to the circumstances surrounding ITT's actions. Normally, a corporation is free to adopt a classified board structure. In fact many companies, including Hilton, have classified boards. As long as the classified board is adopted in the proper manner, whether through charter amendment, changes in the by-laws of a company or through shareholder vote, it is permissible. However, Blasius illustrates that even if an action is normally permissible, and the board adopts it in good faith and with proper care, a board cannot undertake such action if the primary purpose is to disenfranchise the shareholders in light of a proxy contest. [*Citation omitted.*] Thus, while ITT could normally adopt a classified board or issue a dividend of shares creating ITT Destinations, it cannot undertake these actions if the primary purpose is to disenfranchise ITT shareholders in light of Hilton's tender offer and proxy contest.

As a board would likely never concede that its primary purpose was to entrench itself, this Court must look to circumstantial evidence to determine the primary purpose of ITT's action touching upon issues of control. While none of the following factors are dispositive, collectively they eliminate all questions of material fact, and demonstrate that the primary purpose of ITT's Comprehensive Plan was to disenfranchise its shareholders.

i. Timing

The intent evidenced by the timing of the Comprehensive Plan is transparent. Although ITT claims that a spin-off or sale was contemplated before Hilton's tender offer, it makes no mention of when the board determined to move from an annually elected board to a classified board. Moreover, all aspects of ITT's Comprehensive Plan were formulated against the backdrop of Hilton's tender offer and proxy contest, and the Plan was not announced until well after Hilton's initial tender offer. Finally, this major restructuring of ITT was announced and to be implemented in a little over two months, and designed to take effect less than two months before the annual meeting was to be held at which shareholders would have the opportunity to vote on an annually elected rather than a classified board.

ii. Entrenchment

The ITT directors who are approving the Comprehensive Plan are the same directors who will fill the classified board positions of ITT Destinations. ITT and its advisors recognized from the outset that they were vulnerable because they did not have a staggered board of directors. The members of ITT's board are appointing themselves to new, more insulated positions, and at least seven of the eleven directors are avoiding the shareholder vote that would otherwise occur at ITT's 1997 annual meeting. While companies may convert from annual to classified boards, as Blasius illustrates, the rub is in the details. It is the manner of adopting the Comprehensive Plan with its provision for a new certified board comprised of incumbent ITT directors which supports the conclusion that ITT's Plan is primarily designed to entrench the incumbent board.

iii. ITT's Stated Purpose

ITT has offered no credible justification for not seeking shareholder approval of the Comprehensive Plan. ITT simply claims that it wants to "avoid market risks and other business problems." [*Citation omitted.*] Such vague generalizations do not approach the required showing of a reasonable justification other than entrenchment for the board's action. Simply stating that its "advisors" suggested a rapid implementation of the Comprehensive Plan, without pointing to a specific risk or problem, is insufficient to meet ITT's burden.

iv. Benefits of Comprehensive Plan

ITT argues that there are economic benefits to the Comprehensive Plan, and general benefits of the classified board provision for ITT Destinations. That may be true, but the additional benefits of a plan infringing on shareholder voting rights do not remedy the fundamental flaw of board entrenchment.

v. Effect of Classified Board

The classified board provision for ITT Destinations under ITT's Comprehensive Plan ensures that ITT shareholders will be absolutely precluded from electing a majority of the directors nominated under Hilton's proxy contest at the 1997 annual meeting. Such a Plan, coupled with ITT's vehement opposition to Hilton's tender offer, is inconsistent with ITT's earlier argument that a delay of the 1997 annual meeting from May to November would afford shareholders additional time to inform themselves and more fully consider the implications of their vote for directors at the 1997 annual meeting.

ITT's position is particularly anomalous given the fact that when ITT previously split the company in 1995, it sought shareholder approval. While shareholder approval may not be absolutely required to split ITT now anymore than it was in 1995, the fact that the ITT board decided to subject the 1995 split of the company to a shareholder vote is strong evidence that the primary purpose of its attempts to implement the Comprehensive Plan prior to the 1997 annual meeting is to entrench the incumbent ITT board.

vi. Failure to Obtain an IRS Opinion as to Effects of the Comprehensive Plan

ITT is not seeking an Internal Revenue Service opinion regarding the tax consequences of the three-way split of ITT under the Comprehensive Plan. It is doubtful that an Internal Revenue Service opinion on the matter could be obtained before ITT's 1997 annual meeting. Furthermore, there are serious questions as to the extent to which implementation of the Comprehensive Plan will constitute a taxable event to ITT and its shareholders, or the extent to which Hilton would incur adverse tax consequences if it attempted to takeover ITT Destinations once the Comprehensive Plan is implemented. ITT dismisses these concerns by arguing that its attorneys advise that there are no adverse tax consequences under the Comprehensive Plan. However, the record demonstrates otherwise. ITT's counsel conceded that there is no binding precedent on point and that the issue was not free from doubt. While obtaining a tax opinion from the Internal Revenue Service may not be mandatory, ITT's failure to seriously consider obtaining such an opinion provides additional evidence that ITT's primary intention in implementing the Comprehensive Plan at this time was to impede the shareholder franchise.

2. Other Provisions of the Comprehensive Plan

This Court's analysis regarding the threat to ITT under the first prong of Unocal is equally applicable to the remaining elements of the Comprehensive

Plan. Whether the other aspects of ITT's Comprehensive Plan violate the second step of the Unocal analysis, that is whether they are preclusive or coercive, is problematic. Certainly the record before the Court supports Hilton's contention that the "tax poison pill" relating to its potential purchase of ITT Destinations is preclusive and coercive. Hilton also argues that ITT's Plan is coercive because ITT is offering $70.00 a share for only 26% of the stock. Since the trading value of the stock is $62.00 to $64.00 per share, shareholders will have to tender their shares immediately to avoid a financial loss. These arguments create serious questions as to whether the other elements of the Comprehensive Plan are preclusive and coercive.

The Unocal test is also referred to as a "proportionality test." [*Citation omitted.*] Serious questions remain as to whether the Comprehensive Plan is reasonable in relation to the threat posed by Hilton's offer. . . .

Serious questions exist as to whether the remaining provisions of the Comprehensive Plan are preclusive or coercive, or reasonable responses under Unocal. This Court finds it unnecessary, however, to undertake an exhaustive analysis of the laundry list of issues presented by both parties. The different provisions of the Comprehensive Plan are inextricably related, and this Court has already concluded that the staggered board provision is preclusive and was enacted for the primary purpose of entrenching the current board. Therefore, the entire Comprehensive Plan must be enjoined.

* * * *

IV. CONCLUSION

* * * *

Shareholders do not exercise day-to-day business judgments regarding the operation of a corporation—those are matters left to the reasonable discretion of directors, officers and the corporation's management team. Corporate boards have great latitude in exercising their business judgments as they should. As a result, shareholders generally have only two protections against perceived inadequate business performance. They may sell their stock or vote to replace incumbent board members. For this reason, interference with the shareholder franchise is especially serious. It is not to be left to the board's business judgment, precisely because it undercuts a primary justification for allowing directors to rely on their business judgment in almost every other context. Indeed, as the court in Shoen noted, "one of the justifications for the business judgment rule's insulation of directors from liability for almost all of their decisions is that unhappy shareholders can always vote the directors out of office." *Shoen,* 885 F. Supp. at 1340.

* * * *

ITT strongly argues that its Comprehensive Plan is superior to Hilton's alternative tender offer. This argument should be directed to ITT's shareholders, not this Court.

ITT also claims that it has properly considered other constituencies in responding to Hilton's offer, as it is expressly allowed to do under N.R.S. § 78.138. ITT is correct. Other constituencies may be considered under that provision, but nothing in that statute suggests that the interests of third parties are as important as the right of shareholder franchise. While the two interests are not exclusive, neither are they equal. The right of shareholders to vote on directors at an annual meeting is a fundamental principle of corporate law, and it is not outweighed by the interests listed in N.R.S. § 78.138.

Likewise, the good faith of the ITT board in implementing the Comprehensive Plan does not change this Court's analysis. . . .

The ultimate outcome of the election of directors at ITT's 1997 annual meeting is not a relevant inquiry for this Court. That is something for the shareholders who own ITT to decide when they select the board who will lead the corporation. If a majority of the incumbent ITT board is re-elected after a fully-informed and fair shareholder vote, that board will be free to implement any business plan it chooses so long as that plan is consistent with ITT's charter and by-laws, and governing law.

This Court concludes that the structure and timing of ITT's Comprehensive Plan with its classified board provision for ITT Destinations, is preclusive and leaves no doubt that the primary purpose for ITT's proposed implementation of the Comprehensive Plan before the 1997 annual meeting is to impermissibly impede the exercise of the shareholder franchise by depriving shareholders of the opportunity to vote to re-elect or to oust all or as many of the incumbent ITT directors as they may choose at the upcoming annual meeting. It has as its primary purpose the entrenchment of the incumbent ITT board. As a result, the Court concludes that Hilton has prevailed on the merits of its claim for permanent injunctive relief.

IT IS THEREFORE ORDERED that Hilton's Motion for Permanent Injunctive Relief . . . is granted to the extent that ITT is hereby enjoined from implementing its Comprehensive Plan announced July 15, 1997.

IT IS FURTHER ORDERED that ITT's annual meeting shall be held no later than November 14, 1997.

* * * *

F. State Takeover Statutes

Several states have attempted to regulate aspects of the takeover process, either with respect to price and/or changes in control. The *CTS* case below involves a challenge to an Indiana "control-share-acquisition" statute, which required a person acquiring control in an Indiana corporation to obtain the approval of a disinterested majority of the other shareholders before that person could vote.

CTS Corp. v. Dynamics Corporation of America

481 U.S. 69, 107 S. Ct. 1637, 95 L. Ed. 2d 67 (1987)

JUSTICE POWELL delivered the opinion of the Court.

[This case]. . . present the questions whether the Control Share Acquisitions Chapter of the Indiana Business Corporation Law, Ind. Code § 23–1–42–1 *et seq.* (Supp. 1986), is pre-empted by the Williams Act, 82 Stat. 454, as amended, 15 U. S. C. §§ 78m(d)–(e) and 78n(d)–(f) (1982 ed. and Supp. III), or violates the Commerce Clause of the Federal Constitution, Art. I, § 8, cl. 3.

I

A

On March 4, 1986, the Governor of Indiana signed a revised Indiana Business Corporation Law, Ind. Code § 23–1–17–1 *et seq.* (Supp. 1986). That law included the Control Share Acquisitions Chapter (Indiana Act or Act). Beginning on August 1, 1987, the Act will apply to any corporation incorporated in Indiana, § 23–1–17–3(a), unless the corporation amends its articles of incorporation or bylaws to opt out of the Act, § 23–1–42–5. Before that date, any Indiana corporation can opt into the Act by resolution of its board of directors. § 23–1–17–3(b). The Act applies only to "issuing public corporations." The term "corporation" includes only businesses incorporated in Indiana. See § 23–1–20–5. An "issuing public corporation" is defined as:

"a corporation that has:

"(1) one hundred (100) or more shareholders;

"(2) its principal place of business, its principal office, or substantial assets within Indiana; and

"(3) either:

"(A) more than ten percent (10%) of its shareholders resident in Indiana;

"(B) more than ten percent (10%) of its shares owned by Indiana residents; or

"(C) ten thousand (10,000) shareholders resident in Indiana." § 23–1–42–4(a).

The Act focuses on the acquisition of "control shares" in an issuing public corporation. Under the Act, an entity acquires "control shares" whenever it acquires shares that, but for the operation of the Act, would bring its voting power in the corporation to or above any of three thresholds: 20%, 331/3%, or 50%. § 23–1–42–1. An entity that acquires control shares does not necessarily acquire voting rights. Rather, it gains those rights only "to the extent granted by resolution approved by the shareholders of the issuing public corporation." § 23–1–42–9(a). Section 23–1–42–9(b) requires a majority vote of all disinterested[2] shareholders holding each class of stock for passage of such a resolution. The practical effect of this requirement is to condition acquisition of control of a corporation on approval of a majority of the pre-existing disinterested shareholders.

The shareholders decide whether to confer rights on the control shares at the next regularly scheduled meeting of the shareholders, or at a specially scheduled meeting. The acquiror can require management of the corporation to

---

2 "Interested shares" are shares with respect to which the acquiror, an officer, or an inside director of the corporation "may exercise or direct the exercise of the voting power of the corporation in the election of directors." § 23–1–42–3. If the record date passes before the acquiror purchases shares pursuant to the tender offer, the purchased shares will not be "interested shares" within the meaning of the Act; although the acquiror may own the shares on the date of the meeting, it will not "exercise . . . the voting power" of the shares.

As a practical matter, the record date usually will pass before shares change hands. Under Securities and Exchange Commission (SEC) regulations, the shares cannot be purchased until 20 business days after the offer commences. 17 CFR § 240.14e–1(a) (1986). If the acquiror seeks an early resolution of the issue—as most acquirors will—the meeting required by the Act must be held no more than 50 calendar days after the offer commences, about three weeks after the earliest date on which the shares could be purchased. See § 23–1–42–7. The Act requires management to give notice of the meeting "as promptly as reasonably practicable . . . to all shareholders of record as of the record date set for the meeting." § 23–1–42–8(a). It seems likely that management of the target corporation would violate this obligation if it delayed setting the record date and sending notice until after 20 business days had passed. Thus, we assume that the record date usually will be set before the date on which federal law first permits purchase of the shares.

hold such a special meeting within 50 days if it files an "acquiring person statement,"[4] requests the meeting, and agrees to pay the expenses of the meeting. See § 23–1–42–7. If the shareholders do not vote to restore voting rights to the shares, the corporation may redeem the control shares from the acquiror at fair market value, but it is not required to do so. § 23–1–42–10(b). Similarly, if the acquiror does not file an acquiring person statement with the corporation, the corporation may, if its bylaws or articles of incorporation so provide, redeem the shares at any time after 60 days after the acquiror's last acquisition. § 23–1–42–10(a).

B

On March 10, 1986, appellee Dynamics Corporation of America (Dynamics) owned 9.6% of the common stock of appellant CTS Corporation, an Indiana corporation. On that day, six days after the Act went into effect, Dynamics announced a tender offer for another million shares in CTS; purchase of those shares would have brought Dynamics' ownership interest in CTS to 27.5%. Also on March 10, Dynamics filed suit in the United States District Court for the Northern District of Illinois, alleging that CTS had violated the federal securities laws in a number of respects no longer relevant to these proceedings. On March 27, the board of directors of CTS, an Indiana corporation, elected to be governed by the provisions of the Act, see § 23–1–17–3.

Four days later, on March 31, Dynamics moved for leave to amend its complaint to allege that the Act is pre-empted by the Williams Act, 15 U. S. C. §§ 78m(d)–(e) and 78n(d)–(f) (1982 ed. and Supp. III), and violates the Commerce Clause, Art. I, § 8, cl. 3. Dynamics sought a temporary restraining order, a preliminary injunction, and declaratory relief against CTS' use of the Act. On April 9, the District Court ruled that the Williams Act pre-empts the Indiana Act and granted Dynamics' motion for declaratory relief. 637 F.Supp. 389 (ND Ill. 1986). Relying on Justice White's plurality opinion in *Edgar v. MITE Corp.,* 457 U.S. 624 (1982), the court concluded that the Act "wholly frustrates the purpose and objective of Congress in striking a balance between the investor, management, and the takeover bidder in takeover contests." 637 F.Supp., at 399. A week later, on April 17, the District Court issued an opinion accepting Dynamics' claim that the Act violates the Commerce Clause. This holding rested on the court's conclusion that "the substantial interference with interstate commerce created by the [Act] outweighs the articulated local benefits so as to

---

[4] An "acquiring person statement" is an information statement describing, *inter alia,* the identity of the acquiring person and the terms and extent of the proposed acquisition. See § 23–1–42–6.

create an impermissible indirect burden on interstate commerce." *Id.,* at 406. The District Court certified its decisions on the Williams Act and Commerce Clause claims as final under Federal Rule of Civil Procedure 54(b). *Ibid.*

* * * *

[The Court of Appeals for the Seventh Circuit affirmed the judgment of the District Court.]

II

The first question in [this case] is whether the Williams Act pre-empts the Indiana Act. As we have stated frequently, absent an explicit indication by Congress of an intent to pre-empt state law, a state statute is pre-empted only

" 'where compliance with both federal and state regulations is a physical impossibility . . .,' *Florida Lime & Avocado Growers, Inc. v. Paul,* 373 U.S. 132, 142–143 (1963), or where the state 'law stands as an obstacle to the accomplishment and execution of the full purposes and objectives of Congress.' *Hines v. Davidowitz,* 312 U.S. 52, 67 (1941) . . . ." *Ray v. Atlantic Richfield Co.,* 435 U.S. 151, 158 (1978).

Because it is entirely possible for entities to comply with both the Williams Act and the Indiana Act, the state statute can be pre-empted only if it frustrates the purposes of the federal law.

A

Our discussion begins with a brief summary of the structure and purposes of the Williams Act. Congress passed the Williams Act in 1968 in response to the increasing number of hostile tender offers. Before its passage, these transactions were not covered by the disclosure requirements of the federal securities laws. [*Citation omitted.*] The Williams Act, backed by regulations of the SEC, imposes requirements in two basic areas. First, it requires the offeror to file a statement disclosing information about the offer, including: the offeror's background and identity; the source and amount of the funds to be used in making the purchase; the purpose of the purchase, including any plans to liquidate the company or make major changes in its corporate structure; and the extent of the offeror's holdings in the target company. [*Citation omitted.*]

Second, the Williams Act, and the regulations that accompany it, establish procedural rules to govern tender offers. For example, stockholders who tender their shares may withdraw them while the offer remains open, and, if the offeror has not purchased their shares, any time after 60 days from commencement of the offer. . . . The offer must remain open for at least 20 business days. . . . If more shares are tendered than the offeror sought to purchase, purchases must be made on a pro rata basis from each tendering shareholder. . . . Finally, the offeror must pay the same price for all purchases; if the offering price is increased before the end of the offer, those who already have tendered must receive the benefit of the increased price. . . .

B

The Indiana Act differs in major respects from the Illinois statute that the Court considered in *Edgar v. MITE Corp.,* 457 U.S. 624 (1982). After reviewing the legislative history of the Williams Act, Justice White, joined by Chief Justice Burger and Justice Blackmun (the plurality), concluded that the Williams Act struck a careful balance between the interests of offerors and target companies, and that any state statute that "upset" this balance was pre-empted. *Id.,* at 632–634.

The plurality then identified three offending features of the Illinois statute. Justice White's opinion first noted that the Illinois statute provided for a 20-day precommencement period. During this time, management could disseminate its views on the upcoming offer to shareholders, but offerors could not publish their offers. The plurality found that this provision gave management "a powerful tool to combat tender offers." *Id.,* at 635. This contrasted dramatically with the Williams Act; Congress had deleted express precommencement notice provisions from the Williams Act. According to the plurality, Congress had determined that the potentially adverse consequences of such a provision on shareholders should be avoided. Thus, the plurality concluded that the Illinois provision "frustrate[d] the objectives of the Williams Act." *Ibid.* The second criticized feature of the Illinois statute was a provision for a hearing on a tender offer that, because it set no deadline, allowed management " 'to stymie indefinitely a takeover,' " *id.,* at 637 (quoting *MITE Corp. v. Dixon,* 633 F.2d 486, 494 (CA7 1980)). The plurality noted that " 'delay can seriously impede a tender offer,' " 457 U.S., at 637 (quoting *Great Western United Corp. v. Kidwell,* 577 F.2d 1256, 1277 (CA5 1978) (Wisdom, J.)), and that "Congress anticipated that investors and the takeover offeror would be free to go forward without unreasonable delay," 457 U.S., at 639. Accordingly, the plurality concluded that this provision conflicted with the Williams Act. The third troublesome feature of the Illinois statute was its requirement that the fairness of tender offers would be reviewed by the Illinois Secretary of State. Noting that "Congress intended for investors to be free to make their own decisions," the plurality concluded that " 'the state thus offers investor protection at the expense of investor autonomy—an approach quite in conflict with that adopted by Congress.' " *Id.,* at 639–640 (quoting MITE *Corp. v. Dixon*, *supra*, at 494).

C

As the plurality opinion in *MITE* did not represent the views of a majority of the Court, we are not bound by its reasoning. We need not question that reasoning, however, because we believe the Indiana Act passes muster even under the broad interpretation of the Williams Act articulated by Justice White in *MITE*. As is apparent from our summary of its reasoning, the overriding concern of the *MITE* plurality was that the Illinois statute considered in that case operated to favor management against offerors, to the detriment of shareholders. By contrast, the statute now before the Court protects the independent shareholder against the contending parties. Thus, the Act furthers a basic purpose of the Williams Act, " 'plac[ing] investors on an equal footing with the takeover bidder,' " *Piper v. Chris-Craft Industries, Inc.,* 430 U.S., at 30 (quoting the Senate Report accompanying the Williams Act, S. Rep. No. 550, 90th Cong., 1st Sess., 4 (1967)).

The Indiana Act operates on the assumption, implicit in the Williams Act, that independent shareholders faced with tender offers often are at a disadvantage. By allowing such shareholders to vote as a group, the Act protects them from the coercive aspects of some tender offers. If, for example, shareholders believe that a successful tender offer will be followed by a purchase of nontendering shares at a depressed price, individual shareholders may tender their shares—even if they doubt the tender offer is in the corporation's best interest—to protect themselves from being forced to sell their shares at a depressed price. As the SEC explains: "The alternative of not accepting the tender offer is virtual assurance that, if the offer is successful, the shares will have to be sold in the lower priced, second step." [*Citations omitted.*] In such a situation under the Indiana Act, the shareholders as a group, acting in the corporation's best interest, could reject the offer, although individual shareholders might be inclined to accept it. The desire of the Indiana Legislature to protect shareholders of Indiana corporations from this type of coercive offer does not conflict with the Williams Act. Rather, it furthers the federal policy of investor protection.

In implementing its goal, the Indiana Act avoids the problems the plurality discussed in *MITE*. Unlike the *MITE* statute, the Indiana Act does not give either management or the offeror an advantage in communicating with the shareholders about the impending offer. The Act also does not impose an indefinite delay on tender offers. Nothing in the Act prohibits an offeror from consummating an offer on the 20th business day, the earliest day permitted under applicable federal regulations, see 17 CFR § 240.14e–1(a) (1986). Nor does the Act allow the state government to interpose its views of fairness between willing buyers and sellers of shares of the target company. Rather, the Act allows *shareholders* to evaluate the fairness of the offer collectively.

D

The Court of Appeals based its finding of pre-emption on its view that the practical effect of the Indiana Act is to delay consummation of tender offers until 50 days after the commencement of the offer. . . . As did the Court of Appeals, Dynamics reasons that no rational offeror will purchase shares until it gains assurance that those shares will carry voting rights. Because it is possible that voting rights will not be conferred until a shareholder meeting 50 days after commencement of the offer, Dynamics concludes that the Act imposes a 50-day delay. This, it argues, conflicts with the shorter 20-business-day period established by the SEC as the minimum period for which a tender offer may be held open. [*Citation omitted.*] We find the alleged conflict illusory.

The Act does not impose an absolute 50-day delay on tender offers, nor does it preclude an offeror from purchasing shares as soon as federal law permits. If the offeror fears an adverse shareholder vote under the Act, it can make a conditional tender offer, offering to accept shares on the condition that the shares receive voting rights within a certain period of time. The Williams Act permits tender offers to be conditioned on the offeror's subsequently obtaining regulatory approval. [*Citations omitted.*] There is no reason to doubt that this type of conditional tender offer would be legitimate as well.

Even assuming that the Indiana Act imposes some additional delay, nothing in *MITE* suggested that *any* delay imposed by state regulation, however short, would create a conflict with the Williams Act. The plurality argued only that the offeror should "be free to go forward without *unreasonable* delay." 457 U.S., at 639 (emphasis added). In that case, the Court was confronted with the potential for indefinite delay and presented with no persuasive reason why some deadline could not be established. By contrast, the Indiana Act provides that full voting rights will be vested—if this eventually is to occur—within 50 days after commencement of the offer. This period is within the 60-day period Congress established for reinstitution of withdrawal rights in 15 U. S. C. § 78n(d)(5). We cannot say that a delay within that congressionally determined period is unreasonable.

Finally, we note that the Williams Act would pre-empt a variety of state corporate laws of hitherto unquestioned validity if it were construed to pre-empt any state statute that may limit or delay the free exercise of power after a successful tender offer. State corporate laws commonly permit corporations to stagger the terms of their directors. [*Citations omitted.*] By staggering the terms of directors, and thus having annual elections for only one class of directors each year, corporations may delay the time when a successful offeror gains control of the board of directors. Similarly, state corporation laws commonly provide for cumulative voting. [*Citation omitted.*] By enabling minority shareholders to assure themselves of representation in each class of directors, cumulative voting provisions can delay further the ability of offerors to gain untrammeled authority over the affairs of the target corporation. [*Citation omitted.*]

In our view, the possibility that the Indiana Act will delay some tender offers is insufficient to require a conclusion that the Williams Act pre-empts the Act. The longstanding prevalence of state regulation in this area suggests that, if Congress had intended to pre-empt all state laws that delay the acquisition of voting control following a tender offer, it would have said so explicitly. The regulatory conditions that the Act places on tender offers are consistent with the text and the purposes of the Williams Act. Accordingly, we hold that the Williams Act does not pre-empt the Indiana Act.

III

As an alternative basis for its decision, the Court of Appeals held that the Act violates the Commerce Clause of the Federal Constitution. We now address this holding. On its face, the Commerce Clause is nothing more than a grant to Congress of the power "to regulate Commerce . . . among the several States . . .," Art. I, § 8, cl. 3. But it has been settled for more than a century that the Clause prohibits States from taking certain actions respecting interstate commerce even absent congressional action. . . .

A

The principal objects of dormant Commerce Clause scrutiny are statutes that discriminate against interstate commerce. [*Citations omitted.*] The Indiana Act is not such a statute. It has the same effects on tender offers whether or not the offeror is a domiciliary or resident of Indiana. Thus, it "visits its effects equally upon both interstate and local business," [*Citation omitted.*]

Dynamics nevertheless contends that the statute is discriminatory because it will apply most often to out-of-state entities. This argument rests on the contention that, as a practical matter, most hostile tender offers are launched by offerors outside Indiana. But this argument avails Dynamics little. "The fact that the burden of a state regulation falls on some interstate companies does not, by itself, establish a claim of discrimination against interstate commerce." *Exxon Corp. v. Governor of Maryland,* 437 U.S. 117, 126 (1978). . . . Because nothing in the Indiana Act imposes a greater burden on out-of-state offerors than it does on similarly situated Indiana offerors, we reject the contention that the Act discriminates against interstate commerce.

B

This Court's recent *Commerce Clause* cases also have invalidated statutes that may adversely affect interstate commerce by subjecting activities to inconsistent regulations. [*Citations omitted.*] The Indiana Act poses no such problem. So long as each State regulates voting rights only in the corporations it has created, each corporation will be subject to the law of only one State. No principle of corporation law and practice is more firmly established than a State's authority to regulate domestic corporations, including the authority to define the voting rights of shareholders. *See* Restatement (Second) of Conflict of Laws § 304 (1971) (concluding that the law of the incorporating State generally should "determine the right of a shareholder to participate in the administration of the affairs of the corporation"). Accordingly, we conclude that the Indiana Act does not create an impermissible risk of inconsistent regulation by different States.

C

The Court of Appeals did not find the Act unconstitutional for either of these threshold reasons. Rather, its decision rested on its view of the Act's potential to hinder tender offers. We think the Court of Appeals failed to appreciate the significance for Commerce Clause analysis of the fact that state regulation of corporate governance is regulation of entities whose very existence and attributes are a product of state law. As Chief Justice Marshall explained:

"A corporation is an artificial being, invisible, intangible, and existing only in contemplation of law. Being the mere creature of law, it possesses only those properties which the charter of its creation confers upon it, either expressly, or as incidental to its very existence. These are such as are supposed best calculated to effect the object for which it was created." *Trustees of Dartmouth College v. Woodward,* 4 Wheat. 518, 636 (1819).

. . . . Every State in this country has enacted laws regulating corporate governance. By prohibiting certain transactions, and regulating others, such laws necessarily affect certain aspects of interstate commerce. This necessarily is true with respect to corporations with shareholders in States other than the State of incorporation. Large corporations that are listed on national exchanges, or even regional exchanges, will have shareholders in many States and shares that are traded frequently. The markets that facilitate this national and international participation in ownership of corporations are essential for providing capital not only for new enterprises but also for established companies that need to expand their businesses. This beneficial free market system depends at its core upon the fact that a corporation—except in the rarest situations—is organized under, and governed by, the law of a single jurisdiction, traditionally the corporate law of the State of its incorporation.

These regulatory laws may affect directly a variety of corporate transactions. Mergers are a typical example. In view of the substantial effect that a merger may have on the shareholders' interests in a corporation, many States require supermajority votes to approve mergers. See, *e. g.,* 2 MBCA § 73 (requiring approval of a merger by a majority of all shares, rather than simply a majority of votes cast); RMBCA § 11.03 (same). By requiring a greater vote for mergers than is required for other transactions, these laws make it more difficult for corporations to merge. State laws also may provide for "dissenters' rights" under which minority shareholders who disagree with corporate decisions to take particular actions are entitled to sell their shares to the corporation at fair market value. . . . By requiring the corporation to purchase the shares of dissenting shareholders, these laws may inhibit a corporation from engaging in the specified transactions.

It thus is an accepted part of the business landscape in this country for States to create corporations, to prescribe their powers, and to define the rights that are acquired by purchasing their shares. A State has an interest in promoting stable relationships among parties involved in the corporations it charters, as well as in ensuring that investors in such corporations have an effective voice in corporate affairs.

There can be no doubt that the Act reflects these concerns. The primary purpose of the Act is to protect the shareholders of Indiana corporations. It does this by affording shareholders, when a takeover offer is made, an opportunity to decide collectively whether the resulting change in voting control of the corporation, as they perceive it, would be desirable. A change of management may have important effects on the shareholders' interests; it is well within the State's role as overseer of corporate governance to offer this opportunity. The autonomy provided by allowing shareholders collectively to determine whether the takeover is advantageous to their interests may be especially beneficial where a hostile tender offer may coerce shareholders into tendering their shares.

Appellee Dynamics responds to this concern by arguing that the prospect of coercive tender offers is illusory, and that tender offers generally should be favored because they reallocate corporate assets into the hands of management who can use them most effectively.[13] [*Citations omitted.*] As indicated *supra,* . . . Indiana's concern with tender offers is not groundless. Indeed, the potentially coercive aspects of tender offers have been recognized by the SEC . . . and by a number of scholarly commentators. . . . The Constitution does not require the States to subscribe to any particular economic theory. We are not inclined "to second-guess the empirical judgments of lawmakers concerning the utility of legislation," [*Citation omitted.*] In our view, the possibility of coercion in some takeover bids offers additional justification for Indiana's decision to promote the autonomy of independent shareholders.

Dynamics argues in any event that the State has " 'no legitimate interest in protecting the nonresident shareholders.' " . . . . Dynamics relies heavily on the statement by the *MITE* Court that "insofar as the . . . law burdens out-of-state transactions, there is nothing to be weighed in the balance to sustain the law." 457 U.S., at 644. But that comment was made in reference to an Illinois law that applied as well to out-of-state corporations as to in-state corporations. We agree that Indiana has no interest in protecting nonresident shareholders *of nonresident corporations.* But this Act applies only to corporations incorporated in Indiana. We reject the contention that Indiana has no interest in providing for the shareholders of its corporations the voting autonomy granted by the Act. Indiana has a substantial interest in preventing the corporate form from becoming a shield for unfair business dealing. Moreover, unlike the Illinois statute invalidated in *MITE,* the Indiana Act applies only to corporations that have a substantial number of shareholders in Indiana. . . . . Thus, every application of the Indiana Act will affect a substantial number of Indiana residents, whom Indiana indisputably has an interest in protecting.

---

[13] It is appropriate to note when discussing the merits and demerits of tender offers that generalizations usually require qualification. No one doubts that some successful tender offers will provide more effective management or other benefits such as needed diversification. But there is no reason to *assume* that the type of conglomerate corporation that may result from repetitive takeovers necessarily will result in more effective management or otherwise be beneficial to shareholders. . . .

D

Dynamics' argument that the Act is unconstitutional ultimately rests on its contention that the Act will limit the number of successful tender offers. There is little evidence that this will occur. But even if true, this result would not substantially affect our Commerce Clause analysis. We reiterate that this Act does not prohibit any entity—resident or nonresident—from offering to purchase, or from purchasing, shares in Indiana corporations, or from attempting thereby to gain control. It only provides regulatory procedures designed for the better protection of the corporations' shareholders. . . . The very commodity that is traded in the securities market is one whose characteristics are defined by state law. Similarly, the very commodity that is traded in the "market for corporate control"—the corporation—is one that owes its existence and attributes to state law. Indiana need not define these commodities as other States do; it need only provide that residents and nonresidents have equal access to them. This Indiana has done. Accordingly, even if the Act should decrease the number of successful tender offers for Indiana corporations, this would not offend the Commerce Clause.

IV

On its face, the Indiana Control Share Acquisitions Chapter evenhandedly determines the voting rights of shares of Indiana corporations. The Act does not conflict with the provisions or purposes of the Williams Act. To the limited extent that the Act affects interstate commerce, this is justified by the State's interests in defining the attributes of shares in its corporations and in protecting shareholders. Congress has never questioned the need for state regulation of these matters. Nor do we think such regulation offends the Constitution. Accordingly, we reverse the judgment of the Court of Appeals.

It is so ordered.

* * * *

JUSTICE SCALIA, concurring in part and concurring in the judgment.

I join Parts I, III-A, and III-B of the Court's opinion. However, having found, as those Parts do, that the Indiana Control Share Acquisitions Chapter neither "discriminates against interstate commerce," . . . nor "create[s] an impermissible risk of inconsistent regulation by different States," . . ., I would conclude without further analysis that it is not invalid under the dormant Commerce Clause. While it has become standard practice at least since *Pike v. Bruce Church, Inc.,* 397 U.S. 137 (1970), to consider, in addition to these factors, whether the burden on commerce imposed by a state statute "is clearly excessive in relation to the putative local benefits," *id.,* at 142, such an inquiry is ill suited to the judicial function and should be undertaken rarely if at all. This case is a good illustration of the point. Whether the control shares statute "protects shareholders of Indiana corporations," . . . or protects incumbent management seems to me a highly debatable question, but it is extraordinary to think that the constitutionality of the Act should depend on the answer. Nothing in the Constitution says that the protection of entrenched management is any less important a "putative local benefit" than the protection of entrenched shareholders, and I do not know what qualifies us to make that judgment—or the related judgment as to how effective the present statute is in achieving one or the other objective. . . .

* * * *

I also agree with the Court that the Indiana Control Share Acqusitions Chapter is not pre-empted by the Williams Act, but I reach that conclusion without entering into the debate over the purposes of the two statutes. The Williams Act is governed by the antipre-emption provision of the Securities Exchange Act of 1934, 15 U. S. C. § 78bb(a), which provides that nothing it contains "shall affect the jurisdiction of the securities commission (or any agency or officer performing like functions) of any State over any security or any person insofar as it does not conflict with the provisions of this chapter or the rules and regulations thereunder." Unless it serves no function, that language forecloses pre-emption on the basis of conflicting "purpose" as opposed to conflicting "provision." Even if it does not have literal application to the present case (because, perhaps, the Indiana agency responsible for securities matters has no enforcement responsibility with regard to this legislation), it nonetheless refutes the proposition that Congress meant the Williams Act to displace *all* state laws with conflicting purpose. And if any are to survive, surely the States' corporation codes are among them. It would be peculiar to hold that Indiana could have pursued the purpose at issue here through its blue-sky laws, but cannot pursue it through the State's even more sacrosanct authority over the structure of domestic corporations. Prescribing voting rights for the governance of state-chartered companies is a traditional state function with which the Federal Congress has never, to my knowledge, intentionally interfered. I would require far more evidence than is available here to find implicit pre-emption of that function by a federal statute whose provisions concededly do not conflict with the state law.

I do not share the Court's apparent high estimation of the beneficence of the state statute at issue here. But a law can be both economic folly and constitutional. The Indiana Control Share Acquisitions Chapter is at least the latter. I therefore concur in the judgment of the Court.

* * * *

JUSTICE WHITE, with whom JUSTICE BLACKMUN and JUSTICE STEVENS join as to Part II, dissenting.

The majority today upholds Indiana's Control Share Acquisitions Chapter, a statute which will predictably foreclose completely some tender offers for stock in Indiana corporations. I disagree with the conclusion that the Chapter is neither pre-empted by the Williams Act nor in conflict with the Commerce Clause. The Chapter undermines the policy of the Williams Act by effectively preventing minority shareholders, in some circumstances, from acting in their own best interests by selling their stock. In addition, the Chapter will substantially burden the interstate market in corporate ownership, particularly if other States follow Indiana's lead as many already have done. The Chapter, therefore, directly inhibits interstate commerce, the very economic consequences the Commerce Clause was intended to prevent. The opinion of the Court of Appeals is far more persuasive than that of the majority today, and the judgment of that court should be affirmed.

* * * *

NOTES AND QUESTIONS

1. Following the *CTS* decision, a number of states adopted anti-takeover legislation of various forms. New York adopted a "third generation" anti-takeover statute in 1985 (N.Y. Bus. Corp. Law § 912) which requires a five-year waiting period for any person acquiring a 20% or more interest in a New York corporation before that person may engage in a "business combination" with that corporation, unless that person obtained approval from the corporation's board of directors prior to acquiring the 20% interest. Delaware's statute (DGCL § 203) requires a three-year waiting period before any person acquiring 15% of a Delaware corporation may engage in a (narrowly defined) business combination, unless that person acquires 85% of the corporation in a single transaction or if that person obtains approval of two-thirds of the disinterested shareholders and approval of the board of directors.

2. In *Amanda Acquisition Corp. v. Universal Foods Corp.*, 877 F.2d 496 (7th Cir. 1989), *cert. denied,* 493 U.S. 995 (1989), the Seventh Circuit upheld a Wisconsin statute that provided a similar delay for a would-be acquirer of a Wisconsin corporation. Do these waiting period statutes seem to benefit the shareholders?

3. If you represented a board that was deciding whether to waive the protections provided by such a statute, by what standard would their decision be evaluated?

Index

References are to Pages

PARTNERSHIPS

PRINCIPALS